How College Affects Students

Volume 3: 21st Century Evidence That Higher Education Works

D1567575

How College Affects Students

Volume 3

21st Century Evidence That Higher Education Works

Matthew J. Mayhew
Alyssa N. Rockenbach
Nicholas A. Bowman
Tricia A. Seifert
Gregory C. Wolniak
With Ernest T. Pascarella and Patrick T. Terenzini

JB JOSSEY-BASS™
A Wiley Brand

Published by Jossey-Bass
A Wiley Brand
One Montgomery Street, Suite 1000, San Francisco, CA 94104–4594—www.josseybass.com

Jossey-Bass books and products are available through most bookstores. To contact Jossey-Bass directly call our Customer Care Department within the U.S. at 800-956-7739, outside the U.S. at 317-572-3986, or fax 317-572-4002.

Wiley publishes in a variety of print and electronic formats and by print-on-demand. Some material included with standard print versions of this book may not be included in e-books or in print-on-demand. If this book refers to media such as a CD or DVD that is not included in the version you purchased, you may download this material at http://booksupport.wiley.com. For more information about Wiley products, visit www.wiley.com.

Library of Congress Cataloging-in-Publication Data

Pascarella, Ernest T.
How college affects students : a third decade of research / Ernest T. Pascarella,
Patrick T. Terenzini.— 2nd ed. (Already cataloged)
p. cm.
Includes bibliographical references and index.
ISBN 0-7879-1044-9 (alk. paper)
1. College students—United States—Longitudinal studies. 2. College graduates—
United States—Longitudinal studies. I. Terenzini, Patrick T. II. Title.
LA229.P34 2005
378.1'98'0973—dc22
Volume 3: ISBN 9781118462683 (paperback)

Cover image: ©malija/iStockphoto
Cover design: Wiley

Printed in the United States of America
FIRST EDITION
PB Printing   10 9 8 7 6 5 4 3 2 1

To our loved ones.

CONTENTS

LIST OF FIGURES AND TABLES

FIGURES

TABLES

ACKNOWLEDGMENTS

The nearly four-year journey to the third volume of *How College Affects Students* involved many individuals who dedicated their time and talents to supporting our efforts. First and foremost, this opportunity would not exist if not for the guidance and wisdom of Ernest Pascarella and Patrick Terenzini. Their generosity, humility, and grace are unparalleled in this and (we suspect) other related fields, as these scholars gently guided the management and ultimate execution of this product, which was the most challenging any of us has ever attempted. In our moments of doubt, Ernie and Pat provided the type of support only they, as the architects of volumes 1 and 2, could: flavoring criticism with praise and using the wisdom gained from lessons learned to guide some innovations punctuated throughout this volume. Ernie and Pat, thank you!

We are immensely grateful for the significant contributions of our graduate research assistants: Paulina Abaunza, Marc Lo, Benjamin Selznick, and Tiffani Williams at New York University; Laura Dahl at The Ohio State University; Rebecca Crandall, Tara Hudson, and Shauna Morin at North Carolina State University; Vivienne Felix at Bowling Green State University; KC Culver at the University of Iowa; David Aderholdt, Christy Oliveri, and the wonderful students in the College Students course during spring 2015 at Montana State University; and Alicia Kruisselbrink Flatt, Qin Liu, and Monica Munaretto at the University of Toronto. Many thanks also to Laura Davis, assistant director of the Center for Research on Higher Education Outcomes at New York University. Together they were an exceptional team, and devoted countless hours to collecting, organizing, and abstracting more than ten thousand studies, as well as preparing the final manuscript for publication. This volume would not have been possible without their enthusiasm, skill, and creativity.

We also value the support offered by our institutions and departments by way of scholarly leave time and graduate research assistants. Library services provided by our institutions, particularly the expertise and insight of librarians specializing in postsecondary education, were invaluable as we proceeded to assemble the vast array of articles and books for our review.

Many colleagues and mentors cheered us on over the years and imparted essential wisdom, advice, and encouragement along the way—too many to list here. Furthermore, this volume represents the work of thousands of gifted researchers who committed their scholarship to the cause of studying college impact. Their contributions have substantially advanced the field empirically and theoretically over the past decade. We also appreciate the multitude of college students who willingly gave of their time and candidly shared their experiences and perspectives across thousands of research studies.

Above all, we are indebted to our loved ones—to friends and family members who believed in us and the importance of this volume, who listened to our perpetual musings about the shaping influences of college in students' lives, who inspired us to keep moving forward, and who graciously accepted years of sacrificed evenings and weekends that went into writing this volume. All told, this work rests on many shoulders, and we are truly humbled by the generosity shown by those who took part in the journey with us.

ABOUT THE AUTHORS

Matthew J. Mayhew is the William Ray and Marie Adamson Flesher Professor of Educational Administration with a focus on Higher Education and Student Affairs at The Ohio State University. He received his BA from Wheaton College, Illinois, his master's degree from Brandeis University, and his PhD from the University of Michigan. Before coming to OSU, he served as an associate professor at New York University and an administrator at Fisher College and the University of North Carolina at Wilmington.

He has focused his research on examining the relationship between college and its influence on student learning and democratic outcomes. To support the study of college and its impact on student development and learning, he has been awarded over $14 million in funding from sources including the U.S. Department of Education, the Ewing Marion Kauffman Foundation, the Merrifield Family Trust, and an anonymous non-religiously affiliated organization with interests in social cooperation. He has been on the editorial boards of the *Journal of Higher Education, Research in Higher Education*, and the *Journal of College Student Development*. He recently received the American Educational Research Association Religion and Education SIG Emerging Scholar Award.

Alyssa N. Rockenbach is professor of higher education at North Carolina State University. She received her BA in psychology from California State University, Long Beach, and her master's degree and PhD in higher education from the University of California, Los Angeles.

Her research focuses on the impact of college on students, with particular attention to spiritual development, religious and worldview diversity in colleges and universities, campus climate, and gendered dimensions of the college student experience. Her current work includes a multimillion-dollar initiative, Cooperation in a Pluralistic World: A National Study of College Students' Engagement with Religious Diversity, in partnership with the Interfaith Youth Core and Matthew Mayhew. She serves on the editorial boards of *Research in Higher Education* and *Journal of Higher Education*, and has been honored with national awards, including the American College Personnel Association Emerging Scholar Award, and the American Educational Research Association Religion and Education SIG Emerging Scholar Award.

Nicholas A. Bowman is an associate professor of higher education and student affairs as well as the director of the Center for Research on Undergraduate Education at the University of Iowa. He received his BA from the University of California, Los Angeles, as well as two master's degrees and a PhD from the University of Michigan. Before working at the University of Iowa, he was a postdoctoral research associate at the University of Notre Dame and an assistant professor at Bowling Green State University.

His research has examined issues of college diversity, religion/worldview, outcome assessment, college rankings and prestige, and student success. He serves on the editorial boards of *Review of Educational Research*, *Research in Higher Education*, *Journal of Higher Education*, and *Journal of College Student Development*. He has had over 50 peer-reviewed journal articles published since 2008, and he received the Promising Scholar/Early Career Award from the Association for the Study of Higher Education in 2012.

Tricia A. Seifert is an associate professor of adult and higher education at Montana State University and has a faculty appointment at the Ontario Institute for Studies in Education at the University of Toronto. She received her BA in sociology and political science from Illinois Wesleyan University, her master's degree in college student services administration from Oregon State University, and her PhD in counseling, rehabilitation, and student development (student affairs administration and research emphasis) from the University of Iowa.

Her research examines postsecondary organizational cultures and structures, as well as student experiences associated with learning and success. She serves as the *Journal of College Student Development*'s associate editor for international research and scholarship and is past associate editor for *New Directions for Institutional Research* and Faculty in Residence for ACPA's Commission for Global Dimensions of Student Development. She received the Award of Honour from the Canadian Association of College and University Student Services in 2015 and the Emerging Scholar Award from ACPA in 2010.

Gregory C. Wolniak is director of the Center for Research on Higher Education Outcomes and associate professor of higher education at New York University. He received his BS in economics from Iowa State University, MA in economics from University of Illinois at Chicago, and PhD in social foundations of education from the University of Iowa. Before coming to NYU, he was senior research scientist at NORC at the University of Chicago.

His research centers on examining the socioeconomic effect of college, with a focus on the factors that influence students' pathways into college and the career and economic effects of college. He serves on the editorial boards of *Research in Higher Education*, *Journal of Higher Education*, and *Sociology of Education* and has occupied primary roles on numerous privately and publicly funded higher education studies, including the Spencer Foundation, the National Science Foundation, and the U.S. Department of Education.

Ernest T. Pascarella is professor and the Mary Louise Petersen Chair in Higher Education at the University of Iowa. He received his AB degree from Princeton University, his master's degree from the University of Pennsylvania, and his PhD from Syracuse University. Before coming to Iowa in 1997 he spent 20 years as a faculty member at the University of Illinois at Chicago.

He has focused his research and writing for the past 35 years on the impact of college on students and student persistence in higher education. He is consulting editor for the *Journal of Higher Education* and has been on the editorial boards of the *Review of Higher Education* and the *Journal of College Student Development*. He has received a number of awards from national associations for his research. These include the research awards of the Association for Institutional Research, Division J of the American Educational Research Association, the Association for the Study of Higher Education, the American College Personnel Association, the National Association of Student Personnel Administrators, and the Council of Independent Colleges. In 1990, he served as president of the Association for the Study of Higher Education and in 2003 received the Howard R. Bowen Distinguished Career Award from ASHE.

Patrick T. Terenzini is distinguished professor and senior scientist emeritus in the Center for the Study of Higher Education at Pennsylvania State University. He received his AB degree in English from Dartmouth College, his MAT degree in English education from Harvard University, and his PhD in higher education from Syracuse University. Before coming to Penn State, he served as a faculty member and administrator at Dean College (Massachusetts); Syracuse University; the University at Albany, SUNY; and the University of Georgia.

For more than 40 years, he has studied the effects of college on student learning and development, persistence, and educational attainment, and low-income and first-generation students. He has published more than 140 articles in refereed journals and made more than 200 presentations at national and international scholarly and professional conferences. The Exxon Foundation, U.S. Office of Education, National Science Foundation, College Board, Lumina Foundation, Spencer Foundation, and Alfred P. Sloane Foundation have provided financial support for his research. He has been a consulting editor for *Research in Higher Education* for more than thirty-five years and served as editor in chief of *New Directions for Institutional Research* for over a decade. He has also been associate editor of *Higher Education: Handbook of Theory and Research* and an editorial board member for *Review of Higher Education*. He has received research awards from the Association for the Study of Higher Education, the Association for Institutional Research, American Society for Engineering Education, American College Personnel Association, and National Association of Student Personnel Administrators. He received the Outstanding Service Award and the Distinguished Career Award from the Association for Institutional Research. He is a past president of the Association for the Study of Higher Education.

CHAPTER ONE

Studying College Outcomes in the 2000s

Overview and Organization of the Research

The purpose and value of higher education are under fire. As national confidence in the aims of higher education and the subsequent value of degree attainment erode (see Arum & Roksa, 2011, 2014), scholars interested in college and its influence on students are faced with a series of emergent challenges, ranging from the decoupling of the once tightly held belief that participation in higher education was the primary means for learning and thus social mobility to ontological questions about learning itself: Is learning about making money? Why is learning important if it does not lead to financial gain? Indeed, some students are paid to forgo college-going for pursuing entrepreneurial start-ups. Peter Thiel, founder of the Thiel Foundation, an organization that pays up-and-coming entrepreneurs to leave formal education, noted, "University administrators are the equivalent of mortgage brokers, selling you a story that you should go into debt massively, that it's not a consumption decision, it's an investment decision. Actually, no, it's a bad consumption decision. Most colleges are four-year parties" (Jenkins, 2010, p. A.13). This comment exemplifies the emergent American learning conundrum: How utilitarian and pragmatic does learning need to be in order to hold value in and to American society? Is higher education an investment in one's future or a consumable good of questionable value?

In light of these questions and challenges, educators from across disciplines are designing and executing rigorous college impact studies that draw on the scholarly work of generations past to further develop a robust understanding of college as critical to not only the learning enterprise but to other social and economic factors as well. Rather than shy away from the difficulties of studying outcomes that many think are ineffable and even irrelevant, these scholars are approaching the study of college impact with the thoroughness needed to appraise historic claims regarding the roles and purposes of higher education and the innovation needed to tackle questions once believed too challenging to address. Our aim in this volume is not to provide silver-bullet answers to these pressing and difficult questions but to review carefully the evidence for helping educators make claims about college and its impact on students.

Conceptually, this volume is based on Astin's (1984) framework for understanding how college affects students. Put simply, this framework deconstructs the college experiences into three discrete categories: inputs, environments, and outcomes. Inputs include demographic characteristics, academic preparedness, and predispositions that students bring with them to campus (e.g., race, high school grade point average, SAT scores, degree aspirations, and academic motivation, to name a few). Environments include, but are not limited to, institutional cultures and climates and specific educational experiences designed to shape students in some meaningful way. Outcomes relate to the attitudes (e.g., student satisfaction), aptitudes (e.g., critical thinking), and behaviors (e.g., departure) that students exhibit as a result of going to college.

Of critical importance to this review is how these categories work together to explain college and its effects on students. When organizing studies, we based our review on two relationships: that which we call "general" to describe the relationship between environments and outcomes (i.e., how exposure to and participation in college generally affect all college students) and that which we call "conditional" to underscore the relationship between environments and outcomes as it relates to student inputs (i.e., how exposure to and participation in college experiences affect students differentially based on students' input characteristics).

Figure 1.1 is a graphic representation of Astin's model. These relationships are represented by the dotted arrows in the figure. Note that the relationship between inputs and outcomes is displayed with a solid arrow to reflect that the review did not focus on studies that examined this relationship.

Figure 1.1 Astin's Framework (1984) for Understanding College and Its Influence on Students

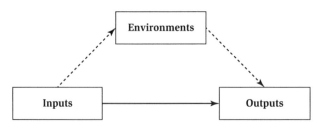

With this conceptual map as our guide, we used the organizational framework developed by Ernest Pascarella and Patrick Terenzini (1991, 2005) to synthesize the many thousands of empirically based articles designed to better understand college and its relationship to student outcomes. Building on the generous work of many scholars and employing the organizational framework used in the previous two volumes of this work, we addressed each of these six issues for each set of outcomes: the development of verbal, quantitative, and subject matter competence; cognitive skills and intellectual growth; psychosocial change; attitudes and values; moral development; educational attainment and persistence; career and economic impacts of college; and quality of life after college. Specifically, we adopted Pascarella and Terenzini's six-question framework for organizing the literature within each chapter. This framework, which developed out of previous work by G. Gurin (1971), Nucci and Pascarella (1987), and Pascarella (1985), asks six basic questions that serve as the organizing feature for each chapter:

1. What evidence is there that individuals change during the time in which they are attending college?

2. What evidence is there that change or development during college is the result of college attendance?

3. What evidence is there that attending different kinds of postsecondary institutions have a differential influence on student change and development during college?

4. What evidence exists that engaging in different experiences in the same institution are associated with student change and development during college?

5. What evidence is there that the collegiate experience produces conditional, as opposed to general, effects on student change or development?

6. What are the long-term effects of college?

Question 1, which we sometimes refer to by the shorter phrasing of "change during college," refers to whether change occurred while students were exposed to postsecondary education. Question 2, regarding the net effects of college, focuses on whether the change is attributed to postsecondary exposure, as opposed to precollege characteristics, maturation, or other noncollege experiences. Question 3, between-college effects, explores the degree to which institutional conditions (e.g., size, control, geographic location) or organizational characteristics (e.g., average level of peer cognitive development, whether the school is bureaucratic or collegial, structural diversity of the faculty) have an influence on the learning and development of the student. Question 4, within-college effects, summarizes the articles that address student change as a function of exposure to or participation in specific collegiate experiences. Question 5, conditional effects of college, gauges the extent to which the relationship between student change and any given college experience differs based on student characteristics, such as race, gender, or academic major. Question 6, long-term effects of college, addresses the duration or permanence of the college influence based on student's postcollege activities, attitudes, beliefs, and behaviors. Table 1.1 summarizes the framework used to guide this review.

Table 1.1 Overview of Review Framework

	Conceptual Orientation	Shorthand	Description	Example Research Question
Question 1	General	Change during college	Whether change occurred while in college	Do college students demonstrate gains in moral development during college?
Question 2	General	Net effects of college	Whether the change can be attributed to college-going, as opposed to maturation, for example	Does moral development occur as a result of college-going, accounting for a host of potential confounding influences?
Question 3	General	Between-college effects	Whether the change can be explained by institutional conditions, organizational characteristics, and/or peer socialization	What role does institutional type and public (versus private) control play in shaping students' moral development?
Question 4	General	Within-college effects	Whether the change can be explained by exposure to and participation in specific educational experiences	How does participation in a service-learning experience influence moral development?

(continued)

Table 1.1 Overview of Review Framework (continued)

	Conceptual Orientation	Shorthand	Description	Example Research Question
Question 5	Conditional	Conditional effects of college	Whether the change that occurs as a result of participation in any given college experience differs based on student inputs such as race, gender, living status	Does the relationship between participating in a service-learning experience and moral development differ between residential and commuter students?
Question 6	General	Long-term college effects	If the changes due to college are sustained after graduation	Are the moral development gains made during college sustained beyond graduation?

Building on these six questions used to frame the literature, we organized studies within each question based on themes emerging from the articles reviewed for each chapter. This decision came from our collective value to review articles in the spirit in which they were written. We wanted to stay as close to the authors' intentions as possible. Of course, this decision produced a distinctive set of challenges regarding structural continuity across chapters. For example, for the within-college effects section of each chapter, some authors studied honors colleges while others did not; some articles discussed interactional diversity while others examined quality of diversity interaction or non-classroom-based diversity peer interaction; some studies investigated work on campus while others reflected interest in part-time employment. Given these and the many more examples of themes that emerged from the studies themselves, we chose not to try to force articles into categories for the sake of consistency across chapters; rather, we let the literature base specific to the chapter's focus inform the organization of that chapter, at least to some degree. Similarly, a number of outcomes examined in the literature do not fit neatly and discretely into one chapter or another. For example, one could argue that a self-reported gain in general education is a measure of the general skills, like verbal and quantitative competence, that students develop in college; a parallel argument could advance that this is a reflection of students' academic and intellectual self-concept. We shaped our review with the authors' intentions in mind while recognizing the potential overlap between researchers' definitions of outcomes and the conceptual outcome framework used in the book.

HOW THE LITERATURE HAS CHANGED

Since the first volume of this book was published (Pascarella & Terenzini, 1991), terms and definitions continue to change at a remarkable pace. Words like *how*, *college*, *affect*, and *students* have taken different meanings in the higher education research context since the beginning of the century. For example, with the advent and momentum of computer-mediated distance education, for-profit institutions, and massive open online courses (MOOCs), "college," as we know it today, has moved beyond chartered boundaries to be more inclusive than ever before. As the college experience extends its reach, its "effects" are more difficult than ever to ascertain; indeed, new methods are continuously being offered and refined to manage issues with studying students in their natural, albeit nonrandom, learning environments. Finally, there are many definitions of *student*: Is a student someone enrolled in one MOOC? A degree program? A certification program? A GRE course offered at an institution? Since these words—*how*, *college*, *affects*, *students*—underlie the syntheses provided in this volume, we consider the meaning of each to discuss trends in the literature since the previously published volume (Pascarella & Terenzini, 2005) and to note where this volume departs from those previously written.

How: Changes in the Ways College May Have Influenced Students

Based on the rich 30-plus years of research linking college-going to development and change across a variety of domains, scholars have moved from empiricism to assumption: rather than question if college-going has an influence on students, scholars assume that the relationship exists and subsequently focus on investigating the specific practices and psychological mechanisms responsible for student change. In other words, since the previous volume, scholars are asking more questions about *why* college affects students than *if* college affects students. Such a trend presented a particular set of challenges for this review, including how to speak to change over time with very few longitudinal designs that tracked students over multiple time points, address the net effects of college-going as so few studies compared students to their peers who did not attend college, and evaluate and summarize the theoretical claims across the empirical studies.

Another disruption in our understanding of the "how" comes in the form of the many competing approaches designed to interrogate college and its effects on students. Clearly, the frameworks researchers use to position their inquiries into college and its effects on students play a role in the questions researchers ask and their subsequent choices regarding data and methods of analysis. Like previous volumes, we overrepresented studies that adopted a positivist or post-positivist paradigm for asking questions about college and its effects on students. Perhaps this overrepresentation is an artifact of the types of studies that are published in most peer-reviewed journals. Alternatively, the overrepresentation may result from our decision to review only the studies that measured the relationship between college and its effects on students. Either way, we own that our collective perspective also informed our approach to this review from its conceptualization to its organization.

Like its predecessors, this review theoretically draws from many disciplines for studies and explanations of the relationship between college and students. Each chapter tended to rely on certain disciplinary perspectives based on the material published on the chapter's subject; for example, chapters focused on outcomes with developmental dimensions often drew from psychology, while those that emphasized earnings were based largely in economic studies. Due to the distinctiveness that each theoretical perspective offered for making meaning of empirical findings, we decided to discuss the theoretical underpinnings of each outcome within its related chapter and to provide a review of only the theories that this volume's researchers most often used to frame their inquiries. To be clear, *this volume is not intended to cover, or even mention, all theories, conceptualizations, and frameworks that have informed higher education scholarship since its inception.* Instead, we provided brief overviews of these elements as contextual support for conclusions offered by the authors of the articles reviewed in this volume. Placing the theoretical overview section within each chapter marks a departure from previous efforts where an overview of guiding theory for all chapters was offered in Chapter 2.

Turning to our approach to the literature review, we gave greater weight to issues of design over analysis when making decisions about article inclusion and subsequent exposition (see Rubin, 2008). When compared to articles that used cross-sectional designs, articles that included research designs that were longitudinal and included a pretest and a comparison group, or that were quasi-experimental (e.g., propensity score or regression discontinuity) were relied on more heavily as evidence of particular empirical trends. Due to our collective commitment to help readers understand the criteria we used for reviewing and ultimately including articles in this volume and marking a departure from previous volumes, we included a detailed methodological overview as a methodological appendix in this review.

Of course, the issue of survey fatigue also has made making claims about college and its effect on students more problematic. Technological advances in data collection and control have equipped scholars and institutional researchers with the infrastructure needed to support more institution-specific data collection efforts. Although we encourage these practices as they lead to data-driven decisions administrators can use to ameliorate institutional practices, we also recognize that the proliferation of these data collection efforts makes multi-institutional research efforts more challenging. Survey fatigue presented another issue that complicated the "how" with regard to understanding college and its effects on students.

College

What is college? Since its inception, higher education in the United States has been in constant evolution. The particular sociohistoric and political location in which this volume was drafted marks no exception to this trend. However, in the 10 years since the previous volume was published, a number of developments have changed the way that many understand and relate to college and student experiences therein.

The term *college* is complicated. For example, in the United States, *college* could refer to higher education in general, a single institution within the higher education system (e.g., Pomona College), or a subunit within a larger university system (e.g., College of Business within the University of Iowa). In other countries, the term *college* carries different meanings, often reflecting each nation's interest in, values concerning, and organization of higher/postsecondary/tertiary education (Jones, 2012). Despite the challenges that accompany different interpretations of college, especially across national borders, we broadened the scope of this review to include relevant college impact research executed in Australia, New Zealand, the United Kingdom, and Canada. Marking a departure from previous efforts, the inclusion of studies from these countries as part of an expanded scope of the review reflects an acknowledgment that higher education has become much more internationalized since the previous volume's publication (Altbach & McGill Peterson, 2007; Guruz, 2008; Knight, 2008) and that much could be learned from understanding student experiences outside the United States. Acknowledging and appreciating the differences in these countries' respective approaches to higher education, we selected these nations based on their use of English as the primary language for instruction and research dissemination, as well as their historic grounding in the Oxford-Cambridge residential colleges model.

The technological movement has advanced the notion of college from being a context bound by geographic borders to one that is essentially borderless, with many individuals claiming student status without having set foot on a college campus (Selino, 2013). Indeed, even President Obama has enacted policies that challenge the notion of equating college with a degree, as involvement in at least one year has taken federal priority over four-year degree completion (e.g., Complete College America, 2011, 2012, 2013). With the increasingly widespread and mobile nature of Internet technologies and social media shifting the landscape for educational delivery, technology has complicated research on college and its effects on students by challenging assumptions that any scholar could ever isolate the effects of any measured experience on any student outcome.

The movement toward integration of the college experience has changed the research landscape, as evidence-based best practices (e.g., service-learning, living-learning communities; see Kuh, 2008) often reflect integrated educational delivery models designed in an effort to educate the whole student. What is service-learning? What is a living-learning community? Are these academic, social, or functional experiences (see Milem & Berger, 1997)? To date, despite a robust research base on these topics, few practices have attained definitional consensus. As a result, the college experience itself has become harder to define, making the study of a presumed best practice for its influence on college student learning more challenging.

The changing nature of the peer environment has rendered historic higher education vernacular increasingly difficult to understand. For example, what do we mean by *college major*? A series of courses tightly threaded together by a common academic interest? A means for generating a pseudo-academic cohort effect by engaging students with common interests around a set of ideas presented sequentially in the curriculum? Another way of grouping students, similar to identity patterns based on social identity group organization or residence hall participation? Again, these questions provided some conceptual challenges to researchers interested in unpacking college experiences as a set of embedded peer networks and to us as we confronted some organizational obstacles in deciding where to discuss peer effects in each chapter.

Similar challenges emerged from studies that linked faculty practice to student outcomes. Who are the faculty who have the greatest impact on students? Are these adjunct faculty? Faculty who teach more courses? Faculty who engage students in undergraduate research opportunity programs? To complicate matters further, faculty practice sometimes is mediated fully through a particular delivery mechanism: authors may study an educational context (e.g., diversity course) for its association with a particular outcome without specifically examining the practice within that context. Given these and the many other issues that remain unmentioned, it is often difficult to draw conclusions about the potential impact of faculty behaviors on students.

Affects

Given the explosion of research on college and its effects on students over the past decade, the use of causal language has been increasingly scrutinized in making claims about college and its relationship to college student learning and development. In tandem with criticism about causal language, questioning such verbs as *affects* and, to some degree, *influences* (Swanson, 2010, 2012), many scientists have also questioned the use of the term *quasi-experimental*, even for research that uses longitudinal designs with control or comparison groups. Unless researchers can randomly assign students into a certain educational experience (i.e., experimental) or methodologically make adjustments to samples through the use of propensity scores or regression discontinuity (i.e., quasi-experimental), causal claims about college and its relationship to students must be made cautiously or, in some cases, not at all. The disruption concerning what constitutes a quasi-experimental design marks a point of departure in our synthesis of the literature when juxtaposed against previous reviews. In addition to being more thoughtful in our use of terms like *affects* and *influences*, we were equally careful to use the term *quasi-experimental* only in studies with adjusted sample designs.

As with previous volumes, *affects* is a term reserved for studies that measure the relationship between college experiences and outcomes, not necessarily for studies that use college students as samples of convenience for examining relationships between certain phenomena or for scholars only interested in how outcomes differed among certain student characteristics, like race or high school achievement. In short, all of the studies reviewed for this volume involved researchers' empirical attempt to link educational experiences to student outcomes.

What do we mean by a college experience *affecting* students? Most of the studies reviewed for this volume used developmental language for making meaning of college and its impact on students: we use phrases like "helping students make cognitive gains," "more likely to demonstrate gains in pluralism orientations," and "make moral gains" as communicative proxies for college's impact on students. When the studies depart from developmental frames, we aimed to use the authors' voices to describe the kind of learning or achievement, if any, that occurs and its relationship to college-going. Examples include "helping students achieve outcomes related to critical thinking" to "outcomes with moral dimensions."

Students

Who a college student was, is, and is becoming plays a central role in framing this review. As stated in previous volumes, the demographic characteristics of college-going students continue to rapidly change, forcing us to reconsider the ways we have traditionally defined the college student. According to the U.S. National Center for Educational Statistics, the percentage of undergraduates of color has risen from 29.2% in 2000 to 39.7% in 2012 (U.S. Department of Education, National Center for Education Statistics, 2015). Given these shifting characteristics, especially as they relate to students' racial identities, comparisons between studies conducted in the 1990s with those reviewed in this volume must be interpreted cautiously.

Similarly, more international students are enrolling in U.S. higher education institutions than ever before (Institute of International Education, 2012). Institutions continue to expand their reach into international markets through strategic partnerships with global partners and increase revenue streams through recruiting more international students to campus in order to remain globally relevant and economically viable (Altbach & McGill Peterson, 2007; American University Office of Institutional Research and Assessment, 2014; Guruz, 2008; University of California Office of the President, 2015; University of Notre Dame, 2013). Given this increase of international students, college impact researchers are beginning to be more attentive to other variables (e.g., English as a second language) that may exert influence on either the college experience or the student outcome.

Related to these complications are notions of multiple, intersecting identities for college students. With a greater number of students coming to college more cognizant of their multiple identities and/or more familiar with the lexicon used to describe intersecting identities, it is important to understand that the effects of "race" or "worldview" or "sexual orientation" may involve intersections across these characteristics. Moreover, we were cautious in our use of terms that sidestep these intersecting realities and tried to shy away from using terms like "controlling for race" because they, although technically correct, probably do not provide the most accurate picture of student experience. How can anyone really control for race? In addition, because the research reviewed was broadened to include studies outside the United States, it is necessary to be cognizant of how perceptions of identity are deeply rooted in the unique history, culture, and systemic social structure of the various international postsecondary contexts reviewed.

Another complication arises when trying to capture the experience of the traditional college student. Traditional-aged college students are now a minority of undergraduates in U.S. postsecondary education, as Pascarella and Terenzini (2005) predicted in the previous volume. In short, we attempted to include studies that spoke to the undergraduate experience of all students, regardless of age, college choice, degree aspiration, or preferred mode of educational delivery (e.g., online). In doing so, we hope to extend the reach of this volume to any person interested in undergraduate postsecondary education.

VOLUME 3: RESEARCH FROM THE 21ST CENTURY

This volume adheres closely to the guidelines provided in previous iterations of *How College Affects Students* (1991 and 2005). As such, we echo the sentiments expressed in 1991 and 2005, respectively. This book is an attempt to synthesize the college impact research evidence that has accumulated since the review period of the 2005 publication. At times, we relied on articles from previous decades to frame arguments made by the authors whose work is reviewed in this volume. This review covered articles written between 2002 and 2013. In addition, we included some articles published from 2014, depending on the time that the chapter was written. This approach was consistent with the previous volumes' presentation of the evidence.

In terms of focus, this book collected information from over 10,000 sources of literature. Of those pieces, 1,848 peer-reviewed articles served as the foundation for this synthesis. Unlike previous volumes, we chose not to include conference papers or dissertations due to the overwhelming number of quality-controlled research published over the past decade. Articles were located in journals representing an array of audiences. Every article identified as relevant (i.e., it addressed some aspect of "college effects" on students) was initially reviewed and flagged for potential use for this review. In addition to this approach, we located articles through the use of search engines such as Google Scholar, ERIC, and PsycInfo, among others. In addition, we conducted a hand-search of general higher education journals (e.g., *Journal of Higher Education, Research in Higher Education, Review of Higher Education*, along with some other journals (e.g., *Journal of College Student Development, Review of Educational Research, Journal of College Student Retention*). Also, we conducted forward searches in Google Scholar to see who cited eligible articles. After articles were identified as relevant, we scoured that article's references as a means for tracking down other cited works germane for this review. Once the articles were compiled, they were then organized based on chapter focus. On completion of this step, articles were then systematically coded based on their fit within (and often across) the six-question framework offered by Pascarella and Terenzini (1991, 2005) as part of their syntheses and methodological quality.

Exemplary studies of college impact received greater weight in our review of the literature. Specifically, we placed an emphasis on studies that used research designs that permitted stronger causal conclusions (i.e., experimental, quasi-experimental, and nonexperimental with rigorous analytical controls), obtained multi-institutional samples, conducted multilevel analyses (when appropriate), explored direct and indirect effects (when appropriate), employed a longitudinal design, and used well-validated measures of outcomes and experiences. In subsequent chapters, we cite studies that contain a variety of methodological characteristics, but we generally describe the findings of stronger research in greater detail, and we use considerable caution when evaluating the results of studies that meet few of these criteria.

To provide readers context for understanding our approach to weighing the evidence provided in this volume, we offer some points about measuring and modeling the student outcomes represented and reviewed in Chapters 2 through 9 of this book. Although technical in some regards, this strategy enables readers to make meaning of the research designs and numbers derived for this volume. We begin with a brief discussion of the complexities involved with measuring student change as a result of exposure to and participation in post-secondary education. We then discuss issues of whether and when effects are practically meaningful, and we provide guidelines for making these decisions.

Measuring and Modeling Student Outcomes

The measurement of changes in student outcomes is more complicated than one might expect. Direct measures of change necessarily involve collecting data on the same students (or institutions) on two or more occasions in time and then comparing the outcomes at these different time points. However, longitudinal data collection (with or without random assignment) presents some logistical difficulties: (1) students' data from the pretest must be linked to their responses

on the posttest(s), which requires keeping track of students' personal information; (2) many students who completed the pretest may drop out, transfer, or
simply not respond to the posttest; (3) collecting data multiple times requires
more human and financial resources than conducting a single data collection;
(4) the time between the pretest and posttest may be too short for the expected
effect to occur; and (5) the primary results from longitudinal analyses cannot be
determined until two or more waves of data collection have occurred. To allevi-
ate these challenges, some college impact studies conduct a single cross-sectional
assessment. This may be less problematic for outcomes that do not have a true
pretest (e.g., college satisfaction, perceptions of campus climate), but this is
certainly a concern for determining changes in cognitive, attitudinal, and psychosocial outcomes. Researchers who administer a single questionnaire often
ask students for an estimate how much they have changed on a variety of outcomes, which serves as a proxy for longitudinal measures of growth.

Although college student self-reported gains are often interpreted as if they
reflect changes in student outcomes over time (Gonyea & Miller, 2011), considerable evidence suggests that this is not the case. If these self-reports were
accurate, there should be a strong correlation between students' self-reported
gains on a particular outcome and longitudinal changes on a well-validated
measure of that same outcome. Across a variety of outcomes, the correlations
between longitudinal and self-reported gains on the same construct are consistently weak and are often not significantly different from zero (Bowman, 2010a,
2011b; Bowman & Brandenberger, 2010; Gosen & Washbush, 1999; Hess &
Smythe, 2001). In addition, the variables that significantly predict longitudinal
growth (e.g., college experiences, student demographics, institutional attributes) are often nonsignificant—and sometimes even significant in the opposite
direction—when predicting self-reported gains for the same construct
(Anaya, 1999; Bowman, 2010a; Bowman & Brandenberger, 2010; Porter, 2013).
Earlier research has established consistent biases in self-reported growth among
college students and older adults, such that people tend to overestimate how
much their skills and abilities have changed, yet underestimate how much their
attitudes have changed (Conway & Ross, 1984; Goethals & Reckman, 1973;
Markus, 1986; McFarland & Ross, 1987; M. Ross, 1989). A meta-analytic review
further suggests that people may be somewhat accurate in reporting their current knowledge, whereas they are highly inaccurate at reporting changes in
knowledge over time (Sitzmann, Ely, Brown, & Bauer, 2010). In short, using
student self-reported gains as a proxy for college impact may yield substantially
flawed results.

That said, longitudinal studies that use objective assessments also face some
difficulties for measuring changes in student outcomes. Perhaps the most
important concern is students' effort on assessments that have substantial cognitive demands, such as critical thinking instruments. If students do not exert
considerable effort, then the results of these assessments may be questionable.
Indeed, providing monetary incentives for student performance results in

higher test scores than providing no incentive (for a meta-analysis, see Duckworth, Quinn, Lynam, Loeber, & Stouthamer-Loeber, 2011). In addition, both telling students that their test scores will be used as a means of assessing the quality of their institution or assessing their own skills result in better performance than telling students that their responses are simply part of a research project (Liu, Bridgeman, & Adler, 2012; also see Wise & DeMars, 2005). Although the impact of different motivational conditions is concerning, there are at least two ways in which these problems can be at least partially remedied. First, researchers or administrators can frame the purpose of the study carefully to increase student motivation (i.e., the results will be used not only for research purposes, but also for assessing individual students or the institution as a whole). Second, a variety of techniques are available for identifying unmotivated test takers, especially when the exams are administered via computer (e.g., Swerdzewski, Harmes, & Finney, 2011; Wise & Kong, 2005). Finding and removing unmotivated students from the sample can lead to more accurate conclusions about student performance.

Additional difficulties may occur when attempting to estimate the overall impact or net effect of college, since a decrease or increase in some outcome measure during the college years does not necessarily suggest that college contributed to that increase or decrease. To address this college impact question, one would need to explore whether changes in college students' outcomes differ from those of people who are the same age but not in college (which is why this book distinguishes between "change during college" and "net effects of college"). One example is particularly illustrative. A number of studies found a decline in religious behaviors during the college years, such as attending religious services, frequency of prayer, discussing religion, and perceiving oneself as religious (e.g., Bryant, Choi, & Yasuno, 2003; also see Pascarella & Terenzini, 1991). This result, which merely reflects change during college, can be interpreted as demonstrating that college attendance has a secularizing effect. However, Uecker, Regnerus, and Vaaler (2007) examined a large sample of young adults who did and did not attend college so that they could accurately assess the net effects of college. Both college students and noncollege adults declined on several measures of religiosity, but these decreases were actually greater among young adults who were not attending college. Thus, simply exploring change during college as a proxy for net effects can yield conclusions that are exactly the opposite of those obtained when using appropriate noncollege comparison groups.

A final issue with measuring and modeling college outcomes is that some dependent variables are not continuous, whereas many statistical analyses make assumptions that are violated when the distribution of the outcome is not at least approximately normal. These nonnormal outcomes occur because variables can be dichotomous (a student graduates or does not), categorical (a student could remain at the same institution, transfer to another institution, or drop out of college entirely), ordinal (a student might respond to the perceived importance of a life goal on a four-point scale from "not at all important" to "essential"), or a count of the number of times an event occurs (a student could take no diversity courses, one course, two courses, and so on). These types of outcomes can be modeled successfully through the use of logistic, multinomial, ordinal logit, and Poisson regression, respectively (for more information, see Agresti, 2013; Long, 1997; Smithson & Merkle, 2013; Xie & Powers, 2008). These treatments of categorical and limited dependent variables can then be incorporated within some of the statistical techniques discussed in the appendix, such as multilevel modeling, structural equation modeling, and quasi-experimental analyses.

Practical and Statistical Significance

When considering research or assessment results, various stakeholders seek to answer a fundamental question: Are these effects meaningful? The vast majority of research studies emphasize one definition of meaningful, which is whether the results are statistically significant at some specific threshold of confidence (most commonly, $p<.05$). Statistical significance is arguably necessary to determine whether an effect is meaningful, since it suggests whether a particular finding is unlikely to have occurred by chance. However, it is also crucial to decide whether a finding is not only "real" (nonrandom), but also whether it is practically meaningful. Some national studies of higher education collect data on tens of thousands of students; because statistical tests are sensitive to the sample size, a result could be statistically significant while also being very small and therefore having little practical importance. For example, within a sample of 10,000 students, a seemingly trivial correlation of .02 would be statistically significant at $p<.05$. Many people would likely agree that this correlation is not meaningful in practice. Thus, given that higher education researchers, practitioners, and policymakers all want to create change that improves student outcomes, statistical and practical significance are both necessary for determining the importance of a finding.

This point brings up the difficult issue of how to determine whether an effect is substantively or practically meaningful. Any answer to this question depends on a variety of circumstances. First, obtaining a reasonable return on the investment of human and financial resources when making a change in institutional practices is a valid and important consideration. For example, a reasonably small effect might be considered worthwhile if it were obtained through minor and virtually cost-free adjustments in teaching or academic advising practices, but not if a proposed change was to open a comprehensive student success center that required numerous new employees and expensive facilities. Second, how much attention a relationship deserves is shaped in part by the rigor of the study that produced it. For instance, an effect size from a randomized experiment is probably more worthy of attention than one of similar size found in a study with fewer controls for potentially confounding variables, because more rigorous designs will often provide a more accurate estimate of a causal relationship. Third, in a somewhat related point, some outcomes have no true pretest (e.g., college satisfaction, perceptions of campus climate). Because the pretest is often strongly related to the posttest, there is more variance to be explained by within- and between-college attributes for outcomes that have no true pretest. Fourth, some outcomes are more stable over time than others, so the same effect size is more impressive when it occurs for a less malleable outcome than for a variable known to fluctuate greatly. Fifth, the length of time between an experience and the outcome is also a relevant consideration. It certainly seems reasonable to expect a larger impact of service-learning (or any other experience) when civic engagement is measured in the next semester rather than several years after college graduation. Sixth, predictor variables can be dichotomous or continuous. It is therefore difficult, for example, to directly compare the size of effects for a dichotomous and a continuous independent variable predicting the same outcome. In short, the meaningfulness of the magnitude of an effect should be considered contextually to some extent.

Despite these complexities, college impact researchers need to have some basis for determining what constitutes a practically meaningful effect. We offer a discussion of this issue and provide specific recommendations. We necessarily discuss some statistical detail, because these guidelines are provided for specific statistical results. We hope that these recommendations will be widely used by researchers, who can then interpret the magnitude of these effects to better inform practice.

Effect Size Guidelines

Many social science studies use Cohen's (1988) general guidelines for effect sizes. Cohen frequently notes that researchers should not rely too heavily on these guidelines since they are general and provided for all behavioral sciences, which clearly includes a large and diverse array of disciplines and fields of study. These guidelines are also frequently misused not only through overreliance, but also through incorrect interpretation of the actual text. Most notably, Cohen suggests specific values for "small," "medium," and "large" effects, but he is often miscited as providing ranges of values for these criteria. He also provides guidelines for various types of effect sizes; we will focus on those that are most relevant to college impact research. A Cohen's d is the standardized difference between the means of two groups; this statistic is calculated as the difference of the means divided by the pooled standard deviation (i.e., the standard deviation for both groups combined). These guidelines state that a difference of .2 standard deviations is small, .5 is medium, and .8 is large. For correlation coefficients (which are ideal for indicating the simple relationship between two continuous variables), Cohen asserts that a small effect is a correlation of .1, medium is .3, and large is .5. He also provides guidelines for the variance explained (or R-squared) of a multiple regression analysis that includes multiple independent variables predicting an outcome variable; these are approximately .02 for a small effect, .13 for medium, and .26 for large.

Because these guidelines are not specific to higher education and there is little other basis for determining the magnitude of effects in college impact research, we propose revised guidelines. We do so while recommending substantial caution about the use of these figures. We have already noted some reasons that one would consider the same effect size to be more practically meaningful in one context than another, including the cost of the intervention, the methodological rigor of the study, the stability of the outcomes examined, and the length of time between the experience and outcome. We provide guidelines for measures of effect size that we believe are particularly relevant to college impact research, including Cohen's *d*, multiple regression coefficients, and delta-*p* (which we define later). We also describe two conditions that *must* exist for the appropriate use of these effect sizes. First, these conditions are designed to describe the findings *only* from studies that used well-conducted experimental designs, quasi-experimental designs, and other multivariate analyses (e.g., regression, hierarchical linear modeling) that contain a set of rigorous control variables (i.e., which must include pretests when examining outcomes that could have a pretest). Stated differently, these guidelines are *not* appropriate for nonexperimental analyses that omit key predictors that are necessary to isolate the relationship between the experience of interest and the outcome.

Second, to compare the magnitude of effects for multivariate analyses within and across studies, all continuous variables (both dependent and independent) should be standardized with a mean of zero and a standard deviation of one, whereas dichotomous variables should not be recoded. This transformation ensures that unstandardized coefficients (i.e., for regression, multilevel modeling, structural equation modeling) for dichotomous independent variables predicting continuous outcomes are analogous to Cohen's *d*s (adjusting for all other variables in the model), whereas unstandardized coefficients for continuous independent variables predicting continuous outcomes are analogous to standardized regression coefficients or beta weights (Cohen, Cohen, West, & Aiken, 2003). This recoding of continuous predictors may be especially important for analyses predicting noncontinuous outcomes, because the coefficients from these analyses (e.g., odds ratios, delta-*p*s) depend on the coding values of the independent variable, and there are no coefficients from these analyses that are analogous to standardized regression coefficients. The unstandardized coefficients for all predictors should then be reported, and other coefficients should be provided when appropriate or helpful (e.g., delta-*p* for logistic regression). We feel that these coding and reporting choices are important regardless of whether the authors of a study choose to use these effect-size guidelines, since these will allow other researchers to easily compare the magnitude of effects across studies.

In a couple of circumstances, results of studies that do not use these coding practices can be subsequently converted to appropriate effect sizes. For studies that use unstandardized continuous variables, researchers can use the standard deviations to calculate what the results would have been if the variables were standardized before being included in the analyses. To accomplish this task, researchers must use the standard deviations provided in a descriptive table (or elsewhere) for this transformation to occur. In addition, standardized regression coefficients when both the predictor and outcome are continuous will not be affected by our recommended coding, since these coefficients convey the relationships in terms of standard deviations by definition.

We also point out that our recommendations are not based on an exhaustive quantitative synthesis of the literature. Theoretically, one could record and analyze the tens of thousands of results that we summarize in this volume and create guidelines that are solely based on that empirical analysis. Such a synthesis would not only prove extraordinarily time-consuming, but it would also require that a sufficient number of studies have met the methodological standards and provided effect sizes that fit the specifications described here. That empirical approach would also need to determine how to define these guidelines within the sea of results. For instance, would a "large" effect size be defined as the cutoff for the top 5% of effect sizes for all eligible studies? The top 20%? How would one justify this decision? As an alternative approach, we rely on our own experience in conducting this research as well as existing literature. For instance, What Works Clearinghouse (2014) claims that "effect sizes of .25 standard deviations or larger are considered to be substantively important" (p. 23). Valentine and Cooper (2003) assert that effect sizes are generally smaller in education research than in other fields, which is consistent with Cohen's (1988) view:

> Thurstone once said that in psychology we measure [people] by their shadows. As the behavioral scientist moves from [her/his/their] theoretical constructs, to their operational realization in measurement and subject manipulation, very much "noise" (measurement unreliability, lack of fidelity to the construct) is likely to accompany the variables (p. 79).

That is, we can generally expect to find smaller effect sizes when examining real-world aspects of the college experience—in which curricula, cocurricular programs, and institutional missions are also implemented with varying degrees of effectiveness and measured with some degree of error—as predictors of real-world outcomes. Perhaps most important of all, adopting such a set of guidelines, while highly mathematical and "scientific," would also require overlooking or ignoring a vast number of relevant studies that fail to meet those criteria. In our view, as in Pascarella and Terenzini's (1991, 2005) two volumes, there is simply no substitute for judgment in developing the kinds of research syntheses that we provide in subsequent chapters. Thus, we provide estimates of effect sizes where appropriate, and we also rely heavily on the canons of good research and our professional training and experiences in making judgments about "the weight of evidence" in our summaries and conclusions.

With these caveats in mind, our guidelines for "small," "medium," and "large" effect sizes are presented in Table 1.2. Consistent with Valentine and Cooper's (2003) observation, our recommendations for Cohen's d or the standardized mean difference (small = .15, medium = .30, and large = .50) are smaller than those that Cohen (1988) provided. However, we believe that a ½ standard deviation causal effect of a college experience on a meaningful college outcome certainly qualifies as "large." Similar to Cohen's guidelines, these figures are not minimum thresholds or specific ranges (which imply a false precision); for instance, we feel that effects of .28 and .34 standard deviations are both approximately "medium" (since they are both close to .30), while .40 standard deviations could be described as "between medium and large" in magnitude. These values for Cohen's d could come from a simple mean comparison (for experimental studies *only*) or from an unstandardized regression coefficient when the predictor is dichotomous and the outcome is continuous and standardized (for quasi-experimental or rigorous multivariate analyses *only*).

Cohen (1988) and others do not provide any guidance about the magnitude of standardized regression coefficients (although there is some tentative advice about translating between these multivariate statistics and raw correlations; see Peterson & Brown, 2005). Therefore, we are not able to draw on previous guidelines to supplement our thinking about the magnitude of the link between a continuous predictor and a continuous outcome. If we use a formula to convert a standardized mean difference to a point-biserial correlation (see Lipsey & Wilson, 2001), then a "large" Cohen's d of .5 corresponds to a correlation of .24 (if the sample sizes in the two groups are equal), .22 (if 70% of participants are in one group), or .20 (if 80% of participants are in one group). Moreover, as Lipsey and Wilson note, dichotomizing what is actually a continuous construct will result in a smaller effect size; this concern seems applicable in many cases in which students participate in a particular experience to a varying extent. Therefore, .2 seems reasonable as a "large" standardized regression coefficient. Using the same ratios as for Cohen's d, .06 and .12 seem reasonable as "small" and "medium" effect sizes for standardized regression coefficients, respectively.

For determining the impact of college on a dichotomous outcome, we prefer the use of the delta-p statistic to the odds ratio because this value can be interpreted more easily than the odds ratio (for more information, see Cruce, 2009; Petersen, 1985). Delta-p is the change in the probability of having a "1" on the dependent variable (rather than "0") that corresponds to a one-unit change in the independent variable. This probability change also depends on the values on the independent variables; therefore, to provide this estimate for the "average" participant, delta-p is often calculated for a participant who has the mean value on all predictors. It is more difficult to provide a delta-p value that is informed by the other effect size recommendations, since there is no way to determine the "variance explained" for a dichotomous outcome. Informed by Cohen's (1988) discussion of the h statistic and our own experiences, we propose that a "large" delta-p is .15. That is, an effect of a college experience is large if it corresponds to a 15 percentage point change in the probability of a dichotomous outcome occurring (e.g., college graduation). Using the same proportions as for the other effect size metrics, delta-ps of .05 and .09 would be

Table 1.2 Overview of Guidelines for Effect Size Metrics in College Impact Research
When Key Conditions Are Met

Metric	Explanation and Use	Small	Medium	Large
Cohen's *d* (standardized mean difference)	Difference between two groups when predicting a continuous outcome variable (this metric should also be used for dichotomous predictors and a continuous outcome in multivariate analyses)	.15	.30	.50
Standardized regression coefficient	Relationship between a continuous predictor and a continuous outcome in a multivariate model (unstandardized coefficients and Cohen's *d* guidelines should be used if the predictor is dichotomous)	.06	.12	.20
Delta-*p*	Change in probability when predicting a dichotomous outcome in a multivariate model (for both dichotomous and continuous predictors)	.05	.09	.15

Note. These guidelines should be used only when a study meets the following conditions. First, the study employs an experimental design, quasi-experimental design, or rigorous multivariate analyses (with appropriate control variables, including a pretest). Second, for Cohen's *d* and delta-*p*, continuous dependent and independent variables are standardized with a mean of zero and a standard deviation of one, whereas dichotomous variables are not transformed. The values for delta-*p* should also be used for average marginal effects. These effect size guidelines should be considered in the context of relevant study features, such as the overall rigor of the study, the financial return on investment, the malleability of the outcome, and the length of time between the experience and outcome.

then considered "small" and "medium," respectively. These same values for delta-*p* should also be used for average marginal effects, which similarly provide the effect of a one-unit change in the independent variable on the dependent variable.

Summary

This section provided an overview of some of the challenges regarding the valid measurement of student outcomes and changes in these outcomes and determining whether effects have practical significance for higher education professionals and policymakers. We also offered effect size guidelines for college impact studies so that people who produce and use this research can have a common understanding of what constitutes a small, medium, and large effect of college. We hope that this discussion provides the needed context for helping readers understand the weight of the evidence considered in this volume.

CHAPTER CONCLUSION

This chapter provided an overview of the organization of this volume, the changing higher education landscape as a pretext for understanding some of the choices authors made in their lines of inquiry, some of the challenges with measuring and modeling student outcomes, and some methodological innovations with regard to making meaning of the numbers used as evidence for the claims in the book. Indeed, writing a book of this scope requires attention to detail without losing sight of some of the larger questions facing higher education stakeholders.

To accomplish the former, we offer Chapters 2 through 9, which are organized by student outcome areas: the development of verbal, quantitative, and subject matter competence (Chapter 2); cognitive and intellectual development (Chapter 3); psychosocial change (Chapter 4); attitudes and values (Chapter 5); moral development (Chapter 6), educational attainment and persistence (Chapter 7); career and economic impacts of college (Chapter 8); and quality of life (Chapter 9). The methodological appendix at the end of the book further illustrates some of the details important for making meaning of chapter content.

In order to address some of the larger issues facing higher education stakeholders, we have provided two summary chapters. Chapter 10 summarizes points consistently raised across all chapters. In Chapter 11, we discuss our work's implications for policymakers, researchers, and practitioners. It is our hope that a variety of stakeholders interested in higher education will use this volume to create and optimize contexts for student success.

CHAPTER TWO

Development of Verbal, Quantitative, and Subject Matter Competence

Completing a higher education credential, whether a diploma, certificate, or a degree, means little if students do not also gain in knowledge and skills. Since publication of the previous volume (Pascarella & Terenzini, 2005), the degree to which students achieve designated learning outcomes has become a topic of greater public conversation (Ewell, 2009; McClaran, 2013). Perspectives from this conversation have often advanced a skills deficit among recent higher education graduates (Borwein, 2014; Economist Intelligence Unit, 2014). Research on employer perceptions of college graduates has fueled the media's portrayal of the skills shortage (Hart Research Associates, 2008, 2010). Yet the question that this raises is how college or university attendance influences graduates' knowledge and skills development in the most academic areas: verbal skills and literacy, quantitative reasoning and numeracy, and subject matter competency, defined by the discipline or field studied. This chapter examines this set of outcomes using the six-question framework introduced in Chapter 1.

MEASURES OF STUDENT LEARNING

Central to this chapter are measurements of student learning with respect to verbal and quantitative competence. We prioritized studies that used objective measures of these competencies. Of the research reviewed, instruments typically used in measuring student verbal and quantitative skill development included ACT's Collegiate Assessment of Academic Proficiency (CAAP), Educational Testing Services' (ETS) Proficiency Profile, and, to a lesser extent, the standardized tests for graduate school admission: the Graduate Record

Examination (GRE), Medical College Admissions Test (MCAT), and the Law School Admissions Test (LSAT). The CAAP measures general cognitive learning in college, and consists of five modules, four of them relevant to this chapter: reading comprehension, mathematics, writing skills, and science reasoning (critical thinking measured by the CAAP and broader notions of cognitive development are covered in Chapter 3). The CAAP reading comprehension module has items that assess inference, reasoning, and generalizing. The mathematics module emphasizes quantitative reasoning and measures a student's ability to solve mathematical problems. The writing module measures students' understanding of the conventions of standard written English in usage and mechanics and rhetorical skills, and, finally, science reasoning measures scientific reasoning skills embedded in content drawn from biology, chemistry, physics, and the physical sciences.

The ETS proficiency profile measures four academic achievement skill areas, three of them relevant to this chapter: reading, writing, and mathematics. The reading questions sample content from the humanities, social sciences, and natural sciences. The writing questions measure sentence-level skills, including grammatical agreement and sentence organization, and the mathematics test measures a range of skills from mathematics terminology to interpreting scientific measurement scales (Educational Testing Service, 2010; Lakin, Elliott, & Liu, 2012). Previous analyses of the Proficiency Profile (Lakin et al., 2012) support its use to measure higher education outcomes regardless of students' cultural backgrounds.

This chapter also reviews research that has examined college experiences associated with self-reported gains in general education, learning and intellectual development, and several more refined self-reported gains scales. Two of the most widely used college experience surveys are the College Student Experiences Questionnaire (CSEQ) and the National Survey of Student Engagement (NSSE). The CSEQ consists of three scales relevant to this chapter that yield self-reported gains in understanding the arts and humanities, understanding science and technology, and thinking and writing skills (Flowers, 2004a, 2004b; Kuh, 1999; Whitt, Edison, Pascarella, Terenzini, & Nora, 1999). Each scale consists of several Likert-type items, combined for a total score. Flowers (2004b), described the scales as follows. The Understanding Arts and Humanities scale (five items) assessed students' perceptions of how much they gained during college in understanding literature, philosophy, and the arts (e.g., "developing an understanding and enjoyment of art, music, and drama" and "broadening your acquaintance and enjoyment of literature"). The Understanding Science and Technology scale (three items) assessed students' perceptions regarding how much they gained during college in understanding scientific and technological ideas (e.g., "understanding the nature of science" and "understanding new scientific and technical developments"). The Thinking and Writing Skills scale (four items) assessed students' perceptions of how much they gained during college in writing and thinking skills (e.g., "writing clearly and effectively" and "ability to think analytically and logically").

The NSSE is designed to assess how students engage in what have been defined as empirically based good practices in undergraduate education (Chickering & Gamson, 1987, 1991) and what they gain from these experiences (Kuh, 2001; Umbach, Palmer, Kuh, & Hannah, 2006). Fifteen items are presented to respondents to self-assess the extent to which their experience at their institution contributed to their knowledge, skills, and personal development in a number of areas. Three factors resulted from a principal components analysis (Kuh, 2001). Germane to this chapter is the four-item scale of general education that includes gains in writing clearly and effectively, speaking clearly and effectively, thinking critically and analytically, and analyzing quantitative problems. Other research using NSSE self-reported gains has added items such as students' self-assessments of acquiring a broad general education, acquiring job- or work-related knowledge and skills, using computing and education technology, and working effectively with others (see Nelson Laird & Cruce, 2009) to develop a broader measure of general education.

The subject matter competence outcomes referenced in the chapter are largely student grades in the course where the experience or different learning environment was encountered. For example, in a biology course where the efficacy of graded online homework was examined, it would be common for students' quiz and final exam performance to be the outcome measure. We distinguish between student grades as a measure of subject matter competence in a specific course and students' overall or cumulative grades. As noted in the previous volumes (Pascarella & Terenzini, 1991, 2005), a multitude of factors may influence student cumulative grade point average extraneous to what one learns in college. For this reason, we maintain the perspective advanced by Pascarella and Terenzini (2005) that cumulative grades are an indicator of students' internalization of academic norms and institutional requirements and provide an additional dimension of the college experience where students may demonstrate different levels of competence and achievement.

SCOPE OF RESEARCH

Since publication of the previous volume, the scholarship of teaching and learning (SoTL) has grown exponentially. We view this as an exciting milestone for higher education. It suggests that in addition to the scholarship of discovery, integration, and application, the fourth form of scholarship, the scholarship of teaching (Boyer, 1990), is being taken seriously by the professoriate. Ernest Boyer in his revolutionary book, *Scholarship Reconsidered* (1990), noted that great teachers spark "active, not passive learning and encourage students to be critical, creative thinkers, with the capacity to go on learning after their college days are over" (p. 24). As such, pedagogical procedures must not be left to chance but "carefully planned, continuously examined, and relate directly to the subject taught" (Boyer, 1990, p. 24). The scholarship of teaching, then, involves faculty within and across disciplines sharing the results of such continuous examination with their peers. The scope of available research ranges widely, from multidisciplinary and interdisciplinary journals of education to teaching within a specific subject area or field. No fewer than 482 SoTL journals are in circulation, including 42 interdisciplinary SoTL journals, 90 in the arts and humanities, and 19 in engineering (University of Central Florida, Faculty Center for Teaching and Learning, n.d.).

Along with the process outlined in Chapter 1, we examined articles that had cited research reviewed in the previous volume, with the restrictions that articles had to have examined some college impact with postsecondary students in the United States, Canada, United Kingdom, Australia, or New Zealand between 2002 and 2012–2013 on outcomes aligned with verbal, quantitative, or subject matter competence. We prioritized meta-analyses, multi-institutional research using a pretest/posttest design, particularly those that used an objective measure of the outcome (as opposed to a self-reported gain), studies conducted at single institutions employing an experimental or quasi-experimental design, and articles published in peer-reviewed journals. All articles that fit and were in scope were abstracted, and a secondary keyword search by relevant outcomes was conducted to ensure comprehensiveness.

THEORETICAL OVERVIEW

Recognizing that a full discussion of the family of learning theories is beyond the scope of this chapter, a brief review of relevant theory is beneficial. Modern learning theories, especially active, experiential, and collaborative learning theory (see Kolb, 1984; Prince & Felder, 2006), have their roots in the educational theories of John Dewey, Lev Vygotsky, and Jean Piaget, some of the most influential learning theorists of the 20th century. Rooted in pragmatism, Dewey's theories and ideas (1938) about a democratic and civil society are steeped in the assertion that genuine education, and therefore learning, occurs through direct experience. He noted that traditional teaching and learning often took place in situations where rote memorization was emphasized, devaluing students' personal experiences. Severing the learning experience from students' real lives resulted in boredom and a lack of engagement in learning. Dewey critiqued the traditional school, an institution with its own rules and regulations, as foreign to children and very different from other institutions, such as the family. He asserted that the didactic method of teaching subjects and concepts directly from books and elders/teachers presented knowledge as static and unchanging. Yet according to Dewey, knowledge is constantly produced; theories and concepts are developed, modified, or rejected, and these processes are influenced by the historical time period. All told, knowledge is not fixed but constructed.

Building on the notion that knowledge is constructed, Piaget's (1954) theory of cognition postulated that development results from one's interaction with the world based on past experience. Piaget developed his theories from studying his children from infancy along with other children in Switzerland. The theory of cognitive development is based on adaptive processes in which children transition between assimilation and accommodation. The assimilation proposition holds that people develop cognitive schemas through which they view the world and any new information is adapted to fit within these schemas. Thus, the new information is assimilated with the old way of thinking, and the child is at a place of equilibrium. When a new object or situation occurs that does not fit with the existing schema, the child experiences disequilibrium. Accommodation is the process by which the schema is altered to deal with the new object or situation. Three major tenets of Piaget's theory are (1) knowing results from the interaction between self and environment, (2) development occurs through the progressive and gradual reorganization of structures in order to make sense of the world, and (3) learning happens when a motivated learner resolves the discrepancies between what is known and the new information that does not fit with prior knowledge (Kurfiss, 1988; Piaget, 1954).

Researching and writing in Russia in the 1920s and early 1930s, Lev Vygotsky, whose seminal work was translated into English in 1978, emphasized the social factors that contribute to cognitive development. Specifically, Vygotsky advanced that children and adults learn best when they are challenged just enough so that they may accomplish a learning task with the appropriate supports. Defined as the zone of proximal development, it is the distance between students' current development and their potential development, which can be achieved with the guidance of an adult or more knowledgeable other. Vygotsky advocated teaching students concepts and tasks slightly above their current abilities through the use of support at appropriate points in order to help students along. The zone of proximal development has been compared to scaffolding by other researchers (Wood, Bruner, & Ross, 1976) who theorized that providing students with challenging tasks along with supports, such as peer tutoring and teacher supports, will result in the highest level of learning. Vygotsky asserted that traditional education, which assesses students' developmental levels and provides education appropriate for the current level, actually lags behind and is ineffective in furthering student development.

Kolb's theory of experiential learning (1984) developed in part out of Piaget's theory of development and other major research on cognitive development. Experiential learning combined models of human cognition and growth with developmental theories. Similar to previous learning theorists such as Dewey and Piaget, Kolb grounded his theory on the concept of experience: people, he wrote, learn through direct experience. Kolb proposed a circular and continual learning cycle consisting of four stages. Concrete experience occurs, which then results in observing and reflecting. On the basis of these direct observations and thoughts, concepts and abstractions are developed, which are then tested in new situations. Subsequently, the process starts over again. Kolb combined this learning model with theories of personality, advancing that learners need four types of abilities: concrete experience, reflective observation, abstract conceptualization, and active experimentation. In order to use these abilities, Kolb theorized that one must constantly move back and forth between being an actor and an observer, between involvement and reflection, commenting, "Learning is the process whereby knowledge is created through the transformation of experience" (1984, p. 38).

Inductive teaching and learning is rooted in the developmental constructivist theories of Dewey (1938), Piaget (1954), Vygotsky (1978), and Kolb (1984), beginning with the real, practical, and specific—a problem to solve, data to interpret, or a case study to analyze—and then moving to the abstract (Prince & Felder, 2006). Traditional, or deductive, teaching begins with the theoretical or the abstract, and then moves into the specific and inductive, a method that relies on the often incorrect assumption that students will be motivated to learn facts and theories despite having not yet learned why they are important or how they may be put to use (Prince & Felder, 2006). Inductive teaching and learning is also student or learner centered, so that students take on more of the responsibility of their own learning (Prince & Felder, 2006). In addition, inductive and constructivist learning is characterized by collaborative, cooperative, and active learning techniques used to promote the co-construction of knowledge through peer discussion, problem solving, and small group–based learning (Prince & Felder, 2006).

At the core, learning and development theories emphasize learning through experience, from which the modern concept of experiential and active learning manifests. In addition to experience, they focus on the importance of challenge in the learning process, along with appropriate support, which can and should be provided by peers. The current movements in peer support in the form of peer tutoring, reciprocal tutoring, and peer teaching are based in the theory that more advanced peers can assist students' learning and development. In addition, active learning and cooperative learning focus on the importance of the social aspects of learning and suggest that an interactive and engaged classroom may be much more effective than lecturing. These concepts are grounded in principles advanced by Vygotstky (1978) and Piaget, who proposed that students were not blank slates but people with prior experiences that needed to be acknowledged in order for them to become engaged learners (Kurfiss, 1988; Piaget, 1954). The learning theories reviewed in this section form the basis for much of the research examining the relationship between environments and experiences cultivated in and out of the classroom and student learning.

CHANGE DURING COLLEGE

Conclusions from the 1990s

Relatively few studies published in the 1990s specifically examined change during college. Of those that did, they tended to be cross-sectional, comparing freshman (or first-year) to senior (or final-year) students, and were often based on data from a single institution. Cross-sectional studies are limited due to the potential differential selection over time, with fewer of the least academically able students persisting into the final-year cohort. Few studies from the 1990s were longitudinal and examined outcomes relevant to this chapter. Within this small body of literature, researchers tended to examine two areas: knowledge gain and knowledge retention. In general, Pascarella and Terenzini (2005) concluded that students make statistically significant gains in verbal and quantitative competence over their college tenure (varying from 28 percentile points in English to 21 percentile points in mathematics), largely realized in the first two years of college. In terms of knowledge retention, Semb and Ellis's (1994) meta-analysis found that students retain about 70 to 85% of the knowledge gained during college, depending on whether the task was related to recognition, recall, or cognitive skills. Despite knowledge gains and knowledge retention, Pascarella and Terenzini (2005) cautioned that the absolute level of knowledge acquisition in terms of prose, document (the ability to understand applications, forms, and schedules), or quantitative literacy might be lacking. With only about 50% of college graduates functioning at the most proficient level across key areas of verbal and quantitative competence (Barton & LaPointe, 1995), Pascarella and Terenzini (2005) concluded, "Understanding the proficiency of college graduates on absolute standards of subject matter competence and academic skills may be equally if not more important than knowing how much they change or grow during college" (p. 145).

Evidence from the 2000s

Pascarella and Terenzini (2005) noted less evidence in the 1990s with respect to change during college on verbal, quantitative, and subject matter competence than in the previous volume (Pascarella & Terenzini, 1991). Given the public discourse questioning the value of higher education and students' development of designated learning outcomes (Arum & Roksa, 2011; Ewell, 2009; McClaran, 2013), it may be surprising how few studies examined the extent to which students change during college with respect to verbal, quantitative, and subject matter competence. We found no studies that presented unconditioned descriptive evidence detailing students' longitudinal change from first year in college or university to their final year. Rather, national and international research studies have examined adults' literacy and numeracy skills by level of educational attainment. In this regard, the evidence compares adults who have selected to pursue and completed some level of postsecondary education to those who have not. This is not the same as longitudinal change but instead measures the difference in outcomes between these two self-selected groups, a form of change as a result of college or university attendance.

The 2003 National Assessment of Adult Literacy (Kutner et al., 2007) assessed the ability of a nationally representative sample of U.S. adults 16 years and older to use written and numeric information in a variety of workplace, family, and community settings. Findings showed that adults with higher levels of educational attainment had greater literacy in terms of their ability to search, understand, and use information from prose texts like news stories and instructional materials, as well as documents like job applications, payroll forms, and transportation schedules. Educational attainment was also associated with greater quantitative literacy, defined as the knowledge and skills necessary to identify and perform computations required to balance a checkbook, figure a tip, or determine the amount of interest on a loan. The study also found that adults who received their college degree at an age indicative of continuous postsecondary enrollment had higher levels of prose, document, and quantitative literacy than adults who completed their college degree at an older age (Kutner et al., 2007), lending some support to the assertion that continuous study is associated with greater verbal and quantitative competence than interrupted or delayed postsecondary study.

While the percentage of adults with a bachelor's degree increased from 1992 to 2003, the average prose and document scores decreased with each degree level over this decade, although quantitative literacy scores did not differ between adults at these two time points (Kutner et al., 2007). This leaves one to question what has taken place at colleges and universities in the previous decade to precipitate a decline in prose and document literacy. This is perhaps best answered by comparing adults who have completed a two-year, four-year, and graduate degree to those who have a high school diploma or equivalent at the two time periods. Among those who have not completed any level of higher education, approximately 5% of adults in 1992 and 2003 scored proficient in prose literacy. Although there was not a statistically significant difference between the percentage of adults in 1992 and 2003 with a two-year degree who were proficient in prose literacy, 31% of adults with a bachelor's degree in 2003 were proficient compared to 40% of adults in 1992; and 41% of adults with graduate studies or a graduate degree in 2003 were proficient compared to 51% of adults in 1992. This pattern of difference between high school graduates and adults with post-secondary degrees (two-year, four-year or graduate) is similar for document literacy as well. This is noteworthy in that a more diverse student body attended U.S. colleges and universities during that decade than had attended previously (Hudson, Aquilino, & Kienzl, 2005). The percentage deemed "proficient" has decreased, which may be due to increased access to postsecondary education for students with a broader range of precollege academic preparation. If equity is to be more than access, however, the fact that less than one-third of American adults with a bachelor's degree are proficient in prose and quantitative literacy and one-quarter are proficient in document literacy may be reason for concern.

More recently, the Program for the International Assessment of Adult Competencies (PIACC) assessed literacy, numeracy, and problem solving in technology-rich environments among adults in 33 countries. Literacy referred to reading vocabulary, sentence comprehension, and basic passage comprehension. Numeracy assessed respondents' "ability to access, use, interpret, and communicate mathematical information and ideas, to engage in and manage mathematical demands of a range of situations in adult life" (Organisation for Economic Co-operation and Development, 2012, cited in Goodman, Finnegan,

Mohadjer, Krenzke, & Hogan, 2013, p. 2). Problem solving in technology-rich environments was defined as "using digital technology, communication tools, and networks to acquire and evaluate information, communicate with others, and perform practical tasks" (Organisation for Economic Co-operation and Development, 2012, as cited in Goodman et al., 2013, p. 2). In the United States, 6% of adults completing high school reached the highest literacy level (level 4/5) versus 24% of adults with a bachelor's degree, consistent with the PIACC international average for bachelor's degree holders. Four percent of adults completing high school reached the highest numeracy level compared to 18% of those with a bachelor's degree. The PIACC international numeracy average for bachelor's degree holders was 24%, indicating the U.S. percentage was 25% lower than the international average. Finally, only 4% of U.S. high school diploma holders scored in the highest level for problem solving in technology-rich environments compared to 12% of bachelor's degree holders, 1% less than the PIACC international average (Goodman et al., 2013).

These general findings in which bachelor's degree holders have greater proficiency than high school completers also held for respondents in Australia (Australian Bureau of Statistics, 2014), Northern Ireland (Department for Employment and Learning, 2013), and for literacy in Canada and England (numeracy and problem solving in technology-rich environment scores were not included) (Department of Business Innovation & Skills, 2013; Programme for the International Assessment of Adult Competencies in Canada, n.d.). Although the desired or expected amount of change as a result of attending college and university may be up for debate (see Arum & Roksa, 2011), findings from the United States and other international contexts are unequivocal: greater educational attainment is associated with greater levels of verbal skills and literacy, as well as quantitative skills/literacy and numeracy. It is important to note that none of these international studies actually examined students' longitudinal change during postsecondary education. Rather this body of literature examined "change" during college by comparing adults with different levels of educational attainment and identifying this as the unconditioned difference in verbal, quantitative, and subject matter competence.

NET EFFECTS OF COLLEGE

It's one thing to say that students change as a result of attending college or university; it is another to say that attending college or university "caused" the change. The thorny challenge of identifying causation within college impact research was identified in Chapter 1. We know that students who attend and complete a higher education degree are a select group who differ in systematic ways from their peers who did not pursue a college or university credential. In the absence of randomly assigned control groups that account for these selection effects, it is difficult to ascertain whether change between the first year and final year of postsecondary education is attributable to college or students' maturation. As Pascarella and Terenzini (2005) noted, change due to maturation could manifest as a result of exposure to work, travel, personal reading, and a variety of other experiences—influences quite apart from postsecondary attendance. In cross-sectional studies, the internal validity concerns are even greater. In addition to maturation, any change in student learning and development may be due to differential recruiting standards for successive cohorts and the natural attrition of less capable students in the senior (or final) year sample.

Studies that attempt to isolate the net effects of postsecondary attendance on learning and development are more complex in design and scope than those that simply examine change during college or learning differences by level of educational attainment. Ideally, they would compare a randomly assigned group who attended and completed college to a randomly assigned group who did not. Yet these kinds of randomized control trials are not practical within college impact research. In light of less-than-ideal design conditions, research that seeks to partition the effects of college from maturation typically compares groups that differ in exposure to postsecondary education and employs a variety of measures to control statistically for differences between groups. The methodological appendix describes in detail the variety of research designs and statistical methods used in college impact research and how these methods have evolved since the publication of previous volumes (Pascarella & Terenzini, 1991, 2005).

Conclusions from the 1990s

The previous volume was limited in the number of studies that looked at the net effects of college on the development of verbal, quantitative, and subject matter competence. Flowers, Osterlind, Pascarella, and Pierson (2001) examined freshman-to-senior differences on subject areas within the College Basic Academics Subjects Examination (CBASE) and found that seniors, compared to freshmen, had gains of 22 percentile points in English, 13 percentile points in mathematics, 18 percentile points in science, and 18 percentile points in social studies. The authors noted that these relative differences were lower than previous studies due to the extensive controls employed. Another study evaluated the net effects of college on the Armed Forces Qualifying Test between people who had completed a bachelor's degree and those who had a high school diploma and found a 10 percentile point advantage for those with a bachelor's degree (Myerson, Rank, Raines, & Schnitzler, 1998). Finally, the previous volume noted that more than three-quarters of the studies that examined the net effects of college on verbal and quantitative competence found the largest gains during the first two years of college (Pascarella & Terenzini, 2005). This effect was attributed to the fact that verbal and quantitative competencies are most germane to and developed through general core or breadth requirements.

Evidence from the 2000s

No studies in the 2000s compared the learning and development of students enrolled in college from their peers who did not go to college, having accounted for students' background characteristics. For this reason, it is difficult to ascertain whether exposure to and participation in postsecondary opportunities has an impact on student learning and development. However, other studies attempted to examine learning and development among students enrolled in college. Depending on the research study, researchers operationalized exposure to postsecondary education as credit hours completed, class standing (freshman/first year, sophomore, junior, senior/final year), or as a comparison between freshman and senior students. Consistent with the results from Pascarella and Terenzini's reviews (1991, 2005), we found that exposure to postsecondary education had a positive association with student learning and development, controlling for a multitude of potentially confounding influences.

Across the multi-institutional student sample from the NSSL, Bray, Pascarella, and Pierson (2004) found credit hours completed had a small positive relationship with third-year reading comprehension (effect size = .05), controlling for a host of student background characteristics. Using standardized assessments for reading, writing, math, and critical thinking, Lakin et al. (2012) found that credit hours had a positive association with all four measures of student learning, with standardized regression coefficients ranging from 0.27 in math to 0.39 in reading. Although limited by the cross-sectional nature of its design, the Lakin et al. (2012) study has strong external validity in that it examined data from 30 two-year and four-year postsecondary institutions, in 20 U.S. states, for over a decade. Using the same outcome instrument, Liu and Roohr (2013) conducted an analysis that spanned a decade of students attending 13 community colleges from eight U.S. states. Controlling for GPA, hours worked, age, transfer status, English language learner, sex, and race, they found that credit hours completed was associated positively with students' ETS Proficiency Profile total score and all subscale scores, but effects were small, with standardized regression coefficients varying from 0.03 for writing and math to 0.04 for reading and the total score (Liu & Roohr, 2013).

Other research has used students' self-reported gains in general education or intellectual skills as measured through cross-sectional administrations of the NSSE or CSEQ to investigate the net effects of college. In examining the relationship between greater exposure to postsecondary education as measured by class standing and students' overall gains score on the CSEQ, Kuh and Gonyea (2003) found a consistently larger effect size for sophomores (effect size = .25), juniors (effect size = .33), and seniors (effect size = .39) compared to freshmen. However, the Kuh and Gonyea study did not take into account students' level of engagement or integration into the campus environment. Studies that have controlled for students' engagement or integration have found class standing indirectly associated with self-reported gains in learning and intellectual development, with part of the effect mediated by students' integration (Pike, Kuh, & Gonyea, 2003) or engagement (Lundberg, 2003). Upper-level students are more integrated in and engaged with the campus, suggesting a mechanism by which exposure to postsecondary education results in differential self-reported learning gains.

Although the weight of the evidence demonstrates greater exposure to postsecondary education is associated with student learning gains, particularly as it pertains to verbal, quantitative, and broadly defined general education knowledge and skills, the direct effect is fairly small (see, for example, the small effect size of .05 for reading comprehension as reported in Bray et al., 2004) and is mediated to a great extent by students' integration and engagement. This leads one to wonder whether different learning environments (attending a more selective institution or research university compared to a liberal arts college) or experiences (participating in small group learning or contributing to a faculty member's research) are associated with verbal and quantitative skill development and subject matter competence. These questions frame the literature review presented in the next two sections.

BETWEEN-COLLEGE EFFECTS

Conclusions from the 1990s

Pascarella and Terenzini's 2005 synthesis reviewed studies of between-college effects on the development of verbal, quantitative, and subject matter competence across three categories: institutional characteristics, institutional type, and institutional environment. Despite a larger body of evidence to review than the 1991 volume, research on between-college effects in the 1990s was inconsistent, with results either small in magnitude or not statistically significant. Pascarella and Terenzini (2005) noted that the examination of between-college effects has been complicated due to the increasing number of students who transfer between colleges during postsecondary study.

Much of the research from the 1990s on institutional characteristics used aggregate measures of institutional SAT and ACT standardized test scores to operationalize institutional selectivity. Using this measure of selectivity and controlling for student characteristics, the weight of the evidence found little to no significant positive impact of selectivity on student learning. In general, how selective an institution is had no effect on students' scores on the Medical College Admissions Test, the Law School Admissions Test, the quantitative score on the Graduate Record Examination, and the three subscores on the National Teacher Examination once differences in student body characteristics were taken into account (Pascarella & Terenzini, 2005). Another institutional characteristic, institutional size, had a small positive association with students' GRE quantitative scores and National Teacher Examination communication skills and professional knowledge after controlling for student background characteristics (Astin & Astin, 1993; Opp, 1991).

Institutional type was defined in several different ways: two-year institutions versus four-year institutions, Historically Black Colleges and Universities (HBCUs) versus predominantly white institutions (PWIs), women's colleges versus coeducational institutions, and by Carnegie classification. Controlling for student background characteristics, the effect of attending a two-year institution on first-year gains was very similar when compared with four-year institutions (Pascarella & Terenzini, 2005), suggesting that community colleges may be realizing their mandate as democratizing institutions (see Dowd, 2003, for a discussion of community college's equity mandate). Moreover, despite their fairly substantial resource disadvantage, HBCUs appeared to provide positive environments to foster student subject matter competence and academic skills. Yet little evidence suggested that women's colleges had statistically significant advantages in women's knowledge gains. Finally, classifications that distinguish higher education institutions as research universities, comprehensive colleges, and liberal arts colleges had no consistent or definitive relationship with student learning (Pascarella & Terenzini, 2005).

Finally, research examined the relationship between aggregate student perceptions of the institutional environment and verbal, quantitative, and subject matter competence. In general, environments that emphasized scholarship and learning, distinct from measures of institutional selectivity, were associated positively with student verbal, quantitative, and subject matter competence, and environments relatively free of prejudice and discrimination were particularly effective in fostering learning among African American students (Pascarella & Terenzini, 2005).

It is important to note that the previous volume concluded that many operationalizations of between-college effects had no significant relationship with student knowledge gains and the magnitude of findings in studies that found statistically significant results were often small. Student transfer and attendance at multiple institutions certainly compounds the challenge of isolating between-college effects, as Pascarella and Terenzini (2005) noted. Without adequate controls for the confounding influence of attending multiple institutions, estimating between-college effects adequately and accurately is difficult. The multiple-attendance issue notwithstanding, Pascarella and Terenzini (2005) concluded that "similarities in between-college effects substantially outweigh the differences" (p. 590).

Evidence from the 2000s

As noted in the previous volume, student transfer complicates researchers' ability to accurately assess the extent to which student learning differs based on institutional characteristics. Acknowledged as a challenge and complication in the 2005 book, student transfer—as one of many paths to degree completion noted by Adelman in *The Toolbox Revisited* (2006)—has become commonplace, with 37% of American students in the six-year cohort who began in 2008 transferring at least once during their college career (Shapiro, Dundar, Wakhungu, Yuan, & Harrell, 2015). Thus, students' concurrent or consecutive attendance at multiple institutions confounds between-college differences. Despite the public and policymakers' interest in comparing outcomes between institutions (Benjamin, 2008; U.S. Department of Education 2006), we alert readers to the difficulty inherent in such an analysis and the potential public policy implications of applying such findings carelessly.

We follow the approach of examining between-college effects from the previous volume (Pascarella & Terenzini, 2005) and review the literature as it pertains to the relationships between the following institutional characteristics and student verbal, quantitative, and subject matter competence: selectivity, institutional type, and institutional environment.

Selectivity. The research published since 2002 that examines the association between selectivity and students' verbal, quantitative, and subject matter competence was largely limited to cross-sectional studies using students' self-reported gains and yielded mixed findings. Lundberg (2012) found that selectivity had a small positive association with students' self-reported gains in general education controlling for student gender and first-generation status as well as institutional type and environments, using data from the 2004 administration of the NSSE. However, Kuh and Gonyea (2003) found no association between selectivity and students' self-reported overall educational gains from 300,000 students who completed the CSEQ between 1984 and 2002, taking into account student characteristics, perceptions of the institutional environment, and college experiences. Using a multilevel model from a subsample of the student data in the Kuh and Gonyea (2003) study, Hu and Kuh (2003a) found a small negative association, with a standardized regression coefficient of .03, between selectivity and the overall self-reported gain items from the CSEQ. Even so, they found no difference between selectivity and gains in general education or science and technology, controlling for institutional type and perception of institutional environment. Other research investigating the link between selectivity and student learning among specific student demographic groups has also resulted in mixed findings (Kim, 2002a, 2002b; Lundberg, 2007, 2010). Given the inconsistent associations, it appears little evidence supports the view that selectivity is related to measures of students' self-reported gains in general education or science and technology.

Institutional Type. The U.S.-based college impact research examining institutional type has continued to compare two-year and four-year institutions, but much of the research has distinguished between four-year institutions by Carnegie classification (research, comprehensive, or baccalaureate) or institutional mission (e.g., Historically Black Colleges and Universities, work colleges that require students to work at the institution, women's colleges). We review the literature on institutional type from these various perspectives.

Two-Year versus Four-Year. In a cross-sectional study using self-reported gains on items that measure a range of general education domains, Knight (2009) found a significant mean difference in learning gains favoring students at four-year institutions who completed the NSSE versus students at two-year colleges who completed the comparable Community College Survey of Student Engagement. Liu and Roohr (2013) added substantially to this line of inquiry by controlling for student characteristics, using a standardized measure of student learning, and comparing cross-sectional estimates over a decade. In a 10-year cohort study comparing community colleges to other institutional types on reading, writing, and math scores from the ETS Proficiency Profile, Liu and Roohr (2013) found a series of divergent patterns where four-year institutions did not always perform as well as two-year institutions in terms of student learning. Controlling for number of credit hours, research universities outperformed community colleges on all measures, with the largest difference apparent in mathematics from 2001 ($d = 0.23$) to 2010 ($d = 0.50$). However, comprehensive colleges and liberal arts colleges' advantage over community colleges narrowed considerably over the decade. By 2010, community colleges significantly outperformed liberal arts colleges ($d = 0.11$ for reading) and did not differ in writing and math. Although this set of comparisons confounds the two-year/four-year distinction by Carnegie classification, the evidence suggests students at four-year institutions have higher scores than their peers at two-year colleges, but the gap has narrowed over time and in limited situations has favored learning in two-year colleges. A major limitation of the Liu and Roohr (2013) study was the lack of control for students' precollege academic ability, as this is likely a substantial confounding variable in student attendance at a community college and may have underestimated the difference between student learning at two-year versus four-year institutions.

Carnegie Classification. Other research has examined institutional type differences among four-year institutions as differentiated by Carnegie classification(s) (see Lundberg, 2003, 2012; Pike et al., 2003). Most of this research has used students' self-reported gains in general education or intellectual development, or both, as measured by items on the NSSE or CSEQ. In addition, this research is complicated by the variety of strategies used to categorize baccalaureate colleges by the Carnegie Classification in recent years (Carnegie Foundation for the Advancement of Teaching, 2001, 2006, 2011). Controlling for student background characteristics, Kuh and Gonyea (2003) found, compared to doctoral-extensive universities, students at baccalaureate liberal arts and baccalaureate general institutions had slightly lower self-reported gains in overall education; no differences surfaced between students at doctoral-intensive and master's- granting universities. Examining data from a subset of the sample used by Kuh and Gonyea (2003) and investigating the subscales from the CSEQ, Hu and Kuh (2003a) found lower average scores for students at doctoral universities and selective liberal arts colleges on self-reported gains in science and technology compared to their peers at comprehensive colleges or universities, but no difference in general education, accounting for student characteristics. Demonstrating the variation in operationalizing measures (both outcomes and institutional type), Pike et al. (2003) found that students at baccalaureate liberal arts colleges reported the greatest self-reported gains in general education but identified no differences by other institutional types based on the 2000 Carnegie Classification. Meanwhile, Lundberg (2012) found no difference in self-reported gains in general education across institutional type from students who completed the NSSE in 2004. Variation in how institutions were classified, which institution type was used as the reference group, and outcome measures used yields a body of evidence with inconclusive results.As noted in the section detailing the net effects of college, student integration and engagement play an important role in the outcomes of college. As Pascarella and Terenzini (1991, 2005) concluded in their discussion of between-college and within-college effects, it appears that what students do in college is more important than the type of institution they attend. Lundberg's findings (2003) demonstrated the role student engagement plays in mediating the effects of institutional type on an overall measure of self-reported gains in learning, with research universities having a small negative indirect effect and comprehensive college or university having a small positive indirect effect compared to all other institution types, which included doctoral universities and liberal arts colleges.

We found two studies that permitted an examination of differences in an objective measure of mathematical knowledge by institutional type. Yetter and colleagues (2006) examined the extent to which students at a liberal arts college (which served a nontraditional student body in which many students worked full time) differed from their peers attending two land-grant universities in terms of solving a complex, well-structured problem-solving task in elementary set theory. Students at the liberal arts college scored significantly lower than students at the two universities. As reviewed earlier, Liu and Roohr (2013) investigated mathematics, reading, and writing scores by Carnegie type, although they did not assess statistically significant differences except with respect to community colleges. With that limitation acknowledged, they found that research universities consistently scored higher than comprehensive colleges and liberal arts colleges in math, reading, and writing (Liu & Roohr, 2013). In both studies, without controls for educational ability, it is not possible to determine if differences in student learning by institutional type are a function of institutional type as defined by Carnegie Classification or different educational abilities of the student body.

Control. In addition to institutional type, research has examined the relationship between other institutional characteristics and students' self-reported gains in general education and cognitive development. In the most expansive examination (300,000 students attending 300 four-year colleges from 1984 to 2002), Kuh and Gonyea (2003) found no difference by control (whether an institution was public or private) on students' self-reported overall education gains. Among students of color who took the CSEQ between 1999 and 2001, there was no difference in self-reported gains in general education or science and technology between students at private and public institutions, but there was a small negative difference between students attending public versus private institutions (with a standardized regression coefficient of $-.05$) on self-reported gains in intellectual skills, taking into account student characteristics and college experiences.

Institutional type differences overall suggest that students with equal exposure to postsecondary education attending four-year institutions (compared to two-year institutions) have higher scores on objective measures of verbal and quantitative knowledge and skills. However, without controlling for students' precollege academic ability, it is difficult to ascertain whether this is an institutional or selection effect. Institutional type differences within four-year colleges are inconsistent and seem to hinge on the categorization of institutional type and operationalization of the outcome. Finally, we found inconsistent evidence to suggest that institutional control (whether public or private) was associated with students' self-reported learning gains, net of background characteristics and experiences. It may be that these institutional characteristics are too removed from the learning process to have an influence on student learning (Ro, Terenzini, & Yin, 2013). The next section examines the extent to which between-college effects may exist when examining a more proximal measure of institutional type, a stated mission.

Mission. We refer to institutional mission in this regard as a stated commitment to provide education for a specific demographic of students (e.g., women's colleges, HBCUs) or to organize the educational environment in a particular way (e.g., curricular or philosophical mission). For example, at a work college, student work is a required and integrated core component of the work-learning-service program (Electronic Code of Federal Regulations, 2015). Generally institutional characteristics more directly related to the learning environment are associated with relevant student learning outcomes.

Work colleges have received relatively little scholarly attention, perhaps because only seven federally recognized work colleges exist across the United States. In the sole study examining this small cluster of institutions, Wolniak and Pascarella (2007) used a retrospective longitudinal study to examine the differences between work colleges, other liberal arts colleges, and regional comprehensive institutions on a number of learning outcomes among three alumni cohorts. Controlling for a variety of confounding influences, students at work colleges reported modest to large differences in their perception of their college's contribution to their orientations toward learning and developing intellectual skills than their peers at liberal arts colleges (effect size = .25) and regional institutions (effect size = .38) as well as greater scientific and quantitative skills than their peers at liberal arts colleges (effect size = .25).

Although single-sex institutions are declining in overall number in North America (Renn, 2014), women's colleges have played an integral role in providing equitable educational opportunities for women. However, the evidence in terms of attending a single-sex institution on students' verbal and quantitative skills and broader general education gains is mixed. Among women from 86 private postsecondary institutions in the United States who completed the Cooperative Institutional Research Program (CIRP) survey between 1987 and 1991, attending a women's college had no effect on women's analytical and problem-solving skills, controlling for other institution-level and individual-level variables (Kim, 2002a). However, among women who completed the 2000 NSSE, both first-year and senior women who attended women's colleges reported greater gains in general education and analyzing quantitative problems than their female peers who attended a coeducational institution (Kinzie, Thomas, Palmer, Umbach, & Kuh, 2007). Among African Americans, students who reported attending a single-sex institution reported stronger writing ability than their peers who attended a coed institution, controlling for institutional average writing ability, selectivity, and whether the institution was an HBCU or PWI (Kim, 2002b), although similar analyses examining math ability found no difference. Taken together, the inconclusiveness of these findings leads us to wonder whether students who attend a single-sex institution differ in their verbal, quantitative, and subject matter competence.

A fairly extensive body of literature has examined the contributions of minority-serving institutions to the American postsecondary landscape, particularly in terms of cultivating a socially and psychologically supportive environment for student success (see Gasman, Baez, & Turner, 2008). Several studies examined the extent to which students from historically underrepresented racial/ethnic groups attending institutions with a larger proportion of students of that racial/ethnic group differ in verbal and quantitative competence than their peers at predominantly White institutions (PWIs). Although the findings are mixed, controlling for background characteristics, the weight of the evidence suggests that students who enroll at minority-serving institutions perceive greater gains than their peers at PWIs.

In an interesting study that examined simultaneously two manifestations of unique institutional mission, HBCU versus PWI and single sex versus co-ed, Kim (2002b) found that African American students attending an HBCU compared to a PWI reported no differences in self-perceived math or writing ability, controlling for institutional average outcome ability, selectivity, single-sex institution status, and other student characteristics; however, when single-sex institution was omitted from the regression equation, a small positive association between attending an HBCU and writing ability emerged. These results suggest that for African American students, more important than attending an HBCU was attending a single-sex institution, whether it was an HBCU or not. Among African American women, attending an HBCU was associated positively with students' analytical and problem-solving skills, controlling for institutional- and individual-level variables (Kim, 2002a), although the relationship was reduced to nonsignificance when internal measures of the college environment were taken into account.

Other research has found that African American students attending an HBCU compared to a PWI reported greater self-reported gains on understanding the arts and humanities, understanding science and technology, intellectual development and writing skill, and acquiring a broad general education, controlling for a multitude of factors (Flowers, 2002; Nelson Laird, Bridges, Morelon-Quainoo, Williams, & Salinas Holmes, 2007). Similar differences were identified between Hispanic students who attended a Hispanic-serving institution (HSI) versus a PWI, but in fewer areas and with lower magnitudes than African American students attending an HBCU (Nelson Laird et al., 2007). With few exceptions, the evidence suggests that students enrolled at institutions where the student body is of similar racial/ethnic background feel they receive a better education as reflected by self-reported gains.

Institutional Environment. The institutional characteristics reviewed to this point have focused on dimensions relatively difficult to alter readily, as bodies outside the immediate institutional context (e.g., boards of governors/regents/trustees or state legislatures) typically make such a determination. Institutional environment, however, is within the purview of institutional administrators, faculty, staff, and students to shape. This section describes the relationships between various dimensions of institutional environment on verbal, quantitative, and subject matter competence, as well as broader gains in general education.

Having previously described the differences in student learning by institutions that have a stated mission to educate specific demographics of students, a number of studies examined relationships between measures of structural diversity or institutional emphasis on cross-racial interaction and learning outcomes. Structural diversity is the numerical representation of diverse groups, for example, the proportion of Caucasian, African American, or Latino/a students on campus (Bowman, 2011a; Gurin, Dey, Hurtado, & Gurin, 2002). A structurally diverse student body does not, however, necessarily result in meaningful intergroup interactions. Informal interactional diversity (Gurin et al., 2002) is the frequency and quality of intergroup interactions outside of the classroom. Finally, classroom diversity consists of learning about diverse people/groups, or content knowledge, with diverse peers in the classroom (Bowman, 2011a; Gurin et al., 2002). Controlling for student and institutional characteristics, Lundberg (2012) found a small positive association between institutional emphasis on interactional diversity and self-reported gains in general education in a sample inclusive of all students, as well as more focused analyses on Native Americans (Lundberg, 2007) and students of color (Lundberg, 2010).

Still other research has examined the relationship between institutional environment with respect to student engagement and personal relationships with student learning. Although typically employing a number of control variables to account for student and other institutional characteristics, virtually all of the literature in this area used cross-sectional designs and some measure of self-reported gains. Controlling for an array of factors, average student campus involvement at the institutional level was associated with self-reported gains in general education (Umbach & Wawrzynski, 2005). Moreover, at institutions where greater student-faculty interaction exists (Nelson Laird & Cruce, 2009) and faculty use active and collaborative learning techniques, challenge students academically, emphasize higher-order cognitive activities, and the faculty culture emphasizes best practices (Umbach & Wawrzynski, 2005), students reported significantly greater gains in general education.

Umbach and Wawrzynski's study (2005) examined dimensions of faculty members' use of challenge and support in the educational arena. Several cross-sectional studies examined the relationship between institutional challenge and support and students' self-reported learning gains, with findings that suggest a more positive role for institutional challenge and scholarly emphasis (Hu & Kuh, 2003a; Kim, 2002a) than support and personal relations

(Hu & Kuh, 2003a; Lundberg, 2012). Nuancing the difference between a supportive campus environment and one that emphasized personal relations, Lundberg found that a supportive campus environment was associated positively with self-reported gains in general education (Lundberg, 2012), but that institutions that emphasized personal relations had lower overall mean scores for students' self-reported gains in general education, science and technology, and intellectual development—a finding that replicated Hu and Kuh's research (2003a). With employers commenting on the state of graduates' career-readiness (Hart Research Associates, 2010), it is interesting that Hu and Kuh (2003a) found no relationship between an institution's vocational and practical emphasis and students' self-reported gains in general education, science and technology, or intellectual development. Finally, Berger (2002) examined the relationship between organizational culture (bureaucratic, collegial, political, symbolic, and systemic) and students' self-perceived change in knowledge and skills (defined as gains in writing, reading and math) at six religiously affiliated institutions. He found systemic and symbolic environments (defined as those that view the organization and its subunits in terms of their interactions with one another and the external environment and those that focus on the role of symbols in creating meaning within an organization, respectively) were associated negatively with student change in knowledge and skills, controlling for student characteristics and experiences.

In summary, the between-college characteristics most difficult to alter (institutional type and control) had generally inconsistent and trivial effects on students' verbal, quantitative, and subject matter competence. Institutional mission, as reflected by curricular or philosophical emphasis or service to particular populations, while somewhat mixed, had small but generally positive associations with students' self-reported learning gains. Institutional environments that emphasize scholarly and intellectual pursuits were associated positively with student learning, controlling for student characteristics. Most of the research that examined the relationship between institutional environment and learning outcomes did so by aggregating student responses at the individual level and assigning this as a measure of environment, emphasis, culture, or climate at the institutional level. This is a functional approach to estimating between-college effects but is imperfect in that it minimizes variation among student experiences. We address this limitation in the next section by reviewing literature that has examined the richness of the individual student experience in college and university.

WITHIN-COLLEGE EFFECTS

Conclusions from the 1990s

The previous volume of *How College Affects Students* found hundreds of studies that evaluated within-college effects on the development of verbal, quantitative, and subject matter competence. Based on the research reviewed, Pascarella and Terenzini (2005) advanced these conclusions:

1. Undergraduate students had greater gains in knowledge in subject matter areas aligned with their major field of study. Students also had more academic skills in their area of study as well.

2. Regarding class size, larger class sizes negatively affected student's grades; however, some studies using standardized measures found no significant differences for students in small or large classes.

3. The type of instruction affects students' subject matter competence positively. Different pedagogical approaches evaluated included learning for mastery, computer-assisted instruction, active learning, collaborative learning, cooperative learning, small-group learning, and supplemental instruction with advantages over traditional teaching methods ranging from 10 percentile points for active-learning methods to 25 percentile points for learning for mastery. Research on problem-based learning and learning communities was in a nascent stage but suggested great promise. Positive gains were associated with peer tutoring, reciprocal teaching, attributional retraining, concept-knowledge maps, and the one-minute paper.

4. There tended to be no differences between students who engaged in distance learning and those who attended traditional face-to-face classes in terms of subject matter competence, although much of this research was challenged due to the selection bias.

5. Behavior of instructors had positive effects in the areas of preparation and organization, clarity and comprehensibility, availability and helpfulness, quality of and frequency of feedback, and concern for and rapport with students.

6. Time on task can take many forms but broadly consists of the extent to which students engage in activities that "reinforce and extend the formal academic experience" (Pascarella & Terenzini, 2005, p. 149). The greater the quality of student engagement in educationally purposeful activities (e.g., library use, research with a faculty member, writing experiences), the more a student will learn.

7. Several conclusions pointed to the effects of students' lifestyle outside the classroom. Student engagement outside the classroom had positive associations with student learning. On-campus living had no significant influence on knowledge gained; however, the interactions with peers, staff, and faculty that are engendered when living on campus were associated positively with student learning. Extracurricular involvement mostly had a positive impact on student learning, except for student athletes and students in fraternities and sororities. Part-time work on- or off-campus showed no significant effect on student learning.

Evidence from the 2000s

Without a doubt, college impact research has grown in terms of understanding the practices and conditions that promote students' verbal, quantitative, and subject matter competence. Given that the largest body of evidence examines within-college effects, we organize the chapter from those aspects furthest from faculty members' and students' control (largely administrative decisions) to pedagogical decisions within a faculty member's purview to decisions made autonomously by the student. Although we found fewer multi-institutional studies using objective measures of reading, writing, and math as in the previous volume (Pascarella & Terenzini, 2005), the scholarship of teaching and learning has given rise to a multitude of journals that publish research examining the efficacy of various teaching and learning approaches in the discipline. Journals like *Teaching Sociology* and the *Journal of Engineering Education* routinely publish research conducted within faculty members' classrooms that employ experimental or quasi-experimental designs to investigate the effectiveness of a particular teaching approach on course learning and understanding within a discipline. These studies permit us to discuss findings in terms of plausible causal differences. However, the strength of the internal validity within these studies is typically offset by limited external validity in that they tend to have been conducted at a single institution and in a single classroom, in which are almost always self-selected students. We endeavored to balance rigorously designed research with generalizability and highlight meta-analyses where possible.

Class Size and Design. Increasing enrollments at many institutions raise questions about how many students can be placed within a class before the sheer number detracts from students' ability to learn. This question has been taken up by a number of research studies, largely at single institutions. In the main, class size has a negative association with course grades, controlling for student and institutional characteristics (Arias & Walker, 2004; Bandiera, Larcinese, & Rasul, 2010; Cheng, 2011; Delucchi, 2007; Kokkelenberg, Dillon, & Christy, 2008). Two studies examined this question in greater depth. Cheng (2011) examined student course grades from 24 departments at a single institution, noting the greatest distribution in course grades was in those courses with the fewest students; the variation in course grades lessened as the class size increased. Moreover, the relationship between class size and student learning varied by the magnitude of the size increase and discipline. Eleven of the 24 disciplines showed negative effects when increasing class size by 50 students, and more negative associations between class size and course grades surfaced in courses and departments related to the sciences (Cheng, 2011). Similarly, in a sample of university students in the United Kingdom, Bandiera et al. (2010) found the effect of class size on student grades was significant only for the smallest and largest range of class sizes. Student test scores were most affected when class sizes were reduced from the mid-30s to below 20 and by not allowing class size to rise to more than 100 students. The key message from this study seems to be that students do better in seminar-size classes

(20 or fewer students), but in situations when that is not feasible, student course achievement is not hindered by larger classes provided they are smaller than 100 students. It is at the point of extremely large classes that class size matters the most.

Classroom design may engender spirited conversation on campuses that are building new classrooms or renovating old spaces. In the past decade, a number of research studies have examined the impact of active learning classrooms, defined as spaces that typically feature tables with movable seating to facilitate small group work and often additional learning technologies such as whiteboards, wireless Internet access, and student computer-projection (Baepler, Walker, & Driessen, 2014). Comparing grades between students who were in classrooms with tables, a studio environment, or individual desks, Espey (2008) found no difference in students' grades in a natural resource economics course once student GPA was taken into account. However, across several institutions and disciplines ranging from physics to biology, studies employing quasi-experimental design and accounting for students' precollege academic preparation as measured by the ACT found consistent positive effects of courses using an active learning classroom design—rather than a traditional desk or forward-facing table design—on student course grades and conceptual understanding (Brooks, 2011; Dori & Belcher, 2005; Walker, Brooks, & Baepler, 2011; Whiteside, Brooks, & Walker, 2010). As higher education institutions continue to create spaces that promote active learning and the development of community, we expect growth in this line of inquiry.

Pedagogical Approaches and Instructional Techniques. Faculty may draw from a variety of pedagogical approaches and instructional techniques to teach course content, as well as disciplinary-based thinking skills, attitudes, and values. In this section, we synthesize a vast literature that has examined the relationship between these approaches and techniques and students' verbal, quantitative, and subject-matter competence. A unifying theme across is that students appear to benefit from opportunities to co-construct the learning environment and classroom experience. Students also make learning gains when they are encouraged to use past experiences as a means to teach peers and situate their own learning, consistent with the learning theories highlighted at the beginning of the chapter.

Technology-Assisted Instruction and Assessment. Pascarella and Terenzini (2005) noted the potential for computers and related information technologies "to transform fundamentally the nature of teaching and learning in postsecondary education" (p. 97). From MIT's introduction of OpenCourseWare in 2001 and the rise of the massively open online course (MOOC) to the conversations surrounding the value of a "flipped classroom" (Bishop & Verleger, 2013), it is clear that postsecondary education has moved into a digital and virtual age. This has resulted in researchers using varying definitions for what constitutes online learning. McFarland and Hamilton (2005/2006) discussed this body of research and noted the variations can alternatively mean

1. A course having materials delivered online that meets synchronously and regularly, perhaps in a chat room, moderated by the instructor;

2. A course having materials delivered online that never meets synchronously and the student learns completely independent of a live instructor;

3. A course delivered by videoconferencing, where a live instructor is lecturing in one location and students are viewing the lecture in another location (most often referred to as "distance learning"). (p. 25)

In a meta-analysis examining online learning, Means, Toyama, Murphy, and Baki (2013) defined *online learning* as "learning that takes place entirely or significantly over the internet" (p. 6) and *blended learning* as "learning through a combination of online and face-to-face experiences" (p. 6). The variations within these two definitions and the myriad of others used underscore the challenge of synthesizing this literature. Given this breadth and variation, we discuss technology-assisted instruction and assessment in terms of meta-analyses that have examined general engagement with online learning as well as specific studies that have investigated technology as a means of instructing, providing support and building community, assessing learning and providing feedback, disseminating and retrieving information, and distracting students from learning.

General Engagement with Online Learning. Tamim, Bernard, Borkhovski, Abrami, and Schmid (2011) conducted a second-order meta-analysis (a meta-analysis of 25 meta analyses comprising 1,055 primary studies) and found "the average student in a classroom where technology is used will perform 12 percentile points higher than the average student in the traditional setting that does not use technology to enhance the learning process" (p. 17). In meta-analyses that have examined technology use for different purposes (see also Schmid et al., 2009), Tamim and colleagues found that technology used for cognitive support was more effective in enhancing student learning than technology used to deliver content or instruction.

In many cases, it is difficult to isolate what among the technologically assisted features contributed to student learning. It may be the structured interaction with peers, availability of online tutors, practice assessments, or web-based information and resources that are associated with course learning (Johnston & Olekalins, 2002; Rodgers, 2008) or gains in general education (Chen, Lambert, & Guidry, 2010). In less rigorously designed studies, as Pascarella and Terenzini (2005) acknowledged, results may also be attributable to students' self-selection into mode of instruction. Recognizing the difficulty in isolating the effectiveness of specific technology components, Tamim and colleagues (2011) found that studies that examined multiple uses of technology in a class setting demonstrated greater learning gains than situations in which technology was not used.

Instruction. Perhaps the area of research that has garnered the greatest attention has been studies investigating the extent to which technology-assisted instruction improves student verbal, quantitative, and subject matter competence.

Several meta-analyses and single-institution studies have been conducted with this aim. With few exceptions (Arbaugh et al., 2009), this research has found that students who complete coursework through online instruction as opposed to traditional face-to-face methods did not differ in their course learning (Ashby, Sadera, & McNary, 2011; Bernard et al., 2004; Collins & Pascarella, 2003; Lou, Bernard, & Abrami, 2006; Zhao, Lei, Yan, Lai, & Tan, 2005) and in some cases learned more (Gratton-Lavoie & Stanley, 2009; Shachar & Neumann, 2003; Sosa, Berger, Saw, & Mary, 2011; Trenholm, 2006), although the issue of self-selection is often the determining factor (Driscoll, Jicha, Hunt, Tichavsky, & Thompson, 2012; McFarland & Hamilton, 2005/2006). In the most rigorous meta-analysis to date, in which only studies that used experimental or quasi-experimental designs were included, Means and colleagues (2013) examined 21 studies of undergraduate students in purely online, blended formats versus face-to-face instruction. They found that students whose course was taught purely online or using a blended format learned more than their peers in traditional face-to-face courses, with a medium effect size of .31. In the full set of studies reviewed, Means et al. (2013), however, found no difference in student learning in studies that compared purely online to traditional face-to-face instruction but a medium positive effect in which students in blended learning environments learned more than their peers in traditional environments. Moreover, in the full set of studies, Means and colleagues found that pedagogical approaches moderated the online learning effect, with collaborative instruction and expository instruction, in which the instructor presents content and creates opportunities for learners to engage with one another in discussing and making meaning of course concepts, having significantly stronger positive relationships with student achievement than independent, active online learning.

These findings support the caution issued by Jaggars and Bailey (2010) that "without additional supports, online learning may even undercut progression among low-income and academically underprepared students" (p. 1), highlighting the necessity for educators teaching online to support learners and build community. Online learning has the potential to increase access to post-secondary education to historically underserved populations. However, as Means and colleagues' research demonstrates, the learning environment and experience cannot be left for individual learners to navigate and engage alone.

Cognitive Support and Community. Several meta-analyses have examined the practices and conditions within online learning environments to identify those associated with increased student learning. A limitation of this research is that it tended to aggregate results across all learning contexts (K–12, under-graduate, and graduate), but the findings are useful in evaluating and interpreting research that has examined similar questions at single institutions.

Bernard and colleagues (2009) examined different practices within the online learning environment as moderator variables and found that student-student engagement (defined as students collaborating closely with one another to discuss course material compared to independent online work) and student-content engagement (defined as students actively engaging with course content using various multimedia presentations compared to reading course content posted online) had greater influences on student achievement than student-teacher interaction (defined as high levels of synchronous and asynchronous instructor interaction compared to limited asynchronous instruction interaction).

These findings supported previous results from an earlier meta-analysis by Lou et al. (2006) in which student-student interaction (defined in terms of face-to-face contact and participation in asynchronous listserv or discussion board) as well as student-teacher interaction (face-to-face meetings) predicted distance education students' achievement. The weight of the evidence clearly indicates that the emphasis on active engagement with course content (e.g., searching for additional resources, solving simulation tasks, engaging in virtual reality scenarios) and intentional, designed collaboration between students is critical for online learning environments to achieve superior student outcomes (Andresen, 2009; Borokhovski, Tamim, Bernard, Abrami, & Sokolovskaya, 2012; Butler & Butler, 2011; Cain & Pitre, 2009; Stark-Wroblewski et al., 2008).

Feedback and Assessment. Several single-institution studies examined how computer-mediated and technology-enhanced feedback improved student course learning (Hundhausen, Agarwal, Zollars, & Carter, 2011; Kellogg, Whiteford, & Quinlan, 2010; Post, & Whisenand, 2005). Dynamic, detailed and immediate feedback was associated with engineering students' greater problem-solving accuracy and maintenance of a higher level of performance even after being switched back to the "no feedback" condition (Hundhausen et al., 2011). Similarly, students in a first-year composition course at a single institution in the United States who received automated continuous feedback on their writing performance showed fewer errors in mechanics, usage, grammar, and style in a transfer essay written two weeks later, although they did not differ in the holistic scoring of the essay than their peers who received only intermittent or no feedback (Kellogg et al., 2010).

Feedback comes in multiple forms, including the questions that peers ask of one another in discussion forums. The use of online scaffolding to assist students in generating questions to peers' posts increased the frequency of student questioning behavior but did not improve the quality of questions or students' course learning (Choi, Land, & Turgeon, 2005). Consistent with the notion that online instructors must be intentional in crafting the virtual learning environment, Choi et al. (2005) concluded, "Further study should focus on the quality improvement of peer-generated questions while considering adaptive and dynamic forms of scaffolding and intermediate factors such as prior knowledge, metacognition, task complexity, and scaffolding type" (p. 483). Other research has examined the timing (asynchronous versus synchronous) and volume of feedback in online environments. Schellens and Valcke (2005, 2006) found that students participating in asynchronous discussion forums were more task oriented in their communication and had higher levels of knowledge creation and that the greater volume of discussion within a forum was related to higher levels of knowledge construction.

Several studies examined the use of clickers and online quizzes to provide students with feedback on their knowledge and understanding of course concepts. Across several quasi-experimental single-institution studies, biology students' use of clickers was associated with higher grades (Levesque, 2011), as well as knowledge and retention of the course concepts that had been taught using clickers, although there was no difference in overall grades (Crossgrove & Curran, 2008). In addition to providing instructors with immediate feedback, clickers seem to be a means by which to maintain students' attention and focus on course materials (Mayer et al., 2009). In studies across disciplines, sustained engagement with computer-mediated assessments was associated with better course grades (Angus & Watson, 2009; Burridge & Öztel (2008); Hagerty & Smith, 2005; Luyben, Hipworth, & Pappa, 2003; Pennebaker, Gosling, & Ferrell, 2013). However, Lyke and Frank (2012) found no difference in scores between students who completed psychology quizzes online rather than in person. Time on task may be the causal mechanism operating in a number of the studies that examined computer-mediated and technology-enhanced assessment and feedback.

Information Dissemination and Retrieval. With new technology-enhanced devices entering the market on a regular basis, several studies investigated the relationship between the technology-enhanced medium, like an electronic reader or Quick Response (QR) code, and student learning. In both cases, there was no difference in reading comprehension between students reading a book and those who read text from an e-reader (Schugar, Schugar, & Penny, 2011) or in access to additional digital material using QR codes (Chen, Teng, Lee, & Kinshuk, 2011). In a multi-institutional cross-sectional study, Strayhorn (2006) found, taking into account student characteristics, that searching the Internet for course material, using a computer to analyze data, and using an index or database to find material were associated with the sum of all general education gains among students who completed the CSEQ in 2003–2004. Conversely, Lundberg (2010) found among students of color who had completed the CSEQ between 1999 and 2001 using computers for academic purposes was associated negatively with self-reported gains in general education but positively with self-reported gains in science and technology. Together, this body of evidence lends support to the hypothesis that it is not the computer as the medium but the time on task required to engage with technology-based content that enhances student learning.

Distraction. Much has been written about the emergence of "digital natives" and their use of technology-based devices for communication, connection, and learning (see Junco & Mastrodicasa, 2007; Palfrey & Gasser, 2008). In an area of research that will likely see far more investigation in the coming years, we found two studies that examined the extent to which engaging with technology distracts students in developing their verbal competence, specifically reading comprehension.

Tran, Carillo, and Subramanyam (2013) hypothesized that simultaneously engaging in a secondary online communication task would impair content learning in a primary academic learning task. Contrary to prediction, for the easy reading comprehension and recall task, participants who simultaneously engaged in a primary learning task and a secondary communication task performed significantly better than participants who completed the two tasks sequentially. No difference in scores emerged for the more difficult task. Although this study suggests a counterintuitive benefit for multitasking, Tran et al. (2013) found a negative relationship between respondents' scores on a self-reported measure of multitasking and reading comprehension on both the easy and difficult tasks.

In another experimental study, students who were assigned the instant messaging multitasking condition in which they conversed with one person while reading passages of varying difficulty, performed no worse than their peers on reading comprehension (Fox, Rosen, & Crawford, 2009). However, in a separate analysis, minutes spent instant messaging daily were associated with lower reading comprehension scores (Fox et al., 2009). These studies may be limited in their generalizability due to the experimental conditions but suggest a threshold by which students' use of other technological devices to multitask hinders learning. Given recent research examining cell phone use and grade point average (see Lepp, Barkley, & Karpinski, 2014), we expect continued research interest in assessing the relationship between students' technology use and specific academic skills.

Learning for Mastery. Learning for mastery is the quintessential manifestation of time on task. Students do not progress through course material until they have mastered earlier concepts. In the main, with one exception (Posner, 2011), the research suggests that learning for mastery—by which students are required to engage with course material in an ongoing fashion until they have achieved concept mastery—was associated positively with student quantitative and subject matter competence. Silverman and Seidman (2011) found that students enrolled in the Math My Way course, which required a daily commitment to complete the 10 modules in which arithmetic and prealgebra are collaboratively taught using peer tutors and a learning for mastery approach, had higher cumulative math GPA scores over two years than their peers who had not taken the course. A limitation of Silverman and Seidman's (2011) research was the lack of control for group differences (e.g., student age, percentage Hispanic, and number of unit hours enrolled in a basic skills math course).

In a single-institution, quasi-experimental study across eight college algebra courses (four assigned to the treatment condition and four to the control), Hagerty and Smith (2005) found students using Assessment and Learning in Knowledge Spaces (ALEKs—a mastery learning-type online assessment tool) outperformed other students by 8% on average on their postsemester summative assessment, although the drop, failure, withdrawal (DFW) rate for the ALEKs group was slightly larger than the traditional course. Finally, "Keller's personalized system of instruction," grounded in personalized instruction and mastery learning, was implemented in a biology course at a single community college in Texas. Course content was provided mainly through written materials, with the classroom session used mostly for motivation. Students determined their individual rates of progress through the materials. Overall, students showed improved scores from baseline attempt to best score, with number of attempts associated positively with students' best score. All students showed mean learning gains of at least 40% over baseline (Fike et al., 2011).

Attributional Retraining. Attributional retraining (AR) is an intervention strategy designed to change students' thoughts and sense-making regarding what causes their success or failure (Stewart et al., 2011). We found several studies that specifically examined attributional retraining in terms of course performance. In a pre/post quasi-experimental study, Perry, Stupnisky, Hall, Chipperfield, and Weiner, (2010) found students in the AR group had higher test scores and course grades than those in the control group, particularly among students of low and average initial performance. Perhaps most important, AR appeared to be particularly effective among students who were either overly optimistic but used maladaptive explanations for poor academic performance or had a high failure avoidance orientation. In both cases, AR assisted students in developing more constructive and adaptive explanations that resulted in improved academic course performance (Boese, Stewart, Perry, & Hamm, 2013; Haynes, Ruthig, Perry, Stupnisky, & Hall, 2006).

Active Learning. Active learning is generally defined as any method that engages students meaningfully in the learning process, requiring them to think about and reflect on what they are doing in relationship to the course content (Prince, 2004). *Inductive teaching and learning* has been used as an umbrella term for many forms of active learning. Whereas traditional didactic methods of teaching tend to be deductive and begin with theory and then progress to application, inductive teaching begins with the application as a motive for students to learn the theory (Prince & Felder, 2006, 2007). Prince and Felder describe problem-based learning, discovery learning, project-based learning, case-based teaching, and other inquiry methods as forms of inductive teaching in which students hold much of the responsibility for learning and actively co-construct knowledge in making sense of their experiences.

A large body of research has examined and compared students in active learning courses to those in traditional didactic classrooms. Although much of the research does not specify the full variety of methods instructors have used to create an active classroom environment, they often include student-centered classroom activities, frequent clicker response questions, and small-group discussions, among others.

Across active learning methods and disciplinary fields of studies, the weight of the evidence has found students who actively engage in the learning process gained greater subject matter competence (Armbruster, Patel, Johnson, & Weiss, 2009; Cheng, Thacker, Cardenas, & Crouch, 2004; Deslauriers & Wieman, 2011; Ernst & Colthorpe, 2006; Freeman et al., 2007, 2014; Knight & Wood, 2005; Maskiwicz, Griscom, & Welch, 2012; Strauss & Terenzini, 2007; Walker, Cotner, Baepler, & Decker, 2008; Wilke, 2003) and were more adept at higher order thinking in the discipline (Jensen & Lawson, 2011; Richmond & Kindelberger Hagan, 2011) than their peers who were less actively engaged in their learning.

In the most thorough meta-analysis of active learning in the science, technology, engineering, and mathematics (STEM) disciplines, Freeman and colleagues (2014) found that students' average examination scores increased by about 6% in active learning environments compared to lecture-based environments, and students in lecture-based environments on average were 1.5 times more likely to fail. Moreover, Freeman et al. (2014) found that active learning was associated with increased student achievement in classes of all sizes but had the greatest effect in courses of 50 or fewer students.

Employing active learning methods effectively requires careful attention, intention, and structure on the part of the instructor. Having found no significant difference in biology knowledge by level of active learning employed by the instructors in a multi-institutional study, Andrews, Leonard, Colgrove, and Kalinowski (2011) concluded the necessity of training educators to use active learning methods effectively.

Small Group, Cooperative, and Collaborative Learning. Researchers have defined *cooperative learning* as students working together to pursue common goals that may be assessed individually or as a group, and *collaborative learning* as students working with and teaching each other through focused exploration of course material (Pascarella & Terenzini, 2005; Prince, 2004). In general, this body of research consistently has found that cooperative and collaborative learning contributed to student gains in verbal, quantitative, and subject matter competence and broad measures of general education (Anderson, Mitchell, & Osgood, 2005; Berger, 2002; Cabrera et al., 2002; Cortright, Collins, & DiCarlo, 2005; Delucchi, 2007; Gaudet, Ramer, Nakonechny, Cragg, & Ramer, 2010; Ge & Land, 2003; Hazel, Heberle, McEwen, & Adams, 2013; Johnson, Archibald, & Tenenbaum, 2010; Preszler, 2009; Stump, Hilpert, Husman, Chung, & Kim, 2011; Yamarik, 2007).

In a meta-analysis of 37 studies, Tomcho and Foels (2012) examined group processes and collaborative learning activities in terms of student learning gains in undergraduate psychology and found a large positive association (effect size = .49). However, not all group processes and collaborative learning activities contributed equally or even positively to student learning. Contrary to the authors' hypotheses, group size, task complexity, and prelearning activities had no effect on student learning outcomes. Overall, group activities of shorter duration, with higher levels of interdependence among group members and without group presentation or peer assessment, were associated with improved learning outcomes (Tomcho & Foels, 2012).

Findings from Tomcho and Foels's (2012) meta-analysis suggest the importance of structure in the small collaborative, cooperative learning group experience. Yetter and colleagues (2006) found that students in an unstructured collaborative setting scored significantly lower than their peers who worked individually. Supporting these findings, research that has examined various structured means of engagement and collaboration, like the Belvedere constraint-based group discussion tool (Cho & Jonassen, 2002), scaffolded and threaded online discussions (Oh & Jonassen, 2007), and the focused interactive learning technique (Harton Richardson, Barreras, Rockloff, & Latane, 2002), to name a few, has found that students benefit from structured approaches in developing advanced levels of thinking, problem solving, and subject matter competence. In addition to structuring collaborative learning environments effectively, researchers have articulated the importance of instructors to convey expectations for student engagement in active learning activities clearly (Walker et al., 2008). Researchers have also pushed for future research to identify the optimal "ratio of collaborative to traditional techniques that is most beneficial for college student learning" (Gubera & Arguete, 2013, p. 651).

Problem-Based Learning. Prince (2004) defined *problem-based learning* (PBL), a common technique of inductive teaching, as an instructional method in which problems provide the context and motivation for students' self-directed learning, often in collaborative and cooperative groups. Although PBL's roots are in the field of medicine, it is now used across disciplinary domains.

In a meta-analysis of 41 studies, students who experienced PBL developed greater skills in applying knowledge than peers in traditional classrooms, with a large positive association (effect size = .46), but PBL was found to have no effect on students' course content knowledge. The nonsignificant effect on content knowledge resulted from the varying effects by year of study, with negative effects for students in their second year that become positive in studies of third-year students and did not differ for students in subsequent years (Dochy, Segers, Van den Bossche, & Gijbels, 2003). However, studies that allowed a period of time to pass before measuring knowledge found that PBL had a small positive association (effect size = .14), indicating that students in PBL environments remember more of the knowledge acquired in the class setting (Dochy et al., 2003). In a follow-up study, Gijbels, Dochy, Van den Bossche, and Segers, (2005) found that PBL had the most positive effects when the focal constructs being assessed were at the level of understanding principles that link concepts. Walker and Leary (2009) examined the effectiveness of PBL across disciplines and found a generally small positive effect ($d = .13$) but one that varied considerably by discipline ($d = .64$ for teacher education; $d = .045$ for engineering).

Like other forms of active learning, PBL challenges students, as evidenced in students' lower self-reported gains despite higher scores on objective measures of problem-solving and knowledge transfer (Yadav, Subedi, Lundeberg, & Bunting, 2011). Although students find PBL challenging but worthwhile (Grade, Gouldsborough, Sheader, & Speake, 2009), they have noted that PBL is more time-consuming (Steck, DiBiase, Wang, & Boukhtiarov, 2012) and requires an instructor who serves in a critical role, moving between groups, clarifying the task, and providing support (Prince & Felder, 2006). As Chernobilsky, Dacosta, and Hmelo-Silver (2004) concluded, "Interaction itself does not assure that the ideas being generated will reach a high level of knowledge and language development" (p. 347).

Without sufficient shared knowledge before solving the problem, groups may simply list or mention concepts without meaningfully applying them to the problem. The weight of the evidence suggests the benefits of PBL in advancing students' ability to apply course concepts. The opportunity for further research is to identify the necessary precursor stages of shared knowledge development and how to scaffold the exercise for maximum learning.

Case Study. We identified research across a range of disciplines that examined the extent to which subject-matter competence was enhanced as a result of students engaging in a real life case study, which provides students with a particular instance to analyze and apply course concepts and principles. The weight of the evidence suggests gains not only in subject matter knowledge (Qureshi, Cosine, & Rizvi, 2013; Waples, Antes, Murphy, Connelly, & Mumford, 2009), but also in higher-order thinking (Chaplin, 2009; Karantzas et al., 2013; Rybarczyk, Baines, McVey, Thompson & Wilkins, 2007; Yadav & Beckerman, 2009) and communication skills (Noblitt, Vance, & Smith, 2010) within the discipline. Lundeberg and Yadav (2006) concluded, "The higher the level of knowledge and thinking required on the assessment task, the more likely that case-based teaching will produce greater gains in student understanding" (p. 10). Consistent with our review of other active learning methods, constructing effective case study experiences requires instructors to "balance structure and direction on the one hand, with flexibility and self-direction on the other" (Ormrod, 2011, p. 198).

Experiential Labs. Experiential labs vary in their application based on discipline. In the sciences and engineering, students may manipulate equipment and other matter to test hypotheses or observe disciplinary properties in action. In the social sciences and humanities, experiential labs might take the form of ethnographic fieldwork or games and simulations in which disciplinary concepts are examined. Across disciplines and in two-year as well as four-year institutions, students in classes where they had the opportunity to engage in inquiry-based experiential labs had greater subject matter competence than their peers (Ball, Eckel, & Rojas, 2006; Bhathal, Sharma, & Mendez, 2010; Dickie, 2006; Durham, McKinnon, & Schulman, 2007; Emerson & Taylor, 2004; Luckie et al., 2004; Myers & Burgess, 2003; Pedersen, 2010; Sirum & Humburg, 2011).

With the availability of remote lab apparatus increasing (see Western Interstate Commission for Higher Education, 2015), Corter, Esche, Chassapis, Ma, and Nickerson (2011) extended this line of inquiry by examining the extent to which learning differed by hands-on/physical or remote data collection and whether the lab was conducted individually or with others. In the multiyear, randomized study, they found that students participating in hands-on labs showed a large advantage over those who received group data collection instructions, while students collecting data individually did better in the remotely operated lab format. Overall, students experiencing the lab in hands-on format had higher mean scores than students experiencing the remote labs, who, in turn, scored higher than students experiencing simulations. In another study that inquired how the context of an experiment was related to student learning, Carter and Emerson (2012) used a quasi-experimental design to investigate whether any difference in students' economic course scores on the Test of Understanding in College Economics (TUCE) existed between in-class experiments and computerized online experiments. They found no difference in student achievement, but students in the in-class condition had more favorable views of the experimental pedagogy and reported higher levels of peer interaction.

Service-Learning. Bringle and Hatcher (1995) distinguish academic service learning from volunteerism and community service, stating that the former is a

> "course-based, credit-bearing educational experience that allows students to (a) participate in an organized service activity that meets identified community needs and (b) reflect on the service activity in such a way as to gain further understanding of course content, a broader appreciation of the discipline, and an enhanced sense of civic responsibility" (p. 112).

Volunteering and community service are designed to meet the needs of the community agency or clients, but do not explicitly connect to credit-bearing experiences.

Since publication of the previous volume, the interest in service-learning has risen exponentially, although the research is not consistent in distinguishing between academic service-learning (experiences expressly associated with a course) and service-learning (not part of a course but intentionally designed with learning outcomes). In 11 studies of undergraduate students across disciplines with a variety of outcomes (self-reported gains, assignment scores, exam scores, posttest cognition measures), service-learning had medium-sized effects, with a weighted mean effect size of .33, which varied by self-report ($d = .37$) and more objective learning measures (exams and student assignments; $d = .31$) (Warren, 2012). A meta-analysis of 62 studies (of which 68% focused on undergraduate students) found a similar mean effect size ($d = .31$) across a multitude of outcomes (Celio, Durlak, & Dymnicki, 2011). In a related meta-analysis including K–12 and adult learners, Conway, Amel, and Gerwien (2009) found the effect of service-learning on academic and learning outcomes had a mean weighted effect size of .43 but with substantial variation in findings.

Concept Maps and Graphic Organizers. Concept maps, also referred to as knowledge maps, are students' representation of ideas as node-like assemblies that may be labeled or unlabeled, and with or without arrows indicating direction (Nesbit & Adescope, 2006). In a meta-analysis of postsecondary studies that examined the efficacy of constructing concept maps for promoting students' content acquisition and mastery, Nesbit and Adescope (2006) found a large mean effect size of .77; in postsecondary studies that examined studying concepts, they found a moderate effect size of .36. Lim, Lee, and Grabowski (2009) examined the difference in course learning between constructing a concept map versus simply studying one and found that students who generated their own concept map had greater knowledge acquisition than their peers who studied an expert-generated map. Part of the explanation for this difference may lie in the active amount of time on task and the student effort required to make meaning of the content in constructing the concept map. Berry and Chew (2008) found that the number of concept maps constructed, as well as the number of nodes per map, were associated with enhanced performance in a psychology course. Yet Stull and Mayer's (2007) findings suggested that an upper-bound threshold may exist at which point constructing a concept map or graphic organizer results in extraneous cognitive load.

In general, concept mapping was found to benefit learners across subject areas and settings (Nesbit & Adescope, 2006). In comparison with reading text passages, attending lectures, or discussing in groups, concept mapping was more effective in influencing knowledge acquisition, retention, and transfer (Bahr & Dansereau, 2005; Chularut & Debacker, 2004; Nesbit & Adescope, 2006; Stull & Mayer, 2007).

Graphic organizer (GO) is a more expansive term for concept maps in that they also include outlines, flowcharts, time lines, and tables as a means of showing "relationships among concepts or processes by means of spatial position, connecting lines and intersecting figures" (Nesbit & Adescope, 2006, p. 413). In addition to graphically presenting conceptual relationships, GOs can also be used to reflect the organizational patterns of a text (such as cause and effect, comparison and contrast, problem and solution), which when recognized by a student, facilitates reading comprehension (Jiang & Grabe, 2007). Because of the variations in GO, it has been difficult to determine if they consistently foster student learning (Manoli & Papadopoulou, 2012).

Despite this mixed evidence, individual research studies have examined the timing of graphic organizer presentation within a text and the contexts in which graphic organizers are used to assist learning. Robinson, Corliss, Bush, Bera, and Tomberlin (2003) found that presenting more substantial graphic organizers before the text enabled students to recall more broad-based course principles, learn concept relations, and apply knowledge in new situations better than presenting smaller graphic organizations throughout the text. Trumpower and Goldsmith (2004) investigated the extent to which graphic organization presented in alphabetical order, randomly, or conceptually based on disciplinary experts' knowledge influenced psychology students' knowledge structures and performance. Although there were no differences in definitional knowledge between the three groups, students in the expert group scored higher on conceptual knowledge and on a task that required transfer of knowledge from one procedure to another than their peers whose graphic organization was presented either randomly or alphabetically. Extending this finding to chemistry, Stroud and Schwartz (2010) found that metaphorical graphics aided students in developing a deeper understanding of the behavior and reactivity, but not the physical properties, of a selected set of chemical elements.

Reflective, Linguistic, Aesthetic, and Arts-Based Approaches. A number of studies examined teaching techniques that use reflective writing, linguistic devices, and other arts-based approaches to foster student verbal, quantitative, or subject matter competence. Reflective writing is used as a means for students to detail conceptual understanding in their own words (Fulwiler & Young, 1982). Linguistic approaches may use mnemonic and other linguistic devices to facilitate student subject matter mastery, while aesthetic and arts-based approaches invite students to role-play or draw their understanding of course concepts. We review these different approaches.

Writing to learn (WTL) has gained in popularity in the past decade. Fulwiler and Young (1982) defined *writing to learn* as a means "to objectify our perceptions of reality; the primary function of this 'expressive' language is not to communicate, but to order and represent experience to our own understanding" (p. x). Several studies examining the efficacy of writing to learn have originated within the science disciplines, suggesting that WTL has been used to advance institutional writing across the curriculum objectives. The evidence base largely derives out of single-institution quasi-experimental studies with mixed results. Although a number of studies found enhanced subject matter knowledge in courses ranging from ecology (Balgopal & Wallace, 2009) to physics (Hand, Gunel, & Ulu, 2009) to psychology (Stewart, Myers and Culley, 2010), particularly among nonscience majors (Klein, Piacente-Cimini, & Williams, 2007), others have found no difference (Armstrong, Wallace, & Chang, 2008; Fry & Villagomez, 2012).

Despite the mixed findings, researchers have advanced WTL provides students with an opportunity to practice their metacognitive and reflective thinking skills by putting information in their own words and integrating concepts (Kalman, 2011; Ziegler & Montplaisir, 2012). The efficacy of the approach appears to rely on instructors' explicitly teaching students when and how to use different metacognitive strategies (Armstrong et al., 2008).

Instructional techniques also include unique ways instructors may employ language and literary devices to facilitate student verbal, quantitative, and subject matter knowledge. For example, Stalder and Olson (2011) found the use of mnemonics aided in statistical concept recall. Clement and Yanowitz (2003) examined the use of analogy to relate information from a source text to that of an unfamiliar target text. Students were able to use analogy from the source text to understand the target text within a different context. Another study (Schoerning, 2014) compared students across two microbiology course formats; in one course, students used the traditional microbiology vocabulary, while in the other course, their peers learned microbiology using plain-English equivalent terms. The latter group performed better on written exams that assessed higher-order abilities such as applying and analyzing course content. The plain-English group gained similar lower-order knowledge. The findings from these studies suggest learning gains may be due to students' ability to use neural networks to ground new learning (Schoerning, 2014). Yet, in order for these devices to be employed effectively, students must have some level of prior knowledge from which to build and develop their understanding (Braasch & Goldman, 2010).

Other research has examined the timing of writing and literary devices as instructional techniques. Thiede and Anderson (2003) examined the effect of having students write a summary immediately following reading a passage or delaying the summary writing (compared to no summary) on test performance and metacomprehension accuracy (defined as the correlation between students' perceived comprehension and test performance). Students who wrote their summary after a length of time did not differ from nonsummarizers on test performance but scored higher than either group in metacomprehension accuracy, suggesting that summarizing after a period of time allowed students to digest, reflect on, and comprehend the written text. In a related study, Anderson and Thiede (2008) found that students who wrote summaries after delay detailed the gist of the text as opposed to focusing on the details, the former being associated with higher levels of metacomprehension accuracy. Together, these findings suggest that delayed summary writing provides students with an opportunity to "see the forest through the trees."

Finally, innovative teaching techniques have used arts-based approaches, including role-play and drawing, to facilitate subject matter knowledge acquisition. Building on previous research from the 1990s, Elliot (2010) used role play in an immunology classroom and found it equally effective for both participants and observers, with greater gains realized in basic recall of immunology content than the application of knowledge. Van der Veen (2012) incorporated drawing and self-reflection in a physics classroom as a means to help students, particularly historically underrepresented students in higher education, overcome disciplinary language barriers and increase knowledge of physics concepts.

Evidence from these studies provides empirical support for those who advance the need to infuse the arts and aesthetic studies into the broader STEM agenda (STEM to STEAM, 2015), as a means for students to develop both natural technical knowledge as well as creative perspectives (Sousa & Pilecki, 2013).

Question Prompts. Asking questions is part of an instructor's deliberate practice, in that questions invite students to engage their understanding of course material and demonstrate disciplinary skills while receiving feedback, hallmarks of pedagogies associated with constructivist learning and formative assessment (Deslauriers, Schelew, and Wieman, 2011). Research in the past decade has examined different forms of questioning, ranging from scaffolded question prompts to comparisons between types of question prompts. In general, students who were prompted to consider, reflect on, and engage with course material, such that they were practicing subject matter–based reasoning and problem solving showed greater gains than peers who were not prompted (Chen, 2010; Deslauriers et al., 2011; Ge & Land, 2003; Scarboro, 2004; Steif, Lobue, Kara, & Fay, 2010).

Difficulty of course content seems associated with the effectiveness of different types of question prompts. Scaffolded question prompts were associated positively with students' reading comprehension for difficult passages but yielded no difference in comprehension for easier passages (Chen et al., 2011). Students in an engineering exploration course who were prompted to evaluate arguments for solutions to an ethics case and those who generated and supported their own solutions developed stronger arguments and more supported solutions than their peers who simply summarized different perspectives, theoretical approaches, and ethical canons (Jonassen et al., 2009). Moreover, certain types of prompts appear associated with different types of outcomes. In two related single institution studies among preservice teachers, there was no difference in conceptual knowledge between students who received a knowledge-integration prompt and those who received a problem-solving prompt, but students who received the former made efforts to identify major concepts and their relationships for solving the ill-structured problem, while the latter made greater efforts to construct solutions and explicitly provide arguments for subsequent implementation (Chen & Bradshaw, 2007). Again in a sample of preservice teachers, Chen (2010) found that students who received integration, procedure, and a combination of integration and procedure prompts had higher problem-solving scores than their peers who did not receive a question prompt. Supporting previous research (Chen & Bradshaw, 2007), integration question prompts were most effective in the problem representation phase of problem solving, while procedural prompts were most effective in the solution development phase (Chen, 2010).

Homework. At some level, homework is the ultimate means by which to increase students' time on task. Doing homework, whether online or on paper, for a grade or ungraded, requires students to engage with course content beyond the classroom domain. Across research designs, students who completed homework received higher grades than those who did not (Dillard-Eggers, Wooten, Childs, & Coker, 2011; Grodner & Rupp, 2013; Kitsantas & Zimmerman, 2009; Riffell & Sibley, 2005; Trost & Salehi-Isfahani, 2012; Wooten & Dillard-Eggers, 2013).

Some studies have investigated the extent to which homework's relationship with student achievement was due to it being graded. With few exceptions (Geide-Stevenson, 2009), the results suggest that graded homework (compared to ungraded homework) is associated with greater course achievement (Cheng, Thacker, Cardenas, & Crouch 2004; Grove & Wasserman, 2006; Emerson & Mencken, 2011; Pozo & Stull, 2006), although students in the graded homework condition did not differ in scores on a standardized measure of disciplinary knowledge in economics (Emerson & Mencken, 2011).

Still other research has examined if the effect of homework completion varies by format: online or paper. The results suggest no difference (Bonham, Deardorff, & Beichner, 2003; Marshall, 2009; Mathai & Olsen, 2013). Despite parity in course achievement, Bonham and colleagues advanced the idea that the "additional support and feedback enabled by the medium [online] may be of real value" (p. 1066). Because of its preprogrammed nature, online homework provides the opportunity for students to receive immediate feedback while reducing instructor workload. Timely feedback is an important means by which to provide encouragement and spur student motivation and is not to be overlooked considering that part of the relationship between homework completion and student achievement was attributed to students' increased self-efficacy for learning and perceived responsibility (Kitsantas & Zimmerman, 2009).

Types of Assessment. Like homework, researchers have been interested in understanding how the frequency of assessments and collaborative assessment (compared to individual assessment) relates to student learning. Recent research has found frequent student engagement, typically with online quizzes, associated with improved student achievement in many subject matter domains (Angus & Watson, 2009; Freeman, Haak, & Wenderoth, 2011; Haak, HelleRisLambers, Pitre, & Freeman, 2011; McGuire & MacDonald, 2009). The notion of continuous assessment in the form of daily quizzes (as opposed to regularly spaced assessments) was associated with higher posttest grades in a mathematics for calculus course (Shorter & Young, 2011). Again, this suggests that time on task, practicing disciplinary skills, and using disciplinary knowledge are associated with subject matter competence.

An area that has received a great deal of research focus in the past decade is the effectiveness of collaborative/group assessment compared to individual assessment with respect to subject matter achievement. As postsecondary enrollment has increased, assessing student learning in ways that are pedagogically effective yet efficient has become necessary. In studies across disciplines, students who completed exams together or whose scores were pooled to form a group score generally do as well as or better than their peers tested individually (Bloom, 2009; Cortright, Collins, Rodenbaugh, & DiCarlo, 2003; Gaudet, Ramer, Nakonechny, Cragg, & Ramer, 2010; Kapitanoff, 2009; Keselyak, Saylor, Simmer-Beck, & Bray, 2009; Leight, Saunders, Calkins, & Withers, 2012; Meseke, Bovée, & Gran, 2009; Peck, Stehle Werner, & Ralrigh, 2013; Sandahl, 2010; Slusser & Erickson, 2006; Srougi, Miller, Witherow, & Carson, 2013; Woody, Woody, & Bromley, 2008; Zipp, 2007), although findings were mixed in terms of the value of collaborative testing for retention of class material. The fact that students in collaborative assessment environments appear to do as well as their peers assessed individually may be a boon to instructors who are looking for efficiencies in student learning assessment. However, if the goal is to enhance course achievement by drawing on the benefits of collaborative learning, future research should examine the mechanisms operating within collaborative examination environments associated with increased retention of course content (see Bloom, 2009; Cortright et al., 2003)

In summary, the literature in the past decade has solidified the knowledge base that students learn more when actively engaged in the learning process through any number of means and methods. Opportunities for students to engage with course concepts such that they are routinely practicing disciplinary skills in using disciplinary knowledge are associated positively with subject matter competence. As evidenced by the substantial variation in effect sizes for service-learning on academic outcomes, future research would be well advised to examine the efficacy of active learning techniques by learning context and/ or identify the mechanisms within the active learning environment associated with greater learning gains.

Teacher Behaviors. Historically, higher education faculty have tended to be trained as researchers in their discipline and, to a lesser extent, as disciplinary educators (Wulff & Austin, 2004). Honing the teaching craft takes time and often requires pursuing professional development opportunities provided by a center of teaching and learning, center for faculty excellence, and the like. Lambert, Terenzini, and Lattuca (2007) found that the degree to which engineering faculty reported engaging in professional development activities was positively associated with students' self-reported engineering design and analytical skills, controlling for a host of student and institutional factors. The prevalence and expansion of such centers on postsecondary campuses suggests that being a good teacher is not an inherent trait but that the principles underlying good teaching can be taught, a conclusion advanced by Pascarella and Terenzini in both earlier volumes (1991, 2005). This next section reviews literature that has examined these behaviors.

Preparation and Organization. Research from the 2000s has found that effective instruction, defined by the extent to which faculty members are prepared and organized in the presentation of course content, is associated with students' verbal, quantitative, and subject matter competence. In a series of studies using data collected through the National Study of Student Learning, instructor organization/preparation was associated positively with standardized measures of reading comprehension and mathematics (Bray et al., 2004; Whitt, Pascarella, Elkins Nesheim, Marth, & Pierson, 2003). These findings were extended in a multi-institutional study of engineering students in which instructor clarity and organization were related to self-reported engineering analytical skills, controlling for student and institutional characteristics (Strauss & Terenzini, 2007). Schonwetter, Clifton, and Perry (2002) provided the strongest evidence suggesting a direct influence between instructor organization and student subject matter competence. In a randomized experimental design, instructor organization positively predicted students' perceived learning, as well as an objectively measured assessment of their economics learning, controlling for students' content familiarity and high school GPA (Schonwetter et al., 2002).

Clarity and Expressiveness. Related to instructor preparation and organization is the degree to which faculty members are clear and expressive in their presentation of course material (Bray et al., 2004). Lambert and colleagues (2007) found that clarity of teaching was associated positively with self-reported engineering analytical skill, net of student and institutional characteristics. Again, Schonwetter and colleagues (2002) conducted the most rigorous examination of instructor expressiveness and student learning using a randomized experimental design. Although instructor expressiveness influenced students' perceived learning from the economics lecture, expressiveness had no impact on an objectively measured assessment of learning from the lecture, accounting for students' content familiarity and high school GPA (Schonwetter et al., 2002).

Feedback. Instructor feedback has many facets: individual or collective, developmental in focus or abbreviated, immediate or delayed. Research from the 2000s examined all of these facets pertaining to the relationship between instructor feedback and students' verbal, quantitative, and subject matter competence.

Gallien and Oomen-Early (2008) found in a single-institution study of students enrolled in online health courses that those who received individualized feedback rather than collective feedback (which summarized the class performance and detailed ways to improve) had higher academic performance. Among preservice teachers' lesson plan development, instructor feedback (referred to as teacher evaluation) was related to significantly greater improvement in students' lesson plans than when students were evaluated by their peers (Ozogul & Sullivan, 2009). However, once relevant training and practice in the evaluation process were added, no differences were found between the feedback provided by the instructor and that provided by peers, with both groups improving (Ozogul & Sullivan, 2009).

The depth of instructor feedback was examined in an experimental study at a large research intensive university in Canada and found that while developed feedback (defined as asking questions for clarification on student work) was helpful and perceived as fair, it did not have a significant effect on students' written performance compared to students who received short, terse comments on their writing (McGrath, Taylor, & Pychl, 2011). Finally, an experimental study of engineering students examined the effect of immediacy of feedback on problem-solving for problems that required a near transfer of knowledge, defined as problems similar in structure to the examples discussed in instruction but different in surface information, than those who required a more extensive transfer (Moreno, Reisslein, & Ozogul, 2009). Students who received feedback immediately after attempting each problem-solving step outperformed students who received feedback only at the end of the process on problems that required a near transfer of knowledge. The two groups did not differ on problems that required more extensive knowledge transfer (Moreno et al., 2009).

Findings from single-institution experimental and quasi-experimental studies support the conclusions from two cross-sectional multi-institutional studies of engineering students (Lambert et al., 2007; Strauss & Terenzini, 2007) where instructor interaction and feedback were associated positively with gains in self-reported engineering analytical skills, taking into account student and institutional characteristics. Students appreciate knowing if they are on track, and timely feedback provides needed assessment and evaluation of student effort and understanding.

Holistic Good Teaching. A number of studies used a more holistic notion of good teaching as opposed to separately operationalized instructor behaviors. From multi-institutional pretest/posttest research conducted in the United States in which effective teaching was associated with an objective measure of reading comprehension (Bray et al., 2004; Cruce, Wolniak, Seifert, & Pascarella, 2006) but not with mathematics knowledge (Cruce et al., 2006) to two studies from Australia where good teaching was associated with students' disciplinary knowledge, communication, and problem-solving skills (Lizio & Wilson, 2004; Smith & Bath, 2006), students learn more from teachers who motivate them to do their best work, make an effort to understand students' difficulties, explain content well, make courses interesting, and give helpful feedback.

Combining these teacher behaviors with research-based pedagogy is the foundation of deliberate practice (see Ericsson, Krampe, & Tesch-Römer, 1993). In a study of a Canadian institution's large-enrollment science course, the quasi-experimental design compared student course learning between a section taught by a highly experienced content instructor who lectured but did not use research-based pedagogy and a less experienced content instructor who used pedagogy based on cognitive psychology and physics education informed by the Carl Wieman Science Education Initiative (CWSEI) at the University of British Columbia (2007–2015). Students in the treatment group were engaged in their instructors' "deliberate practice" (Deslauriers et al., 2011, p. 862) such that students responded to a series of challenging questions and tasks that required physicist-like reasoning and problem solving while receiving frequent feedback. The difference in test scores between the two classroom conditions yielded a 2.5 effect size advantaging the treatment group, the largest ever observed for an educational intervention. Deslauriers and colleagues eschew the notion of a single instructional best practice, asserting, "The educational benefit does not come primarily from any particular practice but rather from the integration into the overall deliberate practice framework" (p. 862). Research and results from CWSEI across seven science disciplines is compelling and demonstrates that the principles of good teaching informed by research-based pedagogy can be taught.

Peers as Teachers and Learners. Peers are a valuable source for supported teaching and learning during college (Astin, 1993; Keup, 2012; Pascarella & Terenzini, 2005). Not only do the students being taught or mentored benefit, but the student tutors, mentors, and teachers benefit as well. The value that peers bring to the learning milieu is not a new notion. Vygotsky (1978) identified peers as sources of learning support and guidance in his theory of the zone of proximal development. Since peers are closer to a student's own experience and stage of development, students may listen to and learn more easily from a peer. Peer support can take the form of learning communities (Goldman, 2012; Kuh, 2008; Zhao & Kuh, 2004), tutoring (Ashwin, 2003; Preszler, 2009), and supplemental instruction (Moore & LeDee, 2006; Ogden, Thompson, Russell, & Simon, 2003), to name a few.

Learning Communities. At their most basic level, learning communities attempt to leverage shared or collaborative learning and connected learning across a student community (Pascarella & Terenzini, 2005). This may be accomplished by having the same students take multiple courses or two connected courses together, often with a common theme, and broadly linking two or more fields of inquiry (Andrade, 2007; Brower & Inkelas, 2010; Inkelas & Weisman, 2003). Some studies have found positive effects on general education outcomes for learning community students (Goldman, 2012; Kuh, 2008; Zhao & Kuh, 2004). Zhao and Kuh (2004) examined NSSE data and found that first-year (effect size = .36) and senior students (effect size = .24) in learning communities reported greater gains in general education than their peers who were not in a learning community. The 2007 Annual Report published by the NSSE highlighted specific features of the learning community that contributed to the self-reported gains in general education outcomes. These included integrating learning across the learning community courses, especially through assignments, and required out-of-class activities. Goldman (2012) studied students in a first-year learning communities program in a large research-intensive university in Canada and found that learning community students performed better academically in their core courses than students not in a first-year community, controlling for both high school grades and high school attended.

Other research has found the relationships between learning community participation and general education gains are largely due to increased levels of engagement and relatedness to the campus community. Rocconi (2011) found a negative direct effect of learning community membership on self-reported gains in general education, but it was offset by the positive indirect effect through increased student engagement. Similarly, Beachboard, Beachboard, Li, and Adkison (2011) found a positive mean difference in students' academic development by learning community participation. However, controlling for student background characteristics, learning community participation was not associated with academic development, but relatedness (defined as feelings of belongingness and connectedness with others) was associated positively with academic development (Beachboard et al., 2011). Students in the learning communities reported higher levels of relatedness to faculty and students, providing further evidence of the indirect effects of learning community participation. Both the Rocconi (2011) and the Beachboard et al. (2011) studies illustrate the systemic nature of learning and that a sole focus on direct effects can mislead researchers and policymakers as in both cases, students in the learning communities reported greater engagement and relatedness, which were, in turn, associated positively with student learning.

Other studies, mostly of single courses or at single institutions, have not found significant differences in outcomes between learning community participants and their nonparticipating peers. For example, Boise State University's STRETCH program links two related English courses together, creating a cohort (Peele, 2010). Faculty ratings of portfolios from student in the STRETCH program did not differ significantly from the ratings of the mainstream English portfolios (Peele, 2010). Despite similar writing performance, students in the learning community commented that the increased student-faculty interaction was one of the program's most productive features.

Overall, few studies have specifically examined academic/subject matter learning outcomes. However, from the studies reviewed, it would appear that studies of larger samples tended to find positive effects of learning communities on general education gains. There also appeared to be many mediating factors, such as support received and relationships developed more easily as a result of learning community participation, which are associated with academic knowledge gains.

Peer Tutoring. Peer tutoring is defined as members with the same

"social standing educating one another when one peer has more expertise or knowledge" and may include "continuing classroom discussions, developing study skills, evaluating work, resolving specific problems, and encouraging independent learning" (Colvin, 2007, p. 166).

Reciprocal teaching has more focused objectives, with students working together and with a teacher to better comprehend textual material through predicting, questioning, clarifying, and summarizing (Yang, 2010). Multiple studies have examined the efficacy of peer tutoring and reciprocal teaching with regard to course grade improvement, subject matter understanding, problem solving related to the subject or course, and subject matter retention.

Studies investigating the effects of peer tutoring and reciprocal teaching at the course level across disciplines have found positive benefits in general (Ashwin, 2003; Karantzas et al., 2013; Krych et al., 2005; Lundberg, 2003; Preszler, 2009). A single institution study in the United Kingdom found a statistically significant positive correlation between attendance at peer support sessions and end-of-year performance in mathematics, statistics, and chemistry courses (Ashwin, 2003). Munley, Garvey, and McConnell (2010) found that the dichotomous peer support participation measure was not associated with course grade in economics but that the continuous measure of tutorial hours predicted improved course performance, with about 10 hours of weekly tutoring over a 14-week semester needed for a change in letter grade.

In an interesting study that examined mutual benefit, Krych and colleagues (2005) examined peer or reciprocal teaching in an anatomy course and found that students reported increased understanding of anatomy concepts in the teacher role, increased understanding and retention in the learner role, and increased long-term retention of the teaching topic. In addition, the teacher role resulted in a significantly higher understanding and retention of material compared to the learner role, pointing to the reciprocal benefits for peers as teachers.

Other research has examined peer review, a more focused form of peer tutoring and teaching, with mixed results. Walvoord, Hoefnagels, Gaffin, Chumchal, and Long (2008) found students in a zoology course did not improve in either their technical writing skills or their ability to convey scientific understanding through essay writing over the course of the term using the Calibrated Peer Review™ tool (an online tool used to integrate writing into the classroom). Nevertheless, Gunersel and Simpson (2009) found that students improved in writing skills and reviewer competency with repeated use of calibrated peer review. Springer and Pear (2008) studied the effects of another online peer review system and found that students in self-paced courses who used peer reviewers obtained higher final exam scores than students who did not use peer reviewers or used them less. Conversely, Covill (2010) found no difference between students who engaged in formal peer review, formal self-review, or no review in the quality of their final paper in a writing course. Trautmann

(2007) found that students who engaged in peer review made significantly more revisions than those who were assigned to the self-review condition. Moreover, Trautmann found that receiving peer suggestions was more influential in triggering students to revise their papers than writing reviews for others.

These inconclusive results suggest careful consideration must be paid in creating the conditions and scaffolding the objectives of peer teaching and tutoring such that reciprocal benefits as teacher and learner can be realized. Future research may examine peer tutoring and review under a variety of conditions to investigate which conditions are associated with greater gains in verbal, quantitative, and subject matter competence.

Supplemental Instruction. Supplemental instruction (SI), an academic assistance program developed at the University of Missouri—Kansas City in 1973, consists of peer-assisted study sessions where peers who have previously taken the course and done well facilitate sessions to help students develop strategies to learn and understand the course content (International Center for Supplemental Instruction, 2015). Supplemental instruction is different from many peer learning and tutoring programs because the course, rather than the student, is targeted. Courses that have historically had 30% or more students receive grades of D, F, or withdraw are deemed high risk and may be identified as supplemental instruction courses (Pascarella & Terenzini, 2005).

In a recent meta-analysis, Dawson, van der Meer, Skalicky, and Cowley (2014) analyzed 29 studies examining the effectiveness of SI from 2001 to 2010. Course grades, the most common measure of effectiveness in these SI studies and the only outcome for which effects could be calculated, had effect sizes ranging from .29 to .60, consistent with previous research (U.S. Department of Education, 1995). One of the challenges in identifying the effects of SI is the self-selection bias of those who choose to participate. Controlling for students' high school GPA and SAT scores, Rath, Bayliss, Runquist, and Simonis (2012) found that SI was effective in increasing student achievement in both introductory courses of general and organic chemistry, but not in either of the follow-up courses. Hensen and Shelley (2003) and Oja (2012) found similar results, controlling for precollege academic ability.

Several studies found positive effects for supplemental instruction, especially in courses with students who were conditionally admitted to the institution or deemed at risk on matriculation. Ogden et al. (2003) conducted a single-institution study examining the effects of self-selecting into SI in a political science course and found conditionally admitted students (those in a learning support program or who were English language learners) had higher grades compared to conditionally admitted non-SI students and grades similar to the traditionally admitted non-SI students. No difference existed between the traditionally admitted SI students versus traditionally admitted non-SI students.

Moore and LeDee (2006) studied the effects of SI in an introductory biology course for students in developmental education. Although first-year SI students earned similar grades as the non-SI students, the grade distributions were different. SI students earned fewer Ds and Fs than non-SI students (Moore & LeDee, 2006).

The SI students who earned As and Bs had similar admissions scores as those that earned Ds and Fs, but their academic behaviors were different, including attending class at higher rates, submitting more work for extra credit, and attending more help sessions and office hours than the non-SI students (Moore & LeDee, 2006). This may indicate that SI-assisted students tend to engage in positive academic behaviors, thereby improving their academic performance. But due to students' ability to self-select into SI in both of these studies, it is difficult to untangle the extent to which these findings are due to the SI intervention or the fact that more academically motivated students opt into SI.

This section detailed the valuable role peers can play as teachers, mentors, and, in the words of Vygotsky (1978), a "more knowledgeable other." Either through being part of a learning community, tutoring, teaching reciprocally, or as supplemental instruction leader, peers can help their classmates master course concepts and gain academic skills. Student learning cannot be left to chance, though, and peers as teachers require appropriate support and scaffolding as they assist their fellow classmates in understanding challenging course material.

Program of Study. "What are you going to study?" is one of the most commonly asked questions of students beginning their postsecondary education. Building on previous conceptual frameworks of college impact, Terenzini and Reason (2012) posit that academic and cocurricular programs, policies, and practices are the three primary factors within the organizational context that contribute to educational outcomes. The program of study, particularly as it pertains to academic major or program, is a critical component of a student's educational experience and contributes to students' development of subject matter competence (Pascarella & Terenzini, 2005). We review literature that has examined several components within students' programs of study, including the academic major, broader coursework patterns, developmental coursework, honors coursework, as well as paths to completing one's degree/credential with respect to verbal, quantitative, and subject matter competence.

Academic Major. Consistent with previous volumes (Pascarella & Terenzini, 1991, 2005) and with few exceptions (Gratton-Lavoie & Stanley, 2009; Johnson & Kuennen, 2004), we found that students tended to gain in subject matter competence in areas closely associated with their field of study (Carter & Emerson, 2012; Herzog, 2011; Sanders-Dewey & Zaleski, 2009; Strauss & Terenzini, 2007). For example, Herzog (2011) found that students who studied social sciences, health sciences, or humanities had lower GRE longitudinal quantitative gains scores and lower self-reported gains in math and quantitative skills compared to their peers who studied physical sciences or business.

Challenging the notion that quantitative competence is primarily the domain of math and science majors, however, Kinzie and colleagues (2007) found that while math and sciences majors reported greater gains in quantitative skills in their first year of college than their social sciences peers, no difference between majors was found among senior students attending women's colleges. Although more research is needed to identify the potential mechanisms, these findings suggest the environment at women's colleges may serve to neutralize students' perceptions that only those in majors with a strong quantitative foundation gain in math and quantitative skills during college.

In a study that used the NSSE self-reported gains items to create outcome indices reflective of different Holland academic environments, Pike, Smart, and Ethington (2012) found that Holland environments positively predicted learning outcomes most associated with those environments: students in investigative environments reported higher gains in investigative outcomes than students from other Holland environment types; students in social environments reported higher gains in social outcomes; and so forth. They tested Holland's theory further, hypothesizing that environments vary in their expectations, norms, and values with respect to forms of engagement, and thus the relationship between environment and outcome may be mediated through forms of engagement. On the contrary, Pike and colleagues (2012) found very limited evidence that the effect of Holland environment on outcomes was mediated by engagement characteristics.

Beyond subject matter competence, a number of correlational studies examined how self-reported gains in general education differed by academic major. Controlling for a host of characteristics, only students majoring in engineering reported greater gains in general education than business students, who reported greater gains than their peers in all other fields (Nelson Laird & Cruce, 2009). Compared to students in preprofessional majors, those in math and science reported a small, positive difference (effect size = .15) in their gains in overall education; no differences surfaced between students majoring in preprofessional fields, humanities, social sciences, or business, nor did undecided students or those in multiple majors differ in gains from students in other majors (Kuh & Gonyea, 2003). Lundberg (2003) found similar results.

It is difficult to make conclusive statements given that researchers used different majors as the reference category, but the findings suggest that those studying in fields with a more quantitative focus report greater gains in general education as measured by the self-reported items on the NSSE and CSEQ. In one of the few studies that examined this question with a sample from women's colleges, Kinzie et al. (2007) found that seniors who majored in the humanities, math and science, or professional areas, compared to social sciences majors, reported lower general educational gains. Kinzie and colleagues' (2007) findings for women's colleges run counter to other research, which invites speculation about whether the environment at women's colleges contributes to this difference.

Coursework Patterns. In addition to academic major, students may be exposed to different patterns of coursework or accumulation of experience within certain broad disciplinary areas. Several research studies examined the effects of sequencing coursework on students' verbal, quantitative, and subject matter competence and found specific sequences associated with greater course achievement (Barron & Apple, 2014; Johnson & Kuennen, 2004; Matz, Rothman, Krajcik, & Banaszak

Holl, 2012). For example, students who took an integrated sequence of statistics and research methods in consecutive semesters outperformed peers who did not take the integrated coursework in course grades for both courses and the subtests for statistics and methods in the Area Concentration Achievement Test (ACAT), a standardized test of psychology domain knowledge (Barron & Apple, 2014). Matz and colleagues (2012) examined the extent to which concurrent enrollment in a chemistry lecture and lab courses improved student subject matter competence and found that concurrent enrollment was associated with improved grades for all but students with the highest placement scores at entry. Results from both studies suggest the potential value in identifying learning-enhancing course sequences.

Other research has examined the overall benefit of cumulative course work within certain disciplinary areas on student verbal and quantitative skills. Herzog (2011) found that the number of math courses taken was associated positively with students' longitudinal gains in GRE quantitative scores, as well as self-reported gains in quantitative skills and math. Bray et al. (2004), however, found no relationship between the number of courses taken in mathematics, social sciences, technical, preprofessional areas, or arts and humanities with students' end-of-third-year reading comprehension, but coursework in natural sciences and engineering had a small positive relationship (effect size = .05). Herzog's results follow what might be expected based on research examining academic major: students gain in areas where their course work is mostly closely aligned. However, it is noteworthy that Bray and colleagues found reading comprehension associated with taking natural sciences and engineering courses, but not arts and humanities courses. Although this could be an artifact of the pretest/posttest research design employed and potential ceiling effects in reading comprehension among students who took large numbers of arts and humanities courses, future research may examine relationships between disciplinary coursework and verbal, quantitative, and subject matter competence to identify the mechanisms by which course-taking patterns shape student learning and development.

Developmental Coursework. Although in decline since the 1999–2000 academic year, 24% of students enrolled at two-year colleges and 21% of students enrolled at four-year colleges in 2007–2008 reported taking remedial courses (Snyder & Dillow, 2011, table 241). Since publication of the previous volume, there has been tremendous interest in the effectiveness of developmental (also referred to as remedial) education to strengthen students' academic skills in reading, writing, and math, enabling students to successfully complete college-level course work and ultimately earn a credential.

The number of students attending U.S. postsecondary institutions who arrive underprepared for postsecondary study (Attewell, Lavin, Domina, & Levey, 2006; Bailey, 2009), coupled with the cost of providing developmental education (Goudas & Boylan, 2012), has largely driven this interest. Much of this research has examined outcomes such as number of credits earned, attrition, transfer, and college graduation (Attewell et al., 2006; Bahr, 2012;

Bettinger & Long, 2005; Calcagno & Long, 2008; Martorell & McFarlin, 2011) —valuable outcomes but not within this chapter's scope. We review the research that has specifically examined the effects of developmental education on course achievement and measures of verbal, quantitative, and subject matter competence.

The literature points to educators' and policymakers' concern that developmental education may not be achieving its objectives (Bailey, 2009; Goudas & Boylan, 2012). The research findings we reviewed were inconsistent in part because developmental education varies considerably in its execution (Bailey, 2009). Recognizing this variability, several studies highlighted the positive benefits of developmental courses in English (with an emphasis on reading and writing) in terms of verbal and subject matter competence (Crews & Aragon, 2004; Goen-Salter, 2008; Goldstein & Perin, 2008; Rochford, 2003; Moss & Yeaton, 2006; Southard & Clay, 2004). Less convincing and consistent evidence was found with respect to mathematics developmental coursework. Researchers have found the majority of community college students who take developmental math fail to achieve college-level math competency (Bahr, 2007, 2008b; Bailey, Jeong, & Cho, 2010). Although students who were required to take developmental math and did so had slightly lower economics course achievement than those who were college-math-prepared at the outset, they scored higher than their peers who were required to take developmental math but had not done so (Johnson & Kuennen, 2004).

These findings highlight the key challenge to developmental education: the actual completion of developmental course work. Using data from the Achieving the Dream study of community colleges in the United States, Bailey (2009) noted the gap between referral to and enrollment in developmental course work: 21% of students referred to developmental math and 33% of students referred to developmental reading did not enroll in the recommended course work within three years of initial registration. Of those students who do enroll, completion of the developmental course work varies considerably, with only 30% passing all of the developmental math courses in which they enroll (Attewell et al., 2006) and even fewer completing the full sequence of developmental coursework to which they are recommended (Bailey, 2009). It is difficult for developmental education to achieve its objectives if the students for whom the intervention is most suited fail to enroll and among those who do enroll, fail to complete the suggested progression of developmental coursework.

The delay and duration of developmental courses in both writing and math is related to students' success in college coursework, with students who require greater levels of remediation (a longer duration) more likely to delay beginning the sequence and less likely to pass the first course (Bahr, 2012). This has resulted in educators' testing and evaluating multiple approaches to developmental education, including avoidance models (i.e., dual enrollment, early college high schools, summer bridge programs), acceleration models (fast-tracked, self-paced, and modularized developmental course work), contextualized models (where students are integrated into their program of study while completing developmental coursework, which may also include learning communities), and student support models (see Zachry Rutschow & Schneider, 2012, for a full description of models and examples).

Several studies suggest promising possibilities. Within the acceleration model, Silverman and Seidman (2011) found students enrolled in the intensive Math My Way course (two hours a day, five days a week for 10 modules) had higher math scores over two years than their peers who had not taken the intensive course. From the contextualized approach, Jenkins, Speroni, Belfield, Jaggars, and Edgecombe (2010) found students mainstreamed into English 101 and who concurrently enrolled in a companion course were more likely to pass college introductory English 101 and 102 than students not in the program, but these benefits did not have long-term effects with respect to other college-level courses and persistence. Compounded by the challenges that delayed and lengthy-duration course work present, developmental education is plagued by inconsistent effectiveness in preparing students for success in college-level coursework and degree completion.

Honors Participation. Contrary to the richness of research findings in the K–12 sector, there is a dearth of research examining the influence of participating in an honors college or program within the postsecondary setting (Rinn, 2007). Part of this challenge lies in defining what constitutes an honors program in the postsecondary environment as these programs vary highly in design, duration, structure, eligibility, and other dimensions. Another challenge is the inherent selection effects that threaten the internal validity of such studies. The problem of unequal groups is a major limitation of studies that examine the differences in course achievement between students in a traditional versus honors course of the same disciplinary content (see Ogilvie & Reza, 2009). Moreover, one might expect a reduced effect of honors participation on verbal, quantitative, or subject matter competence when examined within a pretest/posttest design, due to regression to the mean or ceiling effects. However, in a multi-institutional longitudinal design, Seifert, Pascarella, Colangelo, and Assouline (2007) found that students who participated in an honors program scored marginally higher in their first year of college in mathematics knowledge (effect size = .16) and reading comprehension (effect size = .07), accounting for student characteristics, college experiences, and institution attended. Holding constant student characteristics and college experiences, Herzog (2011) found honors participation was associated with self-reported quantitative gains, results that were consistent with the self-reported gains in analytical and problem-solving skills among a sample of women's college students (Kim, 2002a). However, Herzog did not uncover differences between honors participants and nonparticipants in self-reported math gains or the GRE quantitative score. The weight of the evidence favoring honors program participation suggests that these programs may provide a desired community of intellectually compatible peers (Hébert & Reis, 1999, as cited in Ogilvie & Reza, 2009) and a setting in which students do not feel stigmatized as a result of their giftedness (Cross, Coleman, & Stewart, 1993, cited in Ogilvie & Reza, 2009).

Paths to Program of Study Completion. This section reviews the literature that has examined a variety of paths students may take in completing their program of study and credential. These paths include part-time/full-time enrollment, repeating and transferring courses, and changing academic major.

The prototypical college student of the past, a White, male student who enrolls the fall after high school graduation, lives on campus, and goes to college full time, is no longer the norm. In the United States, part-time attendance at postsecondary institutions has steadily increased over the past 15 years (U.S. Department of Education, 2014a). Several studies in the 2000s investigated the extent to which attending part time versus full time resulted in lower academic achievement. In general, attending part time was associated with lower self-reported gains in general education due to lower levels of campus engagement (Lundberg, 2003), although this relationship did not hold in a sample of Native American students (Lundberg, 2007). Similarly, among students attending women's colleges, full-time enrollment was associated positively with self-reported gains in general education for first-year and senior students but had no effect on self-reported gains in quantitative skills for either group (Kinzie et al., 2007). In related studies that accounted for the relationship between current hours enrolled and student grade in an economics course, Carter and Emerson (2012) found a negative association where Emerson and Taylor (2004) found no relationship. The inconsistent findings may be due to the variation in the regression models used but also suggests that too little (part-time) or too much (heavier class load) enrollment intensity may hinder student achievement. Students may be overburdened with expectations from outside work or family responsibilities, in the case of part-time students, or from too many courses with multiple demands and assignments to focus and achieve optimally.

Given the prevalence of students attending multiple institutions, several studies have investigated the extent to which transfer is related to students' verbal, quantitative, and subject matter competence, with inconclusive results. Students who transferred reported weaker gains in general education, controlling for student background and institutional characteristics (Kuh & Gonyea, 2003; Nelson Laird & Cruce, 2009). However, in a sample of students from women's colleges, transfer status was unrelated to self-reported gains in general education or quantitative skills among first-year and senior students (Kinzie et al., 2007). Finally, Liu and Roohr (2013) found students who had transferred to a community college from another institution outperformed their community college peers on objective measures of reading, writing, and math, controlling for GPA, credit hours, hours worked, gender, and race. The weight of the evidence regarding part-time enrollment and transfer status seems to suggest that any negative effects these paths to program of study completion may have on student learning may be mediated by meaningful engagement with the campus community.

The last series of paths to completion we encountered focused on the effects of repeating a course or changing major on student learning. Controlling for student background characteristics, repeating a course had no relationship with students' GRE quantitative score or self-reported gains in quantitative skills or math (Herzog, 2011). Emerson and Mencken (2011) found similar results with regard to students' economic knowledge gains measured by the Test of Understanding in College Economics. Although repeating a course appeared to have no negative effects with students' quantitative and subject matter competence, Herzog (2011) found that changing major had a small but statistically significant negative relationship with students' self-reported gains in quantitative skills and math but, interestingly, no association with the objective measure of quantitative ability.

Academic Challenge, Effort and Engagement. Everyone has heard the old saying, "You get out of life what you put into it." Much the same can be said about postsecondary education. Robert Pace (1979) operationalized this premise in the CSEQ's quality-of-effort measures. Moreover, the premise served as the foundation for Astin's theory of student involvement (1999) and one of its key postulates: "The amount of student learning and personal development associated with any educational program is directly proportional to the quality and quantity of student involvement in that program" (p. 519). With this in mind, the next section examines student involvement, engagement, and effort in the postsecondary environment.

Drawing from Nevitt Sanford's (1967) theory of challenge and support, instructors' high expectations and academic challenge must be accompanied by support in order to yield commensurate student effort. In this spirit, we review research that has examined the relationships between academic challenge and student effort with respect to verbal, quantitative, and subject matter competence.

Using pretest/posttest data from the NSSL and accounting for student background characteristics, college experiences, and a parallel pretest of the outcome measure, Cruce et al. (2006) found no relationship between student reports of classroom academic challenge and high expectations, defined as self-reported academic effort and involvement, number of essay exams in courses, emphasis on higher-order examination questions, use of computers, number of textbooks or assigned readings, and number of term papers or other written reports, and mathematics knowledge or reading comprehension. Using the self-reported gains items on the NSSE to create outcome measures based on Holland environments, Pike et al. (2012) found the extent to which students reported being asked to engage in higher-order thinking was related positively to investigative, artistic, social, and enterprising learning outcomes, taking into account a number of potentially confounding factors.

Student effort lies on the other side of the challenge/expectations coin. The weight of the evidence is clear: the more effort students expend in their courses pays off in increased competence, whether measured by self-reported gains in general education (Rocconi, 2011), changes in knowledge over four years (Berger, 2002), or Holland-type outcomes: investigative, artistic, social, and enterprising (Pike et al., 2012). Moreover, student effort as defined by self-reported hours per week studying or use of study skills has been associated with higher course performance (Johnson & Kuennen, 2004; Stump et al., 2011).

Involvement in Academic Activities. A number of studies have examined student engagement in academically related activities through a composite survey measure, often referred to as academic engagement, involvement, or the total sum of participation in enriching educational experiences. Using this encompassing notion of academic engagement, the weight of the evidence suggests a generally positive relationship with students' self-reported gains in academic competence (Reason, Terenzini, & Domingo, 2006), general education (Lundberg, 2010), or learning and intellectual development, but one indirectly mediated through students' integration experiences (Pike & Kuh, 2006; Pike et al., 2003). Perhaps not quite as broad-based as academic engagement, Harper and Lattuca (2010) defined the cocurriculum as out-of-class experiences such as participation in internships, design competitions, and professional associations related to a students' discipline and found a unique relationship with students' self-reported ability to apply engineering skills in a multi-institutional student sample from ABET-accredited engineering programs across the United States. Using the same dataset, other researchers examined individually the experiences comprising the cocurriculum measure and found participation in internships, design competitions, and professional engineering associations each uniquely associated with students' self-reported engineering design and analytical skills (Lambert et al., 2007, Strauss & Terenzini, 2007).

Library. The college or university library is central to any postsecondary institution, and a small body of research has examined the relationship between students' library experiences and verbal, quantitative, and subject matter competence. A couple of studies specifically examined the extent to which academic experiences connected with library use were associated with student learning. Using data from the pretest/posttest NSSL study, Bray et al. (2004) found that student course learning experiences, library experiences, or required writing assignments had no unique relationships with end of third-year reading comprehension. Narrowing the demographic focus of the research, Flowers (2004b) found that academic experiences connected to using the library (e.g., finding interesting material by browsing the stacks) and in their courses (e.g., doing additional readings on topics introduced and discussed in class) were positive predictors of African American students' self-reported gains in understanding arts and humanities, understanding science and technology, and thinking and writing skills. Conversely, Kuh and Gonyea (2003) found no relationship between library experiences and overall self-reported gains in education among a racially/ethnically diverse sample. The mixed evidence provides support for Matthews's recommendation (2012) that library use data need to be combined with institutional data to assess relationships with critical postsecondary outcomes like persistence and graduation, as well as direct measures of student learning.

Work-Integrated Learning. Internships, co-ops, and placements are out-of-class experiences often referred to as work-integrated learning (WIL) and aim to improve students' employment opportunities and labor market outcomes after college (Sattler & Peters, 2013). Rarely are work-integrated learning experiences connected with a single course; rather, they typically are done as part of a student's broader postsecondary experience. As such, researchers have examined their effects in terms of students' program of study outcomes, like GPA or, in the United Kingdom, students' degree mark (e.g., classification of students' performance in their program of study defined as first-class honours, second-class honours, upper division, etc.). Although distally related to the outcomes central to this chapter, the evidence on the influence of work-integrated learning on academic achievement related to students' overall program of study performance is fairly consistent, with several studies from the United Kingdom finding positive effects on degree mark (Gomez, Lush, & Clements, 2004; Green, 2011; Mandilaras, 2004; Mansfield, 2011; Rawlings, White, & Stephens, 2005; Reddy & Moores, 2006, 2012; Surridge, 2009). Similar findings were ascertained in the United States (Blair, Millea, & Hammer, 2004). Although Lucas and Tan (2007) acknowledged improved academic performance for WIL students, they suggested it was due to improved interpersonal and intrapersonal skills. Recognizing that interpersonal skills are essential to communicating effectively, the focus group findings from a U.K. university shed light on how WIL opportunities had a positive influence on students' academic performance. WIL students commented, "I learned loads of communication skills," and, "You do learn to talk to people a lot better in lots of different ways," and that the experience strengthened their "sentence construction" and "letter writing" (Reddy & Moores, 2006, p. 557). However, like many other high-impact practices, the quality in which WIL experiences are constructed and supervised is instrumental in their effectiveness (Kuh, 2008). In the case of WIL, communicating learning objectives and developing meaningful opportunities with workplace supervisors as well as ensuring close supervision and mentoring in the placement appear to be important characteristics for a quality WIL experience (Sattler & Peters, 2013).

Study Abroad. Despite the increased emphasis and encouragement for students to study abroad (for example, see the *100,000 Strong Educational Exchange Initiatives* sponsored by the U.S. Department of State, n.d.), the research community has rarely examined the effect of participating in study abroad on academic outcomes beyond foreign language acquisition (Sutton & Rubin, 2004).

In one of the largest studies to focus on more general academic outcomes, the University System of Georgia Learning Outcomes of Students Studying Abroad Research Initiative (GLOSSARI) compared a group of study-abroad students to a matched convenience sample of students who did not study abroad and found no difference in students' communication skills, controlling for self-reported GPA (Sutton & Rubin, 2004). In looking at one of the high-impact practices, Kuh (2008) found that seniors who studied abroad had greater self-reported gains in general education, taking into account student background and institutional characteristics.

Herzog (2011) found study abroad had no significant relationship with the objective GRE quantitative score or self-reported gains scores in quantitative or math. Similarly, Strauss and Terenzini (2007) found no difference between engineering students who studied abroad and those who did not in their self-reported engineering analytical skills.

Synthesizing the literature on the effects of study abroad on academic outcomes over the past two decades, Twombly, Salisbury, Tumanut, and Klute (2012) concluded that little consistent evidence exists to suggest that students who study abroad are advantaged in their verbal, quantitative, or subject matter competence. Although not germane to this chapter, it is possible that study abroad as a high-impact practice has greater contributions to developing students' attitudes and values, particularly intercultural competence and self-efficacy, as well as critical thinking, intellectual curiosity, adaptability, skills, and dispositions students need to navigate a different country and language.

Interactions and Research with Faculty. A key component of the educational experience is the interactions students have with their instructors. Interestingly, the evidence regarding interactions with faculty and student verbal, quantitative, and subject matter competence is inconclusive. Some evidence pointed to positive relationships between interactions with faculty and self-reported gains in general education (Nelson Laird & Cruce, 2009; Rocconi, 2011). Other studies focused on students' self-assessment in analytical and clear thinking skills, clear and effective writing, and ability to read and comprehend academic material (Kim & Sax, 2011), and some studies examined outcomes within the field of engineering (Lambert et al., 2007; Strauss & Terenzini, 2007). Researchers have examined student-faculty interaction within specific student subsamples as well. Flowers (2004b) found that discussing ideas for a term paper or class project, as well as career plans and ambitions, was associated positively with African American students' self-reported gains in understanding arts and humanities, understanding science and technology, and thinking and writing skills. Similarly, the student-faculty relationship composite measure was associated positively with students' intellectual ability (Kim, Chang, & Park, 2009). Among women, interactions with faculty had a positive association with analytical and problem-solving skills, controlling for other institution and individual-level factors (Kim, 2002a).

Despite these positive associations, a fair body of evidence has found that interacting with faculty has no association with student verbal, quantitative, and subject matter competence. Herzog (2011) found no relationship between student-faculty interaction and the GRE quantitative score on two measures of self-reported gains in math or quantitative skills. Mixed results surfaced in a single-institution study in an introductory sociology course in which interacting with the instructor was negatively associated with students' second exam scores but had no effect on an integrated data analysis assignment, controlling of other factors (Driscoll et al., 2012). This pattern of nonsignificant, and in some cases negative, relationships also emerged in studies addressing self-reported gains in intellectual growth (Strauss & Volkwein, 2002) and general education (Lundberg, 2012). Investigation of self-reported gains based on the Holland environments revealed nonsignificant relationships for the artistic and social outcomes and negative relationships for the investigative and enterprising outcomes (Pike et al., 2012). Although the weight of the evidence fails to find positive relationships between interactions with faculty and verbal, quantitative, and subject matter competence, such interaction may be educationally relevant for outcomes reviewed in subsequent chapters.

The research has varied considerably in how interactions with faculty have been operationalized, from composite measures that largely capture the frequency with which students interact with faculty (see Carini, Kuh, & Klein, 2006) to student perceptions of the quality of the student-faculty relationship (see Kim et al., 2009). This could contribute to the inconsistent findings, but it is likely that the approach of including multiple measures of good practices in undergraduate education as defined by Chickering and Gamson (1987, 1991)—academic challenge, active and collaborative learning, student-faculty interactions—significantly reduces the possibility of finding a unique relationship between student-faculty interaction and student learning if measures of good practices are substantially correlated. Seifert and colleagues (2008) aimed to address this limitation in modeling the systemic nature of liberal arts experiences, although this approach has the counterchallenge for practitioners and policymakers in knowing where to focus institutional effort and energy.

Engaging with faculty members in their research is one type of interaction that has received a great deal of attention in the research community and associated consistently with enhanced student learning. This is one of the high-impact practices identified by Kuh (2008), as it was associated positively with self-reported gains in general education among senior students who completed the NSSE, accounting for student and institutional characteristics. Flowers (2004b) also found that working with a faculty member on a research project had a strong positive relationship with African American students' self-reported gains in understanding science and technology. Lopatto (2004) examined evaluations from students who engaged in faculty research at 41 institutions in the United States. Students reported, as a result of their research experience with faculty, that they better understood the research process and how scientists work on real problems and learned lab techniques, but they reported fewer gains in oral presentation and science writing (Lopatto, 2004).

Similar results differentiating among personal/professional gains, thinking and working like a scientist, and improved communication were found in a qualitative analysis of students who participated in faculty research at three U.S. liberal arts colleges (Seymour, Hunter, Laursen, & DeAntoni, 2004). Other studies examined the effect of conducting research as a part of a single institution's nursing course in New Zealand and found that the experience resulted in higher overall course grades (Niven, Roy, Schaefer, Gasquoine, & Ward, 2013) and students feeling more comfortable in searching and reviewing literature in biology, scientific writing, proposing research questions, and designing and developing and experimental research plan (Stanford & Duwel, 2013).

Academic Skills Courses. From institution to institution, academic skills courses are referred to by different names but are geared toward improving students' skills and knowledge toward success in their academic pursuits through study skills workshops, learning strategies, use of mnemonic devices, note-taking training, and time management.

In a meta-analysis, Robbins, Oh, Le, and Button (2009) found that academic skills courses had a moderate effect on course grades (effect size = .32). The direct effect of academic skills interventions on course grades was 30% larger than its indirect effects mediated by motivational control (effect size = .13) and emotional control (effect size = .10). In a meta-analysis examining the construct validity of student reports on study habits, skills, and attitude inventories, Credé and Kuncel (2008) found work methods, study habits, and study orientation to have the strongest effects on students' performance in individual classes, and these constructs were weakly correlated with general cognitive ability and academic achievement in high school. Together, the findings from these meta-analytical studies suggest that study habits, skills, and attitudes can be taught so as to have a positive impact on student verbal, quantitative, and subject matter competence.

Social and Extracurricular Engagement. Student engagement outside the classroom often complements their engagement in course-based pursuits. We review the breadth of the research that has examined how social and extracurricular engagement, as diverse as affiliating with a fraternity or sorority to working during college, relates to students' verbal, quantitative, and subject matter competence.

Interactions with and Support from Peers. A great deal of college impact research has examined the effects of peer support and peer interactions in college on student learning, and includes evidence from a large meta-analysis (Robbins et al., 2009), data from the National Study of Student Engagement (Cruce et al., 2006; Pike et al., 2003; Pike & Kuh, 2005; Roconni, 2011), and many other data sources (Carini et al.; Flowers, 2004b; Lundberg, 2003; Smith & Bath, 2006; Strauss & Volkwein, 2002).

Robbins and colleagues (2009) conducted a meta-analysis with 107 studies, in which they examined the effects of first-year experience interventions—quintessential initiatives designed largely to introduce students to their peers, foster interaction, and develop a supportive network—on course grades, GPA, and retention. The effect of first-year-experience interventions on course grades was small (effect size = .03) and mediated mostly by the extent to which these programs help students develop motivational control. A small correlation is to be expected given that these interventions are largely intended to facilitate socioacademic adjustment as opposed to directly influencing course performance. The mediating factor of motivation control suggests the efficacy of first-year-experience programs in developing students' "on-task attention during skill maintenance and transfer" (Kanfer et al., 1996 cited in Robbins et al., p. 1167), critical for subject matter competence development.

Beyond the structured peer interaction of many first-year-experience initiatives, multiple studies have examined the effects of informal peer interactions on learning gains, nearly all with positive results (see Berger, 2002, for a divergent example). In one of the few multi-institutional pretest/posttest studies examining verbal and quantitative competence using objective measures, Cruce et al. (2006) found interactions with peers had a small positive effect on mathematics knowledge in first-year students, controlling for a number of student characteristics and a pretest mathematics score; however, there was no effect on reading comprehension.

Other research has largely relied on cross-sectional research designs using self-reported gains measures often from the NSSE or CSEQ. Rocconi (2011) found self-reported interactions with peers had a positive association with self-reported gains in general education. In two studies, involvement and engagement, as measured by the NSSE, were found to have an impact on learning in a positive manner (Pike & Kuh, 2003; Pike et al., 2003). In another study, using data from the CSEQ, Lundberg (2003) found that peer discussion had a positive effect on self-reported gains on a broad-based learning measure. In addition, Flowers (2004b) found that African American students' personal experiences were associated positively with self-reported gains in understanding arts and humanities, understanding science and technology, and thinking and writing skills, although discussing why some groups get along and others do not was not particularly influential. Strauss and Volkwein (2002) used data from a survey from 51 participating SUNY institutions and found that peer interaction had a positive prediction of self-reported intellectual growth in the presence of extensive controls. Finally, a single-institution study in Australia found a learning community (defined as student perceptions of the extent to which they felt part of a group committed to learning, were able to explore academic interests with staff and students, explored ideas confidently with other people, and felt they belonged to the university community) had moderate positive effects (effect size = .39) on students' communication and problem-solving abilities and their disciplinary knowledge and skills (Smith & Bath, 2006).

Residence. We found few studies that expressly examined verbal, quantitative, or subject matter competence with respect to campus residence. More commonly, cross-sectional studies using data from students who at different times completed one of the major college impact surveys (NSSE, CSEQ, or HERI surveys) examined the extent to which living on campus (compared to commuting) was associated with self-reported gains in general education. Within this body of research, the findings from the 2000s were largely inconsistent. Pike and Kuh (2005) found that living on campus had a positive direct and indirect (through integrative experiences) effect on students' self-reported gains in learning and intellectual development. This was further supported by Lundberg's (2003) analysis in which commuting (not living on campus) had a negative indirect effect on gains in a broad-based learning measure. This contrasts with Flowers (2004a) and Lundberg (2007), who found no difference in self-reported learning gains between resident students and commuters among African

American and Native American students, respectively. Finally, Nelson Laird and Cruce (2009) found that students who commuted to campus reported greater gains in general education than those who lived in residence, controlling for student and institutional characteristics.

The discrepancy between these findings may be a result of the examination of indirect effects. Students who live on campus tended to report greater integrative experiences that are associated with gains in general education (Pike & Kuh, 2005). The data suggest that students who live on campus are in a position, largely due to proximity, to engage academically and socially with faculty, staff, and peers and thus perceive greater gains in learning and intellectual development.

Fraternity and Sorority Participation. The evidence with respect to the relationship between fraternity/sorority membership (affiliation) and students' verbal, quantitative, and subject matter competence and general education is inconsistent, in part due to the differences between studies using self-reported gains and more objective measures of student learning.

Pike (2003) found no difference between affiliated and unaffiliated first-year students in terms of self-reported gains in academic development but greater self-reported gains among senior fraternity/sorority affiliated students. A similar pattern was found by Kinzie and colleagues (2007) and in the presence of more stringent statistical controls; senior affiliated women attending women's colleges reported greater gains in quantitative skills although no difference in general education. Asel, Seifert, and Pascarella (2009) in a single-institution study found no differences in perceptions of the contributions of the undergraduate experience to growth in general/liberal arts competencies between affiliated and unaffiliated first- and senior-year students. Although Thompson, Oberle, and Lilley (2011) found no difference among affiliated and unaffiliated students' reading comprehension test scores, another study examining end-of-course grades across 20 courses at a single institution found that affiliated students had lower course grades, controlling for many precollege characteristics and students' participation in peer tutoring (Munley, Garvey, & McConnell, 2010).

In what has been the most rigorous examination to date, Routon and Walker (2014) used propensity score matching with first-year and senior data collected by the Higher Education Research Institution and found no difference between affiliated and unaffiliated men and women on the GRE, LSAT, GMAT, and MCAT. Given the media profile that fraternity and sorority members' actions have consistently attracted, the debate on the benefit and detriment that fraternities and sororities have with respect to student learning and development will likely continue. However, with respect to students' verbal, quantitative, and subject matter competence, the evidence suggests minimally that student involvement in fraternities/sororities does not hinder student learning.

Intercollegiate Athletics and Recreation. Since publication of the previous volume (Pascarella & Terenzini, 2005), several national scandals involving intercollegiate athletics programs have focused the U.S. media and the public's attention, making Pascarella and Terenzini's (2005) statement identifying intercollegiate athletics as "one of the salient filters through which the public view American postsecondary education" (p. 126) as prescient today as a decade ago. In light of the scandals, several of which dealt specifically with issues of academic integrity, the National Collegiate Athletic Association's (NCAA) clear expectations for student athletes' enrollment, cumulative grade point averages, and progress toward degree are particularly noteworthy (see NCAA, n.d.). Several studies have examined male and female athletes' academic ethic, motivation, and overall achievement (Gaston-Gayles, 2004; Gottschalk & Milton, 2010). Fewer studies, however, have examined the verbal, quantitative, and subject matter competence of student athletes.

Student athletes may be discussed as a single entity; however, the research in this area frequently delineated between male and female intercollegiate athletes, those in higher profile (typically revenue-generating) compared to lower profile (typically non-revenue-generating) sports, and the national division in the United States in which the student athlete competes (recognizing the experiences of students in Division I athletics may differ in systematic ways from students competing in Division III).

Using the NSSE and accounting for student background characteristics, Umbach and colleagues (2006) found that being an athlete had a positive relationship with self-reported gains in general education for men, although no significant difference was evident between female athletes and nonathletes. The significant difference for men, however, was reduced to nonsignificance once controls for athletic division were added to the regression model. Compared to their peers attending Division 3 institutions (the only NCAA division in which institutions are not able to give athletic scholarships), male and female students at institutions where athletic scholarships are available reported lower gains in general education (Umbach et al., 2006). Gayles and Hu (2009) used data from the Basic Academic Skills Study administered by the NCAA and found that although student athletes in higher-profile sports did not differ from their peers in lower-profile sports in terms of self-reported gains in communication and learning skills, the relationship between writing papers and completing reading assignments and gains in communication and learning skills was smaller in magnitude for athletes in higher-profile sports. Gayles and Hu (2009) recommended that future research examine the mechanisms for why writing and reading assignments would have a reduced positive influence on student learning for student athletes in higher-profile sports.

In an experimental study conducted at a Division III selective liberal arts college, Moore (2011) found no difference between athletes and nonathletes in course grade in economics. This study also examined the effects of different group composition characteristics on individual student grades and found that having an athlete in one's group also had no effect on student course grade.

Given the number of major building and renovation projects that have occurred to student recreational facilities, particularly in the United States in the past decade (see the *Chronicle of Higher Education's* Campus Architecture Database for listing of projects), we expected a greater volume of research examining the extent to which these investments are associated with student learning.

Herzog (2011) found a positive association between fitness center use and GRE longitudinal quantitative gains. In a more nuanced correlational study using data from African American students who completed the CSEQ between 1990 and 2000, Flowers (2004b) found that using gym facilities for individual activities, as well as being a spectator at a college athletic event, was associated positively with self-reported gains in understanding arts and humanities and gains in thinking and writing skills. The study found no association between using the facilities for sports that require more than one person or playing on an intramural team and these outcomes, taking into account student and institutional characteristics. Flowers also found that setting goals for athletic performance in some skill was related positively to self-reported gains in understanding arts and humanities, science and technology, and thinking and writing skills.

Employment during College. Researchers have often used work during college as a control variable because, by its nature, time spent working is time not spent studying, and thus may confound the relationship under examination. This was the case with the research reviewed for this volume; work during college was used as a control variable in all studies examining the relationship between postsecondary experiences and students' verbal, quantitative, and subject matter competence. However, given the number of students who work during college, we found it important to review this research. It is also worthy of note that work during college can take different forms, from federally funded work-study to working off campus part time or full time.

Given such wide variation in the operationalization of work during college, the mixed evidence concerning the relationship between work during college and student learning may be expected. In several cross-sectional multi-institutional studies, working during college was associated positively with self-reported gains on measures of general education and quantitative and subject matter competence, accounting for an array of student and institutional characteristics (Herzog, 2011; Kim, 2002a; Strauss & Terenzini, 2007). However, in studies with a standardized measure of reading comprehension, economics subject knowledge (Test of Understanding in College Economics or TUCE), or course performance, the relationship between working in college and student verbal, quantitative, and subject matter competence was non-significant (Bray et al., 2004; Carter & Emerson, 2012; Driscoll et al., 2012; Emerson & Mencken, 2011). Interestingly, in a series of single-institution studies within economics courses, hours worked had both a positive association with final exam score (Gratton-Lavoie & Stanley, 2009) as well as a negative association with course performance in microeconomics (Johnson & Kuennen, 2004) and a standardized measure of economic subject knowledge (TUCE) (Emerson & Taylor, 2004). In a more nuanced approach to examining student work, Lundberg (2004) examined whether amounts of off-campus employment differed in their relationship to students' self-reported gains in a broad-based measure of learning. Despite being less involved with faculty and peers, there were no differences in self-reported learning gains between those who did not work, those who worked 20 hours or fewer, and those who worked more than 20 hours. Given the increasing cost of higher education, it seems that more students will need or will choose to work during college. The weight of the evidence seems to suggest that working during college does not hinder student verbal, quantitative, or subject matter competence.

Attendance at Cultural Events. A couple of studies examined the effect of attending cultural events on students' self-reported gains based on items from the CSEQ. Among students of color who took the CSEQ between 1999 and 2001, Lundberg (2010) found that attending a fine arts event had a positive association with self-reported gains in general education, but a negative association with intellectual skills and no association with gains in science and technology. However, among African American students, attending art, music, and theater events and performances had positive relationships with students' gains in understanding arts and humanities, but only attending a concert or other music event had positive associations with gains in multiple areas: arts and humanities, understanding science and technology, and thinking and writing skills (Flowers, 2004b).

Participation in Socialization and Self-Management Programs. Socialization programs, which may be named differently from institution to institution, aim to orient students to the campus and socialize students to the norms and expectations that differentiate postsecondary study from high school or other learning environments. Self-management programs often focus on improving students' abilities to manage emotions through anxiety reduction, stress management, and self-acceptance. Robbins and colleagues' (2009) meta-analysis found that self-management experiences were associated positively with course grades (effect size = .18), although Kim and Hodges (2012) found no significant difference in the success in online remedial math achievement between students who watched videos focused on emotion control, a component within a self-management initiative, and those who did not. Despite no difference in math achievement, those who watched the emotion control videos reported more positive emotions, enjoyment, pride, and motivation with respect to math. These findings support Robbins et al.'s (2009) results that some of the effect of self-management programs on course grades is mediated by motivational and emotional control factors.

Diversity Experiences. Distinct from structural diversity, diversity experiences refer to students' interactions with others who differ from themselves in terms of race, ethnicity, sexual orientation, religion, and personal beliefs, as well as their interactions with diverse perspectives inside the classroom through readings, media, and discussion with instructor and peers. In the main, interacting with people from different races and cultures was associated with greater self-reported gains in broad measures of general education, academic competence, and intellectual development and ability, accounting for a multitude of student and institutional characteristics (Hu & Kuh, 2003; Reason et al., 2006).

ɔ perspectives in discussions or writing assignments within
ciated positively with students' self-reported gains in general
ɪgh the frequency of having serious conversations with stu-
ɔnt race/ethnicity had no relationship (Lundberg, 2012).

f Supportive Campus Environment. Students' perceptions of a
ɪpus environment can take many forms. Although the specific
ɪg a supportive campus environment vary by college experience
ʃu... ɪdy of research in this area often defined it as the extent to which
students perceive their institution as providing the support needed to succeed
academically, cope with nonacademic responsibilities, and thrive socially, and in
which relationships with students, faculty, and administrative personnel were
characterized as supportive, helpful, and considerate. Students' perceptions of a
supportive campus environment associated positively with gains in academic
competence (Reason et al., 2006), general education (Pike et al., 2003), learning
and intellectual development (Pike & Kuh, 2005), broad-based learning
(Lundberg, 2003), Holland-based outcomes associated with investigative, artistic,
social and enterprising learning environments (Pike et al., 2012), as well as in
academic gains for students at both two-year and four-year institutions
(Knight, 2009).

Perceptions of a supportive campus environment can also be defined in
terms of students' perceptions of tolerance, a climate low in prejudice, in which
diversity of ideas, people, and perspectives is valued. Interestingly, Strauss and
Volkwein (2002) found a negative relationship between climate of perceived
tolerance and self-reported intellectual growth in the presence of extensive controls, and no relationship between climate for fostering diversity and climate for
perceived low prejudice and the self-reported intellectual growth measure. This
runs counter to the positive relationship found between cross-racial interaction
and students' diversity experiences and gains in general education and intellectual development (Chang et al., 2006). Moreover, it is at odds with findings
from a sample of engineering students in which perceptions of program openness to new ideas and people, as well as perceptions of the campus's diversity
climate, was associated positively with students' self-reported engineering
design and analytical skills (Lambert et al., 2007). Consistent with the arguments advanced by Gurin et al. (2002) and the amicus briefs filed in support of
the University of Michigan in the *Gratz v. Bollinger* (2003) U.S. Supreme Court
case, the weight of the evidence suggests that perceptions of a supportive campus environment, particularly one that is inclusive and values the contributions
of a diverse student body, contributes significantly to students' educational gains.

The research that examined the relationship between experiences and verbal, quantitative, and subject matter competence, in the main, found that students make the greatest gains when they are actively involved in the learning
process. Whether collaborative assignments and assessments, case studies, or
concept maps, educators can use a wide variety of in- and out-of-class
pedagogies and instructional techniques to engage students to think, question,

reason, and communicate as they develop verbal, quantitative, and subject matter competence. Yet consistent with the premise of the scholarship of teaching and learning, creating a rich learning environment and the experiences therein cannot be left to chance but must be carefully considered and thoughtfully employed—tasks, technologies, and tendencies that educators can learn.

CONDITIONAL EFFECTS OF COLLEGE

Conclusions from the 1990s

The previous volume noted the substantial growth in studies that examined conditional effects and identified these studies as tending to focus on how the net effects, between-college effects, and within-college effects differed by student characteristics. Pascarella and Terenzini (2005) also commented on the difficulty in replicating conditional effects results, given the variation in samples. To that end, they prioritized research on conditional effects that were replicated and those that had either strong theoretical foundations or implications for policy.

The majority of the conditional-effects research reviewed either examined how college varied in its effects by either student demographic characteristics (typically gender or race) or student learning styles. In studies examining net effects by gender, the weight of the evidence found that college had the largest net effects on men. Studies that evaluated race found contradicting results about net gains from freshman to senior year. The conditional effects for between-college effects examined institutional selectivity and institutional type. The influence of attending a selective institution seemed to have general rather than conditional effects because no differences between men and women or by race were found. When evaluating institution type, attending a two-year institution prior to a four-year institution had positive effects on reading comprehension and mathematics for African American students, but negative effects for white students (Pascarella, Edison, Nora, Hagedorn, and Terenzini, 1995/1996). Finally, the within-college conditional effects evaluated learning style, student characteristics, and academic and social effort and involvement. Student learning styles were examined with respect to teaching approaches, and studies found that students realized greater learning gains when exposed to instruction that matched their learning style. The previous volumes were tentative in their conclusions given that a number of the conditional effects reviewed relied heavily on single studies that had not been replicated.

Evidence from the 2000s

Similar to the within-college effects research that has grown in the past decade, so too has the research examining conditional effects of postsecondary education on students' verbal, quantitative, and subject matter competence.

We herald this as a positive development within educational research as it suggests that researchers have realized that environments and experiences may have differential benefits and drawbacks for different kinds of students. It rejects the notion of finding a silver bullet and acknowledges the uniqueness of individual learners. Yet this proliferation of conditional effects research makes a tidy synthesis more challenging. Like the previous volume, we emphasize studies that have made a concerted effort to identify the presence of a conditional effect, those that have been replicated by other research, and those with strong theoretical grounding or the potential for informing policy or both. Consistent with the previous volume, our review focuses on how the between-college effects and the within-college effects of college differ by student demographic characteristics, academic ability, and learning style.

Net Effect Differences by Student Background Characteristics. Several studies examined the extent to which exposure to postsecondary education related to differential verbal, quantitative, and subject matter competence by student demographic characteristics, specifically race and international student status. Flowers and Pascarella (2003) found that being African American had a negative effect on a standardized measure of reading comprehension in students' first year of college, taking into account student background characteristics and college experiences. This negative relationship increased in magnitude in the third year, an indication that the net effect of college attendance on reading comprehension was attenuated for African American students compared to their White peers. Holding constant a multitude of student demographic and college experience measures, the White student sample self-reported greater freshman to senior gains in science and technology and intellectual and writing skills than African American students (Flowers, 2003). In studies examining how exposure to postsecondary education differed in its effects on self-reported learning gains in samples of Native American and students of color, respectively, Lundberg (2007) found that among Native American students who took the CSEQ between 1998 and 2001, year in school was associated positively with gains in academic learning. Lundberg (2010) found no difference in self-reported gains in general education for students of color during the same approximate time frame. However, when narrowing the focus to more specific subscales within the CSEQ, year in school was associated positively with self-reported gains in science and technology and intellectual skills (defined as, for example, writing, speaking, thinking analytically, and analyzing quantitative problems) for students of color (Lundberg, 2010).

Lakin and colleagues (2012) found that credit hours completed was associated positively with student learning, but the relationship differed for students who spoke English as their first language and those who were English language learners, with the latter group showing smaller gains in test scores across credit hours completed. Reading scores over time (measured by credit hours completed) differed the most between English language learners and native speakers; there was more consistent growth in math scores between the two groups. Examining self-reported gains in general education, Zhao, Kuh, and Carini (2005) found being an international student (compared to a U.S. domestic student) had a larger positive effect for first-year students (effect size = .16) than for seniors (effect size = .11) but that this effect differed by the international students' race. Although there was no testing of the statistical difference between subsample effects, Zhao and colleagues (2005) found a negative effect (effect size = −.35) for Asian international student (compared to Black international students) in the first year but that the effect decreased slightly in magnitude by the senior year (effect size = −.29). Black international students in their first year reported greater gains in general education than their White international peers but this difference was non-significant in the senior year (Zhao, and colleagues, 2005).

With few exceptions, much of the research in this area used self-reported gains. Consistent with the previous volume, we conclude that it is difficult to distinguish how much of the net differences by student background characteristics are true differences and how much is an artifact in sample attrition and/or the reporting tendencies and dispositions for self-assessment among different racial/ethnic groups.

Between-College Effects

Student Background Characteristics by Institutional Selectivity and Type. The persistent achievement gap between students of different racial/ethnic groups has prompted a number of studies to examine the extent to which attendance at institutions of varying types has effects that differ by students' race/ethnicity. Given the interest in institutional ratings and selectivity, Lundberg (2012) directly examined whether selectivity and institutional type had differential relationships with verbal, quantitative, and subject matter competence for students of different races/ethnicities. Drawing a stratified random sample of students by race/ethnicity from the NSSE database, Lundberg (2012) found that selectivity was associated positively with self-reported gains in general education for Asian/Pacific Islanders but no relationship surfaced for African American, Native American, White, or Hispanic students. In the same study, Lundberg (2012) found that attending a master's institution (compared to a baccalaureate institution) had positive effects on self-reported gains in general education for White students only; no other differences by institutional type were found. Knight (2009) examined the two-year/four-year distinction in the United States and found that while students attending two-year colleges (compared to four-year institutions) reported lower self-reported academic gains overall, White students, continuing-generation students (compared to first-generation students), and men reported even fewer gains.

Hu and Kuh (2003b) extended this area of research by examining the extent to which differential effects of student experiences by institutional type were further complicated by students' race/ethnicity. They found that interactional diversity experiences had larger effects for White students than students of color on self-reported gains in general education among those who attended doctoral-extensive institutions and general colleges. Moreover, interactional diversity experiences had a larger effect on the self-reported gains in science and technology for White students at liberal arts colleges; yet no difference was found between interactional diversity experiences and overall self-reported gains for White students and students of color at master's universities. It is interesting that Hu and Kuh found that interactional diversity had the strongest relationship with measures of self-reported student learning for White students. This may be due to the fact that students of color, attending postsecondary institutions where they remain underrepresented, exist in a constant state of interactional diversity, whereas for many White students, these interactions may be the first time they have interacted with students of color. These findings are complicated by variation in effects by institutional type. Interactional diversity experiences may be particularly influential for White students at liberal arts colleges where the residential nature of the campus provides for more extended interaction or at larger doctoral-extensive institutions that may have greater a number of students from different races and ethnicities making interaction possibilities more numerous.

Experiences by Institutional Type. Examining experiences associated with Chickering and Gamson's (1987, 1991) good practices in undergraduate education, Pike et al. (2003) found no differences in the relationship between student experiences and self-reported gains in learning and intellectual development among students enrolled at institutions that differed by Carnegie type. With the exception of interactions with peers having a more positive effect on math knowledge for students enrolled in a community college compared to other institutional types, Cruce et al. (2006) suggested general relationships, rather than those conditioned by institutional type, between effective teaching and interaction with faculty, challenge and high faculty expectations, and a composite measure of good practice and measures of student learning.

Student Background Characteristics by Institutional Mission and Environment. Several other studies examined differential relationships between institutional mission and environment and students' verbal, quantitative, and subject matter competence by student background characteristics. In a study of three cohorts of students (1970s, 1980s, and 1990s) who attended a work college compared to a liberal arts college or a regional institution, Wolniak and Pascarella (2007) found no difference in the effect of attending a work college by student cohort or gender in students' self-reported intellectual skills and learning orientations. However, among students from lower-income families, students who attended a work college (versus a liberal arts college) reported greater gains in scientific and quantitative skills but no difference with alumni who attended a regional institution. No differential effect of attending a work college on these outcomes was found for students from higher-income families (Wolniak & Pascarella, 2007).

Lundberg (2012) found that a supportive campus environment was associated positively with self-reported gains in general education for students of all racial groups, but the effect had the greatest magnitude for Native American students. Although no tests were conducted to ascertain statistically significant difference between these effects, given the dearth of research on Native American students' experiences and outcomes in postsecondary education (see Shotton, Lowe, Waterman, & Garland, 2013), this finding suggests that a supportive campus environment is of particular importance to Native American students, a racial/ethnic group that is grossly underrepresented in U.S. postsecondary environments. Although Lundberg's findings are situated within the U.S. context, these findings may resonate in other contexts in which indigenous students have been historically underrepresented.

Institutional emphasis on interactional diversity is one manifestation of a supportive campus environment, particularly for students of different racial and ethnic identities. Yet controlling for student and institutional characteristics, Lundberg (2012) found an institutional emphasis on interactional diversity was positively related with self-reported gains in general education for Asian/Pacific Islanders but had no statistically significant relationship for African American, Native American, White, or Hispanic students. Given the positive association between average perceptions of a supportive campus environment and self-reported gains in general education for students of color (Lundberg, 2012), it is surprising that average perceptions of institutional emphasis on interactional diversity, arguably a dimension of supportive campus environment, was associated with students' self-reported gains in general education for only a single racial/ethnic group.

Considering the notion of challenge and support, supportive campus environments and supportive relationships may be more effective for some students and less effective for others. Using data from the NSSL, Whitt and colleagues (2003) examined the relationship between a host of institutional environments and objective measures of reading, math, and science reasoning among men and women. Average supportive relationships were associated negatively with first-year mathematics and second-year science reasoning for men, but these relationships were not significant for women. Interestingly, a chilly institutional climate for women had a positive relationship with women's first-year mathematic skills yet was not associated with women's third-year reading comprehension. By contrast, a chilly institutional climate for women had no effect on men's first-year mathematics but a positive relationship with men's third-year reading comprehension. Recognizing the public and governmental focus on increasing the proportion of women in STEM fields and men's success in postsecondary education in general, it would be worthwhile to replicate these findings in samples of current students.

In summary, research examining how attendance at different types of postsecondary institutions varies in its effects on student learning for different kinds of students is in its early stages. We cannot draw firm conclusions when much of the research is yet to be replicated with different samples. Given the interest in institutional comparisons, we expect this line of inquiry will grow in the next decade. Yet we caution researchers and policymakers that students' subsequent and concurrent attendance at multiple institutions makes discerning institutional effects extremely challenging.

Within-College Effects

Student Demographic Characteristics. Altering institutional type is rare; even changing institutional culture and emphasis is a time-consuming process. For the average educator committed to enhancing learning environments and experiences, examining the effectiveness of one's pedagogical approach and practice on the verbal, quantitative, and subject matter competence for all students is a logical starting place. A tremendous number of studies have investigated different facets of an active learning pedagogy compared to the more traditional didactic lecture style of teaching and the extent to which effects on student learning varied by student demographic characteristics.

Dochy and colleagues (2003) conducted a meta-analysis assessing the effect of problem-based learning (one form of active learning) on students' knowledge and skills by year in postsecondary. They found that the benefit of problem-based learning courses versus a traditional lecture course on student knowledge (defined as an assessment that measures knowledge of disciplinary facts, concepts, and principles) did not manifest positively until the third year, when all students are more likely to be asked to apply their knowledge. Those who had practice doing so through PBL were thus advantaged. Dochy et al. (2003) found consistently positive effects of PBL on student skills (defined as knowledge application), albeit of different magnitude, for all years.

Although not detrimental to any student demographic group, the differential positive benefits of active learning on student learning outcomes by student demographic characteristics are inconclusive. Two quasi-experimental subject matter–focused studies (Haak et al., 2011; Preszler, 2009) found that women and underrepresented minority students realized greater course outcomes and retention as a result of engaging in active learning environments than their peers. Malone and Speith's (2012) findings lend support to this notion; they found that women in the team-based learning (TBL) group scored significantly higher than men in the TBL condition and higher than those in the traditional lecture class. Yet Stump and colleagues (2011) found in a study of mechanical and aerospace engineering students that while women engaged in significantly more informal collaboration than males, there was no difference in course grade by gender. Similarly, Cabrera and colleagues (2002) found that cooperative learning had less of an impact on White women and minority students' self-reported gains in appreciation of science and technology than it did on White men's self-reported gains.

Moving beyond the defined context of peer interactions within a collaborative learning setting, these findings have been replicated by research that has found a more global measure of interacting with peers associated positively with math knowledge and reading comprehension for men but no effect for women (Cruce et al., 2006; Whitt et al., 2003). Lundberg (2003) found the positive relationship between peer discussion and self-reported gains on a broad-based measure of student learning to be the weakest among students 30 years old or older.

Earlier in this chapter, we discussed institutional emphasis of interactional diversity; here we highlight studies that have examined individual students' interactions with diverse peers. Gurin and colleagues (2002) examined the differential unique effects of classroom diversity, as well as informal interaction by race/ethnicity, in terms of students' academic skills. Classroom diversity, controlling for informal interaction, had the strongest positive effect on self-reported change in academic skills for Latino students, a positive effect for White students, no effect for Asian American students, and a negative effect for African American students. In contrast, informal interaction was associated positively with academic skills for all racial ethnic groups, but the effect was strongest for Latino and African American students (Gurin et al., 2002). Using a different subsample from the CIRP and different operationalization of the outcome measure, Lundberg (2012) found that classroom diversity was associated positively with Asian/Pacific Islanders, White, and African American students' self-reported general education gain, but had no effect on Hispanic and Native American students. The varied results by racial/ethnic group may be related to the extent to which students' interactions with peers who differ from them are perceived positively and take place within an institutional environment that is welcoming, inclusive, and low in prejudice.

Research has also focused on the differential influence student-faculty interaction may have on student learning by student demographic characteristics. Effective teaching and interactions with faculty had a positive effect on math knowledge for women but a negative effect for men (Cruce et al., 2006). These findings lend support to other research that found relationships with faculty and administration had the strongest association with self-reported gains for students who were 30 or older (Lundberg, 2003). Student-faculty interaction also had a positive effect for part-time students in another study, mitigating some of the direct negative effect that part-time enrollment has on self-reported gains in general education (Nelson Laird & Cruce, 2009). The confluence of these findings may be due to the fact that women are more likely to be enrolled part time and older than average (U.S. Department of Education, 2013b, 2014a)

Several studies have examined whether forms of online instruction have differential effects on course learning for men and women (Gratton-Lavoie & Stanley, 2009; Rodgers, 2008; Spradlin & Ackerman, 2010). The weight of the evidence is inconclusive with research studies challenged by the difficulty in developing equivalent groups for rigorous analysis (Gratton-Lavoie & Stanley, 2009). Although Spradlin and Ackerman (2010) found no gendered conditional effects of computer-assisted instruction in their quasi-experimental study in a developmental math course, Rodgers (2008) found a slight negative conditional effect for engaging with the e-learning modules for women and international students on their final grade in data analysis skills and statistics. In a study examining the effectiveness of an online mastery learning system (Assessment and LEarning in Knowledge Spaces or ALEKS), there was no difference, however, between traditional-age and nontraditional-aged students on the pre/post gains in college algebra between those who used ALEKS compared to traditional texts (Hagerty & Smith, 2005). The inconsistent findings suggest that more research is needed to understand how students from different demographic groups engage the e-learning context.

Inconclusive conditional effects by race and gender were also found for the influence of research-related faculty interaction, participation in faculty research, and conducting experiments in the classroom on subject matter competence. Although engaging in research with a faculty member had overwhelming benefits for all students irrespective of gender or race/ethnicity (Lopatto, 2004), research-related interactions with faculty did not enhance students' perceptions of communication skills among African American students, but this relationship was positive for other racial/ethnic groups (Kim & Sax, 2009). From a different inquiry perspective, Emerson and Taylor (2004) found the use of experiments in an economics course mitigated the male advantage on a standardized measure of economics knowledge but had detrimental effects for students of color.

Student Ability and Learning Style. Much of the research that has examined conditional effects has looked at how experiences differ in magnitude by different demographic characteristics. The inconclusive findings from much of the previous section may be due to the fact that the emphasis on demographic characteristics may be misplaced. Focusing on these differences may obscure other factors more salient to the way students experience and engage with the postsecondary environment. This section reviews research that has examined differential effects of student experiences on verbal, quantitative, and subject matter competence by student academic and intellectual ability and learning styles.

Researchers have examined the extent to which active learning approaches are differentially beneficial to students of varying ability levels. Studies have investigated a range of techniques used within the active learning paradigm from generating questions (Berry & Chew, 2008), to small group instruction and assignments (Gaudet et al., 2010; Srougi, Miller, Witherow, & Carson, 2013), to engaging in inquiry-related activities (Hu, Kuh, & Li, 2008). In the main, the evidence suggests that students of all ability levels benefit from the active learning approach, but it has compensatory effects in that students with lower initial ability and more limited backgrounds benefit more (Berry & Chew, 2008; Ernst & Colthorpe, 2006; Gaudet et al., 2010). Moreover, research has begun to examine the contexts by which active learning is most effective for different groups of students. In a quasi-experimental investigation of inquiry instruction and group composition, Jensen and Lawson (2011) found that lower-reasoning students had higher achievement when placed within heterogeneous groups in the didactic condition but did even better in homogeneous groups within the inquiry-based condition. Contrary to Vygotsky's propositions for a more advanced peer to assist students in their zone of proximal development, these results found that students in the active learning environment benefited more from active exploration with similar-ability peers.

Self-regulated learning may contribute to the benefits realized in other active learning techniques, like concept mapping. In a quasi-experimental study involving 269 students in a semester-long introductory philosophy course, Harrell (2011) investigated the effect of teaching argument diagramming (AD), defined as a visual representation of the content and structure of an argument, on students' scores on argument analysis tasks. Scores of the lower-achieving students who were taught AD increased significantly more than the scores of lower-achieving students who were not taught AD, although scores between the treatment and control groups did not differ for the higher-achieving students. Another study examining reading comprehension and recall found that students with lower verbal ability who developed concept maps performed better than lower-ability peers who used a summarization technique, whereas higher-verbal-ability students performed better using summarization than concept mapping (Roberts & Dansereau, 2008).

Other research has examined student engagement with experiments as another form of active learning and its differential effects by student learning style. In a quasi-experimental study comparing the effectiveness of experiments in micro- and macroeconomics courses for students with different learning styles, Durham et al. (2007) found that performance on all microeconomic concepts was significantly higher for multimodal and kinesthetic learners (who were 87% of the sample) in the course using experiments than for visual, aural, and read-write learners who did as well in the traditional lecture/discussion method. In terms of macroeconomic concepts, with the exception of those who preferred a read-write learning style, all learners in the course using experiments showed significant gains in content knowledge, ranging from 7 to 16 percentile points. Emerson and Taylor's (2007) results lend further support. Although all students in the course that employed experiments scored higher on a standardized measure of economics subject knowledge (TUCE) than their peers in the traditional section, students in the experiments course who were more concrete and factual in their learning tended to have lower achievement on the TUCE than their peers who were more abstract thinkers.

Active learning is one of a constellation of good practices in undergraduate education identified by Chickering and Gamson (1987, 1991). Studies have also examined the conditional effects of a broader base of good practices on verbal, quantitative, and subject matter competence and how these effects may differ for students of varying precollege academic ability. A composite measure of good practice (including effective teaching and interaction with faculty, interaction with peers, and academic challenge and high expectations of faculty) was associated with gains in math knowledge for students who scored below the mean on a precollege measure of math knowledge (Cruce et al., 2006).

The vast majority of conditional effects research examined the extent to which college experiences differ in their effects by student background characteristics. The evidence from studies that looked at the differential effects of college experiences on verbal, quantitative, and subject matter competence by gender or race was largely inconclusive. More consistent were the findings that examined how college experiences differ in their effects for students with varying precollege academic ability and learning styles. In general, active learning pedagogy and instructional techniques benefit not only all students but particularly those who begin college the least academically prepared and those who are multimodal or kinesthetic learners (the majority of students). We expect the focus on conditional effects to continue in future research. Based on these findings, it seems more productive to examine the differential relationships of pedagogy and instructional techniques to student characteristics most germane to students' learning capacity, precollege academic ability, and learning style.

LONG-TERM EFFECTS OF COLLEGE

Conclusions from the 1990s

Volume 2 of *How College Affects Students* found that college graduates were more likely to participate in activities that assisted in the further acquisition of knowledge. Studies evaluated such factors as using the Internet, continuing education, leisure reading, creative writing, reading books, and reading newspapers. Not only did college graduates engage in these activities at a higher rate, they were more efficient at acquiring knowledge from these tasks. In addition to efficiency, Pascarella and Terenzini (2005) acknowledge that greater access to these sources of information may have played a role in these findings.

Evidence from the 2000s

Consistent with findings from previous volumes (Pascarella & Terenzini, 1991, 2005) and discussed earlier in this chapter, higher levels of educational attainment are associated with greater prose, document, and quantitative literacy (Kutner et al., 2007). Verbal and quantitative competence in this respect has implications for how graduates acquire knowledge later in life—hence education's long-term effects. Using data from the nationally representative National Assessment of Adult Literacy, Kutner et al. (2007) found that adults with higher levels of prose and document literacy were more likely to obtain information about current events, public affairs, and government matters from a variety of print and nonprint sources. Kingston, Hubbard, Lapp, Schroeder, and Wilson (2003) also discerned that years of education were associated positively with newspaper reading.

    The means by which college graduates obtain information is critical in terms of their ability to acquire accurate information. Consistent with an earlier study by the same authors cited in the previous volume (Pascarella & Terenzini, 2005), Drew and Weaver (2006) examined campaign issue knowledge leading up to the 2004 presidential campaign in the United States. Controlling for political party, age, gender, income, employment, campaign interest, and exposure and attention to a variety of media, years of formal education was second only to Internet exposure in its positive association with campaign issue knowledge. Building on this finding, Wei and Hindman (2011) examined the 2008–2009 American National Election Studies Panel Study data to examine if years of education and use of new media (the Internet) versus old media (TV, radio, and newspapers) was associated with greater knowledge of the U.S. political system. Accounting for gender, age, race/ethnicity (White versus person of color), income, and party affiliation, higher degrees of educational attainment were associated positively with political knowledge, but only as it pertained to differential Internet use. Those with higher levels of education, who also had a higher rate of Internet use, had greater political knowledge than those with lower levels of education who used the Internet an equal amount. As more news outlets transition to having solely an online presence, and given the fact that the Internet allows for custom-tailored content acquisition, access to digital information may exacerbate rather than reduce inequalities. College graduates, who have greater verbal and quantitative competence, may simply be more adept in selecting, sifting, and effectively using information encountered on the Internet.

Consistent with Pascarella and Terenzini (2005), we found that college graduates experience the long-term effects of college through a more productive use of information sources. The advantage graduates have in using information has implications for how they engage with their family and their communities. We consider this notion of intergenerational transmission between educated parent and child, as well as how educational attainment is associated with health literacy, behavior and outcomes, as well as civic and community engagement in Chapter 9.

CHAPTER SUMMARY

Change during College

Although the previous volume noted the dearth of research that has examined change during college with regard to verbal, quantitative, and subject matter competence, we found perhaps even fewer studies with this aim published since then. Those reviewed were international in scope and assessed the difference in proficiency levels for prose, document, quantitative literacy and numeracy, as well as problem solving in technology-rich environments, between those who pursued postsecondary education and those who did not. This unconditioned examination of educational attainment and measures of verbal and quantitative competence is less than ideal but permits tentative conclusions with respect to postsecondary exposure and these outcomes. Specifically, bachelor's degree holders had consistently higher levels of proficiency than their peers with a high school credential. Among bachelor's degree holders in the United States, 24% had the highest literacy level, 18% had the highest numeracy level, and 12% scored in the highest level for problem solving in technology-rich environments. Although educational attainment was associated positively with greater proficiency in these areas in the United States, Australia and New Zealand, Canada, and the United Kingdom, with less than one-third of U.S. bachelor's degree holders scoring in the highest proficiency level, the absolute standard of knowledge may not be sufficient for success today or in the future. Given the increasing cost of postsecondary education across the countries reviewed in this volume, these findings may fuel the fire of those who question the value of higher education.

Net Effects of College

The weight of the evidence demonstrates that greater exposure to postsecondary education is associated with students' gains in verbal, quantitative, and subject matter competence, although much of this research is limited by cross-sectional designs. Despite the positive net effect of attending college on student learning gains, the direct effect is small, with the association between completed credit hours ranging from an effect size of .05 for third-year reading comprehension (Bray et al., 2004) to .03 standardized regression coefficients for writing and math (Liu & Roohr, 2013). Much of the effect of exposure to postsecondary education on student learning appears to be mediated by students' integration and engagement. As students gain postsecondary exposure, they become more integrated and engaged with the environment, which is associated positively with a number of academic skills and self-reported gains in general education (Lundberg, 2003; Pike et al., 2003).

Between-College Effects

As noted in the previous volume, between-college-effects research has become increasingly complicated due to the prevalence of students attending multiple institutions during their postsecondary study. Although policymakers' and the public's appetite for institutional comparison seems fairly insatiable, we found few, if any, studies that accounted for the confounding factor that multiple attendance may have on estimations of between-college effects. Recognizing the methodological limitation inherent in this research, a number of studies examined a host of institutional characteristics, including selectivity, size and control, and institutional type (defined by two-year/four-year, Carnegie classification, and mission), as well as institutional environment.

With the ubiquity of institutional ranking schemes by *U.S. News & World Report*, Shanghai Jiao Tong University Academic Ranking of World Universities, and the *Times* Higher Education Supplement Rankings of Universities, to name a few, the desire for institutional comparison has perhaps never been greater. In the United States, institutional selectivity has been a key feature on which to compare institutional performance. Given the inconsistent associations, our review supports the conclusion from the 2005 volume: little evidence suggests that selectivity is related to measures of students' self-reported gains in learning, let alone verbal, quantitative, or subject matter competence measured by standardized tests. This finding, which has been consistent over the past 40 to 50 years, has implications for college choice, family finances, and public policy, particularly as students, their families, and policymakers deal with the differential allocation of resources to publicly supported institutions. Accounting for student background characteristics, the weight of the evidence simply does not support students' or policymakers' beliefs that a selective admissions process enhances student learning.

Institutional type is another common feature by which to compare and distinguish institutions. The evidence from the 2000s is mixed with respect to two-year/four-year differences. In studies using self-reported gains measures, students at four-year institutions appeared to be at an advantage in general education gains. However, findings from a ten-year multi-institutional review using objective measures of students' verbal and quantitative competence suggested the type of four-year institution plays an important role (Liu & Roohr, 2013), with research universities performing considerably better than community colleges in reading and math, and the advantage held by comprehensive colleges and liberal arts colleges narrowing considerably from 2000 to 2010. Although four-year institutions maintained higher scores, it is difficult to assess the true difference between two-year and four-year institutions without taking into account students' ability.

The body of research that examined distinctions by Carnegie classification was largely inconclusive. Much of the research investigated students' self-reported gains in general education, and the findings varied depending on whether liberal arts colleges were grouped as baccalaureate liberal arts colleges or separated into those that are selective. In the couple of studies that used objective measures of students' verbal and quantitative competence, research universities appeared to have higher outcome scores (Liu & Roohr, 2013; Yetter et al., 2006). But without accounting for students' educational ability, it is difficult not to attribute these differences to selection effects. Lundberg (2003) accounted for student precollege ability and college engagement and found much of the institutional difference mediated by the latter factor. The two studies that examined control and size found no evidence to support associations between these measures and student learning.

As noted earlier in the chapter, these measures of institutional type (two-year/four-year; Carnegie classification; public/private; large/small) may be too distal to accurately characterize institutional learning environments. A body of research also examined institutional mission as a conceptualization of institutional type and found modest evidence to suggest that students who enroll at institutions with specific missions (i.e., work colleges, minority-serving institutions) realize greater learning gains than their peers at institutions with more broad-based missions, yet even some of these differences are reduced to nonsignificance when institutional environments like scholarly emphasis is considered (see Kim, 2002a). Although the evidence with respect to women's colleges was less conclusive, students attending a work college (compared to a liberal arts or comprehensive regional institution) and African American and Hispanic students attending minority-serving institutions reported greater gains in academic skills and general education than their peers. These findings are largely consistent with conclusions from the previous volume.

Finally, several studies examined institutional environment as it related to institutional emphasis with respect to interactional diversity, student engagement, and personal relationships, as well as scholarship and learning. In each case, institutional emphases were associated with student gains in general education. Although a slightly different approach to conceptualizing institutional environment than in the 2005 volume, the conclusions are similar. The evidence suggests institutional environments—rather than more traditional institutional descriptors—that support students to interact meaningfully with those who differ from themselves; cultivate supportive relationships among students, staff, and faculty; and encourage students to engage in academically purposeful activities are associated with greater gains in verbal and quantitative competence, as well as general education.

Between-college-effects research examines institutional characteristics that vary considerably in the degree to which campus stakeholders have control. Selectivity, control (whether public or private), size, and institutional type (two-year/four-year, Carnegie Classification, and mission) are largely determined by those beyond the campus borders. From this perspective on examining between-college effects, findings from the 2000s are largely consistent with the research over the past four decades (Bowen, 1977; Pascarella & Terenzini, 1991, 2005), and warrants the conclusion Pascarella and Terenzini (2005) advanced in the previous volume: "Similarities in between-college effects substantially outweigh the differences" (p. 590). Yet if one considers between-college-effects research in terms of institutional environment—a matter over which students, staff, and faculty have greater control—we find where one attends college makes a considerable difference in terms of experiencing a learning environment conducive to growth in verbal and quantitative competence and broad-based measures of general education. This gives new meaning to Pascarella and Terenzini's (2005) conclusion that what you do in college matters more than where you go. Reframed, the weight of the evidence based on the institutional environment research suggests that what one does in college multiplies in its effect when everyone is also doing it.

Within-College Effects

Consistent with the previous volume (Pascarella & Terenzini, 2005), we reviewed hundreds of studies that evaluated the relationship between a host of student experiences during postsecondary education and development of verbal, quantitative, and subject matter competence. The volume of research within this question of the Pascarella and Terenzini (1991, 2005) framework has grown exponentially in the past decade, as evidenced by nearly 500 journals that focus broadly on education issues and the scholarship of teaching and learning. Within this enormous body of evidence, two key messages resonate across the research reviewed. Supportive of the family of learning theories that postulate the importance of valuing students' prior experience and engaging learners through present experience (Dewey, 1938; Kolb, 1984; Piaget, 1954; Vygotsky, 1978), our review found conclusive, nearly incontrovertible evidence that students learn the most when they are actively engaged in the learning process. Whether learning in collaborative groups or through a simulation in the classroom, students who take part as active and engaged learners gain more from the educational experience than their peers' more passive approach. Relatedly, the more time students put into the learning enterprise, the more they realize in terms of enhanced verbal, quantitative, and subject matter competence. Although few studies expressly examined the relationship between time on task and student learning, virtually all of the pedagogical approaches, instructional techniques, and forms of engagement reviewed for this chapter require that students expend time and effort. Following the outline of the chapter, the following general conclusions appear warranted:

1. Although we did not review research that examined the effects of class size on standardized measures of student learning, evidence from studies using other measures published during the 2000s supports conclusions from the previous volume that class size has a negative association with student course achievement. Current research suggests these effects are particularly negative for courses in the science disciplines and when classes rise to more than 100 students.

2. We have entered a digital era of postsecondary education, and there is no turning back. The weight of the evidence suggests that technology-assisted instruction and assessment may be a boon to student learning, with a 12 percentile point increase for student course achievement in environments where technology was used in the classroom. In order to realize superior learning outcomes, it is necessary that online learning environments emphasize students' active engagement with course content and intentionally encourage collaboration between students and instructor. Whereas the previous volume noted the inherent internal validity issues of self-selection into online learning environments, recent research has used more rigorous research designs and estimation techniques to account for this threat to internal validity, increasing our confidence in the trustworthiness of these findings.

3. As noted in the previous volume, innovative pedagogical approaches used in the classroom setting have clear and consistent relationships with student learning. We reviewed experimental and quasi-experimental research that compared active learning approaches to more traditional didactic, lecture-based teaching and found that student verbal, quantitative, and subject matter competence was enhanced with few exceptions. The gains in learning varied by approach and across discipline. Problem-based learning resulted in 5 percentile point gains overall but varied from 2 to 24 percentile points depending on the discipline. Active learning resulted in a 6% higher exam score for

students in STEM fields. Small group, cooperative, and collaborative learning produced 19 percentile point gains in psychology. On average, across disciplines, participating in service-learning resulted in a 14 percentile point advantage.

4. Students learn more from instructors who are prepared and organized, are clear and expressive, and provide timely feedback. One might consider these dimensions of holistic good teaching as part of a deliberate practice framework. In either case, students gain more in verbal, quantitative, and subject matter competence from instructors who learn these behaviors and employ them in their classrooms. Students also benefit from various instructional techniques, many of which require students to actively engage with course material. These include creating concept maps, summary writing, drawing, responding to question prompts, and completing homework and frequent short assessments.

5. Peers also play an important role as teachers and fellow learners in the postsecondary milieu. We found peer tutoring and supplemental instruction effective in fostering students' verbal, quantitative, and subject matter competence. Supplemental instruction specifically had effects that ranged from 11 percentile to 23 percentile point increases in course achievement, but the findings should be considered with caution given the selection effect that plagued many of these studies. Empowering peers to teach peers requires instructors to carefully and thoughtfully train students to take on such roles, but our review suggest students realize benefits from both teacher and learner roles.

6. Consistent with previous volumes, students realize the greatest gains in knowledge and subject matter areas aligned with their major field of study or in areas where they have substantial credit. Extending past research, we found preliminary evidence to suggest that learning-enhanced sequencing of courses, defined as identifying courses that help or hinder students in subsequent courses, may be a worthwhile pursuit at the institutional level. Although we found positive effects of honors program participation for the most academically gifted students, controlling for student background characteristics and college experiences, the research on developmental coursework for those with the greatest academic need was inconsistent. Some promising practices exist, but they are challenged by students' delay in enrolling (or even failure to enroll) in the recommended coursework and the lengthy duration of the developmental sequence. Also, the fact that few research studies have found long-term effects suggests that developmental education is challenged to realize its objectives if those are articulated solely as preparing students to complete college-level coursework.

7. The body of evidence with respect to academic effort and engagement is consistent: students benefit greatly in developing subject matter

competence when they expend effort and engage meaningfully in academically purposeful activities. Whether participating in design competitions, joining a student chapter of a professional association, or doing an internship, involvement that aligns with students' field of study is associated with positive gains in verbal, quantitative, and subject matter competence.

8. Student engagement and interactions outside the classroom in social and extracurricular pursuits also consistently contribute to student learning. Although living on campus has little direct influence on students' verbal, quantitative, and subject matter competence, it has positive indirect effects through the increased relationships that students develop with other students, staff, and faculty. These relations, whether defined as interacting with peers or students' perceptions of a supportive campus climate, have positive relationships with students' self-reported gains in general education and more objective measures of student learning. Despite the media's attention to fraternities/sororities and intercollegiate athletics, we found little research to suggest that students are penalized in terms of their self-reported gains in general education, verbal, or quantitative skills or standardized measures taken for graduate school admission as a result of these associations and involvement. Finally, given the increasing number of students who work during college, it is perhaps refreshing to find the effects largely inconclusive. This may be due to the variability in student work such that any influence is effectively eliminated. Or, as the previous volume suggested, working during college may help students organize their time such that it results in enhanced student learning.

Overall, findings from the within-college effects section epitomize the phrase, "You get out of it, what you put in," and suggest an absolute need for postsecondary educators to articulate through recruitment materials, socialize students upon matriculation, and reiterate regularly throughout students' program of study the critical role students play in their own learning. If, as Woody Allen asserts, "eighty percent of success is showing up," then the other 20% is being fully present to actively engage. However, it is not enough to show up and be ready to play the part if the stage doors are locked. The weight of the evidence demonstrates that postsecondary education as theater has many actors, and students are only part of the company. Instructors and administrators perform key roles in setting the stage and directing the play. It is incumbent on them to create conditions such that students seize the opportunity to act.

Conditional Effects

Like the previous volume, the number of studies examining conditional effects has grown substantially. This suggests a positive trajectory within educational research in understanding how environments and experiences may differ in their effects for different kinds of students. In the main, conditional effects research largely examined student by net effects of college, student by between-college effects, and student by within-college effects. Consistent with the previous volume, given the preponderance of cross-sectional research in this domain, we conclude it is difficult to distinguish the extent to which net differences by student background characteristics reflect differences that are more than systematic dispositions for self-assessment that vary by gender and race. Research that examines how attending different types of postsecondary institutions varies in effects on student learning for different kinds of students is in its early stages. We cannot draw firm conclusions when much of the research is yet to be replicated with different samples. Yet two studies found that the effects of good practices in undergraduate education (Chickering & Gamson, 1987, 1991) on student learning did not vary by institutional type; they benefit students irrespective of where students attend. Given the interest in institutional comparisons, we expect this line of inquiry will grow in the next decade.

The overwhelming majority of conditional effects research examined the extent to which college experiences, that is, within-college effects, vary in their relationships to outcomes by student background characteristics. This body of research largely examined these differences by student demographic characteristics and, to a lesser extent, learning styles and precollege academic ability. The findings with regard to how postsecondary experiences differ in their effects by student demographic characteristics were largely inconclusive. The conditional effects research with regard to learning styles and precollege ability was more consistent in its results. Several studies found that students realized the greatest learning gains when the instructional approach matched their preferred learning style. Finally, the evidence suggests that students of all ability levels benefit from the active learning approaches and general good practices in undergraduate education (see Chickering & Gamson, 1987, 1991), but these have compensatory effects in that students with lower initial ability benefit more.

Long-Term Effects

A key conclusion from the previous volume was that postsecondary exposure had long-term impacts on graduates' lives after college. With respect to the verbal, quantitative, and subject matter competence students develop in college, we conclude in similar fashion. The difference in prose, document, and quantitative literacy associated with educational attainment manifests in graduates' engaging in markedly different ways in terms of productive use of information, especially as news moves to the Internet. We discuss in subsequent chapters how the more educated have greater access to resources and information, as well as the ability to use that information more effectively, and the implications for college graduates' health, their engagement with their communities as citizens, and the intergenerational benefits they pass onto their children.

CHAPTER CONCLUSION

This chapter focused on the general educational skills associated with a postsecondary education: verbal and quantitative competence as well as specific subject area achievement. While these skills and subject matter knowledge are important, they are certainly not the only outcomes associated with a college education. Developing students' ability to think critically and gain cognitive skills are frequently cited as key college outcomes. We employ the six-question framework to examine these outcomes in Chapter 3.

CHAPTER THREE

Cognitive and Intellectual Development

Nowhere has higher education been more scrutinized than in its ability to help students make cognitive gains. As Arum and Roksa (2011) assert, "In terms of general analytic competencies assessed, large numbers of US college students can be accurately described as academically adrift. They might graduate, but they are failing to develop the higher-order cognitive skills that it is widely assumed college students should master. These findings are sobering and should be a cause for concern" (p. 121). This statement reflects a growing concern over the value and purposes of higher education, particularly as they relate to helping students develop the cognitive and intellectual skills needed to address the many complex issues facing us now and in the future.

This past decade evidenced an increase in the number of studies that examine college and its influence on intellectual and cognitive development. Several reasons may explain the noticeable surge. Perhaps the most intuitive, intellectual and cognitive growth, is conceptually facile—a broad and accessible form of learning for most people, from federal policymakers to parents considering the value of higher education. As such, more private and public resources have been committed to defining, measuring, and assessing cognitive dimensions of learning than perhaps any other form (see Council for Aid to Education, 2015; National Science Foundation, 2015; Rhodes, 2010). Accrediting bodies have more formally recognized the need for creating performance indicators related to college-going and its association with intellectual and cognitive learning dimensions. In 2005, the Council for Higher Education Accreditation (CHEA) established the CHEA Award for Outstanding Institutional

Practice in Student Learning Outcomes specifically to recognize high impact practices:

> Colleges, universities, programs, faculty, higher education associations and accrediting organizations all focus on the importance of learning outcomes, evidence of student learning and communication with students and the general public about the results of efforts to improve student performance. Student learning outcomes are an important part of the public discourse on higher education, accreditation and quality assurance (Council for Higher Education Accreditation, 2015, para. 1).

At the institution level, intellectual and cognitive growth is often situated as central to any college's mission, with many organizational units within the institution charged with leveraging resources to help students make gains along these lines. Given the host of reasons for their importance, development in these areas remains areas of consideration for many theorists, whose interests lie in describing and often differentiating many cognitive and intellectual dimensions, including postformal reasoning (i.e., epistemic beliefs, reflective judgments) and critical thinking disposition and skills. Each is described in the next section.

THEORETICAL OVERVIEW

Postformal Reasoning

Research on cognitive development has been conducted for nearly 50 years, originating with studies conducted by William Perry in the 1950s (see Perry, 1970). Perry's work laid the foundation for the empiricism of many contemporary scholars with similar interests, such as Belenky, Clinchy, Goldberger, and Tarule (1986), Baxter Magolda (1992), Kegan (1994), and King and Kitchener (1994). They used his work to reposition and refine lines of inquiry investigating students' postformal reasoning, including epistemic beliefs, the contexts in which these beliefs are nurtured, and how these beliefs inform the process of meaning making. As generally explained by these scholars, postformal reasoning is a dimension of cognition that involves the ability to competently and carefully weigh available evidence from multiple viewpoints in the process of making informed decisions and solving problems. Postformal reasoning development theories explore students' underlying assumptions about the nature and certainty of knowledge, often referred to as their personal epistemology (Hofer & Pintrich, 2002). Researchers have studied how these assumptions inform students' abilities to make decisions.

The personal epistemology of college students generally evolves from assuming that the certainty of knowledge is context independent, something to be learned through exposure to external authorities, to context related, where the self-in-situation plays a larger role in knowledge construction

(Baxter Magolda, 1999).[1] Development involves "taking responsibility to explore what one does not understand, working to see the big picture, realizing that knowledge evolves, and viewing learning as a lifelong process" (Baxter Magolda, 2004, p. 2). In positioning context as the catalyst for constructing personal opinions and belief systems, the developed student derives "judgments from personal experiences, evidence from other sources, and from the perspectives of others" (King & Baxter Magolda, 2005, p. 577). These students replace their knowledge construction systems based on biases and unchallenged paradigms with sophisticated forms of evidence, constructed by grounding judgment in the nexus of personal experiences, diversified information sources, and perspective taking. Students who adopt this new approach to evaluating what constitutes evidence use it to justify their viewpoints and take a stand on controversial issues (Guthrie, King, & Palmer, 2000). Minnich (2003) describes these students as "open-minded, reflective, challenging—. . . more likely to question than to assert, inclined to listen to many sides, [and] capable of making sensitive distinctions that hold differences in play rather than dividing in order to exclude" (p. 20).

A defining element of what constitutes personal epistemology is reflective judgment: "the ways that people understand the process of knowing and in the corresponding ways that they justify their beliefs about ill-structured problems" (King & Kitchener, 1994, p. 13). While most problems are well structured and dualistic (i.e., one solution exists for every problem), ill-structured problems are more complex in that multiple solutions may exist for any given dilemma. For example, how do we eradicate poverty in our country? How do we maintain our existing economic infrastructure in a global market with competing ideologies? The reflective judgment model developed by King and Kitchener (1994) provides a developmental framework that empowers educators with the tools needed to understand the processes students use for wrestling with questions like these.

The reflective judgment model is composed of seven stages, which are "distinct but developmentally related sets of assumptions about the process of knowing (view of knowledge) and how it is acquired (justification of beliefs)" (King & Kitchener, 2002, p. 39). The first three stages reflect *prereflective thinking*, where students experience problems as dualistic, with a clear right and wrong answer. Students demonstrating prereflective thinking rely quite heavily on authority as evidence for drawing conclusions when faced with an ill-structured problem. *Quasi-reflective thinking* consists of stages 4 and 5, where students recognize that knowledge contains elements of some uncertainty (King & Kitchener, 2002). Quasi-reflective thinkers attribute such uncertainty "to missing information or to methods of obtaining the evidence. Although they use evidence, they do not understand how evidence entails a conclusion (especially in light of the acknowledged uncertainty), and thus tend to view judgments as highly idiosyncratic" (King & Kitchener, 2002, p. 40). *Reflective thinking* (the last two stages) continues to allow for uncertainty but is not arrested by it. Such a stance "is based on criteria such as the evaluation of evidence, consideration of expert opinion, adequacy of argument, and implications of the proposed solutions" (Kitchener & King, 1990, p. 160). Using these criteria, individuals make judgments they feel are the most reasonable.

The breadth and depth of research on reflective judgment have been significant, providing greater validity to King and Kitchener's reflective judgment model. In their broad review of the literature, Pascarella and Terenzini (1991) concluded that the model was "the best known and most extensively studied" (p. 123) covering adult cognitive development, demonstrated by numerous articles and its extensive use in practice across the country.

What is perhaps most surprising is that despite these growing numbers, this volume's review of the studies of college-going on intellectual and cognitive development is only loosely based in appropriate developmental theories that, ironically, were often designed to explain college and its influence on students' learning along cognitive dimensions. It appears as though studies of cognitive growth have focused more on constituent dimensions related to critical thinking tendencies, dispositions, and skills than on postformal reasoning, epistemic reasoning, or reflective judgment. So profound is this movement toward the former that rather than adopt the previous volume's strategy of bifurcating some findings into those related to critical thinking versus postformal reasoning (see Pascarella & Terenzini, 2005), we decided to group all studies of intellectual and cognitive growth. This emerging trend also explains our approach to reviewing the cognitive theories in this chapter; we will give more consideration to theories that explain college-going and its influence on critical thinking than to those that link participation in college to postformal dimensions of cognitive growth.

Critical Thinking

No common theory or framework has been used to cast critical thinking, especially as a collegiate outcome. Common to the many scholarly approaches that attempt to define critical thinking is the ontological assumption that critical thinking is a construct that exists and therefore can be measured (see Pascarella and Terenzini, 1991). It is also assumed that the construct can develop over time, whether through maturation or exposure to a catalytic context. The assumption guiding this review is that one such context—exposure to and participation in college or its set of embedded experiences—has the potential to help students develop their critical thinking capacities.

Taking these assumptions into account, we use a guiding definition offered by Pascarella and Terenzini (1991), that educators want students to:

> process and utilize new information; communicate effectively; reason objectively and draw objective conclusions from various types of data; evaluate new idea and techniques efficiently; become more objective about beliefs, attitudes, and values; evaluate arguments and claims critically; and make reasonable decisions in the face of imperfect information. These and related general cognitive skills are a particularly important resources for the individual in a society and world where factual knowledge is becoming obsolete at an accelerated rate (pp. 114–115).

Given the variety of elements expressed in this idea and to remain consistent with how we describe cognitive effects, we have adopted many ways of communicating about college and its effects on students' cognitive and intellectual development. We use the following language to capture these ideas: "critical thinking capacities," "cognitive gains," "cognitive outcomes," "cognitive skills," "intellectual development," "cognitive development," and "develop along cognitive dimensions." Of course, the authors of the articles reviewed for this chapter may have chosen different, and often more appropriate, language to discuss development of the "cognitive kind," but in order to make this review more accessible, we consolidated the language to fit the nomenclature designed for this chapter's purposes.

CHANGE DURING COLLEGE

Conclusions from the 1990s

Evidence from the 1990s suggested that cognitive development was associated with college-going. Through a combination of a careful review of the empirical work and meta-analytic procedures, Pascarella and Terenzini (2005) were able to conclude that approximately 63% to 90% of the change in critical thinking skills and postformal reasoning skills occurred by the sophomore year. Best estimates of the typical performance of college students demonstrated that seniors had an advantage over incoming students of .50 of a standard deviation (19 percentile points) in critical thinking skills; of .90 of a standard deviation (32 percentile points) in reflective thinking and problem solving; of 2 standard deviations (48 percentile points) in epistemological sophistication; and of .50 of a standard deviation (19 percentile points) in critical thinking disposition.

Evidence from the 2000s

Change over One Year. Turning to first-year change during college, Pascarella, Blaich, Martin, and Hanson (2011) and Bowman (2010a) used the same dataset to examine critical thinking growth among first-year students. Pascarella et al. (2011) found that their sample of 923 college students made an average gain of .11 of a standard deviation in critical thinking scores during the first year in college; this marked a 4 percentile point increase in critical thinking scores. Similarly, in his investigation of postformal reasoning and critical thinking among first-year students, Bowman (2010a) reported small effect sizes (Cohen's $d = .04$) for critical thinking score gains among his sample of 3,072 first-year students; this represented a 2 percentile point increase.

Change over Two Years. Interestingly, Arum and Roksa (2011) administered the Collegiate Learning Assessment to students after two years of exposure to college; students made an average gain of .18 of a standard deviation in critical thinking scores. This marked a 7 percentile point increase in critical thinking scores for students after two years in college.

Change over Four Years. The magnitude of cognitive change during college is difficult to assess, as few studies longitudinally reported critical thinking changes over the course of the traditional four-year college experience. An exception to this trend, the longitudinal study performed by Pascarella, Blaich, Martin, and Hanson (2011) examined critical thinking growth for 923 students enrolled at 17 four-year institutions across 11 states over two points: a cohort of students was assessed when they first arrived at college (fall 2006) and at the end of their senior year (spring 2010). Students made average gains of .44 of a standard deviation in critical thinking scores from the first to the fourth year in college; this estimate represented a 17 percentile point increase in critical thinking scores since these students entered college. Arum and Roksa (2011) also used data from the Council for Aid to Education's Collegiate Learning Assessment Longitudinal Project (2005–2007). They found that among 2,322 undergraduate students enrolled in one of 24 institutions, students made average gains of .47 of a standard deviation in critical thinking scores after four years of exposure to college. This represents an 18 percentile point increase in critical thinking scores since these students entered college. Other four-year studies of change over time were performed as well, although the change occurred in cohorts of students in the 1990s (see Keen, 2001). Cross-sectional studies (see Saavedra & Saavedra, 2011; Strauss & Volkwein, 2002) support this trend, with seniors scoring higher on critical thinking measures than first-year students.

NET EFFECTS OF COLLEGE

Conclusions from the 1990s

Over the three decades of research covered in the previous volumes (see Pascarella and Terenzini, 1991, 2005), one conclusion was inescapable: cognitive gains among college students are uniquely attributable to enrollment in postsecondary education. Summarily, the first three years of college improved critical thinking skills by .55 of a standard deviation (20 percentile points) and reflective thinking skills by .90 of a standard deviation (32 percentile points).

Evidence from the 2000s

In this decade of research, no literature was uncovered that addressed the cognitive development of college students versus non–college goers. As a result, we were not able to calculate the net effects of college-going on students' cognitive or intellectual development.

Given the number of studies examining college-going and its influence on cognitive development, research in this area has become increasingly complicated, with more researchers interested in uncovering the experiences and mechanisms responsible for this change. As the emphases for most of the empirical work in this area, the research on these experiences and mechanisms is discussed at great length in the "Between-College Effects" and "Within-College Effects" sections of this chapter.

BETWEEN-COLLEGE EFFECTS

Conclusions from the 1990s

Findings from the previous volumes (Pascarella & Terenzini, 1991, 2005) indicated that very few significant or consistent differences exist between colleges in terms of students' general cognitive development. However, among noteworthy results were studies that found that single-sex institutions more positively affected women's cognitive growth than their coeducational peers, Historically Black Colleges and Universities (HBCUs) are more conducive to self-reported gains in critical thinking, and community colleges foster the same level of critical thinking growth in first-year students as their four-year peers. In addition, Pascarella and Terenzini (2005) noted that one discovery that warranted ongoing conversation was the role that institutional environment played on cognitive development. Scholars apparently embraced this charge; many studies in this volume attempted to explain environmental influence on helping students make cognitive gains.

Evidence from the 2000s

With more advanced statistical techniques used to account for students nested within educational context came a surge of studies designed to explain, at least partially, the influence of institutional conditions and aggregated environmental perceptions on cognitive development. Among the series of studies that empirically examined between-college effects, three (Carini, Kuh, & Klein, 2006; Kugelmass & Ready, 2011; Strauss & Volkwein, 2002) used hierarchical linear modeling, which adjusts parameter estimates based on the nonrandom clustering patterns of college students within a particular educational context. Using this correlation-based technique, these authors substantiated the important role context played in shaping cognitive development among students, with reported intraclass correlation coefficients ranging from 3.0% to 23.0%. (Note that when pretest cognitive controls were included at the student level, intraclass correlations reached 8%). These statistics indicate that administrators have the potential of enacting practices that will help students develop along cognitive dimensions and that not all development can be explained by individual-level differences, including race, aptitude, socioeconomic status, and the levels of cognitive development students bring to campus.

Institutional Conditions

Selectivity. Of these conditions, institutional selectivity exerted the most influence on cognitive development, although effect magnitudes were small. Pascarella, Wolniak, Seifert, Cruce, and Blake (2005) studied the link between institutional selectivity and good practices in undergraduate education. Interestingly, the authors estimated the average critical thinking scores of students as an operational proxy for institutional selectivity and used this manipulated metric as a determinant of a variety of good educational practices. They authors concluded "that institutional selectivity does indeed count in terms of fostering good practices in undergraduate education . . . [but] may not count very much" (p. 278). Selectivity was also found to share a small and positive association with the cognitive gains demonstrated or reported by students in studies by Kugelmass and Ready (2011) and Pascarella et al. (2005).

Institutional Type. Turning to institutional type, scholars continued to explore whether cognitive gains were associated with distinctive educational contexts (see Arum & Roksa, 2011; Chang, Denson, Sáenz & Misa, 2006; Inkelas, Soldner, Longerbeam, & Leonard, 2008; Keen, 2001; Kugelmass & Ready, 2011; Loes, Pascarella, & Umbach, 2012; McCormick, Pike, Kuh, & Chen, 2009; Pascarella & Blaich, 2013; Pascarella et al., 2005; Umbach, 2006), such as two-versus four-year institutions (Strauss & Volkwein, 2002), and HBCUs versus predominantly White institutions (Kugelmass & Ready, 2011). For example, Strauss and Volkwein (2002) compared student self-reported intellectual performance among 7,658 second-year students enrolled at two- or four-year institutions and found that after controlling for a host of covariates, students enrolled in four-year institutions scored significantly higher than those enrolled at the two-year institutions. Turning to HBCUs, Kugelmass and Ready (2011) found no effects of attending an HBCU on cognitive development, after controlling for relevant covariates.

In addition, McCormick et al. (2009) examined self-reported cognitive gains as a function of Carnegie Classification Systems, the 2000 edition versus the 2005 edition. In the context of the 2000 edition, students enrolled at doctoral/research extensive, doctoral research intensive, or master's I and II institutions were more likely to self-report cognitive gains than students enrolled at baccalaureate colleges–general institutions. In the context of the 2005 edition, more self-reported cognitive gains were associated for students at institutions in the 25th percentile ACT score for entering undergraduates, with higher part-time enrollment as a percentage of full time equivalent, and/or where the percentage of undergraduate major fields in which graduate degrees were also awarded. Negative effects were noted for students enrolled at institutions with higher percentages of undergraduates who live in college-owned, -operated, or -controlled housing; at institutions with greater percentages of undergraduate majors in the arts and sciences; and greater percentages of entering transfer students.

In a study designed to address the extent to which liberal arts colleges enhanced intellectual and personal development, Pascarella et al. (2005) reported that "only chance" (p. 52) critical thinking score differences were found between students attending liberal arts college and students attending research universities and regional institutions. However, after accounting for selectivity, significant critical thinking differences were found for students enrolled at selective liberal arts institutions when compared to students attending research universities and regional institutions, with students at selective liberal arts colleges being advantaged by .13 of a standard deviation.

Institutional Size and Location. Similarly, two studies investigated cognitive development and its association with institutional size and location. In their multilevel examination of racial and ethnic disparities in collegiate cognitive gains, Kugelmass and Ready (2011) studied 35,323 seniors nested within 245 colleges and universities and found modest associations between senior scores on the Collegiate Learning Assessment (CLA) and institutional size, with larger sizes being related to higher CLA scores (effect size = .07), after accounting for the influence of many relevant covariates. However, this result was not found in Strauss and Volkwein's (2002) study, where institutional size failed to reach statistical significance.

Turning to location, Kugelmass and Ready (2011) reported a statistical relationship between senior scores on the CLA and institutional location, with students enrolled in a suburb or small town scoring higher on the CLA than those enrolled in an institution within an urban context. Effects of geographic location were also noted in Arum and Roksa's (2011) study: students enrolled in schools in the West made significantly more cognitive gains than those enrolled in schools in the North. The significant relationships between institutional location and CLA scores must be interpreted with caution, as institutions were not randomly considered as part of this sample; perhaps nonurban institutions and those located in the West had more resources than the other schools in this sample.

Institutional Control. Within many of these studies were institution-level variables that failed to reach statistical significance. In the study that examined institutional control and its relationship to cognitive development, Kugelmass and Ready (2011) reported no significant associations. The same pattern of nonsignificance is reported by Strauss and Volkwein (2002) who attempted to examine wealth and complexity for their potential influence on cognitive development.

Institutional Commitment to Diversity/Structural Diversity of Institution. Complicating the idea of between-college effects were studies that examined how students perceive their institution and its commitments. A couple of studies investigated an institution's structural diversity as a potential determinant of cognitive growth. Among 1,354 first-year students enrolled at one of 19 institutions, Loes et al. (2012) found that increases in the numerical proportion of students of color on campus were negatively associated with cognitive development. This effect was more pronounced among the 271 students of color in the study; first-year students of color who enrolled in colleges that were less structurally diverse made more cognitive gains than students of color enrolled in colleges that were more structurally diverse. Given the small institutional and student sample size, the authors were not able to account for subgroup (e.g., African American) differences in either the variable measuring structural diversity or the race indicator; doing so may shed light on this counterintuitive finding.

The Kugelmass and Ready (2011) study was of particular interest due to its multilevel examination of racial and ethnic disparities in collegiate cognitive gains. The battery of modeled institutional covariates included the percentage of African American enrollment, the percentages of Hispanic enrollment, HBCU classification, student-related expenditures as a percent of total expenditures per FTE, total Pell Grant award to institutions divided by the total number of enrolled students, total expenditure divided by total number of enrolled students, median SAT score, institutional size, institutional control, whether the majority of students lived on campus, and whether the institution was rural or urban. After controlling for a host of student-level covariates, results indicated modest associations between senior scores on the CLA and the racial and ethnic institutional composition, with effect sizes reaching -.068 for African American enrollments and .043 for Hispanic enrollments, respectively. This indicates that increased African American enrollments are associated with lower CLA scores, while increased Hispanic enrollments are associated with higher CLA scores.

Resource Allocation. Malleable organizational characteristics were also examined for their influence on cognitive development. For example, the amount of resources spent on students was the subject for one study that found a significant relationship between resource allocation and students' intellectual and cognitive gains. Kugelmass and Ready (2011) studied 35,323 seniors nested within 245 colleges and universities and found that both institutional-related expenditures (effect size = .13) and student-related expenditures were related to higher test scores on the CLA (effect size = .02), *ceteris paribus.*

Learning Productivity. Cognitive development was also examined as a partial function of learning productivity: "The combination of student engagement in educationally purposeful activities and the gains they make in a range of desired outcomes of college" (Kuh & Hu, 2001, p. 2). Carini et al. (2006) used this coding scheme for comparing to institutions in the low-productivity group (n = 11) to those in the high group (n = 3) and reported that institutions in the high group had significantly stronger relationships between student engagement and critical thinking. Of course, the small institutional sample sizes in each category indicate that results from this study should be interpreted cautiously.

Peer Socialization: Aggregated Perceptions. Many scholars investigated aggregated student perceptions as potential determinants of cognitive gains. After accounting for a number of relevant variables, Chang et al. (2006) reported two socialization effects: the first suggested that the more women an institution enrolled, the less each student developed along cognitive dimensions; the second suggested that campuses which enrolled more students who, on average, pursued civic goals were more likely to report cognitive gains among its student population. Also, Jessup-Anger (2012) used average peer effects to examine "how an overall ethos marked by the liberal arts experiences" (p. 453) helped explain two dimensions of cognitive development: the need for cognition and the inclination to inquire. Controlling for theoretically related variables of interest, she found that the average score for perceptions of academic challenge had a significant and positive effect on one measure of cognition (need for cognition) and the average score for out-of-the-class contact with faculty exerted a positive effect on another cognitive measure (inclination to inquire).

Across these studies and consistent with the findings from previous decades is the notion that socialization plays an important role in helping students make cognitive gains. Unlike previous reviews, we are able to make more substantive claims about the effects of socialization based on how it was studied, with more scholars examining student averages (e.g., average perception of academic challenge, students' average report of pursuing civic goals) and their role in explaining cognitive development.

Summary

Between-college effects remain important considerations for policymakers and educators interested in cognitive and intellectual development. Results from this volume suggest that results were mixed for institutional variables, such as selectivity, institutional type, size, location, and control. As the variables least susceptible to change, they often are included in statistical models as a means for controlling for their influence on other college experiences and on cognitive and intellectual development.

Among the organizational characteristics most likely to change, several were worth noting. It appears that an institution's expenditure strategy is associated with intellectual and cognitive gains among its students, with the amount of resources allocated directly to students sharing a significant and positive relationship with intellectual and cognitive growth. Of similar interest were the findings related to peer socialization factors and their role in explaining intellectual and cognitive growth: an individual student's intellectual and cognitive development was affected by participating in institutions that students perceived to be academically rigorous, embodied more of a liberal arts emphasis, had a greater proportion of students interested in pursuing civic goals, encouraged more out-of-class faculty contact, and enrolled a fewer number of women. While some findings were more controversial than others, the surge of studies of between-college effects is a welcome addition to the literature reviewed for this volume.

WITHIN-COLLEGE EFFECTS

Conclusions from the 1990s

Consistent in both prior volumes of *How College Affects Students* was the prevalence of scholarship pertaining to within-college effects on cognitive and intellectual skills. In the 2005 synthesis, Pascarella and Terenzini drew many conclusions relating cognitive development to aspects of the college experience. To summarize, cognitive and intellectual development was associated with: (1) college major, although a modicum of evidence suggested that specific reasoning skills differed by field; (2) enrollment in natural science courses; (3) participation in an interdisciplinary or integrated core curriculum that built connections across courses and disciplines; (4) the intentional use of technology to support learning activities, research, or the mastery of a computer program language itself; (5) participation in cooperative learning groups; (6) instruction in critical thinking or problem solving; (7) active learning; (8) level of individual effort (e.g., hours studied per week, number of nonassigned books read, writing experiences, library use, and course learning activities); (9) social interactions that connected or reinforced ideas from academic experiences or presented diverse interests, values, political beliefs, and cultural norms; (10) student-faculty interactions outside the classroom that connected back to the academic experience; and (11) diversity experiences and service learning experiences.

Evidence from the 2000s

Due to the explosion of questions designed to examine within-college effects and their influence on intellectual and cognitive development, we decided to organize this section into four overarching categories: campus climate, curricular experiences, faculty-and-student relationships, and cocurricular experiences. Campus climate studies examined students' perceptions and experiences of a particular institution's atmosphere (Peterson, Marx, & Clark, 1978) and how they were associated with cognitive development. The articles reviewed for the curricular experience section of this chapter included studies that examined academic major, course-related interventions, integrated academic interventions (e.g., liberal arts experiences, first-year experiences, residential colleges, learning communities, honors programs, and research mentorship programs). The faculty-and-student relationship section covered general relationships and teaching behaviors, such as scaffolding, feedback and reflection, and student behaviors, like texting in class. The section on cocurricular experiences included articles that addressed club and organizational involvement, diversity-related events and dialogues, fraternity and sorority life, residential living, working, registration and library use, general peer interactions, and diverse peer interactions.

Based on the sheer volume of studies reviewed for this section, we also wanted to provide a table of the variables authors considered important for examining any given college experience and its influence on cognitive development. Table 3.1 provides a list of these variables complete with citations.

Campus Climate. In general, climate refers to the internal environment or atmosphere of a college or university. Efforts to assess an institution's climate focus on a variety of topics (Peterson & Spencer, 1990), with the study of different kinds of climates being inherently multidimensional (Hurtado, 1992; Hurtado, Milem, & Allen, 1995). Dimensions of a campus climate were examined for their potential influence on intellectual and cognitive growth.

Campus climates that students perceived and experienced as challenging, scholarly, and intellectual were positively associated with the cognitive gains demonstrated and reported by students. Specifically, climates of academic challenge and support were positively related to gains in the cognitive and intellectual development in McCormick et al.'s (2009), Reason, Terenzini, and

Table 3.1 Covariates with Citations

Covariate	*Citations*
Race	Arum & Roksa, 2011; Boulton-Lewis, Wilss, & Lewis, 2003; Bowman, 2009; Brint, Cantwell, & Saxena, 2012; Cabrera et al., 2002; Flowers & Pascarella, 2003; Gurin, Dey, Hurtado, & Gurin, 2002; Hu & Kuh, 2003b; Inkelas et al., 2006; Jessup-Anger, 2012; Kim & Sax, 2009; Kugelmass & Ready, 2011; Loes, Pascarella, & Umbach, 2012; Mayhew, Wolniak, & Pascarella, 2008; McCormick, Pike, Kuh, & Chen, 2009; Nelson Laird, 2005; Pascarella & Blaich, 2013; Pascarella, Palmer, Moye, & Pierson, 2001; Pike & Kuh, 2005; Pike, Kuh, & McCormick, 2011; Pike, Kuh, McCormick, Ethington, & Smart, 2011; Seifert, Pascarella, Colangelo, & Assouline, 2007; Strauss & Volkwein, 2002; Umbach, 2006
Gender	Ahuna, Tinnesz, & VanZile-Tamsen, 2011; Al-Fadhli & Adbulwahed, 2009; Arum & Roksa, 2011; Bauer & Liang, 2003; Bowman, 2009; Brint, Cantwell, & Saxena, 2012; Cabrera, Crissman, Bernal, Nora, Terenzini, & Pascarella, 2002; Chan, Ho, & Ku, 2011; Chang, Denson, Sáenz, & Misa, 2006; Clifford, Magdalen, & Kurtz, 2004; Dugan, Kusel, & Simounet, 2012; Gayles & Hu, 2009; Halawah, 2006; Hayek, Carini, O'Day, & Kuh, 2002; Inkelas et al., 2006; Jessup-Anger, 2012; Kim, 2002a; McCormick, Pike, Kuh, & Chen, 2009; Pascarella & Blaich, 2013; Pascarella, Palmer, Moye, & Pierson, 2001; Pierson, Wolniak, Pascarella, & Flowers 2003; Pike, 2000, 2003; Pike & Kuh, 2005; Pike, Kuh, & McCormick, 2011; Sax, Bryant, & Harper, 2005; Seifert, Pascarella, Colangelo, & Assouline, 2007; Shibley, Milakofsky, Bender, & Patterson, 2003; Strauss & Volkwein, 2002; Tümkaya, 2012; Whitt, Pascarella, Nesheim, & Marth, 2003; Vogt, 2008
Socioeconomic status	Ahuna, Tinnesz, & VanZile-Tamsen, 2011; Arum & Roksa, 2011; Brint, Cantwell, & Saxena, 2012; Cheung, Rudowicz, Lang, Yue, & Kwan, 2001; Cheung, Rudowicz, Kwan, & Yue, 2002; Kim, 2002a, b; Pascarella, Pierson, Wolniak, & Terenzini, 2004; Pascarella, Wolniak Pierson, & Terenzini, 2003; Pierson, Wolniak, Pascarella, & Flowers 2003; Pike & Kuh, 2005; Pike, Kuh, & McCormick, 2011; Pike, Kuh, McCormick, Ethington, & Smart, 2011; Seifert, Goodman, Lindsay, Jorgensen, Wolniak, Pascarella, & Blaich, 2008; Seifert, Pascarella, Colangelo, & Assouline, 2007; Whitt, Pascarella, Nesheim, & Marth, 2003; Williams & Hellman, 2004
Nationality	Ahuna, Tinnesz, & VanZile-Tamsen, 2011; Zhang, 2004; Zhang & Lambert, 2008; Zhang & Watkins, 2001

(continued)

Table 3.1 Covariates with Citations (continued)

Covariate	Citations
Precollege cognitive ability/ academic achievement	Arum & Roksa, 2011; Brint, Cantwell, & Saxena, 2012; Cabrera, Crissman, Bernal, Nora, Terenzini, & Pascarella, 2002; Inkelas, Johnson, Lee, Daver, Longerbeam, Vogt, & Leonard, 2006; Inkelas, Soldner, Longerbeam, & Leonard, 2008; Kim, 2002; Loes, Pascarella, & Umbach, 2012; Martin, Hevel, Asel, & Pascarella, 2011; McCormick, Pike, Kuh, & Chen, 2009; Nelson Laird, 2005; Pascarella & Blaich, 2013; Pierson, Wolniak, Pascarella, & Flowers 2003; Rickles, Schneider, Slusser, Williams, & Zipp, 2013
English language proficiency	Arum & Roksa, 2011; Hayes & Devitt, 2008; Lombard & Grosser, 2008; Lun, Fischer, & Ward, 2010; Umbach, 2006
Year in school	Burbach, Matkin, & Fritz, 2004; Cheung, Rudowicz, Kwan, & Yue, 2002; Friedman, 2004; Haw, 2011; Hayek, Carini, O'Day, & Kuh, 2002; Hayes & Devitt, 2008; Inkelas, Johnson, Lee, Daver, Longerbeam, Vogt, & Leonard, 2006; Jessup-Anger, 2012; Lampert, 2007; Macpherson, 2002; Pike, Kuh, & McCormick, 2011; Wise, Lee, Litzinger, Marra, & Palmer, 2004; Zhang, 2004
Within-college academic ability or achievement	Ahuna, Tinnesz, & VanZile-Tamsen, 2011; Arum & Roksa, 2011; Borg & Stranahan, 2010; Bradley, Sankar, Clayton, Mbarika, & Raju, 2007; Coutinho, Wiemer-Hastings, Skowronski, & Britt, 2005; Downing, 2009; Harrell & Bower, 2011; Hayward, Blackmer, & Raelin, 2007; Inkelas, Soldner, Longerbeam, & Leonard, 2008; Kim & Sax, 2009; Pascarella & Blaich, 2013; Pierson, Wolniak, Pascarella, & Flowers 2003; Stupnisky, Renaud, Daniels, Haynes, & Perry, 2008; Strauss & Volkwein, 2002; West, Toplak, & Stanovich, 2008; Whitt, Pascarella, Nesheim, & Marth, 2003; Williams, Oliver, & Stockdale, 2004
Major	Ahuna, Tinnesz, & VanZile-Tamsen, 2011; Arum & Roksa, 2011; Brint, Cantwell, & Saxena, 2012; Cheung, Rudowicz, Kwan, & Yue, 2002; El Hassan & Madhum, 2007; Hayes & Devitt, 2008; Lampert, 2007; Pike, Kuh, & McCormick, 2011; Pike, Kuh, McCormick, Ethington, & Smart, 2011; Nelson Laird, Shoup, Kuh, & Schwarz, 2008; Porter, 2013; Reason, Terenzini, & Domingo, 2006; Strauss & Terenzini, 2007; Tümkaya, 2012; Wettstein, Wilkins, Gardner, & Restrepo, 2011; Zhang & Lambert, 2008

Domingo's (2006), and Carini et al.'s (2006) respective samples. Similar results were found by Arum and Roksa (2011), who reported a positive relationship between cognitive gains and student reports that faculty held them to high standards. In addition, Carini et al. (2006) found that students at campuses perceived to be scholarly and intellectual were significantly more likely to make cognitive gains.

Three studies examined students' perceptions of and experiences with the campus climate for diversity and cognitive change. Chang, Astin, and Kim (2004) and Chang et al. (2006) developed a measure that approximated "the overall campus quality for sustaining positive race relations" (p. 437) in order to examine the educational benefits of sustaining cross-racial interactions among undergraduates. In each study, sustaining positive race relations was positively related to intellectual ability (Chang et al., 2004) and cognitive development (Chang et al., 2006). Specifically, in the 2006 study, Chang et al. investigated the cognitive development of 19,667 students nested within 227 four-year institutions. Controlling for a host of institutional and student-level variables, including a pretest, the authors found that a student's individual perception of campus quality for sustaining positive race relations was positively associated with that student's cognitive development. Of particular note is that the relationship between individual perceptions of campus climate and cognitive development varied significantly by institution. Offering contradictory evidence, Strauss and Volkwein (2002) reported a negative relationship between climate of perceived tolerance and the cognitive development in their student sample.

Results were mixed with regard to student perceptions of their climate as placing a value on active and collaborative learning. Interestingly, while a climate reflecting active and collaborative learning was significantly related to cognitive outcomes for students in McCormick et al.'s (2009) study, the same dimension was not significant in Carini et al.'s (2006) study.

To summarize, controlling for the influence of a number of factors, authors who examined campus climates for their influence on cognitive development uncovered many interesting findings. In particular, two stories emerged from this collection of studies. First, the more that students experienced their college as academically challenging or rigorous, the more likely those students were to report or demonstrate intellectual and cognitive gains. The second emergent narrative involved diversity climates: students who perceived their campus as taking an active role in sustaining positive race relations were more likely to develop along intellectual and cognitive lines. Together, these findings suggest that each institution has the ability, if not responsibility, to engineer its campus climate in ways that challenge students and support positive cross-race relations in efforts to help student make intellectual and cognitive gains.

Curricular Interventions. Given the rich history of scholars tasked with understanding the curricular practices that might engender cognitive development, many experimental and quasi-experimental studies have been designed to examine the specific role that practice exerted on cognitive gains. The breadth and depth of study in the area of critical thinking practice spans many disciplines, including history (see Reed & Kromrey, 2001) and electrical engineering (see Moreno, Reisslein, & Ozogul, 2009), as well as many theoretical models (see Marra & Palmer, 2004), philosophical approaches to pedagogy (see Angeli & Valanides, 2009), and typologies (see Capt & Oliver, 2012; Hu & McCormick, 2012; Kuh & Hu, 2001)—too many to carefully describe in this volume.

Several studies have examined critical thinking course-taking experiences as they related to intellectual and cognitive development. Overall, van Gelder (2007) estimated that the average gain for students enrolled in a single-semester critical thinking course was .3 of a standard deviation based on a meta-analysis performed by Alvarez (2007). Course-taking experiences reviewed for this volume included structural features, like class size (Hayes & Devitt, 2008) and type (i.e., subject matter versus general critical thinking contexts; see Angeli & Valanides, 2009) as well as course materials specifically designed to help students develop their critical thinking skills (see Cruce, Wolniak, Seifert, & Pascarella, 2006; Renaud & Murray, 2007). Clearly these elements are challenging to study but provide insight into course-taking behaviors and their influence on helping students make cognitive and intellectual gains.

Liberal Arts Experiences.   One study examined liberal arts experiences and their potential influence on cognitive development. Seifert et al. (2008) longitudinally examined 909 first-year students in an effort to understand the effects of liberal arts experiences on liberal arts outcomes, two of which had explicitly cognitive dimensions: effective reasoning/problem solving and inclination to inquire/lifelong learning. Although the authors found no significant effects of liberal arts experiences on effective reasoning/problem solving, students' liberal arts experiences affected their inclination to inquire/lifelong learning orientations by .24 of a standard deviation after controlling for other confounding influences.

Academic Major.   As in previous volumes, many studies have examined variables, like academic major, as part of larger efforts to understand college and its effects on cognitive development. Interestingly, major was examined in two ways: through examining students within major (Kim & Sax, 2011; Kugelmass & Ready, 2011) or by including major as a model covariate (Arum & Roksa, 2011; Hayes & Devitt, 2008; Nelson Laird, Shoup, Kuh, & Schwarz, 2008; Pike & Killian, 2001; Pike, Kuh, & McCormick, 2011; Wettstein, Wilkins, Gardner, & Restrepo, 2011). Of course, some studies used samples drawn from certain majors as samples of convenience to test hypotheses unrelated to college impact (Thorpe & Loo, 2003).

Small proportions of the variance in intellectual and cognitive development could be explained by the "students-nested-within-major" (or field) term. The intraclass correlation coefficients for studies with a pretest measure or proxy ranged from 1.1% (see Kugelmass & Ready, 2011) to 6.7% (see Kim & Sax, 2011). This indicates that under 10% of the variance in cognitive development, within studies with a pretest measure or proxy, could be explained by students' academic major. Moreover, Kugelmass and Ready (2011) demonstrated that a much larger proportion of variability exists among students within fields within the same institution (at least 75%), while less than a quarter lies between institutions. Taken together, these metrics indicate that intellectual and cognitive development are likely more a function of practices within each major or field than between majors and fields.

Evidence from this review suggests that direct studies comparing one major to another have given way to more nuanced studies of disciplinary context and the roles that transparency and support within these contexts play in influencing cognitive development. For example, in their multilevel examination of the role that academic major plays in explaining the relationship between student-faculty interaction and cognitive skills, Kim and Sax (2011) studied 43,014 students from 119 academic majors across nine campuses. The results of this study suggested that the relationship between students' interactions with faculty on cognitive skills indeed varied by academic major. The relationship of general faculty contact and cognitive skills was significantly stronger in fields such as Chinese language/literature, microbiology, and nutrition sciences than in fields such as information science/studies, cell/cellular biology, and minor areas of social sciences. The relationship between student research engagement with faculty and cognitive development was stronger in the fields of Hispanic-American/Chicano studies, geography, and microbiology and least within mass communication/media studies, biotechnology, and minor areas of social sciences.

Of course, other studies informed the relationship between academic major and cognitive development. Pike et al. (2011) examined major as a predictor of high-order thinking skills among first-year students and seniors, respectively, and found that first-year students in arts and science majors were significantly more likely to report higher-order thinking skills than students not in arts and science; this result did not hold for the sample of seniors. Similar results were reported by Arum and Roksa (2011), who found that students majoring in math, science, social science, or the humanities make greater gains on the CLA than students majoring in business, and by Wettstein et al. (2011), who found that seniors with a strong science background (they had completed over 10 credits in science) had significantly higher critical thinking scores than peers with a weaker science background. Brint et al. (2012) examined the analytical and critical thinking skills of over 16,000 students in the University of California system; they found that when compared to social science majors, higher critical thinking scores were associated with physical science, life science, and engineering and lower scores were associated with the arts. When compared to students who major in sociology, those majoring in philosophy, history, biology, and chemistry had higher analytical and critical thinking scores, while those majoring in English and foreign language had significantly lower scores. Others also reported differences in intellectual and cognitive gains based on academic major (Lampert, 2007; Reason et al., 2006). Offering competing evidence, Hayes and Devitt (2008) reported no significant differences in critical thinking scores for food science majors when compared to other majors.

Perhaps more important than the observation that these notable differences exist are the reasons that these differences exist across fields. These reasons are the subject of inquiry for many field scholars, including Kim and Sax (2011); Pike and Killian (2001); Pike et al. (2011); Nelson Laird, Shoup, Kuh, and Schwarz (2007); and Brint et al. (2012). Specifically reported by Kim and Sax (2011) and supported by the Pike and Killian (2001), the amount of support an academic unit received may be more important than the unit itself when attempting to explain the role discipline plays on cognitive development. The relationship between student-faculty interaction and cognitive skill development tends to be greater in academic majors where students (1) have more open channels of communication with faculty; (2) are treated more equitably and fairly by faculty; (3) obtain more prompt and useful feedback on student work by faculty; (4) clearly understand well-articulated program requirements, rules, and policies; and (5) are asked to examine and consider other methods and conclusions, incorporate ideas from different courses, generate new ideas, and use facts and examples to support their viewpoints (Kim & Sax, 2011). These dimensions underscore the results of the Nelson Laird, Bridges, Morelon-Quainoo, Williams, and Salinas Holmes (2007) study that showed the relationship between academic discipline, deep learning approaches, and gains in personal and intellectual development.

To summarize, academic major has been the subject of many studies that examined college and its relationship to cognitive development. More often than not, authors included academic major as a control variable in an effort to study some other college experience and its association with helping students make cognitive gains. In addition, authors often did not study academic major in similar ways, with some grouping arts and science majors together and others separating them, for example. Given these differences, it is difficult to conclude that one major is better than any other at helping students make cognitive gains. Rather, it appears that the amount of support faculty members receive in their major or department for enacting practices intended to spur critical thinking may be more important than the major and department itself.

Course Structure. How faculty structure their courses was the subject of two studies designed to examine students' cognitive development. Although they did not control for the influence of relevant covariates, Hayes and Devitt (2008) found a significant difference in the critical thinking scores of students assigned to small compared with large recitation sections; students in the small sections had higher critical thinking scores than those in the larger sections. Similarly, Lyke and Kelaher Young (2006) discovered a relationship between cognitive skills and how instructors structured a class: for example, instructors who "find out what students are interested in" (p. 482) are more likely to have students report cognitive gains than instructors who "emphasize grades" (p. 482). Given the limited scope of these studies, results should be interpreted cautiously.

Critical Thinking Courses. A number of studies examined critical thinking courses and their influence on cognitive development. The authors of these studies used quasi-experimental and experimental designs to assess the role that participation in critical thinking courses played on helping students develop along cognitive dimensions. For example, using a sample of 144 undergraduate students, Angeli and Valanides (2009) performed an experimental study designed to assess three approaches instructors have taken toward teaching critical thinking: a general approach that teaches general critical thinking skills separately from subject matter (e.g., lecture, discussion, no reflection); an infusion approach, which teaches subject-specific critical thinking skills (e.g., lecture, discussion, reflection, and dialogue with researcher); and an immersion approach, where students "are prompted to consider, analyze, and evaluate different points of view" (p. 324) (e.g., no lecture, reflection, Socratic questioning with researcher). Results indicated that approach significantly mattered, with Cohen's d reaching 1.10 standard deviations for the infusion group and .99 of a standard deviation for the immersion group when each was compared to the mean critical thinking performance of the control group representing the general approach to critical thinking.

Other examples of quasi-experimental and experimental designs were offered by Borg and Stranahan (2009), Rickles, Zimmer Schneider, Slusser, Williams, and Zipp (2013), Williams, Oliver, and Stockdale (2004), Barnett and Francis (2012), and Reid and Anderson (2012). Borg and Stranahan (2009) studied the cognitive gains of 147 students enrolled in one of two sections of a Principles of Economics course; after controlling for a host of covariates, the authors found an instructor effect for the experimental course and attributed these effects to differences in pedagogical approaches, including textbook choices and course assessments.

Turning to sociology courses, Rickles et al. (2013) examined four sections of an introduction to sociology course; the four sections were taught by two instructors, with one class for each instructor serving as the experimental section and one class for each instructors serving as the control section. The design elements for all sections were the same, with one exception: for the experimental sections, instructors focused on the critical thinking assignments, which are described in detail in the article. Controlling for relevant covariates, being in the experimental section had a significant impact on critical thinking at the semester's end.

In a business environment, Reid and Anderson (2012) assessed the critical thinking development of students enrolled in one of three sections of a senior-level capstone course in business administration. One of these sections served as the control group, while two served as the experimental, with the treatment "incorporating critical thinking skills into the weekly case study analyses" (p. 56). Problems with data collection for the control group forced the authors to examine only the development of students in the treatment conditions; these students' critical thinking scores positively changed from pretest to posttest.

Turning to psychology courses, Williams et al. (2004) and Barnett and Francis (2012) examined if questions designed to spur cognitive development exerted any significant influence. Williams et al. (2004) examined the critical thinking development of more than 200 students enrolled in one of five sections of a human development course by administering a treatment to a random group of students in each section. The treatment specifically incorporated critical thinking practice questions to accompany the core course concepts. The authors found positive treatment effects for psychological critical thinking, measured by the Psychological Critical Thinking Instrument (Lawson, 1999) designed to assess subject matter critical thinking, but not for generic critical thinking, measured by the Watson-Glaser Critical Thinking Appraisal (Watson & Glaser, 1994).

Barnett and Francis (2012) performed another classroom-based, quasi-experimental, longitudinal design to test if the use of higher-order thinking questions influenced critical thinking development. Three sections of an educational psychology course were randomly assigned to one of three experimental conditions: condition A students were assigned multiple-choice items that measured facts from the chapter; condition B students were assigned quizzes with two or three essay questions that required critical thinking about the chapter; and condition C students were assigned quizzes with essay questions, but items required only fact-based knowledge. Condition B students scored significantly higher in critical thinking ability.

Diversity Coursework. A series of studies examined the influence of diversity course taking and cognitive development. In his meta-analytic approach that investigated the role of college diversity experiences on cognitive development, Bowman (2010b) examined results from 17 studies. He found that diversity coursework participation was positively associated with cognitive development, but to a lesser degree than other diversity-related experiences, such as frequency of interpersonal interactions reported by students. Similarly, Gurin et al. (2002) synthesized data from a national study of 11,383 students from 184 institutions and a Michigan study of 1,582 students and found that participation in classroom diversity courses was positively associated with the cognitive development of Latino/a students (effect sizes ranged from .13 to .14) and White students (effect sizes ranged from .03 to .16). However, for African Americans, there was a positive association between cognitive measures and diversity course taking in the Michigan study (effect sizes ranged from .17 to .23) but a negative relationship in the national study (effect size $= -.13$).

Wang and Rodgers (2006) examined cognitive development as it related to students' enrollment in social justice–oriented service-learning courses. Students were enrolled in one of six service-learning courses; three of these courses had a social justice emphasis. After controlling for age, class rank, and gender, the authors found a treatment effect for students enrolled in the service-learning courses with the social justice emphases. Similarly, other studies reported that student experiences with diversity coursework, including perceptions of diversity in the curriculum at liberal arts colleges (Umbach & Kuh, 2006), level of integration of diversity into coursework (Carini et al., 2006), and participation in diversity experiences (Jessup-Anger, 2012) were statistically related to cognitive gains.

In an effort to understand how many diversity courses are needed to influence cognitive development, Bowman (2009) and Nelson Laird (2005) designed studies to assess diversity saturation, that is, the number of diversity courses needed to help students make cognitive gains. Bowman (2009) studied the effects of taking diversity courses on the cognitive development of 3,000 first-year students at 19 institutions. Through the use of a longitudinal design, he found that after controlling for a host of covariates, taking at least one diversity course had effects on students' desires to engage in effortful thinking, but not on their critical thinking skills. He attributes these mixed findings to either testing differences (the measure for need for cognition was subjective while the measure for critical thinking was more objective) or the "possibility that diversity courses contribute to cognitive skills in particular domains" (p. 191). In a similar effort, Nelson Laird, Engberg, and Hurtado (2005) examined the critical thinking of 289 students at the University of Michigan. Through the implementation of a cross-sectional design that used cut-off scores to compare students with higher critical thinking scores to students with lower critical thinking scores, they found that the number of diversity courses taken was statistically related to critical thinking, with an effect size of .14.

Contradicting evidence is offered by Loes, Saichaie, Padgett, and Pascarella (2012) who performed a longitudinal study that examined classroom diversity (number of courses taken in the first year of college that focus on diverse cultures and perspectives, number of courses that focus on women/gender, number of courses that focus on equity and justice) and its effects on the cognitive development of 1,354 first-year students enrolled at one of 19 institutions. The authors found no effects of first-year diversity course taking on cognitive development.

Online Courses. Online courses were examined for their influence on cognitive development. Butchart et al. (2009) reported a .45 of a standard deviation pre- to posttest improvement in critical thinking for students who took an online course, although they did not control for many relevant covariates. Williams and Hellman (2004) assessed self-regulation for online learning between 708 first- and second-generation college students enrolled in courses delivered online from a rural regional university. Controlling for the effects of comfort level, the authors found that online learning environments disadvantaged first-generation students by 2.8 percentile points in terms of self-regulated learning when compared to their second-generation counterparts. Treffinger and Schoonover (2012) compared the "orientation to change" (p. 2) of 112 distance learners to 3,325 higher education students and a worldwide database of 27,351 students. According to the authors, this orientation measures students who "use their creative and critical thinking in ways that others clearly recognize as relevant and useful" (p. 2). The authors found that the distance education group did not show significant differences on the measure than either the higher education students or those represented in the worldwide database.

Integrated Academic Experiences. Integrated academic experiences refer to college opportunities that are intended to formally instruct students but may not readily fit into the structure of a course. These experiences include student participation in first-year experience programs, residential colleges, learning communities, honors programs, and research mentorship programs.

The wide variety of these integrated academic experiences resulted in an equally varied number of strategies adopted for pulling studies together. Although this idea of "integrated" was used to justify the need for studies of particular experiences, it was never directly measured but assumed to be the theoretical basis for linking a particular experience to intellectual and cognitive development.

One study examined the effects of integrated academic experiences on athletes' cognitive development. After controlling for a host of relevant covariates, Gayles and Hu (2009) found that athletes' cognitive skills were related to their participation in "academic related activities" (p. 321), an integrated measure including reading textbooks and articles, writing a paper with more than eight pages, and doing extras that showed their commitment to being a good student. This study serves as an important reminder of the difficulties that accompany providing a review of this magnitude: sometimes the ways authors measured constructs, especially among specific student populations, like athletes, rendered organizational strategies more challenging.

First-Year Experiences. Several scholars sought to understand the effects of first-year experiences on intellectual and cognitive development. In their examination of academic competence in the first-year in college, Reason et al. (2006) examined the survey responses of nearly 6,700 students and 5,000 faculty members on 30 campuses nationwide. They found that students' self-reported gains on a measure of academic competence were related to institutions where faculty perceived that their institution's first-year courses, programs, and service were integrated, coordinated, intentional, and active and frequently participated in development activities related to first-year students. Interestingly, the authors found a negative relationship between students' cognitive gain scores and faculty who perceived that their institutions were effective in keeping faculty informed of the services to which they could refer students who were having academic and social difficulties.

Turning to quasi-experimental studies, Wise, Lee, Litzinger, Marra, and Palmer (2004) designed a longitudinal study to assess the impact of a collaborative first-year design course, which featured "hands-on team projects that require complex problem solving on the part of the student" (p. 105), on the intellectual development of 21 undergraduate engineering students. The authors found "that some curricular changes such as active learning classrooms with team projects can have a positive effect on this development, but the advantage does not last without further experiences that further support the new modes of thinking" (p. 109).

Residential Colleges. Another curricular innovation examined for its potential influence on cognitive outcomes was the residential college, where "administrators and faculty purport to create the atmosphere of a small liberal arts college while still offering students the resources of the large university" (Jessup-Anger, 2012, p. 342). In her study of 24 residential colleges, Jessup-Anger found that 8.8% of the variance in one measure of cognition and 5.3% of the variance in another measure of capacity for lifelong learning could be explained by variations between the residential colleges. Although these percentages are relatively small, they provide some evidence for residential college educators interested in linking participation in residential colleges to cognitive and intellectual growth; there is some room for designing opportunities within these learning environments that may help students make gains along these lines.

Learning Communities. Learning communities were also investigated for their relationship to intellectual and cognitive development. Walker (2003) examined the effects of participation in learning communities on cognitive abilities that included critical thinking and analytical problem solving. She found that students in communities with a "yearlong sequence of theme-orientated courses that were team-taught and that included interdisciplinary lectures and small seminars" (p. 11) were significantly more likely to report cognitive gains than students who did not participate in these communities.

Similarly, Pike et al. (2011) examined participation in a learning community as a determinant of high-order thinking skills among first-year students and seniors, respectively. He found that participation in a learning community was associated with .31 of a standard deviation increase in higher-order thinking for first-year students and .39 of a standard deviation increase in higher-order thinking of seniors. Additionally, in their study of the effects of participation in living-learning programs on cognitive complexity, McCormick et al. (2009) reported that a composite measure, "enriching educational experiences" (p. 165) (e.g., learning community, study abroad, independent study), was significantly related to self-reported cognitive gains. On the other hand, Inkelas et al. (2006) reported no significant differences in cognitive development between students in the living-learning communities versus those in traditional residence halls.

Honors Programs. One study explored the effects of participation in honors programs on cognitive and intellectual development. Seifert et al. (2007) examined the effects of honors program participation on students' first-year cognitive outcomes. After controlling for a host of covariates, the authors found that honors program participants scored .14 of a standard deviation higher on the composite cognitive measure of learning and .09 of a standard deviation higher on the critical thinking measure than did their nonhonors peers.

Research Mentorship. Two studies attempted to examine the relationship between research mentorship and critical thinking skills. In their study of 58,281 students who participated in the 2006 University of California Undergraduate Experience Survey, Kim and Sax (2009) found that "students' experience of assisting faculty with research as a volunteer, for course credit or for pay (i.e., research-related faculty contact) significantly and positively predicted their . . . gains in critical thinking" (p. 447), after controlling for a host of covariates. Specifically, research-related faculty contact was positively related to gains in critical thinking for: Latino/as (effect size = .04), Asian Americans (effect size = .02), Whites (effect size = .04), males (effect size = .03), females (effect size = .03), middle-class students (effect size = .02), upper-class students (effect size = .04); non-first-generation students (effect size = .03), and first-generation students (effect size = .03). Although not directly measured, the faculty-student mentoring relationship was likely a reason why Zydney,

Bennett, Shahid, and Bauer (2002) examined differences in alumni-reported cognitive gains as a result of participation in an undergraduate research opportunities in engineering; these authors also reported a positive and significant relationship between cognitive gains and participation in this research opportunity program.

The research on integrated academic interventions indicates that they seem to influence the cognitive development of undergraduate students, especially those that students found challenging and rigorous, like an honors program and opportunities to work with faculty on research. While results were mixed across many of these experiences, when they were significant, their influence was notable, with effect sizes ranging from .14 to .24. Authors who found significant effects between these experiences and cognitive development often mentioned the notion of academic challenge in describing why they thought the experience had a positive association. As Arum and Roksa (2011) suggested, "Having faculty who hold high expectations . . . focus[es] attention on the fact that students benefit when they are in instructional settings where faculty demand and students engage in rigorous academic endeavors" (p. 129).

Summary. To summarize, curricular interventions appear to be a very effective way of helping students make intellectual and cognitive gains. Courses with specific emphases on developing critical thinking were the most effective; indeed, entire curricula have been designed for the purposes of spurring intellectual and cognitive gains among undergraduate students. Diversity course taking also had some influence, although questions remain regarding the number of courses needed to maximize developmental gains. Surprisingly, online course taking neither advantaged nor disadvantaged students in terms of their cognitive and intellectual development.

Researching and reviewing curricular interventions remains challenging for a host of reasons. Although scholars ask research questions designed to understand the effects of taking a particular course on intellectual and cognitive development, they often cannot randomly assign students into courses, making findings subject to criticisms regarding selection and treatment (e.g., the same teacher cannot be in the same place at the same time) bias. Another challenge involves the entanglement of course taking with teacher behavior; for this review, we attempted to differentiate between content and practice when necessary, but like the authors of these studies, we found it immensely challenging to do so. We turn now to a discussion of faculty-and-student relationships, including discussions of teacher and student behaviors.

Faculty-Student Relationship. The relationship between students and faculty remains critical for helping students make cognitive gains. Consistent with previous volumes, the literature about the faculty-to-student exchange is complex, ranging from faculty approaches to teaching to faculty-student out-of-class relationships. The relationship also serves as the cornerstone for the educational practices used in the classroom. For this reason teaching behavior is included in this section as well.

General Positive Relationships with Faculty in and out of Classroom. General and positive interactions with faculty were related to cognitive gains across a variety of studies, such as the meta-analysis performed by Gellin (2003), and samples, including the athletes studied by Gayles and Hu (2009), the African American students investigated by Flowers (2004b), and the undergraduates examined by McCormick et al. (2009) and Kim and Sax (2009).

Course-related student-faculty interactions are those that occur within curricular spaces. For example, Umbach and Wawrzynski (2005) found that faculty perceptions of and experiences with course-related interactions were statistically related to students' self-reported learning gains in a factor called "general education" (p. 164) which encompassed many items, with one being "thinking critically and analytically" (p. 182).

In addition, course-related student-faculty interactions based on students' perceptions and experiences was found to be significantly and positively associated with the critical thinking gains of Kim and Sax's (2009) sample of 58,281 University of California students and the intellectual development of Strauss and Volkwein's (2002) sample of 7,658 State University of New York students. For example, after controlling for a host of covariates, Kim and Sax (2009) found that course-related student-faculty interaction was positively associated with cognitive development for each of the following groups: Latino/as (effect size = .10), Asian Americans (effect size = .11), males (effect size = .11), females (effect size = .06), lower-class students (effect size = .11), middle-class students (effect size = .07), upper-class students (effect size = .08), non-first-generation students (effect size = .08), and first-generation students (effect size = .11).

Turning to out-of-classroom faculty-student relationships, while Sax, Bryant, and Harper (2005), and Jessup-Anger (2012) found that talking with faculty outside class was associated with self-reported changes in critical thinking, Umbach and Wawrzynski (2005) found the opposite: out-of-classroom interactions with faculty were not related to self-reported critical thinking gains.

Teaching Behaviors. As with previous volumes, many studies that attempted to isolate a particular teaching behavior (e.g., active learning, reflection) for its influence on cognitive development used experimental designs aimed at evaluating the efficacy of a particular educational practice over another (see Moreno et al., 2009; Schutte, 2007). Emerging from these studies is the idea that feedback and reflection are critical elements for spurring cognitive gains. As these practices continue to be studied, more detailed information on what constitutes effective feedback and reflection mechanisms is being documented.

Faculty-Initiated Practices: Academic Challenge, Emphasis on Higher-Order Cognitive Activities, Importance Placed On Enriching Educational Activities, and Culture of Best Practice. How faculty members approached and reported their classroom practice was a particular focus of scholarly inquiry in the 2000s. Wyre's (2012) quasi-experimental, longitudinal study of 733 community college students was designed to explore if students' epistemic reasoning strategies were influenced by whether faculty were trained in metacognitive enrichment. Results suggested that "teaching students to think critically changes the students' personal epistemologies effectively adding metacognitive enrichment speeds up the process" (p. 1002).

Similarly, Reed and Kromrey (2001) designed a quasi-experimental, longitudinal study to test the effects of faculty's use of Paul's model (a critical thinking teaching tool) among 52 community college students enrolled in a history course. Two of the sections of the course received the treatment, faculty use of Paul's model (see Reed & Kromrey for a fuller description of this model), and two of the sections did not. Results showed that faculty use of Paul's model was effective for helping students develop critical thinking, as measured by the Document Based Question section of an AP Examination in US History (Spoehr & Fraker, 1995) and the Ennis-Weir Critical Thinking Essay Test (Ennis & Weir, 1985), but not the Critical Thinking Dispositions Inventory (CCTDI; Facione & Facione, 1992) or a content exam.

Results from Umbach and Wawrzynski's (2005) study of 20,220 first- and 22,033 senior-year students enrolled at one of 137 institutions showed similar trends. Specifically, 14,336 faculty from the same sample of institutions also participated in this study. Unique to this study was the merging of faculty and student data in an effort to explain the effects of faculty practices on students' cognitive development, which included a self-reported gain measure of critical thinking. The authors found that after controlling for a host of institutional-level, student-level, and faculty-level covariates, student self-reported gains in critical thinking were positively and significantly related to (1) faculty who introduced challenging tasks and assignments as part of the classroom experience, (2) faculty who had course-related interactions with students, (3) faculty who used collaborative learning techniques in class, (4) faculty who placed an emphasis on higher-order cognitive activities, (5) faculty who emphasized the importance of enriching educational activities (e.g., study abroad), and (6) faculty who worked on a campus with a culture of best practice.

Finally, in an examination of the relationship between the cognitive level of professor discourse and the cognitive gains of students, Ewing and Wittington (2009) observed 12 professors and their respective approaches to teaching. They found that faculty members were not teaching students in ways that challenged them; in fact, the level of cognitive challenge that these professors introduced in the classroom matched, as opposed to exceeded, the level of cognition that students demonstrated. This particular finding suggests the need for faculty to challenge students academically by developing learning objectives and appropriate educational supports that exceed students' cognitive levels. For learning to occur, faculty need to locate the sweet spot with regard to challenging students: providing nonchallenging environments may bore students but providing overly challenging environments may scare students away (see Bandura, 1977).

Perceptions of Good Teaching. Good teaching was also the subject of many studies designed to understand cognitive development. Cruce et al. (2006) longitudinally examined the cognitive development of 2,474 first-year students. The authors found that a composite measure of good practice, including perceptions of effective teaching and interactions with faculty, was associated with greater critical thinking gains, after controlling for students' precollege characteristics, institutional type, and other first-year experiences. Relatedly, another measure of instructor efficacy was reported to be statistically related to need for cognition, after controlling for precollege and related experience-based covariates in a longitudinal study of 405 undergraduate students (Mayhew et al., 2008). Good practices, including perceptions of teaching quality or faculty use of e-mail, were also related to higher critical thinking scores in Carini et al.'s (2006) sample of undergraduate students, in Jessup-Anger's (2012) study of residential college students, and in Walker's (2003) sample of learning community students.

Feedback and Reflection. Educators have examined the role and type of feedback and reflection for their potential in spurring students' cognitive development. Interestingly, scholars varied widely in their approach to and definitions of feedback and reflection. Some emphasized the timing of feedback offered (Arend, 2009; Hattie & Timperley, 2007) and others the type of feedback given (Butchart et al. 2009; Hattie & Timperley, 2007; Hayes & Devitt, 2008; Moreno et al., 2009; Sharma & Hannafin, 2004).

Some studies have approached cognitive and intellectual development from the perspective of helping students develop their problem-solving skills. For example, in an effort to move students from solving fully worked out problems to solving problems independently, Moreno et al. (2009) used randomized controlled trials to study the effects of different forms of scaffolding and feedback on the problem-solving abilities of 232 college students. In one condition, students were provided with step-by-step (i.e., scaffolding) feedback as they "independently solved multi-step problems" (p. 83); in the other, students were given feedback that encouraged them to compare their solutions to those of a worked-out problem. The authors found that students in the latter condition were better able to problem-solve independently than students in the former condition. In another example, Bixler and Land (2010) adopted a posttest-only control group design to investigate the relationship between question prompts (i.e., scaffolding) and problem-solving outcomes. Results showed that students randomly assigned to the treatment condition with the question prompts were significantly more likely to have higher problem-solving performance scores than students assigned to the control condition.

A number of studies examined the feedback/reflection relationship as a condition for cognitive growth. Schutte (2007) examined 63 business majors, or those considering business majors, to assess the use of guided reflection in an experiential education setting as a "means of cognitive development" (p. 120). Through the use of a mixed-method, control group study, Schutte compared no reflectors to low and high reflectors and found that when compared to no reflectors, both low and high reflectors benefited the most when they used feedback to rethink their reflections. The idea of feedback and reflection as a pedagogical strategy for encouraging critical thinking was also supported by the work of Angeli and Valanides (2009), Arend (2009), Bunch (2005), Burbach,

Matkin, and Fritz (2004), Choi et al. (2005), Iwaoka and Crosetti (2007), and Sharma and Hannafin (2004).

With regard to feedback, the studies of online courses may offer a distinctive perspective. Of the studies reviewed here (see Arend, 2009; Choi et al., 2005; Sharma & Hannafin, 2004), the authors validated that cognitive outcomes were associated with the feedback strategies instructors used for involving the students. Succinctly put with regard to faculty feedback, Arend (2009) notes, "Critical thinking appears to be best encouraged among students when a more consistent emphasis is placed on the discussions, and when the instructor's facilitation is less frequent but more purposeful" (p. 1).

Collaborative Learning Facilitation. Some scholars examined cognitive and intellectual development and their relationship to collaborative learning. Collaborative learning practice was the subject of Cabrera et al.'s (2002) study of 2,050 second-year students enrolled at one of 23 institutions and of Umbach and Wawrzynski's (2005) study of 42,249 students enrolled at one of 137 colleges. For both studies, items of collaborative learning practices included information on how faculty used groups as a mechanism for teaching course material. Both studies also used self-reported gains as proxies for cognitive development. Across these studies, collaborative learning practices and techniques were positively associated with cognitive skills. These results echo findings reported by Walker (2003) and Kim and Sax (2011): students who discussed course content with other students were more likely to report cognitive gains. Contradicting evidence was provided by Arum and Roksa (2011), who reported that cognitive gains were negatively and significantly related to the number of hours students spent studying with each other.

Diverse Peer Interaction Facilitation. Two studies examined race-related diverse interactions in the classroom and their role in influencing cognitive development. In a study that examined educational practice on life long learning orientations, Mayhew et al. (2008) found that negative interactions with diverse peers were negatively related to the development of a dimension of cognition (i.e., need for cognition) after controlling for precollege and related experience-based covariates in a longitudinal study of 405 undergraduate students. Similarly, in his study of 289 students, Nelson Laird (2005) found that critical thinking was not related to the number of diverse peer interactions students had but rather the quality of those interactions, with more negative diverse peer interactions resulting in lower critical thinking scores. Taken together, these studies suggest that leaving classroom-based diverse peer interactions to chance has the potential to attenuate cognitive development.

Student Course-Related Behaviors.

Time Spent Preparing for Class. Several studies examined student-related behaviors for their influence on intellectual and cognitive development. Arum and Roksa (2011) found that cognitive gains were associated with whether students took both a course where they reported reading more than 40 pages a week and a course where they reported writing more than 20 pages the previous semester. Similar effects were noted by Carini et al. (2006), whose sample reported positive relationships between the amount of reading and writing required and critical thinking. Kim and Sax (2011) found that a positive association between general academic engagement (e.g., studying and other academic activities outside of class) and development of scholarship (e.g., extensively revised a paper at least once before submitting it to be graded) was related to cognitive development. Cabrera et al. (2002), Wolniak et al. (2001), Reason et al. (2006), and Walker (2003) reported a positive relationship between the number of hours students studied per week and cognitive abilities, including analytical skills, preferences for higher-order cognitive abilities, academic competence, and critical thinking. Offering contrasting evidence, Loes et al. (2012) found that time spent preparing for class was negatively associated with the cognitive development of first-year students who were less prepared for college.

Texting. In an effort to understand how texting shaped perceived cognitive learning, Wei, Wang, and Klausner (2012) developed a theoretical model that assessed the relationships between self-regulation, use of text messaging during class, sustained attention, traditional academic and performance, and perceived cognitive learning. Based on the information received from 190 undergraduate students recruited from a small university in the Northeast, the authors found that "self-regulated students are less likely to text during class and are more likely to sustain their attention on classroom learning, which, in turn, facilitates cognitive learning" (p. 185).

Summary. The weight of the evidence suggests that good teaching matters with regard to helping students make cognitive gains. Elements of good teaching associated with students' cognitive development included the faculty member's ability to design courses with assignments and examples that ask students to think critically about discipline-specific, course-related material; challenge students by requiring them to read more than 40 pages a week and write more than 20 pages; effectively structure race-related conversations in ways that students experience as productive; provide critical and thoughtful feedback throughout the course of a semester; and offer opportunities for students to reflect meaningfully on materials presented in class.

In addition, faculty need to be attentive to how students work together in class. While results were mixed with regard to collaborative learning practices and their influence on learning, findings were consistent regarding classroom-based diverse peer relationships: the quality of diverse peer interaction matters more than that the interactions occur. Finally, faculty need to structure environments that minimize student distraction and avoid allowing students to text in class, for example. The successful execution of these educational practices appears more important to helping students make cognitive gains than student enrollment in a particular course of set of courses.

Cocurricular Engagement. Terenzini, Pascarella, and Blimling (1996) stated, "It seems reasonable to suggest, however, that formal extracurricular activities may have an indirect effect on learning gains through the kinds of interpersonal contacts and interactions they create between students and faculty members and between students and their peers" (p. 155). This statement continues to describe the small but important relationship between cocurricular engagement and cognitive development. Although participation in certain cocurricular programs and activities was examined to some degree (see Gellin, 2003; Flowers, 2004b; Nelson Laird, 2005; Pike, 2003), more often informal peer effects were investigated for their influence on cognitive development (see Gellin, 2003; Flowers, 2004b; Bowman, 2010b; Gayles & Hu, 2009).

Club and Organizational Involvement. From the number of studies that examined club and organizational involvement, results were mixed with regard to the relationship of involvement to cognitive growth. For example, Gellin's (2003) meta-analysis of the literature from 1991 to 2000 examined the effect of undergraduate student involvement on critical thinking. He found that on average, undergraduate students involved in a variety of activities outside the classroom experienced a .14 effect gain in critical thinking compared to students who were not involved. More specifically, effect gains of .11 were related to undergraduate students who were involved in clubs and organizations. Supporting these results were those reported by Strauss and Volkwein (2002), who found a positive association between social and community involvement and intellectual growth, and by Chang et al. (2006), who reported a positive relationship between high levels of campus involvement and cognitive gains.

Flowers (2004b) examined the academic and social development of 7,923 African American students from 192 postsecondary institutions. As part of the study, Flowers investigated four cocurricular spaces (i.e., experiences with art, music, and theater; experiences in the student union; experiences with athletic and recreation facilities; and involvement in clubs and organizations) on a series of scales that together formed academic and social development. With respect to the subscale analyses, results were mixed, with some experiences reported as positive and others negative.

Finally, negative relationships between participation in social activities and critical thinking were observed in Bauer and Liang's (2003) study of 265 first-year students at a mid-Atlantic doctoral extensive university. A composite measure, *Quality Effort in Personal/Social Activities* (p. 281), had six subscales: Dormitory/Fraternity/Sorority, Student Union, Clubs and Organizations, Personal Experiences, Student Acquaintances, and Athletic/Recreation Facilities. After controlling for a host of covariates, the authors found a negative and significant relationship between their composite measure and critical thinking. In short, students who put more effort into social activities tended to have lower scores on the critical thinking measure.

Diversity-Related Events and Dialogues. One study of 1,582 University of Michigan students examined the influence of the number of multicultural events attended and participation in a dialogue group on dimensions of cognitive growth. Controlling for a host of covariates, including the number of informal interactions with diverse peers and diversity course taking, Gurin et al. (2002) found that attending diversity-related events and dialogues was positively associated with the cognitive development self-reported by African

Americans (effect sizes ranging from .17 to .23), Asian Americans (effect sizes ranging from .16 to .29) and White students (effect size ranging from .09 to .13).

Fraternity and Sorority Life. Mixed results were also found for studies of fraternity and sorority membership and its influence on cognitive growth (see Arum & Roksa, 2011; Gellin, 2003; Inkelas et al., 2006; Martin, Hevel, Asel, & Pascarella, 2011). In his examination of the critical thinking scores of 289 students at one institution, Nelson Laird (2005) found that involvement in fraternities or sororities was negatively related to critical thinking, after controlling for a host of covariates. Arum and Roksa's (2011) longitudinal study showed similar effects, with number of hours being spent in fraternities and sororities sharing a negative relationship with posttest scores on the Collegiate Learning Assessment. However, a study by Pike (2003) suggested that Greek affiliation had weak but positive relationships with cognitive outcomes.

Residence. Living on campus had some influence on the cognitive development of students. In Gellin's (2003) meta-analysis of the effect of undergraduate student involvement on critical thinking, he found that on average, the most important involvement activity related to cognitive development was students' housing choices: living on campus was positively associated with critical thinking (effect size .23). This finding resonates with Pike and Kuh's (2005) and Reason et al.'s (2006) studies that found an association between intellectual development and residential living. Offering contrasting evidence, Loes et al. (2012) found that living on campus was negatively associated with the cognitive development of first-year students highly prepared for college.

Working. Many scholars have studied work as it relates to the cognitive development of students. For most of these studies, examination of work-life was peripheral to the central research questions; this may be why results are mixed. While Brint et al. (2012) and Walker (2003) report negative relationships with work and cognitive and intellectual development, others report positive relationships (Gellin, 2003; Kardash, 2000; Kim & Sax, 2011; Strauss & Terenzini, 2007; Zydney et al., 2002). To complicate matters further, it appears as though working on- versus off-campus may make a difference by way of cognitive development; Arum and Roksa (2011) reported that working off-campus was negatively related to cognitive gains but working on-campus was positively related to the same gains.

Registration and Library Use. Two studies examined cognitive outcomes with what Berger and Milem (2000) call "functional experiences" (p. 319)—those that capture ways of participating in campus life that are neither academic nor social. Strauss and Volkwein (2002) found that satisfaction with facilities was positively associated with intellectual growth, while satisfaction with registration and billing procedures was negatively associated. Flowers (2004b) investigated the effects of library experiences on these self-reported gains and found positive effects for students who used the library as a quiet place to read and study material and asked the librarian for help finding material on some topic.

Peer Interactions: General. Informal discussions with peers were statistically related to cognitive growth for students across a number of studies. Both Gellin (2003) and Bowman (2010b) performed meta-analyses that included interactions with peers as determinants of cognitive growth; both noted positive effects. Carini et al. (2006) and Strauss and Volkwein (2002) echoed these findings; "receiving strong peer support" (p. 148) was positively associated with critical thinking and intellectual development. Additional evidence is provided by the athletes in Gayles and Hu's (2009) study, the African American students in Flowers's (2004b) study, the first-year students in Reason et al.'s (2006) study, and the residential college students in Jessup-Anger's (2012) study. Across all of these studies, the authors suggest that general interactions with peers are important for cognitive growth; by way of these experiences, students "may be exposed and open to a variety of viewpoints" (Gellin, 2003, p. 754).

Peer Interactions: Diverse. Diverse peer interactions and their relationship to cognitive outcomes was the subject of many scholarly undertakings, including a meta-analysis by Bowman (2010b), two longitudinal analysis (Gurin, Dey, Hurtado, and Gurin, 2002; Loes, Pascarella, Umbach, 2012), and a cross-sectional study by Reason et al. (2006). Bowman's (2010b) meta-analysis of 17 studies explored the relationship between diversity experiences and cognitive development. Of all the examined experiences, including participation in diversity coursework, diversity workshops, and interactions with nonracial diversity, the frequency of interpersonal interactions with racial diversity was most strongly related to cognitive development.

In their synthesis of a national study of 11,383 students from 184 institutions and a Michigan study of 1,582 students, Gurin et al. (2002) found that informal interactions for diverse others were positively associated with the cognitive development self-reported by African Americans (effect sizes ranging from .17 to .21), Latino/as (effect size = .21, national study only), Asian Americans (effect size ranging from .10 to .16), and White students (effect size ranging from .05 to .16), after controlling for a host of relevant covariates.

Contradictory evidence is offered by Loes et al. (2012). In this longitudinal study, cognitive development shared no significant relationships with interactional diversity or diverse peer friendships. Loes et al. (2012) note that "in the presence of statistical controls for all other variables in the model, neither classroom diversity nor interactional diversity had more than a chance estimated impact on critical thinking skills" (p. 14).

Summary. The weight of the evidence is mixed regarding cocurricular experiences and their relationship to cognitive development. Studies of formal cocurricular experiences, including participation in clubs and organizations, fraternity and sorority life, living on-campus, and working, were mixed, with some reporting positive associations and others showing negative relationships. On the contrary, studies of general informal peer interactions were conclusive: all studies of general informal interactions provided evidence of their positive relationship to cognitive development. Studies of diverse informal peer interactions were less conclusive, with some studies reporting positive associations with cognitive development and others showing negative relationships.

CONDITIONAL EFFECTS OF COLLEGE

Conclusions from the 1990s

In the 2005 synthesis, Pascarella and Terenzini observed a significant increase in empirical studies of the conditional effects of college on cognitive growth from the first volume. Among the most common findings in this growing body of evidence were differential effects based on race and gender. Generally White students possessed an advantage over Black students in years one and three and Latino/a students in year one. While institutional characteristics were found not to play a role in cognitive gains, environmental factors emphasizing cognitive attributes evidenced a greater effect for Latino/a students. Course-taking patterns, Greek involvement, studying with peers, enrollment level, and engagement in volunteer work or diversity activities all differed in magnitude in predicting gains for students of color versus White students. These findings were similar for women as compared to men at four-year colleges; men had significantly greater gains in critical thinking skills from academic and social involvement. However, living oncampus was a stronger predictor of end-of-third-year critical thinking skills for women than for men. Regarding institutional type, women evidenced greater critical thinking gains in four-year institutions, while men evidenced greater gains at community colleges. Finally, some evidence was found that cooperative learning may promote more complex cognitive functioning and that academic-social engagement in college may have a stronger effect on general cognitive development for students with relatively low-tested academic ability.

Evidence from the 2000s

How does the relationship between cognitive development and any given college experience differ based on some other characteristic? Many scholars have adopted varying strategies for examining these relationships. Some have included cross-product terms (e.g., race by classroom diversity course) in statistical models predicting cognitive outcomes and then used the information derived from these estimates to divide samples into subgroup categories (e.g., African American, White) and rerun analyses. Others have not created cross-product terms but tested differences in slopes between subgroups (i.e., are the cognitive gains associated with being Asian American and participating in a living-learning program similar to those associated with being Native American and participating in a living-learning program?). Still others have tested how organizational characteristics (e.g., enrollment at a HBCU) explained subgroup differences (e.g., the gaps between Latino/a and White student cognitive gains). All of these approaches are offered in the spirit of trying to answer these two questions: Who benefits from the experiences intended to spur cognitive development? Do all students equally benefit from participating in those experience?

In previous volumes, conditional effects were reported through the use of four categorical types: students by net effects of college, students by between-college effects, students by within-college effects, and instructional approaches. For this volume and given our emphasis on attempting to provide insights into the "Who benefits?" question, we chose to organize studies based on students' self-identified identity patterns. We begin with an understanding of the relationship between cognitive and intellectual development, examined college experiences, and self-identified race.

African Americans. A series of studies examined the relationship between college and its embedded experiences on cognitive outcomes and how this relationship or set of relationships influenced the experiences of African American students, when compared to their White peers. In their study of 35,000 college seniors from 250 institutions, Kugelmass and Ready (2011) found that, compared to White students' cognitive and intellectual development, African American students were .17 of a standard deviation lower from the beginning to end of four years of college—a 6.8 percentile point difference. The authors found that on average, the initial African American/White achievement gap (effect size = 1 standard deviation difference in initial SAT scores between African American and White students) widened somewhat during the course of undergraduate study as measured by the Collegiate Learning Assessment. However, additional analyses indicated that this gap was significantly reduced as institutions enrolled more high-achieving African American students (effect size = .11) and as students enrolled in a greater number of HBCUs (effect size = .10). In other words, for African American students, "attending college with other African American students appears to afford some benefits, but this positive relationship depends on the academic characteristics of other [African American] students at the institution" (p. 340).

The authors also found that African American students appear to benefit somewhat more from additional budgetary outlays (effect size = .16) compared to White students attending the same institution. This gap also served as a theme in Arum and Roksa's (2011) study of college and its effects on cognitive development.

Turning to climate perceptions, Flowers and Pascarella (2003) examined the cognitive development of African American and White students from 18 four-year institutions over three time points. Main effects indicated that White students made significantly higher cognitive gains in college than African American students: .21 of a standard deviation higher from first to third year, translating into a 7.9 average percentile point difference. To explain these main effects, the authors examined the relationship between a series of experiences, race, and cognitive development and found one significant interaction effect germane to this review: a race by average scholarly/intellectual emphasis at institution attended effect. On splitting the samples into African American and White, respectively, the estimated effect of the average scholarly/intellectual emphasis at the institution attended at end-of-third-year critical thinking was more negative for African American students (effect size = −1.26) than for White students (effect size = −.01), but was statistically nonsignificant for both samples. This finding suggests that an academic climate with a scholarly and intellectual emphasis may exert a stronger influence on the cognitive gains for African Americans when compared to their White peers.

Latino/as. Scholars have also deepened their understanding of the college experiences that influence the cognitive development of Latino/as compared to their White peers. In their study of 35,000 college seniors from 250 institutions, Kugelmass and Ready (2011) found, on average, a gap between Latino/a and White cognitive achievement, as measured by the Collegiate Learning Assessment, with Latino/a students at a .06 standard deviation (2.4 percentile point) disadvantage when compared with their White peers. That gap is drastically reduced after adjusting for precollege ability as measured by the SAT-a result indicating that Latino/a students make cognitive gains at a rate similar to demographically comparable White students. Further analyses indicated that the Latino/a/White gap was reduced even further after accounting for other student-level characteristics. In short, Latino/a students make more cognitive gains at institutions that enroll high-achieving Latino/a students and at residential colleges, but make fewer gains at colleges in rural when compared to suburban areas.

Students of Color. In the absence of cell counts that allow for subgroup analyses and in acknowledgment of some of the limitations that come with such an approach (see Teranishi, Ceja, Antonio, Allen, & McDonough, 2004), some scholars used categories like "students of color" or "minorities" to understand how college experiences and their influence on cognitive and intellectual development differed by race.

In terms of between-college effects, one study examined the relationships between between-college variables (i.e., institutional diversity and structural diversity) and cognitive development and race. In their study of the effects of diversity-related experiences on first-year critical thinking, Loes et al. (2012) divided their sample between White students and their peers of color, after calculating interaction effects between race and other diversity-related experiences in the model. The authors reported a negative and significant relationship between the structural diversity of the institution attended and the critical thinking development among the 271 students of color in the sample.

Four studies examined curricular elements, their relationships to cognitive development, and if these relationships differed by race. In terms of general academic experiences, Loes et al. (2012) reported that first-year students of color who took courses with emphases in the liberal arts were less likely to make cognitive gains than students of color who did not take courses that emphasized the liberal arts.

In his examination of race and its influence on the relationship between diversity course taking and cognitive development, Bowman (2009) reported that when compared to White students, students of color did not receive any significant benefits from taking diversity coursework. Also, Cabrera et al.'s (2002) study of 2,050 second-year college students found that cooperative learning practices were statistically related to a self-reported gains in analytical reasoning for minority students when compared to White students. Taken together, these studies indicate the increasing need to innovate across the curriculum and in the classroom. As student demographics consistently change, faculty need to be strategic about their classroom practice. Who benefits from taking diversity courses and engaging in certain educational experiences should remain an important consideration for educators interested in creating effective learning environments poised to spur cognitive development.

Turning to cocurricular experiences, Loes et al. (2012) found that living on campus was negatively associated with the cognitive development of first-year students and that this effect was most pronounced among the 271 students of color in the sample. Holding all other variables constant, first-year students of color who lived on campus were significantly less likely to make cognitive gains than students of color who lived off campus. Such a finding warrants further exploration as increasing resources continue to be allocated toward residential programming for first-year students.

Whites. Although the White student experience dominates the empirical research narrative of college impact work, a series of studies examined how certain diversity-related experiences influenced the cognitive development of White students specifically. Turning to course taking, two studies examined the relationship between course taking and cognitive development and how that relationship informs the White student experience. In his examination of race and its influence on the relationship between diversity course taking and intellectual and cognitive development, Bowman (2009) reported that when compared to students of color, White students who enrolled in two diversity courses experienced greater cognitive gains. Further analyses indicated that White students who took one, two, or three or more diversity courses experienced greater gains in need for cognition than White students who enrolled in no such courses. This result suggests that "students from some privileged groups actually receive larger benefits from diversity coursework" (p. 189).

Contradictory evidence was provided by Loes et al. (2012). After testing for an interaction effect between race and classroom diversity on critical thinking indicators, the authors divided the sample and reran models based on students' self-identified race. The authors found no significant relationship between classroom diversity and critical thinking among the 1,083 first-year White students in the sample.

Turning to informal diverse peer interactions, Loes et al. (2012) investigated critical thinking as it was associated with the relationship between race and interactional diversity, "the extent of participation in diversity-oriented experiences and discussions with diverse peers" (p. 8). After finding a significant interaction effect between race and interactional diversity, the authors divided the sample and found that interactional diversity was positively and significantly associated with critical thinking gains among first-year White students.

Gender. Scholars have also examined how college influences the cognitive and intellectual development of students based on their gender identification patterns. Seifert et al. (2007) examined the effects of honors program participation on students' first-year cognitive outcomes and found that men who participated in the honors program scored 2.3 percentile points higher on the composite cognitive measure than men not involved in an honors course. Turning to engagement with faculty, Sax et al. (2005) reported that the impact of general faculty support on self-reported changes in critical thinking was stronger for men than for women. Contrarily, for the same sample, the authors found that the impact of challenging a professor's ideas in class on self-reported changes in critical thinking was stronger for women than for men. By way of practice, Cabrera et al.'s (2002) study found that effects for cooperative learning and its relationship to cognitive development was stronger for White women than White men, but effects of hours spent studying on the same measure of cognitive development was more pronounced for White men than White women. Of course, these studies serve as another reminder of curricular and pedagogical practices that occur in the context of exchange—between faculty and students and among peers—and that these exchanges, if not managed thoughtfully, might be gendered, silencing voices that have historically and socially been oppressed.

Socioeconomic Status. Scholars examined socioeconomic status (SES) and its relationship to college's effects on students' cognitive and intellectual growth. Two studies examined the effects of course taking on cognitive development and whether this relationship differed among students from different socioeconomic backgrounds.

In their examination of the efficacy of participating in an honors program, Seifert et al. (2007) found that high-SES first-year students who participated in the honors program scored 1.5 percentile points higher on a cognitive measure than lower-SES students who did not participate in the honors program.

In his examination of diversity-course taking frequency and intellectual and cognitive development, Bowman (2009) reported that students from low-income families experienced larger cognitive gains from taking diversity coursework than did other students. To summarize, Bowman (2009) notes:

"Taking diversity courses is not associated with any cognitive benefits for students from high-income backgrounds. In contrast, for students from middle- or lower-income families, significant gains in need for cognition accrue from taking one, two, or three or more diversity courses. . . . Moreover, for these less affluent students, taking two diversity courses is associated with greater critical thinking gains" (p. 190).

Taken together, the results also remind educators to critically question educational practices. What constitutes effective practice? For whom are these practices effective?

First-Generation Students. The college experiences that influence the cognitive and intellectual development of first-generation college students has newly emerged as a topic of interest for college impact scholars. In terms of two- versus four-year institutional type, Pascarella et al. (2003) examined the cognitive skills of 144 college students attending one of five community colleges. Controlling for a host of covariates, they found that when compared to students whose parents were both college graduates, first-generation college students made significantly larger cognitive two-year gains.

One study examined curricular experiences and their influence on cognitive development and if this relationship differed between first-generation college students and their peers whose parents attended some college. Controlling for a variety of relevant variables, Pascarella, Pierson, Wolniak, and Terenzini (2004) found that when compared to students whose parents had at least some college education, first-generation students' higher end-of-year cognitive scores were positively associated with higher cumulative grades and the more nonassigned books these students read.

Turning to the cocurriculum, Pascarella et al. (2004) explored many experiences for their relationship to cognitive development and if this relationship was conditioned on first-generation status. Greater higher-order thinking scores for first-generation college students were positively associated with more extracurricular involvement, Greek affiliation, and volunteer work but were negatively related to the number of hours worked per week. With so many distinctive patterns of relationships, it is clear that more evidence is needed to understand the distinctive context of the first-generation college student.

Precollege Preparation and Ability. A handful of studies investigated the relationship between participation in higher education and cognitive outcomes and if this relationship varied by students' precollege academic ability or preparation. The first study examined institutional type differences. Loes et al. (2012) found that when compared to less academically prepared first-year students enrolled at liberal arts colleges, cognitive gains among less academically prepared first-year students were positively associated with attending a research university but negatively associated with attending a regional university.

One study examined the critical thinking development of first-year students as it related to precollege academic preparation and time spent preparing for class. Loes et al. (2012) found that time spent preparing for class shared a significant and negative relationship with the critical thinking development of less academically prepared first-year students.

Turning to diversity experiences, Loes et al. (2012) found that interactional diversity and its relationship to first-year students' cognitive gains varied by precollege preparation. Students with lower precollege preparation made significantly greater cognitive gains through exposure to and interaction with diverse peers than students with higher precollege preparation. This relationship was also supported in the work of Carini et al. (2006), who found that low-ability students appeared to receive the greatest benefits, by way of critical thinking, when diversity was integrated into the coursework. These authors also found that lower-ability students made greater cognitive gains through an increased frequency of student-faculty interactions and assignments that encouraged reading and writing.

Peer support seemed especially important for low-ability students as they made cognitive and intellectual gains. For example, Cruce et al. (2006) found that peer interactions had a more profound and significant effect on the post-test critical thinking scores of first-year students with below-average precollege critical thinking scores than students with higher-than-average precollege thinking skills. Quality peer relationships and being in a supportive campus climate also were associated with the critical thinking gains reported by lower-ability students in Carini et al.'s (2006) study.

Athletic Profile Status. In their study of the influence of student engagement and sport participation on college outcomes among Division I student athletes, Gayles and Hu (2009) found that the interaction between participation in academic-related activities and profile of sport (i.e., football would be considered high profile while soccer would be considered low profile) were significant for influencing learning and communication skills. In other words, "Academic related activities such as writing papers and completing reading assignments had a smaller effect on reported gains in learning and communication skills for athletes in high profile sports compared to athletes in low profile sports" (p. 329). To explain these findings, the authors suggest that educators interested in spurring cognitive gains offer different educational opportunities for athletes in high- versus low-profile sports.

Summary. The weight of the evidence suggests that the relationship of cognitive development to college is complicated, often conditioned by students' self-reported race, gender, socioeconomic status, academic ability, first-generation status, and even sports profile. The message from these collective results is that educators must continue to innovate by creating and assessing climates, programs, classrooms, and activities designed to spur cognitive growth. What may have worked in the past may not be working now or in the future as student demographics continue to change at a rapid pace. Educators must always remember to critically and routinely question their educational environments and practices to ensure that their reach does not help a few to the detriment of the many or spur learning for those already in privileged positions to the detriment of those historically marginalized and underserved.

LONG-TERM EFFECTS OF COLLEGE

Conclusions from the 1990s

Consistent with their 1991 synthesis, Pascarella and Terenzini's (2005) synthesis found that alumni regarded college as having had an impact on their cognitive development and thinking skills. They concluded that college promoted development; however, continued cognitive and intellectual development was contingent on the levels of intellectual stimulation and challenge postcollege.

Evidence from the 2000s

The long-term effects of college on cognitive development have rarely been the subject of scholarly inquiry, at least over the past decade. In their study of whether older adults are wiser than younger adults, including college-aged students, Ardelt (2010) surveyed 477 undergraduate college students and 178 adults older than 52 years of age. On a measure of wisdom, college-educated older adults scored significantly higher than college-aged students. Interestingly, older adults scored the same as college-aged students.

In a retrospective study on the influence of undergraduate research opportunities in engineering on a host of cognitive development single-item indicators, such as solving problems independently, analyzing literature critically, and tolerating ambiguity, Zydney et al. (2002) used a comparative design that matched 229 alumni who were involved in the undergraduate research program during college with those not involved in the program. The authors concluded that when compared to their counterparts, program alumni "reported significantly greater enhancement of important cognitive and personal skills" (p. 156).

CHAPTER SUMMARY

Theoretical Overview

The weight of the evidence suggested that scholars have distanced themselves from studies of postformal reasoning for those related to other dimensions of cognitive and intellectual development, such as critical thinking, critical thinking dispositions, need for cognition, and self-reported gain scores. Compared to reviews from previous decades, this volume's synthesis included articles with very few references to Perry's scheme (1968, 1981), reflective judgment (King & Kitchener, 1994), or epistemic reflection (Baxter Magolda, 1992).

Many reasons for this distancing can be posited. Recent evidence suggests that perhaps epistemic reasoning is subject to more change after the undergraduate experience, well into graduate school and beyond (see Owen, 2011). Still, others might suggest that some measures of cognition are too cumbersome to administer to students, especially in an assessment environment wrought by survey fatigue. We suspect that this distancing is not due to theoretical inconsistencies or challenges, but may be due to convenience, as the availability and widespread use of empirically validated measures focuses nearly exclusively on critical thinking. Of course, many dangers accompany trading theory for efficiency. Are the best questions about cognitive and intellectual development being asked? How are policies and practices concerning college and its effects on this form of development being misguided by an almost singular focus on critical thinking?

The weight of the evidence also suggests that, when compared to previous volumes, more scholars from disciplines outside higher education are interested in college and its effects on cognitive and intellectual development. Examples range from sociologists adopting a college-impact framework for examining change over time to engineering educators whose commitment toward problem-based inquiry has led to a surge of studies that investigated highly specific aspects of pedagogical practice (e.g., forward versus backward fading). Certainly these emerging efforts should be welcomed and embraced by scholars within the field of higher education, as expanding, interdisciplinary interests often ameliorate research endeavors.

Change during College

Consistent with previous volumes, the weight of the evidence supports the notion that participation in higher education is strongly and positively associated with cognitive and intellectual growth during college. Results from this chapter show that changes in cognitive development occurred as a result of college-going, with one-year exposure to college associated with an average gain of .11 of a standard deviation in critical thinking scores or a 4 percentile point increase in critical thinking scores. Two years of college also made a difference, with average gains in critical thinking reaching .18 of a standard deviation or a 7 percentile point percentage increase. Four-year average gains ranged from .44 to .47 of a standard deviation or a 17 to 18 percentile point increase from the first to the fourth year of college. Indeed, participation in higher education promotes cognitive growth.

These findings are consistent with the results reported in previous volumes. Across many longitudinal efforts that used many measures to assess cognitive and intellectual development, positive change was observed as students steadily progressed through their college experience. This change is not trivial, as many higher education stakeholders have suggested in recent years.

Net Effects of College

As opposed to results in previous volumes, we cannot make any conclusive statements about the net effects of college-going on cognitive and intellectual development. No studies reported in this volume included research designs of college-going versus non-college-going students. Without this comparison group, estimating net effects was not possible. As scrutiny about the value and purposes of participation in higher education will likely continue, funding agencies should be willing to allocate resources to empirical efforts designed to assess college versus non-college goers along cognitive dimensions.

Between-College Effects

Another means of unpacking the degree to which cognitive and intellectual development occurred involved scholars' use of multimodeling techniques to understand between-college effects. Specifically, we learned that significant but modest proportions of the variance in cognitive growth could be explained by institutional differences, with reported intraclass correlation coefficients ranging from 3.0% to 23.0%. These statistics indicate that colleges have the potential to create and enact policies that influence the cognitive development of their students and provide a context for researchers to begin to analyze cognitive development as a learning process, albeit a complex and systemic one.

Like previous syntheses, we found that cognitive and intellectual gains were associated with distinctive types of learning environments. In terms of institutional selectivity and its potential influence on cognitive and intellectual development, results were mixed, with some studies reporting small to moderate associations between selectivity indicators and cognitive gains with effect sizes reaching .13 for students enrolled in highly selective liberal arts colleges, while others reporting no such associations. Interestingly, the authors represented in this volume examined selectivity using a variety of measurement and analytical strategies, including the average amounts of cognitive growth occurring at any given institution and externally derived ranking scores. Perhaps the mixed results reported in this volume of research are an artifact of the different approaches scholars have adopted in measuring selectivity. Either way, accounting for selectivity in studies of cognitive development remains important theoretically, as it helps differentiate cognition from ability and aptitude.

Turning to institutional type, results from this decade of research showed that by itself, type rarely explained differences in cognitive and intellectual growth. Consistent with research presented in previous volumes, it remains challenging to support any conclusive statement about the relationship between cognitive development and institutional type, even when type was examined by Carnegie Classification.

Also consistent with previous volumes was the lack of consistent findings associating cognitive gains with other institutional characteristics, such as size, location, and control. Perhaps the lack of interest in variables of this kind is due to their static, immutable nature. Even if the weight of the evidence would support that cognitive development was statistically related to location—for example, how could institutional stakeholders use these findings? Change locations? Questions like these have recently been explored empirically by scholars who have developed typologies for examining institutional characteristics and their effects on student outcomes (see Ro, Terenzini, & Yin, 2013). While some institutional characteristics are malleable and open to change (e.g., mission statement, curricular requirements, numerical proportion of faculty of color on campus), others (e.g., geography region, control) are not, making results of investigations into the latter more informative and less instructive.

In their previous volume, Pascarella and Terenzini (2005) noted that ongoing conversations concerning how specific aspects of an institution's environment shaped cognitive development were warranted. Apparently scholars embraced this charge, as many studies in this volume attempted to explain environmental influence on helping students make cognitive gains. Included within this set of influences were student perceptions of an institution's commitment to diversity, allocation of resources, and peer socialization processes.

New to this volume were the studies that examined students' cognitive development as a function of an institution's commitment to diversity, assessed through student perceptions or through the numerical proportion of students of color or women on campus. Like institutional type, results were complicated with regard to these relationships. For students in some samples, the numerical proportion of students of color on campus was negatively related to cognitive growth, while for students in other samples, the relationship between the structural diversity of the student body and cognitive growth was more positively related. Specifically, students enrolled in institutions with a greater proportion of African American students were disadvantaged by .07 of a standard deviation, while students enrolled in institutions with a greater proportion of Latino/a students were advantaged by .04 of a standard deviation. Findings like these remain challenging to interpret, especially in the absence of representative institutional samples. Clearly more studies are needed to understand the complicated relationship that structural diversity shares with student cognitive development. That said, perhaps more important than the numerical representation of students of color on campus is how institutions structure and support meaningful engagement across race for all students.

Also new to this volume are studies that explored resource allocations and their relationship to students' cognitive development. The weight of the evidence suggests that holding all factors constant, the amount of resources spent on students was associated with gains in critical thinking, with effect sizes ranging from .02 to .13. Spending money on students matters in terms of helping them develop along cognitive dimensions.

Finally, a number of peer socialization effects were examined for their influence on students' cognitive and intellectual development. The weight of the evidence in this area emerged from studies that were grouped based on their authors' analytical approaches to examining student perceptions; by modeling an aggregated measure of student perceptions, authors could make inferences about an institution's climate and its effects on students' cognitive development. Greater cognitive gains were associated with institutions that enrolled students who (1) perceived their college as sustaining positive cross-race interactions, (2) pursued civic goals, (3) experienced their institution as academically challenging, and (4) reported greater amounts of out-of-class faculty interactions.

Within-College Effects

Consistent with findings reported in previous volumes, specific climate dimensions were explored for their likely influence on cognitive and intellectual development. Unlike the peer socialization effects discussed in the "Between-College Effects" section of this chapter, the climate perceptions analyzed in the "Within-College Effects" section were based on individual (as opposed to aggregated) student perceptions and experiences. Although authors varied in their understanding and use of the term *climate*, the weight of the evidence suggests that certain campus features were associated with cognitive gains.

Based on the weight of the evidence, the most important climate dimension that shared positive associations with cognitive gains was students' perceptions of the climate as scholarly and intellectual—faculty holding students to higher standards. Students who felt academically challenged were more likely to make cognitive gains.

The weight of the evidence also indicated that some dimensions of a campus climate were negatively associated with cognitive and intellectual development. In both longitudinal and cross-sectional studies, perceptions of the campus as tolerant were negatively associated with intellectual and cognitive gains. These results resonate with findings presented by scholars interested in tolerance and diversity (see Engberg & Mayhew, 2007); the most developed critical thinkers may be those most equipped to pick up on expressed prejudices and microaggressions on campus. Thus, one might expect higher critical thinking scores to be more closely aligned with perceptions of intolerance on campus.

Turning specifically to diversity climates and their effects on intellectual ability and cognitive development, a series of studies showed that sustaining positive race relations or less chilly climates for women was positively related to intellectual ability and cognitive development. Of particular note is that the relationship between individual perceptions of a campus's ability to sustain quality race relations and cognitive development varied significantly by institution. These findings suggest that each institution has the responsibility to see that its campus climate uniquely supports positive and cross-race relations in an effort to support cognitive development.

Unlike previous volumes, more scholars examined the liberal arts experience for its potential in explaining cognitive and intellectual development. Results were inconclusive with regard to these experiences and their influence on cognitive and intellectual gains, although effect sizes reached .24 for exposure to and participation in liberal arts experiences and their influence on intellectual and cognitive gains. To complicate matters further, there is some evidence to suggest that first-year students of color who took courses with emphases in the liberal arts were less likely to make cognitive gains than students of color who did not take courses that emphasized the liberal arts. These mixed and perhaps deleterious effects might be explained by some conceptual and operational confusion regarding the liberal arts, as authors sometimes confused enrollment in a liberal arts college with exposure to and participation in a liberal education. Although definitional consensus is challenging, without some consistency regarding use of terms, drawing conclusions across studies will remain challenging.

Results on academic major were mixed with regard to discipline or major and its influence on cognitive development; however, emerging research suggests that cognitive and intellectual development within major is less about choice of major and more about how faculty within majors are supported to help students make cognitive gains. Consistent with findings from previous volumes, small proportions of variance in cognitive development could be explained by nesting students within major or field; intraclass correlation coefficients for studies of cognitive development with a pretest measure or proxy ranging from 1.1% to 6.7%. Other evidence demonstrated that a much larger proportion of variability in cognitive and intellectual development exists among students within field at the same institution (at least 75%). These results initially suggest that academic major might be too gross of an indicator to examine as a mechanism for cognitive growth; instead, scholars may want to investigate the particular practices within any given major (e.g., course requirements, credit hours, delivery modes) for their influence on helping students make cognitive gains.

Unlike previous volumes, evidence from this review suggests that direct studies comparing one major to another have given way to more specific studies of disciplinary context and the roles that transparency and support within these contexts play in influencing cognitive development. The amount of support an academic unit received may be more important than the unit itself when attempting to explain the role discipline plays on cognitive development. The relationship between student-faculty interaction and cognitive skill development tends to be greater in academic majors where students (1) have more open channels of communication with faculty; (2) are treated more equitably and fairly by faculty; (3) obtain more prompt and useful feedback on work by faculty; (4) clearly understand well-articulated program requirements, rules, and policies; and (5) are asked to examine and consider other methods and conclusions, incorporate ideas from different courses, generate new ideas, and use facts and examples to support their viewpoints.

Two interesting results emerged regarding course structure. Although effects were small, class size seemed to matter, with students in the small sections having higher critical thinking scores than those in the larger sections. Similarly, instructors more interested in learning than grades seemed to encourage more critical thinking from their students. These findings should be interpreted cautiously, however, given the limited scope of the studies where these results are reported.

The effects of taking critical thinking courses on cognitive and intellectual development were modest to very strong, with reported effect sizes reaching up to 1.1 of a standard deviation change in critical thinking as a result of taking a course in critical thinking. The weight of the evidence suggests that context-specific critical thinking content and materials are better than context-general materials at promoting cognitive development. Using discipline-specific content as a mechanism for engaging students to consider, analyze, and evaluate evidence from a variety of perspectives is important for spurring cognitive and intellectual growth.

Consistent with other volumes, results are inconclusive with regard to diversity course taking and its influence on intellectual and cognitive development. First, discrepancies emerged between studies that sought to understand if cognitive gains were related to the number of diversity courses taken, with some evidence suggesting that one course may have a small to moderate (effect size = .14) influence on growth and competing evidence showing that educators should encourage students to enroll in as many diversity courses as possible to spur cognitive and intellectual development. Second, some of the evidence showed that intellectual and cognitive development was related to diversity course taking, albeit to a lesser degree than participating in other diversity-related experiences, like diverse peers interactions. Third, the evidence suggested that diversity course taking may spur cognitive growth differentially, based on student self-identification patterns. Although taking diversity courses was effective for first-generation students, students from lower socioeconomic backgrounds, and White students, it had little to no influence on the cognitive development of students of color.

The weight of the evidence showed that intellectual and cognitive development was more related to the nature and quality of the diverse peer interaction in the classroom as opposed to the quantity or frequency of these interactions. Facilitating and negotiating positive and productive diverse peer interactions in the classroom can be an effective means for spurring dissonance, which often leads to cognitive gains; however, if faculty fail to support these interactions properly (i.e., students experience these interactions as hostile, symbolic, or overly fatiguing), then these exchanges may push students to resolve the engendered cognitive dissonance by retreating to stereotype. While diverse peer interactions can be a catalyst to promote cognitive dissonance, leaving such interactions to chance has the potential to attenuate many of the benefits espoused by the higher education community.

New to this volume was the number of studies designed to examine online course taking for its effects on students' cognitive and intellectual development. The dearth of research comparing online course taking to traditional face-to-face course taking was surprising given the surge of online environments offered to students. Interestingly, the studies that examined online courses seemed to focus more on the practices within the courses than comparing these courses with more traditional courses. From the evidence, it appears as though online course taking gives no advantage or disadvantage to students by way of helping them make cognitive and intellectual gains.

The weight of the evidence suggests that first-year experiences have an influence on cognitive and intellectual development. Exposure to college was associated with an average gain of .11 of a standard deviation or a 4 percentile point increase in critical thinking scores. Potential greater movement could occur for first-year students enrolled at institutions with coherent first-year courses, programs, and activities and with professional opportunity enhancement programs designed specifically for faculty who teach first-year students. The evidence suggests that participation in first-year innovations like honors programs may help first-year students make between a 5 to 6 percentile point increase in cognitive and intellectual gains.

Other related course experiences exerted influence on students' intellectual and cognitive growth. Beginning with the residential college experience designed to integrate the small institution feeling of a liberal arts schools with the resources of a larger institution, evidence showed only 8.8% of the variance in the cognitive outcomes was explained by between-residential-college effects. This suggests that most of the variability in the cognitive outcome measures was explained by what was happening within each residential college, leaving administrators with creative room to design these experiences according to the specific needs of the students enrolled at the institution.

Quasi-experimental and cross-sectional studies validated that the adjusted effects for participation learning communities were small to moderate, ranging from .31 to .39 of a standard deviation. That said, one study showed no differences in cognitive and intellectual development for students enrolled in a learning community versus those enrolled in traditional residence halls.

Undergraduate research opportunities that gave students access to collaborate with faculty on empirical projects also influenced intellectual and cognitive gains. Although the magnitude of effects was relatively small, ranging between .02 and .04, effects held for a variety of subgroups, including Latino/as, Asian Americans, Whites, men, women, middle-class students, upper-class students, non–first-generation students, and first-generation students. Perhaps these opportunities exemplify the dimensions of the learning experience that students need to help them develop intellectually and cognitively. By offering a structured opportunity that challenges students through involving them in collaborative work with faculty, educators may be able to spur cognitive growth.

To a much greater degree than the previous volume, results from this volume suggest that teaching behaviors were critical to cognitive and intellectual development. Based on experimental and quasi-experimental studies, the weight of the evidence suggests that feedback and reflection are vitally important for faculty who want to help their students make cognitive and intellectual gains. To spur cognitive and intellectual growth feedback needs to be a central component of the student-faculty classroom exchange, not merely a mechanism for evaluating student performance. By providing feedback throughout the course of the semester, faculty encourage reflection and can set appropriate expectations for individual students. Perhaps it is in these engagements that students locate their sense of academic challenge and effective student-faculty relations – both shown to have influence over intellectual and cognitive development.

Similar to previous volumes, a series of other educational practices were important for helping students develop along intellectual and cognitive lines. In short, good teaching matters. Consistent with findings from the previous volumes, good teaching practice is critically important for helping students make intellectual and cognitive gains. What is good teaching? Synthesizing findings from the studies reported in this volume, we offer that students' cognitive and intellectual gains were related to faculty who:

1. Were trained in metacognitive enrichment and/or application of critical thinking modules,
2. Worked on a campus with a culture of best teaching practices,

3. Had high expectations for student performance,

4. Introduced challenging tasks and assignments as part of the classroom experience,

5. Had course-related interactions with students,

6. Used appropriate collaborative learning techniques in class,

7. Placed an emphasis on higher-order cognitive activities,

8. Emphasized the importance of enriching educational activities (e.g., study abroad),

9. Were perceived by students to be good teachers, and

10. Served as research mentors to students.

For efficiency, these practices were offered in a list for educators interested in helping their students make cognitive gains. That said, the importance of good teaching as it relates to cognitive growth cannot be understated and should serve as a cornerstone for policies related to college-level teaching and learning.

Like previous volumes, but to a greater extent in terms of representation in this volume, students' course-related behaviors were examined for their link to intellectual and cognitive development. Net all other potential influences, the weight of the evidence suggests that the more time students prepare reading and writing for class, the greater their intellectual and cognitive gains. Frequent reading and writing may refine students' abilities to evaluate competing truth claims and critically question what is known; as their skills become more sophisticated, cognitive development occurs. Additionally, frequent reading and writing assumes that faculty will be engaged in the learning process. It is hard to imagine a scenario where students' weekly writing is not being used as a feedback mechanism for faculty and a resultant reflection opportunity for students. Symbolically, preparing for class through reading and writing might be one way that students gauge faculty expectations for performance and, to a greater extent, their institutions as holding high academic standards.

Results were mixed with regard to students working collaboratively on course work. Like previous volumes, this review suggests that collaborative learning shares some relationship with cognitive and intellectual growth; however, that relationship is complicated by the findings that suggest that collaborative learning environments may be a more effective pedagogical technique for helping historically underrepresented students (students of color and women) make cognitive gains than for students historically in the statistical majority (White students and men). Faculty should provide oversight into the collaborative work of students; leaving group formation to chance or letting teams work together on group assignments with minimal oversight may put some students at risk for not making the most effective use of their opportunities to learn from their peers.

Texting in class was found to be negatively related to cognitive and intellectual development. Allowing students to distract themselves from the learning process may be impeding their abilities to make cognitive gains. Extrapolating principles from this study, faculty need to be strategic regarding students' use of technologies in the classroom.

Cocurricular experiences ranged from planned to serendipitous, with many effects similar to those reported in previous volumes. One meta-analytic study reported that on average, undergraduate students involved in a variety of activities outside the classroom experienced a .14 effect gain in critical thinking. The same study reported that effect gains were related to undergraduate students who were involved in clubs and organizations (effect size reaching .11). Despite these reported gains, other studies were not as positive with regard to participation in clubs and its effects on cognitive and intellectual growth. Taken together, results were mixed for studies of club participation, mostly due to the random ways clubs were grouped together as a means of measuring cocurricular involvement.

One organization consistently studied for its impact on cognitive and intellectual development is fraternity and sorority life. As in previous volumes, findings were inconclusive.

As in previous studies, cognitive and intellectual development was associated with having positive interactions with peers. The weight of the evidence, including two meta-analyses, longitudinal and cross-sectional studies, all maintain that for cognitive and intellectual development, peer effects remain strong. The adjusted effects hold for population-specific studies of athletes, African American students, first-generation students, and residential college students.

Not all peer effects are created equal. Mixed results emerge for informal diverse peer interaction effects and cognitive development. Meta-analyses and cross-sectional studies indicated that effects for diverse peer interactions were quite strong; however, results from three longitudinal analyses showed otherwise, with no significant effects reported. Of course, measurement issues remain challenging for assessing diverse peer interactions, as many scales did not readily specify whether these interactions were diverse by way of race, gender, or otherwise; continue to assess frequency as opposed to quality of interaction; and struggled with mixing items that assess diverse peer interactions in the classroom versus those occurring outside class.

Consistent with previous volumes, residential status on campus was studied for its potential in influencing students' cognitive and intellectual development. In one synthesis of multiple studies, it was reported that living-on was associated with a .23 effect gain in critical thinking. Despite this report and those from supporting cross-sectional studies, a longitudinal study found no relationship between living status and intellectual and cognitive development. Over the past three decades, the role of living on campus as it relates to intellectual and cognitive development has seemingly become less important, perhaps because of changing student demographics or emergent learning needs (i.e., more time on task) of this generation of student.

In line with previous volumes, the weight of the evidence suggests that results were mixed with regard to working while enrolled and its relationship to intellectual and cognitive development. For most of these studies, examination of work-life was peripheral to the central research questions, so little is offered by way of explaining why work would or would not be related to cognitive and intellectual development. To complicate matters further, it appears as though working on versus off campus may make a difference by way of cognitive development, as the same longitudinal study reported that working off campus was negatively related to cognitive gains but working on campus was positively related to the same gains. As attending college becomes more expensive, it is reasonable to assume that more students will work, either on or off campus. Campus educators may want to find ways to increase on-campus employment opportunities, as many may be designed in ways that facilitate cognitive and intellectual growth.

New to this volume were the few studies that investigated functional areas and their relationship to cognitive and intellectual gains. Apparently satisfaction with facilities was positively related to intellectual growth, but satisfaction with registration and billing were negatively related. Also, one study reported a relationship between cognitive and intellectual growth and use of the library, specifically with regard to students who went to the library as a quiet place to read and study material and who asked librarians for help finding material on some topic. However, given the dearth of research in the area, these results are offered cautiously.

Conditional Effects

The weight of the evidence suggests that scholars have responded positively to Pascarella and Terenzini's (2005) call for more studies of conditional effects, especially as they related to explaining cognitive and intellectual development. At the heart of methodological considerations and analytical strategies designed to examine conditional effects is the researcher's attempt to answer the question, "Who benefits? from experiences thought to be associated with cognitive growth" For example, there are times when evidence may suggest that diversity course taking is statistically and positively related to helping students make cognitive gains. Conditional effects analyses allow educators to ask and answer important follow-up questions. In terms of helping students make cognitive gains, does diversity-course taking benefit all students equally? If not, who benefits from enrolling in these courses? Given the focus on the "Who benefits?" question, we organized this section on conditional effects as potential answers to that question.

African Americans. The weight of the evidence suggests that with regard to cognitive development, college is hard-wired for White student success compared with African American students. Compared to White students' cognitive and intellectual development, African American students were disadvantaged by .17 to .21 of a standard deviation from the beginning to end of three to four years of college, a 6.8 to 7.9 percentile point disadvantage. On average, when compared to White students, African American students began college with significantly lower scores on measures of aptitude and intellectual and cognitive development, with one study reporting one full standard deviation separating African American and White students on the SAT.

Evidence has shown that this initial gap widens during the course of study for African American students when compared to White students (effect size = −.17). Enrollment of high-achieving African American students (effect size = .11), attending an HBCU (effect size = .10), and additional budgetary outlays specifically directed to academic support for all students (e.g., faculty development centers, teaching and learning centers, and academic support staff) (effect size = .16) helped to reduce these gaps, but not entirely.

Taken together, these trends suggest that when compared to White students, African American students have been and continue to be disadvantaged in college. In response to the "who benefits" question, it appears as though White students benefit in terms of intellectual and cognitive development, perhaps to the detriment of African American students.

The norms that accompany the American postsecondary experience were created in ways to privilege Whites. What educators need to address is how these norms are being sustained and reproduced through existing policy and practice. Evidence from this volume suggests that disrupting norms may require allocating more resources to faculty development centers, teaching and learning centers, and academic support staff. Evidence also suggests that educators may want to encourage African American students to attend HBCUs or other institutions that enroll high-achieving African American students. Of course, the notion of 'high achieving' also deserves serious consideration, especially in light of the voluminous research that critically questions traditional collegiate success metrics.

Latino/as. The weight of the evidence suggests is a gap between Latino/a and White cognitive achievement. Compared to White students' cognitive and intellectual development, Latino/a students were disadvantaged by .06 of a standard deviation from the beginning to end of college, a 2.4 percentile point disadvantage.

Although initial differences in cognitive and intellectual measures for Latino/a and White students were reported, evidence showed that certain characteristics and college experiences helped reduce the gap to nonsignificance. Latino/a students make more cognitive gains at institutions that enroll high-achieving Latino/a students and at residential colleges, but fewer gains at colleges in rural when compared to suburban areas. Supporting some of these results, certain college experiences also help Latino/a students develop along cognitive and intellectual lines. These experiences included increased research-related faculty contact, increased course-related faculty contact, increased informal interactions with diverse peers, and increased participation in classroom diversity courses.

Students of Color. The relationship between cognitive development and collegiate experiences differ for students of color when compared to their White peers. Interestingly, the weight of the evidence suggests that participating in diversity-related course experiences has little to no net benefit in helping students of color make cognitive and intellectual gains. Alternatively, when compared to White students, cognitive and intellectual growth among students of color was related to faculty's use of collaborative learning practices in the classroom, not participating in liberal arts courses, and living off campus.

Whites. A series of studies examined how certain experiences influenced cognitive development for White students when compared to students who self-identified with another race. By way of cognitive and intellectual development, the weight of the evidence suggested that White students disproportionally benefited from diversity experiences, including informal diverse peer interactions, taking diversity courses, and interactional diversity. Other experiences related to White students' cognitive and intellectual growth included increased research-related contact with faculty. Who are diversity-related experiences designed to benefit? If diversity experiences are not equally benefiting all students, then what types of learning environments would? Should and can benefiting all students equally be a goal of any educational experience? Questions will become increasingly important to answer as policymakers and practitioners sustain and recast arguments for the important role that structural diversity plays in shaping the collegiate educational environment.

Gender. The weight of the evidence showed that the relationship between college and its effects on students' cognitive and intellectual growth was gendered. In one examination of the effects of honors program participation on students' first-year cognitive outcomes it was found that men who participated in the honors program were advantaged by .16 of a standard deviation on a composite cognitive measure than men not involved in an honors program, after controlling for a host of relevant covariates. Specifically, when compared to the cognitive and intellectual gains reported by women, the same gains for men were related to increased general faculty support and a greater number of hours spent studying.

Certain experiences were specifically related to the intellectual and cognitive development of women, when compared with men. These included more instances of challenging a professor's ideas in class and being in more cooperative learning environments.

Socioeconomic Status. The weight of the evidence suggests that the relationship between certain educational experiences and cognitive and intellectual development varies based on an individual's socioeconomic status. Curricular benefits extended to students from higher socioeconomic backgrounds, as participation in an honors program spurred the cognitive gains of these students by .12 of a standard deviation or 4.7 percentile points more than did participation in the same program for students from lower socioeconomic backgrounds. Clearly educators need to be attentive to creating experiences that benefit the economically underprivileged. Only through careful studies of conditional effects can we hope to grasp the level of additive advantage we continue to offer our wealthiest students.

First-Generation Status. New to the research reviewed in this volume were studies specifically designed to examine college and its impact on cognitive and intellectual development and how this relationship varied by first-generation college student status. The weight of the evidence suggests that this group, first-generation college students, is one that has its own distinctive perspective on the postsecondary experience, with many relationships conditioned based on first-generation status. When compared to students whose parents had at least some college, first-generation students' cognitive and intellectual gains were related to (1) attending a two-year institution, (2) higher cumulative grades, (3) more extracurricular engagement, (4) fewer number of hours of work per week, (5) more number of nonassigned books read, (6) Greek affiliation, and (7) volunteer participation.

Precollege Preparedness and Ability. The evidence suggests that lower-ability students gain more from many of the practices well documented for their effects on helping students make cognitive gains. On the curricular front, educators should be aware that diversity course taking, increased faculty-student interactions, more time spent preparing for class, and more time reading and writing seemed to influence the cognitive development of low-ability students when compared to their high-ability peers. In addition, it appears as though peer support resonates strongly with low-ability students; the weight of the evidence suggests that quality of peer support, including diverse peer interactions, exerts influence over their cognitive gains.

Athletic Profile Status. New to the research published since 2005 was emerging literature on the profile of a particular sport and how that profile explains the relationship between college-going and cognitive and intellectual development. In short, academic activities like writing papers and completing reading assignments had more profound effects on the cognitive and intellectual development of athletes in low-profile sports than in high-profile sports.

Long-Term Effects of College

Consistent with previous efforts, this review found that alumni regarded college as having had an impact on their cognitive development and thinking skills. Once again it appears that although college promoted intellectual and cognitive development, continued gains were contingent on the levels of intellectual stimulation and challenge after college.

CHAPTER CONCLUSION

Central to the higher education learning enterprise is the idea that participation in postsecondary education should engender intellectual and cognitive growth. Given the importance of this fundamental relationship, many higher education stakeholders, ranging from policymakers to graduates, feel particularly vested in understanding if college-going leads to learning, which is often closely identified with cognitive and intellectual gain. This chapter provides compelling evidence that participation in postsecondary education matters with regard to helping students make such gains.

As part of the responsibility for providing robust evidence for making such claims, learning must be considered as more than content mastery and cognitive and intellectual growth, but as a mosaic comprising many learning dimensions, including psychosocial change, the subject of the next chapter. Only when we begin to understand learning as a complex process will we be able to speak to all the potential higher education brings its citizenry.

Notes

1. It is important to highlight that personal epistemology focuses on how people think about complex problems, not what they think about those problems. For cognitive and educational psychologists studying personal epistemology, there are no right or wrong answers to any given problem; what emerges as critical is how an individual reasons when faced with a problem or question. Persons with more complex thinking on a topic often hold the same position as another person with less advanced thinking, but the rationale behind their position is much more developed. See King and Kitchener (1994) for more on these distinctions.

2. Scores of scholarly approaches spanning many disciplines have been used to understand cognition (e.g., its development, potential for measurement). From these disciplines, we have learned much about cognitive development and its relationship to the need for cognition, higher-order thinking skills, self-regulatory behaviors, intellectual development, academic and social development, and many more. With each of these ideas comes nuanced and important theoretical distinction between what and how cognition is studied. A thorough review of all of these ideas extends beyond the purview of this review.

CHAPTER FOUR

Psychosocial Change

The purpose of a college education is multifaceted. To some, the goals are instrumental in nature and do not extend far beyond acquiring the skills necessary to successfully enter the workforce and attain economic stability. To others, a college education is a purely academic endeavor, a stepping-stone on the way to mastering disciplinary knowledge, earning top grades, and perhaps seeking a graduate-level degree. Regardless of the individual student's path or purpose, we contend that the traditional outcomes of college—knowledge acquisition, academic achievement, degree attainment, and occupational success—are a central part of a college education but do not entirely fulfill what it means to be an educated person. In our view, a liberal education demands more: growth in self-understanding; development of personal, intellectual, cultural, and social interests; critical reflection on one's worldview, attitudes, and values; cultivation of moral and ethical standards; and preparation for global citizenship in a diverse nation and world. Recognizing the merit in these holistic aims, we devote this and the next two chapters to reviewing what we have learned at the beginning of a new century about the innumerable ways in which college experiences shape psychosocial development, attitudes and values, and moral reasoning.

The review of psychosocial development—in accordance with the two previous volumes (Pascarella & Terenzini, 1991, 2005)—is based on change in the "self system," a notion coined by Inkeles (1966) that covers a significant body of research aligned with identity formation and development of multiple social identities. In addition to the self system, Inkeles (1966) described relational systems—essentially how individuals understand and engage other people, conditions, and institutions in the world around them. Within the relational dimension are students' connections to peers; orientations to authority figures; and relationships to close friends, partners, and others. A number of psychosocial categories extend from this system: perceptions of the academic and social self relative to peers, autonomy and independence, personal adjustment and psychological well-being, and general personal development.

In an effort to feature research attentive to self and relational systems, this chapter is organized around seven broad topics: identity development (including development in four specific domains: racial and ethnic identity; gender identity; gay, lesbian, and bisexual identity; religious and spiritual identity); academic self-concept; social self-concept and interpersonal relationships; leadership skills; autonomy, independence, locus of control, and self-efficacy; psychological well-being; and general personal development. Unlike the previous volumes, we have grouped social self-concept with interpersonal relations because most of the literature in this area pertains to how adept students believe themselves to be as they interact with others. Studies of self-esteem, given their focus on students' sense of worth, are included with the empirical literature that has emerged in the last 10 years around psychological well-being. In many studies, "personal and social development" is a construct that reflects how well students understand themselves and others. Because this construct transcends many categories, we include these studies within our discussion of general personal development. We begin with a brief review of relevant theory to ground the discussion of psychosocial change and the impact of collegiate experiences on development along myriad dimensions.

THEORETICAL OVERVIEW

Foundational Theories

Many psychosocial development theories have their roots in the classic work of Erik Erikson (1959, 1963, 1968), who characterized successive stages through which individuals pass as they undergo age-related biological and psychological changes. According to Erikson, when individual changes converge with demands in the sociocultural environment, particular challenges—or "crises"—confront the individual and inspire a period of decision making from among available alternatives. *Identity versus identity confusion*, the fifth stage in Erikson's theory, was deemed as the foremost developmental task of traditional-age college students. As such, many psychosocial theories framing studies of college impact are attuned to issues of identity formation, including particular domains of identity such as race, gender, and sexuality.

Another abiding theoretical influence that maintains a visible presence in many identity-related studies of college students is Marcia's (1966, 1980) typological portrayal of four distinct identity statuses. Marcia delineated two critical tasks in identity formation. The first task, exploration, entails active consideration and making choices about possible courses of action. The second task, commitment, involves investing in the chosen path across occupational, political, religious, and sexual domains. Marcia proposed that "identity-diffused" individuals are neither in a period of exploration nor have they made commitments, and "foreclosed" individuals establish commitment without undergoing a period of exploration. Those in "moratorium" are actively exploring identity alternatives, while "identity-achieved" individuals satisfactorily explored options prior to formulating commitments. Marcia acknowledged that identity achievement is not necessarily static; individuals can cycle through periods of exploration and commitment throughout the life span.

The pioneering student development theory contributions of Chickering (1969) and Chickering and Reisser (1993) have been at the heart of many studies of psychosocial change. The seven vectors—achieving competence, managing emotions, moving through autonomy to independence, developing mature interpersonal relationships, establishing identity, developing purpose, and developing integrity—proposed by Chickering (1969) and refined by Chickering and Reisser (1993) were not intended as lockstep sequential stages, but as spiraling steps toward greater complexity in identity, relationships, beliefs, and values. Importantly, the vectors present a holistic vision of student development, blending cognitive and affective tasks and individuation and community with others.

Self-authorship theory, a pivotal holistic framework from the cognitive-structural family of theories, was foundational to plentiful studies throughout the 2000s, particularly those addressing issues of authority dependence, autonomy, and internality.[1] The notion of "self-authorship" stems from Kegan's (1982, 1994) five "orders of consciousness," which represent phases that individuals negotiate over their life span as they make sense of themselves, their relationships with others, and the world around them. Kegan's fourth order of consciousness, self-authorship, signifies a shift from reliance on external to internal sources of influence and meaning making. Epistemological ("How do I know?"), intrapersonal ("Who am I?"), and interpersonal ("How do I relate to others?") dimensions undergo change as individuals self-author and ultimately begin to coordinate their beliefs, values, identity, and relationships (Baxter Magolda, 2001, 2008, 2009; Kegan, 1982, 1994).

Baxter Magolda (2001, 2009) traced the self-authorship journeys of 80 traditional-age college students from 1986 to 1989 and continued to follow 30 of the individuals for 27 years, into their mid-forties. Based on longitudinal evidence, she ascertained three meaning-making structures that become cognitively, intrapersonally, and interpersonally more complex from one to the next. The first structure is marked by reliance on *external authorities* who prescribe formulas for knowing and relating that individuals follow uncritically. Eventually individuals recognize the shortcomings of formula following, begin to question authorities, and enter the second meaning-making structure, the *crossroads*. In the crossroads, individuals wrestle with conflicts between external voices and the internal voice emerging within. The third meaning-making structure on the other side of the crossroads is self-authorship—the point at which individuals internally direct their beliefs, sense of self, and relationships with others. Baxter Magolda, King, Taylor, and Wakefield (2012) depicted 10 nuanced positions, demonstrating that there are in fact differing levels within each meaning-making structure. Furthermore, Baxter Magolda's (2008, 2009) follow-up with study participants later in life yielded additional insight about three elements of self-authorship as individuals age. We discuss these elements in greater depth in the section of this chapter on long-term effects.

The concept of psychosocial identity development has evolved over time such that phenomena that were once principally studied from the lens of psychology are now observed from sociological frames as well (Jones & Abes, 2013). Sociological perspectives are, by and large, based on the proposition that college is not merely an individual experience but an inherently social process that extends beyond psychological and cognitive changes (Kaufman, 2014). Indeed, developmental models focused exclusively on the individual's internal world fall short of elucidating the role of external factors provoking change. In the end, "relying solely on developmental or sociological models may lead to misstatements concerning the origins of student change and growth" (Pascarella & Terenzini, 2005, p. 52).

A core sociological principle is the notion of symbolic interactionism (see Blumer, 1969; Charon, 2009). According to Blumer (1969), the behaviors of people involve an interpretive process in which meanings emerge from social interactions. Bringing this concept into the student identity sphere, Kaufman (2014) distinguishes college students' personal and social identities, noting, "It is one thing to feel that you are a friendly or hard-working college student, but unless others ascribe or reflect this identity back to you it is unlikely that your self-avowals will go very far" (p. 37). Sociological frameworks also prove useful for understanding how students connect to and identify with social groups (Torres, Jones, & Renn, 2009). In short, "Sociological approaches to identity help to explain, from a broader perspective than does psychology, the forces that act on individuals as they make their way into adulthood and form self-concepts of, allegiances to, and aspirations toward various identities" (Torres et al., 2009, p. 579). Many of the theories described in this chapter have an individual developmental emphasis, but also reflect an amalgam of paradigmatic assumptions that draw from both psychological and sociological roots.

Dimension-Specific Theories

Against the backdrop of classic psychological and sociological frameworks, a variety of theory bases are useful for conceptualizing how students develop specific social identities (related to race, gender, sexuality, and faith), contend with the intersections among multiple identities, develop as citizens who contribute to their communities, and cultivate a sense of well-being in the midst of developmental and life challenges. Given that most studies fall into one or more of these categories, we review theory pertinent to each.

Racial/Ethnic Identity Theories. Multiple models depicting racial and ethnic identity development informed empirical investigations through the 2000s.

One of the foundational frameworks, Cross's (1991, 1995) Model of Nigrescence, portrayed five stages of Black identity development to explain "how assimilated Black adults, as well as deracinated, deculturalized or miseducated Black adults are transformed by a series of circumstances and events into persons who are more Black or Afrocentrically aligned" (Cross, 1991, p. 190). The first stage, *preencounter*, is marked by a Eurocentric worldview and potentially anti-Black attitudes among individuals for whom Black identity lacks salience or is stigmatizing. In the subsequent stage, *encounter*, a significant event or series of events culminates in awareness of racial realities, an array of felt emotions, and reconsideration of preencounter beliefs. *Immersion-emersion*, the third stage, is denoted by strongly identifying with and solely valuing Blackness and eventually shifting toward more moderated beliefs and emotions that reflect greater complexity and balance. During the fourth stage, *internalization*, individuals achieve greater stability and serenity as they adopt personally relevant understandings of Blackness and exhibit openness in reconstructed relationships with people of other races and cultures. Finally, stage 5, *internalization-commitment*, involves acting on commitments in an effort to address the challenges faced by Blacks and other racial/ethnic communities. In sum, achieving nigrescence corresponds to living in accordance with one's values and internalized Black identity.

Helms (1995) constructed a racial identity model applicable to multiple groups—Latinos/as, Asians, Native Americans, and African Americans—with six statuses that parallel Cross's stages. *Conformity* is characterized by assimilation to White norms and disregard for one's racial identity and community. *Dissonance* arises as individuals are exposed to new ideas or circumstances that challenge and call into question conformist beliefs. In the *immersion* period, individuals reject Whiteness and idealize their own racial group as they learn about and strive to cultivate a transformed racial identity. *Emersion* entails committing to the values, beliefs, and actions of one's racial group and forging an emotional connection to the community. Individuals reinforce their commitments during *internalization*, and they become adept at critically reflecting on their own racial group in addition to the dominant group. Finally, *integrative awareness* corresponds to presenting a positive racial identity and resisting undermining forces in the environment. Helms (1990) also conceptualized a six-status White racial identity model to elucidate the process of abandoning racism (through *contact*, *disintegration*, and *reintegration*) and subsequently defining a nonracist White identity (involving *pseudo-independence*, *immersion/emersion*, and *autonomy*).

Other studies that we review in this chapter adopted Phinney's (1989, 1992, 1993) model of ethnic identity development. Resonant with Erikson's and particularly Marcia's earlier work, Phinney observed that ethnic identity formation is a function of identity exploration—learning about the history and traditions of the ethnic group—and identity commitment—achieving a secure sense of identification with the ethnic group (see also Phinney & Ong, 2007). Three stages illustrate the evolution of ethnic identity. At the *diffusion-foreclosure* stage, the individual has generally no interest in ethnicity and has forged an identity based on external sources of influence, such as family members or dominant (often negative) societal views. *Moratorium*, the second stage, entails a growing consciousness (and consequently charged emotions) and ethnic identity search and exploration to understand the meaning of one's ethnic identity and membership within the group. Finally, at the *identity-achievement* stage, the individual moves beyond the dissonance of the second stage, finds a sense of peace, and establishes a personal ethnic identity and ethnic group commitments.

Multiracial Identity Theories. By the 2000s, the theoretical landscape addressing racial and ethnic identities had expanded tremendously to include frameworks attuned to the identity development of multiracial people (see Kilson, 2001; Poston, 1990; Rockquemore & Brunsma, 2002; Root, 1990; Wallace, 2001, 2003; Wijeyesinghe & Jackson, 2001). Renn (2000, 2003, 2004, 2008) drew on these theory bases, ecological perspectives, and data from 56 students attending six institutions to bring attention to five nonlinear identity patterns germane to the lives of mixed-race college students.

Students adopting the first pattern hold a *monoracial identity* and choose to identify with one heritage over the others. The second pattern, holding *multiple monoracial identities*, involves shifting allegiances to different heritage groups depending on situational factors. Students assume a *multiracial identity*, equivalent to identification with any other racial group, in conjunction with the third pattern. Students exhibiting the fourth pattern take on an *extraracial identity* as they deconstruct race and refuse to identify with any recognized racial category. Finally, the fifth pattern stresses holding a *situational identity*, in which the individual's racial identity is stable but fluidly expressed such that some identity elements are more apparent than others in certain contexts.

Renn's use of human ecology frameworks (e.g., Bronfenbrenner, 1979, 1993) to understand how multiracial identities evolve marks another significant contribution to the student development theory base. Ecological lenses enable an intricate exploration of "the influences of individuals (person), their interactions with the environment and the responses they provoke from the environment (process), their interactions within immediate settings (context), and changing sociocultural influences on development (time)" (Renn, 2003, p. 387). Moreover, in ascertaining multiple layers of influence—from the most immediate microsystems of classes and friendship groups to the most distal macrosystems consisting of cultural norms and historical events—Renn maximized ecological frameworks to portray nuanced identity pathways of mixed-race college students. Later in the chapter, we highlight the influential people and contexts that shaped identity formation among these students.

Gender Identity Theories. Theoretical and empirical advances pertaining to gender identity development among women were sparse through the 2000s, resulting in few additions to Josselson's (1987, 1996) landmark study of women's identity formation during and subsequent to the college years and

Baxter Magolda's (1992) study of gendered patterns in students' ways of knowing and intellectual development. The few studies conducted did not generally consider change over the college years or college effects. Instead, most studies were limited to exploring associations between gender identity and measures of well-being (Constantine & Watt, 2002; Gillen & Lefkowitz, 2006; Leavy, Gnong, & Ross, 2009; Vaccaro, 2011; Watt, 2006), academic behaviors (Marrs, Sigler, & Brammer, 2012), and racial identity (Vaccaro, 2011; Watt, 2006; Winkle-Wagner, 2009).

Other research depicted the identity challenges of women students, particularly as they pertained to issues of authority, autonomy, connection, voice, and sense of competence. Among the challenges, Sengupta and Upton (2011) noted interpersonal (e.g., experiences of disconnection, lack of positive affirmation from others, frustration with authorities, and problems with developing relationships), intrapersonal uncertainties (doubting one's own ability to give and receive knowledge), and practical realities involving financial struggles.

With the exception of a few studies that considered gender role attitudes (see summaries of Bryant, 2003, and Sax, 2008, in Chapter 5), we identified no research in the 2000s that examined college effects on feminist identity development. Some scholars reflected on theories of feminist identity constructed in the 1980s (see Moradi, Subich, & Phillips, 2002) and the relationship between feminist identities and measures of well-being (see Saunders & Kashubeck-West, 2006).

There was a surge of research in the 2000s on masculine gender identities among college men (Davis, 2002; Edwards & Jones, 2009; Harper & Harris, 2010; Harris, 2008, 2010; Harris & Harper, 2008, 2014; Harris & Struve, 2009; Laker & Davis, 2011; Peralta, 2007, Steinfeldt, Steinfeldt, England, & Speight, 2009; Steinfeldt & Steinfeldt, 2012), including a number of studies that explored this phenomenon among men of color (Baber, Aronson, & Melton, 2005; Brown, 2005; Dancy, 2012; Ford, 2011; Harper, 2004; Harris, Palmer, & Struve, 2011; Jackson & Wingfield, 2013; Shek & McEwen, 2012; Strayhorn & Tillman-Kelly, 2013; Tatum & Charlton, 2008).[2] This line of scholarship has pointed to intersectional issues in men's lives by integrating issues surrounding masculinities with race, sexuality, class, disability identity, and other identity dimensions (see the edited works of Harper & Harris, 2010, and Laker & Davis, 2011). Harris and Barone (2011) further observed that sustained misconceptions abound regarding the problems facing men in higher education (e.g., underachievement, violence, homophobia) and advocated for an anti-deficit framework (see Harper, 2004, 2006) "to learn how men who transcend hegemonic masculinity . . . make the most of their college experience (in the face of social forces and pressures that encourage them to do otherwise)" (p. 60).

With a couple of exceptions (e.g., Harper, Harris, & Mmeje, 2005; Edwards & Jones, 2009), the empirical evidence concerning masculinities outpaced theoretical developments. Accordingly, Harris (2010) noted,

> Models that seek to explain college men's gender identity development are largely absent in the published college student development

research. Even recent studies . . . focus primarily on describing gender-related conflicts and challenges among college men rather than a process of masculine identity development in college (p. 298).

Harris (2010) proposed a conceptual model detailing contextual influences—precollege gender socialization, aspects of the campus culture, campus and academic involvement, and interactions with male peer group interactions—that challenged or reinforced men's notions of masculinity.

Although more research on transgender students emerged in the 2000s relative to earlier decades, gender identity development tended not to be the focus. Studies were attuned to transgender students' needs on campus (Beemyn, 2012) and differences in perceptions, engagement, and outcomes for transgender students compared to their cisgender peers (Dugan, Kusel, & Simounet, 2012) rather than college impact. Some theoretical work exists regarding transgender identity development among young adults (see Pollock & Eyre, 2012), but we were unable to identify empirical studies or theoretical accounts in the higher education context exploring the impact of college on students' transgender identities.

Lesbian, Gay, and Bisexual Identity Theories. Over the last decade, research on college students' sexual identities has undergone considerable theoretical advances and shed new light on how students of diverse sexualities experience their campuses. Much of this work builds on the foundational theories of Cass (1979, 1984) and D'Augelli (1994). Cass proposed a six-stage model reflecting the transition from *unexamined heterosexuality* through stages of *identity comparison* (consideration of a gay or lesbian identity), *tolerance* (commitment to a gay or lesbian identity and exploration of community), *acceptance* (validation from and preference for gay and lesbian community), *pride* (coming out and rejecting of heterosexism), and *synthesis* (greater trust of supportive heterosexuals and congruence between personal and public identities). Subsequent theoretical developments led to D'Augelli's model (1994), which portrayed lesbian, gay, and bisexual (LGB) development as malleable and socially constructed, unfolding in six identity processes: exiting heterosexual identity, cultivating an internalized and personal LGB identity status, developing an LGB social identity in the context of a supportive network, coming out to parents and family members, establishing intimacy as an LGB person, and engaging in social and political action in collaboration with the LGB community.

Queer theory has a visible presence in contemporary studies of sexuality. As a poststructural perspective, queer theory "examines, challenges, and deconstructs social norms attached to gender and sexuality" (Jones & Abes, 2013, p. 197). Moreover, queer theory addresses the interplay between social identities and context; involves resisting heteronormative oppression; and emphasizes intersectionality among social identities, performativity (ongoing and fluid expression of identities), and becoming (continuous identity evolution without a fixed end point; Jones & Abes, 2013).

Although important advances have been made theoretically and empirically, studies have tended not to emphasize the direct impact of college on LGB identity development. In our view, post-positivist and linear assessments of identity formation that trace initial LGB identity at the beginning of college through the college years in an effort to find clear evidence of "developed" LGB identity outcomes are inconsistent with current theoretical perspectives—and, we surmise, with students' lived experiences. In subsequent sections, we review research during the 2000s that attended to college engagement, meaning making, and intersectional phenomena to reflect LGB students' lives in a way that measurement of lockstep changes in identity categories cannot. Much of this work is delineated in later sections on multiple identities, intersectionality, and between-college effects.

Spirituality and Faith Development Theories. Classic theories of faith development have informed studies of college students' spirituality and religiosity over the last decade. Fowler (1981) envisioned a stage model of faith development spanning from infancy to adulthood. He defined *faith* as "the most fundamental category in the human quest for relation to transcendence" (p. 9) and represented its relational, affective, and cognitive facets, unfolding with greater complexity, across the sequence of stages. His notion of *individuative-reflective faith*, stage 4, typified the processes of critically reflecting on beliefs and moving away from authority dependence toward independent constructions of faith characteristic of traditional-age college students.

Parks (2000) defined *faith* "as the activity of seeking and discovering meaning in the most comprehensive dimensions of our experience" (p. 7). She balanced cognitive and affective domains in her theory and accounted for the effects of interpersonal, social, and cultural influences on faith development. Parks proposed four stages—*adolescent/conventional*, *young adult*, *tested adult*, and *mature adult*—each comprising three forms that change from stage to stage. Forms of knowing emphasize the cognitive-structural aspects of faith development; forms of dependence have to do with the ways in which relationships and feelings about authority influence faith; and forms of community represent interpersonal connections and social or cultural contexts for faith development.

Recent developments in research and theory have stressed the breadth of religious and worldview diversity among college students and are more critical of earlier theories that have an embedded Christian bias (Siner, 2015). For example, Small's (2011) work on faith frames shares the narratives of atheists, Muslims, Jews, and Christians, showcasing the issues, beliefs, and experiences central and unique to each frame. Others have critiqued forms of religious and Christian privilege evident in higher education (see Goodman & Mueller, 2009; Seifert, 2007) with arguments that have served as the backdrop for much of the research detailing the nuanced experiences of religious minority and nonreligious students described throughout this chapter.

Multiple Identities, Intersectionality, and Critical Lenses. Concerted efforts to advance theory through the 2000s have given way to new lenses for understanding students' multiple identities and the intersections among them. Jones and McEwen (2000) used a grounded theory approach and interview data from 10 female participants to propose their Model of Multiple Dimensions of Identity, which "depicts a core sense of self or one's personal identity. Intersecting circles surrounding the core identity represent significant identity dimensions (e.g., race, sexual orientation, and religion) and contextual influences (e.g., family background and life experiences)" (p. 401).

Several years later Abes and Jones (2004) studied the multiple identity dimensions of 10 lesbian women to explicate how sexuality interfaced with other social identities. As the narratives of the women unfolded in interviews, the authors ascertained that lesbian identity construction entailed cognitive, intrapersonal, and interpersonal processes, akin to Baxter Magolda's (2001, 2008, 2009) notions of self-authorship. Further, the content of the women's lesbian identities depended on the ways in which their meaning-making structures (i.e., how reliant the women were on external formulas versus the internal voice) filtered contextual influences such as social norms, stereotypes, family background, and peer culture. Meaning-making structures ranged from externally oriented ("formulaic") to tentatively internal ("transitional") to internally defined ("foundational"). As meaning making became increasingly complex, the women were able to more judiciously filter contextual influences on their sexuality and its relationship to other social identity dimensions.

In light of Abes and Jones's (2004) findings, Abes, Jones, and McEwen (2007) proposed a Reconceptualized Model of Multiple Dimensions of Identity that included a meaning-making filter. The filter was depicted visually between contextual influences (i.e., peers, family, norms, stereotypes, sociopolitical conditions) and self-perceptions of multiple identity dimensions (i.e., gender, race, class, religion, and sexual orientation). Individuals exhibiting formulaic meaning-making capacity tend to have a more porous filter; contextual influences make a significant impression on their perceptions of self. However, the filter is typically much less permeable among those who engage in foundational (i.e., self-authored) meaning making; contextual factors are less influential in shaping intersections among multiple identity dimensions. The addition of meaning-making capacity to the model provided a way to conceptualize "not only *what* relationships students perceive among their personal and social identities, but also *how* they come to perceive them as they do" (Abes et al., 2007, p. 13).

Reliance on intersectional frameworks to study college students' identities became more prevalent through the 2000s.[3] Intersectionality is concerned with not only the relationships among multiple identities, but also with how those identities are situated and shaped within larger social structures of power, privilege, and oppression (Strayhorn, 2013; Torres et al., 2009). Strayhorn (2013) explained, "Intersectionality advances a more poignant and complex narrative that rejects simple summations or serial recollections of what it is like to be *Black*, then *lesbian*, then *woman*, in favor of thick, rich descriptions (or robust estimates) of multiple constructed realities" (p. 7). Torres and colleagues (2009) contended that intersectionality is an apt lens for studying identity development and is advantageous practically in that it brings "a focus on identity (e.g., dynamics of race, class, gender) to a full range of questions relevant to student development, such as retention, student involvement, campus community, and equity" (p. 588).

We came across many studies in our review in which both qualitative and quantitative researchers employed an array of intersectional lenses in their scholarship. Often scholars connected intersectionality to other theoretical perspectives, including queer theory (which entails deconstructing social norms related to gender and sexuality; Jones & Abes, 2013), critical race theory (which emphasizes race and racism as fundamental dimensions of identity and as intersecting with other social identities; Jones & Abes, 2013), and quantitative criticalism (which involves using data to advance models attuned to nuanced experiences of underrepresented groups, between- and within-group differences, and social and educational inequities; Stage, 2007).

Leadership Identity Theories. Studies of leadership identity and skill development during the 2000s primarily referenced the Social Change Model of Leadership (Higher Education Research Institute, 1996) and the Leadership Identity Development Model of Komives and colleagues (see Komives, Longerbeam, Owen, Mainella, & Osteen, 2006; Komives, Owen, Longerbeam, Mainella, & Osteen; 2005). Foundational to socially responsible leadership are seven core values. As Dugan and Komives (2010) described, "These values operate at the individual level (consciousness of self, congruence, commitment), the group level (collaboration, common purpose, controversy with civility), and the societal level (citizenship). Collectively, they contribute to an eighth leadership value of change for the common good" (pp. 526–527).

Komives and colleagues' Leadership Identity Development Model portrays leadership identity evolving across six successive stages. In the first stage, *awareness*, individuals begin to recognize that leadership is occurring elsewhere, and they tend to associate leadership with historical, national, and authority figures. Stage 2, *exploration/engagement*, is characterized by peer interactions, friendship development in group settings, and opportunities to seek out interests. In the *leader identified* phase, stage 3, individuals assume a leader-centric view and believe leaders necessarily hold formal positions. As part of stage 4, *leader differentiated*, individuals become open to the notion that non-positional group members can also be leaders and come to see leaders as facilitators of group processes as well as community builders. Once in the *generativity* period, stage 5, individuals have the "ability to look beyond themselves and express a passion for their commitments and care for the welfare of others (Komives et al., 2006, p. 411). Finally, at stage 6, *integration/synthesis*, individuals express confidence in their leadership across varied contexts, recognize they can lead without holding a positional leadership role, are open to continual growth as a leader, and are committed to congruence between their values and actions.

Psychological Well-Being and Thriving. Heightened attention to students' emotional, social, and physical wellness was apparent in the student development literature through the 2000s. Appearing in many of these studies was Ryff's (1989) conception of psychological well-being (PWB), which includes six dimensions: functioning autonomously and making decisions, mastering one's environment, seeking opportunities for personal growth, maintaining positive relations with others, having a sense of life purpose, and engaging in self-acceptance and positive thinking. Bowman (2010d) explained that PWB is theoretically rooted in the classic works of Maslow (self-actualization), Erikson (psychosocial development), and Jung (individuation) and is distinct from other common indicators often associated with wellness, such as self-esteem, life satisfaction, happiness, and locus of control.

Another concept, *thriving*, emerged in the student development literature in the 2000s. Schreiner (2010a) defined thriving as

> the experiences of college students who are fully engaged intellectually, socially, and emotionally. Thriving college students not only are academically successful, they also experience a sense of community and a level of psychological well-being that contributes to their persistence to graduation and allows them to gain maximum benefit from being in college (p. 4).

Thriving is multifaceted and consists of five dimensions: engaged learning, academic determination, positive perspective, diverse citizenship, and social connectedness (Schreiner, 2010a, 2010b, 2010c, 2013, 2014).

As evidenced even in this brief review, the basis for understanding college students' psychosocial change is theoretically rich and ever evolving. The theory-based literature is substantial; we encourage readers interested in deepening their knowledge to consult the work of individual theorists, as well as the detailed reviews provided elsewhere (e.g., Evans, Forney, Guido, Patton, & Renn, 2010; Jones & Abes, 2013) and in the previous volumes (Pascarella & Terenzini, 1991, 2005).

This theoretical overview provides context for understanding how scholars have tended to conceptualize identity development and other forms of psychosocial change during college. Yet there is a crucial distinction between using theory to inform a study and actually testing theoretical conjectures empirically. For the most part, the psychosocial research we reviewed was not designed to test directly the merits of a given theory. Instead, scholars tended to use theory to develop measures and analytical models reflective of theoretical concepts. We note throughout the chapter the instances in which scholars were guided by particular theories in devising studies and collecting, analyzing, and drawing conclusions from their data.

CHANGE DURING COLLEGE

Conclusions from the 1990s

Much of the psychosocial research prior to 1990s was theoretically grounded in Eriksonian conceptions of developmental tasks through the life span, with particular emphasis on the crisis characterizing the fifth stage of identity versus identity confusion (Pascarella & Terenzini, 1991, 2005). This crisis period, signified by consideration of and decisions around possible identity commitments, was deemed central to the development of traditional-age college students. Erikson's principles prevailed in the theoretical literature in the 1990s as well—but without significant empirical advancement—and attended to identity formation in general or particular identity dimensions, such as race/ethnicity, gender, or sexual orientation.

The impact of college on racial and ethnic identity development garnered further empirical attention in the 1990s and supported earlier scholarship that was largely theoretical. Even so, studies in this domain of identity were primarily descriptive in the past decade, uncovering within- and between-group differences and correlational patterns between racial identity and psychosocial dimensions. Studies of change in racial identity status among African American students generally showed no change from the freshman to senior year.

Although the previous volumes did not report on college effects related to gender identity, Pascarella and Terenzini (2005) reviewed the small number of studies that considered gay and lesbian identity development. At the time of the previous review, some understanding of gay, lesbian, and bisexual identity formation was beginning to emerge, but many questions remained regarding whether "coming out" in college was a function of maturation or the greater degree of personal freedom and support available on campus. Other areas of inquiry left untapped concerned the unique developmental pathways potentially traversed by students identifying as lesbian, bisexual, or gay.

Prior to the 1990s, studies documented declines during college in the importance students attributed to religion. Yet the small body of research in the previous decade clarified that religious identities were generally refined during college—not necessarily abandoned—as students' faith became more complex, personally relevant, and internalized. Pascarella and Terenzini (2005) noted generalizability problems in these studies based on small samples.

Turning to self-concept, the literature base was noticeably smaller in the 1990s compared to previous decades. Inconsistent terminology made synthesis of findings somewhat challenging. Pascarella and Terenzini (2005) observed that researchers often conflated notions of "self-concept" (i.e., self-perceptions that are shaped through experience with the environment and significant others, as well as comparisons to peers) and "self-esteem" (i.e., self-evaluations to an internalized ideal, as well as one's sense of personal worth and ability). Among the many manifestations of self-concept, research in the previous decade emphasized both academic and social indicators. Student evaluations of their academic abilities became more positive over time; however, average changes were quite small and masked the shifting of individual students between categories of self-appraisal. Some students became less inclined to rate their academic abilities positively, while others became more positive. The net result of this movement was a very small self-assessed increase in academic ability. Earlier research also detected some nonlinearity in change, with declines in academic self-concept between high school and the sophomore year and recovery of confidence later in college. The reasons behind these shifts were debatable according to Pascarella and Terenzini's (1991, 2005) two earlier reviews, but may have been the result of students adjusting to a new peer group or becoming increasingly determined to succeed.

Unlike academic ability, students became less confident in their mathematical competence—although the change was quite small in magnitude and reports of average change also masked individual movement. Few studies in the 1990s examined changes in social self-concept. In general, students' perceptions of their social skills (e.g., popularity, social self-confidence) declined somewhat between high school and college but rebounded by the sophomore year, resulting in positive change. As with academic self-concept, the net change was quite small. Other research in the 1990s based on self-reported gains was inconclusive on the issue of whether students' interpersonal relationships improved and matured. The literature was somewhat clearer on the question of leadership skill development and generally showed growth, albeit modest, in leadership abilities over time.

The review of research in the past decade also examined literature depicting changes in the degree to which students believed themselves—rather than external influences—to be in control of their own lives. Pascarella and Terenzini (2005) elucidated the meanings of several terms used in the literature. Autonomy or independence is the level of freedom from others' (e.g., parents', peers', institutions') influence that students feel in choosing their attitudes, values, and behaviors. Locus of control equates to students' self-directedness and beliefs about how outcomes are determined: by external forces (e.g., others, luck, chance, fate) or individual actions. Self-efficacy (Bandura, 1994, 1997) reflects whether students believe they are capable of performing at a designated level and able to influence life events. Regarding independence, research in the 1990s demonstrated that students generally became more independent from parents during the college years, but the studies were based on small, single-institution samples. Likewise, other studies of students' autonomy, including independence from peers, suggested growth but on the basis of samples with limited generalizability. Studies in the 1990s identified increases during college in self-directedness and internal locus of control.

A few studies in the 1990s examined self-esteem, a cornerstone of psychological well-being, which reflects students' personal sense of worth and competence relative to their own internal standards. Educational attainment and self-esteem were highly correlated in studies prior to 2003—although some evidence pointed to declines in self-esteem among lower division students, likely concurrent with the initial drop in self-concept as students began college.

Regarding general personal development, the few empirical investigations in the 1990s were fairly consistent in showing positive change, but were not without methodological limitations. Many of the studies relied on students' self-reported changes, which is problematic given that students tend to believe that they have developed personally and socially during college and often overestimate growth when asked to evaluate their own progress. Studies were also limited by survey questions asking students to compare themselves to the peer group. Peer group comparisons are a moving target because of compositional changes over the years as students withdraw and leave behind increasingly competent peers. Pascarella and Terenzini (2005) estimated first- to senior-year gains in self-understanding, a measure of personal development, at .17 of a standard deviation. Studies tended to depict dips in first-year students' self-understanding but noted that gains in subsequent years compensated for initial declines.

Evidence from the 2000s

In addition to limited evidence regarding general identity shifts during college, scholars in the 2000s brought to light changes in racial/ethnic, religious, and spiritual identities and attended to other psychosocial dimensions, such as academic self-concept, social self-concept, and interpersonal relationships; leadership skills; autonomy, independence, locus of control, and self-efficacy; and psychological well-being.

Identity Development. Most of the advances in research on psychosocial identity development through the 2000s concerned specific identity dimensions rather than general measures of identity formation. A series of studies conducted by Luyckx and colleagues (Luyckx, Goossens, Soenens, & Beyers, 2005; Luyckx, Goossens, & Soenens, 2006; Luyckx, Klimstra, Schwartz, & Duriez, 2013) with samples of college students in Belgium is the exception. The longitudinal studies were based in Marcia's (1966) foundational notions of exploration (questioning various identity options) and commitment (forging convictions and beliefs), but with the added theoretical assertion that both processes cannot be construed as end points. The dual-cycle model of identity formation proposed by Luyckx and colleagues accounts for Marcia's classical paradigm of commitment formation, in which young adults explore a breadth of identity alternatives and form initial commitments. The second cycle, though, entails evaluating commitments through a subsequent period of in-depth exploration and identification with the commitments one has made (Luyckx et al., 2005). The dual-cycle model casts commitment formation as an iterative process through which young adults can develop further insight into commitments as they continue to explore. In the event the commitments established are not satisfying, "the process possibly cycles back to a renewed broad exploration of other possible commitments" (Luyckx et al., 2006, p. 367).

Upon assessing 400 students across four time points in the first two years of college, Luyckx et al. (2006) observed positive gains, on average, in three of the four identity dimensions (exploration in breadth, commitment making, and exploration in depth), but overall declines (and considerable fluctuations between time points) in identification with commitment. Explaining the findings, Luyckx et al. (2006) concluded, "Fluctuations could very well be an important mechanism inherent in commitment evaluation. It could be precisely this fluctuation that constitutes the outcome of a continuous, iterative evaluative process" (p. 377).

A subsequent three-wave longitudinal study of 456 college students conducted by Luyckx et al. (2013) identified somewhat different trajectories, with declines in commitment making and both exploration categories and slight increases in identification with commitment over time. In addition, the researchers traced changes in another dimension, ruminative exploration (i.e., difficulties in finding satisfying answers to questions of identity), which remained stable across three time points. The differences in findings relative to Luyckx et al. (2006) may be the result of a shorter time frame (the first year of college) and smaller intervals between time points. The Luyckx et al. (2013) study may have captured nuances distinctive to the first year of college.

Other than the collection of studies generated by Luyckx and colleagues, which were longitudinal but with limited generalizability, very little research over the past 10 years has concentrated on general identity development. Yet some progress has been made in terms of characterizing developmental patterns associated with particular social identities. We found no studies of change involving gender identity or sexual orientation, but some evidence attentive to changes in racial, ethnic, and religious identities.

Racial and Ethnic Identity. A handful of studies in the 2000s that examined students' racial and ethnic identity development produced mixed results.[4] Although the studies generally involved smaller samples with limited institutional representation, most employed a longitudinal design, constituting a marked improvement over studies of racial/ethnic identity change in the 1990s. Pascarella and Terenzini (2005) identified only two studies of racial/ethnic identity change, and both utilized cross-sectional designs.

Several studies conducted during the 2000s found no evidence of maturation, revealing nonsignificant differences in identity processes (e.g., search, commitment) between time points or significant regression from one period to the next. Fuller-Rowell, Ong, and Phinney (2013) followed a sample of 97 Latino college students attending an urban university and found no significant overall increase in ethnic identity commitment (sense of attachment and ties to one's ethnic group) across the study's eight consecutive semesters.

Tsai and Fuligni (2012) assessed students' ethnic self-labeling, as well as Phinney's (1992) notions of ethnic identity search and belonging, in a panel of students surveyed in the last year of high school and again in the second year of college. The researchers began with a sample of high school seniors attending three high schools and ultimately tracked the identity development of 458 students who matriculated to 106 two- and four-year colleges. Students' preference for pan-ethnic labels (e.g., "Asian," "Latino") or American labels (e.g., use of the term "American" with or without a pan-ethnic label) did not change significantly across two years, nor were there normative changes in students' ethnic belonging (e.g., feeling good about one's cultural or ethnic background). Despite null results on the self-labeling and belonging dimensions, the students exhibited declines in ethnic search during the first two years of college (e.g., spending time learning about one's ethnic group, including history, traditions, and customs). Affirming consistencies in identity over time, Worrell, Mendoza-Denton,

Telesford, Simmons, and Martin (2011) also reported stability in racial identity attitudes in their study of African American college students.

Another study did find evidence of ethnic identity development. In their longitudinal investigation involving 175 diverse college students attending a public university in California, Syed and Azmitia (2009) examined changes in ethnic identity exploration and commitment from the beginning of college through the senior year. Upon constructing a series of multilevel models to assess group-level and individual-level variation, the researchers identified from the unconditional models a net increase over time of one-half a standard deviation in exploration and approximately one-third a standard deviation in commitment. At each time point, ethnic minority students exhibited higher levels of exploration and commitment than White students did, but there were no significant between-group variations in the rate of change. The researchers attributed growth in exploration and commitment to consciousness-raising experiences during the transition to college.

Two other population-specific studies went beyond assessing levels of exploration, commitment, and self-labeling across time, and assigned students to identity statuses. These studies confirmed that identity statuses are quite fluid, and often (but not always) change resembles maturation. Scottham, Cooke, Sellers, and Ford (2010) examined the ethnic identity development of 204 African American students from three universities in a two-wave panel study. Over the first year of college, one-third of the sample maintained the same identity status, and approximately two-thirds of this group was classified as "achieved." The remaining two-thirds of the sample exhibited movement across the two time points. Forty percent of the group matured according to Phinney's (1992) model, while the others regressed. All told, the researchers contended,

> the fact that two thirds of the sample in the present study moved from one identity status to another within the period of study reinforces the conclusion of other studies that the freshman year of college is a period of identity transition for many ethnic minorities (p. 35).

Moreover, this study challenged the assumption of lockstep movement from earlier to later stages present in many ego identity development models. In reality, multiple pathways are possible, including progression across the stages, regression to earlier stages, and recycling (whereby individuals cycle through earlier stages across the life span).

In a similar vein, Syed, Azmita, and Phinney (2007) studied the trajectories of 128 Chicano/Latino first-year college students attending two public universities and did not find significant changes in average levels of ethnic identity exploration and commitment from the fall to spring semester. However, examining mean changes alone masked substantial individual-level change. The results of cluster analyses revealed significant shifts in identity status. As participants began college, they were equally distributed across three statuses (although slightly more students fell into the moratorium category than the achieved and unexamined categories). In the spring term, most participants were either in the moratorium or achieved statuses, with few remaining in the unexamined status. Further analysis of individual change underscored considerable variability, with some participants maintaining their status ($n = 66$), others maturing ($n = 48$), and a few regressing ($n = 14$). The researchers emphasized "the malleability of the ethnic identity statuses during this developmental period, even for those who initially were ethnic identity achieved" (pp. 170–171).

Inconsistent findings across the six longitudinal studies of ethnic identity change during the 2000s may be the consequence of nuances in the relatively small participant and institutional samples. Moreover, studies of average change in identity processes such as exploration and commitment may not have been adequately sensitive to the considerable variety in individual trajectories of change. When shifts in identity status were the focus of a given study, evidence of maturation and stability—and sometimes regression—became more readily apparent.

Religious and Spiritual Identity. Research dedicated to examining religious and spiritual change during the college years grew exponentially throughout the 2000s. Advances in this line of inquiry began with a national study of college student spirituality conducted by Astin, Astin, and Lindholm (2011) at the UCLA Higher Education Research Institute.[5] The researchers attended to the multifaceted nature of spirituality and religiosity and traced changes in 10 dimensions from students' first to third years of college. The multiyear longitudinal study involved 136 colleges and universities and more than 14,000 students. Although some dimensions reflect attitudes and values—better suited to the next chapter—others are more closely linked to identity.

Importantly, Astin and colleagues were conscientious in distinguishing spiritual development from religious change. They addressed multifaceted indicators of spirituality, including the extent to which students sought answers to existential questions (spiritual quest), maintained a sense of calm and centeredness (equanimity), exhibited openness to other religions and cultures (ecumenical worldview), and treated others with care and compassion (ethic of caring and charitable involvement). Religiousness was marked by students' commitment to religious beliefs and engagement in religious practices (e.g., attending religious services).

Overall, the evidence suggested positive spiritual change from the first year of college to the junior year. For example, students became more inclined toward high levels of "spiritual quest" (i.e., actively pursuing answers to existential questions about life's meaning and purpose) the longer they were in college. Close to one-quarter (24%) of first-year students had "high" scores on the spiritual quest measure, and the proportion of high scorers rose to one-third (33%) by the junior year. Patterns of individual change also provided evidence of spiritual growth. Approximately half of the sample maintained similar scores on spiritual quest (52%), but twice as many students became more inclined toward spiritual quest (32%) than less inclined (16%). Another key spiritual identity measure, equanimity, reflects the degree to which students were able to find meaning in times of hardship, felt at peace and centered, and felt good about the direction in which their lives were headed. Similar to spiritual quest, students in the Astin et al. (2011) study demonstrated, on average, higher levels of equanimity from the first year to the third year of college, as the percentage of high scorers increased from 19% to 23%.

One caveat to understanding spiritual gains during college is the fact that students may not perceive growth relative to their peers. In one study based on pilot data collected as part of the UCLA spirituality project, Bryant (2007) found that both men and women became increasingly prone to report "integrating spirituality into my life" is "essential" from the first to the third year of college, with a 4 percentile point increase for men and an 8 percentile point increase for women. However, when asked to rate their spirituality compared to peers, students became less inclined to rate their spirituality as "above average" or "highest 10%," as reflected by a 7 percentile point decline for men and a 10 percentile point decline for women. It may be that students became more critical and self-reflective about what constitutes spiritual development the longer they were in college.

Relative to spiritual gains, religious development was less apparent during the college years, according to studies conducted over the last decade. A study early in the 2000s that relied on self-reported changes in religious beliefs and convictions indicated that students, for the most part, perceived they had either maintained (48%) or strengthened (38%) their beliefs (Lee, 2002b). Subsequent longitudinal studies helped to provide a more robust account of patterns in students' religiosity over time, revealing a predominant pattern of religious stability. Religious commitment—a measure from the Astin et al. (2011) study that reflects the extent to which students followed religious teachings in everyday life, found religion to be personally helpful, and gained personal strength by trusting in a higher power—remained relatively steady over the first three years of college. According to Astin et al. (2011), just under one-quarter (23%) of first-year students and juniors scored highly on the measure of religious commitment. Furthermore, fewer than 30% of students changed in their level of religious commitment from the first to the third year of college, and only 1% exhibited change between the extremes (from high to low levels of commitment or vice versa). Paralleling consistency in religious commitment, very little change in religious skepticism occurred, with 19% of students exhibiting high scores on the measure in the first year of college and 20% by the third year.

Some appreciable changes in religiosity were apparent on two other measures: religious engagement and religious struggle. Students became demonstrably less religiously engaged, as depicted by substantial declines in the rate of frequent religious service attendance (44% in the last year of high school to 25% in the third year of college) and a doubled rate of nonattendance (from 20% to 38%). Declines in other forms of religious engagement (e.g., praying, reading sacred texts) were smaller, typically in the range of 2% to 4% (Astin et al., 2011). However, students reported more religious struggle, as signified by feeling unsettled about religious matters, disagreeing with family about religious matters, and feeling distant from God, the longer they were in college. The percentage of high scorers on the religious struggle measure rose by 5 percentile points (9% to 14%). A smaller longitudinal study of religious change identified similar patterns to the Astin et al. study, with students exhibiting aggregate declines in religious behaviors during college but consistency in the importance they placed on religion (Stoppa & Lefkowitz, 2010). Nonetheless, the researchers cautioned that assessments of average change might have masked individual-level change and reported that religious behaviors remained more stable at the individual level compared to belief importance, which fluctuated over time.

Academic Self-Concept, Social Self-Concept, and Interpersonal Relationships. Although numerous studies addressed academic self-confidence in the 2000s, most of the attention was placed on within-college effects rather than the degree of change. Standing as the exception, Sax (2008) conducted a national study of the gender gap in college using data derived from the Cooperative Institutional Research Program.[6] In her analysis of more than 17,000 college students, she observed that first- to fourth-year changes in self-rated academic self-concept varied depending on the measure in question. The most demonstrable shifts occurred in intellectual self-confidence and writing ability, with 11 to 16 percentile point increases in the proportion of students rating their aptitude as "above average" or "highest 10%" when asked to compare themselves to their peers. Akin to the small positive changes noted by Pascarella and Terenzini (2005) in their previous review, changes in self-rated academic ability were quite a bit smaller than intellectual and writing ability—in the range of a 2 percentile point increase. Also consistent with research through the 1990s, both women and men—but especially women—became less inclined to rate their mathematical ability as "above average" or "highest 10%," as indicated by a 3 to 6 percentile point drop. Changes in self-rated drive to achieve and competitiveness were positive but quite small, approximately 4 percentile points at most. Given that most changes in academic self-concept were rather modest, it is intriguing that students in the same cohort perceived considerable changes in their abilities when asked to report gains in the fourth year of college. More than 90% of students reported "stronger" or "much stronger" abilities in the areas of critical thinking, analytical and problem-solving skills, general knowledge, and knowledge of a particular field. Students were slightly less confident that their writing ability (81% to 82%) and reading skills (66% to 68%) were "stronger" or "much stronger." Another small-sample longitudinal study based on 147 students at three universities in England reported declines in academic self-concept in the first year of college among women but not among men (Jackson, 2003). The women's declining self-concept may have been attributable to adjustment challenges unique to the first year of college. As Pascarella and Terenzini (2005) concluded, loss of academic confidence in the first year of college is often followed by gains in subsequent years.

The findings from a qualitative investigation help to make meaning of the differential patterns of change across multiple measures of academic self-concept and the nonlinear patterns of change that may occur depending on the timing of the assessment. Kaufman and Feldman (2004) observed that although college overall improved intellectual identities within their sample of more than 80 college students, evaluations of their abilities relative to peers resulted in felt deficiencies. Students expressed concerns about not measuring up to peers in their intelligence and knowledge. The researchers questioned assumptions that intellectual identity formation moves forward in a progressive direction during college, noting that even though "college does attempt to instill in students some degree of intellectual self-worth, such outcomes are not mechanically ordered simply because the student moves from one grade level to the next" (p. 477).

Our search for studies of social self-confidence and interpersonal development produced little evidence of change in these dimensions, again because studies of this nature tended to focus on within-college effects instead. Sax (2008), however, reported considerable growth across four years of college on a measure of social self-confidence, with an estimated 16 to 17 percentile point positive shift in students rating themselves in the "highest 10%" and "above average" relative to peers. Foubert, Nixon, Sisson, and Barnes (2005) found that students became slightly more inclined toward mature interpersonal relationships during college, but their sample and effect sizes were quite small.

Leadership Skills. Two national, longitudinal studies examined shifts in leadership self-confidence and associated skills. Sax (2008) identified noteworthy growth from the first year of college to the fourth year in students' leadership orientation, with men exhibiting positive change in this domain more so than did women. Students became increasingly likely to rate themselves as "above average" or in "the highest 10%" compared to peers on public speaking ability, with an increase of 10 percentile points for women and 17 percentile points for men, and leadership ability, with an increase of 6 percentile points for women and 11 percentile points for men.

Other analyses of leadership gains were conducted using data from the Wabash National Study of Liberal Arts Education, which tracked students across the first year of college and from the first to the fourth year of college.[7] Relying on measures from the socially responsible leadership scale, Shim (2013) found positive shifts in women's growth in consciousness of self (i.e., awareness of the beliefs, values, attitudes, and emotions that motivate taking action) and change (i.e., the ability to adapt to evolving environments while preserving core functions of the group). However, both women and men declined in their level of commitment (i.e., the energy and passion that motivates service to collective efforts and their outcomes) during the first year of college. Assessments of first- to fourth-year change on a holistic measure of socially responsible leadership resulted in an estimated positive change in the range of .37 of a standard deviation (O'Neill, 2012). In the main, when change is evaluated across four years of college, students appear to become more inclined toward leadership.

Autonomy, Independence, Locus of Control, and Self-Efficacy. Studies of change in autonomy and independence were few and far between. Standing as one exception, Baxter Magolda et al. (2012) examined changes in authority dependence in conjunction with the Wabash National Study as they followed 228 students who attended six institutions from the first to the second year of college. They reported a substantial decline in students' reliance on external sources for making meaning of knowledge, self, and relationships at the same time that many students shifted toward internal resources for meaning making. Overall, most students (63%) exhibited more complex meaning making over time; 18% did not change; and 19% regressed in their meaning-making complexity. Generally patterns pointed to decreased authority dependence even though many students still approached meaning making with some degree of reliance on external reference points. A single-institution study also discerned positive change, albeit slight, in academic autonomy from the first to the senior year (Foubert et al., 2005).

Few studies of self-efficacy and locus of control surfaced. Those that did tended to focus on the impact of a particular intervention (e.g., studying abroad, engaging in a writing or journaling intervention, participating in an orientation program, taking a course). Although most implemented a pre/posttest design (rarely an experimental design), these studies were based on small samples of students at single institutions and had other design limitations, such as insufficient controls for confounding college experience variables, which precluded adequately addressing change or effects.

Psychological Well-Being. Given recent evidence that college students' emotional health has been declining across successive cohorts of entering first-year students (Eagan et al., 2014), studies of the factors that contribute to and undermine well-being have been on the rise during the 2000s. Not only do students come to college with more stress than ever before (Eagan et al., 2014), levels of stress, anxiety, and depression may increase during college. For instance, Sax, Bryant, and Gilmartin (2004) found that emotional health declined and depression increased across the first year of college for both women and men. Although women generally had lower levels of psychological well-being than men did, men's depression increased at a faster rate across the first year, narrowing the gender gap to some degree. Similarly, a small-sample longitudinal study showed declines in self-esteem across the first year of college, as well as significant individual variability in initial self-esteem levels and rates of change (Shim, Ryan, & Cassady, 2012). This problem is not unique to U.S. college students, as other longitudinal data from the United Kingdom confirmed similar patterns of change, especially in the first semester of university (Bewick, Koutsopoulou, Miles, Slaa, & Barkham, 2010).

Despite concerning trends among cohorts of entering first-year students and marked declines in well-being in the first year of college, Sax (2008) found marginal changes in emotional health from the first to the fourth year of college. For instance, women in her longitudinal analysis became slightly more likely to rate their physical health as "above average" or "highest 10%" compared to peers, and men became slightly less likely to do so. Nevertheless, changes were trivial, in the range of 1 to 2 percentile points. Changes in self-rated emotional health, with negligible declines for women and slight increases for men, also indicated consistency, at least on average. Both groups became somewhat more inclined to say they were "frequently" overwhelmed, but again the percentage changes were quite small, in the range of 1 to 5 percentile points. Differences in the rate of change across the first year of college versus four years of college may be rooted in a number of factors beyond college enrollment and could include maturation, college withdrawal (i.e., those who remain by the fourth year may have higher levels of psychological well-being), or experiences unrelated to college. Importantly, on all measures, women's well-being registered lower than men's, and the first- to fourth-year gender gap widened on self-rated emotional health.

In addition to evidence that shows some differential changes by gender, other student characteristics play a role in patterns of change in psychological well-being, especially among students with marginalized identities. For example, Bowman and Small (2012) found that declines in hedonic well-being (defined as experiencing positive emotions and satisfaction) may be more pronounced among certain groups, particularly those with marginalized social identities, including Black/African American students, American Indian/Native American students, Latino/Chicano students, Asian American/Pacific Islander students, and those with parents who have less education. Confirming some of Sax's findings, Bowman and Small noted declines in hedonic well-being were more pronounced among women than men.

Drawing on data from the UCLA Spirituality in Higher Education project, Park and Millora (2010) examined first- to third-year changes in psychological well-being in a large sample of diverse students. Low levels of well-being increased over time, and changes were greater for students of color than White students. Moreover, high levels of well-being decreased quite dramatically. Rates of decline were similar for Asian American and White students (10 percentile points) and most pronounced for Latino/a (18 percentile points) and Black students (22 percentile points).

In addition to differential patterns of change by race and gender, sexual orientation may also shape the degree of change in well-being, although the existing evidence has limited generalizability. Kirsch, Conley, and Riley (2015), upon comparing matched samples of heterosexual and LGB students during the first year of college, found that both groups of students were subject to significant increases in psychological distress across the first semester. Yet LGB students' levels of stress were consistently higher, marked by greater cognitive and affective vulnerabilities and compromised social well-being, relative to their heterosexual peers.

In sum, very little research through the 2000s considered general identity formation but did elucidate patterns of change in racial/ethnic, spiritual, and religious identity dimensions. When it comes to racial/ethnic identity, fluctuations in exploration, commitment, and identity status are apparent at the individual level, while consistent patterns are more difficult to discern when change is assessed in the aggregate. Students make considerable gains during college on multiple measures of spirituality, while religious commitments remain stable and religious engagement declines. Students also make gains on several self-concept measures—intellectual and writing abilities, social self-confidence, and leadership skills—and become less reliant on external authorities in their meaning making. Although downward shifts in psychological well-being are apparent in the first year of college, changes on well-being indicators from the first- to fourth-year of college are marginal by comparison.

NET EFFECTS OF COLLEGE

Conclusions from the 1990s

What impact does college attendance have net of other influences such as normal maturation or sociohistorical factors? In their previous reviews, Pascarella and Terenzini (1991, 2005) characterized the challenges inherent in isolating the net effects of college. Rigorous designs are required to untangle the effects of college from other forces that affect change. Ideally, designs should involve comparisons of development between people with no exposure to college and those who attended college. But given that such data are typically not available, other approaches have been employed, such as examining the impact of the degree of college exposure [e.g., see Astin's (1993) notions of extensity (length of time in college) and intensity (depth of engagement in college experiences)] in models that control for pretest measures of the outcomes in question, age (to control for maturation), and other demographic variables. Moreover, changes within a cohort can be compared to changes across cohorts to assess whether sociohistorical factors are at play.

In light of these challenges, the evidence through the 1990s was inconclusive regarding whether general or specific forms of identity development (e.g., racial and ethnic identity, sexual orientation, religious identity) were due to college rather than maturational or sociohistorical forces. Other studies that controlled for precollege self-concept, other confounding factors, and degree of exposure to college (i.e., both extensity and intensity) showed college had net positive effects on academic self-concept and net negative effects on mathematical self-concept. Although studies in the previous decade indicated positive net effects of college on interpersonal skills, the validity of the studies was questionable in the absence of controls for factors such as maturation. Other research demonstrated that college did have a net positive effect on leadership skills given controls for precollege characteristics and age. In addition, the limited number of studies on locus of control generally conveyed that students became more self-directed with more exposure to college. Very few studies of self-esteem were available in the 1990s, and while overall they suggested college might have had a net impact on self-esteem, the studies used dated samples, samples with limited generalizability, and inadequate controls.

Evidence from the 2000s

In our review of research from the 2000s, we uncovered scant evidence of overall net effects, as most studies of psychosocial development emphasized within-college effects. As a result, we comment briefly on two categories of net effects that received at least some attention in the research literature: racial/ethnic identity and religious identity.

Identity Development

Racial and Ethnic Identity. We identified no studies of acceptable rigor that demonstrated a net effect of college on racial and ethnic identity development. Most studies were limited to cross-sectional designs that considered differences in identity statuses between cohorts or longitudinal designs without adequate controls for maturation (e.g., age) and that failed to examine differences in development by degree of college exposure. One study alluded to the potential of net effects of college by comparing patterns in racial identity development across the lifespan (Yip, Seaton, & Sellers, 2006). Grounded in Phinney's (1992) model of ethnic identity development, the study included just under 1,000 African American adolescents, college students, and adults, and revealed that adolescents were more likely to be in moratorium and less likely to have an achieved identity status relative to college students and adults. Moreover, the college students and adults had a higher propensity toward the achieved status than the diffused, foreclosed, and moratorium statuses. Thus, the study suggested progression toward more mature statuses as people moved beyond adolescence, but college impact, maturation, and cohort effects could not be disentangled given the cross-sectional design and absence of control variables.

Religious and Spiritual Identity. For the most part, studies through the 2000s of the distinctive dimensions of religiosity and spirituality (e.g., Astin et al., 2011) were attuned to change over time and between- and within-college effects rather than the net impact of college. The assumption undergirding most of the existing research was that college *does* make a difference in spiritual and religious growth; scholars studying these dimensions sought to identify those experiences most associated with change.

Whether young adults undergo similar transformations because of non-college forces has received little attention in the literature with a few exceptions. The National Study of Youth and Religion (NSYR) traced religious development in a large sample of approximately 2,500 participants that included both college-going young adults and individuals who did not go to college. The study showed that religious declines were actually more prevalent among young adults who did not attend college (Smith & Snell, 2009). Moreover, continuity in religious identity was the prevailing pattern in emerging adulthood regardless of college attendance (Smith & Snell, 2009). Thus, even though it is often taken for granted that college has liberalizing effects, modest changes in religious identity are difficult to pin on attending college alone.

Other studies corroborated these findings (Uecker, Regnerus, & Vaaler, 2007), and some introduced additional nuances. Two studies illuminated positive associations between educational level and church attendance (Brown & Taylor, 2007; McFarland, Wright, & Weakliam, 2010), but one of the investigations revealed associations between educational attainment and lower inclinations to pray and view the Bible as the literal word of God (McFarland et al., 2010). Hill (2009) studied the impact of educational attainment on religious participation using data from the National Longitudinal Study of Youth and controlled for age, period, and pretest measures of religious participation. Although enrolling in college came with temporary modest declines in religious participation compared to students who never enrolled in college, graduating from college had a positive net effect on religious participation. Yet a closer look at the data revealed that highly engaged religious service attenders enrolled in and graduated from college to a greater extent than individuals who were less inclined to attend religious services. This pattern led Hill to conclude, "Educational attainment is both a result of, as well as a cause of, higher religious participation during adolescence and young adulthood" (p. 523).

BETWEEN-COLLEGE EFFECTS

Conclusions from the 1990s

There was scarce empirical attention to the impact of institutional characteristics on identity development through the 1990s. Some studies examined racial identity development at Historically Black Colleges and Universities (HBCUs) versus predominantly White institutions (PWIs), but these studies generally did not conclude that institutional type was a factor in differential identity development. Likewise, research in the previous decade affirmed that between-college characteristics, such as size, type, control, mission, and selectivity, were not reliable predictors of other dimensions of psychosocial identity change among students.

Some studies showed that particular types of institutions—women's colleges, HBCUs, and structurally diverse institutions—enhanced students' academic and social self-concept. In terms of other relational measures, much of the research in the 1990s examined leadership skills rather than interpersonal relations, and for the most part showed that first- to senior-year changes in leadership skills were not predicated on institutional type, control, or size after adjusting for pre-college traits and college experiences. Studies of changes in students' self-directedness showed either no effect of attending a community college versus a four-year institution or an advantage for students attending a community college, particularly in the first year. Most of the limited research on self-esteem in relation to institutional characteristics considered the impact of attending a women's college—and, in the main, that research revealed null effects after controlling for other factors. As with many of the other indicators of psychosocial change, significant between-college effects were rare in studies assessing general personal development. All told, when effects on multiple indicators of psycho-social identity were identified, they were typically small and often indirect.

Evidence from the 2000s

Studies of between-college effects from the 2000s addressed several categories of identity development (i.e., racial and ethnic identity; gay, lesbian, and bisexual identity; religious and spiritual identity). In addition, the research literature covered many relevant psychosocial dimensions (i.e., academic self-concept, social self-concept, and interpersonal relationships; leadership skills; autonomy, independence, locus of control, and self-efficacy; psychological well-being; general personal development).

Identity Development

Racial and Ethnic Identity. Few studies in the 2000s considered the impact of between-college characteristics on racial and ethnic identity development. Two studies, both with cross-sectional designs, compared levels of racial identity salience (Steck, Heckert, & Heckert, 2003) and Cross's notion of "internalization" (Spurgeon & Myers, 2010) between students attending HBCUs and PWIs. In both cases, African American students attending PWIs scored higher on the measures of salience (the centrality of race to one's sense of self) and internalization (effort to resolve dissonance and experience inner peace and pride in one's race) than their peers attending HBCUs. Spurgeon and Myers (2010) estimated an effect size of .31 of a standard deviation in comparing the two groups' degree of internalization. Although limited by small participant and institutional sample sizes, as well as designs that did not enable assessments of change over time, the evidence pointed to the possibility that students strengthen their racial identity as a strategy for coping with environments where students of color are in the minority.

Three other studies similarly considered the structural diversity context of institutions in relation to ethnic identity development but did not use institutional identity (PWI or HBCU status) as the measure of context. The first of the three studies provided qualitative evidence that diverse campus environments yielded evolution in racial identity. According to Santos, Ortiz, Morales, and Rosales (2007), who interviewed 103 students at two diverse universities in Southern California, ethnically diverse universities attended by participants provided an optimal context for cultivating ethnic awareness and attaining a positive ethnic identity. However, two other studies (Syed et al., 2007; Tsai & Fulingi, 2012) found no effect of context (measured as the concentration of Latinos in the community in Syed et al., 2007, and college ethnic composition in Tsai & Fulingi, 2012) on changes in racial identity status (Syed et al., 2007) and ethnic search (Tsai & Fulingi, 2012), respectively.

Finally, Tsai and Fulingi (2012) examined differences in ethnic self-labeling, search, and belonging in a longitudinal study of two- and four-year college students. They found that students' self-labeling (i.e., choosing pan-ethnic labels and/or American labels) did not change significantly across time and that change did not vary by college type. However, at both times, students in four-year colleges were more inclined to choose American labels than students attending two-year colleges. Greater declines over time in ethnic search and belonging occurred among students attending two-year institutions relative to their four-year counterparts.

Taken together, the evidence about between-college effects on ethnic and racial identity development continued to be sparse in the 2000s, as in earlier decades. The structural diversity of an institution may play a role in promoting racial identity development, particularly when students of color find themselves in the minority. In addition, ethnic identities may evolve somewhat differently in four-year institutions and community colleges. Given methodological limitations and inconsistencies in the findings across studies, these conjectures remain tentative.

Gay, Lesbian, and Bisexual Identity. We identified no reliable studies that examined between-college effects on gender identity, but a small number of qualitative studies provided limited evidence of institutional effects on gay and lesbian identity development. Much of this work pointed to the importance of affirming environments that were proactively inclusive and free of homophobia and heterosexism. In such contexts, queer students were more likely to have the resources necessary to find empowerment for self-acceptance, coming out, and negotiating multiple identities (Stevens, 2004). Holland and Holley (2011), in their qualitative study, determined that gay men attending a traditional women's college (which only in recent decades began admitting men) experienced a sense of belonging and the freedom to perform gay identities in supportive institutional spaces that consisted of a high percentage of women and lacked confining heterosexual masculine norms. Conversely, a study of gay and bisexual men attending an HBCU revealed that the men felt others validated their racial identities on campus, but validation of their diverse sexual identities was less consistent. The campus environment shaped the expression and level of importance attributed to sexual identity because "being gay or bisexual carried certain ramifications, which required the participants to be particularly thoughtful about how they got involved, who they dated, and in whom they confided" (Patton, 2011, p. 95). Likewise, lesbian women attending an HBCU "were insiders of the campus environment because of their race. However, when either raced or gendered experiences conflicted with their lesbian identity, they became outsiders where being Black and female translated into being heterosexual" (Patton & Simmons, 2008, p. 212).

Although we did not find any research linking experiences with faith-based colleges and universities with sexual identity development, one study identified a primarily negative climate for students of minority sexual identities or with same-sex attractions at Christian institutions, which may have had implications for identity exploration and expression (Yarhouse, Stratton, Dean, & Brooke, 2009). Thus, evidence from this small fund of qualitative research suggests that the degree to which students of minority sexualities express and centralize their sexual identities is largely tied to the campus's cultural norms and degree of support for students presenting various identity dimensions.

Religious and Spiritual Identity. Institutional type and control have been associated with religious and spiritual identity development in a handful of studies. For the most part, such studies have denoted higher levels of religiosity and spirituality at religious institutions, but there are additional nuances. Bowman and Small (2010) analyzed longitudinal data from the UCLA spirituality project and reported the highest levels of spiritual development (e.g., identifying as a spiritual person and engaging in spiritual quest) among students at non-Catholic religious institutions (most of which were Protestant), followed by Catholic institutions and then secular schools, respectively. In a similar vein, a subsequent study using the same dataset pointed to greater gains in religiosity among students attending Protestant institutions than other types of campuses (Small & Bowman, 2011).

Another longitudinal study further unpacked the religious college effect by distinguishing among types of Protestant institutions. In that analysis, the modest negative impact of the number of years enrolled in college on religious service participation was more pronounced at mainline Protestant, Catholic, and nonreligious private institutions compared to evangelical institutions and public colleges and universities (Hill, 2009). At first glance, this may seem counterintuitive, but Hill attributed these effects to "Catholic and mainline Protestant institutions less successfully providing a shared moral order that legitimates religious language, motive, and behavior when compared to conservative Protestant colleges" (p. 515). Alternatively, non-evangelical religious institutions may encourage critical reflection on religious faith, leading some students to shift their perspectives on the importance of religious service participation. At public institutions, Hill argued, ethnic and religious pluralism may have served to activate religious identity, particularly among students with minority worldviews. The inconsistencies in the findings reported by Small and Bowman and Hill are likely due to differences in outcome measures (Bowman and Small used multifaceted religious and spiritual constructs in their work, while Hill focused on religious service participation), institutional classification (Hill distinguished evangelical schools from other Protestant institutions), and differences between the institutional samples in the respective studies.

Other evidence shows that institution type may also open the door for some of the more challenging aspects of spiritual development. Bryant and Astin (2008) concluded, based on their analysis of longitudinal pilot data associated with the UCLA spirituality project, that attending a religious college (whether Catholic, Protestant, or evangelical) was associated with a higher degree of spiritual struggling, with effects in the range of .06 to .09 of a standard deviation.

Beyond the religious affiliation of the institution, another aspect of institutional identity—whether the campus is an HBCU or a PWI—may be relevant to spiritual identity. A two-institution study of African American college students found higher levels of spirituality at the PWI in the study relative to the HBCU, leading the researchers to conclude "that African Americans matriculating at PWIs use spirituality as a coping mechanism to deal more effectively with life's stressors" (Weddle-West, Hagan, & Norwood, 2013, p. 310). However, the study involved a relatively small sample and had a cross-sectional design, so this association awaits further validation in subsequent research.

The advantage to religious and spiritual development among students attending religious institutions—particularly campuses that are conservative Protestant or evangelical—may be tied to aspects of the peer and faculty culture at Protestant schools. When these factors are introduced in models, they tend to reduce the effects of institutional type and control. Several studies uncovered significant effects of peer and faculty environments. For example, Astin et al. (2011) estimated a small effect (in the range of .06 of a standard deviation) of the average faculty focus on spirituality, a measure derived directly from a survey of faculty at the institutions in the sample, on students' growth in spiritual quest. Regarding measures of religious development, the average religious engagement of students attending the institution predicted a moderate increase—of .12 of a standard deviation—in individual students' levels of religious engagement (Astin et al., 2011). Lee (2002b) found a small association between the frequency of religious service attendance among peers and students' self-rated growth in religious beliefs and convictions, although the outcome measure in this case reflected students' own assessments of their religious change. Also, on campuses where more students held an ecumenical worldview, which is a measure of openness to and acceptance of people of diverse religions and cultures (Small & Bowman, 2011), or were very religiously engaged (Astin et al., 2011), religious struggles tended to be greater among individual students.

Academic Self-Concept, Social Self-Concept, and Interpersonal Relationships. A few institutional structural characteristics exert influences, albeit typically small, on measures of academic self-concept. We found almost no evidence supporting similar effects on social self-concept or interpersonal relationships. The size of an institution, as reflected by the number of full-time undergraduates, had a negative impact on students' scholarly (i.e., academic, intellectual, and writing) self-confidence and self-rated drive to achieve, according to Sax's (2008) longitudinal study. Another study of more than 7,000 students, also longitudinal in nature, concluded that the research emphasis of an institution had a small positive impact on students' intellectual self-concept (Cole, 2007).

Several studies attended to institutional structure as reflected by the student populations served. A multi-institutional study involving more than 7,000 African American college students and 207 institutions revealed that attendance at HBCUs was associated positively with students' self-perceived gains in intellectual and writing skills. However, standardized effects were quite small (between .03 and .07 of a standard deviation) in the presence of controls for age, socioeconomic status, and other collegiate environmental and experiential variables—and might have been reduced to nonsignificance without reliance on measures of self-report (Flowers, 2002). A smaller-scale study with limited generalizability corroborated Flowers's findings in denoting higher levels of academic self-concept among students who attended an HBCU (Cokley, 2002). More recently, Cuellar (2014) presented evidence supporting the benefits students derive from attending minority-serving institutions. In the well-controlled longitudinal analysis involving more than 2,000 Latino/a students, she reported small positive effects, estimated at .07 of a standard deviation, of attending an Hispanic-serving institution (HSI) on academic self-concept.

Other effects identified in several longitudinal studies alluded to the impact of peer culture on self-concept. Sax (2008) reported negative effects of the average socioeconomic status of the student body on students' math self-concept. Beyond demographic qualities of peers, average peer behaviors and attitudes may also shape self-concept, particularly those having to do with diversity engagement, civic values, and general investment in college life. According to Denson and Chang (2009), the average level of curricular diversity engagement on campus had a positive impact on students' self-assessed changes in their academic skills (e.g., general knowledge, problem solving, critical thinking, writing skills), holding constant student characteristics and other college experience variables. Although the institutional and student sample was large, the pretest measure used in the model was a proxy for academic skills, which may have inflated the magnitude of the effects uncovered. Finally, the inclinations of students to express commitment to civic goals and be involved in campus life exerted positive influences on students' gains in intellectual and social self-confidence, after controlling for student characteristics and pretested outcome measures (Chang, Denson, Sáenz, & Misa, 2006). However, the average tendency of the student body to hold part-time jobs on campus reduced self-confidence.

Leadership Skills. Institutional effects on leadership identity and skills, as well as proclivities for socially responsible leadership, are generally trivial in comparison to within-college effects (Dugan, Kodama, & Gebhardt, 2012; Dugan & Komives, 2010). Although the evidence is not definitive, there are a few between-college effects worth noting. Students who attended institutions with large undergraduate enrollments experienced a weakened sense of leadership identity in Sax's longitudinal study (2008). However, the average faculty focus on spirituality at an institution promoted student leadership development in Park and Millora's (2012) analysis of data from the UCLA Spirituality in Higher Education project. Two other studies attested to the potential cultivation of leadership skills in work colleges, where students are assigned jobs according to their interests and campus and community needs, and women's colleges. Wolniak and Pascarella (2007) examined collegiate outcomes in a sample of alumni and found that attending a work college was strongly associated with entrepreneurial and leadership skills relative to liberal arts and regional colleges, holding constant demographic variables and relevant college experiences. Effects ranged from .34 to .46 of a standard deviation. Furthermore, in her international study of women's colleges in nine countries, Renn (2012) documented the opportunities for leadership development in institutional contexts where "women step in and get things done" (p. 186) as part of student government, student publications, and other organizations.

Autonomy, Independence, Locus of Control, and Self-Efficacy. There was a dearth of evidence substantiating between-college effects on students' self-directedness and locus of control. We found only one reliable study that presented any significant effects. Bowman (2010d) analyzed longitudinal first-year student data from the Wabash National Study and reported more growth in autonomy among students attending community colleges compared to those attending liberal arts colleges. Importantly, his models controlled for appropriate confounding influences. With this study as the exception, little attention was directed to the institutional qualities associated with students' growth in autonomy, self-efficacy, and sense of control over their lives and accomplishments.

Psychological Well-Being. Two well-controlled longitudinal studies identified small positive associations between institutional selectivity and well-being (Bowman & Small, 2012; Park & Millora, 2012). Both studies were based on the same dataset derived from the UCLA spirituality project, but they used different outcome measures, eudaimonic well-being (a measure of social self-confidence, cooperativeness, and understanding of others; Bowman and Small, 2012) and psychological well-being (a measure of self-rated emotional health and *not* feeling depressed, stressed, or overwhelmed; Park & Millora, 2012). Selectivity effects did not hold in another study based on the same dataset (Park & Millora, 2010), likely due to differences in the models. The small magnitude of the effects makes them tenuous and easily reduced to nonsignificance in the presence of other variables that are more proximal to students' sense of well-being. Other institutional qualities that played a positive role in students' well-being, according to some longitudinal studies, included the research emphasis of the institution (Bowman, 2010d; Martin, Hevel, Asel, & Pascarella, 2011) and the average faculty focus on spirituality at an institution (Park & Millora, 2012). Alternately, the level of religious engagement among students on campus was linked to declines in psychological well-being (Park & Millora, 2012).

Findings pertaining to the impact of attending HBCUs on wellness are mixed and based on data with limited generalizability. A small-sample study involving just over 200 African American male students attending either an HBCU or PWI revealed higher levels of social self-wellness among the HBCU students, but higher levels of physical self-wellness among the PWI students (Spurgeon & Myers, 2010). In a related study involving the same sample, Spurgeon (2009) found that students at the HBCU reported higher levels of friendship, love, sense of control, and gender identity development than students at the PWI. However, the PWI students reported higher levels of sense of worth. Similar to findings around ethnic identity development in the PWI context, cultivating a sense of worth may be an important contributor to coping with identity-related challenges and marginalization in the PWI environment.

In a similar vein, qualitative research attended to the psychological consequences of privilege disparities in different types of institutional environments. Aries and Seider (2005) interviewed 30 low-income students attending an elite liberal arts college or a state college and discovered greater difficulties associated with social class for the students at the elite institution than the state college, where class differences were less salient. In addition, the researchers noted that first-generation students with the least cultural capital were subject to an array of negative emotions, ranging from feelings of intimidation to inadequacy and uneasiness.

General Personal Development. Analysis of large-sample, cross-sectional data centered on students' self-reported gains in "personal development" and "personal and social competence" revealed two between-college qualities associated with students' impressions that they have grown: institutional emphasis on interactional diversity and perceptions of a supportive campus environment (Lundberg, 2012; Reason, Terenzini, & Domingo, 2007). Other effects on general personal development were linked to institutional emphasis and mission. Work colleges, where students perform jobs to gain professional experience and meet campus and community needs, had a strong effect relative to regional colleges—estimated at .73 of a standard deviation—on personal and spiritual orientations of students after accounting for other confounding variables (Wolniak & Pascarella, 2007). Some studies ascertained positive effects of attending HBCUs (relative to PWIs) on overall development (e.g., acquiring a broad general education, thinking critically and analytically, understanding oneself and people of other racial and ethnic backgrounds, developing a personal code of values and ethics, and contributing to the welfare of one's community; Nelson Laird, Bridges, Morelon-Quainoo, Williams, & Salinas Holmes, 2007), personal and social development (e.g., developing values and ethical standards; understanding other people; and getting along with different kinds of people; Flowers, 2002), and life satisfaction (Constantine & Watt, 2002) of African American students. Nelson Laird and colleagues (2007) added that attending Hispanic-serving institutions (HSIs) benefited the overall development of Hispanic students. Another study observed that students attending single-sex institutions reported greater gains in understanding self and others than students attending coeducational institutions, holding constant individual and institutional characteristics (Kinzie, Thomas, Palmer, Umbach, & Kuh, 2007). These studies had their share of design weaknesses, including reliance on cross-sectional data, self-reported gains, and samples with limited generalizability. Moreover, in some instances, effects were small in magnitude or would have been smaller given the presence of pretested outcome measures in the models.

A few consistent findings pertaining to between-college effects on psychosocial change surfaced in our review. Aspects of the institutional diversity climate—for instance, whether students of minority identities are present on campus or whether campus norms support students of diverse identities—are important for racial/ethnic and lesbian, gay, and bisexual identity development. Religious and spiritual development may unfold differently depending on the institutional identity of the campus, but these effects may be indirect, as features of the peer and faculty culture have more pronounced influences. Various facets of peer and faculty culture also shape students' self-concept and well-being.

WITHIN-COLLEGE EFFECTS

Conclusions from the 1990s

Scholarship attentive to identity development in the 1990s distinguished a variety of within-college experiences associated with growth along general and specific identity dimensions. For instance, research on the effects of community service or service-learning (which entails integrating service experiences with formal curricular experiences) revealed some evidence to suggest that such involvement may enhance identity clarification and self-awareness. Women's studies courses and programs with gender-focused content also appeared to generate identity transformation, including feminist identity development, but many of the studies in the 1990s lacked controls for self-selection. Other academic experiences that had the potential to shape identity included senior capstone courses, multiracial/multiethnic classrooms, diversity courses, supportive faculty who encouraged self-discovery, and study abroad experiences.

The majority of studies detailing the effects of academic experiences on identity formation were qualitative and based on single-campus investigations with limited generalizability. Very little research about the impact of out-of-class experiences on identity formation was available in the 1990s, although Rhoads (1997) showed that student activism could enhance racial/ethnic, gender, and sexual identity formation. Studies in the 1990s also underscored the experiences in college with the potential to activate racial and ethnic identity development: programs focused on intergroup relations and conflict, racial and ethnic student organizations, and multicultural training activities.

The weight of the evidence in the 1990s pointed to the greater impact of college experiences on developing students' positive self-concepts relative to structural or organizational characteristics (e.g., institutional type, control, size, selectivity). Research attentive to within-college effects on academic self-concept was fairly comprehensive in the previous decade. Based on studies primarily out of the Higher Education Research Institute, the import of peer and faculty interactions in relation to positive change in academic self-concept was quite clear. With appropriate confounding factors taken into account, socializing with peers, tutoring other students, discussing course content with other students, participating in student government, and engaging in campus protest all improved academic self-concept. As with peer interactions, talking with faculty outside class, interacting with supportive faculty who provided intellectual challenge, being a guest in a faculty member's home, and teaching or conducting research with faculty were beneficial with respect to students' academic self-concept.

A common theme in much of the research detailing peer and faculty interactions in relation to academic self-concept was exposure to difference. Encountering new knowledge, ideas, beliefs, and walks of life appeared to stimulate reflection that in turn brought about new ways of thinking about the world and others. For instance, service work and service-learning, discussions with peers of another racial/ethnic group, ethnic studies courses, and cultural awareness workshops resulted in net gains in academic self-concept. Compared to academic self-concept, the review of research through the 1990s had much less to contribute to our understanding of college effects on social self-concept.

Although the literature on interpersonal relationships grew in the 1990s, much of the evidence was mixed. For instance, studies of the impact of community service activities and service-learning on interpersonal skills illuminated some net benefit; however, whether service-learning had a unique effect over and above general volunteer activities was unclear. Small gains in interpersonal skills were experienced by fraternity and sorority members and by intercollegiate athletes relative to peers, but some research suggested no improvement in interpersonal skills resulting from co-curricular engagement. Generally interactions with other students—perhaps more so than interactions with faculty—promoted growth in interpersonal skills.

Regarding leadership skills, several studies in the 1990s supported a positive relationship between service activities and leadership, although service-learning may not have afforded advantages over general volunteer activities. Studies of educational programs and classes focused on leadership development consistently underscored the benefits of such interventions for students' leadership skills. The research on intercollegiate athletic participation and involvement in intramural sports from the 1990s was inconsistent in affirming a connection between sports engagement and leadership skill development. Participation in racial/ethnic organizations (including Black fraternities and sororities) may have affected leadership skills positively, but some of this impact was likely tied to self-selection, as students with preexisting leadership proclivities were probably drawn to this type of involvement. Many of the effects identified in the literature reflected the positive impact on leadership development of students' interactions with their peers and, to a lesser extent, faculty.

The findings from the 1990s regarding the impact of within-college experiences on autonomy and locus of control presented certain inconsistencies. Some studies examined the impact of volunteer activities and service-learning in relation to internal attributions for academic success and self-efficacy. The mixed reports, when considered together, suggested that service connected to academic learning may have had a greater impact than general volunteer activities, but this conclusion was tentative. Other academic experiences that appeared to have a positive influence on dimensions of independence included the number of courses taken, the quality of instruction, study-abroad participation, and leadership experiences. Peer interactions and extracurricular activities shaped students' sense of autonomy positively, while the effects of fraternity and sorority involvement and living on campus were less convincing. Male intercollegiate athletes made gains, accounting for other factors, in internal locus of attribution for academic success relative to students who were not intercollegiate athletes.

Studies of within-college effects on self-esteem, an indicator of psychological well-being, were decidedly mixed. Whether certain instructional approaches, such as clustered courses, service-learning, or supplemental instruction, improved self-esteem during college was unclear. However, compared to traditional pedagogies, active and collaborative instructional practices fostered self-esteem, and so did opportunities to connect informally with faculty.

Research from the 1990s based on self-reported gains emphasized that the degree of effort students invested in academic and social activities contributed to gains in personal development. Peer interactions were the predominant reason behind gains in personal development—and the impact of faculty interactions was indeterminate. Other college experiences that held promise for personal development included learning through active and collaborative instruction, living on campus, joining a fraternity or sorority, and studying abroad. However, controlling for precollege characteristics in this set of studies was atypical, so effect sizes were likely overestimated.

Evidence from the 2000s

Studies of within-college effects through the 2000s did not attend to general identity development, as in years past, but did address the formative role of collegiate experiences in shaping particular social identities (i.e., racial and ethnic identity, gender identity, religious and spiritual identity). Moreover, scholars examined within-college effects on other cornerstone dimensions of psychosocial development: academic self-concept; social self-concept and interpersonal relationships; leadership skills; autonomy, independence, locus of control, and self-efficacy; psychological well-being; and general personal development.

Identity Development
Racial and Ethnic Identity. Exposure to diversity in college has been linked to racial and ethnic identity outcomes in a number of studies. Although diversity experiences typically spur racial/ethnic identity development, these studies are limited by design and often generalizability, which tempers the conclusions that can be drawn.

On the whole, curricular, co-curricular, and interactional diversity engagement appears to benefit identity development. One study highlighted small effects of all three forms of engagement. The cross-sectional investigation included just over 5,000 students attending 14 institutions participating in the pilot of the

Diverse Learning Environments survey (Hurtado, Ruiz, & Guillermo-Wann, 2011). The researchers found that several aspects of the college experience had small effects on racial identity salience, that is, how often students thought about their race or ethnicity. Following controls for demographic and precollege socialization variables, three aspects of diversity engagement exhibited small effects on racial identity salience: taking classes that contained material and pedagogy focused on issues of diversity and equity, participating in campus-facilitated diversity activities (e.g., population-specific center activities, debates or panels about diversity issues) and engaging in conversations outside class related to racial or ethnic diversity.

While Hurtado and colleagues included multiple forms of diversity engagement in their models, other scholars centered their attention on particular experiences: intergroup dialogue, peer engagement, critical incidents, support and validation, and participation in population-specific organizations. Two studies explored the impact of intergroup dialogue on ethnic identity development. Although the studies employed distinctive paradigmatic assumptions and research designs, both provided a longitudinal view of development and affirmed the utility of intergroup dialogue in promoting students' ethnic identity.

In the first of the two studies—an experimental investigation involving nine universities—Nagda, Gurin, Sorensen, and Zúñiga (2009) found statistically significant effects of intergroup dialogue on "intergroup understanding," which included a measure of "identity engagement," or students' proclivities to consider and learn about their group identity and the relationships among group members' perspectives. Although effects sizes were not reported (limiting our ability to assess the magnitude of the effect), students were randomly assigned to the intervention and control groups and measures of identity development were pre- and post-tested.

The second study, a qualitative investigation of both inter- and intragroup dialogue, involved 31 students at a small, private, liberal arts college in the northeast. Researchers demonstrated using a pre-dialogue/post-dialogue research design the personal transformations of participating students who exhibited growth in the saliency and complexity of their racial identity, sense of wholeness, and self-esteem (Ford & Malaney, 2012).

The researchers of both studies offered precise definitions and emphasized the critical components of intergroup dialogues. Ford and Malaney (2012) characterized intergroup dialogue as a "facilitated, face-to-face encounter that aims to cultivate meaningful engagement between members of two or more social identity groups that have a history of conflict" (p. 16). In intragroup dialogue, Ford and Malaney (2012) wrote, "Students meet together to explore common experiences, issues of privilege and oppression, and the meaning of their racial group membership" (p. 16). According to Nagda et al. (2009), the three essential components of dialogue are structured interaction (e.g., small group of students and equal representation of at least two social identities), active and engaged learning, and facilitated learning environments.

Interacting with a diverse peer group is relevant to identity development, according to several qualitative studies (Maramba & Velasquez, 2012; Renn, 2008; Torres, 2003). Renn's (2004) study of 56 multiracial college students attending six institutions established the significance of peer culture—especially cultures that challenge rigid racial categories and support boundary crossing—as an impetus to multiracial identity construction. Even so, Peterson and Hamrick (2009) provided evidence that diverse environments and peer groups, particularly those that disrupt privilege, do not uniformly enhance racial identity development for students with privileged identities. Based on their study of seven White men attending an HBCU, the researchers observed tendencies of their participants to self-censor in class and disengage from social opportunities. Such protective strategies may have undermined the exploration and commitment necessary for mature White racial consciousness (Peterson & Hamrick, 2009).

Several studies pointed to the transforming effects of "critical incidents." Even negative experiences, such as encountering and confronting racism or a negative campus climate, have been shown to inspire racial and ethnic identity development or the salience of one's ethnic identity (Hurtado et al., 2011; Kellogg & Lidell, 2012; Kim & Lee, 2011; Pasupathi, Wainryb, & Twali, 2012; Torres, 2003). In fact, "discrimination and bias in the college environment" was among the strongest predictors of racial identity salience—with an effect size of .18 of a standard deviation—according to Hurtado et al. (2011). Consistent with theoretical notions of "encounter" (Cross, 1991, 1995) and "dissonance" (Helms, 1995), we can deduce from such evidence that difficult experiences may catalyze racial consciousness and propel identity development.

Importantly, supportive contexts and people are vital contributors to identity development as well, especially as students navigate critical incidents and racial discrimination. For example, Maramba and Velasquez (2012) highlighted the meaningful contribution of a summer bridge program to their participants' ethnic identity development, and Hurtado et al. (2011) identified a small association between "academic validation" (e.g., having contributions valued in class, receiving feedback from instructors that helped the student judge progress) and racial identity salience. Renn (2004) recognized the value in supportive multiracial faculty role models in the identity formation of multiracial students, as well as the import of affirming classroom experiences where "opportunities to engage in academic work in the area of identity provided meaningful settings to think, read, hear, and talk about important issues related to identity" (p. 250).

Another form of student engagement, participation in population-specific organizations, has been identified in myriad studies as supporting the identity development of students of color. The existing quantitative research is somewhat mixed, however, and it is unclear whether participation in identity-based groups enhances identity development over and above other forms of campus engagement. Sidanius, Van Laar, Levin, and Sinclair (2004) found that ethnic organization membership was a significant predictor of ethnic identity, defined as importance of and closeness to one's ethnic group, and activism among minority students in the senior year of college, given controls for pretest measures of ethnic identity and activism. Effect sizes were moderate and in the range of .10 to .13 of a standard deviation. By contrast, membership in Greek organizations was not associated with senior-year ethnic identity and activism among White students, following controls for pretest measures. Although Sidanius et al. relied on data from only one institution, more than 2,000 students participated across five waves of data collection.

Another quantitative study underscored the importance of general extracurricular engagement but did not find unique effects of ethnic organization participation on identity development, leading the researchers to conclude "Engagement in campus activities, regardless of whether they are ethnically related, facilitate search about the meaning of one's ethnic group membership during college" (Tsai & Fulingi, 2012, p. 62). Importantly, though the study was longitudinal, pretests for outcome measures were not included in the models. The disparate results of Sidanius et al. (2004) and Tsai and Fulingi (2012) may be tied to differences in design, with the inclusion of pretest measures in the former and various indicators of extracurricular engagement in the latter. As well, Tsai and Fulingi's (2012) study was based on a smaller participant sample but included a more representative set of colleges and universities than Sidanius et al. (2004). The studies also used different measures of ethnic identity.

A number of qualitative studies by and large support the role of population-specific organizations and spaces in the identity development of students of color. The evidence is predominantly focused on Latino/a students, with a couple of exceptions. In a phenomenological study of seven men taking part in a Latino fraternity at a Hispanic-serving institution, Guardia and Evans (2008) found that the familial atmosphere, sense of Latino unity, and opportunities to acquire Spanish language skills in the organization helped members to explore and identify with the broader Latino/a community.

Case and Hernandez (2013), in a qualitative investigation at a predominantly White faith-based college, explored the ethnic identity development of 30 Latino/a college students who had participated in an ethnic leadership program. Students at each class level exhibited important developmental milestones. First-year students reported that the leadership program helped to broaden their understanding of ethnic identity, such that they experienced awakening, pride, and affirmation. Sophomores expressed an elevated ethnic consciousness, came to value others' ethnicity, and reflected on the significance of giving back to their communities. Juniors moved toward identity acceptance and began engaging their ethnic identities on a regular basis. Seniors emphasized their contributions as bicultural leaders, which involved employing skills that were transferable to a variety of leadership contexts. In an earlier study, Torres (2003) found similarly positive indicators of personal growth and identity development among Latinos/as participating in Latino organizations. Reiterating and broadening these findings to other groups, Maramba and Velasquez (2012) noted that many participants in their sample of 19 students of color at a large, public PWI recognized the influence of ethnic student organizations in supporting their ethnic identity development.

Finally, Renn (2004), in her study of multiracial students, affirmed that the presence of a public multiracial space on campus—whether temporary or ongoing, formal or informal—prompted identification with a multiracial identity and served as a supportive resource.

Gender Identity. Although we found no studies linking college experiences to gay and lesbian development or to women's identity development, the literature has broadened substantially through the 2000s to include investigations of men and masculinities.

Specific contexts in higher education, namely fraternities and college athletics, have been identified in some studies as reinforcing patriarchal and hegemonic masculinity (Harris & Struve, 2009; Steinfeldt & Steinfeldt, 2012; Tatum & Charlton, 2008). Despite these potentialities, other studies, many of them qualitative, looked to the ways that peer environments can engender positive masculine identities. For instance, in their study of 50 fraternity men from around the country, Harris and Harper (2014) underscored the conditions that facilitate constructive masculinity, including first, authentic acceptance of core organizational values (e.g., respect, character, integrity) by a critical mass of men in the local chapter and national association and, second, student leaders who model positive masculine behaviors and hold others accountable.

Jackson and Wingfield (2013) examined peer influences on masculinities in a campus organization for Black men. Men serving in leadership roles in the organization used anger constructively to encourage brotherhood and professionalism and to motivate "men to adopt a more 'respectable' form of black masculinity that was restrained, even-keeled, and perhaps most importantly, served as a foil to the commonplace representations of black men" (p. 289). Likewise, McClure (2006) found that fraternity membership for Black men supported their development of complex masculine identities consistent with both Afrocentric (emphasizing cooperation, connection, and emotional honesty) and mainstream (emphasizing individuality and self-sufficiency) models of masculinity.

Another study of more than 500 football players found some support for the reinforcement of hegemonic masculinity in college football—but also evidence to the contrary. Specifically, senior football players were less inclined than their freshmen, sophomore, and junior teammates to endorse norms protecting their heterosexuality. Senior football players, argued the researchers, had been socialized for a longer period of time in football but actually conformed the least to the homophobic facets of traditional masculinity (Steinfeldt & Steinfeldt, 2012). However, the study's cross-sectional design and lack of controls for other college influences limited the conclusions. All told, the weight of the evidence disrupts to some degree the assumption that predominantly male environments are bastions of hegemonic masculinity and reveals the ways that such contexts can be harnessed to promote constructive identity development among men. Such environments may prove especially fruitful for identity formation among men of color who are actively navigating the intersections of their racial and gender identities.

Beyond the influence of peer environments, other qualitative research emphasized the important role of friends, faculty, and student affairs staff in shaping masculinities among college men (Dancy, 2012). Campus involvement, academic engagement, and diversity engagement with peers are also noteworthy influences. Harper's (2004) study of 32 high-achieving African American men attending six public universities highlighted the relationship between active campus involvement—particularly leadership in minority student organizations—and healthy masculine identities. Edwards and Jones (2009) conducted a grounded theory study of men's performance of masculinity and noted academic courses as playing a powerful role in developing students' awareness of inauthentic masculinity and fostering new avenues for expressing their masculinities.

Rich diversity on campus was identified in some studies as offering men the opportunity for interactions with peers—through various forms of campus involvement and leadership—who provided broader possibilities for masculine expression (Harris, 2010; Harris & Struve, 2009). Dancy (2012) attested to the value in communities external to the college as sites of learning as well, where men drew "nearer to understanding self, work, and the world, which are critical manhood concepts" (Dancy, 2012, p. 123).

Other research called attention to conditions—campus climate and traditionally oriented peers—that restrict men's masculine expression. In a qualitative study of six White gay men attending a public university in the Midwest, Anderson-Martinez and Vianden (2014) observed the importance of campus climate for the participants' gender identity expression. The men in the study did not feel free to express their unique masculinities given the pressures to measure up to masculine norms and heteronormative conventions. Davis (2002) also identified restrictions on gender expression among men in her qualitative study who were concerned that their sexual orientation would be questioned if they exhibited traditionally feminine behaviors. Indeed, male peer groups played an important role in men's lives, often constraining masculine performance to limited and stereotypical conceptions of manhood (Tatum & Charlton, 2008). Summing up negative peer influences and the reason behind them, Harris and Harper (2008) contended, "Men's adherence to unproductive masculine conceptions such as sexism, homophobia, violence, and anti-intellectualism are often requisite for their access to male peer groups" (p. 29). Thus, to belong, men may feel the need to perform masculinity in a traditional and stereotypical manner.

Religious and Spiritual Identity. Studies that drew on longitudinal and generalizable data offered new insight through the 2000s about various within-college effects on indicators of religious and spirituality identity. Holding constant pretest measures and student characteristics, some academic majors appear to influence religious and spiritual identity development, according to Astin and colleagues' (2011) national study of college student spirituality. The magnitude of effects they estimated were rather small in most instances. Some evidence suggests secularizing effects of science and engineering, but not unequivocally. Engineering students became slightly less religiously engaged during college compared to students in other majors, according to Astin and colleagues. Yet Scheitle (2011), using the same national dataset as Astin et al. (2011), provided evidence that natural science majors do not undergo religious and spiritual changes that distinguish them from students in most other majors. In fact, where he found differences, it was usually students in the other major exhibiting religious and spiritual declines. Only business majors became less religiously skeptical than natural science majors across three years of college. Otherwise, compared to students majoring in natural sciences, social science majors became less religiously committed, engineering and mathematics majors became less engaged in spiritual questing, and arts and humanities majors encountered more religious struggles (Scheitle, 2011).

On the issue of religious or spiritual struggle, other analyses based on various datasets generated by the UCLA spirituality project confirmed a few additional differences by academic major. While students who majored in business tended to have fewer religious struggles than their peers (Astin et al., 2011), students who majored in English (Astin et al., 2011) and psychology had more. Again, effects were small. Using cross-sectional data with limited generalizability, Mayhew and Bryant Rockenbach (2013) identified negative relationships between majoring in social science/education or business and worldview commitment, a measure attuned to the commitments students make to their worldview following a period of significant reflection and exploration of alternative perspectives.

A number of college experiences influence religious and spiritual identity development. The UCLA Spirituality in Higher Education project (Astin et al., 2011) provided the most comprehensive review of within-college effects given controls for pretest measures, student characteristics, academic major, and institution-level variables. One of the most consistent patterns identified was the vital role of religious and spiritual conversations with others on campus, particularly those with faculty. Faculty encouragement to search for meaning and purpose and discuss religion and spirituality had a noteworthy impact on many outcomes, including spiritual quest, equanimity, religious commitment, religious engagement, religious skepticism, and religious struggle (Astin et al., 2011; Small & Bowman, 2011). In a related study involving the same data source, Bowman and Small (2010) found that faculty support for religious/spiritual development was moderately associated with gains in spiritual identification and spiritual quest. Interestingly, such encouragement promoted gains in key dimensions of growth, as well as dimensions of struggle and critique of religious concepts. Discussions about religion with professors, peers, and staff had moderate to strong relationships with spiritual quest, religious commitment, religious engagement, and religious struggle (Astin et al., 2011). In addition, talking with faculty outside class exhibited a small association with religious engagement (Astin et al., 2011).

Beyond the important role of faculty, academic pursuits also bear some modest connections to religious and spiritual identity development. According to

Astin and colleagues (2011), engaging in group projects was associated with growth in equanimity, and students' time investment in studying was connected to increases in both spiritual quest and equanimity. In addition, interdisciplinary courses provoked religious struggle, while religious studies courses enhanced religious engagement. Study abroad had small effects on two religious and spiritual identity dimensions; although studying abroad spurred religious struggle, such experiences also yielded growth in equanimity (Astin et al., 2011).

Several co-curricular and social experiences contribute to students' development of equanimity: engaging in leadership training, devoting time to clubs and groups, and socializing with different racial/ethnic groups. Moreover, students' helping behaviors, such as community service and volunteer work, donating money to charity, and helping friends with personal problems, exhibited various positive effects (most small) on spiritual quest, equanimity, religious engagement and commitment, and religious struggle (Astin et al., 2011).

Some activities counteract the generally positive direction of religious and spiritual change during college. In Astin and colleagues' study, partying and drinking had negative, though modest, effects on religious commitment and engagement, and time spent playing video games had a moderately negative impact on equanimity. Astin et al. (2011) observed only one positive effect in this set of college experiences: drinking furthered religious struggle.

Features of the campus religious and spiritual climate, as perceived by individual students, have implications for religious and spiritual identities. While students' perceptions of a divisive climate (i.e., separation of and conflict between people of diverse faiths and worldviews on campus) related positively to their worldview commitment, coercion (i.e., experiencing religious pressure on campus) exhibited a negative relationship with commitment (Mayhew & Bryant Rockenbach, 2013). Although a coercive climate appeared to create uniformly unfavorable conditions for worldview commitment, divisiveness may have stimulated "retreating to pre-existing psychological commitments or stereotypes when confronted with and threatened by difference" (Mayhew & Bryant Rockenbach, 2013, p. 78). Much of the research on the campus climate for religious diversity conducted during the time of our review was emergent and relied on cross-sectional data with limited generalizability. Therefore, we await future studies before drawing definitive conclusions.

Several religious experiences support students' religious and spiritual identities. According to Astin and colleagues' longitudinal study, religious mission trips enhanced equanimity and (especially) religious engagement. Participating in campus religious organizations was associated with religious commitment and religious engagement and seemed to stave off religious skepticism. Bowman and Small (2010) and Small and Bowman (2011) also documented the effects of religious involvement on religious and spiritual development using an overall measure of engagement that evidenced a strong association, estimated at approximately one-half of a standard deviation, with spiritual identification and religious commitment. In addition, they found a more moderate association between religious engagement and spiritual quest, estimated at .11 of a standard deviation. Moreover, their work pointed to the role of religious engagement in minimizing religious skepticism by a considerable degree, as shown by an effect size of close to one-half of a standard deviation. Spiritual practices, such as self-reflection, meditation, yoga, prayer, religious singing/ chanting, and reading sacred texts or other spiritual books, generally supported religious and spiritual development in Astin and colleagues' study.

A few other studies with some methodological limitations revealed more about religious experiences that promote commitment and struggle. Religious and spiritual co-curricular engagement provided considerable support for students' worldview commitment based on Mayhew and Bryant Rockenbach's (2013) small-sample, cross-sectional study. Likewise, Lee (2002b) underscored the strong relationship between religious service attendance and students' perceptions of gains in their personal religious beliefs and convictions, but the self-reported outcome measure was a noted limitation of the study. Religious experiences that may be unsettling to students, namely converting to another religion or spiritual questing, produced spiritual struggles among students in Bryant and Astin's (2008) analysis, but a pretest measure of spiritual struggle was not included in the model.

A series of qualitative studies corroborated quantitative evidence regarding the role of various college experiences in the religious and spiritual identity transformations that students undergo. Aligning with the primarily quantitative research base on spiritual development, Small's (2011) qualitative investigation of students' faith frames highlighted the value of interacting with religiously diverse peers and enrolling in religion courses for spiritual growth. Many qualitative studies attended to the trajectories of particular religious and social identity groups. For instance, Lee (2002a) examined shifting religious identities of Catholic students in her narrative analysis, and found evidence to support the notion that social and academic communities in college, particularly those that are diverse, can provoke questioning, shifts in social views, independence, and a renewed self-understanding of one's religious identity. Peek (2005) postulated that independence from parents, exposure to Muslim peers, and involvement in Muslim student organizations are important motivators in choosing a Muslim religious identity. Similarly, Stubbs and Sallee (2013) underscored the relevance of social networks, living arrangements, and situational American or Muslim cultural expectations in shaping the identity navigation of Muslim students. Reiterating the role of religious communities and peer relationships, Bryant (2011a) traced self-authored faith development of evangelical college students over several years and found that provocative encounters with friends who did not share their faith and both positive and negative experiences in religious communities inspired faith development. Common themes across these studies emphasize the provocative role that diverse peers networks and academic and religious communities can play in helping students identify, redefine, and own their faith commitments.

Some aspects of spiritual development have implications for related dimensions and other outcomes altogether. For instance, experiencing spiritual struggles had a negative impact on perceptions of one's religious and spiritual growth in one study (Bryant & Astin, 2008). Importantly, Astin and colleagues (2011) reported that spiritual development during college yielded gains in other traditional outcomes, such as academic performance, degree aspirations, leadership development, and self-esteem.

Academic Self-Concept

College Major. Few studies in the period we reviewed devoted significant attention to the impact of college major on academic or intellectual self-concept, and for the most part they treated major as a control variable. In investigations that did report effects, they were usually small. Generalizable and longitudinal studies observed positive effects of majoring in business on intellectual self-concept and negative effects of majoring in history or political science (Cole, 2007). Majoring in psychology resulted in a lower levels of math self-confidence (Sax, 2008). Cross-sectional evidence indicated that when students experienced congruence between their personality type and disciplinary environment, they reported gains in self-perceived outcomes relevant to the environment. For example, students whose personalities fit "investigative" environments described growth in their quantitative, analytical, and critical thinking skills; those whose personalities resonated with "artistic" environments believed they had made gains in writing and speaking skills (Pike, Smart, & Ethington, 2012).

Residence. Whether students' place of residence has any impact on academic self-concept is debatable, and we did not locate longitudinal studies with sufficient controls to verify significant effects in one direction or another. A cross-sectional analysis detected negative effects of living on campus on students' self-reported gains in quantitative, analytical, and critical thinking skills (Pike et al., 2012). Yet a quasi-experimental study of data from the National Study of Living-Learning Programs, involving four institutions and over 5,000 students, revealed higher levels of academic self-confidence among those students in the living-learning program relative to students living in traditional residence halls (Inkelas, Vogt, Longerbeam, Owen, & Johnson, 2006). There is reason to believe, however, that self-selection bias may explain this effect, as students in the living-learning community had higher levels of academic aptitude and achievement than their counterparts, and precollege academic self-confidence was not controlled in the analyses. Also limited by its cross-sectional design and dependence on students' self-evaluations, another study determined that first-year and senior-year participants in learning communities made gains in general education (Zhao & Kuh, 2004).

Peer and Faculty Engagement. Several studies affirmed the positive effects of peer engagement on intellectual and academic self-concept measures. Effects on these measures—most of which reflected students' perceptions of themselves compared to peers—were typically small in studies with longitudinal designs. Gains in intellectual self-concept were in part a function of discussing courses with other students and tutoring other students (Cole, 2007). Tutoring other students also boosted students' math self-concept and drive to achieve in Sax's (2008) study, and participating in student clubs or groups or socializing with other students advanced drive to achieve (Sax, 2008) and academic self-concept (Kim & Sax, 2014), respectively.

Corroborating these findings, participating in student clubs and groups improved self-rated academic ability and achievement orientation in one small-scale study (Berger & Milem, 2002). One unusual finding surfaced in Cole's (2007) longitudinal analysis: studying with other students reduced intellectual self-confidence. Explaining the counterintuitive finding, Cole surmised that students developed more realistic self-appraisals in study sessions with their peers.

Some analyses considered specific populations. African American students accrued benefits to their intellectual self-concept when they had discussions, studied, and worked in groups with peers (Cole, 2011). Latino/a students became more academically confident when they discussed course content with students outside of class and tutored another student (Cuellar, 2014). Moreover, discussing course content with other students had a stronger effect on students attending Hispanic-serving institutions (HSIs; institutions in which the full-time student population is at least 25% Latino/a and 50% low-income) than emerging HSIs (institutions on the path to becoming an HSI).

Many research studies were attentive to the various ways faculty have an impact on students' academic self-concept. Several longitudinal studies based on data from the Cooperative Institutional Research Program assessed the influence of nuanced interactional qualities. According to these investigations, talking with faculty outside class had a small impact on students' scholar self-concept (e.g., self-rated academic ability, intellectual self-confidence, and writing ability compared to peers; Sax, 2008; Sax, Bryant, & Harper, 2005). Challenging a professor's ideas in class had a moderate effect, estimated at .10 to .14 of a standard deviation, on similar measures, variously described as "scholar self-concept" (Sax, 2008; Sax et al., 2005), "intellectual self-concept" (Cole, 2007), and "academic self-concept" (Kim & Sax, 2014). Feeling supported by faculty enhanced students' scholar self-concept, self-rated drive to achieve, and self-rated competitiveness, with moderate to strong effects on these measures (Sax, 2008; Sax et al., 2005). Other experiences associated with small-to-medium gains in academic or intellectual self-concept included having been a guest in a professor's home (Kim & Sax, 2014), asking a professor for advice outside class (Kim & Sax, 2014), having course-related faculty contact (Cole, 2007), and having a mentoring relationship with a faculty member (Cole, 2007). Faculty who expect excellence from students may also stimulate intellectual gains, as cross-sectional evidence underscored the strong effects of academic challenge on self-reported gains in general education (Lundberg, 2012).

Some forms of faculty engagement have a marginal negative impact on intellectual self-concept: feeling bored in class, feeling faculty didn't take one's comments seriously, and receiving advice and critique from faculty (Cole, 2007). Pike et al. (2012) reported that student-faculty interaction negatively influenced students' self-perceived "investigative" gains in analytical, quantitative, and critical thinking skills, which counters much of the other evidence. However, it may be that students who sought help from faculty with analytical and quantitative course work were struggling with the content and therefore had lower assessments of their own competence.

When students participate in faculty research and other projects overseen by faculty, they tend to make gains, but not uniformly. Research with faculty furthered students' self-rated competitiveness to a small degree, and completing independent study projects helped students develop their scholar self-concept and drive to achieve in Sax (2008) and Sax and colleagues' (2005) longitudinal analyses. Hu, Kuh, and Li (2008), in their study of students' self-reported intellectual gains, discovered that inquiry-oriented activities, such as working with faculty on research projects or completing experiments or projects using scientific methods, exerted a small negative effect on students' self-assessed gains in general education—perhaps because such experiences entail considerable disciplinary focus. Even so, students who engaged in inquiry-based activities believed they developed intellectually and gained further knowledge of science and technology.

Some studies addressed how faculty influence students of color. In a small-sample but well-controlled study, Cole (2011) pointed to the positive effects of faculty support and encouragement on African American students' intellectual self-concept. Núñez (2009) used longitudinal data and reported similar effects of faculty interest in student development on Latino/a students' academic self-confidence. One cross-sectional investigation of a small sample of African American college students found that caring faculty make a difference in promoting students' academic self-concept (Cokley & Chapman, 2008). Effects are in the opposite direction when interactions are less optimal. Cuellar (2014) revealed that feeling intimidated by professors had a medium negative effect on Latino/a students' academic self-concept. Subsequent analyses illuminated that feeling intimidated by faculty had a particularly strong effect on Latino/a students attending non-HSIs versus HSIs or emerging HSIs. Without the buffer of institutional support from a campus dedicated to serving Hispanic students, faculty intimidation is particularly deleterious.

Academic Engagement. Academic, intellectual, and scholarly self-concept were predicated on academic engagement experiences such as devoting time to studying and taking honors courses, according to two longitudinal investigations (Kim & Sax, 2014; Sax, 2008). Taking honors courses also enhanced students' drive to achieve, and using personal computers furthered students' math self-concept and competitiveness (Sax, 2008). However, attending classes or labs (surprisingly) had a small negative effect on academic self-concept in Kim and Sax's study. Cross-sectional evidence provided some parallel insight. When students invested a great deal of effort in their courses, they tended to report gains in investigative (analyzing quantitative problems and thinking critically) and artistic (writing and speaking effectively) domains (Pike et al., 2012). However, Pike and colleagues also deduced that collaborative learning had positive effects on investigative gains, but negative effects on artistic gains.

Some studies considered effects for specific populations. Academic engagement played a generally positive role in African American students' self-reported gains in understanding arts and humanities, understanding science and technology, and thinking and writing skills (Flowers, 2004b). In particular, Flowers observed small positive effects of using the library and engaging in course learning on students' perceptions of their academic growth. Adding to the evidence that investment in learning is advantageous for students of color, Núñez (2009) found that frequent studying enhanced Latino/a students' academic self-confidence by a significant margin.

Diversity Engagement. Exposure to diversity, whether as part of the formal curriculum or informal social experiences, has been linked in a number of studies to students' intellectual self-perceptions. According to one well-controlled longitudinal study that asked students to compare their academic abilities to those of their peers, curricular diversity exerted a small influence on several related outcomes, including students' self-rated drive to achieve, intellectual self-confidence, competitiveness, academic ability, and writing ability (Denson & Chang, 2009). Even larger effects of diversity course work—in the range of .16 of a standard deviation—were observed in relation to Latino/a students' self-referential academic confidence (Núñez, 2009). On the other hand, Sax (2008) found in her longitudinal analysis that a more narrowly focused self-concept measure—math confidence—was weakened by taking ethnic studies courses. In addition to the longitudinal evidence, cross-sectional research showed classroom diversity made a positive impression on students' perceptions that they had made gains in general education knowledge (Lundberg, 2012) and in their problem-solving, critical thinking, and writing skills (Denson & Chang, 2009).

More studies reported effects of interactional diversity, measured in various ways to reflect students encountering peers of different racial/ethnic backgrounds and points of view in class, co-curricular activities, or social settings. On the whole, longitudinal studies with ample controls for confounding variables indicated such interactions enhanced academic and intellectual self-confidence (Chang, Astin, & Kim, 2004; Chang et al., 2006; Denson & Chang, 2009; Kim & Sax, 2014) and related outcomes, such as self-rated drive to achieve, competitiveness, academic ability, and writing ability (Denson & Chang, 2009). When interactions are negative in quality, though, academic self-confidence may be substantially derailed, as Núñez (2009) discovered in her longitudinal study of Latino/a students. Cross-sectional investigations affirmed these effects, showing how interactional diversity improved students' self-reported growth in general education, science and technology, and intellect (Hu & Kuh, 2003b; Luo & Jamieson-Drake, 2009). Across all studies, effects ranged from small to large, but were typically smaller in the more robust studies with pre/posttest designs.

Other Sources of Impact. A handful of other effects were reported in some studies. Overall, engagement is beneficial: being involved on campus exerted a moderate positive effect on intellectual self-confidence in Chang et al.'s (2006) study. Taking part in demonstrations and exercising and playing sports were associated with first- to senior-year gains in self-rated drive to achieve (Sax, 2008). However, watching television reduced drive to achieve (Sax, 2008). Two leadership-related activities—participating in student government and leadership training—resulted in gains in students' self-rated competitiveness (Sax, 2008). The amount of time students spent working on campus may have interfered with academics, as such experiences exerted small negative effects on academic self-concept (Kim & Sax, 2014).

The remaining evidence regarding the impact of an array of co-curricular experiences on academic self-concept came from studies based on small samples or that relied on self-reported gains collected at one point in time. In one small-sample study, Berger and Milem (2002) ascertained differences in the effects of various types of community service engagement on students' self-rated academic ability and achievement orientation. Religious community service was negatively associated with both measures of academic self-concept, holding constant student characteristics, pretested outcome measures, and other college involvement variables. Type of service was more predictive of outcomes than the frequency of participation. In another study based on self-reported gains, fraternity or sorority membership predicted students' self-reported growth in general education (e.g., acquiring a broad general education, writing clearly and effectively), although effect sizes were quite small (Hayek, Carini, O'Day, & Kuh, 2002). Some limited cross-sectional evidence from students attending highly selective institutions suggested committed athletics participation was related to lower levels of academic self-concept (i.e., reflective of skills such as writing ability, foreign language ability, analytical ability, and quantitative skills; Aries, McCarthy, Salovey, & Banaji, 2004). Nevertheless, peer and academic engagement may help to cultivate academic self-perceptions among athletes. Comeaux, Speer, Taustine, and Harrison's (2011) cross-sectional study of over 100 first-year athletes attending four NCAA Division I public universities demonstrated that developing friendships with other athletes who valued education and were committed to fostering their academic talents was associated with athletes' academic self-concept given controls for student characteristics.

Social Self-Concept and Interpersonal Relationships. Research delineating within-college effects on social self-confidence and relational maturity was less plentiful than research examining academic self-concept. As with intellectual self-concept, general involvement on campus bore a moderate relationship to social self-confidence, according to some longitudinal and generalizable evidence (Chang et al., 2006). Two longitudinal investigations identified small-to-medium effects of cross-racial interactions (e.g., in class, in dating relationships, while dining, and while studying) on social self-confidence in models that controlled for pretests (Chang et al., 2004, 2006). Furthermore, a meta-analysis of 62 studies indicated that service-learning had significant positive effects on attitudes toward self (.28 of a standard deviation) and social skills (.30 of a standard deviation; Celio, Durlak, & Dymnicki, 2011).

Other cross-sectional studies posited that living on campus produced small gains in social outcomes (understanding self and others; Pike et al., 2012), but living-learning communities did not impart differential benefits in interpersonal self-confidence to living-learning participants versus those who lived in traditional residence halls (Inkelas et al., 2006). Other findings from Pike and colleagues (2012) indicated social benefits among students investing effort in their courses and majoring in a social discipline. In addition, two measures of the campus climate were advantageous to social gains: the interpersonal environment and support for student success. Reiterating the importance of a welcoming and supportive environment for social gains, a small-scale longitudinal study linked sense of belonging on campus to students' perceptions of their social competence (Pittman & Richmond, 2008).

Leadership Skills

Faculty Engagement and Mentoring. Faculty interactions and mentoring inspire leadership development according to several studies. The nature of the interactions most conducive to leadership formation present somewhat of a dualistic picture: students who sought faculty support and advice made gains in leadership skills, but so did students who challenged professors' ideas in class (Sax, 2008; Sax et al., 2005). The effects that materialized in Sax and colleagues' analyses persisted in the presence of controls for confounding influences, including pretested outcome measures. Other cross-sectional research attended to the qualities of mentoring that facilitate socially responsible leadership development. According to the Multi-Institutional Study of Leadership (Campbell, Smith, Dugan, & Komives, 2012), mentoring by student affairs professionals (compared to faculty) exhibited a small positive relationship with college leadership outcomes. Even more vital than who served as mentor, though, was the type of mentoring students received. Mentoring for leadership empowerment and (especially) mentoring for personal development were both associated with leadership outcomes. In addition, the effects of mentoring for personal development on leadership development were stronger when faculty, rather than student affairs professionals, served as mentors (Campbell et al., 2012). Qualitative investigations reinforced the significance of adult mentors and role models in students' leadership development (Komives et al., 2005; Renn & Bilodeau, 2005).

Diversity Engagement. Compelling evidence supports the positive impact of diversity experiences, broadly defined, on leadership development. In a well-controlled study based on longitudinal data from the Wabash National Study, Parker and Pascarella (2013) estimated that diversity experiences, such as having serious conversations with students of a different race or ethnicity, attending a debate or lecture on a current political or social issue, and sharing personal feelings and problems with diverse students, exerted large positive effects, of nearly one-quarter of a standard deviation, on socially responsible leadership development. Other longitudinal findings identified small positive effects of various types of curricular, cocurricular, and interactional diversity on leadership development, including socializing with other racial groups (Park & Millora, 2012), participating in intergroup dialogue and other extracurricular diversity events (Hurtado, 2005), and taking diversity courses (O'Neill, 2012).

Other studies with cross-sectional designs echoed these findings. A consistent predictor of leadership capacity was having sociocultural conversations with peers, according to the Multi-Institutional Study of Leadership (Dugan et al., 2012; Dugan & Komives, 2010). Dugan and Komives (2010) explained that conversations spanning many dimensions of difference from multiculturalism to politics provided "a platform for the development of listening skills, clarification of personal values and perspectives, and social perspective taking" (p. 539). Sociocultural conversations consistently predicted leadership outcomes for students of various races (Dugan et al., 2012), and among women in STEM majors such conversations, along with students' sense of belonging, exerted moderate effects in support of women's leadership self-efficacy (Dugan, Fath, Howes, Lavelle, & Polanin, 2013). Finally, interracial interactions corresponded to greater perceived gains in leadership skills in a study of alumni reflecting retrospectively on their college experiences (Luo & Jamieson-Drake, 2009).

Two additional points are noteworthy. First, the quality of diversity interactions shape leadership development over and above the frequency of the interactions. Hurtado (2005) observed small adverse effects of negative diversity interactions on leadership skills, while positive interactions fostered leadership skills. Second, students who have positive interactions with diverse peers on a regular basis benefit the most. Bowman (2013b) found that first-year students with low or moderate levels of diversity interactions exhibited very little growth in leadership (and even declines), whereas those with high levels of engagement showed considerable gains. In fact, the leadership skill difference between students who had interracial interactions very often versus rarely was .43 of a standard deviation. In sum, the more students engage diversity, the better prepared they are as leaders.

Academic and Cocurricular Engagement. Several studies affirmed the value of academic engagement for leadership development. Sax (2008) observed greater leadership self-concept gains from the first to fourth year among students who studied with others. A holistic measure of liberal arts experiences, which consisted of a variety of academic engagement indicators from faculty and peer contact to deep approaches to learning, made a strong impression on socially responsible leadership among students participating in a cross-sectional pilot of the Wabash National Study (Seifert et al., 2008). The strength of the effects may have been reduced had pretest measures been included in the models. However, later longitudinal evidence from Wabash, with the requisite controls, confirmed that liberal arts indicators indicative of deep engagement in learning were indeed strong contributors to socially responsible leadership, including academic challenge and high expectations, reflective learning, active and collaborative learning, and integrative learning (O'Neill, 2012). All effect sizes ranged from .20 to .29 of a standard deviation. Corroborating Wabash evidence concerning reflective learning, Park and Millora (2012) examined longitudinal data and reported that engaging in self-reflection and participating in courses that included reflective writing and journaling enhanced leadership development.

Leadership development is also attributable to involvement in a number of co-curricular and extracurricular activities. Most of these effects tended to be small in magnitude and included membership in student organizations and community service participation or service-learning (Dugan et al., 2012, 2013; Dugan & Komives, 2010; Hurtado, 2005; O'Neill, 2012; Park & Millora, 2012; Sax, 2008). Moreover, Kilgo, Sheets, and Pascarella (2015) reported conservative estimates of high-impact practices, derived from models with stringent controls, using longitudinal data from the Wabash National Study. According to their assessment, internship experiences exerted modest effects, in the realm of one-tenth of a standard deviation, on socially responsible leadership. Sax (2008) determined that gains in leadership self-concept were most prevalent among students who participated in student government, Greek organizations, and leadership training.

Other evidence about the benefits of individual leadership experiences came from cross-sectional and qualitative investigations. Dugan et al. (2011) suggested that several social change model leadership outcomes (individual, group, societal, and change for the common good) were attributable to individual leadership experiences. Leadership experiences that were linked to all four domains of the social change model included attending leadership conferences and participating in leadership lectures and workshops, but the effects were quite small.

An array of qualitative investigations supported much of the evidence we have presented to this point: adult mentors and role models, supportive peers, reflective learning, and meaningful involvement are central to the leadership development process. In their grounded theory study, Komives et al. (2005) described the evolution of students' leader identity as a transition from leader-centric perceptions to understanding leadership as inherently collaborative and relational. Those experiences that inspired clarification of values and commitments, skill procurement, and understanding of self and diverse others were pivotal forces in leadership development. An intervention associated with leadership courses—personal growth projects—also fostered leadership development when such projects introduced students to novel experiences, engendered reflection, and encouraged application of learning to other aspects of life (Odom, Boyd, & Williams, 2012).

Studies of specific sub-populations affirmed progressive stages of leadership development and the forms of engagement that fostered growth and integration of social and leader identities. For example, Renn and Bilodeau (2005) traced leadership development among LGB students and demonstrated that interacting with adult and peer mentors, engaging in LGB organizations, exercising leadership roles, and becoming involved in leadership conferences were important contributors to students' development. Subsequently, Renn (2007) described an involvement-identity cycle in which students who were increasingly involved in leadership further embraced a public LGB identity, as well as merged their sexual and leader selves to reflect three distinct identities: LGB leader, LGB activist, or queer activist. Further qualitative evidence suggested that student leaders of identity-based organizations experienced their psychosocial (e.g., race, ethnicity, gender, sexual orientation) and leadership identities as salient and either merged ("gay leader," "Latina activist") or parallel (Renn & Ozaki, 2010).

Other specific initiatives aimed at leadership development may prove fruitful for enhancing merged social and leader identities. For example, a study of Native American students posited that through a leadership conference, Native students developed their leadership because of opportunities to construct a positive self-image, build community, and learn from Native role models (Minthorn, Wanger, & Shotton, 2013).

Other Sources of Impact. We located a handful of studies addressing leadership development through athletics participation, and the evidence is rather mixed. The one study based on longitudinal and generalizable data indicated that overall, athletic involvement had marginal positive effects on leadership development (Park & Millora, 2012). It may be, though, that active leadership while playing sports makes a stronger impression. In a small-sample longitudinal study, leadership gains were more pronounced in one playing season when students served as team captain (Grandzol, Perlis, & Draina, 2010). The level of sports participation may also be a factor. Comeaux and colleagues' (2011) cross-sectional study of a small sample of first-year athletes demonstrated that revenue-generating athletics participation (men's football and basketball) was associated with leadership skills. Still, effects may depend on gender, as other cross-sectional research based on military college students showed that varsity athletic participation had a negative impact on women's leadership (Shepherd & Horner, 2010). Finally, when sports participation makes a difference in leadership skills, the impact may be attributable to any number of experiences afforded to participants, including organizing and planning, balancing roles, and problem solving, according to one qualitative study (Hall, Scott, & Borsz, 2008).

Several other studies identified some disparate effects involving college major (Dugan et al., 2013), scholarship programs (Hu, 2011), working (Salisbury, Pascarella, Padgett, & Blaich, 2012), and religious and spiritual activities (Rennick, Toms Smedley, Fisher, Wallace & Kim, 2013), many of which were indirect and mediated by academic, cocurricular, and peer engagement. As a noteworthy counterpoint to the wealth of evidence about the benefits of engagement, forms of disengagement, such as watching television, contributed to declines in leadership self-confidence in one longitudinal investigation (Sax, 2008).

Autonomy, Independence, Locus of Control, and Self-Efficacy. Much of the research that emerged through the 2000s regarding students' development of autonomy and independence was framed by self-authorship theory and probed how students become cognitively, intrapersonally, and interpersonally self-directed. This research, most of it qualitative, illuminated intricate pathways that students navigate as they grow less reliant on external voices and more attuned to internal reference points in their ways of knowing, relating, and understanding themselves.

Provocative moments, defined as experiences of significant disequilibrium, are important to catalyzing self-authorship (Pizzolato, 2005). Provocative moments come in many forms. Many studies allude to the importance of encounters with diversity and multiple perspectives in reducing authority dependence and inspiring more complex meaning-making approaches (Barber, King, & Baxter Magolda, 2013; Baxter Magolda et al., 2012; Bryant, 2011a). In a study of first-year students, academic work introduced students to different points of view, which led to dissonance when multiple views came into conflict. Dissonance also emerged when educators pushed first-year students to assume responsibility for their own learning and when peers did not live up to expectations (Baxter Magolda et al., 2012).

Extending beyond the first year of college, Barber et al. (2013) followed a sample of college students attending six institutions across three years to examine the experiences closely associated with self-authorship. They focused their analysis on 30 students who had made the most significant progress. Echoing the study of first-year students (Baxter Magolda et al., 2012), a host of noteworthy factors fostered self-authorship, including experiences with dissonance related to academic coursework, leadership or work roles, relationships with others that prompted identity exploration and refinement, academic and social encounters that stimulated engaging and evaluating multiple perspectives (e.g., studying abroad, taking diversity courses, having roommate conflict), and major life events (e.g., deaths of friends and family members). Interactions with others on campus were salient in students' self-authoring, specifically, faculty who showed confidence in students' abilities and supportive peers who helped them process dissonance and encouraged them to be assertive in relationships.

Other studies identified additional nuances in the provocation that can motivate self-authoring. Pizzolato, Nguyen, Johnston, and Wang (2012) described identity dissonance, "a mismatch between participants' and others' perceptions of key characteristics of their identities" (p. 666), and relational dissonance, "[struggling] to balance personal, relational, and cultural consequences of meaning making" (p. 667), as pivotal in the self-authoring of diverse college students. Moreover, the researchers noted that the diverse participants in their study often confronted more than the "Who am I?" question in moments of dissonance; they also wrestled with the "Who are we?" question in making meaning of their racial or ethnic group membership. Psychological contexts (e.g., familial, cultural, collegiate) influenced and constrained how these students navigated intrapersonal, epistemological, and interpersonal dimensions of their lives. All told, relationships are key to initiating and progressing toward self-authorship. Both provocateurs and supporters have a role to play in this process (Pizzolato, 2003).

Pizzolato (2005) further contended that certain motivational conditions, namely volitional efficacy—belief that one can enact goal-directed behaviors even in the midst of challenge—and self-regulation, help students make the most of provocative experiences. Without volitional efficacy, students give others too much control over their behaviors; they may not be able to harness provocative experiences to recast their ways of knowing, relationships with others, and understanding of themselves.

Developmentally effective experiences (DEEs; see King, Baxter Magolda, Barber, Brown, & Lindsay, 2009) also inspire self-authorship largely because of their provocative qualities. Two studies, involving a cross-sectional, mixed-methods design and interviews with students at four diverse institutions, described an array of DEEs: interactions with diverse others (through friendships, living arrangements, and co-curricular activities); academic, political, and current events discussions with friends or in class; and negative experiences and relational challenges. In all, such experiences facilitated self-authorship by increasing students' awareness of and openness to diversity, encouraging exploration of the basis for beliefs and choices, cultivating a sense of identity to guide choices, and enhancing awareness of and openness to responsibility for learning. Importantly, students' reactions to developmentally effective experiences—and thereby pathways to development—were defined by their meaning-making orientations, whether external, internal, or a combination of both (Barber & King, 2014; King et al., 2009). Barber and King (2014) went on to identify two of the DEEs, being exposed to new ideas, situations, and people and experiencing discomfort leading to action, as resonant of Sanford's (1962, 1967) notions of "challenge," and the final DEE, relying on organizational structures or routines, as commensurate with his concept of "support." The researchers concluded that together, challenge and support established a strong context for learning, but that either one could spark development. All students were driven toward development by initial encounters with new perspectives, beliefs, cultures, and situations (the first DEE), but then continued toward self-authorship along distinctive trajectories imbued with either challenge (the second DEE, acting to resolve discomfort) or support (the third DEE, seeking structures to cope). Importantly, students tended to engage in strategies to resolve discomfort or seek structures to cope on their journey toward self-authorship along pathways that varied by their level of readiness or meaning-making orientation. Students who followed external formulas often took different routes from students who were at the crossroads.

Other qualitative studies and some limited quantitative evidence illuminated a variety of experiences that further self-authorship, gains in autonomy, and attributions for academic success. One study revealed that an academic advising intervention based on the learning partnerships model (LPM) helped students make progress toward self-authorship (Pizzolato & Ozaki, 2007). The advising program accomplished the three tenets of the LPM by validating students' capacity to know, situating learning in students' experiences, and defining learning as mutually constructing meaning. Jones and Abes (2004) explored the process by which service-learning motivates self-authorship and underscored how service-learning inspired students to integrate in their sense of self a commitment to helping others through service. They also became more efficacious, believing themselves able to learn about the circumstances of others and engage in socially responsible work.

Turning to the quantitative evidence, Bowman (2010d) found a variety of factors that contributed to students' gains in autonomy in the first year of college: working on or off campus more than 20 hours a week, good relationships with other students, and in-class challenge. Other effects were negative: drinking alcohol one or two times a week and having occasional or frequent negative experiences with diversity. Another study limited to first-year students revealed that, controlling for the pretest, student characteristics, institutional measures, and college experiences, effective teaching and interactions with faculty resulted in large gains, estimated at .16 of a standard deviation, in internal locus of attribution for academic success (Cruce, Wolniak, Seifert, & Pascarella, 2006).

Self-authorship is a long journey. Although college students generally become less authority dependent and develop new insight, many continue to rely on external voices and do not always resolve challenges in ways that yield new meaning-making strategies (Baxter Magolda, 2001; Baxter Magolda et al., 2012). Because most students do not achieve self-authorship in college, we discuss post-college self-authoring later in the chapter.

Psychological Well-Being

Residence. Evidence from several longitudinal studies convincingly details challenges to students' psychological well-being that stem from living on campus. Well-controlled analyses of longitudinal data from the Wabash National Study observed first-year declines in psychological well-being—a measure of autonomy, environmental mastery, personal growth, positive interpersonal relationships, purpose in life, and self-acceptance—linked to living in a residence hall (Bowman, 2010d; Martin et al., 2011; Padgett, Johnson, & Pascarella, 2012) or a fraternity/sorority house (Bowman, 2010d). Padgett and colleagues estimated the magnitude of the negative effect of residence hall living at .16 of a standard deviation. Potentially illuminating some of the mechanisms behind this negative effect, Sax, Bryant, and Gilmartin (2004) specified problems in one's place of residence as having a uniformly negative impact on emotional health in the first year of college. Importantly, all three studies were limited to first-year students, who may be particularly vulnerable to declines in well-being because of adjusting to new peers and living arrangements, not to mention the academic demands of college.

Peer and Faculty Engagement. The quality of peer interactions makes an impression on psychological well-being according to several rigorous studies. When students experienced positive and influential relationships with peers, their well-being flourished in studies of first-year outcomes (Bowman, 2010d; Martin et al., 2011; Padgett et al., 2012). Padgett and colleagues estimated the positive effect of peer interactions on well-being at one-fifth of a standard deviation. Enjoying a student support network also resulted in emotional health gains in Sax and colleagues' (2004) longitudinal study of first-year students. Socializing with peers invigorated first- to fourth-year gains in emotional health and reductions in feeling overwhelmed (Sax, 2008). A small-scale study with limited generalizability upheld these patterns; perceived support from friends lowered levels of depressive and somatic symptoms (Wang & Castañeda-Sound, 2008). Negative peer interactions can be harmful, however. Peer pressure undermined first-year students' emotional health in Sax and colleagues' (2004) study, and evidence from a study with limited generalizability also attributed friendship conflict to adjustment problems in the first year (Swenson, Nordstrom, & Hiester, 2008).

A parallel phenomenon exists for students' engagement with faculty. When faculty devote time to interacting with students, challenge and maintain high expectations of students, provide support and honest feedback, and practice good teaching, students make gains in psychological well-being and emotional health, holding constant other factors (Bowman, 2010d; Martin et al., 2011; Padgett et al., 2012; Sax, 2008; Sax et al., 2005). However, when faculty do not take students' comments seriously, students become more overwhelmed (Sax et al., 2005). In all cases, effects tended to be small to medium.

Diversity Engagement. Bowman (2010c, 2010d, 2013b) conducted several studies, using longitudinal data from the Wabash National Study, which drew connections between diversity engagement and psychological well-being in the first year of college. He observed, first, that the quality of diverse interactions affects well-being, with positive interactions spurring gains and frequent or even occasional negative interactions contributing to declines (Bowman, 2010d). Particular types of engagement—curricular and social—are also of consequence. Taking into account other variables critical to psychological well-being, diversity course work exerted a positive influence on well-being, but greater gains were realized for students more invested in diversity course work. Compared to taking one diversity course, taking two or three courses were each associated with gains in psychological well-being of about .10 of a standard deviation (Bowman, 2010c). Taking only one diversity course (compared to none), however, did not translate into well-being gains, perhaps because such experiences created disequilibrium that was not resolved until additional diversity courses were taken. In a similar fashion, the positive relationship between interracial interactions and psychological well-being was stronger at higher levels of engagement (Bowman, 2013b). Put differently, the difference in psychological well-being between students who rarely had diversity interactions versus those who had them "very often" was more than a quarter of a standard deviation.

Academic and Cocurricular Engagement. A few longitudinal studies, most based on generalizable data, identified associations between psychological well-being and an array of academic and cocurricular engagement factors. In two studies that drew on data from the Cooperative Institutional Research Program, studying and doing homework exacerbated students' feelings of being overwhelmed (Sax, 2008) and made a small to moderate negative impression on psychological well-being (Park & Millora, 2012). To this, Park and Millora (2012) added self-reflection as a contributor to declines in well-being, perhaps because reflection became ruminative among students already struggling with mental health challenges.

The effects of engaging in community service were mixed according to another study that was longitudinal but had limited generalizability. Berger and Milem (2002) determined that academic community service was associated positively with psychological wellness, while off-campus community service had the opposite effect, controlling for student characteristics, pretest measure, and other college involvement variables. Yet other forms of engagement—collaborative learning and participating in clubs and groups—were related positively to wellness gains in their analysis.

Other evidence of engagement as a positive force in students' well-being came from a cross-sectional analysis based on the Wabash National Study pilot. In that investigation, a combination of liberal arts experiences—representative of academic and cocurricular engagement, deep learning strategies, and influential encounters with faculty, peers, and diversity—were linked to myriad psychological well-being indicators, including autonomy, positive relationships with others, environmental mastery, personal growth, life purpose, and self-acceptance. Effect sizes ranged from .13 to .24 of a standard deviation, but were probably larger in magnitude than they would have been had pretest measures been incorporated within the models (Seifert et al., 2008).

Religious and Spiritual Experiences. Religious and spiritual aspects of students' lives also feature as contributors to students' well-being. Data from the UCLA Spirituality in Higher Education project were mined to uncover these effects. Bowman and Small (2012) examined hedonic well-being (obtaining psychological pleasure and avoiding pain) and eudaimonic well-being (living life to the fullest, maintaining good relationships, and feeling a sense of competence). Holding constant a variety of demographic and precollege characteristics (including pretest measures), the researchers found that religious engagement had a positive influence on both hedonic and eudaimonic well-being, but effects were small, in the range of .05 to .06 of a standard deviation. Conversely, when students had spiritual difficulties in life, such experiences eroded their psychological well-being, self-esteem, and physical health, according to one investigation (Bryant & Astin, 2008). Further evidence showed that spiritual quest and religious struggle together had negative effects on psychological well-being, in the range of .08 to .24 of a standard deviation—and these effects were consistent across students of diverse races/ethnicities (Astin et al., 2011; Park & Millora, 2010). On the other hand, equanimity, a measure reflective of feeling at peace and centered even in times of hardship, was associated positively and uniformly with well-being, with effect sizes estimated at .13 to .28 of a standard deviation (Astin et al., 2011; Park & Millora, 2010). Other data from a small-sample longitudinal study showed the strong negative effects of spiritual struggle following a personal loss on adjustment (Wortmann, Park, & Edmondson, 2012).

Intercollegiate Athletics and Recreation. Across several longitudinal and cross-sectional studies, participating in intercollegiate athletics (Aries et al., 2004; Park & Millora, 2012) and playing sports and exercising (Sax, 2008; VanKim & Nelson, 2013) supported students' psychological wellness. Clarifying the mechanisms behind this effect, a national cross-sectional study of more than 14,000 college students revealed that part of the relationship between vigorous physical exercise and well-being was explained by higher levels of socializing among students who exercised (VanKim & Nelson, 2013). Another caveat to these generally positive findings came from a study of male athletes. When men in college football restricted their emotions in interactions with male peers, they tended to have lower levels of life satisfaction (Steinfeldt, Wong, Hagan, Hoag, & Steinfeldt, 2011).

Campus Climate. Limited evidence suggests that when students feel their campus is supportive (Pascarella, Seifert, & Blaich, 2010)—and when they experience a sense of fit at their institution (Gilbreath, Kim, & Nichols, 2011)—their psychological well-being tends to be higher. However, most of the evidence details the often harmful effects that hostile campus climates have on students of marginalized identities. Quite a few studies emerged in the 2000s, although many were based on small samples and had other design limitations. Even so, when they are taken together, several conclusions materialize. Studies of students of color undisputedly connected perceptions of campus racial tensions, negative views of campus climate, racial harassment and discrimination, and race-related stress to higher levels of psychological distress, suicidal ideation, stress, anxiety, and depression, and to lower levels of self-esteem, well-being, and life and health satisfaction (Arbona & Jimenez, 2014; Buchanan, Bergman, Bruce, Woods, & Lichty, 2009; Byrd & McKinney, 2012; Griffin, Chavous, Cogburn, Branch, & Sellers, 2011; Hwang & Goto, 2009; Neville, Heppner, Ji, & Thye, 2004; Prelow, Mosher, & Bowman, 2006; Yoo & Lee, 2008). Two other studies found that lesbian, gay, bisexual, queer, and transgender students who perceived discrimination and experienced microaggressions and victimization on campus reported lower levels of college adjustment (Schmidt, Miles, & Welsh, 2010) and higher levels of psychological distress (Woodford, Kulick, Sinco, & Hong, 2014). Further evidence showed that part of the reason sexual minority college students experienced higher levels of depression and anxiety had to do with the higher levels of personal hostility, incivility, and heterosexist harassment they encountered (Woodford, Han, Craig, Lim, & Matney, 2014).

Effects of campus climate work in the other direction as well. Some evidence suggested that sense of community on campus was an important contributor to adjustment (i.e., lower levels of depression and higher self-esteem) for students of color (Rivas-Drake, 2012), and social support appeared to benefit college adjustment among LGBT students in another study (Schmidt et al., 2010).

Other Sources of Impact. Other within-college factors associated with students' psychological well-being have surfaced in several additional investigations. Partying behaviors, including drinking alcohol, reduced wellness in two longitudinal studies (Bowman, 2010d; Sax, 2008). However, participating in a fraternity or sorority was unrelated to psychological well-being in another analysis (Martin et al., 2011). Difficult life events, from experiencing financial problems to suffering from a personal illness or injury, had deleterious consequences for emotional health and well-being (Park & Millora, 2012; Sax et al., 2004). In addition, the personal problems of friends undermined the well-being of students who offered help (Park & Millora, 2012). Engaging leisure activities that offer fulfillment, such as reading, helped students to feel less overwhelmed in Sax's (2008) longitudinal study, but disengaging activities, from watching television to using the Internet as a coping strategy, reduced students' physical health and well-being, according to some other evidence (Gordon, Juang, & Syed, 2007; Sax, 2008).

Some studies considered the impact of interventions (e.g., involving writing, physical activity, counseling) on students' well-being. Most implemented pre/ posttest designs, but varied in quality, as few used experimental designs or controlled for other confounding variables, and most were based on small samples of students at one institution.

General Personal Development. The remaining studies depicting within-college effects on personal development often resorted to analyzing students' self-reported gains on holistic inter- and intra-personally oriented measures such as "personal and social development" or "practical competence." We caution readers that many of the effects delineated in this section should not be deemed causal given tendencies toward cross-sectional designs.

Living arrangements may influence general personal development. In one study, living on campus was negatively related to self-reported "enterprising" gains—essentially a measure of competence in working effectively with others and acquiring work-related skills (Pike et al., 2012). However, learning communities appeared to enhance students' beliefs that they had grown personally, socially, and practically, according to Zhao and Kuh (2004).

Faculty interactions and academic challenge were linked to self-reported gains in personal development and practical competence (Lundberg, 2012). Particular learning strategies that faculty employ in their interactions with students also emerged as correlates of personal development. Two studies revealed positive associations between cooperative learning practices and self-reported growth in personal development and "enterprising" abilities (Cabrera et al., 2002; Pike et al., 2012). Perhaps because of the focused and disciplinary-specific nature of faculty research, inquiry-oriented activities bore a small negative relationship with self-reported gains in personal development in another study (Hu et al., 2008).

Diversity experience most often has a favorable influence on students' self-reported personal development, with one exception. Two studies found associations between interactional diversity and self-reported gains in personal development and personal and social competence (Hu & Kuh, 2003b; Reason et al., 2007). Lundberg (2012) also connected self-reported gains in personal development to exposure to classroom diversity. However, serious conversations with students of a different race or ethnicity were negatively related to personal development in Lundberg's study, perhaps a reflection of the unsettledness that students often face when challenged by diverse peers.

The weight of the evidence revealed that multiple forms of engagement, whether cognitive, academic, co-curricular, or out of class, corresponded to students' reporting growth in personal, social, and practical competence domains (Pike et al., 2012; Reason et al., 2007). Some studies emphasized particular types of engagement. For example, a meta-analysis of 40 studies examined the effects of service-learning on holistic student development (Yorio & Ye, 2012). The researchers estimated the effects of service-learning on "personal insight" (e.g., identity, awareness of oneself, self-efficacy, self-esteem, determination, persistence, career aspirations) at .28 of a standard deviation. In addition, participating in Greek organizations related to self-reported gains in personal and social development and practical competence, according to Hayek et al. (2002). Pike (2003) also reported a positive but weak relationship between Greek participation and personal development. A smaller scale single-institution study generated longitudinal evidence to show that a greater degree of investment in student organizations—joining or leading rather than simply attending a meeting—was associated with modest first-year to senior-year gains in a number of personal development domains (e.g., establishing and clarifying purpose, educational involvement, career planning, life management, and cultural participation; Foubert & Grainger, 2006).

When students perceive that their institution supports student success and challenges them, they report greater growth in their personal, practical, and social competence (Pike et al., 2012; Reason et al., 2007). What is more, institutional environments with more seamless academic and student affairs structures may also be of benefit to students' holistic growth. Personal development, defined as connecting in- and out-of-class experiences, thinking critically, taking responsibility for learning, and understanding self and others, was fostered when students participated in academic and student affairs partnership programs, according to a qualitative study of 18 institutions (Nesheim et al., 2007).

Other research considered personal and social development for particular student populations. For instance, findings from one study observed that male and female athletes reported greater gains in personal, social, and practical development than did non-athletes (Umbach, Palmer, Kuh, & Hannah, 2006). The self-reported personal and social development of African American students was predicated on a number of in-class and out-of-class experiences in Flowers's (2004b) analysis. Effects were numerous, but the domains with the greatest number of significant, albeit small, associations included course learning (e.g., integrating ideas from various sources into a paper; trying to explain course materials to another student) and personal experiences (e.g., discussing intergroup dynamics with other students; identifying with a character in a book or movie). Among community college students, perceived gains in personal and social development were moderately associated with the degree of effort students expended academically (i.e., in the library, course work, writing, and clubs) and socially (with other students). Also, perceptions of the institution and their courses as stimulating, challenging, and worthwhile predicted students' self-reported gains in personal and social development (Ethington & Horn, 2007). Finally, interactions with faculty and staff were important for women's self-understanding and development of personal and professional identities, according to a qualitative study of women attending two Catholic women's colleges (Ropers-Huilman & Enke, 2010).

In sum, persuasive evidence has documented that a host of within-college experiences directly shape psychosocial outcomes. Across outcomes, the experiences that surfaced as the most influential were faculty engagement, peer interactions, and encounters with diversity in formal and informal settings. Studies generally concurred that adverse experiences with faculty, peers, or diversity undermine psychosocial development as much as constructive experiences promote identity, self-concept, and well-being. "Constructive experience," though, has multiple meanings. Supportive people and contexts in students' lives foster growth, but so do individuals and environments that provoke students to confront new ideas, navigate novel situations, dismantle assumptions, and refine beliefs about themselves and others.

CONDITIONAL EFFECTS OF COLLEGE

Conclusions from the 1990s

Studies of conditional effects were rare prior to the 2000s. Most of the evidence in the previous decade pointed to general rather than gendered conditional effects of college on identity development, with the exception of some indication of differential effects of fraternity or sorority membership by gender. Otherwise, whether identity development varied by gender and race/ethnicity (or any other institutional or student characteristic) was unknown as of the 1990s.

Evidence from the 1990s revealed that some college experiences influenced self-concept in different ways for different students. For instance, the impact of racial/ethnic diversity in the friendship group differentially affected the intellectual self-confidence of African American and White students. Moreover, women majoring in math-intensive fields made greater gains in math self-confidence than did men in the same fields, which was likely the result of an environment where others shared women's talents and interests. In some other disciplinary environments—those deemed social (emphasizing mentoring, helping others, friendliness)—women's gains in skills and abilities congruent with these fields were smaller than men's gains. Finally, intercollegiate athletic participation had a stronger effect on African American students' social and academic self-concept relative to their White peers.

Although rigorous studies surfaced in the 1990s addressing conditional effects of college on locus of control, many findings were not replicated. Some studies considered whether and how the overall impact of college attendance is conditional on gender, race, and attendance at four-year versus two-year institutions. These studies generally found that students of different genders, races, and institutional types moved toward internality to a similar degree during college. However, the effect of different experiences, such as specific forms of curricular and extracurricular engagement, on internal locus of attribution did vary by the type of college attended, race, gender, age, and first-generation status. For example, among first-year students attending community colleges, honors program participation, age, fraternity or sorority membership, hours worked, and teachers' instructional skills and clarity had stronger positive effects on internality relative to those attending four-year institutions. First-generation students also appeared to make greater gains in internal locus of attribution for academic success than their non-first-generation peers due to a variety of academic and extracurricular forms of involvement in the second and third years of college. Some experiences, though, had a stronger negative effect of internality among first-generation students compared to their peers: number of hours worked and volunteer work.

Finally, some research indicated that college attendance had a stronger impact on self-esteem among women compared to men. Nevertheless, models suggesting as much left important confounding factors uncontrolled, so the conjecture was tentative as of the last decade.

Evidence from the 2000s

Identity Development. We located few studies addressing the differential effects of college on identity development. Although no studies explored varied collegiate effects on gender identity or sexual orientation that were dependent on student characteristics, a small fund of evidence considered racial-ethnic and religious-spiritual identities.

Racial and Ethnic Identity. Only two studies of racial and ethnic identity development considered conditional effects and both were based on small samples. In their longitudinal investigation of just under 100 Latino college students attending a large, urban university, Fuller-Rowell et al. (2013) identified a significant interaction between perceived discrimination by faculty, students, and staff on campus and national identity (as measured by the degree to which students endorsed values of mainstream American society and felt a part of American culture) in relation to ethnic identity commitment, or sense of attachment to one's ethnic group. Among students with low levels of national identity, perceived discrimination had a positive influence on ethnic identity commitment during college. By contrast, those with a stronger national identity experienced the opposite effect, with discrimination curbing growth in ethnic identity commitment by almost one-third of a standard deviation across four years of college. The researchers surmised that American prejudices toward certain ethnic groups and nationalities were particularly harmful to identity commitments among members of ethnic groups that identified strongly with American values and society. A cross-sectional study involving a relatively small sample of ethnic-minority and ethnic-majority college students found that discrimination narratives bore a stronger relationship to ethnic identity exploration and pride among ethnic-minority students compared to their majority peers (Pasupathi et al., 2012), consistent with the notion that difficult experiences can at times catalyze identity development among students of color.

Religious and Spiritual Identity. Most of the research delineating conditional effects of college on religious and spiritual identities was attuned to religious or worldview identification. For instance, Bowman and Small (2010) examined college effects on spiritual identification and spiritual quest for "double religious minority students," whose religiously minoritized identity is twofold: on the college campus and within mainstream society. Their carefully controlled models revealed moderate to strong institutional effects conditioned by worldview. Specifically, double religious minority students who attended Catholic institutions experienced sharper declines in spiritual identification and spiritual quest than mainline Protestant students attending Catholic institutions. Furthermore, born-again Christians attending non-Catholic religiously affiliated institutions experienced more dramatic declines in spiritual identification than did mainline Protestants. Catholic students were also uniquely affected by institutional context; at secular schools, Catholic students experienced greater gains in spiritual quest than did mainline Protestants.

In a subsequent study, Small and Bowman (2011) determined that institutional religious affiliation and aggregate measures of students' openness to religious diversity on campus differentially affected student religiosity in ways that varied by student worldview. As one example, attending an institution where students embraced religious diversity reduced the religious commitment of evangelicals compared to mainline Protestants. Small and Bowman surmised that evangelical students, who traditionally hold to particular truth claims, may have been especially challenged in environments marked by an ethos of religious pluralism. Also indicative of the unique ways that campus climate may shape religious outcomes, a cross-sectional study with limited generalizability furthered the argument that students of different religious backgrounds respond to climate dimensions uniquely. In that study, religious majority students (who identified with a Christian tradition) tended to have higher levels of worldview commitment than nonreligious students when they perceived their campus as religiously divisive and when they engaged in co-curricular religious and spiritual activities (Mayhew & Bryant Rockenbach, 2013). It may be that divisiveness introduced challenge—thereby intensifying Christian students' determination to maintain beliefs—and religious activities reinforced those commitments.

A particular type of religiosity—religious service participation—was the focus of other studies. According to some evidence, institutional type differentially affected the religious service participation of students with varying worldviews. For example, declines in religious service participation were less dramatic among Catholic students attending evangelical and Catholic institutions relative to non-Catholics. However, declines in religious participation were steeper for Black Protestant students attending evangelical colleges compared to students of other worldview identities (Hill, 2009).

In addition to conditional effects of institution type, net effects of attending college on religious outcomes also differed by worldview. Graduating from college did not provide the same boost in religious service participation among White Protestant students compared to students of other worldviews. Conversely, gains in religious service participation due to graduating from college were stronger for Black Protestants than peers of other worldviews (Hill, 2009). McFarland et al. (2010) also detected conditional effects of educational attainment on religiosity. In their study, higher levels of educational attainment corresponded to greater religiosity for certain groups—evangelical Protestants, Black Protestants, and Catholics. The same effects did not hold, however, for mainline Protestants and the nonaffiliated. We can deduce from these studies that students' worldview identities inform how their religious proclivities are influenced by certain institutional contexts and attending college overall.

Beyond religious identification, the effects of college on spiritual development also vary to some extent by gender (Bryant, 2007). Having many friends of the same religion bolstered students' commitment to integrating spirituality into their lives and their spiritual self-concept, holding constant confounding factors, but the effects were stronger among women than men. For men, certain intellectual pursuits—majoring in science and spending time studying and doing homework—were associated with declines in spirituality during college (Bryant, 2007).

Academic Self-Concept

Gender. Sax (2008) reported numerous conditional effects by gender involving multiple measures of academic self-concept. In some cases, the magnitude of effect was different for women and men; in other instances, effects were unique to one group. Women who attended institutions with a larger proportion of female faculty and who participated in racial/cultural awareness workshops made greater gains in their scholar orientation. It may be that such institutional and engagement factors shaped women's perceptions of the campus as a welcoming and supportive place for women and people of color, and thereby inspired confidence in their own scholarly abilities. Men's scholar self-confidence was more closely tied to academic major: Majoring in history and political science advanced men's scholar orientation, whereas majoring in science and math reduced their scholar self-concept. Sax (2008) attributed men's loss of confidence to the competitive nature of the STEM fields. Men's scholarly self-confidence was also uniquely (and positively) influenced by attending institutions with a strong party culture and working full time.

Women's math self-concept grew at larger campuses where a sizable percentage of students majored in science, math, and engineering. Moreover, majoring in business, engineering, physical sciences, math, statistics, computer science, and education, as well as studying with other students, facilitated women's math self-concept. Importantly, faculty had an important part to play: when faculty did not take women's comments seriously, their math self-concept declined. The set of effects germane to men's math self-concept were largely in the reverse, with negative effects surfacing for majors and peer group factors and positive effects for faculty characteristics and interactions. Majoring in English or humanities, history or political science, and journalism or communications—and being exposed to an artistic peer group—undermined men's math self-concept. By contrast, the percentage of women faculty at the institution, participating in faculty research, and receiving faculty support improved men's math self-concept (Sax, 2008).

Self-rated drive to achieve—a measure that asked students to compare themselves to peers—was affected by a unique set of institution-level predictors for each gender. Women benefited from a higher percentage of women faculty on campus, but wealthier peer cultures reduced achievement drive. For men, materialism of the peer group enhanced drive to achieve, while a peer group that prized understanding of others lowered men's drive to achieve. Other within-college experiences produced differential effects by gender. Although studying and doing homework, challenging professors' ideas, and social diversity experiences affected drive to achieve for both groups positively, effects were stronger for men. Women benefited more than men did from faculty providing honest feedback. Other gendered patterns involved college major. Majoring in the biological sciences enhanced drive to achieve among women, while majoring in the fine arts heightened drive to achieve among men. Conversely, majoring in psychology or social sciences weakened drive to achieve among men.

Race/Ethnicity. Some studies through the 2000s examined whether college effects on academic self-concept varied by race and ethnicity. Although many significant effects were observed, conclusions remain tentative because the data sources were cross-sectional or not generalizable. Many of the outcome measures in the cross-sectional studies were acquired from students' perceptions of their own growth. In one investigation, interactional diversity had stronger effects on White students' self-reported gains in general education, science, and technology than students of color (Hu & Kuh, 2003b). Lundberg (2012) reported an array of race-related conditional effects involving institution type, interactional diversity, and classroom diversity on self-reported gains in general education. Those effects that were at least moderate in magnitude included the stronger effects of institutional diversity emphasis and selectivity on general education gains among Asian/Pacific Islanders, and the stronger effects of classroom diversity on the general education gains of African Americans, Asian/Pacific Islanders, and Whites, compared to other groups.

Differential effects of faculty and peer engagement transpired in two other studies. In one large-scale but cross-sectional analysis, the effects of student-faculty interactions (e.g., working on faculty research, discussing career plans with faculty) made a stronger impression on self-reported intellectual gains among White and Asian American students relative to African American and Latino/a students. Even so, discussions of academic work tended to be consistently effective in shaping students' self-perceived intellectual gains (Einarson & Clarkberg, 2010). Furthermore, longitudinal data from a well-controlled single-institution study showed that friendship group degree aspirations contributed to first- to third-year gains in intellectual self-concept among White students, but friendship groups with higher SAT scores reduced White students' intellectual self-concept. The friendship group's intellectual self-confidence and degree of racial/ethnic diversity promoted the intellectual self-concept of students of color (Antonio, 2004). In the end, these two studies suggest, albeit tentatively, that students of different races/ethnicities are uniquely sensitive to distinctive aspects of peer and faculty contexts as they develop academic self-perceptions.

Other Conditional Effects. Other effects conditional on certain student and disciplinary characteristics were reported in two studies. Inquiry-oriented activities, such as participating in faculty research, were negatively associated with students' self-reported gains in general education but associated positively with students' perceptions of their intellectual development, according to one study. However, these effects were significant only among middle- and high-performing students. Students with lower levels of academic performance did not appear to experience such effects (Hu et al., 2008).

Kim and Sax (2014) examined the conditional effects of student-faculty interaction on students' academic self-concept by major using longitudinal data. Their well-controlled models revealed that the positive effects of having been a guest in a professor's home were comparatively weaker in investigative fields (e.g., biology, chemistry, mathematics) and enterprising fields (e.g., business administration, finance, journalism) than in social fields (e.g., philosophy, sociology). The positive relationship between being a guest in a professor's home and academic self-concept was also stronger in departments where students were satisfied with mentor accessibility and there were more students of color.

Leadership Skills

Gender. According to Sax's (2008) longitudinal study of the gender gap in higher education, certain types of involvement in college uniquely shaped women's propensity for leadership during college: taking honors courses, attending racial/cultural awareness workshops, and socializing with friends. Women majoring in business tended to experience growth in leadership, whereas the opposite effect occurred for women majoring in the biological sciences. Men's leadership was strengthened at institutions with a higher proportion of female faculty and when they worked full time. Paralleling the negative effects of biology environments for women's leadership, majoring in certain science and math fields tended to curb men's leadership development (Sax, 2008).

Two other studies examined longitudinal data from the Wabash National Study to identify the presence of some gendered effects on leadership development during the first year of college. Shim (2013) reported negative effects of attending liberal arts colleges and regional universities (versus research universities) on certain measures of socially responsible leadership, and some of these negative effects were stronger for or unique to men. Peer relationships had nearly consistent positive effects on men's and women's socially responsible leadership, although in some instances, effects were non-significant for women or slightly stronger for men. Surprisingly, leadership training and cocurricular activities had very little impact on socially responsible leadership. Positional leadership experiences had some small effects, but these were inconsistent across the measures of socially responsible leadership and typically varied by gender: positional leadership experiences enhanced men's self-awareness and women's collaborative and group facilitation skills. Other factors—faculty relationships, diverse peer interactions, and volunteering— exerted nearly uniform positive influences on measures of socially responsible leadership regardless of gender. Martin, Hevel, and Pascarella (2012) discovered some gendered effects of Greek membership on socially responsible leadership. Fraternity men excelled beyond non-fraternity men on the values of citizenship and change, while sorority women had an advantage over non-sorority women on common purpose and citizenship.

Race/Ethnicity. The impact of college experiences on capacity for socially responsible leadership differed in some ways by race in two studies (Dugan et al., 2012; Kodama & Dugan, 2013). For example, membership in student organizations uniquely predicted leadership capacity among African American/ Black and Asian Pacific American students. Moving from membership to leadership roles is not beneficial for all students, however. Holding leadership positions in student organizations was negatively related to socially responsible leadership among African American/Black students and positively related to leadership among multiracial students. Community service engagement corresponded to socially responsible leadership for all racial groups with the exception of African Americans. Finally, mentoring effects differed by subpopulation: mentoring by faculty supported the leadership development of White, African American/Black, and Asian Pacific American students; mentoring by student affairs professionals inspired leadership among multiracial students; and mentoring by other students encouraged leadership capacity among Latino/as. In all cases, effects were small in magnitude, estimated at .04 to .07 of a standard deviation (Dugan et al., 2012).

In a related study, Kodama and Dugan (2013) demonstrated that the predictors of leadership self-efficacy—that is, students' beliefs about their abilities to be successful leaders—also varied by race to a certain extent. Community service engagement predicted leadership self-efficacy only for African Americans, Asian Pacific Americans, and multiracial students, and mentoring by student affairs professionals supported leadership self-efficacy uniquely for African Americans. Working on campus negatively influenced the leadership self-efficacy of Asian Pacific Americans, while working off-campus inhibited the leadership self-efficacy of Latinos/as and multiracial students. Internship experiences were linked positively to leadership self-efficacy among multiracial students, and formal leadership program participation advanced Latino/a leadership self-efficacy. Again, all effects were small in magnitude. These findings highlight differences in the student engagement strategies that practitioners may employ to develop leadership self-perceptions among diverse students.

Autonomy, Independence, Locus of Control, and Self-Efficacy. Very little research addressed conditional effects of college on students' autonomy and self-directedness, with a few exceptions. According to quantitative evidence, several collegiate experiences exerted positive effects on internal locus of attribution for academic success uniquely among first-generation college students: the number of mathematics, social sciences, and arts and humanities courses taken; course-related interactions with peers; academic effort and involvement; and extracurricular involvement. However, hours worked and volunteering had a negative influence on first-generation students' internal attributions. For students whose parents had postsecondary education, these effects were generally negative or null, but the effects of volunteering on internal attributions were positive (Pascarella, Pierson, Wolniak, & Terenzini, 2004). The fact that volunteering had different implications for first-generation students versus their continuing-generation peers raises questions about the encounters that students may be having in these settings and how to ensure that service work is a constructive endeavor for students who are the first in their family to attend college.

Some qualitative evidence alluded to differential pathways to self-authorship for students with certain characteristics. High-risk college students and those with marginalized racial/ethnic and sexual identities may self-author earlier than students from privileged backgrounds as a result of processing provocative interpersonal experiences prior to or during college, encountering racism and undergoing development in other identity domains, such as sexuality (Abes & Jones, 2004; Pizzolato, 2003; Torres & Hernandez, 2007). Subsequent research showed that marginalizing experiences had a tendency to weaken high-risk students' self-authorship in the first year of college. However, problem-focused coping strategies helped students' self-authoring capacities reemerge as they adapted to their new environment (Pizzolato, 2004).

Psychological Well-Being

Gender. Sax and colleagues (Sax, 2008; Sax et al., 2004, 2005) uncovered a number of differential effects of college on indicators of psychological wellness. One investigation considered emotional health in the first year of college. In that analysis, socializing with friends and integrating successfully into campus life had distinctly positive effects on women's emotional health, but frequent off-campus e-mail communications and feeling bored in class detracted, overall, from women's emotional health. These experiences had no statistically significant impact on men, underscoring the vital role of support and integration on campus for women's well-being (Sax et al., 2004).

Subsequent analyses examined changes in several measures of wellness—emotional health, physical health, and feeling overwhelmed—from the first to fourth years of college (Sax, 2008; Sax et al., 2005). Engaging communities were important to fostering women's emotional health. Joining a sorority or attending an institution where many students lived on campus gave women's emotional health a boost. Contrarily, disengaging experiences, such as watching television, undermined women's emotional well-being. Engagement was also important for men's emotional health, specifically living on campus and participating in intercollegiate sports. Moreover, environmental factors were relevant to men's well-being. Men's emotional health was strengthened at institutions with a high proportion of female faculty, but was weakened when they majored in the physical sciences, a finding that deserves further inquiry given concerns about the chilly climate in the sciences uniquely affecting women (Sax, 2008). Sax (2008) also determined that religious service attendance supported gains in emotional health for both women and men, but gains were more apparent for men. However, another cross-sectional study that addressed broader forms of spiritual and religious engagement than merely religious service participation indicated such activities appeared to have greater positive benefits for women's psychological health relative to men's (Rennick et al., 2013).

For both women and men, participating in intercollegiate sports or regular exercise contributed to increased physical health, but the positive effects were stronger for men. Women were uniquely influenced, for better or worse, by faculty. When women received honest feedback from faculty, their physical health improved; however, feeling their comments were not taken seriously by faculty degraded women's sense of physical health. For men, physical health self-ratings declined when they majored in social sciences and took women's studies courses. A similar pattern emerged in Bowman's (2010c) analysis of longitudinal data from the Wabash National Study. Men's psychological well-being was reduced when they took one diversity course (versus no courses or two courses). Exposure to social science, women's studies, and diversity courses presents students with opportunities to confront privilege, a process that may prove difficult for students—in this case, men—with privileged statuses. Bowman's study demonstrated that effects on well-being are most pronounced when students are first introduced to diversity concepts.

Moving to the factors associated with students' feelings of being overwhelmed, one measure of faculty engagement—challenging a professor's ideas in class—had contrasting ramifications for women and men. Challenging professors reduced men's overwhelmed feelings, but incited further stress among women. Certain majors—physical science, engineering, social sciences, and women's studies—generated greater feelings of stress in women over time. Many of these majors are academically demanding, and some (such as women's studies) provoke consciousness raising that may be stress inducing for women. Exercising and sports curtailed overwhelmed feelings among women, while less-than-healthy patterns of partying did not provide the same sort of stress release and actually perpetuated women's overwhelmed feelings.

Watching television reduced stress for men, but participating in racial/cultural awareness workshops—again, potentially a consciousness-raising and privilege-confronting experience—increased men's overwhelmed feelings. Reiterating the typically unique and often beneficial effects for men of campuses with a high proportion of female faculty, Sax (2008) revealed such campuses lowered men's stress.

Race/Ethnicity. Diversity experiences are associated with differential gains in psychological well-being in ways that depend on race and ethnicity. For instance, in Bowman's (2013b) study, the benefits of interracial interactions and overall diversity interactions on psychological well-being were stronger among students of color relative to White students. In another investigation focused expressly on diversity course-taking patterns, Bowman (2010c) determined that White students experienced well-being gains of .10 to .11 of a standard deviation from taking two or three courses (versus one). Contrary to Bowman's hypothesis, White students did not appear to undergo a reduction in well-being because of initial exposure to one diversity course. However, students of color had lower levels of well-being, in the range of about one-fifth of a standard deviation difference, when they took one diversity course (compared to no courses), and they did not benefit appreciably by taking two or three courses. Bowman surmised that diversity courses, particularly those at the introductory level, may be discouraging or stressful to students of color if peers in the class behave insensitively.

Religious and spiritual experiences were linked in two studies to differential gains in psychological well-being dependent on race and ethnicity. Using longitudinal data from the UCLA Spirituality in Higher Education project, Park and Millora (2010) reported that going on a religious mission trip uniquely fostered well-being among Black students, and religious engagement supported well-being for White and (especially) Asian American students. To this, Rennick and colleagues (2013) added, based on their cross-sectional analysis, that the time students devoted to spiritual and religious engagement had greater positive benefits for African American students compared to other groups. The consensus across the two studies, albeit highly tentative, seems to be that African American students in particular may benefit emotionally from religious and spiritual involvement.

Park and Millora (2010) identified a few other conditional effects as well. Attending nonsectarian institutions (versus public) had a negative effect on well-being for Latinos/as. Major choice appeared to have conditional effects on well-being by race, but effects were generally small, and no clear pattern was discernable. College experiences exerting at least moderate effects on psychological well-being included the positive effect of performing community service for Black students and the negative effect of joining a social fraternity or sorority for Latinos/as.

Another holistic domain of wellness, "thriving," was the focus of Schreiner's (2014) research. She examined the unique pathways to thriving among students of color using data from more than 30,000 students attending 100 campuses in the United States, Canada, and Australia. Reiterating some of the conclusions from research on traditional measures of psychological well-being, four facets of the college experience—campus involvement, student-faculty interaction, spirituality, and the sense of community on campus—appeared to operate differently in the lives of students of color. For Asian American and Latino/a students, campus involvement was not a direct contributor to thriving, but for African American students, campus involvement, particularly leadership experience, was most critical to thriving. Quality faculty interactions—rather than merely the frequency of such interactions—promoted thriving among students of color. Corroborating the work of Park and Millora (2010) and Rennick et al. (2013), spirituality was important to advancing thriving among all racial/ethnic groups, but was a particularly strong contributor to the thriving of African American students. Finally, sense of community led to thriving for all students, but the pathway to community varied across groups. For Latino/a students, sense of community was enriched by involvement, for African American students by spirituality, for Asian American students by fit within their major, and for White students by interactions with faculty.

Other research underscored the effects of campus climate dimensions on the wellness of students of color and students exhibiting different levels of racial identity development, but the evidence comes from studies with some design limitations. Racial harassment appeared to have stronger negative effects on the psychological well-being of Black and multiracial students relative to White students, according to a single-institution study with a cross-sectional design (Buchanan et al., 2009). In a another study of just under 200 African American college students, Banks and Kohn-Wood (2007) identified conditional effects of racial discrimination on depressive symptoms based on racial identity profile. Students who prioritized blending in with the mainstream and emphasized shared human qualities rather than race (i.e., those who had an "integrationist" racial identity profile) were most affected by discrimination, as evidenced by their increased depressive symptoms. The researchers wrote, "When faced with racial discrimination, members of this group may be more strongly affected than members of other [racial identity profiles] because of the strong desire to connect with the mainstream" (p. 349). Brittian et al. (2013) found that the impact of ethnic identity affirmation (positive feelings about one's ethnic identity) on anxiety, self-acceptance, and self-esteem was moderated by university ethnic composition. Specifically, the positive relationships between ethnic identity affirmation and wellness measures were more pronounced at institutions with low ethnic composition than high ethnic composition. In sum, ethnic identity affirmation may have been a more salient contributor—in essence a buffer—to well-being in the absence of significant campus diversity.

Two other studies, though, contested the notion that a strong ethnic identity buffers students' experiences with discrimination and helps them to preserve their well-being. In a small-sample study, Yoo and Lee (2005) found that Asian American students who professed a strong ethnic identity experienced a buffering effect only when racial discrimination was low, but not when it was high.

Even students who strongly identified with their ethnic identity had difficulty maintaining their well-being in overtly discriminatory environments. Related evidence by Yoo and Lee (2008), based on a small-sample dataset and quasi-experimental design, showed that Asian Americans' ethnic identity commitments actually strengthened the negative impact of racial discrimination on situational well-being. Perhaps students with strong ethnic identity commitments find themselves exerting energy as they resist and combat discrimination in a way that lowers their well-being.

Other Conditional Effects. A few additional conditional effects involving religion/worldview and first-generation status surfaced in the 2000s. Bowman and Small (2012) found that "double religious minority" students—whose religiously minoritized identity is twofold: on the college campus and within mainstream society—experienced reductions in eudaimonic well-being (i.e., social self-confidence, cooperativeness, and understanding of others) when they attended religiously affiliated institutions versus secular institutions. The researchers explained, "Because many Christian colleges and universities in the U.S. incorporate Christianity extensively into the curriculum and co-curriculum . . . religious minority students may feel socially isolated in institutions that practice and privilege Christianity" (p. 502). In another investigation, spiritual struggle stemming from personal loss had a particularly strong association with posttraumatic stress and depressive symptoms among Catholics (versus Protestants), but the findings were generated from a small sample of college students (Wortmann et al., 2012).

Data from the Wabash National Study elucidated conditional effects of peer and faculty interactions on well-being in accordance with students' status as first generation in college. The positive effect of peer interactions on well-being was more than twice as strong for first-generation students relative to students whose parents had some college. In addition, good teaching interactions with faculty had no statistically significant impact on well-being among first-generation students, but had positive effects for all other students (Padgett et al., 2012).

General Personal Development. Some cross-sectional evidence reliant on students' self-reported gains in "self-development" (e.g., growth in self-esteem, self-confidence, independence) revealed small associations between students' perceptions of their development and interactions with faculty, accounting for student background characteristics and relevant college experience variables. The effect of faculty interactions varied to some degree by race. Discussing course selection with faculty had a uniformly positive influence, but there were differences in the effects of some types of interaction by race. For example, African American students benefited from working on research with faculty, but effects on self-development were negative for all other groups. Likewise, discussing career plans was associated with self-reported gains only for White and Asian American students. Interacting at social events with faculty exerted a moderate impact on Latino/a students' self-development, but effects were mixed for all other groups (Einarson & Clarkburg, 2010). Lundberg (2012) reiterated that faculty engagement as a whole had effects on students' self-reported gains in personal development that were conditional on race. All told, faculty-student interaction benefited the perceived personal development of African Americans, Asian/Pacific Islanders, and Hispanics.

In addition to faculty effects, Lundberg (2012) identified differential effects of diversity experiences on students' self-reported personal development and practical competence. Regarding personal development gains, serious conversations with students of other races negatively affected Hispanics, and classroom diversity benefited Native Americans and Asian/Pacific Islanders while diminishing the personal development of Hispanics. With respect to other indicators of personal growth, institutional diversity emphasis furthered White students' practical competence. Classroom diversity had negative effects on practical competence among Whites and Hispanics but positive effects for African Americans. Serious conversations with students of another race or ethnicity had positive implications for the practical competence of Hispanics.

Finally, Hu et al. (2008) reported that the negative effects of inquiry-oriented activities (e.g., participating in research with faculty) on students' personal development existed only for middle- and high-performing students. Students with lower levels of academic performance did not indicate similar declines in conjunction with inquiry-oriented activities.

Taken together, the evolving literature detailing the conditional effects of college on psychosocial development has grown tremendously in the new century. Some of the most compelling findings have to do with the influence that faculty, peers, and institutional and disciplinary climates have on students with differential levels of privilege. For example, direct interactions with faculty can improve or undermine women's self-concept and well-being, while the proportional representation of women faculty on campus usually bodes well for men's outcomes. Compared to their peers, first-generation students and students of color also appear to respond differently on many outcomes to certain types of engagement and campus environments or climates. Experiences that provoke students to confront social inequalities and challenging diversity issues seem to unsettle students with privileged identities. Many of the findings we reviewed require replication and further interpretation. Identifying what effects are conditional is an important first step, but making meaning of them—understanding why—will be essential to advancing research and practice.

LONG-TERM COLLEGE EFFECTS

Conclusions from the 1990s

The most persuasive evidence prior to the 2000s about the long-term effects of college on identity development came from studies of self-authorship and women's identity formation. Baxter Magolda (2001) traced the journeys of 101 students over time and delineated their progress to self-authorship cognitively, intrapersonally, and interpersonally, revealing how those domains of meaning-making continued to evolve and interact into adulthood. Informed by Erik Erikson's fifth developmental crisis (identity versus identity confusion) and Marcia's (1966, 1980) theory of identity development, Josselson's (1973, 1996) study of college women from the senior year through their forties revealed four pathways to identity formation that reflected the extent to which women had explored identity alternatives and forged commitments: *Guardians* maintained unexamined commitments; *Pathmakers* committed to an identity after a period of exploration; *Searchers* persisted in active identity exploration but without forging a commitment; *Drifters* did not explore or make identity commitments.

A paucity of evidence supported long-term college effects with respect to other psychosocial outcomes, with a few exceptions. Some research identified positive effects of college on intellectual self-confidence five years after college and overall self-confidence eleven years after college, due in part to interactions with diverse peers while a student. Other evidence suggested that intercollegiate athletic participation influenced social self-concept in the long term, with some noticeable differences by race/ethnicity. The influence of college on leadership development endured 5 to 15 years after graduation. Furthermore, the long-term effects on leadership of attending a women's college over a co-ed institution were likely indirect, due to the unique leadership experiences available to women at women's colleges.

Research through the 1990s was consistent in specifying that college had long-term effects on locus of control or self-directedness. In addition, participation in service-learning and community service activities appeared to relate to self-efficacy nine years after college, accounting for relevant confounding factors. As to whether college affected psychological well-being based on indicators of self-esteem in the long-term, the findings from the 1990s were largely mixed, with some studies showing no enduring impact and others (particularly those regarding the impact of women's college attendance) failing to disentangle the effects of college, maturation, and sociohistorical conditions.

Evidence from the 2000s

Long-term effects of college fell into several categories consistent with the organization of this chapter: academic self-concept; autonomy, independence, locus of control, and self-efficacy; and psychological well-being. However, no studies examined identity development or any other psychosocial outcomes after college.

Academic Self-Concept. One study of the long-term effects of college on academic self-concept examined the effects of attending an HBCU (versus an historically White college or university) on African American graduates. Using data from 1,069 African American respondents, Kim (2002b) constructed models to predict academic self-concept relative to peers. Controlling for various student- and institution-level variables, attending an HBCU had no impact on gains in self-rated academic ability, writing ability, or math ability nine years after entering college. Kim surmised that African American students are poised to succeed academically in the long term regardless of whether they attend an HBCU or predominantly White institution. Despite the generalizability of the data and the longitudinal design, the study was conducted early in the 2000s and thus represents a cohort that attended college several decades ago. Given the dated sample and the lack of corroboration from similar research, we caution readers against drawing definitive conclusions regarding the long-term impact of HBCUs on academic self-concept.

Autonomy, Independence, Locus of Control, and Self-Efficacy. Upon following 30 of her original participants into their thirties and forties, Baxter Magolda (2008, 2009) identified three elements of self-authorship that for the most part were characteristic of those who self-authored in the years after they graduated college. The first position, *trusting the internal voice*, involved participants feeling empowered to internally direct their responses to external events. Although many realities were beyond their control, they took ownership of their emotional reactions and meaning-making processes. In addition, participants moved beyond mere awareness of the internal voice: they began to exhibit confidence in the epistemological, intrapersonal, and interpersonal dimensions of their development across multiple contexts, from the workplace to personal relationships. As they developed greater consciousness of the internal voice and engaged in exploration, participants sometimes ventured through the "shadowlands," marked by periods of uncertainty and distress. However, personal reflection and support from others facilitated resolution of struggle in these difficult seasons.

Once they came to trust their internal voices, participants shifted to *building an internal foundation*, or core framework, to direct their actions and responses to the external world. As they endeavored to align their ways of knowing, identity, and relationships with the internal voice, a cohesive foundation began to take shape, although participants continued to refine their foundation as their efforts to live it out resulted in feedback from others and excursions through the shadowlands.

Securing internal commitments signified moving from knowing about one's internal foundation to living consistently with the commitments it represented. In trusting and solidifying core convictions, participants found they could act on them freely, as though they were second nature. Yet participants remained open to learning and continued to cycle through building confidence and creating foundations as they grew in wisdom and appreciation of the "dynamic process of living their internally authored systems" (Baxter Magolda, 2008, p. 281).

How might experiences in college contribute to self-authoring after college? Baxter Magolda (2009, 2014) put forth the Learning Partnerships Model (LPM), based on her longitudinal investigation, to shed light on the factors that inspired movement through the crossroads and ultimately toward self-authorship. She affirmed the importance of "learning partners," whether peers, professors, advisors, or mentors, who support students' cultivation of the internal voice by "respecting their thoughts and feelings, thus affirming the value of their voices; helping them view their experiences as opportunities for learning and growth;

and collaborating with them to analyze their own problems, engaging in mutual learning with them" (Baxter Magolda, 2009, p. 251). In addition, learning partners challenge learners by helping them to appreciate the complexity of major life decisions (and the drawbacks of simplistic solutions), urging them to pay attention to and heed their own voices as they journey through life, and emboldening them to offer their expertise as they work interdependently with others.

Psychological Well-Being. Adding to what we know about the long-term effects of HBCUs on college outcomes, Price, Spriggs, and Swinton (2011) examined self-image—a measure reflective of self-esteem and Black identity—among Black Americans after college. Based on their propensity score matching estimates involving three decades of data from the National Survey of Black Americans, the researchers determined that psychological outcomes were generally more favorable among graduates of HBCUs, which in turn had positive implications for labor market outcomes. Other factors that positively shaped psychological outcomes of Black graduates who participated in the National Longitudinal Study through the 1970s and 1980s included the percentage of Black students attending an institution, with an effect on self-esteem estimated at one-fifth of a standard deviation, and institutional selectivity, with an effect on self-esteem estimated at .17 of a standard deviation. Similar effects of institutional characteristics on post college self-efficacy did not materialize (Oates, 2004).

In addition to institutional characteristics, friendships and collegiate experiences have the potential to make an enduring impact on well-being, but the evidence is limited to just two small-scale studies. Martínez Alemán (2010) explored the significance of collegiate female friendships during the post-college years and found through her qualitative longitudinal study that such friendships continued to provide women with similar benefits for their personal development as they had during college, particularly in the areas of well-being (through stress and anxiety reduction) and self-authorship.

In addition, diversity engagement makes an impression on student well-being in the long term. Using longitudinal, albeit single-institution, data collected during the first year, the senior year, and 13 years after college, Bowman, Brandenberger, Hill, and Lapsley (2011) ascertained that racial/cultural workshops and ethnic studies courses had small indirect effects on measures of personal growth and identified/engaged purpose 13 years after college. The effects that surfaced were mediated by prosocial orientation in the senior year, which directly influenced both measures of well-being.

CHAPTER SUMMARY

Change during College

Most U.S.-based research was attuned to specific identity dimensions rather than to identity formation generally. Studies involving international samples concluded that identity formation may entail dual-cycles of exploration and commitment. Once initial commitments are formed, students may turn to further in-depth exploration before identifying with their commitments.

Although more studies of racial identity development, many of them longitudinal, emerged in the 2000s relative to the previous decade, this area of research produced some mixed results. The inconclusive findings may be the consequence of small participant and institutional samples. In addition, resorting to estimates of average change may have masked considerable individual movement between identity statuses. In fact, when identity status changes were examined, transitions—often maturation, but sometimes regression—became apparent. Most of the research in the 2000s addressing racial identity formation considered relationships between identity and other psychosocial measures (e.g., well-being).

According to recent national longitudinal research on religious and spiritual development, students exhibit growth on measures of spiritual quest and equanimity, but become more reserved about whether they are "spiritual" relative to their peers—potentially because they grow to be more reflective over time about what constitutes a "spiritual person." Religious commitment remains relatively stable during the first three years of college, but religious engagement—especially religious service participation—drops precipitously. Students also come to encounter difficulties in their religious lives, as indicated by increases in religious struggles the longer students are in college.

Regarding changes in academic self-concept, the most demonstrable shifts seem to occur in intellectual self-confidence and writing ability, with 11 to 16 percentile point increases in the proportion of students rating their aptitude as "above average" or "highest 10%" relative to peers. Paralleling the small positive changes reported by Pascarella and Terenzini (2005) in their earlier review, changes in self-rated academic ability are notably smaller than intellectual and writing ability. Another consistency with research through the 1990s is that both women and men—but especially women—become less confident in their mathematical ability. Although most changes in academic self-concept are rather modest, students report substantial growth in their academic abilities and knowledge when asked to evaluate overall gains in the fourth-year of college.

We found few studies of social self-confidence and interpersonal development, but longitudinal evidence posited noteworthy first- to fourth-year growth of 16 to 17 percentile points on a measure of social self-confidence. Students also appear to become more confident in their leadership orientation, with men exhibiting positive change in this domain more so than women do from the first to fourth year. Although growth across the first year in socially responsible leadership is less than consistent, assessments of first- to fourth-year change in a holistic measure of socially responsible leadership revealed an estimated positive change in the range of .37 of a standard deviation. Studies of autonomy and independence were few in number, but one in-depth assessment pointed to decreased authority dependence even though many students still relied to varying degrees on external sources of influence.

Over the years, the emotional health of entering first-year students has been declining. In response, many studies emerged in the 2000s to address this pressing issue. Deteriorating emotional health may be largely a first-year phenomenon, as longitudinal evidence pointed to only marginal changes in emotional health from the first to the fourth year of college. However, on all measures, women's well-being was lower than men's, meaning that the first- to fourth-year gendered wellness gap widened. Students of marginalized racial and sexual identities appear to suffer lower levels of well-being, and sometimes the rate of downward shifts in well-being is more pronounced for these groups.

Net Effects of College

We encountered similar problems as in previous reviews with the quality of evidence claiming college impact net of normal maturation or sociohistorical factors. As in the 1990s, our review is inconclusive given the difficulty in untangling college effects from other influences. Overall, no studies of acceptable rigor convinced us of a net effect of college on racial and ethnic identity development. However, research attentive to religious change was more compelling because of the availability of data sources that made it possible to compare college attenders with non-attenders. According to that literature, religious declines tend to be more prevalent among young adults who do not attend college, and rather than religious change, continuity in religious identity is more often the norm. What is more, highly engaged religious service attenders enroll in and graduate from college to a greater extent than individuals who rarely attend religious services, meaning that the relationship between educational attainment and religious participation is bidirectional: each behavior reinforces the other.

Between-College Effects

As with the evidence presented in previous reviews (Pascarella & Terenzini, 1991, 2005), studies of between-college effects often reveal that structural characteristics make a minor impact on outcomes when other within-college experiences are taken into account. Research approximating the effects of college on racial identity had its share of limitations, but indicated that racial identity salience and internalization may be somewhat higher among students of color attending predominantly White institutions, perhaps because students strengthen their racial identity as a strategy for coping in environments where they feel marginalized. Other findings posited that ethnic identities may evolve differently in four-year institutions versus community colleges. However, the methodological limitations and inconsistencies across studies leave open many questions.

No studies of sufficient quality examined between-college effects on gender identity. Nevertheless, a handful of qualitative investigations underscored the importance of affirming and inclusive environments for the identity development and expression of students with minority sexualities.

In terms of religious and spiritual development, some reliable studies reported higher levels of religiosity and spirituality at religious institutions.

Protestant institutions, especially those with an evangelical identity, promote religious and spiritual identity outcomes more so than other types of institutions. Religious colleges also appear to stimulate religious and spiritual struggles, but it is possible that this effect, as well as the others, is indirect, mediated by peer and other cultural influences at religious institutions. Supporting this point, the degree of religiosity and spirituality in the peer group and faculty culture tends reduce to nonsignificance the effects of institutional affiliation.

Some institutional structural qualities, such as size (negative) and research emphasis (positive), exert influences, albeit typically small, on measures of academic self-concept. Minority-serving institutions have small positive effects on academic and intellectual self-concept, but some of the evidence comes from studies with limited generalizability and reliance on self-reported gains. Stronger evidence emerged in the 2000s delineating the impact of peer culture—as reflected by peers' diversity engagement, civic values, and general investment in college life—on gains in academic self-concept.

In the main, institutional effects on leadership identity and skills, as well as inclinations for socially responsible leadership, are generally trivial in comparison to within-college effects. However, some limited evidence indicated that leadership skills may be cultivated at work colleges, women's colleges, and institutions where faculty are spiritually oriented.

We uncovered little evidence substantiating between-college effects on students' self-directedness and locus of control. However, as in Pascarella and Terenzini's (2005) previous review, more growth in autonomy may occur among students attending community colleges compared to those attending liberal arts colleges.

Although the average faculty focus on spirituality at an institution affords benefits to students' wellness, the level of religious engagement among students on campus may weaken psychological well-being. Findings attributing student wellness to attending HBCUs are mixed and based on data with limited generalizability—researchers found some wellness advantages conferred in HBCUs and some in PWIs. Qualitative research attended to the psychological consequences of privilege disparities in different types of institutional environments, showing that elite institutions may engender feelings of intimidation and inadequacy in low-income and first-generation students.

Large-sample, cross-sectional data revealed positive associations between students' impressions that they have made personal gains and institutional diversity emphasis and perceptions of a supportive campus environment. Other studies indicated positive effects on personal development of attending work colleges, HBCUs, Hispanic-serving institutions, and women's colleges.

Within-College Effects

Studies of within-college effects on identity in the 2000s attended to particular identity domains rather than general identity formation. Several studies denoted that exposure to diversity in college has favorable implications for racial and ethnic identity outcomes. Generally, curricular, cocurricular, and interactional diversity engagement appears to benefit racial identity development. Moreover, experiences with intergroup dialogue, peers, critical incidents, support and validation, and population-specific organizations may further identity progression, but some of the evidence is inconclusive. Even difficult encounters, such as confronting discrimination and negative campus climate factors, may catalyze racial consciousness and advance identity gains. Even so, supportive spaces and people are critical contributors to identity development as well.

Although research devoted to explicating women's identity development was nearly nonexistent in the 2000s, the literature base has broadened immensely to include studies of men and masculinities. According to the wealth of evidence, some environments, including fraternities and college athletics, reinforce patriarchal and hegemonic masculinity. Nonetheless, numerous qualitative studies examined how peer environments foster masculine identities. The conclusions from these studies show that peer contexts can promote identity development among men and may prove especially beneficial for identity formation among men of color as they negotiate the intersections between their racial and gender identities. Some studies highlighted the relevant role of friends, faculty, and student affairs staff in helping college men to construct masculinities. Campus involvement, academic engagement, and diversity engagement with peers are also promising sources of influence when they introduce men to the multifaceted possibilities for expressing masculinity.

Research addressing religious and spiritual development underscored that the effects of major on spirituality are generally small and that there is some veracity to the secularizing effects of majoring in science and engineering, but not indisputably. Faculty encouragement of religious and spiritual discussions has a noteworthy impact on many outcomes, with effects ranging from .08 to .17 of a standard deviation for spiritual quest, equanimity, religious commitment, religious engagement, religious skepticism, and religious struggle. Student engagement in helping behaviors, such as community service and volunteer work, donating money to charity, and helping friends with personal problems, has various small to medium positive effects on spiritual quest, equanimity, religious engagement and commitment, and religious struggle. On the other hand, partying and drinking have negative, though modest, effects on religious commitment and engagement, and time spent playing video games has a moderately negative impact on equanimity. Features of the campus religious and spiritual climate may affect religious and spiritual development, but at the time of our review, this evidence was limited to small-sample, cross-sectional data. Qualitative studies led to much the same conclusions as quantitative inquiries, suggesting the importance of exposure to peers of diverse religious backgrounds in furthering religious and spiritual identity development. Importantly, spiritual development produces gains in many traditional outcomes of college, including academic performance, degree aspirations, leadership development, and self-esteem.

Few studies in 2000s devoted significant attention to the impact of college major on academic or intellectual self-concept, and whether students' place of residence has any impact on academic self-concept is debatable in the absence of compelling longitudinal research. However, peer engagements, from tutoring other students to engaging in clubs or groups to socializing, are reliable contributors to intellectual and academic self-concept. Many rigorous studies delineated the impact of quality faculty interactions and found positive effects of quite a few indicators on academic and intellectual self-concept: talking with faculty outside class, challenging a professor's ideas, feeling supported by faculty, being a guest in a professor's home, asking a professor for advice outside class, having course-related faculty contact, and having a mentoring relationship with a faculty member. Conversely, some forms of faculty engagement have a small negative impact on intellectual self-concept: feeling bored in class, feeling faculty didn't take one's comments seriously, and receiving advice and critique from faculty. Some studies addressed how faculty affect students of color, stressing the importance of faculty support for intellectual self-concept gains. Academic, intellectual, and scholarly self-concept also grow when students devote time to studying and taking honors courses. Moreover, exposure to diversity has been connected in a number of studies to students' intellectual self-perceptions. Curricular diversity enhances students' self-rated drive to achieve, intellectual self-confidence, competitiveness, academic ability, and writing ability. Longitudinal studies typically indicated that informal and co-curricular diversity interactions boost academic and intellectual self-confidence. Studies of social self-confidence and relational maturity were fewer in number than those examining academic self-concept. Several factors—general involvement on campus, cross-racial interactions, and service-learning—appear to benefit social skills.

Research affirmed that faculty interactions and general mentoring facilitate leadership development. Interestingly, the types of interactions propelling leadership include students feeling supported by faculty *and* challenging professors' ideas in class. Mentoring for leadership empowerment and personal development also appears to stimulate leadership outcomes. Various types of curricular, co-curricular, and interactional diversity engagement advance students' leadership. As one example, having sociocultural conversations with peers increases leadership capacity. Importantly, the quality of diversity interactions and the degree of diversity exposure are relevant to leadership outcomes. Students with low or moderate levels of diversity interactions tend to grow very little in their leadership skills (and may even regress), whereas high levels of engagement produce considerable gains. Certain types of engaged learning in environments that are academically rigorous contribute to socially responsible leadership, including reflective learning, active and collaborative learning, and integrative learning. Leadership development is also associated with involvement in a number of cocurricular and extracurricular activities, such as student organizations, community service or service-learning, student government, Greek organizations, and leadership training and conferences. The evidence regarding the impact of athletic participation on leadership is mixed. Several other studies brought to light some other effects involving college major, scholarship programs, working, and religious and spiritual activities, but most of these were indirect and mediated by academic, co-curricular, and peer engagement.

Studies in the 2000s addressing students' development of autonomy and independence dealt primarily with self-authorship and how students become cognitively, intrapersonally, and interpersonally self-directed. This largely qualitative literature base consistently pointed toward the role of provocative moments in catalyzing self-authorship, as well as experiences with dissonance related to academic courses; leadership or work roles; relationships with others that prompt identity exploration and refinement; academic and social encounters that stimulate engaging and evaluating multiple perspectives; and major life events. Developmentally effective experiences—interactions with diverse others; academic, political, and current events discussions with friends or in class; and negative experiences and relational challenges—also motivate self-authorship given their provocative qualities. In terms of the quantitative evidence, many factors contribute to students' gains in autonomy in the first year of college: working on or off campus more than 20 hours a week, quality relationships with other students, and in-class challenge. Moreover, effective teaching and interactions with faculty produce large effects, estimated at .16 of a standard deviation, on internal locus of attribution for academic success.

Evidence from several longitudinal studies is relatively conclusive in conveying that living on campus and having problems in one's place of residence undermine emotional health in the first year of college. In addition, the quality of peer interactions is important to psychological well-being, according to several studies. Whereas positive and influential relationships with peers improve wellness outcomes, negative peer interactions can be emotionally destructive. Likewise, when faculty interact with students, provide challenge and set high expectations, offer support and honest feedback, and practice good teaching, students' psychological well-being and emotional health improve. Yet when faculty do not take students' comments seriously, students become more overwhelmed. Other evidence shows that the quality of diverse interactions affects well-being, with positive interactions inciting gains and frequent or even occasional negative interactions contributing to declines. Diversity course work and interracial interactions have overall positive influences on well-being, but are more effective at higher levels of engagement. Some experiences, such as studying, doing homework, and engaging in self-reflection, make students feel overwhelmed and less psychologically healthy. On the other hand, many religious and spiritual aspects of students' lives, with the exception of spiritual struggles, foster students' well-being. According to several longitudinal and cross-sectional studies, participating in intercollegiate athletics and playing sports and exercising further psychological wellness, but effects may be indirect and mediated by peer engagement. Hostile campus climates have harmful effects on the wellness of students with marginalized identities. Finally, partying behaviors, including drinking alcohol, correspond to reductions in wellness.

Other evidence pertaining to general personal and social development or practical competence emphasizes the positive influence of faculty interactions, diversity experiences, and perceptions of a supportive and challenging institutional environment. All told, engagement, spanning cognitive, academic, co-curricular, or out-of-class forms, corresponds to students' reporting growth in personal, social, and practical competence domains. Service-learning promotes "personal insight," with an estimated effect size derived from a meta-analysis of .28 of a standard deviation.

Conditional Effects of College

Compared to the 1990s, scholarship in the latest decade has undergone extensive advances in the study of conditional effects. While no studies examined differential collegiate effects on gender identity or sexual orientation, others considered racial/ethnic and religious-spiritual identities.

Just two small-sample studies of racial and ethnic identity development addressed conditional effects. They showed that discrimination can curb ethnic identity development in some circumstances, especially among students who value mainstream cultural values. For other students, facing discrimination can catalyze identity development.

Most of the research attentive to conditional effects of college on religious and spiritual identities examined differences by religious or worldview identification. Double religious minority students—those who are minorities on campus and in society at large—attending Catholic institutions experience more pronounced declines in spiritual identification and spiritual quest than do mainline Protestant students attending Catholic institutions. What is more, attending an institution where students embrace religious diversity weakens the religious commitment of evangelicals compared to mainline Protestants. Graduating from college does not provide the same boost in religious service engagement among White Protestant students compared to students of other worldviews. On the contrary, gains in religious service participation because of graduating from college tend to be stronger for Black Protestants than peers of other worldviews. Some limited evidence contended that peer groups and disciplinary environments have different effects on spiritual gains for women and men.

Regarding academic self-concept, women who attend institutions with a larger proportion of female faculty and who participate in racial/cultural awareness workshops make greater gains, relative to men, in their scholar orientation. Men's scholar self-confidence, conversely, is more closely linked to their academic major. Women's math self-concept surges in campus contexts where a sizable percentage of students major in science, math, and engineering. Moreover, majoring in business, engineering, physical sciences, math, statistics, computer science, or education and studying with other students improve women's math self-concept. Faculty are important contributors to women's confidence in their math skills: when faculty do not take women's comments seriously, their math self-concept drops. Men's math self-concept, on the other hand, is negatively affected by certain majors and peer group factors and positively affected by faculty characteristics and interactions. Some evidence emerged in the 2000s regarding race-related college effects on academic self-concept, but conclusions were tentative because the data sources were cross-sectional and often not generalizable.

Certain forms of involvement in college uniquely influence women's propensity for leadership during college, including taking honors courses, attending racial/cultural awareness workshops, and socializing with friends. Men develop leadership skills at institutions with a higher proportion of female faculty. With respect to socially responsible leadership, positional leadership experiences engender men's self-awareness and women's collaborative and group facilitation skills. Other factors—from faculty relationships to diverse peer interactions and volunteering—exert similar positive influences on measures of socially responsible leadership regardless of gender. Still, the impact of college experiences on capacity for socially responsible leadership differs in some ways by race.

Studies of self-authorship contended that high-risk college students and those with marginalized racial/ethnic and sexual identities have a propensity to self-author—as a result of provocative interpersonal experiences prior to or during college, racism, and development in other identity domains—earlier than students from privileged backgrounds. Related to evidence Pascarella and Terenzini (2005) presented in the last review, several academic and co-curricular experiences exert positive effects on internal locus of attribution for academic success uniquely among first-generation college students. However, volunteering has a negative impact on first-generation students' internal attributions, unlike their peers whose parents attended college. For that group, the effects of volunteering on internal attributions are positive.

Numerous conditional effects surfaced related to well-being. Community can be important to fostering women's emotional health. Joining a sorority or attending an institution where many students live on campus supports a positive trajectory in women's emotional health. Alternatively, disengaging experiences, such as watching television, make a negative impression on women's emotional well-being. Engagement is also worthwhile for men's emotional health, specifically living on campus and participating in intercollegiate sports. Moreover, environmental factors—such as attending an institution with a high proportion of female faculty—invigorate men's well-being. Women are uniquely influenced by direct encounters with faculty. When women receive honest feedback from faculty, their physical health improves; however, feeling their comments are not taken seriously by faculty is ultimately degrading to women's sense of physical health. For men, physical health self-ratings decline when they major in social sciences and take women's studies courses, perhaps because these environments encourage men to confront their own privilege. Regarding the factors associated with students' feelings of being overwhelmed, challenging a professor's ideas in class has opposing effects for women and men: it reduces men's overwhelmed feelings but breeds further stress among women.

Diversity experiences affect psychological well-being in ways that depend on race and ethnicity. Overall diversity interactions have stronger effects on psychological well-being among students of color relative to White students. The effects of course-taking patterns are decidedly different, though. White students incur no losses in their well-being after initial exposure to one diversity course. However, students of color have lower levels of well-being, about one-fifth of a standard deviation difference, upon taking one diversity course (compared to no diversity courses), and they do not benefit in any noticeable way from taking two or three courses. Other studies showed that campus climate may uniquely affect the wellness of students of color, but whether a strong ethnic identity buffers students' experiences with discrimination and helps them to preserve their well-being has mixed support in the literature. A counterpoint to evidence regarding experiences and environments that have negative effects on well-being, African American students, according to several studies, thrive psychologically when they have religious and spiritual experiences.

A few additional conditional effects related to religion/worldview and first-generation status were identified in the 2000s. Double religious minority students—who are minorities on campus and in the society at large—experience lower levels of well-being, probably due to their lack of privilege, when they attend religiously-affiliated institutions versus secular institutions. Furthermore, the positive effect of peer interactions on well-being is more than twice as strong for first-generation students relative to students whose parents attended college.

Limited cross-sectional evidence based on students' self-reported gains in "self-development" uncovered small associations between students' perceptions of their development and interactions with faculty, but those effects vary to a certain extent by race. The effect of diversity experiences on general measures of personal development vary to some degree by race as well.

Long-Term College Effects

Evidence pertaining to long-term effects of college on psychosocial identity was sparse through the 1990s, but provided some insight into self-authorship and women's identity formation. Continuing the line of evidence involving self-authorship, Baxter Magolda (2008, 2009) offered further nuance in articulating three positions within the self-authored meaning-making structure, including trusting the internal voice (feeling empowered to internally direct responses to external events), building an internal foundation (establishing a core framework to direct actions and responses to the external world), and securing internal commitments (moving from knowing about one's internal foundation to living consistently with the commitments it represents). In addition, Baxter Magolda offered further specification about the learning partnerships—with peers, professors, mentors, and others—most conducive to self-authorship.

Other research on post-college outcomes was quite limited. One study reported null effects of attending an HBCU on long-term gains in self-rated academic, writing, and math ability nine years after entering college, but we cannot draw many conclusions based on one study consisting of graduates who attended college decades ago. As a counterpoint, other research determined that psychological outcomes are generally more favorable among graduates of HBCUs, which bodes well for graduates' labor market outcomes. Some evidence suggested that the racial composition of the institution (i.e., the percentage of Black students attending) and institutional selectivity shape the self-esteem of Black graduates down the line. Studies with limited generalizability highlighted the enduring value of friendships for women's personal development and well-being after college and the long-term (indirect) effects of diversity engagement (e.g., racial/cultural workshops and ethnic studies courses) on well-being for all students.

CHAPTER CONCLUSION

The major themes surfacing from our review of more than a decade of investigations into students' identity formation, self-concept, leadership, autonomy, and well-being show that the most pronounced changes stem from positive, engaging, and even challenging interactions with peers and faculty, as well as significant exposure to diversity in curricular, cocurricular, and social contexts. Broad patterns in college impact become more nuanced as student characteristics—gender, race, worldview, and first-generation status—come into contact and interact with college experiences. Structural qualities of the institution provide the backdrop but are not often the direct cause of students' psychosocial change. As students grapple with multiple and intersecting aspects of their identities, they tend to grow more assured of their intellectual and interpersonal abilities and gradually become more internally directed in their decision making.

In the next chapter, we shift to questions revolving around attitude and value formation during the college years: How do students' attitudes toward civic, political, and diversity issues shift and why? What do students value in their religious and spiritual lives, and how does college influence these domains? To what extent do students develop values commensurate with lifelong learning during college?

Notes

1. Cognitive-structural theories depict how individuals change in their thinking, reasoning, and meaning making (Evans, Forney, Guido, Patton, & Renn, 2010).

2. Much of this research detailed men's conceptualizations of masculinity, as well as masculine expression and performance in relation to sexualities, societal gender role norms, college sport participation, sexual violence, academic motivation and behaviors, and the college environment (Anderson-Martinez & Vianden, 2014; Baber, Aronson, & Melton, 2005; Brown, 2005; Davis, 2002; Edwards & Jones, 2009; Ford, 2011; Harper, 2004; Harris, 2008, 2010; Harris & Harper, 2014; Harris, Palmer, &

Struve, 2011; Harris & Struve, 2009; Jackson & Wingfield, 2013; Leaper & Van, 2008; Locke & Mahalik, 2005; Marrs, Sigler, & Brammer, 2012; Sáenz, Bukoski, Lu, & Rodriguez, 2013; Steinfeldt & Steinfeldt, 2012; Steinfeldt, Wong, Hagan, Hoag, & Steinfeldt, 2011; Stephens & Eaton, 2014; Strayhorn & Tillman-Kelly, 2013; Tatum & Charlton, 2008). Other work has considered the repercussions for health and wellness of various (often socially prescribed and hegemonic) expressions of masculine gender identity and male gender role conflict (Blanco & Robinett, 2014; Blazina, Settle, & Eddins, 2008; Ford, 2011; Gillen & Lefkowitz, 2006; Groeschel, Wester, & Sedivy, 2010; Harris & Harper, 2008; Helme, Cohen, & Parrish, 2012; Levant, Wimer, & Williams, 2011; Mahalik, Lagan, & Morrison, 2006; Oliffe et al., 2010; Pederson & Vogel, 2007; Peralta, 2007; Shek & McEwen, 2012; Steinfeldt, Steinfeldt, England, & Speight, 2009; Steinfeldt, Wong, Hagan, Hoag, & Steinfeldt, 2011; Thompkins & Rando, 2003).

3. Torres, Jones, and Renn (2009) note that intersectional frameworks are informed in large part by critical legal studies (see Crenshaw, 1989, 1991) and feminist scholarship focused on women of color (see Collins, 2000; Dill, McLaughlin, & Nieves, 2007; Dill & Zambrana, 2009).

4. A much larger body of research considered how ethnic identity development relates to other psychosocial and academic measures, such as self-esteem (Hesse-Biber, Livingstone, Ramirez, Barko, & Johnson, 2010; Jaret & Reitzes, 2009; Rivas-Drake, 2012; Shek & McEwen, 2012; Watt, 2006; Yuh, 2005), mental health (e.g., stress, anxiety, depressive symptoms, suicidal ideation, psychological well-being; Arbona & Jimenez, 2014; Banks & Kohn-Wood, 2007; Brittian and colleagues, 2013; Brittian, Umaña-Taylor, & Derlan, 2013; Ghavami, Fingerhut, Peplau, Grant, & Wittig, 2011; Gilbert, So, Russell, & Wessel, 2006; Hovey, Kim, Seligman, 2006; Iturbide, Raffaelli, & Carlo, 2009; Iwamoto & Liu, 2010; Johnson & Arbona, 2006; Rivas-Drake, 2012; Schmidt, Piontkowski, Raque-Bogdan, & Ziemer, 2014; St. Louis & Liem, 2005; Syed et al., 2013; Walker, Wingate, Obasi, & Joiner, 2008; Whittaker & Neville, 2009; Worrell, Mendoza-Denton, Telesford, Simmons, & Martin, 2011; Yip, Seaton, & Sellers, 2006), physical health (Schmidt, Piontkowski, Raque-Bogdan, & Ziemer, 2014), religious orientation (Sanchez & Carter, 2005), college adjustment (Anglin & Wade, 2007; Rivas-Drake & Mooney, 2009; Watson, 2009), interpersonal development (Watt, 2006), leadership skills (Dugan, Kodama, & Gebhardt, 2012), and academic success (Chavous, Rivas, Green, Helaire, 2002; Cokley & Chapman, 2008; Jaret & Reitzes, 2009; Robichaud & Soares, 2014). However, this scholarship generally did not address the impact of college.

5. The UCLA Spirituality in Higher Education project was the first of its kind to examine spiritual development in a national sample of college students. The researchers initiated the project with a longitudinal pilot study of 3,680 students from 46 institutions who were surveyed in 2000 (the first year of college) and again in 2003 (the junior year). In 2004, the national study launched with the administration of the College Students' Beliefs and Values Survey (CSBV) to 112,232 entering first-year college students attending 236 institutions from around the country. A subsample of students attending 136 of the original institutions in the study responded to the follow-up CSBV in their junior year, resulting in a final sample of 14,527 students. The research team developed 10 scales reflective of students' religious and spiritual qualities to examine the institutional factors and collegiate experiences most conducive to development (Astin, Astin, & Lindholm, 2011).

6. Sax's (2008) national longitudinal study of the gender gap in college examined the conditional effects of collegiate environments and experiences on academic, identity, and attitudinal outcomes among women and men, controlling for student characteristics and pretest measures. The sample consisted of more than 17,000 students (and approximately 200 colleges and universities) who participated in the 1994 Cooperative Institutional Research Program (CIRP) Freshman Survey and the 1998 College Student Survey (CSS) administered by the UCLA Higher Education Research Institute.

7. The Wabash National Study of Liberal Arts Education was a multi-institutional longitudinal study designed to assess the academic and nonacademic collegiate experiences that contribute to liberal learning outcomes (e.g., effective reasoning, lifelong learning orientation, intercultural effectiveness, leadership), holding constant confounding influences (e.g., precollege measures of liberal learning outcomes, student demographic characteristics). Students attending 19 institutions participated in the study across three waves of data collection: fall 2006 (beginning of the first year of college), spring 2007 (end of the first year of college), and spring 2010 (end of the fourth year of college). Findings pertaining to change across the first year of college include 3,100 students; findings reflective of change from the first- to fourth-year of college include 2,200 students (Pascarella & Blaich, 2013).

CHAPTER FIVE

Attitudes and Values

Higher education in the United States has historically played a vital role in helping college students reflect on and refine their attitudes, values, and beliefs, and the importance of this role continues into the present. If one of the central aims of higher education is to cultivate citizens equipped to contend with the major social, political, and economic challenges of their time, attention to attitudinal change and value commitment is a necessary part of assessing the college experience. Over the past 10 years, the evidence of college impact on a wide range of attitudinal and value indicators has surged—some of it confirming earlier reviews and some of it extending into new territory altogether.

As discussed in the previous volumes (Pascarella & Terenzini, 1991, 2005), we encountered some challenges accompanying much of the research detailing the effects of college on students' attitudes and values. The first challenge has to do with considerable variation in the approaches to defining and operationalizing concepts. Researchers through the 2000s tended to use the terms *values*, *attitudes*, and *beliefs* interchangeably and devised numerous multifaceted constructs and scales to capture students' perspectives. Readers will notice that some studies attend to specific points of view directed at certain social issues, but the trend in the past decade has been to devise more global measures reflective, for instance, of students' overarching commitment to civic and community values or their orientation toward diversity.

The second challenge is that the connection between attitudes, values, and behaviors across many of the studies is difficult to discern. Can we assume that the values students claim to hold—their commitment to helping others or their desire to promote racial understanding—will manifest in their actions and behaviors? We sought evidence to address this question, but studies that connect values and behaviors in this regard are uncommon. In addition, some behaviors, such as required volunteering, may not necessarily reflect deeply held, intrinsic commitments.

The third challenge, as we have addressed elsewhere in this volume, is identifying the unique role of college in shaping attitudes and values over and above the impact of maturation, generational, or historical factors. Design limitations often make it difficult to isolate the factors producing attitudinal change.

The fourth main challenge is that scholars studying attitudes and values differ in their approach to examining change; some examine change at the level of the individual, while others examine changes in cohorts over time. Unless otherwise noted, our review emphasizes how individual students change in their attitudes and values during college. Throughout the chapter, we caution readers when research design limits the inferences that can be made.

We have organized our review of the extensive literature on attitudes and values into seven distinctive categories: sociopolitical, civic, and community attitudes and values; racial/ethnic and cultural diversity attitudes; gender-role attitudes; attitudes toward lesbian, gay, bisexual, and transgender people; religious and spiritual attitudes and values; educational and occupational attitudes and values; and understanding and interest in the arts. Most studies we reviewed fall into one of these overarching topics. Given that the research on sociopolitical attitudes and values was intertwined with civic and community attitudes and engagement—because of measures that combine indicators of social and political activism—we consider them together in the same section. Diversity outcomes have become more complex, reflecting broader openness to diverse people and viewpoints. Thus, the category from Pascarella and Terenzini's (2005) previous volume, racial/ethnic attitudes, has expanded to encompass a larger domain of outcomes. We begin with an overview of theoretical perspectives that guided many studies addressed in this chapter.

THEORETICAL OVERVIEW

Weidman's (1989) model of undergraduate socialization is one of the foundational conceptual models depicting the process by which college students develop proclivities toward certain values, aspirations, and career and lifestyle choices. The model integrates both sociological and psychological elements that shape socialization outcomes. Weidman assumes that students come to college with specific preferences and aptitudes and are influenced by socioeconomic factors and normative pressures prior to college from parents and other reference groups (e.g., peers). These precollege characteristics and pressures predispose students to gravitate toward certain collegiate contexts and experiences, including normative academic (e.g., institutional mission, major department) and social (e.g., residence, organizations, peer groups) contexts and socializing forces (e.g., interpersonal interactions, intrapersonal processes, and academic and social integration). These contexts and processes in turn affect the normative pressures that students encounter, which inspire values, aspirations, and preferences. The model also assumes that parents and non-college reference groups continue to have a socializing influence on students during the college years. In the end, students must find strategies to balance normative influences with personal goals and values. Many longitudinal studies of attitudinal and value development apply similar theoretical ideas in modeling change. Most, for example, control for student background characteristics in order to attend to the effects of context and student experiences on particular outcomes.

Much of the literature through the 2000s considered attitudinal change as a function of exposure to diverse viewpoints, novel experiences, and people from other cultures and walks of life. Several theory bases have been used to frame this research. The perspectives of Allport (1954) and Pettigrew (1998) appear in a number of studies attentive to diversity attitudes. Allport's (1954) contact hypothesis surmises that stereotypes manifest where there is little or no personal contact between groups. At a minimum, proximity helps to dismantle negative intergroup perceptions because it establishes an opportunity for minority and majority groups to come into contact. Prejudice, however, cannot be entirely overcome by diminishing spatial distance. Rather, according to Allport, four conditions determine the quality of interactions and facilitate bias reduction. First, the individuals coming into contact need to have equal status in the encounter. Second, shared goals and collaboration, as well as active effort to achieve those goals, is essential. Third, individuals must work together interdependently, relying on group cooperation rather than competition to achieve goals. Finally, authority support for the intergroup contact, including accompanying laws or social norms, is necessary for prejudice reduction.

Pettigrew (1998) expanded Allport's conditions to four processes that support the reduction of bias: learning about the out-group and correcting negative views, changing behavior as a precursor to attitude change, generating affective ties, and reappraising in-group norms and customs. Moreover, Pettigrew emphasized the importance of a fifth condition, the opportunity for the individuals coming into contact to become friends, as an essential element for prejudice reduction. Pettigrew also underscored strategies by which contact effects could generalize to other situations involving the entire out-group or other out-groups not involved in the encounter. Many of the studies we review in this chapter, particularly those focused on diversity experiences and outcomes, draw on the tenets of Allport's contact hypothesis and Pettigrew's work on bias reduction.

More recently, psychologists and social psychologists have put forth frameworks that characterize the intricate processes by which intergroup biases are reduced. Although comprehensive coverage of this substantial literature is beyond the scope of this theoretical overview, two models illustrate emerging concepts. Dovidio et al. (2004) examined educational interventions designed to reduce intergroup bias and introduced a model purporting that exposure to curricular diversity content and contact with diverse peers activate cognitive and affective processes that influence how individuals conceive of and relate to other groups.

Another emergent theory, the categorization-processing-adaption-generalization (CPAG) model (Crisp & Turner, 2011), highlights the mediating processes that lead to greater cognitive flexibility in social and cultural diversity attitudes. The model suggests that diversity exposure must challenge stereotyped assumptions and that individuals must be motivated to resolve inconsistencies between stereotyped expectations and new information. If challenge and motivation are present, individuals can engage in inconsistency resolution and adapt their perceptions of other groups. With repeated diversity encounters, generalized cognitive flexibility becomes more likely.

Other recent scholarship builds on Kegan (1994) and Baxter Magolda's (2001, 2008, 2009) self-authorship framework toward a model of intercultural maturity development. *Intercultural maturity* is defined as "complex understanding of cultural differences (cognitive dimension), capacity to accept and not feel threatened by cultural differences (intrapersonal dimension), and capacity to function interdependent[ly] with diverse others (interpersonal dimension)" (King & Baxter Magolda, 2005, p. 274). Further investigation of intercultural maturity (King, Baxter Magolda, & Massé, 2011) yielded several conclusions about the types of reactions that students have in response to the discomfort wrought by contact with diverse peers. The first type of reaction, reflective of an early level of intercultural maturity, *being stuck*, is a reality for students who articulate dissonance but do not take additional steps toward engaging productively with people of other backgrounds. The second type of reaction, *continued questioning*, an intermediate level of intercultural maturity, fosters some exploration of diversity with peers, but to a moderate degree. The third type of reaction, representing an advanced level of intercultural maturity, is *new insights*, whereby students are able to harness the challenge of dissonance in reframing their perspectives. The voluminous research on attitude change—particularly those studies pertaining to diversity-related outcomes—is attuned to holistic outcome measures (cognitive, interpersonal, and intrapersonal). In addition, the literature reveals intricate and often indirect mechanisms, similar to those identified by King and colleagues, by which college influences attitudes and values. Typically, challenge and subsequent disequilibrium—and the ability to make meaning of those experiences—are central to developing new perspectives and reframing values and commitments.

All told, the theories highlighted in this brief review reflect many of the guiding assumptions embedded in studies of college students' attitude and value development. However, relying on theory to contextualize a study does not equate to testing theory in an empirically rigorous manner. In much of the research we reviewed, theoretical concepts informed measures, analytical models, and data interpretations. Only in a handful of studies—most of which queried the impact of diversity experiences on student attitudes—were theories explicitly tested.

CHANGE DURING COLLEGE

Conclusions from the 1990s

Evidence from the 1990s pointed overall to positive shifts associated with educational attainment on measures of students' understanding of democratic processes, voting and other forms of political participation, and endorsement of civil liberties. College-going also led to increases in social activism and liberalism, but findings from the 1990s revealed smaller changes between the first and senior years than in previous decades. Rates of civic engagement, such as community service participation, appeared to increase with higher levels of educational attainment, but Pascarella and Terenzini (2005) underscored the considerable differences in participation rates by the type of service work in question. Longitudinal data generally supported upward shifts in students' commitment to and engagement in serving their communities, with estimates of the change ranging from one-quarter to one-third of a standard deviation. Earlier studies also revealed that students tended to become increasingly empowered to enact social change—and exhibited greater social efficacy—the longer they were in college.

Regarding racial/ethnic attitudes, research in the 1990s was consistent in illuminating growth in racial understanding, increased commitment to racial equality, and prejudice reduction across the college years. Even so, changes across time were not dramatic, often in the range of 4 percentile points (or .09 of a standard deviation). Akin to progressive shifts in racial/ethnic attitudes, gender-role egalitarianism, reflected by attitudes toward pay equity, women's roles in the home, and date rape, rose according to national longitudinal data by anywhere from 4 to 11 percentile points from the first year to the senior year. Moreover, liberal views on these issues were already well established in the first year of college. The limited evidence in the 1990s regarding attitudes toward lesbian, gay, and bisexual people showed generally progressive changes as students grew in their knowledge and acceptance of diverse sexualities and became less homophobic. Although studies were single institution and cross-sectional, reductions in homophobic attitudes amounted to approximately one-half to two-thirds of a standard deviation.

Despite indications of college's liberalizing effects on religious values, evidence in the 1990s began to disrupt this general assumption. Though nationally representative studies were sparse and rather mixed, they showed students becoming slightly more committed to their religious convictions and to integrating spirituality into their lives. In sum, Pascarella and Terenzini (2005) concluded that change in religious values during college may equate to refining and reexamining rather than relinquishing.

Regarding educational, occupational, and aesthetic values, the weight of evidence in the past decade held that students became more likely to find intrinsic value in education and express intrinsic occupational motivations over the course of college. Furthermore, they became less inclined toward instrumental and extrinsic educational and occupational values. Although less attention was devoted to studying college students' interests in the arts in the 1990s than in previous decades, the small number of studies largely concurred that students' artistic interests increased from the first year to the senior year.

In the end, conclusions from Pascarella and Terenzini's (2005) previous review show college students becoming more engaged in their communities and growing somewhat more liberal and progressive across a variety of socio-political indicators. Despite these trends, religious and spiritual convictions may change in quality but not necessarily to the extent that might be expected in light of the assertion that college is ultimately liberalizing. Finally, students come to favor the intrinsic worth of their education, become less externally motivated in their occupational values, and grow more interested in the arts.

Evidence from the 2000s

Sociopolitical, Civic, and Community Attitudes and Values. Studies of socio-political attitudes and values through the 2000s affirmed rather modest changes across time on measures of overall political orientation and specific attitudinal measures. Data from the Wabash National Study of Liberal Arts Education provided longitudinal evidence from more than 3,000 first-year students attending 19 institutions that personal political views were virtually unchanged from the beginning to the end of the first year (Pascarella, Salisbury, Martin, & Blaich, 2012). Sociopolitical change tends to be more detectable in studies that follow students for a longer period of time, but even then changes are not substantial (Rude, Wolniak, & Pascarella, 2012). Sax (2008) drew on national, longitudinal data from the Cooperative Institutional Research Program (CIRP) freshman survey and the College Student Survey (CSS) follow-up of seniors. She found that changes in political orientation during college were not particularly strong in magnitude. Students shifted slightly away from characterizing their political orientation as "middle of the road," but only by 3 percentile points. The percentage of students identifying as "conservative" showed trivial change, but more students identified as "liberal" from the first to fourth year of college by a small margin of 5 percentile points.

Sax (2008) also monitored shifts in specific political attitudes. Students tended to move away from classically liberal assertions that suggest the government should have more oversight of social problems. For instance, both women and men became *less* likely during college to agree that "the federal government is not doing enough to control pollution," with a decline of 7 percentile points. Declines were also apparent for other indicators of classic liberalism, such as "wealthy people should pay a larger share of taxes" (6–7 percentile points), "the federal government should raise taxes to reduce the deficit" (6–9 percentile points), and "the federal government is not protecting consumers" (13–15 percentile points). Regardless, students tended to grow increasingly permissive in many attitudes reflective of individual rights and freedoms. Over time, more students came to support legalized abortion (3–6 percentile points), casual sex (7–17 percentile points), and legalized marijuana (7–9 percentile points). Across such measures, women's liberalization was more pronounced than men's. Data from a single-institution longitudinal study affirmed permissive trends, as students grew in their level of tolerance from the first year to the senior year. Reiterating that changes are typically modest, effect sizes were quite small (Foubert, Nixon, Sisson, & Barnes, 2005).

When it comes to measures of political engagement and associated attitudes, change most often follows a negative trajectory or is minimal. Sax (2008) reported that students became slightly less committed to political engagement over four years of college, with small downward shifts in both the importance attributed to keeping up to date with political affairs (1–2 percentile points) and having frequent political discussions (3–4 percentile points). Modest declines also occurred in the importance to students of influencing the political structure, which dropped by 3 percentile points for women and 7 percentile points for men.

The picture becomes more complicated with the emergence of holistic measures of civic attitudes and values in the 2000s. As a general rule, civic and community attitudes and behaviors include students' sense of social responsibility, social activism, volunteering, and orientation toward improving the welfare of others. Yet some researchers collapsed political and social activism into a single construct, and inconsistencies in operationalization make comparisons across studies challenging. Some evidence parallels reports of decline or minimal change in political orientation and engagement during college. For instance, Pascarella et al. (2012), using longitudinal data from the Wabash National Study, found that students became less socially and politically active in the first year of college. Other reports, also based on Wabash, estimated a first- to fourth-year decline of .13 of a standard deviation in political and social involvement, an overarching measure of whether students assigned importance to "influencing the political structure," "influencing social values," and "becoming a community leader," among other values (O'Neill, 2012).

Nonetheless, the direction of change depends in large part on the items in question. Several studies stressed growth in civic attitudes and values. In their national survey of college students' beliefs and values, conducted in conjunction with the UCLA Spirituality in Higher Education project, Astin, Astin, and Lindholm (2011) collected data from more than 14,000 students attending 136 college and universities. Change from the first to third year of college on the measure, "ethic of caring" ("sense of caring and concern about the welfare of others and the world," p. 64) followed a generally positive trajectory, on average, with the percent of high scorers on the measure nearly doubling across three years from 14% to 27%. Other longitudinal data from the UCLA Higher Education Research Institute also pointed to gains on a measure of "social agency" (values such as keeping up to date with political affairs, participating in community action programs, influencing social values, and helping others), with an increase in the percentage of high scorers of nearly 11 percentile points across the first year and 13 percentile points from the first to fourth year. In short, growth was most dramatic in the first year of college (O'Neill, 2012).

Studies that delve into changes on individual items from holistic scales may aid in disentangling what appears on the surface to be contradictory evidence. Astin and colleagues (2011) examined one such measure, "charitable involvement," which reflected whether students volunteered, donated money, and helped friend with problems. All told, Astin et al. reported waning commitments to charitable involvement from the first to third year of college. Specifically, 12% of students scored highly on this measure as they began college; by the end of the junior year only 9% did. Unpacking the measure, Astin et al. observed more students donating money to charity, helping friends with personal problems, and aspiring to participate in community action programs the longer they were in college. The slight overall decline, explained in large part by reduced community service participation, was likely the result of competing demands for students' time as they took on new responsibilities as college students. Similarly, Sax (2008) found that students became more interested in helping others in difficulty, an item in her social activism construct. Changes were marginal on questions about influencing social values and participating in community action programs. A common denominator linking most studies is evidence of student growth on indicators that reflect the humanitarian values of helping and caring. When other political and civic behaviors and attitudes are considered—volunteering, community action, general social values, and political engagement—findings are often more mixed.

Racial/Ethnic and Cultural Diversity Attitudes. Studies of students' attitudes toward race and their general openness to diverse cultures and perspectives were plentiful throughout the 2000s, following an upsurge in diversity-related research that gained momentum in the 1990s (Pascarella & Terenzini, 2005). This research documented only modest growth in diversity outcomes and even declines, countering expectations that college-going produces progressive ideologies. Students are inclined toward optimistic portrayals of their development. To illustrate, the majority of students in Sax's (2008) national longitudinal study reported growth in their cultural awareness when asked as seniors to describe how they changed on such indicators as "understanding social problems of the nation," "ability to get along with other races," and "knowledge of people from other races." However, self-reported estimates of change overstate actual gains in cultural awareness, according to accompanying evidence. When scores on pre/posttest measures were compared in the same cohort, a different pattern emerged. Students assigned more importance to "helping to promote racial understanding" as first-year students than as seniors, though the decline was marginal for women and only 3 percentile points for men.

Other studies reveal that even positive changes are typically minimal. Using longitudinal data from the Preparing Students for a Diverse Democracy project involving 10 institutions and more than 4,600 students, Engberg and Hurtado (2011) examined the development of students' pluralism orientation (i.e., ability to see multiple perspectives, openness to having one's views challenged, and tolerance of others with different beliefs). From the first to the second year of college, students' pluralism levels changed very little on average, although most groups, with the exception of Asians, who experienced slight declines, grew slightly more pluralistic. Researchers conducting the Wabash National Study (O'Neill, 2012) included in the battery of assessments they administered the Miville-Guzman Universality-Diversity scale, which measured first- to fourth-year gains of .13 of a standard deviation in an overall measure of Diversity of Contact (i.e., interest in and commitment to participating in diverse, intentionally focused social and cultural activities), Relativistic Appreciation (i.e., appreciation of both similarities and differences in people and the impact of diversity on one's self-understanding and personal growth), and Comfort with Differences (i.e., degree of comfort with diverse individuals").

Other evidence from the Wabash National Study calls attention to negative patterns of change. O'Neill (2012) reported a slight drop by .13 of a standard deviation in openness to diversity and challenge, a measure of openness to cultural and racial diversity and the extent to which the student enjoys being challenged by different perspectives, values, and ideas. Likewise, Rude et al. (2012) found that racial attitudes do not necessarily become more progressive during college. Similar to Sax's (2008) findings, students became less committed to promoting racial understanding from the first year to the fourth year of college. The mean decline across the time points occurred despite the fact that students became more liberal in their political orientation. In sum, although students tend to report increases in their level of cultural awareness when asked to assess how they have changed, analysis of longitudinal data shows minimal change over time, including, for some measures, slight declines.

Gender-Role Attitudes. Very little research in the 2000s considered changes in gender-role attitudes during college. Sax's (2008) study of the gender gap in college is one of the exceptions. According to her analysis of the 1994–1998 cohort, few students, especially women, agreed with the notion that "the activities of married women are best confined to home and family." The small proportion of students who endorse traditional gender roles may be a reflection of increasing gender-role progressivism in the society at large and pressure from peers to adopt egalitarian attitudes. Furthermore, the number of students who agreed with this measure dropped from the first to the fourth year of college. Sax reported that the decline was more pronounced for men than women, which caused a narrowing of the gender gap in gender-role traditionalism. A study of another cohort (1996–2000) followed by the UCLA Higher Education Research Institute also reiterated patterns of slight decline in gender-role traditionalism (Bryant, 2003). Although few studies in the 2000s examined changes in gender-role attitudes during college, some provided evidence that such attitudes influence other attitudinal and values outcomes, including domestic violence beliefs (Berkel, Vandiver, & Bahner, 2004; Nabors & Jasinski, 2009; Yamawaki, Ostenson, & Brown, 2009) and career and family aspirations (Colaner & Giles, 2008; Colaner & Warner, 2005; Kaufman, 2005).

Attitudes toward Lesbian, Gay, Bisexual, and Transgender People. Contemporary cohorts of first-year college students by and large support civil rights for lesbian, gay, bisexual, and transgender (LGB) people. According to data from the CIRP Freshman Survey, 82% of entering first-year students in 2014 favored marriage rights for same-sex couples (Eagan et al., 2014), and 83% supported the rights of gay and lesbian people to legally adopt children in 2013 (Eagan, Lozano, Hurtado, & Case, 2013). Endorsement of LGB civil rights on the part of incoming first-year cohorts has tended to increase dramatically across time, sometimes by as much as 6 or 7 percentile points over just two years.

Studies that examine attitudinal changes within cohorts are few and far between, however. Reflecting first- to fourth-year changes in attitudes toward homosexuality in the mid- to late-90s, Sax (2008) found students generally grew less likely to agree that "homosexual relations should be prohibited," with declines in the range of 12 percentile points for men and 8 percentile points for women. Because women began college with more progressive views than men, this shift meant that the gender gap narrowed over time. Arguably, patterns of change today may look very different given the rapid shifts in social opinions. In a recent cross-sectional and single-institution study, students with more years in college generally had more favorable LGB attitudes than students with fewer years, implying positive attitude change over the college years, holding constant gender, race, religion, and political orientation (Holland, Matthews, & Schott, 2013). Future longitudinal and multi-institutional studies assessing the same students across time are needed to substantiate these findings.

Religious and Spiritual Attitudes and Values. When asked to describe how their religious convictions had changed, over one-third of seniors (35–40%) in Sax's (2008) national longitudinal study claimed their religious beliefs had grown "stronger" or "much stronger." Again, the reliability of students' self-reported gains is questionable; when growth occurs based on pre/posttest data, it is often more modest than students' self-reported growth estimations.

On a number of measures, religious and/or spiritual attitudes and values do change to some degree. Sax (2008) found that "developing a meaningful philosophy of life" became more important to students over time, with increases in the range of 8 to 10 percentile points. Students also tend to become more inclined in the first three years of college toward an ecumenical worldview, which is a spiritual measure of "seeing the world as an interconnected whole . . . and feeling a personal connection with, and acceptance of, all other beings" (Astin et al., 2011, p. 67). According to Astin and colleagues affiliated with the UCLA Spirituality in Higher Education project, growth on this measure was moderate when considering the percentage of high scorers. Thirteen percent of students scored high on ecumenical worldview in the first year of college, and this percentage grew to 18% by the end of the junior year. Gehrke (2014) used the UCLA spirituality dataset to examine ecumenical development by racial/ethnic identity and determined that Asian American students exhibited the greatest changes from the first to third year of college, followed by Whites, Latinos/as, and African Americans, respectively.

Another construct monitored by Astin and colleagues (2011), religious/social conservatism, reflects conservative views on abortion, casual sex, atheism, as well as inclinations to proselytize and see God as a father figure. Overall, students became less religiously and socially conservative during college. Among the eight items in the measure, only one increased from the first to third year: viewing God as a father figure. The percentage of students with such an image of God grew from 37% to 41%. The greatest decline on any given item in the scale was the 8-point drop observed for the percentage of students *dis*agreeing with legalized abortion (48% to 40%). Consistent with Sax's (2008) earlier findings about individual rights and freedoms, this study suggests that while students may become more permissive of personal choices, they also strengthen their religious views in some areas.

Finally, Scheitle (2011) examined how student views on the relationship between science and religion changed during college using longitudinal data from the UCLA spirituality project. In general, students moved away from perceiving a conflict between religion and science and toward perceiving the independence of or collaboration between the two domains.

The weight of the evidence affirms that students' religious and spiritual attitudes and values tend to shift in a pluralistic direction and away from religious and social conservatism during the college years. Moreover, students grow less inclined to view science and religion as oppositional. Many students maintain that their religious convictions have been strengthened during college, but these self-reported gains are tempered by evidence suggesting changes that are more moderate.

Educational and Occupational Values. Findings about changes in educational values are somewhat mixed according to national longitudinal data. Although modest first- to fourth-year increases of nearly one-third of a standard deviation have been reported in measures reflective of enjoying and investing effort in thinking (O'Neill, 2012), declines in other measures of motivation and lifelong learning have been reported. For instance, habits of mind—behaviors and traits associated with academic success and lifelong learning—declined from the beginning to the end of the first year (O'Neill, 2012). Academic motivation, as reflected by one's willingness to work hard for intrinsic reasons and enjoyment of challenge, also decreased, on average, from the first to fourth year by .37 of a standard deviation (O'Neill, 2012).

In addition to changes in orientations to learning, occupational values also shift during college, and some gendered patterns surfaced in Sax's (2008) longitudinal study. Reflecting their growing "status striver" orientation, men came to value "obtaining recognition from colleagues" to a greater degree during college. Changes on this item were marginal for women. However, women, but not men, became more inclined to report "raising a family" was "very important" or "essential" to them. Regarding declines in various values, both groups, but especially women, became less concerned with being successful in business. First- to fourth-year drops were consistent for all students in valuing financial wealth and making theoretical contributions to science. In the main, changes in occupational values reflect declining materialism in some respects, although men become more concerned with obtaining recognition than women.

Understanding and Interest in the Arts. Sparse research through the 2000s presented evidence pertaining to students' artistic proclivities. Sax (2008) found that students tended to become more artistically inclined from the first to fourth year of college, as illustrated by positive shifts on measures of creativity and artistic ability relative to peers. They also became slightly more inclined to say that writing original works and creating artistic works were "very important" or "essential" to them. The only other evidence supporting artistic growth comes from a qualitative study of students' identity formation in college, which suggested that educational attainment leads students to become increasingly "cosmopolitan." In the words of the researchers, "They are forming a sense of themselves as being 'college-educated'—becoming individuals who are cultured rather than uncultured, cosmopolitan rather than provincial. The realm here is that of a loose conjunction of aesthetic appreciation, sophistication of tastes, and diversity of worldview" (Kaufman & Feldman, 2004, p. 484).

NET EFFECTS OF COLLEGE

Conclusions from the 1990s

The evidence we have presented to this point regarding change during college cannot be used to infer that college is the cause underlying shifts in students' attitudes and values. In addition to college experiences, a number of other factors may be at work, including changes due to maturation, as well as episodic events and sociohistorical trends that may uniquely affect individuals living in a particular time. Many of the conclusions drawn in the review of 1990s research (Pascarella & Terenzini, 2005) relied on studies that demonstrated gains or declines in students' perspectives after controlling for demographic characteristics, attitudes and values assessed when students first entered college, and length of time and degree of involvement in college. Few studies estimated net effects with the more convincing approach of comparing college attenders to non-attenders.

Pascarella and Terenzini (2005) reported mixed findings with respect to the net effects of college on sociopolitical attitudes in large part due to differences in measurement across studies. College had very little impact on political orientation once other characteristics were taken into account, and small net effects on liberalism may have been rooted in societal changes. Research in the past decade gave some merit to college's effects on myriad social and political attitudes and engagement, as well as knowledge of the government. Yet some of the benefits conferred by educational attainment on political engagement may have been indirect via the occupational and social networks accessed by college-educated people. Consistent evidence supported the net effect of college on civic and community involvement, but effects depended on the type of civic activity in question. Likewise, findings from studies of racial/ethnic attitudes revealed the positive net effects of college, in the presence of control variables, on an array of outcomes such as openness to diversity, cultural awareness, commitment to racial understanding, and acceptance of other races and cultures. Growth in gender egalitarianism also appeared to be influenced by college, controlling for other factors, as reflected by feminist attitudinal indicators regarding pay equity, women's roles, and date rape. The previous review did not identify studies addressing the net effects of college on attitudes toward LGB people, nor did any rigorous studies surface articulating the net effects of college on religious and spiritual attitudes and values.

Continuing the theme introduced in the previous section, net college effects on educational values resulted in students becoming more intrinsically oriented toward the value of a good education and less focused on the monetary benefits of college. Some dualities were apparent in the net effects of college on occupational values, with educational attainment exerting positive influences on both extrinsic values (e.g., "getting ahead") and intrinsic values (e.g., finding interesting work and feeling free to use one's talents). Research addressing students' aesthetic interests was generally inconclusive about the source of impact, which likely had to do with a variety of maturational, peer group, and college involvement influences.

Evidence from the 2000s

Scant research in the 2000s examined the net effects of college on students' attitudes and values in a compelling and rigorous manner. Drawing on disciplines beyond education, political science researchers provided some important insights on how the college-going population differs from non-attenders on measures of civic engagement, while sociologists of religion examined religious liberalism.

Sociopolitical, Civic, and Community Attitudes and Values. The long-standing conclusion that educational attainment has net positive effects on measures of civic participation has been challenged by recent evidence. Through the early 2000s, positive net effects of education were mostly uncontested, as Hillygus (2005) argued: "Education has consistently been found to increase political participation, electoral turnout, civic engagement, political knowledge, and democratic attitudes and opinions" (p. 25). In one of the earlier studies, Dee (2003) examined the effect of enrolling in college (two-year or four-year) on voter participation and volunteerism. The measure of educational exposure had some limitations; participants who were classified as college attenders were those who had accumulated a large number of undergraduate credits. College attendance had strong effects on voter participation—increasing participation by 21 to 30 percentile points—but small effects on the probability of volunteering. Although this study used instrumental variables to more convincingly estimate the effects of educational attendance, pretest measures of civic inclinations were not included in models.

Studies that emerged later in the 2000s were more critical of earlier evidence. Hillygus (2005) suggested that much of the research on which the education effect conclusion is based "lacks a definitive explanation as to the explicit mechanism by which education influences political behavior. Too many studies blindly include education in the regression model, assuming a purely linear and additive relationship, and failing to explain why it matters" (p. 26). Indeed, when more rigorous approaches were taken to examine the net effects of college on measures of citizenship and civic engagement, the findings were mixed. Kam and Palmer (2008) used propensity score matching to examine the impact of college on political participation in a sample of 3,250 college attenders and non-attenders between 1965 and 1973. With the matching process accounting for pre-adult experiences in the senior year of high school, they found no effect of college on political participation. They explained that college is in actuality a proxy for previous life experiences and values that drive educational attainment and subsequent civic outcomes. The time period studied makes the findings less relevant to contemporary college students, but some research suggests that college effects may be even smaller in more recent cohorts. Long (2010) compared the effect of years of education on a number of outcomes across different cohorts tracked in federal education datasets: the National Longitudinal Study, High School and Beyond, and the National Education Longitudinal Study. While each additional year of education raised the likelihood of voting, the effect of education on registering to vote diminished with each subsequent cohort.

The debate over the "education effect" continued in 2011 when two studies (Henderson & Chatfield, 2011; Mayer, 2011) challenged Kam and Palmer's (2008) approach and implemented a variety of matching strategies to reduce bias. In both instances, the researchers uncovered positive effects of education on political engagement. For example, Mayer (2011) found that postsecondary education contributed to an "18% increase in voter turnout, a 10% increase in individuals contacting public officials, and a 6% increase in participation at demonstrations, protests or rallies" (Mayer, 2011, p. 640). Explaining the different conclusions in the set of studies, Mayer (2011) contended that confounding variables produced biases in Kam and Palmer's estimates of college effects. Furthermore, Henderson and Chatfield (2011) argued that propensity scores based on too many variables may also have resulted in inaccurate estimates. Although bias cannot be removed entirely, Henderson and Chatfield (2011) cautioned against discounting years of evidence in light of the findings of a single study.

At the heart of the matter was disagreement over the optimal strategy for balancing treatment and control groups to mimic the gold standard of a randomized experiment. The authors disagreed over the appropriate robustness checks and sensitivity analyses necessary to assess whether balance had been achieved. Kam and Palmer (2011) responded to their critics and analyzed another longitudinal dataset, High School and Beyond, which provided more balance between treatment and control groups. In so doing, the researchers replicated their original findings: that higher education had no significant impact on political participation, again challenging conventional wisdom. They concluded,

> There are severe selection issues that characterize the decision to attend and complete higher education. Because of these issues, previous empirical findings (upon which the conventional wisdom rests) cannot be interpreted as providing an unbiased causal estimate of the relationship between higher education and political participation (p. 662).

Religious and Spiritual Attitudes and Values. We identified two dependable studies of net college effects on religious and spiritual attitudes and values, and both used longitudinal data from the National Study of Youth and Religion. Hill (2011) found more decline in "super-empirical Christian beliefs" (i.e., belief in God, a judgment day, an afterlife, angels, demons, and the possibility of miracles) among college attenders and college graduates than those who never attended college, accounting for race/ethnicity, gender, age, relational closeness to parents, census region, and type of residence. Although there was no significant effect of attending college on identifying as "spiritual, but not religious," college graduates became more likely to affirm that congregations are an important part of being religious, compared to individuals who never attended college. Furthermore, relative to non-attenders, college graduates became increasingly tolerant of the notion that it is acceptable to pick and choose beliefs. In short, net college effects on beliefs depended mostly on the principle in question, but showed students refining their convictions in some ways because of college attendance.

Mayrl and Uecker (2011) challenged the contention that college-going liberalizes students' religious beliefs. They incorporated additional measures reflective of social networks in their models, leading to some different conclusions than Hill drew. Compared to non-attenders, college students were no more likely to become religiously liberal over time. The researchers considered measures such as belief in a personal God, belief in supernatural occurrences, religious doubts, beliefs about proselytizing, religious inclusivity, religious individualism (i.e., believing one can pick and choose beliefs), and religious independence (i.e., identifying as "spiritual but not religious"). On all measures, the effect of college-going was statistically nonsignificant once controlling for demographic characteristics and other relevant covariates. Mayrl and Uecker asserted that changes in religious beliefs among emerging adults have more to do with social networks, such as attending religious services and having friends of the same religion, than college-going. Moreover, they surmised, "Self-segregation of students into 'moral communities' on campus may effectively undercut any 'cultural broadening' effect of college, and thus any additional propensity for religious liberalization" (p. 202). They also found that college-going may have more protective effects on conservative Protestants, but more liberalizing effects on mainline Protestants, perhaps due to the predispositions toward liberal or conservative conceptions of religion that students bring with them to college or "divergent socializing patterns" (p. 201) each group manifests when they matriculate.

Summing up the weight of the evidence, in their synthesis of research on college student religiosity, Mayrl and Oeur (2009) contended that college does not promote apostasy per se. Rather, "the question is now less about whether students' religious commitments are maintained or abandoned, and more about whether they are ignored or reconstituted during the college years" (p. 265).

BETWEEN-COLLEGE EFFECTS

Conclusions from the 1990s

The review of college impact research in the past decade (Pascarella & Terenzini, 2005) concluded that structural characteristics of an institution, namely size, mission, and control, had minimal impact on sociopolitical and civic outcomes. However, the faculty and peer culture of an institution tended to have a more pronounced effect, particularly in the areas of sociopolitical orientations and attitudes, such as social activism, political engagement, liberalism, and support for individual freedoms.

Most structural characteristics of an institution also had little bearing on students' racial/ethnic attitudes. Structural diversity—or the racial composition of the campus—had some effect on outcomes, but in an indirect manner through the opportunities for exposure to diversity in the curriculum and peer group afforded by structurally diverse institutions. Attending women's colleges (versus coeducational colleges) had small effects on women's racial/ethnic attitudes, but similar effects were not observed for African American students attending Historically Black Colleges and Universities (HBCUs) versus predominantly White institutions. Campus climate and perceived faculty support for diversity and multiculturalism were positively linked to students' openness to diversity, commitment to promoting racial understanding, and cultural awareness. However, few studies provided any evidence about between-college effects on gender-role, LGB, and religious attitudes in the 1990s. Some studies connected attending an HBCU to African American students' educational, occupational, and artistic values and attending two-year colleges to learning orientations toward self-understanding, but otherwise structural characteristics of institutions had little impact on value outcomes.

Evidence from the 2000s

Sociopolitical, Civic, and Community Attitudes and Values

Structural Characteristics. Public or private control of the institution, size, and selectivity play small roles in civic and political engagement, with a few studies finding significant effects, typically favoring private institutions of lower selectivity. Sax (2008) found that attending public universities reduced students' social activism, while Lott (2013) reported that private institutions enhanced civic values (e.g., goals to influence the political structure, clean up the environment, participate in community action programs). Regarding institutional size, volunteerism tended to be higher at smaller institutions and at institutions not located within large cities (Cruce & Moore, 2007), although Lott (2013) found marginal positive effects of institution size on civic values. Selective institutions undermined civic values according to two studies (Astin and Antonio, 2004; Lott, 2013).

The findings regarding structural diversity's relationship to sociopolitical and civic outcomes are somewhat mixed. In one longitudinal study with ample controls for confounding variables, Rhee and Kim (2011) found small positive effects of institutional structural diversity, a measure of the percentage of minority students on campus, on civic values. Likewise, controlling for student characteristics and precollege liberalism, the percentage of students of color at the institution attended exerted a marginal positive effect on liberalism in the first year of college (Pascarella et al., 2012). However, the structural diversity of the institution attended did not affect voting in another longitudinal study (Wolfe & Fletcher, 2013).

Institutional Mission. Institutional mission plays an important role in fostering citizenship values and behaviors, according to a number of studies. One investigation assessed alumni perceptions of their institution's contributions to outcomes and identified work colleges—where students are assigned jobs to integrate work into the educational experience and meet campus and community needs—as having a significant impact on citizenship and global orientations compared to regional and liberal arts colleges. Effects ranged from .56 to .71 of a standard deviation (Wolniak & Pascarella, 2007). Data drawn from the National Survey of Student Engagement revealed that first-year students attending single-sex institutions self-reported greater gains in their willingness to contribute to the welfare of their community than students attending coeducational institutions, holding constant individual and institutional characteristics (Kinzie, Thomas, Palmer, Umbach, & Kuh, 2007). The religious mission of an institution also fosters civic outcomes, as Astin and Antonio (2004) reported in their study of character development. Using longitudinal data from the Cooperative Institutional Research Program, the researchers found positive effects of attending Catholic and Protestant colleges on civic and social values. The impact of the religious mission of the institution, though, was indirect and mediated by students' curricular and cocurricular activities, which, in turn, directly influenced civic outcomes. Cruce and Moore (2007) echoed these findings using data from two National Survey of Student Engagement cohorts (2004 and 2005) to examine volunteerism in the first year of college. Attending public institutions or private independent institutions related to lower levels of volunteerism in the first year of college compared to private religious institutions.

Although attending work colleges, women's colleges, and religious institutions appears to benefit civic outcomes, mission as reflected by an institution's for-profit status may have deleterious consequences, according to an analysis of data from the Beginning Postsecondary Students Longitudinal Study. Students who attended for-profit colleges and community colleges began college with similar levels of civic mindedness. However, those who attended the for-profit colleges (versus the community colleges) lost ground on many measures of civic mindedness, including registering to vote, voting, talking about politics, making financial contributions, writing letters to public officials, and volunteering. The magnitude of effects, however, was rather small. In reflecting on the ramifications of educational institutions oriented toward profit, the researchers concluded, "An unintended consequence of focusing solely on economic goals may be the undermining of social ones. . . . Students attending such schools will be less well prepared for citizenship and community participation" (Persell & Wenglinsky, 2004, p. 352).

Other research has examined the impact of the institutional emphasis (e.g., liberal arts, research) on measures of political orientation. Hanson, Weeden, Pascarella, and Blaich (2012), in their analysis of longitudinal data from the Wabash National Study, found positive effects from the first to the senior year of attending liberal arts colleges on liberalism. Under the most stringent set of controls with confounding collegiate influences held constant, the effect of attending a liberal arts institution on liberalism was quite modest, at .09 of a standard deviation. Another study based on the same data source focused on first-year student gains in liberalism and found a negative effect of attending a research university versus a liberal arts college (Pascarella et al., 2012). Although not a traditional institutional emphasis by way of liberal arts or research focus, a spirit of collaboration on campus may enhance civic outcomes, according to some qualitative evidence involving 18 institutions. The campuses all had academic and student affairs partnerships, thereby creating environments that fostered students' civic engagement, as reflected by their community service involvement and community activism (Nesheim et al., 2007).

Peer and Faculty Socialization. Other dimensions of the campus environment, namely characteristics and behaviors of the student body and pedagogical emphases, influence prosocial values and behaviors. Astin et al. (2011) used longitudinal data from the UCLA Spirituality in Higher Education project to examine between-college effects on students' charitable involvement and ethic of caring. Given controls for student characteristics, anticipated major, and place of residence, between-college variables had generally small effects on both measures. For instance, the degree to which faculty employed student-centered pedagogy propelled development on both dimensions, while the average level of religious engagement on campus was associated with increases in charitable involvement. Contrarily, the average liberalism on campus resulted in lower levels of charitable involvement over time. Institutional type and affiliation variables were not significantly related to the outcomes in the presence of variables that more directly approximated aspects of campus life (such as liberalism and religious engagement).

Facets of the peer environment have fairly pronounced effects on students' political orientation and sociopolitical attitudes. For instance, in Sax's (2008) longitudinal study, the average liberalism of the peer group at an institution furthered individual students' liberal political orientation and their support for individual rights and freedoms (regarding abortion, marijuana, casual sex, and LGB rights).

Racial/Ethnic and Cultural Diversity Attitudes

Structural Diversity. A number of studies have considered the effects of structural diversity on changes in racial and cultural attitudes, finding that most effects are positive but indirect, operating through interactions with diverse peers and curricular and cocurricular diversity experiences. For instance, Pike, Kuh, and Gonyea (2007) used cross-sectional data from the National Survey of Student Engagement to identify indirect effects of student body diversity, which increased the likelihood of interactional diversity and thereby gains in understanding people from diverse backgrounds. Other work did not illuminate indirect mechanisms but posited that attending an institution with a higher percentage of Hispanic students reduced White students' perceived social distance from Hispanics (Fischer, 2011).

Some research examined interaction, rather than attitudes and values, as the outcome. Given that diversity interactions foster positive outcomes, as plentiful evidence presented in the "Within-College" section attests, it is worthwhile to probe the underlying mechanisms by which structural diversity affects interactions and, consequently, attitudinal outcomes. Chang, Astin, and Kim (2004) analyzed national longitudinal data to demonstrate the strong positive relationship, equating to one-quarter of a standard deviation, between structural diversity (the percentage of students of color on a campus) and cross-racial interactions (e.g., dating, dining with, studying with, interacting in class with students of other races). By far, this was the strongest relationship between institution-level measures and interracial interactions. Park (2012) later added that the racial diversity of the institution increased the likelihood of developing friendships across race among students who participated in the National Longitudinal Study of Freshmen. Sáenz (2010) drew a similar conclusion in that the percentage of nonwhite students at an institution predicted positive cross-racial interaction, although effects were small and particular to White students.

Other structural characteristics appear to matter as well. Pike and colleagues (2007) observed strong effects of the percentage of female students on campus and modest effects of the percentage of full-time students on campus on students' self-perceived gains in understanding of diverse others. In the end, the characteristics of the student body influence the behaviors and attitudes of individual students.

Peer Socialization. Not only do structural characteristics of the institution have some bearing on outcomes; the effects of average peer attitudes and behaviors are also noteworthy. In one study, the average level of cross-racial interaction engaged in by students at an institution exerted a strong influence, of nearly one-third of a standard deviation, on individual students' self-assessed growth in openness to diversity, accounting for student characteristics and college involvement variables (Chang, Denson, Sáenz, & Misa, 2006). Echoing these findings, Denson and Chang (2009) later determined that the average level of curricular diversity engagement and the average level of cross-racial interaction at an institution had a positive impact on students' self-assessed change in knowledge of people of different races and cultures and ability to get along with people of other races/cultures. Denson and Chang also pointed to an important caveat: the effects of students' individual level of cross-racial interaction mattered more to furthering the outcome at institutions where cross-racial interaction was lower on average. In sum, on campuses where students do not engage diversity to a significant degree, it is even more imperative that students individually reach across racial lines. Regarding specific race-related attitudes, Park (2009) found that peer opposition to affirmative action on a campus reinforced these beliefs at the individual level.

Other Institutional Factors. Other institutional characteristics also make an impression on racial and cultural attitudes. Sax (2008) reported that attending public universities reduced students' commitment to promoting racial understanding. Whereas private institutions, liberal arts colleges, and urban institutions generally had positive effects on the outcomes, selectivity had a negative effect. Astin and Antonio (2004) also reported negative effects of selectivity on cultural awareness. In only one instance did selectivity advance progressive attitudes; Park (2009) found institutional selectivity reduced opposition to affirmative action. Further complicating the question of how institutional selectivity influences students, but also highlighting a possible mechanism for negative effects, White male views on contemporary racism differed according to institutional context in Cabrera's (2014) qualitative study. At the academically nonselective institution, participants tended to be apathetic on matters of race, while students at the academically selective and more racially diverse campus angrily asserted their positions. Men attending the selective and racially diverse institution "could not avoid issues of race, and they also tended to exist in academically competitive environments where they sometimes felt their social standing was threatened by race-conscious policies such as affirmative action" (p. 777). Thus, to the extent that selective institutions breed a sense of competition among students, students of privileged identities may be skeptical of diversity policies and practices.

Attitudes toward Lesbian, Gay, Bisexual, and Transgender People. Evidence regarding between-college effects on attitudes toward LGB people is extremely limited. One study of just under 700 students attending six liberal arts colleges found that attitudes toward lesbian, gay, and bisexual people were less positive at institutions with Greek organizations (Hinrichs & Rosenberg, 2002). Although the study used a variety of scales to assess attitudes and controlled for gender, age, and sex-role attitudes, it was not longitudinal. Given the dearth of evidence, questions remain regarding how institutional qualities influence students' support for LGB people and their civil rights.

Religious and Spiritual Attitudes and Values. Findings pertaining to between-college effects on religious and spiritual attitudes and values address three distinct outcomes: ecumenical worldview, religious/social conservatism, and beliefs about the relationship between religion and science. Astin et al. (2011) identified modest effects of institution-level measures in their national longitudinal study of college student spirituality. Ecumenical worldview, an outcome that taps into students' acceptance of and sense of connectedness to others of diverse cultures and beliefs, was influenced by the quality of the campus environment more so than institutional type—and even then effects were small, in the range of .05 to .06 of a standard deviation. Positive effects surfaced for average diversity advocacy on campus, average religious engagement, and the proportion of students living on campus. To this, Mayhew's (2012b) subsequent analysis added that the average level of religious struggle of peers on campus positively influenced the ecumenical worldview development of individual students, with an effect size of .10 of a standard deviation. Moreover, the average level of ecumenical worldview of students at the institution and the religious identity of the institution (Catholic or "other" religious affiliation) enhanced ecumenical worldview in the junior year. At institutions where many students had religious struggles, ecumenical gains tended to be greater for students at evangelical institutions than at either public or other religiously affiliated institutions.

The average level of peers' religious/social conservatism—defined as conservative views on abortion, casual sex, and atheism, as well as inclinations to proselytize and see God as a father figure—predicted increases on this measure for individual students, controlling for student characteristics, anticipated major, and place of residence (Astin et al., 2011). Hill (2011) approximated between-college effects on a related measure of traditional religious views to determine the impact of elite institutions on such beliefs in a large, longitudinal dataset. He discovered that elite colleges had a more pronounced negative impact on "super-empirical Christian beliefs" (i.e., belief in God, a judgment day, an afterlife, angels, demons, and the possibility of miracles). Compared to those who never attended college, elite college attenders became almost one-half of a standard deviation less conventional in their beliefs. Similar patterns were observed for non-Christian super-empirical beliefs (i.e., belief in reincarnation and astrology), with students attending elite colleges declining more in their beliefs than students who never attended college. Furthermore, compared to non-attenders, students attending religious colleges became more inclined over time to agree that congregations are an important part of being religious.

Two population-specific studies affirmed the contrasting effects of secular and evangelical institutions on students' traditional religious beliefs. A study of Protestants showed that educational attainment was associated with liberal theological views, but the liberalizing impact of higher education was unique to those in the sample who attended secular institutions (Reimer, 2010). Railsback's (2006) descriptive analysis of the identity changes among born-again Christian students affirmed the tendency for students attending evangelical colleges (relative to other types of institutions) to maintain or strengthen their religious convictions. However, the analysis did not include controls for other confounding factors, and some models involved students' self-reported gains.

Finally, Scheitle (2011) used data from the UCLA Spirituality in Higher Education project to examine the predictors of students' views on the relationship between science and religion. He reported the somewhat counterintuitive finding that students attending religiously affiliated institutions were *less* inclined than those attending secular institutions to shift their views toward perceiving conflict between religion and science and siding with religion.

Educational and Occupational Values

Institutional Mission. Most of the research detailing between-college effects on lifelong learning orientations pointed to the influence of institutional mission, with greater gains occurring within liberal arts colleges, community colleges, and work colleges. Nelson Laird, Seifert, Pascarella, Mayhew, and Blaich (2014) examined the effects of deep approaches to learning on lifelong learning orientations (e.g., effortful thinking and positive attitudes toward literacy) among first-year college students who had participated in the Wabash National Study. Compared to liberal arts colleges, attending a research university had small to medium negative effects on effortful thinking and positive attitudes toward literacy, while attending a regional university had a small negative effect on positive attitudes toward literacy. Further analysis of these relationships from the first to the fourth year of college yielded evidence of indirect effects. Specifically, the positive effects of attending a liberal arts institution were mediated through clear and organized classroom instruction and deep approaches to learning, such as reflective learning and integrative learning (Pascarella, Wang, Trolian, & Blaich, 2013).

Unlike research and regional institutions, attending a community college (compared to a liberal arts college) had a strong positive effect, equating to .14 to .18 of a standard deviation, on effortful thinking in Nelson Laird and colleagues' (2014) study, as well as earlier investigations that drew on data from the Wabash National Study (Padgett, Goodman, Johnson, Saichaie, Umbach, & Pascarella, 2010; Padgett, Johnson, & Pascarella, 2012). Providing a contrast to longitudinal data supporting gains in effortful thinking among students attending community colleges, Cox's (2009) qualitative analysis illuminated utilitarian approaches to education among students attending a community college, distinguishing these approaches from students with educational advantages in other types of postsecondary institutions. She noted,

> Students' decisions in pursuing instrumental goals led to gaps of various degrees between their espoused goals and actual career trajectories. Perhaps most unfortunately, students' instrumental approaches decreased their learning opportunities despite their intentions to acquire meaningful and valuable career-related knowledge. Both phenomena illuminate fundamental differences between their way of doing college and the instrumentalism applied by more advantaged students in higher status postsecondary sites (p. 380).

Together, the nuanced qualitative evidence along with the generalizable data point to some complexities, which leads to a "both/and" conclusion.

Instrumentalism may be a necessity for students whose livelihood depends on education as a pathway to vocational advancement, but their experience in community college has other benefits, as demonstrated by their growing enjoyment of effortful thinking.

Another unique institutional context, the work college, has a significant impact on learning orientations. At work colleges students are assigned jobs in an effort to integrate educational experiences with campus and community needs. An important feature of these work experiences is that they are not only required; they are meaningful. The work students engage in makes significant contributions integral to the functioning of the institutional community. According to data collected from alumni, these institutions, relative to regional and liberal arts colleges, had a significant impact on perceptions that the college contributed to students' engagement in lifelong learning and appreciation of literature and the fine arts. The magnitude of effects ranged from .25 to .42 of a standard deviation (Wolniak & Pascarella, 2007).

Structural Diversity. A final institutional characteristic, structural diversity, exerted a marginal positive influence on positive attitudes toward literacy. This finding came from longitudinal data focused on the first year of college and analyses that controlled for the pretest measure, student background characteristics, institutional variables, and student experiences (Loes, Salisbury, & Pascarella, 2013).

WITHIN-COLLEGE EFFECTS

Conclusions from the 1990s

The college impact literature through the 1990s examined numerous environmental and experiential influences on students' attitudes and values. Many assessments credited faculty and peer engagement, diversity exposure, and high-impact curricular and cocurricular practices (such as service-learning) for gains in civic and political outcomes, diversity and gender-role attitudes, and educational and occupational values.

The review of research in the previous decade uncovered little evidence that academic major influences sociopolitical and civic outcomes. The exceptions were majoring in engineering or taking courses in quantitative fields, which tended to reduce commitments to social activism and liberalism, as well as majoring in social sciences, which advanced civic and community engagement. Evidence regarding the impact of service-learning, courses that integrate service into course content, was quite conclusive and underscored the benefits for innumerable civic and political outcomes, ranging from sense of social responsibility and helping orientation to understanding social and economic inequities. Whether service empowered students' sense of citizenship confidence and self-efficacy was unclear. General volunteering also benefited students' civic development, but required service often had the opposite effect. Other curricular and cocurricular experiences, such as women's and ethnic studies courses and diversity workshops, inspired movement toward political liberalism, but the directionality of the relationships was indeterminate in many studies. Engaging diverse peers and perspectives informally and through cocurricular offerings, as well as participating in learning communities and collaborative learning, propelled gains in students' orientation to community and civic engagement. Peer interactions had demonstrable effects on many measures of students' civic and political development, but the purported conservative impact of fraternity and sorority membership on students was tentative in the absence of convincing causal evidence. Participation in Greek organizations, though, did support student gains in civic and community attitudes and behaviors.

A variety of academic majors, namely business, nursing, science, and engineering, exerted negative influences on students' racial/ethnic attitudes. While living on campus appeared to promote positive diversity attitudes, fraternity and sorority engagement undermined such values. As noted in the between-college section, structural diversity was identified in the last decade as supportive of interracial interactions and friendship formation. In turn, diversity engagement yielded many positive outcomes with respect to racial awareness and understanding. An array of course and cocurricular experiences that expose students to diversity—for instance, women's and ethnic studies courses, racial and cultural diversity workshops, diversity discussions in the classroom, and interactions with instructors of color—strengthened students' openness to diversity and related racial attitudes. Pascarella and Terenzini (2005) noted, though, that the direction of causality was unclear in the existing research at the time. Service-learning, leadership training, and study abroad also produced small positive effects on diversity outcomes, but Pascarella and Terenzini (2005) cautioned that much of the research detailing study abroad effects on intercultural knowledge and understanding was not methodologically strong. Some evidence linked participation in non-revenue-producing intercollegiate athletics to declines in openness to diversity.

Research through the 1990s generally supported the positive effects of women's studies courses on gender-role egalitarianism and feminist attitudes, although some studies had methodological limitations. Workshops on gender violence also positively shaped attitudes, but the longevity of the impact was unclear. Some evidence revealed that gender-role ideologies may have become more conservative in the context of fraternity and sorority membership. Whereas feminist perspectives were often associated with curricular and cocurricular opportunities, progressive LGB attitudes were engendered through interpersonal interactions with lesbian, gay, and bisexual people, according to some studies in the past decade. Further, interventions (e.g., workshops and speaker panels) reduced homophobia and improved acceptance, but many studies lacked rigorous designs and did not attest to whether attitude changes were sustained in the long term. Findings pertaining to the effects of Greek membership on gender-role and LGB attitudes were inconclusive.

Compelling evidence in the past decade highlighted the impact of academic major on educational values. Humanities majors experienced the greatest declines in extrinsic orientation to education relative to social science and physical science majors, but business majors tended to become more extrinsically oriented. Regarding other collegiate experiences, fraternity and sorority members became more inclined toward extrinsic educational values than independent students, but men in revenue-producing sports became more committed to learning for self-understanding during college. Limited research in the 1990s examined within-college effects on students' interest in the arts, but some studies did show that artistic students in artistic disciplinary environments underwent growth in their artistic values. Even so, students with incongruent personality types also benefited artistically in such environments, suggesting that positive outcomes do not uniformly depend on person-environment congruence.

Evidence from the 2000s

Paralleling and building on research from earlier decades, scholars through the 2000s brought to light the role of myriad collegiate influences in students' attitudinal and values development. To some extent, studies contributed further evidence regarding the effects of within-college disciplinary and residential contexts, but more concerted attention was devoted to other factors: peer and faculty influences, diversity exposure, and service-learning and other high-impact experiences.

The following review of each outcome category is organized by type of environment or experience. Contextual influences—reflecting various environments students may encounter in their majors, courses, and places of residence—are described first in each section, followed by shaping experiences students have as they engage peers and faculty and become involved in other aspects of campus life. We emphasize the types of student engagement that produced the most meaningful effects for a given outcome.

Sociopolitical, Civic, and Community Attitudes and Values. Research detailing within-college effects on sociopolitical, civic, and community attitudes and values comprehensively addresses numerous potential influences, including disciplinary (college major and courses) and residential contexts and five additional categories of student engagement: peer and faculty engagement; diversity engagement; community service and service-learning; involvement in student government, student organizations, leadership, and political activities; and fraternity and sorority participation.

Academic Major and Courses. A few national studies reported the effects of college major on various aspects of civic and community attitudes and engagement. Overall, majoring in science detracted from civic values (e.g., influencing the political structure, influencing social values, helping others who are in difficulty; Rhee & Kim, 2011) and had a null relationship with volunteering (Cruce & Moore, 2007). Rhee and Kim (2011) controlled for confounding covariates in estimating the negative effects of majoring in natural science or engineering (compared to all other majors) on civic values at .13 of a standard deviation. However, majoring in social science supported gains in civic values (Lott, 2013) and majoring in education was associated with volunteering (Cruce &

Moore, 2012). Regarding political engagement, majoring in history or political science resulted in gains, while majoring in the health professions contributed to declines (Sax, 2008). Some evidence supported the benefits to students of transcending disciplinary boundaries, as taking interdisciplinary courses promoted character development, according to Astin and Antonio (2004).

Residence. Some limited evidence, primarily drawn from cross-sectional analyses of data from the National Survey of Student Engagement, suggests that living on campus—and particularly in learning communities—promotes volunteerism in the first year of college (Cruce & Moore, 2007, 2012). Cruce and Moore (2012) controlled for high school volunteerism and other student characteristics and estimated that first-year learning community members had a probability of volunteering that was 23 percentile points greater than nonmembers. Although the effect size was strong in magnitude, we caution against assuming causality, particularly given that self-selection issues may have biased the analysis. One of the potential mechanisms that may explain the impact of living in residence halls or learning communities is the interaction that occurs between students living in close quarters. In a single-institution study that implemented a quasi-experimental panel design with matching procedure, Klofstad (2010) reported that "civic talk" between roommates, defined as the frequency of discussing politics and current events, influenced civic participation (i.e., involvement in voluntary civic organizations) in the first year of college, which led to increased civic participation several years later.

Peer and Faculty Engagement. Evidence supports the civic benefits to students of engaging with their peers in academic contexts. Based on data from the Cooperative Institutional Research Program, Rhee and Kim (2011) reported a small effect of academic peer interaction on civic values. Particular types of cocurricular engagement, which arguably entail peer engagement and interactions with diverse peers, prompt development of civic and community values, but we reserve discussion of those experiences for later sections.

Compelling evidence has emerged through the 2000s regarding the shaping influence that faculty have on students' civic development and political attitudes and behaviors. Importantly, the latest research has taken care to explicate the qualities of faculty engagement most relevant to student outcomes. As a result, we now have more definitive understanding that the frequency of interacting with faculty is less important than the nature of those interactions and the pedagogical strategies faculty employ in the classroom.

Rhee and Kim (2011) reported a small effect of time spent meeting with faculty on students' civic values in their analysis of longitudinal data, but evidence from other studies helps to shed light on those experiences with faculty that have the most pronounced effects. These analyses revealed small-to-moderate positive effects of various forms of faculty engagement on becoming politically involved, including talking with faculty outside class (.06 of a standard deviation) and challenging a professor's ideas in class (.12 of a standard deviation). General expressions of support by faculty exerted moderate to strong effects (of .11 to .17 of a standard deviation) on students' development as social activists, including their commitment to influencing political and social values, helping others in difficulty, and participating in community action programs (Sax, 2008; Sax, Bryant, & Harper, 2005). Astin and Antonio (2004) affirmed that having faculty provide emotional support enhances students' "character development," a construct featuring civic and social values, as well as volunteerism.

Other civic outcomes, students' charitable behaviors (e.g., whether students volunteer, donate money, and help friend with problems), and ethic of caring are strongly influenced by the spiritual support that faculty provide students. Astin, Astin, and Lindholm (2011) conducted a national longitudinal study of student and faculty spirituality and controlled for confounding influences in identifying positive effects on caring behaviors and values of faculty encouraging spiritual discussions and students' discussing religion with professors and others on campus (with effects ranging from .13 to .23 of a standard deviation). Fleming, Purnell, and Wang (2013) drew on the same dataset to contrast different dimensions of faculty mentoring and pedagogy on students' ethic of caring and discovered rather small effects of academic/career mentoring and student-centered pedagogy on the outcome relative to strong effects (nearly one-quarter of a standard deviation) of ethical and spiritual mentoring. Furthermore, they reported the relationship between ethical/spiritual mentoring and an ethic of caring as particularly strong at public institutions.

In addition to spiritual mentoring, reflective practices, such as writing and journaling, encourage development of an ethic of caring (Astin et al., 2011; Park & Millora, 2012) and social justice learning (Mayhew & DeLuca Fernández, 2007). Likewise, data from the Wabash National Study reiterated that reflective learning strongly supports students' political and social involvement, and so do several other pedagogical strategies, including active and collaborative learning; academic challenge and high expectations; and integrating ideas, information, and experiences. The Association of American Colleges & Universities reported effect sizes for these high-impact practices in the range of .20 to .29 of a standard deviation following rigorous efforts to control for confounding variables (O'Neill, 2012).

Diversity Engagement. Considerable research has provided convincing evidence that diversity experiences, variously defined as curricular, cocurricular, and interactional encounters with diversity, play a promising role in the development of civic attitudes, values, and behaviors. In a comprehensive review of this literature, Bowman (2011a) reported generally positive relationships between college diversity experiences and civic engagement, with an average effect size of .11 across 180 effects generated from 29 distinct samples. In only seven instances were effect sizes negative, while 22 were positive and greater than .20. Based on an unconditional HLM model, Bowman estimated a significant positive effect of college diversity experiences on civic engagement of .16 of a standard deviation. Effect sizes tended to be greater in studies of self-reported gains (compared to studies using longitudinal methods) and when the type of diversity experience was interpersonal in nature (compared to diversity course work, cocurricular diversity, or intergroup dialogue). Moreover, effect sizes were larger when the outcome reflected diversity-related civic outcomes (e.g., cultural knowledge or understanding) rather than other types of civic attitudes (e.g., importance of social action).

A closer look at the evidence reveals that curricular diversity experiences influence a range of civic outcomes. Studies based on longitudinal data show that taking ethnic or women's studies courses influence such outcomes as character development (Astin & Antonio, 2004) and civic values (Lott, 2013). In addition to diversity-focused content, the pedagogical practices implemented in such courses may explain their influence. Mayhew and DeLuca Fernández (2007) examined the impact of diversity-related pedagogical practices on social justice learning in a sample of 423 undergraduate students. With student race and gender held constant, courses involving intergroup dialogue, general diversity discussions, and opportunities for reflection exerted a positive influence on social justice learning.

The values cultivated in diversity courses appear to empower students to act on their new knowledge. Although their work was limited to a single institution, Zúñiga, Williams, and Berger (2005) showed modest effects (approximately one-tenth of a standard deviation) of taking diversity courses on students' motivation to promote inclusion and social justice by challenging others on racially/sexually derogatory comments and joining organizations that promote cultural diversity. Another smaller investigation at a single institution also supported the positive effects that diversity courses tend to have on students' commitment to social action and intent to end social injustices (Nelson Laird, Engberg, & Hurtado, 2005).

The magnitude of diversity course effects remains unclear. In some instances, effect sizes are rather small (Engberg & Mayhew, 2007; Hurtado, 2005; Pascarella et al., 2012), but in others, the effects are larger (Denson & Bowman, 2013; O'Neill, 2012). Differences in effect sizes may be attributable to nuances across samples, extensiveness of controls for relevant covariates, and measurement variations. For example, smaller effect sizes were noted when the analysis was focused on first-year students; effects were larger when follow-up data on fourth-year students were analyzed.

General diversity experiences—occurring as part of cocurricular programs, extracurricular activities, or socializing with peers of diverse racial and ethnic groups—have demonstrable effects on a wide range of civic and political outcomes. Studies have illuminated positive effects of exposure to racial, ethnic, and cultural diversity beyond the curriculum on social activism commitments (Sax, 2008), civic values and interests (Chang et al., 2004; Rhee & Kim, 2011), political and social involvement (O'Neill, 2012; Pascarella et al., 2012), motivation to promote inclusion and social justice (Zúñiga et al., 2005), character development (Astin & Antonio, 2004), and an ethic of caring (Astin et al., 2011). Some studies pointed to the modest positive impact of racial/cultural awareness workshops (Sax, 2008) and interactional diversity (Pascarella et al., 2012) on gains in political liberalism. Effect sizes in most of these studies ranged from medium (.09 to .13 of a standard deviation; Astin et al., 2011; Chang et al., 2004; Pascarella et al., 2012; Rhee & Kim, 2011; Zúñiga et al., 2005) to large (.27 to .29 of a standard deviation; O'Neill, 2012; Pascarella et al., 2012).

Other evidence attended to the *quality* of diversity interactions. Using longitudinal data derived from ten public universities, Hurtado (2005) illuminated the import of positive diversity interactions in developing efficacy for social change, concern for the public good, and belief in the importance of civic contributions. Positive interactions contributed to gains even after accounting for whether students were engaged in extracurricular diversity activities. Effects of positive exchanges were small to medium, in the range of .06 to .11 of a standard deviation. In addition, negative diversity interactions had small adverse effects on all outcomes. In their single-institution study of Australian students, Denson and Bowman (2013) affirmed the significance of interactional quality. Interestingly, both positive and negative diversity interactions prompted civic participation, but negative diversity interactions undermined students' sense of civic duty. Indeed, qualitative findings support the notion that in some instances, negative encounters can motivate social action. Hernandez (2012) shared the narratives of Latina women, underscoring how politicized peer groups and communities on campuses—and even encounters with racism— help to engender political consciousness and activism.

What are the mechanisms by which diversity experiences affect civic outcomes? Bowman and Brandenberger (2012) addressed this question in their investigation of the effects of diversity experiences, including encountering "the unexpected," on orientation toward equality and social responsibility, which reflects attitudes and values centered on helping others and recognizing and denouncing social inequality. Though their study was based on a small number of students at one religious institution, they used a longitudinal design and surveyed students at the beginning and end of a service-learning course. Using structural equation modeling and controlling for a pretest measure, they learned that positive diversity experiences contributed to students' "experiencing the unexpected," which in turn yielded feelings of belief challenge and subsequently stronger commitments to equality and social responsibility orientation. The researchers concluded that diversity experiences must be novel or surprising in some regard in order to shape student development.

In another small-sample longitudinal study attuned to the mechanisms producing certain outcomes, Bowman and Denson (2011) identified the importance of interracial emotional connections as a mediating influence between interracial interactions and civic outcomes. Positive diversity interactions contributed to positive interracial emotional connections (e.g., sharing feelings, closeness, friendship), which in turn directly influenced civic participation and sense of civic duty. The emotionality of the exchanges completely mediated the relationship between having the interactions and the outcomes. The evidence supporting complex processes behind the impact of diverse exchanges on civic development points to the meaningful role of experiencing the unexpected and forging emotional connections in motivating commitment to social and civic responsibility. However, further efforts to replicate these intricate mechanisms using generalizable data are warranted.

Community Service and Service-Learning. Service work, whether as part of a formal curricular experience (i.e., service-learning) or other endeavors of students to serve their communities, is positively tied to civic gains. Several national longitudinal studies point to the benefits of volunteering for social activism orientation (Sax, 2008), character development (Astin & Antonio, 2004), an ethic of caring (Astin et al., 2011), and civic values (Lott, 2013).

Similar to Pascarella and Terenzini's previous review, the evidence supporting the impact of service-learning on civic and community outcomes is quite substantial and overwhelmingly emphasizes the benefits of this high-impact practice. Two relatively recent meta-analyses provided a synopsis of this extensive literature. In the first, a meta-analysis of 62 studies, Celio, Durlak, and Dymnicki (2011) estimated that service-learning had significant effects on civic engagement on the order of one-quarter of a standard deviation. We caution readers that this analysis of close to 12,000 students included populations other than undergraduates, though the majority (68%) were at the undergraduate level and effects tended to be stronger for that population. A subsequent meta-analysis of 40 studies examined the effects of service-learning on "understanding of social issues," a measure reflective of two dimensions, social attitudes and civic responsibility. They estimated an effect size for understanding of social issues at .34 of a standard deviation. Service-learning experiences involving reflections through discussion had a stronger effect on understanding of social issues (.42 of a standard deviation) than written reflections (.22 of a standard deviation).

Regarding the evidence from specific studies, Rhee and Kim (2011) found that curricular community service engagement had a positive influence on civic values (e.g., influencing the political structure, influencing social values, helping others who are in difficulty), holding constant the pretest measure, student characteristics, institutional variables, and student engagement, with standardized coefficients in the range of .08 to .28 of a standard deviation. Hurtado (2005) found that service-learning exerted small to medium effects on students' concern for the public good and belief in the importance of making civic contributions from the first to the second year of college. Astin and colleagues (2011) determined that growth in students' ethic of caring was in part a function of engaging in course-related community service (.12 of a standard deviation). Other studies involving smaller samples mostly reiterated the findings of the more generalizable research (Spiezio, Baker, & Boland, 2005; Wilson, 2011).

Service-learning generates moderate gains in political and social involvement, according to data from the Wabash National Study (O'Neill, 2012). Also underscoring the potential political outcomes of service-learning, one small-scale study (Seider, Gillmor, & Rabinowicz, 2012) found participating in a service-learning program with social justice aims had a small effect on students' expected political voice (e.g., expectations to contact a public official to express opinion, take part in a protest, campaign for a political cause). However, standing as one of the few adverse effects that we identified, service-learning had a small negative association with voting in Hurtado's (2005) study.

A caveat to the general principle that service-learning universally promotes social justice values comes from Mayhew and DeLuca Fernández (2007), who concluded that service-learning experiences entailing negative interactions with diverse peers produced negative effects on social justice learning. Qualitative research distinguished between civic and social justice outcomes, finding that service-learning participants generally increased their awareness of inequality, commitment to civic engagement, and multicultural skills (e.g., empathy, patience, reciprocity, respect), but only some individuals became committed to social justice activism (Einfeld & Collins, 2008).

Finally, the benefits of service-learning are not unique to undergraduates attending four-year institutions. Civic gains also appear to extend to students in community colleges. Prentice (2007) collected pre- and post-course data from students engaged in service-learning as well as non-participants at a sample of eight community colleges. Accounting for pretest levels of civic engagement, service-learning participants made greater gains in civic engagement (a measure of political and community awareness and participation) than non-participants did. Service-learning effects for students in community colleges were most pronounced in the areas of participatory citizenship (e.g., volunteering for a campaign) and justice-oriented citizenship (e.g., organizing a group in the community to address a problem), especially when students had taken two or more service-learning courses (Prentice, 2007).

Student Government, Student Organizations, Leadership, and Political Activities. Particular forms of cocurricular engagement help to foster civic and political values and behaviors. Longitudinal evidence shed light on the liberalizing effects of participating in organized demonstrations from the first to the fourth year of college (Sax, 2008). Taking part in organized demonstrations also may reinforce other forms of political engagement (Sax, 2008). On the other hand, student government and student organization participation appear to have opposite, though small, effects on political orientation and attenuate slight trends toward liberalism in the first year of college (Pascarella et al., 2012).

Despite the divergent political effects of participating in organized demonstrations and student government, according to generalizable, longitudinal data (Lott, 2013; Rhee & Kim, 2011), both forms of engagement support the development of civic values (e.g., influencing the political structure, influencing social values, helping others who are in difficulty, becoming involved in programs to clean up the environment, developing a meaningful philosophy of life, participating in a community action program, helping to promote racial understanding). Student government effects are small compared to the strong impact of participating in protests (Rhee & Kim, 2011). Astin and colleagues (2011) added that student government participation and participating in student organizations made moderate to strong impressions on the charitable behaviors (e.g., volunteering, helping) of college students in their longitudinal study of college students' beliefs and values. Finally, leadership training furthers character development (Astin & Antonio, 2004), charitable involvement (Astin et al., 2011), an ethic of caring (Astin et al. 2011), and general civic values (Lott, 2013), with reported coefficients in the range of .16 to .19 of a standard deviation. It may be that general engagement in college is characteristic of students who want to be involved in making a difference in their communities. Aligning with this hypothesis is evidence from Sax (2008), who showed that students who were more invested in college activities, from student clubs to studying and doing homework, became more committed to social activism (e.g., commitment to helping others in difficulty, influencing social values, participating in community action programs). However, those who were disengaged, as indicated by such activities as frequently watching television, became less oriented toward social activism over time.

Fraternity and Sorority Participation. Participating in fraternities and sororities appears to exert a slight negative effect on liberalism, irrespective of other student and institutional characteristics, according to a study focused on first-year students. Few studies, though, have examined the political ramifications of Greek membership on student development. A small body of literature suggested that civic gains associated with participating in Greek organizations are largely behavioral; students who belong to fraternities or sororities tend to volunteer more than students who do not (Astin et al., 2011; Cruce & Moore, 2007, 2012; Hayek et al., 2002). Cruce and Moore (2012) estimated that Greek affiliates had a probability of volunteering that was 22 percentile points greater than non-affiliates in the first year of college. The evidence linking fraternity and sorority membership to volunteerism has some methodological challenges that limit our ability to infer causality. The literature does not provide compelling evidence that Greek organizations foster civic attitudes and values.

Other Sources of Impact. Other experiences that are connected to political and citizenship gains include athletic participation, religious and spiritual engagement, studying abroad, and working. With respect to political attitudes, two experiences curb liberalism. Sax (2008) observed that attending religious services had negative effects on students' support of individual freedoms (casual sex, substance use, and abortion). Other evidence—including one longitudinal study of first-year students and one cross-sectional study of students attending selective institutions—connected athletic participation with conservative political views, controlling for other confounding variables (Aries et al., 2004; Pascarella et al., 2012).

Spiritual practices such as meditation, prayer, and religious/spiritual reading had moderate effects on end-of-the-third-year charitable involvement and ethic of caring in Astin and colleagues' (2011) longitudinal study of college students' beliefs and values. In Astin and Antonio's (2004) analysis, participation in religious services and activities motivated character development, a holistic construct reflecting civic and social values, as well as volunteerism. Related findings by Drezner (2013) highlighted the role of the African American church in inspiring philanthropic giving among students in his qualitative study. Students in the study "frequently mentioned that their involvement in the church taught them the importance of giving; in essence, the African American church was exhibiting, through pastoral conversations and observations, a form of philanthropic modeling" (p. 377).

Limited evidence also suggests studying abroad has a positive influence on civic values, such as attributing importance to influencing the political structure, becoming involved in programs to clean up the environment, and participating in community action programs (Lott, 2013). A study of short-term immersion trips, which included both service-learning and studying abroad, found such experiences helped to foster meaning making of social issues, stereotypes, and privilege. Immersion primed learning because it exposed students to the world "beyond the bubble," encouraging boundary crossing (from familiar to unfamiliar) and personalizing the lived experiences of others (Jones, Rowan-Kenyon, Ireland, Niehaus, & Skendall, 2012).

Other studies have uncovered small positive effects of working (both on and off campus) to social and political activism (Pascarella et al., 2012), as well as volunteerism (Cruce & Moore, 2007). Perhaps forging a sense of responsibility as employees inspires students to consider and broaden their commitments to improving their communities.

Finally, some evidence helps to make meaning of the interrelationships between civic values and behaviors. According to Bryant, Gayles, and Davis (2012), cultivating social activism values (e.g., commitment to reducing pain and suffering in the world, influencing the political structure, becoming a community leader, helping to promote racial understanding) is a critical precursor to engaging in civic behaviors (volunteering; donating money, clothing, or food; helping friends with personal problems). Other evidence is consistent with the proposition that values shape subsequent actions; according to Cruce and Moore (2012), students with high levels of civic mindedness are more inclined to volunteer.

Racial/Ethnic and Cultural Diversity Attitudes. Representative of research from the early 2000s and prior, Engberg's (2004) review of studies on racial bias reduction revealed, on the whole, positive effects of educational interventions as varied as multicultural courses, diversity workshops, peer-facilitated interventions, and service interventions. Fifty-two findings were positive, fourteen were mixed, and seven were null. Engberg noted conceptual, methodological, measurement, and analytical flaws in many studies, including models that left confounding variables uncontrolled. As a result, the weight of the evidence seemed to support the effectiveness of educational interventions in reducing racial bias, but not without a number of caveats and unanswered questions. Research conducted later in the 2000s, if not entirely conclusive, made further inroads in determining which college experiences have the greatest impact on racial and cultural attitudes.

Academic Major. Researchers tended not to address in great detail the impact of college major on racial/ethnic and cultural diversity attitudes and directed their attention instead to collegiate experiences, primarily diversity engagement, most germane to attitudinal change. Although college major was included in many models, it was typically construed as a control variable and effects were not reported. There is some longitudinal evidence that majoring in engineering reduced students' commitment to promoting racial understanding (Sax, 2008).

Residence. Similar to college major, few studies reported on the effects of students' place of residence on diversity attitudes, even though many studies controlled for residence. Two longitudinal studies with large samples of college students reported medium to large effects of living on campus, but the effects were in opposing directions. According to Chang et al. (2006), living on campus contributed to first- to fourth-year gains of .14 of a standard deviation in self-reported openness to diversity (i.e., knowledge and acceptance of different races and cultures). However, Padgett et al. (2012) identified negative effects (estimated at .16 of a standard deviation) of first-year students' on-campus living on intercultural effectiveness and universal-diverse orientation (a multidimensional measure of diversity of contact, relativistic appreciation, and comfort with differences). We surmise that Padgett and colleagues' finding, which holds weight given careful controls for preexisting proclivities toward diversity, may reflect the unique impact of living on campus for first-year students. Encountering diverse perspectives and peers in close quarters may initially engender negative attitudes among students who are perhaps having these experiences for the first time. Experiences that disrupt and unsettle students early in college may become more normalized in subsequent years.

Not all residential life experiences are equal in their impact, according to limited evidence drawn from the National Study of Living-Learning Programs. Inkelas, Vogt, Longerbeam, Owen, and Johnson (2006) pointed to higher levels of diversity appreciation among students who participated in living-learning programs relative to those in traditional residence halls. Yet the researchers cautioned readers about inherent self-selection bias, as several indicators pointed to higher levels of academic aptitude and achievement among the living-learning program participants than their peers in other residence halls. The study was also cross-sectional; preexisting diversity orientations were not taken into account when comparing the two groups, further limiting causal inferences.

Peer and Faculty Engagement. General involvement on campus and interactions with peers cultivate openness to diversity on campus, with effects ranging from medium to strong, according to two longitudinal studies (Chang et al., 2006; Cruce, Wolniak, Seifert, & Pascarella, 2006). We delve further into possible peer effects—particularly those involving diversity interactions—in subsequent sections.

Credible evidence supports the positive impact that faculty have on diversity outcomes by way of their interactions with students and pedagogical strategies. Discussions with faculty who held different views made a small impression on first- and fourth-year gains in commitment to promoting racial understanding

(Rude et al., 2012). A number of other longitudinal studies, many drawn from Wabash National Study data, focused on first-year gains or gains through the senior year. Those investigations connected diversity outcomes such as universality-diversity, intercultural competence, and openness to diversity and challenge with a variety of pedagogical practices, including academic challenge and high expectations (O'Neill, 2012; Padgett et al., 2012; Seifert et al., 2008), effective teaching (Cruce et al., 2006; Padgett et al., 2012; Seifert et al., 2008), active and collaborative learning (Cabrera et al., 2002; Kilgo, Sheets, & Pascarella, 2015; O'Neill, 2012; Seifert et al., 2008), integrative learning (O'Neill, 2012; Salisbury, An, & Pascarella, 2013; Seifert et al., 2008), and reflective learning (O'Neill, 2012). Effects, particularly those representing high-impact pedagogical strategies, were typically at least medium in magnitude, and some were quite large.

Diversity Engagement. A considerable supply of research highlights the gains in positive racial/ethnic and cultural attitudes stemming from diversity engagement. Exposure to curricular diversity has been linked to attitudinal outcomes in a number of studies. Taking courses on diverse cultures and perspectives contributed to first- and fourth-year net gains, in the range of .06 to .14 of a standard deviation, in commitment to promoting racial understanding, according to data from the Wabash National Study (Rude et al., 2012). Based on another longitudinal dataset, Sax (2008) affirmed the positive impact of ethnic studies courses on the same outcome: commitment to promoting racial understanding. Fourth-year gains on two other measures—universality-diversity (diversity of contact, relativistic appreciation, and comfort with differences) and general openness to diversity and challenge—were also a function of students' investment in diversity courses, with effects in the medium to strong range (O'Neill, 2012).

Using Wabash data but focusing on the first year of college, Bowman (2010c) contrasted different levels of diversity course engagement to find that taking two diversity courses (versus one) was associated with moderate gains (.12 to .13 of a standard deviation) in comfort with differences, relativistic appreciation, and diversity of contact. Taking three diversity courses (versus one) was linked to even stronger patterns of growth in comfort with differences (.24 of a standard deviation) and relativistic appreciation (.15 of a standard deviation), but the advantage of greater investment in taking diversity courses was only marginal for the diversity of contact dimension.

Concerning another set of outcomes from a different data source, Hurtado (2005) observed small-to-medium effects of diversity courses on gains in cultural awareness, recognition of racial inequality as a societal problem, perspective-taking, and pluralistic orientation. In another multi-institutional study, Denson and Chang (2009) identified a strong association (.22 of a standard deviation) between curricular diversity engagement and students' self-assessed change in knowledge of and ability to get along with people of different races and cultures. Reliance on students' self-reported gains may have amplified the magnitude of the effect. The weight of the evidence from large-scale studies points to a moderate impact of curricular diversity exposure on a variety of racial/ethnic and cultural attitudes, but these effects tend to be even stronger at higher levels of engagement. Other smaller-scale studies affirm our conclusions regarding the positive effects of diversity course participation (Denson & Bowman, 2013; Engberg & Mayhew, 2007; Zúñiga et al., 2005). These studies were generally well constructed and longitudinal in design despite having limited generalizability.

Several studies identified attitudinal benefits—albeit often small in magnitude—attributable to participating in intergroup dialogue. Based on her analysis of longitudinal data from ten public institutions, Hurtado (2005) reported positive effects of intergroup dialogue on perspective taking and pluralistic orientation. In a carefully designed small-sample study, Gurin, Nagda, and Lopez (2004) compared 87 students who had participated in an intergroup relations program to 87 non-participants. The two groups were matched on a number of demographic characteristics and whether they lived on campus, and models controlled for first-year predispositions toward the outcome measures. Gurin and colleagues reported that the intergroup relations program participants scored higher as seniors than non-participants on a variety of attitudinal measures: enjoying learning about the experiences and perspectives of other groups, thinking about memberships in various groups, and learning about other racial/ethnic groups and their contributions to American society. Participants also exhibited greater democratic diversity sentiments (perspective taking, sense of commonality in work and family values with other groups) than non-participants.

Some research assessed the effects of intergroup dialogue on *behaviors* that are consistent with attitude change. Specifically, Alimo (2012) explored the influence of race-related intergroup dialogue on the development of confidence and frequency of engagement in behaviors congruent with being a White racial ally (e.g., self-directed actions such as recognizing and challenging one's own biases and language; other-directed actions such as challenging others' derogatory comments; and intergroup collaborative actions such as working with others to promote diversity). Nine institutions and more than 300 students were part of the experimental study, which entailed stratified random assignment with controls for pretested outcome measures and college involvement variables. Although levels of confidence in performing ally-consistent behaviors did not differ significantly between the treatment and control groups, Alimo observed that dialogue participants engaged more frequently in *actual* ally behaviors, holding constant other covariates, although effect sizes were small in magnitude.

Many studies have affirmed the positive impact of interacting with diverse peers on myriad attitudinal outcomes. Researchers have illuminated the benefits of both cross-racial interactions, as well as general engagement with peers of diverse backgrounds and perspectives. Using longitudinal data on first-year students from the Wabash National Study, Bowman (2013b) reported "overall diversity interactions" (e.g., had discussions regarding intergroup relations with diverse students, had meaningful and honest discussions about issues related to social justice with diverse students) and interracial interactions (e.g., made friends with a student whose race was different from your own, had serious conversations with a student from a different race or ethnicity than your own) had moderate to strong positive effects on "intercultural effectiveness," a measure reflecting understanding of similarities and differences across people and groups, level of comfort with diverse individuals, and interest in diverse cultural and social activities. Other studies have identified significant positive effects of diverse peer interactions—variously operationalized as cross-racial interactions, interracial friendships, and general interactional diversity—on commitment to promoting racial understanding (Rude et al., 2012), motivation to reduce prejudice (Zúñiga et al., 2005), self-reported growth in openness to diversity (Chang et al., 2006), self-assessed change in knowledge and ability to get along with of people of different races and cultures (Denson & Chang, 2009), and self-reported gains in diversity competence (Hu & Kuh, 2003b). With the exception of Rude and colleagues' analysis, these studies had some design limitations: some were multi-institutional but cross-sectional, while others were longitudinal but used small samples or self-reported gains. As a result, effect sizes varied tremendously, from .07 to .09 of a standard deviation in Rude and colleagues' analysis using longitudinal, multi-institutional data and controls for pretested outcome measures, to .17 to .42 of a standard deviation in studies relying on students' assessments of their own growth.

"Diversity experiences," broadly defined, are noteworthy in impact when considered holistically. For example, evidence from the Wabash National Study estimated effects of diversity experiences on first-year student gains in intercultural effectiveness and universal-diverse orientation at .17 of a standard deviation (Padgett et al., 2012). Salisbury, An, and Pascarella (2013) reported diversity experiences uniformly influenced first- to fourth-year gains on all intercultural competence sub-scales, including diversity of contact, relativistic appreciation, and comfort with difference, with effects ranging from .13 to .27 of a standard deviation in their rigorously controlled analysis. Finally, Gurin and colleagues (2004) considered longitudinal data involving 1,670 University of Michigan students to examine the impact of a culmination of diversity experiences (i.e., intergroup dialogue, multicultural events, curricular diversity experiences) on a variety of democratic diversity outcomes. Some conditional effects transpired, as discussed later in the chapter, but all groups grew in their sense of mutuality as reflected by participating in their own and other groups' activities and learning about other groups. All groups also became more inclined to believe that differences do not inevitably lead to divisiveness. However, diversity experiences tended to diminish learning about their own group's contributions to society. Given the strength of effect sizes in these studies, there appears to be value in sustained diversity engagement.

The effects of diversity engagement have been well-substantiated, but several other studies attest to the importance of the *quality* of interactions. According to Hurtado's (2005) longitudinal investigation of the diversity experiences of more than 4,400 students attending 10 public universities, positive diversity interactions generally had small-to-medium effects on cultural awareness, acknowledgment of the problems of racial inequality in society, perspective taking, comfort with racially diverse peers, and pluralistic orientation. Yet negative diversity interactions weakened gains on these outcomes. Importantly, the significant effects of interactional quality persisted over and above the effects of frequency of diversity interactions and participation in extracurricular diversity events, which generally had positive effects on outcomes as well. Three other studies supported the importance of interactional quality (Denson & Bowman, 2013; Engberg, 2007; Engberg & Hurtado, 2011).

Bowman and Denson (2011) examined the process by which quality interracial interactions affect outcomes and identified the mediating influence of cross-racial emotional connections. Across all three diversity outcomes (interaction confidence with people from diverse cultures, open-mindedness in and enjoyment of cross-cultural engagement, and respect for cultural differences), positive diversity interactions contributed to positive interracial emotional connections (sharing feelings, closeness, friendship), which in turn directly influenced the three outcomes. The emotionality of the exchanges completely mediated the relationship between having the interactions and the outcomes. Negative emotional reactions to interracial exchanges generally resulted in poorer diversity outcomes, although the role of emotion as a mediator of the relationship between negative cross-racial interactions and attitudinal outcomes was somewhat inconsistent.

Given that diversity interactions yield consistent positive effects on student outcomes, what are the student-level conditions that facilitate such interactions? In addition to the evidence supporting between-college influences on cross-racial interaction, such as structural diversity, as we discussed earlier in the chapter, other research sheds light on how the individual student's experience may promote diversity engagement. Sáenz (2010) used longitudinal data from the Preparing Students for a Diverse Democracy project, which included 4,600 students from nine campuses, to determine the predictors of positive cross-racial interactions (CRI) during college. In addition to myriad precollege factors that resulted in subsequent positive CRI, collegiate conditions also enhanced the likelihood of such encounters. Sáenz uncovered medium-to-large effects of socializing, living with people from different backgrounds, and participating in diversity co-curricular activities on positive CRI. Relatedly, Park (2012) detected negative effects of religious identity salience and engagement in campus religious and ethnic organizations on the likelihood of developing interracial friendships. A smaller scale longitudinal study of just over 300 students at one institution showed that intergroup friendship formation between White and African American first-year students was predicated on having a roommate (versus no roommate), having a roommate of another racial group, and the frequency of on-campus intergroup contact (Schofield, Hausmann, Ye, & Woods, 2010).

Diversity experiences in the first year of college are predictive of later experiences, pointing to the importance of students engaging diversity early on

(Bowman, 2012). Bowman observed that positive diversity interactions in the first year related to positive interactions and engagement in diversity coursework in the fourth year. Moreover, diversity course taking in the first year yielded later investment in diversity courses. Even so, diversity course work early in college did not guarantee subsequent positive diversity interactions. Some students actually had more negative diversity interactions following their participation in diversity courses—perhaps because of challenging racism or engaging in more activism and encountering hostile responses as a result, or simply because diversity course work in the first year sensitized students and made them more aware of racism. Some of the findings pertaining to the effects of early negative interactions challenged assumptions, in that these experiences were associated with increased participation in diversity course work later in college and did not reduce positive diversity interactions. At first glance, such findings appear counterintuitive and challenge evidence from other studies. However, Bowman surmised that early negative experiences may be developmentally meaningful, inspiring student learning so long as the proper institutional support is in place to help students make sense of their negative experiences.

Other Sources of Impact. Evidence regarding the impact of fraternity and sorority membership on diversity-related attitudes and values is decidedly mixed. In one longitudinal study of first-year college students, Martin, Hevel, Asel, and Pascarella (2011) determined participation in Greek organizations had essentially no effect on students' intercultural effectiveness; however, in a study that used a holistic measure of first-year students' diversity orientation (e.g., contact with, appreciation of, and comfort with diversity), Greek membership had a positive association with the outcome, controlling for other confounding influences (Padgett et al., 2012). Two other studies detected negative effects. Sax (2008) indicated that joining a Greek organization reduced gains in the commitment to promoting racial understanding from the first to fourth year of college (Sax, 2008), while Sidanius, Van Laar, Levin, and Sinclair (2004), through their single-institution panel study, found that participation in Greek organizations among White students enhanced their ethnic prejudice, perceived group conflict, and opposition to diversity on campus. As a potent contrast, they also discovered that participation in ethnic organizations among minority students had no relationship to attitudes on race-related social policy (e.g., diversity on campus and affirmative action) or ethnic prejudice, but did relate to some extent to perceived group conflict. The researchers concluded, "Among Whites, membership in fraternities and sororities appeared to produce even more ethnocentric, conflict-inducing, and exclusionary effects than membership in ethnic student organizations produced among minority students" (p. 107).

Kilgo and colleagues (2015) illuminated the benefits of studying abroad for students' universality-diversity orientation and openness to diversity and challenge, estimating medium-to-large effects in the range of .10 to .21 of a standard deviation. However, whether study abroad effectively shapes diversity outcomes to the same degree as other diversity experiences has been debated in another recent study that took a closer look at the subscales that comprise universality-diversity orientation (referred to by the researchers as "intercultural competence"). Salisbury and colleagues (2013), employing rigorous controls for precollege characteristics, pretested outcome measures, college experiences, and a propensity score to account for selection bias, revealed that study abroad participation had a strong positive impact, estimated at nearly one-quarter of a standard deviation, on one dimension of intercultural competence in the senior year: diversity of contact (e.g., interest in learning about other cultures, attending events to get to know people of other racial backgrounds). Compared to other diversity experiences that have uniformly positive effects on multiple measures of intercultural competence, the impact of study abroad appears limited by comparison, leading Salisbury and colleagues to conclude,

> If study abroad only influences diversity of contact but has no effect on growth along other domains, then study abroad by itself may not be as transformative as previously claimed. Alternatively, if increasing diversity of contact is a necessary precursor for substantive comfort with difference and relativistic appreciation of cultural difference, then educators cannot discount the potential educational importance of study abroad (p. 15).

Other evidence shows that student perceptions of their campus matter for diversity-related attitudes and values. Harper and Yeung (2013) found positive effects on openness to diversity of students' awareness of mentoring programs on campus for minority students. However, believing the university spent too much time on diversity issues was negatively related to openness to diversity. Effects were moderate to large. Also alluding to the effects of campus perceptions, Denson and Bowman (2013) identified small negative effects of perceived differences between the high school and university cultural composition on students' interaction confidence across cultural differences. Though both studies were longitudinal, they were based on single institutions, limiting generalizability.

Several other collegiate experiences have been linked to diversity attitudes and values. For instance, undergraduate research exerted a moderate positive first- to fourth-year influence on two measures of intercultural effectiveness: universality-diversity and openness to diversity and challenge. In addition, internship experiences had a modest positive impact on universality-diversity (Kilgo et al., 2015). Community service participation and service-learning have small effects on diversity outcomes (O'Neill, 2012; Sax, 2008), and taking part in demonstrations enhances students' commitment to promoting racial understanding (Sax, 2008). Finally, some limited evidence has associated working off campus to small positive increases in intercultural effectiveness and universality-diversity orientation (Padgett et al., 2012).

Gender-Role Attitudes. Research exploring within-college effects on students' gender-role ideologies was sparse through the 2000s. Drawing from a few multi-institutional studies, it appears that certain types of faculty engagement exert a small positive influence on progressive gender-role attitudes, especially when faculty provide honest feedback to students and intellectual challenge and stimulation (Bryant, 2003; Sax, 2008; Sax et al., 2005). Women's studies courses (Bryant, 2003; Stake, 2007), general exposure to co-curricular diversity programs (i.e., racial and cultural awareness workshops), and social experiences with peers of diverse backgrounds and perspectives (Bryant, 2003; Sax, 2008) yielded positive change in progressive gender-role attitudes and feminist activism in some studies. Contrastingly, the influences of religious friends tended to shift gender-role views in a traditional direction (Bryant, 2003).

Attitudes toward Lesbian, Gay, Bisexual, and Transgender People. Few studies examined the impact of college on students' attitudes toward lesbian, gay, bisexual, and transgender people, although research has emerged addressing the impact of "framing factors" (e.g., religiosity, personal worldview, political orientation) and the intersections among these factors. Multi-institutional studies that centralize college effects are rare, with some of the most rigorous evidence coming from the Preparing Students for a Diverse Democracy project involving nine institutions and more than 4,700 students who responded to surveys during their first and second years of college. Engberg, Hurtado, and Smith (2007) characterized positive lesbian, gay, and bisexual attitudes as being accepting and supportive of LGB people and believing the romantic relationships of LGB people are as acceptable as those of heterosexual couples. They controlled for a variety of confounding variables, including pretested attitudes, and identified small positive effects of curricular diversity and informal interactions across race on positive attitudes. These findings signify that diversity exposure in one domain (e.g., race) has the potential to stimulate positive attitudes in another domain (e.g., sexuality). The strongest effects on attitudes, however, came from interpersonal interactions with LGB peers, which had a large standardized effect of .22 of a standard deviation. Reflective of framing factors, religious engagement resulted in more negative attitudes toward LGB people. Every unit increase in religious engagement generated a .18 standard deviation decline in positive attitudes.

Engberg and colleagues also uncovered some of the indirect mechanisms by which collegiate experiences shape attitudes. Identity centrality is the extent to which students reflect on multiple social identities. When students experienced curricular diversity, informal cross-racial interactions, and LGB peer interactions, they tended to exhibit more pronounced degrees of identity centrality, which in turn propelled positive attitudes. Another mediating influence, intergroup anxiety, was reduced by interacting with LGB peers, and lower levels of anxiety contributed to positive attitudes. Engberg and colleagues also noted accentuation effects, in that preexisting inclinations to either support or feel anxious about LGB people were generally reinforced by college and peer engagement decisions. One other longitudinal study involving a large sample revealed the small-to-medium effects that general support from faculty may have on students' acceptance of LGB relationships (Sax et al., 2005).

Most of the remaining studies attending to college students' LGB attitudes were smaller in scale, based on cross-sectional data, or less rigorously controlled. The studies affirm the findings of Engberg and colleagues and thus bolster the evidence that interpersonal interactions, including friendships and familial relationships, make the greatest difference in attitudes (Hinrichs & Rosenberg, 2002; Wolff, Himes, Kwon, & Bollinger, 2012; Woodford, Atteberry, Derr, & Howell, 2013; Woodford, Silverschanz, Swank, Scherrer, & Raiz, 2012; Worthen, 2012). On the contrary, framing factors, such as religious worldview, are foundational to LGB attitudes and generally have a negative influence (Hinrichs & Rosenberg, 2002; Swank, Woodford, & Lim; 2013; Woodford et al., 2013). Other collegiate effects, such as discussions of LGB issues in class, speaker panels, and ally training programs, inform attitudes as well (Hinrichs & Rosenberg, 2002; Kwon & Hugelshofer, 2012; Worthen, 2011, 2012), but gains were typically smaller in magnitude than direct engagement with LGB people.

In addition, some evidence showed that the effects of exposure to LGB course content were null in the presence of demographic and attitudinal controls (Woodford et al., 2013), and some courses enhanced knowledge of human sexuality but did not produce attitude change toward same-sex sexual orientation and gender confirmation surgery for transgender individuals (Noland, Bass, Keathley, & Miller, 2009). Other cross-sectional research conducted at one public university suggested that disciplinary cultures may have an impact on attitudes, with students majoring in business and education expressing less favorable attitudes toward LGB people than those in the arts and sciences (Holland et al., 2013). Indicative of the effects that nondiscriminatory campus climates may have on attitudes, Worthen (2011, 2012) reported that the mere presence of ally training on campus related to positive attitudes among students who had an awareness of the program's existence.

Qualitative studies reinforced the attitudinal benefits of cocurricular and interactional engagement. One study of sexual orientation intergroup dialogue courses demonstrated that students developed more affirming and less stereotyped perceptions of LGB people, better understanding of heterosexual privilege and heterosexism, and greater appreciation of the intersectionality of social identities. Moreover, students who participated exhibited behavioral shifts such as challenging the prejudices of others and taking steps to learn more and serve as allies (Dessel, Woodford, Routenberg, & Breijak, 2013). Another study identified several factors as influential in attitude formation, including having normalizing experiences in childhood, engaging with LGB peers in high school and college, empathizing with the struggles and successes of LGB peers, and resisting discriminatory attitudes expressed by others (Stotzer, 2009).

Research on college students' LGB attitude formation is still in the early stages. Moving forward, longitudinal research with generalizable samples will advance our understanding of the collegiate forces most conducive to encouraging progressive attitudes toward LGB people. Given rapid societal changes as well as major developments in LGB civil rights in recent years, attitudinal dynamics among college students are increasingly salient.

Religious and Spiritual Attitudes and Values. Most of the research concerning within-college effects on religious and spiritual attitudes and values has considered whether college experiences inspire students' openness to religious and worldview diversity. Astin et al. (2011) based their examination of ecumenical worldview—"seeing the world as an interconnected whole . . . and feeling a personal connection with, and acceptance of, all other beings" (p. 67)—on national longitudinal data from the UCLA Spirituality in Higher Education project. They learned that experiences in college contributed more substantially to ecumenical worldview than between-college indicators. Those experiences exerting medium to strong influences (in the range of .12 to .21 of a standard deviation) on ecumenical worldview, following controls for student characteristics, anticipated major, and place of residence, and institution-level characteristics, included having faculty encourage search for meaning and purpose and religious and spiritual discussions, socializing with different racial groups, helping friends with personal problems, and spiritual engagement (e.g., self-reflection, meditation, and religious/spiritual reading).

Further research on students' openness to religiously and culturally diverse people brought to light the potential for religious and spiritual struggles to provoke acceptance. Early indications of this relationship came from the pilot data collected as part of the UCLA spirituality project. In that analysis, Bryant and Astin (2008) reported that struggling spiritually had a positive association with students' perceptions that their acceptance of others of different faiths grew stronger during college. The findings, though, were correlational and based on self-reported gains. In a later study with more adequate controls for precollege predispositions toward struggle and ecumenism, Bryant (2011b) examined the mechanisms by which college experiences trigger spiritual struggles and subsequent openness to religious diversity. She observed that academic encounters with religion and spirituality (in class and with faculty), challenging cocurricular experiences, and perceptions of a favorable campus climate for spiritual expression positively influenced ecumenical worldview in the junior year. Importantly, these first- to third-year effects were partially mediated by religious and spiritual struggles. However, religiously reinforcing experiences tended to undermine ecumenical worldview. Bryant explained, "Religious/spiritual struggles have promising developmental implications for students' pluralistic competence, despite the difficult emotions that likely go hand-in-hand with struggling" (p. 456). Mayhew (2012b), in a study based on the same dataset, substantiated the effects of academic and social experiences on ecumenical worldview development. Curricular and cocurricular opportunities to learn about religious and spiritual matters supported gains in ecumenism, with standardized effects of .17 of a standard deviation. Spiritual struggles also predicted gains in ecumenical worldview, as reflected by a medium-to-large effect of .16 of a standard deviation.

Other research, albeit using cross-sectional data and a two-institution sample, determined that ecumenical orientation (students' interest in, openness to, and engagement with worldviews other than their own) is predicated on features of campus climate and religious diversity engagement. That is, students who felt supported and safe to express their worldviews on campus, had provocative experiences that challenged their assumptions of others' worldviews, and took courses designed to enhance their knowledge of other religious traditions tended to have higher levels of ecumenical orientation, holding constant other student characteristics (Bryant Rockenbach & Mayhew, 2013).

Other religious and spiritual outcomes that received some attention in the 2000s included religious/social conservatism, developing a meaningful philosophy of life, and views on the relationship between science and religion. Experiences in college that made a moderate to large impact on religious/social conservatism (conservative views on abortion, casual sex, atheism, and inclinations to proselytize and see God as a father figure) consisted of participating in a campus religious organization, praying, religious singing and chanting, reading sacred texts, and reading other religious and spiritual materials. Declines in religious/social conservatism were most prevalent among students who partied and drank alcohol (Astin et al., 2011). What is more, exposure to secular theories in higher education settings may be at work in liberalizing theological views, according to one study of Protestant individuals (Reimer, 2010).

Developing a meaningful philosophy of life was a function of a number of college experiences, including challenging professors' ideas in class, attending racial/cultural awareness workshops, spending time exercising and playing sports, and volunteering. Joining a fraternity or sorority and watching television undermined gains in procuring a meaningful life philosophy (Sax, 2008; Sax et al., 2005).

Scheitle (2011) used UCLA spirituality data to examine the predictors of students' views on the relationship between science and religion and discovered that college major had a significant influence, even when accounting for pretested perspectives and other student characteristics. Relative to natural science majors, students majoring in social sciences, education, or business and those who were undecided tended to become more inclined during college toward perceiving conflict between science and religion and siding with religion.

Educational and Occupational Values

Academic Major. Only Sax (2008) identified significant effects of college major on students' occupational values. In her longitudinal study, students' commitment to making a theoretical contribution to science was fostered in large part by academic major, specifically the health professions, physical sciences, and biological sciences. We uncovered no other evidence regarding the ways in which academic major shapes educational values.

Residence. Although some longitudinal evidence shows that living on campus exerts a medium-to-strong negative influence on lifelong learning orientations, specifically positive attitudes toward literacy in the first-year of college (Padgett et al., 2012), other evidence, though limited, posits that living-learning communities show promise in terms of instilling intrinsic educational values.

Based on pilot data from the National Study of Living-Learning Programs, which involved four institutions and more than 5,000 students, Inkelas et al. (2006) used a quasi-experimental design to compare students who were part of living-learning residences to a randomly selected comparison group of students living in traditional residence halls. They found a higher level of interest in sustained intellectual challenge and self-perceived growth in liberal learning (e.g., appreciation of a broad education; enjoyment of art, music, and cultural diversity; openness to different views) among students in the living-learning program relative to the control group. However, the researchers acknowledged the problem of self-section bias, with those in the living-learning program evidencing higher levels of academic aptitude and achievement than their counterparts. Moreover, the study did not examine changes in outcome measures over time.

Evidence from a longitudinal investigation with ample controls strengthens the argument that living-learning communities have an impact on lifelong learning orientations. Loes, Saichaie, Padgett, and Pascarella (2012) identified positive effects of participating in a living-learning community on positive attitudes toward literacy, estimated at .08 of a standard deviation.

Peer and Faculty Engagement.   Researchers examined longitudinal data from the Wabash National Study to probe college effects on the inclination to inquire and lifelong learning, which they defined as effortful thinking and positive attitudes toward literacy. Across several studies, the effects of peer interaction were somewhat inconsistent, which may be the result of differences in the models and measures. Two studies reported small negative effects of influential peer interactions (i.e., positive peer engagement and co-curricular involvement) on students' effortful thinking in the first year of college, but no effect of such interactions on positive attitudes toward literacy (Martin et al., 2011; Padgett et al., 2012). In another Wabash study, also of first-year college students, meaningful discussions with diverse peers (regarding intergroup relations, social justice issues, and personal feelings and problems) made a small positive impact on effortful thinking (Padgett et al., 2010). In a study of "good practices" that drew on longitudinal data from the National Study of Student Learning, Cruce et al. (2006) determined that interactions with peers, as reflected by cooperative learning, course-related and non-course-related peer interaction, quality of peer interactions, and cultural and interpersonal involvement, exerted small-to-medium positive effects on first-year gains in learning for self-understanding and preference for higher-order cognitive tasks. The weight of the evidence, albeit a bit inconclusive, suggests that peer interaction effects on lifelong-learning orientations are generally small in magnitude during the first year of college and are positive when there is an element of diversity engagement in the interaction, a topic that we cover in greater detail in a subsequent section.

Only Sax's (2008) longitudinal study provided insight with respect to peer effects on occupational values. She reported that students develop a "status striver" orientation (e.g., attributing importance to being well-off financially, obtaining recognition from colleagues, becoming an authority in one's field) when they study often with other students and engage in partying behaviors.

Faculty have the potential to significantly influence students' educational values. Analyses of longitudinal data in multiple studies illuminated the benefits of experiencing academic challenge, high expectations, good teaching, and quality interactions with faculty on gains in such lifelong learning orientations as effortful thinking, positive attitudes toward literacy, and academic motivation (Cruce et al., 2006; Loes et al., 2012, 2013; Martin et al., 2011; O'Neill, 2012; Padgett et al., 2010, 2012). Effects were generally in the small-to-moderate range. Indeed, professors play an important role in developing students' orientations to learning, and specific strategies on the part of faculty have bearing on outcomes. Loes et al. (2012) found that teacher organization contributed to gains in effortful thinking, and instructor clarity and prompt feedback resulted in gains in both effortful thinking and positive attitudes toward literacy (effects ranged from .04 to .08 of a standard deviation).

When faculty encourage deep approaches to learning, students grow in their intrinsic educational values. For example, several studies reported medium-to-strong effects of reflective learning, active and collaborative learning, higher-order learning, and integrative learning on various lifelong learning orientations, such as effortful thinking, positive attitudes toward literacy, and academic motivation (Kilgo et al., 2015; Nelson Laird et al., 2014; O'Neill, 2012). Nelson Laird and colleagues (2014) explored these dynamics in greater detail to find that integrative learning (e.g., working on a paper or project that required integrating ideas or information from various sources, including diverse perspectives in class discussion or writing assignments) and reflective learning (e.g., examining the strengths and weaknesses of one's views on a topic or issue, trying to better understand someone else's views by imagining how an issue looks from his or her perspective) were the most salient contributors to effortful thinking and positive attitudes toward literacy, with effects in the range of .07 to .11 of a standard deviation.

All told, many of these faculty behaviors and pedagogical strategies constitute core liberal arts experiences. One study devised a holistic "liberal arts" measure, which exerted a powerful influence, of one-quarter of a standard deviation, on lifelong learning orientations toward effortful thinking and literacy (Seifert et al., 2008). However, the study was based on pilot data from the Wabash National Study, so the sample size was smaller and pretest measures were not available.

Almost no research addressed the role of faculty engagement in shaping occupational values. Sax (2008) found that interacting with faculty—talking with them outside class or challenging them in class—contributed to increases in status striving in her longitudinal study. Academic engagement supervised by faculty, such as participating in faculty research and independent study projects, supported students' development of a scientific orientation.

Diversity Engagement. Although one study showed that curricular diversity had no impact on positive attitudes toward literacy (Loes et al., 2013), effects of diversity courses on effortful thinking and academic motivation were positive, according to longitudinal evidence from the Wabash National Study. O'Neill (2012) reported first- to fourth-year gains in effortful thinking and academic motivation of .05 and .08 of a standard deviation, respectively, among students who took diversity courses. Bowman (2010b) focused on first-year students and found that taking one or more diversity courses (compared to none) was associated with at least a .12 standard deviation increase in effortful thinking, accounting for the pretested outcome, student characteristics, and college engagement measures.

As we alluded to previously in our discussion of peer engagement, co-curricular and interactional diversity have a positive impact on lifelong learning orientations. Data from the Wabash National Study support this conjecture. Small positive effects of diversity experiences on first-year gains in effortful thinking and positive attitudes toward literacy were reported by Padgett et al. (2012). Likewise, Loes et al. (2013) indicated that both diversity workshop experiences and interactional diversity produced small gains of about .06 of a standard deviation on positive attitudes toward literacy. Controlling for confounding influences, first- to fourth-year gains in effortful thinking and academic motivation were even larger than in the first year among students who had diversity experiences (approximately .14 of a standard deviation; O'Neill, 2012).

Bowman (2013b) presented further evidence that the effect of interracial interactions on intellectual engagement becomes stronger at higher frequencies of diversity interaction. Bowman's study drew on several first-year cohorts that had participated in the Wabash National Study between 2006 and 2009; the full sample represented 49 institutions and more than 8,000 students. Interracial interactions—making friends with a student of a different race, having serious conversations with a student from a different race or ethnicity—and overall diversity interactions—having discussions regarding intergroup relations with diverse students, having meaningful and honest discussions about issues related to social justice with diverse students—produced positive small to medium effects on intellectual engagement (effortful thinking) in the first year of college, holding constant student background characteristics, college engagement, and pretested inclinations toward effortful thinking. Importantly, the effect of interracial interactions on intellectual engagement became more pronounced at higher frequencies of diversity interaction. Students with rare interracial interactions had less growth in intellectual engagement than those with regular, sustained interactions; the difference in growth between the two groups was nearly one-third of a standard deviation.

Other Sources of Impact. Several additional collegiate experiences have been linked to educational and occupational values. Data from the Wabash National Study indicated that participation in first-year seminars exerted a small total effect on effortful thinking (.08 of a standard deviation), but further analysis deemed the effect indirect and mediated by first-year student exposure to the pedagogical strategies discussed earlier: integrative learning (e.g., integrating ideas, information, and experiences) as well as academic challenge and effort (Padgett, Keup, & Pascarella, 2013).

Kilgo et al. (2015), in a study that thoroughly controlled for confounding influences and pretested predispositions, identified considerable first- to fourth-year gains of .11 to .16 of a standard deviation in effortful thinking among students who participated in undergraduate research, internships, and capstone courses or experiences. Moreover, undergraduate research experiences exerted positive effects, estimated at .18 of a standard deviation, on positive attitudes toward literacy.

Evidence supporting the effects of volunteering and service-learning on educational values is inconsistent. The meta-analysis of 62 studies performed by Celio et al. (2011) approximated an overall effect size of .28 of a standard deviation regarding the impact of service-learning on attitudes toward school and learning. The studies were not solely focused on undergraduates; however, effects at the undergraduate level tended to be stronger compared to other populations. Analyses of data from the Wabash National Study showed volunteering and service-learning having no impact on effortful thinking, but service-learning exerted small positive effects on first- to fourth-year growth in academic motivation (O'Neill 2012). In another analysis, Kilgo and colleagues determined that service-learning had a moderate negative impact on first-year students' effortful thinking.

Fraternity and sorority membership conferred neither advantages nor disadvantages when it came to first-year students' orientation toward lifelong learning (effortful thinking and positive attitudes toward literacy), according to Martin et al. (2011), but hours worked on campus had small positive associations with gains in effortful thinking and literacy attitudes across the first year of college (Martin et al., 2011; Padgett et al., 2012).

The only evidence on other factors affecting occupational values comes from Sax's (2008) longitudinal study. A status-striver orientation (e.g., commitment to being well-off financially, obtaining recognition from colleagues, becoming an authority in one's field) was reinforced by joining a Greek organization, but fraternity and sorority membership reduced students' scientific orientation.

Understanding and Interest in the Arts. Very little research through the 2000s provided additional insight beyond previous reviews on the collegiate experiences that develop students' understanding and interest in the arts. What we do know based on longitudinal evidence reported in Sax's (2008) study of the gender gap in college is that direct exposure to college experiences associated with the arts (e.g., majoring in the arts or humanities) enhances students' artistic orientation. Moreover, exposure to new ideas through reading, social exchanges with diverse peers, and organized demonstrations exerts a positive influence on students' artistic sensibilities. Interacting with professors outside class, as well as challenging professors in class, contributes to gains in artistic orientation as well (Sax, 2008; Sax et al., 2005).

Results from an earlier study provided additional insight and highlighted the gains that students make when they engage with their peers in cooperative settings. Accounting for precollege academic ability, student demographic characteristics, and hours spent studying, cooperative learning practices (i.e., the frequency with which students engaged in group projects, class discussions, and study groups) was positively associated with students' self-reported second-year gains in art appreciation, with a standardized effect of .25 of a standard deviation. The data came from more than 2,000 second-year students attending 23 colleges and universities who had participated in the National Study of Student Learning (Cabrera et al., 2002).

A qualitative study of students' identity formation in college reiterated the importance of peer engagement, particularly with peers of diverse backgrounds, in fostering aesthetic development. Kaufman and Feldman (2004) found college students becoming increasingly "cosmopolitan," and participants in the study attributed changes in large part to diversity exposure during college, the wide variety of cultural leisure opportunities provided, and an educated and cosmopolitan peer group.

Clearly, within-college experiences make their mark on many domains of attitudinal and values development. As with psychosocial growth, peers and (especially) faculty have a demonstrable impact on students. The research since 2002 has further clarified the intricate mechanisms by which diversity-related factors foster certain attitudes and values. However, not all effects are universal; next, we turn to the question of conditional effects to reveal how student characteristics such as gender and race interact with college experiences in influencing attitudinal and values outcomes.

CONDITIONAL EFFECTS OF COLLEGE

Conclusions from the 1990s

Compared to earlier decades, more studies through the 1990s considered whether the effects of college were conditional on student characteristics. Initial evidence posited that some college effects depend on gender and racial identity. For example, perceived institutional support for diversity had stronger effects on women's openness to diversity than men's, while men's openness to diversity was more profoundly affected by interpersonal interactions. In addition, although perceiving the campus environment as nondiscriminatory strengthened positive racial attitudes among all students, the effects appeared to be greater for students of color than White students. Racial or cultural awareness workshops also improved racial attitudes for all students, but in this case, the effects were stronger for White students. Fraternity and sorority membership had opposing effects on racial attitudes, improving openness to diversity for students of color and reducing openness for White students. Some evidence on openness to diversity showed first-generation students benefiting from academic engagement to a greater degree than students whose parents went to college.

Findings were mixed regarding the impact of women's studies courses on gender-role ideologies. In some instances the impact was similar across gender but in other instances different for men, either furthering or weakening men's feminist attitudes relative to women's.

Other evidence showed that the effects of academic major on students' educational and artistic values varied by students' personality characteristics and fraternity or sorority membership. At the time of the previous review, Pascarella and Terenzini (2005) contended that the study of conditional effects was, in the main, unexplored territory. Since that time, our understanding of conditional effects has expanded tremendously, as we detail in the following section.

Evidence from the 2000s

Sociopolitical, Civic, and Community Attitudes and Values

Gender. The evidence that college effects on sociopolitical dimensions and civic values and behaviors are conditional on gender rests for the most part on Sax's (2008) comprehensive study of the gender gap in higher education. In that study, based on more than 17,000 college students surveyed at the beginning of their first year and again in their senior year, Sax identified college experiences with effects that were stronger for or unique to one group versus the other.

Regarding the sociopolitical domain, differences in college impact were evident along three key dimensions: political orientation; classic liberalism; and permissive attitudes toward abortion, sex, marijuana, and homosexuality. Sax learned that attending religious services tended to curb the liberalizing effects of college on students' political orientation, and this was especially true for women. Also for women, majoring in the social sciences, taking women's studies courses, working part time on campus, and engaging in hedonistic behaviors (e.g., partying, drinking) inspired liberalism. Majoring in business or journalism, participating in student government, and joining a sorority had the opposite effect for women. Among men, majoring in English or the humanities, talking with faculty outside class, and participating in intercollegiate athletics resulted in greater leanings toward liberalism, but attending public universities and watching television curbed liberal inclinations (Sax, 2008, Sax et al., 2005). Pascarella et al. (2012) added that interactional diversity had stronger effects on first-year gains in liberalism among men than women.

Classic liberalism, or views that support government intervention and regulation, was positively influenced by a variety of institutional characteristics and collegiate experiences: the percentage of women faculty and women undergraduates on campus, the average political liberalism of the peer group on campus, taking ethnic and women's studies courses, feeling supported by faculty, and social diversity experiences. However, classic liberalism was negatively influenced by peer tendencies toward science and gender-role traditionalism, majoring in business, and attending religious services. In all instances, the effects were stronger among men than women (Sax, 2008; Sax et al., 2005). Some effects on classic liberalism were unique to women, including the positive influence of talking with faculty outside class and the negative effects of taking leadership training and joining a sorority. Smaller campuses where students had, on average, a compassionate orientation toward understanding others uniquely facilitated men's classic liberalism (Sax, 2008; Sax et al., 2005).

Regarding support for individual freedoms related to abortion, sex, marijuana, and homosexuality, Sax (2008) found such views were fostered among women when they majored in social sciences, enrolled in ethnic studies courses, had social diversity experiences, spent time in student clubs or groups, studied with other students, took part in demonstrations, and received honest feedback from faculty. However, exercising and sports participation resulted in lower levels of support for individual freedoms among women, and when faculty did not take women's comments seriously, women tended to develop more conservative views about casual sex. Working and reading for pleasure promoted men's support for individual freedoms and so did being exposed to a compassionate peer group and feeling that faculty did not take their comments seriously. Furthermore, when faculty provided honest feedback about abilities, men developed more critical attitudes toward date rape (Sax, 2008; Sax et al., 2005).

The weight of the evidence with respect to the sociopolitical domain suggests that men's attitudes are more strongly influenced than women's by structural characteristics of the institution, such as the percentage of women faculty on campus, and the general orientation of the student body, for example, the degree of gender-role progressivism or humanitarian concern exhibited by students on the whole. The conservatism of the immediate peer group in contexts such as Greek organizations, student government, and leadership training more often emerge as conservative influences in women's lives than in men's. Liberalism is generally enhanced by diversity exposure and reduced by religious engagement, but differential effects are evident depending on the outcome in question. Likewise, interactions with faculty most often stimulate liberal attitudes for students of both genders (again, depending on the outcomes), but this is not always the case for women.

Sax (2008) examined two areas related to civic outcomes: political engagement and social activism orientation. Several cocurricular activities were predictive of students' gains in political engagement (defined, for example, as discussing politics and keeping up to date on political affairs), including participating in student clubs, participating in student government, and tutoring other students, but these experiences tended to have stronger effects on men than women. Moreover, engaging faculty and taking ethnic and women's studies courses enhanced political engagement, but especially for men. Conversely, attending a residential campus, where many students live on campus, had a positive influence on women's political engagement but the opposite effect on men. Other peer factors also uniquely affected women. On campuses where students were wealthier and intellectually confident, women became more politically engaged, and similar effects were apparent among women who spent more time each week partying. Majoring in journalism enhanced women's political engagement, while majoring in engineering detracted from engagement. For men, spending more time studying exerted a positive impact on political engagement, but majoring in physical sciences, math, computer science, or psychology produced the opposite effect (Sax, 2008; Sax et al., 2005).

Disciplinary cultures had unique effects on women's social activism orientation. Majoring in social sciences resulted in first- to fourth-year gains in social activism for women, but majoring in business or attending institutions with science and engineering emphases reduced it. Perceiving that faculty did not take their comments seriously increased women's commitment to social activism, perhaps because such encounters motivated women to advocate for others who experienced mistreatment and victimization. Living on campus and holding a part-time job off campus also spurred women's activist commitments. However, participating in a sorority decreased inclinations toward activism. Social activism among men was facilitated on smaller campuses with larger numbers of students majoring in education. Likewise, when men worked on independent study projects and when they challenged a professor's ideas in class, they grew in their commitment to shape social and political changes (Sax, 2008; Sax et al., 2005).

All told, men's political engagement is more often than women's predicated on co-curricular activities, diversity-related coursework, and faculty engagement. Peer group characteristics, as reflected by average tendencies of the student body on campus, have a more demonstrable impact on women's political engagement. Certain disciplinary environments also appear to affect men and women uniquely. Faculty affect students' social activism in ways that depend on gender: women who do not feel faculty take them seriously engage in more social activism; men tend to do so when they challenge a professor's ideas in class.

Race/Ethnicity. A small number of studies identified conditional effects of interactional, cocurricular, and curricular diversity engagement on civic outcomes by race. Positive effects were observed for White students across most outcomes; fewer significant effects surfaced for Latino/a students. For instance, Gurin, Dey, Hurtado, and Gurin (2002) used longitudinal data to demonstrate the strong positive impact of informal diversity interactions on students' citizenship engagement regardless of race. However, the impact of classroom diversity experiences was inconsistent, with positive, albeit small, effects for only White students. In another study, Gurin, Nagda, and Lopez (2004) analyzed longitudinal data from one institution and observed that diversity experiences (i.e., intergroup dialogue, multicultural events, curricular diversity experiences) were universally related to engagement in campus political activities, but the relationship between diversity experiences and community service participation was significant for White, African American, and Asian American students only.

More recently, Bowman (2013a) examined the effects of interacting with specific racial/ethnic groups on a number of student outcomes using a multi-institutional, longitudinal dataset. With controls in the models for student characteristics, institution type, other relevant college variables, and pretested outcome measures, Bowman found generally positive effects of diversity interactions on intentions to volunteer after college. Specifically, positive effects were observed for Asians when they interacted with Blacks, for Blacks when they interacted with Hispanics, and for Whites when they interacted with Asians and Hispanics. No effects were significant for Hispanics, and one negative effect emerged: for Blacks when they interacted with Whites. Difficult intergroup dynamics between Black and White students, framed by a long history of oppression, may explain the tendency for this type of interaction to weaken Black students' interest in postcollege service work.

Political Orientation and Interest. Some limited evidence suggests that college effects on civic outcomes depend on political orientation and level of political interest. In general, effects are stronger for conservative students and those with lower levels of political interest. For instance, in one robust study, classroom diversity had stronger positive effects on orientation toward social and political activism among conservative/far right and middle-of-the-road first-year students than liberal first-year students (Pascarella et al., 2012). In another study with limited generalizability, Beaumont, Colby, Ehrlich, and Torney-Purta (2006) examined across multiple institutions the impact of 21 educational interventions that all included at least one "pedagogy of engagement" (e.g., extensive student discussion or reflection, politically related internships, interaction with activists or political leaders as guest speakers, service-learning projects). According to comparisons of pre/posttest data, the intervention enhanced students' politically engaged identity when they had low initial political interest. For students of differing initial interest levels, the intervention increased foundational political knowledge and political influence and action skills, but effect sizes were larger for those with low initial interest in politics. Finally, among those with low levels of initial political interest, the intervention enhanced both expected participation in conventional electoral activities and expected participation in political voice activities.

Other Conditional Effects. Two other noteworthy findings involve athletic participation and academic aptitude. First, Gayles, Bryant Rockenbach, and Davis (2012) tested their model of Civic Values and Behavior and learned that although athletes (particularly football and basketball players) were less involved than their non-athlete peers in charitable behaviors (e.g., volunteering, helping friends, donating), the effects of college on civic values and behaviors did not differ between athletes and non-athletes. Consequently, the researchers concluded, "Athletic involvement is not a deterrent [to civic value development] among student athletes when other promising involvements are available" (p. 551). Second, according to a longitudinal study of first-year students' political attitudes and engagement, interactional diversity had stronger effects on liberalism among students with lower standardized test scores than students with higher test scores (Pascarella et al., 2012).

Racial/Ethnic and Cultural Diversity Attitudes. Engberg's (2004) review of research on racial bias reduction synthesized studies from the 1990s through the beginning of the 2000s; he concluded that educational interventions such as multicultural courses, diversity workshops, peer-facilitated interventions, and service interventions typically had positive effects on racial attitudes. The fund of research was not entirely conclusive, however; 52 findings were positive, 14 were mixed, and 7 showed no effect of the intervention. The conditional effects observed across the studies most often involved race, with White students benefiting from interventions more than students of color, especially when receiving diversity workshops and training. Women also appeared to benefit from interventions more than men, or to change in their racial attitudes over time to a greater extent. Research through the 2000s has produced further evidence about the differential effects of college on diversity outcomes by gender, race, socioeconomic status, and academic major. Moreover, some evidence purports that the college conditions supporting cross-racial interactions and friendships depend on student characteristics.

Gender. Sax (2008), in her longitudinal study of the gender gap, determined that women's commitment to promoting racial understanding was closely tied to major choice. Whereas majoring in English or humanities and social sciences furthered these commitments among women in her multi-institutional sample, majoring in business, physical sciences, math, statistics, or computer science stymied growth. Among men, diversity and faculty engagement were particularly important. For instance, attending racial/cultural awareness workshops, having social diversity experiences, receiving honest feedback from faculty, talking with faculty outside class, and feeling generally supported by faculty had stronger positive effects on men's desire to promote racial understanding than women's. In all instances, effects were weaker or nonexistent for women. Importantly, institution-level effects were also noteworthy in their impact on men's racial values. Large, selective institutions—and those with a larger percentage of students of color—had negative ramifications for men's commitment to racial understanding. Yet the percentage of women undergraduates on campus enhanced men's commitment. Here we see the limits of compositional diversity: without social and cocurricular engagement across lines of racial difference, men do not develop positive values and, in fact, may regress even in structurally diverse environments (Sax, 2008; Sax et al., 2005). On a related note, Bowman (2010c) found in his multi-institutional longitudinal study that the effects of diversity courses varied by students' gender privilege. Initial exposure to course content focused on diversity appeared to disrupt attitudinal development among students with more privilege. Specifically, men's relativistic appreciation was weakened when they took one diversity course (versus no diversity courses).

Race/Ethnicity. Some studies suggest White students gain the most from interactional, cocurricular, and curricular diversity compared to their peers of color. Bowman (2010c), for instance, reported unique effects for White students in his analysis of diversity course effects on attitudes. White students who took two diversity courses (compared to one) exhibited gains in the range of .15 to .17 of a standard deviation in comfort with differences, relativistic appreciation, and diversity of contact. Taking three courses (versus one) also improved White students' comfort with differences (by .27 of a standard deviation) and relativistic appreciation (by .12 of a standard deviation). Taking no diversity courses (versus one) reduced diversity of contact (by .11 of a standard deviation) for White students. Students of color experienced the greatest gains, reaching .29 of a standard deviation, in diversity of contact when they took three diversity courses (versus one). Otherwise, effects of diversity courses were minimal for students of color. Three other studies showed greater gains for White students than students of color on such outcomes as perspective taking, sense of commonality with other groups, self-reported growth in cultural awareness and acceptance of other races, and self-reported growth in diversity competence as a result of various diversity experiences (e.g., intergroup dialogue, multicultural events, curricular diversity experiences, interactional diversity); however, these studies had some design limitations involving generalizability or reliance of self-reported gains (Gurin et al., 2002, 2004; Hu & Kuh, 2003b).

Two studies focused explicitly on the factors conducive to generating positive racial attitudes among White students. Fischer (2011) used data from the five-wave National Longitudinal Study of Freshmen, involving nearly 4,000 students attending 28 selective institutions, to examine the effects of college experiences on White students' racial attitudes. Controlling for student characteristics, pretested outcome measures, and the percentage of Black students on campus, the findings were generally consistent with the contact hypothesis. That is, participating in extracurricular activities wherein Blacks or Asians were the majority reduced Whites students' perceived social distance from Blacks and Asians, respectively. Although having a Black roommate reduced stereotypes, participating in extracurricular activities in which Latinos/as were in the majority increased stereotypes among White students. Finally, White students' self-reported contact with Asian, Black, and Hispanic peers generally reduced their sense of social distance from other groups and stereotypes.

Some qualitative evidence coincides with the findings of Fischer. Cabrera (2012) explored the ways in which White men engage and struggle with their Whiteness and found that the development of racial cognizance was often predicated on cross-racial friendships and multicultural education. Cabrera argued that the education of White students should not rest on the shoulders of students of color, which makes identifying the most effective forms of multicultural education all the more important. Specifically, Cabrera noted the importance of

> humanizing pedagogy . . . in which the participants did not simply absorb the numbers regarding racial inequality but in which their professors placed a human face on the social problem. . . . They did not become experts on the subject of race but rather became aware of their personal ignorance (p. 395).

Personal minority experiences of some of the men also helped participants develop empathy because "awareness of systemic oppression . . . allowed them to draw parallels between their experiences and those of racial minorities" (p. 394).

Other studies show greater gains in diversity outcomes associated with collegiate experiences for students of color, in some cases because White students' race ideologies and willingness to confront privilege are resistant to change. Harper and Yeung (2013) identified aspects of campus climate that had a general impact on students' openness to diversity. Yet they also reported several medium to strong positive effects of diversity experiences that uniquely contributed to gains in openness to diversity among students of color, including interacting with a heterogeneous friendship group, taking diversity courses, engaging diverse students socially, and perceiving that the university encourages formation of ethnic and religious support networks. Similar effects did not extend to White students. Because the longitudinal data were drawn from one public research university, the findings may reflect nuances of the particular campus. A mixed-methods study, again conducted at one institution, found few predictors of race ideology among White men compared to men of color. Only discussions of racial/ethnic issues related to a more progressive race ideology among White men after holding constant the pretested outcome measure. Nevertheless, a handful of experiences influenced the race ideology for men of color. Racial/ethnic diversity courses and discussing racial/ethnic issues led to more progressive race attitudes, whereas interacting with Whites and having more White individuals in the friend group led to less progressive race attitudes for men of color. Cabrera (2011) summarized,

> The intersection of being white and being male was strongly related to subscribing to hierarchy-enhancing racial ideologies. . . . White men are the beneficiaries of both white privilege and male privilege. . . . They were also a group of students who were generally immune to influence in their racial ideologies during the first year of college. . . . The college environment generally functioned as a reification of the racial status quo as it left these white male students insufficiently challenged ideologically regarding issues of race (p. 88).

Some studies display more complex patterns, wherein conditional effects differ by the experiences and outcomes in question. Bowman (2013a) examined the effects of interacting with specific racial/ethnic groups on sense of closeness to other races, ease of getting along with people of other races, and tendency to blame people of color for their life outcomes. The findings portrayed Asian students as benefiting more than other groups from interactions across race. In addition, interracial interactions reduced Asian and White students' tendencies to blame people of color for their life outcomes. Interacting across race facilitated a sense of closeness to other races for all groups except for Whites. Overall, patterns of interracial impact were less clear for Blacks and Hispanics. Engberg and Hurtado (2011) identified an amalgam of conditional effects on pluralism orientation in their examination of data from the Preparing Students for a Diverse Democracy project. A clear pattern was not immediately evident, but their work illustrated that the differential impact of diversity experiences on student development is anything but straightforward. For example, participating in co-curricular diversity activities benefited only White students, and diversity courses benefited only Latino/a students. Intergroup learning (motivation to engage in reciprocal learning around social identity differences) boosted pluralism for all groups with the exception of Latinos/as. Finally, negative cross-racial interactions weakened pluralism orientation for Whites and Asians, and intergroup anxiety weakened pluralism for all groups except for Latinos/as.

The impact of quality cross-racial interactions on attitudes toward one racial/ ethnic population can also generalize to other groups, a process known as secondary transfer effect (STE). These effects do not hold for all racial groups, however. Bowman and Griffin (2012) used data from the National Longitudinal Survey of Freshmen and controlled for a variety of covariates, including student characteristics, college experiences, and pretested outcome measures, to uncover positive secondary transfer effects among Asian, Black, and Hispanic college students but not among Whites. Mediation analyses demonstrated that secondary transfer effects were largely explained by attitude changes toward the primary out-group, supporting the notion of "attitude generalization" (see Pettigrew, 2009), in which contact with a primary group improves attitudes, and those attitudes generalize to a secondary out-group. STEs were most pronounced when the primary and secondary groups were similar in social status.

Socioeconomic Status. Some collegiate effects on racial and cultural attitudes depend on income level and first-generation status. Students from wealthier backgrounds benefited more from diversity courses than did their low- and middle-income peers in Bowman's (2010c) analysis of data from the Wabash National Study. Specifically, students with family incomes of at least $100,000 per year grew more than their less wealthy counterparts in their comfort with differences and relativistic appreciation (i.e., appreciation of both similarities and differences in people and the impact of diversity on their self-understanding and personal growth) when they took two diversity classes (versus one), with gains of at least .40 of a standard deviation. Also, pointing to the potential disequilibrium that comes from initial diversity exposure, particularly for students with privilege, taking only one course (versus none) resulted in a greater decrease in relativistic appreciation for wealthy students compared to low- and middle-income students.

Other studies based on the Wabash National Study and the National Study of Student Learning brought to light effects conditioned on first-generation status. Padgett et al. (2012) found that the effects of interactions with peers on first-year gains in intercultural effectiveness and universal-diverse orientation were stronger among first-generation students relative to students whose parents had some college or a bachelor's degree or higher. Furthermore, Pascarella, Pierson, Wolniak, and Terenzini (2004) reported that second-year openness to diversity and challenge was influenced positively by the number of term papers or written reports completed and by Greek affiliation among first-generation students, but effects were generally in the opposite direction for students whose parents had postsecondary education. Conversely, volunteer work exerted negative effects on first-generation students' second-year openness to diversity, but positive effects for other students whose parents had high levels of postsecondary education. Third-year openness to diversity and challenge for first-generation students was predicated on the average level of precollege cognitive development among students at the institution, credit hours completed, and academic effort or involvement. By contrast, average cognitive development of students at the institution had a negative effect on openness to diversity among students whose parents had a high level of postsecondary education, and volunteer work had a positive effect.

Other Conditional Effects. Some effects of diversity engagement on attitudes depend on precollege exposure to diversity and academic major, according to two rigorous studies. Bowman and Denson's (2012) study pointed to the stronger positive effects of diversity interactions (e.g., frequency of interactions with four major racial/ethnic groups) on affirming that people of other races are hard-working and getting along with people from other racial groups among students with more precollege exposure to diversity. The researchers surmised that students with fewer precollege diversity interactions may be less prepared for exposure to diversity in college, resulting in interactions that are "more tense, more superficial, and/or less interpersonally engaging than those of students who have more experience with diversity" (p. 420).

Engberg (2007) designed a model of pluralistic skill development and examined path differences by academic major. Several consistent relationships surfaced. Structural diversity had a significant indirect influence on pluralism orientation via positive interactions across race and subsequent intergroup learning (motivation to engage in reciprocal learning around social identity differences). Effects were somewhat stronger for arts/humanities and engineering majors, but generally held for other academic majors as well. The episodic effects of 9/11 and associated campus events related to the tragedy also had an impact on students' engagement in other diversity activities and positive interracial interactions—which together influenced pluralism. Only business majors did not experience this series of effects on their pluralism development. Cocurricular diversity experiences produced largely indirect effects on pluralism that were mediated by intergroup learning, and these effects were observed for arts/humanities, social science, engineering, and education/social work majors. The effects of diversity courses differed across major, with direct effects on pluralism orientation observed only for engineering and life science majors. Effects for other groups were largely indirect and mediated by intergroup learning. Intergroup anxiety weakened pluralism orientation, although effects were not consistent by academic major. Positive interactions across race, however, helped to attenuate intergroup anxiety, while negative interactions resulted in higher levels of anxiety.

Conditional Effects of College on Cross-Racial Interaction and Diversity Engagement. We have discussed the collegiate conditions and experiences that facilitate cross-racial interactions given that such interactions have promising effects on attitudinal change. Some of the factors that bring about (or deter) cross-racial interactions are dependent on student characteristics. Using a longitudinal dataset, Bowman (2012) found that structural diversity supported the development of White students' close interracial friendships and romantic relationships with partners of other races. What is more, structural diversity had greater impact on close interracial friendship development among Whites at higher levels of campus diversity. The effects operated independent of institutional size, student demographic traits, and experiences with interracial friendships prior to college. However, structural diversity did not appear to have an impact on cross-racial relationship formation among Black and Hispanic students. Patterns for Asian students were less clear, as structural diversity reduced their interracial friendship development; however, the negative effect was weaker at higher levels of diversity. Replicating Bowman's findings using another longitudinal dataset, Wolfe and Fletcher (2013) found that the diversity of the institution attended was predictive of cross-racial friendship formation in college, but only for White students. Relatedly, structural diversity enhanced both positive and negative interactions across race only for White students in Engberg and Hurtado's (2011) study of pluralism orientation. Even so, they also found benefits of structurally diverse environments for students of color. Specifically, Asian and Latino students experienced fewer negative interactions in diverse campus environments.

We speculate that other factors may be at work to explain why students of color may not be forming cross-racial friendships even with institutional conditions that appear to support friendship development. Structural diversity does not automatically ensure a campus environment that is welcoming and inclusive, nor does it guarantee that student interactions across diversity will be positive. Students who have experienced racial microaggressions or marginalization in their lives may be more sensitive to these dynamics—and therefore cautious in their friendship formation—compared to students with racial privilege.

Two other studies looked beyond structural characteristics to determine whether certain individual-level experiences furthered diversity engagement. As detailed earlier in the chapter, Sáenz (2010) used longitudinal data from the Preparing Students for a Diverse Democracy project to examine the predictors of positive cross-racial interactions (CRI) during college. He found medium to large effects on positive CRI of socializing with other students, living with people from different backgrounds, and participating in co-curricular diversity activities. In addition to these general effects, Sáenz reported an array of conditional effects. For instance, majoring in engineering negatively affected positive CRI among nonwhites in primarily White environments. Segregated college experiences, such as participating in Greek life, also had deleterious effects on positive CRI—but only among Whites in primarily White college environments. Similarly, living in culturally themed environments reduced the likelihood of positive CRI among nonwhites in primarily White environments. Diversity-related experiences also had some differential effects. Joining an organization focused on cultural diversity enhanced positive CRI for White students in primarily minority environments, while enrolling in diversity courses had a negative effect on positive CRI among nonwhites in primarily White environments. Opportunities for classroom engagement with diverse peers promoted positive CRI for Whites in primarily minority environments and nonwhites in both primarily White and minority environments. In sum, positive CRI is a function of several factors: the type of activity in which students engage, the compositional diversity of the institution, and the individual student's racial identity.

In another study, Bowman (2012) found that early experiences with diversity in college resulted in different levels of senior-year diversity engagement that depended on race and gender. For instance, the relationship between positive diversity interactions and later negative interactions was stronger for women and students of color than men and White students. Bowman speculated that having a minoritized status might lead women and students of color to perceive some of their interactions with majority students in a negative light. Although negative diversity experiences generally led to greater investment in diversity courses later on, this effect was weaker among students of color, perhaps because students of color doubted that diversity course work would teach them anything new beyond their existing awareness of power and privilege. The link between early and later diversity experiences in college did not, however, depend on students' openness to diversity. In other words, requiring diversity course work may foster engagement in diversity and subsequent outcomes regardless of students' initial interest.

Gender-Role Attitudes. Only two studies attended to conditional effects of college on gender-role attitudes. In the first of the two studies, faculty engagement had opposing effects on the gender ideologies of women and men (Sax, 2008; Sax et al., 2005). That is, participating in faculty research increased gender-role traditionalism among women but fostered progressivism among men. Sax (2008) postulated,

> Working with faculty on research exposes women to the long hours and heavy workload often necessary to gain professional success, at least in academia, causing some to question how they themselves would be able to balance a professional career with raising a family (p. 154).

Talking with faculty outside class had a similar conservative effect on women. In both instances, though, effects were small in magnitude.

Other experiences, according to Sax and colleagues, curtailed gender-role traditionalism among women, including attending a residential campus, enrolling in honors courses, challenging professors' ideas in class, and spending time partying and drinking. Peer effects for men were particularly noteworthy; men became more traditional in their gender-role attitudes when exposed to a peer group with a traditional mindset and when they participated in fraternities. However, living on campus, taking ethnic studies courses, attending racial/cultural awareness workshops, and feeling supported by faculty enhanced men's gender-role progressivism.

Bryant (2003) also found different effects of college on women's and men's gender-role ideologies. Independent of student background characteristics and other college experiences, women became more progressive when they lived on campus and took ethnic studies courses. Men became more progressive when they majored in humanities, participated in leadership training, and spent time studying and doing homework, but more traditional when they had many male friends. Effect sizes were generally quite small in all instances.

Some effects differed across Sax's and Bryant's studies (e.g., living on campus and taking ethnic studies courses promoted progressivism for women in one study and progressivism for men in the other), which may be attributable to cohort effects. However, the weight of the evidence points to consistent patterns in terms of faculty engagement, which supports progressivism among men and traditionalism among women, and peer effects, which typically shift men's ideology in a conservative direction.

Attitudes toward Lesbian, Gay, Bisexual, and Transgender People. Almost no research addressed conditional effects of college on attitudes toward LGB people. One exception was Worthen's (2014) study, which revealed that the effects of athletic participation and Greek membership on LGB attitudes in some ways depended on gender. Male athletes and fraternity members had generally unsupportive attitudes. Women's participation in athletics was unrelated to their LGB attitudes, while sorority membership predicted some positive attitudes. Knowing personally lesbian, gay, and bisexual people and levels of religiosity mediated these relationships. These findings have limited generalizability given that the data were drawn from two universities and just under 1,000 students. In addition, the cross-sectional design hampers our ability to infer causal effects.

Religious and Spiritual Attitudes and Values. Several conditional effects were observed in studies that traced students' development of an ecumenical worldview and meaningful life philosophy. Most of the conditional effects pertained to differences by religion, gender, and race.

Religion/Worldview. As discussed earlier in the chapter, Bryant (2011b) identified the positive influences of encountering religion and spirituality in academic contexts, challenging cocurricular experiences, and perceptions of a favorable campus climate for spiritual expression on first- to third-year gains in ecumenical worldview. Religiously reinforcing experiences tended to undermine ecumenical worldview. Many of these effects were partially mediated by religious and spiritual struggles. In a subsequent study, Bryant (2011c) tested the validity of the model by race, gender, and worldview. The model was generally applicable to students of different genders and racial/ethnic groups, but was a weaker approximation of the experiences of religious minority and non-religious students relative to Christians. Challenging cocurricular activities and religiously reinforcing experiences exhibited stronger effects on the ecumenical worldview development of religious minority students compared to Christian students. Attributing these differences to their minority status in society and higher education institutions, Bryant observed,

> Religious majority students have the privilege of finding support for their 'normative' worldview in a variety of contexts—perhaps even in conjunction with challenging co-curricular experiences and academic encounters. Religious minority students, on the other hand, must move between worlds with exceedingly distinct worldview assumptions; it is probable that the contrast between their religious reinforcers and

challenging co-curricular experiences are more pronounced than is the case for religious majority students for whom the contrast may exist, but to a lesser degree (p. 476).

The greatest differences in the model parameters were between nonreligious students and their religious peers. In fact, none of the college experiences in the model, save for religious reinforcers, predicted ecumenical worldview for nonreligious students, leaving many unanswered questions regarding the process by which nonreligious students develop openness to diverse perspectives.

We have reviewed the findings of Bryant Rockenbach and Mayhew (2013), which showed that the ecumenical orientation of college students is affected by features of the campus climate. Students in their study who felt supported and safe to express their worldviews on campus, had provocative experiences that challenged their assumptions of others' worldviews, and took courses designed to enhance their knowledge of other religious traditions tended to have higher levels of ecumenical orientation, accounting for other student characteristics. Yet space for support and spiritual expression was especially important for fostering ecumenical orientation among nonreligious students (relative to religious students). Although research on non-religiously affiliated students is still in the early stages, campuses that welcome self-expression of nonreligious viewpoints may help atheist, agnostic, and other nonaffiliated students feel more open about engaging the perspectives of diverse peers.

Gender. Limited evidence exists regarding gendered collegiate effects on religious and spiritual attitudes and values. In Sax's (2008) analysis, women who attended non-Catholic religious institutions and received honest feedback from faculty made greater gains than peers in their development of a meaningful philosophy of life. Majoring in physical sciences, math, statistics, or computer science had the opposite impact on women. In addition, although general faculty support and social diversity experiences contributed to gains in cultivating a meaningful life philosophy for all students, the effects were stronger among men. Moreover, men's commitment to developing a meaningful philosophy of life was undermined by attending public institutions and majoring in engineering or social sciences.

Further illuminating gendered effects, the average religious struggle at an institution had a differential effect on women's and men's ecumenical worldview development in Mayhew's (2012b) study. Although women made greater gains in ecumenical worldview during college than men, the gender gap was reduced slightly by peer effects. That is, men attending institutions where peers frequently struggled with religious issues tended to deepen their ecumenical perspectives to a greater degree than men attending institutions where religious struggling was not so prevalent.

Race/Ethnicity. Gehrke (2014) used data from the UCLA Spirituality in Higher Education project to examine the impact of prosocial involvement on ecumenical worldview development and uncovered many effects that were conditional on race/ethnicity. Accounting for student characteristics, high school involvement, and the pretested outcome measures, he reported several differential effects of institutional measures: Latino/a students' ecumenical development was more pronounced at private nonsectarian institutions, Black students' ecumenical development was enhanced at Catholic institutions, and selective institutions had a tendency to undermine Asian and Latino/a ecumenism. A variety of prosocial involvement experiences bolstered ecumenical development, but typically only for certain groups. Participating in leadership training supported ecumenical development for Asians, Latinos/as, and Whites; participating in organized demonstrations supported ecumenism for Blacks, Latino/as, and Whites; and discussing politics supported ecumenism for Asians and Whites. Participating in student government exerted a negative influence on ecumenism for Asians and Latino/as. Finally, some experiences produced opposite effects for certain groups. For instance, working on a political campaign fostered ecumenism among Blacks and Asians but reduced ecumenism for Latino/as and Whites. Also, volunteer work supported ecumenical development for Asians but diminished ecumenism for Blacks. Gehrke concluded with practical advice for educators:

> Practitioners tasked with developing training experiences related to diversity, pluralistic understanding, and spirituality should seek to utilize aspects of student activism, leadership, political engagement, and service in order to foster meaningful outcomes for their students. However, as these experiences are not consistently positive for all groups of students, student affairs practitioners are urged to explore individual motivations of students they work with to better understand how their experiences contribute to their development of an ecumenical worldview (p. 688).

Educational and Occupational Values. A range of conditional effects—most often associated with gender, race, and socioeconomic status—surfaced in our review. The findings of numerous studies showed that college influences on such outcomes as effortful thinking, positive attitudes toward literacy, and various occupational orientations depend on student characteristics.

Gender. Faculty engagement has distinctive influences on men's and women's educational values. Specifically, men experienced greater gains than women in their positive attitudes toward literacy when exposed to high expectations and challenge from faculty in a longitudinal analysis performed by Cruce et al. (2006). Women's gains in literacy attitudes were more pronounced than men's when they encountered effective teaching.

A number of differential effects by gender were delineated by Sax (2008) in predicting the occupational values of status striving and orientation toward science. In materialistic peer environments and in business departments, students became more inclined toward status striving (e.g., commitment to being well-off financially, obtaining recognition from colleagues, becoming an authority in one's field). However, effects were stronger for men than women. Among women, religious influences (e.g., attending religious services and non-Catholic religious institutions) reduced status-striving tendencies. Yet peer environments where students drank, smoked, and partied enhanced women's status striving, as did frequent television watching. For men, engaging peers in social settings furthered status striving, but independent activities, such as reading for pleasure, had the opposite effect. Environmental influences also played a role in status striving uniquely for men, with majoring in education and attending an institution where many students majored in the social sciences diminishing status striving, but majoring in the fine arts (surprisingly) enhancing striving. Compared to women, talking with faculty outside class, challenging a professor's ideas in class, and feeling supported by faculty had stronger effects on men's status striver orientation than women's (Sax et al., 2005).

Commitment to making contributions to science was cultivated in honors courses and in conversations with faculty outside class, but these effects were stronger for men than women. Moreover, men's scientific orientation was stimulated in environments with a larger percentage of female faculty and in instances where faculty did not take their comments seriously. Nonacademic pursuits that might reflect intellectual curiosity and experimentation—reading for pleasure and partying behaviors—were associated with men's gains in scientific orientation, but watching television had a negative impact. Men's scientific orientation was undermined in highly intellectual peer environments, which Sax (2008) surmised may be the result of men questioning their scientific abilities in the presence of a very capable peer group. Alternatively, such peer groups may simply help men widen the range of intellectual possibilities available to them. Among women, peer effects prevailed when it came to goals to make contributions to science. A peer group with a stronger science orientation and studying with other students resulted in gains in science orientation for women (Sax, 2008; Sax et al., 2005).

Race/Ethnicity. Research from the Wabash National Study pointed to stronger effects of diversity courses and overall diversity interactions (e.g., having discussions regarding intergroup relations with diverse students; having meaningful and honest discussions about issues related to social justice with diverse students) on first-year gains in effortful thinking among White students relative to students of color (Bowman, 2010c, 2013b). However, some experiences are of greater benefit to students of color. In particular, first-year gains in positive attitudes toward literacy were more substantial for students of color than their counterparts when they were exposed to effective teaching and interactions with faculty (Cruce et al., 2006).

Socioeconomic Status. The impact of college on educational values is not uniform for students with different levels of socioeconomic privilege. In some instances, students with lower levels of privilege gain the most from their experiences. According to Bowman (2010c), the effects of taking one or three diversity courses (versus none) on first-year students' effortful thinking were weaker among higher-income students than their lower- or middle-income peers. Yet other evidence shows that students whose families have had more exposure to postsecondary education stand to make greater gains in their educational values. In a longitudinal study of first-year students, Padgett et al. (2012)

determined that diversity experiences had more pronounced effects on effortful thinking among students whose parents had at least some college (versus first-generation students). In addition, the effects of good teaching interactions with faculty on effortful thinking were stronger among students who were *not* first-generation college attenders (similar differential effects of non-classroom faculty interactions were identified by Padgett et al., 2010). Padgett and colleagues (2012) connected their findings to the tenets of social capital theory, suggesting, "Upon entrance to college first-generation students are not as well equipped as their peers to derive the potential developmental benefits that stem from interactions with an institution's faculty" (p. 261).

Adding to what we know about the differential effects of diversity engagement and faculty interactions on educational values for students of distinctive socioeconomic backgrounds, further evidence points to contrasting influences of other collegiate experiences on lifelong learning orientations that depend on students' first-generation status. According to data from the National Study of Student Learning, an array of experiences uniquely influenced first-generation students' learning orientations. First-generation students' learning for self-understanding was positively influenced by the number of credit hours completed, course-related peer interactions, the number of non-assigned books read, the number of term papers or written reports, and the average precollege cognitive development of students at the institution, and negatively influenced by the number of technical/pre-professional courses taken. Regarding preference for higher-order cognitive tasks, extracurricular involvement, the number of non-assigned books read, and Greek affiliation had positive effects for first-generation students, while hours worked had a negative effect. Among students whose parents had attended college, only volunteer work surfaced as a positive force that furthered learning for self-understanding and preference for higher-order cognitive tasks (Pascarella et al., 2004).

Other Conditional Effects. Finally, some research shows that the effects of faculty engagement on learning orientations depend on institution type and level of academic preparation. To be more precise, challenge and high expectations of faculty exerted stronger effects on positive attitudes toward literacy among students attending community colleges, Historically Black Colleges, regional institutions, and research universities than students attending liberal arts colleges (Cruce et al., 2006). In addition, teacher effects appear to be conditional on level of academic preparation such that teacher support had a slightly negative effect on effortful thinking among students with lower standardized test scores compared to their higher-scoring counterparts (for whom effects were null; Loes et al., 2012).

Understanding and Interest in the Arts. Only Sax's (2008) study of the gender gap in college illuminated conditional effects involving understanding and interest in the arts. Using computers produced opposite effects by gender, effectively strengthening men's orientation to the arts and weakening women's. Engaging activities, such as working on independent study projects and exercising or playing sports, provided the creative space for women's artistic orientation to thrive, whereas talking with faculty outside class exerted a stronger effect on men's artistic orientation than women's. For men, scientific environments (e.g., majoring in the physical sciences or attending an institution with a large number of science majors) curtailed artistic orientation. In addition, men who received grants and scholarships tended to see reductions in their artistic orientation, perhaps because such awards directed men to other intellectual rather than purely artistic pursuits (Sax, 2008; Sax et al., 2005).

LONG-TERM COLLEGE EFFECTS

Conclusions from the 1990s

According to the review of research in the 1990s, the long-term effects of college on sociopolitical attitudes and behaviors were well established in the literature (Pascarella & Terenzini, 2005). College effects endured when it came to voting and other aspects of political participation, as well as engagement in civic and community groups. Changes in sociopolitical attitudes during college typically stabilized after graduation and were reinforced in supportive social and occupational environments. Net increases in intrinsic educational and occupational values, along with corresponding net decreases in extrinsic values, were maintained after college. Pascarella and Terenzini (2005) also highlighted direct and indirect effects of college on attitudinal outcomes in the long term. To be sure, college directly influenced students' social and political values. However, indirectly, college-going afforded graduates with access to social networks that further shaped their attitudes and values. The evidence was lacking or inconclusive with respect to long-term college effects on several specific attitudinal dimensions: racial/ethnic, gender-role, and LGB attitudes.

Evidence from the 2000s

The majority of the studies we reviewed examined postcollege civic outcomes (e.g., volunteering, commitment to serving the community) and a few considered political attitudes and diversity outcomes. We identified no studies detailing long-term college effects—those effects sustained for one year or more—on gender-role attitudes, attitudes toward LGB people, religious and spiritual attitudes and values, educational and occupational values, or understanding and interest in the arts. Unlike most of the studies in the 1990s, researchers tended to go beyond examining net effects of college in the long term. Rather, they attended to particular aspects of college-going—institutional characteristics and collegiate experiences—to draw conclusions about not only whether college has an impact but also how it does.

Sociopolitical, Civic, and Community Attitudes and Values

Institutional Characteristics. The long-term impact of institutional quality, size, and public or private designation on political and civic outcomes is somewhat unclear given inconsistencies across studies. Selectivity, a traditional measure of college quality, had varied effects on voter participation in the long term that depended on cohort. One study revealed negative effects of selectivity on voter participation (Long, 2010), but other research found no impact of selectivity on voter turnout and political engagement in the long term (Hillygus, 2005). Moreover, while one study reported no effect of school size on political engagement (Hillygus, 2005), another (Ishitani & McKitrick, 2013) identified positive effects of attending larger institutions on civic engagement. Although both studies followed students three to four years after graduation from college, the inconsistency between them may reflect measurement differences. Hillygus's analysis was limited to political involvement, while Ishitani and McKitrick examined a more holistic measure that included a combination of political and community engagement indicators.

The public or private status of an institution also has some impact on graduates' political participation (i.e., volunteering for a campaign, attending a political rally or meeting, contributing money to a campaign, writing a letter to a public official) in the long term. Lott, Hernandez, King, Brown, and Fajardo (2013) used data from the Baccalaureate and Beyond Longitudinal Study and employed Holland's theory of person-environment fit to discern institutional effects. Based on a sample of more than 5,000 respondents who had attended 501 institutions, they learned that average political participation did not vary significantly between individuals who attended public or private institutions ten years after college; however, they did observe differences in the short term, favoring public institution graduates one year after graduation. Contrarily, civic engagement, the broader measure Ishitani and McKitrick (2013) constructed to reflect both political and community participation, was negatively affected in the long term by attending public institutions.

Academic Major. Disciplinary influences have surfaced in a number of studies. Majoring in business, science, and engineering tended to weaken civic outcomes. The effects of majoring in social sciences were somewhat inconsistent across studies. Evidence regarding the long-term effects of business and economics course-taking patterns and majors on political attitudes and civic engagement comes from Allgood, Bosshardt, van der Klaauw, and Watts's (2012) study of more than 2,000 participants. Controlling for demographic characteristics (including wealth and property ownership) and college GPA, the number of economics courses taken and majoring in economics or business increased the likelihood of joining the Republican Party. Course-taking patterns also drove attitudes in that individuals who had taken more economics courses in college preferred less government regulation and intervention. Business majors did not differ substantially from other majors on these attitudes, but they were less likely to volunteer than other majors and to vote in the 2000 presidential election. Economics majors were no different from other majors in terms of their civic participation. Several additional studies observed the negative influences of majoring in business on postcollege outcomes such as voting (Hillygus, 2005) and measures of overall political engagement and civic involvement (Astin et al., 2006; Ishitani & McKitrick, 2013).

Other work highlighted the contrasting post-college influences of majoring in the sciences and social sciences on political engagement (i.e., voting and participation in political activities). Hillygus (2005) used data from Baccalaureate and Beyond to examine the political engagement of individuals who graduated in 1992–1993. More than 3,800 individuals were interviewed for the first time in 1993, again in 1994, and once more in 1997 (four years after receiving the bachelor's degree). Controls for student characteristics and post-college variables were included in the models. The number of social science credits earned positively predicted both voting and participation in political activities, while the number of science credits earned had a negative effect on voting. Hillygus explained,

> Even if participation in an educational community—a classroom, a department, or a university—is an important connective mechanism between higher education and participation . . . the specific content of education (both in college and before) is also critical. The findings suggest that an educational system geared towards developing verbal and civic skills can encourage future participation in American democracy (p. 41).

Some similar findings were reported by Ishitani and McKitrick (2013), who, upon examining more holistic conceptions of civic participation in their longitudinal study, found that majoring in engineering, math, and physical sciences (compared to education) had negative effects on postcollege civic engagement (e.g., volunteering, voting, attending to the news, engaging in the community). They also discovered negative effects of applied social sciences on civic engagement, but null effects for social sciences, in contrast to the positive findings of Hillygus. A few other effects of college major were observed as well, including the negative effects of majoring in the arts and humanities (Ishitani & McKitrick, 2013), and the positive effects of majoring in history or political science on postcollege civic engagement (Astin et al., 2006).

Lott and colleagues (2013) lent further complexity to our understanding of long-term effects of college major on political participation. They examined disciplinary influences by modeling the effects of course-taking patterns and also considered whether disciplinary effects depended on the institution's public or private status. Most effects extended one year after college. Only majoring in business had a significant, direct negative effect on political participation 10 years after college—and only for graduates of public institutions. Models controlled for participant demographics, values, and prior political participation. The results highlighted the importance of considering how the additional layer of institutional ethos may act in concert with disciplinary contexts to shape students' political engagement in the long term.

Diversity Experiences. Not only do diversity interactions influence students while they are in college; such effects also appear to shape students in the years after graduation. Using longitudinal data collected during the first year, senior year, and 13 years after college, Bowman, Brandenberger, Hill, and Lapsley (2011) examined the long-term effects of diversity interactions in college on volunteering in adulthood. They found that racial/cultural workshops and ethnic studies courses had small indirect effects on volunteer work participation 13 years after college. Prosocial orientation in the senior year directly influenced later volunteer work. Although the sample was small and based on only one institution, such long-term follow-ups are quite rare. Other longitudinal evidence based on more representative samples confirmed the positive, long-term impact of enrolling in ethnic studies courses on graduates' civic engagement (Astin et al., 2006). Furthermore, a qualitative investigation supported the long-term impact of dialogue experiences on a variety of civic outcomes (Diaz & Perrault, 2010). At the heart of growth in civic commitments was personal transformation, with "individuals becoming more intellectually curious (as in learning about other cultures and histories), cognitively sophisticated (as in media literacy), more emotionally empathic toward others (as in respecting multiple truths), and more skilled in communicating across differences" (p. 41).

Curricular and co-curricular diversity interactions appear to have a lasting impact on civic outcomes, but structural diversity produces inconsistent effects on civic behaviors in the long term. Using data from the Beginning Postsecondary Students' Longitudinal Study (1996/2001), which tracked students from the first year of college and included two follow-ups (in 1998 and 2001), Hinrichs (2011) estimated effects on civic outcomes for non-Hispanic White students attending four-year institutions. Five years after entering college, the share of underrepresented minorities at the institution and the degree of racial variety had essentially no effect on voting in the 2000 election. However, holding constant demographic and institutional characteristics, high school diversity, state of residence, and state of the institution, the share of underrepresented minorities on campus exerted a negative effect on community service participation. The dynamics behind this effect are unclear and provide an opportunity for further investigation into the ways in which campus structural diversity and racial climate motivate (or reduce) graduates' inclinations to serve their communities.

Community Service and Service-Learning. Studies of the long-term effects of service work on civic outcomes pointed to the importance of reflection and intrinsic factors in motivating future commitments to civic engagement. Astin and colleagues (2006) followed a national, longitudinal sample of more than 8,400 individuals from 229 colleges and universities who were initially surveyed as entering first-year students in 1994, again as seniors in 1998, and six years after college in 2004. The goal of the postcollege follow-up was to examine the long-term effects of college on civic engagement and sense of civic responsibility. The researchers noted substantial declines in community service participation during and after college: 80% of respondents volunteered in their last year of high school, but this percentage dropped to 74% by the senior year of college and to 68% after college. Perhaps shifting roles related to family obligations and workforce participation reduce time for volunteering and civic engagement.

Regarding the effects of service on long-term college outcomes, Astin and colleagues found that service-learning exerted small effects (on the order of .03 to .04 of a standard deviation), over and above generic service participation and other student and institutional characteristics, on 3 of 13 civic outcomes they examined, including civic leadership, charitable giving, and overall political engagement. The effects of general community service were typically stronger than service-learning, ranging from .03 to .15 of a standard deviation, and held even when accounting for student characteristics, institutional characteristics, service-learning, reflection, and other college activities. Importantly, the effects of service-learning and general community service were partially mediated by reflection on the service experience with peers and professors. Beyond service participation, the researchers found positive post-college effects on civic outcomes of taking interdisciplinary courses, attending religious services, and participating in student government (in addition to some effects of college major and diversity courses, as already noted).

Qualitative research supported the findings of Astin and colleagues in terms of the benefits of service participation for students' civic development. Iverson and James (2013) concluded that change-oriented service-learning helped students to develop more complex understandings of citizenship, increase their citizenship self-efficacy, and enhance their awareness of self in relation to their communities.

Bryant Rockenbach, Hudson, and Tuchmayer (2014) drew attention to distinctions among various types of service work and motivational factors in examining college effects on service behaviors after college. Using national data from the Beginning Postsecondary Students Longitudinal Study and controlling for pretest levels of citizenship, as well as hours worked weekly after college, the researchers found that the intensity of service during college and volunteering with children conferred both extrinsic (vocational and career advancement) and intrinsic (social consciousness and compassion) benefits. Helping individuals and communities in need was more strongly associated with intrinsic benefits than extrinsic benefits, and volunteering with religious organizations was uniquely associated with intrinsic benefits. Required service afforded primarily extrinsic benefits. Importantly, intrinsic benefits from service experiences exerted a positive effect on life goals oriented toward meaning, purpose, and service, which enhanced the intensity of service after college. Extrinsic benefits of service, however, undermined such life goals (thereby exerting negative indirect effects on postcollege service). The researchers concluded,

> Encouraging 'internal' benefits of service participation over and above
> benefits such as resume-building and skill expansion can develop
> students' commitment to meaning, purpose, and citizenship. . . .
> [Service] experiences should begin and end with an emphasis on the
> deeper meaning and other-focus of service rather than on the utilitarian
> ways that participation may benefit the individual student (p. 331).

Relatedly, Soria and Thomas-Card (2014) found in their sample of more than 7,800 students attending nine public research universities that service motivations were predictive of the desire to serve after college. Several intrinsic motivators were related to future desires to serve: belief in the particular cause, commitment to being a good citizen, and intent to change conditions in the community. Some extrinsic motivations were also at work: desire to develop leadership skills, opportunity to learn new things, and academic requirements. Being required by one's fraternity or sorority to serve, however, was negatively related to the desire to serve after college.

Racial/Ethnic and Cultural Diversity Attitudes. Two studies examined post-college diversity outcomes, and both demonstrated how the effects of college diversity experiences extend into life after college. According to the first study (Jayakumar, 2008), cross-racial interaction during college exerted a direct medium effect on post-college pluralistic orientation. As well, taking ethnic studies courses during college predicted pluralistic orientation in the long term, but to a somewhat lesser degree. Indirectly, the structural diversity of a campus and the campus racial climate promoted cross-racial interactions, thereby influencing pluralistic perspectives in the long term (Jayakumar, 2008).

Bowman and colleagues (2011) followed students 13 years after college to investigate the long-term effects of diversity interactions in college on recognition of racism in adulthood. They found that racial/cultural workshops and ethnic studies courses had small indirect effects on measures of racism recognition 13 years after college. Effects of workshops on racism recognition were mediated by prosocial orientation in the senior year, which had a direct effect of .17 of a standard deviation on postcollege racism recognition. These findings highlight the importance of diversity exposure in college to enhance students' openness and compassion toward people of other cultures and viewpoints. Interactions with diverse peers and curricular and co-curricular opportunities to explore diversity issues help shape graduates' abilities to recognize injustice and engage others constructively in the years after college.

CHAPTER SUMMARY

Change during College

Many of the patterns observed in the 1990s have persisted through the 2000s, particularly in relation to students' growing commitments to individual freedoms and humanitarian values while in college. However, whether civic behaviors (e.g., political engagement, volunteering) become more prevalent from the first to senior year, as noted in the previous decade of research (Pascarella & Terenzini, 2005), is questionable given recent evidence. Changes in political orientation reported since 2002 are relatively small across the college years, suggesting slight movements toward liberalism. Nevertheless, liberal shifts reflect students' growing support for individual freedom (involving abortion, marijuana, and casual sex) rather than classically liberal views regarding government intervention. The fact that students become less supportive of government interventions from the first to fourth year of college raises the possibility that college may influence their skepticism, but the reasons behind this pattern await further inquiry.

A number of studies in the 2000s focused on holistic sociopolitical outcome measures, many of which combined indicators of social activism and political engagement. As a result, definitive conclusions are difficult to draw, as some studies reported growth and others declines, depending on the nature of the measure. At the same time, with closer consideration of the components comprising holistic measures, certain patterns of change are evident. Political engagement—students' desire to influence the political structure, intent to keep up to date with political affairs, and frequency of political discussions—declines by a small margin. Community service engagement wanes as well, a likely result of competing demands for students' time. Yet students become more inclined toward an ethic of caring and increasingly value helping others during the college years. In fact, the percentage of students exhibiting a caring orientation nearly doubles from the first to the third year of college.

Although students are fairly convinced that their cultural awareness grows substantially during college, longitudinal evidence shows that changes are less dramatic than students assume and sometimes contradict presuppositions of positive change. Small increases of a little more than one-tenth of a standard deviation have been reported on measures of universality-diversity (e.g., diversity of contact, relativistic appreciation, and comfort with differences). Students' pluralistic orientation (e.g., ability to see multiple perspectives; ability to work cooperatively with diverse people) also increases to a small degree. On the contrary, students become somewhat less committed during college to promoting racial understanding, and their openness to diversity drops by a small margin (.13 of a standard deviation).

Evidence supporting slight positive changes resonates with research in the 1990s, but the negative findings are cause for concern and challenge the assumption that college-going necessarily leads to progressive racial attitudes. We recommend that scholars and campus leaders, in their research and practice, address factors that may deter growth in diversity attitudes. Perhaps negative campus racial climates and conflict-filled interpersonal exchanges leave students feeling unresolved about whether they are able to contribute to racial understanding in society and form relationships across racial and cultural differences.

The small number of studies devoted to examining gender-role attitudes over the last decade is consistent with research in the previous decade: students exhibit progressive gender-role ideologies as they begin college, and these attitudes are reinforced during college. Research on student attitudes toward LGB people also supports the patterns that surfaced in studies from the 1990s. All told, college students not only express wide support for LGB civil rights from the outset of college; they deepen these commitments and become less homophobic across the college years. Nevertheless, we caution readers that the source of students' changing attitudes toward LGB rights is unclear; history effects and college effects may be confounded given rapid societal shifts over the past decade.

Research on religious and spiritual attitudes and values in the 1990s gave way to some evidence that religious change during college is more complex than previously assumed. College students do not lose their religious convictions over time; rather, they may revisit and redefine them. New evidence in the 2000s supports these conjectures. Specifically, students become more pluralistic as they progress through college and develop greater openness to religious diversity and appreciation of human interconnectedness. For the most part, students become less religiously and socially conservative and able to conceptualize an independent or cooperative relationship between religious and scientific domains.

The latest findings pertaining to educational and occupational values, akin to previous decades of research, point to students' growing more intrinsically motivated and less materialistic. For instance, students generally become more likely to enjoy and invest effort in thinking by approximately one-third of a standard deviation and less concerned with being well-off financially. Counter-evidence also exists, however, as illustrated by declines in habits of mind and academic motivation, and by men's increased need for recognition from colleagues after four years of college. Finally, the scant evidence regarding students' growth in artistic interests and cosmopolitanism affirms many decades of research that drew the same conclusions.

Net Effects of College

Studies of net effects were few and far between through the 2000s, but several rigorous studies, many using quasi-experimental methods that simulated randomized experiments, called into question assumptions that college fosters civic engagement and religious liberalism. Scholars debated the effects of educational attainment on political involvement, with some studies showing no effect of college following matching procedures to account for the pre-adult differences between college attenders and non-attenders, and others showing fairly significant gains among college attenders relative to their counterparts on measures of voting, contacting public officials, and participating in protests or rallies. The weight of the evidence across many decades supports college effects on many measures of civic and political engagement (Pascarella & Terenzini, 2005); however, with methodological advancements, scholars have become more scrupulous in accounting for selection bias, and we expect the "education effect" will continue to be scrutinized in coming years. Whether and how education motivates civic and political engagement remains an important area of inquiry for educational researchers. Questions that have emerged in the past decade demand attention from scholars committed to examining these crucial issues.

Other rigorously conducted research, though limited in quantity, contested conventional wisdom regarding the liberalizing effects of college on religious beliefs. In fact, college attenders and non-attenders do not differ at all across many religious indicators when other covariates, such as religious social networks, are taken into account. In the end, we identified compelling work about civic behaviors and religiosity, but no new evidence of net effects on particular attitudinal domains, including views on racial/ethnic diversity, gender equality, and LGB rights. Nor did we come across studies investigating the net effects of college on educational, occupational, and artistic values. Many of these issues have been covered in depth over the decade, but researchers have been less concerned with net effects and directed their attention to the impact of specific collegiate experiences on outcomes and whether and how such effects depend on student characteristics.

Between-College Effects

Similar to earlier reviews, the impact of structural characteristics on sociopolitical and civic outcomes is minimal, and some studies have produced inconsistent findings regarding the effects of institutional type, size, selectivity, and structural diversity. The research is more conclusive on the issue of institutional mission, which plays an important role in fostering citizenship values and behaviors. The weight of the evidence points to positive effects on civic outcomes of attending work colleges, women's colleges, and religious institutions and negative effects of attending for-profit institutions. Evidence from other robust analyses also indicates modest growth in political liberalism among students attending liberal arts colleges. However, in some of these studies, the magnitude of effects is small or based on students' self-reported gains, and some effects may be indirect, mediated by curricular and co-curricular opportunities or emphases at the institution. Akin to the conclusions from Pascarella and Terenzini's (2005) previous review, peer and faculty culture matter more to outcomes than basic structural characteristics. The average tendency for faculty to use student-centered pedagogies at an institution furthers students' charitable behaviors and caring orientation, and the average religiousness of the student body contributes to higher levels of charitable engagement among individual students. Furthermore, the average liberalism exhibited in the peer environment detracts from charitable behaviors but exerts a positive effect on students' liberal attitudes.

Research in the 2000s was consistent with the previous decade in terms of observing primarily indirect effects of structural diversity on racial/ethnic and cultural attitudes. The extent to which an institution is structurally diverse establishes potential for students to encounter diverse peers and curricular and co-curricular diversity offerings, which in turn can influence attitudinal outcomes. A number of studies examined the mechanisms by which the proportional representation of diverse groups supports cross-racial interactions and friendship formation. The peer culture also makes an impression on racial/ethnic attitudes at the individual level. At institutions where students regularly engage diversity formally through curricular choices or informally through peer relationships, individual students tend to have more positive racial attitudes, holding constant other confounding factors. Other structural characteristics of the institution play a modest role, and some evidence suggests that institutional selectivity undermines positive attitudes toward diversity.

Very little research had anything conclusive to add to reviews from previous decades regarding the between-college effects on students' gender-role ideologies or attitudes toward LGB people. However, as demonstrated in many other attitudinal studies, religious perspectives are shaped for the most part by aspects of the peer culture and institutional emphases rather than by structural qualities. At institutions where students are religiously engaged and also undergoing religious struggles, individual students have a greater propensity to develop an ecumenical worldview. At institutions where students are religiously conservative, individual students become more conservatively oriented.

Institutional emphasis has a meaningful relationship to lifelong learning orientations, such as enjoyment of effortful thinking and positive attitudes toward literacy. Convincing evidence suggests that the effect of liberal arts colleges on these domains is at least partially mediated by clear and organized classroom instruction and practices at liberal arts institutions that encourage deep approaches to learning. Pascarella and Terenzini's (2005) review of 1990s research indicated that attending community colleges promotes students' orientation to learning for self-understanding. Research in the 2000s draws related conclusions. Although some evidence suggests that community college students take a utilitarian approach to their education, this reality is coupled with a growing enjoyment of effortful thinking associated with attending a community college. In addition, students who attended work colleges perceive their experiences as contributing to their engagement in lifelong learning and appreciation of literature and fine arts. Beyond this relationship, we found little evidence of between-college effects on students' aesthetic sensitivities.

Within-College Effects

Resonating with Pascarella and Terenzini's (2005) earlier review, majoring in science, according to a few national studies, is negatively related to civic values, but majoring in social sciences often reaffirms students' commitments to improving their communities. Although studies focused on the role of disciplinary and residential subcultures were few in number, more convincing evidence purports that faculty engagement, regardless of discipline, exerts a positive influence on students' political engagement, social activism and civic values, ethic of caring, and civic and charitable behaviors. Research through the 2000s went beyond examining the frequency of student-faculty interactions to identify particular qualities of the interaction as nuanced as feeling supported by faculty, challenging professors' ideas in class, being mentored by faculty, and engaging in religious and spiritual discussions with faculty. Also, the positive effects of pedagogical practices that are often under the purview of faculty, such as student-centered teaching, reflective practices, academic challenge, and active and collaborative learning, surfaced as important factors in students' citizenship development.

Abundant and fairly conclusive evidence supports the effects of diversity experiences on civic and political outcomes. A comprehensive meta-analysis estimated such effects as medium to large (.16 of a standard deviation;

Bowman, 2011a). A closer examination of specific studies revealed that the effect sizes of curricular diversity engagement varied tremendously, probably due to differences across samples, variations in accounting for confounding influences, and inconsistencies in measures. Medium-to-large effects of diversity experiences in general, and cocurricular activities and interactions with diverse peers in particular, surfaced in many studies. The interactional quality and associated emotions attached to diversity exchanges are noteworthy in their impact and likely part of the indirect mechanisms by which diversity experiences further civic and political development.

Beyond diversity, other engaging experiences relate to civic outcomes: service work, political activism, cocurricular activities, and spiritual engagement. As the review of research in 1990s attested, a good amount of evidence verifies that service work tends to inspire civic and community values and behaviors. However, new evidence is more limited in substantiating the implications of service involvement for political engagement and deeper social justice learning. While participating in protests and student government have opposing influences on liberalism, both experiences relate to gains in civic values. Furthermore, leadership training is closely associated with the development of civic values, but Greek membership may attenuate liberalism (compared to non-Greek students) and have little impact on attitude change. Participating in fraternities and sororities is at most associated with volunteerism, but whether civic values are cultivated as a result is debatable. We advise further investigation into whether higher levels of volunteering contribute to changed values among fraternity and sorority members. A small number of studies linked citizenship gains to religious and spiritual engagement, studying abroad, and working, and other evidence pointed to the importance of nurturing civic values as a precursor to civic actions.

Much of the research on racial/ethnic and cultural attitudes confirms and extends findings from the previous decade. Little research attended to the effects of college major, but some evidence alluded to the possibility that majoring in engineering may weaken commitments to promoting racial understanding (a finding in need of replication). The effects of residential experiences on racial/cultural attitudes were indeterminate, but the evidence was clearer about practices and pedagogical strategies that faculty may employ to boost students' intercultural competence and openness to diversity: providing opportunities for academic challenge and high expectations, integrative learning, reflective learning, and active and cooperative learning. In addition, curricular diversity engagement consistently relates to gains in a variety of diversity outcomes. Effect sizes vary by study, but tend to be at least medium, and gains are even greater at higher levels of curricular engagement. The effects of intergroup dialogue on attitudes and ally behaviors are often positive but small in magnitude. Aligned with evidence that curricular diversity engagement generates positive diversity outcomes, interacting with others of diverse racial and cultural backgrounds facilitates attitudinal change. Research through the 2000s has drawn convincing conclusions about the importance of interactional quality. Mere frequency of interacting is less important than the emotions (positive or negative) cultivated in the exchange. Even so, some research alludes to the disequilibrium wrought by negative encounters with diversity that may have developmental benefits. Given that the benefits of cross-racial interactions stand on solid evidence, a good number of studies have investigated diversity engagement and interracial friendships to identify student-level conditions that foster (e.g., diversity engagement early in college, living with people from other backgrounds) or impede (e.g., participation in religious organizations, Greek organizations) these interactions.

Research on the impact of fraternity and sorority membership on diversity outcomes is rather mixed, with some studies pointing to positive effects, others suggesting null effects, and still others suggesting negative effects. On the whole, engagement in Greek organizations appears to translate into few benefits when it comes to diversity attitudes—and in some instances it may produce more negative effects. The effectiveness of study abroad has also been recently challenged, although some positive effects have also been identified.

Studies on gender-role attitudes through the 2000s were rare. The few studies conducted pointed to the positive influences that faculty, women's studies courses, and diversity experiences can have on gender-role progressivism. Religious friends, however, induce more traditional attitudes toward gender roles. Based on the existing evidence, curricular and co-curricular influences on LGB attitudes are generally favorable, but the strongest effects tend to be interactional in nature. Interacting with peers of diverse races and sexualities and knowing someone who is lesbian, gay, bisexual, or transgender by far makes the greatest difference when it comes to attitude change. Contrarily, religious influences tend to engender negative attitudes toward LGB people. The emergent nature of this research base leaves many questions for future inquiry: How do students negotiate religious values and positive attitudes toward LGB people when conflicts arise between the two? How do aspects of the campus climate shape students' LGB attitudes? How do LGB students of different identities perceive one another, and what factors foster favorable attitudes? What collegiate structures and experiences contribute to positive exchanges and friendship formation between students of different sexualities?

Much of the research conducted on religious and spiritual attitudes and values through the 2000s focused on the process by which college shapes students' ecumenical orientation, or openness to diverse religions and worldviews, as well as religious/social conservatism. When students turn outward and engage faculty and diverse peers, they tend to develop an ecumenical worldview. Spiritual struggle partially mediates the relationship between exposure to diversity and other challenging co-curricular experiences and ecumenical worldview. Deeper engagement in one's religious community and practice, however, tends to increase religious/social conservatism. Even so, some spiritual practices support both ecumenism and conservatism (e.g., reading religious and spiritual materials).

Few studies addressed the role of disciplinary and residential contexts in educational and occupational values development. Unlike research from the 1990s, few effects of college major on educational and occupational values were identified; one exception is the positive influence of majoring in the sciences on the desire to make a theoretical contribution to science, holding constant other variables that influence values. Living on campus exerts a negative influence on positive attitudes toward literacy, but participating in living-learning communities generally enhances enjoyment of challenging intellectual pursuits and positive attitudes toward literacy.

Engaging with peers has mixed effects on educational values. In some studies, gains in effortful thinking are disrupted by peer interactions; however, effects are positive when students have meaningful discussions with diverse peers. Moreover, when other outcomes are considered (i.e., learning for self-understanding and preference for higher-order tasks), peer interactions support gains. In both social and academic contexts (studying and partying), peer interactions encourage a status striver orientation. Peer effects are also apparent in studies of diversity experiences. While the positive effects of diversity engagement on educational values are typically small to moderate in magnitude, interactional diversity has a stronger effect on effortful thinking among students who have frequent interactions with diverse peers. The effects of peer engagements in certain contexts, such as Greek organizations, are unclear. For the most part, joining Greek organizations is unrelated to educational values but associated with certain occupational values: fraternity and sorority membership increases status striving but reduces science orientation.

Research through the 2000s concerning educational and occupational values focused primarily on the ways in which quality faculty interactions, academic challenge and high expectations, and various teaching and learning strategies strengthen such lifelong learning orientations as effortful thinking and positive literacy attitudes. Most effects were medium to strong. Moreover, certain practices often facilitated by faculty, including undergraduate research, internships, and capstone courses/experiences, have a positive impact on effortful thinking. Service-learning, however, had mixed effects across various studies that depended on the sample (e.g., first-year students versus fourth-year students) and the measure (e.g., academic motivation, effortful thinking).

Studies of students' artistic development were uncommon through the 2000s. However, some work confirmed that majoring in the arts or humanities, encountering new ideas through reading, interacting socially with diverse peers, participating in organized demonstrations, interacting with faculty, and learning in cooperative settings foster students' artistic orientation.

Conditional Effects of College

Research through the 2000s made significant progress in terms of distinguishing how college effects on attitudes and values vary by student characteristics. Many collegiate effects on sociopolitical outcomes are conditional on gender. The evidence points to stronger effects of institutional structural characteristics and the general orientation of the student body on men's attitudes than women's. For women, the conservatism of the immediate peer group, for instance, in sororities, student government, and leadership training, is more germane to developing conservative attitudes. Liberalism tends to be amplified by diversity exposure and weakened by religious engagement, but gendered effects occur across outcomes. In addition, interactions with faculty bring about liberal attitudes for students of both genders, but this pattern is not universally true for women. With respect to political engagement, men are more prone than women to become politically active when they engage in cocurricular activities, diversity-related coursework, and faculty interactions. Aspects of the peer group, that is, the average tendencies of the student body on campus, have stronger effects on women's political engagement than men's. Disciplinary environments play a distinctive role in women's and men's political engagement, and faculty effects are unique as well: women who do not feel faculty take them seriously engage in more social activism, but men tend to do so when they challenge a professor's ideas in class.

A few studies ascertained conditional effects of various interactional, cocurricular, and curricular diversity engagement on civic outcomes that depended on race. Positive effects, in the main, were observed for White students across most outcomes. However, fewer significant effects materialized for Latino/a students. Limited evidence purports that college effects on civic outcomes are stronger for conservative students and those with lower levels of political interest. College does not appear to differentially affect civic values of athletes and non-athletes, but diversity effects on liberalism may be more pronounced for students with lower standardized test scores.

With respect to diversity attitudes, evidence in the 2000s addressing gender-related conditional effects showed women's racial understanding is closely tied to major choice, while men's is predicated on faculty engagement and a number of institutional characteristics. Furthermore, poorer outcomes for men than women transpire when their privilege is disrupted by taking a diversity course. Regarding conditional effects by race and ethnicity, some studies confirm that benefits of diversity experiences are greater for White students; however, recent work has illuminated further nuances. Conditional effects by socioeconomic status, including income level and first-generation status, also show that students with privilege tend to benefit in their diversity attitudes when their privilege is challenged (e.g., in diversity courses, when volunteering). Even so, a variety of cocurricular experiences, particularly academic engagement and exposure to peers with high levels of cognitive development, uniquely help first-generation students develop openness to diversity. Precollege exposure to diversity and academic major also shape the ways in which diversity experiences affect diversity attitudes. Some studies show that the predictors of cross-racial interactions (which subsequently influence attitudes) differ by race and ethnicity.

Very little research through the 2000s attended to conditional effects of college on gender-role attitudes, but some limited evidence showed that collegiate experiences affect women and men in different ways. Participating in research with faculty has the opposite effect, encouraging traditionalism among women and progressivism among men. Spending time exclusively with other men tends to increase men's gender-role traditionalism. No conclusive evidence emerged in our review regarding conditional effects of college on students' attitudes toward LGB people.

A number of effects that were dependent on religion, gender, and race emerged in studies that examined students' development of an ecumenical worldview and a meaningful life philosophy. Comparisons of models focused on ecumenical development by religious worldview revealed that developmental processes may look quite different for nonreligious students compared to their religious peers. To some extent, the process of ecumenical worldview development is a function of gender and racial identity. The level of religious struggle at an institution has stronger effects on men's ecumenism, and prosocial involvement has a host of differential effects on ecumenical worldview by race.

A consistent theme regarding gendered college effects on occupational orientations is the unique way that faculty engagement affects women and men, showing effects that are usually stronger for men. On the topic of race-related conditional effects on educational values, diversity course work and overall diversity interactions have stronger effects on White students' effortful thinking than students of color. However, effective teaching and interactions with faculty have stronger effects on positive attitudes toward literacy among students of color compared to their White peers. Effects of college on intrinsic educational values also vary by socioeconomic indicators. The effects of diversity courses on effortful thinking are weaker for higher-income students. However, diversity experiences tend to encourage effortful thinking to a greater extent for students whose parents have attended college (compared to first-generation students). In sum, understanding the effects of diversity experiences requires considering multiple aspects of socioeconomic status because income level and parents' education level result in different types of conditional diversity effects, at times, but not consistently, favoring those in the privileged status. For first-generation students, academic engagement facilitates gains in learning for self-understanding and preference for higher-order cognitive tasks; for students whose parents had postsecondary experience, volunteering relates to gains in learning orientations.

Very limited evidence identified conditional effects of college on artistic orientations but did seem to indicate that engaging activities, including working on independent study projects and exercising or playing sports, opened the door to women's artistic exploration, whereas talking with faculty outside class had stronger effects on men's artist orientation. In addition, scientific environments and receiving grants and scholarships tended to reduce men's artistic proclivities.

Long-Term College Effects

Research identifying the enduring effects of college on attitudes and values had little to contribute by way of evidence for long-term effects on gender-role, LGB, and religious attitudes. New data about postcollege trends in educational, occupational, and aesthetic values were also lacking over the past 10 years. Instead, researchers emphasized the variety of ways in which college shapes sociopolitical and civic attitudes and behaviors and also highlighted some support for the enduring impact of college on diversity outcomes. Previous reviews of research (Pascarella & Terenzini, 2005) concluded that net effects in the long term were evident, especially for sociopolitical, civic, educational, and occupational values. However, research through the 2000s lends new insight by focusing on particular aspects of the college experience that make the most impact rather than the general enduring effect of "going to college."

Whether institutional characteristics influence political and civic outcomes in the long term is debatable according to mixed findings from various studies. The influence of selectivity, size, and public or private status on students' civic values and behaviors depends on the outcome measure. There was quite a bit of variation from study to study, with some studies focused on political engagement and others on broader and more inclusive civic constructs.

The weight of the evidence is clearer when it comes to the long-term effects of college major, as majoring in business, science, and engineering have a tendency to undermine civic development, and these effects persist after graduation. Other evidence shows that disciplinary impact on political engagement varies by institution type, which suggests that multiple contextual layers are at work in shaping outcomes in the long term. Although the effects of structural diversity on political and civic engagement after college are inconsistent, curricular and co-curricular diversity experiences in college, such as participating in racial/ethnic diversity courses and taking ethnic studies courses, have small, often indirect, effects on civic engagement.

Community service engagement is another facet of the collegiate experience that appears to have an enduring impact on students' civic outcomes after they graduate. The effects of service-learning are generally quite small in magnitude— and often smaller than generic community service participation—but are apparent for such outcomes as civic leadership, charitable giving, and overall political engagement. Reflection on service experiences in discussions with peers and faculty is a critical mediating influence between service participation and long-term outcomes. Furthermore, the type of community service students engage in during college and the benefits they draw from their experiences play a role in commitments to service engagement after college. Students who reap internal benefits from service—when they become more socially conscious and other-focused through their service work—tend to volunteer at higher rates after college. However, when benefits of college service are largely external, emphasizing vocational advancement, rates of service engagement after college decline. In sum, cultivating intrinsic values and motivations is worthwhile in order to ensure graduates' continued commitments to their communities.

Finally, limited evidence in the 2000s supported the prevailing effects of diversity experiences, including cross-racial interactions, racial/cultural diversity workshops, and ethnic studies courses, on postcollege pluralistic orientation and recognition of racism. Some evidence shows these effects are indirect, mediated by prosocial orientation in the senior year of college. Moreover, structural diversity and campus climate may affect pluralistic orientation, but indirectly through their impact on cross-racial interactions.

CHAPTER CONCLUSION

Collegiate influences that have the greatest impact on students' changing attitudes and values can be characterized as experiences that draw them into meaningful interactions with faculty and diverse peers and present them with novel learning opportunities to cultivate new insight. Broader institutional qualities more distant from students' day-to-day experiences on campus matter insomuch as they create a context for shaping interactions and learning to occur. Although patterns of and predictors of change vary based on gender, race, religious affiliation, first-generation status, and other student characteristics, students overall become more humanitarian and intrinsically oriented in their values, as well as more progressive in some (but not all) political, religious, and social justice attitudes. In the next chapter, we shift focus to explicate how collegiate conditions and experiences shape moral reasoning.

CHAPTER SIX

Moral Development

S ince its inception, higher education has shared a tumultuous relationship
with moral development. Should moral development be a central or
peripheral focus of higher education? What role does morality play in
how institutions are governed? Although discussing each of these considerations falls outside the scope of this chapter, a review of the past decade of
research on college and its influence on moral development suggests that
higher education scholars are becoming increasingly interested in this relationship, much more so than in previous decades.

A series of hypotheses could be offered for the marked increases in higher
education scholarship along this reemerging research line. As nations have
moved toward increasing dissatisfaction with the costs of college, more people
are questioning the value of higher education, including its central purposes,
its role in society, and its place in shaping a global citizenry; each of these has
arguably moral considerations. As a result, national and state legislatures
(e.g., Michigan) responded, often passing acts designed to keep moral development at the center of conversations about higher and postsecondary education.
Extending this notion, many organizational bodies with a vested interest in
higher education have included moral criteria in rubrics intended to measure
institutional effectiveness. For example, in 2002, the Association of American
Colleges & Universities (AAC&U) (2002) called for liberally educated students
to become empowered, informed, and responsible learners charged with
"maintaining the integrity of a democratic society" (p. xii). The AAC&U further
charged institutions with providing educational environments that fostered
"responsibility for society's moral health and for social justice" among students
(p. xii). Given renewed emphasis on understanding the moral dimensions of

postsecondary and higher education, scholars have designed more studies to examine the relationship between college-going and moral development. In this chapter, we review the evidence of empirical studies that have linked collegiate experiences to moral development.

Many definitions of the concept of moral development have been and will continue to be offered—too many to enumerate in this review. Moral development in the college impact literature is often construed as a process that moves from simple to complex, as Dorough (2011) notes:

> Moral development refers to the process whereby people form a progressive sense of what is right and wrong, proper and improper. As implied by the term development, human moral sense is commonly seen to involve a movement from simple and finite definitions of right and wrong to more complex ways of distinguishing right from wrong. (p. 59)

As opposed to some advancement on a standard scale of moral rightness, where some arbitrary external authority is used to cast some individuals and their decisions as more morally right than other, moral development is located within and facilitated by the individual, whose growth along moral lines moves from less to more sophisticated, either over time or, as this review suggests, as a result of exposure to and participation in higher education.

THEORETICAL OVERVIEW

The preponderance of evidence from the 2000s emerged from scholars who adopted Kohlbergian and neo-Kohlbergian frames for understanding moral reasoning development and its relationship to college-going. Though certainly others, most notably Gilligan (1982) and Turiel (1998, 2002), have questioned and continue to scrutinize the paradigmatic and gendered theoretical assumptions that underscore these frames (e.g., Is morality a measurable construct? Is the theory universally applicable?), the Kohlbergian and neo-Kohlbergian understandings of morality and its subsequent measurement dominate the research landscape with regard to college and its impact on students.

Consistent with the parameters articulated in Chapter 1 of this volume, we provided only overviews of frameworks and theories that authors used to address their lines of inquiry. To reiterate, this strategy was adopted to provide context for the articles reviewed and for efficiency. By no means does it suggest that Kohlbergian theories and frameworks, as examples, are superior or that other perspectives are flawed; the excellent work of Carol Gilligan (1982), for example, remains critical for understanding the moral development of women, particularly as it was the first to introduce the idea of the caring voice—how women differentially approach issues with moral undertones (see Evans, Forney, Guido, Patton, & Renn, 2010, for an excellent review of this and other theories related to student development). Although exemplary, Gilligan's theory falls outside the scope of this volume as it was rarely used to explain college and its effects on moral development. We now turn to a brief overview of the frames offered for making meaning of the studies reviewed for this chapter.

Kohlbergian Approaches

From a phenomenological perspective, Kohlberg understood the study of moral reasoning as a relevant construct for inquiry apart from moral behavior, noting that "such [moral] judgments must be seen as meaningful in their own terms, in some sense at face value, rather than treated as mere reflections or expressions of irrational feelings, unconscious motives, or external forces" (Colby & Kohlberg, 1987, p. 1). Kohlberg also adopted a constructivist approach to development where "the individual is always inventing or constructing new responses to each situation encountered" (Colby & Kohlberg, 1987, p. 4). This approach enabled Kohlberg to create a sequential stage theory to describe the development of moral reasoning: "Each new stage of development represents a qualitative reorganization of the individual's pattern of thought, with each new re-organization integrating within a broader perspective the insights achieved at the prior stages" (p. 5).

Based on these philosophical precepts, Kohlberg (1981) put forward four governing principles that he said characterized the sequential-stage developmental model of moral reasoning. First, characterizing development as stages implies qualitative differences in modes of reasoning (e.g., two people at different stages may share similar values, but their way of thinking about these values are qualitatively different). Second, each stage forms a structured whole (i.e., each stage represents a whole way of thinking about moral issues where a change in stage implies a restructuring of how one thinks about moral issues). Third, stages form an invariant sequence (i.e., a person cannot reason at a stage 4 level without first passing through stage 3). Fourth, stages are hierarchical integrations (e.g., when a person's thinking develops from one stage to the next, the higher stage reintegrates the structures found at lower stages). From these principles, Kohlberg developed his cognitive-developmental theory of moralization (Kohlberg, 1976), a theory that explains how individuals develop their understandings of justice. His theory can be briefly summarized in the following way:

> Development is described as proceeding through six stages embedded within three levels. The first two stages (Level 1) are considered preconventional. At this level, moral reasoning is highly egocentric in that it is based on the person's concerns for his or her own interests and for those of specific others the individuals might care about. At Level II (Stages 3 and 4), conventional moral reasoning takes over. The reasoning is based on a concern with maintaining the social order. Moral judgments are guided by obedience to rules and meeting the expectations of others, particularly those in positions of authority. The orientation toward maintaining the system is replaced at Level III (stages

5 and 6) by a postconventional or principled perspective. The basis of this kind of reasoning is a view of morality as a set of universal principles for making choices among alternative courses of action that would be held by any rational moral individual (Pascarella, 1997, pp. 48–49).

Germane to this review is the notion that Kohlberg (1981) developed his theory of moral reasoning with an eye toward educational practice. Originally he intended his model to be used to inform pedagogical considerations; however, after working with educators, he grew into an understanding that the relationship between theory and practice was indeed reciprocal: "The relationship between psychology and education must be a two-way street. . . . Individual moral action usually takes place in a group or context and that context usually has a profound influence on the moral decision making of individuals" (Kohlberg, 1981, pp. 37–38). This insight is particularly relevant to this review as we highlight studies that examined college contexts for their influence on the moral development of students.

In many ways, Kohlberg defined what moral reasoning is and how it develops, especially in adolescence and adulthood. By grounding theoretical constructs in philosophical precepts and systematically researching these constructs, Kohlberg legitimized the study of moral reasoning as a meaningful construct in its own right. Kohlberg also defined the construct of moral reasoning to include structures and patterns of thought as opposed to thought content, and he established principles for understanding development as a function of the individual's ability to construct and reconstruct new moral responses to different environmental cues. These principles enabled him to not only clarify the assumptions surrounding the use of stagelike models to explain development but also propose stages for moral reasoning development.

Neo-Kohlbergian Approaches

The neo-Kohlbergians, frequently associated with James Rest and his colleagues, argued in favor of theoretical consideration of moral reasoning development, yet believed it should be described using a framework of three schemas. They extended the Kohlbergian understandings of developmentally sequenced and structured patterns of thought by using the following three schemas:

1. The personal interests schema where individuals justify their reasoning strategies based on personal stakes—that the decisions made will have personal lasting consequences for the decisions they make (see Rest, Narvaez, Bebeau, & Thoma, 1999).

2. The maintaining norms schema, where individuals adopt reasoning strategies based on "maintaining the existing legal system, maintaining existing roles and formal organizational structure" (Bebeau & Thoma, 2003, p. 19).

3. The postconventional schema, where individuals organize information about making moral decisions based on how social norms may be biased, often at the expense of others and therefore make decisions based on moral criteria (e.g., respect for human rights), moral ideals for organizing society (e.g., reciprocal, transparent, and open for critique) for organizing society, and moral purpose (e.g., the intention for the social mechanism as the means for understanding justice, rather than the existence of the mechanism itself) (Rest et al. 1999).

The neo-Kohlbergian approach to the study of moral reasoning development stems from scholarly attempts to place decision making in the context of the decision being made. By organizing moral development into a series of schemas, neo-Kohlbergians distance themselves from the stage model that Kohlberg proposed, thereby making theoretical room for explaining movement among the schema: individuals may be using Personal Interests scheme in one context and Maintaining Norms in another. What remains important is that these schema retain structure and are developmentally sequenced; with increasing sophistication in reasoning strategies comes more prevalent use of the postconventional scheme. In short, developmental movement between these schema reflects a shift for organizing thoughts on justice from those that serve the self to those that recognize the self in relation to other.

The Four Component Model

Grounded in the work of Kohlberg, the four component model (4CM) was developed by James Rest (1986) who explained the production of moral behavior as it related to four components with distinctive properties. By "imagining what courses of action are possible and tracing the consequences of action in terms of how each action would affect the welfare of each party involved" (Rest, Thoma, & Edwards, 1997, p. 5), the first component, moral sensitivity, enables individuals to interpret situations as moral. Component 2, moral judgment or reasoning, addresses the reasoning strategies individuals use to "determine that one course of action in a particular situation is morally right and another course of action is wrong" (Rest et al,, 1997, p. 5). Component 3, moral motivation, describes why individuals might choose a moral or non-moral alternative, especially when said choice involves sacrifice or hardship. Moral character, component 4, involves "figuring out the sequence of concrete actions, working around impediments and unexpected difficulties, overcoming fatigue and frustration, resisting distraction, and allurements, and keeping sight of the eventual goal . . . to execute and implement a plan of action" (Rest et al., 1997, p. 15). Rest (1986) describes how the four components work together to produce moral behavior. In so doing, the 4CM expands theories of moral development beyond the traditional way of thinking about behavior production (i.e., thought to action) to include other psychological processes (i.e., sensitivity, motivation, and character) that contribute to a fuller understanding of the psychology behind the production of moral behavior.

Most of the research reviewed for this volume examined moral *reasoning* development and its relationship to participation in higher education. The focus on moral reasoning is likely due, at least in some part, to the availability, widespread use, and psychometric foundations of the moral reasoning measure (i.e., Defining Issues Test-1 and Defining Issues Test 2; see Rest, 1984; Rest et al., 1999) that was based largely on Kohlbergian theory. Although other measures exist (Lind, 2008; Sirin, Brabeck, Satiani, & Rogers-Serin, 2003), the DIT1 and DIT2 have remained consistently reliable and valid, weathering nearly 40 years of scholarly scrutiny. Most frequently, scholars use these instruments to measure moral reasoning as an outcome in its own right; however, some scholars, including those whose work is represented in this chapter, have incorporated the DIT1 or DIT2 in a research design that asks how college influences moral reasoning in ultimate hopes of explaining moral behaviors, such as cheating.

In any case, it should be clear that the authors of the measures of moral reasoning never intended that they be used as a measure of the moral domain in its entirety; rather, they were designed to capture the reasoning strategies individuals employ when faced with a moral dilemma. Furthermore, the measures were constructed to assess the principles or organizational strategies individuals use when faced with a moral decision and not the decision itself. Many of the studies reviewed for this volume used moral reasoning as a proxy for moral development but were not necessarily explicit about it. To be transparent and streamline the information contained in a review of this magnitude, we often do the same in spirit of remaining close to the authors' original intentions.

Summary

This review cannot capture all of the complexities and nuances of arguments about moral development. Phenomenological explanations of what morality is and if and how it can be developed vary within and between disciplines. Some authors suggest that the essence of morality is at least partially structural and thus open for development and subsequent measurement (Colby & Kohlberg, 1987; Rest, 1979); others maintain that morality is more organic, too ineffable to be developed or measured (see arguments by Walker, 2002); still others take a different position, arguing that moral reasoning development is not a stand-alone construct, but rather a reflection of other attributes such as verbal ability and cognitive development (see Lubinski, 2004; Sanders, Lubinski, & Benbow, 1995; cf. Thoma, Derryberry, & Narvaez, 2009 for discussion of this debate).

These differences noted, the dominant paradigm for understanding college and its effects on students is based on Kohlbergian understandings of justice, where an individual moves from reasoning about justice based on principles that serve oneself to those that serve known others to those that serve anonymous others. Of course, the Kohlbergian frame for understanding moral reasoning has and continues to be scrutinized for its gendered origins (see Gilligan, 1982), culturally neutral stance (Crain, 1985), position that reasoning rationally leads to behavior (Haidt, 2001; Lickona, 1991), and deficiencies in explaining real-life and daily decision-making (Krebs & Denton, 2005; Parke,

Gauvain, & Schmuckler, 2010; Turiel, 1998, 2002; Turnbull & Carpendale, 2001). Nevertheless, the Kohlbergian understanding of moral reasoning remains the dominant paradigm that scholars have used to examine college and its effects on moral development.

Most of the studies reviewed for this chapter use this developmental theoretical orientation for making meaning of college and its impact on students. We use phrases like "helping students make moral reasoning gains," "more likely to demonstrate gains in moral reasoning," and "make moral gains" as communicative proxies for colleges' impact on students' justice orientations, from egocentric principles that serve the self to expanded societal frames that serve anonymous others. When authors depart from Kohlbergian frames, we do our best to describe the kind of moral development, if any, that occurs and its relationship to college-going.

Germane to scholars interested in moral reasoning is the theoretical link between moral processes and moral behaviors, like cheating (McCabe, Treviño, & Butterfield, 2001). Although not all authors used the four component model to establish these relationships, its brief discussion was intended to help readers make theoretical connections between and among all dimensions of moral growth, with particular attention to the link between reasoning and behavior.

We now turn to the review of studies that examined exposure to and participation in postsecondary education and their relationship to the moral development of undergraduate students. We begin by reviewing the studies that explored change during college.

CHANGE DURING COLLEGE

Conclusions from the 1990s

Evidence from the 1990s suggested that morally related outcomes were achieved as a result of college-going, although most of the research suggested that developmental gains were small, with specific respect to moral reasoning (see Pascarella & Terenzini, 2005). Small as it was, the move from the conventional moral reasoning stage to the principled stage was a nontrivial one, with students moving from reasoning strategies that positioned rules, laws, and norms as the organizational means for maintaining the structure of society among all members, even those unknown, to strategies that recognized that some rules, laws, and norms designed to maintain social order often infringed on, if not compromised, certain human rights and civil liberties (see Rest et al., 1999).

These claims emerged from evidence based on the use of longitudinal studies, cross-sectional reports comparing first-year to senior scores on measures related to moral development, and studies that used college students as samples of convenience to explore relationships between different dimensions of moral development, such as moral reasoning and action, as examples. These types of studies also provided the evidence for the findings reviewed for this volume.

Evidence from the 2000s

Moral development has been linked to college-going, with increasing exposure to college leading to greater gains in moral development. Although no published studies were experimentally designed to make causal claims about college-going and moral development, many studies have been able to examine differences in moral development based on year in school, through the use of longitudinal research designs (Mayhew & Engberg, 2010; Mayhew & King, 2008; Mayhew, Seifert, & Pascarella, 2010, 2012; Mayhew, Seifert, Pascarella, Nelson Laird, & Blaich, 2012) or cross-sectional designs that account for year in school as a covariate of interest (Bascom, 2011; Harding, Mayhew, Finelli, & Carpenter, 2007; Maeda, Thoma, & Bebeau, 2009; Lau, Caracciolo, Roddenberry, & Scroggins, 2011; Lau & Haug, 2011; You & Penny, 2011).

The weight of evidence in this decade of research reveals that moral gains for students represented from 2002 to 2012 was considerably smaller than in the preceding decade. In this review, students made average gains of .58 of a standard deviation in moral reasoning scores from the first to the fourth year in college when compared to the average four-year gain from research conducted in the 1990s, which was estimated at .77 standard deviations (Pascarella & Terenzini, 2005).

As in previous studies, this movement occurred mostly between conventional to postconventional ways of organizing information when faced with moral dilemmas. As students progressed through college, their reasoning strategies became more sophisticated, moving from patterns of thought that prioritized societal norms, rules, and policies as vehicles for maintaining society's structure to patterns of thought that recognized the arbitrary and sometimes compromised nature of some of these norms, rules, and policies.

Due to the difficulties inherent in studying students in their natural, albeit nonrandom environments, researchers have not been able to assess directly college's effects on moral development. This said, all studies reviewed showed that moral growth can and does occur during college, mostly due to exposure to certain experiences with moral or social justice emphases, or both.

The magnitude of change is subject to empirical scrutiny, as few studies longitudinally assessed moral development over the course of the college experience. An exception, a longitudinal study conducted by Pascarella, Blaich, Martin, and Hanson (2011) examined moral growth for 923 students enrolled at 17 four-year institutions across 11 states over three time points: a cohort of students was assessed when they first arrived at college (fall 2006), after their first year in college (spring 2007), and at the end of their senior year of college (spring 2010). During the first year in college students made an average gain of .32 of a standard deviation in moral reasoning scores; this marked a 13 percentile point increase in moral reasoning score for students during their first year in college. Additionally, students made average gains of .58 of a standard deviation in moral reasoning scores from the first to the fourth year in college; this estimate represented a 22 percentile point increase in moral reasoning scores during the four years of college. Cross-sectional studies (Bascom, 2011; You &

Penny, 2011) support this trend, with seniors scoring higher than first-year students within certain institutions.

NET EFFECTS OF COLLEGE

Conclusions from the 1990s

Most of the evidence of growth was demonstrated in the previous volume (see Pascarella & Terrenzini, 2005) through estimates of movement based on meta-analytic procedures. Even with this sophisticated approach, movement along moral growth trajectories was difficult to ascertain based on how authors defined variables. Across these reviews, moral gains were reported between .28 and .34 of a standard deviation, indicating a small-to-moderate net effect of college on moral reasoning gains.

Evidence from the 2000s

Based on the 30-plus-year history of research linking college-going to moral development, scholars have moved from empiricism to assumption. In short, our review uncovered no new evidence that speaks to the net effects of college on moral development.

Rather than question if college-going has an influence on moral development, scholars assumed this relationship existed and focused instead on investigating the specific practices and psychological mechanisms that influence this change. Although this level of specificity is relatively new with regard to the proliferation of empirically based articles, the exploration of practices and mechanisms as growth catalysts to moral change finds theoretical support in the work of Kohlberg, Rest, and their contemporaries. This shift to specificity represents a migration from examining the net effects of college on moral reasoning development to investigating more between and within-college effects: What is happening during the college experience that contributes to moral growth?

BETWEEN-COLLEGE EFFECTS

Conclusions from the 1990s

Studies from the 1990s provided initial evidence of between-college differences in two domains: principled moral reasoning and moral behavior. To the first, the authors (Pascarella & Terrenzini, 2005) built on a dataset generated by McNeel (1994) to detect differences in moral reasoning across three institutional types: liberal arts colleges, Bible colleges, and large public universities. The results determined that the largest freshman-to-senior gains in moral reasoning were made by students at private liberal arts colleges (.87 of a standard deviation, 31 percentile points), followed by students at large public universities (.62 of a standard deviation, 23 percentile points). Students attending Bible colleges demonstrated, on average, the smallest moral reasoning gains during their time in college (.13 of a standard deviation, 6 percentile points). Corroborating these findings, Good and Cartwright (1998) reported similar results using a sample containing one institution of each type.

To the second, moral behavior, McCabe and Treviño (1993, 1996, 1997; McCabe, Treviño, & Butterfield, 1999) found that regardless of institutional factors such as selectivity and size, institutions with honor codes or honor systems experienced less academic dishonesty than institutions without such systems based on students' self-reports. Furthermore, a number of multi-institutional studies conducted in the 1990s by McCabe and colleagues found that a student was significantly more likely to admit (anonymously) engaging in academic dishonesty if he or she had observed another student cheating; a student was less likely to make such an admission if he or she believed that other students would disapprove of cheating behavior.

Evidence from the 2000s

Among the series of studies that examined between-college effects (Mayhew, Seifert, & Pascarella, 2010, 2012), two (Maeda et al., 2009; Mayhew, 2012a) used hierarchical linear modeling, which accounts for the nonrandom clustering patterns of college students within a particular educational context. Using this technique, Mayhew (2012a) and Maeda et al. (2009) substantiated the important role of context (e.g., institutional type, geographic region) in shaping moral reasoning development among students, with estimates suggesting that moral reasoning gains can be at least partially explained by contextual-level differences.

Mayhew (2012a) examined if institutional type differences played an important role in understanding the developmental trajectories of 1,469 first-year students enrolled at one of 19 institutions. Developmental gains in moral reasoning were most pronounced for students enrolled at liberal arts colleges, followed by those enrolled at regional universities, followed by those enrolled at research universities, and finally by those enrolled at community colleges. After controlling for selectivity as well as a number of theoretically related covariates, students enrolled in liberal arts colleges were statistically more likely to make moral development gains than those enrolled at community colleges.

Maeda et al. (2009) examined the moral reasoning development of 7,462 students enrolled at one of 65 institutions in 28 states; between-college variables included region, political climate, religious affiliation, region by political climate, academic ranking of institution (or Carnegie Classification), and academic major. For the purposes of this review, only one variable, region, reached statistical significance, indicating that students in institutions in the nine southern states were less likely to make moral gains than students in institutions in the other regions. Maeda et al. (2009) emphasized the importance of context for future studies, noting, "It seems clear that by ignoring the context in which the data were collected we run the risk of a biased, incomplete picture of individual moral judgment development" (p. 245). Supporting findings from between-college analyses, results from both studies highlight the critical role that context plays in explaining the student development in moral domains.

Scholars who investigated college and its effects on student cheating also explored between-college effects (Arnold, Martin, Jinks, & Bigby, 2007; Harding, et al., 2007; Mayhew, Hubbard, Finelli, & Harding, 2009; McCabe & Bowers, 2009; McCabe et al., 2001, 2002; Passow, Mayhew, Finelli, & Carpenter, 2006; Stephens, Young, & Calabrese, 2007). Notably, McCabe et al. (2002) examined the impact of honor codes and student perceptions of academic dishonesty and behavior among samples of undergraduate students enrolled in 21 institutional environments that "spanned a spectrum of size, residential character, and admissions policies" (p. 364). Of particular importance to this review was the authors' coding of institutions into three distinctive categories: institutions with traditional honor codes, modified honor codes, and no honor codes.[1] The authors found that the level of dishonesty was highest at schools without honor codes, moderate at modified code schools, and lowest at schools with traditional honor codes.

Similarly, Arnold et al. (2007) explored the academic honesty of 695 students as it related to college honor code adoption and institutional size (small, medium, and large). By comparing students enrolled at Character Building Colleges (CBCs)[2] with honor codes to their peers enrolled at Traditional Colleges (TCs) with no honor codes, students from CBCs were less likely to help another student cheat than those from TCs.[2] In addition, students from CBCs reported feeling more likely they would get caught cheating than students from TCs.

Arnold et al. (2007) also found that students enrolled in small schools were more likely to report cheating than those from medium-sized institutions, and that students from large institutions reported feeling more likely to get away with cheating than their peers enrolled at small or midsized institutions. Similar findings were reported by Stephens et al. (2007), in their study of digital versus conventional cheating. They found that when compared to students enrolled in a large public institution, those in the small private institution in their study were significantly more likely to report feeling as though students cheated on their campus. Perceptions of peer cheating increased between .20 and .30 of a standard deviation between students who attended the private small institution, when compared to those who enrolled in the large public school. With regard to cheating behaviors, institutional conditions and policies may make a difference, as students in institutions with features that increase the potential for peer accountability (character-building missions and institutional size) were less likely to engage in cheating behaviors.

WITHIN-COLLEGE EFFECTS

Conclusions from the 1990s

Evidence from the previous volumes suggested that several within-college effects exerted influence on moral outcomes. Moral reasoning gains were associated with participation in curricular experiences with ethical components, social justice emphases, or service-learning dimensions. Similarly, moral outcomes were related to experiences that exposed students to different perspectives, most notably through role-taking activities or diverse peer networks.

Since the publication of the previous volume, research examining college and its influence on moral reasoning development has yielded varied results: some contexts have been effective in promoting moral reasoning among college students, and others have not. In two comprehensive literature reviews examining the relationship between moral reasoning and the collegiate contexts intended to spur its development, King and Mayhew (2002, 2005; see also Mayhew & King, 2008) attributed these mixed results to a number of theoretical and methodological issues: (1) a failure to use theory and relevant college impact frames to effectively ground discussions of college and its influence on moral reasoning; (2) too few thorough investigations into the context-specific mechanisms (e.g., educational practices) responsible for developmental gains in moral reasoning among college students; (3) a lack of rigorous designs (e.g., including meaningful comparison or control groups in data collections and analyses); (4) sample sizes too small to make accurate inferences about subgroup differences; and (5) methodological elements (e.g., statistically accounting for selection bias, adjusting standard errors for students in their natural learning environments) needed to substantiate claims regarding college and its influence on moral reasoning development. Due to these limitations, researchers and practitioners have struggled to develop, sustain, and assess evidence-based contexts or interventions designed to either influence moral reasoning development or understand its role in predicting moral behaviors, such as student cheating.

Evidence from the 2000s

Because of the shift toward within-college effects, scholars studying college students' moral reasoning development have embedded effect results within queries exploring the relationship between practice/process and moral development while drawing on expanded notions of student inputs and higher educational experiences in the new decade (see Stewart, 2012). A review of these studies suggests that empirically based questions designed to address the effects of any given college experience and its influence on moral development have included the covariates presented in Table 6.1.

The remainder of this section reviews a number of collegiate interventions considered in the literature as sources of influence on within-college moral development. These interventions include curricular elements (major, course type); faculty-to-student relationship (general, academic challenge, good teaching, assessments, active learning, reflection, critical thinking, integration of learning, cognitive disequilibrium); and cocurricular engagement (e.g., service-learning). The ordering of this section is structured to reflect patterns in how moral reasoning development was studied in the 2000s, with a primary emphasis on within-classroom practices, especially nuances in faculty practice, and a secondary emphasis on moral development in cocurricular spaces.

Table 6.1 Covariates with Citations

Covariate	*Citations*
Institutional type	Mayhew, 2012a; Mayhew, Seifert, & Pascarella, 2010, 2012
Geographic location of institution	Maeda, Thomas, & Bebeau, 2009
Year in school	Bernacki & Jaeger, 2008; Derryberry, Mulvaney, Brooks, & Chandler, 2009; Derryberry, Snyder, Wilson, & Barger, 2006; Lau, Caracciolo, Roddenberry, & Scroggins, 2011; Lies, Bock, Brandenberger, & Trozzolo, 2012; Maeda, Thomas, & Bebeau, 2009; Martin, Hevel, Asel, & Pascarella, 2011; Mayhew & Engberg, 2010; Mayhew & King, 2008
Gender	Arnold, Martin, Jinks, & Bigby, 2007; Barber & Venkatachalam, 2013; Bascom, 2011; Bowman, 2009; Derryberry, Mulvaney, Brooks, & Chandler, 2006; Derrbyberry. Mulvaney, Brooks, & Chandler, 2009; Grunwald & Mayhew, 2008; Hurtado, Mayhew, & Engberg, 2012; Lau & Haug, 2011; Mayhew & King, 2008; Mayhew, Seifert, & Pascarella, 2010, 2012; Mayhew, Seifert, Pascarella, Nelson Laird, & Blaich, 2012; Wilhelm, 2004
Race	Bowman, 2009; Hurtado, Mayhew, & Engberg, 2012
Income	Bowman, 2009
Political identification	Lies, Bock, Brandenberger, & Trozzolo, 2012; Maeda, Thomas, & Bebeau, 2009; Mayhew & King, 2008; Thoma, Derryberry, & Narvaez, 2009
Academic ability or achievement	Mayhew & King, 2008; Mayhew, Seifert, & Pascarella, 2010; Mayhew, Seifert, Pascarella, Nelson Laird, & Blaich, 2012; Olafson, Schraw, Nadelson, & Kehrwald, 2013; Passow, Mayhew, Finelli, Harding, & Carpenter, 2006; Yardley, Rodriguez, Bates, & Nelson, 2009
Precollege moral reasoning	Bowman, 2009; Martin, Hevel, Asel, & Pascarella, 2011; Mayhew, 2012a; Mayhew, Seifert, & Pascarella, 2010, 2012; Mayhew, Seifert, Pascarella, Nelson Laird, & Blaich, 2012

Curricular Interventions. In line with the trend of moving toward more nuanced explorations of the college environment and its influence on moral development, many of the studies included in this review adopted an expanded approach to investigating curricular interventions through the use of research designs that examined the efficacy of major and course type (e.g., diversity courses, challenge courses) and their influence on gains in moral reasoning development. In terms of courses, Mayhew and King (2008) suggested that reviews of these classroom-based interventions be grouped into two categories: those with explicit moral foci (e.g., ethics courses) and those with more implied moral emphases (e.g., social justice courses). To complicate matters, many of these studies not only investigated courses as they influenced moral outcomes, but included examinations of educational practices within those courses in relation to moral development. For this review, we sought to differentiate between content and practice when necessary.

Academic Major. Consistent with previous volumes, academic major was considered as a college experience studied for its relationship to moral outcomes, including reasoning and cheating. Many studies used samples based on major (Clarkeburn, Downie, Gray, & Matthew, 2003; Passow et al., 2006; Schmidt, McAdams, & Foster, 2009; Wilhelm, 2004; Yang & Wu, 2009), while others sampled from across the institution and compared respondents across majors (Barber & Venkatachalam, 2013; Derryberry et al., 2006; Harding et al., 2007; Lau & Haug, 2011; Livingstone, Derryberry, King, & Vendetti, 2006; Seider, Gillmor, & Rabinowicz, 2011; Wilhelm, 2004).

From these studies, business majors remained less likely to engage in moral behaviors than students in other majors. For example, Rettinger and Jordan (2005) studied cheating attitudes and behaviors among 151 sophomores, juniors, and seniors at a Jewish university. The authors found that business students self-reported cheating more frequently than liberal arts students enrolled in Jewish studies and general college courses. In addition, business students justified cheating to a greater degree than did their peers in the liberal arts. Similar findings were reported by Lau and Haug (2011), with business students having a higher tolerance for cheating than nonbusiness students.

Not only were moral outcomes less prevalent among business majors, but positive outcomes also appeared less frequently among engineering majors when compared to humanities majors (Harding et al., 2007), among education majors when compared to liberal arts majors (Derryberry et al., 2006), and among science students when compared to non-science students (Lau & Haug, 2011). In addition, Yardley et al. (2009) performed a study among 273 alumni who provided retrospective reports of cheating behaviors during their attendance at a large Western university. Although 82% of the sample self-reported cheating, most alumni indicated that they cheated more in their major classes due, in large part, to the belief that other students were also cheating, as well as to the social pressures that accompany helping friends succeed. The pronounced influence of the social pressure to cheat was also the subject of studies conducted by Rettinger and Kramer (2009) and Lucas and Friedrich (2005).

Morally Explicit Courses. A series of studies has examined courses with curricula that emphasized morally explicit content and its influence on moral reasoning development (Grunwald & Mayhew, 2008; Mayhew & King, 2008; You & Penny, 2011) and attitudes toward ethics (Lau et al., 2011). Mayhew and King (2008) longitudinally assessed and compared students enrolled in courses with explicitly moral content (contemporary moral problems and moral choice) to students enrolled in a control course, Introduction to Sociology. After controlling for a host of covariates, the authors found an accentuation effect for students who participated in the morally explicit courses: students enrolled in these courses tended to enter the courses at more advanced levels of moral reasoning and evidenced higher gain scores as a result of participation than students in the control course. When compared to students in the control course, students in the morally explicit courses made a .13 of a standard deviation gain or a 5.2 percentile point increase in moral reasoning scores by the end of the semester. To explain, the authors offer: "Courses that include explicit moral content may give students more practice wrestling with moral issues, as well as a vocabulary and concepts that assist in the development of their moral reasoning" (p. 34).

Morally Implied Courses. Scholarship on this topic also investigated moral reasoning gains resulting from participation in courses with implied moral emphasis, including intergroup dialogue courses (Grunwald & Mayhew, 2008; Mayhew & Engberg, 2010; Mayhew & King, 2008); religious courses (Rettinger & Jordan, 2005); general diversity courses (Bowman, 2009; Hurtado et al., 2012); service-learning courses (Mayhew & Engberg, 2010; Mayhew & King, 2008); courses that that helped students understand the historical, political, and social connections of past events (Mayhew, Seifert, & Pascarella, 2010, 2012); general science courses (Aalberts, Koster, & Boschhuizen, 2012); a fifteen-week physical education challenge course program (Smith, Strand, & Bunting, 2002); courses that feature geographic knowledge and literacy (Bascom, 2011); and distance education courses (Walker, 2010).

Among the course-taking experiences with implied moral content, diversity courses were examined for their potential influence on moral development indicators. For example, Hurtado et al. (2012) compared the moral reasoning scores of students enrolled in diversity courses with those enrolled in a business course; the authors found that through gains in critical thinking, students enrolled in the diversity courses achieved higher moral reasoning scores than those in the business course. The students in the diversity courses made .13 of a standard deviation gain, or a 5 percentile point increase when compared to students in the business course. In addition, the authors found that students who had taken diversity courses before enrolling in either the diversity course or the management course were significantly more likely to make moral reasoning gains, with effect sizes for "previous diversity course enrollment" reaching .10. The authors note that moral reasoning gains may occur through "exposing students to course content that addresses power, oppression, and the origins of contemporary social issues" (p. 219).

Similarly, Mayhew, Seifert, and Pascarella (2012) examined the influence of diversity course taking on moral reasoning development by investigating the growth trajectories of two types of first-year students: those who were transitioning between moral development stages and those who were consolidated within a stage. For students in transition, diversity course taking exhibited a small but significant effect on moral reasoning development, with effect sizes reaching .13; no effects of diversity course taking were found on the moral reasoning development of consolidated students. Explaining the differences, the authors noted that "students in moral transition might be more developmentally ready for and receptive to negotiating the disequilibrium and discomfort that often arise when discussing contested diversity issues" (p. 36).

Offering competing evidence, in his longitudinal study of over 3,000 students enrolled in one of 19 institutions, Bowman (2009) reported that diversity course taking was not associated with moral reasoning growth among first-year students. In a related study that included two diversity-related courses in the context of examining those with implied moral content, Grunwald and Mayhew (2008) used propensity score analyses to compare students in morally explicit and morally implied courses to those enrolled in a control course. No significant differences were reported between courses that had a moral emphasis and those that did not.

Beyond diversity courses, other classroom experiences were noted for their relationship to the moral gains demonstrated by students. In a study of first-year moral reasoning development, Mayhew et al. (2010) found that students were more likely to make moral reasoning gains when enrolled in courses that addressed the historical, political, and social connections of past events, with effect sizes reaching .06. To explain this finding, the authors suggest that engaging students "in critical dialogue with the past" (p. 379) may promote more developed forms of moral reasoning as students situate themselves as participants in broader historical and sociopolitical contexts. With regard to cheating, a difference was noted for students enrolled in distance education from those enrolled in traditional education within the same college or university. Walker (2010) examined the cheating intention and behaviors of students enrolled in either a traditional business or online business course. He found that distance students plagiarized to a significantly lesser degree than traditional students and had lower rates of verbatim and extensive plagiarism.

Summary. The weight of the evidence suggests that curricular experiences influence moral development. Students who major in business are less likely to make moral gains than students from other majors. These students also appear to have higher cheating tolerance than students from other majors.

Course taking also exerted influence on moral outcomes, albeit to varying degrees. Courses explicitly designed to help students make moral gains were the most effective, with students in the morally explicit courses making a .13 standard deviation gain or a 5.2 percentile point increase, in moral reasoning scores from the beginning to the end of the semester. Courses with more implied moral foci exhibited mixed results, with some studies suggesting no relationship between taking these courses and moral reasoning development and others suggesting small but significant relationships, with effect sizes ranging between .06 and .13.

Faculty-Student Interaction. The relationship between students and faculty remains related to moral development. However, the recent emergence of literature about educational practices and their influence on morally related outcomes has led to a surge of studies on the faculty-to-student dynamic, including examinations of faculty and student relationship quality, perceptions of and experiences with academic challenge in the classroom, perceptions of good teaching, teaching quality, perceptions of faculty use of assessments, and experiences with different pedagogies that faculty have adopted for use in the classroom. Scholars have frequently examined these faculty behaviors for their roles in directly spurring moral growth and indirectly influencing the achievement of moral outcomes.

General Positive Relationships with Faculty. Positive relationships between students and faculty generally facilitate moral development. Lau et al. (2011) designed a study to examine students' perceptions of the roles faculty play in shaping ethical beliefs. The authors determined that "faculty and instructors' influence can be exerted through their ability to help students develop values in their classes, to incorporate ethics training into classes, and to enforce ethical standards onto their students" (p. 10). Mayhew and King (2008) found similar results in a longitudinal study of undergraduate students: perceptions of positive faculty relationships were related to moral reasoning gains when enacted in classes with explicit or implied moral content.

Stearns (2001) examined students enrolled at a large regional university in the West to determine the relationship between academic dishonesty and student's evaluative perceptions of their course instructors. The author found that students who cheat tend to have lower evaluations of instructors. Similarly, in order to test the effects of two types of instructor-initiated practices on student-related attitudes and behaviors related to cheating, Spear and Miller (2012) examined three groups of students: one enrolled in a course where the instructor used fear-based strategies to deter cheating, one enrolled in a course that used moral-based strategies to deter cheating, and a control group. Students enrolled in the course where the instructor used fear-based techniques were significantly less likely to cheat than those in the control course; no significant differences were found between students in the course with the instructor who used moral strategies and the control group of students. Moreover, in their examination of faculty roles as predictors of student cheating, Lau and Haug (2011) examined students and their perceptions of faculty involvement on its relationship to student ethics. Here too the authors concluded that faculty involvement (e.g., direct incorporation of ethics into course, enforcement of ethical standards) mattered regarding effective ethics education.

Academic Challenge. How students perceive and experience academic challenge on campus tends to influence moral development (Lau et al., 2011; Martin et al., 2011; Mayhew et al., 2010; McKibban, 2013; Smith et al., 2002; Stearns, 2001). In their study of the effects of fraternity and sorority affiliation during the first year in college, Martin et al. (2011) found that, when compared to unaffiliated students, students in fraternities or sororities who experienced their learning environments as academically challenging were advantaged by .12 of a standard deviation in terms of moral reasoning development. In their study of 1,469 first-year students enrolled in one of 17 institutions, Mayhew et al. (2010) found that students' perceptions of academic challenge were also related to moral reasoning gains but not as strongly (effect size = .06). The authors concluded that the frequency with which faculty challenge students (e.g., through asking thought-provoking questions, encouraging students to apply course content to an actual problem, creating learning environments that encourage defended argumentation) has a positive influence on undergraduates' moral reasoning development.

Of additional interest was the study by Smith et al. (2002), who examined the efficacy of a physical challenge course on moral reasoning development. By longitudinally comparing students enrolled in the challenge course with peers enrolled in general physical education courses, the authors found a small effect for participation in the challenge program, which introduced moral concepts through a series of trust-building exercises. The authors explain, "Challenge course programs can provide the unstructured environment to practice problem solving and critical thinking, thus leading to improvement in ethical and moral behavior" (p. 279).

Finally, with regard to cheating, McKibban (2013) assessed the relationship between 3,151 students' perceptions of the classroom environment and academic honesty. These students were enrolled in over 100 classes, which were used as the unit of analysis. The authors found that courses perceived to be less challenging or where not enough material was presented were those in which students cheated to a greater degree.

Good Teaching. Perceptions of good teaching and teaching quality have been linked to moral development. To develop a holistic picture of the relationship between teaching and moral sensitivity development, Smith and Bath (2006) performed a cross-sectional study of moral sensitivity among three cohorts of students: 2,622 first-year students, 1,949 students in their final year of college, and 673 students in their final year of pursuing post-graduate coursework. Through the use of hierarchical linear modeling, the authors found a significant relationship between perceptions of good teaching and indicators of teaching quality and moral sensitivity scores. In addition, Mayhew et al. (2010) also found that perceptions of good teaching were statistically related to moral reasoning gains among students enrolled at one of 17 institutions, with effect sizes reaching .06.

Active Learning. Active learning strategies enacted by faculty have been studied as a possible influence on moral reasoning development. In a study of students enrolled in courses with explicit or implied moral content, Mayhew and King (2008) found that active learning promoted moral growth, regardless of course type. Another study, conducted by Hurtado et al. (2012), found that participation in a diversity course was linked to active learning, which in turn was related to the critical thinking skills needed to spur moral reasoning development. The effect size for the indirect effects for active learning on moral reasoning gains through critical thinking reached .04. These findings are consistent with other studies that highlight a positive association between student participation in the learning process, such as through exercises that encourage perspective taking, and moral reasoning development. (Clarkeburn et al., 2003; Rettinger, Jordan, & Peschiera, 2004; Rettinger & Kramer, 2009; Yang & Wu, 2009).

Cognitive Dissonance, Disequilibrium, Disruption. Although the relation-ship between cognitive dissonance and moral reasoning was never directly measured, it has served as the underlying psychological mechanism theoreti-cally noted for movement along moral development lines (see Kohlberg Rest) and empirically offered as the reason for moral change. In particular, the pro-cess of disruption was the subject of four articles (Mayhew & Engberg, 2010; Mayhew et al., 2010, 2012; Spear & Miller, 2012), each explaining that moral growth occurred due to the cognitive dissonance often spurred by encounters with difference. Across these studies, the authors imply that such dissonance, when properly supported, leads to moral reasoning development among stu-dents. For example, in their study of diverse peer interactions, Mayhew and Engberg (2010) argued that leaving diverse peer interactions to chance or pro-viding such opportunities in unstructured environments had the potential to attenuate moral reasoning development; the small but significant effect of course-related negative diverse peer interactions on moral reasoning gains reached .21.

Similarly, in their study of moral reasoning among first-year students, Mayhew et al. (2010) reported that moral reasoning gains could be attributed to learning environments and practices that provided opportunities for students to consider issues of fairness from broadened, less-egocentric perspectives: expos-ing students to practices and assessments that disrupted existing schema asso-ciated with egocentric frames for understanding justice. In their study of fear as a catalyst of cognitive dissonance, which influences moral reasoning develop-ment, Spear and Miller (2012) summarized: "Specifically, we anticipated that instructors who made direct anti-cheating appeals to their students would pro-mote cognitive dissonance in their students" (p. 205). Although assessed indi-rectly by way of peer interactions and curricular practices, studies discussing cognitive dissonance found it to be a catalyst for moral development.

Reflection. A series of studies interrogated reflection as a catalyst for moral growth. Some of these studies were classroom based, where students were asked the degree to which faculty encouraged them to reflect on materials (Mayhew & King, 2008; Juujarvi, Myyry, & Pesso, 2010; Schmidt et al., 2009), while others measured students' reflection abilities and their relationship to moral reasoning development (Mayhew, Seifert, Pascarella, Nelson Laird et al., 2012). In their evaluation of the deliberate psychological education model (DPE: Mosher & Sprinthall, 1971) for its efficacy in helping business students make moral reasoning gains, Schmidt et al. (2009) examined four sections of a course that focused on business ethics, of which one was randomly assigned the DPE. Although the DPE has many component parts, reflection is at its core. The authors found small to moderate effect sizes for the course section that received the treatment; students in the treatment section differed by a .49 standard deviation or 6.9 percentile points across three moral reasoning meas-ures than students in the control section.

Mayhew and King (2008) found that reflection by itself was not sufficient to promote moral reasoning, but was moderately correlated with development when enacted in courses with explicit (i.e., moral psychology, moral philosophy) or implied (e.g., service-learning) moral content. Alternatively, Mayhew, Seifert, Pascarella, Nelson Laird et al., (2012) did not find a significant relationship between reflective learning, one of the subscales of measure designed to assess deep learning, and moral reasoning gains. Despite scholars' hypotheses that moral reasoning development is strongly linked to reflection (see Juujarvi et al., 2010), it appears as though the relationship is a bit tenuous, probably due to the different ways reflection has been examined.

Integration of Learning. As educators advocate for more integrated approaches to learning (Barber, 2012, 2014; Baxter Magolda, 1999, 2001; Lattuca, 2001), recent studies have investigated integrated learning experiences as potential sources of moral growth. Specifically, three studies have examined this relationship: the first through a direct assessment of the relationship between integrated and moral learning and the second and third through inferences after moral growth was observed for students enrolled in a senior capstone experience (Craig & Oja, 2013) and students enrolled in a learning community (Smith & Bath, 2006).

The first study, by Mayhew, Seifert, Pascarella, Nelson Laird et al. (2012) examined 1,457 students enrolled in one of 19 institutions and found a relationship between moral reasoning gains and a deep learning practice, integrated learning, where educators taught students to integrate information from varied sources and perspectives and then to use the resulting frameworks as the basis for making moral decisions. The effects were small but significant, with sizes reaching .10. The second study, performed by Craig and Oja (2013), determined through a case study whether a 14-week internship experience modeled on the integrated learning framework produced changes in moral reasoning among undergraduate students enrolled in a recreation management program at a public university; through a paired sample *t*-test, the authors noted an increase in moral reasoning scores as a result of participation in this capstone experience. Although no comparison group was used to test whether gains were resultant from participation in the program or maturation, effect sizes were strong, reaching .70 for the sample. Finally, Smith and Bath (2006) found a significant relationship between participation in a learning community and moral sensitivity scores.

Critical Thinking. The relationship between critical thinking and moral reasoning development was the subject of many studies, with some arguing that critical thinking be included as a control variable in order to isolate the influence of the environment on moral development (Grunwald & Mayhew, 2008; Mayhew & Engberg, 2010; Mayhew & King, 2008; Mayhew, Seifert, & Pascarella, 2010, 2012; Mayhew, Seifert, Pascarella, Nelson Laird et al., 2012) and others suggesting that the environment influences moral development through exposing students to activities which induce critical thinking (Aalberts et al., 2012; Hurtado et al., 2012). For example, Hurtado et al. (2012) studied students enrolled in either a diversity or management course. They found that students enrolled in the diversity course were more likely to acquire critical thinking skills, which eventually led to moral reasoning development. Effect sizes for the relationship between critical thinking and moral reasoning reached .21.

Assessments. How faculty members assessed students also informed their moral development, mostly as it related to cheating attitudes, perceptions, and behaviors. Several authors determined that the types of assessment matter with regard to influencing outcomes related to cheating (Brent & Atkisson, 2011; Harding et al., 2009; Mayhew et al., 2009; Passow et al., 2006; Stephens et al., 2007; Walker, 2010). To understand how students made meaning of cheating, Passow et al. (2006) investigated whether student cheating varied as a function of type of assessment (homework versus exam cheating). From this study, the authors learned that students differed in their perceptions of what constituted cheating; subsequently, their decisions to cheat were different depending on the context in which the cheating took place, with students more likely to cheat on homework than on exams. Extending this work, Harding et al. (2008) provided an empirically tested theoretical framework for distilling the underlying psychological mechanisms involved in students' decisions to cheat in homework and exam contexts. They found that students' expressed cheating intentions effectively explained student cheating in both contexts. Although students may approach cheating differentially, based on the type of assessment being administered, the relationship between cheating intentions and behaviors remains strong and consistent across assessment contexts.

Interestingly, this line of inquiry has also been used to relate cheating outcomes to learning context, including traditional versus Internet plagiarism and conventional versus digital cheating on assignments and exams (Stephens et al., 2007). In their study, Stephens et al. found that slightly more students reported engaging in digital plagiarism (e.g., cutting and pasting from the Internet) than conventional plagiarism, with effect sizes reaching .02. The findings regarding context, technological versus traditional, and its role in explaining differential attitudes toward or engagement in cheating behaviors were also supported by the work of Lau et al. (2011) and Walker (2010): students make different ethical considerations based on the context in which the choice is being made. Notably, Walker (2010) found that the use of Turnitin, a popular digital platform aimed at deterring plagiarism, did not serve as a comprehensive deterrent to this specific form of cheating.

Summary. Faculty-to-student relationships continue to dominate the research landscape with regard to understanding college and its effects on moral outcomes, including cheating. Overall, perceptions of good practice influence moral reasoning development to a small but significant degree, with effect sizes reaching .06. In order of magnitude, results indicated that moral outcomes have the strongest relationships with the following educational practices: reflection (.49), critical thinking (.21), diverse peer interactions (.21), academic challenge (from .06 to .12), integration of learning (.10), and active learning (.04).

It appears that context matters with regard to students' ethical considerations and engagement in cheating behaviors. Students feel differently as well as make different choices about cheating based on the context in which the decision or behaviors takes place. Overall, students perceive that exam cheating is the worst form of cheating and may cheat more in digital learning environments when compared to traditional learning environments, although certainly more research needs to be done in these areas. We turn now to our review of cocurricular experiences and their effects on moral outcomes.

Cocurricular Engagement. Moral development shares a relationship with cocurricular engagement despite its radical difference in operation across studies, including informal interactions with peers (Mayhew et al., 2010), number of work hours and number of reported television hours (Bascom, 2011), fraternity and sorority membership (Harding et al., 2007; Martin et al., 2011; McCabe & Bowers, 2009; Passow et al., 2006); and participation in service-learning experiences (Bernacki & Jaeger, 2008; Lies et al., 2012; Seider et al., 2010, 2011; Scott, 2012). For example, Mayhew et al. (2010) found a significant but small effect (.04) between moral reasoning development and the degree to which students had had meaningful interactions with each other, after controlling for a host of covariates. Another example from this series of studies is Bascom's (2011) examination of the relationship between geographic knowledge and moral sensitivity. As part of this study, Bascom found that developing a sense of issues as moral was positively associated with more hours worked and fewer hours of watching television per week.

Some researchers examined participation in fraternities and sororities in relation to cheating. McCabe and Bowers (2009) examined the relationship between student cheating and college fraternity or sorority membership among fraternity/sorority members enrolled in one of nine institutions; the authors found that fraternity/sorority members and residents were more likely to cheat than independent students. Similar results were embedded in the study of engineering students and college cheating in Harding et al.'s (2007) and Passow et al.'s (2006) studies, which found that students who participated in fraternities and sororities were more likely to cheat than unaffiliated students. A notable exception to these results was reported by Martin et al. (2011), who found no significant results between fraternity/sorority membership and unaffiliated students, although the authors only examined first-year students. With the exception of fraternity and sorority membership, the dearth of studies in this area echo King and Mayhew's (2002) observations that the effects of most aspects of the cocurriculum (e.g., leadership positions) on morally-related outcomes remain largely unexplored.

Service-Learning. Service-learning remains an engaging area for scholars interested in moral outcomes (Bernacki & Jaeger, 2008; Grunwald & Mayhew, 2008; Lies et al., 2012; Mayhew & Engberg, 2010; Mayhew & King, 2008; Ruso, 2012; Seider et al., 2010). That said, results remain mixed as to the efficacy of these experiences in engendering growth along moral dimensions. For example, Lies et al. (2012) examined the effects of off-campus service-learning on the moral reasoning development of 144 college students. The authors grouped students into a treatment group of students who participated in service-learning and a control group of students not participating in service-learning. On average, participants in the service-learning group made .41 of a standard deviation or a 7 percentile point average gain over students in the non-service-learning group. The authors suggested that "service-learning experiences with different community immersion structures have moral implications (as is often assumed but not often measured)" (p. 197).

On the contrary, Bernacki and Jaeger (2008) explored the influence of service-learning on moral development and moral orientation of 46 undergraduate students enrolled at a Catholic university in the U.S. Northeast. They grouped students into treatment and control conditions and found no effects on moral reasoning or orientation for participation in the service-learning course. However, based on another assessment, the authors reported that students who completed the service-learning course were significantly more likely to perceive positive changes in themselves than students enrolled in the traditional course.

A literature review by Scott (2012) examined the intersection between service-learning and moral growth, suggesting that Rest's (1986) four dimensions of moral maturity—moral sensitivity, moral judgment, moral motivation, and moral character—be considered as outcomes of service-learning experiences. Scott ended his discussion in a positive tone, noting, "A review of the moral dimensions explored in this volume highlights the potential for moral growth in the context of service-learning relationships" (p. 35). Because the results appear mixed with regard to service-learning and its relationship to moral outcomes, scholars need to continue efforts in this area.

Summary. The weight of the evidence suggests that cocurricular experiences exert influence on moral development. Informal interactions with peers also had small but significant effects on the moral reasoning development of first-year students, with effect sizes reaching .04. Across the studies of service-learning, results were mixed; however, when effects were significant, they reached .41, giving students in service-learning environments a 7 percentile point advantage in making moral gains when compared with students not in these environments.

CONDITIONAL COLLEGE EFFECTS

Conclusions from the 1990s

In Volume 2, very few if any studies of conditional effects on moral development via a measured dimension of the college environment were noted. One study was reported (Rykiel, 1995). Without another to support findings, questions remain with regard to interpretations of meaning outside the context of other evidence.

Evidence from the 2000s

Although this decade saw a surge of more sophisticated research on college and its effects on moral reasoning development, few studies reported conditional effects. Mayhew et al. (2010) tested a series of first-year college experiences for their influence on the development of moral reasoning and how this relationship differed among a host of student characteristics. The authors reported no significant relationships among these variables; results, they said, were "general rather than conditional" (p. 376).

As an exception, Bowman's (2009) study longitudinally examined the relationship between diversity course taking and moral reasoning development and whether this relationship differed by race, gender, or family income. He found significant interactions between income and diversity course work on moral reasoning development. While taking two courses benefited the moral reasoning development of high-income students when compared to less affluent students, taking three or more courses was associated with greater gains in moral reasoning for lower-income students, when compared to high-income students.

LONG-TERM EFFECTS OF COLLEGE

Conclusions from the 1990s

In previous volumes, little to no evidence was reported for the long-term effects of college on moral reasoning gains. With the exception of Mentkowski and Associates (2000) and Astin, Sax, and Avalos (1999) who studied morally related gains over time beyond college, the knowledge base following students during and beyond college was scant at best. While one study suggested that moral gains continued beyond the college years (Astin et al., 1999), the other (Mentkowski & Associates, 2000) reported that the moral growth during college was at least maintained five years out of college, without much growth (about .18 of a standard deviation).

Evidence from the 2000s

Much like findings on conditional effects, long-term effects of college on moral reasoning scores were not examined as an area of inquiry.

CHAPTER SUMMARY

Theoretical Developments

Theoretical frameworks for understanding moral development have been expanded and refined since the last versions of this volume were published. One noteworthy theoretical shift has involved the use of neo-Kohlbergian, as opposed to Kohlbergian, approaches to describing the moral reasoning process. Movement away from stages to schemas theoretically distances scholars from trite oversimplifications of individuals' reasoning strategies to explanations that are more complex, particularly by the way of the nuances individuals often invoke when making moral decisions (see Rest, 1999).[3] Although these theoretical shifts are important for contextualizing the evidence provided in this review, understanding the origins of Kohlbergian thought remains critical for researchers interested in college and its effects on students. As Narvaez (2005) summarizes, "Critics have pointed out the oversimplified perspectives and globality of their [Piaget and Kohlberg] theories, noting that the view from the ground is much more complicated and messy. Yet there is more empirical support for Kohlberg's general theory than ever before" (p. 119).

In light of this claim, educators may want to consider the importance of developmental movement along Kohlbergian and neo-Kohlbergian dimensions. Specifically, what can educators do to help students develop reasoning strategies from justifying choices based on maintaining rules, laws, and norms to appropriately disrupting them, especially when their sustenance and reproduction are biased in favor of some to the detriment of others? Educational contexts designed to support this theoretical movement would help students develop a respect for human rights; a robust understanding of the benefits of a participatory society that is transparent, inclusive, and open to scrutiny; and the skills needed to critically examine the intentions and expressions of any social arrangement. Of course, helping students understand when the amalgam of these developmental milestones should express themselves in action would be equally important, as both an educational objective and another means for studying the relationship between reasoning and behaviors.

Change during College

As with previous syntheses, the evidence suggests that change in moral development occurs during college. As this trend had been well established through decades of research through a series of meta-analyses (see McNeel, 1994; Nucci & Pascarella, 1987; Pascarella & Terenzini, 2005) and longitudinal quasi-experimental designs comparing college with noncollege goers (Rest, 1979), this decade of research supported these general findings.

Evidence was provided from a longitudinal study that examined students' moral growth over three time points: beginning of college, end of the first year of college, and during the senior year. Drawing from these data, Pascarella, Salisbury, and Blaich (2011) reported that an average gain of .32 of a standard deviation in moral reasoning scores was demonstrated for students during their first year in college; this marked a 13 percentile point increase in moral reasoning score for students during their first year in college. In tandem, students made average gains of .58 of a standard deviation in moral reasoning scores from the first to the fourth year in college; this estimate represented a 22 percentile point increase in moral reasoning scores since these students entered college. Given decades of consistent findings confirming that college influences moral development, scholars have initiated more specified research to understand the extent to which this development occurs.

Net Effects of College

There were no studies of the net effects of participation in higher education and moral development. Of course, the dearth of information in this area is cause for concern as national confidence in higher education continues to erode.

Although no net effects were directly observed, to begin unpacking the extent to which moral growth occurs, many scholars initiated studies that found that college-going was related to moral development, net of other important characteristics. Through examining numerous empirically based questions designed to address the net effects of college and its influence on moral development and moral action through cheating, we determined that such work needs to account for the following covariates in order to clearly elucidate the relationships between educational environments and moral development outcomes: institutional type, geographical location of institution, year in school, gender, race, political identification, and academic ability or achievement. While the magnitude of influence of each of these characteristics varies across research questions and design, we found that four were particularly noteworthy due to theoretical considerations underlying the study and measurement of moral development: gender, political identity, verbal ability or level of cognitive development, and year in school.

Between-College Effects

One means of unpacking the extent to which development occurred involved addressing between-college effects: the institutional conditions, organizational characteristics, and average peer perceptions and experiences that may have exerted influence on explaining moral reasoning development. With a relatively large 18% variance in moral development being explained by these types of institutional characteristics, it seems reasonable to suggest that institutions may have more influence on moral reasoning development than many other outcomes reviewed in this volume. In practice, this result empowers institutions to think differently about moral dimensions of their mission. Perhaps institutions should consider enacting policies that help students build character and, consistent with the underlying tenets of most theories on moral development, frame their college experience as an opportunity to gain the skills necessary to make positive changes in society.

Like previous syntheses, we found that outcomes associated with moral development were related to distinctive types of learning environments. In terms of institutional type, students enrolled in liberal arts institutions were more likely to develop along moral dimensions than students attending community colleges. Also, colleges located in the nonsouthern regions of the country were more likely to enroll students with higher moral reasoning scores. The size of the institution played a role in influencing both moral reasoning and cheating behaviors, with students at smaller institutions more likely to develop along moral dimensions than students at larger schools.

Institutions with honor codes and Character Building Colleges tended to have fewer problems with academically dishonest behaviors. Taken together, these studies emphasize the need to understand the role that organizational characteristics can play in influencing moral development, with some (e.g., honor codes) malleable and able to be designed and others (e.g., size, geographic location) more immutable, less susceptible to change.

Within-College Effects

As in the preceding volumes, the literature on within-college effects continued to dominate the research landscape in terms of college and its influence on outcomes related to moral development. As a result, we present the following general conclusions:

1. Academic major remained a topic of importance among empiricists interested in helping students achieve moral gains. As in previous volumes, we found that business majors were less likely to report or achieve moral outcomes than students from other majors. Also noteworthy was the emergence of several new studies among engineering educators who found that engineering students differentially approached cheating based on the type of assessment being administered. These findings remind educators that context remains important for students as they make meaning about moral behaviors like cheating.

2. A growing number of studies investigated curricular interventions as vehicles for helping students achieve gains along moral dimensions. We found that two types of courses, those with explicit moral content and those with an implied moral focus (e.g., diversity courses), were instructive for understanding student moral growth. Students enrolled in courses with explicit moral content were more likely to make moral gains than those in other types of courses, including students enrolled in courses with implied moral emphases. Students in the morally explicit courses made a .13 standard deviation gain or a 5.2 percentile point increase in moral reasoning scores from the beginning to the end of the semester. Results were mixed for students who enrolled in courses with more implied moral foci, like diversity courses, with some studies suggesting no relationship between taking these courses and moral reasoning development and others suggesting small to moderate but significant relationships, with effect sizes ranging between .06 and .13.

3. Emerging evidence on the role that distance education played in deterring cheating showed that method of assessment delivery (i.e., digital vs. traditional) might influence students' ethical considerations.

4. Evidence suggested that the faculty-to-student relationship remained important to consider as a determinant of moral development in college. Overwhelmingly, the evidence showed that faculty practices are the key

to unlocking student moral growth potential. This finding persists in terms of the general relationships faculty shared with students, the practices that faculty enacted in courses, and the gains faculty helped students make in other learning dimensions that influenced moral gains. More specifically, we found that

a. Moral outcomes were associated with students' general perceptions of experiences with faculty members, especially with regard to their teaching quality, with effect sizes reaching .06. Indeed, when these perceptions and experiences were positive, they even deterred course-related cheating behaviors among students.

b. Academic challenge was also associated with moral gains, with effects ranging from .06 to .12. Students who perceived that course work was challenging were likely to make moral gains.

c. Good teaching was related to development among outcomes with moral dimensions.

d. The type of assessment faculty used as a part of the course experience influenced students' moral behaviors, with students more likely to cheat on homework than on tests.

e. Moral gains were noted among students enrolled in courses where faculty enacted practices that encouraged active learning (.04), reflection (.49), and the development of critical thinking skills (.21).

f. Negative diverse peer interactions in the classroom had negative but significant net effects on moral reasoning gains (.21). Faculty should consider if and how cross-race interactions are occurring in class, develop strategies for minimizing the likelihood of nonproductive interactions, and appropriately support all students who wrestle with issues of race by being attentive to the group norms that underlie the learning context.

g. Evidence began to show a positive relationship between integrated learning experiences and moral outcome achievement, with effect sizes reaching .10. Specifically, three studies have examined this relationship: the first through a direct assessment of the relationship between integrated and moral learning and the second and third through inferences offered to explain relationships among other variables, after moral growth was observed.

h. Although never directly measured, the relationship between cognitive dissonance and moral reasoning has served as the underlying psychological mechanism theoretically noted for movement along moral development lines and empirically offered as the reason for moral change.

5. We found mixed evidence regarding service-learning and its relationship to moral outcomes. While some scholars continue to assume that some relationship between service-learning and moral development must

exist, our review suggests otherwise: some studies showed a positive relationship, with effect sizes reaching .49, and others reported no relationship at all.

6. With the exception of studies of fraternity and sorority membership, there was a dearth of studies relating specific cocurricular experiences to moral gains. Among the studies of fraternities and sororities, three of four found significant and positive relationships between membership in these organizations and academic dishonesty like cheating. One study did not support the idea that fraternity and sorority membership was related to academic dishonesty.

Conditional Effects of College

Like the previous volumes, very few, if any, studies of conditional effects on moral development using a measured dimension of the college environment were noted. Although this decade saw a surge of more sophisticated research on college and its effects on moral reasoning development, only a few studies reported conditional effects. Among these studies, only one conditional effect was reported: taking diversity courses has differential effects on the moral development of students based on their level of income, with higher-income students benefiting more from taking two courses and lower-income students benefiting more from taking three or more courses.

Long-Term Effects of College

Consistent with previous volumes, no evidence was provided concerning the long-term effects of college on moral reasoning scores. Part of the issue may be in finding students after they graduate; indeed many researchers have had to hire firms to locate recent alumni (see New, 2013). Also, many of the instruments used to measure morally related outcomes are cumbersome to administer and cognitively demanding to take. Whatever the issue, nothing in this review suggests that we know anything more from research conducted in the 2000s about morally related outcomes from college to postgraduate years.

CHAPTER CONCLUSION

Embedded in the missions of higher education institutions is the idea that students should graduate with a sense of citizenry, with the responsibility to use their education as a platform for making the world a better place. The weight of the evidence in this review suggests that exposure to and participation in higher education remains influential in shaping students' moral development. As a result of college-going, students' reasoning patterns became more complex, evolving from understanding justice as something that is based on normed definitions of rules and policies to framing justice as something principled, intended to critically scrutinize the source, appropriations, and equitable administrations of rules and policies.

Of increasing importance and as evidenced by this review, is how institutions approach their responsibilities in helping student make moral gains. Indeed, results indicated that institutions should feel empowered to create or rethink existing policy and practice as they relate to shaping the moral dimensions of the college student experience. In particular, classroom-based practices that students experienced as challenging, active, integrative, and reflective were related to moral growth. In addition, faculty need to consider the group norms that underlie the course experience; classroom-based cross-race interactions left to chance or inappropriately supported were found to have negative influences on moral gains.

Graduating students with a sense of citizenry is critical if we are to meet the needs of the twenty-first century. We turn next to a review of studies designed to inform the graduation process: factors that contribute to helping students persist through their educational journeys and complete their college degrees. Examining this challenge remains vital, as educators argue that college degrees serve as conduits for economic mobility and often, more important, as platforms for social change.

Notes

1. According to the authors, modified honor codes "seem to focus on two strategies. First, the institution, through any number of mechanisms (e.g., integrity rallies, presidential involvement, integrity seminars), clearly communicates to its students that academic integrity is a major institutional priority. Second, students are given a significant role in both the judicial or hearing body on campus and in developing programs to inform other students about the purposes of the code, its major components, enforcement strategies, and so forth. This often includes programming to convince students that academic integrity is something to be valued. And while we are not aware of any modified codes that mandate them, several modified codes allow the possibility of unproctored exams or the use of a pledge at an instructor's option. The single most important thing modified codes may do, however, is focus a campus's attention on the issue of academic dishonesty and clearly communicate to students that integrity is an institutional priority" (McCabe et al., 2002, pp. 362–363).

2. Character Building Colleges, according to the authors, are "recognized by the John Templeton Foundation for their character development programs" (Arnold et al., 2007, p. 4) and have honor codes.

3. For a discussion of this and other differences between Kohlberg and the neo-Kohlbergians approaches, see an excellent review offered by Rest and colleagues (1999) and more recently by Darcia Narvaez (2005).

CHAPTER SEVEN

Educational Attainment and Persistence

Attending college and obtaining a postsecondary degree are both associated with a variety of financial and personal benefits throughout one's life after college (see Chapters 8 and 9). The positive effects of education on economic outcomes are also apparent at the national level: countries with well-educated populations tend to fare better in terms of economics and well-being (Organisation for Economic Co-operation and Development, 2013). Some have argued that increasing the number of college-educated adults is necessary to prepare the United States for continued economic prosperity; this push for bolstering postsecondary attainment has even become the primary mission of the Lumina Foundation (2014) and other organizations. College attrition and a lack of access to higher education can be quite costly not only for societies, but also for colleges and universities (which often invest substantial resources into recruiting students and promoting their success) and for families and students (who may accrue substantial debt during college without the financial benefit associated with receiving a degree or certificate). Therefore, it is critical to understand the factors that shape college student persistence and graduation. What types of institutions are most effective at promoting educational attainment? And which college experiences increase the likelihood of degree completion?

Before discussing the empirical literature on this topic, a brief review of relevant theory is informative. We start by discussing Tinto's (1987, 1993) influential theory, given its near-paradigmatic status in higher education (Braxton, Sullivan, & Johnson, 1997). According to Tinto, students' precollege family backgrounds, skills and abilities, and prior schooling all affect their entering levels of goal commitment (to the outcome of degree completion), institutional commitment (to their current college or university), and educational intentions (regarding departure from that college or from college in general). These initial postsecondary commitments and intentions also interact with commitments that are external to the college environment. Students' entering predispositions then lead to experiences within the academic and social systems of the institution (e.g., faculty/staff and peer interactions, extracurricular activities), and experiences within these two systems may influence each other. Such experiences lead to students' integration (or lack thereof) within the social and academic environment of the institution. In later versions of his theory, Tinto notes that students could fit well within some part of the campus (but not necessarily the whole), which would still serve the positive function of college integration. These two forms of integration, along with students' current external commitments and their commitments and intentions on entering college, all shape their subsequent goal commitment, institutional commitment, and intentions. Students' subsequent intentions and commitments then lead to a departure decision.

Although Tinto's theory is often used and widely cited, it is also frequently critiqued; Museus (2014) provides a summary of four main criticisms of this theory. First, Tinto argued (particularly in earlier work) that students needed to leave behind their precollege communities and cultures to adapt successfully to college. This assertion was seen as being particularly problematic for students of color, whose cultures may differ notably from those of their institutions (e.g., Rendón, Jalomo, & Nora, 2000; Tierney, 1992). Second, some have asserted that the theory places too much emphasis on students' role in adjusting to college and not enough on institutions' responsibility to help students succeed (e.g., Bensimon, 2007; Rendón et al., 2000). Third, some research has found that academic and social integration are not strongly related to student success (e.g., Braxton, Hirschy, & McClendon, 2004; Braxton & Lien, 2000; Swail, Redd, & Perna, 2003) and that some measures of integration may overlook forms of engagement that are more common among students of color (e.g., Hurtado, 1994). The final critique focuses primarily on research based on applications of Tinto's work: academic and social integration are often defined through behavioral measures, which overlooks the fact that these were intended to be psychological constructs (see Bowman & Denson, 2014; Braxton Sullivan, & Johnson, 1997; Hurtado & Carter, 1997). As a result of these criticisms, a number of alternative theories of college student departure have been provided, and Tinto also revised his work to address some of these issues.

Interestingly, while other theories generally seek to avoid these critiques, many of them share one or two key attributes of Tinto's theory. First, the theories often take an interactionist approach by positing that the intersection of student and institutional attributes, along with students' perception of that (in)congruence, shapes college attrition (Bean & Eaton, 2000; Braxton, Hirschy, & McClendon, 2004; Kuh & Love, 2000; Museus & Quaye, 2009; Stage & Hossler, 2000). Second, they often contain constructs that are also used in

Tinto's theory, including social and academic integration, goal and institutional commitment, and intent to persist (Bean & Eaton, 2000; Braxton et al., 2004; Cabrera, Nora, & Castañeda, 1992; Nora & Cabrera, 1996; Swail, Redd, & Perna, 2003; for a review, see Museus, 2014). Given the prevalence of these constructs in theory and research, we draw on these in our review without making a priori assumptions about which theory or theories may best account for student retention, persistence, and graduation.

In this chapter, we discuss literature on educational attainment, typically defined as obtaining a postsecondary degree. We also discuss research on persistence toward a degree, which includes continued enrollment at an institution, continued enrollment in higher education, and completion of a course with a passing grade. Clearly, continued enrollment and successful course completion are integral to the attainment of a postsecondary credential. We focus almost exclusively on studies that predicted actual student behavior (e.g., graduation, retention) rather than intent to persist, since using intent to persist can yield different findings from using persistence and other enrollment outcomes (e.g., Pan, 2011; Schreiner & Nelson, 2013), and higher education stakeholders are clearly interested in students' behavior rather than simply their intentions. For consistency, we use the terms *persistence* to describe continued enrollment in higher education (regardless of whether this occurs at one or more institutions) and *retention* to describe continued enrollment within the same institution (this is sometimes referred to as *institutional persistence*). This choice of language is not always consistent with the language in the studies that we discuss. We also include research in which transfer from a two-year to a four-year institution (i.e., *upward transfer*) is the primary outcome, since this is a necessary step toward the attainment of a bachelor's degree for students who do not start at a four-year college. Because of the nature of college attendance and completion, this chapter covers four categories of effects: between college, within-college, conditional, and long term.

BETWEEN-COLLEGE EFFECTS

Conclusions from the 1990s

Considerable prior research examined whether and how institutional attributes predict retention, persistence, and graduation. The largest and most consistent findings occurred for attending a two-year versus four-year school. Pascarella and Terenzini (2005) concluded that two-year colleges provided democratization benefits insofar as they attracted students who may not have attended college at all, and they provided attainment opportunities for those students. At the same time, among students who were interested in pursuing a bachelor's degree, they concluded that attending a two-year institution instead of a four-year institution reduced the chances of bachelor's degree completion by 15 to 20 percentage points. They also noted that virtually all of this disparity occurred because students at two-year schools often did not transfer successfully to four-year schools; students who did transfer were about as likely to graduate as similar students who started at four-year institutions.

Other between-college differences generally had smaller effect sizes. The second-most consistent effect occurred for institutional quality or selectivity, which was defined in terms of students' average admissions test scores, high school GPA, or high school rank. Attending a more selective institution was directly associated with a greater likelihood of persistence and degree completion. These effects were intertwined with students' college experiences, and the magnitude of this relationship was reasonably small. The effects of other between-college characteristics were generally quite small or inconsistent. African American students at predominantly Black schools (relative to predominantly White schools) and female students at women's colleges (relative to coeducational colleges) tended to fare better, with these patterns likely explained by more supportive environments and interpersonal interactions for these students. Attending a private (versus public) institution and a school with a smaller (versus larger) student body both had small, inconsistent positive relationships with persistence and attainment that appeared to be explained by other institutional factors and by students' interactions with faculty and peers.

Evidence from the 2000s

Two-Year versus Four-Year Institutions. In Pascarella and Terenzini's (1991, 2005) reviews, starting at a four-year college or university (rather than a two-year institution) had the largest effect of any other institutional characteristic on students' attainment of a bachelor's degree. We draw our current estimate of this effect primarily from studies that used nationally representative or state unit-record data, compared students at four-year colleges to those at two-year colleges who were interested in obtaining a bachelor's degree, and used quasi-experimental designs and numerous control variables to account for self-selection into these institutional types (Alfonso, 2006; Doyle, 2009a; Long & Kurlaender, 2008; Reynolds, 2012; Sandy, Gonzalez, & Hilmer, 2006). Similar to Pascarella and Terenzini's (2005) previous estimate, starting at a four-year institution appears to result in a 15 to 25 percentage point greater likelihood of bachelor's degree completion than starting at a two-year institution. A number of additional studies also obtained similar substantive results (Christie & Hutcheson, 2003; Novak & McKinney, 2012; Paulsen & St. John, 2002; Roksa, 2011; Stratton, O'Toole, & Wetzel, 2007, 2008). This research generally controlled for a variety of student demographics, family attributes, high school preparation, and academic achievement.

Some research has explored the processes through which this large disparity can be explained. Clark (1960) famously described the "cooling out" function of community colleges, in which students with aspirations to obtain (at least) a bachelor's degree are counseled to reduce these aspirations as a result of insufficient preparation, ability, or resources. Leigh and Gill (2004) provide direct evidence of this phenomenon in their examination of the National

Longitudinal Survey of Youth. Specifically, two-year students reduce their desired education level during college more so than four-year students do, and this pattern is larger for students with lower academic ability.

One proposed mechanism for this aspirational reduction occurs through interactions with academic advisors, who could directly suggest that students' aspirations are unrealistic and should be revised. Therefore, Bahr (2008a) explored the relationship between advising and attainment within a statewide sample of California community college students. When controlling for sex, race, age, socioeconomic status, academic goals, and academic preparation, interactions with academic advisors were positively related to successful math remediation (for those who needed it) and transferring to a four-year institution. Moreover, these relationships were stronger for students with greater remedial needs, which further runs contrary to the cooling-out effect of academic advisors. It is certainly possible that highly motivated students are likely to seek out advising in the first place, but these findings suggest that, at a minimum, community college advising does not appear to inhibit students' progression toward a four-year degree. In sum, although cooling out does appear to occur at two-year colleges, academic advising may not cause this phenomenon.

Furthermore, some scholars note that any potential cooling-out effect of community colleges (relative to four-year institutions) may be offset by the democratizing effect of attending a community college (versus no college at all). Specifically, two-year colleges provide additional access to higher education, so their presence leads to increases in educational attainment among students who might not have otherwise attended college. Controlling for a variety of precollege characteristics (including standardized test scores and desired education level), Leigh and Gill (2003) replicate the cooling-out effect, as they show that starting at a two-year college results in 0.7 to 1.0 fewer years of education than starting at a four-year college. In addition, they found that attending a two-year college results in 1.1 to 1.8 more years of education than not attending a two-year college at all. Therefore, they conclude that the democratization effect outweighs the cooling-out effect, demonstrating that community colleges bolster educational attainment overall. Similar patterns are also apparent when examining two-year college attendance and desired education levels (Leigh & Gill, 2004).

Starting at a two-year college also does not appear to reduce the likelihood of graduation among students who transfer to a four-year institution with a large number of credits. Melguizo and colleagues (2011) used nationally representative data from the U.S. Department of Education to compare the graduation outcomes of students who started at a four-year institution and those who transferred as incoming juniors. These two groups of students differ in a variety of ways; those who transferred are more likely to be Hispanic/Latino, have lower average precollege preparation and involvement, are more likely to be employed, and have lower degree expectations (Melguizo, Kienzl, & Alfonso, 2011). However, when adjusting for these and other student characteristics, transfer students are as likely to receive a bachelor's degree as nontransfer students (Adelman, 2006; Melguizo & Dowd, 2009; Melguizo et al., 2011). Interestingly, when examining this relationship for Hispanic students specifically, Melguizo (2009) found that Hispanic transfer students were less likely than nontransfers to earn a degree in the earlier High School and Beyond dataset, but no significant differences were observed in the later National Education Longitudinal Study dataset. Given the modest sample sizes and limited number of control variables, these findings for Hispanic students should be viewed cautiously. Moreover, the findings for entering juniors do not necessarily apply to students with fewer credits, as Ishitani (2008) observed that students who transfer as sophomores and juniors are less likely to drop out of a four-year university than those who transfer as first-year students.

To understand the relationship between college enrollment and attainment, it is important to consider the multiple paths through which students navigate institutions to graduation. Specifically, transferring from a two-year to a four-year institution is only one type of transfer; students may also transfer from a two-year to two-year or a four-year to four-year college (often known as lateral transfer) or from a four-year college to a two-year college (often known as reverse transfer). Some students enroll concurrently (or co-enroll) at multiple institutions at the same time, and/or they "swirl" by alternating courses at two or more institutions in different semesters. According to Peter, Cataldi, and Carroll (2005), more than 40% of entering postsecondary students attend more than one institution, and more than 10% of all students are co-enrolled at some point.

Two rigorous studies have found that co-enrollment is positively related to persistence and degree attainment among students who started at both two- and four-year institutions (Crisp, 2013; Wang & McCready, 2013). Both of these studies matched co-enrolled and other students on a variety of attributes, including demographics, precollege academic preparation, college grades, college experiences, and other aspects of college enrollment (e.g., delayed entry into college). A propensity score analysis of dual enrollment in college classes while in high school also found that this practice is associated with greater degree attainment (An, 2013). While the mechanism that explains this relationship is unclear, co-enrollment and dual enrollment may provide opportunities for students to take coursework in an expedient manner; for instance, a student could obtain a course from a second institution if it is either not available at the first school or offered at an inconvenient time.

However, students who engage in lateral or reverse transfer from four-year institutions certainly do not fare better than those who do not transfer, and they may have lower attainment outcomes. For instance, when controlling for a variety of student precollege and college characteristics, Li (2010) found that students who engaged in lateral transfer were much less likely to obtain a bachelor's degree within six years than students who did not transfer or stop out. These findings are almost certainly overestimates of the true relationship, since the comparison group does not include students who stop out and then return to the same school, and students who transfer are less likely to graduate in a timely manner than those who do not (DesJardins, Kim, & Rzonca, 2003). In fact, Adelman (2006) found that engaging in four-year to four-year transfer did not reduce the likelihood of bachelor's degree attainment (within eight years of students' high school senior year) relative to students who did not transfer, reverse transferred, or who swirled among institutions. Once again, issues with the referent group prevent strong conclusions from being drawn about lateral transfer.

Institutional Quality. Attending a prestigious college or university is highly valued in U.S. society, as evinced by the extensive discussion around two high-profile U.S. Supreme Court cases regarding the use of affirmative action at the University of Michigan and the University of Texas. Considerable research has explored whether two commonly used indicators of institutional "quality"—selectivity and faculty-student ratio—predict greater degree attainment. Relevant studies often measure selectivity using the average SAT or ACT score among entering first-year students, a widely available measure for four-year institutions. Overall, we find that attending a more selective institution notably increases the probability of bachelor's degree attainment. Alon and Tienda (2005) explored this issue using three large datasets, two of which contain nationally representative populations of K–12 students (High School and Beyond [HS&B] and National Education Longitudinal Study [NELS]) and a third that included only students at selective colleges and universities (College and Beyond [C&B]). Alon and Tienda used several different analyses to match students on the probability of their attending a selective institution, including multiple measures of social class, high school characteristics, and academic preparation, along with race, sex, region, and athletic participation. Attending a selective institution is associated with a greater likelihood of graduation within all analyses and datasets; these estimates vary considerably across samples, ranging from fairly modest (5–7 percentage points in the selective C&B dataset) to fairly large (18 percentage points in the HS&B dataset) to somewhere in the middle (11–12 percentage points in NELS). The latter two estimates are consistent with Melguizo's (2008) finding of 13 to 15 percentage points for attending a college that is within the three top Barron's selectivity categories relative to attending the least selective four-year institutions. Thus, as Long (2008) states succinctly, "There is solid evidence of positive effects of college quality on college graduation" (p. 588).

This effect may be at least partially explained by higher social and academic engagement at more selective schools. Virtually all researchers that do not include student involvement in their statistical models has found positive effects of institutional selectivity on graduation, even when controlling for a range of institutional and student attributes (Adelman, 2006; Brand & Halaby, 2006; Chen & St. John, 2011; Cragg, 2009; Gansemer-Topf & Schuh, 2006; Ishitani, 2006; Kim, Rhoades, & Woodard, 2003; Long, 2008; Melguizo, 2008, 2010; Melguizo & Dowd, 2009; Oseguera, 2005; Oseguera & Rhee, 2009; Ryan, 2004; Schudde, 2011; Scott, Bailey, & Kienzl, 2006; Shin, 2010; Smith, 2013;

Webber & Ehrenberg, 2010; Wilson, 2007; Zhang, 2009). A quantitative meta-analysis of institutional selectivity and retention observed a mean bivariate correlation of .20 across six studies that contained 11,482 students (Robbins et al., 2004). In fact, having a test score that is higher than the vast majority of other students within one's college or university is associated with lower persistence (Niu & Tienda, 2013) and graduation (Cragg, 2009); this finding is consistent with benefits of attending more selective schools. Conversely, studies that include measures of campus involvement as independent variables typically do not detect any significant relationship for selectivity predicting persistence and graduation (Chen, 2012; Fischer, 2007; Li, 2010; Lohfink & Paulsen, 2005; Schreiner & Nelson, 2013; Titus, 2006a, 2006b). These patterns are fairly consistent regardless of students' race/ethnicity (Alon & Tienda, 2005; Fischer, 2007; Melguizo, 2008), first-generation status (Lohfink & Paulsen, 2005), and institutional type (research/doctoral, master's, and liberal arts; Zhang, 2009).

Within studies that examine several enrollment outcomes, students who attend selective institutions are less likely to transfer than those at less selective schools (Allen, Robbins, Casillas, & Oh, 2008; Goldrick-Rab & Pfeffer, 2009; Kalogrides & Grodsky, 2011). This lack of transfer may also be explained by greater social and academic engagement at selective institutions. In addition, institutional selectivity is related positively to institutional financial resources; as a result, selective institutions may provide better support services for their students, which may also contribute to retention (versus transfer or dropout).

Moreover, selectivity appears to have a nonlinear relationship with educational attainment. Although the specific selectivity categories differ somewhat across studies, the effect of attending one of the most selective institutions is similar to the next highest level of selectivity, with much of the drop-off occurring for less selective and nonselective institutions (Melguizo, 2008, 2010; Smith, 2013; Titus, 2006a, 2006b). Consistent with this view, Alon and Tienda (2005) found the smallest effects of selectivity when examining the College and Beyond dataset, which consists entirely of selective institutions.

In addition to institutional selectivity, a second common indicator of "quality" is the student-faculty ratio. This figure is often reported and used on institutional websites and in college rankings and listings. The assumption is that attending an institution with a lower student-faculty ratio (i.e., a large number of faculty members relative to the number of students) will result in a better undergraduate experience as a result of increased faculty-student interaction, a decreased workload for faculty (which would therefore leave more time to devote to effective teaching), or both. Attending an institution with a more favorable student-faculty ratio appears to result in a greater likelihood of graduation. Long (2008) used the National Education Longitudinal Study to explore the likelihood of earning a bachelor's degree when controlling for various demographics, family characteristics, high school characteristics, precollege achievement indicators, and neighborhood characteristics. He also used several different quasi-experimental analyses to remove the potential impact of self-selection as indicated by various student characteristics. Overall, a 1 standard deviation improvement in student-faculty ratio was associated with a 6 to 9 percentage point increase in graduation, and attending a four-year institution in the top 25% of student-faculty ratio was associated with a 13 to 19 percentage point increase relative to attending a four-year school in the bottom 25%.

These estimates may be somewhat high, as they did not adjust for any other institutional attributes. Studies that included other institutional predictors found positive results for student-faculty ratio predicting graduation rates at community colleges (Jacoby, 2006) and doctoral universities (Goenner & Snaith, 2004) and for bachelor's degree attainment among Black students (Wilson, 2007). In contrast, Scott et al. (2006) did not find that student-faculty ratio significantly predicted six-year graduation rates. Chen (2012) also found no significant effect of student-faculty ratio on dropout when including academic integration and college GPA (along with various other student and institutional variables) as additional predictors, but these two academic variables predicted a lower chance of dropout. Thus, a more favorable student-faculty ratio may provide greater opportunities for academic engagement and achievement, which may then lead to improved educational attainment.

Overall, both institutional selectivity and faculty-student ratio are related positively to degree attainment, with the more consistent and robust findings occurring for selectivity. It should be briefly noted that more indirect proxies for quality are unrelated to educational attainment and success (e.g., faculty salary, tuition; Hoffman & Oreopoulos, 2009b; Long, 2008).

Institutional Expenditures and Resources. In an era of economic scarcity for many colleges and universities, the appropriate allocation of institutional financial resources has become especially important. A number of studies have explored the relationship between various types of institutional expenditures and educational attainment. To adjust for the link between institutional size and expenditures, most research has examined the expenditures either per full-time-equivalent (FTE) student or as a percentage of total expenditures.

Overall, the available evidence suggests that institutional expenditures may have some effects on degree attainment at four-year institutions (albeit with some inconsistency in the results) but virtually no effect at two-year institutions. In one notable study, Webber (2012) explored whether changes in the amount of an institution's expenditures in several areas predicted changes in graduation among students attending four-year Ohio public institutions; this examination of within-institution change helps avoid concerns that institutions differ in many ways other than their expenditures. The analyses of about 95,000 undergraduates also accounted for a variety of student characteristics, including race/ethnicity, gender, age, test scores, and undergraduate major. As expected, changes in instructional expenditures (e.g., for faculty and teaching) predicted graduation; for each additional $100 per FTE student that an institution spent on instructional expenditures, the probability of graduation increased by 3.9 percentage points. These relationships were especially pronounced for students with above-average ACT scores (6.5 percentage points) and for science, technology, engineering, and mathematics (STEM) majors (7.7 percentage points). Increased expenditures on student services (e.g., student affairs and registrar) did not significantly predict graduation for the entire sample, but they did predict improvements among students with below-average ACT scores (4.1 percentage points per additional $100 per FTE student). These less-prepared students may obtain greater benefits because they either receive more of these services or they exhibit greater gains from the same amount of experience with student services. No significant relationships were found for academic support (e.g., libraries and academic computing).

Some types of instructional expenditures were related positively to institutional retention and graduation rates in several additional studies (Gansemer-Topf & Schuh, 2006; Ryan, 2004; Scott et al., 2006; Webber & Ehrenberg, 2010), but research that used student-level data from the Beginning Postsecondary Students Longitudinal Study (BPS:96/01) found no significant relationships (Chen, 2012; Titus, 2006a, 2006b, 2006c). The latter studies included student variables that may explain the link between instructional expenditures and degree attainment (e.g., college GPA, academic integration and involvement), which may reflect indirect effects. Moreover, institutional grants (i.e., for student financial aid) are positively associated with graduation in institution-level analyses (Gansemer-Topf & Schuh, 2006) but not in student-level analyses (Titus, 2006a, 2006b, 2006c).

As with instructional expenditures, Titus's analyses control for multiple variables that likely account for at least part of the relationship between institutional expenditures on grants and degree completion, including unmet financial need, hours spent working, and socioeconomic status. Administrative expenditures (e.g., for administration and legal services) are negatively related to graduation in some research (Gansemer-Topf & Schuh, 2006; Titus, 2006c), but these are nonsignificant elsewhere (Ryan, 2004; Titus, 2006a, 2006b). Research expenditures are generally unrelated to graduation when using a traditional level of statistical significance ($p < .05$; Kim et al., 2003; Titus, 2006a, 2006b, 2006c; Webber & Ehrenberg, 2010).

The picture is even murkier for student services and for academic support. Some studies found positive associations between student services expenditures and institutional retention and graduation (Chen, 2012; Webber, 2012; Webber & Ehrenberg, 2010), while others found no significant link with attainment (Ryan, 2004; Titus, 2006a, 2006b, 2006c), and Gansemer-Topf and Schuh (2006) found a negative relationship. Chen's study may be particularly noteworthy, as she observed a relationship between student services and a reduced likelihood of dropout even when controlling for key explanatory factors, including students' college grades and their academic and social integration into the university. For academic support, some evidence suggests a positive relationship (Gansemer-Topf & Schuh, 2006; Ryan, 2004), but other studies have found no overall effect (Chen, 2012; Webber & Ehrenberg, 2010), and Webber's (2012) rigorous examination of changes in expenditures found no significant results within the whole sample or for various student subgroups. Both student services and academic support may contribute to degree attainment, but more evidence is needed.

It is perhaps not surprising that four-year institutions' total expenditures are often positively related to graduation when accounting for various other predictors (Goenner & Snaith, 2004; Morrison, 2012; Titus, 2006a, 2006b, 2006c), since schools with more resources are likely in a much better position to address the needs and interests of a variety of students. However, the total amount of expenditures, as well as the type of expenditure, has virtually no impact on the outcomes of community college students (Bailey, Calcagno, Jenkins, Leinbach, & Kienzl, 2006; Bailey, Jeong, & Cho, 2010; Calcagno, Bailey, Jenkins, Kienzl, & Leinbach, 2008; Clotfelter, Ladd, Muschkin, & Vigdor, 2013). This lack of relationship may occur because many community college students do not intend to obtain a degree. In addition, community colleges generally have much more modest financial resources available to them than do four-year institutions, so there may be limited variation in these institutional expenditures with which to explain student outcomes.

Tuition. Rising tuition costs have received a great deal of public attention and scrutiny. Over the past 40 years, the inflation-adjusted total for tuition and fees has more than tripled at four-year public and private nonprofit institutions, and this figure is now about two and a half times larger at public two-year institutions (College Board, 2014). While the increased cost of college may be a substantial barrier to college attendance, the research strongly suggests that tuition does not affect the persistence and degree attainment of students who are already enrolled in college.

Tandberg and Hillman (2014) examined the extent to which changes in a state's public tuition predict changes in bachelor's degree completion. Because they used a panel analysis to explore variation over time, their results controlled for all differences that exist across state public higher education systems. Changes in the public in-state tuition at four-year and at two-year schools were unrelated to bachelor's and associate's degree completion. Conducting an institution-level fixed-effects panel analysis, Zhang (2009) also found that changes in in-state tuition and fees were unrelated to changes in six-year graduation rates at four-year public universities; subgroup analyses found this nonsignificant pattern was consistent regardless of institutional type and level of state funding.

The vast majority of additional studies have identified no significant relationship between tuition and educational attainment (Bailey et al., 2006, 2010; Calcagno, Crosta, Bailey, & Jenkins, 2007a, 2007b; Calcagno et al., 2008; Chen & St. John, 2011; Dowd & Coury, 2006; Mamiseishvili, 2012; Titus, 2006a; Ver Ploeg, 2002; Wilson, 2007). The research that has identified significant relationships for tuition has mostly used institution-level data, and these find inconsistent results across analyses within the same study (Jacoby, 2006; Long, 2008; Porchea, Allen, Robbins, & Phelps, 2010; Scott et al., 2006; Shin, 2010). In fact, most of the occasional significant findings indicate that tuition is positively associated with persistence and attainment. These positive results probably occur because these models insufficiently account for differences across institutions and students. Consistent with this explanation, both Zhang (2009) and Tandberg and Hillman (2014) also found significant positive relationships before they implemented fixed-effects analyses.

The strong evidence for a lack of influence of tuition may be surprising given the seemingly intuitive role that finances play in educational decision making. However, the extent to which students pay for some or all of the stated tuition price varies dramatically both within and across institutions. Therefore, although there is seemingly no effect of tuition, net price (i.e., how much students actually pay for their enrollment) may affect retention and persistence. In addition, tuition may strongly influence students' decisions about which college to attend or whether to attend college at all, whereas the studies reviewed here almost exclusively examine whether students who have already enrolled in college progress in their degrees.

Institutional Racial and Gender Characteristics. Minority-serving institutions have long played an important role in educating students from marginalized racial and ethnic groups. Most research on this topic has examined Historically Black Colleges and Universities (HBCUs).

We find that students attending HBCUs fare at least as well as those at predominantly White institutions in terms of degree attainment. To explore this issue, Wilson (2007) examined two nationally representative samples (one collected earlier and one more recently) of African American students who attended an HBCU or another institution. She used several statistical techniques and various precollege control variables, including gender, family income, parental education, two-parent household, SAT/ACT score, high school GPA, and state economic indicators. In virtually all analyses, HBCU attendance was unrelated to stop out and six-year graduation; the lone exception was that students starting at HBCUs in the early 1980s were 5.5 percentage points more likely to graduate than those attending other institutions. In contrast, no significant effect was apparent for students starting in the mid-1990s.

Other studies predicting graduation and persistence have obtained mixed results, with some obtaining positive results for HBCU attendance (Bailey et al., 2006; Ryan, 2004; Webber & Ehrenberg, 2010), and others finding no relationship (Kim & Conrad, 2006; Lohfink & Paulsen, 2005; Titus, 2006c). Sibulkin and Butler (2005) conducted analyses separately by gender and observed a positive association for black women but not for black men. Moreover, the very limited amount of research on other types of minority-serving institutions has found no link between attending a tribal college and community college graduation rates (Bailey et al., 2006) or Hispanic-serving institutions and persistence within a STEM major (Chang, Cerna, Han, & Saenz, 2008). Attending a single-sex college is also unrelated to graduation (Kim & Conrad, 2006). In making sense of their results and others, Kim and Conrad show that HBCUs are underfunded relative to other four-year institutions, so they argue that HBCUs are effective in promoting degree attainment, since they achieve similar or better graduation outcomes with less funding.

Other research has examined the proportion of female students and students from various racial/ethnic groups. Because black, Hispanic, and American Indian students have lower graduation rates than White students (e.g., Radford, Berkner, Wheeless, & Shepherd, 2010), it is not surprising that the proportion of students of color, along with the proportions of students from each of these three racial minority groups, is often negatively related to institutional graduation rates (Cragg, 2009; Ehrenberg & Zhang, 2005; Jacoby, 2006; Morrison, 2012; Ryan, 2004; Scott et al., 2006; Webber & Ehrenberg, 2010). Although women graduate at a higher rate than men (Radford et al., 2010), the proportion of women has an inconsistent relationship with graduation rates in institutional analyses (Bailey et al., 2006; Calcagno et al., 2008; Cragg, 2009; Scott et al., 2006; Webber & Ehrenberg, 2010).

To determine whether the student body composition affects attainment above and beyond students' characteristics, data from individual students are needed to fully understand this dynamic. However, such research yields inconsistent results. Most studies that simply examine the percentage of students of color and attrition/graduation have found no association (Chen, 2012; Gross, Torres, & Zerquera, 2013; Robbins, Allen, Casillas, Peterson, & Le, 2006), a negative association (Kim et al., 2003), or a mix between the two (Jaeger & Eagan, 2009; Schreiner & Nelson, 2013). In contrast, Titus (2006a) found that an index that accounts for the heterogeneity among several racial/ethnic groups is positively related to three-year persistence, and Porchea et al. (2010) found that the percentage of students of color is associated with greater retention (versus dropout) among community college students. The findings using student-level data for the proportion of women are also decidedly mixed (Kim et al., 2003; Schreiner & Nelson, 2013; Titus, 2006a).

To better understand these representation effects, the more important issue may be the alignment between student body characteristics and students' own identities. As Gurin (1999) and others have argued, students of color may particularly benefit from attending college with a critical mass of fellow students so that they are less likely to feel isolated or tokenized on campus. Some limited evidence supports this assertion. Oseguera (2005) examined a broad range of precollege variables, college plans, and institutional attributes as predictors of six-year graduation among students from several racial/ethnic groups. She found that the proportion of Asian students predicted a greater likelihood of Asian students' graduation in all models, and the proportion of Hispanic students was associated with greater graduation rates for Mexican and Black students in most models. However, this study used a stepwise regression procedure that sometimes entered highly correlated variables into the same analysis (e.g., overall proportion of students of color and proportions of Hispanic and Asian students), which makes it difficult to interpret the findings. In addition, Garcia (2013) found that the proportion of Latino students and Latino faculty and staff was unrelated to Latino graduation rates, but this paper examined only institution-level effects and included few control variables.

Institutional Location. Urbanicity, which describes the geographical location of the institution, is typically used as a control variable in educational attainment research. Drawing conclusions about urbanicity is complicated both because the term is defined differently across studies and the amount of research literature is modest. Given the contradictory and often nonsignificant findings, it appears that urbanicity may be unrelated to attainment when controlling for other relevant predictors. Within the California community college system, urbanicity is unrelated to associate's degree completion (Jaeger & Eagan, 2009), but students attending rural campuses are less likely than those at suburban campuses to transfer to a four-year institution (Eagan & Jaeger, 2009).

Within a sample of 28 highly selective institutions, Fischer (2007) found that attending an institution within a city is inversely related to persistence for White students but not for Asian American, Hispanic/Latino, or black/African American students. This finding broaches the possibility that urbanicity may interact with other student characteristics in shaping attainment, but this single result is insufficient to draw strong conclusions. Institution-level analyses predicting graduation rates yield mixed findings; these sometimes show no significant differences by urbanicity (Calcagno et al., 2008; Jacoby, 2006); lower rates for urban schools than for suburban schools, with no differences between suburban and rural institutions (Bailey et al., 2006); or higher rates for urban public schools than for nonurban public schools (Scott et al., 2006). In sum, the lack of consistent results makes this relationship ambiguous.

Institution Size. Institution size is often defined in terms of the number of undergraduate students or the number of FTE undergraduates (adjusting for the fact that part-time attendees take fewer classes). Overall, size appears to have no unique effect on educational attainment, although there is some possibility of a small negative effect at two-year institutions. Offering perhaps the best support for a (modest) negative relationship, Jaeger and Eagan (2009) examined associate's degree completion within five years using statewide unit-record data for California community college students whose stated intentions and course-taking patterns evinced a strong desire to obtain this degree. Their multilevel analyses controlled for various student characteristics (race, gender, age, citizenship, financial aid, major, part-time attendance, grades, course work with part-time faculty) and institutional characteristics (state and local revenues, campus urbanicity, representation of students of color, and part-time faculty). Multiple models identified significant, negative relationships between the number of FTE students and associate's degree completion, but this effect was small (0.2 percentage points per 100 FTE students).

Most studies that examined institution-level data obtained negative relationships for size and community college graduation or transfer rates (Bailey et al., 2006; Calcagno et al., 2008; Jacoby, 2006), but others found no relationship

(Clotfelter et al., 2013) or a mix of nonsignificant and positive results (Wassmer, Moore, & Shulock, 2004). In addition, most studies that examined student data at two-year institutions found no significant effect on transfer, retention, and persistence (Eagan & Jaeger, 2009; Niu & Tienda, 2013; Robbins et al., 2006), along with occasional positive effects on successful remediation and transfer (Bailey et al., 2010; Porchea et al., 2010). As Ro, Terenzini, and Yin (2013) argued, distal institutional factors may exhibit indirect effects on student outcomes through their impact on student experiences. In this instance, students at smaller institutions may be likely to have more frequent and meaningful engagement with faculty and fellow students. However, Ro et al. found little support for this assertion in terms of size predicting several forms of student engagement. Moreover, the student-level analyses in the studies already noted generally did not include such predictors in their models; the student variables instead largely consisted of precollege characteristics, including demographics, high school experiences, and noncognitive attributes.

At four-year colleges and universities, the bulk of the evidence suggests no significant relationship between institutional size and persistence and graduation (Allen et al., 2008; Chen, 2010; Cragg, 2009; Fischer, 2007; Goenner & Snaith, 2004; Niu & Tienda, 2013; Oseguera, 2005; Oseguera & Rhee, 2009; Robbins et al., 2006; Robbins, Lauver, Le, Davis, Langley, & Carlstrom, 2004; Titus, 2006a, 2006c). The studies that do find significant effects are mixed between relationships that are positive (Lohfink & Paulsen, 2005; Morrison, 2012; Ryan, 2004; Scott et al., 2006) and negative (Ishitani & DesJardins, 2002; Kim & Conrad, 2006; Li, 2010). In sum, institutional size appears to have little to no effect on educational progress and attainment.

Institutional Control and Type. When accounting for other institutional and student attributes, attending a public institution is associated with similar transfer behavior, retention, persistence, and graduation as attending a private institution (Byun, Irvin, & Meece, 2012; Chen, 2012; Chen & DesJardins, 2008, 2010; Chen & St. John, 2011; Goldrick-Rab & Pfeffer, 2009; Ishitani & DesJardins, 2002; Kim & Conrad, 2006; Li, 2010; Melguizo, 2008; Melguizo & Dowd, 2009; Niu & Tienda, 2013; Novak & McKinney, 2011; Oseguera & Rhee, 2009; Rhee, 2008; Robbins et al., 2006; Schreiner & Nelson, 2013; Schudde, 2011; Somers, Woodhouse, & Cofer, 2004; Stratton et al., 2007, 2008; Titus, 2006c; Wilson, 2007). Some occasional studies have shown statistically significant relationships, but these findings are mixed among general student populations (Cragg, 2009; Dwyer, McCloud, & Hodson, 2012; Morrison, 2012; Titus, 2006a) and even among first-generation students (Ishitani, 2006; Lohfink & Paulsen, 2005). Scott et al. (2006) explored the attributes of public and private institutions in some detail. Within a sample of 1,621 four-year institutions, they noted that private colleges have higher unadjusted graduation rates than public colleges (57% versus 45%, respectively), but this disparity is explained primarily by differences in student characteristics. That is, private colleges tend to have students with greater academic preparation as well as lower proportions of student groups who generally have lower graduation rates (commuters, nontraditional age, men, racial minorities, and part-time students). In short, students do graduate at higher rates at private than at public institutions, but this pattern is explained by factors other than institutional control itself.

Other forms of institutional type have received less empirical attention, including religious affiliation, research emphasis, and degrees offered or emphasized. The few studies of institutional religious affiliation have been mixed, finding no significant effect (Ryan, 2004), an overall positive effect of attending religiously affiliated institution (Scott et al., 2006), or inconsistent effects that depend on students' race and the control variables in the analysis (Oseguera, 2006). As described later in more detail, any potential impact of religious affiliation may be explained through the fit between student and institutional beliefs (see Morris, Beck, & Mattis, 2007; Morris, Beck, & Smith, 2004; Morris, Smith, & Cejda, 2003; Patten & Rice, 2009).

Summarizing the results of the remaining type indicators is complicated by the use of divergent definitions of institutional type and choice of outcomes. For instance, among certificate or associate's degree-granting institutions, Bailey et al. (2006) found that certificate degree-oriented colleges and technical colleges had higher graduation rates than those that focus on associate's degrees, whereas Wassmer et al. (2004) found that the proportion of degrees awarded in general studies or liberal arts/sciences (i.e., nonapplied programs) was sometimes positively related to the proportion of students transferring to a four-year institution. This apparent discrepancy probably occurs because these latter two-year degree programs are often intended to prepare students to obtain a four-year degree (and therefore upward transfer), whereas the certificate-focused and technical colleges are preparing students for shorter-term credentials (they plan to receive only that degree). Consistent with this assertion, students attending two-year vocational-technical colleges are more likely to obtain a degree without transferring than those at two-year junior or community colleges (Porchea et al., 2010). Among four-year institutions, attending a doctoral or research-intensive university is sometimes associated with greater persistence and graduation, but this finding varies within and across studies (Gross et al., 2013; Madgett & Belanger, 2008; Somers et al., 2004; St. John, Hu, Simmons, Carter, & Weber, 2004; St. John, Musoba, & Simmons, 2003). These findings may also be explained by differences in institutional selectivity, which was not included as a predictor within this research.

State Policies and Resource Allocations. Although most between-college effects are associated with specific institutional attributes, state policies and resources may also shape educational attainment, particularly for public institutions. The two policies discussed here are explicitly designed to increase degree completion at specific colleges and universities and for the state as a whole: articulation agreements and performance-based accountability.

Articulation policies are generally intended to allow students to transfer coursework from a public two-year college to a public four-year institution (and sometimes among two-year and among four-year institutions) with little or no loss of credits in this transition. In theory, such policies could reduce the time to degree (since students would not need to retake courses that did not transfer successfully) and improve graduation rates (since students will have a shorter and more direct path to satisfying degree requirements). Although articulation agreements can occur between two institutions, the research described here examined whether state-level articulation policies predict baccalaureate degree completion. Through several studies exploring this issue, Roksa found no evidence that articulation policies improve bachelor's degree attainment. For instance, Roksa (2010) used a nationally representative sample of college students and controlled for a variety of student characteristics (demographics, academic preparation, family attributes, timing and continuity of college enrollment) and state contextual variables (level and types of funding, type of governing board, economic indicators, and geographic region). Attending college in a state with an articulation policy was not related to bachelor's degree attainment. These nonsignificant findings are also replicated when restricting the sample to students who transferred from a two-year to a four-year institution (Roksa, 2006; Roksa & Keith, 2008), predicting associate's degree attainment or transfer to a four-year school (Roksa, 2006), and primarily focusing on state-level patterns (Roksa, 2009).

Another increasingly prevalent state policy is the use of performance funding, which often employs six-year graduation rate as a key indicator of institutional success. These policies base the state budget allocation to a public university, in part or in whole, on one or more measures of institutional performance. The logic is that these strong incentives will encourage institutions to take greater and more effective steps to improve their outcomes. However, the few studies of this policy suggest that these funding policies have little or no impact on institutional graduation rates.

Tandberg and Hillman (2014) examined a 20-year period during which some states enacted performance funding policies and others did not; the consideration of this time frame allowed them to explore whether the implementation of performance-based funding led to subsequent increases in bachelor's degrees at public colleges and universities in those states. After accounting for other state-level changes in higher education attributes, economics, and demographics, they found no overall main effect of introducing performance-based funding on bachelor's degrees awarded. More detailed analyses found that performance funding was positively related to degree completions in the seventh, eighth, and eleventh years after implementation of this policy. While it is unclear why these particular years exhibit positive effects, the results suggest that institutional efforts to improve graduation in response to performance funding may take quite a while to realize benefits, if such benefits occur at all. Shin (2010) also found that performance funding had small yet significant effects on institutional graduation rates, whereas studies with smaller sample sizes found no significant results (Sanford & Hunter, 2011; Shin & Milton, 2004).

A final topic pertains not to a specific policy, but to whether the amount and type of state funding affects degree completion. Overall, the research suggests that state funding for higher education is positively related to bachelor's degree attainment, and supporting need-based aid may be a particularly effective form of support. In a noteworthy analysis, Titus (2009) examined whether changes in state funding predict changes in the number of bachelor's degrees awarded per enrolled student. This analysis controlled for a variety of potential confounding state-level factors, including tuition rates, enrollment at public and private colleges, per capita spending on K–12 education and other areas, and economic indicators. Increases in both the amounts of state per-capita appropriations for higher education and the "need-based aid per undergraduate enrollment [have] a positive ... influence on bachelor's degree production within a state" (p. 456). Zhang (2009) and Shin (2010) also found that increased state appropriations per FTE student received by a public four-year institution are associated with improved six-year graduation rates. Analyses of student-level data that control for student attributes, as well as state and institutional characteristics, provide support for the positive role of state funding for higher education generally and financial aid specifically (Chen & St. John, 2011; Jaeger & Eagan, 2009; Roksa, 2010; Titus, 2006b). These findings are consistent with the apparent impact of overall institutional expenditures noted earlier and the receipt of need-based aid discussed later.

WITHIN-COLLEGE EFFECTS

Similar to the reviews of Pascarella and Terenzini (1991, 2005), we found that the between-college effects are generally quite modest in size or non-significant (with a couple of notable exceptions for attending a four-year college and institutional selectivity). This finding is also consistent with Berger and Milem's (2000) theoretical framework, which posits that the link between institutional characteristics and student outcomes is mediated by student experiences and peer group characteristics. In other words, the effects of between-college attributes on educational attainment (among other outcomes) are largely explained by differences in students' within-college experiences and perceptions. Therefore, considering the variation that occurs within institutions (and types of institutions) is critical to understanding the factors that may affect retention, persistence, and graduation. Given the massive volume of literature in this area, we have divided this portion into several domains of within-college effects that are generally the same as previous volumes of *How College Affects Students*: academic performance, programmatic interventions, financial aid, experiences with faculty members, interactions with peers, residence, learning communities, academic major, and general academic and social integration/involvement.

Academic Performance

College grades do not necessarily indicate student learning during college or any objective level of achievement or mastery. Instead, grades are shaped by a variety of attributes, including students' own precollege academic preparation, motivation, innate ability, and cultural capital; students' performance relative to that of their peers (especially when courses are graded on a curve); instructors' teaching performance, preferences, and biases; and the fit between the learning and teaching styles of students and instructors. However, grades are the primary means through which instructors offer quantifiable feedback on student performance and therefore students can make judgments about their academic performance (and perhaps ability). Moreover, grades are a high-stakes form of individual assessment, since they can be used for awarding academic honors, placing students on academic probation or dismissing them, and informing graduate schools and employers about student performance. As a result, the relationship between grades and educational attainment has been frequently examined.

Pascarella and Terenzini (2005) concluded that college academic achievement was the strongest within-college predictor of educational attainment. Our study also supports this conclusion, as college grades are consistently and strongly related to retention, persistence, and graduation in both national and single institutional studies. Grades are associated with educational attainment even in research that controls for a broad array of precollege attributes (including high school GPA and high school strength of curriculum), between-college attributes (such as institutional selectivity), and college experiences and perceptions (both academic and social in nature). This finding is consistent for different groups of students and institutions; specifically, the relationships between college GPA and attainment are at least as strong for first-generation as for continuing-generation students (Lohfink & Paulsen, 2005; Somers et al., 2004); for Asian American, Black, and Latino students as for White students (Baker & Robnett, 2012; Hausmann, Ye, Schofield, & Woods, 2009; St. John, Paulsen, & Carter, 2005); and at four-year colleges as at two-year colleges (Allen & Robbins, 2010; Arbona & Nora, 2007). Results are also similar regardless of the urbanicity of students' precollege environments (Byun et al., 2012) and students' in-state residency status (Singell & Waddell, 2010). Additional research also observed positive relationships in online courses (Cochran, Campbell, Baker, & Leeds, 2014; Dupin Bryant, 2004; Harrell & Bower, 2011), for international students at U.S. institutions (Mamiseishvili, 2012), and at Canadian universities (Wintre & Bowers, 2007). Moreover, although Pascarella and Terenzini (2005) found some evidence that the link between grades and retention/persistence is stronger in the first year than in subsequent years, more recent studies suggest that these relationships are similar regardless of students' year in college (DesJardins, McCall, Ahlberg, & Moye, 2002; Ishitani, 2003, 2008; Schreiner & Nelson, 2013; St. John et al., 2003).

What exactly drives this strong relationship between grades and educational attainment? One possible mechanism is that low grades can lead to academic dismissal. Consistent with that explanation, students with low grades are much less likely to persist or graduate than those with average grades, whereas the difference between students with average versus high grades is much more modest (Chen & DesJardins, 2008; Ishitani & DesJardins, 2002; Somers et al., 2004; St. John et al., 2003, 2005; Stratton et al., 2008). An upward trend in grades is also associated with an increased probability of graduation (Adelman, 2006), which suggests that students who start with low grades and improve can pull themselves into good academic standing and therefore be more likely to graduate.

Involuntary academic dismissals, however, cannot explain differences in the likelihood of graduation between students with average and high college grades. Instead, Stinebrickner and Stinebrickner (2012) posit that students receive feedback on their academic skills through their grades, and the resulting changes in self-perceptions of their own skills inform retention and persistence decisions. These authors conducted a simulation study with a single institutional sample that explored the relationships of grades, changes in self-perceptions of academic ability, and dropout; they find that "dropout between the first and second years would be reduced by 40% if no learning occurred about grade performance/academic ability" (p. 707). Other studies provide indirect support for this assertion. For instance, Hu, McCormick, and Gonyea (2012) show that students' self-reported gains during college and their college grades each uniquely predict retention, which suggests that both the perceptions of growth (as indicated by a composite of self-reported gains in various areas) and performance (as indicated by grades) may be important.

In contrast, objective measures of growth on several constructs, such as critical thinking and need for cognition, are generally unrelated to retention when controlling for other variables (Hu et al., 2012; Wolniak, Mayhew, & Engberg, 2012). Students with lower GPAs are more likely to transfer from a four-year school to a two-year school (Goldrick-Rab & Pfeffer, 2009; Kalogrides & Grodsky, 2011), which implies that lower-performing students may feel that they would benefit from moving to a less academically competitive campus. Overall, lower grades are associated with a greater chance of leaving one's current institution; this relationship is even stronger for dropping out completely than for transferring or stopping out temporarily (Allen et al., 2008; Herzog, 2005; Kalogrides & Grodsky, 2011; Stratton et al., 2008).

Programmatic Interventions

Pascarella and Terenzini (2005) found positive effects for four types of academic interventions: remediation, supplemental instruction, first-year seminars, and comprehensive retention and support programs. We review recent literature on remediation and first-year seminars, along with student services (including supplemental instruction and comprehensive retention programs that make use of such services). Relative to prior reviews, the evidence since 2002 provides somewhat weaker support for the potential impact of these interventions (with the notable exception of comprehensive programs).

Remediation. Students often enter postsecondary institutions without having obtained sufficient academic preparation in one or more areas (e.g., math, reading, and writing). Some estimates suggest that over two-thirds of students entering two-year colleges and 40% of those entering open-access four-year colleges take at least one remedial (also known as developmental) course, and many more students need remediation but do not enroll in these courses (Jaggars & Stacey, 2014). Therefore, the efficacy of remediation in preparing students to continue and succeed in college-level course work is critically important. Determining the causal impact of remediation is quite difficult, because enrolling in a remedial course by definition means that a student is underprepared for college and therefore less likely to graduate. As a result, research risks underestimating the effects of remediation, since it is difficult to disentangle eligibility for remediation from any potential benefits of taking remedial courses. Therefore, quasi-experimental methods are particularly important for understanding these relationships.

Jaggars and Stacey (2014) systematically reviewed eight rigorous studies of community college students to provide insights from research whose designs might provide the strongest causal conclusions. All but one of these studies used regression discontinuity analyses that compared students who were just below or above the cutoff for needing remediation, while the other study used instrumental variable analyses to determine causal effects. Although this review has the substantial strength of examining only quasi-experimental research, its primary drawback is that most of these studies have not undergone a rigorous peer-reviewed journal publication process, since they are working papers (Boatman & Long, 2013; Calcagno & Long, 2008; Scott-Clayton & Rodríguez, 2012), dissertations (Dadgar, 2012; Xu, 2013), or book chapters (Bettinger & Long, 2005). Across a variety of desired outcomes (persistence, passing the corresponding college-level course, total credits earned, and transferring to a four-year institution), most of the observed relationships for remediation are nonsignificant, and significant negative effects of remediation are more prevalent than significant positive effects.

Published quasi-experimental research of remediation that includes students at four-year institutions (and therefore not eligible for inclusion in the prior systematic review) offers somewhat more favorable results, although these are still mixed. In Bettinger and Long's (2009) study that uses instrumental variable analyses, students at Ohio public institutions who take remedial coursework are more likely to drop out during their first year than those who do not, but they are ultimately less likely to drop out after five years and more likely to receive a bachelor's degree.

At a single public university, Lesik's (2007) regression discontinuity analyses suggest that students who take remedial math courses have greater retention than those who do not take such courses, and this relationship is similar in magnitude across several years of college. In contrast, propensity score analyses of a nationally representative dataset suggest that enrolling in either at least one or at least three remedial courses is associated with a lower chance of degree attainment at four-year institutions but not at two-year institutions (Attewell, Lavin, Domina, & Levey, 2006). Moreover, research that uses multiple regression or related statistical techniques to control for potential confounding variables consistently finds that remedial course work is either unrelated or negatively related to retention, persistence, and degree completion (Attewell, Heil, & Reisel, 2011; Calcagno et al., 2007; Dowd & Coury, 2006; Duggan, 2004; Gross et al., 2013; Herzog, 2005; Ishitani, 2006; Mamiseishvili, 2012; McKinney & Novak, 2012; Roksa, 2006, 2010; Somers et al., 2004; Wang, 2009).

Understanding the difficulties that remedial students face may be helpful in improving their educational attainment. Notably, community college students who were successfully remediated (i.e., they complete a college-level course in that subject) exhibit similar educational outcomes to students who never took remedial coursework (Bahr, 2008b, 2010b; also see Southard & Clay, 2004). Students who successfully finish their remedial coursework have high pass rates within the first college-level course in that subject, and these rates are similar regardless of the number of previous remedial courses taken (Bailey et al., 2010). However, the primary challenge is achieving successful progression through relevant coursework. Within a sample of over 250,000 first-time, credential-seeking students at 57 community colleges, only about half of the students who were referred to the most advanced remedial math or reading class successfully completed that course. Moreover, students who were referred to take three remedial courses were quite unlikely to complete the sequence successfully (29% for reading and 17% for math; Bailey et al., 2010; also see Bahr, 2007, 2010a, 2012).

Perhaps surprisingly, the low sequence completion rates identified by Bailey et al. (2010) are not primarily due to students' failing or withdrawing from remedial courses; instead, most noncompleters either did not enroll in any remedial coursework or did not enroll in a subsequent remedial course needed to complete the sequence. Furthermore, among the students who completed the remedial sequence, about one-third did not enroll in the initial college-level course for which they had been remediated. As a potential explanation for some of these patterns, Bahr (2012) found that some students tend to drop out after each successive semester, so the fact that students spend time taking remedial courses increases the time spent in college and therefore increases the likelihood of attrition. These challenges may be compounded by the presence of multiple skill deficiencies. According to Bahr's (2007) analysis of California community colleges, the likelihood of successful remediation in one subject is reduced even more if that student also needs remediation in a second subject.

If the research finds that remediation generally does not help students persist and graduate, then an important question remains: Are some approaches to remediation more successful than others? One intriguing experimental study examined an accelerated program that occurred at three institutions in the City University of New York (CUNY) system (Scrivener & Weiss, 2013). Community college students who needed one or two remedial courses and had low family incomes were randomly assigned to participate in the Accelerated Study in Associate Programs (ASAP) or regular coursework. Participation in ASAP had a number of requirements: students were required to enroll full time in coursework, take a noncredit ASAP seminar in their first year (which included topics such as goal setting and academic planning), register for block-scheduled classes in the first year (which often included the remedial course and the ASAP seminar), and meet regularly with an academic advisor and a career/employment counselor. Students were also encouraged to take their remedial courses early and to graduate with their associate's degree within three years. In exchange for participation, the services and benefits students received were also substantial. They worked with ASAP advisors who had much smaller caseloads of students, had tutors dedicated to the program, had any shortfall between their financial aid and their tuition and fees waived by the college, and received free public transportation and free textbooks (conditional on meeting program requirements).

The overall impact of this program was substantial. After the fourth semester, relative to students in the control group, ASAP students were about 10 percentage points more likely than to be enrolled at a CUNY institution, they had earned about eight additional credits, and they were about 6 percentage points more likely to have received a degree (14.5% versus 8.7%). Data on graduation rates after two and a half years were available for about one-third of the sample (i.e., students who had started their program earlier). The differences in associate degree attainment between ASAP and non-ASAP students were even more pronounced: 33.3% versus 18.2%. The following quotation nicely summarizes the significance of these results:

> To the authors' knowledge, ASAP's increases are larger than the effects of any other community college program that has been studied to date using a large-scale, rigorous experimental design. These findings provide some confirmation of a hypothesis suggested by earlier research: in order to *substantially* boost students' success, *comprehensive, extended* interventions may be needed. (Scrivener & Weiss, 2013, p. 9)

Other research provides support for some of the specific features of remedial coursework used in this intervention. The accelerated nature of the program is likely beneficial. As discussed later, full-time enrollment is a strong and consistent predictor of academic progress and attainment (e.g., Doyle, 2009b). Moreover, ASAP students' frequent enrollment in short-term intersession courses may have also been beneficial. Sheldon and Durdella (2010) examined the relationship between the length of remedial courses (a usual 15- to 18-week format versus condensed eight- to nine-week and five- to six-week versions) and the likelihood of passing the course. Although the analyses did not control for any differences in student populations, within-group comparisons showed large and substantially greater course completions when enrolling in short-term remedial courses regardless of students' gender, race/ethnicity, age, and GPA. These patterns were particularly large for English: 87% of students in eight- to nine-week courses received a passing grade, followed by 76% of those in five- to six-week courses and just 57% in traditional 15- to 18-week courses. It also appears that many students took remedial and college-level courses concurrently, which may also be beneficial.

Although Worley (2003) examined only descriptive statistics, she observed that students who enrolled concurrently in college-level and remedial courses earned far more credits over three years than students who enrolled in only remedial courses or students who placed into remediation but did not take any remedial courses. These patterns were similar regardless of the amount of remediation required. Enrolling early in the first remedial course also predicted a greater likelihood of remediation even when controlling for demographics, level of remediation needed, academic goals, remedial course grades, and other enrollment characteristics (Bahr, 2010a). The use of advising and comprehensive learning communities may also promote postsecondary attainment (e.g., Bahr, 2008a; Visher, Butcher, & Cerna, 2012). Finally, as discussed in detail later, the need-based financial aid in this program likely played a role as well (see Goldrick-Rab, Harris, & Troestel, 2009; Hossler, Ziskin, Gross, Kim, & Cekic, 2009; Welbeck, Diamond, Mayer, & Richburg-Hayes, 2014).

A noteworthy challenge for institutions that wish to offer some version of the ASAP program is the substantial time required of its students. People who need full-time employment to support their families would have difficulty attending this type of accelerated program. Indeed, the average age of students who entered the study was 21.5 years old; few participants were married or had children, and most lived with their parents (Scrivener & Weiss, 2013). As a result, this program may be less feasible for students who are older and have greater need to provide financial support to others. Of course, supporting this program financially also constitutes a barrier, since colleges and universities— or perhaps state or federal legislators—would have to provide substantial additional resources. An earlier version of this program was deemed cost effective in terms of the resources needed per college graduate (Levin & Garcia, 2012), so this approach may be more plausible in states that have performance-based funding models in which state support is partially or fully based on successful course and degree completion.

First-Year Seminars. Many institutions use first-year seminar courses (also referred to as first-year experience courses) as one means of helping students adjust to college academically and sometimes socially. The function and form of these courses (extending even to the number of credits offered) can vary considerably. Many first-year seminars specifically address knowledge and skills that may contribute to success, such as goal setting, study skills, campus resources, transition issues, and so on. Other courses focus on specific academic topics of interest, and sometimes these two functions are combined into a single course. Similar to student services, these are intended to promote successful college adjustment and ultimately educational attainment. In many cases, class sizes for these courses are small, especially relative to those in many introductory courses at large institutions.

An experimental study explored whether randomly assigning community college students to a first-year seminar was associated with a variety of positive outcomes (Rutschow, Cullinan, & Welbeck, 2012). This course focused not only on building academic skills, but also on addressing socioemotional needs through students' reflection about their past history and future goals as well as taking responsibility for their own learning. Although this student success course improved several desired learning outcomes among students who were initially low in these attributes (e.g., self-management, emotional intelligence, interdependence, orientation toward lifelong learning), it had no significant effect on credits attempted, credits earned, course pass rates, or retention. Supplemental analyses found some positive effects for only the first cohort in students' second semester, but virtually all of these benefits had vanished by the third postprogram semester.

Contrary to these non-significant results, several studies that carefully matched students on their precollege and entering characteristics (i.e., by conducting propensity score matching analyses) have generally found positive relationships for first-year seminar attendance. Clark and Cundiff (2011) used these analyses to compare students who did or did not take a first-year seminar course but were equally likely to have enrolled. This single-institution study matched students on an array of relevant variables, including high school grades, standardized test scores, motivation, institutional commitment, personality traits, mental health, and demographics. The first-year seminar had small class sizes and was intended to introduce students to both the academic and social life of the university. Within two different types of propensity score analyses, students who took this first-year seminar were more likely to return in their second year (although the results were only marginally significant in both analyses). In another examination of a first-year seminar at a medium-sized public university, Schnell and Doetkott (2003) matched students on a smaller number of variables (ACT scores, high school class rank, college major, and size of high school graduating class). They found that students who took the seminar were significantly more likely to be retained in each of their first four years of college than matched students who did not take the seminar. Tuckman and Kennedy (2011) also matched students on precollege variables (enrollment term, gender, ethnicity, age, high school class rank, standardized test scores) and found that students in the first-year seminar had higher retention and graduation than matched students who chose not to take it. Perhaps importantly, Rutschow et al.'s (2012) experimental study examined students at a two-year college, whereas the quasi-experimental studies all examined four-year institutions. As a result, it is unclear whether the disparate findings can be attributed to the research design, the institutional type, course content, or some other difference.

Studies that use multivariate analyses that are not quasi-experimental find a mix of positive and nonsignificant relationships (Hendel, 2007; Jamelske, 2009; Miller, Janz, & Chen, 2007; Schnell, Seashore Louis, & Doetkott, 2003; Singell & Waddell, 2010), as do studies that examine simple bivariate relationships between seminar participation and retention/graduation (Barton & Donahue, 2009; Lang, 2007). The link between seminars and attainment seems to be similar regardless of the type of course, such as focusing on general college transition versus a specific academic theme (Friedman & Marsh, 2009) or whether it has a residential component (Singell & Waddell, 2010). The two studies that examined graduation outcomes (as opposed to retention) both obtained significant, positive relationships (Lang, 2007; Schnell et al., 2003).

Robbins, Oh, Le, and Button (2009) conducted a meta-analytic review of the relationship between first-year experience courses and retention. Within their sample of 32 studies that contained 41,434 participants, they identified a significant, positive correlation between first-year experience and retention ($r = .095$). They also conducted meta-analytic path analyses to explore the extent to which this relationship is mediated or explained by three forms of student "control" or mastery: motivational (e.g., motivation, academic goals, institutional commitment), emotional (e.g., stress, self-efficacy, personal adjustment), and social (e.g., social support, social involvement). Part of the link between these seminars and retention is explained by motivational and social control, but a direct relationship persists even when including these variables. An important note of caution is that this quantitative meta-analysis used raw correlations, which do not adjust for student self-selection into these experiences or the potential impact of other college experiences. Therefore, these may be more useful in providing insights into potential underlying processes of first-year seminars rather than definitively determining a causal impact of these courses.

Student Support Services. Colleges and universities typically offer a range of support services to students, including academic advising, tutoring, and structured mentoring; supplemental instruction is also a specific form of student support associated with a particular course. These services are often designed with the specific intention of ultimately improving student retention and graduation by facilitating a smoother academic and social transition. Several randomized experiments have explored the impact of offering additional student services; the exact results are difficult to compare directly across studies, since the specific services often differ (both within and across service areas), and modest financial incentives were sometimes used to motivate students to participate. Students are also offered the opportunity to use these services, with some students opting not to do so. Within this research, Bettinger and Baker (2014) identified the strongest and most lasting effects. Their intervention used a private coaching service that was operated external to the participating colleges. Trained coaches contacted their students by phone, e-mail, text, and social networking sites, and their interactions ranged from brief contacts to in-depth meetings. These coaches' goal

> was to encourage persistence and completion by helping students find ways to overcome both academic and "real-life" barriers and to identify strategies for success by helping students use resources and advocate for themselves. The company hopes that coaches provide informed, empathetic support separate from students' academic and personal lives. (p. 6)

Coaches were generally successful in interacting with students: about 94% of students who were assigned a coach had at least one substantive meeting, and 77% received at least five contacts from their coach. Relative to students in the control group, students who were assigned a coach were 5.2 percentage points more likely to persist through 12 months (the length of the coaching program), 3.4 percentage points more likely to persist through 24 months, and 4.0 percentage points more likely to receive a degree.

Other experiments found much more modest (if any) effects. Angrist, Lang, and Oreopoulos (2009) examined the impact of different interventions among entering first-year students at a primarily commuter university: (1) peer advising about academics and college transition as well as class-specific study skills lessons; (2) substantial financial incentives for achieving strong grades (the required college GPA differed depending on high school grades, but students received $1,000 for reaching the lower threshold, and $5,000 for reaching the higher one); and (3) the combination of these two interventions. Unfortunately, most students who were assigned to receive services never actually participated; in the first intervention, only about 21% contacted their peer advisor, and 12% attended a study-skills session. Relative to the control condition, only the combination of student services and financial incentives had an impact on the number of credits earned and the likelihood of being on probation or withdrawal, and the significant effects were only among female students. Another experiment that examined outreach for engaging in academic advising showed no effects on credit hours earned, terms enrolled, or graduation, but this may be due to the fact that the additional outreach barely had any significant effect on the number of advising appointments (Schwebel, Walburn, Klyce, & Jerrolds, 2012).

Another experimental intervention employed a combination of peer mentoring and first-year orientation among business majors (Sanchez, Bauer, & Paronto, 2006). This effort had no impact on graduation within the major or from the institution within four years, but this could have been at least partially the result of a small sample size ($N = 110$ participants across both conditions at the study's outset). A fairly modest intervention at two community colleges had students meet with a college counselor at least twice a semester during students' first year in exchange for a $150 stipend for each semester (Scrivener & Weiss, 2009). This program had significant effects on retention in the second and third semesters (of about 7 and 4 percentage points, respectively), but this difference became nonsignificant in the 4th through 6th semesters. Another program sought to promote use of student services by randomly assigning mentors to remedial math courses that would provide information about available campus resources to the whole class and help individual students who needed assistance. This program increased the proportion of students who used the Center for Learning Excellence on campus, but it yielded no significant impact on successful remedial course completion, credits earned, or retention (Visher et al., 2010).

Why were the effects in Bettinger and Baker (2014) stronger and longer lasting than those in other experimental studies? Multiple factors may explain this disparity. First, the coaches in the external organization were carefully selected and extensively trained, and they received considerable feedback on their performance. This extensive use of information and training for continuous improvement is arguably rare at many colleges and universities, and these efforts may have resulted in higher quality interactions. Supporting this possibility, Sanchez et al. (2006) observed significant correlations between perceived peer mentoring quality and subsequent college graduation, which means that some mentors or coaches may be much more effective than others. Second, although students were randomly assigned to have access to additional services or to experience greater communication about those services, students in some studies were simply unlikely to participate (Angrist et al., 2009; Schwebel et al., 2012; Visher et al., 2010). This disengagement presents a notable challenge for institutions that wish to promote retention through increased services. Perhaps not coincidentally, the other study with reasonably promising results also had high uptake rates, and it accomplished this by providing nontrivial monetary incentives for attending advising sessions (Scrivener & Weiss, 2009). Third, the college coaching focused on skills and knowledge that should extend beyond the intervention (e.g., advocating for oneself and navigating college resources). Scrivener and Weiss observed positive effects on retention up to one semester after the advising program, but these differences dissipated thereafter, which suggests the importance of interventions that are continuous and carefully designed to have lasting effects.

The mixed effects of student services in experimental research diverge from findings obtained from other studies. Non-experimental research has consistently identified positive effects of various student services, including academic advising (Bahr, 2008a; Bai & Pan, 2009; Robbins et al., 2009; Swecker, Fifolt, & Searby, 2013), Student Support Services programs (Fike & Fike, 2008), tutoring and skill development (Higgins, 2004; Laskey & Hetzel, 2011; Robbins et al., 2009; van der Sluis et al., 2013), mentoring (Reyes, 2011; Salinitri, 2005), and disability services (Pingry O'Neill, Markward, & French, 2012). Clearly, given the disparity between the experimental and nonexperimental results, it seems that self-selection into these services accounts for at least some of the positive relationships. This possibility was explored directly through a national evaluation of Student Support Services (SSS), which is a federally funded program that provides a variety of supports to students who are from low-income families, are first-generation college students, or have disabilities. Overall, SSS enrollment was not directly related to credits earned, retention, persistence, or graduation (Chaney, 2010), but students who enrolled in this program were not required to participate in any services at all. Therefore, additional analyses examined the frequency of engagement with services, and it used propensity score matching in some analyses to account for potential self-selection. The results depended somewhat on the individual analysis, with many results indicating positive effects of SSS services. When considering participation in all student services (not just those specific to SSS), even the multilevel, propensity score analyses yielded significant positive results: bachelor's degree attainment for the average SSS participant was 11 percentage points higher than for matched students who had received no supplemental services.

While the findings for student services are complicated, the literature seems to support some conclusions. By itself, participation in a particular student service may be unlikely to yield substantial improvements in attainment, but the most effective educational interventions may be those that integrate a number of support services or other components (e.g., Scrivener & Weiss, 2013). This assertion is consistent with findings from a multisite study of learning communities that will be discussed later in more detail (Visher et al., 2012). Moreover, participating in a comprehensive first-year success program that combined a first-year seminar, shared residence halls, peer advising, and tutoring was positively related to college graduation (Noble, Flynn, Lee, & Hilton, 2007). Chaney (2010) also found that certain combinations of student services seemed particularly associated with student success. Moreover, the quality of these services may play a key role; for instance, one might assume that a required mentoring program may be effective only if the mentor and mentee establish a strong relationship (see Bettinger & Baker, 2014; Sanchez et al., 2006).

Finally, one specific type of student service that has received a fair bit of direct attention is supplemental instruction. Dawson, van der Meer, Skalicky, and Cowley (2014) define supplemental instruction (SI) as "an academic support program that employs successful later-year tertiary students to facilitate peer-learning sessions mostly attached to high-risk courses.... SI is currently offered internationally to hundreds of thousands of students each year" (pp. 609–610). The courses in which SI is offered tend to be introductory in nature and have high failure rates. In their systematic review, Dawson and colleagues found that students who participate in SI are less likely to fail the course than those who do not participate. However, an important concern is whether students who choose to take advantage of this supplemental instruction are more academically motivated or capable than those who choose not to do so. Interestingly, SI students are no more qualified—and sometimes significantly less qualified—than their peers in terms of their standardized test scores (Congos & Mack, 2005; Hensen & Shelley, 2003; Peterfreund, Rath, Xenos, & Bayliss, 2008), precollege academic achievement (Terrion & Daoust, 2012), and their predicted course GPA (based on test scores, high school GPA, and first-year college GPA; Ogden, Thompson, Russell, & Simons, 2003). SI session attendance is positively related to receiving a passing course grade even when controlling for a host of precollege variables and attributes of the SI sessions (Cheng & Walters, 2009). While other studies generally used few control variables, they identified sizable positive relationships with course pass rates across a variety of academic subjects and student populations (Bowles, McCoy, & Bates, 2008; Congos & Mack, 2005; Fayowski & MacMillan, 2008; Henson & Shelley, 2003; Meling, Mundy, Kupczynski, & Green, 2013; Ogden et al., 2003; Oja, 2012; Peterfreund et al., 2007; Rath, Peterfreund, Xenos, Bayliss, & Carnal, 2007).

Some limited research has examined outcomes that extend beyond the course that offered supplemental instruction. Perhaps the strongest study was conducted by Terrion and Daoust (2011) at a single Canadian university. They identified a control group that was similar to the SI group not only on precollege achievement but also on seven different measures of academic motivation. Although the sample was reasonably small ($N = 184$), SI students were more likely to persist to the second year than non-SI students. In contrast, Oja (2012) found that hours attending SI did not predict retention to the following semester when controlling for cumulative GPA. Moreover, Ogden et al. (2003) observed that retention for SI students did not differ significantly from that of non-SI students, which may have been at least partially attributable to small sample sizes. In sum, it seems likely that supplemental instruction may affect performance within that course, but it is less clear whether it affects overall retention or overall persistence in higher education.

Financial Aid

Research on the impact of financial aid on educational persistence and attainment may be simultaneously more voluminous and more contradictory in its findings than for any other topic. Several qualitative review articles have attempted to make sense of this literature and offer directions for future research (e.g., Goldrick-Rab et al., 2009; Hossler et al., 2009; Welbeck et al., 2014). Pascarella and Terenzini (2005) concluded that students who received aid were at least as likely as other students to persist and graduate, with the strongest evidence of benefits associated with receiving grants and scholarships. The impact of aid is particularly difficult to examine, in part because eligibility for merit- or need-based aid is often determined by precollege factors that are strongly related to persistence and graduation. Therefore, this chapter focuses primarily on studies that have used rigorous experimental and quasi-experimental designs to isolate causal effects.

Some experimental research on financial aid has examined performance-based scholarships, which are given to students only if they achieve certain thresholds for credit completion and grades within those courses. MDRC, a nonprofit research organization that focuses on improving the lives of people with low incomes, has administered such scholarship programs in seven states (Patel, Richburg-Hayes, de la Campa, & Rudd, 2013). The program characteristics varied across states, including the maximum scholarship amount ($1,000–$4,000), program duration (one semester to two years), eligibility criteria (which usually included age and family income, among other factors), and academic benchmarks necessary to receive the funding (which often included a combination of credits successfully completed and grades achieved in one or more courses). In all states, students at participating two-year institutions were randomly assigned to be eligible for performance-based scholarships or not be eligible. At the end of the first year, students who were eligible for the scholarships had completed one to three credits more than students who were not eligible for the scholarship, and they were also more likely to have met the academic benchmarks required for scholarship receipt within their state. The program also reduced loan debt by several hundred dollars the first year. However, the findings for retention and persistence were mixed. In most states, the program had no significant impact on persistence to the second year. However, in Ohio (which has the longest follow-up period), students who were eligible for the scholarship were more likely to have completed a degree or certificate program after two or three years of college than those who were not eligible for the scholarship (after the third year, these figures were 26.9% versus 23.3%, respectively). In Louisiana, assignment to the scholarship program also predicted greater enrollment in the third and fourth semesters, even though the scholarships were only offered in the first two semesters (Scrivener & Coghlan, 2011).

Two other experimental studies have examined the impact of student scholarships on achievement and persistence outcomes. In a study of a single Canadian university, Angrist et al. (2009) found that being offered a combination of a performance-based scholarship and academic support services was associated with higher grades, more credits earned, and a lower likelihood of being on probation or having withdrawn in the first and second years of college. However, receiving this scholarship without the academic support was unrelated to student success, and subgroup analyses revealed that this intervention affected only female students' outcomes.

Goldrick-Rab et al. (2012) examined a need-based scholarship program for Pell-eligible students attending Wisconsin public universities. In the first three semesters, students who were offered a $3,500 scholarship had higher grades, more credits earned, and greater retention than similar students who were not offered the scholarship; for instance, students who were offered the scholarship were 2.5 percentage points more likely to return in the second year. However, these differences were largely nonsignificant in semesters four to six, even though students were eligible to receive the scholarship for up to 10 semesters. Finally, several strong quasi-experimental studies have found that receiving grants and scholarships—whether need based, merit based, or a combination of the two—is positively related to college persistence and graduation (Alon, 2007, 2011; Castleman & Long, 2013; Dynarski, 2009; Henry, Rubenstein, & Bugler, 2004; Scott-Clayton, 2011).

Across at least 75 additional studies that examined the link between financial aid and attainment, the results vary dramatically. For instance, some studies have found that work-study is positively related to persistence and degree attainment (Chen, 2012; Chen & DesJardins, 2008; Cragg, 2009; DesJardins & McCall, 2010; Johnson, 2008; Lohfink & Paulsen, 2005; Somers et al., 2004; Stratton et al., 2008; Wohlgemuth et al., 2007), whereas others have found it is negatively related (DesJardins et al., 2002; Singell, 2004; Singell & Waddell, 2006) or unrelated (Chen & DesJardins, 2010; Dowd, 2004; Dowd & Coury, 2006; Eagan & Jaeger, 2009; Gross, 2011; Gross et al., 2013; Ishitani, 2006; Jaeger & Eagan, 2011; Paulsen & St. John, 2002; Stratton, O'Toole, & Wetzel, 2007). On the whole, given that many studies tend to underestimate the impact of eligibility for need-based aid on reducing the likelihood of graduation (Alon, 2005), it seems that work-study may have an overall positive effect on persistence and degree attainment. Research is also divided on whether loans predict greater persistence and attainment (Chen, 2012; Chen & DesJardins, 2008, 2010; DesJardins et al., 2002; DesJardins & McCall, 2010; Dowd, 2004; Gross, 2011; Singell, 2004; Singell & Waddell, 2010; Somers et al., 2004; St. John et al., 2004), lower outcomes (Cragg, 2009; Dowd & Coury, 2006; Johnson, 2008; Stratton et al., 2008; Wohlgemuth et al., 2007; Wolniak et al., 2012), or no systematic difference (Alon, 2007; Eagan & Jaeger, 2009; Gross et al., 2013; Herzog, 2005; Ishitani, 2006; Jaeger & Eagan, 2009; Lohfink & Paulsen, 2002; St. John et al., 2003, 2005; Stratton et al., 2007). In general, subsidized loans appear to have a greater benefit than unsubsidized loans (Chen, 2012; Chen & DesJardins, 2010; Herzog, 2005; Singell, 2004). Moreover, the relationship between financial aid and attrition does not vary strongly by students' year in school; if there is any systematic pattern, this relationship might be slightly stronger later in college (Chen & DesJardins, 2008, 2010; DesJardins, Ahlburg, & McCall, 2002a, 2002b; Wohlgemuth et al., 2007).

The processes through which financial aid affects educational outcomes are likely complex and multifaceted (for reviews, see Goldrick-Rab et al., 2009; Hossler et al., 2009). However, the extent to which students have unmet need (i.e., a gap between the financial resources available to them and the total cost of college) may play an important role. Research has consistently found that unmet need predicts greater attrition and lower attainment when controlling for numerous other factors (Bresciani & Carson, 2002; Chen & St. John, 2011; Herzog, 2005; Kuh, Cruce, Shoup, Kinzie, & Gonyea, 2008; Titus, 2006b, 2006c). Therefore, greater attention to unmet need, along with the extent to which several sources of financial aid may reduce unmet need, may yield important insights.

Another important issue is whether grants and scholarships (i.e., financial assistance that is not repaid) are more effective at promoting persistence and graduation than loans. Of course, grants and scholarships may also play a role in encouraging students to attend college or to attend a particular institution, a question that is beyond the scope of this chapter. The available evidence is mixed, but it provides some support for grants and scholarships being more influential. This issue was examined directly through studies of debt-reduction programs in several Canadian provinces that replaced loans with need-based grants (also known as bursaries) but did not increase the total amount of financial aid that students received. These studies compared students who received bursaries with students who would have been eligible for the bursaries but had attended college before the bursary program began. Across several degree programs (ranging from two-year diplomas to four-year degrees), students who received the bursary in Manitoba were 10 to 11 percentage points less likely to have left college than those who did not receive the bursary (McElroy, 2005). However, within a study with a similar design for a bursary program in New Brunswick, McElroy (2008) found that receiving the bursary did not reduce the likelihood of leaving college. She posited two potential reasons for the discrepancies across studies: (1) the New Brunswick bursary was largely ineffective at reducing student debt, which was believed to be a primary mechanism through which this intervention operated, and (2) the proportion of students who left college in New Brunswick was much lower than in Manitoba, so the lack of group differences may reflect a ceiling effect in college persistence. A third study examining multiple grant programs suggested that debt-reduction programs may be effective only when students' unmet need is low (CEISS, 2004). A simulation study provides some support for the efficacy of replacing loans with equal amounts of grants and scholarships (DesJardins et al., 2002b), and educational debt is inversely associated with persistence and degree completion (although this relationship is curvilinear; see Dwyer et al., 2012; Somers et al., 2004).

Finally, some evidence suggests that the simple act of applying for financial aid may promote educational attainment, since applying for financial aid often results in receiving additional aid, and students may see their applying as an indication of their commitment to the importance of college. Assessing the causal effect of applying for aid is challenging, because students who apply may differ from those who do not in ways that are important yet difficult to measure (e.g., motivation, cultural capital, expectation of receiving aid). To examine the potential impact of financial aid, Singell (2004) modeled both students' enrollment and retention at a public flagship university, since unobserved characteristics that lead to enrollment may also contribute to retention. This analysis found that submitting a Free Application for Federal Student Aid (FAFSA) was positively related to retention even when controlling for various observed and unobserved characteristics (i.e., those that are not included in the statistical model). Other studies also found a positive and substantial relationship between applying for aid and subsequent retention and persistence (Gross, 2011; McKinney & Novak, 2012; Novak & McKinney, 2011). However, this relationship may be an overestimate, as students who already intend to drop out will be less likely to apply for aid in the first place.

Employment

Many students work part time or full time while pursuing a degree. Clearly, working during college has the potential to affect students' finances as well as the amount of time available to spend on academics and other endeavors. It appears that working extensively decreases the likelihood of persistence and degree attainment. Several studies found that full-time employment is associated with a lower likelihood of retention, persistence, and graduation (Martinez, Sher, Krull, & Wood, 2009; Sibulkin & Butler, 2005; Somers et al., 2004). Research that examines the curvilinear relationship between hours worked and attainment consistently finds that attainment diminishes at some point (except for Kuh et al., 2008), but the exact number of hours varies across studies. Raley, Kim, and Daniels (2012) and Roksa (2011) found diminished persistence and degree attainment starting at 35 hours per week, while Attewell et al. (2011)

found that this occurred at either 15 or 30 hours per week (depending on institutional type), and Bozick (2007) found a negative relationship for more than 20 hours per week (the highest category in the study). On the low end, Titus (2006a, 2006b) found reduced persistence for students working more than 20 hours per week as well as working 11 to 20 hours per week relative to not working at all. Alfonso, Bailey, and Scott (2005) measured employment intensity through the proportion of time that students worked while attending school; students who worked more than 75% of the time had lower degree attainment than those who worked less than 25% of the time (including students who did not work at all). Within this research, only Martinez et al. (2009) and Roksa (2011) found that working modest amounts predicted better outcomes than not working at all.

Given this apparent curvilinear relationship, it is not surprising that the simple linear relationship for the number of hours worked or a dichotomous measuring of having any employment are often nonsignificant, along with some significant negative results (Arbona & Nora, 2007; Beeson & Wessel, 2002; Chen & DesJardins, 2010; Cragg, 2009; Dowd & Coury, 2006; Ewert, 2010; Hagedorn, Maxwell, & Hampton, 2002; Herzog, 2005; Leppel, 2002; Lohfink & Paulsen, 2005; McKinney & Novak, 2012; Nakajima, Dembo, & Mossler, 2012; Porchea et al., 2010; Schreiner & Nelson, 2013; St. John et al., 2005; Titus, 2004; Wang, 2009, 2012; Woosley, 2003). Working on campus may provide a benefit to students, since on-campus employment is sometimes positively related to retention and graduation (Adelman, 2005; Beeson & Wessel, 2002; Christie & Hutcheson, 2003; Herzog, 2005). Whether students worked on or off campus does not predict retention or persistence when controlling for time spent working and other measures (Nakajima et al., 2012; Titus, 2004, 2006a, 2006b). A better test of these differential relationships would be to examine the number of hours worked on campus and off campus as separate variables. The vast majority of studies did not distinguish between on- and off-campus employment, so additional evidence is needed to draw stronger conclusions about possible differential effects.

Experiences with Faculty

Pascarella and Terenzini (2005) concluded that student interactions with faculty were positively related to persistence and graduation, and simply perceiving that faculty members are available and interested in students' success may have also been influential. Below, we discuss three areas of research on faculty and educational attainment: the quality and quantity of faculty interactions, characteristics of faculty members, and the teaching format through which faculty offer their courses.

Faculty-Student Interactions. Experiences with faculty can take a variety of forms, with the most common form of interaction generally occurring through instruction in formal coursework. Across several studies, students' perceptions of the quality of teaching are consistently related to retention and persistence.

Within a large Canadian university, Hoffman and Oreopoulos (2009b) examined the link between various indicators of an instructor's teaching quality (including individual student perceptions and the average perception in that course) and dropping the course. Even when using fixed effects to draw comparisons within the same academic year, course, student, and time of day, instructor effectiveness was consistently associated with lower rates of course withdrawal. Using the Wabash National Study, two articles found that perceived teaching clarity and organization predict greater retention when controlling for various precollege attributes and college experiences, and this relationship is explained by increases in college grades and overall college satisfaction (Pascarella, Salisbury, & Blaich, 2011; Wolniak et al., 2012). At both Canadian and American institutions, perceived quality of instructors and instruction predicts lower attrition (Madgett & Belanger, 2008; Schreiner & Nelson, 2013).

The overall frequency of interactions with faculty has also been examined, and this research often identified no significant relationship with retention or graduation (Cragg, 2009; Crissman, 2002; Hausmann et al., 2009; Wolniak et al., 2012). In addition, perceived faculty concern about students did not significantly predict retention (Hausmann et al., 2009; Otero, Rivas, & Rivera, 2007). Faculty interactions could occur for a variety of purposes, ranging from meaningful engagement about intellectual topics to assisting and counseling students who have performed poorly in coursework. As a result, the presence of certain faculty interactions may be caused by academic struggle, so a negative relationship with attainment could be observed for some students even if the interactions themselves are not detrimental.

Faculty Characteristics. A number of studies have examined whether the characteristics of faculty predict educational attainment. Several national studies provide strong evidence that exposure to part-time faculty leads to a decreased likelihood of graduation. Ehrenberg and Zhang (2005) used panel analyses to explore whether changes in an institution's faculty composition predict changes in six-year graduation rates. As a result of this methodological approach, these findings cannot be attributed to any stable differences across institutions. They found that increases in the percentage of part-time faculty are associated with reduced graduation rates regardless of institutional control (public and private) or type (doctoral, master's, and liberal arts). Moreover, increases in the percentage of non-tenure-track faculty also predict decreased graduation at both public and private schools and at doctoral and master's institutions (but not liberal arts colleges). These findings occurred even while also controlling for changes in the number of total faculty and various attributes of the student body (e.g., demographics and academic preparation). At two-year institutions, Eagan and Jaeger (2009) simultaneously examined both students' exposure to part-time faculty in their coursework as well as the overall representation of part-time faculty at the institution as predictors of transferring to a four-year institution; Jaeger and Eagan (2009) performed similar analyses predicting associate's degree completion. In both studies, students' personal experiences with part-time faculty predicted a lower likelihood of transferring and degree completion even when controlling for various other student and institutional attributes in multilevel models. Jaeger and Eagan (2009) also identified a significant, negative association between part-time faculty representation and associate's degree completion, whereas Eagan and Jaeger (2009) found no such relationship for college transfer. Jaeger and Eagan (2011) extended these findings by using instrumental variable analyses predicting first-year retention. They found that exposure to graduate instruction, non-tenure-track full-time instruction, and other contingent faculty instruction was inversely associated with retention at most institutional types, although these relationships were actually positive at doctoral-intensive schools.

The conditions under which these results were replicated (or not) in other studies provide insight into the potential mechanisms that may explain these effects. For instance, Jacoby (2006) and Calcagno et al. (2008) obtained similar findings for graduation rates in nationally representative samples, as did Jaeger and Hinz (2008) for part-time faculty exposure and retention at a single research-extensive institution. Academic integration may explain the link between the proportion of part-time faculty and student attrition, since the two multi-institutional studies that found no relationship between part-time faculty and attrition included measures of academic integration within their multivariate models (Chen, 2012; Porchea et al., 2010). Porchea et al. also included a variable measuring commitment to the goal of college graduation and examined a sample with a modest number of institutions ($N = 21$), which creates a lower possibility of finding significant differences across schools. Many part-time and non-tenure-track faculty experience low pay and heavy teaching workloads (as many part-time faculty teach at multiple institutions; see Kezar & Sam, 2010; Wagoner, 2008), so these faculty members may be less able to engage with students or assign meaningful assignments that would require extensive grading. Interestingly, these effects of part-time faculty exposure do not appear to be related to academic performance in a particular course, given that faculty characteristics are generally not associated with successful course completion (Fike & Fike, 2007; Hoffman & Oreopoulos, 2009a, 2009b), and non-tenure-track and part-time faculty assign grades that are at least as high as their tenure-track colleagues (Fike & Fike, 2007; Hoffman & Oreopoulos, 2009b; Johnson, 2011).

Course Delivery Format. Since Pascarella and Terenzini's (2005) review, one of the most salient changes in higher education has been the proliferation of online coursework, which sometimes consists of fully online degree programs. The evidence about the relation between online course work and student success is generally limited to course-based outcomes (e.g., percentage of students with passing grades).

Bowen, Chingos, Lack, and Nygren (2013) examined the impact of offering a statistics course in a traditional face-to-face format versus a hybrid format (with mostly online instruction and assignments, along with one hour per week of face-to-face instruction). The 605 participants attending one of six four-year universities were randomly assigned to one of the two course delivery formats. They found "that students are not harmed by this mode of instruction in terms of [course] pass rates, final exam scores, and performance on a standardized assessment of statistical literacy" (p. 94). However, students who chose to participate in the study differed in numerous ways from nonparticipants who were taking the same course but did not agree to participate in the study, so it is unclear whether the results might generalize to other students.

The findings from other research on this topic are mixed. In a remedial algebra course at a large, urban community college, students in the face-to-face sections had higher course completion rates than those in the hybrid and online sections even when controlling for learning style, race/ethnicity, gender, and age (Zavarella & Ignash, 2009). Conversely, at a different large, urban community college, students who took an online course in their first semester were more likely to be retained to their second semester and their second year when controlling for demographics, remedial coursework, student support services, receiving financial aid, and hours enrolled and dropped in their first semester (Fike & Fike, 2008). The inclusion of the hours dropped may be somewhat problematic, since online students might be more likely to drop the course, which then leads to lower retention at the institution. Several studies find either no difference or lower passing rates among online students (Ashby, Sadera, & McNary, 2011; Frydenberg, 2007; Hachey, Wladis, & Conway, 2012; Stillson & Alsup, 2003), but the lack of control variables makes it difficult to draw any conclusions about whether these findings would persist when examining comparable groups of students.

A number of studies have examined predictors of successfully completing online coursework. Consistent with research on postsecondary attainment in general, college grades are the most consistent predictor of successful online course completion across these studies (Aragon & Johnson, 2008; Boston, Ice, & Burgess, 2012; Boston, Ice, & Gibson, 2011; Dupin Bryant, 2004; Harrell & Bower, 2011). Hachey et al. (2012) found that previous online coursework taken did not predict online course success or retention, but successful completion of previous online coursework was strongly predictive of both outcomes (also see Dupin Bryant, 2004). Moreover, Hachey et al. found that students who were unsuccessful in previous online course work had significantly lower course completion and retention than students with no previous online course work experience at all. Also similar to general findings for educational attainment, taking a heavier course load is positively related to successful online course completion (Aragon & Johnson, 2008; Boston et al., 2012; Boston, Ice, & Gibson, 2011). Another consistent finding was that online course participation (as indicated by discussion posts read, content pages viewed, posts created, and overall activity) predicted greater successful course completion (Davies & Graff, 2005; Finnegan, Morris, & Lee, 2008; Morris, Finnegan, & Wu, 2005). Engagement with the online software is often necessary for success as a course requirement or to prepare for assignments, so lower online engagement may directly cause course failure. However, many students unofficially "withdraw" from the course through discontinuing their participation without necessarily submitting a formal withdrawal form (Hyllegard, Deng, & Hunter, 2008), so a lack of online participation may best be considered an indicator of previous (unofficial) withdrawal rather than a predictor of future non-completion.

Interactions with Peers

Consistent with Pascarella and Terenzini's (2005) earlier conclusion, research since 2002 finds that quality interactions and relationships with college friends are often positively related to retention and persistence. For instance, Fischer (2007) used a sample of 28 selective institutions to examine informal on-campus ties (a combined measure of the number of close campus friends and time spent with friends and spent partying) and off-campus ties (indicated by the frequency of contacting off-campus friends and the number of visits home during the first year) as predictors of persistence to the end of the third year of college. When controlling for demographics, precollege academic preparation, academic adjustment to college, campus racial climate, and institutional characteristics, informal on-campus ties were positively related to persistence among Asian American, Black, Latino, and White students, whereas off-campus ties predicted lower persistence among Black and White students. Offering some interesting support for the role of campus relationships, students at a small Christian university who used Facebook primarily to connect with other students at that college were more likely to be retained than those who used Facebook primarily to connect with people outside of their college (Morris, Reese, Beck, & Mattis, 2009). However, this study did not use any control variables when assessing this relationship. Multivariate analyses in other studies have found time spent socializing on campus with friends predicts greater retention (Otero et al., 2007), and having high-quality campus friendships and relationships also predicts retention (Wolniak et al., 2012). It appears that the quality of these relationships matters more than the quantity, since the number of campus friends is generally unrelated to retention (Crissman, 2002; Swenson Goguen, Hiester, & Nordstrom, 2010).

If peer relationships in college have a causal impact on retention and persistence, then this relationship is likely explained by social integration and institutional commitment. For instance, the number of Facebook friends attending the student's college predicts social adjustment, which then predicts retention (Gray, Vitak, Easton, & Ellison, 2013). Perhaps not surprisingly, the total number of Facebook friends did not significantly predict college adjustment. Hausmann et al. (2009) also found that the quality of peer group interactions predicts a sense of belonging, which is then positively related to retention. Studies that included a measure of institutional commitment or social integration in the analyses did not find a direct, significant relationship between the quality of peer relationships and retention (Madgett & Belanger, 2008; Morris, Beck, & Smith, 2004), since these constructs likely explain any effect of peer relationships.

Perceptions of the campus climate also appear to have an indirect effect on retention and graduation. Although these perceptions are often influenced by institutional and historical factors (Milem, Chang, & Antonio, 2005), engagement with other students arguably plays the strongest role in shaping these views. Johnson, Wasserman, Yildirim, and Yonai (2014) conducted structural equation modeling analyses separately for White students and students of color at a selective research university. For both groups of students, overall perceptions of the campus environment (as welcoming, friendly, respectful) predicted institutional commitment, which then led to retention to the second year. Moreover, observed racism on campus predicted worse perceptions of the campus environment and greater academic stress among students of color, while opportunities for diversity interactions predicted more positive campus environment perceptions and lower stress regarding social integration among White students. Stress was inversely related to institutional commitment for both groups. Similarly, Museus, Nichols, and Lambert (2008) found that satisfaction with the campus racial climate predicted greater institutional commitment among students from all racial/ethnic groups, and it predicted greater goal commitment among Black, Latina/o, and White students. Fischer (2007) found that perceptions of the campus racial climate were associated with college satisfaction for all racial/ethnic groups, and college satisfaction predicted greater persistence. Climate also had a significant, direct relationship with persistence among Black and Hispanic/Latino students when controlling for a variety of precollege attributes and college experiences, but these relationships became marginally significant when college satisfaction was added to the model.

Providing further support for the potential indirect role of campus climate, studies directly predicting retention that included overall satisfaction or sense of belonging in the analyses identified no significant relationship for climate (Baker & Robnett, 2012; Soria & Stebleton, 2012). Satisfaction with the racial climate and the overall campus climate, however, predicted greater degree attainment within two national studies that did not control for such intermediate variables (Schreiner & Nelson, 2013; Titus, 2006a).

Residence

Many of the colleges and universities with the highest retention and graduation rates are primarily residential, but students at these institutions differ in numerous ways from those at other institutions. Therefore, within-school comparisons of students who live on campus and those who do not are likely to lead to the most valid conclusions. Through their review of prior literature, Pascarella and Terenzini (2005) concluded that on-campus residence appeared to be positively related to attainment, but this evidence was not particularly strong.

In perhaps the best examination of this topic to date, Schudde (2011) conducted propensity score matching analyses using the nationally representative Education Longitudinal Study (ELS:2002) federal dataset. To adjust for the propensity to live on campus, she matched students on a variety of measures, including demographics; high school course work, academic performance, and extracurricular activities; reasons for college choice; finances; and college/ university attributes. In the most rigorously matched analysis, students who live on campus were 3.3 percentage points more likely to return for their second year than those who lived off campus, whereas other matching analyses within this study placed this estimate at 4.2 percentage points. Moreover, this finding is not the product of institutional differences in residentiality; in fact, multiple studies that simultaneously examine students' individual living situations and the proportion of students who live on campus have found that students' place of residence predicts degree completion, but the institutional measure does not (Oseguera & Rhee, 2009; Wilson, 2007).

It appears that living on campus may affect retention and graduation primarily through promoting social integration or involvement. With the exception of studies by Titus (2004, 2006b, 2006c) that use the same dataset, research that has included social integration variables finds no significant relationship between campus residence and attainment (Gray et al., 2013; Lohfink & Paulsen, 2005; Mamiseishvili, 2012; Robbins et al., 2009). In contrast, research that does not include social integration measures—but does incorporate numerous other control variables, such as precollege attributes, institutional characteristics, financial resources, and college GPA—has almost exclusively found positive relationships for campus residence (Bozick, 2007; Gross et al., 2013; Herzog, 2005; Jaeger & Eagan, 2011; Jamelske, 2009; Johnson, 2008; Jones-White, Radcliffe, Huesman, & Kellogg, 2010; Paulsen & St. John, 2002; Somers et al., 2004). Thus, these findings provide intriguing, albeit indirect, evidence that living on campus promotes social integration, which then promotes retention. The presence of significant relationships even when controlling for college GPA suggests that academics may play less of a role (if any) in explaining this relationship.

Learning Communities

Broadly defined, learning communities consist of small cohorts of students who take two or more courses together. In most cases, learning communities also involve some level of collaboration among instructors of those courses. However, learning communities can vary considerably in their intensity, such as length of time, coordination or integration across courses, number of courses, presence of a residential component, presence of a particular theme for the community, and so on. Pascarella and Terenzini (2005) concluded that both residential and nonresidential learning communities promoted academic and social integration, which may have then led to retention.

In the current review period, MDRC used an experimental design to examine learning community outcomes at six community colleges; half of participating students were randomly assigned to a first-semester learning community that linked a developmental (remedial) course to another course. These programs varied in their intensity; two programs emphasized curricular integration, and one of them also provided extra support services through tutors, advising, book stipends, and additional funding for participating in intersession courses.

Multiple evaluations showed positive effects for the most comprehensive program (at Kingsborough College in New York City). After two years, students who were assigned to learning communities in that program earned more credits, were more likely to progress through developmental English requirements, and reported a greater sense of integration and belonging to college than those who were not (Scrivener et al., 2008). After six years, participants had earned an average of 4.0 more credits, were 5.0 percentage points more likely to be enrolled consistently (without stopping out), and were 4.6 percentage points more likely to have received a degree from any institution (Sommo Mayer, Rudd, & Cullinan, 2012). In many cases, the size of these group differences increased over time, even though the learning community occurred only in the first semester.

However, when examining all six learning communities simultaneously, Visher, Weiss, Weissman, Rudd, and Wathington (2012) found much more modest effects in students' first three semesters: learning community students earned an additional one-half credit overall and one-half credit in the developmental subject, but there were no differences in persistence. The disparities between Kingsborough College and other institutions may have occurred because that learning community had much greater intensity in its implementation, including the provision of various student services. Moreover, the modest findings may be attributed to the implementation of these programs: "Few learning communities achieved a level of integration that would meet the standard of an ideal learning community" (p. ES-8).

Nonexperimental research on learning communities has almost uniformly found positive relationships with grades, retention, and graduation (with the exception of Bai & Pan, 2009). The contexts of these studies include academic-year residential programs (Jones-White et al., 2010; Stassen, 2003), those that are organized by field of study (Hill & Woodward, 2013; Stassen, 2003), those at two-year colleges (Popiolek, Fine, & Eilman, 2013), and those at four-year institutions (Hotchkiss, Moore, & Pitts, 2006; Mangold, Bean, Adams, Schwab, & Lynch, 2002). In a format somewhat akin to a learning community, enrolling concurrently in a chemistry lecture and corresponding laboratory section is associated with lower withdrawal rates from that lecture than enrolling exclusively in the lecture (Matz, Rothman, Krajcik, & Banaszak Holl, 2012). Although some evidence suggests that program intensity plays a key role in shaping outcomes, Stassen (2003) found that living-learning community participation had similar relationships with students' first-year GPA and retention across three programs with divergent levels of coordination and intensity. It is possible that the residential component of these programs facilitates substantial meaningful engagement among students regardless of the nature and extent of the curricular integration. Stassen also found that students in living-learning communities were more academically integrated across a variety of indicators than other students, but few differences existed for social integration. Perhaps consistent with this role of campus integration, Jones-White et al. (2010) found that engaging in living-learning communities predicted graduation from students' initial four-year institution, but it was not related to receiving a two- or four-year degree from another institution. In sum, it appears that learning communities that provide opportunities for meaningful engagement, whether through structured curricula or informal interactions, may promote student achievement and retention.

Summer bridge programs often take the form of a learning community in which the same cohort of students completes multiple courses together. These programs are generally designed to improve the transition to college for underrepresented or underprepared students. Before their first semester or quarter of general enrollment, students participate in summer courses or other programs designed to prepare them for college. These can take the form of remedial courses, general college-level courses, and learning about the transition to college (including available support resources).

The most rigorous study of summer bridge programs was conducted by MDRC (Barnett et al., 2012); a randomized experiment occurred at two open-access four-year institutions and six two-year colleges in Texas. This summer bridge program lasted four to five weeks and involved developmental coursework in at least one subject area (math, writing, or reading), academic support, and direct guidance about "college knowledge" to help aid students' transition to higher education. However, the long-term impacts of this program were negligible. Summer bridge students passed their first math or writing course at higher rates than nonbridge students early in college, but this difference became nonsignificant after two years. There were also no significant differences in the number of credits attempted, number of credits earned, and persistence in college over two years.

Nonexperimental studies have provided mixed results. Cabrera, Miner, and Milem (2013) examined a voluntary six-week summer bridge program at the University of Arizona that included taking academic courses, living in residential halls, engaging in social activities, and learning about support services on campus. They compared program participants to nonparticipants who were similar in terms of gender, race/ethnicity, and Pell eligibility. When controlling for demographics, high school preparation, and high school performance, summer bridge students were more likely to be retained to the second year than nonparticipants. However, other single-institution studies provided weaker support for the efficacy of these programs. Allen and Bir (2012) found that students who voluntarily enrolled in a summer bridge program earned more credits, had higher first-year GPAs, and were more likely to return for their second year than nonparticipants who were similar in terms of their high school GPA and gender. However, no multivariate analyses were conducted, so student self-selection may account for these findings. When examining a summer bridge program for conditionally admitted students, Walpole et al. (2008) found that participating students had similar credits earned and retention rates as nonparticipants who were matched on their SAT scores.

From this limited evidence, it is difficult to determine the impact of summer bridge programs. Perhaps not coincidentally, the two studies that examined students who could choose whether to participate showed the greatest gains. This could be construed as implying the efficacy of voluntary bridge programs, which could reinforce the fact that students in required programs often need greater special assistance and are less prepared than other students. Conversely, this pattern could also suggest that self-selection drives group differences, since students who are highly motivated and financially secure are probably more likely to choose to spend at least a month of their summer to participate in bridge programs. In the Barnett et al. (2012) study, students had all volunteered to join the program, but they were then randomly assigned to participate or not, so self-selection was not a concern. However, this program was nonresidential, and it is possible that extended engagement with fellow students outside the classroom is necessary to realize the full benefits of summer bridge programs.

Academic Major

It is difficult to discern whether undergraduate major might have any significant influence on retention, since students who gravitate toward different majors likely differ in a variety of ways, and experimental and quasi-experimental research designs to explore field of study are often not feasible. Pascarella and Terenzini (2005) concluded that students majoring in the sciences, engineering, business, and health-related fields were more likely to persist and graduate than similar students in other fields.

In our review, community college students who enroll in vocational or occupational majors are less likely to receive a degree or successfully complete remedial course work than students who enroll in academic majors (Alfonso et al., 2005; Bailey et al., 2010; Jaeger & Eagan, 2009). However, these two groups of students may differ in important ways that were not adequately measured in these studies (e.g., precollege academic motivation). The findings for four-year institutions are less consistent; in fact, several studies from one author using the same dataset yielded conflicting results about whether undeclared students are less likely to persist than students who had declared a major in their first year (Titus, 2004, 2006a, 2006b). Additional studies also obtained mixed results about whether undeclared students have lower attainment, with some research finding no difference between declared and undeclared students (Burgette & Magun-Jackson, 2009; McKinney & Novak, 2012), and others observed group differences that depend upon students' race/ethnicity and year in college (St. John et al., 2004) as well as institutional type (Jaeger & Eagan, 2011).

Among students who identified a major, some research did not find any significant differences based on students' major or field of study (Chen, 2012; Cochran et al., 2014; Donhardt, 2013; Hendel, 2007). When significant differences were observed, students who majored in business, engineering, and health sciences tended to have the highest retention rates, whereas students in the humanities tended to have among the lowest rates (Chen & DesJardins, 2010; DesJardins et al., 2003; Jaeger & Eagan, 2011; St. John et al., 2004; Wohlgemuth et al., 2007). Interestingly, the majors with the highest retention rates explicitly prepare students for high-paying jobs, so it is possible that these students become more motivated to complete their degree, since graduation could have a substantial financial payoff. Students who have stronger entering academic preparation and motivation may also gravitate toward these fields, but many of these studies account for students' achievement before and during college, so this self-selection may not be a problem.

Other research has examined the extent to which congruence between students' interests and their undergraduate major predicts college success. As measured by Holland's (1997) occupational types, interest-major congruence is sometimes associated with greater retention and degree completion when controlling for precollege characteristics (Allen & Robbins, 2010; Leuwerke, Robbins, Sawyer, & Hovland, 2004; Tracey & Robbins, 2006). Furthermore, undergraduate majors vary in the extent to which students have divergent interest profiles; that is, some majors have students with profiles that are more similar to one another, whereas others have students with a broader range of profiles. As one might expect, the link between interest-major congruence and retention is strongest in majors that have little variation in the interest profiles of their students (Tracey, Allen, & Robbins, 2012).

Social and Academic Integration/Involvement

Social integration and academic integration are included in various models of college student departure (e.g., Bean & Eaton, 2000; Braxton et al., 2004; Cabrera et al., 1992; Museus, 2014; Nora, 2004; Tinto, 1993). Tinto differentiated between two types of academic integration. *Structural academic integration* refers to the extent to which students meet their institution's expectations of academic performance, as often indicated by college grades. As summarized earlier, college GPA is a strong and consistent predictor of postsecondary attainment. *Normative academic integration* measures the extent to which a student fits within the academic environment of the institution. In Tinto's formulation, social integration reflects the congruence between the student and the institution's social system. As discussed earlier, relevant theory typically frames integration as a psychological construct, whereas research that claims to measure integration often measures student involvement in various activities (Bowman & Denson, 2014; Braxton et al., 1997; Hurtado & Carter, 1997). Therefore, we attempt to differentiate between psychological integration and behavioral involvement whenever possible in this discussion. Pascarella and Terenzini (2005) found that academic and social involvement exerted positive and significant effects on persistence and graduation, and at least some of these effects may have occurred through increasing students' institutional commitment.

Since this earlier review period, three quantitative meta-analyses have synthesized the literature on integration/involvement and persistence. Robbins et al. (2004) examined the relationship between social involvement (i.e., "the extent that students feel connected to the college environment; the quality of students' relationships with peers, faculty, and others in college; the extent that students are involved in campus activities," p. 267) and the number of semesters enrolled in college. Across 36 studies that examined 26,263 participants, the average correlation between these constructs was .166. Within a meta-regression analysis that controlled for socioeconomic status, high school GPA, and standardized test scores, this relationship dropped slightly to an adjusted correlation of .134. In another meta-regression analysis that added other psychosocial predictors (academic goals, academic self-efficacy, social support, and institutional commitment), this relationship dropped considerably to .053, which suggests that one or more of these variables explains much of the link between social involvement and persistence.

A second meta-analysis examined social and academic integration and three student success outcomes: college GPA, intent to persist, and actual persistence (Pan, 2010). Her systematic review examined 71 studies with 74,009 participants for academic integration and 79 studies with 77,812 participants for social integration. However, most of this research did not examine persistence directly. Among the 32 studies that explored academic integration and actual persistence, the average correlation was .16, while the average correlation between social integration and persistence across 36 studies was slightly lower ($r = .12$). Interestingly, the relationship between academic integration and intent to persist ($r = .13$) is similar to that for actual persistence. In contrast, the link between social integration and intent to persist is much higher ($r = .32$), which suggests that students may explicitly consider social dynamics in their conscious decision-making process.

The most recent meta-analysis, conducted by Credé and Niehorster (2012), included only studies that examined social and academic adjustment using the Student Adaptation to College Questionnaire (Baker & Siryk, 1984). A benefit of using this instrument is that the items more directly assess the extent to which students are integrated within their institution socially and academically (rather than simply involved). Given the relatively narrow scope of this meta-analytical review, the sample sizes are notably smaller than for the previous two syntheses (11 studies with 3,672 students for social adjustment predicting retention, and 13 studies with 4,116 students for academic adjustment predicting retention). The average correlation for academic adjustment ($r = .18$) is similar to the academic adjustment figure for Pan's (2010) study, but the result for social adjustment ($r = .23$) is higher than the social results obtained by Pan and by Robbins et al. (2004). A meta-regression analysis found that these relationships were virtually unaffected by controlling for standardized test scores and high school GPA, so these results do not appear to be attributable to differences in precollege achievement.

These meta-analyses come with an important caveat: they all used simple bivariate correlations between integration and persistence. Credé and Niehorster (2012) and Robbins et al. (2004) avoided this problem to some extent by conducting meta-regression analyses, which are designed to simulate what would occur in a multiple regression analysis using the studies within the meta-analytical sample. By doing so, they provided support for theories of college student departure that propose institutional commitment as a mediator of the link between social involvement or integration and persistence (Bean & Eaton, 2000; Nora, 2004; Tinto, 1993). For Robbins et al., the relationship between involvement and persistence decreased substantially when they added institutional commitment, along with other factors, as predictors in their meta-regression analysis. Furthermore, when predicting persistence using meta-regression analyses and controlling for high school grades and admissions test scores, Credé and Niehorster found that institutional attachment was a stronger predictor than academic adjustment, social adjustment, and personal-emotional adjustment, especially when including all of these variables in the same model. Providing support for the presence of additional indirect relationships, multiple meta-analyses have found positive (albeit modest) correlations between integration and college GPA (Richardson, Abraham, & Bond, 2012; Robbins et al., 2004), which is then strongly related to educational persistence and attainment.

Given the use of raw correlations and meta-analytic samples of studies that largely occurred before 2003, a systematic review of more recent studies is needed. A great deal of research on this topic used the nationally representative Beginning Postsecondary Students (BPS) federal datasets (from either 1990–1994 or 1996–2001), so these studies therefore often contained very similar indices of social involvement (e.g., participation in fine arts activities, intramural sports, varsity sports, school clubs, going places with friends from school) and academic involvement (e.g., participated in study groups, met with an academic advisor, had social contact with faculty, talked with faculty about academic matters outside class). Interestingly, even studies that used the BPS dataset and had similar involvement measures and analytic samples (i.e., students who started at four-year institutions) obtained disparate results. Some articles identified positive relationships for social and/or academic involvement (e.g., Chen, 2012; Chen & St. John, 2011; Museus et al., 2008), whereas others found no significant relationships (e.g., Chen & DesJardins, 2010; Dowd, 2004; Ishitani & DesJardins, 2002).

The quality and nature of students' involvement may play a key role in determining its relationship to college attrition. In general, national studies that do not use BPS data have found positive relationships between social engagement and persistence, whether this experience takes the form of general involvement (Wang, 2009; Woosley, 2003), peer interactions and friendships (Fischer, 2007; Wolniak et al., 2012), or cocurricular activities (Fischer, 2007; Kuh et al., 2008; Wolniak et al., 2012). Although peer interactions and cocurricular activities are included in the BPS social integration index, the BPS measures these in a fairly narrow manner and combines them with other indicators that occur among a small proportion of college students (e.g., participation in varsity sports). Moreover, the relationship between social integration and persistence is sometimes nonlinear, but the nature of this association varies across studies. While some research suggests that high social engagement may be beneficial (Hu, 2011; Stratton et al., 2007), others have found that simply exceeding minimal levels is associated with persistence with little potential benefit for additional engagement (Kuh et al., 2008; Li, 2010; for combined social and academic involvement, see Leppel, 2002).

The results for normative academic integration/involvement and persistence are also mixed between positive and nonsignificant relationships, and the uneven results occur for studies that do and do not use the BPS dataset. It appears that college GPA may explain at least part of the relationship between academic integration/involvement and retention, since students with effective academic behaviors and adjustment tend to receive higher grades, which then leads to persistence. Consistent with this explanation, most studies that include a continuous college GPA measure in the analyses find no significant relationship for academic integration (Chen, 2012; Chen & DesJardins, 2010; Chen & St. John, 2011; Dowd, 2004; Fischer, 2007; Hoffman & Lowitzki, 2005; Kuh et al., 2008; Li, 2010; Lohfink & Paulsen, 2005; Pan & Bai, 2010; Settle, 2011), whereas those that do not often find positive relationships (Bai & Pan, 2009; Chen & DesJardins, 2008; Hu, 2011; Hu & McCormick, 2012; Ishitani & DesJardins, 2002; Museus et al., 2008; Stratton et al., 2007; Woosley, 2003). Wolniak et al. (2012) provide more direct evidence for this pattern. In analyses that do not include college GPA as a predictor, perceiving quality teaching is positively associated with retention, but this relationship becomes nonsignificant when college GPA is added to the model. That is, college GPA explained the relationship between a form of academic integration and retention. Offering further support, Hoffman and Lowitzki (2005) found no significant relationship between academic involvement and retention in a multivariate model, but involvement predicted greater academic achievement, which then predicted a greater likelihood of retention.

Student Groups. Some research has examined engagement in formal cocurricular activities, including athletics and student organizations. When examining educational attainment, Pascarella and Terenzini (2005) found mixed results for athletic participation, while Pascarella and Terenzini (1991) identified a positive relationship for extracurricular activities. At many institutions, varsity student-athletes are highly integrated into the campus through their extensive involvement with their sport and their team, and many institutions provide additional services for student-athletes (e.g., tutoring). Two single-institution studies at large universities have found that varsity athletes are more likely to be retained when controlling for demographics, precollege preparation, financial aid, and other factors. Wohlgemuth et al. (2007) observed a significant effect only in the first year, whereas DesJardins et al. (2003) found similar relationships for student-athlete status across seven years of college. Although intramural sports may also involve some modest integration into the campus social environment, engagement in this activity does not significantly predict bachelor's degree completion (Byun et al., 2012; Cragg, 2009).

Participation in campus student organizations is positively related to retention and graduation (Cragg, 2009; Crissman, 2002; Kuh et al., 2008) as well as reenrollment at the same university after stopping out (Woosley, 2004). Studies that conducted subgroup analyses often found significant relationships only for certain groups, such as students from rural precollege environments (Byun et al., 2012), Latino students (Baker & Robnett, 2012), and continuing-generation students (Lohfink & Paulsen, 2005). Interestingly, some of these significant subgroup findings occurred even when controlling for satisfaction with social, academic, and financial aspects of college (Baker & Robnett, 2012; Lohfink & Paulsen, 2005), although it is likely that satisfaction at least partially explains any relationship between student clubs and educational attainment. Kuh et al. also found that spending 6 to 20 hours per week in cocurricular activities is about as strongly related to retention as is spending more than 20 hours per week. Therefore, if cocurricular activities have a causal impact on college enrollment, then engaging very heavily may not be more effective than engaging a moderate amount.

Student-Institution Fit. Other research has more directly examined the definition of integration as the extent of fit or match between the individual and the institution. Several studies have done so within the context of religiously affiliated institutions, finding that retention is greater among students who personally identify with the religious affiliation of the university (Patten & Rice, 2009), who hold similar worldviews as their faculty and classmates (Morris, Beck, & Mattis, 2007) and who feel that they fit spiritually on their campus (Morris et al., 2004). Across six Canadian universities, both quantitative and qualitative measures of perceived institutional fit predict greater student retention (Wintre et al., 2008). However, these studies have at least two noteworthy shortcomings. First, they typically include few (if any) additional variables that may also explain student persistence (e.g., students with stronger high school GPAs may generally experience greater fit). Second, with the exception of Patten and Rice (2009), these studies assess students' perceptions of their own fit with the institution. These perceptions may be largely informed by their satisfaction with their educational experience rather than any objective level of fit (e.g., that compares students' desired institutional attributes with the attributes of their current institution).

Two other studies used different measures to explore the potential role of fit. Mattern, Woo, Hossler, and Wyatt (2010) used data on high school students' college preferences obtained when they took the SAT, and they linked these preferences with the characteristics and outcomes at the postsecondary institutions that they ultimately attended. Attending an institution that matched students' high school preferences for campus size and year (two-year vs. four-year) were both positively related to graduation, but several other fit dimensions were nonsignificant (e.g., distance from home, institutional control). As these authors note, students may not know what they want from a college when they are still in high school; moreover, these broad institutional characteristics may not be central to the cultural aspects of colleges and universities that are most relevant to student-institution fit.

In another study, Cragg (2009) examined the potential role of academic match (as indicated by the difference between a student's SAT score and the institutional average score) and affordability match (sum of financial aid and estimated family contribution minus cost of attendance). Affordability match did not significantly predict graduation. However, the numerical results for academic match provided in this article's tables contradict each other. The reported delta-p values provide support for a match explanation (graduation is lower among students who are 200 points above or below the institutional average), whereas the reported odds ratios are consistent with a selectivity explanation (attending a more selective school uniformly improves the likelihood of graduation). In sum, student-institution fit may play a role in promote attainment, but the evidence to date is neither particularly strong nor clear.

Enrollment Intensity. Arguably, one form of academic integration occurs through the intensity and continuity of student enrollment. At a minimum, attending college full time or taking a larger number of credits seems likely to contribute to the timeliness of degree completion (Roksa & Keith, 2008), since students should accumulate credits more quickly. In addition, enrollment intensity may lead to improved educational attainment for multiple reasons. First, students who accrue credits more slowly through part-time enrollment may perceive that they are making slow progress toward their postsecondary goals, which may be discouraging and lead to attrition. Second, factors external to college (e.g., work and family responsibilities, financial difficulties) can cause students to withdraw during or after any given semester, so enrolling in a greater number of semesters, as part-time students must generally do, increases the length of time and therefore the number of opportunities for students to leave school (see Bahr, 2012). Third, students who attend full time likely experience college as more central to their lives than do part-time students; as a result, part-time students may be more likely to leave, since they are less integrated or invested psychologically into college. Pascarella and Terenzini (2005) found strong evidence that interrupted enrollment decreased the likelihood of graduation, but they did not review evidence regarding the number of credits enrolled per semester.

To examine the link between enrollment intensity and degree progress, Doyle (2011) examined community college students who were intending to receive a bachelor's degree within the nationally representative Beginning Postsecondary Students (BPS:96/01) dataset. He used propensity score analyses to match students on a composite of 45 different variables, including demographics, high school characteristics, financial aid, reasons for college choice, type of degree program, and college remedial coursework. Even when matching to account for self-selection, he found "a linear relationship between credits taken and eventual transfer to a four-year college" (p. 191). Doyle (2009b) also conducted propensity score analyses using statewide data from public institutions in Tennessee. Students at two-year colleges who took at least 12 credit hours in their first semester were 11 to 15 percentage points more likely to transfer to a four-year institution than matched students who took fewer than 12 credits. Differences were also significant, albeit somewhat smaller, for examining cutoffs for taking at least nine credits (10–13 percentage points) and at least six credits (8–11 percentage points).

Consistent with these quasi-experimental findings, multivariate studies have frequently found a positive, significant relationship between full-time postsecondary attendance and student retention, persistence, upward transfer, and degree completion (Adelman, 2006; Byun et al., 2012; Calcagno et al., 2007a, 2007b; Eagan & Jaeger, 2009; Eddy, Christie, & Rao, 2006; Haynes Stewart et al., 2011; Jaeger & Eagan, 2009; Kalogrides & Grodsky, 2011; Kuh et al., 2008; McKinney & Novak, 2012; O'Toole, Stratton, & Wetzel, 2003; Paulsen & St. John, 2002; Porchea et al., 2010; Roksa, 2006, 2010; Roksa & Calcagno, 2010; Roksa & Keith, 2008; Somers et al., 2004; St. John et al., 2004; Taniguchi & Kaufman, 2005; Wang, 2012). Research that exclusively conducted institution-level analyses also found that the proportion of full-time students is positively associated with graduation rates (Bailey et al., 2006; Scott et al., 2006; Zhang, 2009). Among the studies that found no significant relationship, most of these had reasonably small sample sizes, which reduces the statistical power for identifying any potential differences (Dowd & Coury, 2006; Duggan, 2004; Mamiseishvili, 2012; Robbins et al., 2009; Sibulkin & Butler, 2005; Wang, 2009).

Another form of enrollment intensity is reflected by the continuity of enrollment in college. For various reasons, students may choose to stop out by not enrolling for one or more nonsummer terms and then either reenrolling at the same institution or taking courses at another institution. Not surprisingly, being continuously enrolled is strongly related to educational progress and attainment. Two studies examined the magnitude of this effect using nationally representative datasets and controlling for various demographics, precollege academic preparation, degree aspirations, and college achievement.

Wang (2012) found that community college students who were continuously enrolled were 31 percentage points more likely to transfer to a four-year institution than those who were not, and Li (2010) found that students who transferred from one four-year institution to another with no interruption were 38 percentage points more likely to receive a bachelor's degree than those who stopped out while transferring between four-year institutions. Research on this topic has found uniformly strong, positive effects of continuous (versus interrupted) enrollment on associate and bachelor's degree completion (DesJardins, Ahlberg, & McCall, 2006; Donhardt, 2006; Ishitani, 2006; Roksa, 2006, 2010; Roksa & Keith, 2008). Continuous enrollment is also associated with a shorter time to degree (Roksa & Keith, 2008), and multiple stop-outs appear to further diminish students' chances of graduation (DesJardins et al., 2006).

CONDITIONAL EFFECTS OF COLLEGE

A critical question regarding within- and between-college effects is the extent to which these findings might generalize (or not) to different institutions or different student populations. Will a particular educational experience be more or less effective in different contexts? When considering the research evidence on this issue, Pascarella and Terenzini (2005) found few replicable conditional effects in their review; in fact, one of their main findings was that the apparent impact of attending a two-year versus four-year institution was similar regardless of students' race/ethnicity and gender. The only conditional effect that was replicated to some extent was that living on campus, particularly in a living-learning community, appeared to be particularly beneficial for students of color and students who had below-average predicted success. However, the conclusions from that section were tentative, especially given that the two conditional effects identified in Pascarella and Terenzini (1991) were not subsequently replicated during the review period of the second volume.

Considerable research in the 2000s examined within- and between-college effects among subgroups of students and institutions. In most cases, no statistical tests were conducted to determine whether the relationship for one group was significantly different from that of the other group. Moreover, a large number of apparent group differences did not replicate in other research; for instance, depending on the study, the link between financial aid and attainment is larger, smaller, or about the same in students' earlier and later years in college (Chen, 2012; Chen & DesJardins, 2008, 2010; DesJardins et al., 2002b; DesJardins & McCall, 2010; Ishitani, 2003, 2006; Ishitani & DesJardins, 2002). Therefore, we used similar criteria to those of Pascarella and Terenzini (1991, 2005) in determining whether to discuss conditional effects as meaningful: (1) the statistical relationship for college impact must be significant for at least one of the subgroups or the overall sample, (2) the ratio of the coefficients between subgroups must be at least 2:1 (or the coefficients are different in sign), and (3) the same differential pattern must appear in multiple studies.

Many of the systematic conditional effects occurred for financial aid. Need-based grants are more strongly related to stopout and graduation for students from lower-income backgrounds than for those from relatively higher-income backgrounds (Alon, 2011; Castleman & Long, 2013; Chen, 2012; Chen & DesJardins, 2008, 2010) as well as for first-generation than for continuing-generation students (Lohfink & Paulsen, 2005). Merit aid is also more strongly associated with reduced stop-out for lower-income students than for higher-income students (Chen, 2012; Chen & DesJardins, 2010), and debt is more strongly associated with attrition for first-generation than for continuing-generation students (Somers et al., 2004). Conditional effects are also apparent for race/ethnicity: Black and Latino students appear to benefit more from receiving grants than do White students (Chen, 2012; Chen & DesJardins, 2008; Melguizo, 2008; St. John et al., 2004). Findings for other racial/ethnic groups and other types of aid are inconsistent across studies, but they trend toward all groups of students of color benefiting more from all types of aid. Therefore, financial aid (and particularly grants) may play an important role in promoting equitable attainment outcomes by socioeconomic status and race/ethnicity. Financial aid is also more positively related to persistence and graduation at two-year than at four-year institutions (Attewell et al., 2011; CEISS, 2004);

among four-year schools, need-based aid is more positively associated with retention and graduation at less selective than at more selective institutions (Attewell et al., 2011; Goldrick-Rab et al., 2012).

Multiple factors may account for these conditional effects. Students from lower-income backgrounds are more likely to depend heavily on their aid— regardless of whether it is awarded on need, merit, or other criteria—to stay enrolled from semester to semester than are students with greater financial resources. As a result, aid may be especially influential for less affluent students. The disparate findings by first-generation status and race/ethnicity may be proxies for these financial dynamics, since this research did not examine conditional effects by social class and race simultaneously. Furthermore, it is possible that students from marginalized and historically underrepresented backgrounds may view aid as more important in their college decision and persistence process independent of financial need. Differential patterns by institutional type may also simply reflect the greater proportion of students from lower-SES backgrounds and students of color at two-year and less selective four-year institutions. For all of these conditional effects, the relationships are more positive for groups of students and types of institutions that generally have lower retention and graduation rates, so ceiling effects for higher-achieving populations may play some role in shaping these conditional effects.

In general, first-year seminars are more strongly related to college retention and graduation among students who were less successful academically. Schnell et al. (2003) examined the interaction between high school ranking and seminar participation; they found that the differential outcomes between students who took the course and those who did not were particularly large among students who were ranked toward the bottom half of their high school (but not in the bottom 10%). In addition, within a carefully matched sample, Tuckman and Kennedy (2011) found that students who were in poor academic standing in their first college semester (below a 2.0 college GPA) seemed particularly likely to benefit from seminar participation. Similar to the conditional effects for financial aid, multiple explanations are possible, since lower-achieving students are clearly at greater academic risk and therefore have greater room for improvement. In addition, the learning strategies and other content of these first-year seminars may be especially helpful for students who are initially lower achieving, since these students likely have more to learn from such courses.

In another conditional effect that was replicated in multiple studies, racial climate was negatively and significantly related to retention and persistence among students of color, but not White students (Fischer, 2007; Johnson et al., 2014). Museus et al. (2008) also found that racial climate was more strongly related to institutional commitment among Blacks than Whites, although the direct paths from climate to degree completion were generally quite small. These differences do not appear to reflect a general sensitivity to the college context among students of color, since the link between perceptions of the overall campus environment and retention was positive for both students of color and White students (Johnson et al., 2014). At predominantly White institutions, a hostile racial climate often occurs primarily by excluding or marginalizing students of color (see Harper & Hurtado, 2007), so these differential relationships by race/ethnicity should not be surprising.

Finally, among the few studies that compared students by enrollment intensity, college GPA is more strongly related to persistence among students who are attending full time than those attending part time (McKinney & Novak, 2012; Stratton et al., 2007). The potential reasons for this disparity are unclear. Students who attend part time often have more responsibilities outside of school, so external factors may play a greater role in their attrition behavior, whereas college-related factors may be less important. In these two samples, college grades were at least as high among part-time students as full-time students, but these differences did not seem large enough to affect the relationship between GPA and persistence.

LONG-TERM EFFECTS OF COLLEGE

Chapter 8 describes the long-term economic and career effects of educational attainment, and Chapter 9 describes the quality of life after college. In addition to these personal benefits, a person's educational attainment may also affect the education of one's children. Any such impact could occur through two mechanisms: (1) children of educated parents may be more likely to attend college, and (2) these children may be more likely to persist and graduate among those who do attend college.

Pascarella and Terenzini (2005) found considerable evidence that students with college-educated parents were much more likely to attend college (for recent findings, see Brownstein, 2014). Moreover, parental education is positively related to persistence and graduation in recent research even when accounting for numerous other variables. For instance, Chen and DesJardins (2008, 2010) used event history analyses to explore predictors of student dropout within the nationally representative Beginning Postsecondary Students (BPS:96/01) survey. When controlling for parental income, student demographics (race/ethnicity, age, gender), educational expectations, precollege achievement (high school GPA, test scores), financial aid (Pell grants, loans, work-study), college experiences (academic and social integration, first-year GPA), and institutional control (public/private), students whose parents received at least a bachelor's degree were less likely to drop out than those whose parents had received less education.

This significant finding in the presence of a substantial number of control variables is noteworthy because it would be reasonable to assume, for example, that parental income, college adjustment and achievement, and other factors might explain the link between parental education and persistence. Martinez et al. (2009) explored this issue directly by examining mediators of first-generation college student status and retention. They found that test scores, high school rank, financial aid, employment, and college GPA all significantly explained some (but not all) of the link between parental education and retention. Other research has found that significant relationships for parental education sometimes disappear in statistical models that add student employment (Alfonso et al., 2005; Roksa, 2011) and enrollment intensity patterns (Alfonso et al., 2005; also see Li, 2010). However, the inclusion of additional precollege or college variables does not change this association in other studies (Niu & Tienda, 2013; Novak & McKinney, 2011; Wolniak et al., 2012).

Research exploring this topic often used several distinct levels of parental education as predictors. Overall, these results suggest that having at least one parent obtain a bachelor's degree is the most meaningful cutoff for this long-term transmission of educational attainment (Alfonso et al., 2005; Clotfelter et al., 2013; Cragg, 2009; Ishitani, 2003, 2006; Niu & Tienda, 2013; Porchea et al., 2010; Roksa, 2011; Stratton et al., 2007, 2008; Wilson, 2007). Successfully completing a bachelor's degree is likely integral to developing the social and cultural capital required for passing helpful information along to one's children. The evidence is mixed on whether father's and mother's education are differentially related to their children's attainment. In some instances, father's education significantly and positively predicts outcomes while mother's education does not (Cragg, 2009; Fike & Fike, 2008; Sibulkin & Butler, 2005), whereas Wolniak et al. (2012) observed the exact opposite pattern, and other analyses found that both are positively related or both are nonsignificant (Crissman, 2002; Fike & Fike, 2008; Otero et al., 2007; Sandy et al., 2006; Wilson, 2007). When examined on its own, mother's education is often positively related to attainment (Dowd, 2004; Ishitani & DesJardins, 2002; Kim & Conrad, 2006).

Finally, these intergenerational effects appear to vary depending on the specific indicator of continued postsecondary enrollment. Although parental education frequently predicts retention and persistence to the following year, upward transfer from a two-year college, and degree attainment, it is often unrelated to within-year persistence and retention (Fike & Fike, 2008; Hagedorn et al., 2002; McKinney & Novak, 2012; Novak & McKinney, 2011; Otero et al., 2007; Paulsen & St. John, 2002; St. John et al., 2005). In two studies that examined both within-year and between-year retention among a cohort of entering students (Fike & Fike, 2008; Hagedorn et al., 2002), parental education was positively related to retention to the following year, whereas this relationship was inconsistent for within-year retention. St. John et al. (2003) argue that "within-year persistence is influenced more by a student's financial circumstances" (p. 108), so it appears that any causal impact of parental education is more relevant to between-year decisions.

CHAPTER SUMMARY

Although educational attainment is not necessarily an educational outcome itself, it certainly contributes to a variety of benefits throughout one's life. In addition, nations with well-educated populations tend to fare much better on economic and social indicators. Therefore, understanding the factors that contribute to degree completion is critically important. Our review covers research that predicts not only the attainment of an undergraduate degree or certificate, but also persistence within higher education, retention at a particular college or university, and successful course completion.

Given the widespread use of Tinto's theory for examining college attrition, we felt it was important in this summary to consider (albeit briefly) the extent to which the findings in this chapter are consistent with his work. As discussed more generally in Chapter 11, Tinto's model or framework that hypothesizes relationships among various constructs (as shown in Tinto, 1993, p. 114) is only part of his broader theory. The critiques discussed at the beginning of this chapter focus primarily on elements of his theory that are not part of this schematic diagram. That said, substantial research reviewed in this chapter examined the direct and indirect relationships described in Tinto's model. Numerous assertions from this model were supported: social involvement is associated with social integration, which leads to institutional commitment, which then predicts retention/persistence. Institutional commitment also explains most—and sometimes all—of the relationship between social involvement and retention/persistence, as well as the link between social integration and retention/persistence. However, not all results are consistent with this model. Tinto proposed that normative academic integration explains the link between college GPA and retention. However, from a synthesis of the studies in this review, the opposite may be true: college GPA appears to explain or mediate the relationship between academic integration (or involvement) and subsequent retention/persistence; in fact, college GPA has the strongest within-college effect of the constructs in this review. Research also sheds light into the processes by which grades may cause attrition, which occurs through changes in student self-perceptions as a result of low performance or through involuntary suspension or dismissal. Another important and consistent finding in recent research is that the quality of involvement or engagement (whether academic or social) matters far more than the quantity. This nuance is not readily apparent in Tinto's model, although it is arguably included in the broader theory.

Between-College Effects

Consistent with Pascarella and Terenzini (1991, 2005), we found that the strongest institutional predictor of bachelor's degree completion is whether a student chooses to attend a two-year versus a four-year school. Among students who initially intend to obtain a bachelor's degree, starting at a two-year college reduces the likelihood of receiving that degree by 15 to 25 percentage points versus starting at a four-year college. This result is consistent with long-standing arguments about the role of community college in diverting students from their initial degree aspirations. This effect is driven by the fact that many students at two-year colleges who are seeking a bachelor's degree do not successfully transfer to a four-year institution; in fact, community college transfer students who enter four-year institutions as juniors are as likely to graduate as their peers who started at a four-year school. Importantly, despite this adverse impact on bachelor's degree attainment, two-year colleges provide notable "democratizing" benefits by increasing the attainment of students who otherwise may not have attended college at all.

The enrollment path to a postsecondary degree is often not straightforward; many students transfer laterally among institutions that award the same degree, engage in reverse transfer from a four-year to a two-year school, co-enroll simultaneously at multiple institutions, or swirl between or among institutions in alternating semesters. Overall, co-enrollment at multiple institutions is associated with greater degree completion, whereas both reverse and lateral transfer appear to decrease the likelihood of attainment (although this evidence is mixed).

Two forms of institutional "quality"—selectivity and student-faculty ratio—seem to contribute to greater persistence and completion. These findings occur within numerous rigorous studies that account for precollege academic preparation and achievement, demographics, and other confounding variables. Most of the selectivity benefits come from attending a school that is at least moderately selective versus a school that is open access or largely nonselective. This pattern appears to be partially explained by higher levels of social and academic engagement at more selective institutions. In addition, attending a school with fewer students per faculty member is associated with greater retention and graduation, but these findings are somewhat smaller in size and less consistent than those for institutional selectivity. This relationship may be explained by greater academic engagement and achievement at institutions with more favorable student-faculty ratios.

Total institutional expenditures and state allocations to public institutions appear to contribute to higher graduation rates, especially at four-year institutions. Specific types of institutional expenditures may be beneficial (e.g., instruction, student services, academic support, and institutional grants), but more evidence is needed to draw strong conclusions. The effects of all other between-college attributes are small or non-existent, such as institutional control (public/private), size, religious affiliation, urbanicity, racial/ethnic and gender composition, tuition and fees, and state policies.

Within-College Effects

The modest results for most between-college attributes suggest that students' experiences within a particular institution likely play a much stronger role in shaping persistence and attainment. Of all within-college effects, academic achievement in college has the strongest and most consistent impact on retention, persistence, and graduation within various student populations. This relationship seems to occur through at least two mechanisms. First, some students who are on academic probation may be dismissed from the university or choose to leave before a formal dismissal occurs. Second, students view their grades as a source of feedback about their learning and "ability," so they may choose to switch majors, transfer, or drop out if they come to believe that they are not well-suited for their intended degree.

Several types of curricular programmatic interventions have received substantial attention. The research on remedial or developmental coursework has advanced since Pascarella and Terenzini's (2005) review, as the increased use of rigorous quasi-experimental methods has led to stronger causal conclusions. In general, remediation often appears to have no significant impact on the progression toward and completion of a college degree, especially for students who are just below the threshold of needing any remediation. Students who take remedial course work and achieve college-level competency (by passing the introductory college course) fare as well as students who do not need remediation, but many students who take remedial coursework never achieve that important intermediate outcome. One comprehensive program seems quite promising in promoting persistence and degree completion among students who need remediation; this intervention combines several practices that may each contribute to student success (enrolling full time, taking remedial courses early, enrolling concurrently in remedial and college-level courses, receiving advising and tutoring, eliminating unmet financial need, and participating in a learning community).

First-year seminars (which are commonly offered to help students adjust successfully to college) may improve student retention and graduation, but the evidence is mixed. "Student services" includes a broad array of activities, such as academic advising, tutoring, formal mentoring, and comprehensive programs (e.g., TRiO's Student Support Services). It appears that student services are effective at promoting educational attainment when these services are used within coordinated efforts to improve student success and when the services themselves are high quality. As a specific form of student services, supplemental instruction provides additional academic support in courses (typically large, introductory ones) that are often challenging for students. Engaging in supplemental instruction appears to contribute to greater successful course completion and possibly greater retention.

The literature on financial aid is simultaneously the most voluminous and the most inconsistent of any topic in this chapter. Overall, the best studies generally find that grants and scholarships promote student retention, persistence, and graduation. The results are less clear for work-study and loans, but it seems likely that these also improve persistence and degree completion. Greater amounts of student debt and unmet need appear to reduce educational attainment; indeed, efforts to replace loans with grants and scholarships are sometimes effective in bolstering completion, especially when students have little unmet financial need. Even the act of applying for federal financial aid may improve retention and persistence, whereas working for pay extensively while in college leads to greater student attrition.

Experiences with faculty can occur in a variety of academic and nonacademic settings. Receiving high-quality instruction appears to contribute to students' retention and graduation. In contrast, the impact of the overall frequency of faculty interactions is mixed, which may reflect the fact that faculty-student interaction can occur for a variety of reasons and are not always positive experiences for students. Taking classes from part-time and non-tenure-track faculty seems to reduce retention and graduation. In terms of course delivery, successful course completion is at least as likely in face-to-face as in online courses, with some evidence suggesting less frequent completion of online coursework.

The quality of interpersonal relationships with college peers contributes to greater retention and graduation; this effect is at least partially explained by increased social integration and institutional commitment. However, the mere quantity of campus relationships and interactions with students outside one's own campus do not appear to affect attainment. Positive perceptions of the campus climate likely promote retention, persistence, and graduation, since these seem to promote institutional commitment and college satisfaction. In addition, living on campus appears to promote persistence by contributing to social involvement and integration.

Learning communities generally involve the same students taking two or more courses together. Regardless of whether these occur during the academic year or in a summer bridge program, the results are mixed between positive effects and no effect on retention. Providing opportunities for meaningful engagement outside of course work—which may happen in residence halls, through structured out-of-class activities, and through supplemental student services—may be necessary for learning communities to yield positive outcomes.

Academic major is inconsistently related to retention, persistence, and graduation. When significant differences are observed, students who major in business, engineering, and health sciences tended to have the highest retention rates, whereas students who were undeclared or in the humanities tend to fare the worst. In addition, having an undergraduate major that matches one's vocational interests appears to be beneficial.

Many studies have examined overall social and academic integration, concepts which are central to numerous theories of student attrition. Regardless of whether "integration" is measured in terms of college adjustment (psychological) or student involvement (behavioral), social integration appears to bolster retention, persistence, and graduation, and this effect may be explained by increased institutional commitment. Academic integration also appears to promote attainment through its impact on college GPA. Student-institution fit may play some role in shaping retention, but this relationship is unclear. Participation in student organizations and varsity athletics also seems to increase retention and graduation. Enrollment intensity (attending full time or taking more credits per semester) contributes positively and substantially to retention and degree completion.

Conditional Effects of College

Compared with Pascarella and Terenzini (2005), we identified more instances in which a within- or between-college effect was significantly stronger for one group of students or institutions than another. Similar to their earlier review, we held a high standard for labeling an effect as conditional, including replication of the same finding across multiple studies. In general, financial aid (particularly grants and scholarships) is more positively related to educational attainment among groups that typically have lower overall graduation rates, including students from lower socioeconomic backgrounds, students of color, and students at two-year or less-selective four-year institutions. Moreover, first-year seminars are more positively related to retention and graduation among students who were (initially) less successful academically. In all of these instances, the interventions are more effective for students from disadvantaged or marginalized groups. Campus racial climate has a direct effect on retention and persistence among students of color (but not among White students), consistent with the fact that a hostile racial climate often targets students of color. Finally, college grades are more strongly related to persistence among students who are enrolled full time than those enrolled part time.

Long-Term Effects of College

The long-term intergenerational benefits of college attendance and completion are bestowed through greater educational attainment of one's children. This effect may occur through two mechanisms: (1) children of well-educated parents enroll in college at greater rates, and (2) children of well-educated parents are more likely to persist to graduation, which was the focus of this review. Indeed, students with greater parental education had higher retention, persistence, and graduation, and this relationship was only partially explained by a number of factors, such as standardized test scores, high school achievement, financial aid, and college achievement. Having parents who received a bachelor's degree seems to be the most meaningful educational threshold for the long-term transmission of education to their children.

CHAPTER CONCLUSION

This chapter reviewed between-college, within-college, and conditional effects on retention, persistence, and graduation, along with the long-term intergenerational effects of receiving a postsecondary degree. Some of the strongest effects from Pascarella and Terenzini (1991, 2005) are replicated in this review. These consistent findings include the benefits of starting at a four-year (rather than a two-year) institution and attending a selective institution on subsequent bachelor's degree completion; greater retention and graduation among students whose parents had received a college degree; and the positive impact of various within-college experiences, including earning high grades, receiving financial aid (especially grants and scholarships), living on campus, having meaningful peer interactions and relationships, and experiencing overall social and academic integration and involvement. Other findings from this review contradict conclusions from the earlier reviews, such as the mixed evidence in this volume for some academic programmatic initiatives (e.g., remediation, first-year seminars, learning communities) and faculty-student interaction.

Moreover, comprehensive student success programs (which combine multiple initiatives and experiences) appear to constitute a particularly useful approach for promoting retention, persistence, and graduation. Some new topics were also explored in this chapter. Tuition costs and state policies designed to promote college completion appear to be virtually unrelated to retention and graduation. In contrast, some forms of institutional funding and expenditures seem to promote graduation rates, and attending college full time—or taking a larger number of credits—is strongly and positively related to educational attainment.

For the most part, this chapter and the preceding ones have reviewed dynamics that occur during the college years. This chapter also extended its consideration to whether students successfully obtain a postsecondary degree. The next two chapters focus on outcomes that occur after college: Chapter 8 explores postcollege economic and career outcomes, and Chapter 9 examines the quality of life after college.

CHAPTER EIGHT

Career and Economic Impacts of College

Previous chapters of this book have discussed the vital role higher education plays in cultivating multiple forms of college students' learning and development. Accompanying this multifaceted role is the fact that postsecondary education is driven, at least in some minds, by career and economic considerations, where students access higher education in order to improve their chances for employment or to obtain training to enter a particular occupation or industry. Since the very beginnings of higher education in the United States, colleges and universities have maintained a multifaceted purpose centered on cultivating academic and intellectual skills, as well as developing leaders in key professions and occupations. The substantial investment of individual and social resources, along with the extraordinary commitment of time and money students and their families make to attain a college education, makes students' experiences with higher education a key economic decision. Volumes of empirical studies, policy reports, and texts, including previous volumes of this book, have demonstrated that a college degree is crucial for economic opportunity and financial well-being (Carnevale, Rose, & Cheah, 2011; Pascarella & Terenzini, 1991, 2005; Paulsen & Smart, 2001; Paulsen & Toutkoushian, 2006; Zhang & Thomas, 2005). In fact, college students' decisions to obtain a postsecondary education appear, more than ever before, motivated by occupational factors and the importance of improving the quality of career opportunities. When asked about their reasons for entering college, first-year students have consistently and increasingly conveyed the importance of getting a "better" job over nearly four decades (Eagan, Lozano, Hurtado, & Case, 2013).

Since the previous volume of this book appeared, the United States has experienced the most severe economic recession since the 1930s. While it is too early to ascertain from the research published since 2000 the extent to which the onset of the recession in 2007–2008 may have influenced the effects of college on career and economic outcomes, it appears that college students who graduate during a recessionary cycle may experience lower earnings and be subject to the long-term ramifications of job displacement (Carnevale & Cheah, 2013; Davis & von Wachter, 2011; Kahn, 2010). Coupled with substantial and persistent increases in college tuition and cost of attendance well in excess of inflation (Baum & Ma, 2013), there is heightened interest in understanding career development and employment-based outcomes of students as part of the larger conversation surrounding the quality of postsecondary education. The intensified scrutiny toward the career and economic outcomes of college is evident in federal and state initiatives including the College Scorecard (U.S. Department of Education [USDOE], 2014b) and performance-based funding strategies proposed or implemented in several states that seek to hold postsecondary institutions accountable for their graduates' career trajectories.

It is within this context that we review and synthesize the literature on career and economic impacts of college. From this vast literature, we focus specifically on studies that examine the causal effects of U.S. postsecondary education on three distinct types of outcomes: career development, employment, and earnings. Studies that provide valid estimates of causal effects of college on career and economic outcomes are those that employ experimental, quasi-experimental, and nonexperimental designs with rigorous control variables to distinguish the influence of an educational intervention, experience, or environment from the influence of student differences at college entry and other confounding factors. The strongest designs for estimating causal effects of college on career and economic outcomes tend to draw from multi-institutional samples and employ longitudinal designs. While we favor such studies, we nevertheless incorporate into this review evidence from single-institution studies when the literature on a particular outcome lacks evidence from multi-institutional studies. The bulk of single-institution studies we discuss in this chapter exist within the career development literature; while they tend to focus on only a single institution sample, many are strengthened by the use of experimental design, such as random assignment of students to an intervention. The large majority of studies we review in this chapter draw from large-scale, nationally representative, and longitudinal studies that track students several years beyond college and employ a variety of sophisticated multivariate regression techniques to estimate the effects of college on career and economic outcomes. While other chapters in the book have incorporated college impact research in select international settings, we have focused this chapter on studies of the effects of college on career and economic outcomes within the U.S. context.

THEORETICAL OVERVIEW

The literature on the career and economic impacts of college is framed by theories that draw from economic, sociological, and social-psychological perspectives for understanding the effects of a college education on postcollege earnings, status attainment, and career development. We begin by briefly reviewing relevant theories and theoretical perspectives that frame research on career and economic impacts of college.

Human Capital Theory

Human capital theory presents education alongside a host of other means of improving future earnings such as improving health, family dynamics, child care, and on-the-job training that "influence future monetary and psychic income by increasing resources in people" (Becker, 1993, p. 11). In formalizing human capital theory, Becker makes the following assumptions: (1) schooling results in greater earnings and productivity because it provides "knowledge, skills, and a way of analyzing problems" (p. 19); (2) individuals respond rationally to expected benefits and costs; and (3) firms behave in order to maximize profits. Within this theoretical framework, individual or private benefits from schooling are primarily captured by the earnings that result from schooling, and individuals will invest in schooling to the point where the cost of additional schooling equals the anticipated benefit of the additional schooling (i.e., where marginal costs equals marginal benefits).

Because employers are limited in their opportunity to observe or assess employees' skills or abilities, education provides a valuable signal of workers' ability or level of productivity, which is then rewarded in the labor market through higher starting wages (Spence, 1973). As Stiglitz (1975) suggests, "The reason that the school system is the major screening institution in our society is that this information is a natural by-product of its principle activity of providing knowledge (skills) and guiding individuals into the right occupation" (p. 294). Stiglitz also makes the case that screening workers by education allows for a better matching of individual productive capacities and jobs, a productive occurrence for any employer.

Within the human capital theoretical framework are numerous studies that estimate the earnings premiums, wage differentials, or rates of return associated with an amount of education (e.g., bachelor's degree versus high school diploma) or type of education (e.g., major field of study, quality of institution attended). These studies typically rest on the assumption that education develops productive skills in students, which are subsequently rewarded in the labor market through higher earnings. This assumption has important implications for inferring causality between higher education and economic outcomes.

Status Attainment Theories

The sociological perspective based on status attainment theories place students' pathways into and through college within general models of status attainment and social mobility (Blau & Duncan, 1967; Sewell & Hauser, 1975). This perspective places relatively greater focus on how students are sorted among an array of higher education institutions, the relative influence of individual agency versus social or institutional structures, whether institutional practices reduce or reproduce social inequality, and the extent to which resources are (or are not) equally distributed among students from all socioeconomic and racial/ethnic backgrounds (Alon, 2009; Bastedo & Jaquette, 2011; Grodsky, 2007). In addition to acquiring human capital, postsecondary education exposes students to cultural, informational, and network resources in the development of social capital (Bourdieu, 1986; Coleman, 1988; Glanville & Bienenstock, 2009) that may help students make the transition from college to work in securing the socioeconomic rewards that accompany employment (Greenbank, 2009).

A related concept is that higher education sorts students according to their socioeconomic, cultural, or educational backgrounds rather than changes students' productive abilities. The credentialing or social sorting function of education positions schools as concerned with maintaining dominant and subordinate class structures rather than working to develop productive job skills (Bowles & Gintis, 1976, 2002; Collins, 1979; Rubinson & Browne, 1994). The credentialing interpretations of schooling do not connect labor market earnings to the productivity or expected productivity students may gain while in school. As Bills (2003) states, "Rather than using credentials to secure the most potentially productive workers, employer behavior is in this interpretation non-rational, unreflective, and at least potentially counterproductive" (p. 18). Within a credentialing or sorting framework, career or economic outcomes associated with postsecondary education are the result of students' ascribed backgrounds and less the result of productive skills or aptitudes developed from higher education.

Several career and economic outcomes of college exist within theoretical perspectives rooted in status attainment. Many studies we review in this chapter examine earnings or wage growth (often framed alongside a human capital perspective) conceptualized as status indicators (as opposed to measures of productivity, as is the case with studies rooted in human capital theory). Research in this area also tends to focus on outcome such as occupational status, labor force participation, and job satisfaction, and it concentrates on the effects of a college education in combination with demographic and social class backgrounds, as well as organizational contexts.

Career Development Theories

Several well-defined models or theoretical frameworks articulate the relationship between higher education and dimensions of career development, such as career maturity, identity, self-efficacy, and job attitudes, including the theory of vocational behavior (Holland, 1997), the dispositional theory of job attitudes (Staw, Bell, & Clausen, 1986; Staw & Ross, 1985), and social cognitive career theory (Lent, Brown, & Hackett, 1994).

Holland's (1959, 1985, 1997) theory of vocational behavior has provided insight into the formation of individuals' personalities and the effects they have on vocational involvement, decision making, and job attitudes. Holland's theory is one of personality development in which educational experiences have a central role, where individuals' interests, values, and aspirations interact with different environmental contexts (such as college major and the congruence between majors and jobs) that ultimately shape job attitudes. Holland's work has been widely used to inform research focused on college majors and major-job field congruence in relation to career and economic outcomes, as well as a host of other outcomes related to person-environment fit (Neumann, Olitsky, & Robbins, 2009; Pike, 2006a, 2006b; Pike, Smart, & Ethington, 2012; Smart, Ethington, & Umbach, 2009; Smart, Ethington, Umbach, & Rocconi, 2009; Smart & Umbach, 2007; Wolniak & Pascarella, 2005). In this framework, the alignment between individuals' vocational interests and environments affect the degree of continuity in their occupational decisions, which in turn influence success and satisfaction on the job.

Staw and colleagues' dispositional theory of job attitudes (Staw et al., 1986; Staw & Ross, 1985) contributed the proposition that "people's affective dispositions can be thought of as general tendencies toward positive or negative evaluation of life stimuli—tendencies that should influence the way people perceive work environments during their lives" (Staw et al., 1986, p. 61). Dispositions are important in recognizing the tendencies that may lead a worker to report a level of satisfaction (or dissatisfaction) that remains stable over time and across different employment relationships or work tasks. The satisfaction that employees gain from their jobs is an important determinant of a quality work experience and a quality life experience (Judge & Watanabe, 1993; Mirvis & Lawler, 1984). Gottfredson's (1981, 1996) theory of circumscription and compromise similarly centers on the individual's perceptions of the world of work, in which career choices as well as the stability of career aspirations unfold based on a process of reconciling aspects of one's self-concept with one's perceived aspects of different occupations (Junk & Armstrong, 2010).

In addition, social cognitive career theory (SCCT) builds on Bandura's (1986) social cognitive theory by connecting self-efficacy, outcome expectations, and goals to understand how educational experiences lead to expectations or outcome-related goals (Lent et al., 1994). According to SCCT, people are more likely to pursue occupations for which they believe they have greater likelihood of favorable outcomes, such as employment and satisfaction. The related career self-efficacy theory (Betz & Hackett, 2006) focuses on capacities needed to make career-related decisions. Given the uncertain outcomes that accompany college students' educational decisions, self-efficacy and the ability to identify and work toward a set of goals with the belief of being successful are important determinants of career development and career decision making and have been influential in the evolving role of career centers on many college campuses (Dey & Cruzvergara, 2014). Research in this domain tends to focus on outcomes such as career maturity and career identity development (Betz, 1988; Crites & Savickas, 1996).

The majority of studies on the career and economic impacts of college we have included in this chapter draw from at least one of these three theoretical domains. In Table 8.1 we summarize the literature according to the primary theory (or theories) mentioned in each study. In some cases, researchers address multiple theories in a single study (e.g., human capital and career development), while in other cases, authors do not make explicit that the research builds on a particular theory or theoretical model. It is important to recognize that what is ultimately included or excluded in a research publication is at least partially due to the different publication standards and the blind review process across peer-reviewed journals. Our organization of studies by

Table 8.1 Studies Reviewed by Primary Theoretical Perspective

Theoretical Perspective	Citation
Human capital	Bitzan, 2009; Black & Smith, 2004, 2006; Deil-Amen & Rosenbaum, 2004; Del Rossi & Hersch, 2008; Greenstone & Looney, 2011; Heckman, Lochner, & Todd, 2008; Henderson, Olbrecht, & Polachek, 2006; Hilmer & Hilmer, 2012; Hu & Wolniak, 2010, 2013; Liu, Thomas, & Zhang, 2010; Long, 2008, 2010; Molitor & Leigh, 2005; Neumann, Olitsky, & Robbins, 2009; Oreopoulos & Petronijevic, 2013; Park, 2011; Perna, 2003, 2005; Robst, 2007; Roksa & Levey, 2010; Rumberger, 2010; Strayhorn, 2008; Thomas, 2003; Thomas & Zhang, 2005; Toutkousian, Najeeb Shafiq, & Trivette, 2013; Wolniak & Pascarella, 2007; Wolniak, Seifert, Reed, & Pascarella, 2008; Xu, 2013; Zhang & Thomas, 2005; Zhang, 2005, 2008a, 2008b
Status attainment	Liu, Thomas, & Zhang, 2010; Long, 2008, 2010; Rumberger, 2010; Thomas, 2003; Thomas & Zhang, 2005; Wolniak & Pascarella, 2007; Wolniak, Seifert, Reed, & Pascarella, 2008; Xu, 2013; Zhang & Thomas, 2005; Zhang, 2005g, 2008a
Career development	Blanchard & Lichtenberg, 2003; Diegelman & Subich, 2001; Folsom & Reardon, 2003; Junk & Armstrong, 2010; Neumann, Olitsky, & Robbins, 2009; Reese & Miller, 2006; Scott & Ciani, 2008; Szelenyi, Denson, & Inkelas, 2013
Other (specified)	Flowers, 2004b (Theory of Student Involvement [Astin, 1984]); Taniguchi, 2005 (Life Course Theory [Elder, 1998])
Unknown/ not specified	Flowers, 2002; Gill & Leigh, 2003; Hu & Kuh, 2003b; Hubbard, 2011; Light & Strayer, 2004; Sax & Bryant, 2006

theoretical perspective is based solely on what is explicitly mentioned in each publication in order to provide a general organizational scheme for situating research on the career and economic impacts of college by theoretical perspective.

In the next sections of the chapter, we discuss literature on the career and economic impacts of college. Throughout the chapter, we organize the literature according to studies of career development outcomes (e.g., career maturity, vocational identity, career self-efficacy), employment outcomes (e.g., full-time employment, job satisfaction, occupational status), and earnings (e.g., annual earnings, wage rates, rates of return). Because much of the literature on the career and economic impacts of college focuses on outcomes several years after college, we do not include in this chapter a separate section on long-term effects. Instead, the evidence pertaining to long-term outcomes is synthesized within the other five sections.

CHANGE DURING COLLEGE

Conclusions from the 1990s

The small body of evidence from the 1990s demonstrated that students become more mature, knowledgeable, and focused during college in their thinking about a career, and that college seniors have a more accurate perspective and greater workplace readiness than do students with less exposure to college. By and large, these conclusions were based on students' self-reports and do not rule out the fact that such change during college is anything more than the influence of maturation. This finding also mirrored that of the first volume of this book.

Evidence from the 2000s

Similar to the two preceding volumes, a small body of evidence from the 2000s addresses how students change during college with respect to career and economic outcomes. In part, this paucity is to be expected given the nature of employment and earnings as outcomes, which are not realized until after college. The evidence that does exist in terms of change during college centers on the development of career-related outcomes among college students, such as attitudes, aspirations, and dispositions toward careers.

While several well-designed studies examine career development among college students, we are very limited in the conclusions we can make pertaining to change during college, as nearly all studies focus on specific, time-limited, career-oriented courses or interventions (Diegelman & Subich, 2001; Folsom & Reardon, 2003; Reese & Miller, 2006; Scott & Ciani, 2008) or various experiences and activities (Flowers, 2004b; Sax & Bryant, 2006; Szelenyi, Denson, & Inkelas, 2013) which we discuss in the "Within-College Effects" section. Additional limitations to assessing change during college include the need for baseline (or pretest) measures against which change may be measured. From the literature, we highlight two pretest-posttest, multi-institutional studies of career development of college students.

Sax and Bryant (2006) examine career choices, specifically the changes in sex-atypical career aspirations of men and women. Drawing on longitudinal data of fall 1994 precollege characteristics and attitudes and the 1998 follow-up data, this study assessed change across four years of college among a national sample of more than 17,500 undergraduates. The study's outcome measure was the extent to which men's and women's career choices are atypical for their sex, defined according to percentages of men and women indicating as first-year students that they aspired to the occupation. If, for example, the percentage of women indicating they aspired to a particular occupation was at least twice the percentage of men, that occupation was considered sex atypical for men or female dominated. The results from descriptive analyses indicate that (1) most students entered college predisposed toward careers that were traditional for their gender or gender neutral (a finding that partially reflects how occupations' gender neutrality/atypicality was measured), and (2) over four years of college, roughly one-third of students experienced changing aspirations, typically from gender-neutral to traditional careers. The results from the multivariate analyses uncovered a host of environmental and experiential/involvement measures that predict change toward career sex atypicality; we highlight those findings later in the chapter when discussing within-college effects.

Another pretest-posttest, multi-institutional study on career development was Junk and Armstrong's (2010) examination of the stability of career aspirations among college students. The study examines change in career aspirations over one year among students from seven private liberal arts colleges to test if, or to what extent, dimensions of career aspirations remain stable over the time period studied. Distinct measures of occupational aspirations were constructed to address multiple dimensions, including sex type (the percentage of female employees in a particular occupation), prestige (based on average education and salary levels within an occupational field), and interest-based ratings (based on Holland's realistic, investigative, artistic, social, enterprising, and conventional [RIASEC] typology). Though the data were quite old (collected at two times across 1981 and 1982), the study addresses the complexity of different dimensions of aspirations rooted in self-concept, interest ratings, and prestige. Partial correlations derived from the longitudinal data indicate greater-than-expected stability in expressed career aspirations (as opposed to compromise from initial career aspirations), particularly in terms of interests and prestige dimensions. Examining men and women separately revealed prestige as the most stable dimension among men, and interests as the most stable among women.

The findings build on earlier work by Blanchard and Lichtenberg (2003), who found that as students are faced with varying levels of compromise (the extent to which individuals move away from what are perceived as idealistic to more realistic aspirations) when making career choices, students' interests are the most important decision-making factor in low-compromise conditions, but overshadowed by a career's prestige and sex type (whether one believes a job tends to be done more by women or by men) in moderate- or high-compromise conditions. Whether similar findings exist over four years of college awaits replication.

NET EFFECTS OF COLLEGE

Conclusions from the 1990s

The body of evidence uncovered in the 1990s centered on the effect of college on employment and earnings outcomes. In terms of occupational status, completing a postsecondary degree or certificate provided significant advantages relative to a high school diploma, where the advantages were greater for more advanced degrees. Specifically, completing a bachelor's degree was found to provide significant advantages in occupational status of roughly 0.95 standard deviations (33 percentile points), completing an associate's degree accompanied between 0.24 and 0.44 standard deviations (9 to 17 percentile points) advantage, and other amounts of postsecondary education or sub-baccalaureate credentials such as a vocational degree, license, or certificate resulted in between 0.12 to 0.22 standard deviations (5 to 9 percentile point) advantage.

Evidence also suggested that increases in the amount of postsecondary education increased students' likelihood of employment (or decreased the likelihood of unemployment). In terms of job satisfaction, however, the effect of postsecondary education was mixed; small but somewhat conflicting evidence from the 1990s suggested that the influence of postsecondary education on satisfaction with one's work was likely indirect, acting through factors such as job prestige and earnings, job autonomy, and nonroutine work. Controlling for those factors, the net effect of a college degree on job satisfaction was found to be negative, possibly because education tends to raise expectations toward the intrinsic and extrinsic rewards of one's work.

In terms of earnings, a large body of evidence pointed to the sizable premiums accompanying a bachelor's degree relative to a high school diploma, both in terms of annual earnings (ranging from 37% for men and 39% for women) and hourly wages (28% for men and 35% for women). The size of the effects increased somewhat from the estimates found in the literature from the 1980s. At the sub-baccalaureate level, the net effect on annual earnings of an associate's degree relative to a high school diploma was 17% for men and 27% for women. The effects on hourly wages were similar: approximately 13% for men and 22% for women. Evidence suggested that the earnings effects of an associate's degree were similar for noncredentialed returning adult workers and for continuing high school graduates. In addition, one full-time year of postsecondary enrollment without a degree or certificate was accompanied by an earnings increase of about 5% over a high school diploma. When factoring in the direct and indirect costs of attending college, the private rate of return for a bachelor's degree was estimated to be roughly 12%, ranging from 9% to 16% across studies.

Evidence from the 1990s also pointed to a credentialing or program effect whereby completing a degree yields significantly higher earnings than the equivalent number of college credits without a degree, supporting the notion that colleges and universities function, at least in part, as certifying bodies. At the bachelor's degree level, men earned an average of 15% more and women earned an average of about 12% more than their counterparts who completed four years of college credits without a degree. The credential advantages at the associate's degree level remained a sizable 9% for men and 11% for women.

Evidence from the 2000s

In this section, we summarize the evidence on the net effects of college on career and economic outcomes. Our estimates are based on the average effects (e.g., earnings or wage premiums, rates of return) that accrue to individuals, notwithstanding the type of postsecondary institution attended or one's academic and nonacademic experiences once there (e.g., major field of study, grades, extracurricular involvement). Some estimates we discuss are net of various academic and nonacademic experiences, while other estimates did not control for such factors, potentially masking the unique effect of college by not accounting for variations in between- and within-college effects. We have organized the literature by type of outcome, including employment-related outcomes (workforce participation, occupational status, job satisfaction) and earnings (annual income and hourly wages), with most evidence pertaining to earnings differences by years of higher education or type of postsecondary degree.

Across the studies we have included in this synthesis, the majority draw on publicly available, nationally representative, and predominantly longitudinal data, providing generalizable evidence as to the net effects of college on career and economic outcomes. Table 8.2 summarizes the datasets included in the synthesis.

Employment Outcomes. We uncovered four studies from the first decade of the twenty-first century that produced evidence on the relationships between higher education attainment and aspects of employment, each drawing on nationally representative datasets to estimate the influence of years of higher education or type of postsecondary degree. Each study explored a different employment outcome, as follows.

Long (2010) examined data from multiple nationally representative, longitudinal studies with information on cohorts of students from the 1970s, 1980s, and 1990s. After accounting for a host of confounding factors (demographics, precollege academics and socioeconomics, high school participation, religion, and local labor market and neighborhood characteristics), results indicate that each year of higher education completed (converted into years based on categorical measures of attainment) leads to a small but statistically significant 1.1% increase in the probability of labor force participation 10 years after high school. In other words, completing a bachelor's degree increases the average probability of employment by roughly 4% or more depending on the number

Table 8.2 Primary Data Sources Providing Evidence on the Net Effects of College by Study

Source	Data	Date	Citation
Public	Baccalaureate and Beyond Study (B&B)	1993/1997/ 2003	Zhang, 2008b
	Current Population Survey (CPS)	1999–2003	Bitzan, 2009
		1964–2006	Heckman, Lochner, & Todd, 2008
	High School and Beyond (HSB)	1980/1992	Long, 2008; Perna, 2003
	National Education Longitudinal Study (NELS)	1988/2000	Long, 2010; Perna, 2005; Rumberger, 2010
	National Longitudinal Survey of Youth (NLSY)	1979/1989/ 1996	Gill & Leigh, 2003; Light & Strayer, 2004; Molitor & Leigh, 2005; Roksa & Levey, 2010; Taniguchi, 2005
	National Survey of College Graduates (NSCG)	1993	Robst, 2007
		2003	Del Rossi & Hersch, 2008
Private	ACT Alumni Outcomes Survey	1991–2006	Neumann, Olitsky, & Robbins, 2009
	Appalachian Region Alumni Outcomes Survey	2000	Wolniak, Seifert, Reed, & Pascarella, 2008

of years a student takes to complete his or her degree. Adding evidence on hours worked in relationship to advanced degree attainment among bachelor's degree recipients, Zhang (2008b) found that 10 years after finishing a bachelor's degree, completing a master's degree or a PhD leads to roughly 3% and 6% more hours worked, respectively. Together, these studies demonstrate that higher education degree attainment increases the likelihood and intensity of work.

Focusing on job satisfaction, Perna's (2005) results suggest a positive effect of postsecondary attainment on a dichotomous, overall measure of job satisfaction roughly eight years after high school graduation. The results show that high school graduates who attained bachelor's and advanced degrees were more satisfied with their jobs than high school graduates who completed only some or no postsecondary education. Net of sociodemographic differences, relative to completing no postsecondary education, there appears to be a 6 to 9% increase in the probability of reporting overall job satisfaction for those who complete a bachelor's or advanced degree, respectively. While based on only a single study, evidence of a positive effect of advanced degree attainment on job satisfaction is a departure from the mixed evidence reported in the previous volume of this book.

Additional evidence on the effects of postsecondary degrees on employment outcomes stemmed from Roksa and Levey's (2010) investigation of occupational status. Among bachelor's degree recipients, completing a graduate degree significantly enhanced growth in occupational status across components of the socioeconomic index (Hauser & Warren, 1979). Moreover, the positive effects remained significant in the presence of controls for major field of study and a host of confounding demographic, family, and employment factors.

Earnings. A handful of rigorous studies provided evidence on the extent to which higher education has a positive impact on earnings, either in terms of annual salary or wage rates. The studies we uncovered provide evidence on the earnings effects of years of higher education (Bitzan, 2003; Long, 2010; Neumann et al., 2009; Park, 2011; Rumberger, 2010; Wolniak et al., 2008), as well as attainment of a bachelor's degree (Bitzan, 2003; Gill & Leigh, 2003; Light & Strayer, 2004; Molitor & Leigh, 2005; Perna, 2003, 2005; Taniguchi, 2005), an advanced degree (Bitzan, 2003; Del Rossi & Hersch, 2008; Gill & Leigh, 2003; Molitor & Leigh, 2005; Perna, 2003, 2005; Robst, 2007; Zhang, 2008b), and sub-baccalaureate completion, including an associate's or vocational degree or license/certificate (Bitzan, 2003; Gill & Leigh, 2003; Light & Strayer, 2004; Molitor & Leigh, 2005; Perna, 2003, 2005). In addition to these studies, we benefited from one review of evidence on the economic returns to higher education for individual students (Oreopoulos & Petronijevic, 2013).

Across studies that draw on numerous multi-institutional and representative datasets, and controlling for different sets of variables, it appears that for every year of higher education attained, earnings or wages increase by roughly 0.20 to 0.22 standard deviations (8 to 9 percentile points); a finding that appeared across studies within the first few years of one's career (Rumberger, 2010), and on average, across cohorts of college alumni five to 25 years after college (Wolniak et al., 2008). Studies that provide information for calculating the percent change in earnings demonstrate that earnings increase by approximately 4.8% per year of higher education attained within the first few years following college (based on NELS:88/2000 data capturing information eight years after high school; see Long, 2010), and rising to approximately 7 to 9% decades after college (Neumann et al., 2009; Park, 2011; Wolniak et al., 2008). Compared to the roughly 5% earnings benefit per year of higher education that was found in the 1990s literature, the more recent evidence suggests that the economic effect of an additional year of higher education is holding steady and possibly increasing. Evidence further indicates that the marginal return to higher education is nonlinear, increasing to a maximum level at approximately 16 years of education (Park, 2011), the equivalent to a bachelor's degree.

In terms of postsecondary degree completion, the net effects of college vary based on type of degree attained, with the most consistent evidence pointing to the sizable effect of a bachelor's degree on annual earnings or wages. When compared to individuals with no postsecondary education, the majority of evidence indicates that completing a bachelor's degree leads to a 15 to 27% earnings or wage increase. For example, Perna's (2005) analysis of bachelor's degree completers early in their career (eight years after high school) yielded evidence of a 19% increase in annual income. Gill and Leigh (2003) analyzed data representing individuals in the middle phase of their careers (in their thirties), finding a positive wage effect of completing a bachelor's degree (versus high school diploma) between 22 and 25%. Other studies report somewhat larger differences (Dahl, 2002; Light & Strayer, 2004; Molitor & Leigh, 2005; Perna, 2003; Taniguchi, 2005), most likely attributed to varying levels of control within the statistical models.

At the sub-baccalaureate level, studies focused on the wage rates among individuals in the middle phases of their careers (Gill & Leigh, 2003; Light & Strayer, 2004; Molitor & Leigh, 2005) or on average for a generalizable cross-section of the population (Bitzan, 2009). Together, Gill and Leigh (2003) and Light and Strayer (2004) reported an 11 to 19% wage premium for completing a terminal associate's degree (versus a high school diploma). Bitzan's study of the wage effects of degree completion, controlling for years of education among men, indicated wage effects for credentials of between roughly 5 to 7% for vocational degrees and between 3 and 7% for associate's degrees (versus a high school diploma). Perna (2005) similarly estimated a 4% earnings effect for an associate's degree in the initial years after graduation. Across these studies, associate's and vocational degrees appear to generate 3 to 7% higher earnings, and increasing the more years one spends in the labor market.

By simultaneously examining the effect of vocational or associate's degree attainment and years of education, Bitzan's (2009) study added evidence of credentialing (or "sheepskin") effects. Among a national sample of White and Black men, the earnings effect of a degree or credential significantly and positively increases wages above and beyond the effects of an additional year of education; in addition, the credentialing effects of a bachelor's degree is stronger among White men, whereas the credentialing effect of graduate degrees is stronger among Black men.

Graduate degrees also have a positive influence on career earnings, with considerable variation by type of degree. Among a sample of bachelor's degree completers, Del Rossi and Hersch (2008) present average earnings effects for individuals at various stages of their careers, indicating that an MBA or other master's in business leads to roughly 33% higher earnings than a bachelor's degree, whereas a master's degree in a nonbusiness field accompanies 11% higher earnings. A doctoral degree appears to yield 33% higher earnings, and at the high end of the distribution, an MD and JD accompany a 115% and 71% earnings premium, respectively. Estimates within this range were also reported by Robst (2007), while Molitor and Leigh's (2005) most conservative estimates resulted in roughly a 40% increase in midcareer annual wages based on completing an advanced (greater than bachelor's) degree. Zhang (2008b) also examined bachelor's degree completers, but did so within the early career phase, finding that a combined category of master's and first professional degrees leads to roughly 6% higher earnings four years after a bachelor's degree, which increases to 11% ten years after college graduation. Perna (2005) similarly reported a 5% early career earnings effect for an advanced degree.

Private Rate of Return. The earnings studies we have reviewed provide important evidence of the net monetary benefits resulting from higher education, but they do not formally incorporate the direct and indirect costs of acquiring additional education. Research that does incorporate the full range of costs produces rate of return estimates that accrue to individuals. Rate of return studies are important because they provide students, researchers, and policymakers with a single metric to evaluate the returns on an investment in higher education relative to other investment alternatives and to determine if the return on a college degree is changing over time. For more than 50 years, economists have been examining the rate of return on educational investments based on comparisons of discounted present value costs versus benefits (Hansen, 1963; Schultz, 1963).

The rate of return on a college education is perhaps the best single measure of the economic value of a college education, applicable to decision making in both the public and private sectors. We focus our attention here on the evidence of the private rates of return that accrue to individuals based on their costs incurred and resulting benefits of investing in higher education. Readers interested in a comprehensive and detailed discussion of the concepts and methods related to estimating postsecondary rates of return should refer to Toutkoushian and Paulsen's (2016) *Economics of Higher Education: Background, Concepts, and Applications.*

Rate of return estimates are mathematically complex, requiring a host of assumptions to arrive at a single measure for a given amount of education. Key assumptions include inflation rates, the annual discount rate (the difference in value assigned to money today versus the same amount of money at a future time), direct educational costs (e.g., tuition, fees, books), indirect educational costs (e.g., forgone earnings while enrolled or opportunity costs), the probability of completing a degree, income tax rates for individuals with different levels of education, retirement age, and lifetime annual earnings (Heckman, Lochner, & Todd, 2006; Paulsen & Smart, 2001; Toutkoushian & Paulsen, 2016). Though a variety of methods exist, as described by Heckman et al. (2008), Menon (2003), Psacharopoulos and Patrinos (2004), and Toutkoushian, Najeeb Shafiq, and Trivette (2013), one of the more prevalent approaches is to calculate the internal rate of return (IRR), which is useful for comparing the returns across investment alternatives. The IRR is the rate at which the present value of costs (the current worth of anticipated future spending) on an investment equals the present value of benefits (the current worth of anticipated future earnings).

A small but rigorous literature from the 2000s addresses private rates of return to college. Noting that past earnings estimates of bachelor's degree completion do not take into account the risk of not completing a degree, Toutkoushian et al. (2013) combined graduation and retention data (from the 2011 *Digest of Education Statistics*), cost data (from the College Board's 2012 *Trends in College Pricing*), and earnings and tax data (from the 2011 Current Population Survey) among those 25 to 34 years old to examine the returns to attending college for those who graduated and those who did not. Estimates indicate that the IRR of attending a public college is 14%, ranging from 20% for those who completed a degree to roughly 5% for those who attended but did not complete a degree. The parallel set of estimates for attending a private institution is 12% overall, 15% for degree completers, and 4% for attendees who did not complete a degree. The sizable increase in returns likely reflects unobserved ability and aspirational differences between those who attend and those who ultimately complete a college degree.

Heckman et al. (2008) examined seven decades of CPS data to arrive at IRR estimates of White and Black men across levels of education attainment. The results show that in 2000, after taking into account tuition costs and tax rates, completing 14 versus 12 years of education (comparable to a two-year college degree versus a high school diploma) accompanies roughly a 8% IRR for White men and 12% for Black men. Completing 16 versus 12 years of education (comparable to a four-year college degree versus a high school diploma) yields a 13% IRR for White men and a 16% IRR for Black men. The study did not include a measure of degree completion and therefore does not represent credentialing (or "sheepskin") effects. A key finding is that IRR may be overestimated by up to 5 to 8% if taxes and tuition are not taken into account. Supporting evidence was reported in a 2011 Brookings Institution report that used national data to estimate a 15% rate of return for a two-year college degree (Greenstone & Looney, 2011), leading the authors to note the returns to a college degree range from two to more than five times higher than the individual returns that accompany other kinds of investments, such as the stock market, government bonds, and housing.

Together, evidence from the 2000s suggests a private rate of return to a four-year college education ranges from 12 to 14% on average and may be as high as 15 to 20% when taking into account credentialing effects, as well as investment risk and uncertainty. These estimates are larger than those reported in previous volumes (which ranged from approximately 10% in the 1991 volume to 12% in the 2005 volume). As Pascarella and Terenizini (2005) pointed out regarding the evidence from the 1990s, these estimates tend not to account for all monetary returns such as health care, retirement, stock options, support for continuing professional development, or the option value that accompanies a bachelor's degree (e.g., the option of entering graduate or professional school), leading the authors to consider the estimates to be conservative, lower-bounds figures. Other limitations are addressed in the studies we have reviewed. Toutkoushian et al. (2013), for example, noted that the IRR differences between attending public and private institutions will differ as average earnings differences occur for graduates of public or private institutions. In fact, the approach to accounting for the risk of uncertainty illustrates the conservative nature of estimates that do not take risk into account (a notion formally discussed by Heckman et al., 2006). It may be that the evidence from the most recent decade provides a more accurate depiction of the true rate of return of a college degree. Ultimately, evidence of consistent and sizable rates of return of a college education is a noteworthy finding given the intensity of concern and level of attention centered on college costs. In short, a college education remains an extremely sound investment.

BETWEEN-COLLEGE EFFECTS

Conclusions from the 1990s

At least 50% of the total body of evidence on between-college effects uncovered in the previous volume (Pascarella & Terenzini, 2005) provided estimates of the effects of institutional quality on career and economic returns. Quality was most often measured by way of student-body selectivity and, to a lesser extent, various combinations of academic expenditure per student, reputational ratings, faculty/student ratio, tuition, percentage of faculty with PhDs, and the like. The large volume of evidence in this area highlights scholars' concern in the 1990s over the earnings differences that may be tied to attending different types of postsecondary institutions. The remaining body of evidence from the 1990s on career and economic outcomes focused on the influence of other institutional characteristics, including institutional control (public versus private), Carnegie Classification, institutional size, racial composition, gender composition, two-year versus four-year colleges, and other college environment measures.

A consistent finding was that measures of institutional quality, particularly student body selectivity, tend to have the most pronounced influence on students' subsequent earnings. When *quality* is defined as selectivity, attending a college with a 100-point higher SAT score (or ACT equivalent) is associated with an increase (net of students' precollege characteristics, including preparation and achievement) of about 2 to 4% higher earnings later in life. Besides earnings, the evidence suggested that measures of institutional quality have little more than a trivial direct effect on overall occupational status other than institutions in the upper 1 or 2 percent of the selectivity distribution, which appear to enhance occupational attainment in specific high-status professions such as medicine and law. Attending a selective college appeared to confer a modest net advantage in job attainment and career mobility.

Little empirical evidence demonstrated the influence of other institutional quality measures when institutional selectivity was taken into account. For example, attending a private (versus public) college, an institution's Carnegie Classification, two-year (versus four-year) college, or institution size appeared to have only trivial and nonsignificant net effects on career and occupational outcomes. One exception to this pattern was the evidence that institutional size conferred a small but statistically significant advantage in subsequent earnings, possibly from the greater diversity in major fields of study and broader occupational linkages offered at larger institutions. Another exception was that, controlling for educational attainment, initially attending a two-year college appeared to have a very small, negative effect on subsequent occupational status, though initially enrolling in a two-year college did not seem to confer a significant earnings penalty for students who ultimately had comparable levels of education attainment.

In addition, scholarship in the 1990s yielded reasonably consistent evidence to suggest that non–African American students, particularly men, experience earnings advantages based on attending a racially diverse campus. However, mixed and inconsistent evidence was found for those attending HBCUs, single-sex colleges, or two-year (versus four-year) institutions. Across all college environment measures, the strongest evidence was found to support the notion of "progressive conformity," such that, all else equal, a student's major field of study and career choice are influenced in the direction of the dominant peer group at the institution.

An important, overarching concern that stemmed from the previous volume was that the estimated earnings effects of having a bachelor's degree from a selective institution may be inflated. Studies generally did not control for measures of individual ambition and other unobserved characteristics, which may influence students' pathways into selective colleges and universities, as well as their subsequent productivity and earnings.

Evidence from the 2000s

Building on the scholarship from the 1990s, research from the preceding decade placed considerable attention on examining if differences in students' career and economic outcomes of college may be attributable to the characteristics of institutions attended. While a large share of studies focus on institutional quality or selectivity, the ways in which these constructs are measured and operationalized differ across studies. As discussed in the previous chapters of this volume, numerous methodological challenges accompany the estimation of between-college effects, and three particularly notable challenges accompany the study of career and economic outcomes. First, the influence of the college attended (or some specific institutional characteristic) on students' career and economic outcomes is likely confounded by differences in career-salient characteristics of students at different colleges (e.g., popularity of certain major fields, orientations toward careers, graduate school aspirations). Second, when estimating the monetary returns or earnings premiums associated with attending different kinds of colleges, studies should take into account or somehow at least acknowledge the substantial differences in cost of attendance and average levels of student indebtedness across institutions (Baum & Ma, 2013; Baum & Payea, 2013). Third, estimating between-college effects is complicated by students' transferring institutions, which is increasingly prevalent among U.S. college students (Simone, 2014). Given these challenges, the body of evidence we summarize in this chapter represents studies that met two key criteria: (1) employed methods to partially control or adjust for confounding factors to account for selection and recruitment effects when isolating the effects of institutional characteristics on career and economic outcomes and (2) used large-scale, multi-institutional datasets.

Across the studies we have included in this synthesis, most draw on publicly available, nationally representative, longitudinal data, providing a robust set of estimates on which to identify between-college effects on career and economic outcomes. The data included in this synthesis represent those shown in Table 8.3.

We have organized the evidence according to the institutional characteristics examined, including institutional quality or selectivity, institution type (such as

Table 8.3 Primary Data Sources Providing Evidence on Between-College Effects by Study

Source	Data	Date	Citation
Public	Baccalaureate and Beyond Study (B&B)	1993/1997/ 2003	Bellas, 2001; Liu, Thomas, & Zhang, 2010; Strayhorn, 2008; Thomas, 2003; Thomas & Zhang, 2005; Xu, 2013; Zhang, 2005, 2008b
	High School and Beyond (HSB)	1980/1992	Long, 2008
	National Education Longitudinal Study (NELS)	1988/2000	Long, 2008
	National Longitudinal Survey of Youth (NLSY)	1979/1989/ 1996	Black & Smith, 2004, 2006; Gill & Leigh, 2003; Light & Strayer, 2004
	National Longitudinal Study of the High School Class of 1972 (NLS)	1972/1986	Long, 2008, 2010
Private	Appalachian Region Alumni Outcomes Survey	2000	Wolniak & Pascarella, 2007
	College Student Experience Questionnaire (CSEQ)	1990–2000	Flowers, 2002
	Cooperative Institutional Research Program (CIRP)	1970–1980	Henderson, Olbrecht, & Polachek, 2006
	Gates Millennium Scholars (GMS) Longitudinal Study	2002/2006	Hu & Wolniak, 2010

Carnegie Classification and control), mission (e.g., HBCUs, work colleges), and institutional racial composition. Within each of these sections, we present evidence of between-college effects on career development, employment outcomes, and earnings.

Institutional Selectivity. Research from the 2000s consistently provided evidence that, net of adjustments for students' precollege characteristics, college graduates' career outcomes and particularly earnings are significantly and positively associated with the selectivity of institution attended (Black & Smith, 2004, 2006; Dale & Krueger, 2002;[1] Zhang, 2005, 2008a, 2008b). We benefit from the framing and historical overview of the literature provided by Zhang and Thomas (2005) that outlines the prominent measures of college quality, including average SAT/ACT scores of entering freshmen, tuition, expenditures per full-time-equivalent (FTE) student, and ratings. The most common institutional quality measure found among these studies was Barron's selectivity ratings, which categorizes institutions into six selectivity groups based on entering students' class rank, high school GPA, average SAT scores, and percentage of applicants admitted (Barron's, 2013; Fox, 1993).

In addition to complexities accompanying different approaches to measuring institutional quality, important methodological challenges exist for studying the between-college effects on career and economic outcomes. In particular, research in this area is plagued by selection bias, given the influence that students' educational and socioeconomic backgrounds have on the choice of what college to attend and on subsequent career success. The strongest analytical designs attempt to reduce the influence of self-selection by including as statistical controls a variety of confounding factors—variables such as educational motivation and aspirations—and controlling for typically unobserved characteristics through instrumental variables or various matching strategies. Differences in the timing that earnings data are captured also introduce complexity when synthesizing evidence across studies. Researchers have begun to address these complexities by including multiple measures of institutional quality across numerous follow-ups or cohorts and by using analytical techniques that account for selection effects (Long, 2008, 2010; Thomas, 2003; Zhang, 2005; Zhang & Thomas, 2005). Our review features studies that meet at least one of those criteria.

Employment. Using a constructed college quality index based on several different institutional measures (median freshman SAT/ACT score, percentage of applicants rejected, tuition, ratio of full-time faculty to students, percentage of faculty with a doctorate degree, and Barron's selectivity index), Long (2010) examined data from three nationally representative, longitudinal studies containing information on cohorts of students from the 1970s, 1980s, and 1990s. Holding constant confounding factors (demographics, precollege academics and socioeconomics, high school academics and experiences, religion, and local labor market and neighborhood characteristics), results show a significant negative effect of college quality on labor force participation that was consistent across the three graduation cohorts. Importantly, once the analytic sample was restricted to students not currently enrolled in a postsecondary institution, the effect of college quality failed to reach statistical significance, indicating college quality likely influences graduate school attendance, and therefore negatively influences employment in the years immediately following college. Because college major and degree completion were not factored into the model, the results may be somewhat biased due to omitted variables.

Hours Worked. The number of hours worked following college graduation in relation to institutional quality was the focus of Zhang's (2008b) analysis. Because institutions were grouped according to combined quality (1992–1993 IPEDS and Barron's Profiles of American Colleges) and control (public and private) categories, institutional quality differences could only be inferred within each control group.[2] Among private school graduates, institutional quality had a significant effect on hours worked, which increased the more years that passed following graduation. Roughly 10 years after college graduation and among students who completed their degree between June 1992 and July 1993, those who graduated from a high-quality private institution reported working on average a statistically significant 5.4% more hours per week than graduates of private institutions rated as low quality and 3.6% more hours per week than graduates of middle-quality private institutions. Smaller but still significant differences were evident in 1997, four years after graduation. Among public graduates, no differences were found by institutional quality. Thus, it appears that the effects of institutional quality on hours worked increase the more years one spends in the workforce if one graduated from a private institution.

Job Satisfaction. Little attention has been directed to estimating the between-college effects on job satisfaction, though the work that has been conducted identifies a somewhat complex set of relationships among institutional quality measures, earnings, and dimensions of job satisfaction. Liu et al. (2010) estimated the effects of the same institutional quality and control groupings as Zhang (2008b) on dimensions of job satisfaction, such as satisfaction with pay, fringe benefits, challenge of work, promotion, opportunities to use one's education, and job security. Relying on data roughly 10 years after college graduation and controlling for majors as well as a host of socioeconomic, demographic, and labor market variables (including earnings), results indicate that attending a higher-quality college is negatively related to job satisfaction, particularly those dimensions related to monetary rewards. In fact, graduates of high-quality institutions were roughly 11 percentile points less likely to be satisfied with their pay, relative to graduates of low-quality public institutions, a particularly notable finding given that earnings were included in the model and likely suppressed the effect of institution quality on job satisfaction. Although the data are limited to a single study, their generalizability and the analytic strategy provide strong evidence to suggest that attending a higher-quality college does not necessarily lead to greater job satisfaction. The underlying dynamics of this finding have not been empirically examined. However, it may be that students who attend more competitive and prestigious institutions have higher expectations that are more difficult to achieve once in the workforce, which may erode feelings of job satisfaction. More academically competitive students may also bring to their careers a broader sense of their own options, which may reduce feelings of commitment to a specific job and thus further erode job satisfaction.

Sex-Atypical Career Orientations. Sax and Bryant (2006) found that several different institutional measures had significant effects on students' career choices. Using longitudinal, pretest-posttest data from fall 1994 to 1998, change in students' sex-atypical career choices was measured among roughly 17,500 students at more than 200 colleges and universities. A sex-atypical field was defined as traditionally masculine fields for women and traditionally feminine fields for men. Several institutional quality measures were found to predict change in students' career orientations, controlling for a pretest measure of career orientations and a host of student inputs, financial aid, and college experiences. For women, an institution's student-to-faculty ratio and peers' average years of math and science courses taken in high school significantly increase the odds of selecting a sex-atypical career. For men, attending a more selective institution significantly decreases the likelihood of making sex-atypical career choices.

Earnings. Consistent with earlier editions of this volume, the largest body of research on between-college effects on career and economic outcomes focuses on individual earnings in relation to institutional quality, though several studies also examine the earnings effects of Carnegie Classification, mission, or other measures of institutional type. Long (2008), for example, drew on national longitudinal data containing year 1999 earnings measures and a sample with a median age of 26 to examine the effects of institutional quality on early career earnings. Long examined log-hourly earnings[3] in relation to several measures of institutional quality separately and as an overall college quality index,[4] and used numerous analytic techniques, each with different specifications and degrees of control.[5] The findings illustrate that the effects of college quality on earnings vary substantially based on the model specification and measure of institutional quality. Simply put, when college quality is based on combinations of measures (or an index such as Barron's ratings), studies consistently show significant positive effects on earnings. However, when single measures are used to approximate institutional quality (e.g., full professor salaries, net tuition, mean or median freshman SAT scores), the effects on earnings are much weaker and vary greatly by study. Given that institutional conditions have a multitude of characteristics that determine quality, our conclusions center on studies that have relied on multiple measures or indexes of quality.

For example, when estimating between-college effects for men and women separately, a 1 standard deviation increase in the overall indexed measure of college quality led to a significant 8.5% increase in men's log-hourly earnings (Long, 2008). Alternatively, when college quality was defined as median freshman SAT/ACT scores, the OLS estimate was a smaller, though still statistically significant, 2.1%. When other estimation techniques were used to try to account for selection bias, the magnitude, and at times significance, of the estimated earnings effects differed from the OLS estimates. The differences in estimated effects varied by quality measure and estimation strategy, preventing overall conclusions other than to generally recommend that researchers use multiple strategies when possible to gauge the sensitivity of any given estimate.

When estimating women's log-hourly earnings, Long (2008) found fewer statistically significant effects and showed much greater variation by institutional quality measure and estimation strategy. In fact, the overall quality index did not produce a significant effect on women's log-hourly earnings. Similar results based on different national data were reported by Black and Smith (2004), in which a comparable measure of overall quality yielded a significant positive effect on men's earnings and a nonsignificant effect on women's earnings, with variations identified by analytic method.

Zhang (2005) also examined multiple institutional quality measures on earnings roughly four years after college graduation among terminal bachelor's degree recipients. Differing from Long's (2008) results, Zhang's analyses yielded positive and significant effects of attending higher-quality institutions that proved robust across quality measures in terms of statistical significance and direction, while the size of the effect was sensitive to the particular quality measure examined. For example, the estimated earnings effects (four years after college) of college quality were much higher when using Barron's ratings than when using mean SAT scores. Using Barron's ratings, graduating from high-quality institutions yielded roughly 13 to 18% higher earnings than graduating from a low-quality institution, whereas quality categories based on mean SAT scores yielded earnings differences of only half that magnitude. As mentioned above, given the multifaceted nature of colleges and universities, institutional quality measures based on Barron's ratings provide a more robust estimate of the effects of an institution's overall quality on graduates' earnings.

Examining graduates' earnings and hourly income at multiple time points, Zhang (2008b) analyzed data with institutions again characterized by combinations of institutional quality and control (public versus private). Controlling for demographic and family socioeconomic characteristics, as well as undergraduate GPA, college major, and graduate degree attainment, students who graduated from high-quality institutions (based on Barron's Profiles) earned significantly more than graduates from low-quality public institutions. The magnitude of these differences increased over time: one year after college, graduates from high-quality institutions earned 6 to 8% more than their low-quality counterparts, which increased to 13 to 15% four years after graduation and 16 to 19% 10 years after graduation. Similar though slightly smaller differences were found in terms of hourly income (Zhang, 2008b). Hu and Wolniak's (2010) study of high-achieving minority students six years after high school (within one to two years of college graduation) found a significant 25% earnings advantage among graduates of middle- versus low-selectivity institutions (based on Barron's ratings), but no difference between middle and high selective institutions. The size of this effect may be due to the uniqueness of the sample, which was not generalizable to the full population.

Concentrating on NLS and NELS data, Long (2010) examined the effects of college quality (an index based on Barron's Profiles within three cohorts of high school seniors from 1972, 1982, and 1992, each examined longitudinally) on log-annual earnings 10 years after high school. Findings indicate that annual earnings are positively related to attending a higher-quality college, with effects of a 1 standard deviation increase in college quality ranging from a 2.6% (a 0.026 increase in log-earnings) for the 1970s cohort, to 4.7% and 4.9% for the 1980s and 1990s cohorts, respectively. The increase in effect across cohorts, however, was not statistically significant. College major and degree completion were not factored into the model.

Thomas and Zhang (2005) examined wage growth within four years of college graduation in relation to college quality. They created three categories to capture institutional quality: most competitive or highly competitive (based on a Barron's rating of 4 or greater), very competitive or competitive (Barron's ratings of 2 or 3), and less competitive or noncompetitive (Barron's ratings of 0 or 1). Combined with institutional control (public and private), six groups were created. The study estimated log-annual salary roughly one year after college graduation (in 1994) and four years after college graduation (in 1997), and controlled for a host of demographic, family SES, and academic characteristics (including major field of study); SAT/ACT scores prior to college; and labor market factors. The results indicate a step-wise pattern. Relative to graduates of low-quality public institutions, graduates of middle-quality public institutions reported roughly 11% higher earnings four years after graduation, while graduates of high-quality public institutions reported roughly 20% higher earnings four years after graduation. The pattern was similar among private institutions, where graduates of middle- and high-quality private institutions reported 12 to 20% greater earnings, respectively, than their counterparts who graduated from low-quality private institutions. These earnings differences by institutional quality significantly increased from one to four years after college graduation (e.g., from 5 to 11% among graduates of middle-quality public institutions, 7 to 13% among graduates of middle-quality private institutions, 9.5 to 22% among graduates from high-quality public institutions, and from 7 to 20% among graduates of high-quality private institutions, relative to their counterparts who graduated from low-quality institutions). These results are important in that they identify the possibility that the effect of college quality on earnings increases as more years pass following college graduation. Results of similar magnitude were presented in other studies based on nationally representative data (Thomas, 2003; Zhang, 2005; Zhang & Thomas, 2005).

Mission. We refer to institutional mission as a stated commitment to provide education for a specific demographic of students or to organize the educational environment in a particular way. Among the studies that examine between-college effects on career and economic outcomes were those that focused on the influence of attending HBCUs and work colleges.

Career Development. We uncovered a pair of multi-institutional studies that sought to examine between-college effects on career development outcomes, including vocational preparation and job preparation (Flowers, 2002; Wolniak & Pascarella, 2007). These studies used either cross-sectional (Flowers, 2002) or retrospective longitudinal (Wolniak & Pascarella, 2007) designs to examine aspects of self-reported career development in relation to enrollment at different types of mission-driven institutions. Overall, these studies yielded little evidence that the mission of the institution attended influences career development above and beyond the academic aspects of the college experience, such as grades and major field of study.

Focusing on a scaled measure of students' self-reported gains in vocational preparation, Flowers (2002) combined multiple years of data from 1990 to 2000 to estimate the effects of attending an HBCU versus a predominantly white institution (PWI) among African American students at 207 institutions. Statistically controlling for student background traits, academic experiences (including college major), and students' perceptions of their institutional environment, the results indicate that gains in vocational preparation do not significantly differ based on attending an HBCU versus PWI.

Work colleges were the focus of Wolniak and Pascarella's (2007) multi-institutional study of alumni across three college graduation cohorts spanning three decades: 1974–1976, 1984–1986, and 1994–1996. The study provides estimates of the effects of attending a unique group of work colleges in comparison to private liberal arts colleges and public regional institutions on two scaled measures of job preparation (one based on feeling prepared for one's first job after college, and the other based on feeling prepared for one's current job). Controlling for demographics, precollege characteristics (socioeconomic, academic, and educational aspirations), institutional selectivity, and college graduation, the results suggest that attending a work college is associated with significant advantages over private liberal arts colleges and public regional institutions on both measures of job preparation. However, the differences failed to reach statistical significance once additional variables were added to the model, including college grades, college major, graduate degree attainment, and reported measures of skills and orientation development during college, indicating an indirect influence of these variables on job preparation.

Employment. Wolniak and Pascarella (2007) provide evidence of the differences between work colleges, other liberal arts colleges, and public regional institutions on employment outcomes among three cohorts of graduates who graduated five, fifteen, and twenty-five years prior to participating in the study. The findings indicate that alumni of work colleges were, on average, 1.4 times more likely to report full-time employment compared to liberal arts college alumni. However, this evidence should be interpreted with caution, as the model explained a somewhat small amount of variance (pseudo-R^2 = 0.08), despite numerous statistical controls for demographic, socioeconomic, and educational background characteristics; college education variables; skill and occupational characteristics; and post-college educational attainment and occupational characteristics.

Also examining differences by institutional mission were two studies based on national longitudinal data (Strayhorn, 2008; Zhang, 2008b). Focusing on the hours worked among a nationally representative sample of graduates up to 10 years after college, Zhang found no effects of attending an HBCU, net of institutional selectivity and control. Alternatively, Strayhorn's study of African American college graduates found that HBCU graduates have 0.09 standard deviations higher occupational status (based on socioeconomic codes roughly four years after college graduation).

Earnings. Also addressing differences by institutional mission was Zhang's (2005) examination of the earnings effects of attending an HBCU. Across multilevel and ordinary least square (OLS) estimates, results suggest graduates of HBCUs earn roughly 11% less than other graduates four years after college. However, the statistical significance varied by the analytic method, and a later study by Zhang (2008b) shows no significant differences up to 10 years after college graduation. Together, the evidence suggests that graduating from HBCUs may lead to marginally lower earnings initially after college, with the differences diminishing the more years that pass after college.

Wolniak and Pascarella's (2007) retrospective longitudinal study examined the differences between work colleges, other liberal arts colleges, and regional comprehensive institutions in relation to alumni earnings. Based on an ordinal measure of self-reported earnings (1 = no earnings, to 11 = $125,000 or more) and controlling for a variety of confounding influences, the findings show that work college graduates report a small but significant 0.02 standard deviations lower earnings than their counterparts who graduated from regional public institutions, but they report comparable earnings to alumni from liberal arts colleges. Importantly, the results indicate that relative to both institutional comparison groups, attending a work college significantly limits the accumulation of loan debt. The work colleges examined in the study tend to share a mission centered on work, learning, and service, providing a mechanism for controlling students' costs of attendance and potentially increasing the overall economic value of a degree.

Carnegie Classification

Major-Job Congruence. Xu (2013) used multiple waves of nationally representative B&B data to examine major-job congruence (a measure of how closely related an individual's current primary job is to his or her undergraduate major) among 1992–1993 college graduates who were followed up in 1994, 1997, and 2003. Focusing on STEM and non-STEM graduates separately, between-college effects were estimated by Carnegie type. The results clearly show that students who graduated from institutions categorized as either an associate's college (those with bachelor's degrees accounting for only a small share of all undergraduate degrees) or a specialized institution (distinguished by its concentration of degrees in a single field or set of related fields) are considerably more likely to obtain jobs closely related to their major fields of study than graduates of baccalaureate, master's, or doctoral-granting institutions. The finding may reflect a narrower range of occupational choices students have after completing a bachelor's degree from a more specialized institution and the fact that specialized schools may be more effective at placing graduates in jobs more closely related to their fields of study. Specifically, the results indicate that among non-STEM majors, completing a degree from baccalaureate, master's, or doctoral institutions (versus from an associate's or other specialized institution) significantly reduces the odds of having a job closely related to one's college major by more than 50% (across the comparison categories, the odds ratios (OR) ranged from 0.34 to 0.49). For STEM graduates, having attended a baccalaureate institution (relative to an associate's or specialized institution) lowered the odds having a job closely related to a major by nearly 80% four and 10 years after college (OR = 0.22 and 0.24 in 1997 and 2003, respectively).

Earnings. Carnegie Classification represents another institutional measure examined in relation to postcollege earnings, though the volume of evidence is far smaller than that which focused on institutional quality. In fact, the three studies that examined the earnings effects of Carnegie Classification did so alongside multiple other measures of institutional characteristics. Bellas (2001), Thomas (2003), and Zhang (2005) studied national samples of college graduates within B&B:93/97 data from one to four years after college graduation. Based on a multilevel model, Thomas found that graduates from liberal arts institutions (which were predominantly private and highly selective institutions) experience an earnings disadvantage of roughly 10% compared to graduates from other types of institutions. A possible explanation for this disadvantage is that many graduates of liberal arts colleges transition into graduate school rather than the labor market, which may bias the earnings estimates when based on terminal baccalaureates. Adding evidence to the associations between Carnegie classification and earnings, Zhang's (2005) results show, relative to Liberal Arts II institutions (typically the least selective "liberal arts" category), significant earnings advantages ranging from approximately 6% for graduates from Comprehensive I institutions to nearly 15% for graduates of Doctoral I institutions. Interestingly, Liberal Arts I institutions, which tend to be the most selective institutions among Carnegie Classifications, did not have a significant earnings effect relative to Liberal Arts II institutions, which tend to be the least selective institution type.

Institutional Control (Public versus Private)

Employment. Although linkages between two-year colleges and employers were not directly related to observed employment, we uncovered one study that examined this topic. Deil-Amen and Rosenbaum (2004) conducted a qualitative case study of seven two-year public community colleges relative to seven two-year private occupational colleges. Their study revealed that private two-year occupational colleges actively work with employers to exhibit the qualifications students have developed, effectively mediating the hiring process through established relationships with employers and cultivating a market niche for graduates. The authors used the study to call for similar efforts among public community colleges as a way for low-status schools to make supporting the hiring process an institutional focus to benefit students from lower social backgrounds.

Job Satisfaction. Liu et al. (2010) examined multiple dimensions of job satisfaction in relation to categories of institutions based on combinations of quality and control. Relying on national data roughly 10 years after college graduation, no differences were found between public and private institutions within each institutional quality group.

Earnings and Private Rate of Return. Results based on nationally representative datasets suggest little to no direct earnings effect based on graduating from a public versus private institution. A pair of studies by Zhang (2005, 2008b) drew on B&B data to examine the earnings effects of institutional control based on an institutional classification scheme that included multiple quality measures in combination with institutional control. Across both studies and regardless of the timing of data collection (one, four, or 10 years after college) or method of operationalizing institutional quality (e.g., Barron's ratings or average entering class SAT), no statistical differences were tied to graduating from a public versus private institution when examined within each quality group. However, Thomas (2003) produced contrasting evidence that private school graduates earn roughly 5 to 8% more than public school graduates among middle and highly selective institutions, though the published results do not allow direct comparison to gauge statistical significance of the public versus private school effects. Alternatively, Hu and Wolniak's (2010) study of high-achieving minority students in the years immediately following college graduation found a 10% earnings advantage for graduates of public versus private institutions. This finding stands out from the other studies we reviewed in terms of the size of the effects, and they should be viewed against the knowledge that the sample was not representative of the general population of college students.

Adding important nuance to the earnings differences associated with institutional control are Thomas's (2003) and Toutkoushian et al.'s (2013) efforts to address the cost differences between public and private institutions. Thomas examined debt-to-earnings ratios four years after college graduation, uncovering patterns that suggest statistically significant differences tied to institutional control. Specifically, the debt-to-earnings ratios of private institution graduates were substantially greater than their public institution counterparts, ranging from a 40% greater debt-to-earnings difference for graduates of low-selective private institutions (versus low-selective public graduates) to 55% greater debt-to-earnings differences among graduates of high selective private institution (versus high selective public graduates). Toutkoushian et al. estimated the IRR for students attending private versus public institutions, showing that paying higher tuition and fees drives down the economic value of a degree and that the IRR tends to be lower for attending private relative to public colleges. These findings are particularly important for interpreting the earnings differences tied to public versus private school attendance. Given the cost differences, the economic benefits of attending a public institution may exceed those of attending a private institution.

Institutional Racial Composition. We identified one study that examined the earnings effects of institutional racial composition, defined as the percentage of minority students (Thomas, 2003). Based on nationally representative data and examining a similar set of institutional control and selectivity categories as discussed for Zhang (2005, 2008b), Thomas found that the percentage of minority students at an institution was associated with significantly higher earnings among graduates. Results from a multilevel model that controlled for a variety of important confounding influences suggest that a 10% increase in the racial minority population on a campus is associated with roughly a 3% increase in earnings four years after college graduation.

WITHIN-COLLEGE EFFECTS

Conclusions from the 1990s

The 1990s produced an extensive literature on the career and economic effects of different college experiences within the same institution. The body of evidence highlighted the influence of types of involvement, working during college, and faculty interactions, with the most robust evidence centered on the influence of major field of study and grades.

Career Development. In terms of career development outcomes, specific career-oriented courses or interventions were found to significantly enhance career maturity (an individual's ability to make realistic career decisions), as well as career decidedness (a person's level of certainty in their career choices). In addition, evidence indicated that extracurricular and social involvement during college, including Greek affiliation, as well as involvement in diversity experiences and volunteer service activities, had positive effects on students' self-reported career-related skills and sense of job preparation. This conclusion was limited by the fact that it was based on self-reports and that extracurricular and social involvement had a negligible influence on securing employment or earnings early in one's career.

Specific academic experiences and academic involvement such as cooperative or group learning experiences appeared to significantly influence self-reported career-related skills, such as leadership abilities and the ability to work effectively in groups. Consistent with the 1991 synthesis was the finding that job-relevant skills develop in informal, noninstructional settings. While this conclusion is again limited by relying on self-reports, one of the only longitudinal studies with controls for a host of confounding factors found that students' nonclassroom interactions with peers had a positive effect on perceived gains in career preparation.

In addition, work experience or having an internship during college was found to have a positive influence on development of career-related skills, which appears to be maximized when students' work experiences were related to their major or chosen career. Furthermore, some evidence was found to suggest that interactions with faculty may have a positive influence on students' choice of an academic or scientific research career and development of (self-reported) career-relevant skills.

Employment Outcomes. Several studies from the 1990s pointed to the strong influence of major field of study and college grades on employment outcomes. Undergraduate major appeared to have a significant influence on employment early in one's career, with the greatest influence occurring in the fields with the most direct functional linkage to jobs or occupational sectors (e.g., computer science, social work, nursing, and accounting). Furthermore, fields of study that lead to relatively higher occupational status after college were mathematics- and science-based (e.g., engineering, mathematics, physical sciences, and technical/applied professional fields) and traditionally male-dominated fields.

The influence of achieving higher college grades appeared to increase the likelihood of being employed full time and in a job appropriate to a bachelor's degree early in one's career, though the relationship between grades and job satisfaction or job mobility was unclear. In addition, college grades appeared to predict higher occupational status by roughly 0.10 to 0.20 standard deviations. Work experience or having an internship during college was also found to have a positive influence on the likelihood of being employed immediately after college, particularly for students whose work experiences were related to their major or chosen career.

Earnings. Evidence from the 1990s led to conclusions surrounding the positive earnings effects of certain majors, grades, extracurricular and social involvement, and working during college. Specifically, evidence of economic returns varied by field of study within specific degree programs as well as by gender, making it difficult to form overarching conclusions. For example, women had greater earnings from an associate's degree in business or health fields than from a bachelor's degree in humanities or education, whereas men realized larger economic premiums from an associate's degree in engineering, public service, or vocational/technical areas than from a bachelor's degree in humanities or education. In general, men were overrepresented in major fields of study that were closely linked to the highest-paying occupations (e.g., engineering, mathematics, computers science, preprofessional majors in health sciences such as medicine and dentistry, business/accounting, and several physical sciences), while the opposite was true for women. Furthermore, starting salaries and early career earnings were enhanced by working in a field related to, or congruent with, one's major at the baccalaureate and subbaccalaureate levels.

The 1991 synthesis and evidence from the 1990s supported the conclusion that college grades have a positive effect on earnings. From the 1990s literature, it appeared that the direct effect on earnings of an increase in one grade group (e.g., from a B average to an A average) was estimated at approximately 6.8% above and beyond the effect of educational attainment. Unlike grades, extracurricular and social involvement or work and internship experiences did not appear to influence earnings or earnings growth after college.

An overarching conclusion that stemmed from the 1990s literature was that the within-college effects on career and economic outcomes tended to be larger than corresponding between-college effects. In other words, the choices students make, including their major field of study, the way they allocate time, and the manner by which they engage with the college environment, tend to have a greater influence on subsequent career and economic outcomes than the particular kind of institution attended.

Evidence from the 2000s

Based on our review of the literature from the 2000s, we summarize the evidence on the career and economic outcomes of different experiences within the same institution, controlling for differences in the institution attended. With the exception of research on programmatic interventions in relation to career development outcomes (which tend more often to be based on experiments within single-institutional settings), the datasets listed in Table 8.4 formed the core of the evidence we discuss here due to their national representation, longitudinal design, and breadth of career and economic measures.

We have organized the evidence in this section by the specific educational experience examined (e.g., major field of study, academic achievement, or grades). Within each of those areas, we summarize the evidence according to the outcome examined, including career development (e.g., career maturity, vocational identity), employment outcomes (e.g., employment, occupational status, major-job field congruence, job satisfaction), and earnings (e.g., annual income, wages). Unless noted otherwise, statistical differences cited are from studies that adjusted for students' precollege characteristics relevant to the outcome under study.

Programmatic Interventions. A handful of studies from the 2000s have drawn on single-institutional samples of college students to evaluate specific course interventions on outcomes, such as career maturity, and elements of social cognitive career theory (SCCT) and career decision-making self-efficacy (CDMSE). Though somewhat limited in generalizability due to the single-institutional samples, most of the research we have included in our review employ pretest-posttest, experimental designs, which strengthens the validity of the resulting evidence. In total, the evidence points to significant positive effects of programmatic interventions on a host of career development outcomes.

We benefit from Folsom and Reardon's (2003) comprehensive meta-analysis of career development courses. Their meta-analysis of 46 reports of career courses in college since the 1920s provides a valuable overview of the prevalence and features of career development course. While career courses are quite varied, they are typically designed as interventions, including a systematic approach to delivering career services that often involve academic credit and offer the important advantage (to both students and researchers) of delivering

Table 8.4 Primary Data Sources Providing Evidence on Within-College Effects by Study

	Source	*Date*	*Citation*
Public	American Community Survey (ACS)	2009	Altonji, Blom, & Meghir, 2009
	Baccalaureate and Beyond Study (B&B)	1993/1997/ 2003	Bellas, 2001; Joy, 2006; Liu, Thomas, & Zhang, 2010; Thomas, 2003; Xu, 2013; Zhang, 2008a, 2008b; Zhang & Thomas, 2005
	National Education Longitudinal Study (NELS)	1988/2000	Reynolds, 2012
	National Longitudinal Survey of Youth (NLSY)	1979/1989/ 1996	Altonji, Blom, & Meghir, 2009; Gill & Leigh, 2003; Light, 2001; Light & Strayer, 2004; Molitor & Leigh, 2005; Roksa, 2005; Roksa & Levey, 2010
	National Survey of College Graduates (NSCG)	1993 2003	Robst, 2007 Del Rossi & Hersch, 2008
Private	ACT Alumni Outcomes Survey	1991–2006	Neumann, Olitsky, & Robbins, 2009
	Appalachian Region Alumni Outcomes Survey	2000	Wolniak & Pascarella, 2005; Wolniak, Seifert, Reed, & Pascarella, 2008
	College Student Experience Questionnaire (CSEQ)	1990–2000 1998–2001	Flowers, 2004b, Hu & Kuh, 2003b
	Cooperative Institutional Research Program (CIRP)	1970–1980 1994–1998	Henderson, Olbrecht, & Polachek, 2006 Sax & Bryant, 2006 (with 1998 College Student Survey (CSS) follow-up)
	Gates Millennium Scholars (GMS) Longitudinal Study	2002/2006	Hu & Wolniak, 2010; Melguizo & Wolniak, 2012

career planning services to large numbers of students. Thirty-eight studies examined the effects of career course interventions on outcomes, 15 addressed dimensions of psychosocial change, and a large share employed pretest-posttest and experimental designs.

Despite their varied structure, career development courses tend to have a positive influence on students: 90% of the studies of psychosocial change included in the meta-analysis showed gains in vocational identity, career decision making, or other dimensions, and 87% of the outcomes-based studies (e.g., studies of job satisfaction, choice of major, time to graduation, grades) showed positive effects (Folsom & Reardon, 2003). More specifically, among the studies that contained both a comparison group and pretest-posttest, longitudinal, or quasi-experimental design, career development courses had positive impacts on the following (the parentheses show the number of studies and students represented across all samples, all from Folsom & Reardon, 2003):

- Career planning (three studies, $n = 332$ students)
- Career decidedness/career indecision (eight studies, $n = 1,372$ students)
- Career decision making in relation to selecting a college major (three studies, $n = 1,045$ students)
- Cognitive development or cognitive complexity (two studies, $n = 219$)
- Course or career satisfaction (two studies, $n = 196$)
- Vocational identity or self-knowledge (two studies, $n = 309$)
- Career maturity (two studies, $n = 161$)
- Locus of control and self-efficacy (five studies, $n = 9,551$)
- Retention, graduation, or course withdrawals (three studies, $n = 1088$)

Other single-institution studies generally support Folsom and Reardon's (2003) conclusions. For example, noting that dysfunctional career thoughts influence career indecision, Osborn, Howard, and Leierer (2007) studied 158 first-year students and found that negative career thoughts could be decreased as a result of a six-week, one-credit course, with similar effectiveness as with full semester-long courses. They noted, however, that "further research is needed to determine the influence of a reduction of dysfunctional career thinking on specific desired outcomes such as career decidedness, GPA, career knowledge, and job search plan" (p. 375).

The main tenets of SCCT and CDMSE were supported by a handful of other single-institutional studies. Diegelman and Subich (2001), for example, examined self-efficacy and outcome expectations on a sample of 85 non-psychology students. Using a pretest-posttest design with a presentation and discussion of career opportunities in psychology as the treatment, results support the SCCT hypotheses that self-efficacy and outcome expectations relate positively and significantly to expressed interest in and intent to pursue an undergraduate psychology degree. Results indicated, for example, that increases in outcome expectations for a psychology degree (measured before and after the treatment) increased intent to pursue a psychology degree (change in $R^2 = 0.05$), above and beyond the pretest levels of intent.

In addition, Reese and Miller (2006) and Scott and Cianai (2008) reported the value of semester-long course interventions in which students who complete these types of courses have increased career decision-making ability, particularly through enhanced self-efficacy beliefs. Adding to these findings is evidence from Betz and Borgen's (2009) comparative outcomes study of two online career self-assessments that served as an intervention within a first-quarter survey course. Both of the online interventions significantly increased career decision making efficacy and major decidedness.

Academic Major. The effects of students' major field of study was one of the most heavily researched areas in the 1990s and has remained so. The evidence clearly demonstrates the important influence that academic major has on career and economic outcomes of college, influencing career aspirations, a variety of employment outcomes (e.g., occupational status, job satisfaction), and, to a great extent, postcollege earnings. The studies we uncovered in this area accompanied substantial variation in the treatment of college major, with some using narrowly defined sets of fields of study (Robst, 2007), while others chose to group majors into broader categories such as occupational specificity (Roksa & Levey, 2010) or STEM-related fields (Melguizo & Wolniak, 20012; Xu, 2013). Studies also varied in the approach to address gender differences in both the selection of a major field and later selection of occupational field (Joy, 2006; Roksa, 2005). From a methods standpoint, it is important to address (through statistical control or research design) the fact that students have different propensities for majors at the time they enter college based on their gender, socioeconomic backgrounds, high school course taking, educational and career aspirations, and the like (Crisp, Nora, & Taggart, 2009; Perna, Gasman, Gary, Lundy-Wagner, & Drezner, 2010; Trusty, 2002). Throughout this synthesis, we have given greater weight to studies that estimate the effects of major, controlling for a host of confounding student sociodemographic backgrounds, experiences, and aspirational measures.

Congruence. We uncovered a set of studies that examined the effects of college major on the congruence between field of study and job field, each drawing on national longitudinal data. Variance exists in how researchers operationalize congruence. Researchers tend to rely on an individual's responses to a survey item, such as that contained within the B&B follow-up surveys: "How closely related is this job to your field of study?" with response options of "closely," "somewhat," and "not at all" (Wine, Cominole, Wheeless, Dudley, & Franklin, 2005). However, some have constructed actual or observed measures of congruence. For example, Melguizo and Wolniak (2012) used U.S. Census Industry and Occupation Codes, while Neumann et al. (2009) measured the Euclidean distance between points on a two-dimensional map of career interests and subsequent occupational fields.

Robst (2007) examined data among bachelor's degree holders from the 1993 National Survey of College Graduates to estimate an ordered logit model predicting whether individuals reported working in closely, somewhat, or not-related fields. Controlling for demographics and degree attainment, the evidence indicates significant differences across majors. Using computer and information sciences as the comparison group, the only major that did not accompany significant differences in the likelihood of working in a mismatched occupation was library sciences. In addition, the only major that significantly lowered the likelihood of mismatch (increased the likelihood of a close match) was a major in health professions; relative to computer and information sciences, majoring in health professions resulted in a 0.79 to 0.61 odds of mismatch for men and women, respectively (note that odds less than 1 represent a negative influence). Majors with the highest likelihood of mismatch (lowest likelihood of a close match) were those that cultivate more general skills, including English and foreign languages (OR = 7.81 for men, 4.25 for women), social sciences (OR = 7.46 for men, 4.10 for women), and liberal arts (OR = 10.00 for men, 4.20 for women), indicating that majoring in these fields is associated with four to 10 times higher odds of job mismatch. Aside from these differences, several fields in addition to computer and information sciences had lower likelihood of mismatch (higher prevalence of a close match), which were generally those that develop more specific or applied skills in students, including architecture, business management, engineering, engineering technology, health professions, library science, and, for women specifically, education.

Although her focus was on monetary and sociocultural factors that predict choosing a major-related job 10 years after graduation, Xu (2013) contributed evidence to suggest that factors differ in their influence for STEM versus non-STEM majors. Notably, among non-STEM graduates, women appear more likely than men to work in a congruent occupation, while the opposite was found among STEM graduates, suggesting an important interaction between a STEM major and gender in determining major-job congruence.

Hours Worked. Single-study evidence from Zhang (2008b) suggests that after controlling for demographics, institution attended, and advanced degree attainment, college major does not strongly influence hours worked after graduation within the first 10 years following college. However, the findings do suggest relatively more work hours experienced by business (versus education) majors, and relatively fewer hours of work by health, public affairs, and psychology majors.

Occupational Gender Concentration and Employment Sector. A pair of studies by Roksa (2005) and Joy (2006) contribute evidence on the role of gender in the relationships between college major and employment outcomes. Each study approached gender in different ways. Roksa examined the effects of a major field's gender concentration (percent female within major) on the likelihood of employment in a public, private, or nonprofit sector, as well as the likelihood of employment in a professional or managerial occupation. Focusing on gender concentration within occupations, Joy examined the effects of specific major categories on gender concentration of occupation; those with more than 70% women were considered predominantly female (including clerical, medical, and teaching occupations), while those between 30 and 70% women were considered gender neutral. Both studies drew on nationally representative data that measured individuals at different time points following college graduation (up to 20 years later for Roksa's analyses of NLSY:79/98 data, and one year following college for Joy's analyses of B&B:93/94 data).

Examining the internal versus external rewards associated with different college majors, Roksa (2005) found that majoring in a relatively more female-dominated field significantly increases the likelihood of employment in public and nonprofit organizations and, to a lesser extent, the likelihood of employment in a professional or managerial occupation (indicators of higher status in the occupational hierarchy). Adding to this, Joy (2006) reported that several majors have a positive marginal effect on the probability of entering a female-dominated occupation, including education (47% more likely than business or law majors to enter a female-dominated occupation), health (47%), social sciences (10%), and humanities (10%), while majoring in a science field increases the probability of entering a male-dominated occupation by 32% over business or law majors. Joy summarized: "The uneven effect of college major on occupational differences may stem from the fact that some college majors are closely linked to occupations while others are not. Where the link is strong, choice of college major is a de facto choice of occupation. … Where the link to major is weaker, variation in student's choice of occupation is much wider. … For these occupations, even after controlling for college major and some choice factors, there may still be ample room for employer and individual preferences to shape occupational outcomes" (p. 229). Results from both studies highlight the gendered characteristics of higher education majors and occupations.

Growth in Occupational Status. In the two previous volumes, the evidence was somewhat mixed in terms of the effects of major field of study on students' subsequent occupational status (with the exception of a modest influence of gender concentration), and there was little evidence to suggest that undergraduate major plays a significant role in career mobility or promotion. While we uncovered fewer studies in the 2000s that addressed occupational status and growth over time, the evidence we did find points to a somewhat complex relationship among academic major, occupational specificity, and increased occupational status.

Roksa and Levey's (2010) study focused on two dimensions of occupational status that conform to those developed by Hauser and Warren (1979), including occupational education (the proportion of individuals in each occupation who had completed at least some college) and occupational earnings (the proportion of individuals in each occupation who earned above a specific cutoff). Majors were coded according to occupational specificity based on national data showing the extent to which graduates with a certain major obtain jobs related to their fields of study. For example, if the majority of graduates found jobs related to their major, that major would be considered to have high occupational specificity (e.g., education, health). Alternatively, if a major was distributed across numerous occupations, that major would be considered to have low occupational specificity (e.g., humanities, biological sciences, math and physical sciences, social sciences). Results of using multilevel quadratic growth models of individuals roughly 12 years after earning a bachelor's degree indicate three main findings. First, all else equal, majors with high occupational specificity predict higher occupational status than majors with low occupational specificity. Second, in terms of occupational growth over time, low-occupational-specificity majors had significantly higher growth over time in occupational status than high-occupational-specificity majors. However, even the higher growth did not fully account for status differences between major types up to 12 years after completing a bachelor's degree. Third, holding constant occupational specificity, the percent female in a major field had a significant negative effect on occupational status, particularly as measured by occupational earnings.

Job Satisfaction. We uncovered two studies in the 2000s that estimated the effects of academic major on job satisfaction (Liu et al., 2010; Wolniak & Pascarella, 2005). Together, they present a host of significant relationships between dimensions of job satisfaction and college major.

Drawing on alumni data across 30 institutions up to 25 years after college and controlling for socioeconomic, demographic, and academic characteristics, as well as college selectivity, control, and employment characteristics, Wolniak and Pascarella (2005) tested a causal model in which earnings mediate the effects of majors and major-job field congruence on job satisfaction. Job satisfaction was based on three factorially derived scales measuring alumni satisfaction with their job autonomy, the level of personal fulfillment derived from the job, and the financial characteristics of the job. Majors were coded into eight broad categories. In addition, two measures of major-job field congruence were included in the models, one based on self-reports (on a four-point scale from 1 = not at all related to 4 = highly related), and the other constructed from Holland's six primary types (RIASEC) of majors and occupational categories.

The results demonstrate several significant differences by college major. For example, when controlling for earnings and a variety of confounding factors, no major led to significantly higher satisfaction across each of the three dimensions of job satisfaction, and all estimated effects that were statistically significant were small in magnitude; majoring in an arts and humanities (versus education) field led to 0.07 standard deviations higher satisfaction with job autonomy, and 0.08 standard deviations higher satisfaction with financial characteristics, but no significant difference in satisfaction with personal fulfillment. Furthermore, majoring in a technical field increased alumni satisfaction with financial characteristics of their jobs by 0.07 standard deviations over education majors, and math, computer science, and engineering majors were not significantly different from education majors on any of the three dimensions of job satisfaction. Evident from this study is the significant moderating effect income has on the relationship between college major and job satisfaction, indicating the critical importance of controlling for a job's pay when estimating job satisfaction.

These results were generally supported by Liu et al.'s (2010) study of nationally representative data that captured monetary and nonmonetary dimensions of job satisfaction roughly 10 years after college graduation, which controlled for earnings and quality of institution attended, among many other confounds. While numerous significant differences were reported, the results do not lend themselves to broad conclusions on the general effects of majors on the different dimensions of job satisfaction. Instead, the results show substantial variation in effects of majors on job satisfaction across gender and by race/ethnicity.

Earnings. Consistent with previous volumes of this book, the largest concentration of evidence on the career and economic effects of academic major centers on earnings. Despite the sizable body of evidence, there are at least two notable challenges to drawing conclusions from the literature. First, researchers use a variety of different approaches to operationally defining majors, particularly in terms of the granularity with which fields of study are grouped. Some studies (e.g., Hu & Wolniak, 2010) focus on earnings effects of majoring in a STEM versus non-STEM field, while other studies (e.g., Robst, 2007) examine earnings differences across 23 major categories. Second, datasets differ in terms of the years that have passed since college and therefore reflect earnings at different career stages and confounded by differing sets of work and life experience. In addition to these challenges, while we have selected to review only studies that include a robust set of statistical controls to improve the accuracy of the estimated earnings effects of particular majors and reduce bias, there remain considerable differences in the statistical controls used across studies. Throughout this review, we have assigned greater weight to evidence from studies that include robust statistical controls of factors known to influence both choice of major and subsequent earnings (including sociodemographic characteristics, academic experiences, and work experiences) and that provide estimates of multiple fields of study. The studies we highlight typically are those based on generalizable data from large, multi-institutional, and longitudinal studies. Across the studies we reviewed, three main findings appear.

First, consistent with past volumes, the majors that have the largest effect on earnings are fields with a well-defined body of content knowledge, tend to focus on quantitative or scientific skill development, and have a direct functional alignment with specific occupations. Based on a number of rigorous studies (Altonji et al., 2012; Bellas, 2001; Del Rossi & Hersch, 2008; Hu & Wolniak, 2010; Melguizo & Wolniak, 2012; Robst, 2007; Thomas, 2003; Thomas & Zhang, 2005; Wolniak & Pascarella, 2005; Wolniak et al., 2008; Zhang, 2008b; Zhang & Thomas, 2005), major fields of study that result in the highest earnings include engineering, computer science and information technology, mathematics, and health science, while major fields that lead to the lowest earnings include education and humanities. In the middle of the earnings distribution are public affairs, biological sciences, and social sciences.

Across numerous estimates (Bellas, 2001; Del Rossi & Hersch, 2008; Thomas, 2003; Wolniak et al., 2008; Zhang, 2008b; Zhang & Thomas, 2005), the earnings effect of majoring in engineering (versus education) is 40 to 50%, which appears to be even higher among women (Zhang, 2008a). Computer science and information technology appears to garner similar earnings effects as engineering majors (Robst, 2007). In addition, estimates indicate 30 to 36% higher earnings result from majoring in business (versus education), and 28 to 46% from science and math (versus education). The literature presents substantial variation in the earnings effects of health or health sciences, ranging from 25 to 56% over an education major. While the significant earnings effect of a health-related major is consistent across studies, the large variation across estimates is likely the result of different subfields that researchers have chosen to include in this broad major category.

Second, the earnings differences associated with majors is relatively stable, and in some instances increases, the more years that individuals are in the labor market following college (Altonji et al., 2012; Bellas, 2001; Del Rossi & Hersch, 2008; Hu & Wolniak, 2010; Melguizo & Wolniak, 2012; Robst, 2007; Thomas, 2003; Thomas & Zhang, 2005; Wolniak & Pascarella, 2005; Zhang, 2008b). For example, Zhang's analyses of data one, four, and 10 years after obtaining a bachelor's degree illustrates that an engineering major (compared to an education major) results in roughly 46% higher earnings one year after college, which remains a substantial 42% higher earnings 10 years after college. The effect of majoring in a health sciences field decreases somewhat over the first 10 years following college but remains sizable (from 49% down to 40% earnings advantage over education majors). For other majors, the earnings premium (relative to education) increases significantly from one to 10 years after college, including business (21 to 32%) and social sciences (8 to 20%).

Similar estimates were reported within the first two years after college in Melguizo and Wolniak's (2012) and Hu and Wolniak's (2010) studies of high-achieving minority students. For example, Hu and Wolniak found that majoring in a STEM field results in approximately 9% higher earnings relative to all other majors. However, when compared to the lowest-earning majors (education and humanities), STEM majors had nearly a 42% earnings advantage immediately after college graduation (Melguizo & Wolniak, 2012).

Studies that present earnings effects based on individuals in the mid- to late stages of their career similarly show that engineering and education majors exist on the opposite ends of the earnings distribution (Altonji et al., 2012; Del Rossi & Hersch, 2008; Robst, 2007; Wolniak & Pascarella, 2005; Wolniak et al., 2008). Del Rossi and Hersch provided evidence that field of study for graduate degrees also significantly influences earnings, though the size of the effects tends to be smaller than those accompanying bachelor's degrees. Wolniak et al. added evidence on the mechanism by which majors influence earnings up to 25 years after college, suggesting that the relationship between a college major and subsequent earnings is mediated by education attainment and that the mediating influence differs by major.

Thomas (2003) estimated the effects of college major on debt-to-earnings ratios among bachelor's degree completers. Despite the sizable earnings differences across college majors, only graduates who majored in business had a lower debt-to-earnings ratio than education majors, estimated at 16%. No other college majors were associated with differences in debt-to-earnings ratios, suggesting that students who major in higher-earning fields of study also incur higher levels of debt.

The third main finding is that the earnings premiums across college majors are significantly affected by working in a field that is congruent with one's college major, where the greatest earnings result from majoring in a high-earning field *and* working in a closely related job (Melguizo & Wolniak, 2012; Robst, 2007). Based on self-reported matches between majors and job fields, Robst found that computer and information sciences majors earned significantly more if working in a closely related job versus their counterparts who did not work in a closely related job (28% more among men and a substantial 50% more among women). Among engineering majors, the earnings effects of congruent employment were also large: nearly 28% for men and 32% for women. Melguizo and Wolniak similarly estimated roughly 50% early career earnings differences associated with working in a congruent job among STEM majors. However, among lower-earning fields, including social sciences, working in a congruent job led to roughly 20% lower earnings than working in a job not closely related to the social sciences.

Although it does not specifically address the earnings effects of academic major, a handful of notable studies from the 2000s estimated the direct effects of congruence on earnings based either on self-reported relatedness between majors and job fields (Melguizo & Wolniak, 2012; Robst, 2007) or the connectedness of college students' career interests and their subsequent occupational field (Neumann et al., 2009). In this way, congruence serves as a mechanism through which college major and career orientations influence earnings. Neumann et al. examined ACT Alumni Outcomes Survey data to estimate the earnings effects of congruence between career interests in college and subsequent occupation, based on ACT's World of Work Map, which originated from Holland's RIASEC career typology. Using alumni outcomes data from 1991 to 2006 with extensive information on key areas such as sociodemographics, education attainment, academic achievement, majors, satisfaction, and employment history, Neumann et al. found that a 1 standard deviation increase in job congruence (a 1 standard deviation *closer* connection between career interests and occupational field) resulted in a 5% increase in earnings, where congruence was based on Euclidean distance between points on a two-dimensional space. The magnitude of the earnings effect reported by Neumann et al. was similar in size (roughly three-quarters as large) as the earning effect of an additional year of schooling, demonstrating the important economic impact of aligning interests with occupations.

Robst (2007) similarly contributed evidence that among bachelor's degree holders in various career stages, the average effect of working in a job closely related to degree field (versus not related) yielded a 12.7% wage advantage for men and a 10.6% advantage for women. Melguizo and Wolniak (2012) estimated a much higher 27% earnings advantage among high-achieving minority students who were working in a congruent job in the years immediately after college graduation.

Academic Achievement. Much like degree attainment or years of higher education, college grades provide an accessible measure of college students' overall academic achievement, content knowledge, and academic ability, and they provide a signal of human capital from which employers can base hiring and compensation decisions. While there exist more direct and valid measures of college students' cognitive ability (see Chapter 3), grades provide a relatively accessible metric on which to evaluate students and graduates, and one that has been used often as a predictor or control variable in studies of career and economic outcomes. We review the handful of studies from the 2000s that provide evidence on the effects of grades on employment outcomes and earnings.

Employment Outcomes. The evidence on college grades and employment is mixed in terms of hours worked (Zhang, 2008b) and occupation type (Joy, 2006). The number of hours worked following college graduation roughly one, four, and 10 years after graduating college was the focus of Zhang's analysis of B&B:93/97/03. Results indicate that every unit increase in GPA reduces the number of hours worked by roughly 1% in the first year following college. However, at both of the later time points, GPA did not have a significant effect. This discrepancy may reflect the "option value" that accompanies higher grades and increases the likelihood that higher-achieving students will enter graduate school immediately after college graduation (DesJardins, McCall, Ahlburg, & Moye, 2002; Paulsen & Smart, 2001; Toutkoushian & Paulsen, 2016; Weisbrod, 1962), thereby reducing initial work involvement. Based on the same data as Zhang, Xu (2013) found that higher grades increase the odds of working in a congruent occupation among students who graduated in non-STEM fields but not among STEM graduates.

In terms of the gender concentration of occupations, Joy (2006) found small but significant effects indicating that a 1% increase in college GPA accompanies a 1% greater likelihood of working in a female dominated occupation and a 2% lower likelihood of working in a male-dominated occupation roughly one year after college. Joy also found that a higher GPA was positively related to entering medical, engineering/computer, teaching, clerical, and labor occupations, while negatively related to managerial, sales/technology, and service occupations.

Finally, we found evidence from a single study (Wolniak & Pascarella, 2005) to suggest that college grades may influence dimensions of job satisfaction several years after college even after controlling for income, college major, congruence, and employment characteristics. Specifically, a 1 standard deviation increase in grades was associated with a significant 0.06 standard deviation (2.39 percentile point) higher level of alumni satisfaction with their level of job autonomy.

Earnings. The two previous volumes concluded that college grades had small, positive effects on earnings, noting that grades not only exert a direct influence but also indirectly influence earnings by way of education attainment. The evidence we uncovered from the 2000s is somewhat mixed, suggesting that college grades have at most a small positive influence on earnings after factoring in major field of study, degree attainment, institution attended, and a host of background variables (Donhardt, 2004; Thomas, 2003; Wolniak & Pascarella, 2005; Zhang, 2008b). Donhardt, for example, tracked the employment outcomes of graduates from a single institution, matching administrative enrollment and graduation files from 1989 to 2001 with unemployment insurance files from 1996 to 2001. While the results showed that major, age, and industry have significant earnings effects, college GPA did not. Wolniak and Pascarella also reported nonsignificant earnings effects of GPA up to 25 years after college. Other studies, particularly those based on nationally representative B&B:93 data, have produced somewhat conflicting results. Bellas (2001), Thomas (2003), and Zhang (2008b) each reported an approximate 5 to 6% increase in earnings from a 1 point increase in GPA in the first year following college graduation (Bellas, 2001; Thomas, 2003) and up to 10 years after college (Zhang, 2008b).

Academic Experiences and Involvement. The literature from the 2000s contains multi-institutional studies on the effects of academic experiences and involvement on career development (Flowers, 2004b; Mayhew, Simonoff, Baumol, Wiesenfeld, & Klein, 2012; Sax & Bryant, 2006), as well as evidence from a single study examining earnings (Hu & Wolniak, 2010). Across the research we reviewed, *academic experiences and involvement* refers to specific measures that include course-taking behavior, interactions with faculty, academically oriented interactions with peers through tutoring or studying together, experiences with academic resources such as library services, and pedagogical practices.

Career Development. Evidence from the 2000s illustrates the influence of students' academic experiences and involvement during college and various career development outcomes, including vocational preparation (Flowers, 2004b; Hu & Kuh, 2003b), sex-atypical career choices (Sax & Bryant, 2006), and intentions toward innovation (Mayhew et al., 2012). However, our ability to make general conclusions from this evidence is limited. Although the evidence we identified in this area was based on multi-institutional datasets with well-theorized analytic models, only Sax and Bryant's study included a pretest-posttest design and national data. Nevertheless, each study contributes important information on the plausible effects of academic experiences on college students' career development.

Sax and Bryant (2006) examined career choices, specifically the changes in sex-atypical career aspirations of men and women. Longitudinal data comprising fall 1994 data containing precollege characteristics and attitudes, in combination with data from a 1998 follow-up, allowed change to be assessed across four years of college in a national sample of more than 17,500 undergraduates. The study's outcome was operationalized as percentages of men and women who aspired to particular occupations that were either typical or atypical for their sex. If, for example, the percentage of women was at least twice the percentage of men indicating they aspired to a particular occupation, that occupation was considered sex atypical for men and female dominated.

Controlling for the pretest, a host of precollege input characteristics, financial aid, and environmental and experiential aspects of college, the results indicate that several academic experiences during college significantly influence changes in students' career aspirations and that academic experiences in college affect women and men differently in terms of their career choices. For women, change in career choices toward sex-atypical, nontraditional fields was positively influenced by tutoring other students (OR 1.84), studying with other students (OR 1.62), and enrolling in ethnic studies courses (OR 1.50). Change in career choices away from sex-atypical fields (toward more traditional fields) was negatively influenced by taking honors or advanced courses (OR 0.65). In other words, honors or advance course work promoted movement toward sex-atypical fields and away from more traditional fields. For men, a different set of academic experiences influenced changing career orientations. Movement toward a sex-atypical career choice was significantly influenced by receiving faculty support (OR 1.10) and enrollment in a women's studies course (OR 2.33). Alternatively, more hours per week talking with faculty outside of class was negatively associated with men's movement toward sex-atypical careers (OR 0.59). These behaviors promoted men's movement toward more traditionally masculine fields.

Flowers (2004b) estimated the effects of academic experiences on African American students' reported gains in vocational preparation. The study used a decade's worth of single-year, cross-sectional datasets combined into a single analytic file representing nearly 8,000 African American students; participants were balanced across freshmen through senior status at more than 190 colleges and universities. Flowers estimated the effects of a set of students' academic involvement measures based on library experiences, experiences with faculty, and course learning. Among the multitude of significant effects, most were small in magnitude. Those that were above the "small" effect size of 0.06 standard deviations (see Table 1.2) were concentrated among items that measured experiences with faculty and course learning. Specifically, in terms of faculty contact, significant effects on reported gains in vocational development were associated with asking instructors for course-related information (a 1 standard deviation increase resulted in a 0.10 standard deviation increase in reported gains in vocational preparation) and discussing career plans and ambitions with a faculty member (0.08 SD). In terms of course learning experiences, significant effects were found for thinking about practical applications of course material (0.07 SD) and working on a paper or project that required integrating ideas from various sources (0.07 SD).

Using the same data as Flowers (2004b) but focused on vocational preparation, Hu and Kuh (2003b) examined the effects of interactional diversity, defined as the extent to which students from diverse backgrounds interact in educationally purposeful activities, across more than 50,000 cases spanning 124 institutions. Using a seven-item scaled measure of vocational preparation across several institutional types and controlling for students' gender, race/ethnicity, family SES, year in college, major, institutional control, and selectivity, the results indicate that a 1 standard deviation increase in self-reported interactional diversity is associated with a statistically significant increase in vocational development that ranged from a 0.16 standard deviation increase for students at general colleges to a 0.21 standard deviation increase among students at doctoral intensive institutions (based on the 2000 Carnegie classification).

Mayhew et al. (2012) conducted a senior student survey at five universities of varying types, sizes, and locations, providing initial evidence that educational practices and experiences can effectively increase intentions of students to be innovative and entrepreneurial. Among the 3,700 student participants, after controlling for a set of personality, demographic, educational, and political characteristics, two important involvement- and perceptions-based effects were found: enrolment in an entrepreneurial class and having an instructor use assessments that encouraged innovative approaches to problem solving were significantly and positively related to students' innovative intentions. The findings add to an earlier single-institution study showing that entrepreneurial development may be enhanced by increasing students' general self-efficacy and adaptive goal orientations (Culbertson, Smith, & Leiva, 2011).

Earnings. We uncovered one study that estimated the unique effects of academic involvement on earnings following college. Hu and Wolniak's (2010) study of high-achieving minority students six years after high school—within the initial years following college graduation—estimated the earnings effects of a scaled measure of academic engagement. The scale captured students' frequency of working with other students on school work outside of class, discussing ideas from readings or classes with students outside class or with faculty outside of class, and working harder than anticipated to meet an instructor's expectations. Among the full sample of high-achieving minority students, the scaled measures of academic engagement did not have a significant effect on initial career earnings. However, a small and significant positive effect was found among non-STEM majors, where a one unit increase in the academic engagement scale increased earnings by 1.6%, while evidence to the contrary was found among STEM majors: a one unit increase in academic engagement leads to 1.2% lower earnings.

Social Involvement and Extracurricular Activities. Compared to the prominence of social involvement measures in research on and theories of college student departure, persistence, and completion (as reviewed in Chapter 7), few studies in the 2000s estimated the effects of extracurricular and social involvement on career and economic outcomes. We uncovered six studies containing estimates of the influence of social integration and/or extracurricular activities on career development outcomes (Flowers, 2004b; Linnemeyer & Brown, 2010; Sax & Bryant, 2006; Szelenyi et al., 2013) or earnings (Henderson, Olbrecht, & Polachek, 2006; Hu & Wolniak, 2010).

Career Development. The research on career development in relationship to social and extracurricular behaviors contains a disparate collection of outcomes (such as career identity foreclosure, attitudes toward vocational preparation, and career expectations) as well as a variety of involvement and activity measures (such as athletic involvement, volunteering, experiences in the student union, and exposure to living learning programs). This degree of variation prevented us from drawing general conclusions from the findings and led us to summarize each study, or set of similar studies without making strong empirical linkages across studies.

Linnemeyer and Brown (2010) conducted a cross-sectional comparison of student athletes and nonathletes at a single midwestern institution to test hypotheses that student athletes will score lower on career maturity and report greater identity foreclosure. Career maturity (measured by the Career Maturity Inventory-Revised; Crites & Savickas, 1996) represents the readiness to make career decisions and manage vocational and/or educational development tasks (Savickas, 1984). Identity foreclosure (measured by the Objective Measure of Ego Identity Status; Adams, Shea, & Fitch, 1979) pertains to ideological or occupational commitment in the absence of exploration or planning (Raskin, 1998). Results support the hypothesized relationships: controlling for gender, ethnicity, and year in college, student athletes have lower levels of assessed career maturity and higher levels of identity foreclosure. The findings reinforce the results from a qualitative case-study by Shurts and Shoffer (2004).

Focusing on sex-atypical career choices, Sax and Bryant (2006) found that among women, the number of hours per week using a personal computer has a positive significant effect on change toward sex-atypical career choices, while change in career choices away from sex-atypical fields (or toward more traditional fields) was influenced by volunteering. Among men, change in career attitudes toward a sex-atypical career was significantly influenced by volunteering and greater hours per week watching television, while change in attitudes away from sex-atypical careers (toward more traditionally masculine fields) resulted from more hours a week using a personal computer and relatively more drinking, smoking, and partying-type behavior.

Flowers (2004b) estimated the effects of social involvement and extracurricular activities based on personal experiences with their student union, athletic and recreation facilities, and clubs and organizations. Notable significant effects were found with respect to experiences in the student union; for example, looking at the bulletin board for notices about campus events was associated with reported gains in vocational preparation and with respect to experiences with athletics and recreation facilities, specifically those that involve setting performance goals. The effects for both activities were similar in magnitude: a 1 standard deviation increase was associated with a 0.09 to 0.10 standard deviation increase in reported gains in vocational preparation.

Szelenyi et al. (2013) demonstrated evidence that social activities influence positive career expectations based on a scaled measure of getting a good job, achieving career success, and achieving work-life balance. The study examined 294 women in STEM fields across 34 institutions that participated in the 2004–2007 longitudinal study accompanying the National Study of Living-Learning Programs. Controlling for covariates that align with the SCCT framework, results indicated having discussions about academic and career issues with peers and residing in a STEM-related coeducational (versus women only) living-learning program significantly increased reported expectations for positive career outcomes with sizable effects of 0.27 standard deviations and 0.95 standard deviations, respectively. Positive diversity interactions with peers decrease overall positive expectations (-0.16 SD), while increasing the single component item related specifically to expectations for achieving work-life balance (0.11 SD).

Earnings. Two studies from the 2000s examined the effects of social involvement and extracurricular activities on earnings. One focused on the earnings effects of college athletic participation (Henderson, Olbrecht, & Polachek, 2006), and the other was based on a series of survey items to capture levels of social engagement among four-year, minority college students (Hu & Wolniak, 2010).

Henderson et al. (2006) examined data from the 1970–1971 academic year, with follow-up data collected in 1980, six years after expected graduation. Although the study is dated, it provides evidence of wage differences between former athletes and nonathletes. Once in the labor market, college athletes on average experience a small positive wage benefit, but the earnings advantages vary by occupation and are concentrated among former athletes who reported working in business, manual labor, and military occupations.

More recent evidence resulted from Hu and Wolniak's (2010) study of early-career earnings among high-achieving minority students. Social engagement was measured based on students' reported frequency participating in activities such as working with other students, having discussions with faculty, participating in fraternity/sorority events, and community service activities. When combined into a composite scale measure of social engagement, significant and positive earnings effects were found: a one-unit increase in the social engagement scale resulted in a 1.9% increase in earnings. Similar to the estimated effects of academic engagement, the positive earnings effects of social engagement were concentrated among STEM majors, for whom a one unit increase in student engagement resulted in a 3.7% increase in earnings. Social engagement did not have a significant effect on earnings among non-STEM majors.

Employment during College. We uncovered only a small collection of studies that estimated the effects of working during college on career and economic outcomes. These include Sax and Bryant's (2006) study of changes in career choices and two studies that estimated the effects of working during college, both focused on earnings after college and both relying on NLSY:79 data containing outcomes in the middle phases of individuals' careers (Light, 2001; Molitor & Leigh, 2005).

Career Development. Working part time off campus during college was among the college experience variables that Sax and Bryant (2006) included in their longitudinal study of career choice development toward or away from sex-atypical fields. Estimates show that among women, working part-time off campus has a positive significant effect on change away from sex-atypical career choices or toward more traditional fields. Working did not significantly affect change in career choice of male college students.

Earnings. Molitor and Leigh (2005) estimated the relationship between in-school work experiences and earnings for men who attended two-year and four-year institutions. Controlling for education attainment and years of post-college work experience, among other factors, the results indicate a 4 to 7% increase in annual earnings per year of in-school work experience and showed that the influence is more pronounced among community college students than four-year college enrollees. Rather than isolate models to include only work experience of college-going students, Light (2001) estimated average effects of the years of work experience from the age 16 until the end of schooling, where education attainment was allowed to vary. Based on a male-only sample from nationally representative data, the results demonstrate the importance of including in-school work when estimating the returns from schooling. In fact, the results indicate that not controlling for in-school work may lead to significant overestimation of the returns to schooling. Light (2001) makes the important point that "without controls for in-school work experience, it is incorrect to interpret estimated schooling coefficients as the return to skill acquired strictly via time spent in school" (p. 89). Molitor and Leigh (2005) and Light (2001) together provide evidence that work has a curvilinear effect, such that work experience increases earnings, but the effect diminishes as the amount of work involvement increases.

Institutional Transfer

Earnings. Transfer between institutions, including horizontal transfer (two-year to two-year or four-year to four-year) and vertical transfer (two-year to four-year), is a common experience among college students, with at least one-third of all first-time college students in the mid-2000s transferring or co-enrolling at least once during their postsecondary education (Simone, 2014). While the results that we reviewed are mixed in terms of a discernible negative effect of having attended a two-year college and subsequently transferring to a four-year institution, the weight of evidence suggests there is not a significant effect of transferring institutions after controlling for college type, demographics, and academic backgrounds. According to three studies we uncovered, the earnings effects of a bachelor's or associate's degree did not significantly differ based on transfer behavior (Gill & Leigh, 2003; Light & Strayer, 2004; Thomas, 2003). However, one study found that attending a two-year college reduces the earnings effects of a bachelor's degree, though the effect declines in magnitude and significance after controlling for students' preexisting educational expectations and other individual characteristics (Reynolds, 2012).

Two studies (Gill & Leigh, 2003; Light & Strayer, 2004) analyzed NLSY:79/96 data to address the influence of transferring institutions on subsequent earnings. The sample in both studies contained respondents in their 30s, such that earnings data represent midcareer outcomes. Light and Strayer (2004) classified college students according to degree attainment (no degree, associate's, or bachelor's), and college type (two-year, four-year, or both) to assess wage differences within the population of college-educated workers. Controlling for demographic and academic background characteristics, no significant earnings differences were found between students who completed a four-year degree having attended only one four-year college versus those who first attended a two-year college. Similarly, the earnings effects of an associate's degree did not differ based on transferring between two-year institutions. In both of these cases, transfer did not influence earnings beyond the direct effect of the degree itself, whether an associate's or bachelor's degree. Gill and Leigh also found nonsignificant wage differences between bachelor's degree completers who started at a four-year college versus those who started at a two-year college and transferred to a four-year college.

Reynolds (2012) added important nuance by addressing the cost savings that accompany attending a two-year college relative to a bachelor's degree. Using propensity score matching to address self-selection, Reynolds estimated the treatment effects of two-year college attendance and found that while the present value of the costs of college are significantly reduced by attending a two-year college, the reductions in the present value of future earnings are considerably larger. The results suggest an average treatment effect of attending a two-year college to be a 4% decrease in the returns on a bachelor's degree for men and a 9% decrease for women, driven by the fact that students who start at two-year colleges are less likely to attain bachelor's degree. Relaxing some of the model's assumptions about capital markets and risk aversion for borrowing led Reynolds to note that the cost savings of initially attending a two-year college could outweigh the longer-term labor market disadvantages, making two-year colleges a viable and rational option for students and families who have high concerns over borrowing and face restricted capital markets.

In terms of horizontal transfer between four-year institutions, Light and Strayer (2004) estimated a 6% earnings advantage for students who switched institutions. It may be, as the authors explain, that

> students who switch colleges might (a) succeed in finding a better environment in which to acquire skills, (b) seek a better environment, but discover ex post that they are no better off, or (c) be driven by factors unrelated to skill investment. The first group is more likely than the other to earn a bachelor's degree so the 6 percent wage premium can be viewed as the value of "successful" college matching (Light & Strayer, 2004, p. 764).

CONDITIONAL COLLEGE EFFECTS

Conclusions from the 1990s

The previous volume's synthesis of literature from the 1990s uncovered a set of conclusions on the conditional nature of the influence college has on career and economic outcomes. The weight of evidence pertained to economic advantages, including earnings, economic returns, and private rates of return, while a handful of studies led to relatively weak conclusions regarding employment outcomes. In terms of employment outcomes, a small body of evidence suggested that the increase in occupational status related to bachelor's and associate's degree attainment is conditional on gender, where the effect for men is about two times larger than for women.

A more sizable literature led to several conclusions pertaining to conditional college effects on earnings or economic returns. Earnings premiums accompanying the completion of a bachelor's degree (versus a high school diploma) was roughly the same for men as it was for women, while the premium of completing an associate's degree (versus a high school diploma) for women was 1.5 times as large as it was for men. In terms of race/ethnicity, the net earnings premium of completing a bachelor's degree (versus a high school diploma) was about 1.2 times larger among African Americans than among Whites.

The influence of institutional quality on earnings also appeared conditional on sociodemographic and precollege academic characteristics. African American students specifically and students of color more generally benefited economically from institutional quality or selectivity as much as—and possibly more than—White students, which marks a departure from the conclusions of the 1991 synthesis. In terms of gender, no clear pattern suggests that institutional quality or selectivity led to earnings differences between men and women. The influence of institutional quality is greater for students who transfer into a selective institution versus students who entered directly from high school. Moreover, attending a selective college was found to possibly have the largest influence on earnings for students who, compared to the average student body at selective institutions, had relatively low academic ability or came from families with lower parental income, suggesting a compensatory influence of attending a more selective college.

The earnings effects of both grades and major field of study appeared conditional on demographic characteristics. The positive effect of grades on earnings appeared conditional on gender, with grades affecting earnings for women approximately 1.3 times more than for men. Holding constant other factors, a bachelor's degree in engineering had an impact on earnings that was 1.5 times larger for women than for men, while majoring in mathematics or the physical sciences in a four-year program had an impact on earnings that was 1.75 times larger for women than for men. While notable, the advantages of certain majors on women's earnings are curtailed by the fact that women are less likely than men to enter these fields. Nevertheless, those who do enter such fields appeared to benefit significantly in terms of earnings. Furthermore, African Americans were found to receive relatively smaller economic returns from majoring in a social science field (versus other majors) compared to students belonging to other racial/ethnic groups.

Evidence from the 2000s

This section summarizes the evidence on the conditionality of the effects that college has on career and economic outcomes. We concentrate on describing where research from the 2000s has shown that the evidence discussed in the previous sections (on the net effects of college, between-college effects, and within-college effects) significantly differs by students' background characteristics. The background characteristics we discuss tend to be those that have been shown in past volumes to significantly moderate college effects on career and economic outcomes, such as students' ascribed characteristics (gender, race/ethnicity, socioeconomic status based on parents' education and income levels, and age) and achieved characteristics (academic achievement at college entry). We focus on studies that provide evidence that a college effect is significant for at least one subgroup or the overall sample, where differences are evident between subgroups and similar patterns appear in multiple studies. However, in some cases when the other review criteria are met, we describe conditional effects based on evidence from only a single study and note that the findings await replication.

As with the previous sections of this chapter, the evidence on conditional effects is concentrated on a handful of nationally representative, longitudinal, or multiyear datasets listed in Table 8.5. These data do not provide a complete

Table 8.5 Primary Data Sources Providing Evidence on Conditional College Effects by Study

	Source	*Date*	*Citation*
Public	Baccalaureate and Beyond Study (B&B)	1993/1997/ 2003	Hilmer & Hilmer, 2012; Liu, Thomas, & Zhang, 2010; Xu, 2013; Zhang, 2008a; Zhang & Thomas, 2005
	Current Population Survey (CPS)	1970–2008 1999–2003	Hubbard, 2011 Bitzan, 2009
	High School and Beyond (HSB)	1980/1992	Long, 2010; Perna, 2003
	National Education Longitudinal Study (NELS)	1988/2000	Long, 2010; Perna, 2005; Rumberger, 2010
	National Longitudinal Survey of Youth (NLSY)	1979/1989/ 1996	Taniguchi, 2005
	National Longitudinal Study of the High School Class (NLS)	1972/1986	Long, 2010
	National Survey of College Graduates (NSCG)	1993	Robst, 2007
Private	Appalachian Region Alumni Outcomes Survey	2000	Wolniak & Pascarella, 2007; Wolniak, Seifert, Reed, & Pascarella, 2008
	College Student Experience Questionnaire (CSEQ)	1998–2001	Hu & Kuh, 2003b
	Gates Millennium Scholars (GMS) Longitudinal Study	2002/2006	Hu & Wolniak, 2013

accounting of studies reviewed in this section, but they represent the concentration of evidence from which our conclusions stem. These datasets are repeated throughout the literature in the 2000s because they are uniquely well suited for analyzing conditional effects given their large sample sizes with sufficient power to disaggregate and test for differences across student subgroups, such as gender, race/ethnicity, SES, and the like.

Postsecondary Degree Attainment and Years of Higher Education. The majority of the evidence on the conditional effects of postsecondary degree attainment or years of higher education has focused on earnings. This research has shown that the relationship between attaining different levels of postsecondary education and earnings is conditional on gender (Hilmer & Hilmer, 2012; Hubbard, 2011; Long, 2010; Perna, 2005; Robst, 2007; Rumberger, 2010; Zhang, 2008a), race/ethnicity (Bitzan, 2009; Hilmer & Hilmer, 2012; Perna, 2003; Rumberger, 2010; Zhang, 2008a) and age (Taniguchi, 2005). A set of individual studies have provided further evidence on the gender-conditional nature by which postsecondary attainment affects employment in a field congruent to students' college field of study (Robst, 2007), job satisfaction (Liu et al., 2010), and employment (Long, 2010).

Gender

Major-Job Field Congruence. When estimating the factors that influence college graduates' odds of working in closely, somewhat, or not-related fields relative to their college majors, Robst (2007) found that completing a master's degree (relative to a bachelor's degree) lowers the odds of job mismatch—or raises the odds of close match—significantly more for women than for men (OR = 0.37 versus 0.42), while completing a doctoral degree lowers the odds of working in a mismatched job field significantly more for men than for women (OR = 0.14 versus 0.17). We uncovered no evidence of gender-conditional effects of a bachelor's degree, associate's degree, or two-year college attainment on congruence.

Job Satisfaction. One study presented evidence to suggest that advanced degree attainment influences job satisfaction differently for men than for women. Liu et al.'s (2010) study of graduates roughly 10 years after receiving their degrees indicates that a master's degree has a negative effect on graduates' level of satisfaction with monetary dimensions of their job that is significantly more pronounced among women.

Employment. Evidence from a single study based on data from multiple national longitudinal surveys suggests the effects of an additional year of higher education on labor force participation is conditional on gender (Long, 2010). Controlling for student, family, and neighborhood characteristics and consistent across multiple datasets, estimates show that an additional year of education increases labor force participation by a significant 2 to 3 percent for women, whereas the net effect on men's labor force participation is negligible.

Earnings. Several studies together provide strong evidence that the net earnings effects of degree attainment or years of higher education differs by gender.

Perna (2005) reported that while women make on average significantly less in approximately the first eight years following high school graduation, women receive a higher earnings premium than men for completing some college (versus none), an associate's degree, a bachelor's degree, or an advanced degree. For example, the results indicate that after controlling for race/ethnicity and socioeconomic status, completing a bachelor's degree (versus no postsecondary education) has a negligible influence on earnings among men, whereas women who attain a bachelor's degree earn 45% more than women with no postsecondary education. Similar evidence exists in terms of advanced degree attainment. Hilmer and Hilmer (2012) and Zhang (2008a) added evidence that women also enjoy sizable earnings advantages for completing advanced degrees, where the earnings premium for a master's or first professional degree (relative to a bachelor's degree) is roughly 6 to 9% higher for women in the decade following bachelor's degree completion. In addition, Robst (2007) estimated a 5 to 10% earnings advantage among women for completing a master's or doctoral degree. Similar earnings advantages for women were found in terms of completed years of education (Long, 2010; Rumberger, 2010), whereas completing an additional year of education has a 2.5 times larger impact on women's earnings over the eight years following high school graduation (Rumberger, 2010).

The strong evidence that women realize sizable earnings premiums over men may explain enrollment and graduation trends in recent decades, where nearly two out of every three bachelor's degrees awarded in the United States are granted to women (National Center for Education Statistics, 2010). In other words, demand for higher education may be driven by the higher premiums women receive in the labor market (Chiappori, Iyigun, & Weiss, 2009).[6] Taking this reasoning one step further, Becker, Hubbard, and Murphy (2010) have suggested that the gender differences in enrollments and subsequent earnings premiums are partly the result of noncognitive skills such as self-motivation. In fact, this suggestion has empirical support; noncognitive abilities have been found to be higher on average among women (Heckman, Stixrud, & Urzua, 2006) and to explain a large share of the gender gap in college enrollment (Jacob, 2002).

Race/Ethnicity
Earnings. A collection of studies from the 2000s have demonstrated that the earnings effects of degree attainment or completing additional years of postsecondary education is conditional on students' race/ethnicity. Relative to a bachelor's degree, Hilmer and Hilmer (2012) estimated the salary premium of a master's degree was significantly higher for White than for Black students (13% earnings premium for Whites versus a 1% negative earnings effect for Blacks). Furthermore, the salary effect of completing a professional degree (e.g., MD, JD, DDS, OD, PharmD) relative to a bachelor's degree, while on average is a sizable 28%, appears to be concentrated among White and Black students, while Hispanics and those of other races experienced no significant salary effects from a professional degree. Alternatively, Perna (2003) found

significant earnings effects of completing an advanced degree versus a high school diploma to be greater among Hispanics than among Whites.

Examining the effect of years of education on annual earnings, Long (2010) found that in the more recent cohort of data examined, each additional year of education has roughly twice the effect on annual earnings among Blacks or Native Americans than among Whites. Rumberger (2010) also compared the average earnings effects among racial/ethnic groups and found years of higher education completed to have a significantly larger effect on earnings for Black and Hispanic students than among White and Asian students.

To test for credentialing (or "sheepskin") effects, Bitzan (2009) examined the relative impacts of years of higher education and degree attainment. Testing for differences in the earnings effects between White and Black men, results indicate significant differences in the returns to associate's and bachelor's degrees that favor White men on the order of 4 and 8%, respectively. Alternatively, returns to a doctorate favor Black men by a substantial 18%. Controlling for degree attainment, years of education has significantly larger effects on earnings for White men.

Age

Earnings. Noting the steady increases in the average age of U.S. college students, Taniguchi (2005) examined the possibility of an earnings disadvantage to completing a college degree at a later age. Drawing on nationally representative data, Taniguchi tested for differences in the wages of a national sample of four-year college graduates by age at college graduation. The results indicate that after controlling for confounding ability and work experience factors, graduating at age 25 or older leads to 17 to 18% lower wages compared to those who received degrees at the traditional age of 22 to 24 or at 21 or younger. Additional analyses indicate that the conditional effect of age does not differ by gender.

Institutional Characteristics. A handful of studies from the 2000s have shown the disparate effects that characteristics of the institution attended have on career and economic outcomes based on students' gender (Long, 2010; Zhang, 2008a; Zhang & Thomas, 2005), race/ethnicity (Hu & Kuh, 2003b; Long, 2010; Zhang, 2008a, Zhang & Thomas, 2005), and socioeconomic status (Long, 2010; Wolniak & Pascarella, 2007; Zhang & Thomas, 2005). In many cases the evidence results from a single study and therefore awaits replication.

Gender

Earnings. A small handful of studies produced conflicting evidence that institutional quality affects earnings differently by gender. Using a college quality index based on multiple institutional measures, Long (2010) found a stronger, more positive, and significant relationship for men than for women. However, Zhang and Thomas's (2005) earnings estimates four years after bachelor's degree completion and Zhang's (2008a) earnings estimates roughly 10 years after bachelor's degree completion found no significant gender differences by institutional quality/control groups (e.g., low-quality publics, mid quality publics, mid quality privates).

Race/Ethnicity

Vocational Preparation. We uncovered evidence from a single study to suggest that the relationship between institution attended and vocational preparation is conditional on race/ethnicity. Hu and Kuh (2003b) examined the effects of interactional diversity experiences on self-reported gains in vocational preparation for students attending different Carnegie Classification institution types. Based on 50,000 undergraduates across 124 institutions, the results indicate that within doctoral institutions, students of color reported higher gains in vocational preparation in relation to their experiences with interactional diversity than did White students. No differences were identified across the other institution types.

Job Satisfaction. Liu et al.'s (2010) study of job satisfaction roughly 10 years after college graduation provided partial evidence that the effect of institution attended on monetary dimensions of graduates' job satisfaction is conditional on race/ethnicity. Specifically, the effects of having attended a middle-quality institution (both public and private) as well as high-quality public institutions have significant negative effects on satisfaction with monetary dimensions of their jobs among nonwhite graduates, while having no discernable effect among White graduates. This finding awaits replication.

Earnings. We identified three studies that together provide weak and somewhat mixed evidence that the earnings effects of attending different quality institutions are conditional on race/ethnicity. Zhang (2008a) noted that a significant amount of the race-based earnings gap is explained by institutional type (based on combined categories of institutional quality and control), whereas in contrast, institutional type did not account for the gender gap in earnings. More specifically, Zhang stated that "the variables that contribute to the racial gap are quite different from those that contribute to the gender gap. While most variables that result in the gender gap in earnings are variables of major choices, those that contribute to the racial gap in earnings are largely related to socioeconomic characteristics, including, for example, graduating from highly selective institutions, family income, and students' GPA scores" (p. 68). Long (2010) reported partial evidence that the effect of college quality on earnings differs between Whites and Blacks or Native Americans, but the results vary considerably by cohort studied, making conclusions difficult. Furthermore, Zhang and Thomas (2005) found little evidence to suggest that the earnings effects of institutional quality and control groupings differ between White versus nonwhite students.

Socioeconomic Status

Earnings. Partial evidence suggests that the earnings effect of institutional quality is conditional on students' socioeconomic backgrounds. One of the three cohorts Long (2010) examined yielded relationships between institutional quality and earnings that were stronger among lower-SES students. In other words, attending a high-quality institution appeared to count for more in terms of earnings among low-SES than high-SES students. It may be that lower-SES families may not be able to leverage other resources to compensate for attending lower-quality institutions. This notion is partially supported by evidence from Zhang and Thomas (2005), whose estimates showed that among graduates from low-quality institutions, those from families in the top-third of the income distribution earn significantly more than those from families with incomes in the middle and bottom third, suggesting that family income may compensate for the negative general earnings effect of attending low-quality institutions.

Somewhat contradictory evidence was found by Wolniak and Pascarella's (2007) study of work colleges versus public regional institutions and liberal arts colleges. While graduating from a work college compared to a regional institution had a significantly negative effect on annual salary, the negative effect was most pronounced among alumni from high-income families. In this case, family income did not compensate for the earnings disadvantages tied to the type of institution attended.

College Experiences. Several studies we uncovered indicate that the impacts of a handful of student experiences on career and economic outcomes differ by student's gender. A host of studies provide evidence on the conditional nature of the career and economic influence of course interventions (Scott & Ciani, 2008), academic major (Hilmer & Hilmer, 2012; Liu et al., 2010; Robst, 2007; Wolniak et al., 2008; Zhang, 2008a), and student engagement (Hu & Kuh, 2003b; Hu & Wolniak, 2013).

Gender

Course Interventions. Scott and Ciani (2008) evaluated the effects of a one-credit, semester-long elective undergraduate course on changes in career decision making and vocational identity. Given the strong evidence on the positive career development effects of course-based interventions (discussed in the previous section of this chapter), Scott and Ciani provide new evidence on how gender interacts with factors that influence career decision-making self-efficacy (CDMSE). Findings from the pretest-posttest analyses indicate that men scored higher on the vocational identity scale than women at both time points and demonstrated larger gains. Less consistent gender differences were found across CDMSE subscales (based on Betz, Klein, & Taylor, 1996), though women demonstrated significantly larger postintervention levels of the subscale related to planning. The findings lead to the conclusion that "it is important for those who implement career interventions to be aware of the possible existence of these differences in their own students and find constructive ways to engage men and women in the career exploration process" (p. 282).

Academic Major. A handful of studies from the 2000s have provided evidence that the career and economic effects of academic major are conditional on gender. The evidence we identified concentrates on three outcomes: job satisfaction (Liu et al., 2010), working in a job field congruent with students' college major (Robst, 2007; Xu, 2013), and earnings (Hilmer & Hilmer, 2012; Robst, 2007; Zhang, 2008a).

In terms of job satisfaction, Liu et al. (2010) provide evidence that graduates' satisfaction with the monetary dimensions of their jobs roughly a decade after college is significantly influenced by their college major and that the influence differs between men and women. Specifically, the following majors led to significantly greater satisfaction with monetary job satisfaction among women compared men: business, public affairs, biological sciences, mathematics, social science, history, and humanities. There were no gender differences in the effects of majors on non-monetary dimensions of jobs.

A pair of studies (Robst, 2007; Xu, 2013) provide evidence that the effect of majors on working in a congruent job field is conditional gender. A lack of major-job field congruence, or mismatch, was the focus of Robst's investigation, which found that fields of study have significantly different effects by gender. The degree fields that accompanied the largest differences between men and women are home economics, biological sciences, liberal arts, social science, and mathematics. In each of these cases, the effect of the degree field on job mismatch was larger for men than for women. For example, relative to computer and information sciences, graduating in the social sciences increased the odds of job mismatch by 7.46 among men versus 4.10 among women. In the liberal arts, the differences were even more substantial: OR = 10.00 versus 4.20 for men and women, respectively. Xu similarly found gender-conditional effects of majoring in a STEM versus non-STEM field and working in a closely related job. Roughly 10 years after college, among non-STEM graduates, men are significantly less likely than women to be working in a closely related job field (OR = 0.75); among STEM graduates, men and women did not differ in their odds of working in a closely related field.

We identified four studies that indicate majors carry different economic effects for women than for men (Hilmer & Hilmer, 2012; Robst, 2007; Wolniak et al., 2008; Zhang, 2008a). Several majors accompany significant earnings gains for women over men, including engineering, science, and philosophy/religion/theology. Robst estimated a small but significant 6% earnings advantage for women engineering majors, while Zhang reported a much larger 33% earnings advantage for women engineers. Hilmer and Hilmer found that women who studied the sciences earned nearly 17% more than their male counterparts. And Zhang found that philosophy/religion/theology majors, on average the lowest-earning major, led to women earning 25% more than their male counterparts.

Majors that lead to greater earnings among men include business, social sciences, and mathematics. Hilmer and Hilmer (2012) found that business and social science majors lead to roughly 13 to 14% higher earnings for men than for women. Robst (2007) similarly estimated a 13% higher earnings effects for men than women among social science degree holders, and a smaller but significant 6% higher wage effect for male (versus female) business majors.

Engagement. We uncovered one study indicating the effects of students' academic and social engagement on earnings is conditional on race/ethnicity. Hu and Wolniak's (2013) longitudinal study of high-achieving minorities' transitions from college into the labor market included two scaled measures focused on the frequency and nature of students' activities during college (one academic and one social). The findings show that the earnings effects of both engagement measures significantly differ by gender. In fact, academic engagement is more predictive and has a significantly positive effect on earnings among men but a negligible effect among women, while social engagement significantly influences women's early career earnings but not men's.

Race/Ethnicity

Academic Major. Studies have shown that the effects of college major on career and economic outcomes are conditional on race/ethnicity. We uncovered evidence from three studies in relation to job satisfaction and earnings (Hilmer & Hilmer, 2012; Liu et al., 2010; Zhang, 2008a).

Just as Liu et al. (2010) provided evidence of gender-conditional effects of major on satisfaction with the monetary dimensions of jobs, the evidence also indicates that the effect of major differs between graduates of color and White graduates. Specifically, relative to majoring in education, majoring in business, biological sciences, and social sciences leads to significantly greater satisfaction with the monetary dimensions of jobs among nonwhite versus White graduates. Across all of these cases, the major effect was several times larger among nonwhite than among White students. No racial/ethnic differences were found in the effects of majors on non-monetary job satisfaction.

Two studies provide evidence of racial/ethnic differences in the effects of academic major on earnings. Hilmer and Hilmer's (2012) results indicate that the earnings effect of majoring in a social science (versus computer and information science) was greater among White than among Hispanic and Black students and that the earnings effect of a science major was also significantly higher among White than Hispanic students. Zhang (2008a) did not present detailed estimates on the effects of majors by race/ethnicity but did find evidence that the earnings effects of majoring in business and engineering field significantly contributed to explaining the overall racial/ethnic gap in earnings.

Engagement. Two multi-institutional studies provide evidence on the conditional nature of the effects of student engagement on earnings. Together, the studies focus on aspects of career development (Hu & Kuh, 2003b) and earnings (Hu & Wolniak, 2013).

Interactional diversity, defined as the extent to which students from diverse backgrounds interact in educationally purposeful ways, was the focus of Hu and Kuh's (2003b) examination of self-reported gains in vocational development. While many of the study's findings across numerous other outcomes show White students gain more than nonwhite students from interactional diversity experiences, the opposite was found with respect to vocational preparation.

Specifically, it appears that students of color perceive larger gains in vocational preparation from diverse interactions than their White counterparts.

Similar to the gender-conditional effects we discussed, Hu and Wolniak (2013) also provided evidence that student engagement affects early career earnings differently by race/ethnicity. While their sample is limited by including only students of color, the results present interesting discrepancies between racial/ethnic groups. For example, academic engagement had a positive and significant effect on earnings among Native Americans but a negligible, insignificant effect among Asian Americans. Alternatively, social engagement had a significantly larger positive influence on earnings among Asian Americans than among the other racial/ethnic groups and a negative effect on earnings among Native Americans.

Academic Ability. As was the case in previous volumes, we found few studies that provide evidence of college effects on career and economic outcomes that are conditional on academic ability. From the most recent decade of research, we uncovered only one study that produced somewhat weak and preliminary evidence of a significant effect on career and economic outcomes conditional on students' academic backgrounds. Hu and Wolniak's (2013) investigation of student engagement in relation to early career earnings provided evidence that academic engagement in college exerts a significantly larger effect on earnings for students who entered college with SAT/ACT scores that fall in the middle of the distribution. In fact, evidence suggests that academic engagement negatively influences earnings among the low-ability group (based on SAT/ACT scores), positively influences earnings among the middle-ability group, and has no discernable effect among the high-ability group. These findings await replication.

CHAPTER SUMMARY

This chapter has reviewed and synthesized the literature on career and economic impacts of college. We organized the material according to the book's six-question framework (change during college, net effects of college, between-college effects, within-college effects, conditional effects of college) and in terms of career development outcomes, employment outcomes, and earnings. We did not separately address the long-term effects of college (the sixth question in the framework), given that much of the literature on career and economic impacts is based on outcomes measured several years after college; therefore, evidence of long-term impacts is incorporated into the other five sections.

Change during College

Similar to the two previous volumes, a small body of evidence from the 2000s addressed how students change during college with respect to career development, specifically in terms of career aspirations. The two multi-institutional, longitudinal studies we uncovered indicate that most students entered college predisposed toward careers that were traditional for their gender or were considered gender neutral. In addition, over four years of college, sizable shares of students experience changing aspirations, with movement typically from gender-neutral toward traditional careers. Preliminary evidence on change during the first year of college further indicates that students' career aspirations are more stable in terms of the prestige of an occupational field and in terms of personal interests than in terms of gender concentration. Given the small body of evidence, these findings await replication.

Net Effects of College

The evidence from the 2000s demonstrates clear career and economic benefits of postsecondary education. These benefits include improved likelihood of employment, greater opportunity to work more hours, higher growth in occupational status among bachelor's degree holders, increased probability of overall job satisfaction, and significantly higher earnings and private rates of return.

In the 1990s, an additional year of postsecondary education without a bachelor's degree was associated with a 5% increase in earnings per year of education, and a bachelor's degree was found to boost earnings by roughly 37 to 39%, and wages from 28 to 35% when compared to a high school diploma. Evidence from the 2000s indicates a smaller earnings effect of roughly 20% on annual income and 22 to 25% on wages. Fewer differences were uncovered between the evidence from the 2000s and 1990s with respect to certificate and associate's degrees.

In terms of an additional years of higher education, somewhat larger effects were found in 2000s. Across numerous datasets and based on a variety of estimation techniques, evidence from the 2000s indicates that an additional year of higher education leads to approximately 5% higher earnings within the first few years following college and 7 to 9% higher earnings several years after college, without taking into account whether students completed a degree. Together, these findings may suggest that the labor market is offering more monetary reward per additional year of education, while offering slightly less monetary reward for completed credentials. While only speculative until formally tested, it may be that as the variation in postsecondary, bachelor's-degree-granting programs has increased in the United States, the labor market may have begun placing greater emphasis on years of education completed than on degrees earned.

In terms of the private rate of return for a bachelor's degree or equivalent years of education, evidence indicates a 12 to 14% return on average, with as high as a 15 to 20% return when taking into account credentialing effects as well as investment risk/uncertainty. These findings mark an increase from the 10 to 12% private rate of return reported in previous volumes (Pascarella & Terenzini, 1991, 2005).

Comparisons such as these should be interpreted with caution given the substantial variation in methods. Nevertheless, the apparent downward trend in the net earnings effects of a bachelor's degree is notable, particularly in combination with the apparent upward trend in private rate of return that are based on present value estimates of both educational costs and benefits. The fact that these two figures appear to be converging in magnitude may indicate more careful attention to controlling for costs within the more recent decade's estimated earnings premiums.

Given the sizable and sustained increases in college costs that have occurred since the mid-1990s (Baum & Ma, 2013), it is important to note that on average, an undergraduate degree remains a sound investment. Although this review is focused on how college affects students and thus discussed evidence on the private rates of return, Trostel (2010) importantly notes that total public returns on a college degree are substantially greater than public expenditures. According to Trostel, the public internal rate of return on government funds invested in college students is at least 10% (based on comparisons of government expenditures on higher education relative to the gains in tax revenue). While enrollment trends suggest individuals respond rationally to the private returns through sustained and increasing demand for higher education, the same cannot be said for the public sector where, despite substantial public monetary returns, reduced investment in higher education has been the norm rather than the exception for well over a decade.

Between-College Effects

We uncovered only a pair of studies that sought to examine between-college effects on career development, both relying on multi-institutional, survey-based studies of vocational preparation and job preparation. These studies used either cross-sectional or retrospective longitudinal designs to examine aspects of self-reported career development in relation to enrollment at different types of mission-driven institutions. Overall, we found little evidence to suggest that the type of institution attended influences career development above and beyond the academic aspects of the college experience, such as grades and major field of study.

A handful of studies from the 2000s examined between-college effects on employment-related outcomes, including studies of employment following college, hours worked, job satisfaction, and congruence between major field of study and job field. Among the research we uncovered, institutional quality (such as Barron's index of selectivity) was the most influential factor. However, it appears that the quality of institution attended does not necessarily ensure an advantage in terms of employment or higher levels of job satisfaction. In fact, evidence suggests that graduates of higher-quality institutions are less satisfied with several aspects of their jobs. In terms of congruent employment, evidence from a single study strongly suggests that graduates of associate's or specialized institutions are more likely to work in job fields closely related to their field of study when compared to graduates of baccalaureate, master's, and doctoral institutions.

In terms of the between-college effects on earnings, as in past decades, researchers continued to devote a great deal of effort to accounting for the differences in student characteristics at the point of entering college and the fact that different definitions of college quality may exert substantially different influence across outcomes. In some instances, between-college effects on earnings doubled in magnitude based on different operationalized measures of institutional quality. All else equal, and despite the variability in the estimated magnitudes of the effects, the weight of evidence suggests that attending a higher-quality institution leads to higher earnings following college. In addition, the effects are most pronounced when institutional quality is measured based on an overall college quality index or rating system that combines multiple institutional characteristics (such as entering students' class rank, high school GPA, average SAT scores, and percentage of applicants admitted). In addition, the earnings effects of attending a higher-quality institution increase over time. Evidence suggests that one year after college and controlling for other factors, graduates from high-quality institutions earned 6 to 8% more than their counterparts who graduated from lower-quality institutions. Furthermore, these earnings advantages appear to increase to 13 to 15% four years after graduation and up to 16 to 19% 10 years after graduation. The substantial amount of variation that exists in how institutional quality is operationalized warrants caution when interpreting the estimated earnings effects of attending higher- versus lower-quality institutions.

The results of our review are generally consistent with those reported in the two previous volumes in terms of institutional quality having a positive and significant (if often small) impact on subsequent earnings. However, we believe that too much variation exists across model specification and measures of institutional quality to provide a single estimated effect or to assess whether the evidence from the 2000s (versus the 1990s) indicates larger or smaller earnings advantages accompanying attending higher-quality institutions. In general, we found the more recent decade of research to be increasingly rigorous in terms of methods used to account for selection bias and to control for differences in students' ambition across institutions of differing selectivity and prestige, suggesting greater precision in the estimated effects from the 2000s than previous decades.

With respect to Carnegie Classification and institutional mission, earnings advantages were found for attending a Comprehensive I versus Liberal Arts II institution, and marginally lower earnings were associated with attending a Historically Black Institution relative to other institutions or for attending a work college relative to a regional public institution. These differences quite possibly serve as a proxy for differences in institutional selectivity and do not reflect the quality of education they deliver their students. In fact, this evidence should be interpreted with the knowledge that costs differ substantially across different institution types, and some mission-driven institutions, such as work colleges, significantly limit the accumulation of loan debt.

Finally, institutional control exerts a smaller influence on postcollege earnings than institutional quality, though graduating from a private school appears to lead to slightly higher earnings, but only among higher-quality institutions.

However, the debt-to-earnings ratios of college graduates from private institutions are substantially greater than those who graduate from public institutions.

Within-College Effects

The sizable literature from the 2000s containing estimates of within-college effects on career and economic outcomes presents several conclusions. The following conclusions are arranged by the category of outcome examined.

Career Development

1. Career-oriented courses are effective interventions that appear to have a positive influence on a range of developmental and behavioral outcomes. While varied in design, numerous evaluations have provided evidence that such courses affect outcomes such as career decidedness, locus of control, self-efficacy, and possibly retention and graduation. These studies generally support the main tenets of social cognitive career theory and career decision-making self-efficacy.

2. Academic experiences and involvement appeared to influence a varied set of career development outcomes, including vocational preparation, sex-atypical career choices, and intentions toward innovation. While the evidence in this area addressed unique populations of college students, the evidence across multiple studies points to the important influence of students' interactions with faculty. For example, asking instructors course-related information and discussing career plans with a faculty member improved minority students' sense of vocational preparation. In addition, instructors who encouraged innovative behavior in class stimulated innovative intentions among students. Among male students, talking with faculty outside of class was associated with career aspirations shifting more toward characteristically male career fields.

3. While a handful of studies provide evidence that social involvement and extracurricular activities (such as athletic involvement, volunteering, experiences in the student union, and exposure to living-learning programs) have effects on dimensions of career development (such as career identity foreclosure, attitudes toward vocational preparation, and career expectations), the variables investigated and resulting evidence were too varied to allow general conclusions. Replication of existing studies and efforts to provide conceptual clarity to myriad variables representing the effects of social involvement and extracurricular activities on career development are promising areas for future inquiry.

Employment Outcomes

1. Academic major in college significantly affects students' likelihood of working in a job related to their major. Majors that cultivate more

general skills appear to have relatively higher likelihood of eventual job mismatch (lower likelihood of a close match), while majors that cultivate relatively more specific or applied skills, including STEM fields, appear to have the lowest likelihood of job mismatch (highest likelihood of a close match). In other words, the more specialized and focused the training, the more likely it will lead to close job match.

2. Gender plays an important role in the relationship between college major and employment outcomes. Majoring in a relatively more female-dominated field significantly increases the likelihood of employment in public and nonprofit organizations and possibly the likelihood of employment in a professional or managerial occupation. In addition, majors such as education, health, social sciences, and humanities increase a student's probability of entering a female-dominated occupation immediately following college, while majoring in a science field increases a student's probability of entering a male-dominated occupation. Furthermore, majors with high occupational specificity predict higher occupational status than majors with low occupational specificity, while majors with low occupational specificity demonstrate higher growth in occupational status. Each of these findings, while based on nationally representative data, will benefit from replication.

3. Academic major tends not to significantly affect overall job satisfaction following college, though evidence suggests that certain majors lead to higher levels of specific facets of job satisfaction, such as arts and humanities majors reporting higher satisfaction with their levels of job autonomy relative to education majors. The relationship between a college major and subsequent job satisfaction appears to be significantly mediated by earnings.

Earnings

1. Consistent with the two previous volumes, majors that have the largest effect on earnings are fields that that have a well-defined body of content knowledge, center on quantitative or scientific skills, and have a direct functional alignment with specific occupations. These majors include engineering, computer science and information technology, mathematics, and health science. The lowest-earning fields include education and the humanities. Earnings differences between highest and lowest majors may be as high as 25 to 50%. The sizable earnings effects of major appear to be stable and possibly increasing the more time individuals spend in the labor market following college.

2. Earnings premiums across college majors are positively, significantly, and substantially affected by working in a field that is congruent with one's college major, where the greatest earnings result from majoring in a high-earning field and working in a closely related job. However, as

one might expect, working in a job that is congruent with one's major may lead to lower earnings if one majored in a traditionally lower-earning field. On average, working in a job field that is relatively more congruent with one's college major has a significant positive effect on earnings that appears to be at least as large in magnitude as the earnings effect of completing an additional year of higher education.

3. While the two previous volumes concluded that college grades have a small, positive effect on earnings, evidence from the 2000s is somewhat mixed. Some estimates show that college GPA does not significantly affect earnings, while other estimates indicate that a one point increase in GPA (e.g., from a B average to an A average) was estimated at, on average, approximately 6%, mirroring the conclusions from the 1990s. Overall, the weight of evidence suggests that college grades have at most a small positive influence on earnings after factoring in major field of study, degree attainment, institution attended, and student background characteristics.

4. Controlling for education attainment and years of postcollege work experience, working while in college appears to have a significant and positive effect on subsequent earnings. Preliminary evidence suggests that the earnings effect of working during college may be more pronounced among community college students than among four-year college enrollees and that the positive effect of work experience diminishes as the amount of work involvement increases.

5. Transferring from a two-year to a four-year institution does not have a significant direct effect on earnings. However, horizontal transfer between four-year institutions does appear to have a significantly positive earnings effect, possibly due to achieving a better environmental fit that is more effective at developing the kinds of skills rewarded in the labor market.

Conditional College Effects

Our review of the literature from the 2000s leads to several conclusions about the conditional nature of college effects on career and economic outcomes. While a handful of studies focused on employment outcomes, the weight of evidence is centered on explaining the relationships between postsecondary education experiences and attainment on earnings.

Employment Outcomes. In terms of the net effects of college on employment outcomes, a small body of evidence points to gender differences in the relationship between a postsecondary degree, job satisfaction, gaining employment in a job field that is congruent with one's major, or labor force participation. However, beyond a general conclusion that gender differences appear to exist, the evidence is inconsistent and stems from a small body of studies, preventing us from making more specific conclusions. No racial/ethnic, socioeconomic, age, or academic ability differences were uncovered in terms of the net effects of degree attainment or years of education on career and economic outcomes.

A pair of studies suggests that the type of institution attended affects vocational preparation and job satisfaction among nonwhite students more than among White students. We view this evidence as preliminary and in need of replication. We found no evidence of significant gender, socioeconomic, age, or ability differences in the between-college effects on employment outcomes.

Several gender and racial/ethnic differences were evident in the literature pertaining to the within-college effects on employment outcomes. Single-study evidence that awaits replication has identified possible gender or racial/ethnic differences in the effects of course interventions on career development outcomes and the effects of majors on job satisfaction. For example, one study revealed that several majors appear to lead to higher levels of satisfaction with the monetary aspects of a job among women relative to men (including higher earnings fields such as business, biological sciences, and mathematics, as well as some lower earnings fields such as humanities, all compared against education majors). The same study provided evidence that, relative to education, majoring in business, biological sciences, and social sciences leads to higher satisfaction with the monetary dimensions of jobs among nonwhite versus White graduates. No conditional effects were found with respect to nonmonetary dimensions of job satisfaction. Studies have also shown that academic majors influence employment outcomes differently by students' gender and race/ethnicity. In general, evidence suggests that women who major in non-STEM fields are more likely than men to work in a closely related job.

Earnings. A sizable body of evidence indicates that the net effects of college on earnings are conditional on gender and race/ethnicity, while a single study suggests that earnings effects of postsecondary education are conditional on students' age at graduation. While national reports indicate that women continue to earn less than men on average across all education attainment levels (Julian & Kominski, 2011), the net effects of completing a postsecondary degree has a greater positive impact on women's earnings than on men's earnings. The effects of a bachelor's degree versus no postsecondary education have been found to be as high as 45% greater for women, while studies indicate that the earnings effects of graduate or advanced degrees appear to be 5 to 10% greater for women. These findings differ from the evidence reported in the 1990s, which suggested that the earnings effect of an associate's degree was 1.5 times higher among women than men, whereas gender parity existed in the earnings effects of a bachelor's degree. Thus, the gender-conditional earnings effects of completing a bachelor's degree based on the 2000s literature are roughly similar in size to the gender-conditional earnings effects of completing an associate's degree based on the 1990s literature.

Evidence indicates racial/ethnic differences in the effects of postsecondary degree attainment or years of education. Although the findings as a whole are inconsistent and difficult to generalize, multiple studies indicate that each additional year of education has roughly twice the effect on annual earnings among Black students than among White students. One additional study focuses on age-conditional effects, providing evidence that supports the notion that students who graduate at 25 years or older experience smaller wage effects from a bachelor's degree.

In terms of institution attended, we found only mixed or conflicting evidence that the earnings effects of attending different types of institutions, based on institutional quality indices or by mission, are conditional on gender or race/ethnicity, and partial evidence indicating the effects are conditional on socioeconomic status. Two nationally representative studies show a compensatory relationship between students' SES and the quality of institution attended. Lower-SES students experience larger earnings benefits from attending higher-quality institutions, while higher-SES students experience smaller earnings penalties for attending lower-quality institutions.

A sizable body of evidence shows that the effect of academic major on earnings is conditional on gender and, to a lesser extent, race/ethnicity. Majors that have larger earnings effects among women include engineering and science, as well as philosophy/religion/theology, while majors that lead to greater earnings among men include business and the social sciences.

We found two studies indicating racial/ethnic differences in the effects of major and earnings. The findings are inconsistent in terms of which specific majors influence earnings for different racial/ethnic groups, but they do indicate that academic major contributes to understanding racial/ethnic gaps in earnings. Furthermore, a single study provides preliminary evidence that student engagement in college affects earnings differently across racial/ethnic and academic ability groups, but the findings await replication.

CHAPTER CONCLUSION

Overall, the evidence discussed in this chapter highlights the many ways in which college affects career development, employment, and economic outcomes. What is not captured among these outcomes is whether or how a college education has a lasting influence on students' quality of life following college. Undoubtedly, life after college is characterized in terms of not only time spent working, cultivating careers, and securing financial security for oneself and one's family, but also health, happiness, family well-being, and engagement with one's community. Providing an important and essential accompaniment to the discussion of career and economic outcomes found in this chapter is the review of evidence on how college affects quality of life discussed next in Chapter 9.

Notes

1. An earlier, unpublished version of this study (Dale & Krueger, 1999) was discussed at length in Volume 2 of *How College Affects Students*. The study's key finding was that once student ambition was accounted for (through the average selectivity of the colleges applied to), the positive earnings effects of attending a more selective institution became trivial. The importance of this finding is that it cast doubt on any positive impact of attending elite institutions on subsequent earnings. We do not discuss this study in this chapter, because it was addressed in the previous volume. For the full discussion, see Pascarella and Terenzini (2005).

2. Several studies based on B&B data reviewed in this section define institutional quality based on the following Barron's ratings: highly competitive or high quality (Barron's rating of 4 or greater); very competitive, competitive, or middle quality (Barron's ratings of 2 or 3); and less competitive, noncompetitive, or low quality (Barron's rating of 0 or 1) (Barron's, 2013; Thomas & Zhang, 2005; Zhang, 2005, 2008b).

3. Log transformations make positively skewed earnings distributions more normally distributed and allow estimated effects of a change in an independent variable to approximate a percentage change in earnings. Applying a log transformation of earnings has been standard practice in the economics of education since Mincer's model of earnings was published in 1974. For further reading, see Heckman, Lochner, and Todd (2003) and Mincer (1974).

4. Long (2008) used the following measures of institutional quality: (1) median freshman SAT test score (captures the effects of both selectivity and peer quality) from Barron's data; (2) net price (to capture how much it costs the average student to attend that college) gathered from IPEDS data; (3) average full professor's salary adjusted for living costs (intended to capture faculty quality) gathered from IPEDS data; (4) faculty per student (intended to capture effects of faculty availability and signal smaller class sizes) gathered from IPEDS; and (5) an index of college quality based on a weighted index through principal component analysis of the above four measures, normalized to have a mean of 0 and a standard deviation of 1 (see also Black & Smith, 2004).

5. Long (2008) used four different analytic strategies each with different specifications and degrees of control. The methods employed were ordinary least squares, an instrumental variable approach with average quality of colleges within a certain radius of the student as the instrument for the quality of the college attended, and two approaches aimed at accounting for students' unobserved traits (those believed to be associated with education aspirations): (1) grouping students according to similarities in the colleges applied to and rejected from (see Dale & Krueger, 2002), and (2) narrowing the analytic sample to compare only groups of similar propensities in college application behaviors, comparing those who attended high-quality (top-quartile) colleges versus those that attended lower-quality (bottom-quartile) colleges (see Black & Smith, 2004).

6. Hubbard (2011) provides informative trend estimates on the wage gaps between men and women from 1970 to 2008, though the data and models do not account for aspects of the college experience known to significantly influence employment outcomes.

CHAPTER NINE

Quality of Life after College

In Chapter 8, we described the career and economic benefits of postsecondary attendance. Without a doubt, decisions to pursue a college degree are motivated in large part by students' desires for improved career opportunities and the monetary benefits associated with such opportunities, and rightfully so, given the significant impact that higher education has on career outcomes. Earlier volumes (Pascarella & Terenzini, 1991, 2005) also discussed important nonmonetary benefits of education—health, happiness, community involvement, well-being of children, and the like—as the nonmarket, nonproduction, or nonpecuniary benefits of education (Lochner, 2011; Oreopoulos & Salvanes, 2011), noting that these outcomes are often considered quality of life indicators. Educational attainment is associated with differential life opportunities resulting from higher earnings, occupational prestige, and access to resources, and college graduates' life opportunities, on average, lead to a different quality of life from that of their peers who did not attend college. Recognizing the inherent differences in life opportunities for more versus less educated individuals, research has tended to focused on examining the net effects of college on quality of life measures and has largely come from the fields of economics, epidemiology, demography, and sociology.

Unlike this book's other chapters, in which we review the sizable literature on the between- and within-college effects across different outcomes, only a small body of evidence has addressed these questions in terms of quality of life outcomes. Given that one of higher education's purposes is to educate graduates for engaged citizenship, the paucity of research that has investigated the role that college environments and experiences play in graduates' quality of life after college is puzzling. Although the body of evidence is relatively small, we review and synthesize what literature exists and conclude the chapter by discussing how the relationship between education and quality of life outcomes differs by alumni characteristics—largely gender, race, and age. The latter is a measure of the cohort to which one belongs and thus suggests the long-term effects of college attendance on graduates' quality of life.

THEORETICAL AND METHODOLOGICAL OVERVIEW

Researchers have advanced theoretical propositions and examined the mechanisms linking education to a host of nonpecuniary benefits. Key theories and concepts guiding research on the effects of college on quality of life outcomes include human capital, allocation, and socialization. Relatedly, research has hypothesized the mechanisms by which education operates to promote these outcomes. We discuss each in turn.

The concept of human capital brings forth the notion of capital stemming from the work of classical economists in the eighteenth and nineteenth centuries. Adam Smith (1776) defined capital as

> the acquired and useful abilities of all the inhabitants or members of the society. The acquisition of such talents, by the maintenance of the acquirer during his [sic] education, study, or apprenticeship, always costs a real expense, which is a capital fixed and realized, as it were, in his person. Those talents, as they make a part of his fortune, so do they likewise that of the society to which he belongs (p. 609).

In this statement, Smith clearly articulated the value that human capital developed through education and training has for an individual and acknowledged the societal benefit that derives from an educated populace. Conceptualizing human capital in terms of both individual and social benefits encompasses numerous quality of life outcomes (see Wolfe & Haveman, 2002, for a thorough description of the individual and social dimensions of quality of life outcomes). Building on the previous chapter's discussion of career and economic impacts of college, we adopt a broad notion of human capital to examine individuals' nonmarket returns or quality of life outcomes.

Formally, human capital theory (Becker, 1993; Schultz, 1958) rests on the notion that just as businesses boost productivity by investing in physical capital, individuals enhance their productivity by investing in their own human capital through attaining education or formal training. In the absence of directly observing an individual's productivity, one's education and training become an important signal of the qualities that may be of value to an employer (Spence, 1973, 2002; Stiglitz, 1975). Once hired, the allocation perspective of education (Kerckhoff, 1976; Mirowsky & Ross, 2003) postulates that those with more education gain greater access to higher-status workplace positions and conditions that may be associated with more satisfying, better-paying work with greater autonomy and responsibility. Put simply, the resultant occupational and economic conditions through attained status are associated with better quality of life outcomes. A socialization perspective of education suggests that education enhances one's personal attributes, psychosocial resources, and values (Pallas, 2000), and through such personal development, the more educated have a stronger internal locus of control, self-efficacy, broader social network, and resilience to respond to challenging situations. Those with greater educational attainment are thus able to employ the attributes and resources that yield a higher quality of life. Whether directly related to productivity or as a signal, through allocation or socialization, governments worldwide have justified investment in education as a key means to develop human capital.

Campbell (2006) referred to several ways in which education may affect nonpecuniary outcomes, functioning as an absolute, relative, or cumulative mechanism. Education is an absolute mechanism if it has a direct effect on an outcome, a relative mechanism if it positions or sorts individuals by social status, and a cumulative mechanism if the outcome is conditional on the average educational attainment of one's peer group or locality. The way education has been operationalized as a predictor variable in the literature is related to these different mechanisms, as well as the particular scholar's discipline. First, education has been measured as "years of schooling," a continuous variable that measures formal education completed or contribution to the productive process, akin to an absolute mechanism. Second, research has categorized education based on the degree or credential completed (less than high school, high school diploma, some college, associate's degree, bachelor's degree, graduate degree). This operationalization aligns more closely with the relative mechanism as graduates realize the socioeconomic structural benefits gained from the credential's signaling effect (Feinstein, Duckworth, & Sabates, 2008). Studies that have examined aggregate effects of education on quality of life outcomes, for example at the neighborhood or regional level (see Campbell, 2009; Smets & van Ham, 2013), illustrate education as a cumulative mechanism.

Economists, such as Michael Grossman (2006), have offered three broad explanations for the link between level of education (often defined as years of schooling and in other cases by discrete attainment categories) and quality of life outcomes: efficiency mechanisms, unobserved heterogeneity, and future opportunity costs. Grossman (2006) provides an example of how these explanations operate within the health domain. With respect to efficiency mechanisms, the productive efficiency argument suggests that more educated persons convert inputs more efficiently into a health production function (e.g., through increasing the quantity of health demanded while lowering the quantity of medical care demanded). Some have critiqued assumptions within this argument (see Grossman, 2006, for discussion) and asserted that the allocative efficiency argument better specifies "situations in which the more educated pick a different mix of inputs to produce a certain commodity than the less educated" (Grossman, 2006, p. 587). In the case of health, more educated individuals have greater access to information and thus are in a better position to act in ways to maximize the production function, particularly in terms of smoking, diet, and exercise (Grossman, 2006). Glied and Lleras-Muney (2003), Lange (2011), and McMahon (2009) provide empirical evidence to support the allocative efficiency argument, finding that those with higher levels of education have greater access and ability to act on information that improves their health outcomes.

Unobserved heterogeneity as an explanation posits that education serves as a proxy for unobserved variables such as motivation, dispositions, and tastes (Oreopoulos & Petronijevic, 2013) or what Pierre Bourdieu (1984) referred to as one's habitus, as well as one's time preference (Grossman, 2006). As Becker and Mulligan (1997) noted, "Schooling focuses students' attention on the future" (p. 735) and as such may indicate a greater future orientation. Finally, Cowell (2006) advanced a future opportunity cost explanation in which any future outcome can be influenced by current behavior, such that the more educated person acts today in ways that improve future outcomes. For example, because education raises wages but smoking reduces one's working life and thus the number of years over which one can recoup educational investment, the more educated person sees a disincentive to smoke.

Exposure to postsecondary education and college completion is the quintessential example of the challenge researchers face when trying to estimate causal effects. In examining quality of life measures, researchers have used a multitude of analytical approaches to estimate nonpecuniary returns to college including twin and sibling studies (see Lundborg, 2013; Oreopoulos & Salvanes, 2011), natural experiments (see Grimard & Parent, 2007; Oreopoulos, Page, & Stevens, 2006), and instrumental variables (see Eide & Showalter, 2011, and Price, Price, & Simon, 2011, for critiques of this approach).

In addition to these approaches, researchers have sought to statistically create equivalent groups through propensity score and genetic matching, as well as to identify potential causal mechanisms through the use of structural equation modeling/path analysis and other forms of regression. With all research, the strength of an approach may present a limitation in another regard. For example, the methodological rigor present in twin studies is limited to a small sample of individuals who may not approximate the population to which one wishes to generalize. Conversely, the relationships identified in a nationally representative sample using theoretically based path analyses may still fail to account for an omitted variable. Such are the trade-offs of college impact research, which have been discussed throughout this book. Although new methodological approaches aim to mitigate self-selection bias, only randomized controlled trials can truly make causal claims (see the methodological appendix). We discuss the research in this chapter recognizing the value multiple approaches and samples bring to understanding the impact of postsecondary attendance on one's quality of life after college. While all of the studies we discuss in this chapter have satisfied our criteria for inclusion that is rooted in methodological rigor (see Chapter 1), we focus our review and synthesis of evidence relatively more on studies' findings than on the analytical details leading to those findings and conclusions. Readers interested in the more technical details can find them in the studies cited.

The research we examine in this chapter largely addresses the extent to which quality of life outcomes differ by years of completed formal education or by educational attainment categories (i.e., less than high school, high school graduate, some college, less than four-year degree, bachelor's degree, and graduate degree). We do not review literature from the United States that categorized 12 or more years of schooling as its top category because the category is too broad to support any claims regarding the effects of higher education on quality of life outcomes. There has been a great deal of work examining the relationship between education and quality of life indicators by researchers in the United Kingdom and is thus important to recognize different educational thresholds within that system: primary school (2–5 CSEs), lower secondary (O level), upper secondary (A level), postsecondary/further education/nonuniversity (referred to as "college" in Canada), and completed university/tertiary degree.

CHANGE DURING AND NET EFFECTS OF COLLEGE

Conclusions from the 1990s

The previous volume concluded that the effects of postsecondary attendance on quality of life indicators were complex and varied based on the outcome measure. Overall, the impact of a college education on life satisfaction was inconclusive. Individuals with greater levels of education may qualitatively assess happiness and satisfaction from a more critical or complex perspective than those with less education. However, levels of education appeared to influence life satisfaction and subjective well-being indirectly through increased economic affluence, greater social support networks, and sense of control over one's life, as well as improved perceived health status.

In contrast to life satisfaction, the evidence clearly demonstrated that education has direct and indirect effects on health status. The underlying causes of this link included improved work and economic conditions, healthier lifestyle, greater access to health care and health information, better decisions about one's health from available information, and a time preference that focuses on the future. These causes are consistent with both the allocative efficiency mechanism and unobserved heterogeneity explanations discussed earlier in the chapter.

Education had key indirect effects on health outcomes through lifestyle and health behaviors. For example, educational attainment associated negatively with cigarette smoking, alcohol abuse and dependency, and cholesterol levels. It tended to have a positive relationship with aerobic exercise, a healthy diet, and dietary fiber intake. In addition, studies that isolated the unique or direct effects of college education found individuals who attended or graduated from college had lower risk profiles for both coronary heart disease and cancer, although the relationship with alcohol consumption was far more complicated. Two years of postsecondary education appeared to reduce the probability of alcohol abuse overall, but attending college for a short time may not reduce this probability.

The previous volume also concluded that educational attainment has positive influences on the welfare of children, suggesting education's role in intergenerational legacy, and one's civic and community involvement. For example, a parent's formal education, net of confounding influences, increased the likelihood of the pregnant mother to receive prenatal care. In addition, positive influences were found with respect to parental involvement in a child's school, parental help with homework, and a child's access to technology resources in the home. Parental education was also found to lessen the likelihood of teenage pregnancy and childhood death before age two. Finally, Volume 2 concluded that a college education positively influenced individuals' civic and community involvement. People with a bachelor's degree were more likely to be frequently involved in political activities; knowledgeable about local, regional, national, and international events; engage in cultural events like visiting museums; participate in community groups; and vote in national, state, and local elections.

Evidence from the 2000s

One may question if a conceptual order exists for the quality of life outcomes reviewed in this and the previous volumes. It would seem that access to resources through higher income and greater job satisfaction may lead college graduates to have greater subjective well-being and life satisfaction. Those who are more satisfied with their lives may make more conscientious health decisions. Healthy college graduates may also model positive health behaviors to their children as well as pass on values and dispositions with respect to formal education and civic engagement. In addition to valuing civic engagement, college graduates may contribute more to their community than their noncollege peers. We review the quality-of-life outcomes using this conceptual map.

Subjective Well-Being and Life Satisfaction. Several studies have investigated the relationship between education and subjective well-being, life satisfaction, or happiness and provide empirical evidence to support the theoretical propositions of socialization and allocation discussed earlier in the chapter. Mirowsky and Ross (2007) theorized that education is associated with enhanced quality of life from both a developmental perspective in that practice, training, and learning transform the complex and impossible to something that is perceived as doable; and an achieved status perspective: educated individuals develop the capacity to use information, communicate, negotiate with others, and either plan to avoid or solve problems as they arise. Cuñado and de Gracia (2012) hypothesized that education has an indirect effect on subjective well-being through its positive effects on self-confidence, efficacy, and estimation and pleasure in acquiring knowledge, as well as greater probability of employment, better job quality, higher expected salary and better health—all of which contribute to greater happiness. In the main, past research has found a positive relationship between education and measures of well-being, life satisfaction, happiness, and sense of control (Becchetti, Corrado, & Rossetti, 2008; Blanchflower & Oswald, 2004; Di Tella, MacCulloch, & Oswald, 2003; Mirowsky & Ross, 2007; Oreopoulos & Salvanes, 2011; Schieman & Plickert, 2008). Research has also found that education provides a protective effect against depression (Chevalier & Feinstein, 2006; Kim, 2008; Ross & Mirowsky, 2006; Walsemann, Bell, & Hummer, 2012). Moreover, these relationships hold in samples from the United States and the United Kingdom. Despite the generally positive findings, some studies from Australia found a slight negative relationship between educational attainment and life satisfaction (Dockery, 2010; Headey & Wooden, 2004).

In a sample of 25- to 45-year-olds from the 1972–2000 General Social Surveys in the United States, controlling for a number of background measures and respondent's present income, Oreopoulos and Salvanes (2011) found college graduates reported being roughly 2 percentile points happier than high school graduates. They wrote: "The effect before conditioning on income falls by only one-quarter after conditioning, suggesting that as much as three-quarters of the schooling effect on self-reported life satisfaction is due to nonpecuniary factors" (2011, p. 180). Comparing the relationship between education and happiness in the United States and the United Kingdom, Oreopoulos and Salvanes (2011) also examined data of 25- to 65-year-olds born in the United Kingdom from 1973 to 1998 from the Eurobarometer and found that changes in compulsory schooling (the natural experiment that resulted in some respondents completing more years of schooling) was associated with overall life satisfaction. Although the magnitude of the effect decreased, it remained statistically significant when accounting for respondent's income. While it is difficult to ascertain the effect uniquely attributable to differential exposure to higher education due to the fact that the compulsory schooling change (the natural experiment) existed at the secondary level, Oreopoulos and Salvanes's (2011) findings supported similar results from the British Household Panel study (Becchetti et al., 2008), which found that educational attainment was associated with increased happiness controlling for income. Together, evidence from the United States and United Kingdom bolster conclusions from the World Bank's World Values Survey in which the marginal utility of additional income on happiness was lower for more highly educated people (Castriota, 2006). Becchetti and colleagues (2008) advanced that education "has a Maslow effect on individuals, increasing their immaterial needs and moderating income expectations" (p. 13)

Oreopoulos and Salvanes (2009) examined potential causal mechanisms between education and nonpecuniary outcomes like well-being and life satisfaction. Given the amount of time the average adult spends working, the relationship between educational attainment and having a job that provides a sense of accomplishment, autonomy, opportunity for social interaction, recognition, support from supervisors and coworkers, and favorable working conditions is not trivial and suggests causal mechanisms that connect educational attainment to well-being and life satisfaction. However, these jobs may come with added stressors like greater responsibility, more travel, and expectations for more effort. Cohen and colleagues (2006, cited in Oreopoulos & Salvanes, 2009) examined this possibility and found stress hormones negatively associated with income and schooling, proposing that the additional pressures such jobs possess may be offset by better health and social support. Education was also positively associated with an increased sense of control (Mirowsky & Ross, 2007; Schieman & Plickert, 2008), often defined as the ability to determine positive and negative events and power over life outcomes (Mirowsky & Ross, 2003), as well as reduced depressive symptomatology (Chevalier & Feinstein, 2006; Kim, 2008; Ross & Mirowsky, 2006; Walsemann et al., 2012b). In addition to any societal benefits that may arise from a happier, more subjectively well society, the protective effect education exerts in reducing depression makes Chevalier and Feinstein's (2006) conclusion more prescient: "Due to the high costs of poor mental health, education policies thus have large additional returns" (p. 4).

Research examining the effects of overeducation on life satisfaction and depression notwithstanding (see Bracke, Pattyn, & von dem Knesebeck, 2013; Piper, 2014), two studies conducted in Australia found a negative relationship between education and happiness. Using data from the 1995 year 9 cohort of the Longitudinal Surveys of Australian Youth, Dockery (2010) found that while vocational qualifications had a positive relationship with happiness both during the training period (i.e., college/postsecondary education) and after graduation, university graduates' happiness declined after graduation. At the time of this study, the cohort had been tracked only through their mid–twenties leaving one to question the durability of these findings. Yet results from a household panel dataset from Australia that followed a broader cohort of individuals were strikingly similar. Headey and Wooden (2004) found that although university degree respondents reported less financial stress, they did not differ from high school graduates in life satisfaction and that those with less than a high school diploma, as well as those with a vocational credential/trade qualification, had greater life satisfaction, controlling for gender, age, relationship, employment and disability status. Moreover, Heady and Wooden found no relationship between education and mental health.

With the exception of research from Australia, the weight of the evidence from the United States and the United Kingdom suggests education is associated with higher levels of subjective well-being, happiness, life satisfaction, and sense of control and serves in protective fashion against depression and depressive symptomatology. Studies that have examined causal mechanisms have found these effects largely a result of richer, more satisfying relationships, employment, and working conditions, lending support for both the allocation and socialization perspectives.

Health and Health Behaviors. The relationship between education and health has become so ubiquitous that it is often referred to as the "gradient" (where increased years of schooling are associated with better health outcomes).

Yet the gradient in education-related health inequality is not consistent across countries; it is greater in the United States and the United Kingdom than in Nordic or Western European countries (Jürges, 2009). In addition, while the generally positive relationship between education and health varies in magnitude across countries, it also varies across facets of health. Although an exhaustive review of the education-health nexus is beyond the scope of this chapter, we focus on the most prominent studies that have examined respondents' self-assessment of health, mortality (an objective measure of health), and health behaviors such as smoking, binge drinking, diet, and exercise.

In general, years of education and educational attainment in the form of degree thresholds appeared positively associated with subjective self-assessments of health among respondents in the United States (Fujiwara & Kawachi, 2009; Mazumder, 2008; Oreopoulos & Salvanes, 2011; Prus, 2011; Zajacova, Hummer, & Rogers, 2012). With the exception of Fujiwara and Kawachi (2009), these studies used nationally representative samples of adults. In two studies that examined twin data from the Midlife in the U.S. survey, Lundborg (2013) found, relative to high school dropouts, that people with higher levels of schooling were significantly healthier as measured through their self-reported health and number of chronic conditions. However, high school and college completers did not significantly differ. Fujiwara and Kawachi (2009) operationalized schooling as a continuous measure and found a weak positive relationship between education and perceived global health in the total twin sample but not in separate samples of men and women, which may be an artifact of smaller sample sizes. These findings contrasted with Oreopoulos and Salvanes (2011) who found that bachelor's degree graduates reported being in "very good health" at a much higher proportion than high school graduates, controlling for a multitude of background characteristics and income.

In one of the few studies that examined the relationship between education and self-assessed health across the broadest spectrum of degrees (from less than high school to doctorate), Zajacova et al. (2012a) found descriptively a fairly linear relationship between educational degrees and self-assessed health. After controlling for confounding influences, they found the largest health improvement between associate's degree and bachelor's degree holders.

In educational contexts outside the United States, Prus (2011) examined the degree to which predictors of health differed in magnitude between the United States and Canada. Without controls, a statistically significant difference in self-assessed health existed between Canadian and American respondents who had a high school diploma or less with a greater percentage of Canadians reporting excellent health. No differences were found among those who had postsecondary degrees. Sociodemographic and socioeconomic factors, as well as psychosocial, behavioral risk, and health care access factors had substantial effects on self-assessed health in each country although the magnitude of the effects differed. Accounting for other factors, including income, the relationship between education and health was greater in magnitude in the United States than in Canada (Prus, 2011), lending further support for Jürges's (2009) finding that education-related health inequality varies across countries.

Using data from the General Household Survey for England, Scotland, and Wales to examine the effect of the 1947 and 1972 changes to U.K. compulsory schooling laws, Silles (2009) found additional years of schooling positively related to self-reported health. Estimating across studies in meta-analytical fashion, McMahon and Oketch (2013) found that those with additional years of formal higher education, defined by short-cycle degree completion (similar to two-year degrees in the United States) and bachelor's degree holders in the United Kingdom had better self-assessed health compared to those with less education. In a meta-analysis of studies that have used a self-assessment of health as an outcome variable, Furnée, Groot, and van den Brink (2008) computed a quality adjusted life years (QALY) weight and found a year of education associated with 0.036 QALYs.

One could critique the use of self-assessment of general health measures, preferring mortality as a more objective measure of health. In an interesting study that combined survey measures of health status from the U.S. Panel Study of Income Dynamics data with mortality data, education was associated positively with quality-adjusted life years (0.20–0.38 depending on model; Golberstein, Hirth, & Lantz, 2012). Across a host of studies and analytical approaches in the United States and controlling for a variety of confounding influences, the weight of the evidence suggests an additional year of schooling was associated with reduced mortality/additional years of life (Cutler & Lleras-Muney, 2008; Hadden & Rockswold, 2008; Lillard & Molloy, 2010; Lleras-Muney, 2005; Rogers, Everett, Zajacova, & Hummer, 2010). The evidence is less conclusive in the United Kingdom. Clark and Royer (2010) found no relationship between education and mortality using the natural experiment of two changes in compulsory schooling laws in Britain.

Some research has suggested that the relationship between education and mortality differs by the extent of medical innovation relevant to the health condition, with more educated people responding to these technological advances and acting in precautionary ways (Glied & Lleras-Muney, 2003; Lange, 2011). This research supports the allocative efficiency mechanism (Grossman, 2006) in that more educated people use information more effectively to yield a higher production function. Using information and responding to technological advances presumes an adequate level of health literacy. Results from the National Assessment of Adult Literacy's health literacy tasks (Kutner, Greenberg, Jin, & Paulsen, 2006), which assessed prose, document, and quantitative literacy with respect to health care information and services across clinical, prevention, and navigation of the health system domains, found a clear difference between education level and health literacy in the United States. Fifteen percent of high school graduates had health literacy at a below basic level, whereas 3% of bachelor's degree holders had this literacy level. At the other end of the spectrum, 4% of high school graduates compared to 27% of bachelor's degree holders were proficient in health literacy. While the U.S. study was limited by its descriptive nature, a similar education-health literacy relationship was found in a sample of older adults in Canada, accounting for demographic, socioeconomic, and lifelong learning behaviors (Wister, Malloy-Weir, Rootman, & Desjardins, 2010).

Other research has examined the relationship between education and chronic health conditions, like hypertension. Mazumder (2008) posited that if education is causally associated with better health through access to information that manifests in better decision making, then it should be associated with reduced chronic illness. Using data from the Survey of Income and Program Participation, with the exception of diabetes management, Mazumder found effects of changes in compulsory schooling in the United States at the secondary level to have no consistent effect on several chronic health conditions. Although similar results were found in the United Kingdom in studies using compulsory schooling policy as a natural experiment (Braakman, 2011; Clark & Royer, 2010; Jürges, Kruk, & Reinhold, 2013; Powdthavee, 2010), Dupre (2008) found hypertension and heart attack mortality negatively associated with years of education controlling for behavioral, social, and economic risks among a longitudinal sample of adults in the United States.

Health outcomes often result from health behavior, as is evidenced by the link between smoking and lung cancer. A great deal of research has examined the net effects of education on a variety of health behaviors. These are typically the behaviors included in regression models predicting mortality, which may explain the lack of a direct relationship between education and mortality. We review the literature examining years of education and educational attainment categories as they relate to diet, exercise, and weight in general, as well as smoking and drinking. Among Whites 25 or older, Cutler and Lleras-Muney (2010) found that in the presence of demographic and financial controls, years of education was related to eating fruit and vegetables daily and engaging in moderate and vigorous physical activity. Research from the United Kingdom has found similar associations between years of schooling and diet and exercise (Amin, Behrman, & Spector, 2013; Barker, Lawrence, Woadden, Crozier, & Skinner, 2008; Clark & Royer, 2010). Lending support to the allocative efficiency hypothesis of how information is used to inform health decisions, McKay and colleagues (2006) found in an older adult population that those with less education relied more heavily on doctors, television, and neighbors, while the more educated used a larger resource pool for nutrition information.

Diet and exercise are associated with body mass index (BMI), as well as the likelihood of being overweight or obese. Several studies have examined the relationship between education and these measures of relative weight. Across samples from the United States, Australia, and the United Kingdom, education has been associated with lower BMI and likelihood of being overweight (Amin et al., 2013; Clark & Royer, 2010; Cutler & Lleras-Muney, 2010; Dupre, 2008; Webbink, Marting, & Visscher, 2010). However, the evidence is not as conclusive with respect to the relationship between education and obesity. Clark and Royer (2010) found an inconclusive relationship between schooling and BMI and obesity that varied from negative to nonsignificant depending on the analytical approach. Moreover, gender confounds this general relationship; we discuss the relationship between education and measures of relative weight and its conditional effect for men and women later in this chapter.

Pascarella and Terenzini (2005) found that educational attainment reduced the probability that a person would use tobacco products. More recent research in the United States and the United Kingdom has continued to find the frequency of tobacco use negatively correlated with educational attainment (Amin et al., 2013; Bingham, Shope, & Tang, 2005; Clark & Royer, 2010; Conti, Heckman, & Urzua, 2010; Cowell, 2006; Cutler & Lleras-Muney, 2010; De Walque, 2007, 2010; Dupre, 2008; Grimard & Parent, 2007; Stone, Becker, Huber, & Catalano, 2012; Wetter et al., 2005a, 2005b). However, some researchers have argued that education does not cause this decrease in use; rather, smoking initiation is caused by factors developed in adolescence (Maralani, 2013; Tenn, Herman, & Wendling, 2010). Cowell (2006) asserted that the lower likelihood of smoking supports the future opportunity cost explanation. Given that education increases future wages, engaging in unhealthy behavior reduces the length of one's working life and the opportunity to recoup the investment in education; thus the more highly educated choose not to smoke. One may also assert an allocative efficiency explanation in that those who are more educated access and act on health-related information, which results in their choosing not to smoke.

The previous volume (Pascarella & Terenzini, 2005) also reviewed articles that found educational attainment associated with an increase in the rate of smoking cessation. Supporting previous findings, the research completed in the 2000s has found that educational attainment has a positive correlation with smoking cessation (Cutler & Lleras-Muney, 2010; De Walque, 2007; Margolis, 2013; Wetter et al., 2005a, 2005b). Some researchers argue that this is not caused by educational attainment but rather learning that occurs during adolescence (Maralani, 2013). In a cross-sectional analysis controlling for age, gender, marital status, race, ethnicity, and alcohol use, Wetter and colleagues (2005a) found that respondents who completed college had the highest rate of smoking cessation when compared with those who completed high school or did not complete high school. Examining smokers who quit between 1990 and 1994, the same research group (Wetter et al., 2005b) concluded, "Education was strongly and prospectively associated with smoking cessation" (pp. 458–459).

In a study of 206 women who self-identified as smokers prior to their pregnancy, educational attainment associated positively with quitting smoking on learning of the pregnancy (Higgins et al., 2009). In a longitudinal study looking at more than 16,000 participants 50 to 75 years old, having completed college had a positive effect on smoking cessation for participants in their fifties when diagnosed with a new illness; however, there was no relationship between college completion and smoking cessation for participants in their sixties and seventies upon learning of a new illness (Margolis, 2013). Margolis (2013) hypothesized two possible things could have caused these differences: a decrease in the overall pool of smokers or the perception of future life expectancy by the participant. The latter aligns with the future opportunity cost explanation that Cowell (2006) advanced.

Unlike smoking, educational attainment appears to have a mixed relationship with alcohol use and abuse. Research in the 2000s has shown that educational attainment increases the number of drinks on average a person consumes per week (Bingham et al., 2005; Cutler & Lleras-Muney, 2010; Flowers et al., 2008; Huerta & Borgonovi, 2010; Staff et al., 2010; Zubanov, Webbink, & Martin, 2013). Increased alcohol consumption has been attributed to the social effects of completing a degree, primarily an increase in socioeconomic status, which provides greater income and more opportunities for social drinking (Huerta & Borgonovi, 2010; Stone et al., 2012). Using data from the British Cohort Study, which has followed all children born in Great Britain in one week during 1970, researchers found a positive correlation between college degree completion and alcohol consumption (Bingham et al., 2005; Huerta & Borgonovi, 2010). However, the evidence from the United Kingdom is inconclusive, with some studies finding no difference in alcohol use (Amin et al., 2010) or results that vary based on the analytical approach used (Clark & Royer, 2010).

Binge drinking, or excessive drinking, is defined as having consumed five or more drinks for a person in a single sitting (Naimi et al., 2003); however, it is important to note that many of the articles reviewed had similar but varied definitions. Research completed in the 2000s on binge drinking behaviors found a negative correlation between binge drinking and amount of education a person attained (Bingham et al., 2005; Cutler & Lleras-Muney, 2010; Dupre, 2008; Flowers et al., 2008; Naimi et al., 2003). In a cross-sectional study of over 100,000 people in the United States using the behavioral risk factor surveillance system, Naimi and colleagues (2003) found educational attainment negatively correlated with binge drinking. Another cross-sectional study conducted by Naimi, Nelson, and Brewer (2010) found that college graduates consumed the fewest number of total drinks on average per episode of binge drinking (7.0 drinks) compared to participants with some college (8.0 drinks), high school completers (9.5 drinks), and those with less than a high school diploma (8.7).

Alcohol use disorder (alcohol dependence or alcoholism), is defined by the *Diagnostic and Statistical Manual of Mental Disorders* (American Psychiatric Association, 2013) as the combination of two or more of the following: (mild, two to three drinks; moderate, four to five drinks; severe, six or more drinks): withdrawal symptoms with prolonged abstinence from alcohol, developing a tolerance to alcohol, drinking more than intended, inability to decrease alcohol use, large amounts of time spent doing things that involve alcohol, craving alcohol, impact on major obligations, continued use after negative social implications, and use of alcohol in dangerous environments.

In the previous volume, Pascarella and Terenzini (2005) determined that people who had earned an associate's degree or higher had the lowest risk of developing alcohol dependency than any other group. The research published in the 2000s supports that conclusion, finding college attainment correlated negatively with alcohol dependency (Gilman et al., 2008; Harford, Yi, &

Hilton, 2006; Stone et al., 2012). A 10-year longitudinal study of approximately 8,000 participants between 1984 and 1994 found lower alcohol dependency rates in college degree holders compared to all other groups (Harford, Yi, & Hilton, 2006). Greenfield and colleagues (2003) completed a longitudinal study of 101 people who had undergone rehabilitation for alcohol dependence, looking at the probability of relapse, and found that participants who had some college experience or more had the lowest rate of relapse.

Finally, in a longitudinal study looking at drinking and driving behaviors of 24-year-old participants who completed high school, some college, or completed a college degree, Bingham and colleagues (2005) found men and women who completed a college degree less likely to have driven while drunk. These findings support previous research that reported a negative correlation between driving under the influence and educational attainment (Quinlan et al., 2005).

The majority of research on education and health supports the productive and allocative efficiency hypotheses. Educational attainment is associated with employment status and income, which often results in the more educated having greater access to health insurance and preventative health care (Fletcher & Frisvold, 2009; Mirowsky & Ross, 2003; Ross & Mirowsky, 1999; Schnittker, 2004). Moreover, educational attainment increases access to information and the cognitive ability to use that information to make positive health choices. Although the protective effect of education on hypertension and heart attack incidence was reduced to nonsignificance when mediating behavioral factors were entered into the model, it was because education was associated with each of those factors: negatively associated with smoking, heavy drinking, and obesity (Dupre, 2008). While not testing causal mechanisms, Cutler and Lleras-Muney (2010) tested many mediating factors to account for the education-health relationship and found that income, health insurance, and family background explained 30%, knowledge and measures of cognitive ability accounted for an additional 30%, and social networks another 10%, supporting research done a decade earlier by Ross and Mirowsky (1999). In the presence of an extensive array of control and mediating factors, some portion of the education-health gradient remained. Although the relationship between education and health outcomes is not completely linear (Zajacova, Rogers, & Johnson-Lawrence, 2012), Cutler and Lleras-Muney (2008) presented compelling graphs outlining the relationship across a host of health outcomes in which the impact of years of education is greatest at higher levels and appeared fairly linear from 10 years of schooling and above, controlling for gender and race.

Together, these findings and those of other research (see Cutler & Lleras-Muney, 2003, 2010; Higgins et al., 2009; Lange, 2011; McMahon, 2009) provide strong evidence for both the allocative efficiency explanation, which posits that increased education provides people with greater access to resources and ability to effectively use information from those resources in decision-making, and the socialization explanation, in that the more educated are better able to manage adversity.

This section has largely examined the education-health gradient; rhetorically speaking, what is the relationship between education and health? Given the productive efficiency argument that educational attainment is associated with higher income, an interesting study examined the relationship between income and health and found it varied by level of education. Using data from the Community Tracking Study and the 1972–2000 General Social Survey, Schnittker (2004) found the relationship between education and health most positive among those of lower income, yet the more highly educated had better health at all income levels. This suggests that education has protective health benefits particularly among those with the lowest incomes. Although the prevalence of health conditions decreases as education increases, Zajacova and colleagues (2012) found those with some college but no degree and those with technical/vocational or associate's degrees had a higher prevalence of a range of health conditions than high school graduates and those who had never attended college. This may be due to the type of occupations, particularly in the trades, associated with technical/vocational degrees. Considering the number of U.S. adults pursuing postsecondary study at community colleges—this "glitch in the gradient" with respect to health outcomes, as Zajacova and colleagues (2012) refer to it—is worth further study.

In terms of public policy, a research imperative exists to examine the synergistic relationship of education and income in terms of health outcomes. The challenge of disassociating education and income in terms of health has led researchers in the past decade to use a variety of approaches to identify the causal effects of education on health. In a review of the economics literature with an emphasis on studies that have used instrumental variable or regression discontinuity techniques, Lochner (2011) concluded that additional schooling causes modest improvements in health and small reductions in mortality, although again the instrumental variable approach has tended to use schooling policies typically at the secondary school level; notable exceptions are De Walque (2007) and Grimard and Parent (2007), and not without critique (see Eide & Showalter, 2011). Still, Lochner's (2011) review provides weight to Lundborg's (2013) conclusion: "If schooling has a causal effect on health, policies that strengthen the incentives to obtain a higher education may have beneficial effects for both the productivity of nations and for population health" (p. 698).

Welfare of Children. Parental education has substantial effects on the welfare of children. From birth weight to cognitive development to children's educational aspirations, children benefit from parents who have more years of education and educational credentials. In *Education and the Family*, Feinstein, Duckworth, and Sabates (2008) provide a wealth of evidence to support the association between parents' education and improved outcomes for their children, although they cautiously noted the difficulty in making causal claims. Like other researchers, they highlighted the causal-like mechanisms by which parents education is transmitted: through distal family factors (like family structure and size, income and maternal employment), internal features of the family environment (like parental cognitions, mental health and well-being, and other material resources), and proximal family processes (like parenting style, educational behaviors and language, activities outside the home, and nutrition). Framed by these factors, we review the literature with respect to children's health, learning, and development.

Research has examined the relationship between parents' education and children's health outcomes from birth to adulthood. Using 30 years of Vital Statistics Natality data, Currie and Moretti (2003) found that maternal education improved infant health as measured by birth weight and gestational age. Luo, Wilkins, and Kramer (2006) found similar positive infant health outcomes among babies born to more highly educated mothers in Quebec, Canada; women who had completed community college or some university were less likely to have a preterm birth or stillbirth.

From birth weight to adolescent weight, the influence of parental education is evident. Martin, Frisco, Nau, and Burnett (2012) used hierarchical modeling to examine family and school-level effects on the probability of adolescent overweight. Parents' years of schooling were inversely related to children's overweight, but the magnitude of the effect differed by level of school poverty, with the strongest negative relationship found in the lowest school poverty context. These findings suggest that children who attend richer schools disproportionately realize the protective effects of parents' education. Adolescent overweight is often connected to a lack of physical activity. Sherar, Muhajarine, Esliger, and Baxter-Jones (2009) investigated the relationship between maternal education and the physical activity of girls ages eight to 14. Measuring physical activity by data collected through an Actical accelerometer for seven continuous days, they found that girls whose mothers were university educated were more likely to participate in vigorous physical activity during the weekend and moderate to vigorous physical activity during the weekday commute to school, controlling for other confounding influences.

Finally, the protective effect of parents' education on children's health continues through the life cycle (Ross & Mirowsky, 2011; Walsemann, Ailshire, Bell, & Frongillo, 2012). Ross and Mirowsky (2011) investigated the extent to which parental education was associated with adult children's education and the interaction of these variables on adult children's health. Among adult children who had a college degree, there was no relationship between parent education and the adult child's personal health; however, adult children who were poorly educated and whose parents were also poorly educated experienced a higher level of physical impairment. In other words, parents' education continued to play a role in the health of less-educated adults (Ross & Mirowsky, 2011).

Parents' educational attainment is also associated with children's educational progress and cognitive development. Higher parental educational attainment is associated with greater prose, document, and quantitative literacy, which manifests in parents' engagement with their children and their schooling (Kutner et al., 2007). Using data from the National Assessment of Adult Literacy, Kutner and colleagues found that parents with intermediate or proficient prose literacy scores were more likely to read five days or more per week to their young children and that their children ages of three and five were more likely to know the alphabet. More educated parents also were more likely to talk to their school-age children about things they studied in school and help with homework. These are examples of parent-child interaction that contribute to child cognitions of self-concept of ability and motivations (Feinstein et al., 2008).

Cunha and Heckman (2009) presented a potential explanation between the intergenerational legacy of parents' education and children's development, showing that parenting is the strongest determinant of children's cognitive and noncognitive development. Consistent with Feinstein and colleagues' hypothesized model, learning and development in the home context appeared to be associated with progress in terms of children's formal schooling. Oreopoulos and colleagues (2006) examined the influence of parental compulsory schooling using data from the 1960, 1970, and 1980 U.S. censuses. They found that a one-year increase in education of either parent reduced the probability of child grade retention by between 2 and 4 percentile points.

Parents' education also influences children's educational expectations and subsequent attainment. In addition to providing important financial resources, parents' educational attainment serves as a model for expected behavior (Korupp, Ganzeboom, & Van Der Lippe, 2002; Marjoribanks, 2002; Tierney & Auerbach, 2005; Turley, Santos, & Ceja, 2007; Wells, Seifert, Padgett, Park, & Umbach, 2011). One might recognize this as a "capitals" model in which financial capital is complemented by the social and cultural capital gained through additional years of schooling (Feinstein et al., 2008; McDonough, 1997). A good deal of research has examined the gender-socialization perspective, in which daughters look to their mothers and sons to their fathers in formulating their educational expectations. In the main, this area of research has been inconclusive. Some studies have found evidence consistent with this hypothesis (Buchmann & DiPrete, 2006; Mahaffy & Ward, 2002; Wells et al., 2011), while others maintain that maternal education is as important for sons as for daughters (Korupp et al., 2002).

There is robust empirical evidence that parents' education has a causal impact on children's educational attainment. What is less conclusive is the relative role of maternal and paternal education on children's educational outcomes. Several studies have used the British compulsory schooling change in 1947 and 1974 to examine the causal effect of parents' education on children's educational attainment. Examining the 1947 school-leaving reform, Galindo-Rueda (2003) found positive relationships for both paternal and maternal education on boys' and girls' highest qualifications, although these relationships were reduced to non-significance in the models that used an instrumental variable approach. Chevalier (2004) found positive effects for mothers' and fathers' education on children's education as a result of the 1974 school-leaving reform, but only for natural parents, not stepparents. In general, an additional year of parental education increased the probability that a child would stay beyond the minimum school-leaving age by 4 to 8 percentile points. In addition, Chevalier (2004) provided evidence to support the gender socialization hypothesis of the same-sex parent-child relationship, with maternal education having a stronger effect for daughters' educational attainment and paternal education having a stronger effect for sons' educational attainment.

Other research has used twin studies to examine this relationship and found paternal education has a positive causal relationship with children's educational attainment but maternal education has a marginally negative (albeit typically nonsignificant) relationship with children's educational attainment (Antonovics & Goldberger, 2005; Behrman & Rosenzweig, 2002, 2005). Plug (2004) examined the effect of parental education on a small sample of adoptees from Wisconsin, reasoning that if children share only their home environment (as opposed to genes) with their parents, then any relationship between mothers' and fathers' education and children's education is due to the influences parents have on the home environment. Although Plug used a limited sample, the findings lend further support to Behrman and Rosenzweig's (2002, 2005) research in that accounting for children's inherent abilities and mating patterns, the relationship between mothers' but not fathers' education and children's educational attainment was reduced to nonsignificance. These findings call to mind the cautions Feinstein and colleagues (2008) issued with regard to causal effects. Although maternal education may not have a direct causal effect, it is important to consider how parents' education (maternal and paternal) is associated with a supportive and cognitively stimulating home environment for children.

A cognitively stimulating home environment may be one in which parents talk about current and political events at the local, regional, and national levels. Talking with children and interest in one's community has intergenerational influences on high school children's civic engagement. Using data from the 1996 U.S. Department of Education's National Household Education Survey, controlling for youth and parent characteristics, McIntosh, Hart, and Youniss (2007) found parents' education positively associated with their high school child's political knowledge. Moreover, there was a positive association between youth who reported discussing politics with their parents and youth reports of monitoring the national news, political knowledge, feeling comfortable with writing to a public official or speaking at a public meeting, and serving in their community in the past year. McIntosh and colleagues acknowledged that previous research has suggested that well-educated parents may confer advantage in the political arena to their children through socioeconomic status but also asserted it may be parents with more education who provide their children with a host of sources for civic information "from which to draw in constructing their understanding of the political world" (p. 498).

Community-Civic Involvement. During the early 2000s, several studies addressed the net impact of higher education on civic involvement. These studies tended to cluster community-civic involvement, or civic engagement, into one of two rather distinct categories: political participation and community engagement. Political participation was largely defined in terms of voting behavior, participation in rallies and protests, and calling local and state representatives; community engagement included such activities as volunteering time with various types of community organizations.

Political Participation. Overall, attaining a college education appears to have a positive effect on an individual's level of political participation broadly defined (Campbell, 2009; Dee, 2004; Mayer, 2011; Milligan, Moretti, & Oreopoulos, 2004; Smets & van Ham, 2013; Tenn, 2005). Political participation is most frequently defined as voter participation. Examining self-reported political participation between the United States and United Kingdom, Milligan et al. (2004) found that in the United States, people with more education were more likely to vote. While only 52% of U.S. high school dropouts reported voting, voter participation increased to 67% for high school graduates, 74% for individuals with some college, and 84% for college graduates. In contrast, this relationship between education and voting was not significant in the United Kingdom. However, when accounting for being registered to vote, the effect of education on voting in the United States dropped to less than a third of the estimated effect based on the whole sample (Milligan et al., 2004). The results from the U.S. approach those from the U.K. findings looking at voter registration versus voting, which may indicate that current registration rules serve as a barrier to voting for the less educated (Milligan et al., 2004). Although voting behavior in the United States is conditioned by being registered to vote, in a meta-analysis examining 67 studies from the United States and Europe, Smets and van Ham (2013) found that education had a moderately strong standardized effect of 0.72.

Other research has created indexes of political acts, including attending campaign meetings, displaying bumper stickers, making campaign contributions, and volunteering on a candidate or political organization. (see Campbell, 2009; Kam & Palmer, 2008; Mayer, 2011). The relationship between educational attainment and political acts is inconclusive, appearing to be an artifact of definition and analytical technique.

Kam and Palmer (2008) used two different datasets to examine the relationship between college attendance and political participation before and after propensity score matching. Prior to propensity score matching, statistically significant differences were found between college attendees and those without postsecondary exposure; those attending college averaged 2.79 participatory acts and their nonattending peers averaged 1.43. However, after matching, the authors found no significant group difference, concluding, "The positive relationship between college and political participation derives largely from the pre-adult socialization experiences that propel individuals to pursue higher education, not from the acquisition of higher education per se" (p. 626).

Using a different matching technique on the same datasets, Mayer (2011) found substantial effects of education on political participation. Estimates suggested that postsecondary education increased political participation by about .05 political acts, while the average for the sample was 2.3 acts. Campbell's (2009) findings from the National Civic Engagement Study further contributed to the definitional and analytical complexity of this relationship. Although years of education was associated positively with the electoral index, measured by respondents' actions in terms of displaying buttons, making campaign contributions, and volunteering for a candidate or political organization, it was not predictive of expressive acts including protesting, boycotting, canvassing, and contacting officials, controlling for a contextual measure of education, gender, race, marital status, identification as partisan, residential mobility, and age.

Two studies investigated the notion of education as a cumulative mechanism by examining the extent to which contextual measures (typically aggregated measures of educational attainment at the neighborhood, zip code, or county level) are associated with political participation. In a meta-analysis of voter turnout, Smets and van Ham (2013) found that living in a more highly educated area did not have an influence on individual voter turnout. These findings support research from the United States in which Campbell (2009) found no relationship between individual respondents' years of education, the educational environment, or the interaction between education and educational environment on voting behavior or the expressive index, having accounted for respondent background characteristics. Campbell found, however, a positive association between respondents' years of education and the electoral index at the county and zip code level, although the relationship between an individual's level of education and electoral actions was reduced in magnitude in areas with higher aggregate education levels. In summary, both studies' results are counter to the positive cumulative mechanism explanation discussed already in the chapter, with the contextual effect of education having a limited relationship with political participation.

Although the evidence is somewhat mixed, in the main it suggest a positive relationship between educational attainment and political involvement and voting behavior. However, a more recent study suggests this effect may be diminishing over subsequent decades. In 2010, Long examined the effects of education on likelihood of registering to vote using data from several nationally representative longitudinal cohort-based studies of the United States. Controlling for a host of background characteristics as well as contextual effects at the neighborhood level, results indicated that the effects of education on voter registration have diminished over time (Long, 2010). For the 1970s cohort, each additional year of education increased the likelihood of registering to vote by 3.5 percentile points. This effect fell to 2.8 points for the 1980s cohort and 1.8 points in the 1990s cohort (Long, 2010).

Civic Participation (Volunteering). Similar to the conclusion from the 1990s, the weight of the evidence suggests that college education has a positive effect on the likelihood of contributing one's time and effort toward volunteering and community service (Brand, 2010; Campbell, 2009; Dee, 2004; Gesthuizen & Scheepers, 2012).

Using propensity score matching in a nationally representative longitudinal sample in the United States, Brand (2010) estimated the average effect of college completion on volunteering and found college graduates 2.1 times more likely to volunteer for civic, community, or youth groups than noncollege graduates and 1.7 times more likely to volunteer for charitable organizations or social welfare groups. Although lacking the controls of other research, findings from the National Assessment of Adult Literacy showed educational attainment associated with greater prose, document, and quantitative literacy, which was also positively associated with the likelihood of volunteering with a group or organization and with greater frequency (Kutner et al., 2007). Finally, in a meta-analysis of 37 studies examining social participation from around the world, Huang, Maassen van den Brink, and Groot (2009) found college graduates participated more in social/civic activities (effect size = .026), controlling for gender, family, environment, religion, age, media control, education endogeneity, and average education in the country.

Gesthuizen and Scheepers (2012) examined the relationship between education and volunteerism taking into account mediating variables: TV watching behavior, cognitive competence, occupational status, and worldview (defined as localist, or those who tend to get their information from their close personal network, compared to cosmopolitan or those who get their information from the mass media). Using data from the International Adult Literacy Survey, they defined education as either lower level (early childhood to lower secondary education) or higher education (short term/two-year college programs through graduate-level degrees) and found those with higher education far more likely to volunteer. Despite the somewhat crude means of operationalizing education, the effect of education on volunteering persisted after accounting for the mediating variables. In addition, the authors found the aggregate number of highly educated persons in each country positively associated with volunteer behavior. Although education as a cumulative mechanism was inconsistent in terms of political participation, it appears the contextual effect of education promotes civic engagement.

BETWEEN-COLLEGE EFFECTS

Conclusions from the 1990s

As noted at the outset, far less research examined between-college effects with respect to quality-of-life indicators. The previous volume (Pascarella & Terenzini, 2005) found that two overarching predictors influenced quality-of-life after college. First, some evidence existed to suggest that institutional selectivity had a negative impact on satisfaction with one's life and job. Since there was no control for students' precollege characteristics, it may be that academically selective institutions simply attract students with a more critical perspective. Or it may be that selective institutions help students develop a more critical perspective. Pascarella and Terenzini (2005) reported inconclusive findings with respect to the relationship between institutional selectivity and graduates' community or civic involvement but a small positive association with self-perceived health, largely mediated through healthier lifestyle. Finally, there was evidence that binge drinking behavior was less likely at single-sex versus coed institutions. Pascarella and Terenzini (2005) concluded it is not clear whether this is an artifact of students' precollege characteristics or students' socialization during college, since women attending single-sex institutions were also found to be less likely than their counterparts to binge drink prior to attending college.

Evidence from the 2000s

We found few studies that expressly examined differences in quality-of-life outcomes by the type of postsecondary institution attended, although comparing educational attainment thresholds (vocational diploma/associate's degree compared to a bachelor's degree or more) implicitly compares attendance at two-year versus four-year institutions. The dearth of between-college effects research may be due to the fact that much of the research out of the econometric tradition has focused primarily on estimating the causal effects between education and quality-of-life outcomes. Other research, largely from the sociological tradition, has examined mediating factors and causal-like mechanisms that may explain the nexus between education and quality-of-life outcomes. Differences in college attendance by institutional type, selectivity, and mission may be quite distal in their effects to alumni members' quality of life after college. We review the meager research that has examined differences in quality-of-life measures by these institutional characteristics.

Subjective Well-Being and Life Satisfaction. Few studies have expressly examined the difference in subjective well-being and measures of life satisfaction by type of institution attended. Walsemann, Bell, and Hummer (2012) examined the extent to which depressive symptomatology at midlife was related to educational attainment using data from the National Longitudinal Survey of Youth. They found that attaining at least a bachelor's degree (proxy for four-year institution attendance) by midlife was associated with fewer depressive symptoms, but no relationship existed between educational attainment and depressive symptomatology among those who at age 25 had an associate's degree (proxy for two-year institution attendance) and later attended a four-year institution and attained a bachelor's degree.

Conversely, using a vocational credential as a proxy for attending a technical and further education institution in Australia (similar to a community college in the United States), Dockery (2010) found that respondents who had earned a vocational qualification compared to those who attained a university degree had greater self-assessed happiness. Although Dockery's study was limited in that it did not control for any measure of career (e.g., income, occupational prestige) and tracked respondents only through their mid-twenties, Headey and Wooden (2004) found similar results in a larger sample of Australian adults.

Health and Health Behaviors. Expanding on Ross and Mirowsky's (1999) research examining selectivity and health, Fletcher and Frisvold (2011) examined the nationally representative National Longitudinal Study of Adolescent Health to investigate the relationship between attending a selective college and young adult health behaviors (smoking, binge drinking, marijuana use, obesity, consumption of fast food, and exercise) shortly after college between the ages of 26 and 32. Using ordinary least squares (OLS) regression as well as propensity matching models, institutional selectivity was associated with a reduction in smoking, marijuana use, fast food consumption, and likelihood of being overweight and obese. The positive association between selectivity and binge drinking and exercise was less consistent in magnitude across analytical approaches but remained statistically significant.

Fletcher and Frisvold (2011) continued to examine the causal mechanisms within these relationships and found the competitiveness of the college associated with reductions in smoking and being overweight, as well as associated positively with binge drinking, taking into account respondents' income and marital status. More recently, Fletcher and Frisvold (2014) used sibling data from the Wisconsin Longitudinal Study and compared one sibling who attended a selective college with one who did not. Controlling for parent education, family income, number of siblings in the family, gender, age, birth order, childhood health, and IQ, they found that graduating from a selective college reduced the probability of being overweight in later adulthood by approximately 15%, as well as reduced BMI, but they found no relationship between institutional selectivity and respondents' probability of smoking. In exploring potential causal mechanisms such as income, marriage market outcomes, and health at midlife, the selectivity/college quality-health effect persisted.

Community-Civic Involvement. We uncovered several studies that examined between-college characteristics and civic involvement. The studies vary in terms of the institutional characteristics examined, which make synthesizing across studies difficult. We follow the pattern established in previous chapters, reviewing studies that examined institutional selectivity, type, mission, and other characteristics.

Long (2010) found an effect of college quality, operationalized as Barron's index of selectivity, on the likelihood of registering to vote; however, it differed for each cohort studied. The effect of institutional selectivity on voter registration was negative for the cohort of postsecondary students in the 1990s, positive for the cohort of postsecondary students in the 1980s, and not significant for the cohort of postsecondary students in the 1970s.

Mayer (2011) used propensity score matching to examine the extent to which political participation varied across different institutional types. Those who attended trade or vocational school (versus their pair who did not attend) had a higher participation index, were more likely to vote in the 1972 election, and were more likely to have contacted an official, although they were less likely to have participated in a demonstration. Those who attended college had a higher participation index, were more likely to have voted, and had a higher rate of contacting an official or demonstrating.

Moving from institutional type to institutional mission, Wolniak and Pascarella's (2007) study of work colleges on cohorts from the 1970s, 1980s, and 1990s examined between-college effects on an index measure of citizenship and global orientations, which included items such as the degree to which alumni perceived the institution contributed to their attention to environmental and international issues, positive interactions with people of different races and cultures, and exercising one's rights as a citizen. They found that graduating from a work college had significant positive and substantial total effects compared to liberal arts colleges (effect size = .579) and regional institutions (effect size = .741), with the effects decreasing slightly in magnitude in the presence of background characteristic and college experience controls. Ishitani and McKitrick (2013) examined differences in civic engagement behavior by five institutional characteristics. Using National Education Longitudinal Study of 1988 with follow-up data through 2000, they constructed a broad measure of civic engagement with the following constituent items: read newspapers or magazines (in a typical week), visit a public library (in a typical month), volunteer in youth, civic, or community organization (in the past 12 months), and voted in any election in the past 24 months. Controlling for student background, adult, and academic characteristics, they found attending a public institution negatively associated with civic engagement, institutional size positively associated with civic engagement, and no difference by Carnegie Classification, institutional selectivity or institutional student/faculty ratio.

Given the interest in comparing colleges and universities, there is a paucity of research that has rigorously examined differences in quality-of-life outcomes by a variety of institutional characteristics. With the increased cost of higher education, students, families, and taxpayers may question how graduates who attended different types of institutions fare in terms of their quality of life after college. As stakeholders continue to push for institutional accountability, we expect more research examining these questions in the future.

WITHIN-COLLEGE EFFECTS

Conclusions from the 1990s

Pascarella and Terenzini (2005) identified a number of studies that examined within-college effects on quality-of-life outcomes. First, wellness/health education during college appeared positively associated with good health habits after college. A quasi-experimental study found that students who completed a one-semester health and physical education course during college had greater health knowledge and practiced better health habits than those who did not take this course. Despite the consistent evidence that affiliation with a fraternity or sorority was associated with higher levels of binge drinking during college, research from the 1990s suggested that this negative association was eliminated in postcollege drinking levels for both men and women when accounting for baseline alcohol use. Finally, there is evidence that involvement in racial/ethnic and other diversity experiences during college correlated positively with postcollege civic involvement. Like many other studies of this nature, it is difficult to identify the extent to which this relationship is confounded by graduates' precollege propensity for involvement.

Evidence from the 2000s

Given higher education's purpose to not only educate graduates to contribute to society's economic development but its civic vitality, little empirical research has examined the extent to which experiences during college contribute to graduates' quality of life after college. This could be due to the fact that postsecondary graduates' experience are quite removed from the quality-of-life indicator examined five years to several decades later in life. Research that has examined within-college effects has primarily focused on membership in a fraternity or sorority and alcohol use and the relationship between various postsecondary experiences and community-civic involvement.

Health and Health Behaviors. In a study using longitudinal data from the National Longitudinal Surveys of Youth (NLSY79), Jennison (2004) found that binge drinking during college had a positive effect on later binge drinking and alcohol dependency. Past research has found students involved in certain groups, particularly fraternities and sororities, binge-drink at rates greater than their peers (Larimer, Turner, Mallett, & Geisner, 2004; Park, Sher, Wood, & Krull, 2009; Wechsler, Dowdall, Davenport, & Castillo, 1995).

Connecting patterns of binge drinking in college and fraternity/sorority involvement with alcohol use and dependence after college, Bartholow, Sher, and Krull (2003) conducted one of the most rigorous studies to date examining this relationship seven years after postsecondary completion. Students at a single university were screened for alcoholism among their parents from which a target and control sample was obtained. Students were followed from baseline during their freshman year and in subsequent yearly intervals through the fourth year of college, in year seven after baseline, and 11 years after baseline. The authors created an index of fraternity/sorority involvement ranging from unaffiliated to active member who lived in the chapter house and then multiplied by four years of postsecondary attendance. Despite much heavier drinking during college by those involved with fraternities/sororities, Bartholow et al. (2003) found the decline in heavy drinking after college steepest among those involved with fraternities/sororities, but the effect was most pronounced among men with higher levels of involvement in fraternities/sororities, less so for men with average levels of involvement, and not significant for men with lower levels of fraternity involvement. It may be that within this institution's culture, heavy drinking was normalized among highly involved fraternity men; once removed from this culture, those men decreased their drinking behavior dramatically. The change in heavy drinking from year four to three years postcollege was not significant for women regardless of sorority involvement. These findings suggest that peer culture can powerfully influence (for better or for worse) individual's behaviors.

Community-Civic Involvement. Several studies have examined the long-term effects of college experiences such as study abroad and academic major on community-civic involvement broadly defined.

With respect to study abroad, two studies examined college graduates who studied abroad and their interest in and engagement with local domestic and international civic issues. In the main, the research found studying abroad contributes to graduates' civic engagement after college, but this effect may diminish over time (DeGraaf, Slagter, & Larsen, 2013; Paige, Fry, Stallman, Josic, & Jon, 2009). In a study of a single institution, DeGraaf and colleagues (2013) also found those who had studied abroad fewer than 10 years ago more likely to say they were civically engaged, both domestically (22% versus 9%) and internationally (41% versus 18%), than those who had studied abroad over 10 years ago. Since students' propensity toward domestic and international civic commitment prior to studying abroad were not taken into account, it is difficult to determine causality and rule out the possibility of a selection effect. As is the case for much study-abroad research, the lack of a comparison group and controls for selection effects undermines the ability to associate study-abroad participation with learning outcomes (Twombly, Salisbury, Tumanut, & Klute, 2012).

College major was also investigated in terms of its long-term influence on civic-community involvement. Ishitani and McKitrick (2013) examined the effects of college major on later civic engagement behavior using the National Education Longitudinal Study of 1988 data. Compared to education majors, engineering/mathematics, business, physical science, arts and humanities, and applied social science all had significantly lower estimates for civic engagement, with students in engineering/mathematical programs having scores that were 4.47 points lower on average. Using nationally representative data from the United States and controlling for student background and postcollege characteristics (marital status, further degree attainment, professional occupation and political interest), Hillygus (2005) found the accumulation of social science credits positively associated with political participation and voter turnout. Although humanities and education credits had no association, science and business credits had negative relationships with both political participation and voter turnout. In an earlier study with a broader set of civic outcomes, Nie and Hillygus (2001) found controlling for graduates' background characteristics, college GPA, institutional ranking/quality, and marital status, SAT scores, and, science/engineering credits were negatively associated with political participation, political persuasion, and importance of political influence but had no effect on voting in presidential elections and community service participation. Social science credits were positively associated with political participation, voting in presidential elections, political persuasion, community service participation, and importance of political influence. Humanities credits had no association with any of the political/civic outcomes, and business credits were negatively associated with all of the political/civic outcomes. Finally, education credits had a positive association with the importance of political influence; no association with political participation, political persuasion, or community service participation; and were negatively associated with voting in a presidential election (Nie & Hillygus, 2001). Taken together, the weight of the evidence lends support to Hillygus's (2005) conclusion that "a curriculum that develops language and civic skills, is influential in shaping participation in American democracy" (p. 25). Yet the majors receiving the greatest promotion—science, technology, engineering, and mathematical sciences—and the major that has seen substantial increase in recent years, business, are those that have consistently shown negative relationships with a multitude of postcollege civic outcomes.

In one of the only studies that investigated the relationship between students' involvement during college and their engagement with civic activities after college, Johnson (2004) used data from a cohort study of alumni who attended Appalachian College Association institutions during the 1970s, 1980s, and 1990s to examine relationships between college experiences and participation in cultural and political organizations, as well as service organizations, after college. Participation in college activities had modest positive relationships with both outcomes (.51 and .46 standardized regression coefficients for cultural/political and service organization participation, respectively). Interestingly, alumni perceptions of the extent to which the college contributed to their learning and cognitive development and expanding awareness was associated positively with participation in cultural/political organizations but social responsibility was negatively associated. The extent to which the college experience contributed "entrepreneurial and quantitative skills" had no effect on cultural/political organization participation. In examining participation in service organizations, perceived college contribution to the development of entrepreneurial skills and social responsibility was associated positively, but perceived contribution to expanding awareness had a negative relationship with alumni participation in service activities.

Turning from involvement in one's broader community to involvement with one's alma mater, several studies found that involvement with college activities was positively associated with charitable giving to and volunteering for their institution as an alumnus (Porter, Hartman, & Johnson, 2011; Sun, Hoffman, & Grady, 2007; Weerts & Ronca, 2008). The notion that alumni experience and motivation predicted donation was also found by Weerts and Ronca (2007), who found that "inactive" alumni, defined as those not donating to or volunteering for their institution, were just as likely as "active" alumni to report strong academic and social experiences in college. Where these two groups differed was with regard to involvement experiences as alumni. Active alumni were more likely to have visited the library or attended cultural and athletic events or awards ceremonies at their institution as alumni, and this postcollege involvement with one's alma mater had strong significant effects on giving.

Drilling down to understand the relationship between specific types of student engagement and alumni behavior, Merkel (2013) conducted a qualitative study to understand the relationship between involvement in fraternity/sorority life and alumni giving and involvement and found that students often believed an interest in alumni involvement was what prompted their fraternity/sorority involvement from the beginning. Other students, however, identified their fraternity/sorority experience had negative impact on their relationship with their university due to the fact that the relationship with their fraternity or sorority chapter was seen as the relationship to maintain after graduation.

For all the attention and concern focused on the impacts of college on student learning and development, we found few studies that examined how experiences during college related to graduates' quality of life after college. In the absence of such evidence, the purpose and value of higher education to develop human capital and educate engaged citizens will continue to come under fire (see Arum & Roksa, 2011, 2014), and stakeholders will continue to question if the higher education system is honoring its implicit social contract.

CONDITIONAL EFFECTS OF COLLEGE

The previous volume (Pascarella & Terenzini, 2005) reported no conditional effects for quality-of-life outcomes. Research in this domain has grown in the past decade, with several studies examining how the net effects of educational attainment on subjective well-being, health outcomes, and community-civic involvement differ by respondents' background characteristics.

Evidence from the 2000s

Research that has investigated the differential relationship between education and quality-of-life outcomes has focused primarily on gender, race, and age. While research reviewed in previous chapters has detailed conditional effects by gender and race, age has been less frequently examined. One may consider it a measure of the cohort to which one belongs and thus suggests how the long-term effects of education on graduates' quality of life have varied over time. For example, research may examine how the relationship between years of schooling and mortality and any potential gap differs across cohort. We review the literature that has examined conditional effects using the conceptual map employed throughout the chapter.

Subjective Well-Being and Life Satisfaction. Using data from the General Social Survey (1972–1998), Blanchflower and Oswald (2004) found years of education positively associated with happiness, controlling for income, marital status, age, and employment but with positive effects that were twice as large for women as men and more than twice as large for Whites than Blacks. Although Blanchflower and Oswald compared those with a high school diploma or less to those with some college or more, Ross and Mirowsky (2006) examined how the relationship between education and depression varied between men and women with a college degree and those with less education. Although women tend to experience more depressive symptoms than men, education had a protective effect particularly for women. As level of education increased, a steeper depression gradient existed for women than men, with the gender gap in depression nearly disappearing among those with a college degree or higher.

Chevalier and Feinstein (2006) found similar gendered effects using the British National Child Development survey, a longitudinal dataset with health information from childhood to adulthood. Controlling for a host of factors, education reduced the risk of becoming depressed with even larger effects found for women. Ross and Mirowsky (2006) found two mediating interactions that explained the convergence in the gender gap: education increased work creativity more so in women than men, reducing depression, and the mediating effect of sense of control on depression is stronger for women than men.

Health and Health Behaviors. Research has paid careful attention to the possibility that the relationship between education and health differs in magnitude by a variety of demographic characteristics. In fact, Conti, Heckman, and Urzua (2010) concluded from their findings that uncovered a host of gender differences from British schooling data, "This emphasizes the importance of taking the gender dimension in account when studying health disparities" (p. 16). Although Conti and colleagues' findings were based on a dichotomous measure of respondents who continued after compulsory schooling and those who did not, their admonishment to consider conditional effects is well taken given the multitude of differences research has found between men and women with respect to the effects of education on health.

Consistent with the "healthy" effect of education on depressive symptoms being stronger for women than men (Ross & Mirowsky, 2006), the relationship between education and health appears stronger and more positive for women's self-assessed health than for men (Hill & Needham, 2006) but has a larger effect on reducing mortality in men, particularly in terms of deaths from lung cancer, respiratory disease, stroke, homicide, suicide, and accidents (Ross, Masters, & Hummer, 2012).

Within these conditional effects by gender, other research has found further distinctions by race and marital status. Despite generally improving health over time, particularly for those with a college education, Liu and Hummer (2008) found an increasing probability of college-educated Black women age 42 in 2003 compared to those in 1982 reporting poor or fair health and a decreasing probability of Black women without a high school diploma reporting poor or fair health in the same time frame. This is an example of health convergence among younger adult Black women of differing educational levels. However, using the same dataset but with a different modeling procedure, Zajacova et al. (2012a) found strong evidence for general, rather than conditional, effects of educational attainment on self-assessed health.

We now turn from self-assessment of health to a more objective measure, mortality. Examining data from 1986 to 2006, Montez, Hummer, Hayward, Woo, and Rodgers (2011) modeled the death rate of non-Hispanic, White, and Black men and women by educational attainment and four age groups. Results showed a negative relationship between education and mortality among older ages for White and Black men. Interestingly, among men, only a small difference in mortality existed between those with some college and a high school diploma for those ages 65 to 74 and those ages 75 to 84.

Among White women, those with a college education have a lower mortality risk in every age group compared to their less educated peers, and the educational-health disparity has grown in recent years. These relationships are similar, but to a lesser extent, among Black women with a college degree, although those with some college in the most recent cohort have a mortality rate similar to their high school peers later in life. In the main, these findings are supported by Hadden and Rockswold (2008) who found health inequality grew in the last 15 years of the twentieth century with respect to education's association with reduced mortality.

Other research has examined how the relationship between education and health varies by gender and marital status. Among a sample of White adults, the negative relationship between education and mortality was stronger in magnitude for men than women (Rogers et al., 2010), particularly unmarried men, although no gender differences were found in the gradient among married adults (Montez, Hayward, Brown, & Hummer, 2009). Zajacova (2006) examined the education-mortality gradient among married and divorced adults, finding no difference in the gradient among married men and women but significantly reduced odds of dying for each year of schooling for divorced women, with no effect for divorced men.

In examining the education-health relationship across different cohorts, the research from the United States is conclusive. The health inequality by level of education is largest between those who are middle age and older, but that gap appears relatively stable among younger adults (Goesling, 2007; Liu & Hummer, 2008; Rogers et al., 2010). Mirowsky and Ross (2005) noted that education develops individuals' abilities to gain control over their lives, to which Goesling (2007) added that part of the effect of education on health is also due to the more educated having greater economic resources, engaging in more health-promoting behaviors, and having access to and using health services and medical technology. Yet in examining a latent growth model of U.S. data from the mid-1990s to the early 2000s, Mirowsky and Ross (2008) found that respondents overall reported lower levels of health but those with a high school diploma were more likely to report lower levels of health than respondents with a postsecondary degree. This is notable because lower self-assessed health in the recent age cohort runs in the face of a decreasing age-adjusted mortality rate in the U.S. population (Grossman, 2008).

A tremendous amount of research has examined the conditional net effects of education on a number of health behaviors, specifically diet and relative measures of weight. An interesting study from Saskatchewan, Canada, examined educational level by three different age groups and found the greatest differences in diet by level of education among the youngest cohort; far fewer differences were found between women ages 35 to 54 and 55 to 74 (Hall, Stephen, Reeder, Muhajarine, & Lasiuk, 2003). Within the youngest cohort, women with a college degree had a higher-quality diet than women who had a high school diploma or less, but differences in diet were not consistent between those with some college education and those with a postsecondary degree (Hall et al., 2003). The researchers found similar age cohort differences by education level in terms of obesity, with the greatest prevalence of obesity among women with the lowest level of education in the youngest cohort.

Although not examining women across age cohorts, Lawrence and colleagues (2011) found self-efficacy associated with diet in women in Southampton, England, but with an effect of stronger magnitude among women of lower educational attainment. These findings with respect to education and diet, as well as the mediating role that self-efficacy plays among women, connect to the multitude of other research that has examined the conditional effects of gender on the relationship between education and relative weight as measured by BMI and obesity. These studies in general find that education exerts a positive influence on health behavior.

Several meta-analyses have examined the relationship between education and relative weight (Ball & Crawford, 2005; McLaren, 2007). Both meta-analyses found roughly the same proportion of studies reported a negative relationship between education and BMI in women (nearly two-thirds of the studies have this conclusion) and about half of the studies reported a negative relationship in men. McLaren and Godley (2007) supported these conclusions with data from a Canadian sample.

Although the weight of the evidence is fairly consistent, in one of the few studies that examined a sample with and without estimating twin effects, Webbink and colleagues (2010) found the hypothesized negative relationship between education and weight in the Australian full sample of twins and singletons in 1980, 1988, and 1993, controlling for age, age squared, parental education, and birth weight, although the effect was not significant for women in 1980. Examining the sample of identical twins, the researchers found a negative effect in 1988 and 1993 for men, controlling for birth weight. However, no effect was found among the female twins in the samples.

Similar to the way in which the education-mortality gradient differed by gender and race within gender, the evidence suggests three-way interactions for BMI, a measure of relative weight. Although education was negatively associated with BMI among White women and White men and Black women (Mujahid, Roux, Borrell, & Nieto, 2005), Walsemann, Ailshire, Bell, and Frongillo (2012) found level of education and the rate of BMI change from adolescence to midlife inversely associated among White and Hispanic men and women in general but positively associated among Black women and men. In a study of only women, Lewis and colleagues (2005) found that compared to

White respondents, African Americans had higher BMIs but only at higher levels of education (some college and college degree or more). Walsemann and colleagues (2012a) posit the difference in the direction of the relationship between education and BMI between Black adults and White and Hispanic adults may be due to delayed childbearing and postpartum weight retention for Black women compared to their White peers and that among men of similar education, occupation, and income, Black men are more likely to be physically inactive than their White male counterparts.

Community-Civic Involvement. A few studies examined conditional effects within the constellation of quality-of-life outcomes associated with community-civic involvement. Campbell (2009) examined the extent to which men's and women's individual educational attainment has differential effects in neighborhood contexts that varied in aggregate educational attainment. In communities where there was generally lower educational attainment, the individual respondent's educational attainment had stronger positive effects on civic engagement than in communities where there was higher average educational attainment. This contrasts with findings from previous chapters in which individual action or experience magnifies in its effect when done collectively. From these results, Campbell concluded, "Regardless of the educational environment, a woman's education level has a positive impact on participation in electoral activity. In fact, even though women generally participate less in electoral activity than men, women with advanced degrees in highly educated environments participate at about the same rate as men in an identical context" (Campbell, 2009, p. 783).

Long (2010) added to this body of research in examining the educational effects with voter registration by gender, race, and SES for different student cohorts. Since the 1970s, the education effect on voter registration by gender has reached near parity, with additional education associated with an increased 1.7% likelihood of registering to vote for women and 1.85% likelihood for men. Interestingly, the education effect on voter registration has decreased most among White graduates since the 1970s, though less among African Americans (who have a stronger effect that Whites), but has increased in its effect among Hispanic graduates. Similarly with respect to socioeconomic status, the education effect on voter registration has dropped precipitously since the 1970s among the highest-SES graduates, with the effect nearly five times greater among the lowest-SES graduates in the most recent cohort.

Finally, Brand (2010) examined the extent to which education promotes civic participation among those who are the least likely to attend postsecondary, an estimation of treatment effect heterogeneity. Using data from the U.S. National Longitudinal Survey of Youth 1979 and a series of propensity-matching strata (stratum one was characterized by individuals who, for example, had parents who were high school dropouts, from families of four or more children, or low academic ability; stratum seven was characterized by individuals who, for example, had parents with postsecondary degrees, fewer siblings, or high ability), Brand (2010) found that the effect of college completion on volunteering declined with each increase in propensity stratum. College graduates in stratum one were estimated to be 10 times more likely to volunteer for civic, community, or youth groups than their noncollege peers. In contrast, college graduates did not differ in their volunteering behavior from their noncollege peers in stratum seven. This is perhaps good news for the programs promoting persistence and degree completion among first-generation students (those in the lower strata) in that these students are realizing the civic mission of higher education. Given the nonsignificant difference in volunteer behavior in stratum seven, these findings suggest the opportunity to strengthen the conversation about civic engagement to all students.

CHAPTER SUMMARY

Net Effects of College

Consistent with conclusions from the previous volume, the weight of the evidence suggests that education, whether defined as years of schooling or educational credentials, is associated with improved quality-of-life outcomes across a wide range of areas. Whereas the previous volume (Pascarella & Terenzini, 2005) suggested that those with more education may assess well-being and life satisfaction more critically, we found education positively associated with subjective well-being, happiness, life satisfaction, and sense of control, and it appears to serve in a protective fashion against depression and depressive symptomatology. Studies that have examined causal mechanisms found these effects largely a result of richer, more satisfying relationships, as well as employment and working conditions, lending support for both the allocation and socialization perspectives outlined at the beginning of the chapter.

Although the degree to which causality was established varied by the analytical approach used, the weight of the evidence suggests a clear and positive relationship between education and good health, both self-assessed health and mortality. This relationship is understood across international contexts and is frequently referred to as the education-health gradient. Even under strict causal parameters, Lochner (2011) concluded that additional schooling causes modest improvements in health and small reductions in mortality. The nexus between education and health outcomes is also a function of education's positive association with healthy lifestyle. With few exceptions, more education reduces the likelihood of smoking, increases smoking cessation among those who have smoked previously, contributes to a healthier diet, and increases physical activity. The findings with respect to education's relationship with alcohol use and dependency are mixed, with educational attainment associated with greater alcohol use but negatively associated with binge drinking and alcohol dependency.

Parental education has substantial effects on the welfare of children, serving as an intergenerational transmission of various forms of capital—human (talents or abilities), social (connections), and cultural (values and behaviors)—that manifest in children's health, educational progress, and attainment. From birth weight to childhood health and activity, to long-term health in adulthood, the relationship between parents' education and children's health was consistent with positive associations. Educated parents have the financial and cognitive resources and abilities to cultivate environments inside the home that support children's cognitive and noncognitive development. Although some research questioned the causal effects of maternal education on children's educational trajectories, we remind readers of the caution that Feinstein and colleagues (2008) issued with regard to causal effects. It may be difficult to ascertain a direct causal effect of parents' education (maternal or paternal) on children's educational attainment. However, parental education has been found to have a consistent positive association with the cultivation of a supportive and cognitively stimulating home environment for children.

Similar to the conclusion from the 1990s, the overall evidence suggests that college education has a positive effect on the likelihood of contributing one's time and effort toward volunteering and community service. Without exception, years of schooling and educational attainment associated positively with civic behaviors (including volunteering with charitable organizations or social welfare groups) and higher levels of social trust. Although we found mixed evidence depending on the analytical approach used, we conclude that educational attainment is associated with increased political involvement and voting behavior in the United States, though one recent study suggests this effect may have diminished in recent decades (see Long, 2010). To the extent that postsecondary education is intended to educate students for engaged citizenship, we acknowledge this trend as one to monitor.

Between-College Effects

Given the emphasis on the net effects of college, there is a paucity of evidence on the effects of postsecondary environments and experiences on graduates' quality of life after college. In several cases, a single study examined a specific institutional characteristic, which severely limits our ability to form conclusions with respect to differences in quality-of-life outcomes by Carnegie Classification, public/private distinction, and institutional mission. Alternatively, we can make tentative conclusions based on the handful of studies that examined differences by two-year/four-year institutions and by institutional selectivity. In general, attending a four-year versus two-year institution is associated with increased political activity and fewer depressive symptoms. Whereas the previous volume suggested that differences by institutional selectivity were due largely to selection effects, recent research has used more rigorous analytical methods to isolate the relationship between institutional selectivity and quality-of-life outcomes.

Based on the past decade of research, it appear that institutional selectivity has generally positive associations with health behaviors even in the presence of extensive controlling and matching techniques. Alternatively, institutional selectivity has a negative relationship with voter registration among U.S. graduates from the 1990s and no relationship with civic engagement among alumni. For those interested in studying the impact of different institutional contexts and students' experiences during postsecondary, the paucity of research in this area suggests a fruitful area for further investigation.

Within-College Effects

Research from the 2000s that examined within-college effects on quality-of-life outcomes largely focused on the effects of postsecondary engagement with campus activities, specifically fraternity/sorority involvement, study abroad, and academic major. Involvement with these college activities was positively associated with participation in cultural/political and service organizations, as well as giving to and volunteering for one's alma mater. However, the relationship between fraternity/sorority affiliation and involvement with one's alma mater was more nuanced, with some identifying that maintaining one's connection to the fraternity/sorority chapter after college was more important than their relationship to their alma mater. Given the prevalence of greater alcohol use by fraternity/sorority members during college, other research examined the extent to which these behaviors continued after college. This research found that binge drinking declined considerably over time, with the effect most pronounced among men, who had the highest level of involvement with fraternities. Research on study abroad found that alumni who participated in study abroad were more civically involved than their peers, but this research is often challenged by its inability to distinguish a unique participation effect from a selection effect.

Interestingly, the academic majors that have seen the greatest growth in recent years (business and STEM fields) appear to be associated with graduates having the lowest levels of civic engagement and political participation. This raises the question whether postsecondary education, particularly in the United States, will be successful in realizing its mandate of educating graduates for engaged citizenship in the this century.

Building on the conclusion from the between-college effects section, Desjardins (2008) lamented the dearth of literature examining within-college effects on quality-of-life indicators, namely health, stating, "We know very little about the impact of different curricula on wider society, or about different pedagogical methods and ways of organising and running schools" (p. 31). Although the research from the 2000s was somewhat more expansive than the earlier volume, there is a clear opportunity for college impact research to take this inquiry further.

Conditional Effects of College

Research in the 2000s has carefully examined education's effects on a host of quality-of-life outcomes, particularly with respect to gender, race/ethnicity, and socioeconomic status. In general, research has found that education has a more protective and positive effect for women in terms of depression or happiness than for men. Education also has a greater effect for women's self-assessed health, but that education's effect on reducing mortality was stronger for men than women. Together, these findings may suggest that education serves more as a positive sociological mechanism for women than for men.

Education's gendered effects on both self-assessed health and mortality also vary by race and marital status. Women and men of color (compared to Whites), as well as divorced and single individuals (compared to those who are married), realize different relationships between education and health. An interesting three-way interaction exists between education, gender, and race with the protective effect of education on BMI and obesity. Specifically, based on samples of White, African American, and Hispanic men and women, some studies have found educational attainment associated with higher BMI for African American men and women.

Furthermore, it appears that the educational effect on political participation has greater effects for women than men, while research comparing cohorts of American adults showed that the relationship between education and civic engagement has sharply declined from the 1970s to the 1990s. More recent college graduates (compared to their less educated peers) are less involved politically than college graduates of previous generations. Education's effect on civic engagement has not remained consistent over time, waning in recent decades. If postsecondary education is to serve a role in educating graduates for engaged citizenship, this seems to be a question worth investigating with current and future cohorts across international contexts.

CHAPTER CONCLUSION

This chapter examined the effects of education on quality-of-life outcomes. These included subjective well-being or happiness, health, intergenerational transmission of benefits to children, and civic and community involvement. Across these diverse outcomes, evidence clearly finds that college graduates have an enriched quality of life compared to their less educated peers. Building on the findings discussed in Chapter 8 on the positive effects of a college education on earnings and occupational status, the research discussed in this chapter indicate that graduates' life opportunities are influenced by having more access to resources and an enhanced capacity to effectively use the information provided across a broad set of resources.

Although it is difficult to make causal claims given the evidence, the clear positive effects of education on a vast number of quality-of-life indicators that occurred even after accounting for income and access to and use of greater resources are noteworthy. One would be hard-pressed to identify another institution that has as substantial an influence on overall quality of life as higher education. We discuss the implications of these findings with respect to higher education's ability to meet the mandate set forth by students, families, taxpayers, and other stakeholders in Chapter 10.

CHAPTER TEN

How College Affects Students

A Summary

Chapters 2 through 9 provide an in-depth review of the college impact literature from 2002 to 2013, with each chapter focused on a particular set of outcomes. The chapters are divided into six primary sections:

1. How do students change during the college years? (This is the "change" question.)

2. To what extent are these changes attributable to college attendance as opposed to normal maturation, non-college experiences, or other influences? (This is the "net effects" question.)

3. To what extent are these changes related to characteristics of the institution that students attend? (This is the "between-college effects" question.)

4. To what extent are these changes related to individual students' experiences at a given institution? (This is the "within-college effects" question.)

5. How do these changes vary depending on student and institutional characteristics? (This is the "conditional effects" question.)

6. What are the lasting impacts of college? (This is the "long-term effects" question.)

This chapter offers a summary of the findings from the previous eight chapters. We use these same six questions to organize the content and discuss a variety of outcomes as they pertain to each question. Therefore, this chapter focuses on the sources of impact across a broad range of outcomes; in doing so, we hope to highlight the consistency or inconsistency of effects across numerous different outcomes. We also summarize findings from the two previous volumes of *How College Affects Students* (which reviewed research from 1967 to 1989 and from 1989–1990 to 2001–2002), and we compare our results with these earlier findings.

CHANGE DURING COLLEGE

The two prior reviews by Pascarella and Terenzini (1991, 2005) indicated that college students changed on a large number and variety of outcomes from the first year to the senior year; indeed, they argued that this breadth of change was the most noteworthy feature of their findings. They also suggested that the changes occurred in an integrated manner, such that these were part of a mutually reinforcing network. Moreover, at least in the first volume, the magnitude of change during college was the largest of any of the six types of effects described in their review (e.g., between college, within college), as these changes during college likely reflected the cumulative effects of the wide variety of experiences students had.

This third volume also identifies some large changes during college, especially for improvements in critical thinking skills, moral reasoning, and intellectual and social self-confidence. Although many of the current findings are consistent with the previous volumes, new research has provided greater certainty and nuance to some conclusions, and it has sometimes directly contradicted evidence from earlier years. These findings are discussed in terms of learning and cognitive changes, psychosocial changes, attitudes and values, moral development, and career development.

Learning and Cognitive Changes

Pascarella and Terenzini (1991, 2005) identified sizable gains during college across various types of subject matter knowledge and cognition, including critical thinking skills (.5 to 1 standard deviations [SD]),[1] reflective judgment (about 1 SD), verbal and writing skills (.5 to.75 SD), quantitative skills (.25 to.5 SD), and other subject matter knowledge (around .75 SD). From Volume 1 to Volume 2, the estimates for quantitative reasoning increased and those for critical thinking decreased, whereas estimates for the other outcomes were almost identical across the two volumes.

Very little research in the current review period assessed learning and cognition with objective measures at the beginning and end of college, which is necessary to establish how much change occurs during the college years. Two large-scale studies report gains in critical thinking over four years of college at .44 to .47 SDs, which is quite similar to the results from Volume 2. Cross-sectional research examined differences in adults with different levels of education. In the United States, people who have a bachelor's degree are substantially more likely than people with a high school diploma to be at the highest proficiency level of literacy (24% versus 6%, respectively), numeracy (18% versus 4%), and problem-solving skills (12% versus 4%). An international study obtained even larger gaps for literacy in the United States (31% for a bachelor's degree, 19% for an associate's degree, and 5% for a high school diploma). Sizable disparities by educational attainment are also apparent in Australia, Canada, England, and Northern Ireland. However, it is unclear to what extent these differences reflect changes during college, since students who chose to attend college were almost certainly more proficient (on average) when leaving high school than those who did not attend. The low overall levels of proficiency are also noteworthy, as they suggest that there is considerable room for improvement even among college graduates in obtaining high levels of mastery in these core competencies.

Psychosocial Changes

In Volume 1, some sizable overall changes in psychosocial outcomes were apparent from the first to the senior year, including decreases in authoritarianism and dogmatism (.70–.90 SD), gains in autonomy and freedom from family influences (about .60 SD), greater psychological well-being (.40 SD), and reduced ethnocentrism (.40 SD). Smaller changes were evident for gains in intellectual orientation (.33 SD), internal locus of control (.25–.30 SD), and independence from peer influence and interpersonal relations (.16–.20 SD). Research from Volume 2 was less likely to assess overall change exclusively; studies that did so found modest average shifts in identity complexity, progression through identity stages, academic and social self-concepts, overall self-esteem, and independence. However, these overall trends masked the fact that students sometimes moved in different directions during college, with some exhibiting gains, others showing decreases or regression, and some having no change at all. Studies examining dimensions of identity development, particularly related to race/ethnicity and sexual orientation, flourished during the 1990s. This research found that coming out (revealing one's minority sexual identity) was a significant milestone in forming one's identity and that doing so commonly occurred during the college years.

In the twenty-first century, research in the United States generally focused on specific identity dimensions, particularly racial identity, rather than general identity formation. Consistent with the previous volume, evidence for overall gains in identity during college are mixed, which may reflect the fact that the samples were often small and that a non-trivial proportion of students regressed in their development. Non-U.S. research often finds that identity formation may entail dual cycles of exploration and commitment, and students who make initial commitments may engage in further in-depth exploration before fully identifying with these commitments.

Changes in other psychosocial domains vary considerably by outcome. During the first three years of college, students exhibit increases in spiritual quest (i.e., searching for meaning and purpose in life), equanimity (i.e., having psychological stability and gratitude even when encountering hardship), and religious struggle (i.e., questioning and feeling unsettled about religious beliefs). Over the same time period, religious commitment appears to remain stable, and religious engagement (especially religious service participation) decreases notably. Intellectual self-confidence and perceived writing ability increase considerably (by 11 to 16 percentage points), and overall self-rated academic ability increases slightly, whereas mathematical self-confidence decreases on average (which perhaps reflects a limited need for mathematics within some undergraduate majors).

Some limited research offers support for notable gains over four years in social self-confidence (16–17 percentage points), leadership (.37 SDs), and independence from authority. The number of studies examining student well-being has increased markedly in the twenty-first century; overall, emotional health tends to decline during the college years, but most of the decrease seems to occur during the first year of college. This pattern is contrary to the sizable increases in psychological well-being in the 1990s, but at least some of this divergence may be attributable to the use of different well-being constructs across these studies.

Attitudes and Values

Both Volumes 1 and 2 found that students shifted toward holding more inclusive attitudes and values regarding issues of gender and racial equity, sexual orientation, and religion. They also became more tolerant of others' attitudes and values, as well as more knowledgeable about social and political issues. College attendance appeared to promote community service, awareness and understanding of other cultures, commitment to promoting racial understanding, and frequency of interracial interactions. The only domain in which the two volumes diverged was changes in political orientation: the earlier literature found a shift toward liberal views, whereas research reviewed in Volume 2 found no overall change, with a slight trend toward more polarized views during college.

Evidence from the current review also found that students develop growing commitments to humanitarian values while in college. Small shifts toward liberalism are apparent, but more nuanced findings indicate that these trends vary by attitude. Students' support for individual rights and freedoms increases over time, but their endorsement of government intervention decreases. Contrary to results from the 1990s, political and community engagement actually decrease slightly while in college; however, these conclusions are complicated by the use of different measures, some of which combine various forms of engagement or values.

Some dimensions of cultural awareness increase modestly during college. These attitudes include universality-diversity orientation (which consists of diversity of contact, relativistic appreciation, and comfort with differences), pluralistic orientation (ability to see multiple perspectives and work cooperatively with diverse people), and support for equitable gender roles and the rights of people who identify as lesbian, gay, bisexual, or transgender (LGB) (both attitudes were already supportive when students entered college). Unlike the consistent positive findings for diversity-related outcomes in earlier reviews, students appear to exhibit modest declines in commitment to promoting racial understanding and openness to diversity during college.

Consistent with initial conclusions from more limited evidence in Volume 2, a larger body of research now suggests that religious convictions are often not abandoned during college so much as they are revised and redefined. In general, students' religious attitudes become more pluralistic, they develop a greater appreciation for human connectedness, they perceive less conflict between religion and science, and they become less religiously and socially conservative. Other findings that match conclusions from prior reviews include increases in intrinsic motivation and effortful thinking (albeit countered by some declines in academic motivation and habits of mind), increases in artistic interests and cosmopolitanism, and decreases in materialism.

Moral Development

The previous two reviews strongly suggested that students became much more likely to use principled reasoning to judge moral issues in college. In Volume 2, this difference between first-year students and seniors was a large .77 standard deviations. The primary shift during college was from reasoning that primarily emphasized the role of societal authority (conventional moral reasoning) to applying universal moral principles (principled moral reasoning).

Based on evidence from the twenty-first century, students increase in their principled moral reasoning from the first to the fourth year by .58 SD; the size of this effect is noteworthy, but it is slightly smaller than the estimate of .77 SD from the 1990s. One large-scale study found a .32 SD increase during the first year of college, suggesting that students' early college experiences (including their general education course work) may contribute considerably to the total change during college.

Career Development

The first two volumes reviewed a limited number of studies of students' self-reported career development. The findings suggested that students became more mature, knowledgeable, and focused during college in thinking about their careers, and they developed a more accurate perspective and greater workplace readiness as they progressed through college. However, these findings may simply reflect maturation rather than changes uniquely attributable to the college experience.

The twenty-first-century literature was also quite scarce. According to one study, students often enter college with intentions to join careers that are either gender typical or gender neutral. As they progress through four years of college, many students change their aspirations, often in the direction from gender-neutral to gender-typical occupations. Additional evidence suggests that students' career aspirations may be more stable over time in terms of their occupational prestige and connection to personal interests than for gender concentration. Table 10.1 summarizes the findings and conclusions from the previous two reviews as well as the current volume.

Table 10.1 Change during College: Main Findings

Outcomes	Volumes 1 and 2	Volume 3
Learning and cognitive changes	Substantial increases in critical thinking, reflective judgment, verbal and writing skills, and other subject matter. Sizable (but smaller) increases in quantitative skills.	Substantial increases in critical thinking (very similar to Volume 2). Weak evidence of potentially substantial increases in reading, writing, quantitative, and problem-solving skills across several countries.
Psychosocial changes	Substantial increases in autonomy and psychological well-being; substantial decreases in authoritarianism and ethnocentrism. Smaller increases in self-concept, self-esteem, independence, internal locus of control, and identity development.	Substantial increases in leadership, self-concept, and independence from authority; decrease in emotional health. Increases in spirituality and religious struggle; decreases in religious engagement. Many students either progress or regress in identity development.
Attitudes and values	Increases in tolerance and inclusivity on various attitudes and values. Increases in knowledge of social and political issues and community engagement. Sizable increases in political liberalism in Volume 1, but little or no overall change in Volume 2.	Shifts toward or away from liberal views depend on the attitude or policy. Community engagement may decrease slightly, but evidence is unclear. Religious attitudes become more pluralistic; students revisit and redefine religious views. Most (but not all) attitudes become more supportive of diversity.
Moral development	Substantial increase in using principled moral reasoning to judge moral issues. Upon entering college, using societal authority (conventional moral reasoning) was the normative approach.	Substantial increase in using principled moral reasoning (similar but slightly smaller than that in Volume 2). About half of the increase may occur in the first year of college.

(continued)

Table 10.1 Change during College: Main Findings (continued)

Outcomes	Volumes 1 and 2	Volume 3
Career development	Increases in career maturity, knowledge, and focus; increases in accuracy of perspective and workplace readiness.	Sparse evidence for prevalent changes in career aspirations, often from gender-neutral to gender-typical fields. Aspirations may be reasonably stable for occupational prestige and interests.

NET EFFECTS OF COLLEGE

Although the nature and amount of student change during college is clearly important, an arguably more crucial issue is the extent to which attending college causes students to have different outcomes from those not attending college. College students and other adults may change for all kinds of reasons, including normal maturation and human development, experiences that have nothing to do with college, and general predispositions or proclivity toward change. Therefore, this "net effects of college" question is much more difficult to answer because it requires ruling out these alternative explanations, which generally involves comparing students who attended college with those who did not. Such conclusions can be difficult to draw with certainty, as people who self-select into attending college differ, on average, in numerous ways from those who do not attend.

In the previous two volumes, the evidence on changes in learning and cognition, moral reasoning, and career and economic returns was more extensive and consistent than the evidence for attitudes, values, and psychosocial dimensions. This disparity does not imply that the net impact was inherently larger for these types of outcomes, but stronger conclusions can be drawn for outcomes that received more research attention.

The evidence for net effects in this third volume is quite limited. The few existing studies allow some strong conclusions to be drawn about net effects on religious outcomes, but the findings for political and civic change are mixed. The strongest and most abundant evidence occurs for career and economic impacts, quality of life outcomes, and intergenerational effects of college (passing the benefits of college along to one's children). By definition, these net effects are also long-term effects of college, since they all indicate changes that occur years or decades after graduation. Therefore, the discussion of findings for those outcomes appears in the long-term effects section at the end of this chapter. In this section, we summarize research on learning and cognitive changes, psychosocial changes, attitudes and values, and moral development.

Learning and Cognitive Changes

Pascarella and Terenzini (1991, 2005) found that college had a unique, positive influence on various subject matter and cognitive outcomes, and these findings could not be explained by alternative explanations regarding academic ability, sex, race, or maturation. Volume 2 concluded that college attendance directly contributed to gains in the use of reflective judgment (.90 standard deviations), critical thinking skills (.55 SD), English (.59 SD), science (.47 SD), social science (.46 SD), mathematics (.32 SD), and general verbal and quantitative skills (.25 SD).

In our current review, there is very little evidence regarding net effects, and the available evidence is weak. Several studies of college student samples found positive relationships between exposure to college (measured in terms of years in school and credit hours completed) and student learning (in math, reading, writing, and overall general education skills) that occur even when controlling for precollege characteristics. Although it seems unlikely that people who are not attending college have similar gains in these academic subjects, this research included only college students, so this alternative explanation cannot be ruled out definitively. That said, there is no compelling reason to change the conclusions drawn in syntheses of earlier research.

Psychosocial Changes

In the previous two volumes, general maturation could have explained why students changed on some psychosocial outcomes, particularly various forms of identity or stage development. However, other evidence suggested that college played at least some distinct role in promoting academic and social self-concepts, sense of control over academic performance, and leadership skills. College attendance also resulted in reduced authoritarianism, dogmatism, and ethnocentrism. The results for overall self-esteem and internal locus of control were mixed and may have been indirect through certain college experiences.

As with the earlier reviews, few studies in this volume provide sufficiently strong evidence to estimate the impact of attending college as opposed to maturation or other influences. The one notable exception is for religious identity, since some datasets with these outcomes have followed traditional-age college students and other young adults over time. Research in the late twentieth century observed that students decline in religiosity during college, which some people have interpreted as evidence that college has a secularizing effect. However, according to strong evidence from this review, people who attend college have smaller decreases in religious engagement and identity than those who do not attend college, which suggests that college may actually buffer overall declines in religiosity. One study, adding nuance to this pattern, found that college may have a temporary negative effect on religious participation, but this pattern reverses after students graduate from college.

Attitudes and Values

According to studies from the 1990s, college had unique, positive effects on civic and community involvement, racial understanding, openness to diversity, perception of racism as problematic, and support of gender equity. The findings on other topics conflicted in the two previous volumes. Volume 1 concluded that college may have led students to move toward more open, liberal, and tolerant attitudes and values. In contrast, Volume 2 reviewed studies that either did not identify significant net effects or could not rule out similar societal shifts in attitudes as an alternative explanation.

Although few studies conducted during the review period for this volume explore net effects on attitudes and values, the research uses rigorous quasi-experimental designs and often questions whether college shapes political, civic, and religious beliefs. The results for political and civic outcomes are mixed, with some research finding substantial positive net effects of college and others finding essentially no effect. Thus, we cannot draw firm conclusions, but we believe that these mixed findings and methodological improvements have cast some doubt on previous conclusions. For religious outcomes, one rigorous study found no significant effect of college on changes in a variety of religious attitudinal indicators, such as belief in a higher power, religious doubts, and religious inclusivity. Instead, religious social networks (whether within or outside college) appear to play a key role in shaping religious attitudes and values.

Moral Development

The findings for both previous reviews suggested that college attendance led to increased use of principled moral reasoning, although the exact magnitude of that effect was unclear. Principled moral reasoning was clearly associated with greater moral behavior, but research generally did not explore the direct net effects of college on moral behavior.

However, no research in the period covered by the review for this volume provides direct evidence about the net effects of college on moral reasoning or behavior. Instead, recent research has focused almost exclusively on between-college and within-college predictors of moral outcomes at the expense of understanding the potential overall impact of college. That said, we have no reason to doubt the conclusions drawn in previous syntheses that college attendance may have an effect on moral reasoning and therefore potentially moral behavior. The findings for the net effects of college on all outcomes are summarized in Table 10.2.

Table 10.2 Net Effects of College: Main Findings

Outcomes	Volumes 1 and 2	Volume 3
Learning and cognitive changes	Substantial increases in English, science, social science, critical thinking, reflective judgment, verbal and quantitative skills that are all attributable to college.	Weak evidence shows increases over time in various subject matter areas among college students, but with no comparisons to similar non-college adults.
Psychosocial changes	Increases in self-concept, sense of control, and leadership; decreases in authoritarianism, dogmatism, and ethnocentrism. Weak evidence for identity; mixed results for self-esteem and internal locus of control.	Most research does not support strong claims about net effects that ruled out alternative explanations. However, college clearly buffers the negative trend in religiosity among young adults, such that college students have smaller declines than others.
Attitudes and values	Increases in civic engagement and some positive racial and gender attitudes. Increases in many tolerant and liberal attitudes and values in Volume 1, but no strong conclusions in Volume 2.	Using rigorous research designs, recent studies find mixed results for whether college affects various political and civic outcomes. Other evidence suggests that religious attitudes may not be influenced by college.
Moral development	Increases use of principled moral reasoning; some indirect evidence for increases in moral behavior.	No research in this review directly examined net effects on moral reasoning or behavior.

BETWEEN-COLLEGE EFFECTS

Many countries—including those represented in the review for this volume (Australia, Canada, New Zealand, the United Kingdom, and the United States)—have a diverse array of postsecondary institutions that vary in terms of degrees and fields of study offered, institutional type and control, vocational versus liberal arts emphasis, structural characteristics (size, urbanicity, student demographics), campus climate, and so on. Given this heterogeneity, it may be surprising that the magnitude of between-college effects is generally smaller than for whether someone attends college at all (net effects) and what students do while in school (within-college effects). This conclusion was consistent across both previous volumes (Pascarella & Terenzini, 1991, 2005), despite the fact that substantial differences existed in the entering characteristics of students at different institutions. These modest between-college effects may have occurred because the types of institutional attributes that researchers most frequently considered (such as type, size, and public/private control) would likely have exhibited indirect effects through promoting certain types of college experiences and environments. Moreover, these types of structural characteristics may not have reflected the type of institutional attributes that have the greatest effects on student outcomes.

Of the between-college differences in previous reviews, the postcollege economic and career effects were larger than those for developmental outcomes, such as knowledge acquisition, cognitive skills, psychosocial attributes, attitudes and values, and moral reasoning. This pattern seems reasonable, because attending an institution that is perceived to be more prestigious or rigorous may yield postcollege career benefits above and beyond the learning advantages that those schools presumably provide. In addition, the fact that many students transfer among postsecondary institutions complicates any attempt to estimate the effects of attending a particular type of school.

Consistent with the two prior volumes, we conclude that between-college effects are relatively modest, especially when compared with the overall net effect of college attendance and the within-college effects of specific student experiences. The presence of mostly small or nonexistent findings may not be surprising, since the most commonly examined predictors are structural characteristics of the institution (such as institutional control, type, and selectivity), whose effects are almost exclusively indirect through more proximal institutional environments (such as the overall academic, social, and diversity climate) and individual student experiences (such as academic, social, and extracurricular engagement). There are some notable exceptions to this trend: Attending a four-year versus a two-year institution has a considerable positive effect on bachelor's degree attainment, and institutional selectivity yields sizable benefits for graduation and postcollege earnings.

Since this summary of college effects cuts across all of the previous chapters, the organization of this section follows the type of between-college effect, with all outcomes discussed within each of these subsections. This organization helps clarify what types of between-college attributes are more (or less) consistently associated with various college outcomes, and it allows comparisons of the extent to which a particular between-college effect might foster or constrain some outcomes more than others. Given the large amount of the previous literature on these topics, we also discuss findings from the two prior volumes of *How College Affects Students* within each of these subsections. The categories of institutional effects we discuss are two-year versus four-year, quality, type and control, size, racial and gender characteristics, expenditures and resource allocation, and overall environment.

Two-Year versus Four-Year Institutions

Pascarella and Terenzini (1991, 2005) found that students who sought a bachelor's degree and started at a two-year institution were 15 to 20 percentage points less likely to obtain that degree than similar students who started at a four-year institution.[2] These studies controlled for a variety of confounding factors, including precollege ability and achievement, demographics, and motivation. This disparity was at least partially explained by reductions in educational aspirations among students attending two-year colleges. However, the major challenge for degree completion appeared to be transferring successfully to a four-year institution. Once students made this transition, they were equally likely to graduate with a bachelor's degree as similar students who started at a four-year school (although, not surprisingly, they generally took more time to finish their undergraduate studies).

When accounting for students' entering abilities and other characteristics, prior volumes found that many outcomes of students who started at a two-year institution did not differ from those who started at a four-year institution on many learning outcomes, including reading comprehension, mathematics, science reasoning, writing, and critical thinking. In fact, community college students exhibited greater gains in openness to intellectual and racial/ethnic diversity and in internal locus of control than their four-year counterparts; these findings were particularly strong during the first year of college. Moreover, in a comparison of students with similar educational attainment, attending a two-year college had minimal effects on subsequent earnings and occupational status.

Consistent with earlier research, our current review finds that attending a four-year college has a large effect on educational attainment; recent evidence provides even stronger support for this conclusion using quasi-experimental methods. We have slightly increased the estimated effect and reduced the certainty in the size of the effect: starting at a four-year school leads to a 15 to 25 percentage point greater chance of ultimately obtaining a bachelor's degree than starting at a two-year school. Recent research also replicates earlier findings in that reductions in degree aspirations at two-year institutions appear to explain at least some of this disparity, and students who successfully transfer to a four-year school as a junior are just as likely to graduate as those who started at a four-year school.

Some evidence suggests that students at four-year institutions exhibit larger gains in general education and intellectual growth than those at two-year institutions, but the reliance on self-reported gains (and some contradictory evidence from studies that did not examine change over time) makes these conclusions uncertain. As one illustration of such mixed results for a different outcome, students at four-year colleges are generally more likely to select "American" ethnic self-labels than are students at two-year colleges, but changes in this pattern are unrelated to two-year versus four-year college attendance, and other research related to identity formation yields conflicting findings. Attending a liberal arts college may lead to greater moral reasoning than attending a community college, but the reverse pattern is true for need for cognition and autonomy, such that community college students fare better than those at liberal arts colleges. After attending college, graduates of sub-baccalaureate institutions are considerably more likely to have a job that closely matches their field of study than are graduates of bachelor's, master's, and doctoral institutions.

Institutional Quality

As used in this book and elsewhere, the term *college quality* may be misleading, since this research typically examines institutional selectivity or prestige rather than any objective indicator of the quality of education that students receive. Nonetheless, reviews of the literature before 2002 found that these measures contributed to socioeconomic outcomes, including educational attainment, career, and earnings. Specifically, institutional selectivity had a direct effect on student persistence and degree completion, but these relationships were modest in size and often intertwined with student experiences during college. Institutional selectivity was also associated with greater earnings and, to a lesser extent, with occupational status and career mobility within the middle ranks of an organization. These effects were generally quite small, with the exception of benefits associated with attending a very elite college or university (in the top 1 to 2% of the distribution).

These improved postcollege outcomes appeared to be driven primarily by employers' perceptions of the status of the institution, students' entering characteristics, or both, rather than any actual differences across institutions in cognitive or affective outcomes. Indeed, there was often no significant relationship between admissions selectivity and various learning, cognitive, psychosocial, and attitudinal outcomes. When significant effects of selectivity were observed, these were often small, and better outcomes were sometimes observed at less selective schools. Moreover, some caution about these conclusions is warranted, as many studies did not sufficiently account for potential preexisting differences in motivation or ambition across students entering schools at different levels of selectivity.

Consistent with prior reviews, recent evidence suggests that institutional quality contributes to greater degree completion. This relationship is largest in magnitude when *quality* is defined in terms of selectivity (12–18 percentage points between selective and nonselective); moreover, attending a school that is at least moderately selective seems to be more important than differences between highly and very highly selective schools. Faculty-student ratio also appears to influence graduation, but the effects are somewhat smaller. The impact of institutional quality on degree completion may be largely explained by greater academic and social engagement at higher-quality institutions.

Research also indicates that college quality may contribute to postcollege earnings, especially when an index of multiple institutional characteristics serves as the indicator of quality (rather than relying on a single measure of selectivity or faculty-student ratio). The effect of receiving a degree from a high-quality school becomes larger as students are further away from graduation, with differences increasing after one year (6–8%) to four years (13–15%) to 10 years (16–19%). However, institutional selectivity appears to be inversely related to job satisfaction after graduation; perhaps ironically, this negative effect is most pronounced for satisfaction with pay, although employees from selective schools earn more than their peers from less-selective schools.

The findings for other outcomes are generally inconsistent. Some evidence suggests that selectivity is positively and modestly related to cognitive gains and well-being, but other studies find no significant relationship. Mixed findings for selectivity are also apparent for civic values and behaviors, diversity attitudes, and postcollege outcomes (employment, hours worked, and gender-atypical career choices). Attending a more selective institution is associated with generally positive postcollege health behaviors and outcomes, including less binge drinking, more frequent exercise, and lower rates of obesity. Some research confounds selectivity with institutional type (e.g., comparing doctoral, master's, and baccalaureate institutions), so the unique effects are difficult to discern in these instances. No research examined the link between an unequivocal measure of institutional "quality" and moral development.

Institutional Type and Control

In the prior reviews, the effects of institutional type (e.g., Carnegie Classification) and control (public versus private) were difficult to determine, because these characteristics were often confounded with other institutional attributes, such as selectivity, size, and curriculum. Overall, institutional type and control were often unrelated or modestly related to student outcomes, including psychosocial attributes, attitudes and values, and earnings. Few studies examined relationships with learning and cognitive outcomes. Some significant findings were noteworthy; for instance, small, private liberal arts colleges (including those that are religiously affiliated) seemed to fare better in promoting principled moral reasoning. Among studies that accounted for precollege characteristics, attending a private institution was sometimes associated with greater educational attainment and improved academic and social self-concepts.

In our current review, we also find considerable conflicting evidence and difficulties with disentangling type and control from other between-college attributes. Largely as a result of this issue, we cannot draw any strong conclusions about the role of Carnegie type and control in shaping subject matter competence, cognitive gains, attitudes and values, moral development, and postcollege earnings or job satisfaction. A couple of studies suggest that private institutions may promote greater civic values and social activism relative to public institutions, and attending a liberal arts college appears to result in more liberal attitudes than attending a research university. Institutional control has no significant effect on persistence and degree completion when accounting for other institutional characteristics. Findings for institutional type and education attainment are often unclear. In a notable exception, institutions that focus on providing certificates tend to be more successful in promoting degree completion, whereas those that focus on associate's degrees often promote greater four-year transfer; such patterns are likely consistent with the intended missions of these schools. Moreover, although few studies examined for-profit institutions, attending a for-profit college (versus a nonprofit community college) leads to reductions on various measures of civic mindedness. As one might expect from tuition disparities between public and private institutions, the average debt-to-earnings ratio for graduates of private schools is substantially greater than that of public school graduates.

Meaningful effects were observed in the burgeoning literature on religiously affiliated institutions, which are associated with greater increases in civic and social values, volunteerism, religious and spiritual identity, and (perhaps surprisingly) religious and spiritual struggle. The greater salience of religion at these schools, along with the fact that students may be deeply considering their own views for the first time, likely explains the increases in religious struggle. Strong evidence suggests that these institutional differences can be explained by students' engagement in curricular and cocurricular activities (especially those pertaining to religion and spirituality) and peer effects. Religious affiliation is unrelated to moral development in one study that accounted for other institutional attributes. Moreover, a handful of studies provide inconsistent evidence that religiously affiliated schools may bolster graduation rates, but more research that uses stronger methodologies is needed.

Some limited evidence has identified positive outcomes from attending a work college, in which part-time employment is an institutional requirement; working offsets the costs of college tuition, as well as potentially promoting learning and growth. Relative to other institutional types, work college students report greater net gains in general education and academic skills, citizenship and global orientation, leadership skills, personal development, and full-time postcollege employment. Work college attendance also appears to have a positive, indirect effect on job preparation that is explained by some combination of college grades, major, and occupational development, as well as postbaccalaureate education. However, perhaps reflecting differences in the types of postcollege careers that students seek, work college graduates have lower salaries than graduates of regional public universities but no differences in job satisfaction. Despite the small amount of evidence, the presence of largely favorable findings across various outcomes is noteworthy.

Institutional Size

In most research reported in the first two volumes, the relationships between institutional size and college outcomes were either nonexistent or indirect. Size was often unrelated to attitudes, values, and psychological outcomes. The existing studies suggested that size might have an indirect, negative effect on persistence and degree completion through its relationships with students' perceptions of the institution, faculty and peer interactions, and academic and social involvement. Conversely, size was positively associated with earnings, which may have resulted from the diversity of majors and programs at larger institutions, as well as postcollege networks that these schools often provide. The evidence on size and occupational status was mixed, with some evidence (particularly before 1990) identifying positive relationships.

Taken as a whole, a considerable body of research published since those earlier volumes suggests that there is no relationship between institutional size and graduation, with the slight possibility of a small negative effect at two-year institutions. Inquiry on size and other college outcomes is sparse. Size has no consistent relationship with student learning, cognitive gains, civic growth, and moral development, but size may have a small negative effect on academic self-concept.

Institutional Racial and Gender Characteristics

According to earlier syntheses, attending a Historically Black College or University (HBCU) or a women's college contributed to some improved outcomes. African Americans at HBCUs and women at women's colleges exhibited higher persistence and graduation rates, which appeared to be explained by more supportive faculty, peers, and overall environments at these institutions than at predominantly White and coeducational institutions, respectively. Some evidence also suggested that attending an HBCU or a women's college led to greater career eminence among Black and female graduates, respectively. Findings suggested as well that these institutions might also have provided modest advantages in academic and social self-concepts. In addition, HBCUs appeared to have contributed to greater personal development, while women's colleges may have promoted civic values, desire to influence social conditions, and racial/cultural awareness and appreciation.

Attending an HBCU or women's college, however, was generally unrelated to some other outcomes, including knowledge acquisition, cognitive growth, self-esteem, locus of control, and leadership development. The evidence on occupational status, earnings, and career mobility was often inconsistent and conflicting, so no strong conclusions could be drawn. Evidence from the first volume of *How College Affects Students* suggested that attending a women's college led to notably higher engagement in male-dominated fields, including science, medicine, and engineering, but studies in the second volume were not consistent in their findings. Finally, the overall racial diversity of the student body may have contributed to greater earnings among non-African American students; this dynamic may have occurred because companies tended to value employees who had experience with diversity, and these experiences were much more common on diverse campuses.

In the review for this volume, one primary finding is consistent across a wide array of outcomes: students who attend a minority-serving institution (MSI) or a women's college fare at least as well as students who attend other types of institutions. A couple of positive effects are fairly certain; specifically,

Black/African American and Latino/Hispanic students who attend MSIs report greater gains in general education and academic skills than similar students attending predominantly White institutions, and personal development is greater at HBCUs, Hispanic-serving institutions (HSIs), and women's colleges. However, a host of other relationships are unclear because of the presence of mixed findings (with a combination of positive effects and no significant differences) or substantial limitations in studies that find positive relationships. These ambiguous patterns include results for women's college attendance and perceived learning, the percentage of students of color on campus and socio-political and civic outcomes, MSI attendance and several outcomes (academic and intellectual self-concept, as well as a lack of racial identity salience and internalization), and HBCU attendance and several outcomes (cognitive growth, well-being, and degree attainment). The racial/ethnic and gender composition of the student body do not appear to affect educational attainment in general, but it is unclear whether these attributes may shape the outcomes of specific student groups. Given that MSIs tend to be less well supported financially, one study argued that finding no significant differences—or, across a variety of studies, the inconclusive presence of numerous positive effects—constitutes an impressive accomplishment of these institutions that have fewer resources.

Institutional Expenditures and Resource Allocation

A new topic in this volume is the impact of institutional resources on college students. Some aspects of resource allocation are covered indirectly in the within-college effects section (e.g., the role of financial aid on an individual student's success), but institution-level dynamics certainly merit attention given the increases in accountability demands and decreases in state funding for public colleges and universities. The main overarching finding of this section is that funding matters: total per-student expenditures and state allocations to public colleges and universities both result in higher graduation rates, especially at four-year institutions. State allocations that are targeted toward need-based aid may be especially effective. The findings on other specific types of expenditures and educational attainment are less clear. Instructional expenditures appear to promote graduation, with some mixed support for the positive role of expenditures on student services and academic support. One study suggests that student services expenditures may improve critical thinking skills. If anything, administrative expenditures are negatively related to attainment, perhaps because these resources are not being used to benefit students directly.

Surprisingly, considerable evidence shows that tuition and fees are unrelated to educational attainment. It may be the case that these total figures for tuition and fees are only modestly correlated with the average net price that students actually pay after receiving grants, loans, work-study, and other forms of financial support; this disconnect would obscure the actual role of finances in shaping persistence. Another possibility (which does not contradict the first explanation) is that tuition and fees affect students' decisions of whether to attend college in the first place and which college to attend, whereas these have less of a role in whether students stay in school.

Some limited research has also examined state policy, including the increasing practice of using performance funding, in which a state determines the amount of money provided to each public institution based on one or more measures of institutional performance (such as the number of college graduates and credits completed). The findings of these few studies generally show no significant effects; at most, performance funding may yield very small increases in graduation that begin at least seven years after the policy's creation. State articulation policies that attempt to streamline coursework transfer from two-year to four-year public institutions also appear to have no discernable effect on bachelor's degree attainment.

Overall Institutional Environment

Another domain of institutional characteristics includes the normative attributes of the environment at a particular college or university, which researchers typically measure by average student perceptions of the environment or specific policies that reflect institutional norms (such as an honor code). The examined environmental dimensions varied considerably between the two previous volumes, but Pascarella and Terenzini (1991, 2005) argued that these environments may provide the mechanism through which more distal institutional attributes, such as selectivity or type, might directly influence college outcomes. As a result, they suggested that studying these characteristics may be more fruitful for understanding between-college effects than exploring structural characteristics. According to both reviews, students tended to change their majors and career choices in a direction that mirrored the predominant fields of study at their institution. Moreover, environments that promoted persistence and degree completion among all students were those in which (1) students felt that faculty and the broader institution cared about them and their well-being, (2) having on-campus friendships and attending campus activities were normative, (3) graduation and graduate school attendance rates were high, and (4) racial discrimination and prejudice on campus were infrequent.

Some of these same attributes were also associated with learning in college. For instance, institutions with a scholarly or analytical emphasis promoted learning and general cognitive growth. Moreover, a focus on general education, environments that emphasized frequent interaction and meaningful relationships among faculty and students, and faculty concern about student growth and development were all related to improvements in students' cognitive outcomes. These relationships were independent of an overall scholarly environment.

A host of significant relationships between environmental dimensions and various psychosocial outcomes and attitudes and values was observed. As just some examples, the racial/ethnic diversity of the undergraduate student body led to more frequent intergroup interactions on campus, as well as a greater multicultural orientation on campus, which then led to improved academic and social self-concepts. Moreover, institutional emphases on diversity and multi-culturalism, peer environments, and student beliefs about the sociopolitical attitudes of the faculty were associated with increases in numerous civic attitudes and behaviors. Finally, honor codes were associated with lower levels of self-reported academic dishonesty. It was unclear, however, whether this pattern occurred because the policy improved moral behavior or whether schools with honor policies tended to attract honest students.

Consistent with the previous reviews, this volume found that a variety of institutional environments are associated with student outcomes, and some of these findings are identical to those of earlier research. For instance, institutions that are racially diverse or have high levels of diversity engagement tend to yield improvements in verbal, quantitative, and general education competence; general personal development; identity development and expression for students with minority sexualities; and various attitudes (including those related to race and ethnicity). Average perceptions of a supportive campus environment are associated with gains in subject matter competence, cognitive growth, and personal development.

Environments that encourage academic challenge and engagement also appear to promote learning and cognitive outcomes. Cognitive growth is further bolstered by average intellectual self-esteem, perceptions of a nontraditional curriculum, out-of-class faculty interactions, perceptions that faculty are generally liberal, and pursuing civic goals. Average faculty use of student-centered pedagogies predicts increases in students' charitable behaviors and caring orientation.

In addition to studies exploring institutional religious affiliation, recent research increasingly examined the average religious attitudes and behaviors of students and faculty. Campuses with high student religiosity appear to promote charitable involvement and an ecumenical worldview (i.e., interest in and acceptance of diverse religious/spiritual perspectives), and the average frequency of religious struggle also seems to promote an ecumenical worldview. Interestingly, students' overall religious engagement is associated with decreases in psychological well-being, whereas faculty focus on spirituality predicts greater student wellness. Attending an institution in which entering students are religiously conservative appears to lead to individual students' becoming more conservative over time.

Finally, consistent with previous volumes, institutions with honor codes have lower student self-reports of academic dishonesty, but whether this effect is causal or the result of self-selection is still unclear. Moreover, students at institutions with character development programs (which also have honor codes) are less likely to help another student cheat and more likely to believe that they would get caught cheating.

Table 10.3 provides an overview of the findings and conclusions for between-college effects from all three volumes.

Table 10.3 Between-College Effects: Main Findings

Characteristic	Volumes 1 and 2	Volume 3
Two-year versus four-year	Four-year schools substantially improved bachelor's degree completion; two-year colleges may have increased diversity attitudes and internal locus of control. Learning and cognitive outcomes were similar across school type.	Four-year schools promote much higher bachelor's degree completion among students who want that degree. Two-year graduates have a closer link between field of study and their job. Unclear results for learning and cognitive outcomes.
Quality	Bolstered earnings and career outcomes, especially at very elite schools. Modest positive effects on graduation. Often no relationship with learning, cognition, attitudes, and psychosocial change.	Some sizable positive effects on graduation and earnings that vary with definition of *quality*. Predicts some health behaviors (in different directions). Mixed findings for various other outcomes.
Type and control	Type and control were often conflated with selectivity, size, and curriculum. Most relationships were small or nonexistent, and little research explored learning and cognition.	Same methods problems prevent strong conclusions on numerous topics. Religious schools bolster civic and religious/spiritual outcomes; work colleges may yield gains in psychosocial development and full-time employment.
Size	Size had no consistent link with most outcomes. Size may have had indirect negative effects on attainment and indirect positive effects on earnings.	Size appears to have no effect on graduation. Other inquiry is sparse, with no consistent links (except perhaps negative with academic self-concept).
Racial and gender characteristics	HBCUs and women's colleges promoted graduation, self-concept, and other psychosocial indicators; they appeared to be unrelated to learning, cognition, leadership, and possibly career and earnings.	Attending HBCUs, HSIs, MSIs, women's colleges, or racially diverse schools leads to various outcomes that are at least as favorable as attending other schools; these results are often mixed between positive and no effect.

(continued)

Table 10.3 Between-College Effects: Main Findings (continued)

Characteristic	Volumes 1 and 2	Volume 3
Expenditures and resource allocation	Not reviewed systematically in Volumes 1 or 2.	Total expenditures and state allocations as well as specific expenses that directly support learning and student success promote graduation. Tuition, performance funding, and articulation agreements may not affect graduation.
Overall environment	These proximal environments likely explained the link between structural attributes and desired outcomes. Supportive atmosphere, positive diversity climate, academic environment, and interpersonal engagement fostered positive results for numerous desired outcomes.	The broad-based conclusions from prior volumes, including modest evidence of honor codes reducing dishonesty, are replicated in recent research. Students' aggregate religious attributes also predict religious outcomes, well-being, civic behavior, and political views.

WITHIN-COLLEGE EFFECTS

In Pascarella and Terenzini's (1991, 2005) previous reviews and this review, more research has examined within-college dynamics than any other type of effect. Four key findings from research in the twenty-first century are highlighted here. First, the weight of the evidence is highly consistent with Sanford's (1966) argument about the benefits of providing a balance of challenge and support. Both challenge and support within and outside the classroom are consistently related to greater student learning, growth, development, and success. However, Sanford argues that challenge in the absence of support or extreme levels of challenge can be detrimental, as is true for support in the absence of meaningful challenge. It is probably not a coincidence that diversity experiences and engaged classroom learning, both of which often present salient challenges to students, are among the two most influential types of college experiences in this review (in terms of their consistent, positive relationships across a wide variety of outcomes).

Second, faculty practices are highly influential in shaping student outcomes. The roles of engaged learning and classroom challenge and support are noteworthy; other key influences include engaging in high-quality teaching practices (including clarity and organization), holding students to high standards (arguably a form of challenge), integration of learning within and across courses, tailoring courses to achieve specific intended outcomes (including bolstering critical thinking, moral development, understanding of diversity, and career exploration), and providing meaningful, specific feedback that fosters improvement.

Third, consistent with long-standing arguments from Pace (1982), Astin (1984), Kuh (2003), and others, the quantity and quality of student effort or involvement appear to play a large role in shaping student outcomes. This involvement can occur through cocurricular activities, peer interactions, academic preparation and participation, and engagement in specific educational practices. Of course, some experiences are more influential than others, and a specific experience may affect a relatively narrow or broad range of outcomes. Nonetheless, the bulk of evidence suggests that student involvement generally has positive—or at least not negative—effects on numerous desired outcomes.

Fourth, the improved methodological quality of research is calling into question some previously held conclusions about the impact of college. Some experiences that seemed influential in previous reviews are unrelated to intended outcomes when these were tested more recently with experimental or quasi-experimental studies (specific curricular programs intended to bolster retention constitute perhaps the most notable example). The overall quality of research across domains varied notably; for instance, research on classroom pedagogy frequently employs experimental designs, whereas research on student involvement often uses observational designs and then attempts to adjust for students' precollege characteristics and other college experiences. As a result, we are somewhat cautious in our use of language and note conclusions with very strong empirical support by using *unequivocal*, *certainly*, and other definitive language.

As with the between-college effects section of this summary chapter, the research reviewed falls into several broad categories of college experiences: residence, academic major, academic experiences, interpersonal involvement, extracurricular involvement, and academic achievement. As with between-college effects, we discuss all outcomes simultaneously within each of these experiential sections, and we start each section with findings from the two previous volumes.

Residence

The first volume of *How College Affects Students* concluded that living on campus (versus off campus) was perhaps the most consistent contributor to a range of college outcomes. Across both previous reviews, on-campus residence promoted openness to diversity, as well as positive and inclusive racial/ethnic attitudes. These patterns were stronger within residences that were designed to foster students' interactions with people and ideas that were different from their own. Living on campus also fostered student retention, persistence, and graduation. This relationship appeared to occur through several mechanisms, including greater participation in extracurricular activities, more frequent interactions with peers and faculty, more positive perceptions of the campus environment, and greater satisfaction with the college experience. Participation in a living-learning community seemed to promote educational attainment even more. Moreover, both reviews concluded that living on campus did not have any meaningful direct effect on learning and cognitive outcomes.

The strength and consistency of findings were greater in the first volume, which found positive effects for campus residence on aesthetic, cultural, and intellectual values; liberalization of attitudes and values; self-concepts; intellectual orientation, autonomy, and independence; empathy and ability to relate to others; and use of principled moral reasoning to judge moral issues. In contrast, residence was used less often as a variable of interest in the 1990s, and it was not appreciably related to self-esteem or locus of control. Moreover, research on living-learning communities found stronger evidence for their impact on persistence and degree attainment in the first volume than in the second, but these differences may reflect the fact that the programs examined during the 1990s tended to be less comprehensive in scope than those in prior research.

Continuing the trend from Volume 1 to Volume 2, research examining on-campus residence in the twenty-first century is sparse for most outcomes, and the findings often do not suggest benefits of this experience. Conflicting positive and negative findings are apparent for subject matter competence, cognitive outcomes, and diversity attitudes; the evidence is also inconclusive for educational and occupational values and for academic self-concept. Several studies even suggest that living on campus leads to lower psychological well-being, especially in the first year. In contrast, strong evidence suggests that living on campus contributes to greater retention and graduation (3.3–4.2 percentage points), and this effect appears to be explained by the greater social integration with the institution that may stem from living on campus. Some research also suggests that campus residence may bolster subject matter competence by promoting students' social and academic integration.

Although living on campus provides benefits for educational attainment, it is not clear why the relationships for other outcomes are so modest and inconsistent relative to those in earlier research, especially from the 1970s and 1980s. Some of the reductions in positive effects may be attributable to the improvements in methodology that have occurred over this time, as rigorous studies are better able to adjust for pre-existing differences between residents and commuters within and between institutions. Of course, the actual impact of campus residence may have decreased over time. Living on campus probably used to be a more immersive experience, with students within a residence hall communicating very frequently with one another and going home somewhat rarely. However, residents may be psychologically and physically less immersed on campuses today, given the proliferation and use of technology for communicating frequently with off-campus friends and family, the increase in suite- and apartment-style residence halls that are less conducive to peer interactions, and the greater prevalence of students with their own cars who leave campus on weekends.

In a specific form of campus residence, living-learning communities (LLCs), students live and take some courses together. The existing evidence suggests that LLC participation may contribute to some desired outcomes, including perceived gains in general education, orientation toward intellectual engagement, diversity appreciation, and student retention. Attending a summer bridge program with a residential component, which often takes the form of precollege living-learning communities for underrepresented students, is also often associated with greater retention. In contrast, results for cognitive skills are mixed, and there is no effect for social self-concept. The relatively positive findings for LLCs may be the result of the greater academic and social opportunities that are offered to—and sometimes required of—participating students.

Academic Major

Students' undergraduate major had a notable impact on numerous outcomes according to research in the previous two volumes. Not surprisingly, students made the greatest gains in knowledge and skills in subject matter areas that were consistent with their fields of study. Training in different fields of study also led to the development of different reasoning skills. However, the choice of major was often unrelated to generalized critical thinking and cognitive skills, with the exception that exposure to natural science courses contributed to students' critical thinking. Disciplines also tended to attract certain types of students and then accentuate preexisting differences among those students; some of this research used Holland's model to categorize types of majors and types of outcomes. Thus, for the most part, the effect of major on learning, cognition, and psychosocial growth was specific, rather than general, in nature.

The research on sociopolitical attitudes and values was inconclusive, although some general patterns were present. Students majoring in disciplines that emphasized social service and promoting others' welfare tended to exhibit greater gains in relevant values than students in other fields. Moreover, majoring in engineering and taking many quantitatively focused courses were negatively associated with liberal sociopolitical attitudes, and majoring in business, nursing, science, or engineering was associated with less improvement in racial/cultural attitudes and openness to diversity. Overall, these reviews concluded that the relationships for field of study may be more a product of students who choose those disciplines than the actual disciplinary content or experiences themselves.

Some effects of major field on graduation were also apparent; these appeared to be primarily driven by the favorable economic opportunities associated with a discipline (e.g., sciences, business, engineering, and health) and the culture and climate within a department. Shortly after graduation, students who majored in fields that prepared them for specific occupations or sectors, including computer science, engineering, social work, nursing, and accounting, tended to have a greater probability of securing a job and having a job that was appropriate to their bachelor's degree. In the long term, major field did not appear to have any consistent relationship with career mobility.

Gender dynamics were also apparent for occupational outcomes. According to findings from the second volume, majoring in traditionally male-dominated fields was associated with greater occupational status and earnings. After accounting for confounding characteristics, graduates from the highest-income majors made 25 to 35% more than those from the lowest-income majors. The top earning fields tended to be those that were male dominated and had a specific and well-defined set of knowledge and skills, an emphasis on quantitative or scientific methods, and a close relationship with occupations that had high average earnings. These patterns were more pronounced early in one's career, but the effects persisted long after graduation. One possible exception is that liberal arts degree recipients from selective institutions may have had greater earning potential, given the likelihood that they may have pursued graduate work that ultimately resulted in higher-paying jobs.

In our current review of the research, a great deal of inquiry explores post-college career, employment, and earnings. Undergraduate major has a strong influence on the job that students have after graduation. Graduates generally enter occupations that are consistent with their major, and this correspondence is more pronounced for majors that teach specific, applied skills, such as science, technology, engineering, and mathematics (STEM). Majors with high occupational specificity also tend to lead to higher-status occupations after graduation. Perhaps as a result, the congruence between major and occupation generally contributes to higher earnings (up to 25 to 50%), and this effect may increase over time. However, as one might expect, major-occupation congruence does not always lead to higher earnings, as some majors prepare graduates for relatively low-paying jobs. Consistent with previous volumes, the majors that lead to the greatest earnings have a well-defined body of content knowledge, center on quantitative or scientific skills, and have a direct functional alignment with specific occupations. High-paying majors include engineering, computer science and information technology, mathematics, and health science, while the lower-paying majors are in education and the humanities. Undergraduate major appears to affect specific aspects of job satisfaction (but not overall job satisfaction), and these effects are largely explained by differences in earnings.

Academic major is also associated with a variety of other outcomes during the college years, but the pattern across majors varies considerably depending on the type of outcome. Consistent with Pascarella and Terenzini (1991, 2005), increases in subject matter competence are much greater in areas of study that align with students' undergraduate majors. Some preliminary evidence suggests that careful arrangement of coursework into sequences may improve student learning and that cognitive development tends to be greatest in majors that are well supported by the institution. In contrast to previous reviews, some evidence suggests that growth in general education and cognitive skills is often greater in natural science and engineering majors, followed by social science majors, and then arts and humanities majors. However, these patterns vary somewhat across studies, and the use of self-reported gains casts doubt on these conclusions.

Major is also associated with religious and spiritual change, but the findings vary considerably across outcomes, and the relationships are generally small. Relative to students in other majors, engineering students tend to become less religiously engaged, engineering and mathematics majors tend to become less engaged in spiritual questing, and social science/education and business majors appear to become less committed to their religion or worldview. Moreover, English and social science majors become more religiously skeptical, whereas business majors may become less religiously skeptical and experience less religious struggle. In other psychosocial and value-based outcomes, major seems to be unrelated to self-esteem, and the only significant effect on educational and occupational values is for making a theoretical contribution to science; as one might expect, students majoring in the physical, biological, and health sciences become more likely to hold this value.

As with the prior review, some gendered patterns are also apparent. Academic dishonesty is higher in traditionally male-dominated majors; for instance, business majors exhibit more dishonest behavior, have higher tolerance for cheating, and believe that cheating is more justified than students in other majors. Science and engineering majors also have poorer moral outcomes than humanities and liberal arts majors, in which women tend to be well represented. Not surprisingly, majoring in some female-dominated fields (education, health, social sciences, and humanities) predicts greater likelihood of entering female-dominated occupations, and majoring in science predicts employment in male-dominated occupations. Female-dominated majors also lead to greater chances of employment in public and nonprofit organizations and in professional or managerial roles.

The evidence for academic major and educational attainment is somewhat mixed. While a number of studies find no significant relationship, some evidence suggests that students who have not declared a major are more likely to drop out, perhaps as a result of not having identified a particular career path. Some research also finds no link between a particular field of study and attainment. However, research that identifies significant relationships generally indicates that business, engineering, and health sciences have the highest retention rates, whereas humanities majors have the lowest. Thus, traditionally male-dominated majors tend to have greater persistence with the notable exception of health sciences, in which women have been (and are currently) very highly represented. To the extent that these differences reflect a causal relationship, this finding may be driven by the higher salaries that students may receive when graduating with a bachelor's degree in one of these fields. The other notable finding for educational attainment is that students whose vocational interests and academic major are well aligned (as measured by Holland types) have greater retention and degree completion.

Academic Experiences

The literature on students' academic experiences and subsequent outcomes in the first two reviews was voluminous, and it contained by far more experimental studies than any other topic. As a result of the immense size and scope of this previous research, we take a relatively large amount of space to discuss the findings from the prior reviews before moving on to findings from the twenty-first century. Overall, students' engagement in a variety of academic activities (e.g., library use, individual study, writing papers, reading unassigned books, and completing course assignments) was associated with greater knowledge acquisition and general intellectual growth. Pascarella and Terenzini (2005) argued that this was the key finding of this body of research: the extent to which students were highly engaged in academic opportunities largely determined the benefits that they received.

The pedagogical techniques that instructors used were also consistently related to subject matter learning. In particular, cooperative learning, small-group learning, collaborative learning, active learning, learning for mastery, computer-assisted instruction, and supplemental instruction were all associated with gains relative to traditional approaches. Positive effects for more specific classroom practices were also apparent, including peer tutoring, reciprocal training, attributional retraining, concept-knowledge mapping, and writing one-minute papers. The nature and quality of certain instructor behaviors also appeared to matter, as teacher preparation and organization, clarity, expressiveness and enthusiasm, availability and helpfulness, quality and frequency of feedback, concern for students, and rapport with students were all associated with greater acquisition of course content.

In a couple of instances, the relationship between academic experiences and learning was unclear. Some evidence from the 1990s indicated that class size was inversely related to mastery when defined in terms of grades. However, no such effect was apparent in one study for a standardized measure of knowledge, and earlier research often found no significant effect of class size. Moreover, students seemed to have similar levels of content mastery in distance education and face-to-face classes, but these studies did not sufficiently account for variables that might have reflected students' self-selection into different types of courses.

Several types of academic experiences led to improvements in cognition. The use of computers and computer programming languages was associated with greater general cognitive and critical thinking skills. Explicit instruction on critical thinking and problem solving appeared to bolster these outcomes, although these effects were somewhat modest. Problem-solving skills were also improved by learning in cooperative groups rather than other formats. Some equivocal evidence suggested that service-learning enhanced both cognitive development and course learning, especially when faculty integrated service experiences with course content and provided opportunities for reflection.

The same types of experiences were often associated with changes in psychosocial outcomes as well as in attitudes and values. Diversity-focused coursework promoted identity formation, academic self-concept, self-esteem, internal locus of attribution for success, general personal development, awareness of other ethnic groups and cultures, openness to diversity, desire to promote racial understanding, and dispositions toward community and civic engagement. In addition, service-learning courses appeared to help students define their identities; improve self-esteem, internal locus of control, and interpersonal skills; increase commitments to social justice, activism, and changing social/political structures; and promote a sense of social responsibility and civic engagement. Other influential experiences included having instructors who were women and people of color, taking workshops on social or cultural issues, and engaging with faculty through research and teaching.

Regarding other outcomes, numerous academic programs designed to promote learning, adjustment, and retention were positively associated with student persistence and completion, including first-year seminars, supplemental instruction, academic advising, summer bridge programs, undergraduate research programs, living-learning communities, and active and collaborative pedagogies. Career development courses and other interventions were also effective at promoting aspects of career maturity and development. Instructional interventions that encouraged moral dilemma discussion, used philosophical methods of ethical analysis, or integrated ethical content into professional curricula (among others) were all associated with greater postformal or principled moral reasoning.

Similar to Pascarella and Terenzini's (1991, 2005) previous reviews, an incredible amount of research in the 21st century examined academic experiences, including numerous quantitative meta-analyses and systematic reviews that synthesized various topics. The quality and quantity of this research is greater than that of any other subsection of within-college effects. Overall, this evidence supports the following conclusions:

1. The burgeoning literature on diversity-related coursework suggests that this experience promotes academic ability, writing ability, racial identity development, drive to achieve, intellectual self-confidence, competitiveness, leadership, well-being, personal and social development, civic attitudes and behaviors, positive diversity attitudes, gender-role progressiveness, and LGB attitudes. Diversity courses may also bolster cognitive and moral growth, but these findings are inconclusive.

2. Seemingly irrefutable evidence demonstrates that active and engaged learning practices yield substantial benefits over traditional lecture-based formats in which students passively receive information. These outcomes include greater verbal and quantitative skills, subject matter competence, cognitive and intellectual skills, openness to diversity, intercultural competence, leadership, citizenship, and moral development. Reflective and integrative learning practices also yield gains in leadership, openness to diversity, intercultural competence, citizenship, and moral learning. Moreover, instructional approaches that require

students to engage actively with course materials, including concept maps, summary writing, drawings, question prompts, and homework and frequent short assignments, improve learning.

3. As measured by overall student perceptions and faculty use of specific practices (such as preparation, organization, clarity, and expressiveness), instructional quality enhances learning, cognition, internal locus for success, psychological well-being, emotional health, moral development, retention, and graduation.

4. Forms of academic challenge, including faculty holding high expectations for students and promoting a scholarly environment, contribute to students' cognitive and intellectual skills, leadership, self-authorship, diversity knowledge and proclivities, lifelong learning orientation, autonomy, citizenship development, well-being, and moral growth.

5. Consistent with this finding, students' academic effort and involvement are positively related to desired outcomes, including intellectual and social gains, subject matter competence, personal and social competence, and retention (this last relationship appears to be explained by improvements in college GPA). However, studying and doing homework also have the potential to make students feel overwhelmed and less psychologically healthy.

6. Courses that are tailored toward achieving specific learning outcomes (including cognitive, moral, diversity, and career development) generally succeed in achieving these outcomes, and the effect sizes are sometimes large. Some mixed findings suggest that the relationship depends on the number of courses, type of courses, and student characteristics.

7. Online learning, which has proliferated since the previous review, yields mixed results across outcomes. Online courses may lead to greater content learning and less frequent cheating than face-to-face courses, whereas course format appears unrelated to cognitive growth. Although the evidence for course completion and retention is weak and inconclusive, online course taking does not promote completion, and it may have a detrimental effect.

8. The findings for class size are consistent with the previous volume. That is, class size is inversely related to learning and critical thinking in some studies but not others. In addition to the mixed results, the research is not sufficiently rigorous to draw strong conclusions.

9. On the whole, developmental (remedial) education does not seem to achieve its primary goals of improving academically underprepared students' content mastery and their likelihood of upward transfer, retention, and graduation. Students who successfully achieve remediation (by passing the first non-developmental course in that subject) fare as well as students who did not need remediation, but

developmental education students often do not accomplish that milestone. Some inquiry provides promising results for some developmental education designs, but this research awaits replication and extension.

10. Related to the previous point, comprehensive strategies for promoting student success that combine student services (such as academic advising, tutoring, mentoring) with curricular interventions (such as first-year seminars, learning communities, supplemental instruction, shorter-term developmental courses), financial aid, or other strategies have the potential to dramatically improve retention and graduation. Interestingly, the best evidence simultaneously suggests that some of these practices may not be effective individually, but they may be highly effective when several are implemented in a cohesive package. These integrated programs may also provide other benefits, such as cognitive and intellectual gains.

11. Participating in honors programs and course work seems to yield greater knowledge, learning, and academic and intellectual self-concepts. Learning communities and residential colleges also appear to promote intellectual and cognitive growth, and peer teaching through tutoring and supplemental instruction results in greater subject matter competence. In contrast to previous reviews, the research on learning communities and supplemental instruction as predictors of educational attainment is inconclusive, with a mix of positive and nonsignificant findings.

12. Service-learning appears to bolster learning, social skills, positive self-attitudes, personal insight (identity, self-awareness, self-efficacy), leadership, civic engagement and attitudes, political and social involvement, and diversity attitudes. Structured opportunity for reflection plays a key role in fostering these gains, with some evidence suggesting that verbal reflective discussion is more influential than written reflections. Findings for service-learning are mixed for predicting lifelong learning and moral development.

13. Enrollment intensity (in terms of the number of credits taken per academic term) and enrollment continuity (not stopping out in any academic-year term) both strongly contribute to degree completion and indicators of degree progress.

14. Although financial aid itself is not an academic experience, receiving aid makes it possible to engage in academic work. The research on this topic is voluminous and contradictory, but the best available evidence suggests that grants and scholarships promote retention, persistence, and graduation, along with some weaker evidence that work-study and loans also bolster educational attainment. Student debt and unmet need appear to hinder degree completion.

Interpersonal Involvement

The pre-2002 literature on students' interactions with peers and faculty provided important insights into the nature of interactions that best promoted student outcomes. Although general peer interactions seemed to promote a wide array of attitudes and values, as well as psychosocial and moral outcomes, these effects were particularly strong when students interacted with peers who were different from themselves, discussed issues of difference, and were exposed to ideas that were different from their own. Pascarella and Terenzini (2005) also concluded that peer interactions probably constituted the most powerful influence on persistence through at least two mechanisms: attraction to other students who were similar to themselves in various ways and socialization to peer group norms.

Faculty-student interactions outside the classroom were also associated with various desired outcomes, including cognitive growth, sociopolitical attitudes, career development, and persistence and degree completion. For cognitive and attitudinal outcomes, the effects were generally larger when these interactions focused on academic or intellectual issues. Multiple dynamics appeared to explain the link between faculty interactions and persistence; the two most notable were socializing students to normative values of the academy and promoting a bond between the student and the institution. However, the directionality of the link between faculty interactions and learning or cognitive outcomes was often unclear.

In the review for this volume, the most impressive and consistent findings for any form of interpersonal involvement occur for interpersonal diversity interactions. Strong evidence links these interactions to a wide variety of gains, including those in general education knowledge, academic competence, intellectual ability, cognition, racial identity and consciousness, religious/spiritual identity, positive masculinities, leadership capacity, self-authorship, well-being, personal/social development, civic and political attitudes, gender-role progressivism, LGB attitudes, artistic orientation, ecumenical worldview, and need for cognition (with mixed findings for career development). These effects are generally largest when the interactions are meaningful and positive in nature, and engaging in frequent interactions may be especially important for realizing some of these gains. Although negative diversity interactions can be harmful, such interactions can sometimes bolster student development. This list of positive findings is more impressive than that for general peer interactions, which suggests that the benefits of diversity experiences extend beyond simply those associated with peer engagement.

That said, overall peer interactions (regardless of with whom these interactions occur) probably have the second largest impact of any form of interpersonal experience, since they are positively related to general learning, cognition, racial identity, intellectual/academic self-concept, autonomy, well-being, moral development, retention/graduation, and expected career outcomes (with equivocal findings for need for cognition). The mechanisms through which peer experiences affect students depend somewhat on the outcome. These interactions can help students develop relationships and friendships that facilitate college adjustment, sense of belonging, institutional commitment, and retention; they can provide challenge that spurs various forms of growth and development; and they can make certain behaviors and attitudes seem normative and therefore desirable.

Considerable research in the twenty-first century has explored the potential impact of faculty-student interaction, which appears to promote various indicators of psychosocial change, attitudes and values, moral development, and career aspirations and preparation. The findings suggest that both support and challenge from faculty bolster academic self-concept, leadership, political and civic engagement, and moral development. The frequency of faculty interactions, especially those perceived as positive, are also related to increased psychological well-being, emotional health, general personal and social development, gender-role progressivism, and ecumenical worldview. Perceiving negative interactions with or reactions from faculty leads to some declines in outcomes such as academic self-concept. Faculty encouragement of religious and spiritual discussions appears to shape relevant outcomes, including increases in spiritual quest, equanimity, religious commitment, religious engagement, religious skepticism, and religious struggle. Moreover, attending an institution with a greater proportion of full-time faculty members seems to bolster retention and degree completion; this effect may be explained through greater academic integration with the institution, but it is unclear what behaviors or attributes of full-time faculty are responsible for this increased integration.

Contrary to the prior reviews, faculty interactions are consistently unrelated (at least directly) to retention and graduation, and the evidence is mixed for general education, academic skills, and subject matter competence. Faculty interactions may promote cognitive growth, but some findings also suggest no such relationship. As Pascarella and Terenzini (2005) noted, one of the challenges of determining the impact of faculty is whether faculty interactions lead to student outcomes or vice versa. For instance, some faculty-student interactions are likely spurred by poor performance on an assignment or exam, which either leads students to seek out faculty for assistance or leads faculty to ask those students to come to their office. These interactions would be the result of struggles in learning or cognition rather than the interactions themselves leading to negative outcomes (as some research has suggested).

Cutting across social and academic environments, the fit or match between student and institutional characteristics has received some attention. Although methodological issues prevent us from drawing strong conclusions, most research finds that student-institution fit is positively related to retention and graduation, whether these attributes of fit are specific to religious/spiritual aspects of college or across several academic, social, and environmental domains.

Finally, some research has examined the presence of a generally supportive environment, which may be the result of interactions with students, faculty, and staff members. Perceptions of a supportive environment appear to bolster learning, cognition, identity development, and personal and social development. Perceiving support may be an important prerequisite for students to engage meaningfully in academic and social pursuits that foster growth. Conversely, perceptions of a hostile campus climate—whether specific to diversity or general to the overall institutional milieu—appears to lead to lower intellectual ability, cognitive development, well-being, college satisfaction, institutional commitment, retention, persistence, and graduation.

Extracurricular Involvement

The findings regarding extracurricular involvement varied notably across the types of outcomes, and research from the 1990s focused heavily on exploring three types of involvement: athletic participation, fraternity/sorority affiliation, and paid employment. In general, participation in intercollegiate athletics was negatively associated with learning and cognitive development. However, athletes also fared better than non-athletes on several outcomes, including degree completion, civic values, community orientation, social self-confidence, and interpersonal skills. Athletic participation showed little or no significant relationship for many outcomes, such as moral reasoning, academic dishonesty, leadership skills, internal locus of control, and social and political dispositions.

Research on fraternity/sorority affiliation also exhibited mixed findings across outcomes and only modestly supported some of the conclusions. The strongest conclusions were that fraternity or sorority membership negatively affected racial/ethnic attitudes and openness to diverse ideas and people. In contrast, affiliation was positively related to students' development of interpersonal skills, community orientation, and commitment to civic engagement. Other findings varied over time; the negative effects on knowledge acquisition and critical thinking seemed to dissipate after the first year, and the greater engagement in binge drinking disappeared after college graduation.

Employment had a clear, nonlinear effect on educational attainment, such that working more than 15 to 20 hours a week was associated with a greater likelihood of attrition. Some tentative evidence further suggested that working a small number of hours or doing so on campus was positively related to persistence and completion. A smaller number of studies examined other outcomes; working appeared to contribute to greater career-related skills and employment after college, but also to less principled moral reasoning and lower involvement in community service.

Research in the twenty-first century examined a broader range of involvement. The two experiences that are among the most influential were rarely examined in the prior review: participation in student clubs/groups and religious/spiritual engagement. Overall engagement in student organizations is positively associated with retention/graduation and the development of leadership skills, intellectual and academic self-concept, and positive masculinities (although the evidence for cognitive outcomes is mixed). Participation in ethnic student organizations specifically contributes to some of these same outcomes as well as racial identity development. Religious and spiritual engagement is associated with increased well-being and civic outcomes, and spiritual development may lead to higher grades, degree aspirations, leadership, and self-esteem. These forms of engagement are also positively related to gender-role traditionalism and religious/social conservatism.

Two other extracurricular experiences lead to mostly positive outcomes. Employment is positively related to autonomy, citizenship, moral formation, and post-college earnings. As with the prior review, some tentative evidence suggests that working on campus or in small amounts (no more than 10 hours per week) may promote retention, but working full time or close to full time leads to greater attrition from college. Working off-campus part time may promote gender-typical career choices for women. Results for learning and cognitive gains are inconclusive, but working on-campus may lead to cognitive growth. Community service participation also appears to contribute to student outcomes, including increases in various domains of religion/spirituality, leadership capacity, civic/community values, and orientation toward female-dominated careers; the evidence is less clear for political engagement and social justice learning.

The outcomes of fraternity and sorority membership have become highly contested. The findings in our review are fairly consistent with the previous volume. Fraternity/sorority participation appears to promote leadership capacity and volunteerism, although it may also lead to patriarchal masculinities (among men), less favorable attitudes toward diversity, and greater academic dishonesty. Evidence on several important outcomes is mixed, including learning, academic achievement, cognitive skills, civic attitudes, and educational values. In addition, when measured independently from fraternity/sorority involvement, partying and drinking are associated with reductions in well-being, religious commitment, and religious engagement.

In another controversial domain, varsity athletic participation is associated with greater well-being and retention, as well as lower career maturity and greater patriarchal masculinities among men. We found no consistent relationship of varsity athletics with learning, academic achievement, leadership, and postcollege earnings, which is often inconsistent with the earlier reviews. In a somewhat related set of experiences, exercise and fitness center use appear to be associated with well-being and may even contribute to subject matter competence and career development. However, intramural sports participation is unrelated to bachelor's degree completion.

Finally, for some assorted findings, tutoring other students predicts greater intellectual and academic self-concept, leadership training appears to succeed in promoting leadership capacity and civic values, and cultural event attendance predicts increased understanding of arts and humanities. The link between receiving mentoring and educational attainment is unclear.

Academic Achievement

In both prior reviews, undergraduate grades were identified as the single strongest contributor to persistence and degree completion. Grades in the first year of college were particularly important in predicting persistence, timely graduation, and graduation overall. College GPA also positively affected obtaining employment soon after graduation, occupational status, and earnings; these relationships were both direct and indirect (through improving the likelihood of receiving a degree). Evidence linking grades to job satisfaction and mobility was less clear.

In this third volume, academic achievement once again constitutes the strongest within-college predictor of retention, persistence, and graduation. These findings are consistent across various types of students and institutions, as well as in different countries, and they persist even when accounting for a wide array of precollege and college variables, including academic and social integration. However, contrary to findings from Volume 2, the relationship between grades and attrition is generally consistent regardless of students' year in college. This recent research adds to the prior literature by providing insights into the mechanisms through which this effect likely occurs. Some students achieve grades that are so low that they are academically dismissed from the institution, but this forced attrition clearly does not account for most of the impact of academic achievement. In addition, grades serve as a means through which students receive feedback about their performance and ability, and they make choices about transferring or dropping out based on whether they feel that they can succeed at that institution or in college in general. Considerable direct and indirect evidence provides support for this explanation; one study estimated that this grade feedback mechanism may account for up to 40% of attrition between the first and second year of college.

Contrary to prior conclusions, the evidence for college grades and post-college economic outcomes is often mixed, including for number of hours worked, occupation type, and earnings. Some evidence does suggest that college grades bolster earnings, but other studies find no significant relationship. Moreover, grades may promote job satisfaction after college even when accounting for college experiences and postcollege employment characteristics.

The findings for the wide array of within-college effects for all outcomes are briefly summarized in Table 10.4.

Table 10.4 Within-College Effects: Main Findings

Experiences	Volumes 1 and 2	Volume 3
Residence	In Volume 1, on-campus living had the most consistent positive effects of any college experience on various outcomes. Volume 2 identified some benefits, but fewer than Volume 1 did.	Campus residence promotes retention and possibly promotes learning, but it predicts decreases in psychological well-being. Evidence is mixed for cognition, values, diversity attitudes, and academic self-concept.

(continued)

Table 10.4 Within-College Effects: Main Findings (continued)

Experiences	Volumes 1 and 2	Volume 3
Academic major	Major shaped numerous outcomes, especially earnings, job status, and learning (majors promoted field-specific knowledge and skills). Gender composition of major was often relevant to these effects.	Many findings from prior volumes are replicated, including mixed evidence for cognitive skills and educational attainment. Major may also shape religion, spirituality, and moral reasoning and behavior.
Academic experiences	Active learning approaches, specific teaching practices, and instructional quality all improved learning. Diversity and service-learning courses affected attitudes and psychosocial outcomes. Interventions to promote retention and courses designed to promote specific learning outcomes were generally successful. Overall academic effort and engagement bolstered learning and cognition.	Earlier findings are often replicated, except that evidence for retention-related efforts is now mixed, and diversity courses improve more outcomes. Online courses might promote learning but undermine retention. Remediation is often ineffective, but success strategies that combine student services and curricular approaches can be highly successful. Although not an academic experience itself, financial aid often improves degree completion.
Interpersonal involvement	Peer and faculty interactions promoted a host of desired outcomes. Effects were larger for peer interactions that involved diversity and faculty interactions that focused on academic issues.	Peer interactions, especially across difference, promote numerous desired outcomes. Faculty interactions often seem beneficial, but evidence is mixed for some outcomes. Providing both support and challenge is important.
Extracurricular involvement	Volume 1 found overall level of involvement increased retention and social self-concept. In Volume 2, Greek life, athletics, and paid employment had effects that varied based on the outcome.	Student clubs/groups, religious engagement, paid employment, and community service often improve desired outcomes. Findings for Greek life and athletics are generally consistent with Volume 2.

(continued)

Table 10.4 Within-College Effects: Main Findings (continued)

Experiences	Volumes 1 and 2	Volume 3
Academic achievement	College grades were the strongest contributor to persistence and graduation. GPA also had direct and indirect effects on employment, job status, and earnings.	College grades have the strongest within-college effect on educational attainment. Grades appear to increase job satisfaction; the evidence is mixed for earnings, employment, and type of job.

CONDITIONAL EFFECTS OF COLLEGE

The previous discussion summarizes general findings about different types of effects. However, these findings may vary based on student characteristics, such that students from different groups may experience different amounts of change during college, net effects of attending college, and effects of either attending a particular type of college or having particular experiences during college. The examination of these conditional effects increased substantially in the 1990s relative to earlier decades. Pascarella and Terenzini (2005) reported a large number of results that generally fell into three categories: net effects of college that depended on student characteristics (e.g., demographics, precollege preparation), between-college effects that depended on student characteristics, and within-college effects that depended on student characteristics. Many of these findings were from only one study, and these results often were not replicated across samples. Therefore, this summary of results from the previous two volumes focuses selectively on the results that were replicated multiple times.

According to the earlier reviews, African Americans received greater earnings benefits from receiving a bachelor's degree than did Whites. Women generally had a greater boost in earnings than men from receiving a postsecondary degree or certificate, whereas men received a greater increase in occupational status from postsecondary attainment than did women. For between-college effects, the negative relationship between starting at a two-year (versus a four-year) institution and bachelor's degree attainment was similar regardless of gender and race/ethnicity. College quality had a similar effect on earnings for women and men, and students of color benefited economically from attending a selective institution at least as much as White students. Women and men both exhibited some improved outcomes from having a major in which they were traditionally in the minority. Higher-ability students seemed to benefit more from information technology, whereas lower-ability students may have benefited more from some teaching practices. Finally, with perhaps the strongest evidence of all prior conditional effects, students had much greater knowledge acquisition when they received instruction that matched their preferred learning style than when they did not.

The number of studies and analyses that examined conditional effects ballooned even more in the twenty-first century, with the largest number of conditional effects related to race/ethnicity, gender, socioeconomic status, and academic achievement. Therefore, to keep this review of Volume 3 at a reasonable length and to focus on findings that are more generalizable, we also discuss findings that have received some degree of replication in this summary of recent findings. This standard differs somewhat depending on outcome type. The topics of psychosocial change, attitudes, and values cover such a large range of specific outcomes that we decided that "replication" can occur by finding the same conditional effect on two related outcomes within the same study (as opposed to the same result on the same outcome in different studies). The organization of the summary that follows is intended to illustrate the consistencies and disparities of these conditional effects across outcomes.

Many of the replicated findings from Volumes 1 and 2 were also observed within the research covered in this volume: (1) students learn more when the type of instruction they receive matches their preferred learning style; (2) the impact of institutional type (four-year versus two-year) and selectivity on educational attainment is similar across groups and, if anything, slightly larger for students of color; (3) Blacks receive a substantially larger earnings premium than Whites from years in college (about twice as large) and from degree completion, and (4) women receive greater earnings benefits than men from college graduation. Although this last overall finding is consistent with the prior review, the largest conditional effect of gender is now for bachelor's degrees (45% greater boost for women) with a much smaller disparity for graduate degrees (5–10%). In Volume 2, the most pronounced difference was for associate's degrees (about a 50% greater benefit for women).

One notable pattern in the recent research is that students who have lower academic performance or are from underserved groups often benefit more from a variety of experiences. Specifically, lower-achieving students have greater learning gains than higher-achieving students from participating in some effective classroom practices (similar to prior findings), and first-year seminars may bolster retention and graduation more for students who initially have lower academic performance. In a somewhat related finding, students from several historically underserved groups that have lower retention and graduation rates on average seem to benefit more from financial aid (particularly grants and scholarships), including students from lower socioeconomic backgrounds, students of color, and students attending two-year or less-selective four-year schools. Several academic and cocurricular experiences may have a positive impact only for first-generation students on internal locus for academic success and openness to diversity. Although these conditional patterns help reduce long-standing disparities, the greater earnings premiums for the educational attainment of Blacks and women discussed earlier only partially reduce inequalities in pay relative to Whites and men, respectively. Students from lower socioeconomic backgrounds also experience a larger jump in earnings from attending a selective institution than do their higher-SES counterparts, which suggests the role that these schools can play in fostering social mobility.

These compensatory findings are not universal across outcomes, however, especially when pertaining to race and ethnicity. Studies provide conflicting findings about whether the net effects of college on employment and learning outcomes vary by demographics and academic ability. When examining changes during four years of college, Black, Latino, and Asian American students have smaller cognitive gains than do White students. Moreover, all students generally benefit from campus diversity experiences, but the effects of diversity experiences on cognitive outcomes and of diversity coursework on multiple outcomes are sometimes larger for White students than for students of color. For other race-related experiences and conditional effects, campus racial climate has a direct effect only on retention and persistence among students of color (such that a hostile climate leads to lower attainment), whereas attending an institution with a sizable proportion of high-achieving, same-race peers may bolster the cognitive and intellectual outcomes of Black and Latino students. Clearly, racial dynamics are still salient on campus and play a differential role in shaping student outcomes.

The numerous studies of conditional effects by gender produced a fair number of replicated results within and across studies, but these findings do not seem to fit within a single overarching explanation. Educational attainment appears to affect women more than men in terms of their postcollege well-being and political participation (although the latter disparity appears to be shrinking over time). Moreover, women who feel that faculty do not take them seriously have reduced health and greater political and social engagement, but these patterns do not occur among men. Receiving honest feedback from faculty also predicts improvements in health among women but not men. However, men are sometimes more affected by faculty interactions than women, especially for predicting occupational orientations and racial understanding. Men who challenge faculty in class also have greater social activism and feel less overwhelmed, whereas women who challenge faculty actually feel more overwhelmed. It appears that the type of experience may drive some of these disparate faculty-related results, with negative experiences being more influential for women and challenging faculty more beneficial for men.

Gendered patterns for major also yield some replicated findings, but no overarching explanation seems to account for all of these conditional effects across different outcomes. Academic major predicts changes in scholar self-confidence, math self-confidence, and physical health for men only. In contrast, major is more closely tied to racial understanding among women than men, and women who graduate in a non-STEM major are more likely to take a job that is closely related to their undergraduate major than are men with degrees in non-STEM majors. The link between undergraduate major and postcollege earnings premiums also differs by gender, with women receiving greater benefits from some majors and men achieving greater gains in others. Major could be a source of peer effects that more strongly influence men's self-confidence and physical health. However, that interpretation is inconsistent with other evidence: similar relationships occur across gender for interpersonal experiences (i.e., diverse peer interactions and relationships with faculty) predicting leadership, and larger effects among women are apparent for socializing with friends and taking honors classes predicting leadership capacity.

Conditional effects are also associated with students' religious/worldview identification. Relative to their mainline Protestant peers, students who are religious minorities within the broader society and at their college campus have diminished well-being on religiously affiliated campuses and decreased spiritual outcomes at Catholic schools. Thus, the potential marginalization of students' religions/worldviews on a particular campus may affect their psychosocial (and potentially other) outcomes. Regardless of institution, the development of ecumenical worldview during college appears to differ among religious and non-religious students, and these dynamics may further interact with students' racial and gender identities.

Additional assorted conditional effects pertain to several student and institutional characteristics. Self-authorship tends to occur earlier among racial and sexual minority students and other students who are at risk for attrition, which may be attributable to these students' provocative experiences associated with their identity development. Student experiences with faculty are more strongly related to positive attitudes toward literacy among students of color than White students. The associations between institutional type and graduates' subsequent vocational preparation and job satisfaction are also stronger for students of color than for White students. The link between good practices and learning is generally consistent across institutional type. Finally, among varsity student-athletes, academic activities are more strongly related to cognitive and intellectual outcomes for those in low-profile sports than for those in high-profile sports.

Table 10.5 contains an overview of the conditional effects that had replicated findings.

Table 10.5 Conditional Effects: Main Findings

Characteristic	Volumes 1 and 2	Volume 3
Race/ethnicity	Blacks had greater increases in earnings from a bachelor's degree. Similar effects by race for attending four-year colleges and bachelor's completion as well as school quality and earnings.	Blacks have greater increases in earnings from a bachelor's degree. Similar effects by race for four-year colleges and selectivity on bachelor's completion. Students of color receive greater increases in attainment from financial aid along with other benefits, but also decreased attainment from hostile campus racial climate and lower cognitive gains during college.

(continued)

Table 10.5 Conditional Effects: Main Findings (continued)

Characteristic	Volumes 1 and 2	Volume 3
Gender	Women had greater increases in earnings from college degree; men had greater increases in job status. Similar effects by gender for four-year colleges and bachelor's completion, as well as school quality and earnings. Being in a gender-minority major increased multiple outcomes for men and women.	Women have greater increases in postcollege well-being, political participation, and earnings from a college degree. Similar effects by gender for four-year colleges and selectivity on bachelor's attainment. Effects of faculty experiences and major vary by gender, with patterns depending on the type of experience and the outcome.
Socioeconomic status (SES)	No consistent replicated findings were identified.	Lower-SES students receive greater increases in attainment from financial aid and increased earnings from selective schools; they also receive larger benefits from several academic experiences.
Religion/ worldview	No consistent replicated findings were identified.	Religious minority students have relative decreases in well-being at religiously affiliated schools and in spirituality at Catholic schools. Ecumenical worldview development differs for religious and non-religious students.
Academic ability	Higher-achieving students may have benefited more in learning from technology use; lower-achieving students may have benefited more from some teaching practices.	Lower-achieving students have greater increases in learning from participating in effective classroom practices and greater retention from attending first-year seminars.
Other characteristics	Students had increased learning when instruction matched preferred learning style. Link between four-year school and attribution for academic success was similar by age and entering academic attributions.	Students have increases in learning when instruction matches preferred learning style. Link between classroom practices and learning is similar by institutional type. Self-authorship occurs earlier in college among students who are at-risk for attrition.

LONG-TERM EFFECTS OF COLLEGE

In the previous two reviews, the long-term effects of college attendance and completion were almost uniformly positive across the outcomes that were examined, including cognition, psychosocial dimensions, attitudes and values, moral reasoning, occupation and earnings, quality of life, and even intergenerational transmission of the benefits of college to one's children. In particular, the second volume highlighted mechanisms through which these long-term benefits accrued, and some of these were roughly similar across outcomes. First, postsecondary educational attainment directly led to better employment outcomes and higher earnings. Second, people who graduated from college tended to have different interests, experiences, and opportunities from those who did not, and these post-college experiences then contributed to a variety of outcomes. Such postcollege lifestyle differences could have resulted from different choices that were available to people from various educational backgrounds, whereas others were afforded by college graduates' ability to obtain higher-status occupations that often provided greater self-directedness, health/vacation benefits, and earnings.

For the most part, the findings from this review of long-term effects are generally consistent with those from earlier research in terms of overall patterns and mechanisms that explain those patterns. Recent studies have shifted to pay somewhat more attention to between- and within-college effects rather than net effects (especially for psychosocial change and for attitudes and values), which provides new insights into how specific aspects of the college experience may have a long-term impact. Some recent findings also differ from those of earlier research; for instance, education appears to have a positive impact on several forms of postcollege well-being and satisfaction (whereas little or no total effect was apparent in both prior volumes), and the impact of bachelor's degree attainment on income appears to be smaller than in previous decades. The summary of findings from both previous reviews and the current review is organized by outcome type: socioeconomic, learning and cognitive development, psychosocial change, attitudes and values, moral development, quality of life, and intergenerational effects.

Socioeconomic Outcomes

Volume 2 of *How College Affects Students* provided specific estimates for the impact of educational attainment on socioeconomic outcomes. Receiving a bachelor's degree (versus a high school diploma) resulted in a very high .95 standard deviation (SD) increase in occupational status, 37 to 39% greater earnings, and 28 to 35% higher wages, whereas receiving an associate's degree yielded a .24 to .44 SD improvement in occupational status and about 23% greater earnings (27% for women and 18% for men). A vocational degree or license/certificate provided a .12 to .22 SD increase in occupational status, but earnings differences could not be calculated reliably.

The second volume also determined the credentialing effect of college, which is the increase in earnings associated with degree attainment as opposed to completing the appropriate number of years without receiving the degree (e.g., four years of college credits but no bachelor's). Credentialing effects resulted in 12 to 15% greater earnings at four-year schools and 9 to 11% greater earnings at two-year schools. Even when considering the costs associated with college attendance (e.g., tuition and fees, books, possibly reduced earnings while enrolled in college), bachelor's degree attainment still provided individuals with notable economic benefits (12% return on investment) as well as greater employment stability.

In literature from the twenty-first century, postsecondary education leads to increased economic and career outcomes, including the likelihood of employment, more hours worked per week, occupational status, overall job satisfaction, and earnings. The earnings premiums for associate's degrees, vocational degrees/certificates, and attending one year of college are all similar to those from the previous review. In general, receiving a higher degree is associated with a greater earnings boost, and each year of college attended provides earning benefits as well (5 to 9% per year of college, with larger benefits occurring after college attendance). Compared with the findings from the 1990s, the estimated impact of having a bachelor's degree (versus a high school diploma) is smaller for annual income (20%) and wages (22 to 25%), whereas the estimated return on investment for a bachelor's degree actually increased slightly (12 to 14% and potentially as high as 15 to 20%). While these changes over time might reflect different workforce and market conditions, they could simply be the result of different research methodologies used in these time periods. The convergence between values for earnings/income and return on investment (also known as the private rate of return) may mean that recent research more accurately determines the economic premiums of college attendance and degree attainment. On the whole, an undergraduate degree continues to be a sound economic investment despite increases in tuition at both public and private schools.

Research on graduate degrees and earnings identified effects that differed dramatically by the type of degree, with research finding the lowest gains from non-business master's degrees (11%), followed by MBA and doctorate (both 33%), and then JD (71%) and MD (115%). Similar to undergraduate degrees, the earnings premiums are notably smaller in the first few years after graduation than later in life.

Learning and Cognitive Development

In the first two volumes, the evidence was not always strong methodologically, but it consistently supported the conclusion that college-educated adults had a greater knowledge base and critical thinking skills than those who did not attend college. College attendance appeared not only to increase the capacity for lifelong learning, but it also crystallized the predisposition to engage in lifelong learning and intellectual development. Indeed, the greater participation in post-college learning activities seemed to stem from graduates' access to a combination of greater resources that provide such opportunities (such as books, magazines, travel, computers, and so on) and a greater inclination to seek out learning opportunities that could not be explained by income, occupation, and other confounding factors. The persistence of learning and cognitive gains over time seemed to be largely attributable to differences in these post-college learning behaviors between college and high school graduates.

Research on the long-term effects for learning and cognitive development in the twenty-first century is quite limited, but the findings are consistent with those from previous reviews. Verbal and quantitative competence as well as cognitive skills and tendencies are all stronger among college-educated adults than among adults with a high school diploma; however, these studies provide limited evidence that college attendance itself caused these learning and cognitive differences. Educational attainment is also associated with newspaper reading, and parents with higher education expose their children to substantially more civic information. Moreover, adults with greater literacy levels (who are overwhelmingly more likely to be college educated) engage more frequently in learning-oriented behaviors, including consuming information about current events and public affairs, reading to their children, and helping their children with homework. This evidence provides some support for the assertion that the impact of college is explained, at least to some extent, by greater participation in learning activities and opportunities.

Psychosocial Change

Research in the late twentieth century on long-term psychosocial outcomes was sparse. Studies of identity formation often proposed that identity shifts in college persisted to at least age 30, but it is difficult to disentangle whether these findings were attributable to attending college or to normal maturation and life span development. The limited evidence suggested that college attendance may have had lasting positive effects on self-concept, internal locus of control, and well-being, along with reductions in authoritarianism. Volume 1 found a positive effect on self-esteem, but Volume 2 suggested that no such effect existed. Some of these relationships appeared to be indirect, through greater post-college occupational success.

The evidence on psychosocial outcomes is also quite limited in the twenty-first century. The few available findings—which cover a diverse array of topics—focus primarily on between- and within-college effects rather than net effects. Attending an HBCU instead of a predominantly White institution may contribute to Black graduates' psychological outcomes (such as self-image and self-esteem), which in turn bolster their labor market outcomes. However, HBCU attendance is not related to self-reported subject matter ability relative to one's peers. College curricular and cocurricular diversity experiences among all students predict personal growth and purpose in adulthood, and these relationships are mediated by graduates' prosocial orientation. Additional research explored self-authorship (i.e., the extent to which people define their own beliefs, identity, and social relationships) among college graduates in their forties. Extending prior theory, three additional positions on the self-authored meaning-making structure were defined and delineated: trusting the internal voice (feeling empowered to internally direct responses to external events), building an internal foundation (establishing a core framework to direct actions and responses to the external world), and securing external commitments (moving from knowing about one's internal foundation to living consistently with the commitments it represents).

Attitudes and Values

Both of the first two reviews strongly supported several key conclusions. First, college had a lasting impact on graduates' sociopolitical, cultural, and gender-role attitudes, which generally shifted in a sociopolitically liberal direction during college and remained fairly stable after college. Second, the persistence of these effects appeared to be driven by two mechanisms: (1) college graduates tended to surround themselves with other graduates who shared their views, and (2) college attendance shaped values both directly by providing knowledge of relevant issues and indirectly by providing social and cultural capital. Third, college substantially promoted civic and community involvement, including voting in elections, participating in political activities and discussions, actively engaging in community welfare groups, and committing to community leadership. These patterns were stronger among graduates who had obtained a bachelor's degree than an associate's degree (relative to having a high school diploma). Fourth, college had a sizable impact on occupational values, which were likely reinforced by higher-status postcollege jobs that reflected those values.

Similar to recent research on psychosocial change, inquiry on long-term effects of attitudes and values in the twenty-first century primarily explored between- and within-college factors associated with these postcollege outcomes. At the institutional level, selectivity, size, control, and structural diversity all exhibit mixed findings when predicting long-term civic and political outcomes. Structural diversity and campus climate may promote post-college pluralistic orientation through their roles in increasing cross-racial interaction during college. It is possible that the mixed civic and political findings might be reconciled if future researchers examine indirect effects of institutional characteristics on outcomes that occur through college experiences.

For within-college effects, community engagement during college predicts postcollege civic outcomes, but these findings depend on the nature of the college experience. Students who gain internal benefits from service (such as becoming more socially conscious) tend to continue their community engagement after graduation, whereas this is not the case for students who emphasize external benefits (such as vocational advancement). Moreover, service-learning promotes civic leadership, charitable giving, and political engagement, but students' reflection on their service experiences during the course is crucial for realizing long-term growth.

Experiences with interpersonal, curricular, and cocurricular diversity appear to promote pluralistic orientation and recognition of racism well after college, and these effects are generally mediated by prosocial orientation at the end of college. Racial/cultural awareness workshops and ethnic studies courses may also have indirect effects on civic engagement. Finally, for undergraduate majors, students who receive business, science, and engineering degrees have decreased civic development during college, and these differences persist after graduation.

Moral Development

Volume 1 included the greatest amount of inquiry on moral development, and that review provided strong evidence of the positive influence of college. People who attended college made greater gains in the use of principled moral reasoning during college than those who did not attend, and this gap actually increased during the six years after college. Evidence from Volume 2 provided modest evidence that was consistent with this conclusion: college graduates experienced some growth in moral reasoning after graduation, but it was unclear whether non-college attendees might have similar or different patterns of change over the same time period.

The review in this volume identified no studies that could provide meaningful insight into postcollege moral development. This lack of research may be a result of the time and cognitive demands required for assessing moral reasoning through conventional measures, the difficulty of finding college alumni, and the need to obtain comparable non-college comparison groups to draw strong conclusions about net effects.

Quality of Life

According to evidence from the first two volumes, college appeared to have a positive causal influence on quality of life in adulthood. The strongest evidence pointed to health outcomes: educational attainment reduced the likelihood of specific health problems, risk factors for prevalent diseases, and mortality at any age. In fact, even when accounting for health risk factors and age, college education had a direct effect on reduced mortality. Healthy lifestyle was a major mechanism through which these effects operated, as more educated adults were less likely to smoke cigarettes, abuse alcohol, and have high cholesterol; education also had a positive effect on exercise and a healthy diet. These improvements in lifestyle may have been attributable to people with college degrees having better access to health information and making better health decisions when provided with the same information. Other relevant mechanisms included having occupations and financial resources that facilitated higher-quality health care, as well as having a greater orientation toward planning for the future (including for long-term health outcomes).

Although the research was not quite as strong, evidence from the two prior reviews also suggested that parental education improves children's well-being through greater prenatal care, involvement in children's school, reading to children, and providing access to computer resources. Early studies also suggested that college-educated adults spent a greater proportion of discretionary time and resources on developmentally enriching activities (such as reading and involvement in cultural events and civic affairs), saved a greater percentage of their income, and made more effective long-term investments with their resources. Job satisfaction and overall life satisfaction were not appreciably associated with educational attainment; some evidence suggests that postsecondary degrees simultaneously have positive indirect effects on these forms of satisfaction (through financial resources, the nature of occupational tasks, and internal locus of control) yet negative direct effects (which may be the result of having a more critical perspective or viewing satisfaction in qualitatively different ways).

According to evidence from the current review, higher education (whether defined by number of years or degree attainment) results in a better quality of life across a variety of indicators. In contrast to the prior two volumes, research in the twenty-first century suggests that educational attainment may yield greater subjective well-being, happiness, life satisfaction, and sense of control, as well as protecting against depression and depressive symptomatology. The potential causal mechanisms for these differences include richer and more satisfying interpersonal relationships, as well as more favorable employment and working conditions. It is unclear why these results diverge from those of earlier research, but the apparent prevalence of both social and occupational explanations for this effect on well-being suggests that multiple factors may be responsible (assuming that this divergence over time is not a statistical anomaly).

The strongest evidence from the twenty-first century is consistent with that of previous reviews: postsecondary education contributes to more favorable health outcomes, regardless of whether these are based on self-reports, actual mortality, or other measures. In fact, this pattern is so well established across international contexts that it is called the "education-health gradient." Healthier lifestyles among college-educated adults still play a key role in explaining these dynamics, including lower likelihood of smoking, greater smoking cessation among those who already smoke, a healthier diet, and greater moderate and vigorous exercise. Educational attainment is positively associated with alcohol use, but attainment is negatively related to binge drinking and alcohol dependency.

College education also has a positive effect on engaging in volunteering, community service, and overall social trust. The evidence is somewhat more mixed, but seems to be positive on the whole, for political involvement and voting behavior. One study suggests that this educational benefit may be diminishing over time. We discuss the findings for child welfare in more detail in the next section, but parental education appears to bolster children's short-term and long-term health and educational success.

Intergenerational Effects

The benefits of college may accrue not only to those who attend, but they may also be passed on to the children of college graduates. As discussed in the first two volumes, children of parents with bachelor's degrees were much more likely to earn a bachelor's degree than were students whose parents had not attended college. Similar (but smaller) effects were apparent when comparing students whose parents had some college to students whose parents had no college experience. Parental education also had a notable effect on children's knowledge acquisition, which seemed to be largely explained by differences in the learning capital available in their home environments. Some of these family environment mechanisms (such as involvement in and promotion of children's learning and providing resources for such activities) have been reviewed earlier in this chapter, because intergenerational effects on children's well-being were reviewed within the quality-of-life section in the prior volumes of this book. Early evidence suggested similar intergenerational benefits for children's job status, early career earnings, and (for women) entering a high-paying, male-dominated profession.

Consistent with earlier results, twenty-first-century findings indicate that parental education provides benefits for their children's physical health; these include greater birth weight, childhood health and exercise, and even health in adulthood. Parental education also has positive effects on high school students' civic engagement and political knowledge. Given that college-educated adults are more engaged and informed civically and politically, the link between parent-child political discussions and various child outcomes (including news consumption, political knowledge, and community participation) provides evidence for an indirect effect of intergenerational transmission.

Recent research also provides strong evidence for intergenerational effects of college on children's educational attainment. These benefits may accrue because the children of college-educated parents are more likely to attend college in the first place, and those who attend are more likely to graduate from college than are first-generation college students. In fact, the relationships between parental education and students' retention, persistence, and graduation are only partially explained by standardized test scores, high school achievement, financial aid, and college achievement. It appears that parents' attainment of a bachelor's degree (versus other levels of undergraduate and graduate education) is particularly meaningful for transmitting postsecondary educational benefits to their children.

Table 10.6 provides an overview of findings from all three volumes on long-term effects of college.

Table 10.6 Long-Term Effects of College: Main Findings

Outcomes	Volumes 1 and 2	Volume 3
Socioeconomic	Substantial increases in job status and earnings from bachelor's degree; smaller increases for associate's degree and certificates. Positive credentialing effects on earnings and positive overall return on college investment.	Earlier findings largely replicated, except greater returns on investment and smaller increases in earnings from bachelor's degrees than in prior reviews. College also boosts employment and job satisfaction. Graduate degrees further increase earnings, especially for the MD and JD.

(continued)

Table 10.6 Long-Term Effects of College: Main Findings (continued)

Outcomes	Volumes 1 and 2	Volume 3
Learning and cognitive changes	Modest evidence of increases in knowledge, critical thinking, and lifelong learning (capacity and predisposition).	The limited findings are consistent with earlier reviews, including the role of postcollege participation in learning activities explaining these effects.
Psychosocial changes	Limited evidence suggested college attendance may have increased self-concept, internal locus of control, and well-being, along with decreasing authoritarianism.	HBCU attendance may increase self-image, self-esteem, and labor market outcomes, but not subject matter ability. Diversity experiences indirectly increase personal growth and purpose.
Attitudes and values	Increased civic engagement, liberal attitudes, and occupational values. Changes during college were maintained after college by social networks, social capital, and jobs.	College community engagement and service-learning increase postcollege civic outcomes in certain conditions. Diversity experiences indirectly increase civic and diversity outcomes; academic major also affects civic development.
Moral development	College increased the use of principled moral reasoning.	No research directly examined long-term effects on moral outcomes.
Quality of life	College had direct and indirect effects on improved health; health and well-being benefits extended to graduates' children. College also led to better financial decisions, but it had mixed effects on life and job satisfaction.	Strong evidence replicates the college-related improvement in health outcomes and behaviors across countries. College may also increase community and political engagement, social trust, and several forms of well-being and satisfaction.
Intergenerational effects	Parental education increased children's knowledge, which was explained by providing children with more learning opportunities and resources. Other increases included children's health, adult job status, and early career earnings.	Parental education increases children's health (from birth to adulthood), exercise, and civic outcomes; causal mechanisms from earlier research are replicated. Education also increases children's college attendance and graduation among those who attend.

CONCLUSION

This book, the third volume of *How College Affects Students*, is in fact the fourth attempt to synthesize the enormous body of literature on college students over a given time period. Feldman and Newcomb's 1969 book, *The Impact of College on Students*, was the first of these broad-scale reviews. In some ways, we understand much more about college impact today than we did 10 years, 25 years, and 50 years ago. In particular, the breadth and depth of knowledge are far greater for the effects of college on different groups of students, as well as for certain college experiences, including those related to classroom practices, online learning, religion and spirituality, and diversity. These findings have provided additional insight into the conditions under which college may promote or hinder student outcomes.

The proliferation of stronger research designs and statistical methods has sometimes called into question previous conclusions, some of which seemed well supported by research in earlier systematic reviews. To date, experimental and quasi-experimental studies are often more likely to find no significant relationship than are other studies. This trend has cast doubt not only on findings that have now been examined with these rigorous methods, but also on conclusions regarding issues that have not yet received this greater level of scrutiny. These methodological advances show promise for bolstering the causal claims that we wish to make about how college affects students, but conducting experimental studies on a broad scale (across multiple institutions with large, diverse samples) is quite challenging. Nonetheless, many general conclusions in this volume seem to be well supported by methodologically rigorous research.

Finally, it is important to note that the single strongest predictor of a student's outcomes at the end of college is that student's characteristics on the same construct when entering college. Therefore, while college can (and often does) profoundly shape learning, growth, and development, the precollege environment has a substantial impact on the attributes of college graduates. The large number of significant conditional effects reviewed in this volume highlights the complex interplay between precollege characteristics and college experiences. Given the focus of this book on college impact specifically, the final chapter discusses some of the implications of this body of evidence for improving practice, policy, and research in higher education.

Notes

1. Standard deviations (SD) are used to indicate the size of an effect. In Chapter 1, we proposed effect-size guidelines for within-college and between-college effects, but these may not be applicable to change during college or net effects of college. That said, we believe that the effect sizes reported for learning and cognitive changes—which are generally between 0.5 and 1 standard deviation—should be considered large.

2. In Chapter 1, we proposed guidelines for within-college and between-college effects. For outcomes that have only two options (e.g., graduated or did not graduate), we suggested that a 6 percentage point change is small, 9 is medium, and 15 is large (as one hypothetical example, when accounting for other relevant variables, 65% of people who participated in some experience graduated from college, whereas only 50% of people who did not participate graduated). These guidelines are applicable only for binary outcomes. For outcomes that are continuous (with a categorical predictor), we proposed that .15 standard deviations (SD) is small, .30 SD is medium, and .50 SD is large.

CHAPTER ELEVEN

Implications for Policy, Research, and Practice

The implications from this review are far-reaching for higher education stakeholders. From federal policymakers to research methodologists to practitioners, the review of studies presented in this volume should inform the majority of stakeholders interested in higher education. This volume does not represent everything that stakeholders need to know about college and its influence on students. As acknowledged in the opening chapter, the notion of "college" is not consistent across the postsecondary contexts comprising our review. We have framed this synthesis as an examination of how postsecondary exposure—"college attendance" in American phrasing—affects student learning, development, and lifelong outcomes. For staging this synthesis, we also situated the implications from our review most directly in the American postsecondary context.

We hope decision makers across contexts will use this volume as an empirical road map that shapes national conversations about the values and purposes of higher education, as a data-driven guide that helps scholars improve college impact research, and as a research-based manual that educators use to inform practice. This review has many implications for policy, research, and practice that now we discuss in turn.

IMPLICATIONS FOR POLICYMAKERS

The majority of studies reviewed for this volume examined postsecondary participation for its influence on individual student outcomes. While this strategy offered conceptual clarity and some logistic efficiency to the creation of the volume, we were not able to review studies that examined college and its effects on society. As such, we cannot speak to how college affects states or nations as a whole—which does not mean that these studies do not exist or are unimportant. Legislators should use this volume along with reviews of other relevant topics to help create the best policies for the collective citizenry, as well as individual taxpayers.

The research reviewed informs policymakers in multiple ways. First, the results from this volume answer questions concerning higher education as a social and economic investment. Second, we wanted to use results to inform policymaking decisions in higher education.

Promoting the Public Good

Exposure to and participation in higher education lead to a more engaged citizenry, with the weight of the evidence supporting the notion that college graduates participate in more civic behaviors than their peers who do not attend college. These behaviors include volunteering with charitable organizations or social welfare groups, community service, political involvement, and voting. Disturbingly, more current research suggests that the relationship between college-going and these civic behaviors may be beginning to wane: a study (Long, 2010) examining three cohorts estimates diminishing civic returns over subsequent decades. Of course, this trend is troubling for educators who underscore active participation in democracy as central to the values and purposes of higher education. Perhaps, as evidence in this volume would suggest, distrust in the government has made its way into the college environment to such a degree that students have become more cynical and less optimistic about their ability to effect social change. Alternatively, as institutions focus less on the liberal arts and humanities—even, at some colleges, closing entire departments in these areas—and policymakers incentivize students to major in science, technology, engineering, and mathematics (STEM) fields (see the State of Montana's STEM Scholarship program as one such example), students may have limited exposure to curricula that fosters civic dispositions and commitments. The consequences of such actions may result in graduates who lack a sense of civic urgency or skills for enacting social change through active participation in the democratic process. Several studies found that students who majored in STEM disciplines and business were less likely to engage civically than their peers who majored in the social sciences and education. All higher education stakeholders, policymakers, and institutional educators alike should consider these trends in light of creating an informed and responsible citizenry and may want to take important steps toward reversing them (e.g., reprioritizing curriculum that promotes social advancement).

Participation in postsecondary education is also associated with better health outcomes. The weight of the evidence is conclusive in this regard, with studies consistently establishing the link between college-going and health outcomes, including reduced depressive symptomatology, lower mortality rates, reductions in the likelihood of smoking, increases in smoking cessation among those who have smoked previously, more positive diet choices, and engaging in more moderate and vigorous physical activity. In addition, parents who attended college were more likely to transmit these positive health-related choices to their children. Although some of these positive health and intergenerational transmission benefits are associated with college graduates tending to have higher incomes, education's role in enhanced quality of life persists after accounting for earnings.

Although the social benefits of higher education are not reviewed in this volume, individual benefits accrue in the collective—making investment in higher education a prudent policy decision. As Lundborg (2013) concluded, "If schooling has a causal effect on health, policies that strengthen the incentives to obtain a higher education may have beneficial effects for both the productivity of nations and for population health" (p. 698). Linking higher education to positive personal health and children's outcomes is a critical argument that legislators can use to reestablish the importance of college as pivotal to the welfare of its citizenry.

Legislators should continue to affirm the relevance of the development of moral character as one of the "primary goals in education" (Higher Education Act, 1998). Although questions remain about the extent to which the federal government should be involved at all in the actions of colleges and universities, this volume suggests that postsecondary participation influences the moral development of students. By prioritizing ethics-based education as one of the goals of higher education, policymakers equip accreditation agencies, college administrators, and even faculty with the platform needed to include morally relevant criteria for assessing educational, institutional, and practice-related success. Maintaining the importance of character education would also help educators and students place value on moral dimensions of community citizenship, including academic integrity, responsible drinking, bystander intervention, and creating safe communities.

A Continued Economic Benefit

Consistent with evidence from the previous two volumes, higher education continues to be economically beneficial for students. Whether in terms of an additional year of higher education or completing a certificate, associate, baccalaureate, or graduate degree, the net economic effects of participation in higher education are substantial. In general, receiving a higher degree is associated with a greater earnings boost, and each year of college provides earning benefits as well (5–9% per year of college, with larger benefits occurring further after college attendance). Given the magnitude of the earnings benefits of college over the past three decades, higher education has served an unmatched role in the labor market and continues to do so amid dramatic global, technological, and cyclical economic change. The economic advantages that accompany a higher education provide clear justification for the escalating student demand for higher education in the United States over the past several decades.

The economic benefits of higher education accrue in a variety of ways. People benefit not only through receiving more education (by attending college for more years or completing a degree), but also through the type of education and where they receive it (by majoring in specific fields that prepare students for high-paying jobs, achieving a higher grade point average, or attending a more selective institution). Such benefits also appear to be greater when one's job is congruent with one's major field of study. It appears that transferring from a two- to a four-year institution, an increasingly common occurrence, has little if any negative consequence on postgraduate earnings and may actually increase the returns on an educational investment by lowering the costs. Moreover, the earnings advantages of higher education increase over time as graduates accrue additional years of work experience.

All else equal, students who wish to maximize the earnings benefits of an undergraduate degree should attend the most selective institution to which they are admitted, major in a field that has a well-defined body of content knowledge and tends to center on quantitative and/or scientific skill development, and secure employment in an occupational field closely aligned with their major. Of course, all else is not equal; the sizable differences in costs of attendance and institutions' ability to offer financial aid limit access to segments of the higher education system, particularly the most selective private colleges and universities. It is important to recognize that while the economic advantages resulting from a college degree are substantial, access among students from traditionally underrepresented and lower SES backgrounds remains a significant, systemwide challenge.

For students who participate in higher education, the choices made during college have a larger influence on their postcollege earnings than the decision of which college to attend. For example, while attending a more versus less prestigious institution appears to increase earnings by roughly 15 to 20% ten years after college, majoring in engineering instead of education has twice (about 40 to 50%) the effect on earnings (and even more if students find employment in a closely related field). Similar to the other outcomes discussed throughout this book, the within-college effects on career and economic outcomes exceed the between-college effects.

Increases in college costs warrant continued conversation among policymakers, particularly in relation to postsecondary access, student indebtedness, and the considerable social returns on public monies invested in higher education. However, initial evidence from the twenty-first century indicates that the private rate of return—the economic outcomes that accrue to individual students after taking into account the direct and indirect costs of college attendance—remains high and even slightly above what was reported in past decades. Despite the increasing costs, higher education remains an extremely sound investment on average, with conservative estimates indicating returns on a bachelor's degree of about 12 to 14%.

Moving forward, legislators should fund research on the economic, quality-of-life, and learning returns to educational investments using more complete data, more current data, and more rigorous methodologies. Legislators should also consider funding research on the impacts of college that focus on such an array of outcomes for different types of students. As societies become more complex, more layers of differentiation and potential sources of social and economic inequality emerge (Grusky, 2011). Given the increasingly differentiated higher education system (online degrees, for-profit institutions, expanding fields of study, and greater opportunities for academic and social engagement), future research examining the wide-ranging impacts of higher education should continue to address important questions that ask for whom, within what kind of educational environments, and as a result of which educational experiences are the multitude of benefits associated with college attendance and completion most likely realized.

Research for Policymaking

While this review may help legislators created evidence-informed policy, the volume does not provide an evaluative frame for deciding which policies are better than others or even a directive for good policymaking. Rather, we suggest policymakers consider taking some time to understand college and its effects on the students who directly benefit from federal and state resources; doing so will help officials craft innovative and efficient legislation designed to maximize the potential reach and impact of postsecondary participation. In short, we suggest policymakers adopt a multipronged approach to the study of college and its effects on students.

From rating systems to scorecards, it appears as though policymakers continue with their attempts to provide oversight into issues of quality assurance and accountability for higher education systems. We suggest that legislators include credential completion as just one indicator of student success or institutional effectiveness. Many scholars have designed studies that examine not only that development occurred but where, how, and why it occurred. From these studies, we make the following suggestions for policymakers:

- Adopt a broader view of learning by not, for example, depending on one measure of learning as the sole indicator of success. Results from this review suggest that learning is complex; it comprises content mastery; intellectual, cognitive, and moral development; and psychosocial and attitude change. Who would want to take their children to a doctor who did not understand biology? A therapist who did not appreciate the complexity of the human condition? Vote in an election for officials who cannot see beyond themselves and make decisions for the greater good? The Association of American Colleges & Universities' Liberal Education, America's Promise initiative, and the European Higher Education Area's Tuning Process are initiatives that recognize the complexity of the postsecondary sector and, as a result, the need for a holistic approach to assessment and evaluation.

- Consider the benefits and consequences of accountability efforts that develop and test meaningful performance-based funding indicators. Limited research has examined the effectiveness of using performance-based funding on indicators of institutional performance, such as the numbers of college graduates and credits completed. The limited but methodologically rigorous research to date suggest that these efforts are ineffective. Of course, careful consideration should be given toward lawmakers' understanding and measurement of institutional performance, especially with so much at stake.

- Ensure that the measures used to assess institutional performance are suitable to the diverse types of colleges in the U.S. system. Indeed, a one-size-fits-all approach to creating performance indicators may not capture the complexities, mission, and mandate different types of colleges or universities bring to their distinctive student populations. For example, adding graduate school attendance might be useful as a performance metric for four-year institutions but not for two-year colleges. While articulating sets of performance indicators for every type of institution falls outside the purview of this volume, we suggest that legislators consider students' entering characteristics when assessing or ascribing meaning to institutional effectiveness.

- Think about accountability efforts by funding studies that compare students enrolled in higher education to those who are not. Legislators should consider setting aside funds for social science research specifically designated for understanding how college affects students. We need to be able to longitudinally follow college-going and non-college-going citizens to understand the impact of postsecondary participation on a broadened view of performance, including student learning and development, career and economic outcomes, and long-term quality-of-life measures. Through these funding mechanisms, we can discover what really matters in college. The conclusions that we are able to draw in this volume would not have been possible without the existence of strongly designed research.

In addition to using research to inform accountability conversations, we also offer thoughts related to resource allocation, state articulation agreements, need-based aid, and technology. We now turn to a discussion of each.

Lawmakers should consider providing sufficient resources to public colleges and universities so that they can educate and graduate their students. Over the past several decades, state legislatures have dramatically reduced funding for higher education, and the availability of grants and scholarships (as a proportion of student support for their education) has substantially diminished as well. This review found strong evidence that overall institutional expenditures improve student graduation rates, and the allocation of financial resources to directly support students (through instruction, financial aid, and other areas) also appears to be beneficial. Given the widespread calls for a well-educated workforce, legislators can play an important role in making this goal a reality.

Policymakers may want to develop specific incentives to make more institutions accessible for students from lower socioeconomic backgrounds. Results from this study demonstrated that students who successfully transferred to a four-year institution as juniors were just as likely to graduate as those who started at a four-year college and that completing a bachelor's degree was a strong predictor of social mobility, including economic attainment. In addition, substantial evidence suggests that college attendance itself and engaging in certain college experiences may be most beneficial for the least advantaged, including students from lower socioeconomic backgrounds. Therefore, state legislators should allocate resources to help four-year institutions improve their need-based aid offerings.

State articulation policies that attempt to streamline coursework transfer from two-year to four-year public institutions appear to have no effect on bachelor's degree attainment. Given differences in how states administer these agreements, this finding may not be surprising; however, it may be prudent for state policymakers to keep careful records of agreements that work from those that do not and make resource allocation decisions accordingly. The limited evidence offered in this review substantiated this important claim and did not offer viable solutions to its many accompanying issues.

State allocations that are targeted toward need-based aid may be especially effective in promoting the overall educational attainment within a state's population. As privatization grows and continues to threaten the ability for most families to afford and complete a four-year education (which provides substantial gains in economic mobility and quality-of-life indicators), state legislatures should consider ways to increase monies appropriated for public higher education. Given the development of advanced information technology infrastructures, perhaps states can begin crowdsourcing innovative funding solutions (e.g., the Fund for Wisconsin Scholars) to keep costs down, especially for families with high need.

Given increasing economic issues concerning financing higher education, many institutions offer online education as a means to expand higher education access to college and to do so affordably. Technological advances in educational delivery modes have also reopened issues relating to higher education's strategic partnerships with corporate interests. For example, massive open online courses (MOOCs), which represent one of the most recent online synchronous or asynchronous learning platforms, have gained some popularity as universities leverage their industry networks to partner with the companies that create the platforms. Results from this volume were mixed with respect to online learning and its effects on student outcomes. When compared to students in face-to-face environment, online students were sometimes more likely to gain or minimally not differ in the development of learning outcomes associated with verbal, quantitative, and subject matter competence; they were also just as likely to make intellectual and cognitive gains. However, students in these online environments may have been more likely to drop out of a course. These mixed results suggest that legislators may want to articulate the specific learning objectives they expect online instruction would facilitate and allocate resources for its assessment before implementation on any scale. In addition, policymakers may want to think about regulatory policies to ensure that taxpayer dollars earmarked for higher education purposes are being well spent. While balancing private and public interests is nothing new to higher education policymakers, efficient reviews of the partnerships between higher education institutions and online platform industry providers will become increasingly important given the boom in educational technologies.

Summary

State and federal governments have invested trillions of dollars in the development of human capital. The justification for public support of higher education is rooted in economics and theories of public expenditure that support the use of public resources to lower the individual costs of a college education. This practice will stimulate demand and increase the desirable outcomes from having a population with more advanced education attainment (e.g., better health, greater levels of community service and political involvement). For centuries, education has been recognized as a public good and thus worthy of governmental investment. However, in the past few decades, that perspective has shifted to one that views higher education as an increasingly private commodity. With cuts to governmental support and tuition deregulation across the studies in our review, students and their families are shouldering an ever-increasing portion of the postsecondary cost, resulting for some in potentially debilitating long-term debt (Mitchell & Leachman, 2015). It remains our hope that postsecondary policymakers find a means by which the costs of college-going become less prohibitive so that any student can benefit from participating in higher education.

The evidence provided in this volume suggests that policymakers can take steps toward improving the higher education system. Policymakers may want to consider these possibilities:

- Funding more studies of the net effects of college-going, complete with comparisons between students who go to college with peers who do not.
- Sustaining interests in character education as a federal priority.
- Adjusting the completion agenda to include learning as the defining element of institutional effectiveness and student success.
- Allocating more state resources to institutions for student instruction and financial aid, especially scholarships.

- Developing better strategies for meeting the educational needs, both financially and pedagogically, for low-income students.

- Reconsidering articulation agreements between two- and four-year institutions as the evidence shows they are ineffective in promoting educational attainment.

- Identifying learning objectives associated with online learning environments before rolling them to scale.

These ideas are not intended to be instructive; however, they have emerged from this review as important considerations for policymakers and to some extent the researchers who inform their work. We turn now to a discussion of college impact research and our suggestions for improving practice in this regard.

IMPLICATIONS FOR RESEARCH

In our review of 1,848 studies in this volume, we identified several opportunities where college impact research could better inform and influence research practice in the service of supporting student learning and success. First, we discuss issues regarding the use of theory and literature that authors employed to ground college impact research. Next, we examine methods and analytical choices as they were used to answer questions related to college impact. Finally, we interrogate how higher education researchers discuss findings.

Use of Theory

As theoretical considerations expanded to include a broader array of voices and perspectives, we wanted to be explicit about the role of theory and its use in informing more inclusive conversations about how college affects students. To that end, we begin by situating some assumptions regarding college impact researchers' use of theory, guidelines for how to use theory effectively, and recommendations for theoretical considerations for future researchers interested in college and its impact on students.

How authors approach their lines of inquiry remains a point of interest for college impact and student development. What ontological and epistemic assumptions are authors using to frame their approach to the research questions? How do these assumptions shape methodological and analytical choices? The articles and books reviewed for this volume reflect some of the tensions within these questions. For example, researchers who studied racialized effects of college experiences on student learning often differed in their theoretical orientations to the study of race. From a design perspective, some authors offered research questions about college and its effects on students and then followed with subquestions that reflected interests in conditional effects—for example, how does participation in a living-learning community influence persistence, and does this relationship differ by students' self-reported race? More often than not, these studies examined race as an auxiliary interest, without much theoretical grounding in the critical and social constructions of race. Other authors designed studies that asked questions only of a certain subgroup—for example, how does participation in a living-learning community influence the persistence of Native American students? Questions like these reflect a different orientation to the study of race and are often framed accordingly, through the use of critical race theory, for example.

Recently a group of scholars led by Frances Stage has started to unpack some of these questions, especially as they relate to quantitative research on race-related issues. Adopting what they call a quantitative critical approach (see Stage, 2007), these scholars have called on quantitative researchers to take a series of steps intended to help authors more thoughtfully approach research questions that are examined with quantitative designs. One hope is that quantitative researchers will begin to be explicit about some of the challenges, including whether a construct can be measured, what it means to "control for race," how cell count restrictions may lead to result reporting that obfuscates narratives, and so on. Being more explicit about question origins and methodological and analytical choices will become increasingly important as researchers respond to continued criticisms regarding the values and purposes of higher education.

Theories are rarely tested directly in college impact research. Although theoretical elements (e.g., cognitive dissonance) are offered to explain the relationships among and between tested constructs, these elements are rarely considered and subsequently measured directly. As a result, college impact researchers have little information on why and how constructs relate; they just know whether they do and, in the case of this volume, the magnitude to which they do. Unless theoretical elements are directly tested, authors can only speculate why relationships exist; certainly, finding ways to measure these elements would be a fruitful line of future research. Given the theoretical advances over the past decade in our understanding of various domains of student development (e.g., intersectional psychosocial identities), ample opportunity exists for drawing more rigorous connections between theory and empirical investigations.

In other disciplines that examine postsecondary education's effects on outcomes like health, job satisfaction, and income (e.g., sociology, psychology, economics), researchers appear to frame and test research questions from a position of theory testing and theory building. In this regard, we encourage those who identify primarily as higher education scholars to follow their disciplinary peers by more clearly grounding research in theoretical exploration, verification, and development.

It is important to note that theories differ from frameworks. Although many frameworks and models are used to graphically portray the relationships among constructs and phenomena, theories explain how and why constructs and phenomena relate. Certainly the language of theory will continue to evolve and consensus on its definition will probably never be reached, but college impact researchers should understand the differences among theory, framework, and models so they can add further clarity to the purposes of the research, as well as expand its reach.

In this volume, some theories and frameworks dominated the research landscape, while others were not used to frame inquiry to the same degree as they were in previous volumes. For example, scholars relied heavily upon work by Kohlberg and his contemporaries (see Rest, Narvaez, Bebeau, & Thoma, 1999) and Tinto (1993), whereas use of King and Kitchener's (1994) reflective judgment theory and Gilligan's (1982) moral development model waned. Overreliance on a particular theory or framework has the potential to perhaps reproduce hegemonic norms and thwart innovation; indeed sacrificing good theory for the sake of conceptual and measurement efficiencies may limit our understanding of college and its effects on students. We suggest researchers carefully consider the trade-offs between theories and efficiencies in designing future studies.

Given the growing interdisciplinary scholarly interest in college and its impact on students, authors have asked research questions from, and nuanced by, disciplines that range from sociology to psychology to anthropology. As a field, higher education welcomes these approaches, as we believe learning from one another is critical for more holistic understandings of college and its effects on students. As researchers, we need to be more attentive to work in other fields and how these efforts might shape higher education research questions. Of course, scholars from outside the field would benefit from reading the higher education literature as well. In short, scholars need to be vigilant in reading work from scholars across many disciplines; such a practice will contribute to the quality of the work as well as extend the reach of findings to audiences outside higher education.

Use of Literature

One aim—if not the primary aim—of college impact research is to isolate the extent to which outcomes are influenced by experiences during college. As Smart (2005) notes, "Studies that are not fully grounded in the appropriate research literature lack this substantive and methodological guidance, and are much less likely to be of high quality. In the current vernacular, "you can't make a silk purse out of a sow's ear'" (p. 464).

Researchers may want to approach their use of the literature not only to justify variable selection but to explain how variables worked together to explain certain phenomena. In many ways, much of the research we reviewed in this volume would benefit from more explanation of how variables are interrelated, especially in cases where research questions addressed recursive relationships among constructs to explain the associations between experiences and higher education outcomes. Scholars interested in college impact work should consider being more attentive to the literature in its explanations of the relationships among constructs and variables; again, this approach will lay a better foundation for theory building and informing practice.

Continuing the discussion of variable selection, the studies reviewed from this volume reflected conceptual nuances between organizational variables that were immutable versus those that educators could change. While immutable variables such as institutional size, control, and geographical location continue to dominate the research landscape, others, more susceptible to change and are arguably more important to practice, were also analyzed for their relationship with student outcomes (e.g., whether programs were housed in academic or student affairs, amount of resources allocated toward students, the structural diversity of students on campus). Variable selection practices that represent these distinctions are important as scholars move more toward a multimodeling approach to assessing organizational variables and their effects on students and as high-level administrators increasingly use research to inform practice.

More than ever before, scholars' interest in college and its effects on students involved an examination of functional variables (e.g., ease of registration, library use). Investigations of library use, registration satisfaction, technology adoption, and financial aid ease appeared in predictive models of outcomes and often were statistically related to learning and developmental gains. When researchers consider the variables that comprise the college environment, it will become increasingly important to include variables that have not been previously explored, as long as they are theoretically justified based on the outcome being examined. Berger and Milem (2000) developed a strong theoretical framework for considering these functional variables as they work in concert with more familiar curricular and cocurricular elements to explain student outcomes.

Use of Method

Design. Design is more important than analysis. Through the use of experimental and quasi-experimental designs, scholars interested in higher education research move steps closer to drawing strong causal conclusions regarding the college practices and experiences that are best poised for helping students master content, learn and develop, persist, and make career-related progress. Of course, some research designs are more appropriate than others for assessing college and its influence on students. It appears the best designs (1) emerge from theoretically grounded and thoughtfully considered research questions, (2) are longitudinal, (3) use some form of comparison group (e.g., control group, matched samples), (4) use valid and reliable assessment tools, and (5) collect information on the variables that influence the particular college experience and the outcome. Scholars interested in college and its impact on students should consider implementing designs with these elements.

Similar to findings from previous volumes, a pretest is often the best predictor of the posttest; that is, where students start when they enter college is the best predictor of where they end up. In some ways, the pretest reflects the distinct narrative each student brings to college. The pretest not only embodies any genetic contribution to cognitive and noncognitive factors; it also incorporates the various resources students had available during their precollege years in terms of financial capital for tutoring, social capital in identifying tutors and study groups, and cultural capital as manifest in tastes, dispositions, and values toward academic achievement and postsecondary aspiration. In some ways, the pretest also encapsulates the local and systemic conditions and cultures that may inspire or inhibit students' academic development. The change from pretest to posttest represents how these narratives evolve during college. In short, individual differences will find a way to strongly express themselves no matter what educators do during college. Extending this idea a bit further, the strong relationship between pretest and posttest measures indicates that while we strive to provide equal opportunity and equal support for students during college, trying to ensure equal outcomes at the end of college is much more problematic. For these reasons, we recommend that research on college impact include pretest measures of college outcomes whenever possible, not just as a strong design element but as a means for understanding how educators should think about learning and development. What developmental targets are appropriate? For whom? Questions like these remain central to college impact work and should be thoughtfully considered.

Compared to previous volumes, the evidence presented in this review is more limited, with fewer longitudinal studies of college-going versus non-college-going students with respect to many outcomes. Because of this lack of data, we cannot discuss the net effects of college-going on student outcomes to the same degree as our predecessors did. Although following cohorts of non–college goers is an arduous and costly undertaking, it remains the most effective way of assessing the net effects of college-going. We currently have no way to determine the extent to which postsecondary participation might contribute to people's knowledge, competence, and other outcomes. In a climate in which the cost of postsecondary education has outpaced inflation and the value of higher education has been questioned repeatedly, identifying the net effects of college between those who have attended and those who have not is critical.

Also lacking were longitudinal studies that assessed student growth over three time points or more. Longitudinal studies that accounted for development over multiple time points would have helped in two major ways: we would have been able to (1) have a more robust understanding of long-term college effects, and (2) ascertain whether growth due to participation in a specific college-based intervention was sustained over time. Although costly, longitudinal studies that follow students into their careers would help educators understand the lasting effects of college-going, not to mention help to demystify the college to career link.

Measurement. Many studies reported in this review used self-reported measures of learning gains as proxies for college and its effects on many types of development. In almost every instance, the use of self-reported learning gains enabled authors to execute more cost-effective and expedient research designs, such as cross-sectional studies. Of course, the overuse of these types of studies rendered the process of weighing the evidence more challenging, as effect sizes for experiences in models derived for cross-sectional studies were, on average, quite a bit larger than effect sizes for experiences in models studied with a longitudinal design. Like previous volumes, we gave less weight to effect sizes for experiences examined in cross-sectional studies. Several studies employed self-reported gains measures within a longitudinal context, with respondents indicating the amount they gained from a high school experience serving as a control for one's propensity for reporting gains. Although this may be a more promising research design, studies that used both self-reported gains and more objective measures found more conservative coefficients of college impact for the objective measures. While self-reported gains are an expedient means of collecting data, the limitations in terms of their validity to measure student learning should give higher education stakeholders pause in continuing their unabated use.

Consistent with other volumes, inconclusive results were often associated with scholars' differential use of measures, with some researchers adopting objective measures of outcomes and others employing measures that were more subjective. Use of different types of measures played a role in the effects reported in different studies. For example, measurement mattered for findings on cognitive development. When measured with objective tools, cognitive development was less associated with diversity course taking. This association was stronger, often reaching statistical significance, in studies that included more subjective measures of gains or scales where students could be more susceptible to social desirability. For future college impact work, we urge researchers to use psychometrically rigorous measures of student outcomes.

Another measurement choice that led to confusion was the use of pretest proxies for examining student outcomes. While longitudinal studies are highly preferred to cross-sectional ones, the use of pretest proxies as controls for assessing long-term gains was problematic, especially within the context of calculating and comparing effects across studies. For example, in some studies of intellectual and cognitive growth, scholars used entering SAT or ACT scores as a pretest for outcome measures of critical thinking, like the critical thinking dispositions inventory (Facione & Facione, 1992). To avoid conceptual confusion and subsequent challenges in understanding effect sizes, we encourage researchers to avoid measurement proxies whenever possible, as they may lead to faulty claims about college and its effects on students.

Data Collection. Moving from measurement choice to administration, institutions are asking students to respond to a greater number of surveys. Survey fatigue is negatively affecting response rates, making it increasingly difficult for researchers to make any generalizable statements about college and its effects on students.

Researchers need to design studies that speak to national interests in college and its influence on learning *and* to institutional stakeholders charged with using data to make improvements on specific campuses. In turn, institutional researchers need to manage assessment schedules in ways that allow researchers greater access to students. Although institutions vary in their survey administration abilities, the following techniques have been helpful in improving response rates: use of stratified random sampling to reduce sampling the same students time and time again, delivery mechanism differentiation (i.e., online versus mail), and long-term assessment planning that leads to fewer surveys being administered, to name a few. We urge scholars interested in college impact to work closely with institutional researchers toward survey solutions that will increase response rates. Only by working together can we collect data in a fashion that will provide useful information to improve the college experience for students.

Single institution studies have merit, especially when cast as quantitative case studies of a particular practice or innovation being launched on campus. We suggest that the researchers who design such studies provide detailed information of the campus context in which the study took place. Including relevant institutional facts and figures and detailed information about the campus context may help researchers at similar institutions make empirically based arguments for implementing similar practices and innovations.

Statistical power remained an issue for contextualizing the evidence presented in this volume. Multi-institutional studies need to have sufficient statistical power to make claims about the effects of institutional variables on student outcomes. Similarly, researchers interested in student-level data need to make sure that they design studies with enough statistical power to make claims about subgroup differences when they attempt to explore such dynamics. When collecting their own data, we encourage researchers to perform power analyses in advance to ensure that claims can be made reasonably.

Data Analysis. Much of the evidence provided in this volume came from studies that included research designs intended to account for students within certain contexts, including academic major and institution, as examples. Students' clustering patterns need to be considered in examinations of college and its effects on students. We suggest faculty and graduate students who ask questions calling for quantitative designs to take graduate courses that cover material related to student nesting patterns, as these designs evolve into a research norm for quantitative scholars interested in college and its effects on students.

Use of Results

Having enough information to calculate effect sizes was as pervasive an issue in this volume as it was in the previous one. In order to understand the impact of college on any outcome, researchers needed to provide enough information for effect sizes regarding change during college, between-college effects, and within-college effects. In many instances, researchers did not offer this information at all or offered it in limited amounts (e.g., means and no standard deviations).

To offer some recommendations for good research practice, we ask authors to consider (1) providing means, standard deviations, and sample sizes associated with pretest and posttest scores (so that researchers can determine change over time); (2) standardizing continuous independent and dependent variables in prediction models and reporting unstandardized coefficients in subsequent results sections (which allows interpretation of the effect sizes described in Chapter 1); and (3) reporting effect sizes in results sections (e.g., delta-p for binary outcomes, as also described in Chapter 1).

In the spirit of transparency, we urge researchers to be careful not to overstate results, especially in the context of studies that used nonrepresentative samples. Providing some context for understanding quantitative results may be needed to help researchers make appropriate inferences that are neither dismissive due to small institutional samples nor overstated due to larger, nonrepresentative institutional samples.

How researchers present conditional effects can often lead to unsupported conclusions. Many studies claim to explore whether certain experiences have a differential effect on an outcome as a function of a student characteristic, commonly gender or race. Researchers often conduct conditional effects analysis by disaggregating the sample, reanalyzing the data for each group (e.g., male versus female students), and presenting the coefficients for each. However, without testing to see if the coefficients differ from one another statistically, it is impossible to conclude the effects of experience X are truly larger for group A than group B. We urge college impact researchers to attend to this critical step in examining conditional effects.

Use of Discussion

Hegemonic discussion practices continue to dominate the research landscape, especially as college impact researchers attempt to make meaning of results among subgroup populations. For example, in explanations of race effects, some authors indicted a group of students for their lack of ability to make gains in one form or other: "Asian students should take advantage of programs and services that. . ." Statements from this orientation employ a deficit framework in which students are the actors who must change and adapt. We propose instead that college impact researchers adopt an equity-minded approach in their discussions of racial differences: "Programs and services have consistently failed to attract Asian students" or "Factors outside the student's or institution's control have consistently failed to attract Asian students." Framing racial differences from the perspective of what the institutions or factors beyond the students' or institutions' control are doing or failing to do gives educators more direction as they make decisions to improve campus practice.

Making meaning of conditional effects was a related challenge we encountered across a number of studies. We applaud researchers for their concerted efforts in disaggregating samples to attend to the nuanced relationships between experiences and outcomes for distinctive subpopulations, but this approach often yielded abundant significant effects followed by insufficient discussion of their practical meaning or consequence. Akin to our earlier recommendations regarding theory use, we advocate for theory-driven approaches to examining conditional effects and amplified efforts to articulate and explain the realities they reflect.

Summary

There is always room to consider improving research practice, especially as public scrutiny increases over the purposes and values of higher education. Reviewing this vast array of studies gave us a distinctive perspective on the college impact research landscape, at least with regard to what has been disseminated in this century. From that perspective, we offered suggestions for strengthening scholarship, ranging from recommendations on better use of theory to effective strategies for discussing findings. Collectively, the higher education community can continue making contributions to designing and executing more rigorous studies that will ultimately be used to inform practice.

IMPLICATIONS FOR PRACTICE

The majority of the research reviewed for this volume examined educational environments and experiences inside and outside the classroom where faculty and staff educators foster student learning and development. The implications are far reaching for those who educate students.

Of course, our review was limited, as we discuss implications only in light of published research. Indeed, we appreciate the many undocumented efforts of our administrative coeducators whose work often goes unrecognized. We also offer that some of the implications emerging from this volume may sound trite, oversimplifying the complexities that administrators and educators face when making decisions about their university and the students it serves. Of course, the implications discussed here are not offered as a panacea for the many issues facing institutions today; indeed, educators must contextualize the practice-oriented results to the distinctive narrative and culture of their institution. In doing so, the higher education community can work together to improve the educational conditions and practices for all students.

Evidence from this review suggested that the learning enterprise is becoming increasingly complex, leaving more traditional ways of conceptualizing college and university life sometimes at odds with the realities of what students are actually experiencing. Spurring student learning, development, and persistence is likely to require comprehensive strategies that involve many institutional officers, often not located in one particular unit or functional area. For example, once considered efficacious as involvement spaces where learning was anecdotal and often considered a peripheral by-product to participation in the curriculum, student affairs programs and services have been recast as learning engines, designed to foster learning and development. As a result, we decided to organize this section into themes based on general interests rather than constituency groups: those interested in teaching, persistence and retention, curricular innovations, resource allocation, diversity, and cocurricular engagement.

Teaching

Good teaching matters. It *really* matters. Across all outcomes reviewed in this volume (including those related to persistence and degree attainment), results confirmed that good teaching is the primary means through which institutions affect students. In addition, high-quality instruction was generally more effective in promoting the learning, cognitive, and educational attainment outcomes of students from historically underserved populations than those from majority groups. Importantly, these practices also promote desired outcomes for all students.

What is good teaching? The research contained in this volume included many experimental, quasi-experimental, and correlational studies of teaching behaviors, specifically with regard to helping students make learning and developmental gains. While the correlational studies consistently suggest that academic challenge is critical for helping students make gains in these areas, the experimental and quasi-experimental studies refine the idea of challenge. Indeed, based on the research reviewed in this volume, effective teaching encouraged students to spend time preparing for class, provided students with feedback, gave students opportunities to reflect, and actively engaged students in learning process.

Evidence from this volume suggests that students who experience their institutions as academically challenging are among the most likely to make learning and developmental gains. Although the context for challenge varied among studies included in this review, climates, classrooms, and other experiences that students perceived as academically and appropriately rigorous were closely associated with growth in learning and development. Learning environments that students perceive as too difficult may lead them to retreat from the discomfort rather than productively manage it; however, if enough challenge isn't provided, students may not experience the dissonance needed to make developmental and learning gains (see Sanford, 1967). Locating the sweet spot with regard to academic challenge remains elusive for educators, as student perceptions and experiences of rigor likely vary across institutions, disciplines, and instructors. Keeping abreast of best practice and routine assessments of student climate perceptions and experiences will help educators make data-driven decisions concerning how to make campus experiences challenging but not overwhelming, effective but not easy.

Increasing students' time spent preparing for class was another means toward helping them make learning and developmental gains, as demonstrated by the weight of the evidence provided in this review. Specifically, teachers may want to encourage students to submit weekly reading and writing assignments given their strong association with learning and developmental gains. Students may receive messages about academic challenge through assignments that routinely ask them to produce. Recognizing that all course content does not readily lend itself to these types of assignments, educators in disciplines such as chemistry and physics may consider finding other consistent and developmentally appropriate ways to challenge students (e.g., through lab write-ups and problem sets). Assignments that ask students to apply their learning in disciplinary-appropriate ways through responding to case studies, creating inquiry-based experiments, or engaging in simulations show promise as catalysts for growth.

Another component to good teaching is the role feedback plays in helping students learn and develop. Effective feedback is purposeful and consistent, providing students with comments concerning content (e.g., evaluating students' ideas, directing students to competing sources), logic (e.g., how well the argument is developed), and form (e.g., whether the paper is well written). As examined by many studies in this review, feedback is critical for promoting growth in students in both online and face-to-face learning environments. Summarizing the role of feedback on cognitive and intellectual development, Hattie and Timperley (2007) offered that feedback "is one of the most powerful influences on learning, too rarely occurs, and needs to be more fully researched by qualitatively and quantitatively investigating how feedback works in the classroom and learning process" (p. 104). In short, feedback should not be considered as the end of the student-faculty idea exchange but an integral part of the teaching-learning process; educators may want to reframe their time, with more allocated toward providing effective feedback on student work.

The evidence from this review also demonstrates that educators consider providing more opportunities for thoughtful reflection, as it tends to help students make the most learning and developmental gains. Reflection has been a central component of learning since the beginning of contemporary discourse concerning the philosophy of education (Smith, 2011), so it might seem obvious to encourage that faculty use reflection as a means of helping students learn. Perhaps the results from this review serve as an important reminder that effective reflection as a pedagogical strategy requires careful structure that is "patient and thorough" (Dewey, 1932, p. 204), prompting students to react meaningfully to course material. Reflection may involve more than a journal entry or two; it should challenge students to engage themselves and their relationship to the course material critically.

Across all chapters, active learning had profound effects on helping students achieve desired outcomes. From experiential learning to carefully designed assessments, instructors' active learning strategies equip students with the knowledge and skills needed to make learning and developmental gains. No singular definition or expression of active learning was necessarily more powerful than another. Rather, active learning as a component of a teacher's deliberate practice of inviting students to think and act in ways consistent with disciplinary norms and methods were quite effective at spurring student learning and development. These findings suggest that educators develop active learning techniques, which they may not have experienced themselves as undergraduates or in which they did not receive training during graduate school.

We are not the first to make these claims and will not be the last, but good teaching remains underappreciated, especially at research universities. Perhaps intuitively (but ironically absent in practice at some institutions), educators may consider strategies for hiring good instructors in the first place. As one provost commented, "It's a lot easier to hire a good teacher than to improve a poor one." Departments might also require evidence of teaching abilities (e.g., including teaching a class during the recruitment and selection process) and value such criteria as much they do candidates' research capabilities and performance.

Anybody teaching should be able to demonstrate competencies in teaching. Leaving good teaching to chance or to non-tenure-track faculty perpetuates the narrative that teaching is not valued to the extent that it should be on college campuses, especially at research universities. Of course, prioritizing teaching and providing feedback on teaching in the reward and incentive process are important steps toward improving teaching on campus.

Another way to spur good teaching practice is to provide the necessary support for the growing number of centers for teaching and learning/faculty excellence/faculty development. To a small but significant degree, these support centers have been linked to student intellectual and cognitive development. These services often serve as the hub where instructors discuss pedagogical innovation, test and reflect on new teaching techniques, and are supported in viewing instruction as a lifelong learning endeavor. In all cases, educating the educators will require institutional leaders' commitment to reframe the discourse and value of teaching.

Overwhelmingly, the evidence provided in this and the previous volumes suggest that classroom educators have the greatest impact on student learning, specifically with regard to verbal, quantitative, and subject matter competence and intellectual, cognitive, and moral development. It is the classroom-based teacher who creates the course content designed to help students make learning gains, enacts the practices that maximize learning potentials, and can help students successfully negotiate the tensions that may arise in courses, either through challenging course content or peer responses to that content. Given the clear and strong relationship between good teaching and student learning, we view the need for pedagogical development to be the focus and concern of more than a single unit on campus. Leaders of graduate schools and faculties could require (or, at minimum, strongly recommend) doctoral students who aspire to be educators to complete a sequence of courses that develop pedagogical adeptness. Developing and offering a college teaching certificate provides an opportunity for higher education faculty to collaborate meaningfully with their disciplinary colleagues and counterparts in teaching and learning centers in meeting this pressing need of preparing future teachers.

Persistence and Retention

The recent evidence strongly suggests that institutions create and execute comprehensive retention programs designed for the sole purpose of retaining students. Placing the retention responsibility squarely on one division, unit, or employee does not work, whereas working together across divisions, titles, and roles is necessary. As an institutional priority, retention deserves an institutional response.

Although we recommend a comprehensive retention strategy, perhaps student affairs may want to double-down on its efforts to lead retention efforts through providing innovative formal and informal networking spaces for students. By channeling resources into persistence efforts, student affairs can extend its value to the institution as retention rates continue to dominate national conversations about institutional excellence and quality. Given that student affairs focuses on students, it seems natural for student affairs leaders to coordinate and facilitate the institution's retention efforts, from advising to renovating informal learning spaces in libraries, student unions, and residence halls. Branding student affairs for its critical role as retention agents of universities might also strengthen its position nationally as the public increasingly scrutinizes the resources being spent on college student expenditures, including areas that divisions of student affairs oversee.

One of the key new findings in this volume is that programmatic retention efforts that combine multiple components seem to be far more influential than those that rely on a single initiative. In most instances, these successful programs paired one or more student services (e.g., academic advising, tutoring, mentoring) with one or more additional practices (e.g., learning community, remediation, financial aid). Therefore, colleges and universities need to think systematically about their efforts to promote retention by involving numerous stakeholders in coordinated programs. Offering a variety of programmatic and service options from which students can choose may not be enough; institutions must provide greater structure and coherence through packaged initiatives that deliver direct guidance and support.

Curricular Innovations, including Online Learning Environments

As technologies advance, interest in online education continues to increase. Perhaps due to challenges inherent in designing studies that address the efficacy of online experiences, research yielded mixed results about the influence of online courses on student development and learning. Online courses, when supported properly, may be cost effective and add immediate value to helping students master subject-related material, but the studies we reviewed showed no discernable value of taking these courses on cognitive and intellectual development, and they may even diminish retention in college. Of course, similar to traditional courses, online pedagogies that encourage quality interactions with faculty and peers helped students make subject matter gains, another finding that highlights good teaching. In short, for now, the mode of content delivery seems less important than the way content is being delivered: through quality in-course interactions with peers and faculty. Much more research is needed to substantiate this or any other claims offered about online education, including its economic feasibility.

Curricular innovations tend to advantage those who may need them most: students from lower socioeconomic statuses, with lower incoming academic ability, or from underrepresented social identity groups. Participation in curricular innovations, such as attributional retraining programs and honors programs, is linked to learning, development, and success to a greater degree for these students than for their peers. The irony is that institutions often do not successfully equip students, particularly those who might benefit the most, with the navigational capital (see Yosso, 2005) needed to select into these opportunities, let alone know if they even exist. Even if students know about these opportunities, they may not be able to participate based on a variety of external factors, including work and family responsibilities. If institutions directed their imaginative and creative capacities to the problem, strategies might be developed for increasing the likelihood that those who would benefit the most from these innovations would participate in them. Such a strategy might involve placement of certain students into innovations taught by educators known to be effective teachers and supportive of students with narratives historically underrepresented in the higher education system.

Resource Allocation

The resources spent on students had a profound effect on their learning, development, and success. Budgetary outlays that directly affect students have an influence on their learning and retention. For example, the amount and nature of institutional spending affects student graduation rates, especially at four-year institutions. Total per student expenditures improve student graduation rates and spur gains in cognitive development. Institutions should consider how they allocate their funding; student services and student affairs are often among the first areas to be cut, but evidence on expenditures—as well as various other findings throughout this book—suggests that this may not be a wise strategy if the ultimate goal is to promote student success.

While a detailed account of trends in financial aid policy and the appropriate balance between merit- and need-based aid is beyond the scope of this review, we recognize that this remains a central concern among educators. Results from this review suggest that financial aid (especially grants and scholarships) was generally more effective in promoting learning and educational attainment outcomes among students from historically underserved populations than those from majority groups. Importantly, these practices also promote desired outcomes for all students. Given that financial aid seems to be more effective in promoting both individual and institutional degree completion when this funding does not need to be repaid, institutions should consider investing more heavily in awarding grants and scholarships. Other entities, such as nonprofit organizations and alumni, should also invest in improving financial support for students.

A key challenge for institutional policymakers is to balance trade-offs—or competing goals—when crafting their institution's financial aid policy between increasing profile (i.e., selectivity and rankings), student diversity, or net revenue (Hossler, 2004). Any policy enacted will likely lead an institution closer to one of these and away from another. For example, an institution may prioritize goals related to increasing profile by increasing focus on merit-based aid to attract and ultimately enroll the strongest academic achievement in high school. On average, these students will come from families, communities, and high schools with greater socioeconomic status. Such an institutional policy, while perfectly appropriate for driving profile, may simultaneously reduce enrollment slots available for students who may be willing to pay the full sticker price and reduce the funds available for need-based aid. Financial aid and scholarship monies work for students who need it the most. There is some evidence at both the institutional and student levels that prioritizing need-based aid over merit-based aid, loans, and nonaid expenditures is beneficial for promoting retention, persistence, and graduation overall. Given limited resources, institutions may want to consider shifting some funds from merit-based aid, loans, and non-aid expenditures to need-based aid packages. This approach may increase retention rates for all students, subsequently improve national rankings, and attract more high-achieving students who can pay full freight.

Ultimately the strategy an institution pursues with respect to merit- versus need-based aid should consider such trade-offs and reflect the mission of the institution. Just as a well-articulated, clear institutional mission has a positive influence on student learning and development, we argue that a school's financial aid policy and strategies for managing competing goals of profile, diversity, and revenue should consistently support a clear institutional mission.

In addition, institutions may need to refocus attention around career counseling services given that students' experiences during college substantially influence career development and economic outcomes. Students continue to highlight their desire to achieve "better" jobs as a primary motivation for entering college, and many states and institutions increasingly emphasize career development and employment-based outcomes after graduation as key indicators of the postsecondary "quality" in response to the proposed College Scorecard (USDOE, 2014b) and performance-based funding strategies. Therefore, institutions and students alike will benefit from more intentionality in supporting students in their efforts to pursue and secure jobs related to their majors.

Diversity

Diversity experiences remain a heavily researched area, with related studies spanning most chapters represented in this review. The research covered in this volume suggested that diversity-course taking was often positively associated with outcomes of interest, but not always. To provide further complication, the weight of the evidence also suggested that diversity-course taking may not benefit all students, since they may favor those in historically privileged groups. One plausible evidence-based explanation for this inconclusive pattern is the nature of the diversity course itself; all diversity courses may not be created equally, as instructors' depth and breadth of experiences designing and teaching these courses are likely to vary greatly. Clearly there is no standard approach to teaching diversity courses; however, educators may need to schedule course time for ongoing formative assessments, giving students the chance to articulate their thoughts regarding the course, and then use the information gathered as an opportunity to make course changes if needed.

Consistent with these results, learning and development appeared to be more related to the nature of the diverse peer interaction in the classroom than the number of these interactions. Educators should consider providing students with the opportunity to openly express their racialized identities, engage with other students across lines of difference, and resolve subsequent cognitive disruptions in healthy ways that benefit all students (Shapses-Wertheim, 2014). While diverse peer interactions can be a powerful catalyst to promote cognitive dissonance, leaving these exchanges to chance or providing opportunities in unstructured environments has the potential to attenuate many of the benefits espoused by the higher education community.

Educating about issues relating to diversity takes training and time. Although a few studies indicated a relationship between participation in cocurricular diversity efforts and student growth, the results remained mixed and inconclusive, which may stem from the spectrum of diversity-related programs, dialogues, and activities represented in the volume. Perhaps in contexts where students have repeated exposure to appropriately supported diversity-related materials (e.g., year-long training for resident assistants), educators can sustain the thoughtful work needed to help students productively negotiate some of the cognitive tensions spurred by encounters with difference. When educators do not have the time needed to help students through these encounters and in ways that benefit all students, they may want to reconsider some diversity-related activities and programs (e.g., tunnels of oppression), as they are unlikely to include the support needed for productive exchange to occur.

We were struck by the consistency in the evidence regarding students' engagement with diverse peers. Especially in the areas of psychosocial and attitudinal outcomes, peer interactions in curricular, cocurricular, and informal settings almost uniformly improved outcomes. Quality engagement with peers of diverse racial and ethnic backgrounds, social classes, worldviews, and sexualities inspires positive attitudes in ways that few other educational interventions have the power to do. We therefore suggest that leaders harness the potential that comes with a diverse campus. Rich structural diversity alone does not stimulate personal growth; rather, educators may want to commit to helping students learn how to approach their peers with the goodwill and openness necessary for constructive exchanges to evolve in classroom and out-of-class settings.

Finally, many studies reviewed for this volume examined some aspects of climate as a means for understanding diversity on college campuses. For example, we learned that intellectual and cognitive growth was associated with students' perceptions of their institution's commitment to support cross-race relations. Although debates continue about the design of these studies, we suggest that climate measures be theoretically grounded and empirically validated, as diversity measures consistently need refinement to pick up on the nuances in examining an institution within a particular sociohistorical space.

Cocurricular Engagement

Like its previous iterations, this volume contained results that linked participation in formal cocurricular activities and programs to learning, development, and persistence. The guiding assumption is that students learn and develop in communities outside the classroom—for example, student government, clubs, media, intramural athletics, and competitions associated with major field of study. Given the continuous turnover in the student body by transfer as well as completion, cocurricular educators provide stability, often remaining on the forefront of the innovations needed to help students learn, develop, and persist. These educators are particularly well positioned to design opportunities for students to relate to one another through both formal and informal cocurricular programs and activities. Indeed, students who are involved in any one of the multitude of out-of-classroom experiences on average reported greater social engagement and integration, which had decisively positive benefits toward student persistence.

Cocurricular programming and activities remain important for helping students make learning and development gains, especially for identity-based and psychosocial outcomes. To support the academic mission of the institution, educators interested in the cocurriculum may consider thinking strategically about how their expertise may specifically complement faculty members' skills and abilities with regard to student learning and development, as well as how this expertise may be marshaled to support the broader purposes of higher education. This strategic deployment of expertise may take many forms, but we offer four possibilities:

1. Cocurricular educators have their finger on the pulse of issues facing students and can bring that knowledge and expertise to educating faculty. We suggest these educators harness their knowledge of college students' aspirations, transitions, and experiences and partner with centers for teaching and learning in coconstructing development workshops for anyone who teaches students. Together, their expertise in understanding college students would be complemented by expertise of powerful active learning pedagogy to fundamentally transform learning environments.

2. Cocurricular educators' experience working with the student community places them in a position to assist in ways that support learning and success. For example, these educators may be instrumental in coordinating the logistics of an academic service-learning program, thus contributing to students' subject matter competence. They may also bring knowledge of the local, regional, and national job market to the classroom and help students develop the language to discuss their disciplinary knowledge and skills in transferable contexts. We urge cocurricular educators to speak with faculty members and learn how their expertise could be leveraged to support student learning.

3. Based on their expertise in leadership, cocurricular educators are in a distinctive position to assist the institution in realizing higher education's value and purpose of educating students for engaged citizenship. The focus on subject matter knowledge and generic skill development

with respect to being career ready has left one of most longstanding purposes of higher education without a dedicated champion. Cocurricular educators are often at the center of developing students' notions of citizenship through conversations about community expectations in the residence halls and among student organizations, as well as expectations for academic integrity. We suggest these educators consider taking a lead in the important work of educating students to the rights and responsibilities as citizens of their community and draw on their networks across campus and the community to ensure this critical component of the higher education mission is not left to chance.

4. Cocurricular educators continue to recognize the importance of peer relationships. The weight of the evidence in this volume suggests that the quality of peer relationships is a critical determinant of student learning, development, and persistence. Maximizing the reach of the peer potential should be a consideration for all educators, as the boundaries of the higher education context continue rapid expansion beyond the traditional brick and mortar and as definitions of the college student continue to evolve. As educators, how can we create formal and informal (i.e., networking) engagement opportunities for all students, including those who fall outside what is considered the "traditional student"?

Summary

Ultimately, we hope that the evidence provided in this review will help inform institutional practice. Rather than speaking to specific audiences within university settings, we addressed practices as they relate to interest areas represented within those settings. Echoing the good work of Kuh, Kinzie, Schuh, and Whitt (2011) who argued for a shared vision for student success, this strategy assumes that the best college-based practices are those that draw on the collective expertise across university stakeholders and that the best improvement strategies are comprehensive, bringing together interested parties from across the campus community.

CONCLUSION

As the public increasingly scrutinizes postsecondary education as a vehicle necessary for social and economic growth, empirical reviews like this will become increasingly important for their abilities to provide an evidence-based context for responding to these concerns as well as improving institutional practice. Despite a modicum of evidence to the contrary, college has, is, and will be influential across a host of outcomes, including learning, development, growth, persistence, completion, and financial return on investment. Of course, other indicators are also related to exposure to and participation in higher education; college-going remains influential for life satisfaction, health, and civic engagement. Given the volumes of work that empirically demonstrate the benefits of college-going, policymakers and taxpayers should be encouraged to know that their money is being well spent; indeed, going to college remains a primary means toward creating a successful and informed citizenry.

Educators should consider the evidence in this review as an indication of their success in helping students learn, develop, persist, and complete their education. Of course, some institutional practices, such as those that emphasized good teaching and were experienced by students as academically challenging, were more effective than others. To complicate matters, evidence from this volume suggested that not all practices were equally beneficial for all students. Some served to widen learning gaps between students with privilege and those from historically marginalized groups. Indeed, a critical lesson from this effort is to remind educators to routinely ask critical questions about equity-based practice. Specifically: Who benefits? This question should remain at the forefront of decision making related not only to resource allocation, but to college student learning, development, and retention.

Does college affect students? In a word, yes. We hope that the information provided in this volume has helped provide considerable nuance in answering this important question in detail. College clearly influences student outcomes, ranging from learning and development to economic success and quality of life. We urge policymakers, researchers, and educators to use the empirical arguments developed here to help solve the many issues facing us. Indeed, college matters.

Methodological Appendix: Considerations for Research on College Impact

T he title of this book intentionally contains causal language, because we are interested in understanding how college actually *affects* students. Although we would like to draw causal conclusions, the majority of studies on college students are not well designed for this purpose. This appendix provides an overview of several methodological issues that prevent researchers from identifying causal relationships, along with ways in which these problems can be reduced, if not eliminated. Some of these issues involve the use of statistical analyses and research designs, but this appendix is not intended to serve as a stand-alone resource on either of those technical and complex topics. Instead, it summarizes the general purposes and major analytical limitations of the body of evidence, and it refers readers to detailed discussions of relevant methods in other sources. Chapter 1 also contains relevant discussion of practical versus statistical significance (including effect size guidelines for college impact research) and the measurement of student outcomes.

This appendix serves several purposes. First, it provides readers with a general overview of research methods and analyses employed in many of the studies in this review. Second, the appendix highlights the substantial challenges with conducting research that provides strong causal conclusions about college impact. In doing so, it illustrates the extent to which previous research often has notable limitations, which means that practitioners and researchers should be cautious in their use of these findings. Finally, it provides researchers with a brief overview of methodological approaches that they should consider in their own work to provide the most rigorous possible findings. Certain methods and analyses are quite common in some disciplines and fields of study and not in others. We hope that this discussion will provide additional options to people who are trained within a particular area.

Given the complexity of some of the statistical techniques designed to address these methodological challenges, this appendix contains some discussion that may prove challenging for readers with little or no statistical training. Overall, we hope to provide an overview of some key issues in trying to understand college and its impact on students. First, students have considerable choice in whether to attend college, which college they attend, and what experiences they have while at college. This self-selection can lead to difficulties with determining whether effects are attributable to some aspect of college or to preexisting student characteristics. Second, the effects of college can occur as a result of institutional characteristics or student experiences that vary within an institution; teasing apart these different types of causal factors can prove challenging. Third, some effects of college on student outcomes occur indirectly by influencing some intermediate outcome, which can obscure the results if they are not examined appropriately.

NON-RANDOM ASSIGNMENT OF STUDENTS INTO EXPERIENCES AND INSTITUTIONS

Perhaps the most important problem in drawing causal conclusions is that college students who participate in a particular experience or attend a particular institution (or attend college at all) often differ in important ways from those who do not. In some cases, students are eligible for a program—such as need-based or merit-based scholarships, interventions for at-risk students, and participation in honors or other selective programs—only if they meet certain conditions. For instance, if students in a college honors program have higher college grades and persistence than those who did not participate, then it is a challenge to discern whether these findings are attributable to the honors program itself, differences in students' precollege characteristics (which are likely to be substantial), or participation in other college experiences. The same problem also exists when examining between-college effects: students who attend highly selective institutions differ in many ways from those who attend less selective schools, so how do we know whether any differences in outcomes can be attributed to their attending a particular type of college or university?

Experimental Design

To draw the strongest possible conclusions about college impact, students would be randomly assigned into college experiences through an experimental design, which is sometimes referred to as a *randomized controlled trial* (RCT). That is, students are randomly assigned to being in the treatment condition (e.g., taking course work that involves extensive peer discussion and group work; there may also be multiple treatments within the same experiment) or the control condition (e.g., taking course work in a traditional lecture-based format). If students in the treatment condition fare better on the desired outcomes than those in the control condition, then the researchers can generally be confident in concluding that the group-based pedagogy caused improved outcomes relative to the traditional pedagogy. Experimental design is widely considered the "gold standard" of education and social science research, since the two groups of participants should be essentially identical, except that one group receives the treatment and the other does not. As a result, it is quite likely that any differences in outcomes for the two groups can be attributed to exposure to the treatment versus control conditions (for more information, see Kirk, 2012; Murnane & Willett, 2011; Montgomery, 2012; Schneider, Carnoy, Kilpatrick, Schmidt, & Shavelson, 2007; Shadish, Cook, & Campbell, 2002).

However, research with experimental designs can also encounter at least five different types of challenges. First, not all students who are assigned into the experimental condition may actually participate. This issue can become even more problematic when an experimental intervention has several components; for instance, a program for at-risk students may involve academic advising, tutoring, and workshops, and students may attend each of these to varying degrees. Second, one or more components of the treatment may not be delivered in the intended manner. For instance, the researchers may intend living-learning communities to include components that are carried out in certain ways (e.g., course work that occurs in the residence hall, frequent office hours and opportunities for engagement with faculty members), but these may not occur as intended (or at all). If the registrar accidentally schedules the living-learning courses in another building across campus or the physical space in the residence hall is not suitable for holding those courses, then the study cannot examine the ideal or intended version of the intervention. Third, students in one condition may hear about or receive benefits from students in another condition. For instance, a study examining the impact of lottery incentives for survey participation could randomly assign some students to be entered into a lottery, while others receive no such invitation. If students who do not receive the lottery incentive hear that others have been invited into a lottery, then their perception of unequal treatment may cause them not to complete the survey. Therefore, any differences between the two groups may occur because of reactance of participants in the control condition rather than the lottery causing greater participation in the treatment condition. Fourth, the intervention may be effective for some students but not others. If this is true, then analyses of the entire sample may not find any significant effects at all, or they may understate the amount of impact among the students for whom the treatment is effective (this issue is addressed in more detail later).

The final and perhaps most salient concern deals with logistics and, potentially, ethics. In many instances, it simply may not be feasible to conduct an experiment to test the impact of certain college experiences. For instance, consider the many challenges associated with randomly assigning some students to participate in a fraternity or sorority, whereas other students are randomly assigned not to join—and are actually prevented from joining. Even when randomized studies are possible, they often involve a substantial level of coordination and institutional investment when studying real-world interventions. In short, although experiments are certainly underused in higher education research, viable alternatives are needed for instances in which experiments cannot be conducted.

Quasi-Experimental Designs

Researchers have created a set of designs, often referred to as quasi-experimental methods, to attempt to replicate the results of an experiment when randomization is not possible (for more information, see Morgan & Winship, 2007; Murnane & Willett, 2011; Rosenbaum, 2002, 2009; Schneider et al., 2007; Shadish et al., 2002; Thyer, 2012). Each of these methods takes a different approach at estimating causal effects, and some of these are tailored to addressing a particular way in which participants are assigned to treatment and control conditions. Several of these methods will be discussed briefly below.

Regression Discontinuity. This method is generally considered the most rigorous quasi-experimental approach in terms of its ability to draw strong causal conclusions about the effect of a treatment (Shadish et al., 2002; What Works Clearinghouse, 2014). The approach is ideal when students' assignment into treatment and control groups is based on their score on a single measure (see Bloom, 2009; Flaster & DesJardins, 2014; Imbens & Lemieux, 2008; Lesik, 2008; McCall & Bielby, 2012). For instance, suppose that a need-based scholarship is provided to all students at a public university whose family incomes are below $30,000. Therefore, a student whose family made $29,999 would receive the scholarship, whereas a student whose family made $30,001 would not. A regression discontinuity analysis examines only students who are within a certain range or bandwidth of that cutoff score (e.g., between $28,000 and $32,000) to determine whether the outcomes differ between students who are just below the income cutoff (and therefore receiving the scholarship) and those who are just above the cutoff (and therefore are not). The size of this bandwidth is determined in part by the number of participants who are near that cutoff; the trade-off is that using a smaller income bandwidth means that participants in the two groups are likely to be more similar, but there will be fewer participants in each group and therefore less power to detect statistically significant differences between groups. A key assumption of this analysis is that participants are randomly distributed around the cut point. In other words, it assumes that students and their families are not intentionally manipulating their income to be just below $30,000 so that they qualify for the scholarship.

Figure A.1 provides a visual display of hypothetical results from this regression discontinuity example. The predictor variables in this analysis include the continuous variable on which the cutoff score is based (in this case, family income) as well as a binary variable that indicates the cutoff score (in this case, whether family income is below $30,000). The results in Figure A.1 show that (1) there is generally a positive relationship between family income and intent to persist (the outcome variable), and (2) receiving the need-based scholarship appears to have a positive effect on intent to persist. Formal tests are necessary

Figure A.1 Results of a Hypothetical Regression Discontinuity Analysis for a Need-Based Scholarship with a Family Income Cutoff of $30,000

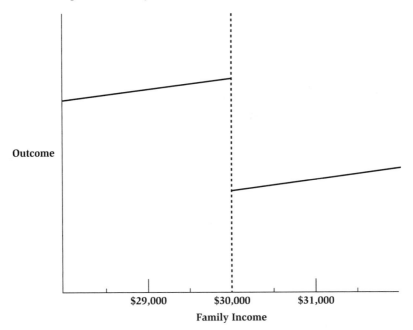

to determine whether these patterns are statistically significant. It is also important to consider whether there are any alternative explanations for these findings before drawing strong conclusions about the impact of the scholarship. For instance, might families receive other forms of financial assistance or benefits if their income is below $30,000? If so, then it would be unclear whether these differences are caused by the scholarship or by these other benefits.

This example of regression discontinuity is an ideal case in a number of ways that are often not true in other circumstances. First, scholarship eligibility is assumed to be determined solely by level of family income. In other circumstances, there may be multiple eligibility criteria, such as having attended an in-state high school. If this were the case, then the same analysis could be performed while limiting the potential sample to students who attended an in-state high school. Moreover, in Figure A.1, the relationship between family income and intent to persist is linear and identical on both sides of the cut point. However, these patterns may not provide an accurate representation of the data; statistical approaches can allow this relationship to be curvilinear and different across the two groups. Finally, and perhaps most importantly, this analysis is best suited for instances in which all students below $30,000 receive the scholarship, whereas all students at $30,000 or above do not. In many potential applications of regression discontinuity, that assumption may not be valid. This institution might offer a few scholarships to students who are above the cutoff for a variety of reasons, ranging from a clerical error to an exception to the usual policy. The presence of such crossover cases requires special attention so that appropriate conclusions are drawn.

Instrumental Variables. It is somewhat rare that students are assigned to college experiences by a cutoff score on a single criterion variable. Instead, their participation in various experiences (including the type of college they attend) often occurs as the result of a number of environmental and individual factors. To examine potential causal effects in these circumstances, the instrumental variable approach relies on a variable that is believed to have a causal effect on the environmental variable of interest (for more information, see Angrist, Imbens, & Rubin, 1996; Bielby, House, Flaster, & DesJardins, 2013; Bowden & Turkington, 1990; Morgan & Winship, 2007). The most important feature of an instrumental variable is that it affects the environmental variable but does not directly affect the outcome. For instance, to estimate the potential effect of years of education on earnings, previous researchers have used tuition at local colleges (among other factors) as an instrumental variable (Angrist & Krueger, 2001; Card, 1999). These instrumental variable analyses assume that lower tuition at nearby colleges would cause people to attend postsecondary education, and their educational attainment would then lead to higher incomes among those students. In addition, they assume that college tuition has no direct effect on earnings; it affects earnings only indirectly by promoting educational attainment (see Figure A.2).

Instrumental variables can take the form of general variation in the environment (e.g., tuition likely varies notably across states or across regions in a state) or a "natural experiment" in which an outside event causes a notable change in events (e.g., a state might decide to offer a sizable new scholarship for some students that could increase their likelihood of attending college). Instrumental variables can also be used to address problems with experimental and regression discontinuity designs. For example, even if students are randomly assigned to treatment and control conditions, some students who are assigned to the treatment may not ultimately participate, especially if doing so requires some action on their part. Therefore, the experimental condition to which students were assigned (sometimes referred to as the *intent to treat*) can serve as the instrumental variable, whereas actually receiving the treatment serves as the environmental variable of interest that may cause a relevant outcome. Moreover, if students do not fall perfectly into the appropriate categories in a regression discontinuity study (i.e., with all students above the cutoff in

Figure A.2 Conceptual Diagram of an Instrumental Variable Analysis

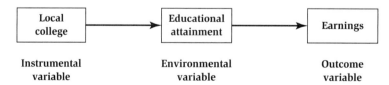

one condition and all students below the cutoff in the other condition), then instrumental variable analyses can similarly be used to examine intent to treat predicting actual treatment, which then predicts the desired outcome.

There are also some concerns about this form of analysis. As noted earlier, the assumption that the instrumental variable does not directly influence the outcome is very important, but this assumption is difficult to demonstrate empirically and often difficult to defend theoretically or conceptually. Moreover, even if the assumption holds, the causal effects are generalizable only to the students whose behaviors are affected by the instrumental variable. Thus, in the preceding example, we would know about the link between education and earnings for people whose college enrollment is affected by local tuition rates, but this relationship may be different for people whose behavior is unaffected by local tuition.

This attribute of instrumental variable analyses leads to two other potential issues. First, the analysis can yield results that are considerably biased if the link between the instrumental variable and the environmental variable of interest is weak. For example, if very few students' college-going behaviors are affected by variation in local tuition rates, then the results are unlikely to be valid, since this analysis would use only data from the small number of people who are potentially affected by the instrumental variable. Second, using different instrumental variables can result in different estimates of the relevant causal relationship, because the results are applicable only to students who are affected by that particular instrumental variable. For instance, the link between education and earnings may be different for students whose college attendance is affected by local tuition rates and for those who are affected by the distance from their current residence to the nearest colleges.

Propensity Score Matching. In many instances, students make their own decisions about the nature and extent of their experiences at their institution—not to mention their choice of institution—which is a process known as *self-selection*. That is, students decide whether and when they want to take a service-learning course, receive supplemental classroom instruction, or work as a resident assistant. As a result, students who choose to engage in an experience likely differ in numerous important ways from those who do not. It seems reasonable to assume, for example, that students who voluntarily take service-learning courses are often more civically engaged and socially conscious before the course even starts than other students.

Propensity score matching is a technique that seeks to account for self-selection effects in estimating the outcomes of college experiences. Specifically, this technique uses variables that occur before the treatment to indicate students' propensity or proclivity to participate in that experience, which is then used to compare students in treatment and control conditions who are equally likely to participate (for more information, see Austin, 2011; Bai, 2011; Guo & Fraser, 2010; Herzog, 2014; Holmes, 2013; Titus, 2007). To create a single score to indicate this propensity, researchers should obtain variables that predict participation in the treatment condition as well as the outcomes of interest. This analysis will only correct self-selection bias that is associated with variables used in the propensity score, so the effectiveness of this procedure depends on the degree to which these variables accurately reflect the process and attributes that predict self-selection. In a study of college service-learning and civic outcomes, for example, these propensity score variables could include pretests of the civic outcomes, prior service-learning course work, undergraduate major, demographics, and openness to diversity, among others. All of these variables should be measured before the treatment so that they accurately reflect students' predisposition to engage in the experience. These variables are then used to predict participation in the treatment through a logistic regression, and each student is given a score representing his or her likelihood of self-selecting into the treatment condition. Then students who received the treatment are matched with students who did not receive the treatment but were equally likely to have participated. Therefore, the analysis compares the outcomes of students who are virtually identical in their predispositions to participate in the treatment (at least in terms of those variables that were included in creating the propensity score). There are many techniques for conducting this matching; regardless of the specific approach, the ultimate goal is to determine whether students who received the treatment exhibit different outcomes from their matched counterparts.

Propensity score matching is more controversial than the other approaches, as some scholars question whether it actually provides better estimates of causal effects than do multiple regression analyses (discussed below). Most notably, a meta-analysis of studies in epidemiology found that propensity score matching yielded only slightly smaller effects than multiple regression, and these two approaches obtained a pattern of significant results that was identical 90% of the time (Shah, Laupacis, Hux, & Austin, 2005; also see Stürmer et al., 2006). Others have found that the quality of the covariates used in the analyses is much more important for removing self-selection bias than is the choice of statistical approach (Cook, Steiner, & Pohl, 2009; Pascarella, Salisbury, & Blaich, 2013; Steiner, Cook, Shadish, & Clark, 2010). In summarizing this debate, Shadish (2013) provides conditions under which propensity score matching is most likely to remove self-selection bias: including key variables in creating the propensity score that affect the selection process, using highly reliable measures, obtaining a large sample size (at least 500 and preferably 1,000 to 1,500), and comparing treatment and control groups that are as similar as possible (so that the propensity score has less bias to reduce).

Multiple Regression Analysis. Perhaps the most common multivariate technique in college student research is multiple regression analysis (for more information, see Allison, 1999; Cohen, Cohen, West, & Aiken, 2003; Garson, 2014; Keith, 2005; Pedhazur, 1997). Among other purposes, multiple regression can be used to estimate the unique relationship between each of the independent variables and a dependent variable while accounting or controlling for the variance explained by all other independent variables in the model. Suppose that a study used standardized test scores and living-learning community (LLC) participation as predictors of college GPA. If both of these predictors were included simultaneously in the multiple regression analysis, the results would indicate the relationship between LLC participation and GPA for students who have the same standardized test scores. In other words, the link between LLC participation and college GPA would account (or control) for the fact that students in the LLC may have had different ACT/SAT scores from those who were not in a LLC. Moreover, a model with high school GPA (HSGPA), standardized test scores, and LLC participation would provide information on the unique relationship for LLC participation (independent of HSGPA and ACT/SAT scores). It could also be used to compare the relative strength of HSGPA versus test scores in predicting college academic achievement (independent of LLC participation). Multiple regression analyses can contain a large number of predictors, especially when there are a large number of participants and the correlations among the predictors are modest.

In college impact studies, the predictors or independent variables in a regression analysis often include one or more college inputs (e.g., demographics, high school experiences and achievement, precollege attitudes and values) and one or more college experiences (e.g., cocurricular involvement, coursework and field of study, interpersonal interactions, perceptions of campus environment). This simultaneous examination of multiple independent variables differs from most quasi-experimental analyses, which are generally designed to provide rigorous estimates of the link between one experience and the outcome. For college student research, multiple regression analyses often isolate the unique relationship between an experience and an outcome by including other college experiences, whereas propensity score matching generally incorporates variables that occur before the college experience of interest (which often precludes the inclusion of other college experiences). Moreover, regression analyses can use dichotomous, ordinal, and continuous predictors, whereas quasi-experimental analyses generally examine the impact of a single dichotomous predictor (treatment versus control condition). The primary drawback of multiple regression is that this approach often yields less accurate estimates of causal effects than do experimental and quasi-experimental analyses.

DIFFERENTIATING BETWEEN-COLLEGE VERSUS WITHIN-COLLEGE EFFECTS

At first glance, it may seem easy to determine whether an outcome can be attributed to one or more characteristics of the student or the school that the student attends. However, in multi-institutional studies, this differentiation can be reasonably difficult. Suppose that a team of researchers obtained institution-level data for hundreds of four-year colleges and universities, and they found a negative relationship between the percentage of students who were eligible for Pell grants and the six-year institutional graduation rate. Does this relationship suggest that (1) Pell-eligible students are simply less likely to graduate, (2) attending an institution with many Pell-eligible students may be detrimental to all students' degree completion, or (3) a combination of the first two possibilities? Unfortunately, this question, as well as many others that focus on between-college effects, cannot be answered only with data at the institutional level. This answer is also not always as straightforward as simply obtaining data on both students and institutions.

A key assumption of multiple regression and some other statistical analyses is that each observation (e.g., an individual student) is independent of all others. However, this assumption is often violated when students within a sample attended different schools, because attending the same institution likely affects a variety of student outcomes. When these institutional influences occur, traditional analyses will often overestimate the statistical significance of certain relationships. As a result, multiple regression analyses may find that some independent variables are significantly related to an outcome, whereas more appropriate analyses would suggest that these same relationships are nonsignificant. To address this issue, research has increasingly employed analyses that can examine data at multiple levels simultaneously.

Multilevel Analyses

Since Pascarella and Terenzini's (1991, 2005) reviews, multilevel analyses have become increasingly common in college student research. Multilevel approaches differentiate between variance in the dependent variable that occurs across groups (e.g., institutions) and within groups (e.g., students at the same institution) so as to estimate more accurately the relationships at each level (for more information, see Heck & Thomas, 2009; Hox, 2010; Raudenbush & Bryk, 2002; Reise & Duan, 2003; Snijders & Bosker, 2012). Within higher education research, multilevel models often fall into one of two types: hierarchical linear modeling (HLM) and econometric panel analyses (Cheslock & Rios-Aguilar, 2011). While considerable overlap exists in these two approaches, HLM often examines nesting of students within institutions (for college impact studies), whereas panel analyses often examine changes in institutional attributes over time.

Hierarchical Linear Modeling. HLM and related techniques are frequently used to explore student and institutional characteristics simultaneously as predictors of an outcome. In a sense, HLM provides a separate multiple regression line for students attending each institution, which serves to differentiate between student-level and institution-level variance. Returning to the earlier example, if each student's Pell eligibility as well as the proportion of Pell-eligible students at the institution were included in the same HLM analysis, then the researchers could disentangle whether the effects occur at the student level or the institution level. Of course, even if the proportion of Pell-eligible students was still a significant predictor, the analysis would still need to include control variables that rule out plausible alternative hypotheses. For instance, schools that have many students from lower socioeconomic backgrounds may receive less funding from their endowments or the state government, and students who attend may have experienced lower-quality secondary school preparation, which could also explain this relationship.

In many HLM analyses, the relationship between a student-level predictor and the outcome is fixed across institutions; that is, the relationship between a college experience and the outcome is modeled as identical at all schools (for an illustration, see Figure A.3). However, this statistical assumption may not be true in practice. It might be the case, for example, that racial diversity workshops have a stronger effect on student attitudes at institutions that have a smaller proportion of students of color, given that White students at these schools have less opportunity to learn from frequent cross-racial interaction. HLM can allow these slopes to vary across institutions to examine whether (1) the relationship between a student-level predictor and the outcome differs significantly across institutions, and (2) the variation in this relationship across schools is associated with institutional characteristics (as described in the diversity workshop example).

HLM can also be used to explore more complex relationships than the two-level example of students within institutions. For researchers who are inter-

Figure A.3 Results of a Hypothetical Hierarchical Linear Modeling Analysis with Students Nested within Institutions

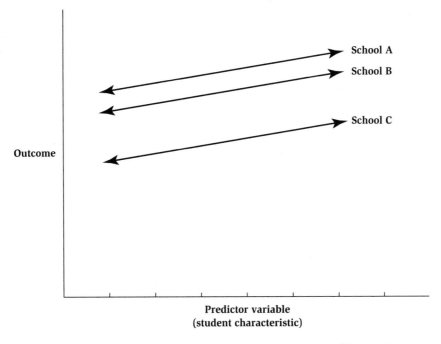

Note: In this example, the slopes are fixed to be identical across institutions; each line provides the predicted value for a given college or university.

ested in the potential impact of state policies on student graduation, HLM can be used to create a three-level model of students within institutions within states. In a longitudinal study that collected student data at several time points or occasions, HLM could be used to examine observations within students within institutions. However, as the number of levels within the analysis increases, researchers need to be increasingly diligent about ensuring sufficient sample size at each level, along with other issues. In addition to these applications within individual studies, HLM can also be used to conduct systematic quantitative reviews (i.e., meta-analyses) of existing research, since many higher education studies provide multiple estimates of the relationships between college experiences and outcomes; therefore, HLM can disentangle the relationships that occur within and across studies.

Panel Analyses. As noted, research that focuses on between-college effects has some notable challenges; these studies must demonstrate not only that an effect occurs between institutions, but also that it is uniquely attributable to that particular between-college characteristic (as opposed to other institutional or state-level factors). One way to help accomplish this task is to examine changes within institutional outcomes over time. Such analyses are inherently multilevel, because observations of these various time points are nested within institutions (i.e., each institution has several measurements of an outcome). Since panel analyses specifically examine between-college changes over time, any observed effects cannot be attributed to stable differences across institutions (e.g., public/private control). This approach is useful because many institutional attributes are generally quite consistent over time (e.g., selectivity). Panel analyses can examine the unique effects of multiple predictors that vary over time in the same model, and some types of analyses can also include within- and between-college predictors simultaneously. As a result, this approach can provide stronger support for causal effects than cross-sectional analyses; indeed, interrupted time series analyses of panel data are often considered to be a form of quasi-experimental analysis.

An important issue to consider is the length of time over which the between-college change should lead to a change in some outcome. For instance, many states have moved toward providing funding for public institutions that is at least partially based on institutional outcomes (e.g., graduation rates). How long after a state changes this funding policy might it take for graduation rates to improve? This lag between changes in the predictor and outcome is important to determine, since a panel analysis must employ a specified length of time. Thus, a nonsignificant result may be obtained not only because there is no actual effect of this change, but also because the amount of lag time that the researchers used was either too short or too long. Given that the appropriate amount of time can be unknown, some studies test multiple lag times to consider how long the effect might take to occur.

Other Approaches for Multilevel Data

Two other techniques for dealing with multilevel data are worth noting. If researchers have student data from multiple institutions but they are solely interested in exploring within-college effects, then they can used fixed effects regression to account for all between-college variability (e.g., Allison, 2009; Goldberger, 1991). As an example, a multiple regression model examining students at four institutions could include dummy-coded variables indicating whether the student attended a particular institution (e.g., school A, school B, and school C, with school D omitted as the referent group). This analysis controls for all possible differences across these schools, so findings for student-related predictors indicate within-school variation in the outcomes. The primary drawback of this approach is that it is not possible to explore the potential effects of between-college characteristics. A second approach is to adjust the standard errors to account for the clustering of students within institutions (Diggle, Heagerty, Liang, & Zeger, 2013; Fitzmaurice, Laird, & Ware, 2004). This adjustment does not involve analyzing the data as multilevel, but it instead seeks to avoid problems with using multiple regression for multilevel data through this statistical adjustment.

Interaction/Moderation Analyses

In the previous section, we provided a hypothetical example of diversity workshops having a stronger relationship with attitude change at campuses that are less structurally diverse. This example is an illustration of when the relationship between a college experience and an outcome may vary depending on an attribute of the student (e.g., gender, race/ethnicity, precollege achievement) or the environment (e.g., institutional demographics, institutional type). We generally refer to this phenomenon as a *conditional effect* in this book; these are also often called *interaction effects* or *moderation effects* (for more information, see Aiken & West, 1991; Hayes, 2013; Jaccard, 1998; Jaccard & Turrisi, 2003; Jose, 2013). Conditional effects can be explored in virtually every form of statistical analysis, whether multilevel or single level. Interactions can occur between institutional and student variables, or they can occur among two (or more) institutional variables or among two (or more) student variables. Exploring conditional effects is critical for determining who might benefit most—or at all—from certain aspects of college. For instance, suppose that participating in a first-year seminar that focuses on college adjustment issues leads to greater retention among students of color, but it has no relationship for White students. If a study exploring these issues occurred at a predominantly White institution, then an analysis that examines the entire sample may obscure the fact that some students receive greater (or any) benefits from this experience.

In an effort to avoid this problem, some higher education studies conduct subgroup analyses, usually separating students into groups by race/ethnicity, socioeconomic status, ability, or gender. While this approach is a good start for exploring conditional effects, additional testing is necessary to determine whether the relationships vary significantly across groups. For instance, even if the link between on-campus living and college satisfaction is similar for students of color and White students, subgroup analyses might find a significant relationship only for White students, since there are more White students (at many institutions) and therefore greater statistical power to detect statistical significance. These group differences can be examined within a single analysis that includes an interaction term, or additional tests can be performed after conducting subgroup analyses to explore potential significant differences across these coefficients (see Cohen et al., 2003).

ESTABLISHING DIRECT VERSUS INDIRECT EFFECTS

Most studies of college impact consider only the direct relationships between some aspect of college and students' subsequent outcomes. However, in some cases, theoretical or conceptual frameworks might suggest the presence of indirect relationships between two variables that occur through one or more additional intervening variables. For instance, the racial/ethnic composition of an institution's student body appears to influence student outcomes, but this relationship occurs only through increased intergroup interaction on campuses with more diverse student populations (Jayakumar, 2008; Pike, Kuh, & Gonyea, 2007). That is, racial/ethnic structural diversity may increase the likelihood of cross-racial interaction (because students have more different-race peers with whom to interact), and cross-racial interaction may lead to desired outcomes (as a result of the cognitive dissonance and resolution process that may stem from these experiences). However, there is no reason to expect a direct relationship between structural diversity and student outcomes, given that increasing cross-racial interaction is the mechanism through which this process is believed to occur (see Gurin, Dey, Hurtado, & Gurin, 2002). Other ways of describing this relationship are that cross-racial interaction mediates the link between structural diversity and student outcomes, and that structural diversity has an indirect effect on student outcomes. Figure A.4 provides an overview of this concept and example.

Figure A.4 Conceptual Overview of Direct and Indirect Effects

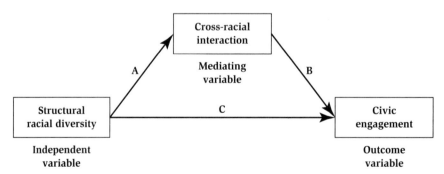

Note: Path C indicates a direct effect of structural racial diversity on civic engagement. An indirect effect for these two variables (via cross-racial interaction) would occur through paths A and B.

Exploring indirect effects is important for both theory and practice. Because many theoretical frameworks posit a string of causal relationships, an examination of these relationships can test whether any effects occur directly, indirectly, or both. Not finding a significant direct relationship that a theoretical framework proposes might suggest a need to revise theory and consider this relationship in developing student experiences. As a concrete example, an institution-wide change in academic advising might not have a direct effect on retention rates as administrators had hoped. However, the new advising policies may have led students to select a major earlier than previously, which promoted greater retention. Or the advising change may lead students to fulfill their degree requirements more quickly, which then leads to reduced time to degree and greater on-time graduation. This finding would be important, since most administrators care about retention, in large part, due to its relationship with subsequent graduation rates and associated financial considerations. Identifying indirect effects also adds to a fuller understanding of the complexity of the college-effects process and (indirectly) to more effective programs. Three different approaches can be used to examine indirect and direct effects: structural equation modeling, mediation analyses, and blocked hierarchical multiple regression.

Structural Equation Modeling

Structural equation modeling (SEM) examines the pattern of relationships among several variables. This analysis can examine both direct and indirect relationships, along with significance tests for both types of effects (for more information, see Hoyle, 2012; Kline, 2010; Raykov & Marcoulides, 2006; Schumacker & Lomax, 2012). One of the benefits of SEM is that it also provides statistics about the extent to which the hypothesized relationships accurately describe the actual results (through goodness-of-fit statistics). For instance, if an SEM analysis contained both intent to persist and actual persistence but the researchers did not include a direct path between these two constructs, then the model would be quite poor, since there is likely a strong relationship between this intention and subsequent behavior. Another benefit of SEM is that it can be used to adjust for measurement error by creating latent constructs, which consist of the items that are intended to measure that construct. That is, the results of SEM analysis with latent constructs represent the relationships if these constructs were measured with perfect reliability. In some ways, SEM represents a combination of factor analysis (items that measure the same construct are grouped together to form a single variable) and multiple regression (one or more constructs are used to predict another construct).

In general, because of their conceptual and analytical complexity, SEM analyses should be fairly parsimonious. Unlike multiple regression, SEM is intended to examine relationships among a fairly small number of constructs. The maximum number of variables depends on a variety of considerations, such as sample size and number of paths in the model. SEM techniques can be combined with other approaches, such as multilevel modeling, to obtain the benefits of both analytical methods. SEM can also be used to conduct analyses that can examine whether and how the relationships among variables differ across groups (e.g., race/ethnicity, gender), and statistical tests can determine whether the paths differ significantly across groups. SEM latent growth models can examine changes in the same measures over time (similar to multilevel models with observations nested within participants).

Mediation Analyses

Although formal mediation analyses are rarely used in college impact studies, they are quite helpful for exploring the extent to which one or more variables (i.e., mediators) explain the relationship between an independent variable and an outcome. This type of analysis is useful for an example already provided in Figure A.4: structural racial diversity (the primary independent variable) leads to cross-racial interaction (the mediator), which then leads to civic engagement (the outcome). The best-known mediation model was proposed in an influential article (Baron & Kenny, 1986). This mediation analysis occurs by conducting three regression analyses: (1) independent variable predicting the mediator, (2) independent variable predicting the dependent variable, and (3) independent variable and mediator simultaneously predicting the dependent variable. A significant mediation result is obtained if the results of the first two analyses are significant and the mediator is significant in the last analysis. Using Figure A.4 as an example, mediation would be established by finding significant relationships for paths A and B as well as for path C (when the mediator is not included in the model).

This work has been extended in some important ways. In more recent formulations, mediation analyses can examine a single mediator or multiple mediators, control variables can be included in any of these steps, and the indirect effect is obtained through a bootstrapping procedure that requires fewer statistical assumptions than previous tests (for more information, see Hayes, 2009, 2013; Preacher & Hayes, 2004, 2008; Shrout & Bolger, 2002). Therefore, unlike SEM, this mediation analysis maintains the benefits of multiple regression (with the potential to include numerous control variables) while still obtaining significance tests for indirect and direct effects. In an analysis with multiple mediators, the total indirect effect (through all mediators) and the indirect effects through each mediator can all be computed. However, the main drawback of this approach relative to SEM is that it examines only the indirect effect of a single independent variable rather than all possible indirect effects in the analysis. Additional indirect relationships can be obtained by re-conducting the analyses using a different independent variable each time.

Blocked Hierarchical Multiple Regression

The name of this analysis (also known as *hierarchical regression* or *blocked regression*) can be confusing, since it is unrelated to the use of *hierarchical* in HLM. Instead, hierarchical regression describes multiple regression analyses in which blocks (or sets) of variables are added to the model in a predetermined sequence of two or more blocks. This practice is common in college impact research, and the sequence of blocks often follows Astin's (1991) Input-Environment-Outcome model to some extent. Therefore, this order often reflects the temporal sequence in which the variables have occurred. That is, input variables (e.g., demographics as well as precollege experiences, achievement, and attitudes) are generally entered in the first block, and college experiences are added to this model in one or more subsequent blocks. In a hierarchical regression, variables that are included in a particular block remain in the analysis when additional variables are added in subsequent blocks. This technique allows estimation of whether the variables after the first block predict the outcome above and beyond the variables that were included in the previous block. This sequencing is designed to control for (or separate) the effects of students' precollege characteristics in order to estimate more accurately and validly the effects of the college experience, over which faculty members and administrators have some programmatic or policy control.

This approach is sometimes used to perform some of the steps of a mediation analysis. For instance, suppose that gender is one of several demographic variables included as predictors of critical thinking skills in block 1, and several college experiences are added to the analysis in block 2. In this hypothetical example, gender is significantly related to critical thinking in the first block, whereas this relationship becomes nonsignificant when college experiences are added in the second block. Therefore, it appears that the college experiences in block 2 explain or mediate the link between gender and critical thinking. This approach can also be used for exploring mediation dynamics that occur solely among college experiences and perceptions. For instance, living in an on-campus residence hall may influence retention by improving students' social and academic integration on that campus. However, living on campus may not be a significant predictor of retention when integration variables are included in the model, because the integration variables explain this underlying process. By adding the independent variables in several blocks of a hierarchical regression (ideally in a sequence specified by student attrition theories), a better understanding of student retention and relevant mediating processes may be obtained.

However, hierarchical regression does not provide as much detail about the mediation process as the analyses that are specifically designed to explore mediation. Specifically, one cannot determine which of the college experiences actually mediate the relationship or the strength of the indirect effect. Therefore, a formal mediation analysis or structural equation model seems preferable when researchers are interested in exploring one or more mediating effects in detail, whereas a blocked hierarchical multiple regression may be preferable when researchers want to understand the relationships for a relatively large number of variables that occur in a temporal or causal sequence.

SUMMARY

This appendix provides an overview of several key challenges for drawing causal conclusions in college impact research: (1) the typical lack of random assignment of students into colleges and universities as well as experiences within those institutions, (2) challenges with differentiating between-college versus within-college effects in multi-institutional studies, and (3) the presence of direct or indirect effects. We hope that researchers consider these challenges as they design more studies that examine college and its effects on students.

REFERENCES

Aalberts, J., Koster, E., & Boschhuizen, R. (2012). From prejudice to reasonable judgment: Integrating (moral) value discussions in university courses. *Journal of Moral Education, 41*(4), 437–455.

Abes, E. S., & Jones, S. R. (2004). Meaning-making capacity and the dynamics of lesbian college students' multiple dimensions of identity. *Journal of College Student Development, 45*(6), 612–632.

Abes, E. S., Jones, S. R., & McEwen, M. K. (2007). Reconceptualizing the model of multiple dimensions of identity: The role of meaning-making capacity in the construction of multiple identities. *Journal of College Student Development, 48*(1), 1–22.

Adams G. R., Shea, J., & Fitch, S. A. (1979). Toward the development of an objective assessment of ego-identity status. *Journal of Youth and Adolescence, 8*(2), 223–237.

Adelman, C. (2005). *Moving into town—and moving on: The community college in the lives of traditional-age students.* Washington, DC: U.S. Department of Education.

Adelman, C. (2006). *The toolbox revisited: Paths to degree completion from high school through college.* Washington, DC: U.S. Department of Education.

Agresti, A. (2013). *Categorical data analysis* (3rd ed.). Hoboken, NJ: Wiley.

Ahuna, K. H., Tinnesz, C. G., & VanZile-Tamsen, C. (2011). "Methods of inquiry": Using critical thinking to retain students. *Innovative Higher Education, 36*(4), 249–259.

Aiken, L. S., & West, S. G. (1991). *Multiple regression: Testing and interpreting interactions.* Thousand Oaks, CA: Sage.

Al-Fadhli, S., & Adbulwahed, K. (2009). Developing critical thinking in e-learning environment: Kuwait University as a case study. *Assessment and Evaluation in Higher Education, 34*(5), 529–536.

Alfonso, M. (2006). The impact of community college attendance on baccalaureate attainment. *Research in Higher Education, 47*(8), 873–903.

Alfonso, M., Bailey, T., & Scott, M. (2005). The educational outcomes of occupational sub-baccalaureate students: Evidence from the 1990s. *Economics of Education Review, 24*(2), 197–212.

Alimo, C. J. (2012). From dialogue to action: The impact of cross-race intergroup dialogue on the development of White college students as racial allies. *Equity and Excellence in Education, 45*(1), 36–59.

Allen, D. F., & Bir, B. (2012). Academic confidence and summer bridge learning communities: Path analytic linkages to student persistence. *Journal of College Student Retention: Research, Theory and Practice, 13*(4), 519–548.

Allen, J., & Robbins, S. B. (2010). Effects of interest-major congruence, motivation, and academic performance on timely degree completion. *Journal of Counseling Psychology, 57*(1), 23–35.

Allen, J., Robbins, S. B., Casillas, A., & Oh, I. (2008). Third-year college retention and transfer: Effects of academic performance, motivation, and social connectedness. *Research in Higher Education, 49*(7), 647–664.

Allgood, S., Bosshardt, W., van der Klaauw, W., & Watts, M. (2012). Is economics coursework, or majoring in economics, associated with different civic behaviors? *Journal of Economic Education, 43*(3), 248–268.

Allison, P. D. (1999). *Multiple regression: A primer.* Thousand Oaks, CA: Pine Forge Press.

Allison, P. D. (2009). *Fixed effects regression models.* Thousand Oaks, CA: Sage.

Allport, G. W. (1954). *The nature of prejudice.* Reading, MA: Addison-Wesley.

Alon, S. (2005). Model mis-specification in assessing the impact of financial aid on academic outcomes. *Research in Higher Education, 46*(1), 109–125.

Alon, S. (2007). The influence of financial aid in leveling group differences in graduating from elite universities. *Economics of Education Review, 26*(3), 296–311.

Alon, S. (2009). The evolution of class inequality in higher education: Competition, exclusion, and adaptation. *American Sociological Review, 74*(5), 731–755.

Alon, S. (2011). Who benefits most from financial aid? The heterogeneous effect of need-based grants on students' college persistence. *Social Science Quarterly, 92*(3), 807–829.

Alon, S., & Tienda, M. (2005). Assessing the "mismatch" hypothesis: Differences in college graduation rates by institutional selectivity. *Sociology of Education, 78*(4), 294–315.

Altbach, P. G., & McGill Peterson, P. (Eds.). (2007). *Higher education in the new century: Global challenges and innovative ideas.* Rotterdam, Netherlands: Sense Publishers.

Altonji, J., Blom, E., & Meghir, C. (2012). Heterogeneity in human capital investments: High school curriculum, college major, and careers. *Annual Review of Economics, 4*, 185–223.

Alvarez, C. M. (2007). *Does philosophy improve critical thinking?* Unpublished master's thesis, University of Melbourne, Melbourne, Australia.

American Psychiatric Association. (2013). *Diagnostic and statistical manual of mental disorders* (5th ed.). Arlington, VA: American Psychiatric Publishing.

American University Office of Institutional Research and Assessment. (2014). *Academic data reference book*. Retrieved from http://www.american.edu/provost/oira/upload/ADRB-2013-14-web-version-Updated.pdf

Amin, V., Behrman, J. R., & Spector, T. D. (2013). Does more schooling improve health outcomes and health related behaviors? Evidence from UK twins. *Economics of Education Review, 35*, 134–148.

An, B. P. (2012). The impact of dual enrollment on college degree attainment: Do low-SES students benefit? *Educational Evaluation and Policy Analysis, 35*(1), 57–75.

Anaya, G. (1999). College impact on student learning: Comparing the use of self-reported gains, standardized test scores, and college grades. *Research in Higher Education, 40*(5), 499–526.

Anderson, M. C. M., & Thiede, K. W. (2008). Why do delayed summaries improve metacomprehension accuracy? *Acta Psychologica, 128*(1), 110–118.

Anderson, W. L., Mitchell, S. M., & Osgood, M. P. (2005). Comparison of student performance in cooperative learning and traditional lecture-based biochemistry classes. *Biochemistry and Molecular Biology Education, 33*(6), 387–393.

Anderson-Martinez, R., & Vianden, J. (2014). Restricted and adaptive masculine gender performance in White gay college men. *Journal of Student Affairs Research and Practice, 51*(3), 286–297.

Andrade, M. S. (2007). Learning communities: Examining positive outcomes. *Journal of College Student Retention: Theory, Research and Practice, 9*(1), 1–20.

Andresen, M. A. (2009). Asynchronous discussion forums: Success factors, outcomes, assessments, and limitations. *Educational Technology and Society, 12*(1), 249–257.

Andrews, T. M., Leonard, M. J., Colgrove, C. A., & Kalinowski, S. T. (2011). Active learning not associated with student learning in a random sample of college biology courses. *CBE-Life Sciences Education, 10*(4), 394–405.

Angeli, C., & Valanides, N. (2009). Instructional effects on critical thinking: Performance on ill-defined issues. *Learning and Instruction, 19*(4), 322–334.

Anglin, D. M., & Wade, J. C. (2007). Racial socialization, racial identity, and Black students' adjustment to college. *Cultural Diversity and Ethnic Minority Psychology, 13*(3), 207–215.

Angrist, J. D., Imbens, G. W., & Rubin, D. B. (1996). Identification of causal effects using instrumental variables. *Journal of the American Statistical Association, 91*(434), 444–455.

Angrist, J. D., & Krueger, A. B. (2001). Instrumental variables and the search for identification: From supply and demand to natural experiments. *Journal of Economic Perspectives, 15*(4), 65–83.

Angrist, J. D., Lang, D., & Oreopoulos, P. (2009). Incentives and services for college achievement: Evidence from a randomized trial. *American Economic Journal: Applied Economics, 1*(1), 136–163.

Angus, S. D., & Watson, J. (2009). Does regular online testing enhance student learning in the numerical sciences? Robust evidence from a large data set. *British Journal of Educational Psychology, 40*(2), 255–272.

Antonio, A. L. (2004). The influence of friendship groups on intellectual self-confidence and educational aspirations in college. *Journal of Higher Education, 75*(4), 446–471.

Antonovics, K. L., & Goldberger, A. S. (2005). Does increasing women's schooling raise the schooling of the next generation? Comment. *American Economic Review*, *95*(5), 1738–1744.

Aragon, S. R., & Johnson, E. S. (2008). Factors influencing completion and noncompletion of community college online courses. *American Journal of Distance Education, 22*(3), 146–158.

Arbaugh, J. B., Godfrey, M. R., Johnson, M., Pollack, B. L., Niendorf, B., & Wresch, W. (2009). Research in online and blended learning in the business disciplines: Key findings and possible future directions. *Internet and Higher Education, 12*(2), 71–87.

Arbona, C., & Jimenez, C. (2014). Minority stress, ethnic identity, and depression among Latino/a college students. *Journal of Counseling Psychology*, *61*(1), 162–168.

Arbona, C., & Nora, A. (2007). The influence of academic and environmental factors on Hispanic college degree attainment. *Review of Higher Education, 30*(3), 247–269.

Ardelt, M. (2010). Are older adults wiser than college students? A comparison of two age cohorts. *Journal of Adult Development, 17*(4), 193–207.

Arend, B. (2009). Encouraging critical thinking in online threaded discussions. *Journal of Educators Online, 6*(1), 1–23.

Arias, J. J., & Walker, D. M. (2004). Additional evidence on the relationship between class size and student performance. *Journal of Economic Education, 35*(4), 311–329.

Aries, E., McCarthy, D., Salovey, P., & Banaji, M. R. (2004). A comparison of athletes and non-athletes at highly selective colleges: Academic performance and personal development. *Research in Higher Education, 45*(6), 577–602.

Aries, E., & Seider, M. (2005). The interactive relationship between class identity and the college experience: The case of lower income students. *Qualitative Sociology, 28*(4), 419–443.

Armbruster, P., Patel, M., Johnson, E., & Weiss, M. (2009). Active learning and student-centered pedagogy improve student attitudes and performance in introductory biology. *CBE-Life Sciences Education, 8*(3), 203–213.

Armstrong, N. A., Wallace, C. S., & Chang, S. (2008). Learning from writing in college biology. *Research in Science Education, 38*(4), 483–499.

Arnold, R., Martin, B. N., Jinks, M., & Bigby, L. (2007). Is there a relationship between honor codes and academic dishonesty? *Journal of College and Character, 8*(2), 1–20.

Arria, A. M., Caldeira, K. M., Vincent, K. B., Winick, E. R., Baron, R. A., & O'Grady, K. E. (2013). Discontinuous college enrollment: Associations with substance abuse and mental health. *Psychiatric Services, 64*(2), 165–172.

Arria, A. M., Garnier-Dykstra, L. M., Caldeira, K. M., Vincent, K. B., Winick, E. R., & O'Grady, K. E. (2013). Drug use patterns and continuous enrollment in college: Results from a longitudinal study. *Journal of Studies on Alcohol and Drug Use, 74*(1), 71–83.

Arum, R., & Roksa, J. (2011). *Academically adrift: Limited learning on college campuses*. Chicago, IL: University of Chicago Press.

Arum, R., & Roksa, J. (2014). *Aspiring adults adrift: Tentative transitions of college graduates*. Chicago, IL: University of Chicago Press.

Asel, A. M., Seifert, T. A., & Pascarella, E. T. (2009). The effects of fraternity/sorority membership on college experiences and outcomes: A portrait of complexity. *Oracle: The Research Journal of the Association of Fraternity/Sorority Advisors, 4*(2), 1–15.

Ashby, J., Sadera, W. A., & McNary, S. W. (2011). Comparing student success between developmental math courses offered online, blended, and face-to-face. *Journal of Interactive Online Learning, 10*(3), 128–140.

Ashwin, P. (2003). Peer support: Relations between the context, process and outcomes for the students who are supported. *Instructional Science, 31*(3), 159–173.

Association of American Colleges and Universities. (2002). *Greater expectations: A new vision for learning as a nation goes to college.* Washington, DC: Association of American Colleges and Universities.

Astin, A. W. (1984). Student involvement: A developmental theory for higher education. *Journal of College Student Development, 25*(4), 297–308.

Astin, A. W. (1991). *Assessment for excellence: The philosophy and practice of assessment and evaluation in higher education.* Westport, CT: American Council on Education/Macmillan.

Astin, A. W. (1993). *What matters in college? Four critical years revisited.* San Francisco, CA: Jossey-Bass.

Astin, A. W. (1999). Student involvement: A developmental theory for higher education. *Journal of College Student Development, 40*(5), 518–529.

Astin, A. W., & Astin, H. S. (1993). *Undergraduate science education: The impact of different college environments on the educational pipeline in the sciences.* Los Angeles, CA: University of California, Graduate School of Education, Higher Education Research Institute.

Astin, A. W., Astin, H. S., & Lindholm, J. A. (2011). *Cultivating the spirit: How college can enhance students' inner lives.* San Francisco, CA: Jossey-Bass.

Astin, A. W., Sax, L., & Avalos, J. (1999). Long-term effects of volunteerism during the undergraduate years. *Review of Higher Education, 22*(2), 187–202.

Astin, A. W., Vogelgesang, L. J., Misa, K., Anderson, J., Denson, N., Jayakumar, U., . . . Yamamura, E. (2006, July). *Understanding the effects of service-learning: A study of students and faculty.* Retrieved from http://www.heri.ucla.edu/PDFs/pubs/reports/UnderstandingTheEffectsOfServiceLearning_FinalReport.pdf

Astin, H. S., & Antonio, A. L. (2004). The impact of college on character development. In J. C. Dalton, T. R. Russell, & S. Kline (Eds.), *Assessing character outcomes in college* (New Directions for Institutional Research No. 122, pp. 55–64). San Francisco, CA: Jossey-Bass.

Attewell, P., Heil, S., & Reisel, L. (2011). Competing explanations of undergraduate noncompletion. *American Educational Research Journal, 48*(3), 536–559.

Attewell, P., Lavin, D., Domina, T., & Levey, T. (2006). New evidence on college remediation. *Journal of Higher Education, 77*(5), 886–924.

Austin, P. C. (2011). An introduction to propensity score methods for reducing the effects of confounding in observational studies. *Multivariate Behavioral Research, 46*(3), 399–424.

Australian Bureau of Statistics. (2014). Education. *Programme for the International Assessment of Adult Competencies, Australia, 2011–12.* Retrieved from http://www.abs.gov.au/ausstats/abs@.nsf/Lookup/4228.0Main + Features502011–12

Baber, W. L., Aronson, R. E., & Melton, L. D. (2005). Ideal and stereotypical masculinity and issues of adjustment to college life for men of color. *Southern Anthropologist, 31*(1–2), 53–73.

Baepler, P., Walker, J. D., & Driessen, M. (2014). It's not about seat time: Blending, flipping, and efficiency in active learning classrooms. *Computers & Education, 78*, 227–236.

Bahr, G. S., & Dansereau, D. F. (2005). Bilingual knowledge maps (BiK maps) as a presentation format: Delayed recall and training effects. *Journal of Experimental Education, 73*(2), 101–118.

Bahr, P. R. (2007). Double jeopardy: Testing the effects of multiple basic skill deficiencies on successful remediation. *Research in Higher Education, 48*(6), 695–725.

Bahr, P. R. (2008a). Cooling out in the community college: What is the effect of academic advising on students' chances of success? *Research in Higher Education, 49*(8), 704–732.

Bahr, P. R. (2008b). Does mathematics remediation work? A comparative analysis of academic attainment among community college students. *Research in Higher Education, 49*(5), 420–450.

Bahr, P. R. (2010a). Making sense of disparities in mathematics remediation: What is the role of student retention? *Journal of College Student Retention, 12*(1), 25–49.

Bahr, P. R. (2010b). Preparing the underprepared. An analysis of racial disparities in postsecondary mathematics remediation. *Journal of Higher Education, 81*(2), 209–237.

Bahr, P. R. (2012). Deconstructing remediation in community colleges: Exploring associations between course-taking patterns, course outcomes, and attrition from the remedial math and remedial writing sequences. *Research in Higher Education, 53*(6), 661–693.

Bai, H. (2011). Using propensity score analysis for making causal claims in research articles. *Educational Psychology Review, 23*(2), 273–278.

Bai, H., & Pan, Y. J. (2009). A multilevel approach to assessing the interaction effects on college student retention. *Journal of College Student Retention, 11*(2), 287–301.

Bailey, T. (2009). Challenge and opportunity: Rethinking the role and function of developmental education in community college. *New Directions for Community Colleges, 145*, 11–30.

Bailey, T., Calcagno, J. C., Jenkins, D., Leinbach, T., & Kienzl, G. (2006). Is student-right-to-know all you should know? An analysis of community college graduation rates. *Research in Higher Education, 47*(5), 491–519.

Bailey, T., Jeong, D. W., & Cho, S. W. (2010). Referral, enrollment, and completion in developmental education sequences in community colleges. *Economics of Education Review, 29*(2), 255–270.

Baker, C. N., & Robnett, B. (2012). Race, social support and college student retention: A case study. *Journal of College Student Development, 53*(2), 325–335.

Baker, R. W., & Siryk, B. (1984). Measuring adjustment to college. *Journal of Counseling Psychology, 31*(2), 179–189.

Balgopal, M. M., & Wallace, A. M. (2009). Decisions and dilemmas: Using writing to learn activities to increase ecological literacy. *Journal of Environmental Education*, *40*(3), 13–26.

Ball, K., & Crawford, D. (2005). Socioeconomic status and weight change in adults: A review. *Social Science and Medicine*, *60*(9), 1987–2010.

Ball, S. B., Eckel, C., & Rojas, C. (2006). Technology improves learning in large principles of economics classes: Using our WITS. *American Economic Review*, *96*(2), 442–446.

Bandiera, O., Larcinese, V., & Rasul, I. (2010). Heterogeneous class size effects: New evidence from a panel of university students. *Economic Journal*, *120*(549), 1365–1398.

Bandura, A. (1977). Self-efficacy: Toward a unifying theory of behavioral change. *Psychological Review*, *84*(2), 191–215.

Bandura, A. (1986). *Social foundations of thought and action: A social cognitive theory*. Englewood Cliffs, NJ: Prentice Hall.

Bandura, A. (1994). Self-efficacy. In V. Ramachaudran (Ed.), *Encyclopedia of human behavior* (Vol. 4, pp. 71–81). New York, NY: Academic Press.

Bandura, A. (1997). *Self-efficacy: The exercise of control*. New York, NY: Freeman.

Banks, K. H., & Kohn-Wood, L. P. (2007). The influence of racial identity profiles on the relationship between racial discrimination and depressive symptoms. *Journal of Black Psychology*, *33*(3), 331–354.

Barber, J. P. (2012). Integration of learning: A grounded theory analysis of college students' learning. *American Educational Research Journal*, *49*(3), 590–617.

Barber, J. P. (2014). Integration of learning model: How college students integrate learning. In P. L. Eddy (Ed.), *Connecting learning across the institution* (New Directions for Higher Education No. 165, pp. 7–17). San Francisco, CA: Jossey-Bass.

Barber, J. P., & King, P. M. (2014). Pathways toward self-authorship: Student responses to the demands of developmentally effective experiences. *Journal of College Student Development*, *55*(5), 433–450.

Barber, J. P., King, P. M., & Baxter Magolda, M. B. (2013). Long strides on the journey toward self-authorship: Substantial developmental shifts in college students' meaning making. *Journal of Higher Education*, *84*(6), 866–896.

Barber, N. A., & Venkatachalam, V. (2013). Integrating social responsibility into business school undergraduate education: A student perspective. *American Journal of Business Education*, *6*(3), 385–396.

Barger, B., & Derryberry, W. P. (2013). Do negative mood states impact moral reasoning? *Journal of Moral Education*, *42*(4), 443–459.

Barker, M., Lawrence, W., Crozier, S., Robinson, S., Baird, J., Margetts, B., & Cooper, C. (2009). Educational attainment, perceived control and the quality of women's diets. *Appetite*, *52*(3), 631–636.

Barker, M., Lawrence, W., Woadden, J., Crozier, S. R., & Skinner, T. C. (2008). Women of lower educational attainment have lower food involvement and eat less fruit and vegetables. *Appetite*, *50*(2), 464–468.

Barnett, E. A. (2011). Validation experiences and persistence among community college students. *Review of Higher Education*, *34*(2), 193–230.

Barnett, E. A., Bork, R. H., Mayer, A. K., Pretlow, J., Wathington, H. D., & Weiss, M. J., . . . Zeidenberg, M. (2012). *Bridging the gap: An impact study of developmental summer bridge programs in Texas*. Washington, DC: National Center for Postsecondary Research.

Barnett, J. E., & Francis, A. L. (2012). Using higher order thinking questions to foster critical thinking: A classroom study. *Educational Psychology: An International Journal of Experimental Educational Psychology, 32*(2), 201–211.

Baron, R. M., & Kenny, D. A. (1986). The moderator-mediator variable distinction in social psychological research: Conceptual, strategic, and statistical considerations. *Journal of Personality and Social Psychology, 51*(6), 1173–1182.

Barron, K. E., & Apple, K. J. (2014). Debating curricular strategies for teaching statistics and research methods: What does the current evidence suggest? *Teaching of Psychology, 41*(3), 187–194.

Barron's. (2013). *Profiles of American colleges 2013* (30th ed.). Hauppauge, NY: Barron's Educational Series.

Bartholow, B. D., Sher, K. J., & Krull, J. L. (2003). Changes in heavy drinking over the third decade of life as a function of collegiate fraternity and sorority involvement: A prospective, multilevel analysis. *Health Psychology, 22*(6), 616–626.

Bartlett, R., Rossen, E., & Benfield, S. (2008). Evaluation of the outcome-present state test model as a way to teach clinical reasoning. *Journal of Nursing Education, 47*(8), 337–344.

Barton, A., & Donahue, C. (2009). Multiple assessments of a first-year seminar pilot. *Journal of General Education, 58*(4), 259–278.

Barton, P., & LaPointe, A. (1995). *Learning by degrees: Indicators of performance in higher education*. Princeton, NJ: Educational Testing Service, Policy Information Center.

Bascom, J. (2011). Geographic literacy and moral formation among university students. *Review of International Geographical Education Online, 1*(2), 92–112.

Bastedo, M. N., & Jaquette, O. (2011). Running in place: Low-income students and the dynamics of higher education stratification. *Educational Evaluation and Policy Analysis, 33*(3), 318–339.

Bauer, K., & Liang, Q. (2003). The effect of personality and precollege characteristics on first-year activities and academic performance. *Journal of College Student Development, 44*(3), 277–290.

Baum, S., & Ma, J. (2013). *Trends in college pricing, 2013*. College Board. Retrieved from http://trends.collegeboard.org/sites/default/files/college-pricing-2013-full-report-140108.pdf

Baum, S., & Ma, J. (2014). *Trends in college pricing, 2014*. College Board. Retrieved from http://trends.collegeboard.org/sites/default/files/2014-trends-college-pricing-final-web.pdf

Baum, S., Ma, J., Pender, M., & Bell, D. (2015). *Trends in student aid, 2015*. College Board. Retrieved from http://trends.collegeboard.org/sites/default/files/trends-college-pricing-web-final-508-2.pdf

Baum, S., & Payea, K. (2013). *Trends in student aid, 2013*. College Board. Retrieved from http://trends.collegeboard.org/sites/default/files/student-aid-2013-full-report-140108.pdf

Baxter Magolda, M. B. (1992). *Knowing and reasoning in college: Gender-related patterns in students' intellectual development*. San Francisco, CA: Jossey-Bass.

Baxter Magolda, M. B. (1999). *Creating contexts for learning and self-authorship: Constructive-developmental pedagogy*. Nashville, TN: Vanderbilt University Press.

Baxter Magolda, M. B. (2001). *Making their own way: Narratives for transforming higher education to promote self-authorship*. Sterling, VA: Stylus.

Baxter Magolda, M. B. (2004). Self-authorship as the common goal of 21st century education. In M. B. Baxter Magolda & P. M. King (Eds.), *Learning partnerships: Theory and models of practice to educate for self-authorship* (pp. 1–35). Sterling, VA: Stylus.

Baxter Magolda, M. B. (2008). Three elements of self-authorship. *Journal of College Student Development, 49*(4), 269–284.

Baxter Magolda, M. B. (2009). *Authoring your life: Developing an internal voice to navigate life's challenges*. Sterling, VA: Stylus.

Baxter Magolda, M. B. (2014). Self-authorship. In C. Hanson (Ed.), *In search of self: Exploring student identity development* (New Directions for Higher Education No. 166, pp. 25–33). San Francisco, CA: Jossey-Bass.

Baxter Magolda, M. B., King, P. M., Taylor, K. B., & Wakefield, K. M. (2012). Decreasing authority dependence during the first year of college. *Journal of College Student Development, 53*(3), 418–435.

Beachboard, M. R., Beachboard, J. C., Li, W. & Adkison, S. R. (2011). Cohorts and relatedness: Self-determination theory as an explanation of how learning communities affect educational outcomes. *Research in Higher Education, 52*(8), 853–874.

Bean, J., & Eaton, S. (2000). A psychological model of college student retention. In J. M. Braxton (Ed.), *Reworking the student departure puzzle* (pp. 48–61). Nashville, TN: Vanderbilt University Press.

Beaumont, E., Colby, A., Ehrlich, T., & Torney-Purta, J. (2006). Promoting political competence and engagement in college students: An empirical study. *Journal of Political Science Education, 2*(3), 249–270.

Bebeau, M. J., & Thoma, S. J. (2003). *Guide for DIT-2*. Unpublished manuscript. University of Minnesota, Minneapolis.

Becchetti, L., Corrado, L., & Rossetti, F. (2008). *Easterlin-types and frustrated achievers: The heterogeneous effects of income changes on life satisfaction* (No. 127). Rome, Italy: Centre for Economic and International Studies.

Becker, G. S. (1993). *Human capital: A theoretical and empirical analysis with special reference to education* (3rd ed.). Chicago, IL: University of Chicago Press.

Becker, G. S., & Mulligan, C. B. (1997). The endogenous determination of time preference. *Quarterly Journal of Economics, 112*(3), 729–758.

Becker, G. S., Hubbard, W. H. J., & Murphy, K. M. (2010). Explaining the worldwide boom in higher education of women. *Journal of Human Capital, 4*(3), 203–241.

Beemyn, G. (2012). The experiences and needs of transgender community college students. *Community College Journal of Research and Practice, 36*(7), 504–510.

Beeson, M. J., & Wessel, R. D. (2002). The impact of working on campus on the academic persistence of freshmen. *Journal of Student Financial Aid, 32*(2), 37–45.

Behrman, J. R., & Rosenzweig, M. R. (2002). Does increasing women's schooling raise the schooling of the next generation? *American Economic Review, 92*(1), 323–334.

Behrman, J. R., & Rosenzweig, M. R. (2005). Does increasing women's schooling raise the schooling of the next generation? Reply. *American Economic Review*, *95*(5), 1745–1751.

Belenky, M., Clinchy, B. M., Goldberger, N. R., & Tarule, J. (1986). *Women's ways of knowing: The development of self, mind, and voice*. New York, NY: Basic Books.

Bellas, M. L. (2001). Investment in higher education: Do labor market opportunities differ by age of recent college graduates? *Research in Higher Education*, *42*(1), 1–25.

Benjamin, R. (2008). The case for comparative institutional assessment of higher-order thinking skills. *Change: The Magazine of Higher Learning*, *40*(6), 50–55.

Bensimon, E. M. (2007). The underestimated significance of practitioner knowledge in the scholarship of student success. *Review of Higher Education*, *30*(4), 441–469.

Berger, J. B. (2002). The influence of organizational structures of colleges and universities on college student learning. *Peabody Journal of Education*, *73*(3), 40–59.

Berger, J. B., & Milem, J. F. (2000). Organizational behavior in higher education and student outcomes. In J. Smart (Ed.), *Higher education: Handbook of theory and research* (pp. 268–338). New York, NY: Agathon Press.

Berger, J. B., & Milem, J. F. (2002). The impact of community service involvement on three measures of undergraduate self-concept. *Journal of Student Affairs Research and Practice*, *40*(1), 85–103.

Berkel, L. A., Vandiver, B. J., & Bahner, A. D. (2004). Gender role attitudes, religion, and spirituality as predictors of domestic violence attitudes in White college students. *Journal of College Student Development*, *45*(2), 119–133.

Bernacki, M. L., & Jaeger, E. (2008). Exploring the impact of service-learning on moral development and moral orientation. *Michigan Journal of Community Service Learning*, *14*(2), 5–15.

Bernard, R. M., Abrami, P. C., Borokhovski, E., Wade, A. C., Tamim, R. M., Surkes, M. A., & Bethel, E. C. (2009). A meta-analysis of three types of interaction treatments in distance education. *Review of Educational Research*, *79*(3), 1243–1289.

Bernard, R. M., Abrami, P. C., Lou, Y., Borokhovski, E., Wade, A., Wozney, L., . . . & Huang, B. (2004). How does distance education compare with classroom instruction? A meta-analysis of the empirical literature. *Review of Educational Research*, *74*(3), 379–439.

Berry, J. W., & Chew, S. L. (2008). Improving learning through interventions of student-generated questions and concept maps. *Teaching of Psychology*, *35*(4), 305–312.

Bettinger, E. P., & Baker, R. B. (2014). The effects of student coaching: An evaluation of a randomized experiment in student advising. *Educational Evaluation and Policy Analysis*, *36*(1), 3–19.

Bettinger, E. P., & Long, B. T. (2005). Remediation at the community college: Student participation and outcomes. *New Directions for Community Colleges*, *129*(1), 17–26.

Bettinger, E. P., & Long, B. T. (2013). Addressing the needs of underprepared students in higher education: Does college remediation work? *Journal of Human Resources*, *44*(3), 736–771.

Betz, N. E. (1988). The assessment of career development and maturity. In W. B. Walsh & S. H. Osipow (Eds.), *Career decision making* (pp. 77–136). Hillsdale, NJ: Erlbaum.

Betz, N. E., & Borgen, F. H. (2009). Comparative effectiveness of CAPA and FOCUS online: Career assessment systems with undecided college students. *Journal of Career Assessment, 17*(4), 351–366.

Betz, N. E., & Hackett, G. (2006). Career self-efficacy theory: Back to the future. *Journal of Career Assessment, 14*(1), 3–11.

Betz, N. E., Klein, K. L., & Taylor, K. M. (1996). Evaluation of a short form of the career decision-making self-efficacy scale. *Journal of Career Assessment, 4*(1), 47–57.

Bewick, B., Koutsopoulou, G., Miles, J., Slaa, E., & Barkham, M. (2010). Changes in undergraduate students' psychological well-being as they progress through university. *Studies in Higher Education, 35*(6), 633–645.

Bhathal, R., Sharma, M. D., & Mendez, A. (2010). Educational analysis of a first year engineering physics experiment on standing waves: Based on the ACELL approach. *European Journal of Physics, 31*(1), 23–35.

Bielby, R. M., House, E., Flaster, A., & DesJardins, S. L. (2013). Instrumental variables: Conceptual issues and an application considering high school course taking. In M. B. Paulsen (Ed.), *Higher education: Handbook of theory and research* (pp. 263–321). Dordrecht, Netherlands: Springer.

Bills, D. (2003). Credentials, signals, screens, and jobs: Explaining the relationship between schooling and job assignment. *Review of Educational Research, 73*(4), 441–449.

Bingham, C. R., Shope, J. T., & Tang, X. (2005). Drinking behavior from high school to young adulthood: Differences by college education. *Alcoholism: Clinical and Experimental Research, 29*(12), 2170–2180.

Bishop, J. L., & Verleger, M. A. (2013, June). *The flipped classroom: A survey of the research.* Paper presented at the ASEE Annual Conference & Exposition, Atlanta, GA.

Bitzan, J. D. (2009). Do sheepskin effects help explain racial earnings differences? *Economics of Education Review, 28*(6), 759–766.

Bixler, B. A., & Land, S. M. (2010). Supporting college students' ill-structured problem solving in a web-based learning environment. *Journal of Educational Technology Systems, 39*(1), 3–15.

Black, D. A., & Smith, J. A. (2004). How robust is the evidence on the effects of college quality? Evidence from matching. *Journal of Econometrics, 121*(1-2), 99–124.

Black, D. A., & Smith, J. A. (2006). Estimating the returns to college quality with multiple proxies for quality. *Journal of Labor Economics, 24*(3), 701–728.

Blair, B. F., Millea, M., & Hammer, J. (2004). The impact of cooperative education on academic performance and compensation of engineering majors. *Journal of Engineering Education, 93*(4), 333–338.

Blanchard, C. A., & Lichtenberg, J. W. (2003). Compromise in career decision making: A test of Gottfredson's theory. *Journal of Vocational Behavior, 62*(2), 250–271.

Blanchflower, D. G., & Oswald, A. J. (2004). Well-being over time in Britain and the USA. *Journal of Public Economics, 88*(7), 1359–1386.

Blanco, J., & Robinett, J. (2014). Leisure helps get the job done: Intersections of hegemonic masculinity and stress among college-aged males. *Journal of Leisure Research, 46*(4), 361–374.

Blau, P. M., & Duncan, O. D. (1967). *The American occupational structure.* New York, NY: Wiley.

Blazina, C., Settle, A. G., & Eddins, R. (2008). Gender role conflict and separation-individuation difficulties: Their impact on college men's loneliness. *Journal of Men's Studies, 16*(1), 69–81.

Bloom, D. (2009). Collaborative test-taking: Benefits for learning and retention. *College Teaching, 57*(4), 216–220.

Blumer, H. (1969). *Symbolic interaction: Perspective and method.* Berkeley: University of California Press.

Boatman, A., & Long, B. T. (2010). *Does remediation work for all students? How the effects of postsecondary remedial and developmental courses vary by level of academic preparation.* Washington, DC: National Center for Postsecondary Research.

Boese, G. D. B., Stewart, T. L., Perry, R. P., & Hamm, J. M. (2013). Assisting failure-prone individuals to navigate achievement transitions using a cognitive motivation treatment (attributional retraining). *Journal of Applied Social Psychology, 43*(9), 1946–1955.

Bonham, S. W., Deardorff, D. L., & Beichner, R. J. (2003). Comparison of student performance using web and paper-based homework in college-level physics. *Journal of Research in Science Teaching, 40*(10), 1050–1071.

Borg, M. O., & Stranahan, H. A. (2010). Evidence on the relationship between economics and critical thinking skills. *Contemporary Economic Policy, 28*(1), 80–93.

Borokhovski, E., Tamim, R., Bernard, R. M., Abrami, P. C., & Sokolovskaya, A. (2012). Are contextual and designed student-student interaction treatments equally effective in distance education? *Distance Education, 33*(3), 311–329.

Borwein, S. (2014). *The great skills divide: A review of the literature.* Toronto: Higher Education Quality Council of Ontario.

Boston, W., Ice, P., & Burgess, M. (2012). Assessing student retention in online learning environments: A longitudinal study. *Online Journal of Distance Learning Administration, 15*(2).

Boston, W. E., Ice, P., & Gibson, A. M. (2011). Comprehensive assessment of student retention in online learning environments. *Online Journal of Distance Learning Administration, 14*(1).

Boulton-Lewis, G., Wilss, L., & Lewis, D. (2003). Dissonance between conceptions of learning and ways of learning for indigenous Australian university students. *Studies in Higher Education, 28*(1), 79–89.

Bourdieu, P. (1984). *Distinction: A social critique of the judgement of taste.* Cambridge, MA: Harvard University Press.

Bourdieu, P. (1986). The forms of capital. In J. G. Richardson (Ed.) *Handbook of theory and research for the sociology of education* (pp. 241–258). Westport, CT: Greenwood.

Bowden, R. J., & Turkington, D. A. (1990). *Instrumental variables* (Economic Society Monographs, Book 8). Cambridge UK: Cambridge University Press.

Bowen, H. R. (1977). *Investment in learning: The individual and social value of American high education*. San Francisco, CA: Jossey-Bass.

Bowen, W. G., Chingos, M. M., Lack, K. A., & Nygren, T. I. (2013). Interactive learning online at public universities: Evidence from a six-campus randomized trial. *Journal of Policy Analysis and Management, 33*(1), 94–111.

Bowles, S., & Gintis, H. (1976). *Schooling in capitalist America: Educational reform and the contradictions of economic life*. New York, NY: Basic Books.

Bowles, S., & Gintis, H. (2002). Schooling in capitalist America revisited. *Sociology of Education, 75*(1), 1–18.

Bowles, T. J., McCoy, A. C., & Bates, S. C. (2008). The effect of supplemental instruction on timely graduation. *College Student Journal, 42*(3), 853–859.

Bowman, N. A. (2009). College diversity courses and cognitive development among students from privileged and marginalized groups. *Journal of Diversity in Higher Education, 2*(3), 182–194.

Bowman, N. A. (2010a). Can first-year college students accurately report their learning and development? *American Educational Research Journal, 47*(2), 466–496.

Bowman, N. A. (2010b). College diversity experiences and cognitive development: A meta-analysis. *Review of Educational Research, 80*(1), 4–33.

Bowman, N. A. (2010c). Disequilibrium and resolution: The nonlinear effects of diversity courses on well-being and orientations toward diversity. *Review of Higher Education, 33*(4), 543–568.

Bowman, N. A. (2010d). The development of psychological well-being among first-year college students. *Journal of College Student Development, 51*(2), 180–200.

Bowman, N. A. (2011a). Promoting participation in a diverse democracy: A meta-analysis of college diversity experiences and civic engagement. *Review of Educational Research, 81*(1), 29–68.

Bowman, N. A. (2011b). Validity of self-reported gains at diverse institutions. *Educational Researcher, 40*(1), 22–24.

Bowman, N. A. (2012). Structural diversity and close interracial relationships in college. *Educational Researcher, 41*(4), 133–135.

Bowman, N. A. (2013a). The conditional effects of interracial interactions on college student outcomes. *Journal of College Student Development, 54*(3), 322–328.

Bowman, N. A. (2013b). How much diversity is enough? The curvilinear relationship between college diversity interactions and first-year student outcomes. *Research in Higher Education, 54*(8), 874–894.

Bowman, N. A., & Brandenberger, J. W. (2010). Quantitative assessment of service-learning outcomes: Is self-reported change an adequate proxy for longitudinal change? In J. Keshen, B. Holland, & B. Moely (Eds.), *Research for what? Making engaged scholarship matter* (Advances in Service-Learning Research, Vol. 10, pp. 25–43). Charlotte, NC: Information Age Publishing.

Bowman, N. A., & Brandenberger, J. W. (2012). Experiencing the unexpected: Toward a model of college diversity experiences and attitude change. *Review of Higher Education, 35*(2), 179–205.

Bowman, N. A., Brandenberger, J. W., Hill, P. L., & Lapsley, D. K. (2011). The long-term effects of college diversity experiences: Well-being and social concerns 13 years after graduation. *Journal of College Student Development, 52*(6), 729–739.

Bowman, N. A., & Denson, N. (2011). The integral role of emotion in interracial interactions and college student outcomes. *Journal of Diversity in Higher Education, 4*(4), 223–235.

Bowman, N. A., & Denson, N. (2012). What's past is prologue: How precollege exposure to racial diversity shapes the impact of college on interracial interactions. *Research in Higher Education, 53*(4), 406–425.

Bowman, N. A., & Denson, N. (2014). A missing piece of the departure puzzle: Student-institution fit and intent to persist. *Research in Higher Education, 55*(2), 123–142.

Bowman, N. A., & Griffin, T. M. (2012). Secondary transfer effects of interracial contact: The moderating role of social status. *Cultural Diversity and Ethnic Minority Psychology, 18*(1), 35–44.

Bowman, N. A., & Small, J. L. (2010). Do college students who identify with a privileged religion experience greater spiritual development? Exploring individual and institutional dynamics. *Research in Higher Education, 51*(7), 595–614.

Bowman, N. A., & Small, J. L. (2012). Exploring a hidden form of minority status: College students' religious affiliation and well-being. *Journal of College Student Development, 53*(4), 491–509.

Boyer, E. L. (1990). *Scholarship reconsidered: Priorities of the professoriate.* Princeton, NJ: Carnegie Foundation for the Advancement of Teaching.

Bozick, R. (2007). Making it through the first year of college: The role of students' economic resources, employment, and living arrangements. *Sociology of Education, 80*(3), 261–285.

Braakmann, N. (2011). The causal relationship between education, health and health related behaviour: Evidence from a natural experiment in England. *Journal of Health Economics, 30*(4), 753–763.

Braasch, J. L., & Goldman, S. R. (2010). The role of prior knowledge in learning from analogies in science texts. *Discourse Processes, 47*(6), 447–479.

Bracke, P., Pattyn, E., & von dem Knesebeck, O. (2013). Overeducation and depressive symptoms: Diminishing mental health returns to education. *Sociology of Health and Illness, 35*(8), 1242–1259.

Bradley, R. V., Sankar, C. S., Clayton, H. R., Mbarika, V. W., & Raju, P. K. (2007). A study on the impact of GPA on perceived improvement of higher-order cognitive skills. *Decision Sciences Journal of Innovative Education, 5*(1), 151–168.

Brand, J. E. (2010). Civic returns to higher education: A note on heterogeneous effects. *Social Forces, 89*(2), 417–433.

Brand, J. E., & Halaby, C. N. (2006). Regression and matching estimates of the effects of elite college attendance on educational and career achievement. *Social Science Research, 35*(3), 749–770.

Braxton, J. M., Hirschy, A. S., & McClendon, S. A. (2004). *Understanding and reducing college student departure* (ASHE-ERIC Higher Education Report 30-3). San Francisco, CA: Jossey-Bass.

Braxton, J. M., & Lien, L. A. (2000). The viability of academic integration as a central construct in Tinto's interactionalist theory of college student departure. In J. M. Braxton (Ed.), *Reworking the student departure puzzle* (pp. 11–28). Nashville, TN: Vanderbilt University Press.

Braxton, J. M., Sullivan, A. V., & Johnson, R. M. (1997). Appraising Tinto's theory of college student departure. In J. C. Smart (Ed.), *Higher education: Handbook of theory and research* (Vol. *12*, pp. 107–164). New York, NY: Agathon.

Bray, G. B., Pascarella, E. T., & Pierson, C. T. (2004). Postsecondary education and some dimensions of literacy development: An exploration of longitudinal evidence. *Reading Research Quarterly, 39*(3), 306–330.

Brent, E., & Atkisson, C. (2011). Accounting for cheating: An evolving theory and emergent themes. *Research in Higher Education, 52*(6), 640–658.

Bresciani, M. J. (2002). A study of undergraduate persistence by unmet need and percentage of gift aid. *NASPA Journal, 40*(1), 104–123.

Bringle, R. G., & Hatcher, J. A. (1995). A service-learning curriculum for faculty. *Michigan Journal of Community Service Learning, 2*(1), 112–122.

Brint, S., Cantwell, A. M., & Saxena, P. (2012). Disciplinary categories, majors, and undergraduate academic experiences: Rethinking Bok's "underachieving colleges" thesis. *Research in Higher Education, 53*(1), 1–25.

Brittian, A. S., Umaña-Taylor, A. J., & Derlan, C. L. (2013). An examination of biracial college youths' family ethnic socialization, ethnic identity, and adjustment: Do self-identification labels and university context matter? *Cultural Diversity and Ethnic Minority Psychology, 19*(2), 177–189.

Brittian, A. S., Umaña-Taylor, A. J., Lee, R. M., Zamboanga, B. L., Kim, S. Y., Weisskirch, R. S., . . . Caraway, S. J. (2013). The moderating role of centrality on associations between ethnic identity affirmation and ethnic minority college students' mental health. *Journal of American College Health, 61*(3), 133–140.

Bronfenbrenner, U. (1979). *The ecology of human development: Experiments by nature and design.* Cambridge, MA: Harvard University Press.

Bronfenbrenner, U. (1993). The ecology of cognitive development: Research models and fugitive findings. In R. H. Wozniak & K. W. Fischer (Eds.), *Development in context: Acting and thinking in specific environments* (pp. 3–44). Hillsdale, NJ: Erlbaum.

Brooks, D. C. (2011). Space matters: The impact of formal learning environments on student learning. *British Journal of Educational Technology, 42*(5), 719–726.

Brower, A. M., & Inkelas, K. K. (2010). Living-learning programs: One high-impact practice we now know a lot about. *Liberal Education, 96*(2), 36–43.

Brown, C., Glastetter-Fender, C., & Shelton, M. (2000). Psychological identity and career control in college student-athletes. *Journal of Vocational Behavior, 56*(1), 53–62.

Brown, E. (2005). We wear the mask: African American contemporary gay male identities. *Journal of African American Studies, 9*(2), 29–38.

Brown, S., & Taylor, K. B. (2007). Religion and education: Evidence from the National Child Development Study. *Journal of Economic Behavior and Organization, 63*(3), 439–460.

Brownstein, D. (2014, April 11). Are college degrees inherited? Parents' experiences with education strongly influence what their children do after high school. *Atlantic.*

Bryant, A. N. (2003). Changes in attitudes toward women's roles: Predicting gender-role traditionalism among college students. *Sex Roles, 48*(3–4), 131–142.

Bryant, A. N. (2007). Gender differences in spiritual development during the college years. *Sex Roles, 56*(11–12), 835–846.

Bryant, A. N. (2011a). Evangelical Christian students and the path to self-authorship. *Journal of Psychology and Theology, 39*(1), 16–30.

Bryant, A. N. (2011b). The impact of campus context, college encounters, and religious/spiritual struggle on ecumenical worldview development. *Research in Higher Education, 52*(5), 441–459.

Bryant, A. N. (2011c). Ecumenical worldview development by gender, race, and worldview: A multiple-group analysis of model invariance. *Research in Higher Education, 52*(5), 460–479.

Bryant, A. N., & Astin, H. S. (2008). The correlates of spiritual struggle during the college years. *Journal of Higher Education, 79*(1), 1–27.

Bryant, A. N., Choi, J. Y., & Yasuno, M. (2003). Understanding the religious and spiritual dimensions of students' lives in the first year of college. *Journal of College Student Development, 44*(6), 723–746.

Bryant, A. N., Gayles, J. G., & Davis, H. A. (2012). The relationship between civic behavior and civic values: A conceptual model. *Research in Higher Education, 53*(1), 76–93.

Bryant Rockenbach, A. N., Hudson, T. D., & Tuchmayer, J. B. (2014). Fostering meaning, purpose, and enduring commitments to community service in college: A multidimensional conceptual model. *Journal of Higher Education, 85*(3), 312–338.

Bryant Rockenbach, A. N., & Mayhew, M. J. (2013). How the collegiate religious and spiritual climate shapes students' ecumenical orientation. *Research in Higher Education, 54*(4), 461–479.

Buchanan, N. T., Bergman, M. E., Bruce, T. A., Woods, K. C., & Lichty, L. L. (2009). Unique and joint effects of sexual and racial harassment on college students' well-being. *Basic and Applied Social Psychology, 31*(3), 267–285.

Buchmann, C., & DiPrete, T. (2006). The growing female advantage in college completion: The role of family background and academic achievement. *American Sociological Review, 71*, 515–541.

Bunch, J. M. (2005). An approach to reducing cognitive load in the teaching of introductory database concepts. *Journal of Information Systems Education, 20*(3), 269–275.

Burbach, M. E., Matkin, G. S., & Fritz, S. M. (2004). Teaching critical thinking in an introductory leadership course utilizing active learning strategies: A confirmatory study. *College Student Journal, 38*(3), 482–493.

Burgette, J., & Magun-Jackson, S. (2009). Freshman orientation, persistence, and achievement: A longitudinal analysis. *Journal of College Retention: Research, Theory and Practice, 10*(3), 235–263.

Burridge, M., & Öztel, H. (2008). Investigating the relationship between student achievement and e-learning: The case of an undergraduate strategic management module. *International Journal of Management Education, 7*(1), 3–11.

Butchart, S., Forster, D., Gold, I., Bigelow, J., Korb, K., Oppy, G., & Serrenti, A. (2009). Improving critical thinking using web based argument mapping exercises with automated feedback. *Australian Journal of Educational Technology, 26*(2), 268–291.

Butler, F. M., & Butler, M. (2011). A matched-pairs study of interactive computer laboratory activities in a liberal arts math course. *Australasian Journal of Educational Technology, 27*(2), 192–203.

Byrd, D. R., & McKinney, K. J. (2012). Individual, interpersonal, and institutional level factors associated with the mental health of college students. *Journal of American College Health, 60*(3), 185–193.

Byun, S., Irvin, M. J., & Meece, J. L. (2012). Predictors of bachelor's degree completion among rural students at four-year institutions. *Review of Higher Education, 35*(3), 463–484.

Cabrera, A. F., Nora, A., & Castañeda, M. B. (1992). The role of finances in the persistence process: A structural model. *Research in Higher Education, 33*(5), 571–593.

Cabrera, A. F., Nora, A., Crissman, J. L., Terenzini, P. T., Bernal, E. M., & Pascarella, E. T. (2002). Collaborative learning: Its impact on college students' development and diversity. *Journal of College Student Development, 43*(1), 20–34.

Cabrera, N. L. (2011). Using a sequential exploratory mixed-method design to examine racial hyperprivilege in higher education. In K. A. Griffin and S. D. Museus (Eds.), *Using mixed-methods approaches to study intersectionality in higher education* (New Directions for Institutional Research No. 151, pp. 77–91). San Francisco, CA: Jossey-Bass.

Cabrera, N. L. (2012). Working through Whiteness: White male college students challenging racism. *Review of Higher Education, 35*(3), 375–401.

Cabrera, N. L. (2014). "But I'm oppressed too": White male college students framing racial emotions as facts and recreating racism. *International Journal of Qualitative Studies in Education, 27*(6), 768–784.

Cabrera, N. L., Miner, D. D., & Milem, J. F. (2013). Can a summer bridge program impact first-year persistence and performance? A case study of the New Start Summer Program. *Research in Higher Education, 54*(5), 481–498.

Cacioppo, J. T., & Petty, R. E. (1982). The need for cognition. *Journal of Personality and Social Psychology, 42*(1), 116–131.

Cacioppo, J. T., & Petty, R. E. (1984). The elaboration likelihood model of persuasion. *Advances in Consumer Research, 11*(1), 673–675.

Cain, D. L., & Pitre, P. E. (2008). The effect of computer mediated conferencing and computer assisted instruction on student learning outcomes. *Journal of Asynchronous Learning Networks, 12*(3–4), 31–52.

Calcagno, J. C., & Long, B. T. (2008). *The impact of postsecondary remediation using a regression discontinuity approach: Addressing endogenous sorting and noncompliance* (No. w14194). Cambridge, MA: National Bureau of Economic Research.

Calcagno, J. C., Bailey, T., Jenkins, D., Kienzl, G., & Leinbach, T. (2008). Community college student success: What institutional characteristics make a difference? *Economics of Education Review, 27*(6), 632–645.

Calcagno, J. C., Crosta, P., Bailey, T., & Jenkins, D. (2007a). Does age of entrance affect community college completion probabilities? Evidence from a discrete-time hazard model. *Educational Evaluation and Policy Analysis, 29*(3), 218–235.

Calcagno, J. C., Crosta, P., Bailey, T., & Jenkins, D. (2007b). Stepping stones to a degree: The impact of enrollment pathways and milestones on community college student outcomes. *Research in Higher Education, 48*(7), 775–801.

Campbell, C. M., Smith, M., Dugan, J. P., & Komives, S. R. (2012). Mentors and college student leadership outcomes: The importance of position and process. *Review of Higher Education, 35*(4), 595–625.

Campbell, D. E. (2006). What is education's impact on civic and social engagement? In R. Desjardins & T. Schuller (Eds.), *Measuring the effects of education on health and civic/social engagement* (pp. 25–126). Paris, France: OECD/CERI.

Campbell, D. E. (2009). Civic engagement and education: An empirical test of the sorting model. *American Journal of Political Science, 53*(4), 771–786.

Capt, R. L., & Oliver, D. E. (2012). Student-centered learning and an emergent developmental student taxonomy. *Community College Journal of Research and Practice, 36*(10), 793–807.

Card, D. (1999). The causal effect of earnings on education. In O. C. Ashenfelter & D. C. Card (Eds.), *Handbook of labor economics* (Vol. 3A, pp. 1801–1863). Amsterdam, Netherlands: Elsevier.

Carini, R. M., Kuh, G. D., & Klein, S. P. (2006). Student engagement and student learning. *Research in Higher Education, 47*(1), 1–32.

Carl Wieman Science Education Initiative at the University of British Columbia. (2007–2015). *Achieving the most effective, evidence-based science education (effective science education backed by evidence)*. Retrieved from http://www.cwsei.ubc.ca/index.html

Carnegie Foundation for the Advancement of Teaching. (2001). *The Carnegie Classification of Institutions of Higher Education, 2000 edition*. Menlo Park, CA: Author.

Carnegie Foundation for the Advancement of Teaching. (2006). *The Carnegie Classification of Institutions of Higher Education, 2005 edition*. Menlo Park, CA: Author.

Carnegie Foundation for the Advancement of Teaching. (2011). *The Carnegie Classification of Institutions of Higher Education, 2010 edition*. Menlo Park, CA: Author.

Carnevale, A. P., & Cheah, B. (2013). *Hard times: College majors, unemployment and earnings*. Washington, DC: Georgetown University Center on Education and the Workforce. Retrieved from https://repository.library.georgetown.edu/bitstream/handle/10822/559308/Unemployment.Final.update1.pdf?sequence=1

Carnevale, A. P., Rose, S. J., & Cheah, B. (2011). *The college payoff: Education, occupations, lifetime earnings*. Washington DC: Georgetown University Center on Education and the Workforce. Retrieved from https://repository.library.georgetown.edu/bitstream/handle/10822/559300/collegepayoff-complete.pdf?sequence=1&isAllowed=y

Carter, L. K., & Emerson, T. L. N. (2012). In-class vs. online experiments: Is there a difference? *Journal of Economic Education, 43*(1), 4–18.

Case, K. F., & Hernandez, R. (2013). "But still, I'm Latino and I'm proud": Ethnic identity exploration in the context of a collegiate cohort program. *Christian Higher Education, 12*(1–2), 74–92.

Cass, V. (1979). Homosexual identity formation: A theoretical model. *Journal of Homosexuality, 4*(3), 219–235.

Cass, V. (1984). Homosexual identity: A concept in need of definition. *Journal of Homosexuality, 9*(2-3), 105–126.

Castleman, B. L., & Long, B. T. (2013). *Looking beyond enrollment: The causal effect of need-based grants on college access, persistence, and graduation* (NBER Working Paper No. w19306). Cambridge, MA: National Bureau of Economic Research.

Castriota, S. (2006). *Education and happiness: A further explanation to the Easterlin Paradox* (Working Paper No. 246). Rome, Italy: Centre for Economic and International Studies.

CEISS. (2004). *The Millennium Bursary in British Columbia: Exploring its impact.* Montreal, QC, Canada: Canada Millennium Scholarship Foundation.

Celio, C. I., Durlak, J., & Dymnicki, A. (2011). A meta-analysis of the impact of service-learning on students. *Journal of Experiential Education, 34*(2), 164–181.

Chan, N. M., Ho, I. T., & Ku, K. Y. I. (2011). Epistemic beliefs and critical thinking of Chinese students. *Learning and Individual Differences, 21*(1), 67–77.

Chaney, B. W. (2010). *National evaluation of Student Support Services: Examination of student outcomes after six years.* Washington, DC: U.S. Department of Education.

Chang, M. J., Astin, A. W., & Kim, D. (2004). Cross-racial interaction among undergraduates: Some consequences, causes, and patterns. *Research in Higher Education, 45*(5), 529–553.

Chang, M. J., Cerna, O., Han, J., & Saenz, V. B. (2008). The contradictory roles of institutional status in retaining underrepresented minorities in biomedical and behavioral science majors. *Review of Higher Education, 31*(4), 433–464.

Chang, M. J., Denson, N., Sáenz, V. B., & Misa, K. (2006). The educational benefits of sustaining cross-racial interaction among undergraduates. *Journal of Higher Education, 77*(3), 430–455.

Chaplin, S. (2009). Assessment of the impact of case studies on student learning gains in an introductory biology course. *Journal of College Science Teaching, 39*(1), 72–79.

Charon, J. M. (2009). *Symbolic interaction: An introduction, an interpretation, an integration.* New York, NY: Pearson.

Chavous, T., Rivas, D., Green, L., & Helaire, L. (2002). Role of student background, perceptions of ethnic fit, and racial identification in the academic adjustment of African American students at a predominantly White university. *Journal of Black Psychology, 28*(3), 234–260.

Chen, C. H. (2010). Promoting college students' knowledge acquisition and ill-structured problem solving: Web-based integration and procedure prompts. *Computers and Education, 55*(1), 292–303.

Chen, C. H., & Bradshaw, A. C. (2007). The effect of web-based question prompts on scaffolding knowledge integration and ill-structured problem solving. *Journal of Research on Technology in Education, 39*(4), 359–375.

Chen, N. S., Teng, D. C., Lee, C. H., & Kinshuk, C. H. (2011). Augmenting paper-based reading activity with direct access to digital materials and scaffolded questioning. *Computers and Education, 57*(2), 1705–1715.

Chen, P. S. D., Lambert, A. D., & Guidry, K. R. (2010). Engaging online learners: The impact of Web-based learning technology on college student engagement. *Computers and Education, 54*(4), 1222–1232.

Chen, R. (2012). Institutional characteristics and college student dropout risks: A multilevel event history analysis. *Research in Higher Education, 53*(5), 487–505.

Chen, R., & DesJardins, S. L. (2008). Exploring the effects of financial aid on the gap in student dropout risks by income level. *Research in Higher Education, 49*(1), 1–18.

Chen, R., & DesJardins, S. L. (2010). Investigating the impact of financial aid on student dropout risks: Racial and ethnic differences. *Journal of Higher Education, 81*(2), 179–208.

Chen, R., & St. John, E. P. (2011). State financial policies and college student persistence: A national study. *Journal of Higher Education, 82*(5), 629–660.

Chen, X., Wu, J., Tasoff, S., & Weko, T. (2010). *Issues tables* (NCES 2010–170 rev.). U.S. Department of Education. Retrieved from http://nces.ed.gov/pubs2010/2010170rev.pdf

Cheng, D. A. (2011). Effects of class size on alternate education outcomes across disciplines. *Economics of Education Review, 30*(5), 980–990.

Cheng, D., & Walters, M. (2009). Peer-assisted learning in mathematics: An observational study of student success. *Journal of Peer Learning, 2*(3), 23–39.

Cheng, K. K., Thacker, B. A., Cardenas, R. L., & Crouch, C. (2004). Using an online homework system enhances students' learning of physics concepts in an introductory physics course. *American Journal of Physics, 72*(11), 1447–1453.

Chernobilsky, E., Dacosta, M. C., & Hmelo-Silver, C. E. (2004). Learning to talk the educational psychology talk through a problem-based course. *Instructional Science: An International Journal of Learning and Cognition, 32*(4), 319–356.

Cheslock, J. J., & Rios-Aguilar, C. (2011). Multilevel analysis in higher education: A multidisciplinary approach. In J. C. Smart & M. B. Paulsen (Eds.), *Higher education: Handbook of theory and research* (Vol. 26, pp. 85–123). New York, NY: Springer.

Cheung, C., Rudowicz, E., Kwan, A. S. F., & Yue, X. D. (2002). Assessing university students' general and specific critical thinking. *College Student Journal, 36*(4), 504–525.

Cheung, C., Rudowicz, E., Lang, G., Yue, X. D., & Kwan, A. S. F. (2001). Critical thinking among university students: Does the family background matter? *College Student Journal, 35*(4), 577–597.

Chevalier, A. (2004). *Parental education and child's education: A natural experiment* (IZA DP No. 1153). Bonn, Germany: Institute for the Study of Labor.

Chevalier, A., & Feinstein, L. (2006). *Sheepskin or Prozac: The causal effect of education on mental health* (No. 2231). Bonn, Germany: Institute for the Study of Labor.

Chiappori, P., Iyigun, M., & Weiss, Y. (2009). Investment in schooling and the marriage market. *American Economic Review, 99*(5), 1689–1713.

Chickering, A. (1969). *Education and identity.* San Francisco, CA: Jossey-Bass.

Chickering, A., & Gamson, Z. (1987). Seven principles for good practice in undergraduate education. *AAHE Bulletin, 39*(7), 3–7.

Chickering, A. W., & Gamson, Z. F. (1991). Appendix A: Seven principles for good practice in undergraduate education. *New Directions for Teaching and Learning, 1991*(47), 63–69.

Chickering, A., & Reisser, L. (1993). *Education and identity* (2nd ed.). San Francisco, CA: Jossey-Bass.

Cho, K. L., & Jonassen, D. H. (2002). The effects of argumentation scaffolds on argumentation and problem solving. *Educational Technology Research and Development, 50*(3), 5–22.

Choi, I., Land, S. M., & Turgeon, A. J. (2005). Scaffolding peer-questioning strategies to facilitate metacognition during online small group discussion. *Instructional Science, 33*(5-6), 483–511.

Christie, R. L., & Hutcheson, P. (2003). Net effects of institutional type on baccalaureate degree attainment of "traditional" students. *Community College Review, 31*(2), 1–20.

Chularut, P., & Debacker, T. (2004).The influence of concept mapping on achievement, self-regulation, and self-efficacy in students of English as a second language. *Contemporary Educational Psychology, 29*(3), 248–263.

Clark, B. (1960). The "cooling out" function in higher education. *American Journal of Sociology, 65*(6), 569–576.

Clark, D., & Royer, H. (2010). *The effect of education on adult health and mortality: Evidence from Britain* (NBER Working Paper No. w16013). Cambridge, MA: National Bureau of Economic Research.

Clark, M. H., & Cundiff, N. L. (2011). Assessing the effectiveness of a college freshman seminar using propensity score adjustments. *Research in Higher Education, 52*(6), 616–639.

Clarkeburn, H. M., Downie, J. R., Gray, C., & Matthew, R. G. S. (2003). Measuring ethical development in life sciences students. A study using Perry's developmental model. *Studies in Higher Education, 28*(4), 443–456.

Clement, C. A., & Yanowitz, K. L. (2003). Using an analogy to model causal mechanisms in a complex text. *Instructional Science, 31*(3), 195–225.

Clifford, J. S., Magdalen, M. B., & Kurtz, J. E. (2004). Personality traits and critical thinking skills in college students: Empirical tests of a two-factor theory. *Assessment, 11*(2), 169–176.

Clotfelter, C., Ladd, H., Muschkin, C., & Vigdor, J. (2013). Success in community college: Do institutions differ? *Research in Higher Education, 54*(7), 805–824.

Cochran, J. D., Campbell, S. M., Baker, H. M., & Leeds, E. M. (2014). The role of student characteristics in predicting retention in online courses. *Research in Higher Education, 55*(1), 27–48.

Cohen, J. (1988). *Statistical power analysis for the behavioral sciences* (2nd ed.). Mahwah, NJ: Erlbaum.

Cohen, J., Cohen, P., West, S. G., & Aiken, L. S. (2003). *Applied multiple regression/ correlation analysis for the behavioral sciences* (3rd ed.). Mahwah, NJ: Erlbaum.

Cohen, S., Doyle, W. J., & Baum, A. (2006). Socioeconomic status is associated with stress hormones. *Psychosomatic Medicine, 68*(3), 414–420.

Cokley, K. (2002). The impact of college racial composition on African American students' academic self-concept: A replication and extension. *Journal of Negro Education, 71*(4), 288–296.

Cokley, K. O., & Chapman, C. (2008). The roles of ethnic identity, anti-White attitudes, and academic self-concept in African American student achievement. *Social Psychology of Education, 11*(4), 349–365.

Colaner, C. W., & Giles, S. M. (2008). The baby blanket or the briefcase: The impact of evangelical gender role ideologies on career and mothering aspirations of female evangelical college students. *Sex Roles, 58*(7-8), 526–534.

Colaner, C. W., & Warner, S. C. (2005). The effect of egalitarian and complementarian gender role attitudes on career aspirations in evangelical female undergraduate college students. *Journal of Psychology and Theology, 33*(3), 224.

Colby, A. & Kohlberg, L. (1987). *The measurement of moral judgment: Theoretical foundations and research validation* (Vol. 1). Cambridge, UK: Cambridge University Press.

Cole, D. (2007). Do interracial interactions matter? An examination of student-faculty contact and intellectual self-concept. *Journal of Higher Education, 78*(3), 249–281.

Cole, D. (2011). Debunking anti-intellectualism: An examination of African American college students' intellectual self-concepts. *Review of Higher Education, 34*(2), 259–282.

Coleman, J. S. (1988). Social capital in the creation of human capital. *American Journal of Sociology, 94*(Suppl.), S95–S120.

Collins, J., & Pascarella, E. T. (2003). Learning on campus and learning at a distance: A randomized instructional experiment. *Research in Higher Education, 44*(3), 315–326.

Collins, P. H. (2000). *Black feminist thought: Knowledge, consciousness, and the politics of empowerment.* New York, NY: Routledge.

Collins, R. (1979). *The credential society: An historical sociology of education and stratification.* New York, NY: Academic Press.

Colvin, J. W. (2007), Peer tutoring and social dynamics in higher education. *Mentoring and Tutoring, 15*(2), 165–181.

Comeaux, E., Speer, L., Taustine, M., & Harrison, C. K. (2011). Purposeful engagement of first-year Division I student-athletes. *Journal of the First-Year Experience and Students in Transition, 23*(1), 35–52.

Complete College America. (2011, September). *Time is the enemy: The surprising truth about why today's college students aren't graduating . . . and what needs to change.* Washington, DC: Author.

Complete College America. (2012, Winter). *Guided pathways to success: Boosting college completion.* Washington, DC: Author.

Complete College America. (2013, October). *The game changers: Are states implementing the best reforms to get more graduates?* Washington, DC: Author.

Congos, D., & Mack, A. (2005). Supplemental instruction's impact in two freshman chemistry classes: Research, modes of operation, and anecdotes. *Research and Teaching in Developmental Education, 21*(2), 43–64.

Constantine, M. G., & Watt, S. K. (2002). Cultural congruity, womanist identity attitudes, and life satisfaction among African American college women attending historically Black and predominantly White institutions. *Journal of College Student Development, 43*(2), 184–194.

Conti, G., Heckman, J., & Urzua, S. (2010). The education-health gradient. *American Economic Review, 100*(2), 234–238.

Conway, J. M., Amel, E. L., & Gerwien, D. P. (2009). Teaching and learning in the social context: A meta-analysis of service learning's effects on academic, personal, social, and citizenship outcomes. *Teaching of Psychology, 36*(4), 233–245.

Conway, M., & Ross, M. (1984). Getting what you want by revising what you had. *Journal of Personality and Social Psychology, 47*(4), 738–748.

Cook, T. D., Steiner, P. M., & Pohl, S. (2009). How bias reduction is affected by covariate choice, unreliability, and mode of data analysis: Results from two types of within-study comparisons. *Multivariate Behavioral Research, 44*(6), 828–847.

Corter, J. E., Esche, S. K., Chassapis, C., Ma, J., & Nickerson, J. V. (2011). Process and learning outcomes from remotely-operated, simulated, and hands-on student laboratories. *Computers and Education, 57*(3), 2054–2067.

Cortright, R. N., Collins, H. L., & DiCarlo, S. E. (2005). Peer instruction enhanced meaningful learning: Ability to solve novel problems. *Advanced Physiology Education, 29*, 107–111.

Cortright, R. N., Collins, H. L., Rodenbaugh, D. W., & DiCarlo, S. E. (2003). Student retention of course content is improved by collaborative-group testing. *Advances in Physiology Education, 27*(3), 102–108.

Council for Higher Education Accreditation. (2015). *Effective institutional practice: CHEA award recipients*. Retrieved from http://www.chea.org/chea%20award/CHEA_Awards_All.html

Coutinho, S. A., Wiemer-Hastings, K., Skowronski, J. J., & Britt, M. A. (2005). Metacognition, need for cognition and use of explanations during ongoing learning and problem solving. *Learning and Individual Differences, 15*, 321–337.

Covill, A. E. (2010). Comparing peer review and self-review as ways to improve college students' writing. *Journal of Literary Research, 42*(2), 199–226.

Cowell, A. J. (2006). The relationship between education and health behavior: Some empirical evidence. *Health Economics*, *15*(2), 125–146.

Cox, R. D. (2009). "I would have rather paid for a class I wanted to take": Utilitarian approaches at a community college. *Review of Higher Education, 32*(3), 353–382.

Cragg, K. M. (2009). Influencing the probability for graduation at four-year institutions: A multi-model analysis. *Research in Higher Education, 50*(4), 394–413.

Craig, P. J., & Oja, S. N. (2013). Moral judgment changes among undergraduates in a capstone internship experience. *Journal of Moral Education, 42*(1), 43–70.

Crain, W. C. (1985). *Theories of development*. Upper Saddle River, NJ: Prentice Hall.

Credé, M., & Kuncel, N. R. (2008). Study habits, skills, and attitudes: The third pillar supporting collegiate academic performance. *Perspectives on Psychological Science, 3*(6), 425–453.

Credé, M., & Niehorster, S. (2012). Adjustment to college as measured by the Student Adaptation to College Questionnaire: A quantitative review of its structure and relationships with correlates and consequences. *Educational Psychology Review, 24*, 133–165.

Crenshaw, K. (1989). Demarginalizing the intersection of race and sex: A Black feminist critique of antidiscrimination doctrine, feminist theory and antiracist politics. *University of Chicago Legal Forum, 139*, 139–167.

Crenshaw, K. (1991). Mapping the margins: Intersectionality, identity politics, and violence against women of color. *Stanford Law Review, 43*, 1241–1299.

Crews, D. M., & Aragon, S. R. (2004). Influence of a community college developmental education writing course on academic performance. *Community College Review, 32*(2), 1–17.

Crisp, G. (2013). The influence of co-enrollment on the success of traditional-age community college students. *Teachers College Record, 115*, 1–25.

Crisp, G., Nora, A., & Taggart, A. (2009). Student characteristics, pre-college, college, and environmental factors as predictors of majoring in and earning a STEM degree: An analysis of students attending a Hispanic serving institution. *American Educational Research Journal, 46*, 924–942.

Crisp, R. J., & Turner, R. N. (2011). Cognitive adaptation to the experience of social and cultural diversity. *Psychological Bulletin, 137*, 242–266.

Crissman, J. L. (2002). The impact of clustering first year seminars with English composition courses on new students' retention rates. *Journal of College Student Retention, 3*(2), 137–152.

Crites, J. O., & Savickas, M. L. (1996). Revision of the career maturity inventory. *Journal of Career Assessment, 4*(2), 131–138.

Cross, W. E., Jr. (1991). *Shades of Black: Diversity in African-American identity.* Philadelphia, PA: Temple University Press.

Cross, W. E., Jr. (1991). The psychology of Nigrescence: Revisiting the Cross model. In J. G. Ponterotto, J. M. Casas, L. A. Suzuki, & C. M. Alexander (Eds.), *Handbook of multicultural counseling* (pp. 93–122). Thousand Oaks, CA: Sage.

Cross, T. L., Coleman, L. J., & Stewart, R. A. (1993). The social cognition of gifted adolescents: An exploration of the stigma of giftedness paradigm. *Roeper Review, 16*(1), 37–40.

Crossgrove, K., & Curran, K. L. (2008). Using clickers in nonmajors and majors-level biology courses: Student opinion, learning, and long-term retention of course material. *CBE-Life Sciences Education, 7*(1), 146–154.

Cruce, T. M. (2009). A note on the calculation and interpretation of the delta-p statistic for categorical independent variables. *Research in Higher Education, 50*(6), 608–622.

Cruce, T. M., & Moore, J. V., III. (2007). First-year students' plans to volunteer: An examination of the predictors of community service participation. *Journal of College Student Development, 48*(6), 655–673.

Cruce, T. M., & Moore, J. V., III. (2012). Community service during the first year of college: What is the role of past behavior? *Journal of College Student Development, 53*(3), 399–417.

Cruce, T. M., Wolniak, G. C., Seifert, T. A., & Pascarella, E. T. (2006). Impacts of good practices on cognitive development, learning orientations, and graduate degree plans during the first year of college. *Journal of College Student Development, 47*(4), 365–383.

Cuellar, M. (2014). The impact of Hispanic-serving institutions (HSIs), emerging HSIs, and non-HSIs on Latina/o academic self-concept. *Review of Higher Education, 37*(4), 499–530.

Culbertson, S. S., Smith, M. R., & Leiva, P. I. (2011). Enhancing entrepreneurship: The role of goal orientation and self-efficacy. *Journal of Career Assessment, 19*(2), 115–129.

Cuñado, J., & de Gracia, F. P. (2012). Does education affect happiness? Evidence for Spain. *Social Indicators Research, 108*(1), 185–196.

Cunha, F., & Heckman, J. J. (2009). Human capital formation in childhood and adolescence. *CESifo DICE Report, 7*(4), 22–28.

Currie, J., & Moretti, E. (2003). Mother's education and the intergenerational transmission of human capital: Evidence from college openings and longitudinal data. *Quarterly Journal of Economics 118*(4), 1495–1532.

Cutler, D. M., & Lleras-Muney, A. (2008). Education and health: Evaluating theories and evidence. In R. F. Schoeni, J. S. House, G. Kaplan, & H. Pollack (Eds.), *Making Americans healthier: Social and economic policy as health policy* (pp. 29–60). New York, NY: Russell Sage Foundation.

Cutler, D. M., & Lleras-Muney, A. (2010). Understanding differences in health behaviors by education. *Journal of Health Economics, 29*(1), 1–28.

Dadgar, M. (2012). *Essays on the economics of community college students' academic and labor market success.* (Doctoral dissertation). Available from ProQuest Dissertations & Theses Global. (UMI No. 3506175).

Dahl, G. B. (2002). Mobility and the return to education: Testing a Roy model with multiple markets. *Econometrica, 70,* 2367–2420.

Dale, S., & Krueger, A. (1999). *Estimating the payoff to attending a more selective college: An application of selection on observables and unobservables.* Unpublished manuscript. Princeton, NJ: Andrew Mellon Foundation.

Dale, S. B., & Krueger, A. B. (2002). Estimating the payoff to attending a more selective college: An application of selection on observables and unobservables. *Quarterly Journal of Economics, 117*(4), 1491–1527.

Dancy, T. E. (2012). *The brother code: Manhood and masculinity among African American males in college.* Charlotte, NC: Information Age.

D'Augelli, A. (1994). Identity development and sexual orientation: Toward a model of lesbian, gay, and bisexual development. In E. Trickett, R. Watts, & D. Birman (Eds.), *Human diversity: Perspectives on people in context* (pp. 312–333). San Francisco, CA: Jossey-Bass.

Davies, J., & Graff, M. (2005). Performance in e-learning: Online participation and student grades. *British Journal of Educational Technology, 36*(4), 657–663.

Davis, S. J., & von Wachter, T. (2011, Fall). Recessions and the costs of job loss. *Brookings Papers on Economic Activity,* 1–72.

Davis, T. L. (2002). Voices of gender role conflict: The social construction of college men's identity. *Journal of College Student Development, 43*(4), 508–521.

Dawson, P., van der Meer, J., Skalicky, J., & Cowley, K. (2014). On the effectiveness of supplemental instruction: A systematic review of supplemental instruction and peer-assisted study sessions literature between 2001 and 2010. *Review of Educational Research, 84*(4), 609–639.

Dawson, T. (2004). Assessing intellectual development: Three approaches, one sequence. *Journal of Adult Development, 11*(2), 71–85.

DeBacker, L., VanKeer, H., & Valcke, M. (2012). Exploring the potential impact of reciprocal peer tutoring on higher education students' metacognitive knowledge and regulation. *Instructional Science, 40,* 559–588.

DeBacker, T. K., & Crowson, H. M. (2006). Influences on cognitive engagement: Epistemological beliefs and need for closure. *British Journal of Educational Psychology, 76,* 535–551.

DeBerard, M. S., Spielmans, G. I., & Julka, D. C. (2004). Predictors of academic achievement and retention among college freshmen: A longitudinal study. *College Student Journal, 38*(1), 66–80.

Dee, T. S. (2003). *Are there civic returns to education?* (NBER Working Paper No. 9588). Cambridge, MA: National Bureau of Economic Research. Retrieved from http://www.nber.org/papers/w9588

Dee, T. S. (2004). Are there civic returns to education? *Journal of Public Economics, 88,* 1697–1720.

DeGraaf, D., Slagter, C., Larsen, K., & Ditta, E. (2013). The long-term personal and professional impacts of participating in a study abroad program. *Interdisciplinary Journal of Study Abroad, 23,* 42–59.

Deil-Amen, R., & Rosenbaum, J. E. (2004). Charter building and labor market contacts in two-year colleges. *Sociology of Education, 77,* 245–265.

Del Rossi, A. F., & Hersch, J. (2008). Double your major, double your return? *Economics of Education Review, 27,* 375–386.

Delucchi, M. (2007). Assessing the impact of group projects on examination performance in social statistics. *Teaching in Higher Education, 12*(4), 447–460.

Denson, N., & Bowman, N. (2013). University diversity and preparation for a global society: The role of diversity in shaping intergroup attitudes and civic outcomes. *Studies in Higher Education, 38*(4), 555–570.

Denson, N., & Chang, M. J. (2009). Racial diversity matters: The impact of diversity-related student engagement and institutional context. *American Educational Research Journal, 46*(2), 322–353.

Department of Business Innovation & Skills. (2013). *The International Survey of Adult Skills 2012: Adult literacy, numeracy and problem solving skills in England.* Retrieved from https://www.gov.uk/government/uploads/system/uploads/attachment_data/file/246534/bis-13–1221-international-survey-of-adult-skills-2012.pdf

Department for Employment and Learning. (2013). *The International Survey of Adult Skills 2012: Adult literacy, numeracy and problem solving skills in Northern Ireland.* Retrieved from https://www.delni.gov.uk/sites/default/files/publications/del/international-survey-adult-skills-2012.pdf

Derryberry, W. P., Jones, K. L., Grieve, F. G., & Barger, B. (2007). Assessing the relationship among Defining Issues Test scores and crystallized and fluid intellectual indices. *Journal of Moral Education, 36*(4), 475–496.

Derryberry, W. P., Mulvaney, R., Brooks, J., & Chandler, C. (2009). Addressing the relationships among moral judgment development, authenticity, nonprejudice, and volunteerism. *Ethics and Behavior, 19*(3), 201–217.

Derryberry, W. P., Snyder, H., Wilson, T., & Barger, B. (2006). Moral judgment differences in education and liberal arts majors: Cause for concern? *Journal of College and Character, 7*(4), 1–10.

Desjardins, R. (2008). Researching the links between education and well-being. *European Journal of Education, 43*(1), 23–35.

DesJardins, S. L., Ahlburg, D. A., & McCall, B. P. (2002a). A temporal investigation of factors related to timely degree completion. *Journal of Higher Education, 73*(5), 555–581.

DesJardins, S. L., Ahlburg, D. A., & McCall, B. P. (2002b). Simulating the longitudinal effects of changes in financial aid on student departure from college. *Journal of Human Resources, 37*(3), 653–679.

DesJardins, S. L., Ahlburg, D. A., & McCall, B. P. (2006). The effects of interrupted enrollment on graduation from college: Racial, income, and ability differences. *Economics of Education Review, 25*, 575–590.

DesJardins, S. L., Kim, D. O., & Rzonca, C. S. (2003). A nested analysis of factors affecting bachelor's degree completion. *Journal of College Student Retention, 4*(4), 407–435.

DesJardins, S. L., & McCall, B. P. (2010). Simulating the effects of financial aid packages on college student stopout, reenrollment spells, and graduation chances. *Review of Higher Education, 33*(4), 513–541.

DesJardins, S. L., McCall, B. P., Ahlburg, D. A., & Moye, M. J. (2002). Adding a timing light to the "tool box." *Research in Higher Education, 43*(1), 83–114.

Deslauriers, L., & Wieman, C. (2011). Learning and retention of quantum concepts with different teaching methods. *Physical Review Special Topics—Physics Education Research, 7*, 1–6.

Deslauriers, L., Schelew, E., & Wieman, C. (2011). Improved learning in a large-enrollment physics class. *Science, 332*(6031), 862–864.

Dessel, A. B., Woodford, M. R., Routenberg, R., & Breijak, D. P. (2013). Heterosexual students' experiences in sexual orientation intergroup dialogue courses. *Journal of Homosexuality, 60*(7), 1054–1080.

de Walque, D. (2007). Does education affect smoking behaviors? Evidence using the Vietnam draft as an instrument for college education. *Journal of Health Economics, 26*(5), 877–895.

de Walque, D. (2010). Education, information, and smoking decisions evidence from smoking histories in the United States, 1940–2000. *Journal of Human Resources, 45*(3), 682–717.

Dewey, J. (1932). *Ethics.* New York, NY: Holt.

Dewey, J. (1938). *Experience and education.* Indianapolis, IN: Kappa Delta Pi.

Dey, F., & Cruzvergara, C. Y. (2014). Evolution of career services in higher education. In K. K. Smith (Ed.), *Strategic directions for career services within the university setting* (New Directions for Student Services No. 148, pp. 5–18). Hoboken, NJ: Wiley.

Di Tella, R., MacCulloch, R. J., & Oswald, A. J. (2003). The macroeconomics of happiness. *Review of Economics and Statistics, 85*(4), 809–827.

Diaz, A., & Perrault, R. (2010). Sustained dialogue and civic life: Post-college impacts. *Michigan Journal of Community Service Learning, 17*(1), 32–43.

Dickie, M. (2006). Do classroom experiments increase learning in introductory microeconomics? *Journal of Economic Education, 37*(3), 267–288.

Diegelman, N. M., & Subich, L. M. (2001). Academic and vocational interest as a function of outcome expectancies in social cognitive career theory. *Journal of Vocational Behavior, 59*, 394–405.

Diggle, P. J., Heagerty, P., Liang, K. Y., & Zeger, S. L. (2013). *Analysis of longitudinal data* (2nd ed.). New York, NY: Oxford University Press.

Dill, B. T., McLaughlin, A. E., & Nieves, A. D. (2007). Future directions of feminist research: Intersectionality. In S. N. Hesse-Biber (Ed.), *Handbook of feminist research* (pp. 629–637). Thousand Oaks, CA: Sage.

Dill, B. T., & Zambrana, R. E. (2009). *Emerging intersections: Race, class, and gender in theory, policy, and practice.* New Brunswick, NJ: Rutgers University Press.

Dillard-Eggers, J., Wooten, T., Childs, B., & Coker, J. (2011). Evidence on the effectiveness of online homework. *College Teaching Methods and Styles Journal, 4*(5), 9–16.

Dochy, F., Segers, M., Van den Bossche, P., & Gijbels, D. (2003). Effects of problem-based learning: A meta-analysis. *Learning and Instruction: The Journal of the European Association for Research on Learning and Instruction, 13*(5), 533–568.

Dockery, A. M. (2010). *Education and happiness in the school-to-work transition.* Adelaide, SA, Australia: National Centre for Vocational Education Research.

Donhardt, G. L. (2004). In search of the effects of academic achievement in postgraduation earnings. *Research in Higher Education, 45*(3), 271–284.

Donhardt, G. (2013). The fourth-year experience: Impediments to degree completion. *Innovative Higher Education, 38*(3), 207–221.

Dori, Y. J., & Belcher, J. (2005). How does technology-enabled active learning affect undergraduate students' understanding of electromagnetism concepts? *Journal of the Learning Sciences, 14*(2), 243–279.

Dorough, S. (2011). Moral development. In S. Goldstein & J. A. Naglieri (Eds.), *Encyclopedia of Child Behavior and Development* (pp. 967–970). New York, NY: Springer.

Dovidio, J., Gaertner, S., Stewart, T., Esses, V., Vergert, M., & Hodson, G. (2004). From intervention to outcome: Processes in the reduction of bias. In W. Stephan & W. Vogt (Eds.), *Education programs for improving intergroup relations* (pp. 243–265). New York, NY: Teachers College Press.

Dowd, A. C. (2003). From access to outcome equity: Revitalizing the democratic mission of the community college. *Annals of the American Academy of Political and Social Science, 586*(1), 92–119.

Dowd, A. C. (2004). Income and financial aid effects on persistence and degree attainment in public colleges. *Education Policy Analysis Archives, 12*(21), 1–33.

Dowd, A. C., & Coury, T. (2006). The effect of loans on the persistence and attainment of community college students. *Research in Higher Education, 47*(1), 33–62.

Downing, K. J. (2009). Self-efficacy and metacognitive development. *The International Journal of Learning, 16*(4), 185–199.

Downing, K., Ho, R., Shin, K., Vrijmoed, L., & Wong, E. (2007). Metacognitive development and moving away. *Educational Studies, 33*(1), 1–13.

Doyle, W. R. (2009a). The effect of community college enrollment on bachelor's degree completion. *Economics of Education Review, 28*, 199–206.

Doyle, W. R. (2009b). Impact of increased academic intensity on transfer rates: An application of matching estimators to student-unit record data. *Research in Higher Education, 50*(1), 52–72.

Doyle, W. R. (2011). Effect of increased academic momentum on transfer rates: An application of the generalized propensity score. *Economics of Education Review, 30*, 191–200.

Drew, D., & Weaver, D. (2006). Voter learning in the 2004 presidential election: Did the media matter? *Journalism and Mass Communication Quarterly, 83*(1), 25–42.

Drezner, N. D. (2013). The Black church and millennial philanthropy: Influences on college student prosocial behaviors at a church-affiliated Black college. *Christian Higher Education, 12*(5), 363–382.

Driscoll, A., Jicha, K., Hunt, A. N., Tichavsky, L., & Thompson, G. (2012). Can online courses deliver in-class results? A comparison of student performance and satisfaction in an online versus a face-to-face introductory sociology course. *Teaching Sociology, 40*(4), 312–331.

Duckworth, A. L., Quinn, P. D., Lynam, D. R., Loeber, R., & Stouthamer-Loeber, M. (2011). Role of test motivation in intelligence testing. *Proceedings of the National Academy of Sciences, 108*(19), 7716–7720.

Dugan, J. P., Bohle, C. W., Gebhardt, M., Hofert, M., Wilk, E., & Cooney, M. A. (2011). Influences of leadership program participation on students' capacities for socially responsible leadership. *Journal of Student Affairs Research and Practice, 48*(1), 65–84.

Dugan, J. P., Fath, K. Q., Howes, S. D., Lavelle, K. R., & Polanin, J. R. (2013). Developing the leadership capacity and leader efficacy of college women in science, technology, engineering, and math fields. *Journal of Leadership Studies, 7*(3), 6–23.

Dugan, J. P., Kodama, C. M., & Gebhardt, M. C. (2012). Race and leadership development among college students: The additive value of collective racial esteem. *Journal of Diversity in Higher Education, 5*(3), 174–189.

Dugan, J. P., & Komives, S. R. (2010). Influences on college students' capacities for socially responsible leadership. *Journal of College Student Development, 51*(5), 525–549.

Dugan, J. P., Kusel, M. L., & Simounet, D. M. (2012). Transgender college students: An exploratory study of perceptions, engagement, and educational outcomes. *Journal of College Student Development, 53*(5), 719–736.

Duggan, M. B. (2004). E-mail as social capital and its impact on first-year persistence of four-year college students. *Journal of College Student Retention, 6*(2), 169–189.

Dupin-Bryant, P. A. (2004). Pre-entry variables related to retention in online distance education. *American Journal of Distance Education, 18*(4), 199–206.

Dupre, M. E. (2008). Educational differences in health risks and illness over the life course: A test of cumulative disadvantage theory. *Social Science Research, 37*(4), 1253–1266.

Durham, Y., McKinnon, T., & Schulman, C. (2007). Classroom experiments: Not just fun and games. *Economic Inquiry, 45*(1), 162–178.

Dwyer, R. E., McCloud, L., & Hodson, R. (2012). Debt and graduation from American universities. *Social Forces, 90*(4), 1133–1155.

Dynarski, S. (2009). Building the stock of college-educated labor. *Journal of Human Resources, 43*(3), 576–610.

Eagan, K., Lozano, J. B., Hurtado, S., & Case, M. H. (2013). *The American freshman: National norms fall 2013.* Los Angeles, CA: Higher Education Research Institute, UCLA.

Eagan, K., Stolzenberg, E. B., Ramirez, J. J., Aragon, M. C., Suchard, M. R., & Hurtado, S. (2014). *The American freshman: National norms fall 2014.* Los Angeles, CA: Higher Education Research Institute, UCLA.

Eagan, M. K., Jr. & Jaeger, A. J. (2009). Effects of exposure to part-time faculty on community college transfer. *Research in Higher Education, 50*(2), 168–188.

Economist Intelligence Unit. (2014). *Closing the skills gap: Companies and colleges collaborating for change.* Indianapolis, IN: Lumina Foundation.

Eddy, P. L., Christie, R., & Rao, M. (2006). Factors affecting transfer of "traditional" community college students. *Community College Enterprise, 12*(1), 73–92.

Educational Testing Service. (2010). *ETS Proficiency Profile user's guide.* Princeton, NJ: Author.

Edwards, K. E., & Jones, S. R. (2009). "Putting my man face on": A grounded theory of college men's gender identity development. *Journal of College Student Development, 50*(2), 210–228.

Ehrenberg, R. G., & Zhang, L. (2005). Do tenured and tenure-track faculty matter? *Journal of Human Resources, 40*(4), 647–659.

Eide, E. R., & Showalter, M. H. (2011). Estimating the relation between health and education: What do we know and what do we need to know? *Economics of Education Review, 30*(5), 778–791.

Einarson, M. K., & Clarkberg, M. E. (2010). Race differences in the impact of students' out-of-class interactions with faculty. *Journal of the Professoriate, 3*(2), 101–136.

Einfeld, A., & Collins, D. (2008). The relationships between service-learning, social justice, multicultural competence, and civic engagement. *Journal of College Student Development, 49*(2), 95–109.

El Hassan, K., & Madhum, G. (2007). Validating the Watson Glaser Critical Thinking Appraisal. *Higher Education, 54*, 361–383.

Elder, G. H., Jr. (1998). The life course and human development. In R. M. Lerner (Ed.), *Handbook of Child Psychology: Volume 1* (pp. 939–991). Hoboken, NJ: Wiley.

Electronic Code of Federal Regulations. (2015). *Title 34: Education subpart C—Work-colleges program.* Retrieved from http://www.ecfr.gov/cgi-bin/retrieveECFR?gp = & SID = 19510d2314b346907b450a1ad4c7244f&mc = true&n = sp34.3.675.c&r = SUB PART&ty = HTML

Elliott, S. L. (2010). Efficacy of role play in concert with lecture to enhance student learning of immunology. *Journal of Microbiology and Biology Education, 11*(2), 113–118.

Emerson, T. L. N., & Mencken, K. D. (2011). Homework: To require or not? Online graded homework and student achievement. *Perspectives on Economic Education Research, 7*(1), 20–42.

Emerson, T. L. N., & Taylor, B. A. (2004). Comparing student achievement across experimental and lecture-oriented sections of a principles of microeconomics course. *Southern Economic Journal, 70*(3), 672–693.

Emerson, T. L. N., & Taylor, B. A. (2007). Interactions between personality type and the experimental methods. *Journal of Economic Education, 38*(1), 18–35.

Engberg, M. E. (2004). Improving intergroup relations in higher education: A critical examination of the influence of educational interventions on racial bias. *Review of Educational Research, 74*(4), 473–524.

Engberg, M. E. (2007). Educating the workforce for the 21st century: A cross-disciplinary analysis of the impact of the undergraduate experience on students' development of a pluralistic orientation. *Research in Higher Education, 48*(3), 283–317.

Engberg, M. E., & Hurtado, S. (2011). Developing pluralistic skills and dispositions in college: Examining racial/ethnic group differences. *Journal of Higher Education*, *82*(4), 416–443.

Engberg, M. E., Hurtado, S., & Smith, G. C. (2007). Developing attitudes of acceptance toward lesbian, gay, and bisexual peers: Enlightenment, contact, and the college experience. *Journal of Gay and Lesbian Issues in Education*, *4*(3), 49–77.

Engberg, M. E., & Mayhew, M. J. (2007). The influence of first-year success courses on student learning and democratic outcomes. *Journal of College and Student Development*, *48*(3), 241–258.

Ennis, R. H., & Weir, E. (1985). *The Ennis-Weir Critical Thinking Essay Test*. Pacific Grove, CA: Midwest.

Ericsson, K. A., Krampe, R. T., & Tesch-Römer, C. (1993). The role of deliberate practice in the acquisition of expert performance. *Psychological Review*, *100*(3), 363–406.

Erikson, E. (1959). Identity and the life cycle. *Psychological Issues Monograph*, *1*, 1–171.

Erikson, E. (1963). *Childhood and society* (2nd ed.). New York, NY: Norton.

Erikson, E. (1968). *Identity: Youth and crisis*. New York, NY: Norton.

Ernst, H., & Colthorpe, K. (2006). The efficacy of interactive lecturing for students with diverse science backgrounds. *Advanced Physiological Education*, *31*, 41–44.

Espey, M. (2008). Does space matter? Classroom design and team-based learning. *Review of Agricultural Economics*, *30*(4), 764–775.

Ethington, C. A., & Horn, R. A. (2007). An examination of Pace's model of student development and college impress. *Community College Journal of Research and Practice*, *31*(3), 183–198.

Evans, N. J., Forney, D. S., Guido, F. M., Patton, L. D., & Renn, K. A. (2010). *Student development in college: Theory, research, and practice* (2nd ed.). San Francisco, CA: Jossey-Bass.

Ewell, P. (2009, November). *Assessment, accountability, and improvement: Revisiting the tension* (NILOA Occasional Paper No. 1). Urbana, IL: University of Illinois and Indiana University, National Institute for Learning Outcomes Assessment.

Ewert, S. (2010). Male and female pathways through four-year colleges: Disruption and sex stratification in higher education. *American Educational Research Journal*, *47*(4), 744–773.

Ewing, J. C., & Whittington, M. S. (2009). Describing the cognitive level of professor discourse and student cognition in college of agriculture class sessions. *Journal of Agricultural Education 50*(4), 36–49.

Facione, P. A., & Facione, N. C. (1992). *The California Critical Thinking Dispositions Inventory*. Millbrae, CA: California Academic Press.

Fayowski, V., & MacMillan, P. D. (2008). An evaluation of the Supplemental Instruction programme in a first year calculus course. *International Journal of Mathematical Education in Science and Technology*, *39*(7), 843–855.

Feinstein, L., Duckworth, K., & Sabates, R. (2008). *Education and the family: Passing success across the generations*. New York, NY: Routledge.

Feldman, K. A., & Newcomb, T. M. (1969). *The impact of college on students*. San Francisco CA: Jossey-Bass.

Fike, D. S., & Fike, R. (2007). Does faculty employment status impact developmental mathematics outcomes? *Journal of Developmental Education, 31*(1), 2–11.

Fike, D. S., & Fike, R. (2008). Predictors of first-year student retention in the community college. *Community College Review, 36*(2), 68–88.

Fike, D. S., Raehl, C. L., McCall, K. L., Burgoon, S. C., Schwarzlose, S. J., & Lockman, P. R. (2011). Improving community college student learning outcomes in biology. *Electronic Journal of Science Education, 15*(1), 1–12.

Finnegan, C., Morris, L. V., & Lee, K. (2009). Differences by course discipline on student behavior, persistence, and achievement in online courses of undergraduate general education. *Journal of College Student Retention, 10*(1), 39–54.

Fischer, M. J. (2007). Settling into campus life: Differences by race/ethnicity in college involvement and outcomes. *Journal of Higher Education, 78*(2), 125–161.

Fischer, M. J. (2011). Interracial contact and changes in the racial attitudes of White college students. *Social Psychology of Education, 14*(4), 547–574.

Fitzmaurice, G., Laird, N., & Ware, J. (2004). *Applied longitudinal analysis*. Hoboken, NJ: Wiley.

Flaster, A., & DesJardins, S. L. (2014). Applying regression discontinuity design in institutional research. In N. A. Bowman & S. Herzog (Eds.), *Methodological advances and issues in studying college impact* (New Directions for Institutional Research No. 161, pp. 3–20). San Francisco, CA: Jossey-Bass.

Fleming, J. J., Purnell, J., & Wang, Y. (2013). Student-faculty interaction and the development of an ethic of care. In A. N. Bryant Rockenbach & M. J. Mayhew (Eds.), *Spirituality in college students' lives: Translating research into practice* (pp. 153–169). New York, NY: Routledge.

Fletcher, J. M., & Frisvold, D. E. (2009). Higher education and health investments: Does more schooling affect preventive care use? *Journal of Human Capital, 3*(2), 144–176.

Fletcher, J. M., & Frisvold, D. E. (2011). College selectivity and young adult health behaviors. *Economics of Education Review, 30*(5), 826–837.

Fletcher, J. M., & Frisvold, D. E. (2014). The long run health returns to college quality. *Review of Economics of the Household, 12*(2), 295–325.

Flowers, L. A. (2002). The impact of college racial composition on African American students' academic and social gains: Additional evidence. *Journal of College Student Development, 43*(3), 403–410.

Flowers, L. A. (2003). Differences in self-reported intellectual and social gains between African American and White college students at predominantly White institutions: Implications for student affairs professionals. *Journal of Student Affairs Research and Practice, 41*(1), 68–84.

Flowers, L. A. (2004a). Effects of living on campus on African American students' educational gains in college. *Journal of Student Affairs Research and Practice, 41*(2), 476–492.

Flowers, L. A. (2004b). Examining the effects of student involvement on African American college student development. *Journal of College Student Development, 45*(6), 633–654.

Flowers, L., Osterlind, S. J., Pascarella, E. T., & Pierson, C. T. (2001). How much do students learn in college? Cross-sectional estimates using the College BASE. *Journal of Higher Education, 72*(5), 565–583.

Flowers, L. A., & Pascarella, E. T. (2003). Cognitive effects of college: Differences between African American and Caucasian students. *Research in Higher Education, 44*(1), 21–49.

Flowers, N. T., Naimi, T. S., Brewer, R. D., Elder, R. W., Shults, R. A., & Jiles, R. (2008). Patterns of alcohol consumption and alcohol-impaired driving in the United States. *Alcoholism: Clinical and Experimental Research, 32*(4), 639–644.

Folsom, B., & Reardon, R. (2003). College career courses: Design and accountability. *Journal of Career Assessment, 11*(4), 421–450.

Ford, K. A. (2011). Doing *fake* masculinity, being *real* men: Present and future constructions of self among Black college men. *Symbolic Interaction, 34*(1), 38–62.

Ford, K. A., & Malaney, V. K. (2012). "I now harbor more pride in my race": The educational benefits of inter- and intraracial dialogues on the experiences of students of color and multiracial students. *Equity and Excellence in Education, 45*(1), 14–35.

Foubert, J. D., & Grainger, L. U. (2006). Effects of involvement in clubs and organizations on the psychosocial development of first-year and senior college students. *NASPA Journal, 43*(1), 166–182.

Foubert, J. D., Nixon, M. L., Sisson, V. S., & Barnes, A. C. (2005). A longitudinal study of Chickering and Reisser's vectors: Exploring gender differences and implications for refining the theory. *Journal of College Student Development, 46*(5), 461–471.

Fowler, J. (1981). *Stages of faith: The psychology of human development and the quest for meaning.* New York, NY: HarperCollins.

Fox, A. B., Rosen, J., & Crawford, M. (2009). Distractions, distractions: Does instant messaging affect college students' performance on a concurrent reading comprehension task? *Cyberpsychology and Behavior, 12*(1), 51–53.

Fox, M. (1993). Is it a good investment to attend an elite private college? *Economics of Education Review, 12*, 137–151.

Freeman, S., Eddy, S. L., McDonough, P. M., Smith, M. K., Okoroafor, N., Jordt, H., & Wenderoth, M. P. (2014). Active learning increases student performance in science, engineering, and mathematics. *Proceedings of the National Academy of Sciences, 111*(23), 8410–8415.

Freeman, S., Haak, D., & Wenderoth, M. P. (2011). Increased course structure improves performance in introductory biology. *CBE-Life Sciences Education, 10*(2), 175–186.

Freeman, S., O'Connor, E., Parks, J. W., Cunningham, M., Hurley, D., Haak, D., . . . & Wenderoth, M. P. (2007). Prescribed active learning increases performance in introductory biology. *CBE-Life Sciences Education, 6*, 132–139.

Friedman, A. (2004). The relationship between personality traits and reflective judgement among female students. *Journal of Adult Development, 11*(4), 297–304.

Friedman, D. B., & Marsh, E. G. (2009). What type of first-year seminar is most effective? A comparison of thematic seminars and college transition/success seminars. *Journal of the First-Year Experience and Students in Transition, 21*(1), 29–42.

Fry, S. W., & Villagomez, A. (2012). Writing to learn: Benefits and limitations. *College Teaching, 60*(4), 170–175.

Frydenberg, J. (2007). Persistence in university continuing education online classes. *International Review of Research in Open and Distance Learning, 8*(3), 1–15.

Fujiwara, T., & Kawachi, I. (2009). Is education causally related to better health? A twin fixed effect study in the USA. *International Journal of Epidemiology, 38*(5), 1310–1322.

Fuller-Rowell, T. E., Ong, A. D., & Phinney, J. S. (2013). National identity and perceived discrimination predict changes in ethnic identity commitment: Evidence from a longitudinal study of Latino college students. *Applied Psychology, 62*(3), 406–426.

Fulwiler, T., & Young, A. (1982). *Language connections: Writing and reading across the curriculum.* Urbana, IL: National Council of Teachers of English.

Furnée, C., Groot, W., & van den Brink, H. M. (2008). The health effects of education: A meta-analysis. *European Journal of Public Health, 18,* 417–421.

Galindo-Rueda, F. (2003). *The intergenerational effect of parental schooling: Evidence from the British 1947 school leaving age reform.* Centre for Economic Performance, London School of Economics, mimeo.

Gallien, T., & Oomen-Early, J. (2008). Personalized versus collective instructor feedback in the online course room: Does type of feedback affect student satisfaction, academic performance and perceived connectedness with the instructor? *International Journal on E-Learning, 7*(3), 463–476.

Gansemer-Topf, A., & Schuh, J. H. (2006). Institutional selectivity and institutional expenditures: Examining organizational factors that contribute to retention and graduation. *Research in Higher Education, 47*(6), 613–642.

Garcia, G. A. (2013). Does percentage of Latinas/os affect graduation rates at 4-year Hispanic serving institutions (HSIs), emerging HSIs, and non-HSIs? *Journal of Hispanic Higher Education, 12*(3), 256–268.

Garson, G. D. (2014). *Multiple regression* (Blue Book Series, 2014 ed.). Asheboro, NC: Statistical Publishing Associates.

Gasman, M., Baez, B., & Turner, C. S. V. (2008). *Understanding minority-serving institutions.* Albany, NY: State University of New York Press.

Gaston-Gayles, J. L. (2004). Examining academic and athletic motivation among student athletes at a Division I university. *Journal of College Student Development, 45*(1), 75–83.

Gaudet, A., Ramer, L., Nakonechny, J., Cragg, J., & Ramer, M. (2010). Small-group learning in an upper level university biology class enhances academic performance and student attitudes toward group work, *PlOS ONE, 5*(12), e15821–e15821.

Gayles, J. G., Bryant Rockenbach, A. N., & Davis, H. A. (2012). Civic responsibility and the student athlete: Validating a new conceptual model. *Journal of Higher Education, 83*(4), 535–557.

Gayles, J. G., & Hu, S. (2009). The influence of student engagement and sport participation on college outcomes among Division I student athletes. *Journal of Higher Education, 80*(3), 315–333.

Ge, X., & Land, S. M. (2003). Scaffolding students' problem-solving processes in an ill-structured task using question prompts and peer interactions. *Educational Technology Research and Development, 51*(1), 21–38.

Gehrke, S. (2014). Dynamics of race and prosocial involvement experiences in developing an ecumenical worldview. *Journal of College Student Development, 55*(7), 675–692.

Geide-Stevenson, D. (2009). Does collecting and grading homework assignments impact student achievement in an introductory economics course? *Journal of Economics and Economic Education Research, 10*(3), 3–14.

Gellin, A. (2003). The effect of undergraduate student involvement on critical thinking: A meta-analysis of the literature, 1991–2000. *Journal of College Student Development, 44*(6), 746–762.

Gesthuizen, M., & Scheepers, P. (2012). Educational differences in volunteering in cross-national perspective: Individual and contextual explanations. *Nonprofit and Voluntary Sector Quarterly, 41*(1), 58–81.

Ghavami, N., Fingerhut, A., Peplau, L. A., Grant, S. K., & Wittig, M. A. (2011). Testing a model of minority identity achievement, identity affirmation, and psychological well-being among ethnic minority and sexual minority individuals. *Cultural Diversity and Ethnic Minority Psychology, 17*(1), 79–88.

Gijbels, D., Dochy, F., Van den Bossche, P., & Segers, M. (2005). Effects of problem-based learning: A meta-analysis from the angle of assessment. *Review of Educational Research, 75*(1), 27–61.

Gilbert, S. C., So, D., Russell, T. M., & Wessel, T. R. (2006). Racial identity and psychological symptoms among African Americans attending a historically Black university. *Journal of College Counseling, 9*(2), 111–122.

Gilbreath, B., Kim, T. Y., & Nichols, B. (2011). Person-environment fit and its effects on university students: A response surface methodology study. *Research in Higher Education, 52*(1), 47–62.

Gill, A. M., & Leigh, D. E. (2003). Do the returns to community college differ between academic and vocational programs? *Journal of Human Resources, 38*(1), 134–155.

Gillen, M. M., & Lefkowitz, E. S. (2006). Gender role development and body image among male and female first year college students. *Sex Roles, 55*(1–2), 25–37.

Gilligan, C. (1982). *In a different voice*. Cambridge, MA: Harvard University Press.

Gilman, S. E., Breslau, J., Conron, K. J., Koenen, K. C., Subramanian, S. V., & Zaslavsky, A. M. (2008). Education and race-ethnicity differences in the lifetime risk of alcohol dependence. *Journal of Epidemiology and Community Health, 62*(3), 224–230.

Glanville, J. L., & Bienenstock, E. J. (2009). A typology for understanding connections among different forms of social capital. *American Behavioral Scientist, 52*(11), 1507–1530.

Glied, S., & Lleras-Muney, A. (2003). *Health inequality, education and medical innovation* (NBER Working Paper No. 9738). Cambridge, MA: National Bureau of Economic Research.

Goenner, C. F., & Snaith, S. M. (2004). Accounting for model uncertainty in the prediction of university graduation rates. *Research in Higher Education, 45*(1), 25–41.

Goen-Salter, S. (2008). Critiquing the need to eliminate remediation: Lessons from San Francisco State. *Journal of Basic Writing, 27*(2), 81–105.

Goesling, B. (2007). The rising significance of education for health? *Social Forces*, *85*(4), 1621–1644.

Goethals, G. R., & Reckman, R. F. (1973). The perception of consistency in attitudes. *Journal of Experimental Social Psychology, 9*, 491–501.

Goldberger, A. S. (1991). *A course in econometrics*. Cambridge, MA: Harvard University Press.

Golberstein, E., Hirth, R. A., & Lantz, P. M. (2012). Estimating the education-health relationship: A cost-utility approach. *BE Journal of Economic Analysis and Policy, 11*(3).

Goldman, C. (2012). A cohort based learning community enhances academic success and satisfaction with university experience for first year students. *Canadian Journal for the Scholarship of Teaching and Learning, 3*(2), 1–19.

Goldrick-Rab, S., Harris, D. N., Kelchen, R., & Benson, J. (2012). *Need-based financial aid and college persistence: Experimental evidence from Wisconsin*. Madison, WI: Institute for Research on Poverty, University of Wisconsin.

Goldrick-Rab, S., & Pfeffer, F. T. (2009). Explaining socioeconomic differences in college transfer. *Sociology of Education, 82*(2), 101–125.

Goldrick-Rab, S., Harris, D. N., & Troestel, P. A. (2009). Why financial aid matters (or does not) for college success: Toward a new interdisciplinary perspective. In J. C. Smart (Ed.), *Higher Education: Handbook of Theory and Research* (Vol. 24, pp. 1–45). New York, NY: Springer.

Goldrick-Rab, S., & Pfeffer, F. T. (2009). Explaining socioeconomic differences in college transfer. *Sociology of Education, 82*(2), 101–125.

Goldstein, M. T., & Perin, D. (2008). Predicting performance in a community college content-area course from academic skill level. *Community College Review, 36*(2), 89–115.

Gomez, S., Lush, D., & Clements, M. (2004). Work placements enhance the academic performance of bioscience undergraduates. *Journal of Vocational Education and Training, 56*(3), 373–385.

Gonyea, R. M., & Miller, A. (2011). Clearing the AIR about the use of self-reported gains in institutional research. In S. Herzog & N. A. Bowman (Eds.), *Validity and limitations of college student self-report data* (New Directions for Institutional Research No. 150, pp. 99–111). San Francisco, CA: Jossey-Bass.

Good, J., & Cartwright, C. (1998). Development of moral judgment among undergraduate university students. *College Student Journal, 32*, 270–276.

Goodman, K. M., & Mueller, J. A. (2009). Invisible, marginalized, and stigmatized: Understanding and addressing the needs of atheist students. In S. K. Watt, E. E. Fairchild, & K. M. Goodman (Eds.), *Intersections of religious privilege: Difficult dialogues and student affairs practice* (New Directions for Student Services No. 125, pp. 55–63). San Francisco, CA: Jossey-Bass.

Goodman, M., Finnegan, R., Mohadjer, L., Krenzke, T., & Hogan, J. (2013). *Literacy, numeracy, and problem solving in technology-rich environments among US adults: Results from the Program for the International Assessment of Adult Competencies 2012. First look. (NCES 2014–008)*. Washington, DC: National Center for Education Statistics.

Gordon, C. F., Juang, L. P., & Syed, M. (2007). Internet use and well-being among college students: Beyond frequency of use. *Journal of College Student Development, 48*(6), 674–688.

Gosen, J., & Washbush, J. (1999). Perceptions of learning in TE simulations. *Developments in Business Simulation and Experiential Learning, 26*, 170–175.

Gottfredson, L. S. (1981). Circumscription and compromise: A developmental theory of occupational aspirations. *Journal of Counseling Psychology, 28*, 545–579.

Gottfredson, L. S. (1996). Gottfredson's theory of circumscription and compromise. In D. Brown & L. Brooks (Eds.), *Career choice and development* (3rd ed., pp. 179–232). San Francisco, CA: Jossey-Bass.

Gottschalk, R., & Milton, P. (2010). Differences in academic success between male and female student-athletes: An exploratory study. *International Journal of Sport Management, 11*, 602–608.

Goudas, A. M., & Boylan, H. R. (2012). Addressing flawed research in developmental education. *Journal of Developmental Education, 36*(1), 2–13.

Grade, R., Gouldsborough, I., Sheader, E., & Speake, T. (2009). Using innovative group-work activities to enhance the problem-based learning experience for dental students. *European Journal of Dental Education, 13*(4), 190–198.

Grandzol, C., Perlis, S., & Draina, L. (2010). Leadership development of team captains in collegiate varsity athletics. *Journal of College Student Development, 51*(4), 403–418.

Gratton-Lavoie, C., & Stanley, D. (2009). Teaching and learning principles of microeconomics online: An empirical assessment. *Journal of Economic Education, 40*(1), 3–25.

Gray, R., Vitak, J., Easton, E. W., & Ellison, N. B. (2013). Examining social adjustment to college in the age of social media: Factors influencing successful transitions and persistence. *Computers and Education, 67*, 193–207.

Grebennikov, L., & Shah, M. (2012). Investigating attrition trends in order to improve student retention. *Quality Assurance in Education: An International Perspective, 20*(3), 223–236.

Green, J. P. (2011). The impact of a work placement or internship year on student final year performance: An empirical study. *International Journal of Management Education, 9*(2), 49–57.

Greenbank, P. (2009). Re-evaluating the role of social capital in the career decision-making behavior of working-class students. *Research in Post-Compulsory Education, 14*(2), 157–170.

Greenfield, S. F., Sugarman, D. E., Muenz, L. R., Patterson, M. D., He, D. Y., & Weiss, R. D. (2003). The relationship between educational attainment and relapse among alcohol-dependent men and women: A prospective study. *Alcoholism: Clinical and Experimental Research, 27*(8), 1278–1285.

Greenstone, M., & Looney, A. (2011, June 25). Where is the best place to invest $102,000–In stocks, bonds, or a college degree? *Brookings.* Retrieved from http://www.brookings.edu/research/papers/2011/06/25-education-greenstone-looney

Griffin, T. M., Chavous, T., Cogburn, C., Branch, L., & Sellers, R. (2011). Dimensions of academic contingencies among African American college students. *Journal of Black Psychology, 38*(2), 201–227.

Grimard, F., & Parent, D. (2007). Education and smoking: Were Vietnam War draft avoiders also more likely to avoid smoking? *Journal of Health Economics, 26*(5), 896–926.

Grodner, A., & Rupp, N. G. (2013). The role of homework in student learning outcomes: Evidence from a field experiment. *Journal of Economic Education, 44*(2), 93–109.

Grodsky, E. (2007). Compensatory sponsorship in higher education. *American Journal of Sociology, 112,* 1662–1712.

Groeschel, B. L., Wester, S. R., & Sedivy, S. K. (2010). Gender role conflict, alcohol, and help seeking among college men. *Psychology of Men and Masculinity, 11*(2), 123–139.

Gross, J. P. K. (2011). Promoting or perturbing success: The effects of aid on timing to Latino students' first departure from college. *Journal of Hispanic Higher Education, 10*(4), 317–330.

Gross, J. P. K., Torres, V., & Zerquera, D. (2013). Financial aid and attainment among students in a state with changing demographics. *Research in Higher Education, 54*(4), 383–406.

Grossman, M. (2006). Education and non-market outcomes. In E. Hanushek & F. Welcoh (Eds.), *Handbook of the Economics of Education* (Vol. 1, pp. 578–633). Amsterdam: Elsevier-North Holland.

Grossman, M. (2008). The relationship between health and schooling. *Eastern Economic Journal, 34,* 281–292.

Grove, W. A., & Wasserman, T. (2006). Incentives and student learning: A natural experiment with economics problem sets. *American Economic Review, 96*(2), 447–452.

Grunwald, H. E., & Mayhew, M. J. (2008). Using propensity scores for estimating causal effects: A study in the development of moral reasoning. *Research in Higher Education, 49,* 758–775.

Grusky, D. B. (2011). Theories of Stratification and Inequality. In G. Ritzer and J. Michael Ryan (Eds.), *The concise encyclopedia of sociology* (pp. 622–624). Oxford, UK: Wiley-Blackwell.

Guardia, J. R., & Evans, N. J. (2008). Factors influencing the ethnic identity development of Latino fraternity members at a Hispanic serving institution. *Journal of College Student Development, 49*(3), 163–181.

Gubera, C., & Aruguete, M. S. (2013). A comparison of collaborative and traditional instruction in higher education. *Social Psychology Education 16*(4), 651–659.

Gunersel, A., & Simpson N. (2009). Improvement in writing and reviewing skills with Calibrated Peer Review TM. *International Journal for the Scholarship of Teaching and Learning, 3*(2), 1–14.

Guo, S., & Fraser, M. W. (2010). *Propensity score analysis: Statistical methods and applications.* Los Angeles, CA: Sage.

Gurin, G. (1971). The impact of the college experience. In S. Withey (Ed.), *A degree and what else? Correlates and consequences of a college education.* New York, NY: McGraw-Hill.

Gurin, P. (1999). Expert report of Patricia Gurin, in *The compelling need for diversity in higher education,* presented in *Gratz et al. v. Bollinger et al.* and *Grutter et al. v. Bollinger et al.* Washington, DC: Wilmer, Cutler, Pickering.

Gurin, P., Nagda, B. R. A., & Lopez, G. E. (2004). The benefits of diversity in education for democratic citizenship. *Journal of Social Issues, 60*(1), 17–34.

Gurin, P., Dey, E. L., Hurtado, S., & Gurin, G. (2002). Diversity and higher education: Theory and impact on educational outcomes. *Harvard Educational Review, 72*(3), 33–66.

Guruz, K. (2008). *Higher education and international student mobility in the global knowledge economy.* Albany, NY: SUNY Press.

Guthrie, V. L., King, P. M., & Palmer, C. J. (2000). Higher education and reducing prejudice: Research on cognitive capabilities underlying tolerance. *Diversity Digest, 4*(3), 10–11, 23.

Haak, D. C., Hille Ris Lambers, J., Pitre, E., & Freeman, S. (2011). Increased structure and active learning reduce the achievement gap in introductory biology. *Science, 332*(6034), 1213–1216.

Hachey, A. C., Wladis, C. W., & Conway, K. M. (2012). Is the second time the charm? Investigating trends in online re-enrollment, retention and success. *Journal of Educators Online, 9*(1), 1–25.

Hadden, W. C., & Rockswold, P. D. (2008). Increasing differential mortality by educational attainment in adults in the United States. *International Journal of Health Services, 38*(1), 47–61.

Hagedorn, L. S., Maxwell, W., & Hampton, P. (2002). Correlates of retention for African American males in community colleges. *Journal of College Student Retention Research, Theory, and Practice, 3*(3), 243–264.

Hagerty, G., & Smith, S. (2005). Using the web-based interactive software ALEKS to enhance college algebra. *Mathematics and Computer Education, 39*(3), 183–194.

Haidt, J. (2001). The emotional dog and its rational tail: A social intuitionist approach to moral judgment. *Psychological Review, 108*(4), 814–834.

Halawah, I. (2006). The effect of motivation, family environment, and student characteristics on academic achievement. *Journal of Instructional Psychology, 33*(2), 91–100.

Hall, K. D., Stephen, A. M., Reeder, B. A., Muhajarine, N., & Lasiuk, G. (2003). Diet, obesity and education in three age groups of Saskatchewan women. *Canadian Journal of Dietetic Practice and Research, 64*(4), 181–188.

Hall, S. L., Scott, F., & Borsz, M. (2008). A constructivist case study examining the leadership development of undergraduate students in campus recreational sports. *Journal of College Student Development, 49*(2), 125–140.

Hand, B., Gunel, M., & Ulu, C. 2009. Sequencing embedded multimodal representations in a writing-to-learn approach to the teaching of electricity. *Journal of Research in Science Teaching, 46*(3), 225–247.

Hansen, W. (1963). Total and private rates of return to investing in schooling. *Journal of Political Economy, 71*, 128–140.

Hanson, J. M., Weeden, D. D., Pascarella, E. T., & Blaich, C. (2012). Do liberal arts colleges make students more liberal? Some initial evidence. *Higher Education, 64*(3), 355–369.

Harding, T. S., Mayhew, M. J., Finelli, C. J., & Carpenter, D. D. (2007). The theory of planned behavior as a model of academic dishonesty in engineering and humanities undergraduates. *Ethics and Behavior, 17*(3), 255–279.

Harford, T. C., Yi, H. Y., & Hilton, M. E. (2006). Alcohol abuse and dependence in college and noncollege samples: A ten-year prospective follow-up in a national survey. *Journal of Studies on Alcohol, 67*(6), 803–809.

Harper, B. J., & Lattuca, L. R. (2010). Tightening curricular connections: CQI and effective curriculum planning. *Research in Higher Education, 51*(6), 505–527.

Harper, C. E., & Yeung, F. (2013). Perceptions of institutional commitment to diversity as a predictor of college students' openness to diverse perspectives. *Review of Higher Education, 37*(1), 25–44.

Harper, S. R. (2004). The measure of a man: Conceptualizations of masculinity among high-achieving African American male college students. *Berkeley Journal of Sociology, 48*(1), 89–107.

Harper, S. R. (2006). Peer support for African American male college achievement: Beyond internalized racism and the burden of "acting White." *Journal of Men's Studies, 1*(4), 337–358.

Harper, S. R., & Harris, F., III. (2010). *College men and masculinities: Theory, research, and implications for practice.* San Francisco, CA: Jossey-Bass.

Harper, S. R., & Hurtado, S. (2007). Nine themes in campus racial climates and implications for institutional transformation. In S. R. Harper & L. D. Patton (Eds.), *Responding to the realities of race on campus* (New Directions for Student Services No. 120, pp. 7–24). San Francisco, CA: Jossey-Bass.

Harper, S. R., Harris, F., III, & Mmeje, K. (2005). A theoretical model to explain the overrepresentation of college men among campus judicial offenders: Implications for campus administrators. *NASPA Journal, 42*(4), 565–588.

Harrell, I. L., & Bower, B. L. (2011). Student characteristics that predict persistence in community college online courses. *American Journal of Distance Education, 25*(3), 178–191.

Harrell, M. (2011). Argument diagramming and critical thinking in introductory philosophy. *Higher Education Research and Development, 30*(3), 371–385.

Harris, F., III. (2008). Deconstructing masculinity: A qualitative study of college men's masculine conceptualizations and gender performance. *Journal of Student Affairs Research and Practice, 45*(4), 453–474.

Harris, F., III. (2010). College men's meanings of masculinities and contextual influences: Toward a conceptual model. *Journal of College Student Development, 51*(3), 297–318.

Harris, F., III, & Barone, R. (2011). The situation of men, and situating men in higher education: A conversation about crisis, myth and reality about male college students. In J. A. Laker & T. Davis (Eds.), *Masculinities in higher education: Theoretical and practical considerations* (pp. 50–62). New York, NY: Routledge.

Harris, F., III, & Harper, S. R. (2008). Masculinities go to community college: Understanding male identity socialization and gender role conflict. In J. Lester (Ed.), *Gendered perspectives on community colleges* (New Directions for Community Colleges No. 142, pp. 25–35). San Francisco, CA: Jossey-Bass.

Harris, F., III, & Harper, S. R. (2014). Beyond bad behaving brothers: Productive performances of masculinities among college fraternity men. *International Journal of Qualitative Studies in Education, 27*(6), 703–723.

Harris, F., III, Palmer, R. T., & Struve, L. E. (2011). "Cool posing" on campus: A qualitative study of masculinities and gender expression among Black men at a private research institution. *Journal of Negro Education, 80*(1), 47–62.

Harris, F. III, & Struve, L. E. (2009). Gents, jerks, and jocks: What male students learn about masculinity in college. *About Campus, 14*(3), 2–9.

Hart Research Associates. (2008). *How should colleges assess and improve student learning?* Washington, DC: Association of American Colleges & Universities.

Hart Research Associates. (2010). *Raising the bar: Employers' views on college learning in the wake of the economic downturn.* Washington, DC: Association of American Colleges & Universities.

Harton, H. C., Richardson, D. S., Barreras, R. E., Rockloff, M. J., & Latane, B. (2002). Focused interactive learning: A tool for active class discussion. *Teaching of Psychology, 29*(1), 10–15.

Hattie, J., & Timperley, H. (2007). The power of feedback. *Review of Educational Research, 77*(1), 81–112.

Hauser, R. M., & Warren, J. R. (1979). Socioeconomic indexes for occupations: A review, update, and critique. *Sociological Methodology, 27*, 177–298.

Hausmann, L. R. M., Ye, F., Schofield, J. W., & Woods, R. L. (2009). Sense of belonging and persistence in White and African American first-year students. *Research in Higher Education, 50*(7), 649–669.

Haw, J. (2011). Improving psychological critical thinking in Australian university students. *Australian Journal of Psychology, 63*, 150–153.

Hayek, J. C., Carini, R. M., O'Day, P. T., & Kuh, G. D. (2002). Triumph or tragedy: Comparing engagement levels of members of Greek-letter organizations and other students. *Journal of College Student Development, 43*(5), 643–663.

Hayes, A. F. (2009). Beyond Baron and Kenny: Statistical mediation analysis in the new millennium. *Communication Monographs, 76*, 408–420.

Hayes, A. F. (2013). *Introduction to mediation, moderation, and conditional process analysis: A regression-based approach.* New York, NY: Guilford Press.

Hayes, K. D., & Devitt, A. A. (2008). Classroom discussions with student-led feedback: A useful activity to enhance development of critical thinking skills. *Journal of Food Science Education, 7*, 65–68.

Haynes, T. L., Ruthig, J. C., Perry, R. P., Stupinsky, R. H., & Hall, N. C. (2006). Reducing the academic risks of over-optimism: The longitudinal effects of attributional retraining on cognition and achievement. *Research in Higher Education, 47*(7), 755–779.

Hayward, L., Blackmer, B., & Raelin, J. (2007). Teaching students a process of reflection: A model for increasing practice-based learning outcomes during cooperative education. *Journal of Cooperative Education and Internships, 41*(1), 35–47.

Hazel, S. J., Heberle, N., McEwen, M. M., & Adams, K. (2013). Team-based learning increases active engagement and enhances development of teamwork and communication skills in a first-year course for veterinary and animal science undergraduates. *Journal of Veterinary Medical Education, 40*(4), 333–341.

Headey, B., & Wooden, M. (2004). The effects of wealth and income on subjective well-being and ill-being. *Economic Record, 80*(s1), S24–S33.

Hébert, T. P. and Reis, S. M. (1999). Culturally diverse high-achieving students in an urban high school. *Urban Education, 34*(4), 428–457.

Heck, R. H., & Thomas, S. L. (2009). *An introduction to multilevel modeling techniques* (2nd ed.). New York, NY: Routledge.

Heckman, J. J., Lochner, L. J., & Todd, P. E. (2003). *Fifty years of Mincer earnings regressions* (NBER Working Paper No. 9732). Cambridge, MA: National Bureau of Economic Research. Retrieved from http://www.nber.org/papers/w9732

Heckman, J. J., Lochner, L. J., & Todd, R. (2006). Earnings functions, rates of return and treatment effects: The Mincer equation and beyond. In E. A. Hanushek & F. Welch (Eds.), *Handbook of the Economic of Education* (Vol. 1, pp. 310–458). Waltham, MA: Elsevier.

Heckman, J., Lochner, L., & Todd, P. (2008). Earnings functions and rates of return. *Journal of Human Capital, 2,* 1–31.

Heckman, J. J., Stixrud, J., & Urzua, S. (2006). The effects of cognitive and noncognitive abilities on labor market outcomes and social behavior. *Journal of Labor Economics, 24*(3), 411–482.

Helme, D. W., Cohen, E. L., & Parrish, A. J. (2012). Health, masculinity and smokeless tobacco use among college-aged men. *Health Communication, 27*(5), 467–477.

Helms, J. E. (1990). *Black and White racial identity: Theory, research, and practice.* Westport, CT: Greenwood.

Helms, J. E. (1995). An update of Helms's White and people of color racial identity models. In J. G. Ponterotto, J. M. Casas, L. A. Suzuki, & C. M. Alexander (Eds.), *Handbook of multicultural counseling* (pp. 181–198). Thousand Oaks, CA: Sage.

Hendel, D. D. (2007). Efficacy of participating in a first-year seminar on student satisfaction and retention. *Journal of College Student Retention, 8*(4), 413–423.

Henderson, D. J., Olbrecht, A., & Polachek, S. W. (2006). Do former college athletes earn more at work? A nonparametric assessment. *Journal of Human Resources, 41*(3), 558–577.

Henderson, J., & Chatfield, S. (2011). Who matches? Propensity scores and bias in the causal effects of education on participation. *Journal of Politics, 73*(3), 646–658.

Henry, G. T., Rubenstein, R., & Bugler, D. T. (2004). Is HOPE enough? Impacts of receiving and losing merit-based financial aid. *Educational Policy, 18*(50), 686–709.

Hensen, K. A., & Shelley, M. C. (2003). The impact of supplemental instruction: Results from a large, public, midwestern university. *Journal of College Student Development, 44*(2), 250–259.

Hernandez, E. (2012). The journey toward developing political consciousness through activism for Mexican American women. *Journal of College Student Development, 53*(5), 680–702.

Herzog, S. (2005). Measuring determinants of student return vs. dropout/stopout vs. transfer: A first-to-second year analysis. *Research in Higher Education, 46*(8), 883–928.

Herzog, S. (2011). Gauging academic growth of bachelor degree recipients: Longitudinal vs. self-reported gains in general education. In N. A. Bowman & S. Herzog (Eds.), *Validity and limitations of college student self-report data* (New Directions for Institutional Research No. 150, pp. 21–39). Hoboken, NJ: Wiley.

Herzog, S. (2014). The propensity score analytical framework: An overview and institutional research example. In N. A. Bowman & S. Herzog (Eds.), *Methodological advances and issues in studying college impact* (New Directions for Institutional Research No. 161, pp. 21–40). Hoboken, NJ: Wiley.

Hess, J. A., & Smythe, M. J. (2001). Is teacher immediacy actually related to student cognitive learning? *Communication Studies, 52*, 197–219.

Hesse-Biber, S., Livingstone, S., Ramirez, D., Barko, E. B., & Johnson, A. L. (2010). Racial identity and body image among Black female college students attending predominantly White colleges. *Sex Roles, 63*(9–10), 697–711.

Higgins, B. (2004). Relationship between retention and peer tutoring for at-risk students. *Journal of Nursing Education, 43*(7), 319–321.

Higgins, S. T., Heil, S. H., Badger, G. J., Skelly, J. M., Solomon, L. J., & Bernstein, I. M. (2009). Educational disadvantage and cigarette smoking during pregnancy. *Drug and Alcohol Dependence, 104*, S100–S105.

Higher Education Research Institute. (1996). *A social change model of leadership development: Guidebook: Version III*. College Park, MD: National Clearinghouse for Leadership Programs.

Hill, J. P. (2009). Higher education as moral community: Institutional influences on religious participation during college. *Journal for the Scientific Study of Religion, 48*(3), 515–534.

Hill, J. P. (2011). Faith and understanding: Specifying the impact of higher education on religious belief. *Journal for the Scientific Study of Religion, 50*(3), 533–551.

Hill, T. D., & Needham, B. L. (2006). Gender-specific trends in educational attainment and self-rated health, 1972–2002. *American Journal of Public Health, 96*(7), 1288–1292.

Hill, W., & Woodward, L. S. (2013). Examining the impact learning communities have on College of Education students on an urban campus. *Journal of College Student Development, 54*(6), 643–648.

Hillygus, D. S. (2005). The missing link: Exploring the relationship between higher education and political engagement. *Political Behavior, 27*(1), 25–47.

Hilmer, M. J., & Hilmer, C. E. (2012). On the relationship between student tastes and motivations, higher education decisions, and annual earnings. *Economics of Education Review, 31*, 66–75.

Hinrichs, D. W., & Rosenberg, P. J. (2002). Attitudes toward gay, lesbian, and bisexual persons among heterosexual liberal arts college students. *Journal of Homosexuality, 43*(1), 61–84.

Hinrichs, P. (2011). The effects of attending a diverse college. *Economics of Education Review, 30*(2), 332–341.

Hofer, B. K., & Pintrich, P. R. (Eds.). (2004). *Personal epistemology: The psychology of beliefs about knowledge and knowing*. Mahwah, NJ: Erlbaum.

Hoffman, F., & Oreopoulos, P. (2009a). A professor like me: The influence of instructor gender on college achievement. *Journal of Human Resources, 44*(2), 479–494.

Hoffman, F., & Oreopoulos, P. (2009b). Professor qualities and student achievement. *Review of Economics and Statistics, 91*(1), 83–92.

Hoffman, J. L., & Lowitzki, K. E. (2005). Predicting college success with high school grades and test scores: Limitations for minority students. *Review of Higher Education, 28*(4), 455–474.

Holland, C., & Holley, K. (2011). The experiences of gay male undergraduate students at a traditional women's college. *Journal of Student Affairs Research and Practice, 48*(2), 173–188.

Holland, J. L. (1959). A theory of vocational choice. *Journal of Counseling Psychology, 6*, 35–45.

Holland, J. L. (1985). *Making vocational choices: A theory of vocational personalities and work environments* (2nd ed.). Englewood Cliffs, NJ: Prentice Hall.

Holland, J. L. (1997). *Making vocational choices: A theory of vocational personalities and work environments* (3rd ed.). Odessa, FL: Psychological Assessment Resources.

Holland, L., Matthews, T. L., & Schott, M. R. (2013). "That's so gay!" Exploring college students' attitudes toward the LGBT population. *Journal of Homosexuality, 60*(4), 575–595.

Holmes, W. M. (2013). *Using propensity scores in quasi-experimental designs.* Thousand Oaks, CA: Sage.

Hossler, D. (2004). Refinancing public universities: Student enrollments, incentive-based budgeting, and incremental revenue. In E. P. St. John & M. D. Parsons (Eds.), *Public funding of higher education: Changing contexts and new rationales* (pp. 145–163). Baltimore, MD: Johns Hopkins University Press.

Hossler, D., Ziskin, M., Gross, J. P. K., Kim, S., & Cekic, O. (2009). Student aid and its role in encouraging persistence. In J. C. Smart (Ed.), *Higher education: Handbook of theory and research* (Vol. 24, pp. 389–425). Dordrecht, Netherlands: Springer.

Hotchkiss, J. L., Moore, R. E., & Pitts, M. M. (2006). Freshman learning communities, college performance, and retention. *Education Economics, 14*(2), 197–210.

Hovey, J. D., Kim, S. E., & Seligman, L. D. (2006). The influences of cultural values, ethnic identity, and language use on the mental health of Korean American college students. *Journal of Psychology, 140*(5), 499–511.

Hox, J. J. (2010). *Multilevel analysis: Techniques and applications.* New York, NY: Routledge.

Hoyle, R. H. (Ed.). (2012). *Handbook of structural equation modeling.* New York, NY: Guilford.

Hu, S. (2011). Reconsidering the relationship between student engagement and persistence in college. *Innovative Higher Education, 36*(2), 97–106.

Hu, S., & Kuh, G. D. (2003a). Maximizing what students get out of college: Testing a learning productivity model. *Journal of College Student Development, 44*(2), 185–203.

Hu, S., & Kuh, G. D. (2003b). Diversity experiences and college student learning and personal development. *Journal of College Student Development, 44*(3), 320–334.

Hu, S., Kuh, G. D., & Li, S. (2008). The effects of engagement in inquiry-oriented activities on student learning and personal development. *Innovative Higher Education, 33*(2), 71–81.

Hu, S., & McCormick, A. C. (2012). An engagement-based student typology and its relationship to college outcomes. *Research in Higher Education, 53*(7), 738–754.

Hu, S., McCormick, A. C., & Gonyea, R. M. (2012). Examining the relationship between student learning and persistence. *Innovative Higher Education, 37*(5), 387–395.

Hu, S., & Wolniak, G. C. (2010). Initial evidence on the influence of college student engagement on early career earnings. *Research in Higher Education, 51*(8), 750–766.

Hu, S., & Wolniak, G. C. (2013). College student engagement and early career earnings: Differences by gender, race/ethnicity, and academic preparation. *Review of Higher Education, 36*(2), 211–233.

Huang, J., Maassen van den Brink, H., & Groot, W. (2009). A meta-analysis of the effect of education on social capital. *Economics of Education Review, 28*(4), 454–464.

Hubbard, W. H. J. (2011). The phantom gender difference in the college wage premium. *Journal of Human Resources, 46*(3), 568–586.

Hudson, L., Aquilino, S., & Kienzl, G. (2005). *Postsecondary participation rates by sex and race/ethnicity: 1974–2003. Issue Brief* (NCES 2005–028). Washington, DC: National Center for Education Statistics.

Huerta, M. C., & Borgonovi, F. (2010). Education, alcohol use and abuse among young adults in Britain. *Social Science and Medicine, 71*(1), 143–151.

Hundhausen, C., Agarwal, P., Zollars, R. & Carter, A. (2011). The design and experimental evaluation of a scaffolded software environment to improve engineering students' disciplinary problem-solving skills. *Journal of Engineering Education, 100*(3), 574–603.

Hurtado, S. (1992). The Campus racial climate: Contexts of conflict. *The Journal of Higher Education, 63*(5), 539-569.

Hurtado, S. (1994). The institutional climate for talented Latino students. *Research in Higher Education, 35*(1), 21–41.

Hurtado, S. (2005). The next generation of diversity and intergroup relations research. *Journal of Social Issues, 61*(3), 595–610.

Hurtado, S., & Carter, D. F. (1997). Effects of college transition and perceptions of the campus racial climate on Latino college students' sense of belonging. *Sociology of Education, 70*(4), 324–345.

Hurtado, S., Mayhew, M. J., & Engberg, M. E. (2012). Diversity courses and students' moral reasoning: A model of predispositions and change. *Journal of Moral Education, 41*(2), 201–224.

Hurtado, S., Milem, J. F., & Allen, W. A. (1995). *The climate for racial/ethnic diversity in higher education institutions: A preliminary report from the Common Destiny Alliance.* A paper presented at the annual One Third of a Nation Conference, American Council on Education, Kansas City, MO.

Hurtado, S., Ruiz, A., & Guillermo-Wann, C. (2011). *Thinking about race: The salience of racial and ethnic identity in college and the climate for diversity.* Los Angeles, CA: Higher Education Research Institute, UCLA.

Hwang, W. C., & Goto, S. (2009). The impact of perceived racial discrimination on the mental health of Asian American and Latino college students. *Asian American Journal of Psychology, S*(1), 15–28.

Hyllegard, D., Deng, H., & Hunter, C. (2008). Why do students leave online courses? Attrition in community college distance learning courses. *International Journal of Instructional Media, 35*(4), 429–434.

Imbens, G. W., & Lemieux, T. (2008). Regression discontinuity designs: A guide to practice. *Journal of Econometrics, 142*(2), 615–635.

Inkelas, K. K., Johnson, D., Lee, Z., Daver, Z., Longerbeam, S. D., Vogt, K., & Leonard, J. B. (2006). The role of living-learning programs in students' perceptions of intellectual growth at three large universities. *NASPA Journal, 43*(1), 115–143.

Inkelas, K. K., Soldner, M., Longerbeam, S. D., & Leonard, J. B. (2008). Differences in student outcomes by types of living-learning programs: The development of an empirical typology. *Research in Higher Education, 49*(6), 495–512.

Inkelas, K. K., Vogt, K. E., Longerbeam, S. D., Owen, J. E., & Johnson, D. (2006). Measuring outcomes of living-learning programs: Examining college environments and student learning and development. *Journal of General Education, 55*(1), 40–76.

Inkelas, K. K., & Weisman, J. L. (2003). Different by design: An examination of student outcomes among participants in three types of living-learning programs. *Journal of College Student Development, 44*(3), 335–368.

Inkeles, A. (1966). Social structure and the socialization of competence. *Harvard Educational Review, 36*(3), 265–283.

Institute of International Education. (2012). *Open doors data: International students.* Retrieved from http://www.iie.org/Research-and-Publications/Open-Doors/Data/International-Students

International Center for Supplemental Instruction. (2016). *Supplemental Instruction (SI) Overview.* Retrieved from http://www.umkc.edu/asm/umkcsi/

Ishitani, T. T. (2003). A longitudinal approach to assessing attrition behavior among first-generation students: Time-varying effects of pre-college characteristics. *Research in Higher Education, 44*(4), 433–449.

Ishitani, T. T. (2006). Studying attrition and degree completion behavior among first-generation college students in the United States. *Journal of Higher Education, 77*(5), 861–885.

Ishitani, T. T. (2008). How do transfers survive after "transfer shock"? A longitudinal study of transfer student departure. *Research in Higher Education, 49*(5), 403–419.

Ishitani, T. T., & DesJardins, S. L. (2002). A longitudinal investigation of dropout from college in the United States. *Journal of College Student Retention, 4*(2), 173–201.

Ishitani, T. T., & McKitrick, S. A. (2013). The effects of academic programs and institutional characteristics on postgraduate civic engagement behavior. *Journal of College Student Development, 54*(4), 379–396.

Iturbide, M. I., Raffaelli, M., & Carlo, G. (2009). Protective effects of ethnic identity on Mexican American college students' psychological well-being. *Hispanic Journal of Behavioral Sciences, 31*(4), 536–552.

Iverson, S. V., & James, J. H. (2013). Self-authoring a civic identity: A qualitative analysis of change-oriented service learning. *Journal of Student Affairs Research and Practice, 50*(1), 88–105.

Iwamoto, D. K., & Liu, W. M. (2010). The impact of racial identity, ethnic identity, Asian values, and race-related stress on Asian Americans and Asian international college students' psychological well-being. *Journal of Counseling Psychology, 57*(1), 79–91.

Iwaoka, W. T., & Crosetti, L. M. (2008). Using academic journals to help students learn subject matter content, develop and practice critical reasoning skills, and reflect on personal values in food science and human nutrition classes. *Journal of Food Science Education, 7*(2), 19–29.

Jaccard, J. (1998). *Interaction effects in factorial analysis of variance.* Thousand Oaks, CA: Sage.

Jaccard, J., & Turrisi, R. (2003). *Interaction effects in multiple regression* (2nd ed.). Thousand Oaks CA: Sage.

Jackson, B. A., & Wingfield, A. H. (2013). Getting angry to get ahead: Black college men, emotional performance, and encouraging respectable masculinity. *Symbolic Interaction, 36*(3), 275–292.

Jackson, C. (2003). Transitions into higher education: Gendered implications for academic self-concept. *Oxford Review of Education, 29*(3), 331–346.

Jacob, B. A. (2002). Where the boys aren't: Non-cognitive skills, returns to school and the gender gap in higher education. *Economics of Education Review, 21*, 589–598.

Jacoby, D. (2006). Effects of part-time faculty employment on community college graduation rates. *Journal of Higher Education, 77*(6), 1081–1103.

Jaeger, A. J., & Eagan, M. K., Jr. (2009). Unintended consequences: Examining the effect of part-time faculty members on associate's degree completion. *Community College Review, 36*(3), 167–194.

Jaeger, A. J., & Eagan, M. K., Jr. (2011). Examining retention and contingent faculty use in a state system of public higher education. *Educational Policy, 25*(3), 507–537.

Jaeger, A. J., & Hinz, D. (2008). The effects of part-time faculty on first semester freshman retention: A predictive model using logistic regression. *Journal of College Student Retention, 10*(3), 33–53.

Jaggars, S. S., & Bailey, T. (2010, July). *Effectiveness of fully online courses for college students: Response to a Department of Education meta-analysis.* Retrieved from http://ccrc.tc.columbia.edu/publications/effectiveness-fully-online-courses.html

Jaggars, S. S., & Stacey, G. W. (2014). *What we know about developmental education outcomes.* New York, NY: Community College Research Center, Teachers College, Columbia University.

Jamelske, E. (2009). Measuring the impact of a university first-year experience program on student GPA and retention. *Higher Education, 57*(3), 373–391.

Jaret, C., & Reitzes, D. C. (2009). Currents in a stream: College student identities and ethnic identities and their relationship with self-esteem, efficacy, and grade point average in an urban university. *Social Science Quarterly, 90*(2), 345–367.

Jayakumar, U. M. (2008). Can higher education meet the needs of an increasingly diverse and global society? Campus diversity and cross-cultural workforce competencies. *Harvard Educational Review, 78*(4), 615–651.

Jenkins, D., Speroni, C., Belfield, C., Jaggars, S. S., & Edgecombe, N. (2010). *A model for accelerating academic success of community college remedial English students: Is the Accelerated Learning Program (ALP) effective and affordable?* (CCRC Working Paper No. 21). New York, NY: Community College Research Center, Columbia University.

Jenkins, H. W., Jr. (2010, October 9). Technology = salvation. *Wall Street Journal*. Retrieved from http://www.wsj.com/articles/SB10001424052748704696304575537882643165738

Jennison, K. M. (2004). The short-term effects and unintended long-term consequences of binge drinking in college: A 10-year follow-up study. *American Journal of Drug and Alcohol Abuse, 30*(3), 659–684.

Jensen, J. L., & Lawson, A. (2011). Effects of collaborative group composition and inquiry instruction on reasoning gains and achievement in undergraduate biology. *CBE-Life Sciences Education, 10*(1), 64–73.

Jessup-Anger, J. E. (2012). Examining how residential college environments inspire the life of the mind. *Review of Higher Education, 35*(3), 431–462.

Jiang, X., & Grabe, W. (2007). Graphic organizers in reading instruction: Research findings and issues. *Reading in a Foreign Language, 19*(1), 34–55.

Johnson, D. I. (2004). Relationships between college experiences and alumni participation in the community. *Review of Higher Education, 27*(2), 169–185.

Johnson, D. R., Wasserman, T. H., Yildirim, N., & Yonai, B. A. (2014). Examining the effects of stress and campus climate on the persistence of students of color and White students: An application of Bean and Eaton's psychological model of retention. *Research in Higher Education, 55*(1), 75–110.

Johnson, I. Y. (2008). Enrollment, persistence and graduation of in-state students at a public research university: Does high school matter? *Research in Higher Education, 49*(8), 776–793.

Johnson, I. Y. (2011). Contingent instructors and student outcomes: An artifact or a fact? *Research in Higher Education, 52*(8), 761–785.

Johnson, M., & Kuennen, E. (2004). Delaying developmental mathematics: The characteristics and costs. *Journal of Developmental Education, 28*(2), 24–29.

Johnson, S. C., & Arbona, C. (2006). The relation of ethnic identity, racial identity, and race-related stress among African American college students. *Journal of College Student Development, 47*(5), 495–507.

Johnson, T. E., Archibald, T. N., & Tenenbaum, G. (2010). Individual and team annotation effects on students' reading comprehension, critical thinking, and meta-cognitive skills. *Computers in Human Behavior, 26*(2010), 1496–1507.

Johnston, C., & Olekalins, N. (2002). Enriching the learning experience: A CALM approach. *Studies in Higher Education, 27*(1), 103–119.

Jonassen, D. H., Shen, D., Marra, R. M., Cho, Y. H., Lo, J. L., & Lohani, V. K. (2009). Engaging and supporting problem solving in engineering ethics. *Journal of Engineering Education, 98*(3), 235–254.

Jones, G. A. (Ed.). (2012). *Higher education in Canada: Different systems, different perspectives*. New York, NY: Routledge.

Jones, S. R., & Abes, E. S. (2004). Enduring influences of service-learning on college students' identity development. *Journal of College Student Development, 45*(2), 149–166.

Jones, S. R., & Abes, E. S. (2013). *Identity development of college students: Advancing frameworks for multiple dimensions of identity*. San Francisco, CA: Jossey-Bass.

Jones, S. R., & McEwen, M. K. (2000). A conceptual model of multiple dimensions of identity. *Journal of College Student Development, 41*(4), 405–414.

Jones, S. R., Rowan-Kenyon, H. T., Ireland, S. M. Y., Niehaus, E., & Skendall, K. C. (2012). The meaning students make as participants in short-term immersion programs. *Journal of College Student Development, 53*(2), 201–220.

Jones-White, D. R., Radcliffe, P. M., Huesman, R. L., Jr., & Kellogg, J. P. (2010). Redefining student success: Applying different multinomial regression techniques for the study of student graduation across institutions of higher education. *Research in Higher Education, 51*(2), 154–174.

Jose, P. E. (2013). *Doing statistical mediation and moderation.* New York, NY: Guilford.

Josselson, R. (1973). Psychodynamic aspects of identity formation in college women. *Journal of Youth and Adolescence, 2*(1), 3–52.

Josselson, R. (1987). *Finding herself: Pathways to identity development in women.* San Francisco, CA: Jossey-Bass.

Josselson, R. (1996). *Revising herself: The story of women's identity from college to midlife.* New York, NY: Oxford University Press.

Joy, L. (2006). Occupational differences between recent male and female college graduates. *Economics of Education Review, 25*(2), 221–231.

Judge, T. A., & Watanabe, S. (1993). Another look at the job satisfaction—life satisfaction relationship. *Journal of Applied Psychology, 78*(6), 939–948.

Julian, T. A., & Kominski, R. A. (2011). *Education and synthetic worklife earnings estimates* (American Community Survey Reports, ACS-14). Washington, DC: U.S. Census Bureau. Retrieved from https://www.census.gov/prod/2011pubs/acs-14.pdf

Junco, R., & Mastrodicasa, J. (2007). *Connecting to the net.generation: What higher education professionals need to know about today's students.* Washington, DC: NASPA.

Junk, K. E., & Armstrong, P. I. (2010). Stability of career aspirations: A longitudinal test of Gottfredson's theory. *Journal of Career Development, 37*(3), 579–598.

Jürges, H. (2009). Healthy minds in health bodies: An international comparison of education-related inequality in physical health among older adults. *Scottish Journal of Political Economy, 56*(3), 296–320.

Jürges, H., Kruk, E., & Reinhold, S. (2013). The effect of compulsory schooling on health evidence from biomarkers. *Journal of Population Economics, 26*(2), 645–672.

Juujarvi, S., Myyry, L., & Pesso, K. (2010). Does care reasoning make a difference? Relations between care, justice and dispositional empathy. *Journal of Moral Education, 39*(4), 469–489.

Kahn, L. B. (2010). The long-term labor market consequences of graduating from college in a bad economy. *Labour Economics, 17*(2), 303–316.

Kalman, C. S. (2011). Enhancing students' conceptual understanding by engaging science text with reflective writing as a hermeneutical circle. *Science and Education, 20*(2), 159–172.

Kalogrides, D., & Grodsky, E. (2011). Something to fall back on: Community colleges as a safety net. *Social Forces, 89*(3), 853–877.

Kam, C. D., & Palmer, C. L. (2008). Reconsidering the effects of education on political participation. *Journal of Politics, 70*(3), 612–631.

Kam, C. D., & Palmer, C. L. (2011). Rejoinder: Reinvestigating the causal relationship between higher education and political participation. *Journal of Politics, 73*(3), 659–663.

Kanfer, R., Ackerman, P. L., & Heggestad, E. D. (1996). Motivational skills & self-regulation for learning: A trait perspective. *Learning and individual differences, 8*(3), 185–209

Kapitanoff, S. H. (2009). Collaborative testing: Cognitive and interpersonal processes related to enhanced test performance. *Active Learning in Higher Education, 10*(1), 56–70.

Karantzas, G. C., Avery, M. R., Macfarlane, S., Mussap, A., Tooley, G., Hazelwood, Z., & Fitness, J. (2013). Enhancing critical analysis and problem-solving skills in undergraduate psychology: An evaluation of a collaborative learning and problem-based learning approach. *Australian Journal of Psychology, 65*(1), 38–45.

Kardash, C. A. M. (2000). Evaluation of an undergraduate research experience: Perceptions of undergraduate interns and their faculty mentors. *Journal of Educational Psychology, 92*(1), 191–201.

Kauffman, D. F., Ge, X., Xie, K., & Chen, C. H. (2008). Prompting in web-based environments: Supporting self-monitoring and problem solving skills in college students. *Journal of Educational Computing Research, 38*(2), 115–137.

Kaufman, G. (2005). Gender role attitudes and college students' work and family expectations. *Gender Issues, 22*(2), 58–71.

Kaufman, P. (2014). The sociology of college students' identity formation. In C. Hanson (Ed.), *In search of self: Exploring student identity development* (New Directions for Higher Education No. 166, pp. 35–42). San Francisco, CA: Jossey-Bass.

Kaufman, P., & Feldman, K. A. (2004). Forming identities in college: A sociological approach. *Research in Higher Education, 45*(5), 463–496.

Keen, C. (2001). A study of changes in intellectual development from freshman to senior year at a cooperative education college. *Journal of Cooperative Education, 36*(3), 37–45.

Kegan, R. (1982). *The evolving self: Problem and process in human development.* Cambridge, MA: Harvard University Press.

Kegan, R. (1994). *In over our heads: The mental demands of modern life.* Cambridge, MA: Harvard University Press.

Keith, T. Z. (2005). *Multiple regression and beyond.* New York, NY: Pearson.

Kellogg, A. H., & Liddell, D. L. (2012). "Not half but double": Exploring critical incidents in the racial identity of multiracial college students. *Journal of College Student Development, 53*(4), 524–541.

Kellogg, R. T., Whiteford, A. P., & Quinlan, T. (2010). Does automated feedback help students learn to write? *Journal of Educational Computing Research, 42*(2), 173–196.

Kerckhoff, A. C. (1976). The status attainment process: Socialization or allocation? *Social Forces, 55*(2), 368–81.

Keselyak, N. T., Saylor, C. D., Simmer-Beck, M., & Bray, K. K. (2009). Examining the role of collaborative assessment in a didactic dental hygiene course. *Journal of Dental Education, 73*(8), 980–990.

Keup, J. (Ed.). (2012). *Peer leadership in higher education* (New Directions in Higher Education, No. 157). San Francisco, CA: Jossey Bass.

Kezar, A. J., & Sam, C. (2010). *Understanding the new majority of non-tenure-track faculty in higher education: Demographics, experiences, and plans of action* (ASHE Higher Education Report Vol. 36, No. 4). San Francisco, CA: Jossey-Bass.

Kilgo, C. A., Sheets, J. K. E., & Pascarella, E. T. (2015). The link between high-impact practices and student learning: Some longitudinal evidence. *Higher Education, 69*(4), 509–525.

Kilson, M. (2001). *Claiming place: Biracial young adults of the post-civil rights era.* Westport, CT: Bergin & Garvey.

Kim, C., & Hodges, C. B. (2012). Effects of an emotion control treatment on academic emotions, motivation and achievement in an online mathematics course. *Instructional Science, 40*(1), 173–192.

Kim, E., & Lee, D. (2011). Collective self-esteem: Role of social context among Asian-American college students. *Psychological Reports, 109*(3), 1017–1037.

Kim, J. (2008). Intercohort trends in the relationship between education and health: Examining physical impairment and depressive symptomatology. *Journal of Aging and Health, 20*(6), 671–693.

Kim, M. M. (2002a). Cultivating intellectual development: Comparing women-only colleges and coeducational colleges for educational effectiveness. *Research in Higher Education, 43*(4), 447–481.

Kim, M. M. (2002b). Historically Black vs. White institutions: Academic development among Black students. *Review of Higher Education, 25*(4), 385–407.

Kim, M. M., & Conrad, C. F. (2006). The impact of historically Black colleges and universities on the academic success of African-American students. *Research in Higher Education, 47*(4), 399–427.

Kim, M. M., Rhoades, G., & Woodard, D. B. (2003). Sponsored research versus graduating students? Intervening variables and unanticipated findings in public research universities. *Research in Higher Education, 44*(1), 51–81.

Kim, Y. K., Chang, M. J., & Park, J. J. (2009). Engaging with faculty: Examining rates, predictors, and educational effects for Asian American undergraduates. *Journal of Diversity in Higher Education, 2*(4), 206.

Kim, Y. K., & Sax, L. J. (2009). Student-faculty interaction in research universities: Differences by student gender, race, social class, and first-generation status. *Research in Higher Education, 50*(5), 437–459.

Kim, Y. K., & Sax, L. J. (2011). Are the effects of student-faculty interaction dependent on academic major? An examination using multilevel modeling. *Research in Higher Education, 52*(6), 589–615.

Kim, Y. K., & Sax, L. J. (2014). The effects of student–faculty interaction on academic self-concept: Does academic major matter? *Research in Higher Education, 55*(8), 780–809.

King, P. M., & Baxter Magolda, M. B. (2005). A developmental model of intercultural maturity. *Journal of College Student Development, 46*(6), 571–592.

King, P. M., Baxter Magolda, M. B., & Massé, J. C. (2011). Maximizing learning from engaging across difference: The role of anxiety and meaning making. *Equity & Excellence in Education, 44*(4), 468–487.

King, P. M., Baxter Magolda, M. B., Barber, J. P., Brown, M. K., & Lindsay, N. K. (2009). Developmentally effective experiences for promoting self-authorship. *Mind, Brain, and Education, 3*(2), 108–118.

King, P. M. & Kitchener, K. S. (1994). *Developing reflective judgment: Understanding and promoting intellectual growth and critical thinking in adolescents and adults.* San Francisco, CA: Jossey-Bass.

King, P. M. & Kitchener, K. S. (2002). The reflective judgment model: Twenty years of research on epistemic cognition. In B. K. Hofer and P. R. Pintrich (Eds.), *Personal epistemology: The psychology of beliefs about knowledge and knowing* (pp. 37–61). Mahway, NJ: Lawrence Erlbaum, Publisher.

King, P. M., & Mayhew, M. J. (2002). Moral judgement development in higher education: Insights from the Defining Issues Test. *Journal of Moral Education, 31*(3), 247–270.

King, P. M., & Mayhew, M. J. (2005). Theory and research on the development of moral reasoning among college students. In J. C. Smart (Ed.), *Higher education: Handbook of theory and research* (Vol. 19, pp. 375–440.) New York, NY: Agathon Press.

Kingston, P. W., Hubbard, R., Lapp, P., Schroeder, P., & Wilson, J. (2003). Why education matters. *Sociology of Education, 76*(1), 53–70.

Kinzie, J., Thomas, A. D., Palmer, M. M., Umbach, P. D., & Kuh, G. D. (2007). Women students at coeducational and women's colleges: How do their experiences compare? *Journal of College Student Development, 48*(2), 145–165.

Kirk, R. E. (2012). *Experimental design: Procedures for the behavioral sciences* (4th ed.). Thousand Oaks, CA: Sage.

Kirsch, A. C., Conley, C. S., & Riley, T. J. (2015). Comparing psychosocial adjustment across the college transition in a matched heterosexual and lesbian, gay, and bisexual sample. *Journal of College Student Development, 56*(2), 155–169.

Kitchener, K. S., & King, P. M. (1990). The reflective judgment model: Ten years of research. In M. L. Commons, C. Armon, L. Kohlberg, F. A. Richards, T. A. Grotzer, & J. D. Sinnott (Eds.), *Adult development* (Vol. 2, pp. 62–78). New York, NY: Praeger.

Kitsantas, A., & Zimmerman, B. J. (2009). College students' homework and academic achievement: The mediating role of self-regulatory beliefs. *Metacognition Learning, 4*(2), 97–110.

Klein, P. D., Piacente-Cimini, S., & Williams, L. A. (2007). The role of writing in learning from analogies. *Learning and Instruction, 17*(6), 595–611.

Kline, R. B. (2010). *Principles and practice of structural equation modeling* (3rd ed.). New York, NY: Guilford.

Klofstad, C. A. (2010). The lasting effect of civic talk on civic participation: Evidence from a panel study. *Social Forces, 88*(5), 2353–2375.

Knight, J. (2008). *Higher education in turmoil: The changing world of internationalization*. Rotterdam, Netherlands: Sense Publishers.

Knight, J. K., & Wood, W. B. (2005). Teaching more by lecturing less. *Cell Biology Education, 4*(4), 298–310.

Knight, W. E. (2009). Student self-reported gains attributed to college attendance: Comparing two-year and four-year students. *IR Applications, 17,* 1–15.

Kodama, C. M., & Dugan, J. P. (2013). Leveraging leadership efficacy for college students: Disaggregating data to examine unique predictors by race. *Equity and Excellence in Education, 46*(2), 184–201.

Kohlberg, L. (1976). Moral stages and moralization: The cognitive-developmental approach. In T. Likona (Ed.), *Moral development and behavior.* New York, NY: Holt, Rinehart, & Winston

Kohlberg, L. (1981). *Essays on moral development: Moral stages and the idea of justice* (Vol. 1). San Francisco, CA: Harper & Row.

Kokkelenberg, E. C., Dillon, M., & Christy, S. M. (2008). The effects of class size on student grades at a public university. *Economics of Education Review, 27*(2), 221–233.

Kolb, D. A. (1984). *Experiential learning: Experience as the source of learning and development* (Vol. 1). Englewood Cliffs, NJ: Prentice Hall.

Komives, S. R., Longerbeam, S. D., Owen, J. E., Mainella, F. C., & Osteen, L. (2006). A leadership identity development model: Applications from a grounded theory. *Journal of College Student Development, 47*(4), 401–418.

Komives, S. R., Owen, J. E., Longerbeam, S. D., Mainella, F. C., & Osteen, L. (2005). Developing a leadership identity: A grounded theory. *Journal of College Student Development, 46*(6), 593–611.

Korupp, S., Ganzeboom, H. B. G., & Van Der Lippe, T. (2002). Do mothers matter? A comparison of models of the influence of mothers' and fathers' educational and occupational status on children's educational attainment. *Quality and Quantity, 36*(1), 17–42.

Krebs, D. L., & Denton, K. L. (2005). Toward a more pragmatic approach to morality: A critical evaluation of Kohlberg's model. *Psychological Review, 112*(3), 629.

Krych, A. J., March, C. N., Bryan, R. E., Peake, B. J., Pawlina, W., & Carmichael, S. W. (2005). Reciprocal peer teaching: Students teaching students in the gross anatomy laboratory. *Clinical Anatomy, 18*(4), 296–301.

Kugelmass, H., & Ready, D. D. (2011). Racial/ethnic disparities in collegiate cognitive gains: A multilevel analysis of institutional influences on learning and its equitable distribution. *Research in Higher Education, 52*(4), 323–348.

Kuh, G. D. (1999). How are we doing? Tracking the quality of the undergraduate experience, 1960s to the present. *Review of Higher Education, 22*(2), 99–119.

Kuh, G. D. (2001). *The National Survey of Student Engagement: Conceptual framework and overview of psychometric properties.* Bloomington, IN: Indiana University Center for Postsecondary Research.

Kuh, G. D. (2003). What we're learning about student engagement from NSSE: Benchmarks for effective educational practices. *Change: The Magazine of Higher Learning, 35*(2), 24–32.

Kuh, G. D. (2008). *High-impact educational practices: What they are, who has access to them, and why they matter.* Washington, DC: Association of American Colleges and Universities.

Kuh, G. D., Cruce, T. M., Shoup, R., & Kinzie, J. (2008). Unmasking the effects of student engagement on first-year college grades and persistence. *Journal of Higher Education, 79*(5), 540–563.

Kuh, G. D., & Gonyea, R. M. (2003). The role of the academic library in promoting student engagement in learning. *College & Research Libraries, 64*(4), 256–282.

Kuh, G. D. & Hu, S. (2001). The effects of student-faculty interaction in the 1990s. *Review of Higher Education, 24*(3), 309–332.

Kuh, G. D., Kinzie, J., Schuh, J. H., & Whitt, E. J. (2011). *Student success in college: Creating conditions that matter.* San Francisco, CA: Jossey-Bass.

Kuh, G. D., & Love, P. G. (2000). A cultural perspective on student departure. In J. M. Braxton (Ed.), *Reworking the student departure puzzle* (pp. 196–212). Nashville, TN: Vanderbilt University Press.

Kurfiss, J. (1988). Intellectual, psychosocial, and moral development in college: Four major theories. In J. P. Balas & J. R. Judy (Eds.), *A handbook on values development and the Lutheran church-related college* (pp. 139–162). Greenville, PA: Thiel College.

Kutner, M., Greenberg, E., Jin, Y., Boyle, B., Hsu, Y. & Dunleavy, E. (2007). *Literacy in Everyday Life: Results from the 2003 National Assessment of Adult Literacy* (NCES 2007–480). Washington, DC: U.S. Department of Education, National Center for Education Statistics.

Kutner, M., Greenberg, E., Jin, Y., & Paulsen, C. (2006). *The Health Literacy of America's Adults: Results From the 2003 National Assessment of Adult Literacy* (NCES 2006–483). Washington, DC: U.S. Department of Education, National Center for Education Statistics.

Kwon, P., & Hugelshofer, D. S. (2012). Lesbian, gay, and bisexual speaker panels lead to attitude change among heterosexual college students. *Journal of Gay and Lesbian Social Services, 24*(1), 62–79.

Laker, J. A., & Davis, T. (Eds.). (2011). *Masculinities in higher education: Theoretical and practical considerations.* New York, NY: Routledge.

Lakin, J. M., Elliot, D. C. & Liu, O. L. (2012). Investigating ESL students' performance on outcomes assessments in higher education. *Educational and Psychological Measurement, 72*(5), 734–753.

Lambert, A. D., Terenzini, P. T., & Lattuca, L. R. (2007). More than meets the eye: Curricular and programmatic effects on student learning. *Research in Higher Education, 48*(2), 141–168.

Lampert, N. (2007). Critical thinking dispositions as an outcome of undergraduate education. *Journal of General Education, 56*(1), 17–33.

Lang, D. J. (2007). The impact of a first-year experience course on the academic performance, persistence, and graduation rates of first-semester college students at a public research university. *Journal of the First-Year Experience & Students in Transition, 19*(1), 9–25.

Lange, F. (2011). The role of education in complex health decisions: Evidence from cancer screening. *Journal of Health Economics, 30*(1), 43–54.

Larimer, M. E., Turner, A. P., Mallett, K. A., & Geisner, I. M. (2004). Predicting drinking behavior and alcohol-related problems among fraternity and sorority members: Examining the role of descriptive and injunctive norms. *Psychology of Addictive Behaviors, 18*(3), 203–212.

Laskey, M. L., & Hetzel, C. J. (2011). Investigating factors related to retention of at-risk college students. *Learning Assistance Review, 16*(1), 31–43.

Lattuca, L. R. (2001). *Creating interdisciplinarity: Interdisciplinary research and teaching among college and university faculty*. Nashville, TN: Vanderbilt University Press.

Lau, L. K., Caracciolo, B., Roddenberry, S., & Scroggins, A. (2012). College students' perception of ethics. *Journal of Academic and Business Ethics, 5*, 1–13.

Lau, L. K., & Haug, J. C. (2011). The impact of sex, college, major, and student classification on students' perception of ethics. *Mustang Journal of Business & Ethics, 2*, 92–105.

Lawrence, W., Schlotz, W., Crozier, S., Skinner, T. C., Haslam, C., Robinson, S., . . . & Group, T. F. C. (2011). Specific psychological variables predict quality of diet in women of lower, but not higher, educational attainment. *Appetite, 56*(1), 46–52.

Lawson, T. J. (1999). Assessing psychological critical thinking as a learning outcome for psychology majors. *Teaching of Psychology, 26*(3), 207–209.

Leaper, C., & Van, S. R. (2008). Masculinity ideology, covert sexism, and perceived gender typicality in relation to young men's academic motivation and choices in college. *Psychology of Men and Masculinity, 9*(3), 139–153.

Leavy, P., Gnong, A., & Ross, L. S. (2009). Femininity, masculinity, and body image issues among college-age women: An in-depth and written interview study of the mind-body dichotomy. *Qualitative Report, 14*(2), 261–292.

Lee, J. J. (2002a). Changing worlds, changing selves: The experience of the religious self among Catholic collegians. *Journal of College Student Development, 43*(3), 341–356.

Lee, J. J. (2002b). Religion and college attendance: Change among students. *Review of Higher Education, 25*(4), 369–384.

Leigh, D. E., & Gill, A. M. (2003). Do community colleges really divert students from earning bachelor's degrees? *Economics of Education Review, 22*(1), 23–30.

Leight, H., Saunders, C., Calkins, R., & Withers, M. (2012). Collaborative testing improves performance but not content retention in a large-enrollment Introductory Biology class. *CBE—Life Sciences Education, 11*(4), 392–401.

Lent, R. W., Brown, S. D., & Hackett, G. (1994). Toward a unifying social cognitive theory of career and academic interest, choice, and performance. *Journal of Vocational Behavior, 45*(1), 79–122.

Lepp, A., Barkley, J. & Karpinski, A. (2014). The relationship between cell phone use, academic performance, anxiety, and satisfaction with life in college students. *Computers in Human Behavior, 31*, 343-350.

Leppel, K. (2002). Similarities and differences in the college persistence of men and women. *Review of Higher Education, 25*(4), 433–450.

Lesik, S. A. (2007). Do developmental mathematics programs have a causal impact on student retention? An application of discrete-time survey and regression-discontinuity analysis. *Research in Higher Education, 48*(5), 583–608.

Lesik, S. A. (2008). Studying the effectiveness of programs and initiatives in higher education using the regression-discontinuity design. In J. Smart (Ed.), *Higher education: Handbook of theory and research* (pp. 277–297). Dordrecht, Netherlands: Springer.

Leuwerke, W. C., Robbins, S. B., Sawyer, R., & Hovland, M. (2004). Predicting engineering major status from mathematics achievement and interest congruence. *Journal of Career Assessment, 12*(2), 135–149.

Levant, R. F., Wimer, D. J., & Williams, C. M. (2011). An evaluation of the Health Behavior Inventory-20 (HBI-20) and its relationships to masculinity and attitudes towards seeking psychological help among college men. *Psychology of Men and Masculinity, 12*(1), 26–41.

Levesque, A. A. (2011). Using clickers to facilitate development of problem-solving skills. *CBE Life Sciences Education, 10*(4), 406–417.

Levin, H. & Garcia, E. (2012). Cost-effectiveness of Accelerated Study in Associate Programs (ASPA) of the City University of New York. New York, NY: Center for Benefit-Cost Studies in Education, Teachers College, Columbia University.

Lewis, T. T., Everson-Rose, S. A., Sternfeld, B., Karavolos, K., Wesley, D., & Powell, L. H. (2005). Race, education, and weight change in a biracial sample of women at midlife. *Archives of Internal Medicine, 165*(5), 545–551.

Li, D. (2010). They need help: Transfer students from four-year to four-year institutions. *Review of Higher Education, 33*(2), 207–238.

Lickona, T. (1991). *Educating for character: How schools can teach respect and responsibility*. New York, NY: Bantam.

Lies, J. M., Bock, T., Brandenberger, J., & Trozzolo, T. A. (2012). The effects of off-campus service learning on the moral reasoning of college students. *Journal of Moral Education, 41*(2), 189–199.

Light, A., & Strayer, W. (2004). Who receives the college wage premium? Assessing the labor market returns to degrees and college transfer patterns. *Journal of Human Resources, 39*(3), 746–773.

Lillard, D., & Molloy, E. (2010). *Live and learn or learn and live: Does education lead to longer lives?* Working paper. Cornell University.

Lim, K. Y., Lee, H. W., & Grabowski, B. (2009). Does concept-mapping strategy work for everyone? The levels of generativity and learners' self-regulated learning skills. *British Journal of Educational Technology, 40*(4), 606–618.

Lind, G. (2008). The meaning and measurement of moral judgment competence: A dual-aspect model. In D. Fasko, Jr. & W. Willis (Ed.), *Contemporary philosophical and psychological perspectives on moral development and education* (pp. 185–220). Creskill, NY: Hampton Press.

Linnemeyer, R. M., & Brown, C. (2010). Career maturity and foreclosure in student athletes, fine arts students, and general college students. *Journal of Career Development, 37*(3), 616–634.

Lipsey, M. W., & Wilson, D. B. (2001). *Practical meta-analysis*. Thousand Oaks, CA: Sage.

Liu, H., & Hummer, R. A. (2008). Are educational differences in US self-rated health increasing? An examination by gender and race. *Social Science and Medicine, 67*(11), 1898–1906.

Liu, O. L., Bridgeman, B., & Adler, R. M. (2012). Measuring learning outcomes in higher education: Motivation matters. *Educational Researcher, 41*(9), 352–362.

Liu, O. L., & Roohr, K. C. (2013). Investigating ten-year trends of learning outcomes at community colleges. *ETS Research Report (RR-13-34)*. Retrieved from https://www.ets.org/Media/Research/pdf/RR-13-34.pdf

Liu, X., Thomas, S., & Zhang, L. (2010). College quality, earnings, and job satisfaction: Evidence from recent college graduates. *Journal of Labor Research, 31*(2), 183–201.

Livingstone, G., Derryberry, W. P., King, A., Vendetti, M. (2006). Moral developmental consistency? Investigating differences and relationships among academic majors. *Ethics and Behavior, 16*(3), 265–287.

Lizio, A., & Wilson, K. (2004). Action learning in higher education: An investigation of its potential to develop professional capability. *Studies in Higher Education, 29*(4), 469–488.

Lleras-Muney, A. (2005). The relationship between education and adult mortality in the U.S. *Review of Economic Studies, 72*(1), 189–221.

Lochner, L. (2011). *Non-production benefits of education: Crime, health, and good citizenship.* (NBER Working Paper No. 16722). Cambridge, MA: National Bureau of Economic Research.

Locke, B. D., & Mahalik, J. R. (2005). Examining masculinity norms, problem drinking, and athletic involvement as predictors of sexual aggression in college men. *Journal of Counseling Psychology, 52*(3), 279–283.

Loes, C., Pascarella, E., & Umbach, P. (2012). Effects of diversity experiences on critical thinking skills: Who benefits? *Journal of Higher Education, 83*(1), 1–25.

Loes, C. N., Saichaie, K., Padgett, R. D., & Pascarella, E. T. (2012). The effects of teacher behaviors on students' inclination to inquire and lifelong learning. *International Journal for the Scholarship of Teaching and Learning, 6*(2). Retrieved from http://digitalcommons.georgiasouthern.edu/ij-sotl/vol6/iss2/7/

Loes, C. N., Salisbury, M. H., & Pascarella, E. T. (2013). Diversity experiences and attitudes toward literacy: Is there a link? *Journal of Higher Education, 84*(6), 834–865.

Lohfink, M. M., & Paulsen, M. B. (2005). Comparing the determinants of persistence for first-generation and continuing-generation students. *Journal of College Student Development, 46*(4), 409–428.

Lombard, K., & Grosser, M. (2008). Critical thinking: Are the ideals of OBE failing us or are we failing the ideals of OBE? *South African Journal of Education, 28*(4), 561–579.

Long, B. T., & Kurlaender, M. (2009). Do community colleges provide a viable pathway to a baccalaureate degree? *Educational Evaluation and Policy Analysis, 31*(1), 30–53.

Long, J. S. (1997). *Regression models for categorical and limited dependent variables.* Thousand Oaks, CA: Sage.

Long, M. C. (2008). College quality and early adult outcomes. *Economics of Education Review, 27*(5), 588–602.

Long, M. C. (2010). Changes in the returns to education and college quality. *Economics of Education Review, 29*(3), 338–347.

Lopatto, D. (2004). Survey of undergraduate research experiences (SURE): First findings. *Cell Biology Education, 3*(4), 270–277.

Lott, J. L., II (2013). Predictors of civic values: Understanding student-level and institutional-level effects. *Journal of College Student Development, 54*(1), 1–16.

Lott, J. L., II Hernandez, J., King, J. P., Brown, T., & Fajardo, I. (2013). Public versus private colleges: Political participation of college graduates. *Research in Higher Education, 54*(8), 895–929.

Lou, Y., Bernard, R. M., & Abrami, P. C. (2006). Media and pedagogy in undergraduate distance education: A theory based meta-analysis of empirical literature. *Educational Technology Research and Development, 54*(2), 141–176.

Lubinski, D. (2004). Introduction to the special section on cognitive abilities: 100 years after Spearman's (1904) "'General intelligence,' objectively determined and measured." *Journal of Personality and Social Psychology, 86*(1), 96–111.

Lucas, G. M., & Friedrich, J. (2005). Individual differences in workplace deviance and integrity as predictors of academic dishonesty. *Ethics and Behavior, 15*(1), 15–35.

Lucas, U., & Tan, P. L. (2007). Developing a reflective capacity within undergraduate education: The role of work-based placement learning. *The higher education academy and charitable trusts of the institute of chartered accountants in England and Wales 2005–2007.* Retrieved from https://www.heacademy.ac.uk/resource/developing-reflective-capacity-within-undergraduate-education-role-work-based-placement

Luckie, D. B., Aubry, J. R., Marengo, B. J., Rivkin, A. M., Foos, L. A., & Maleszewski, J. J. (2012). Less teaching, more learning: 10-yr study supports increasing student learning through less coverage and more inquiry. *Advances in Physiology Education, 36*(4), 325–335.

Lumina Foundation. (2014). *Our work.* Retrieved from https://www.luminafoundation.org/our-work

Lun, V. M. C., Fischer, R., Ward, C. (2010). Exploring cultural differences in critical thinking: Is it about my thinking style or the language I speak? *Learning and Individual Differences, 20*(6), 604–616.

Lundberg, C. A. (2003). The influence of time-limitations, faculty, and peer relationships on adult student learning: A causal model. *Journal of Higher Education, 74*(6), 665–688.

Lundberg, C. A. (2004). Working and learning: The role of involvement for employed students. *Journal of Student Affairs Research and Practice, 41*(2), 400–414.

Lundberg, C. A. (2007). Student involvement and institutional commitment to diversity as predictors of Native American student learning. *Journal of College Student Development, 48*(4), 405–416.

Lundberg, C. A. (2010). Institutional commitment to diversity, college involvement, and faculty relationships as predictors of learning for students of color. *Journal of the Professoriate, 3*(2), 50–74.

Lundberg, C. A. (2012). Predictors of learning for students from five different racial/ethnic groups. *Journal of College Student Development, 53*(5), 636–655.

Lundborg, P. (2013). The health returns to schooling—what can we learn from twins? *Journal of Population Economics, 26*(2), 673–701.

Lundeberg, M. A., & Yadav, A. (2006). Assessment of case study teaching: Where do we go from here? Part I. *Journal of College Science Teaching, 35*(5), 10–13.

Luo, J., & Jamieson-Drake, D. (2009). A retrospective assessment of the educational benefits of interaction across racial boundaries. *Journal of College Student Development, 50*(1), 67–86.

Luo, Z. C., Wilkins, R., & Kramer, M. S. (2006). Effect of neighbourhood income and maternal education on birth outcomes: A population-based study. *Canadian Medical Association Journal, 174*(10), 1415–1420.

Luyben, P. D., Hipworth, K., & Pappas, T. (2003). Effects of CAI on the academic performance and attitudes of college students. *Teaching of Psychology, 30*(2), 154–158.

Luyckx, K., Goossens, L., & Soenens, B. (2006). A developmental contextual perspective on identity construction in emerging adulthood: Change dynamics in commitment formation and commitment evaluation. *Developmental Psychology, 42*(2), 366–380.

Luyckx, K., Goossens, L., Soenens, B., & Beyers, W. (2005). Unpacking commitment and exploration: Preliminary validation of an integrative model of late adolescent identity formation. *Journal of Adolescence, 29*(3), 361–378.

Luyckx, K., Klimstra, T. A., Schwartz, S. J., & Duriez, B. (2013). Personal identity in college and the work context: Developmental trajectories and psychosocial functioning. *European Journal of Personality, 27*(3), 222–237.

Lyke, J. & Frank, M. (2012). Comparison of student learning outcomes in online and traditional classroom environment in a psychology course. *Journal of Instructional Psychology, 39*(4), 245–250.

Lyke, J. A., & Kelaher Young, A. J. (2006). Cognition in context: Students' perceptions of classroom goal structures and reported cognitive strategy use in the college classroom. *Research in Higher Education, 47*(4), 477–490.

Macpherson, K. (2002). Problem-solving ability and cognitive maturity in undergraduate students. *Assessment and Evaluation in Higher Education, 27*(1), 5–22.

Madgett, P. J., & Belanger, C. H. (2008). First university experience and student retention factors. *Canadian Journal of Higher Education, 38*(3), 77–96.

Maeda, Y., Thoma, S. J., & Bebeau, M. J. (2009). Understanding the relationship between moral judgment development and individual characteristics: The role of educational contexts. *Journal of Educational Psychology, 10*(1), 233–247.

Mahaffy, K. A., & Ward, S. K. (2002). The gendering of adolescents' childbearing and educational plans: Reciprocal effects and the influence of social context. *Sex Roles, 46*(11), 403–417.

Mahalik, J. R., Lagan, H. D., & Morrison, J. A. (2006). Health behaviors and masculinity in Kenyan and U.S. male college students. *Psychology of Men and Masculinity, 7*(4), 191–202.

Malone, E., & Spieth, A. (2012). Team-based learning in a subsection of a veterinary course as compared to standard lectures. *Journal of the Scholarship of Teaching and Learning, 12*(3), 88–107.

Mamiseishvili, K. (2012). International student persistence in U.S. postsecondary institutions. *Higher Education, 64*(1), 1–17.

Mandilaras, A. (2004). Industrial placement and degree performance: Evidence from a British higher institution. *International Review of Economics Education, 3*(1), 39–51.

Mangold, W. D., Bean, L. G., Adams, D. J., Schwab, W. A., & Lynch, S. M. (2003). Who goes who stays: An assessment of the effect of a freshman mentoring and unit registration program on college persistence. *Journal of College Student Retention, 4*(2), 95–122.

Manoli, P., & Papadopoulou, M. (2012). Graphic organizers as a reading strategy: Research findings and issues. *Creative Education, 3*(3), 348–356.

Mansfield, R. (2011). The effect of placement experience upon final-year results for surveying degree programmes. *Studies in Higher Education, 36*(8), 939–952.

Maralani, V. (2013). Educational inequalities in smoking: The role of initiation versus quitting. *Social Science and Medicine, 84*, 129–137.

Maramba, D. C., & Velasquez, P. (2012). Influences of the campus experience on the ethnic identity development of students of color. *Education and Urban Society, 44*(3), 294–317.

Marcia, J. E. (1966). Development and validation of ego-identity status. *Journal of Personality and Social Psychology, 3*(5), 551–558.

Marcia, J. E. (1980). Identity in adolescence. In J. Adelson (Ed.), *Handbook of adolescent psychology* (pp. 159–187). New York, NY: Wiley.

Margolis, R. (2013). Educational differences in healthy behavior changes and adherence among middle-aged Americans. *Journal of Health and Social Behavior, 54*(3), 353-368.

Marjoribanks, K. (2002). Family background, individual and environmental influences on adolescents' aspirations. *Educational Studies, 28*(1), 33–46.

Markus, G. B. (1986). Stability and change in political attitudes: Observed, recalled and explained. *Political Behavior, 8*(1), 21–44.

Marra, R., & Palmer, B. (2004). Encouraging intellectual growth: Senior college student profiles. *Journal of Adult Development, 11*(2), 111–122.

Marrs, H., Sigler, E. A., & Brammer, R. D. (2012). Gender, masculinity, femininity, and help seeking in college. *Masculinities and Social Change, 1*(3), 267–292.

Marshall, P. A. (2009). Mastery learning in a sophomore level genetics course using the blackboard course shell. *Journal of the Arizona-Nevada Academy of Science, 41*(2), 55–58.

Martin, M. A., Frisco, M. L., Nau, C., & Burnett, K. (2012). Social stratification and adolescent overweight in the United States: How income and educational resources matter across families and schools. *Social Science & Medicine, 74*(4), 597-606.

Martin, G. L., Hevel, M. S., Asel, A. M., & Pascarella, E. T. (2011). New evidence on the effects of fraternity and sorority affiliation during the first year of college. *Journal of College Student Development, 52*(5), 543–559.

Martin, G. L., Hevel, M. S., & Pascarella, E. T. (2012). Do fraternities and sororities enhance socially responsible leadership? *Journal of Student Affairs Research and Practice, 49*(3), 267–284.

Martinez, J. A., Sher, K. J., Krull, J. L., & Wood, P. K. (2009). Blue-collar scholars? Mediators and moderators of university attrition in first-generation college students. *Journal of College Student Development, 50*(1), 87–103.

Martinez, J. A., Sher, K. J., & Wood, P. K. (2008). Is heavy drinking really associated with attrition from college? The alcohol-attrition paradox. *Psychology of Addictive Behaviors, 22*(3), 450–456.

Martínez Alemán, A. M. (2010). College women's female friendships: A longitudinal view. *Journal of Higher Education, 81*(5), 553–582.

Martorell, P., & McFarlin Jr., I. (2011). Help or hindrance? The effects of college remediation on academic and labor market outcomes. *Review of Economics and Statistics, 93*(2), 436–454.

Maskiewicz, A. C., Griscom, H. P., & Welch, N. T. (2012). Using targeted active-learning exercises and diagnostic question clusters to improve students' understanding of carbon cycling in ecosystems. *CBE-Life Sciences Education, 11*(1), 58–67.

Mathai, E., & Olsen, D. (2013). Studying the effectiveness of online homework for different skill levels in a college algebra course. *PRIMUS, 23*(8), 671–682.

Mattern, K. D., Woo, S. E., Hossler, D., & Wyatt, J. (2010). Use of student-institution fit in college admissions: Do applicants really know what is good for them? *College and University, 85*(4), 18–26.

Matthews, J. R. (2012). Assessing library contributions to university outcomes: The need for individual student level data. *Library Management, 33*(6/7), 389–402.

Matz, R. L., Rothman, E. D., Krajcik, J. S., & Banaszak Holl, M. M. (2012). Concurrent enrollment in lecture and laboratory enhances student performance and retention. *Journal of Research in Science Teaching, 49*(5), 659–682.

Mayer, A. K. (2011). Does education increase political participation? *Journal of Politics, 73*(3), 633–645.

Mayer, R. E., Stull, A., DeLeeuw, K., Almeroth, K., Bimber, B., Chun, D., . . . & Zhang, H. (2009). Clickers in college classrooms: Fostering learning with questioning methods in large lecture classes. *Contemporary Educational Psychology, 34*(1), 51–57.

Mayhew, M. J. (2012a). A multilevel examination of the influence of institutional type on the moral reasoning development of first-year students. *Journal of Higher Education, 83*(3), 367–388.

Mayhew, M. J. (2012b). A multi-level examination of college and its influence on ecumenical worldview development. *Research in Higher Education, 53*(3), 282–310.

Mayhew, M. J., & Bryant Rockenbach, A. N. (2013). Achievement or arrest? The influence of the collegiate religious and spiritual climate on students' worldview commitment. *Research in Higher Education, 54*(1), 63–84.

Mayhew, M. J., & Deluca Fernández, S. (2007). Pedagogical practices that contribute to social justice outcomes. *Review of Higher Education, 31*(1), 55–80.

Mayhew, M. J., & Engberg, M. E. (2010). Diversity and moral reasoning: How negative diverse peer interactions affect the development of moral reasoning in undergraduate students. *Journal of Higher Education, 81*(4), 459–488.

Mayhew, M. J., Hubbard, S. M., Finelli, C. J., & Harding, T. S. (2009). Using structural equation modeling to validate the theory of planned behavior as a model for predicting student cheating. *Review of Higher Education, 32*(4), 441–468.

Mayhew, M. J., & King, P. M. (2008). How curricular and pedagogical strategies affect moral reasoning development in college students. *Journal of Moral Education, 37*(1), 17–40.

Mayhew, M. J., Seifert, T. A., & Pascarella, E. T. (2010). A multi-institutional assessment of moral reasoning development among first-year students. *Review of Higher Education, 33*(3), 357–390.

Mayhew, M. J., Seifert, T. A., & Pascarella, E. T. (2012). How the first year of college influences moral reasoning for students in moral consolidation and moral transition. *Journal of College Student Development, 53*(1), 19–40.

Mayhew, M. J., Seifert, T. A., Pascarella, E. T., Nelson Laird, T. F., & Blaich, C. (2012). Going deep into mechanisms for moral reasoning growth: How deep learning approaches affect moral reasoning development for first-year students. *Research in Higher Education, 53*(1), 26–46.

Mayhew, M. J., Simonoff, J. S., Baumol, W. J., Wiesenfeld, B. M., & Klein, M. W. (2012). Exploring innovative entrepreneurship and its ties to higher educational experiences. *Research in Higher Education, 53*(8), 831–859.

Mayhew, M. J., Wolniak, G. C., & Pascarella, E. T. (2008). How educational practices affect the development of life-long learning orientations in traditionally-aged undergraduate students. *Research in Higher Education, 49*, 337–356.

Mayrl, D., & Oeur, F. (2009). Religion and higher education: Current knowledge and directions for future research. *Journal for the Scientific Study of Religion, 48*(2), 260–275.

Mayrl, D., & Uecker, J. E. (2011). Higher education and religious liberalization among young adults. *Social Forces, 90*(1), 181–208.

Mazumder, B. (2008). Does education improve health? A reexamination of the evidence from compulsory schooling laws. *Economic Perspectives, 32*(2), 2–16.

McCabe, D., & Trevino, L. (1993). Academic dishonesty: Honor codes and other contextual influences. *Journal of Higher Education, 64*(5), 522–538.

McCabe, D., & Trevino, L. (1996, January/February). What we know about cheating in college. *Change, 28*(1), 29–33.

McCabe, D., & Trevino, L. (1997). Individual and contextual influences on academic dishonesty: A multicampus investigation. *Research in Higher Education, 38*(3), 379–396.

McCabe, D., Treviño, L., & Butterfield, K. (1999). Academic integrity in honor-code and non-honor-code environments: A qualitative investigation. *Journal of Higher Education, 70*(2), 211–234.

McCabe, D. L., & Bowers, W. J. (2009). The relationship between student cheating and college fraternity or sorority membership. *NASPA Journal, 46*(4), 573–586.

McCabe, D. L., Treviño, L. K., & Butterfield, K. D. (2001). Cheating in academic institutions: A decade of research. *Ethics and Behavior, 11*(3), 219–232.

McCabe, D. L., Treviño, L. K., & Butterfield, K. D. (2002). Honor codes and other contextual influences on academic integrity: A replication and extension to modified honor code settings. *Research in Higher Education, 43*(3), 357–378.

McCall, B. P., & Bielby, R. M. (2012). Regression discontinuity design: Recent developments and a guide to practice for researchers in higher education. In M. Paulsen (Ed.), *Higher education: Handbook of theory and research* (pp. 249–290). Dordrecht, Netherlands: Springer.

McClaran, A. (2013). New arrangements for quality assurance in higher education. *HEPI Occasional Report (6)*. Oxford, UK: Higher Education Policy Institute.

McClure, S. M. (2006). Improvising masculinity: African American fraternity membership in the construction of a Black masculinity. *Journal of African American Studies, 10*(1), 57–73.

McCormick, A. C., Pike, G. R., Kuh, G. D., & Chen, P. S. D. (2009). Comparing the utility of the 2000 and 2005 Carnegie classification systems in research on students' college experiences and outcomes. *Research in Higher Education, 50*(2), 144–167.

McDonough, P. M. (1997). Choosing colleges: How social class and schools structure opportunity. Albany, NY: SUNY Press.

McElroy, L. (2005). *The Millennium Foundation Bursary in Manitoba: Exploring its impact*. Montreal, Quebec, Canada: Canada Millennium Scholarship Foundation.

McElroy, L. (2008). *The Millennium Bursary in New Brunswick: Impact on debt and persistence*. Montreal, Quebec: Canada Millennium Scholarship Foundation.

McFarland, C., & Ross, M. (1987). The relation between current impressions and memories of self and dating partners. *Personality and Social Psychology Bulletin, 13*(2), 228–238.

McFarland, D., & Hamilton, D. (2005/2006). Factors affecting student performance and satisfaction: Online versus traditional course delivery. *Journal of Computer Information Systems, 46*(2), 25–32.

McFarland, M. J., Wright, B. R. E., & Weakliem, D. L. (2010). Educational attainment and religiosity: Exploring variations by religious tradition. *Sociology of Religion, 71*(1), 1–23.

McGrath, A., Taylor, A., & Pychyl, T. (2011). Writing helpful feedback: The influence of feedback type on students' perceptions and writing performance. *Canadian Journal for the Scholarship of Teaching and Learning, 2*(2), 1–14.

McGuire, M. J., & MacDonald, P. M. (2009). Relation of early testing and incentive on quiz performance in introductory psychology. *Journal of Instructional Psychology, 36*(2), 134–141.

McIntosh, H., Hart, D., & Youniss, J. (2007). The influence of family political discussion on youth civic development: Which parent qualities matter? *PS: Political Science and Politics, 40*(3), 495–499.

McKay, D. L., Houser, R. F., Blumberg, J. B., & Goldberg, J. P. (2006). Nutrition information sources vary with education level in a population of older adults. *Journal of the American Dietetic Association, 106*(7), 1108–1111.

McKibban, A. R. (2013). Students' perceptions of teacher effectiveness and academic misconduct: An inquiry into the multivariate nature of a complex phenomenon. *Ethics and Behavior, 23*(5), 378–395.

McKinney, L., & Novak, H. (2012). The relationship between FAFSA filing and persistence among first-year community college students. *Community College Review, 41*(1), 63–85.

McLaren, L. (2007). Socioeconomic status and obesity. *Epidemiologic Reviews, 29*(1), 29–48.

McLaren, L., & Godley, J. (2009). Social class and BMI among Canadian adults: A focus on occupational prestige. *Obesity, 17*(2), 290–299.

McMahon, W. W. (2009). *Higher learning, greater good: The private and social benefits of higher education*. Baltimore, MD: Johns Hopkins University Press.

McMahon, W. W., & Oketch, M. (2013). Education's effects on individual life chances and on development: An overview. *British Journal of Educational Studies, 61*(1), 79–107.

McNeel, S. (1994). College teaching and student moral development. In J. Rest & D. Narvaez (Eds.), *Moral development in the professions: Psychology and applied ethics* (pp. 26–47). Hillsdale, NJ: Erlbaum.

Means, B., Toyama, Y., Murphy, R., & Baki, M. (2013). The effectiveness of online and blended learning: A meta-analysis of the empirical literature. *Teachers College Record, 115*(3), 1–47.

Melguizo, T. (2008). Quality matters: Assessing the impact of attending more selective institutions on college completion rates of minorities. *Research in Higher Education, 49*(3), 214–236.

Melguizo, T. (2009). Are community colleges an alternative path for Hispanic students to attain a bachelor's degree? *Teachers College Record, 111*(1), 90–123.

Melguizo, T. (2010). Are students of color more likely to graduate from college if they attend more selective institutions? Evidence from a cohort of recipients and nonrecipients of the Gates Millennium Scholars Program. *Educational Evaluation and Policy Analysis, 32*(2), 230–248.

Melguizo, T., & Dowd, A. C. (2009). Baccalaureate success of transfers and rising four-year college juniors. *Teachers College Record, 111*, 55–89.

Melguizo, T., Kienzl, G., & Alfonso, M. (2011). Comparing the educational attainment of community college transfer students and four-year rising juniors using propensity score matching methods. *Journal of Higher Education, 82*(3), 265–291.

Melguizo, T., & Wolniak, G. C. (2012). The earnings benefits of majoring in STEM fields among high achieving minority students. *Research in Higher Education, 53*, 383–405.

Meling, V. B., Mundy, M. A., Kupczynski, L., & Green, M. E. (2013). Supplemental instruction and academic success and retention in science courses at a Hispanic-serving institution. *World Journal of Education, 3*(3), 11–23.

Menon, M. E. (2003). An evaluation of four decades of rate of return analysis in higher education policy making: Weaknesses and future prospects. *Higher Education Policy, 16*(3), 369–384.

Mentkowski, M., & Associates. (2000). *Learning that lasts: Interpreting learning, development, and performance in college and beyond.* San Francisco, CA: Jossey-Bass.

Merkel, R. E. (2013). The influence of sorority and fraternity involvement on future giving. In N. D. Drezer (Ed.), *Expanding the donor base in higher education* (pp. 152–170). New York, NY: Routledge.

Meseke, C. A., Bovée, M. L., & Gran, D. F. (2009). Impact of collaborative testing on student performance and satisfaction in a chiropractic science course. *Journal of Manipulative and Physiological Therapeutics, 32*(4), 309–314.

Milem, J. F., & Berger, J. B. (1997). A modified model of college student persistence: Exploring the relationship between Astin's theory of involvement and Tinto's theory of student departure. *Journal of College Student Development, 38*(4), 387–400.

Milem, H., Chang, M., & Antonio, A. (2005). *Making diversity work on campus: A research-based perspective.* Washington, DC: Association of American Colleges and Universities.

Miller, J. W., Janz, J. C., & Chen, C. (2007). The retention impact of a first-year seminar on students with varying pre-college academic performance. *Journal of the First-Year Experience & Students in Transition, 19*(1), 47–62.

Milligan, K., Moretti, E., & Oreopoulos, P. (2004). Does education improve citizenship? Evidence from the United States and the United Kingdom. *Journal of Public Economics, 88*(9–10), 1697–1695.

Mincer, J. (1974). *Schooling, experience, and earnings.* New York, NY: NBER Press.

Minnich, E. K. (2003). Teaching thinking: Moral and political considerations. *Change, 35*(5),18–24.

Minthorn, R. S., Wanger, S. P., & Shotton, H. J. (2013). Developing Native student leadership skills: The success of the Oklahoma Native American Students in Higher Education (ONASHE) conference. *American Indian Culture and Research Journal, 37*(3), 59–74.

Mirowsky, J., & Ross, C. E. (2003) *Social causes of psychological distress* (2nd ed.). Hawthorne, NY: Aldine De Gruyter.

Mirowsky, J., & Ross, C. E. (2007). Life course trajectories of perceived control and their relationship to education. *American Journal of Sociology, 112*(5), 1339–1382.

Mirvis, P. H., & Lawler, E. E. (1984). Accounting for the quality of work life. *Journal of Occupational Behavior, 5*(3), 197–212.

Mitchell, M., & Leachman, M. (2015). Years of cuts threaten to put college out of reach for more students. *Center on Budget and Policy Priorities.* Retrieved from http://www.cbpp.org/research/state-budget-and-tax/years-of-cuts-threaten-to-put-college-out-of-reach-for-more-students

Molitor, C. J., & Leigh, D. E. (2005). In-school work experience and the returns to two-year and four-year colleges. *Economics of Education Review, 24*(4), 459–468.

Montez, J. K., Hayward, M. D., Brown, D. C., & Hummer, R. A. (2009). Why is the educational gradient of mortality steeper for men? *Journals of Gerontology Series B: Psychological Sciences and Social Sciences, 64*(5), 625–634.

Montez, J. K., Hummer, R. A., Hayward, M. D., Woo, H., & Rogers, R. G. (2011). Trends in the educational gradient of US adult mortality from 1986 through 2006 by race, gender, and age group. *Research on Aging, 33*(2), 145–171.

Montgomery, D. C. (2012). *Design and analysis of experiments* (8th ed.). San Francisco, CA: Jossey-Bass.

Moore, R. L. (2011). The effect of group composition on individual student performance in an introductory economics course. *Journal of Economic Education, 42*(2), 120–135.

Moore, R., & LeDee, O. (2006). Supplemental Instruction and the performance of developmental education students in an introductory biology course. *Journal of College Reading and Learning, 36*(2), 9–20.

Moradi, B., Subich, L. M., & Phillips, J. C. (2002). Revisiting feminist identity development theory, research, and practice. *Counseling Psychologist, 30*(1), 6–43.

Moreno, R., Reisslein, M., & Ozogul, G. (2009). Optimizing worked-example instruction in electrical engineering: The role of fading and feedback during problem-solving practice. *Journal of Engineering Education, 98*(1), 83–93.

Morgan, S. L., & Winship, C. (2007). *Counterfactuals and causal inference: Methods and principles for social research.* New York, NY: Cambridge University Press.

Morris, J., Beck, R., & Mattis, C. (2007). Examining worldview fit and first-year retention at a private, religiously affiliated institution. *Journal of the First-Year Experience & Students in Transition, 19*(1), 75–88.

Morris, J. M., Beck, R., & Smith, A. B. (2004). Examining student-institution fit at a Christian university: The role of spiritual integration. *Journal of Education & Christian Belief, 8*(2), 87–100.

Morris, J., Reese, J., Beck, R., & Mattis, C. (2009). Facebook usage as a predictor of retention at a private four-year institution. *Journal of College Student Retention, 11*(3), 311–322.

Morris, J. M., Smith, A. B., & Cejda, B. D. (2003). Spiritual integration as a predictor of persistence at a Christian institution of higher education. *Christian Higher Education, 2*(4), 341–351.

Morris, L. V., Finnegan, C., & Wu, S. (2005). Tracking student behavior, persistence, and achievement in online courses. *Internet and Higher Education, 8*(3), 221–231.

Morrison, M. C. (2012). Graduation odds and probabilities among baccalaureate colleges and universities. *Journal of College Student Retention, 14*(2), 157–179.

Mosher, R., & Sprinthall, N. A. (1971). Deliberate psychological education. *Counseling Psychologist, 2*(4), 3–82.

Moss, B. G., & Yeaton, W. H. (2006). Shaping policies related to developmental education: An evaluation using the regression-discontinuity design. *Educational Evaluation and Policy Analysis, 28*(3), 215–229.

Mujahid, M. S., Roux, A. V., Borrell, L. N., & Nieto, F. J. (2005). Cross-sectional and longitudinal associations of BMI with socioeconomic characteristics. *Obesity Research, 13*(8), 1412–1421.

Munley, V. G., Garvey, E., & McConnell, M. J. (2010). The effectiveness of peer tutoring on student achievement at the university level. *American Economic Review, 100*(2), 277–282.

Murnane, R. J., & Willett, J. B. (2011). *Methods matter: Improving causal inference in educational and social science research*. New York, NY: Oxford University Press.

Museus, S. D. (2014). The Culturally Engaging Campus Environments (CECE) model: A new theory of college success among racially diverse student populations. In M. B. Paulsen (Ed.), *Higher education: Handbook of theory and research* (pp. 189–227). New York, NY: Springer.

Museus, S. D., Nichols, A. H., & Lambert, A. D. (2008). Racial differences in the effects of campus racial climate on degree completion: A structural equation model. *Review of Higher Education, 32*(1), 107–134.

Museus, S. D., & Quaye, S. J. (2009). Toward an intercultural perspective of racial and ethnic minority college student persistence. *Review of Higher Education, 33*, 67–94.

Myers, M. J., & Burgess, A. G. (2003). Inquiry-based laboratory course improves students' ability to design experiments and interpret data. *Advances in Physiology Education, 27*(1), 26–33.

Myerson, J., Rank, M. R., Raines, F. Q., & Schnitzler, M. A. (1998). Race and general cognitive ability: The myth of diminishing returns to education. *Psychological Science, 9*(2), 139–142.

Nabors, E. L., & Jasinski, J. L. (2009). Intimate partner violence perpetration among college students: The role of gender role and gendered violence attitudes. *Feminist Criminology, 4*(1), 57–82.

Nagda, B. R. A., Gurin, P., Sorensen, N., & Zúñiga, X. (2009). Evaluating intergroup dialogue: Engaging diversity for personal and social responsibility. *Diversity and Democracy, 12*(1), 4–6.

Naimi, T. S., Brewer, R. D., Mokdad, A., Denny, C., Serdula, M. K., & Marks, J. S. (2003). Binge drinking among US adults. *JAMA: The Journal of American Medical Association, 289*(1), 70–75.

Naimi, T. S., Nelson, D. E., & Brewer, R. D. (2010). The intensity of binge alcohol consumption among US adults. *American Journal of Preventive Medicine, 38*(2), 201–207.

Nakajima, M. A., Dembo, M. H., & Mossler, R. (2012). Student persistence in community colleges. *Community College Journal of Research and Practice, 36*(8), 591–613.

Narvaez, D. (2005). The neo-Kohlbergian tradition and beyond: Schemas, expertise and character. In G. Carlo & C. Pope-Edwards (Eds.), *Nebraska Symposium on Motivation, Vol. 51: Moral Motivation through the Lifespan* (pp. 119–163). Lincoln: University of Nebraska Press.

National Center for Education Statistics. (2010). *Digest of Education Statistics*. Washington, DC: U.S. Department of Education. Retrieved from http://nces.ed.gov/programs/digest/d10/tables/dt10_279.asp

National Science Foundation. (2015). *US NSF—Funding*. Retrieved from http://www.nsf.gov/funding/

National Survey of Student Engagement. (2007). *Experiences that matter: Enhancing student learning and success*. Bloomington, IL: Center for Postsecondary Research.

NCAA. (n.d.). *Staying on track to graduate*. Retrieved from http://www.ncaa.org/student-athletes/current/staying-track-graduate

Nelson, K. J., Quinn, C., Marrington, A., & Clarke, J. A. (2012). Good practice for enhancing the engagement and success of commencing students. *Higher Education, 63*(1), 83–96.

Nelson Laird, T. F. (2005). College students' experiences with diversity and their effects on academic self-confidence, social agency, and disposition toward critical thinking. *Research in Higher Education, 46*(4), 365–388.

Nelson Laird, T. F., Bridges, B. K., Morelon-Quainoo, C. L., Williams, J. M., & Salinas Holmes, M. (2007). African American and Hispanic student engagement at minority serving and predominantly White institutions. *Journal of College Student Development, 48*(1), 39–56.

Nelson Laird, T. F., & Cruce, T. M. (2009). Individual and environmental effects of part-time enrollment status on student-faculty interaction and self-reported gains. *Journal of Higher Education, 80*(3), 290–314.

Nelson Laird, T. F., Engberg, M. E., & Hurtado, S. (2005). Modeling accentuation effects: Enrolling in a diversity course and the importance of social action engagement. *Journal of Higher Education, 76*(4), 448–476.

Nelson Laird, T. F., Seifert, T. A., Pascarella, E. T., Mayhew, M. J., & Blaich, C. (2014). Deeply affecting first-year students' thinking: Deep approaches to learning and three dimensions of cognitive development. *Journal of Higher Education, 85*(3), 402–432.

Nelson Laird, T. F., Shoup, R., Kuh, G. D., & Schwarz, M. J. (2008). The effects of discipline on deep approaches to student learning and college outcomes. *Research in Higher Education, 49*(6), 469–494.

Nesbit, J. C., & Adescope, O. O. (2006). Learning with concept and knowledge maps: A meta-analysis. *Review of Educational Research, 76*(3), 413–448.

Nesheim, B. E., Guentzel, M. J., Kellogg, A. H., McDonald, W. M., Wells, C. A., & Whitt, E. J. (2007). Outcomes for students of student affairs-academic affairs partnership programs. *Journal of College Student Development, 48*(4), 435–454.

Neumann, G., Olitsky, N., & Robbins, S. B. (2009). Job congruence, academic achievement, and earnings. *Labour Economics, 16*(5), 503–509.

Neville, H. A., Heppner, P. P., Ji, P., & Thye, R. (2004). The relations among general and race-related stressors and psychoeducational adjustment in Black students attending predominantly White institutions. *Journal of Black Studies, 34*(4), 599–618.

New, J. (2013, April 30). Start-up companies help colleges use social networks to connect with alumni. *Chronicle of Higher Education.* Retrieved from http://chronicle.com/blogs/wiredcampus/start-up-companies-help-colleges-use-social-networks-to-connect-with-alumni/43621

Nie, N., & Hillygus, D. S. (2001). Education and democratic citizenship. In D. Ravitch & J. P. Viteritti (Eds.), *Making good citizens: Education and civil society* (pp. 30–57). New Haven, CT: Yale University.

Niu, S. X., & Tienda, M. (2013). High school economic composition and college persistence. *Research in Higher Education, 54*(1), 30–62.

Niven, E., Roy, D., Schaefer, B. A., Gasquoine, S., & Ward, F. A. (2013). Making research real: Embedding a longitudinal study in a taught research course for undergraduate nursing students. *Nurse Education Today, 33*(1), 64–68.

Noble, K., Flynn, N. T., Lee, J. D., & Hilton, D. (2007). Predicting successful college experiences: Evidence from a first year retention program. *Journal of College Student Retention: Research, Theory and Practice, 9*(1), 39–60.

Noblitt, L., Vance, D. E., & Smith, M. L. D. (2010). A comparison of case study and traditional teaching methods for improvement of oral communication and critical-thinking skills. *Journal of College Science Teaching, 39*(5), 26–32.

Noland, R. M., Bass, M. A., Keathley, R. S., & Miller, R. (2009). Is a little knowledge a good thing? College students gain knowledge, but knowledge increase does not equal attitude change regarding same-sex sexual orientation and gender reassignment surgery in sexuality courses. *American Journal of Sexuality Education, 4*(2), 139–157.

Nora, A. (2004). The role of habitus and cultural capital in choosing a college, transitioning from high school to higher education, and persisting in college among minority and non-minority students. *Journal of Hispanic Higher Education, 3*(2), 180–208.

Nora, A., & Cabrera, A. F. (1996). The role of perceptions of prejudice and discrimination on the adjustment of minority students to college. *Journal of Higher Education, 67*(2), 119–148.

Novak, H., & McKinney, L. (2011). The consequences of leaving money on the table: Examining persistence among students who do not file a FAFSA. *Journal of Student Financial Aid, 41*(3), 5–23.

Nucci, L., & Pascarella, E. (1987). The influence of college on moral development. In J. Smart (Ed.), *Higher education: Handbook of theory and research* (Vol. 3, pp. 271–326). New York, NY: Agathon.

Núñez, A. M. (2009). Modeling the effects of diversity experiences and multiple capitals on Latina/o college students' academic self-confidence. *Journal of Hispanic Higher Education, 8*(2), 179–196.

Oates, G. L. S. C. (2004). The color of the undergraduate experience and the Black self-concept: Evidence from longitudinal data. *Social Psychology Quarterly, 67*(1), 16–32.

Odom, S. F., Boyd, B. L., & Williams, J. (2012). Impact of personal growth projects on leadership identity development. *Journal of Leadership Education, 11*(1), 49–63.

Ogden, P., Thompson, D., Russell, A., & Simon, C. (2003). Supplemental instruction: Short- and long-term impact. *Journal of Developmental Education, 26*(3), 2–6.

Ogilvie, K., & Reza, E. M. (2009). Business student performance in traditional vs. honors course settings. *Business Education Innovation Journal, 1*(2), 31–37.

Oh, S., & Jonassen, D. H. (2007). Scaffolding online argumentation during problem solving. *Journal of Computer Assisted Learning, 23*(2), 95–110.

Oja, M. (2012). Supplemental instruction improves grades but not persistence. *College Student Journal, 46*(2), 344–349.

Olafson, L., Schraw, G., Nadelson, L., Nadelson, S., & Kehrwalkd, N. (2013). Exploring the judgment-action gap: College students and academic dishonesty. *Ethics and Behavior, 23*(2), 148–162.

Oliffe, J. L., Kelly, M. T., Johnson, J. L., Bottorff, J. L., Gray, R. E., Ogrodniczuk, J. S., & Galdas, P. M. (2010). Masculinities and college men's depression: Recursive relationships. *Health Sociology Review, 19*(4), 465–477.

O'Neill, N. (2012). *Promising practices for personal and social responsibility: Findings from a national research collaborative.* Washington, DC: Association of American Colleges & Universities.

Opp, R. (1991). *The impact of college on NTE performance.* (Unpublished doctoral dissertation). University of California, Los Angeles.

Oreopoulos, P., Page, M. E., & Stevens, A. H. (2006). The intergenerational effects of compulsory schooling. *Journal of Labor Economics, 24*(4), 729–760.

Oreopoulos, P., & Petronijevic, U. (2013). Making college worth it: A review of the returns to higher education. *Future of Children, 23*(1), 41–65.

Oreopoulos, P., & Salvanes, K. G. (2009). *How large are returns to schooling? Hint: Money isn't everything* (NBER Working Paper No. w15339). Cambridge, MA: National Bureau of Economic Research. Retrieved from http://www.nber.org/papers/w15339

Oreopoulos, P., & Salvanes, K. G. (2011). Priceless: The nonpecuniary benefits of schooling. *Journal of Economic Perspectives, 25*(1), 159–184.

Organisation for Economic Co-operation and Development. (2013). *Education at a glance 2013: OECD indicators.* Paris, France.

Ormrod, J. S. (2011). Practicing social movement theory in case study groups. *Teaching Sociology, 39*(2), 190–199.

Osborn, D. S., Howard, D. K., & Leierer, S. J. (2007). The effect of a career development course on the dysfunctional career thoughts of racially and ethnically diverse college freshmen. *Career Development Quarterly, 55*(4), 365–377.

Oseguera, L. (2005). Four and six-year baccalaureate degree completion by institutional characteristics and racial/ethnic groups. *Journal of College Student Retention, 7*(1–2), 19–59.

Oseguera, L., & Rhee, B. S. (2009). The influence of institutional retention climates on student persistence to degree completion: A multilevel approach. *Research in Higher Education, 50*(6), 546–569.

Otero, R., Rivas, O., & Rivera, R. (2007). Predicting persistence of Hispanic students in their first year of college. *Journal of Hispanic Higher Education, 6*(2), 163–173.

O'Toole, D. M., Stratton, L. S., & Wetzel, J. N. (2003). A longitudinal analysis of the frequency of part-time enrollment and the persistence of students who enroll part time. *Research in Higher Education, 44*(5), 519–537.

Owen, J. J. (2011). Domain specificity and generality of epistemic cognitions: Issues in assessment. *Journal of College Student Development, 52*(5), 622–630.

Ozogul, G., & Sullivan, H. (2009). Student performance and attitudes under formative evaluation by teacher, self and peer evaluators. *Educational Technology Research and Development, 57*(3), 393–410.

Pace, C. R. (1979). *Measuring quality of effort: A new dimension for understanding student learning and development in college.* Los Angeles, CA: UCLA Laboratory for Research on Higher Education.

Pace, C. R. (1982). *Achievement and the quality of student effort.* Washington, DC: U.S. Department of Education.

Padgett, R. D., Goodman, K. M., Johnson, M. P., Saichaie, K., Umbach, P. D., & Pascarella, E. T. (2010). The impact of college student socialization, social class, and race on need for cognition. In S. Herzog (Ed.), *Diversity and educational benefits* (New Directions for Institutional Research No. 145, pp. 99–111). Hoboken, NJ: Wiley.

Padgett, R. D., Johnson, M. P., & Pascarella, E. T. (2012). First-generation undergraduate students and the impacts of the first year of college: Additional evidence. *Journal of College Student Development, 53*(2), 243–266.

Padgett, R. D., Keup, J. R., & Pascarella, E. T. (2013). The impact of first-year seminars on college students' life-long learning orientations. *Journal of Student Affairs Research and Practice, 50*(2), 133–151.

Paige, R. M., Fry, G. W., Stallman, E. M., Josic, J., & Jon, J. (2009). Study abroad for global engagement: The long-term impact of mobility experiences. *Intercultural Education, 20*(1), 29–44.

Palfrey, J., & Gasser, U. (2008). *Born digital: Understanding the first generation of digital natives.* New York, NY: Basic Books.

Pallas, A. M. (2000). The effects of schooling on individual lives. In M. T. Hallinan (Ed.), *Handbook of the sociology of education* (pp. 499–525). New York, NY: Springer.

Pan, Y. J., & Bai, H. (2010). Testing and estimating direct and indirect effects of an intervention program on college student retention: A structural model. *Enrollment Management Journal, 4*(1), 10–26.

Pan, Y. J. (2010). *Modeling the effects of academic and social integration on college student success: A systematic review* (Unpublished doctoral dissertation). University of Louisville, Kentucky.

Park, A., Sher, K. J., Wood, P. K., & Krull, J. L. (2009). Dual mechanisms underlying accentuation of risky drinking via fraternity/sorority affiliation: The role of personality, peer norms, and alcohol availability. *Journal of Abnormal Psychology, 118*(2), 241.

Park, J. J. (2009). Taking race into account: Charting student attitudes towards affirmative action. *Research in Higher Education, 50*(7), 670–690.

Park, J. J. (2012). When race and religion collide: The effect of religion on interracial friendship during college. *Journal of Diversity in Higher Education, 5*(1), 8–21.

Park, J. J., & Millora, M. L. (2010). Psychological well-being for White, Black, Latino/a, and Asian American students: Considering spirituality and religion. *Journal of Student Affairs Research and Practice, 47*(4), 445–461.

Park, J. J., & Millora, M. L. (2012). The relevance of reflection: An empirical examination of the role of reflection in ethic of caring, leadership, and psychological well-being. *Journal of College Student Development, 53*(2), 221–242.

Park, S. (2011). Returning to school for higher returns. *Economics of Education Review, 30*(6), 1215–1228.

Parke, R. D., Gauvain, M., & Schmuckler, M. A. (2010). *Child psychology: A contemporary viewpoint* (3rd Canadian ed.). Toronto: McGraw Hill-Ryerson.

Parker, E. T., & Pascarella, E. T. (2013). Effects of diversity experiences on socially responsible leadership over four years of college. *Journal of Diversity in Higher Education, 6*(4), 219–230.

Parks, S. (2000). *Big questions, worthy dreams: Mentoring young adults in their search for meaning, purpose, and faith.* San Francisco, CA: Jossey-Bass.

Pascarella, E. (1985). College environmental influence on learning and cognitive development: A critical review and synthesis. In J. Smart (Ed.), *Higher education: Handbook of theory and research* (Vol. 1, pp. 1–64). New York, NY: Agathon.

Pascarella, E., Palmer, E., Moye, M., & Pierson, C. (2001). Do diversity experiences influence the development of critical thinking? *Journal of College Student Development, 42*(3), 257–271.

Pascarella, E., Wolniak, G. C., Seifert, T. A., Cruce, T., & Blaich, C. (2005). *Liberal arts colleges and liberal arts education: New evidence on impacts.* San Francisco, CA: Jossey-Bass/ASHE.

Pascarella, E. T. (1997). College's influence on principled moral reasoning. *Educational Record, 78*(3–4), 47–55.

Pascarella, E. T., & Blaich, C. (2013). Lessons from the Wabash National Study of Liberal Arts Education. *Change: The Magazine of Higher Learning, 45*(2), 6–15.

Pascarella, E. T., Blaich, C., Martin, G. L., & Hanson, J. M. (2011). How robust are the findings of Academically Adrift? *Change: The Magazine of Higher Learning, 43*(3), 20–24.

Pascarella, E. T., Cruce, T., Umbach, P. D., Wolniak, G. C., Kuh, G. D., Carini, R. M., . . . Zhao, C. (2006). Institutional selectivity and good practices in undergraduate education: How strong is the link? *The Journal of Higher Education, 77*(2), 251–285.

Pascarella, E. T., Edison, M. I., Nora, A., Hagedorn, L., & Terenzini, P. T. (1995/1996). Cognitive effects of community colleges and four-year colleges. *Community College Journal, 66*(3), 35–39.

Pascarella, E. T., Pierson, C. T., Wolniak, G. C., & Terenzini, P. T. (2004). First-generation college students: Additional evidence on college experiences and outcomes. *Journal of Higher Education, 75*(3), 249–284.

Pascarella, E. T., Salisbury, M. H., & Blaich, C. (2011). Exposure to effective instruction and college persistence: A multi-institutional replication and extension. *Journal of College Student Development, 52*(1), 4–19.

Pascarella, E. T., Salisbury, M. H., & Blaich, C. (2013). Design and analysis in college impact research: Which counts more? *Journal of College Student Development, 54*(3), 329–335.

Pascarella, E. T., Salisbury, M. H., Martin, G. L., & Blaich, C. (2012). Some complexities in the effects of diversity experiences on orientation toward social/political activism and political views in the first year of college. *Journal of Higher Education, 83*(4), 467–496.

Pascarella, E. T., & Terenzini, P. T. (1991). *How college affects students.* San Francisco, CA: Jossey-Bass.

Pascarella, E. T., Seifert, T. A., & Blaich, C. (2010). How effective are the NSSE benchmarks in predicting important educational outcomes? *Change: The Magazine of Higher Learning, 42*(1), 16–22.

Pascarella, E. T., & Terenzini, P. T. (2005). *How college affects students: A third decade of research* (Vol. 2). San Francisco, CA: Jossey-Bass.

Pascarella, E. T., Wang, J. S., Trolian, T. L., & Blaich, C. (2013). How the instructional and learning environments of liberal arts colleges enhance cognitive development. *Higher Education, 66*(5), 569–583.

Pascarella, E. T., Wolniak, G. C., Pierson, C. T., & Terenzini, P. T. (2003). Experiences and outcomes of first-generation students in community colleges. *Journal of College Student Development, 44*(3), 420–429.

Passow, H. J., Mayhew, M. J. Finelli, C. J, Harding, T. S., & Carpenter, D. D. (2006). Factors influencing engineering students' decision to cheat by time of assessment. *Research in Higher Education, 47*(6), 643–684.

Pasupathi, M., Wainryb, C., & Twali, M. (2012). Relations between narrative construction of ethnicity-based discrimination and ethnic identity exploration and pride. *Identity: An International Journal of Theory and Research, 12*(1), 53–73.

Patel, R., Richburg-Hayes, L., de la Campa, E., & Rudd, T. (2013). *Performance-based scholarships: What have we learned?* New York, NY: MDRC.

Patten, T. A., & Rice, N. D. (2009). Religious minorities and persistence at a systemic religiously-affiliated university. *Christian Higher Education, 8*(1), 42–53.

Patton, L. D. (2011). Perspectives on identity, disclosure, and the campus environment among African American gay and bisexual men at one historically Black college. *Journal of College Student Development, 52*(1), 77–100.

Patton, L. D., & Simmons, S. L. (2008). Exploring complexities of multiple identities of lesbians in a Black college environment. *Negro Educational Review, 59*(3–4), 197–215.

Paulsen, M. B., & Smart, J. C. (Eds.). (2001). *The finance of higher education: Theory, research, policy, and practice.* New York, NY: Agathon.

Paulsen, M. B., & St. John, E. P. (2002). Social class and college costs: Examining the financial nexus between college choice and persistence. *Journal of Higher Education, 73*(2), 189–236.

Paulsen, M. B., & Toutkoushian, R. K. (2006). Overview of economic concepts, models, and methods for institutional research. In R. K. Toutkoushian & M. B. Paulsen (Eds.), *Applying economics to institutional research* (New Directions for Institutional Research No. 132, pp. 5–24). Hoboken, NJ: Wiley.

Peck, S. D., Stehle Werner, J. L., & Ralrigh, D. M. (2013). Improved class preparation and learning through immediate feedback in group testing for undergraduate nursing students. *Nursing Education Perspectives, 34*(6), 400–404.

Pedersen, D. E. (2010). Active and collaborative learning in an undergraduate sociological theory course. *Teaching Sociology, 38*(3), 197–206.

Pederson, E. L., & Vogel, D. L. (2007). Male gender role conflict and willingness to seek counseling: Testing a mediation model on college-aged men. *Journal of Counseling Psychology, 54*(4), 373–384.

Pedhazur, E. J. (1997). *Multiple regression in behavioral research: Explanation and prediction* (3rd ed.). New York, NY: Wadsworth.

Peek, L. (2005). Becoming Muslim: The development of a religious identity. *Sociology of Religion, 66*(3), 215–242.

Peele, T. (2010). Working together: Student-faculty interaction and the Boise State STRETCH program. *Journal of Basic Writing, 29*(2), 50–73.

Pennebaker, J. W., Gosling, S. D., & Ferrell, J. D. (2013). Daily online testing in large classes: Boosting college performance while reducing achievement gaps. *PLOS One, 8*(11), 1–6.

Peralta, R. L. (2007). College alcohol use and the embodiment of hegemonic masculinity among European American men. *Sex Roles, 56*(11–12), 741–756.

Perna, L. W. (2003). The private benefits of higher education: An examination of the earnings premium. *Research in Higher Education, 44*(4), 451–472.

Perna, L. W. (2005). The benefits of higher education: Sex, racial/ethnic, and socioeconomic group differences. *Review of Higher Education, 29*(1), 23–52.

Perna, L. W., Gasman, M., Gary, S., Lundy-Wagner, V., & Drezner, N. D. (2010). Identifying strategies for increasing degree attainment in STEM: Lessons from minority-serving institutions. In S. R. Harper & C. B. Newman (Eds.), *Students of color in STEM: An evolving research agenda* (New Directions for Institutional Research, No. 148, pp. 41–51). San Francisco, CA: Jossey-Bass.

Perry, R. P., Stupnisky R. H., Hall, N. C., Chipperfield, J. G., & Weiner, B. (2010). Bad starts and better finishes: Attributional retraining and initial performance in competitive achievement settings. *Journal of Social and Clinical Psychology, 29*(6), 668–700.

Perry, W. G., Jr. (1968). *Forms of intellectual and ethical development in the college years: A scheme.* New York, NY: Holt, Rinehart, & Winston.

Perry, W. G., Jr. (1970). *Forms of intellectual and ethical development in the college years: A scheme.* New York, NY: Holt, Rinehart, & Winston.

Perry, W. G., Jr. (1981). Cognitive and ethical growth: The making of meaning. In A. W. Chickering (Ed.), *The modern American college* (pp. 76–116). San Francisco, CA: Jossey-Bass.

Persell, C. H., & Wenglinsky, H. (2004). For-profit post-secondary education and civic engagement. *Higher Education, 47*(3), 337–359.

Peter, K., Cataldi, E. F., & Carroll, C. D. (2005). *The road less traveled? Students who enroll in multiple institutions* (NCES 2005-157). Washington, DC: National Center for Education Statistics, U.S. Department of Education.

Peterfreund, A. R., Rath, K. A., Xenos, S. P., & Bayliss, F. (2008). The impact of supplemental instruction on students in STEM courses: Results from San Francisco State University. *Journal of College Student Retention: Research, Theory and Practice, 9*(4), 487–503.

Petersen, T. (1985). A comment on presenting results from logit and probit models. *American Sociological Review, 50*(1), 130–131.

Peterson, R. A., & Brown, S. P. (2005). On the use of beta coefficients in meta-analysis. *Journal of Applied Psychology, 90*, 175–181.

Peterson, R. D., & Hamrick, F. A. (2009). White, male, and "minority": Racial consciousness among White male undergraduates attending a historically Black university. *Journal of Higher Education, 80*(1), 34–58.

Peterson, M. W., & Spencer, M. G. (1990). Understanding academic culture and climate. *New Directions for Institutional Research, 1990*(68), 3–18.

Peterson, P. L., Marx, R. W., & Clark, C. M. (1978). Teacher planning, teacher behavior, and student achievement. *American Educational Research Journal, 15*(3), 417–432.

Pettigrew, T. F. (1998). Intergroup contact theory. *Annual Review of Psychology*, *49*(1), 65–85.

Pettigrew, T. F. (2009). Secondary transfer effect of contact: Do intergroup contact effects spread to noncontacted outgroups? *Social Psychology*, *40*(2), 55–65.

Phinney, J. (1989). Stages of ethnic identity development in minority group adolescents. *Journal of Early Adolescence*, *9*(1–2), 34–49.

Phinney, J. (1992). The Multigroup Ethnic Identity Measure: A new scale for use with diverse groups. *Journal of Adolescent Research*, *7*(2), 156–176.

Phinney, J. (1993). A three-stage model of ethnic identity development. In M. Bernal & G. Knight (Eds.), *Ethnic identity: Formation and transmission among Hispanics and other minorities* (pp. 61–79). Albany: State University of New York Press.

Phinney, J. S., & Ong, A. D. (2007). Conceptualization and measurement of ethnic identity: Current status and future directions. *Journal of Counseling Psychology*, *54*(3), 271–281.

Piaget, J. (1954). *The construction of reality in the child*. New York, NY: Basic Books.

Pierson, C. T., Wolniak, G. C., Pascarella, E. T., & Flowers, L. A. (2003). Impacts of two-year and four-year college attendance on learning orientations. *Review of Higher Education*, *26*(3), 299–321.

Pike, G. R. (2000). The influence of fraternity or sorority membership on students' college experiences and cognitive development. *Research in Higher Education*, *41*(1), 117–139.

Pike, G. R. (2003). Membership in a fraternity or sorority, student engagement, and educational outcomes at AAU public research universities. *Journal of College Student Development*, *44*(3), 369–382.

Pike, G. R. (2006a). Students' personality types, intended majors, and college expectations: Further evidence concerning psychological and sociological interpretations of Holland's theory. *Research in Higher Education*, *47*(7), 801–822.

Pike, G. R. (2006b). Vocational preferences and college expectations: An extension of Holland's principle of self-selection. *Research in Higher Education*, *47*(5), 591–612.

Pike, G. R., & Killian, T. (2001). Reported gains in student learning: Do academic disciplines make a difference? *Research in Higher Education*, *42*(4), 429–454.

Pike, G. R., & Kuh, G. D. (2005). First- and second-generation college students: A comparison of their engagement and intellectual development. *Journal of Higher Education*, *76*(3), 276–301.

Pike, G. R., & Kuh, G. D. (2006). Relationships among structural diversity, informal peer interactions and perceptions of the campus environment. *Review of Higher Education*, *29*(4), 425–450.

Pike, G. R., Kuh, G. D., & Gonyea, R. M. (2003). The relationship between institutional mission and students' involvement and educational outcomes. *Research in Higher Education*, *44*(2), 241–261.

Pike, G. R., Kuh, G. D., & Gonyea, R. M. (2007). Evaluating the rationale for affirmative action in college admissions: Direct and indirect relationships between campus diversity and gains in understanding diverse groups. *Journal of College Student Development*, *48*(2), 166–182.

Pike, G. R., Kuh, G. D., & McCormick, A. C. (2011). An investigation of the contingent relationships between learning community participation and student engagement. *Research in Higher Education, 52*(3), 300–322.

Pike, G. R., Kuh, G. D., McCormick, A. C., Ethington, C. A., & Smart, J. C. (2011). If and when money matters: The relationships among educational expenditures, student engagement and students' learning outcomes. *Research in Higher Education, 52*(1), 81–106.

Pike, G. R., Smart, J. C., & Ethington, C. A. (2012). The mediating effects of student engagement on the relationships between academic disciplines and learning outcomes: An extension of Holland's theory. *Research in Higher Education, 53*(5), 550–575.

Pingry O'Neill, L. N., Markward, M. J., & French, J. P. (2012). Predictors of graduation among college students with disabilities. *Journal of Postsecondary Education and Disability, 25*(1), 21–36.

Piper, A. (2014). Heaven knows I'm miserable now: Overeducation and reduced life satisfaction. *Education Economics, 23*(6), 677–692. doi:org/10.1080/09645292. 2013.870981

Pittman, L. D., & Richmond, A. (2008). University belonging, friendship quality, and psychological adjustment during the transition to college. *Journal of Experimental Education, 76*(4), 343–361.

Pizzolato, J. E. (2003). Developing self-authorship: Exploring the experiences of high-risk college students. *Journal of College Student Development, 44*(6), 797–812.

Pizzolato, J. E. (2004). Coping with conflict: Self-authorship, coping, and adaptation to college in first-year, high-risk students. *Journal of College Student Development, 45*(4), 425–442.

Pizzolato, J. E. (2005). Creating crossroads for self-authorship: Investigating the provocative moment. *Journal of College Student Development, 46*(6), 624–641.

Pizzolato, J. E., Nguyen, T. K., Johnston, M. P., & Wang, S. (2012). Understanding context: Cultural, relational, and psychological interactions in self-authorship development. *Journal of College Student Development, 53*(5), 656–679.

Pizzolato, J. E., & Ozaki, C. C. (2007). Moving toward self-authorship: Investigating outcomes of learning partnerships. *Journal of College Student Development, 48*(2), 196–214.

Plug, E. (2004). Estimating the effect of mother's schooling on children's schooling using a sample of adoptees. *American Economic Review, 94*(1), 358–368.

Pollock, L., & Eyre, S. L. (2012). Growth into manhood: Identity development among female-to-male transgender youth. *Culture, Health and Sexuality, 14*(2), 209–222.

Popiolek, G., Fine, R., & Eilman, V. (2013). Learning communities, academic performance, attrition, and retention: A four-year study. *Community College Journal of Research and Practice, 37*(11), 828–838.

Porchea, S. F., Allen, J., Robbins, S. B., & Phelps, R. P. (2010). Predictors of long-term enrollment and degree outcomes for community college students: Integrating academic, psychosocial, socio-demographic, and situational factors. *Journal of Higher Education, 81*(6), 680–708.

Porter, S. R. (2013). Self-reported learning gains: A theory and test of college student survey response. *Research in Higher Education, 54*(2), 201–226.

Porter, T., Hartman, K., & Johnson, J. S. (2011). Books and balls: Antecedents and outcomes of college identification. *Research in Higher Education, 13*, 1–14.

Posner, M. A. (2011). The impact of a proficiency based assessment and reassessment of learning outcomes system on student achievement and attitudes. *Statistics Education Research Journal, 10*(1), 3–14.

Post, G. V., & Whisenand, T. G. (2005). An expert system helps students learn database design. *Decision Sciences Journal of Innovative Education, 3*(2), 273–293.

Poston, W. S. C. (1990). The biracial identity development model: A needed addition. *Journal of Counseling and Development, 69*(2), 152–155.

Powdthavee, N. (2010). Does education reduce the risk of hypertension? Estimating the biomarker effect of compulsory schooling in England. *Journal of Human Capital, 4*(2), 173–202.

Pozo, S., & Stull, C. A. (2006). Requiring a math skills unit: Results of a randomized experiment. *American Economic Review, 96*(2), 437–441.

Preacher, K. J., & Hayes, A. F. (2004). SPSS and SAS procedures for estimating indirect effects in simple mediation models. *Behavior Research Methods, Instruments, and Computers, 36*(4), 717–731.

Preacher, K. J., & Hayes, A. F. (2008). Asymptotic and resampling strategies for assessing and comparing indirect effects in multiple mediator models. *Behavior Research Methods, 40*(3), 879–891.

Prelow, H. M., Mosher, C. E., & Bowman, M. A. (2006). Perceived racial discrimination, social support, and psychological adjustment among African American college students. *Journal of Black Psychology, 32*(4), 442–454.

Prentice, M. (2007). Social justice through service learning: Community colleges as ground zero. *Equity and Excellence in Education, 40*(3), 266–273.

Preszler, R. W. (2009). Replacing lecture with peer-led workshops improves student learning. *CBE—Life Sciences Education, 8*(3), 182–192.

Price, G. N., Spriggs, W., & Swinton, O. H. (2011). The relative returns to graduating from a historically Black college/university: Propensity score matching estimates from the national survey of Black Americans. *Review of Black Political Economy, 38*(2), 103–130.

Price, J., Price, J., & Simon, K. (2011). Educational gaps in medical care and health behavior: Evidence from US natality data. *Economics of Education Review, 30*(5), 838–849.

Prince, M. (2004). Does active learning work? A review of the research. *Journal of Engineering Education, 93*(3), 223–232.

Prince, M., & Felder, R. (2006). Inductive teaching and learning methods: Definitions, comparisons and research bases. *Journal of Engineering Education, 95*(2), 123–138.

Prince, M., & Felder, R. (2007). The many faces of inductive teaching and learning. *Journal of College Science Teaching, 36*(5), 14.

Programme for the International Assessment of Adult Competencies in Canada. (n.d.). *Key findings*. Retrieved from http://www.piaac.ca/477/Pan-Canadian-Report/Key-Findings/index.html

Prus, S. G. (2011). Comparing social determinants of self-rated health across the United States and Canada. *Social Science and Medicine, 73*(1), 50–59.

Psacharopoulos, G., & Patrinos, H. A. (2004). Returns to investment in education: A further update. *Education Economics, 12*(2), 111–134.

Quinlan, K. P., Brewer, R. D., Siegel, P., Sleet, D. A., Mokdad, A. H., Shults, R. A., & Flowers, N. (2005). Alcohol-impaired driving among US adults, 1993–2002. *American Journal of Preventive Medicine, 28*(4), 346–350.

Qureshi, A., Cozine, C., & Rizvi, F. (2013). Combination of didactic lectures and review sessions in endocrinology leads to improvement in student performance as measured by assessments. *Advances in Physiology Education, 37*(1), 89–92.

Radford, A. W., Berkner, L., Wheeless, S. C., & Shepherd, B. (2010). *Persistence and attainment of 2003-04 Beginning Postsecondary Students: After 6 years* (NCES 2011-151). Washington, DC: U.S. Department of Education.

Railsback, G. (2006). Faith commitment of born-again students at secular and evangelical colleges. *Journal of Research on Christian Education, 15*(1), 39–60.

Raley, R. K., Kim, Y., & Daniels, K. (2012). Young adults' fertility expectations and events: Associations with college enrollment and persistence. *Journal of Marriage and Family, 74*(4), 866–879.

Raskin, P. M. (1998). Career maturity: The construct's validity, vitality, and viability. *Career Development Quarterly, 47*(1), 32–35.

Rath, K., Bayliss, P. A., Runquist, E. & Simonis, U. (2012). Impact of supplemental instruction in entry-level chemistry courses at a midsized public university. *Journal of Chemical Education, 89*(4), 449–455.

Rath, K. A., Peterfreund, A. R., Xenos, S. P., Bayliss, F., & Carnal, N. (2007). Supplemental instruction in introductory biology I: Enhancing the performance and retention of underrepresented minority students. *CBE-Life Sciences Education, 6*(3), 203–216.

Raudenbush, S. W., & Bryk, A. S. (2002). *Hierarchical linear models: Applications and data analysis methods* (2nd ed.). Thousand Oaks, CA: Sage.

Rawlings, P., White, P., & Stephens, R. (2005). Practice-based learning in information systems: The advantages for students. *Journal of Information Systems Education, 16*(4), 455.

Raykov, T., & Marcoulides, G. A. (2006). *A first course in structural equation modeling* (2nd ed.). New York, NY: Psychology Press.

Reason, R. D., Terenzini, P. T., & Domingo, R. J. (2006). First things first: Developing academic competence in the first year of college. *Research in Higher Education, 47*(2), 149–175.

Reason, R. D., Terenzini, P. T., & Domingo, R. J. (2007). Developing social and personal competence in the first year of college. *Review of Higher Education, 30*(3), 271–299.

Reddy, P., & Moores, E. (2006). Measuring the benefits of a psychology placement year. *Assessment and Evaluation in Higher Education, 31*(5), 551–567.

Reddy, P., & Moores, E. (2012). Placement year academic benefit revisited: Effects of demographics, prior achievement and degree programme. *Teaching in Higher Education, 17*(2), 153–165.

Reed, J. H., & Kromrey, J. D. (2001). Teaching critical thinking in a community college history course: Empirical evidence from infusing Paul's model. *College Student Journal, 35*(2), 201–215.

Reese, R. J., & Miller, C. D. (2006). Effects of a university career development course on career decision-making self-efficacy. *Journal of Career Assessment, 14*(2), 252–266.

Reid, J. R., & Anderson, P. R. (2012). Critical thinking in the business classroom. *Journal of Education for Business, 87*(1), 52–59.

Reimer, S. (2010). Higher education and theological liberalism: Revisiting the old issue. *Sociology of Religion, 71*(4), 393–408.

Reise, S. P., & Duan, N. (2003). *Multilevel modeling: Methodological advances, issues, and applications.* Mahwah, NJ: Erlbaum.

Renaud, R. D., & Murray, H. G. (2007). The validity of higher-order questions as a process indicator of educational quality. *Research in Higher Education, 48*(3), 319–351.

Rendón, L. I., Jalomo, R. E., & Nora, A. (2000). Theoretical considerations in the study of minority student retention in higher education. In J. M. Braxton (Ed.), *Reworking the student departure puzzle* (pp. 127–156). Nashville, TN: Vanderbilt University Press.

Renn, K. (2014). *Women's colleges and universities in a global context.* Baltimore, MD: Johns Hopkins University Press.

Renn, K. A. (2000). Patterns of situational identity among biracial and multiracial college students. *Review of Higher Education, 23*(4), 399–420.

Renn, K. A. (2003). Understanding the identities of mixed-race college students through a developmental ecology lens. *Journal of College Student Development, 44*(3), 383–403.

Renn, K. A. (2004). *Mixed race students in college: The ecology of race, identity, and community.* Albany, NY: State University of New York Press.

Renn, K. A. (2007). LGBT student leaders and queer activists: Identities of lesbian, gay, bisexual, transgender, and queer identified college student leaders and activists. *Journal of College Student Development, 48*(3), 311–330.

Renn, K. A. (2008). Research on biracial and multiracial identity development: Overview and synthesis. In K. A. Renn & P. Shang (Eds.), *Biracial and multiracial students* (New Directions for Student Services, no. 123, pp. 13–21). San Francisco, CA: Jossey-Bass.

Renn, K. A. (2012). Roles of women's higher education institutions in international contexts. *Higher Education, 64*(2), 177–191.

Renn, K. A., & Bilodeau, B. (2005). Queer student leaders: An exploratory case study of identity development and LGBT student involvement at a midwestern research university. *Journal of Gay and Lesbian Issues in Education, 2*(4), 49–71.

Renn, K. A., & Ozaki, C. C. (2010). Psychosocial and leadership identities among leaders of identity-based campus organizations. *Journal of Diversity in Higher Education, 3*(1), 14–26.

Rennick, L. A., Toms Smedley, C., Fisher, D., Wallace, E., & Kim, Y. K. (2013). The effects of spiritual/religious engagement on college students' affective outcomes: Differences by gender and race. *Journal of Research on Christian Education, 22*(3), 301–322.

Rest, J. R. (1979). *Development in judging moral issues.* Minneapolis: University of Minnesota.

Rest, J. R. (1984). The major components of morality. In W. Kurtines & J. Gewirtz (Eds.), *Morality, moral development and moral behavior* (pp. 24–38). New York, NY: Wiley.

Rest, J. R. (1986). *Moral development: Advances in research and theory.* New York, NY: Praeger.

Rest, J. R., Narvaez, D., Bebeau, M., & Thoma, S. J. (1999). *Postconventional moral thinking: A neo-Kohlbergian approach.* Mahwah, NJ: Erlbaum.

Rest, J. R., Thoma, S. J., & Edwards, L. (1997). Designing and validating a measure of moral judgment: Stage preference and stage consistency approaches. *Journal of Educational Psychology, 89*(1), 5–28.

Rettinger, D. A., & Jordan, A. E. (2005). The relations among religion, motivation, and college cheating: A natural experiment. *Ethics and Behavior, 15*(2), 107–129.

Rettinger, D. A., Jordan, A. E., & Peschiera, F. (2004). Evaluating the motivation of other students to cheat: A vignette experiment. *Research in Higher Education, 45*(8), 873–890.

Rettinger, D. A., & Kramer, Y. (2009). Situational and personal causes of student cheating. *Research in Higher Education, 50*(3), 293–313.

Reyes, M. E. (2011). A sophomore-to-junior mentoring program that works: The SAM program at the University of Texas Pan American. *Journal of College Student Retention, 13*(3), 373–382.

Reynolds, C. L. (2012). Where to attend? Estimating the effects of beginning college at a two-year institution. *Economics of Education Review, 31*(4), 345–362.

Rhee, B. S., & Kim, A. (2011). Collegiate influences on the civic values of undergraduate students in the U.S. revisited. *Asia Pacific Education Review, 12*(3), 497–508.

Rhoads, R. (1997). Interpreting identity politics: The educational challenge of contemporary student activism. *Journal of College Student Development, 38*(5), 508–519.

Rhodes, T. (2010). *Assessing outcomes and improving achievement: Tips and tools for using rubrics.* Washington, DC: American Association of Colleges & Universities.

Richardson, M., Abraham, C., & Bond, R. (2012). Psychological correlates of university students' academic performance: A systematic review and meta-analysis. *Psychological Bulletin, 138*(2), 353–387.

Richmond, A. S., & Kindelberger Hagan, L. (2011). Promoting higher level thinking in psychology: Is active learning the answer? *Teaching of Psychology, 38*(2), 102–105.

Rickles, M. L., Zimmer Schneider, R., Slusser, S. R., Williams, D. M., & Zipp, J. F. (2013). Assessing change in student critical thinking for introduction to sociology classes. *Teaching Sociology, 41*(3), 271–281.

Riffell, S., & Sibley, D. (2005). Using web-based instruction to improve large undergraduate biology courses: An evaluation of a hybrid course format. *Computers and Education, 44*(3), 217–235.

Rinn, A. N. (2007). Effects of programmatic selectivity on the academic achievement, academic self-concepts, and aspirations of gifted college students. *Gifted Child Quarterly, 51*(3), 232–245.

Rivas-Drake, D. (2012). Ethnic identity and adjustment: The mediating role of sense of community. *Cultural Diversity and Ethnic Minority Psychology, 18*(2), 210–215.

Rivas-Drake, D., & Mooney, M. (2009). Neither colorblind nor oppositional: Perceived minority status and trajectories of academic adjustment among Latinos in elite higher education. *Developmental Psychology, 45*(3), 642–651.

Ro, H. K., Terenzini, P. T., & Yin, A. C. (2013). Between-college effects on students reconsidered. *Research in Higher Education, 54*(3), 253–282.

Robbins, S. B., Lauver, K., Le, H., Davis, D., Langley, R., & Carlstrom, A. (2004). Do psychosocial and study skill factors predict college outcomes? A meta-analysis. *Psychological Bulletin, 130*(2), 261–288.

Robbins, S. B., Allen, J., Casillas, A., Akamigbo, A., Saltonstall, M., Campbell, R., . . . Gore, P. (2009). Associations of resource and service utilization, risk level, and college outcomes. *Research in Higher Education, 50*(1), 101–118.

Robbins, S. B., Allen, J., Casillas, A., Peterson, C., & Le, H. (2006). Unraveling the differential effects of motivational and skills, social, and self-management measures from traditional predictors of college outcomes. *Journal of Educational Psychology, 98*(3), 598–616.

Robbins, S. B., Oh, I. S., Le, H., & Button, C. (2009). Intervention effects on college performance and retention as mediated by motivational, emotional, and social control factors: Integrated meta-analytic path analyses. *Journal of Applied Psychology, 94*(5), 1163–1184.

Roberts, F. W., & Dansereau, D. F. (2008). Studying strategy effects on memory, attitudes, and intentions. *Reading Psychology, 29*(6), 552–580.

Robichaud, M., & Soares, J. A. (2014). The effects of racial self-identity on college GPA and student satisfaction at very selective colleges and universities. *International Journal of Educational Studies, 1*(2), 91–108.

Robinson, D. H., Corliss, S. B., Bush, A. M., Bera, S. J., & Tomberlin, T. (2003). Optimal presentation of graphic organizers and text: A case for large bites? *Educational Technology Research and Development, 51*(4), 25–41.

Robst, J. (2007). Education and job match: The relatedness of college major and work. *Economics of Education Review, 26*(4), 397–407.

Rocconi, L. M. (2011). The impact of learning communities on first year students' growth and development in college. *Research in Higher Education, 52*(2), 178–193.

Rochford, R. (2003). Assessing learning styles to improve the quality of performance of community college students in developmental writing programs: A pilot study. *Community College Journal of Research and Practice, 27*(8), 665–677.

Rockquemore, K. A., & Brunsma, D. L. (2002). *Beyond Black: Biracial identity in America*. Thousand Oaks, CA: Sage.

Rodgers, T. (2008). Student engagement in the e-learning process and the impact on their grades. *International Journal of Cyber Society and Education, 1*(2), 143–156.

Rogers, R. G., Everett, B. G., Zajacova, A., & Hummer, R. A. (2010). Educational degrees and adult mortality risk in the United States. *Biodemography and Social Biology, 56*(1), 80–99.

Roksa, J. (2005). Double disadvantage or blessing in disguise? Understanding the relationship between college major and employment sector. *Sociology of Education, 78*(3), 207–232.

Roksa, J. (2006). Does the vocational focus of community colleges hinder students' educational attainment? *Review of Higher Education, 29*(4), 499–526.

Roksa, J. (2009). Building bridges for student success: Are higher education articulation policies effective? *Teachers College Record, 111*(10), 2444–2478.

Roksa, J. (2010). Bachelor's degree completion across state contexts: Does the distribution of enrollments make a difference? *Research in Higher Education, 51*(1), 1–20.

Roksa, J. (2011). Differentiation and work: Inequality in degree attainment in U.S. higher education. *Higher Education, 61*(3), 293–308.

Roksa, J., & Calcagno, J. C. (2010). Catching up in community colleges: Academic preparation and transfer to four-year institutions. *Teachers College Record, 112*(1), 260–288.

Roksa, J., & Keith, B. (2008). Credits, time, and attainment: Articulation policies and success after transfer. *Educational Evaluation and Policy Analysis, 30*(3), 236–254.

Roksa, J., & Levey, T. (2010). What can you do with that degree? College major and occupational status of college graduates over time. *Social Forces, 89*(2), 389–416.

Root, M. P. (1990). Resolving "other" status: Identity development of biracial individuals. *Women and Therapy, 9*(1–2), 185–205.

Ropers-Huilman, R., & Enke, K. A. E. (2010). Catholic women's college students' constructions of identity: Influence of faculty and staff on students' personal and professional self-understanding. *NASPA Journal about Women in Higher Education, 3*(1), 88–116.

Rosenbaum, P. R. (2002). *Observational studies* (2nd ed.). New York, NY: Springer.

Rosenbaum, P. R. (2009). *Design of observational studies.* New York, NY: Springer.

Ross, C. E., Masters, R. K., & Hummer, R. A. (2012). Education and the gender gaps in health and mortality. *Demography, 49*(4), 1157–1183.

Ross, C. E., & Mirowsky, J. (1999). Refining the association between education and health: The effects of quantity, credential and selectivity. *Demography, 36*(4), 445–460.

Ross, C. E., & Mirowsky, J. (2006). Sex differences in the effect of education on depression: Resource multiplication or resource substitution? *Social Science and Medicine, 63*(5), 1400–1413.

Ross, M. (1989). Relation of implicit theories to the construction of personal histories. *Psychological Review, 96*(2), 341–357.

Routon, P. W., & Walker, J. K. (2014). The impact of Greek organization membership on collegiate outcomes: Evidence from a national survey. *Journal of Behavioral and Experimental Economics, 49*, 63–70.

Rubin, D. B. (2008). For objective causal inference, design trumps analysis. *Annals of Applied Statistics, 2*(3), 808–840.

Rubinson, R., & Browne, I. (1994). Education and the economy. In N. J. Smelser & R. Swedberg (Eds.), *The handbook of economic sociology*. Princeton, NJ: Princeton University Press.

Rude, J. D., Wolniak, G. C., & Pascarella, E. T. (2012, April). *Racial attitude change during the college years*. Paper presented at the annual meeting of the American Educational Research Association, Vancouver, British Columbia, Canada.

Rumberger, R. W. (2010). Education and the reproduction of economic inequality in the United States: An empirical investigation. *Economics of Education Review, 29*(2), 246–254.

Ruso, N. (2012). The role of technology: Community based service-learning projects on ethical development. *Turkish Online Journal of Educational Technology, 11*(3), 375–385.

Rutschow, E. Z., Cullinan, D., & Welbeck, R. (2012). *Keeping students on course: An impact study of a student success course at Guilford Technical Community College*. New York, NY: MDRC.

Ryan, J. F. (2004). The relationship between institutional expenditures and degree attainment. *Research in Higher Education, 45*(2), 97–114.

Rybarczyk, B. J., Baines, A. T., McVey, M., Thompson, J. T., & Wilkins, H. (2007). A case-based approach increases student learning outcomes and comprehension of cellular respiration concepts. *Biochemistry and Molecular Biology Education, 35*(3), 181–186.

Ryff, C. D. (1989). Happiness is everything, or is it? Explorations on the meaning of psychological well-being. *Journal of Personality and Social Psychology, 57*(6), 1069–1081.

Rykiel, J. (1995). The community college experience: Is there an effect on critical thinking and moral reasoning? *Dissertation Abstracts International, 56*, 3824A.

Saavedra, A. R., & Saavedra, J. E. (2011). Do colleges cultivate critical thinking, problem solving, writing, and interpersonal skills? *Economics of Education Review, 30*(6), 1516–1526.

Sáenz, V. B. (2010). Breaking the segregation cycle: Examining students' precollege racial environments and college diversity experiences. *Review of Higher Education, 34*(1), 1–37.

Sáenz, V. B., Bukoski, B. E., Lu, C., & Rodriguez, S. (2013). Latino males in Texas community colleges: A phenomenological study of masculinity constructs and their effect on college experiences. *Journal of African American Males in Education, 4*(2), 82–102.

Salinitri, G. (2005). The effects of formal mentoring on the retention rates of first-year, low achieving students. *Canadian Journal of Education, 28*(4), 853–873.

Salisbury, M. H., An, B. P., & Pascarella, E. T. (2013). The effect of study abroad on intercultural competence among undergraduate college students. *Journal of Student Affairs Research and Practice, 50*(1), 1–20.

Salisbury, M. H., Pascarella, E. T., Padgett, R. D., & Blaich, C. (2012). The effects of work on leadership development among first-year college students. *Journal of College Student Development, 53*(2), 300–324.

Sanchez, D., & Carter, R. T. (2005). Exploring the relationship between racial identity and religious orientation among African American college students. *Journal of College Student Development, 46*(3), 280–295.

Sanchez, R. J., Bauer, T. N., & Paronto, M. E. (2006). Peer-mentoring freshmen: Implications for satisfaction, commitment, and retention to graduation. *Academy of Management Learning and Education, 5*(1), 25–37.

Sandahl, S. (2010). Collaborative testing as a learning strategy in nursing education. *Nursing Education Perspectives, 31*(3), 142–147.

Sanders, C. E., Lubinski, D., & Benbow, C. P. (1995). Does the Defining Issues Test measure psychological phenomena distinct from verbal ability? An examination of Lykken's query. *Journal of Personality and Social Psychology, 69*(3), 498–504.

Sanders-Dewey, N. E. J., & Zaleski, S. A. (2009). The utility of a college major: Do students of psychology learn discipline-specific knowledge? *Journal of General Education, 58*(1), 19–27.

Sandy, J., Gonzalez, A., & Hilmer, M. J. (2006). Alternative paths to college completion: Effect of attending a two-year school on the probability of completing a four-year degree. *Economics of Education Review, 25*(5), 463–471.

Sanford, N. (1962). Developmental status of the entering freshman. In N. Sanford (Ed.), *The American college: A psychological and social interpretation of the higher learning* (pp. 253–282). Hoboken, NJ: Wiley.

Sanford, N. (1966). *Self and society: Social change and individual development.* New York, NY: Atherton.

Sanford, N. (1967). *Where colleges fail: A study of the student as a person.* San Francisco, CA: Jossey-Bass.

Sanford, T., & Hunter, J. M. (2011). Impact of performance-funding on retention and graduation rates. *Education Policy Analysis Archives, 19*(33), 1–27.

Santos, S. J., Ortiz, A. M., Morales, A., & Rosales, M. (2007). The relationship between campus diversity, students' ethnic identity and college adjustment: A qualitative study. *Cultural Diversity and Ethnic Minority Psychology, 13*(2), 104–114.

Sattler, P., & Peters, J. (2013). *Work-integrated learning in Ontario's postsecondary sector: The experience of Ontario graduates.* Toronto, ON, Canada: Higher Education Quality Council of Ontario.

Saunders, K. J., & Kashubeck-West, S. (2006). The relations among feminist identity development, gender-role orientation, and psychological well-being in women. *Psychology of Women Quarterly, 30*(2), 199–211.

Savickas, M. L. (1984). Career maturity: The construct and its measurement. *Vocational Guidance Quarterly, 32*(4), 222–231.

Sax, L. J. (2008). *The gender gap in college: Maximizing the developmental potential of women and men.* San Francisco, CA: Jossey-Bass.

Sax, L. J., & Bryant, A. N. (2006). The impact of college on sex-atypical career choices of men and women. *Journal of Vocational Behavior, 68*(1), 52–63.

Sax, L. J., Bryant, A. N., & Gilmartin, S. K. (2004). A longitudinal investigation of emotional health among male and female first-year college students. *Journal of the First-Year Experience & Students in Transition, 16*(2), 39–65.

Sax, L. J., Bryant, A. N., & Harper, C. E. (2005). The differential effects of student-faculty interaction on college outcomes for women and men. *Journal of College Student Development, 46*(6), 642–657.

Scarboro, A. (2004). Bringing theory closer to home through active learning and online discussion. *Teaching Sociology, 32*(2), 222–231.

Scheitle, C. P. (2011). U.S. college students' perception of religion and science: Conflict, collaboration, or independence? A research note. *Journal for the Scientific Study of Religion, 50*(1), 175–186.

Schellens, T., & Valcke, M. (2005). Collaborative learning in asynchronous discussion groups: What about the impact on cognitive processing? *Computers in Human Behavior, 21*(6), 957–975.

Schellens, T., & Valcke, M. (2006). Fostering knowledge construction in university students through asynchronous discussion groups. *Computers and Education, 46*(4), 349–370.

Schieman, S., & Plickert, G. (2008). How knowledge is power: Education and the sense of control. *Social Forces, 87*(1), 153–183.

Schmid, R. F., Bernard, R. M., Borokhovski, E., Tamim, R., Abrami, P. C., Wade, C. A., . . . & Lowerison, G. (2009). Technology's effect on achievement in higher education: A stage I meta-analysis of classroom applications. *Journal of Computing in Higher Education, 21*(2), 95–109.

Schmidt, C. D., McAdams, C. R., & Foster, V. (2009). Promoting the moral reasoning of undergraduate business students through a deliberate psychological education-based classroom intervention. *Journal of Moral Education, 38*(3), 315–334.

Schmidt, C. K., Miles, J. R., & Welsh, A. C. (2010). Perceived discrimination and social support: The influences on career development and college adjustment of LGBT college students. *Journal of Career Development, 38*(4), 293–309.

Schmidt, C. K., Piontkowski, S., Raque-Bogdan, T. L., & Ziemer, K. S. (2014). Relational health, ethnic identity, and well-being of college students of color: A strengths-based perspective. *Counseling Psychologist, 42*(4), 473–496.

Schneider, B., Carnoy, M., Kilpatrick, J., Schmidt, W. H., & Shavelson, R. J. (2007). *Estimating causal effects: Using experimental and observational designs.* Washington, DC: American Educational Research Association.

Schnell, C. A., & Doetkott, C. D. (2003). First year seminars produce long-term impact. *Journal of College Student Retention, 4*(4), 377–391.

Schnell, C. A., Seashore Louis, K., & Doetkott, C. (2003). The first-year seminar as a means of improving college graduation rates. *Journal of the First-Year Experience & Students in Transition, 15*(1), 53–75.

Schnittker, J. (2004). Education and the changing shape of the income gradient in health. *Journal of Health and Social Behavior, 45*(3), 286–305.

Schoerning, E. (2014). The effect of plain-English vocabulary on student achievement and classroom culture in college science instruction. *International Journal of Science and Mathematics Education, 12*(2), 307–327.

Schofield, J. W., Hausmann, L. R. M., Ye, F., & Woods, R. L. (2010). Intergroup friendships on campus: Predicting close and casual friendships between White and African American first-year college students. *Group Processes and Intergroup Relations, 13*(5), 585–602.

Schonwetter, D. J., Clifton, R. A., & Perry, R. P. (2002). Content familiarity: Differential impact of effective teaching on student achievement outcomes. *Research in Higher Education, 43*(6), 625–655.

Schreiner, L. A. (2010a). The "Thriving Quotient": A new vision for student success. *About Campus, 15*(2), 2–10.

Schreiner, L. A. (2010b). Thriving in the classroom. *About Campus, 15*(3), 2–10.

Schreiner, L. A. (2010c). Thriving in community. *About Campus, 15*(4), 2–11.

Schreiner, L. A. (2013). Thriving in college. *New Directions for Student Services, 2013*(143), 41–52.

Schreiner, L. A. (2014). Different pathways to thriving among students of color: An untapped opportunity for success. *About Campus, 19*(5), 10–19.

Schreiner, L. A., & Nelson, D. D. (2013). The contribution of student satisfaction to persistence. *Journal of College Student Retention, 15*(1), 73–111.

Schudde, L. T. (2011). The causal effect of campus residency on college student retention. *Review of Higher Education, 34*(4), 581–610.

Schugar, J. T., Schugar, H., & Penny, C. (2011). A nook or a book: Comparing college students' reading comprehension level, critical reading, and study skills. *International Journal of Technology in Teaching and Learning, 7*(2), 174–192.

Schultz, T. W. (1958). The emerging economic scene and its relation to high school education. In F. S. Chase & H. A. Anderson (Eds.), *The high school in a new era*. Chicago, IL: University of Chicago Press.

Schultz, T. (1963). *The economic value of education*. New York, NY: Columbia University Press.

Schumacker, R. E., & Lomax, R. G. (2012). *A beginner's guide to structural equation modeling* (3rd ed.). New York, NY: Routledge.

Schutte, K. J. (2007). Journey or destination: A study of experiential education, reflection, and cognitive development. *Journal of Cooperative Education and Internships, 41*(1), 118–129.

Schwebel, D. C., Walburn, N. C., Klyce, K., & Jerrolds, K. L. (2012). Efficacy of advising outreach on student retention, academic progress and achievement, and frequency of advising contacts: A longitudinal randomized trial. *NACADA Journal, 32*(2), 36–43.

Scott, A. B., & Ciani, K. D. (2008). Effects of an undergraduate career class on men's and women's career-decision making self-efficacy and vocational identity. *Journal of Career Development, 34*(3), 263–285.

Scott, J. H. (2012). The intersection of service-learning and moral growth. *New Directions for Student Services*, No. 139, 27–38.

Scott, M., Bailey, T., & Kienzl, G. (2006). Relative success? Determinants of college graduation rates in the public and private colleges in the U.S. *Research in Higher Education, 47*(3), 249–279.

Scott-Clayton, J. (2011). On money and motivation: A quasi-experimental analysis of financial incentives for college achievement. *Journal of Human Resources, 46*(3), 614–646.

Scott-Clayton, J., & Rodriguez, O. (2012). *Development, discouragement, or diversion? New evidence on the effects of college remediation* (NBER Working Paper No. 18328). Cambridge, MA: National Bureau of Economic Research.

Scottham, K. M., Cooke, D. Y., Sellers, R. M., & Ford, K. (2010). Integrating process with content in understanding African American racial identity development. *Self and Identity, 9*(1), 19–40.

Scrivener, S., & Coghlan, E. (2011). *Opening doors to student success: A synthesis of findings from an evaluation at six community colleges*. New York, NY: MDRC.

Scrivener, S., & Weiss, M. J. (2009). *More guidance, better results? Three-year effects of an enhanced student services program at two community colleges*. New York, NY: MDRC.

Scrivener, S., & Weiss, M. J. (2013). *More graduates: Two-year results from an evaluation of accelerated study in associate programs (ASAP) for developmental education students*. New York, NY: MDRC.

Scrivener, S., Bloom, D., LeBlanc, A., Paxson, C., Rouse, C. E., & Sommo, C. (2008). *A good start; Two-year effects of a freshman learning community program at Kingsborough Community College*. New York, NY: MDRC.

Seider, S. C., Gillmor, S. C., & Rabinowicz, S. A. (2010). Complicating college students' conception of the American dream through community service. *Michigan Journal of Community Service Learning, 17*(1), 5–19.

Seider, S. C., Gillmor, S. C., & Rabinowicz, S. (2011). The impact of community service learning upon the worldviews of business majors vs. non-business majors at an American university. *Journal of Business Ethics, 98*(3), 458–504.

Seider, S. C., Gillmor, S. C., & Rabinowicz, S. (2012). The impact of community service learning upon the expected political voice of participating college students. *Journal of Adolescent Research, 27*(1), 44–77.

Seifert, T. A. (2007). Understanding Christian privilege: Managing the tensions of spiritual plurality. *About Campus, 12*(2), 10–17.

Seifert, T. A., Goodman, K. M., Lindsay, N., Jorgensen, J. D., Wolniak, G. C., Pascarella, E. T., & Blaich, C. (2008). The effects of liberal arts experiences on liberal arts outcomes. *Research in Higher Education, 49*(2), 107–125.

Seifert, T. A., Pascarella, E. T., Colangelo, N., & Assouline, S. G. (2007). The effects of honors program participation on experiences of good practices and learning outcomes. *Journal of College Student Development, 48*(1), 57–74.

Selingo, J. J. (2013). *College (un)bound*. Boston, MA: New Harvest.

Selwyn, N. (2008). "High jinks" and "minor mischief": A study of undergraduate students as perpetrators of crime. *Studies in Higher Education, 33*(1), 1–16.

Semb, G. B., & Ellis, J. A. (1994). Knowledge taught in school: What is remembered? *Review of Educational Research, 64*(2), 253–286.

Sengupta, A. S., & Upton, Y. L. (2011). Identity development in college women. In P. A. Pasque & S. E. Nicholson (Eds.), *Empowering women in higher education and student affairs: Theory, research, narratives, and practice from feminist perspectives* (pp. 231–246). Sterling, VA: Stylus.

Settle, J. S. (2011). Variables that encourage students to persist in community colleges. *Community College Journal of Research and Practice, 35*(4), 281–300.

Sewell, W. H., & Hauser, R. M. (1975). *Education, occupation, and earnings: Achievement in the early career.* New York, NY: Academic Press.

Seymour, E., Hunter, A. B., Laursen, S. L., & DeAntoni, T. (2004). Establishing the benefits of research experiences for undergraduates in the sciences: First findings from a three-year study. *Science Education, 88*(4), 493–534.

Shachar, M. & Neumann, Y. (2003). Differences between traditional and distance education academic performances: A meta-analytic approach. *International Review of Research in Open and Distributed Learning, 4*(2), 1–20.

Shadish, W. R. (2013). Propensity score analysis: Promise, reality, and irrational exuberance. *Journal of Experimental Criminology, 9*(2), 129–144.

Shadish, W. R., Cook, T. D., & Campbell, D. T. (2002). *Experimental and quasi-experimental designs for generalized causal inference* (2nd ed.). Boston, MA: Houghton Mifflin.

Shah, B. R., Laupacis, A., Hux, E. J., & Austin, P. C. (2005). Propensity score methods gave similar results to traditional regression modeling in observational studies: A systematic review. *Journal of Clinical Epidemiology, 58*(6), 550–559.

Shapiro, D., Dundar, A., Wakhungu, P. K., Yuan, X., & Harrell, A. (2015, July). *Transfer and mobility: A national view of student movement in postsecondary institutions, Fall 2008 cohort* (Signature Report No. 9). Herndon, VA: National Student Clearinghouse Research Center.

Shapses-Wertheim, S. (2014). *From a privileged perspective: How White undergraduate students make meaning of cross-racial interaction* (Unpublished doctoral dissertation). New York University, New York.

Sharma, P., & Hannafin, M. (2004). Scaffolding critical thinking in an online course: An exploratory study. *Journal of Educational Computing Research, 31*(2), 181–208.

Shek, Y. L., & McEwen, M. K. (2012). The relationships of racial identity and gender role conflict to self-esteem of Asian American undergraduate men. *Journal of College Student Development, 53*(5), 703–718.

Sheldon, C. Q., & Durdella, N. R. (2010). Success rates for students taking compressed and regular length developmental courses in the community college. *Community College Journal of Research and Practice, 34*, 39–54.

Shepherd, R. S., & Horner, D. H. (2010). Indicators of leadership development in undergraduate military education. *Journal of Leadership Studies, 4*(2), 18–29.

Sherar, L. B., Muhajarine, N., Esliger, D. W., & Baxter-Jones, A.D.G. (2009). The relationship between girls' (8–14 years) physical activity and maternal education. *Annals of Human Biology, 36*(5), 573–583.

Shibley, I. A., Jr., Milakofsky, L., Bender, D. S., & Patterson, H. O. (2003). College chemistry and Piaget: An analysis of gender difference, cognitive abilities, and achievement measures seventeen years apart. *Chemical Education Research, 80*(5), 569–573.

Shim, S. S., Ryan, A. M., & Cassady, J. (2012). Changes in self-esteem across the first year in college: The role of achievement goals. *Educational Psychology: An International Journal of Experimental Educational Psychology, 32*(2), 149–167.

Shim, W. J. (2013). Different pathways to leadership development of college women and men. *Journal of Student Affairs Research and Practice, 50*(3), 270–289.

Shin, J. C. (2010). Impacts of performance-based accountability in institutional performance in the U.S. *Higher Education, 60*(1), 47–68.

Shin, J., & Milton, S. (2004). The effects of performance budgeting and funding programs on graduation rate in public four-year colleges and universities. *Education Policy Analysis Archives, 12*(22). Retrieved from http://files.eric.ed.gov/fulltext/EJ852305.pdf

Shorter, N. A., & Young, C. Y. (2011). Comparing assessment methods as predictors of student learning in an undergraduate mathematics course. *International Journal of Mathematical Education in Science and Technology, 42*(8), 1061–1067.

Shotton, H. J., Lowe, S. C., Waterman, S. J., & Garland, J. (Eds.). (2013). *Beyond the asterisk: Understanding native students in higher education.* Sterling, VA: Stylus Publishing.

Shrout, P. E., & Bolger, N. (2002). Mediation in experimental and nonexperimental studies: New procedures and recommendations. *Psychological Methods, 7*(4), 422–445.

Shurts, W. M., & Shoffer, M. F. (2004). Providing career counseling for college student-athletes: A learning theory approach. *Journal of Career Development, 31*(2), 95–109.

Sibulkin, A. E., & Butler, J. S. (2005). Differences in graduation rates between young Black and White college students: Effect of entry into parenthood and historically Black universities. *Research in Higher Education, 46*(3), 327–348.

Sidanius, J., Van Laar, C., Levin, S., & Sinclair, S. (2004). Ethnic enclaves and the dynamics of social identity on the college campus: The good, the bad, and the ugly. *Journal of Personality and Social Psychology, 87*(1), 96–110.

Silles, M. A. (2009). The causal effect of education on health: Evidence from the United Kingdom. *Economics of Education Review, 28*(1), 122–128.

Silverman, L. H., & Seidman, A. (2011). Academic progress in developmental math courses: A comparative study of student retention. *Journal of College Student Retention, 13*(3), 267–287.

Simone, S. A. (2014). *Transferability of postsecondary credit following student transfer or coenrollment* (NCES 2014–163). Washington, DC: National Center for Education Statistics. Retrieved from http://nces.ed.gov/pubsearch

Siner, S. (2015). The evolution of spiritual and faith development theories. In J. L. Small (Ed.), *Making meaning: Embracing spirituality, faith, religion, and life purpose in student affairs.* Sterling, VA: Stylus.

Singell, L. (2004). Come and stay a while: Does financial aid affect retention conditioned on enrollment at a large public university? *Economics of Education Review, 23*(5), 459–471.

Singell, L. D., & Waddell, G. R. (2010). Modeling retention at a large public university: Can at-risk students be identified early enough to treat? *Research in Higher Education, 51*(6), 546–572.

Sirin, S. R., Brabeck, M. M., Satiani, A., & Rogers-Serin, L. (2003). Validation of a measure of ethical sensitivity and examination of the effects of previous multicultural and ethics courses on ethical sensitivity. *Ethics and Behavior, 13*(3), 221–235.

Sirum, K., & Humburg, J. (2011). The Experimental Design Ability Test (EDAT). *Bioscene: Journal of College Biology Teaching, 37*(1), 8–16.

Sitzmann, T., Ely, K., Brown, K. G., & Bauer, K. (2010). Self-assessment of knowledge: A cognitive learning or affective measure? *Academy of Management Learning and Education, 9*, 169–191.

Slusser, S. R., & Erickson, R. J. (2006). Group quizzes: An extension of the collaborative learning process. *Teaching Sociology, 23*, 106–116.

Small, J. L. (2011). *Understanding college students' spiritual identities: Different faiths, varied worldviews.* Cresskill, NJ: Hampton Press.

Small, J. L., & Bowman, N. A. (2011). Religious commitment, skepticism, and struggle among U.S. college students: The impact of majority/minority religious affiliation and institutional type. *Journal for the Scientific Study of Religion, 50*(1), 154–174.

Smart, J. C. (2005). Attributes of exemplary research manuscripts employing quantitative analyses. *Research in Higher Education, 46*(4), 461–477.

Smart, J. C., Ethington, C. A., & Umbach, P. D. (2009). Pedagogical approaches used by faculty in Holland's model environments: The role of environmental consistency. *Journal of Career Assessment, 17*(1), 69–85.

Smart, J. C., Ethington, C. A., Umbach, P. D., & Rocconi, L. M. (2009). Faculty emphases on alternative course-specific learning outcomes in Holland's model environments: The role of environmental consistency. *Research in Higher Education, 50*(5), 483–501.

Smart, J. C., & Umbach, P. D. (2007). Faculty and academic environments: Using Holland's theory to explore differences in how faculty structure undergraduate courses. *Journal of College Student Development, 48*(2), 183–195.

Smets, K., & van Ham, C. (2013). The embarrassment of riches? A meta-analysis of individual-level research on voter turnout. *Electoral Studies, 32*(2), 344–359.

Smith, A. (1776). *An inquiry into the nature and causes of the wealth of nations.* Retrieved from http://www.gutenberg.org/ebooks/3300

Smith, C., & Bath, D. (2006). The role of learning community in the development of discipline knowledge and generic graduate outcomes. *Higher Education, 51*, 259–286.

Smith, C., & Snell, P. (2009). *Souls in transition: The religious and spiritual lives of emerging adults.* New York, NY: Oxford University Press.

Smith, C. A., Strand, S. E., & Bunting, C. J. (2002). The influence of challenge course participation on moral and ethical reasoning. *Journal of Experiential Education, 25*(2), 278–280.

Smith, E. (2011). Teaching critical reflection. *Teaching in Higher Education, 16*(2), 211–223.

Smith, J. (2013). Ova and out: Using twins to estimate the educational returns to attending a selective college. *Economics of Education Review, 36*, 166–180.

Smithson, M., & Merkle, E. C. (2013). *Generalized linear modeling for categorical and continuous limited dependent variables.* Boca Raton, FL: CRC Press.

Snijders, T. A. B., & Bosker, R. (2012). *Multilevel analysis: An introduction to basic and advanced multilevel modeling* (2nd ed.). Thousand Oaks, CA: Sage.

Snyder, T. D., & Dillow, S. A. (2011). *Digest of education statistics* 2010 (NCES 2011–015). Washington, DC: National Center for Education Statistics, Institute of Education Sciences, U.S. Department of Education.

Somers, P., Woodhouse, S., & Cofer, J. (2004). Pushing the boulder uphill: The persistence of first-generation college students. *NASPA Journal, 41*(3), 418–435.

Sommo, C., Mayer, A. K., Rudd, T., & Cullinan, D. (2012). *Commencement day: Six-year effects of a freshman learning community program at Kingsborough Community College*. New York, NY: MDRC.

Soria, K. M., & Stebleton, M. J. (2012). First-generation students' academic engagement and retention. *Teaching in Higher Education, 17*(6), 673–685.

Soria, K. M., & Thomas-Card, T. (2014). Relationships between motivations for community service participation and desire to continue service following college. *Michigan Journal of Community Service Learning, 20*(2), 53–64.

Sosa, G., Berger, D. E., Saw, A. T., & Mary, J. C. (2011). Effectiveness of computer-based instruction in statistics: A meta-analysis. *Review of Educational Research, 81*(1), 97–128.

Sousa, D. A., & Pilecki, T. (2013). *From STEM to STEAM: Using brain-compatible strategies to integrate the arts*. Thousand Oaks, CA: Corwin.

Southard, A. H., & Clay, J. K. (2004). Measuring the effectiveness of developmental writing courses. *Community College Review, 32*(2), 39–50.

Spear, J. A., & Miller, A. N. (2012). The effects of instructor fear appeals and moral appeals on cheating-related attitudes and behavior of university students. *Ethics and Behavior, 22*(3), 196–207.

Spence, M. (1973). Job market signaling. *Quarterly Journal of Economics, 87*(3), 355–374.

Spence, M. (2002). Signaling in retrospect and the informational structure of markets. *American Economic Review, 92*(3), 434–459.

Spiezio, K. E., Baker, K. Q., & Boland, K. (2005). General education and civic engagement: An empirical analysis of pedagogical possibilities. *Journal of General Education, 54*(4), 273–292.

Spoehr, L. W., & Fraker, A. (1995). *Doing the DBQ: Advanced Placement U.S. History Exam*. New York, NY: College Entrance Examination Board and Educational Testing Service.

Spradlin, K., & Ackerman, B. (2010). The effectiveness of computer-assisted instruction in developmental mathematics. *Journal of Developmental Education, 34*(2), 12–18.

Springer, C. R., & Pear, J. J. (2008). Performance measures in courses using computer-aided personalized system of instruction. *Computers and Education, 51*, 829–835.

Spurgeon, S. L. (2009). Wellness and college type in African American male college students: An examination of differences. *Journal of College Counseling, 12*(1), 33–43.

Spurgeon, S. L., & Myers, J. E. (2010). African American males: Relationships among racial identity, college type, and wellness. *Journal of Black Studies, 40*(4), 527–543.

Srougi, M. C., Miller, H. B., Witherow, D. S., & Carson, S. (2013). Assessment of a novel group-centered testing schema in an upper-level undergraduate molecular biotechnology course. *Biochemistry and Molecular Biology Education*, *41*(4), 231–241.

St. John, E. P., Hu, S., Simmons, A., Carter, D. F., & Weber, J. (2004). What difference does a major make? The influence of college major field on persistence by African American and White students. *Research in Higher Education*, *45*(3), 209–232.

St. John, E. P., Musoba, G. D., & Simmons, A. B. (2003). Keeping the promise: The impact of Indiana's twenty-first century scholars program. *Review of Higher Education*, *27*, 103–123.

St. John, E. P., Paulsen, M. B., & Carter, D. F. (2005). Diversity, college costs, and postsecondary opportunity: An examination of the financial nexus between college choice and persistence for African Americans and Whites. *Journal of Higher Education*, *76*(5), 545–569.

St. Louis, G. R., & Liem, J. H. (2005). Ego identity, ethnic identity, and the psychosocial well-being of ethnic minority and majority college students. *Identity: An International Journal of Theory and Research*, *5*(3), 227–246.

Staff, J., Schulenberg, J. E., Maslowsky, J., Bachman, J. G., O'Malley, P. M., Maggs, J. L., & Johnston, L. D. (2010). Substance use changes and social role transitions: Proximal developmental effects on ongoing trajectories from late adolescence through early adulthood. *Development and Psychopathology*, *22*(4), 917–932.

Stage, F. K. (2007). Answering critical questions using quantitative data. In F. K. Stage (Ed.), *Using quantitative data to answer critical questions* (New Directions for Institutional Research, No. 133, pp. 5–16). San Francisco, CA: Jossey-Bass.

Stage, F. K., & Hossler, D. (2000). Where is the student? Linking student behaviors, college choice, and college persistence. In J. M. Braxton (Ed.), *Reworking the student departure puzzle* (pp. 170–195). Nashville, TN: Vanderbilt University Press.

Stake, J. E. (2007). Predictors of change in feminist activism through women's and gender studies. *Sex Roles*, *57*(1–2), 43–54.

Stalder, D. R., & Olson, E. A. (2011). T for two: Using mnemonics to teach statistics. *Teaching of Psychology*, *38*(4), 247–250.

Stanford, J. S., & Duwel, L. E. (2013). Engaging biology undergraduates in the scientific process through writing a theoretical research proposal. *Bioscene: Journal of College Biology Teaching*, *39*(2), 17–24.

Stark-Wroblewski, K., Kreiner, D. S., Boeding, C. M., Lopata, A. N., Ryan, J. J., & Church, T. M. (2008). Use of virtual reality technology to enhance undergraduate learning in abnormal psychology. *Teaching of Psychology*, *35*(4), 343–348.

Stassen, M. L. A. (2003). Student outcomes: The impact of varying living-learning community models. *Research in Higher Education*, *44*(5), 581–613.

Staw, B. M., Bell, N. E., & Clausen, J. A. (1986). The dispositional approach to job attitudes: A lifetime longitudinal test. *Administrative Science Quarterly*, *31*, 56–77.

Staw, B. M., & Ross, J. (1985). Stability in the midst of change: A dispositional approach to job attitudes. *Journal of Applied Psychology*, *70*, 469–480.

Stearns, S. A. (2001). The student-instructor relationship's effect on academic integrity. *Ethics and Behavior, 11*(3), 275–285.

Steck, L. W., Heckert, D. M., & Heckert, D. A. (2003). The salience of racial identity among African-American and White students. *Race and Society, 6*(1), 57–73.

Steck, T. R., DiBiase, W., Wang, C., & Boukhtiarov, A. (2012). The use of open-ended problem-based learning scenarios in an interdisciplinary biotechnology class: Evaluation of a problem-based learning course across three years. *Journal of Microbiology and Biology Education, 13*(1), 2–10.

Steif, P. S., Lobue, J. M., Kara, L. B., & Fay, A. L. (2010). Improving problem solving performance by inducing talk about salient problem features. *Journal of Engineering Education, 99*(2), 135–142.

Steiner, P. M., Cook, T. D., Shadish, W. R., & Clark, M. H. (2010). The importance of covariate selection in controlling for selection bias in observational studies. *Psychological Methods, 15*, 250–267.

Steinfeldt, J. A., Steinfeldt, M. C., England, B., & Speight, Q. L. (2009). Gender role conflict and stigma toward help-seeking among college football players. *Psychology of Men and Masculinity, 10*(4), 261–272.

Steinfeldt, J. A., Wong, Y. J., Hagan, A. R., Hoag, J. M., & Steinfeldt, M. C. (2011). A contextual examination of gender role conflict among college football players. *Psychology of Men and Masculinity, 12*(4), 311–323.

Steinfeldt, M., & Steinfeldt, J. A. (2012). Athletic identity and conformity to masculine norms among college football players. *Journal of Applied Sport Psychology, 24*(2), 115–128.

STEM to STEAM. (2015). Retrieved from http://stemtosteam.org/

Stephens, D. P., & Eaton, A. A. (2014). The influence of masculinity scripts on heterosexual Hispanic college men's perceptions of female-initiated sexual coercion. *Psychology of Men and Masculinity, 15*(4), 387–396.

Stephens, J. M., Young, M. F., & Calabrese, T. (2007). Does moral judgment go offline when students are online? A comparative analysis of undergraduates' beliefs and behaviors related to conventional and digital cheating. *Ethics and Behavior, 17*(3), 233–254.

Stevens, R. A. (2004). Understanding gay identity development within the college environment. *Journal of College Student Development, 45*(2), 185–206.

Stewart, D. L. (2012). Promoting moral growth through pluralism and social justice. In D. Liddell & D. L. Cooper (Eds.), *Facilitating the moral growth of college students in higher education* (New Directions in Student Services No. 139, pp. 63–72). San Francisco, CA: Jossey-Bass.

Stewart, T. L. H., Clifton, R. A., Daniels, L. M., Perry, R. P., Chipperfield, J. G., & Ruthig, J. C. (2011). Attributional retraining: Reducing the likelihood of failure. *Social Psychology of Education, 14*(1), 75–92.

Stewart, T. L., Myers, A. C., & Culley, M. R. (2010). Enhanced learning and retention through "Writing to Learn" in the psychology classroom. *Teaching of Psychology, 37*, 46–49.

Stiglitz, J. E. (1975). The theory of "screening," education, and the distribution of income. *American Economic Review, 65*, 283–300.

Stillson, H., & Alsup, J. (2003). Smart ALEKS . . . or not? Teaching basic algebra using an online interactive learning system. *Mathematics and Computer Education, 37*(3), 329–340.

Stinebrickner, R., & Stinebrickner, T. R. (2012). Learning about academic ability and the college dropout decision. *Journal of Labor Economics, 30*(4), 707–748.

Stone, A. L., Becker, L. G., Huber, A. M., & Catalano, R. F. (2012). Review of risk and protective factors of substance use and problem use in emerging adulthood. *Addictive Behaviors, 37*(7), 747–775.

Stoppa, T. M., & Lefkowitz, E. S. (2010). Longitudinal changes in religiosity among emerging adult college students. *Journal of Research on Adolescence, 20*(1), 23–38.

Stotzer, R. L. (2009). Straight allies: Supportive attitudes toward lesbians, gay men, and bisexuals in a college sample. *Sex Roles, 60*(1–2), 67–80.

Stratton, L. S., O'Toole, D. M., & Wetzel, J. M. (2007). Are the factors affecting dropout behavior related to initial enrollment intensity for college undergraduates? *Research in Higher Education, 48*(4), 453–485.

Stratton, L. S., O'Toole, D. M., & Wetzel, J. M. (2008). A multinomial logit model of college stopout and dropout behavior. *Economics of Education Review, 27*, 319–331.

Strauss, L. C., & Terenzini, P. T. (2007). The effects of students in- and out-of-class experiences on their analytical and group skills: A study of engineering education. *Research in Higher Education, 48*(8), 967–992.

Strauss, L. C., & Volkwein, J. F. (2002). Comparing student performance and growth in two- and four-year institutions. *Research in Higher Education, 43*(2), 133–161.

Strayhorn, T. L. (2006). College in the information age: Gains associated with students' use of technology. *Journal of Interactive Online Learning, 5*(2), 143–155.

Strayhorn, T. L. (2008). Influences on labor market outcomes of African American college graduates: A national study. *Journal of Higher Education, 79*, 28–57.

Strayhorn, T. L. (Ed.). (2013). *Living at the intersections: Social identities and Black collegians.* Charlotte, NC: Information Age Publishing.

Strayhorn, T. L., & Tillman-Kelly, D. L. (2013). Queering masculinity: Manhood and Black gay men in college. *Spectrum: A Journal on Black Men, 1*(2), 83–110.

Stroud, M. J., & Schwartz, N. H. (2010). Summoning prior knowledge through metaphorical graphics: An example in chemistry instruction. *Journal of Educational Research, 103*, 351–366.

Stubbs, B. B., & Sallee, M. W. (2013). Muslim, too: Navigating multiple identities at an American university. *Equity and Excellence in Education, 46*(4), 451–467.

Stull, A. T., & Mayer, R. E. (2007). Learning by doing versus learning by viewing: Three experimental comparisons of learner-generated versus author-provided graphic organizers. *Journal of Educational Psychology, 99*(4), 808–820.

Stump, G. S., Hilpert, J. C., Husman, J., Chung, W. T., & Kim, W. (2011). Collaborative learning in engineering students: Gender and achievement. *Journal of Engineering Education, 100*(3), 475–497.

Stürmer, T., Joshi, M., Glynn, R. J., Avorn, J., Rothman, K. J., & Schneeweiss, S. (2006). A review of the application of propensity score methods yielded increasing use, advantages in specific settings, but not substantially different estimates compared with conventional multivariable methods. *Journal of Clinical Epidemiology, 59*, 437–447.

Sun, X., Hoffman, S. C., & Grady, M. L. (2007). A multivariate causal model of alumni giving: Implications for alumni fundraisers. *International Journal of Educational Advancement, 7,* 307–332.

Stupnisky, R. H., Renaud, R. D., Daniels, L. M., Haynes, T. L., & Perry, R. P. (2008). The interrelation of first-year college students' critical thinking disposition, perceived academic control, and academic achievement. Research in Higher Education, 49(6), 513-530

Surridge, I. (2009). Accounting and finance degrees: Is the academic performance of placement students better? *Accounting Education: An International Journal, 18*(4–5), 471–485.

Sutton, R. C., & Rubin, D. L. (2004). The GLOSSARI project: Initial findings from a system-wide research initiative on study abroad learning outcomes. *Frontiers: The Interdisciplinary Journal of Study Abroad, 10,* 65–82.

Swail, W. S., Redd, K. E., & Perna, L. W. (2003). *Retaining minority students in higher education* (ASHE-ERIC Higher Education Report, 30–2). Hoboken, NJ: Wiley.

Swank, E., Woodford, M. R., & Lim, C. (2013). Antecedents of pro-LGBT advocacy among sexual minority and heterosexual college students. *Sexuality Research and Social Policy, 10*(4), 317–332.

Swanson, E. (2010). Lessons from the context sensitivity of causal talk. *Journal of Philosophy, 107*(5), 221–242.

Swanson, E. (2012). The language of causation. In D. G. Fara & G. Russel (Eds.), *The Routledge companion to the philosophy of language* (pp. 716–728). London, UK: Routledge.

Swecker, H. K., Fifolt, M., & Searby, L. (2013). Academic advising and first-generation college students: A quantitative study on student retention. *NACADA Journal, 33*(1), 46–53.

Swenson Goguen, L. M., Nordstrom, A., & Hiester, M. (2008). The role of peer relationships in adjustment to college. *Journal of College Student Development, 49*(6), 551–567.

Swenson Goguen, L. M., Hiester, M. A., & Nordstrom, A. H. (2011). Associations among peer relationships, academic achievement, and persistence in college. *Journal of College Student Retention, 12*(3), 319–337.

Swerdzewski, P. J., Harmes, J. C., & Finney, S. J. (2011). Two approaches for identifying low-motivated students in a low-stakes assessment context. *Applied Measurement in Education, 24*(2), 162–188.

Syed, M., & Azmitia, M. (2009). Longitudinal trajectories of ethnic identity during the college years. *Journal of Research on Adolescence, 19*(4), 601–624.

Syed, M., Azmitia, M., & Phinney, J. S. (2007). Stability and change in ethnic identity among Latino emerging adults in two contexts. *Identity: An International Journal of Theory and Research, 7*(2), 155–178.

Syed, M., Walker, L. H. M., Lee, R. M., Umaña-Taylor, A. J., Zamboanga, B. L., Schwartz, S. J., . . . Huynh, Q. L. (2013). A two-factor model of ethnic identity exploration: Implications for identity coherence and well-being. *Cultural Diversity and Ethnic Minority Psychology, 19*(2), 143–154.

Szelényi, K., Denson, N., & Inkelas, K. K. (2013). Women in STEM majors and professional outcome expectations: The role of living-learning programs and other college environments. *Research in Higher Education, 54*(8), 851–873.

Tamim, R. M., Bernard, R. M., Borokhovski, E., Abrami, P. C., & Schmid, R. F. (2011). What forty years of research says about the impact of technology on learning: A second-order meta-analysis and validation study. *Review of Educational Research, 81*(1), 4–28.

Tandberg, D. A., & Hillman, N. W. (2014). State higher education performance funding: Data, outcomes, and policy implications. *Journal of Education Finance, 39*(3), 222–243.

Taniguchi, H. (2005). The influence of age at degree completion on college wage premiums. *Research in Higher Education, 46*(8), 861–881.

Taniguchi, H., & Kaufman, G. (2005). Degree completion among nontraditional college students. *Social Science Quarterly, 86*(4), 912–927.

Tatum, J. L., & Charlton, R. (2008). A phenomenological study of how selected college men construct and define masculinity. *Higher Education in Review, 5*, 99–125.

Tenn, S. (2005). An alternative measure of relative education to explain voter turnout. *Journal of Politics, 67*(1), 271–282.

Tenn, S., Herman, D. A., & Wendling, B. (2010). The role of education in the production of health: An empirical analysis of smoking behavior. *Journal of Health Economics, 29*(3), 404–417.

Teranishi, R. T., Ceja, M., Antonio, A. L., Allen, W. R., & McDonough, P. M. (2004). The college-choice process for Asian Pacific Americans: Ethnicity and socio-economic class in context. *Review of Higher Education, 27*(4), 527–551.

Terenzini, P. T., Pascarella, E. T., & Blimling, G. S. (1996). Students' out-of-class experiences and their influence on learning and cognitive development: A literature review. *Journal of College Student Development, 37*(2), 149–162.

Terenzini, P. T., & Reason, R. D. (2012). Rethinking between-college effects on student learning: A new model to guide assessment and quality assurance. In R. Yamada & R. Mori (Eds.), *Quality assurance for higher education and assessment: Higher education policy and quality assurance in globalization* (pp. 7–22). Oslo, Norway: Center for Higher Education and Student Research, Doshisha University.

Terrion, J. L., & Daoust, J. (2012). Assessing the impact of supplemental instruction on the retention of undergraduate students after controlling for motivation. *Journal of College Student Retention: Research, Theory & Practice, 13*(3), 311–327.

Thiede, K. W., & Anderson, M. C. M. (2003). Summarizing can improve metacomprehension accuracy. *Contemporary Educational Psychology, 28*(2), 129–160.

Thoma, S. J., Derryberry, P., & Narvaez, D. (2009). The distinction between moral judgment development and verbal ability: Some relevant data using socio-political outcome variables. *High Ability Studies, 20*(2), 173–185.

Thomas, S. L. (2003). Longer-term economic effects of college selectivity and control. *Research in Higher Education, 44*(3) 263–299.

Thomas, S. L., & Zhang, L. (2005). Post-baccalaureate wage growth within four years of graduation: The effects of college quality and college major. *Research in Higher Education, 46*(4), 437–459.

Thompkins, C. D., & Rando, R. A. (2003). Gender role conflict and shame in college men. *Psychology of Men and Masculinity, 4*(1), 79–81.

Thompson Jr., J. G., Oberle, C. D., & Lilley, J. L. (2011). Self-efficacy and learning in sorority and fraternity students. *Journal of College Student Development, 52*(6), 749–753.

Thorpe, K., & Loo, R. (2003). Critical-thinking types among nursing and management undergraduates. *Nurse Education Today, 23*, 566–574.

Thyer, B. A. (2012). *Quasi-experimental research designs.* New York, NY: Oxford University Press.

Tierney, W. (1992). An anthropological analysis of student participation in college. *Journal of Higher Education, 63*, 603–618.

Tierney, W. G., & Auerbach, S. (2005). Toward developing an untapped resource: The role of families in college preparation. In W. G. Tierney, Z. B. Corwin, & J. E. Colyar (Eds.), *Preparing for college: Nine elements of effective outreach* (pp. 13–28). Albany, NY: State University of New York Press.

Tinto, V. (1987). *Leaving college: Rethinking the causes and cures of student attrition.* Chicago, IL: University of Chicago Press.

Tinto, V. (1993). *Leaving college: Rethinking the causes and cures of student attrition* (2nd ed.). Chicago, IL: University of Chicago Press.

Titus, M. A. (2004). An examination of the influence of institutional context on student persistence at four-year colleges and universities: A multilevel approach. *Research in Higher Education, 45*(7), 673–699.

Titus, M. A. (2006a). No college student left behind: The influence of financial aspects of a state's higher education policy on college completion. *Review of Higher Education, 29*(3), 293–317.

Titus, M. A. (2006b). Understanding college degree completion of students with low socioeconomic status: The influence of the institutional financial context. *Research in Higher Education, 47*(4), 371–398.

Titus, M. A. (2006c). Understanding the influence of the financial context of institutions on student persistence at four-year colleges and universities. *Journal of Higher Education, 77*(2), 353–375.

Titus, M. A. (2007). Detecting selection bias, using propensity score matching, and estimating treatment effects. *Research in Higher Education, 48*, 487–521.

Titus, M. A. (2009). The production of bachelor's degrees and financial aspects of state higher education policy: A dynamic analysis. *Journal of Higher Education, 80*(4), 439–468.

Tomcho, T. J., & Foels, R. (2012). Meta-analysis of group learning activities: Empirically based teaching recommendations. *Society for the Teaching of Psychology, 39*(3), 159–169.

Torres, V. (2003). Influences on ethnic identity development of Latino college students in the first two years of college. *Journal of College Student Development, 44*(4), 532–547.

Torres, V., & Hernandez, E. (2007). The influence of ethnic identity on self-authorship: A longitudinal study of Latino/a college students. *Journal of College Student Development, 48*(5), 558–573.

Torres, V., Jones, S. R., & Renn, K. A. (2009). Identity development theories in student affairs: Origins, current status, and new approaches. *Journal of College Student Development, 50*(6), 577–596.

Toutkoushian, R. K., Najeeb Shafiq, M., & Trivette, M. J. (2013). Accounting for risk of non-completion in private and social rates of return to higher education. *Journal of Education Finance, 39*, 73–95.

Toutkoushian, R. K., & Paulsen, M. B. (2016). *Economics of higher education: Background, concepts, and applications.* Dordrecht, Netherlands: Springer.

Tracey, T. J. G., Allen, J., & Robbins, S. B. (2012). Moderation of the relation between person-environment congruence and academic success: Environmental constraint, personal flexibility, and method. *Journal of Vocational Behavior, 80,* 38–49.

Tracey, T. J. G., & Robbins, S. B. (2006). The interest-major congruence and college success relation: A longitudinal study. *Journal of Vocational Behavior, 69,* 64–89.

Tran, P., Carrillo, R., Subramanyam, K. (2013). Effects of online multitasking on reading comprehension of expository text. *Cyberpsychology: Journal of Psychosocial Research on Cyberspace, 7*(3), article 2.

Trautmann, N. (2007). Interactive learning through web-mediated peer review of student science reports. *Educational Technology Research and Development, 57*(5), 685–704.

Treffinger, D. J., & Schoonover, P. F. (2012). Problem-solving style and distance learning. *Distance Learning, 9*(2), 1–9.

Trenholm, S. (2006). A study on the efficacy of computer-mediated developmental math instruction for traditional community college students. *Research and Teaching in Developmental Education, 25*(2), 68–76.

Trost, S., & Salehi-Isfahani, D. (2012). The effect of homework on exam performance: Experimental results from principles of economics. *Southern Economic Journal, 79*(1), 224–242.

Trostel, P. A. (2010). The fiscal impacts of college attainment. *Research in Higher Education, 51,* 220–247.

Trumpower, D. L., & Goldsmith, T. E. (2004). Structural enhancement of learning. *Contemporary Educational Psychology, 29*(4), 426–446.

Trusty, J. (2002). Effects of high school course-taking and other variables on choice of science and mathematics college majors. *Journal of Counseling and Development, 80,* 464–474.

Tsai, K. M., & Fuligni, A. J. (2012). Change in ethnic identity across the college transition. *Developmental Psychology, 48*(1), 56–64.

Tsui, L. (2002). Fostering critical thinking through effective pedagogy. *Journal of Higher Education, 73*(6), 740–763.

Tuckman, B. W., & Kennedy, G. J. (2011). Teaching learning strategies to increase success of first-term college students. *Journal of Experimental Education, 79,* 478–504.

Tumen, S., Shulruf, B., & Hattie, J. (2008). Student pathways at the university: Patterns and predictors of completion. *Studies in Higher Education, 33*(3), 233–252.

Tümkaya, S. (2012). The investigation of the epistemological beliefs of university students according to gender, grade, fields of study, academic success, and their learning styles. *Educational Sciences Theory & Practice, 12*(1), 88–95.

Turiel, E. (1998). The development of morality. In W. Damon (Series Ed.) & N. Eisenberg (Vol. Ed.), *Handbook of child psychology: Vol. 3. Social, emotional, and personality development* (5th ed., pp. 863–932). New York, NY: Wiley.

Turiel, E. (2002). *The culture of morality*. Cambridge, UK: Cambridge University Press.

Turley, R. N. L., Santos, M., & Ceja, C. (2007). Social origin and college opportunity expectations across cohorts. *Social Science Research, 36*, 1200–1218.

Turnbull, W., & Carpendale, J. I. M. (2001). Talk and social understanding. *Early Education and Development, 12*, 455–477.

Twombly, S. B., Salisbury, M. H., Tumanut, S. D., & Klute, P. (2012). *Study abroad in a new global century: Renewing the promise, refining the purpose* (ASHE Higher Education Report 38-4). Hoboken, NJ: Wiley.

U.S. Department of Education. (1995). Supplemental instruction (SI): Improving student performance and reducing attrition. In G. Lang (Ed.), *Educational programs that work* (21st ed.). Longmont, CO: Sopris West.

U.S. Department of Education. (2006). *A Test of Leadership: CA test of leadership: Charting the future of U.S. higher education*. Washington, DC: Author.

U.S. Department of Education. (2013a). *College scorecard*. Retrieved from http://collegecost.ed.gov/scorecard/index.aspx

U.S. Department of Education. (2013b). *Enrollment component*. Washington, DC: National Center for Education Statistics, Integrated Postsecondary Education Data System.

U.S. Department of Education (2014a). *Fall enrollment survey. IPEDS Spring 2001 through Spring 2014, Enrollment component*. (IPEDS-EF: 90–99). Washington, DC: National Center for Education Statistics, Integrated Postsecondary Education Data System.

U.S. Department of Education. (2015). *Digest of education statistics, 2013* (NCES 2015–011). National Center for Education Statistics, Integrated Postsecondary Education Data System Retrieved from http://nces.ed.gov/programs/digest/d13/tables/dt13_306.10.asp

U.S. Department of State. (n.d.). *100,000 strong educational exchange initiatives*. Retrieved from http://www.state.gov/100k/index.htm

Uecker, J. E., Regnerus, M. D., & Vaaler, M. L. (2007). Losing my religion: The social sources of religious decline in early adulthood. *Social Forces, 85*(4), 1667–1692.

Umbach, P. D. (2006). The contribution of faculty of color to undergraduate education. *Research in Higher Education, 47*(3), 317–345.

Umbach, P. D., & Kuh, G. D. (2006). Student experiences with diversity at liberal arts colleges: Another claim for distinctiveness. *Journal of Higher Education, 77*(1), 169–192.

Umbach, P. D., Palmer, M. M., Kuh, G. D., & Hannah, S. J. (2006). Intercollegiate athletes and effective educational practices: Winning combination or losing effort? *Research in Higher Education, 47*(6), 709–733.

Umbach, P. D., & Wawrzynski, M. R. (2005). Faculty do matter: The role of college faculty in student learning and engagement. *Research in Higher Education, 46*(2), 153–184.

University of California Office of the President. (2015). *Presidential initiatives*. Retrieved from http://www.ucop.edu/initiatives/

University of Central Florida, Center for Teaching and Learning. (n.d.). *SoTL Journals*. Retrieved from http://fctl.ucf.edu/ResearchAndScholarship/SoTL/journals/

University of Notre Dame. (2013). *Enhancement areas: Strategic plan: University of Notre Dame*. Retrieved from http://strategicplan.nd.edu/university-plan/research-scholarship/enhancement-areas

Vaccaro, A. (2011). Toward self-investment: Using feminist and critical race lenses to analyze motivation, self-esteem, and empowerment of women's college students. In P. A. Pasque & S. E. Nicholson (Eds.), *Empowering women in higher education and student affairs: Theory, research, narratives, and practice from feminist perspectives* (pp. 104–120). Sterling, VA: Stylus.

Valentine, J., & Cooper, H. (2003). *Effect size substantive interpretation guidelines: Issues in the interpretation of effect sizes*. Washington, DC: What Works Clearinghouse.

van der Sluis, H., May, S., Locke, L., & Hill, M. (2013). Flexible academic support to enhance student retention and success. *Widening Participation and Lifelong Learning, 15*(2), 79–95.

Van der Veen, J. (2012). Draw your physics homework? Art as a path to understanding in physics teaching. *American Educational Research Journal, 49*(2), 356–407.

Van Gelder, T. (2007). The rationale for Rationale™. *Law, Probability and Risk, 6*, 23–42.

VanKim, N. A., & Nelson, T. F. (2013). Vigorous physical activity, mental health, perceived stress, and socializing among college students. *American Journal of Health Promotion, 28*(1), 7–15.

Ver Ploeg, M. (2002). Children from disrupted families as adults: Family structure, college attendance and college completion. *Economics of Education Review, 21*, 171–184.

Visher, M. G., Butcher, K. F., & Cerna, O. S. (2010). *Guiding developmental math students to campus services: An impact evaluation of the Beacon Program at South Texas College*. New York, NY: MDRC.

Visher, M. G., Weiss, M. J., Weissman, E., Rudd, T., & Wathington, H. D. (2012). *The effects of learning communities for students in developmental education: A synthesis of findings from six community colleges*. New York, NY: MDRC.

Vogt, C. M. (2008). Faculty as a critical juncture in student retention and performance in engineering programs. *Journal of Engineering Education, 97*(1), 27–36.

Vygotsky, L. S. (1978). *Mind in society: The development of higher psychological processes*. Cambridge, MA: President and Fellows of Harvard College.

Wagoner, R. L. (2008). *The current landscape and changing perspectives of part-time faculty* (New Directions for Community Colleges, No. 140). San Francisco, CA: Jossey-Bass.

Walker, A. A. (2003). Learning communities and their effect on students' cognitive abilities. *Journal of the First-Year Experience, 15*(2), 11–33.

Walker, A., & Leary, H. (2009). A problem based learning meta analysis: Differences across problem types, implementation types, disciplines, and assessment levels. *Interdisciplinary Journal of Problem-based Learning, 3*(1), 6–28.

Walker, J. (2010). Measuring plagiarism: Researching what students do, not what they say they do. *Studies in Higher Education, 35*(1), 41–59.

Walker, J. D., Brooks, D. C., & Baepler, P. (2011). Pedagogy and space: Empirical research in new learning environments. *EDUCAUSE Quarterly, 34*(4). Retrieved from http://er.educause.edu/articles/2011/12/pedagogy-and-space-empirical-research-on-new-learning-environments

Walker, J. D., Cotner, S. H., Baepler, P. M., & Decker, M. D. (2008). A delicate balance: Integrating active learning into a large lecture course. *CBE-Life Sciences Education, 7*(4), 361–367.

Walker, L. J. (2002). The model and the measure: An appraisal of the Minnesota approach to moral development. *Journal of Moral Education, 31*(3), 353–367.

Walker, R. L., Wingate, L. R., Obasi, E. M., & Joiner Jr., T. E. (2008). An empirical investigation of acculturative stress and ethnic identity as moderators for depression and suicidal ideation in college students. *Cultural Diversity and Ethnic Minority Psychology, 14*(1), 75–82.

Wallace, K. R. (2001). *Relative/outsider: The art and politics of identity among mixed heritage students.* Westport, CT: Ablex.

Wallace, K. R. (2003). Contextual factors affecting identity among mixed heritage college students. In M. P. P. Root & M. Kelley (Eds.), *Multiracial child resource book: Living complex identities.* Seattle, WA: MAVIN Foundation.

Walpole, M., Summerman, H., Nack, C., Mills, J., Scales, M., & Albano, D. (2008). Bridge to success: Insight into summer bridge program students' college transition. *Journal of First Year Experience and Students in Transition, 20*(1), 11–30.

Walsemann, K. M., Ailshire, J. A., Bell, B. A., & Frongillo, E. A. (2012). Body mass index trajectories from adolescence to midlife: Differential effects of parental and respondent education by race/ethnicity and gender. *Ethnicity and Health, 17*(4), 337–362.

Walsemann, K. M., Bell, B. A., & Hummer, R. A. (2012). Effects of timing and level of degree attained on depressive symptoms and self-rated health at midlife. *American Journal of Public Health, 102*(3), 557–563.

Walvoord, M. E., Hoefnagels, M. H., Gaffin, D. D., Chumchal, M. M., & Long, D. A. (2008). An analysis of calibrated peer review (CPR) in a science lecture classroom. *Journal of College Science Teaching, 37*(4), 66–73.

Wang, C. C. D., & Castañeda-Sound, C. (2008). The role of generational status, self-esteem, academic self-efficacy, and perceived social support in college students' psychological well-being. *Journal of College Counseling, 11*(2), 101–118.

Wang, X. (2009). Baccalaureate attainment and college persistence of community college transfer students at four-year institutions. *Research in Higher Education, 50*(6), 570–588.

Wang, X. (2012). Factors contributing to the upward transfer of baccalaureate aspirants beginning at community colleges. *Journal of Higher Education, 83*(6), 851–875.

Wang, X., & McCready, B. (2013). The effect of postsecondary coenrollment on college success: Initial evidence and implications for policy and future research. *Educational Researcher, 42*(7), 392–402.

Wang, Y., & Rodgers, R. (2006). Impact of service-learning and social justice education on college students' cognitive development. *NASPA Journal, 43*(2), 316–337.

Waples, E. P., Antes, A. L., Murphy, S. T., Connelly, S., & Mumford, M. D. (2009). A meta-analytic investigation of business ethics instruction. *Journal of Business Ethics, 87*(1), 133–151.

Warren, J. L. (2012). Does service-learning increase student learning? A meta-analysis. *Michigan Journal of Community Service Learning, 18*(2), 56–61.

Wassmer, R., Moore, C., & Shulock, N. (2004). Effect of racial/ethnic composition on transfer rates in community colleges: Implications for policy and practice. *Research in Higher Education, 45*(6), 651–672.

Watson, G., & Glaser, E. M. (1994). *Watson-Glaser Critical Thinking Appraisal manual.* San Antonio, TX: Psychological Corp.

Watson, J. C. (2009). Native American racial identity development and college adjustment at two-year institutions. *Journal of College Counseling, 12*(2), 125–136.

Watt, S. K. (2006). The relationship between racial identity attitudes and interpersonal development of African American college peer mentors. *Western Journal of Black Studies, 30*(3), 171–180.

Webber, D. A. (2012). Expenditures and postsecondary graduation: An investigation using individual-level data from the state of Ohio. *Economics of Education Review, 31*, 615–618.

Webber, D. A., & Ehrenberg, R. G. (2010). Do expenditures other than instructional expenditures affect graduation and persistence rates in American higher education? *Economics of Education Review, 29*(6), 947–958.

Webbink, D., Martin, N. G., & Visscher, P. M. (2010). Does education reduce the probability of being overweight? *Journal of Health Economics, 29*(1), 29–38.

Wechsler, H., Dowdall, G. W., Davenport, A., & Castillo, S. (1995). Correlates of college student binge drinking. *American Journal of Public Health, 85*(7), 921–926.

Weddle-West, K., Hagan, W. J., & Norwood, K. M. (2013). Impact of college environments on the spiritual development of African American students. *Journal of College Student Development, 54*(3), 299–314.

Weerts, D. J., & Ronca, J. M. (2007). Profiles of supportive alumni: Donors, volunteers, and those who "do it all." *International Journal of Educational Advancement, 7*, 20–34.

Weerts, D. J., & Ronca, J. M. (2008). Characteristics of alumni donors who volunteer at their alma mater. *Research in Higher Education, 49*, 274–292.

Wei, F. F., Wang, Y. K., & Klausner, M. (2012). Rethinking college students' self-regulation and sustained attention: Does text messaging during class influence cognitive learning? *Communication Education, 61*(3), 185–204.

Wei, L., & Hindman, D. B. (2011). Does the digital divide matter more? Comparing the effects of new media and old media use on the education-based knowledge gap. *Mass Communication and Society, 14*(2), 216–235.

Weidman, J. (1989). Undergraduate socialization: A conceptual approach. In J. C. Smart (Ed.), *Higher education: Handbook of theory and research* (Vol. 5, pp. 289–322). New York, NY: Agathon.

Weisbrod, B. A. (1962). Education and investment in human capital. *Journal of Political Economy, 70*, 106–123.

Welbeck, R., Diamond, J., Mayer, A., & Richburg-Hayes, L., with Gutierrez, M., & Gingrich, J. (2014). *Piecing together the college affordability puzzle: Student characteristics and patterns of (un)affordability.* New York, NY: MDRC.

Wells, R. S., Seifert, T. A., Padgett, R. D., Park, S., & Umbach, P. D. (2011). Why do more women than men want to earn a four-year degree? Exploring the effects of gender, social origin, and social capital on educational expectations. *Journal of Higher Education, 82*(1), 1–32.

West, R. F., Toplak, M. E., & Stanovich, K. E. (2008). Heuristics and biases as measures of critical thinking: Associations with cognitive ability and thinking dispositions. Journal of Educational Psychology, 100(4), 930–941.

Western Interstate Commission for Higher Education. (2015). *North American Network of Science Labs Online*. Retrieved from http://www.wiche.edu/nanslo

Wetter, D. W., Cofta-Gunn, L., Fouladi, R. T., Irvin, J. E., Daza, P., Mazas, C., . . . Gritz, E. R. (2005a). Understanding the associations among education, employment characteristics, and smoking. *Addictive Behaviors, 30*(5), 905–914.

Wetter, D. W., Cofta-Gunn, L., Irvin, J. E., Fouladi, R. T., Wright, K., Daza, P., . . . Gritz, E. R. (2005b). What accounts for the association of education and smoking cessation? *Preventive Medicine, 40*(4), 452–460.

Wettstein, R. B., Wilkins, R. L., Gardner, D. D., & Restrepo, R. D. (2011). Critical thinking ability in respiratory care students and its correlation with age, educational background, and performance on national board examinations. *Respiratory Care, 56*(3), 284–289.

What Works Clearinghouse. (2014). *Procedures and standards handbook* (Version 3.0). Washington, DC: U.S. Department of Education.

Whiteside, A., Brooks, D. C., & Walker, D. C. (2010). Making the case for space: Three years of empirical research on formal and informal learning environments. *EDUCAUSE Quarterly, 33*(3). Retrieved from http://www.educause.edu/ero/article/making-case-space-three-years-empirical-research-learning-environments

Whitt, E. J., Edison, M. I., Pascarella, E. T., Terenzini, P. T., & Nora, A. (1999). Interactions with peers and cognitive outcomes across three years of college. *Journal of College Student Development, 40*(1), 61–78.

Whitt, E. J., Pascarella, E., Elkins-Nesheim, B., Marth, B., & Pierson, C. (2003). Differences between men and women in objectively-measured outcomes, and the factors that influence those outcomes, in the first three years of college. *Journal of College Student Development, 44*(5), 587–610.

Whittaker, V. A., & Neville, H. A. (2009). Examining the relation between racial identity attitude clusters and psychological health outcomes in African American college students. *Journal of Black Psychology, 36*(4), 383–409.

Wijeyesinghe, C. L., & Jackson, B. W. III (Eds.). (2001). *New perspectives on racial identity development: A theoretical and practical anthology*. New York, NY: New York University Press.

Wilhelm, W. J. (2004). Determinants of moral reasoning: Academic factors, gender, richness-of-life experiences, and religious preferences. *Delta Pi Epsilon Journal, 46*(2), 105–123.

Wilke, R. R. (2003). The effect of active learning on student characteristics in a human physiology course for nonmajors. *Advances in Physiology Education, 27*(4), 207–223.

Williams, M. W. M., & Williams, M. N. (2012). Academic dishonesty, self-control and general criminality: A prospective and retrospective study of academic dishonesty in a New Zealand University. *Ethics and Behavior, 22*(2), 89–112.

Williams, P. E., & Hellman, C. M. (2004). Differences in self-regulation for online learning between first- and second-generation college students. *Research in Higher Education, 45*(1), 71–82.

Williams, R. L., Oliver, R., & Stockdale, S. (2004). Psychological versus generic critical thinking as predictors and outcome measures in a large undergraduate human development course. *Journal of General Education, 53*(1), 37–58.

Wilson, J. C. (2011). Service-learning and the development of empathy in U.S. college students. *Education and Training, 53*(2/3), 207–217.

Wilson, V. R. (2007). The effect of attending an HBCU on persistence and graduation outcomes of African–American college students. *Review of Black Political Economy, 34*(1), 11–52.

Wine, J. S., Cominole, M. B., Wheeless, S., Dudley, K., & Franklin, J. (2005). *1993/03 Baccalaureate and Beyond Longitudinal Study (B&B:93/03) methodology report* (NCES 2006–166). Washington, DC: National Center for Education Statistics, U.S. Department of Education.

Winkle-Wagner, R. (2009). *The unchosen me: Race, gender, and identity among Black women in college.* Baltimore, MD: Johns Hopkins University Press.

Wintre, M. G., & Bowers, C. D. (2007). Predictors of persistence to graduation: Extending a model and data on the transition to university model. *Canadian Journal of Behavioural Science, 39*, 220–234.

Wintre, M. G., Knoll, G. M., Pancer, S. M., Pratt, M. W., Polivy, J., Birnie-Lefcovitch, S., & Adams, G. R. (2008). The transition to university: The Student-University Match (SUM) Questionnaire. *Journal of Adolescent Research, 23*(6), 745–769.

Wise, J. C., Lee, S. H., Litzinger, T., Marra, R. M., & Palmer, B. (2004). A report on a four-year longitudinal study of intellectual development of engineering undergraduates. *Journal of Adult Development, 11*(2), 103–110.

Wise, S. L., & DeMars, C. E. (2005). Examinee motivation in low-stakes assessment: Problems and potential solutions. *Educational Assessment, 10*, 1–18.

Wise, S. L., & Kong, X. (2005). Response time effort: A new measure of examinee motivation in computer-based tests. *Applied Measurement in Education, 18*(2), 163–183.

Wister, A. V., Malloy-Weir, L. J., Rootman, I., & Desjardins, R. (2010). Lifelong educational practices and resources in enabling health literacy among older adults. *Journal of Aging and Health, 22*(6), 827–854.

Wohlgemuth, D., Whalen, D., Sullivan, J., Nading, C., Shelley, M., & Wang, Y. (2007). Financial, academic, and environmental influences on the retention and graduation of students. *Journal of College Student Retention, 8*(4), 457–475.

Wolfe, B. L., & Fletcher, J. M. (2013). *Estimating benefits from university-level diversity* (NBER Working Paper No. 18812). Cambridge, MA: National Bureau of Economic Research.

Wolfe, B. L., & Haveman, R. H. (2002, June). Social and nonmarket benefits from education in an advanced economy. In *Conference Series-Federal Reserve Bank of Boston* (Vol. 47, pp. 97–131). Boston, MA: Federal Reserve Bank of Boston.

Wolff, J. R., Himes, H. L., Kwon, E. M., & Bollinger, R. A. (2012). Evangelical Christian college students and attitudes toward gay rights: A California university sample. *Journal of LGBT Youth, 9*(3), 200–224.

Wolniak, G. C., Mayhew, M. J., & Engberg, M. E. (2012). Learning's weak link to persistence. *Journal of Higher Education, 83*(6), 795–823.

Wolniak, G. C., & Pascarella, E. T. (2005). The effects of college major and job field congruence on job satisfaction. *Journal of Vocational Behavior, 67*, 233–251.

Wolniak, G. C., Pierson, C. T., & Pascarella, E. T. (2001). Effects of intercollegiate athletic participation on male orientations toward learning. *Journal of College Student Development, 42*(6), 604–624.

Wolniak, G. C., Seifert, T. A., Reed, E. J., & Pascarella, E. T. (2008). College majors and social mobility. *Research in Social Stratification and Mobility, 26*(2), 123–139.

Wood, D., Bruner, J. S., & Ross, G. (1976). The role of tutoring in problem-solving. *Journal of Child Psychology and Psychiatry, 17*, 89–100.

Woodford, M. R., Atteberry, B., Derr, M., & Howell, M. (2013). Endorsement for civil rights for lesbian, gay, bisexual, and transgender people among heterosexual college students: Informing socially just policy advocacy. *Journal of Community Practice, 21*(3), 203–227.

Woodford, M. R., Han, Y., Craig, S., Lim C., & Matney M. M. (2014). Discrimination and mental health among sexual minority college students: The type and form of discrimination does matter. *Journal of Gay & Lesbian Mental Health, 18*, 142–163.

Woodford, M. R., Kulick, A., Sinco, B. R., & Hong, J. S. (2014). Contemporary heterosexism on campus and psychological distress among LGBQ students: The mediating role of self-acceptance. *American Journal of Orthopsychiatry, 84*(5), 519–529.

Woodford, M. R., Silverschanz, P., Swank, E., Scherrer, K. S., & Raiz, L. (2012). Predictors of heterosexual college students' attitudes toward LGBT people. *Journal of LGBT Youth, 9*(4), 297–320.

Woody, W. D., Woody, L. K., & Bromley, S. (2008). Anticipated group versus individual examinations: A classroom comparison. *Teaching of Psychology, 35*(1), 13–17.

Woosley, S. (2003). How important are the first few weeks of college? The long-term effects of initial college experiences. *College Student Journal, 37*(2), 201–207.

Woosley, S. (2004). Stop-out or drop-out? An examination of college withdrawals and re-enrollments. *Journal of College Student Retention, 5*(3), 293–303.

Wooten, T., & Dillard-Eggers, J. (2013). An investigation of online homework: Required or not required? *Contemporary Issues in Education Research, 6*(2), 189–198.

Worley, J. (2003). Developmental reading instruction, academic attainment and performance among underprepared college students. *Journal of Applied Research in the Community College, 10*(2), 127–136.

Worrell, F. C., Mendoza-Denton, R., Telesford, J., Simmons, C., & Martin, J. F. (2011). Cross Racial Identity Scale (CRIS) scores: Stability and relationships with psychological adjustment. *Journal of Personality Assessment, 93*(6), 637–648.

Worthen, M. G. (2011). College student experiences with an LGBTQ ally training program: A mixed methods study at a university in the southern United States. *Journal of LGBT Youth, 8*(4), 332–377.

Worthen, M. G. (2012). Understanding college student attitudes toward LGBT individuals. *Sociological Focus, 45*(4), 285–305.

Worthen, M. G. (2014). Blaming the jocks and the Greeks? Exploring collegiate athletes' and fraternity/sorority members' attitudes toward LGBT individuals. *Journal of College Student Development, 55*(2), 168–195.

Wortmann, J. H., Park, C. L., & Edmondson, D. (2012). Spiritual struggle and adjustment to loss in college students: Moderation by denomination. *International Journal for the Psychology of Religion, 22*(4), 303–320.

Wulff, D. H., & Austin, A. E. (2004). *Paths to the professoriate: Strategies for enriching the preparation of future faculty.* San Francisco, CA: Jossey-Bass.

Wyre, S. H. (2012). Metacognitive enrichment for community college students. *Community College Journal of Research and Practice, 36*(12), 994–1003.

Xie, Y., & Powers, D. (2008). *Statistical methods for categorical data analysis* (2nd ed.). Bingley, UK: Emerald.

Xu, Y. J. (2013). Career outcomes of STEM and non-STEM college graduates: Persistence in majored-field and influential factors in career choices. *Research in Higher Education, 54,* 349–382.

Yadav, A., & Beckerman, J. L. (2009). Implementing case studies in a plant pathology course: Impact on student learning and engagement. *Journal of Natural Resources and Life Sciences Education, 38*(1), 50–55.

Yadav, A., Subedi, D., Lundeberg, M. A., & Bunting, C.F. (2011). Problem-based learning: Influence on students' learning in an electrical engineering course. *Journal of Engineering Education, 100*(2), 253–280.

Yamarik, S. (2007). Does cooperative learning improve student learning outcomes? *Journal of Economic Education, 38*(3), 259–277.

Yamawaki, N., Ostenson, J., & Brown, C. R. (2009). The functions of gender role traditionality, ambivalent sexism, injury, and frequency of assault on domestic violence perception: A study between Japanese and American college students. *Violence against Women, 15*(9), 1126–1142.

Yang, H., & Wu, W. (2009). The effect of moral intensity on ethical decision making in accounting. *Journal of Moral Education, 38(3),* 335–351.

Yang, Y. F. (2010). Developing a reciprocal teaching/learning system for college remedial reading instruction. *Computers and Education, 55*(3), 1193–1201.

Yardley, J., Rodriguez, M. D., Bates, S. C., & Nelson, J. (2009). True confessions? Alumni's retrospective reports on undergraduate cheating behaviors. *Ethics and Behavior, 19*(1), 1–14.

Yarhouse, M. A., Stratton, S. P., Dean, J. B., & Brooke, H. L. (2009). Listening to sexual minorities on Christian college campuses. *Journal of Psychology and Theology, 37*(2), 96–113.

Yetter, G., Gutkin, T. B., Saunders, A., Galloway, A. M., Sobansky, R. R., & Song, S. Y. (2006). Unstructured collaboration versus individual practice for complex problem solving: A cautionary tale. *Journal of Experimental Education, 74*(2), 137–160.

Yip, T., Seaton, E. K., & Sellers, R. M. (2006). African American racial identity across the lifespan: Identity status, identity content, and depressive symptoms. *Child Development, 77*(5), 1504–1517.

Yoo, H. C., & Lee, R. M. (2005). Ethnic identity and approach-type coping as moderators of the racial discrimination/well-being relation in Asian Americans. *Journal of Counseling Psychology, 52*(4), 497–506.

Yoo, H. C., & Lee, R. M. (2008). Does ethnic identity buffer or exacerbate the effects of frequent racial discrimination on situational well-being of Asian Americans? *Journal of Counseling Psychology, 55*(1), 63–74.

Yorio, P. L., & Ye, F. (2012). A meta-analysis on the effects of service-learning on the social, personal, and cognitive outcomes of learning. *Academy of Management Learning and Education, 11*(1), 9–27.

Yosso, T. J. (2005). Whose culture has capital? A critical race theory discussion of community cultural wealth. *Race Ethnicity and Education, 8*(1), 69–91.

You, D., & Penny, N. H. (2011). Assessing students' moral reasoning of a values-based education. *Psychology Research, 1*(6), 385–391.

Yuh, J. (2005). Ethnic identity and its relation to self-esteem and ego identity among college students in a multiethnic region. *Journal of Applied Social Psychology, 35*(6), 1111–1131.

Zachry Rutschow, E., & Schneider, E. (2012). *Unlocking the gate: What we know about improving developmental education.* New York, NY: MDRC.

Zajacova, A. (2006). Education, gender, and mortality: Does schooling have the same effect on mortality for men and women in the US? *Social Science and Medicine, 63*(8), 2176–2190.

Zajacova, A., Hummer, R. A., & Rogers, R. G. (2012). Education and health among US working-age adults: A detailed portrait across the full educational attainment spectrum. *Biodemography and Social Biology, 58*(1), 40–61.

Zajacova, A., Lynch, S. M., & Espenshade, T. J. (2005). Self-efficacy, stress, and academic success in college. *Research in Higher Education, 46*(6), 677–706.

Zajacova, A., Rogers, R. G., & Johnson-Lawrence, V. (2012). Glitch in the gradient: Additional education does not uniformly equal better health. *Social Science and Medicine, 75*(11), 2007–2012.

Zavarella, C. A., & Ignash, J. M. (2009). Instructional delivery in developmental mathematics: Impact on retention. *Journal of Developmental Education, 32*(3), 2–13.

Zhang, H., & Lambert, V. (2008). Critical thinking dispositions and learning styles of baccalaureate nursing students from China. *Nursing and Health Sciences, 10*, 175–181.

Zhang, L. (2004). The Perry scheme: Across cultures, across approaches to the study of human psychology. *Journal of Adult Development, 11*(2), 123–138.

Zhang, L. (2005). Do measures of college quality matter? The effect of college quality on graduates' earnings. *Review of Higher Education, 28*(4), 571–596.

Zhang, L. (2008a). Gender and racial gaps in earnings among recent college graduates. *Review of Higher Education, 32*(1), 51–72.

Zhang, L. (2008b). The way to wealth and the way to leisure: The impact of college education on graduates' earnings and hours of work. *Research in Higher Education, 49*, 199–213.

Zhang, L. (2009). Does state funding affect graduation rates at public four-year colleges and universities? *Educational Policy, 23*(5), 714–731.

Zhang, L., & Thomas, S. L. (2005). Investments in human capital: Sources of variation in the return to college quality. In J. C. Smart (Ed.), *Higher education handbook of theory and research* (Vol. 20, pp. 241–306). Dordrecht, Netherlands: Springer.

Zhang, L. F., & Watkins, D. (2001). Cognitive development and student approaches to learning: An investigation of Perry's theory with Chinese and U.S. university students. *Higher Education, 41,* 239–261.

Zhao, C. M., & Kuh, G. D. (2004). Adding value: Learning communities and student engagement. *Research in Higher Education, 45*(2), 115–138.

Zhao, C. M., Kuh, G. D., & Carini, R. M. (2005). A comparison of international student and American student engagement in effective educational practices. *Journal of Higher Education, 76*(2), 209–231.

Zhao, Y., Lei, J., Yan, B., Lai, C., & Tan, S. (2005). What makes the difference? A practical analysis of research on the effectiveness of distance education. *Teachers College Record, 107*(8), 1836–1884.

Ziegler, B., & Montplaisir, L. (2012). Examining integrative thinking through the transformation of students' written reflections into concept webs. *Advances in Physiology Education, 36*(4), 307–312.

Zipp, J. F. (2007). Learning by exams: The impact of two-stage cooperative tests. *Teaching Sociology, 35,* 62–76.

Zubanov, N., Webbink, H. D., & Martin, N. G. (2013). The effect of schooling on problem drinking: Evidence from Australian twins. *Applied Economics, 45*(12), 1583–1599.

Zúñiga, X., Williams, E. A., & Berger, J. B. (2005). Action-oriented democratic outcomes: The impact of student involvement with campus diversity. *Journal of College Student Development, 46*(6), 660–678.

Zydney, A. L., Bennett, J. S., Shahid, A., & Bauer, K. (2002). Impact of undergraduate research experience in engineering. *Journal of Engineering Education, 91*(2), 151–157.

NAME INDEX

Page references followed by *fig* indicate an illustrated figure; followed by *t* indicate a table.

Oswald, A. J., 493, 514
Otero, R., 395, 398, 414
O'Toole, D. M., 364, 391, 410
Owen, J. E., 169, 203, 282, 293
Owen, J. J., 144
Ozaki, C. C., 211, 213
Ozogul, G., 62, 120
Öztel, H., 49

P
Pace, C. R., 544
Pace, R. C., 73
Padgett, R. D., 125, 211, 214, 215, 231, 270,
  282, 283, 285, 287, 288, 292–296, 305,
  312, 313, 503
Page, M. E., 490
Paige, R. M., 512
Palfrey, J., 49
Pallas, A. M., 489
Palmer, B., 118*t*, 120, 126
Palmer, C. J., 107
Palmer, C. L., 262, 505
Palmer, E., 117*t*
Palmer, M. M., 25, 39, 191, 219, 265
Palmer, R. T., 165, 245
Pan, Y. J., 363, 388, 401, 405, 407
Papadopoulou, M., 56
Pappa, T., 49
Parent, D., 490, 498, 501
Park, A., 511
Park, C. L., 216–218
Park, J. J., 76, 181, 189, 190, 209–211, 216,
  229, 230, 267, 268, 275, 286, 426*t*
Park, S., 432, 503
Parke, R. D., 336
Parker, E. T., 208
Parks, S., 167
Paronto, M. E., 387
Parrish, A. J., 246
Pascarella, E. T., 3, 6, 11, 12, 14, 18, 19,
  23–25, 29, 32–36, 38, 39, 43–47, 52, 61–63,
  66, 67, 71, 80, 85, 86, 88, 94, 95, 98,
  108–112, 115, 117*t*, 118*t*, 120, 125, 133,
  135–138, 142, 143, 146, 154, 159, 162,
  170–174, 178, 182, 189, 190, 208, 210, 211,
  214, 217, 227, 237, 238, 243, 247, 249, 250,
  253–256, 260, 264–266, 270–272, 276–283,
  285, 287, 288, 293–295, 298, 301, 305, 313,
  314, 319, 321–323, 329, 334, 337–340, 343*t*,
  345, 349, 350, 355, 363, 364, 378–380, 390,
  394–396, 398–400, 403, 404, 407, 409, 411,
  413, 415, 417–419, 421, 425, 426*t*, 431*t*,
  435, 436, 438*t*, 444, 445, 451*t*, 456–458,
  460, 461, 469*t*, 472, 474, 478, 487, 498,
  499, 507, 508, 510, 514, 519, 524, 530,
  533, 534, 540, 543, 547, 549, 550,
  553, 554, 559
Passow, H. J., 341, 343*t*, 344, 351, 352
Pasupathi, M., 196, 222

Patel, M., 51
Patel, R., 390
Patrinos, H. A., 434
Patten, T. A., 376, 408
Patterson, H. O., 117*t*
Patton, L. D., 170, 186, 245, 332
Pattyn, E., 494
Paul, 130
Paulsen, C., 496
Paulsen, M. B., 364, 368, 372, 375, 379, 391,
  392, 394, 400, 407, 408, 410, 411, 414,
  421, 434, 460
Payea, K., 437
Pear, J. J., 65
Peck, S. D., 60
Pedersen, D. E., 54
Pederson, E. L., 246
Peek, L., 202
Peele, T., 64
Pennebaker, J. W., 49
Penny, C., 49
Penny, N. H., 338, 339, 344
Peplau, L. A., 246
Peralta, R. L., 165, 246
Perin, D., 70
Perlis, S., 211
Perna, L. W., 362, 363, 426*t*, 431, 431*t*,
  432–434, 453, 469*t*, 470, 471
Perrault, R., 317
Perry, R. P., 51, 61
Perry, W. G., Jr., 106, 144
Perry, R. P., 118*t*
Persell, C. H., 266
Peschiera, F., 348
Pesso, K., 349
Peter, K., 366
Peterfreund, A. R., 389
Peters, J., 75
Peterson, C., 373
Peterson, M. W., 116
Peterson, P. L., 116
Peterson, R. A., 19
Peterson, R. D., 196
Petronijevic, U., 426*t*, 432, 490
Pettigrew, T. F., 251, 305
Pfeffer, F. T., 368, 375, 380
Phelps, R. P., 371
Phillips, J. C., 165
Phinney, J. S., 163, 174, 175, 183
Piacente-Cimini, S., 57
Piaget, J., 26–28, 99, 355
Pierson, C. T., 32, 33, 61, 117*t*, 118*t*,
  142, 227, 305
Pike, G. R., 33, 37, 68, 73, 74, 77–80, 84, 88,
  96, 112, 117*t*, 118*t*, 120–122, 127, 134, 135,
  203–205, 208, 218, 219, 267, 425
Pilecki, T., 58
Pingry O'Neill, L. N., 388
Pintrich, P. R., 106

SUBJECT INDEX

Page references followed by *fig* indicate an illustrated figure; followed by *t* indicate a table.